W9-BTJ-026

AN INTRODUCTION TO
MEDIEVAL EUROPE

300-1500

AN INTRODUCTION TO
Medieval Europe
300 - 1500

JAMES WESTFALL THOMPSON
SIDNEY HELLMAN EHRMAN PROFESSOR OF EUROPEAN HISTORY

THE UNIVERSITY OF CALIFORNIA

&

EDGAR NATHANIEL JOHNSON
ASSOCIATE PROFESSOR OF HISTORY, THE UNIVERSITY OF NEBRASKA

W · W · NORTON & COMPANY · INC ·

PUBLISHERS · NEW YORK

Copyright, 1937, by

W · W · NORTON & COMPANY, INC.

New York, N. Y.

PRINTED IN THE UNITED STATES OF AMERICA
FOR THE PUBLISHERS BY THE VAIL-BALLOU PRESS

Preface

For this revision of his *History of the Middle Ages, 300-1500*
(W. W. Norton & Company, Inc., 1931), Professor Thompson put
at my disposal a manuscript in which he had made many alterations
from the original text. I am deeply obligated to him not only for the
opportunity presented, but also for the unlimited freedom he granted
me to reorganize, rewrite and expand his manuscript. In so doing I
have tried to remember his maxim that history, in the final analysis,
must be a history of ideas, and that, at the same time, it must
also be refreshed constantly by intimate contact with warm human
beings and the homely facts of daily life. The work on this book is
also to be regarded as, at least in part, an inadequate acknowledgment
of the stimulation and nourishment received from his splendid and
exciting teaching. For his assistance with the proof I am likewise
grateful.

Indeed, so many kind persons have helped to complete this task
that I am under no illusions as to how much of it I have really done
myself. Those who are acquainted with the authors cited in the foot-
notes and bibliography will know to what extent this book is a collection of other writers, whether of their words or ideas. Without wishing to pass on the responsibility for the errors which, despite all care,
still remain in the book, mention must be made of my indebtedness to
Mr. Richard Jobman, who has taken care of many details, and to the
whole staff of W. W. Norton & Company. They, and especially
Mr. R. E. Farlow, will know, I trust, that I am not ungrateful for
the ways in which they have eased my labor. My colleague, Professor
L. B. Smith, has read part of the material on architecture, and was so
gracious as to let me see his notes on architecture. My friend, colleague and chief, Dean C. H. Oldfather, has read the early chapters
pertaining to his field. My friend and colleague, Dr. Glenn W. Gray,
has not only written the two chapters on the constitutional development of England, but he has also taken time from his own work to
read most if not all of the remaining chapters. His extensive learning
is strewn throughout the book. My sister, Mrs. Mildred Bickford, has
buttressed me from the first with invaluable encouragement. She has,

moreover, in countless ways helped to speed on the work. I should not dare to try to evaluate the help my wife has given me, not the least part of which has been the preparation of the Index. Likewise it is impossible for me to measure what I owe to my very dear friend, the late Dr. John Dean Bickford of The Hotchkiss School. From the very first he gave unsparingly of his time, strength, and intelligence to improve the quality of the manuscript. In order, in so far as it was possible, to bring it up to his own high standards of clear, effective and pointed discourse, he subjected it to a rigorous dissection, sentence by sentence, paragraph by paragraph, and page by page. By the time of his death he was reading chapter twenty-four. Whatever this book may contain of clarity, grace, or spark of writing is therefore owing primarily to his alert, uncompromising and devoted criticism, lavishly bestowed.

To the following publishers the book is indebted for permission to quote and use material from authors whose works they have published: The American Historical Review; D. Appleton–Century Co., Inc.; E. Arnold and Co.; The Atlantic Monthly; A. & C. Black, Ltd.; G. Bell & Sons, Ltd.; the Bloch Publishing Co., Inc.; Blue Ribbon Books; the Cambridge University Press; Chatto and Windus; the Clarendon Press; the Columbia University Press; Constable & Co., Ltd.; Covici–Friede, Inc.; F. S. Crofts & Co.; J. M. Dent & Sons, Ltd.; the Dial Press, Inc.; E. P. Dutton and Co.; Ginn & Co.; Harper & Brothers; the Harvard University Press; D. C. Heath and Co.; Henry Holt & Co., Inc.; Houghton, Mifflin Company; George G. Harrap & Co., Ltd.; Alfred A. Knopf, Inc.; Little, Brown & Company; Longmans, Green & Co.; McGraw–Hill Book Co., Inc.; the Macmillan Company; the Medieval Academy of America; Methuen & Co., Ltd.; the Oxford University Press; Prentice–Hall, Inc.; the Princeton University Press; G. P. Putnam's Sons, Inc.; Charles Scribner's Sons; Sheed & Ward, Inc.; the University of California Press; the University of Chicago Press; the University of North Carolina Press; the University of Pennsylvania Press; the University Press of Liverpool; the University of Wisconsin Press; the Yale University Press.

EDGAR N. JOHNSON

Lincoln, May 23, 1937.

Contents

List of Illustrations and Maps

ix

MAPS

Chapter 1

THE GRÆCO-ORIENTAL CONQUEST OF THE ROMAN EMPIRE

HISTORY, it has been remarked, is to the group what memory is to the individual. In order to get at the sources of our own cultural inheritance, we Americans must first go back across the Atlantic. For, in spite of the proclamations of chauvinists concerning the unique quality of the American civilization and the danger of its defilement by immigrants, we are all, unless we are native Indians, either immigrants or descendants of immigrants from Europe or elsewhere. This is not to say that we have not in the course of a comparatively short history developed certain characteristic traits and institutions; but it is to say that beyond a certain short time and a certain shallow depth our history is largely the history of Europe or of European influence. The sources of European civilization are therefore the sources of our own, and to understand ourselves we must understand Europe.

The middle ages in history

The use of the terms "middle ages" and "medieval" is convenient rather than logical or descriptive. The men of those times did not consider their age as middle or medieval; they were living in modern times. Those to whom that age first seemed medieval were the scholars of the renaissance, who, blinded by the radiant dawn of the rediscovered Greek and Roman world, were unmindful of the fact that that dawn came only as a consequence of the activities of a period upon which henceforth they looked back with scorn. We can understand their point of view, but as a result of all that we now know to have happened before them and all that has happened since them we can no longer suppose that their term really means anything in itself.

Expansion of early western European civilization

The geographical setting within which western European civilization first took shape is covered chiefly by present-day Italy, Spain, France, England, Belgium, and Germany. From these areas as centers, with a remarkable expansive strength that has by no means yet seen its limit, it spread in the course of a thousand years, although not always directly, to Ireland, Scotland, Wales, Denmark, Scandinavia, Poland, Czechoslovakia, Austria and Hungary, even beyond Poland along the southern shores of the Baltic and past Italy into the north-western corner of the Balkan peninsula. From one point of view this expansion from definite centers into new areas can be looked upon as a widening of the area of civilization, as the extension of a particular kind of civilization to areas less civilized, or at least differently civilized. It is therefore only a small chapter in the gigantic process of civilizing all mankind.

The early formative period of the west

It is quite impossible to fix any specific date for the beginning of a particular line of western development within the above-mentioned areas. The shift from one age into another is, when looked at closely, gradual and imperceptible. Our prophets always tell us that we are just entering upon a new age. To enclose historical periods within fixed dates is, no matter how convenient, to do violence to historical accuracy and to distort the general picture of slow but ceaseless change. But it is possible to define generally the larger periods within which some of the characteristic features of western history took root. Such a period is that from about A.D. 400 to 800, a period for which has often been especially reserved the epithet "dark ages," again a highly inaccurate term if one looks upon the period as the point of departure for a new growth.

Western Europe built on a Roman foundation

By 400 all Italy, with Rome as capital, had been the cornerstone of the Roman republic and empire for over six hundred years, and the territory of Spain, France, and Belgium had been organized into several Roman provinces for over four hundred and England for only some-what less. The Roman provinces of Rhætia, Noricum, and Pannonia, comprising most of what is now southern Germany, Austria south of the Danube, and most of Switzerland as well, had been subject to Rome only a little less than four hundred years. Within such long periods of time, about equal to or exceeding the chronological length of American history, these areas had naturally been pretty thoroughly Latinized in speech and Romanized in general culture, the degree of Romanization depending for the most part upon the length of time that they had been subject to Roman control. This means that western Europe began to build upon a Roman foundation of long standing. It is therefore necessary to appreciate to some degree the general char-acter of the civilization of that Roman empire of which it was the west-ern half.

Rome's Hellenistic heritage

In the course of its expansion from a small city on the banks of the Tiber to a world state embracing every civilized area that bordered on

the Mediterranean Sea, Rome had become the heir of all that the Mediterranean countries had produced; she had, in fact, become the victim of the superior refinements of the older civilizations in the eastern Mediterranean. When during her desperate struggle with Carthage she was drawn to the east, she entered first into the political, then into the cultural heritage of the succession states into which the empire of Alexander the Macedonian had fallen. A fusion of what the Greeks themselves had achieved with the ancient achievements of the peoples of the valleys of the Nile, the Tigris, and the Euphrates, contemplated and begun by Alexander, took place in the centuries immediately before and after the beginning of the Christian era; and to this Græco-oriental amalgam has been given the term "Hellenistic" to differentiate it from the earlier and more strictly Greek, or Hellenic, civilization. In a sense it was the product of all that civilized man, outside of India and China, had been able to produce hitherto, but in addition it had the freshness and originality, as well as the mellowness, that can come from the mixture of older elements into a new combination.

This Hellenistic world of Egypt, Palestine, Syria, Persia, Asia Minor, Greece, and the islands of the eastern Mediterranean was bound together by a cosmopolitan civilization and the use of Greek as a common language. It was dotted with large, fair cities, old and new, which gave it a strongly urban character. Its rulers were devoted to the cause of learning, and at Alexandria, the crowded scientific and literary capital of this world, there was a state library of some seven hundred thousand rolls for the use of societies of learned men. In the fields of mathematics and science there was such an outburst of activity that only the past hundred years can be compared with it. The *Idyls* of Theocritus and the *Mimes* of Herondas are ingratiating examples of the literature of the Hellenistic period, and its philologists established and handed down the texts of the Greek classics. It produced Epicurus and the founder of Stoicism, Zeno, the "gaunt ascetic Phœnician." Its sculpture reveals a superb mastery of technique and a tendency to theatrical display. In religion it fostered the oriental mystery cults that so strongly influenced the development of Christianity. Indeed, so great was the influence of some aspects of this Hellenistic world upon the Latin western half of the Roman empire that some historians say that Roman civilization is only an imitation of the Græco-oriental east. At all events, Rome's succumbing to eastern influence carries our own beginnings back to the shadowy origins of civilized existence in the valleys of the Nile, the Tigris, and the Euphrates.

It was, however, no unadulterated Græco-oriental culture that Rome handed on to the west, but one conditioned and transformed by the nature and experience of the Romans. The faces of shrewd, hard-headed, practical, even vulgar, Romans that stare at us from the striking portrait busts of Roman sculptors reveal to some extent what the character of this transformation was. The Roman genius lay in the fields of the practical arts, engineering, law, and government. It was a genius that built almost indestructible roads to bind its subjects together and beautiful aqueducts to bring them pure water. In law that genius was supreme: it aimed to give to the whole world justice and security. The Roman, indeed, felt that it was his especial obligation to rule the world. Outside of these realms, in the arts or in religious or philosophic thought, Rome was largely subservient, first to the higher artistic and intellectual culture of old Greece and the Græco-oriental fusion of Hellenism, and in her later declining days, partly in spite of herself, to more purely oriental influences. Her religion assimilated first that of the Greeks and then that of the orient. Her literature owed its beginnings to, and was constantly under the influence of, Greek impulse and example. There was, properly speaking, no Roman philosophy, although in ethics Roman writers perhaps showed some originality. Hence every educated Roman learned his Greek as well as his Latin.

Yet in spite of these borrowings Rome succeeded in imposing upon the western half of her empire, upon Italy, North Africa, Spain, Gaul, and Britain, a definite Roman stamp. She put them through a process of Romanization, not necessarily under compulsion, similar in general character to the Americanization that the European immigrant here undergoes. Just as the immigrant who has prospered in our midst is only too willing to abandon his language, customs, dress, and sometimes even his name in order to appear the more American, so the provincial in the Roman west abandoned his language in favor of Latin, his law in favor of Roman law, his religion in favor of Roman religion. All western Europe became to a certain degree standardized. The analogy with America is, to be sure, by no means perfect, but in substance it is true. The Latin west, attracted by all the advantages that the Roman empire had to offer, a common speech, common religious, commercial, legal, and governmental institutions—a more highly civilized existence, in short—became in time quite contentedly Roman and passed this heritage on to those who followed. Lord Cromer in his *Ancient and Modern Imperialism* has written:

"If we turn to the comparative results obtained by ancient and modern imperialists; if we ask ourselves whether the Romans, with their imperfect means of locomotion and communication, their relatively low standard of public morality, and their ignorance of many economic and political truths which have now become axiomatic, succeeded as well as any modern people in assimilating the nations which the prowess of their arms had brought under their sway, the answer cannot be doubtful. They succeeded far better."

Moreover, Roman influence and power penetrated far beyond the official limits of the empire in the west, filling with dread the painted Picts of Caledonia, and overawing the German tribes of the dark woodlands east of the Rhine and north of the Danube.

During the first two centuries of its history, that is, from the accession of Augustus to the death of Marcus Aurelius in 180, the Roman empire may be said to have realized, if it ever has been realized, that fond dream of patient mankind, a civilized world enjoying the fruits of ordered peace and security. This Roman peace, bestowed for so long a time upon the world surrounding the Mediterranean, has at various times inspired subsequent war-sick ages to strive to regain it and to imitate the machinery by which it was built. Especially after the empire had ostensibly disappeared in the west, the vague memory of those earlier halcyon centuries lingered on to stimulate a revival of empire in a very different form. While early western Europe inherited more than the memory of the empire, yet its actual inheritance came not so much from the empire in its best days as from an empire which in the course of the third, fourth, and fifth centuries had so deteriorated that it was unable in the end to preserve itself. This alteration, collapse, and final disappearance of the Roman empire in the west must be our first concern: western European civilization was built upon shattered foundations.

Indeed, there is much to be said for the idea that at its very outset the Roman empire was really a declining state, built upon the decadent civilizations of the east; that the brilliance of its first two centuries was more apparent than real, and that what ordinarily is called the beginning of decay in the third century was as a matter of fact merely the inability of an already weakened organism to withstand new and unusually difficult strains. Certain it is, on examination of the details in the foundation of Augustus's empire, that there was as much effort to reform and restore to their earlier character what he regarded as

Pax Romana (margin)

Beginning of Roman decline (margin)

undesirable features new in Roman social life as there was to solve old political problems by new methods.

The Augustan political revolution

The phenomenon of dictatorship in the contemporary world offers a clue to the understanding of the shift from republican to imperial institutions in the Roman state. On the other hand, there could be no better preparation for an understanding of modern dictatorship than to study the breakdown of Greek democracy in the century preceding Philip of Macedon and Alexander the Great, or the breakdown of Roman republicanism which led up to Julius Cæsar and his successor Augustus, who assumed as his impressive personal name after 27 B.C. the title *Imperator Cæsar divi filius Augustus,* the August and Divine Emperor and Cæsar, to which official titles were later added. Essentially the foundation of the Roman empire, after almost a century of war between rival provincial governors who had learned to be impatient of republican institutions, meant a return to the very old principle of military dictatorship, which had really been worked out by the despots of the east. Like the modern dictator who wishes to veil the realities of political revolution by preserving all the cabinet offices, reserving the most important for himself, Augustus preserved the magistracies of the Roman republic and held most of them himself. In particular, his control of the army and of finances assured him a monopoly of authority and made him the actual master of the state. To be sure, the senate continued to exist as in theory the chief legislative body of the state, but it had little actual importance except as the highest criminal court. The remainder of the republican administration was likewise retained, but it fell under the emperor's appointive power.

Augustus as a reformer

In addition to these political innovations Augustus felt it necessary to correct certain unfortunate tendencies in Roman society. Like his modern successors he was concerned with preserving the good old stock and the good old virtues. The legions were to be restored to the Roman citizen and cleansed of provincials, and Roman citizenship was to be closed to provincials. Bachelors—and here the modern dictator has imitated him—were to be discouraged by taxation from continuing their lives of celibacy: the true Roman was paterfamilias and his wife the mother of many children. Roman blood was to be kept undefiled, and one might marry only within one's own class. Extravagance and luxury were to be eschewed for the simple virtues of family life. The old Roman peasant proprietor was extolled as a hero by Livy in his new history, and the quiet simplicity of rustic existence was praised by the poet Horace and by Virgil in his *Georgics.* With the aid of literary propaganda Augustus was planning a back-to-the-farm movement.

All this was accompanied by an attempted religious revival of old Roman agricultural festivals, transferred now to the capital itself and put upon the calendar of some priestly college. Evidently Augustus considered that something had been happening to Roman blood, Roman virtues, Roman life, and Roman religion. Was this, after all, the beginning of a decline that he was trying to stem?

Evidence that the new military dictatorship was in essence of eastern origin is supplied by the fact that the new emperor came to be vested with the sanctions of divinity, as was always the case in the east. Julius Cæsar had been deified after his death, and Augustus was his adopted son. Moreover, in gratitude for the relief that Augustus brought to Rome men were ready to look upon him as a savior, a messiah, as others had been looked upon in the east. It was from the east that he received the first request that a specific worship of him be sanctioned. He permitted this worship of himself, not alone but along with the state, personified in the goddess Roma, and it was not long before temples and priesthoods of the new cult were established over the whole empire. Worship of the living emperor was naturally followed by apotheosis at his death. *The worship of the emperor*

A major concern of all absolute monarchs and military dictators is always the choice of a successor. This difficulty in the Roman empire was all the more serious because preservation of the forms of republican government by elected officials precluded simple hereditary succession. Inevitably in such a situation the choice of an emperor rested with any force strong enough to put its candidate in office and keep him there. That force, which was the ultimate basis of Augustus's power, was the military. At first the emperors were put into office by the prætorian guard, the personal guard of the emperor in Rome, but before the first century was over the frontier legions had become aware that they too could make and unmake emperors. Since it seems to belong to human nature to expect rewards for favors, the choice of the prætorians and the legions inclined towards those who were most generous with promises. Since, too, the necessity of increasing the army to protect ever more dangerous frontiers obliged the government to draw more heavily on what might be called the less civilized provinces, and ultimately to depend for troops upon the potential enemy himself, the semicivilized German, there was evident danger that this military control might possibly bring about the ruin of the state. Should the army ever get out of hand, fail in its loyalty to the emperor and the state, and insist upon the fulfillment of its own particular desires, military control might mean anarchy. Indeed, no later than A.D. 68 the troops *Military control of the choice of emperor* of several frontier provinces set up their own candidates and fought the question out among themselves—a return in less than a century to the very anarchy out of which the empire had arisen.

The Emperor Trajan, a Spanish soldier, put a temporary stop to this chaotic system in the second century by adopting his successor as his son and in effect thus establishing the principle of hereditary succession. But by the end of the century the prætorian guard was again in a position to sell the imperial title to the highest bidder. The civil war which was precipitated between the troops of Britain and Pannonia with their respective candidates brought to the throne a North African soldier, Septimius Severus, an army man pure and simple, who ruled by military force and introduced his subordinates into the senate and the civil service. Septimius was the logical product of the Augustan political revolution, the first absolute lord and monarch of a now militarized state. Henceforth for ninety years the disposal of the imperial crown was in the hands of the army. During the thirty-five years after 235 five dozen military pretenders contested for the throne, producing veritable political anarchy at a time when the Roman frontiers were hard pressed. It has been remarked that to accept the emperorship in these days was to impose the sentence of death upon oneself.

Finally Diocletian, who became emperor in 284, made an attempt to cure this chronic disease by setting up a regular plan of succession. His scheme was based upon a complete administrative reorganization of the empire, which by this time had become necessary if it was to be governed at all efficiently. It was clearly recognized by this Illyrian soldier that effective government would require a sharing of responsibility. Imperial authority was therefore to be shared with one other executive of his choice, who was also to have the title of Augustus. In order to encourage able and ambitious men, each Augustus was to choose a subordinate to act as a kind of sub-emperor with the title of Cæsar. The Cæsars were to rise to the place of the Augusti when after twenty years of rule the Augusti had retired, and new Cæsars then were to be appointed. It is extraordinary that a man of Diocletian's experience could have been so ingenuous. He himself abdicated in 305 and retired to private life in his native Illyria, to dabble in gardening and build a palace huge enough to contain the modern town of Spalato. Here he had an opportunity to judge how well his new scheme was working. Immediately there broke out, and continued until 324, a civil war between more Augusti and Cæsars than Diocletian had ever counted on. The ultimate victor in this struggle was another Illyrian, Constantine, whose father had become an Augustus upon Diocletian's retirement, and who after his father's death had himself proclaimed Cæsar in 306 by his troops at York in Britain. After becoming master of the western half of the empire, he cleared the east of his last rival and from 324 to 337 ruled as autocrat of a reunited Roman empire. No new schemes were subsequently evolved to govern the succession. While there was a tendency to accept the hereditary principle, there was no telling what disturbances would arise upon the death of the ruling monarch, and successful generals continued to occupy the imperial throne. Here was a practical problem that the practical Roman could not solve.

It would be difficult to estimate how much this failure impaired the Roman state, but it must not be supposed that this alone was responsible for the complete reorganization of the government undertaken by Diocletian and Constantine. By the end of the third century all the symptoms of what must remain the mysterious collapse of Roman civilization had begun to appear. A century of revolt and civil war was only symptomatic of social, political, and economic ills within, of the whole Mediterranean world's shift to the new religion of Christianity, and of the constant pressure of barbarian German and Persian enemies on the frontier. In a sense the Roman world had completed a cycle in the first three centuries of the empire; now there was need for another savior, another Augustus, if it was to be preserved. That the new reform was undertaken by provincials who had grown up in the army, men to whom Italy and Rome and the feeble republican tradition meant nothing in the face of the immediate problems they were called upon to solve, is indicative of what had taken place since Augustus. Their solution was more government: government of the oriental autocratic type, government sanctioned by the Sun God in the case of Diocletian, by the Christian God in the case of Constantine. Both emperors established their political capitals in the east. Diocletian, anticipating Constantine, set up his at Nicomedia in Bithynia. In 330 Constantine founded a new capital for the reunited empire upon the site of the old Greek colony of Byzantium, a most strategic location, where Europe and Asia are separated only by the narrow straits of the Bosporus. The new capital was given a Greek name, Constantinople—Constantine's city—although its old name never went out of use. Nothing was spared to make the new Rome the rival of the old, and this rivalry, when carried over into the ecclesiastical sphere, was to be of great importance in the history of the Christian Church in both east and west. In fact, the significance of the founding of Constantinople cannot be overemphasized. As Athens had been the center of the

The need for reorganization of the state

The founding of Constantinople

Hellenic world and Alexandria of the Hellenistic world, Constantinople was destined to be the political and cultural capital of the new Byzantine world.

*The adminis-
trative reforms
of Diocletian*

That the Roman empire was in a state of siege on its northern frontier and that this situation could no longer be adequately met from Rome was evident from the nature of the administrative reorganization undertaken by Diocletian. The empire was divided into the four prefectures of Gaul, Italy, Illyricum, and the East,[1] each headed by a prefect. The capital of the prefecture of Gaul was Trier, a most apt center for operations on the Rhine frontier, where today the old Roman gate and the ruins of palatial baths still attest the early importance of the town. Italy's capital was Milan, which commanded every important Alpine pass except the Brenner, and facilitated the throwing of troops into Gaul or, through Verona and the Brenner, against the Danube frontier. Sirmium on the Save River, the capital of the Illyrian prefecture, commanded the lower Danube frontier, while the orient was governed from Nicomedia. These four prefectures were in turn subdivided into thirteen dioceses, each composed of several contiguous provinces and headed by a vicar. The provinces were reduced in size and increased in number to a hundred and twenty. The old Roman city-state, the *civitas*, a specific geographical district governed from an urban center, remained the lowest unit in the administrative system. To limit the power of the heads of the administrative units, from prefecture down to province, military and civil authority was divided between two separate sets of officials. The purpose and the effect of the reorganization was to create a much more highly centralized bureaucracy with the inevitable result of greatly increasing the number of officials. With important exceptions, the local government of the *civitas*, the *curia* or senate of the town from which it was governed, was subordinated to the provincial governor. He, in turn, was responsible to the vicar, the vicar to the prefect, the prefect to the emperor. A newly organized secret service spied on the efficiency of the administration. Nothing was left to local initiative. The self-government of the Roman town, which had been the glory of the earlier empire but which had for some time been losing its autonomy, was now destroyed and the town harnessed to the machinery of a state organized with the military precision of an army.

*Persia the
model for
Diocletian's
court*

It is quite possible that this reorganization of administration was influenced by the practice of oriental empires. Certainly it is analogous to the Persian system of satrapies. It has been said that the contempo-

[1] See map facing p. 1

rary Persian state of the Sassanid emperors was "the precedent and in every respect the model of Diocletian's administrative reforms." At Nicomedia the Lord and God of the Roman empire withdrew into the rarefied atmosphere of a vast palace, standing in an immense "paradise," or park (the Greek word is of Persian origin), like the palaces of Persian monarchs. Here he was surrounded by an officialdom and a new court nobility of carefully graded ranks, who moved in an environment of oriental pomp, ruled by an elaborate etiquette. Gradations in rank were marked by such titles as *illustris* (illustrious), *spectabilis* (notable), *clarissimus* (most distinguished). The emperor was assisted in his government by a consistory, or privy council. Closest to his person stood the grand chamberlain or provost of the sacred bedchamber; just below him, the master of the offices, or chancellor, who was minister of foreign affairs and chief judicial officer. In addition there were the quæstor of the sacred palace, the count of the sacred largesses, and the master of the privy purse, who controlled the management of the imperial crown lands. Two counts of the domestic troops commanded the cavalry and infantry bodyguards of the emperor. The swarm of lesser officials, civil and military, was increased by the large separate staffs of the ministers. Functions pertaining to the person of the emperor were called sacred, and his person was alluded to as The Presence.

Never, not even in Persia or China, did greater divinity surround royalty than in Nicomedia and Constantinople. The awful influence of The Presence permeated not only the court and the capital but the whole empire. On state occasions he was attired in silken robes of blue and gold, to symbolize the sky and the sun; his hair was dressed to imitate the sun and sprinkled with gold; upon his head rested a jeweled tiara; a collar of pearls was around his neck; over his breast flowed necklaces of rubies and emeralds; his fingers wore rings flashing with precious stones; his finger-nails were gilded; his shoes were of red Persian leather with golden soles. He carried a scepter terminating in a gold ball typifying the globe and tipped with a golden eagle, in whose talons was a splendid sapphire, symbolic of the blue of heaven. The throne was an exquisite piece of workmanship in carved precious wood, inlaid with mother-of-pearl and lapis lazuli. It stood upon a dais covered with rare rugs and carpets and was overhung by a great canopy of blue silk representing heaven. The adornment of the throne room suited the magnificence of The Presence. The solemn imperial procession was preceded by the usher of the gold rod, followed by lackeys perfuming the air with attar of roses and fan-bearers stirring it

Diocletian and Constantine in state

with ostrich and peacock feathers. Immediately upon the entrance of The Presence every person in the throne room sank to the floor in oriental obeisance and remained prostrate until The Sacred Presence was seated, when he was permitted to kiss the hem of the imperial robe. Such magnificence must often have been distasteful to Diocletian, the veteran soldier, who had often, wrapped in his old blue army mantle, slept on the ground among his soldiers. But he was aware of the magic spell cast by external symbols of power. Throughout the third century the person of the emperor had continually been exposed to the world, and familiarity had bred contempt; many of the emperors had been assassinated. There was as much need to restore the awe and the majesty of the imperial office and to protect the person of the emperor from a licentious soldiery as there was to reform the administration. The orientalization of the government and the court was simply one part of the great plan of imperial reorganization.

One cannot fully comprehend the reform measures of Diocletian and Constantine without some knowledge of the severe economic depression under which the empire suffered in the third century. In order to provide the additional income necessary to support this large new governmental machine and the considerably increased and reorganized army, Diocletian undertook the first economic survey of the empire to be made since Augustus, which should lay the basis for a new and equitable system of taxation. Peasants were henceforth inseparably attached to the land which they cultivated, and the government saw to it that they could not leave it. Constantine a little later fixed the peasant to the land by law; if he attempted to leave it he was subject to pursuit. Attempts were made to re-establish a sound coinage, after considerable inflation in the course of the third century. As a final effort to stave off economic ruin Diocletian also tried what has always been a temptation to panic-stricken governments, although it has always failed: he established fixed prices for commodities, especially foodstuffs, and even for labor, in order to protect the general public and the government itself against inflated prices and unscrupulous speculators. Unfortunately the efforts of Diocletian and Constantine were not for long successful. The new bureaucracy was able at tremendous cost to keep the state erect for something like two hundred years more, but for about half this period, especially in the west, it was only the semblance of a state that was kept alive. The economic, social, and religious changes which these reforms attempted to check went on unabated as before.

Economic reforms

We must now consider the society of the later Roman empire, inasmuch as in its main features it was the prototype of early western
Europe. Fundamentally the Roman empire rested, as indeed all western European civilization until very recently has rested, upon the work
of the peasants in the fields. Ever since the Punic Wars there had been
a capitalistic development in agriculture, leading to the formation of
very large estates cultivated by slave labor. The development was uninterrupted by the establishment of empire, for Augustus's attempt to
revive the small peasant landowner was unsuccessful. As long as
slaves were plentiful and cheap, slave gangs directed by overseers of
an absentee owner were common. But the last important Roman work
on agriculture, that of Columella in the first century of the empire,
indicates a shift in tendency. To meet the growing scarcity in slaves he
advocated more attention to slave breeding, and a more careful, even
brutal, supervision of those on hand. But at the same time he complained of the absence of Romans from their estates, leaving only
agents in charge, and urged that, to make up for the lack of slaves,
estates should be let on permanent lease to country-bred tenants. This
replacing of large estates cultivated by slaves with estates divided into
many small holdings cultivated by tenants was the first new tendency
of the empire. There was no further development of the large estate
of the earlier type. There was no advance in agricultural skill. A return
was being made to the individual cultivation of the small plot, but
the individual cultivator was now a *colonus*, a tenant of a landed magnate, and no longer an independent peasant owner.

The second transformation was that of Diocletian and Constantine,
just mentioned, which attached the peasantry to their plots on large
estates as serfs, transmitting their servile status to their children. By
the beginning of the fourth century, then, the Roman empire had an
hereditary class of serfs. This transformation is not easy to explain.
In part it came about as a result of the steady attempt of the wealthy
to foreclose mortgages, to force settlement of debts by obliging the
free small owner to exchange the ownership of his land for a tenant
status. In part it was the result of the increasing financial pressure on
a desperate state trying to avoid disaster, which made independent
farming so unprofitable that small owners, willing to do anything to
get rid of ruinous taxes, voluntarily put themselves under the protection of rich landowners of the senatorial class, who knew how to handle
imperial tax collectors and judges. In addition, the general insecurity
brought about by political chaos, civil war, and constant overrunning of

*Late Roman
agriculture*

*The hereditary
serfs*

the frontiers jeopardized any prospect of settled, peaceful agricultural prosperity. The peasants moved to the towns to swell the ranks of the unemployed. Their families were not so large as formerly; the birth rate was steadily declining. Pestilence and famine decimated their ranks. Much land went entirely out of cultivation. Yet the demands of the state were necessarily as great as ever. The vacant lands must be filled up with tenants of any sort at all, and Germans, who knew little about agriculture, were most easily got. To guarantee to society the maintenance of agriculture and to the state its necessary income, the helpless peasant was fixed to the land and put upon the tax register as belonging to it. He was forbidden to leave, and, should he attempt to escape, he could legally be chained like a slave. His only compensation was that thereby he was also guaranteed a livelihood of a sort.

The late Roman villa

With the breakdown of the Roman bureaucracy in the late empire the local magnate assumed private jurisdiction over the tenants of his villa. He became a private governor, an incipient feudal lord; government became a function of land ownership. The medieval manor was already foreshadowed in the organization of the large villa, with its division into land cultivated by dependent tenants and slaves according to a fixed schedule of services, and plots cultivated by the tenants for themselves upon definite shares or rents. The villa became not only the local unit of government but also a practically self-sufficient agricultural unit, producing what it needed and used on the spot. The destructive influence on commerce and industry of such local concentration of production promoted the return to a simplified agrarian economy, in which agricultural products were the chief money.

The Roman town had been hard hit by the crisis in agriculture in the third century. In the earlier centuries of affluence it had developed a local pride, often leading to expenditures beyond its means, which brought in imperial agents to correct municipal finances. The Roman town, moreover, had no such foundation for urban life as the large industrial and commercial middle classes that we know. While industry and commerce had flourished during the first centuries of the empire, by the beginning of the third they were both on the wane. Slave labor for industry was expensive and inefficient. The Mediterranean world offered no opportunities such as the modern world offers to industry

Decline in commerce and industry

for capitalistic development. Inventive genius seemed to have run out, and, with no technical improvements, the quality of goods produced became steadily inferior to meet the needs of a population which had lost its taste or had never been able to acquire any. With the growth of urban life in the provinces industry became localized within the province; with the later development of the large estate it was confined within the villa. Such a situation influenced, of course, the amount of domestic trade carried on within the empire, which, in comparison with the foreign trade—largely in luxuries—had always been more important in Roman commerce. In fact the Roman, although an exacting and even exorbitant interest taker, was never especially interested in trade, which he left largely to the Jew and the Syrian. Consequently the wealth of the middle class in the towns consisted mainly in ownership of small estates, and these, of course, the crisis in agriculture impoverished.

What agriculture did not do to the prosperity of the town the increasing financial needs of the state did do. It is not too much to say that the financial policy of the government succeeded in ruining, or at least making life miserable for, large numbers of the urban middle class, the curial class as it was called, whose members made up the local senate, the *curia*, and occupied the municipal magistracies. Taxes in the earlier empire had not been exorbitant, but in the third century they became so. The creaking economic system and the additional expenses of government made them still higher. In desperation the central government resolved to involve the urban curial class in the business of tax collecting, making them responsible for the collection of the assessment of the *civitas* and obliging them to make good from their own means what they were unable to collect to meet the sum fixed by the state. Since no group of men would voluntarily undertake such a responsibility, it became necessary for the state to force this class to perform the function and to stop any attempt to escape from their unenviable lot by making them virtually an hereditary caste. The son of a member of the *curia* became a member at eighteen; exemption could be got only by those who had large families, who alone were entitled to "honored rest." Those who fled were hunted; if they were not found their property was confiscated and given to their substitutes; if they were found their punishment consisted "in bearing the weight of office for two years." By the middle of the fifth century Roman law had to confess that the curials "have been so oppressed by the injustice of the magistrates and by the venality of the tax gatherers that most of their members have resigned their offices, expatriated themselves, and sought an obscure asylum in some distant province." [2] For many Romans it actually came to seem more desirable to live among barbarians on the frontier than to live at home; there at least they would not be subject to torture in making a declaration of their wealth.

An hereditary middle class

[2] Quoted by D. C. Munro and R. J. Sontag, *The Middle Ages* (1928), p. 10.

*Forced labor
and the heredi-
tary* collegia

Moreover, in addition to taxes the Roman government came more and more to rely upon requisitions of goods and various kinds of forced labor from its citizens, properly termed "liturgies" but popularly regarded as vile burdens. Labor was required to keep up the post roads, and horses to maintain the courier service. Imperial officials and their staffs traveling on government business were entitled to food and lodging in a community. Because of the debased coinage the government was at last obliged to accept raw materials in lieu of taxes, and furnishing means of transport to government warehouses became one of the forced services. From the organizations of independent artisans, the *collegia,* were demanded specified quantities of goods and services; and to assure their receipt the trades were made hereditary callings, from which there was no escape. The metal workers in the imperial munitions factories and workers on the aqueducts were branded to prevent escape. Those who provided entertainment, as well as those who baked bread, for the inhabitants of Rome were organized into hereditary official *collegia.* A society stratified into something like an oriental caste system was in the process of formation.

*Corruption
and ineffi-
ciency of the
administration*

To make matters still worse, taxation rested most heavily on the shoulders of those least able to bear it. The senatorial nobility, the creation of the emperors by appointment and the wealthiest men in Roman society, were generally granted exemption from taxation as part of their title to nobility. The military, and later the Christian clergy, were also exempt. Nor was there anything like an honest system of collecting taxes, for the tax officials became increasingly corrupt. Indeed, as much may be said of the whole later Roman officialdom, even the judicial: it lost sight of its traditions and became more and more incompetent and venal. To protect the people against their own officials the state came as early as the middle of the fourth century to rely upon a new official, the defender, whose duty it was "to act as a father for the people of both country and city, to prevent them from being burdened with taxes, and to protect them against the arrogance of the imperial officials and the shamelessness of judges." [3] But who was to watch the watchers?

*Ammianus
Marcellinus
on Roman
decline*

Strewn through the pages of the last great historian of the Roman empire, Ammianus Marcellinus, who wrote at the end of the fourth century, are observations tending to confirm the general picture sketched above. "It occasionally happened that rich men, relying on the protection of those in office, and clinging to them as the ivy clings to lofty

[3] Quoted in O. J. Thatcher and E. H. McNeal, *Europe in the Middle Age* (1920), p. 19.

trees, bought acquittals at immense prices, and that poor men who had little or no means of purchasing safety were condemned out of hand. . . . He [the emperor] opened the door to plunder, which doors are daily more and more opened by the depravity of judges and advocates, who are all of the same mind and who sell the interests of the poor to the military commanders or the persons of influence within the palace, by which conduct they themselves have gained riches and high rank. . . . The emperor . . . considered nothing but how he might amass money from all quarters without any distinction between just and unjust actions . . . and to this conduct were owing the heavy distresses which afflicted the emperor's subjects, the ruinous titles, privileges and exemptions which alike ate up the fortunes of poor and rich. . . . People were relieved from the burden of transporting the public stores (which often caused such losses as to ruin many families) and also from the heavy income tax. . . . Every class and profession was exposed to annoyance, being called upon to furnish arms, clothes, military engines, and even gold and silver and abundant stores of provisions and various kinds of animals." The natives of Illyria would never have complained "if at a later period some detestable collectors had not come among them, extorting money and exaggerating accusations in order to build up wealth and influence for themselves, and to procure their own safety and prosperity by draining the natives. . . . The misery of these times was further increased by the insatiable covetousness of his [the emperor's] tax collectors who brought him more odium than money. . . . The natives, from weariness of the severe rule under which they were, were eager for any change whatever. . . . Lastly, the burdens of all tributes and taxes were augmented in a manifold degree, and drove some of the highest nobles from fear of the worst to emigrate from their houses. Some also, after being drained to the utmost by the cruelty of the revenue officers, as they really had nothing more to give, were thrown into prison, of which they became permanent inmates. Some, becoming weary of life and light, sought a release from their miseries by hanging themselves. . . . The treasury is empty, the cities are exhausted, the finances are stripped bare." [4]

From such a world people sought escape in amusements and excitements or in the consolations of religion. Without supposing that the city of Rome was in all respects typical of the whole empire, we may quote Ammianus further on what he saw. The city is, he says "declining into old age"; it "has come to a more tranquil time of life." He saw those "who fall away into error and licentiousness, as if a perfect

Ammianus on Rome

[4] Quoted from the translation of Ammianus by C. D. Yonge.

impunity were granted to vice"; those who, "sweating under many cloaks," try "by the continual wriggling of their bodies and especially by the waving of the left hand to make their long fringes and tunics, embroidered in multiform figures of animals and threads of various colors, more conspicuous"; men "who drive their horses . . . with a regular license . . . through the wide streets of the city, dragging behind them large bodies of slaves like bands of robbers." "Houses formerly celebrated for the serious cultivation of becoming studies are now filled with the ridiculous amusements of torpid indolence, reëchoing with the sound of vocal music and the tinkles of flutes and lyres. . . . Women with their hair curled, old enough to have three children, dance on the pavements." When nobles arrive at the bath and find that "any unknown female slave has appeared or any worn-out courtesan, they run up as if to a race, and patting and caressing her with disgusting and unseemly blandishments extol her"; but when one meets these nobles and speaks to them on the street, they "toss their heads like bulls preparing to butt, offering their flatterers their knees or hands to kiss." "Senators when they borrow anything are so humble you would think you were at a comedy . . . when they are constrained to repay what they have borrowed, they become so turgid and bombastic that you would take them for . . . descendants of Hercules." In fact, "friendships at Rome are rather cool, those alone which are engendered by dice are sociable and intimate, as if they had been formed amid glorious exertions and were firmly cemented by exceeding affection." As for the "lazy and idle common people . . . the lower and most indigent class of the populace," they were in Ammianus's opinion no better. "Some spend the whole night in the wine shops. Some lie concealed in the shady arcades of the theatres . . . or else they play at dice so eagerly as to quarrel over them, snuffing up their nostrils and making unseemly noises by drawing back their breath into their noses; or (and this is their favorite pursuit of all others) from sunrise to evening they stay gaping through sunshine or rain, examining in the most careful manner the most sterling good or bad qualities of the charioteers and horses. . . . The Circus Maximus is their temple, their home, their public assembly, in fact their whole hope or desire. . . . And you may see in the forum and roads and streets and places of meeting knots of people collected, quarreling violently with one another and objecting to one another." Some "are continually crying that the republic cannot stand if, in the contest which is to take place, the skillful charioteer whom some individual backs is not foremost in the race. When the wished-for day of the equestrian games dawns, before the sun has visibly risen, they all rush out with headlong haste, as if with their speed they would outstrip the very chariots which are going to race. . . . Among these men are many chiefly addicted to fattening themselves by gluttony, who, following the scent of any delicate food . . . and gliding over the ground on tiptoe, get an entrance into the halls, biting their nails while the dishes are getting cool. Others fix their eyes so intently on the tainted meal which is being cooked that you might fancy Democritus with a number of anatomists was gazing into the entrails of sacrificed victims in order to teach posterity how best to relieve internal pains." This is "greatly at variance with the pursuits and inclinations of that populace of old, whose many facetious and elegant expressions are recorded by tradition and history." "These pursuits and others of like character prevent anything worth mentioning or important from being done at Rome."

The much larger number of people, in Rome and still more *Decay of Roman religion* throughout the empire, who turned for consolation rather to religion did not turn to the old state religion of Rome, but to various newer cults, usually called mystery cults, which were brought in from the east. The official religion had gradually ceased to be of real significance in people's lives. As the state had become more and more urban in character, the old Italian agricultural deities and rites that had been transferred to the city from the country lost contact with the life out of which they had sprung. Moreover, Greek polytheism had been grafted on to Roman polytheism, and the attributes of its gods and the character of its mythology made Roman religion less Roman. Then too, Roman religion had become the peculiar possession of an official priesthood, whose obligation it was to see that the gods were placated in the right fashion at the right time. With all obligations to the gods so punctiliously taken care of, there was no need for the ordinary citizen to concern himself with them or even to participate in the public services devoted to them. Roman religion became stereotyped, formalized, emotionless, delegated to an authoritative priestly class. To be sure, the emphasis which came to be placed on Jupiter as supreme god in the later republic and the new cult of the worship of the emperor still preserved some little vitality in a dying religion, but such vitality as there was was so intimately connected with the worship of the glory of the Roman state—that is, with patriotism—as to have very little proper religious significance. It has already been pointed out that the attempt of Augustus to revive Roman religion was a failure.

The important eastern gods to whom the Roman world surrendered *The oriental* in ever increasing numbers were Magna Mater, the Great Mother of *mystery cults*

Phrygia, often called by her Greek name Cybele, who was worshipped together with her male consort Attis; Atargatis, whom the Romans called the Syrian Goddess, worshipped also with her male consort Hadad; Syrian Baals, such as the ones from Doliche and from Baalbek; the Persian Mithras; the Egyptian Isis and her Osiris; the Hellenistic Adonis, worshipped with Aphrodite; and finally the Jewish Jahveh and the deified Savior Jesus Christ. For the last two a following chapter is reserved, where some attempt will be made to explain their relationship to these other mystery cults and their final victory over them. The general similarity of the worship of the other oriental gods and goddesses makes it possible to discuss them together. Certainly their most fundamental characteristic is the direct appeal to the individual, without qualification of class or race, of their comforting doctrines and their stimulation to religious excitement. They were religions of salvation; their purpose was to save the individual from personal sin and to guarantee him an ultimate escape from the miserable world about him into an immortal after life. To achieve their aim they relied not only upon their teaching but upon an elaborate ritual of worship, which sought to identify the individual with the life of his hero-god and thus to make certain that the fate of the individual should be the same as that of the god: the individual would likewise become divine, blessed, and immortal. It is for this reason that they are called mystery cults, since they aimed by means of secret ritual to bring about an incomprehensible fusion of the lone worshipper with a divine savior. It is therefore characteristic that their heroes, such as Attis, Osiris, and Adonis, were gods who had died and risen again, or like Mithras had come originally from heaven to pass some time on earth, afterwards to return into the ethereal realm of the stars. The believer who followed through the legend of the god as it was presented to him in the ritual of the cult died and rose again with his lord; he partook of the divine essence, he was one with his god. This was very different from the kind of practical, contractual relationship typical of the bond between the ordinary Roman and his god, the idea of which was to give the god something for something specific in return, an appropriate *quid pro quo*.

The organiza-
tion of the
mystery cults

    The organization of these cults was also basically different from that of Roman polytheism. The faithful were grouped together in small bands, religious fraternities and sororities, oriental mystical brotherhoods and sisterhoods. One was initiated into them after passing through several stages, beginning with that of a neophyte. Once admitted into the secrets of the cult as a brother, one was permitted henceforth to witness the services, often held, as in the case of Mithraism, in underground caves or chapels, administered by a special group of priests clad in exotic robes. "The strange masks and robes of the officiants, the weird decorations of the subterranean chamber, which were rendered the more impressive by the flickering half-light of flaming torches, the awe-inspiring character of the rites themselves, the nervous stimulant of the mystic draught of wine and the music with which the service was accompanied" transported the initiate into another world very different from his own humdrum one where he experienced mystical union with his savior. The initiate of the Isis cult in Apuleius's *The Golden Ass* explains: "I approached the borderland of death and . . . when I had been borne through all the realms of nature I returned again; at midnight I beheld the sun blazing with bright light; I entered the presence of the gods below and the gods above and adored them face to face." And Isis promises him: "When thou shalt have run the course of thy life and passed to the world beneath, there too in the very vault below the earth thou shalt see me shining amid the darkness . . . and reigning in the secret domains . . . and thyself dwelling in the fields of Elysium shalt faithfully adore me as thy protector." [5]

It is therefore no cause for wonder if these gods with their new promises and their gorgeous services became so popular as to transform the religious complexion of the Roman world. Nor was it strange that they were taken up by the emperors as patrons and patronesses of their thrones and put upon the official religious calendar. The religions of the east were well suited to a government from the east; the ceremony of eastern monarchy approximated the ceremonies of eastern religions. Indeed, government may almost be said in some of its aspects to have become a religion, and at least one religion, Christianity, certainly became a government.

Epicureanism

The Roman who sought an explanation of the universe and man's relation to it in philosophy rather than in religion had by the beginning of the empire become a materialist and a sceptic. If he adopted the Epicurean view as set forth in Lucretius's poem *De Rerum Natura* (On the Nature of Things), he held that the universe, including man and his soul, was nothing more than a composite of material atoms. Man's chief obligation was to himself, and it consisted in seeking quiet and peace of mind free from all annoyance, pain, fear, and desire. The chief obstacle to that reflective calm was religious superstition, the belief that the gods interfered in the workings of this mundane life to reward the good and punish the wicked, the belief that there was such a thing as

[5] Quoted in C. Bailey, *Phases in the Religion of Ancient Rome*, pp. 200–1.

immortality of the soul to be given or to be denied. The soul, Lucretius held, was nothing but a composite of atoms which were scattered at death, and as for the gods, if such there were, one might be sure that they were too absorbed in their own affairs to bother about the doings of mere men. They were to be conceived as dwelling in the distant spaces between the worlds, living their own perfect kind of Epicurean life (and, it has been suggested, undoubtedly conversing in Greek). It might be well for a good Epicurean to reflect on their idyllic mode of existence and even to imitate them, but he need not worry about them.

Stoicism   Most educated Romans took more kindly to Stoicism, which for the Roman became not only a system of philosophy and practical ethics but something very like a religion. The original Stoic god was the divine spark of reason and order that permeates the universe, of which man contains a particle. It was senseless to combat this divine providence of reason and order, which was the world of nature; man's duty was to live in harmony with it, to expect nothing else, and to remain undismayed by any buffetings he might suffer at its hands. After death the soul of man, the divine particle in him, might expect no sort of personal immortality, but it was assured a final impersonal blending with the divine fiery breath that was god in the universe. Since all men had a part of god in them and were themselves one with the universe, Stoicism preached the brotherhood of man. One must be kind, loyal, and forbearing in one's relations with one's fellow men. As Seneca says, "You must live for others if you wish to live for yourself." A gentle humility is the proper attitude towards those who do you wrong. Moreover, the Stoicism of Seneca and Epictetus tended to make of the divine providence a personal god, who could be communed with and petitioned through humble prayer, and to emphasize the union of that god with man. Epictetus writes: "Have courage to look up to God and say: Deal with me hereafter as Thou wilt, I am one with Thee, I am Thine. I flinch from nothing so long as Thou thinkest it good. Lead me where Thou wilt, put on me what raiment Thou wilt. Wouldst Thou have me hold office, or eschew it, stay or fly, be poor or rich? For all this I will defend Thee before men. . . . What else can a lame old man as I am do but chant the praise of God? . . . As I am a rational creature I must praise God. This is my task and I do it; and I will not abandon this duty so long as it is given me; and I invite you to join me in this same song." [6] Might one not think he were listening to the

[6] Quoted in Bailey, *op. cit.*, p. 239, and W. R. Halliday, *The Pagan Background of Early Christianity*, p. 218.

Psalmist? In the end Stoicism reached a compromise with popular Roman polytheism, which is explained away in allegorical terms, and made its peace with the astrology coming in from the east, whereby one could achieve immortality in the stars.

This last trend in Stoicism was only one more evidence of the turn of the Roman mind away from uncompromising rationalism to magic, superstition, astrology, and mystical religion. Another was the system of philosophy called Neo-Platonism, worked out originally by the Egyptian Plotinus in the third century, which gradually became the most important school of philosophy in the Roman empire. It is perhaps not without point to remark that Plotinus was the philosopher of Rome's first century of major decline. His scheme of things some would call the logical outcome, others the *reductio ad absurdum*, of Plato's philosophy; in either case, Plotinus represents what six centuries of the study of Plato came to. From at least one point of view Plato's influence may be said to have proved unhealthful. He lifted the plane of speculation from the solid and warm bed of earth to the rarefied atmosphere of the clouds. Nothing material was real; it partook of reality only in so far as it was the embodiment of an absolute, abstract idea conceived by the mind of god, himself the supreme absolute idea of the good. These ideas, or more properly forms, were the only realities. Moreover, Plato was a dualist: he conceived of what we call matter and spirit as mutually hostile elements, and in applying this notion to human life he could speak of the antagonism of body and soul, and of the body as being merely the prison of the soul, which somehow the soul must escape. The elements of Plotinus's system are Platonic. What is real is what seems to the modern western mind least real—the world of spirit, idea, reason, incorporeal essence. What seems most real to us, matter, is really nothing until it becomes impregnated with the soul. Human souls are the product of the general soul, the creator of this sensible world about us. But the general soul is itself an emanation from the divine mind or intelligence, which contains all the only real Platonic ideas or forms, according to whose pattern the world of sensible objects is made. Finally, behind the divine mind is the ineffable and absolute abstraction of the one, or the good, or god, as far removed from the intelligence of the ordinary individual as it is possible to be, but a logical necessity from which to start. The object of the soul is to escape the confines of matter and regain the ultimate divine essence from which it came. For all the logical rigidity of the system in detail, Plotinus placed the highest value upon reaching contact with the highest god in the Neo-Platonic trinity through the exercises of

Neo-Platonism

mysticism. The experience of ultimate effacement in contemplation of and union with the one was the all-surpassing glory of life. Plotinus achieved it only four times, we are told by his biographer. Neo-Platonism did not remain the air-tight system that Plotinus contrived, however. In the hands of his pupils and successors Porphyry, Iamblichus, Maximus, and Crysanthius it swiftly descended to the level of the general tendencies and practice of religion and thought in the later Roman empire. It made its compromise with popular religion and, like Stoicism, explained away the gods by allegory. It introduced as mediators between its abstract gods and poor man a host of good and bad demons. Its later practitioners even became wholly devoted to the science of ceremonial magic, which would oblige the gods to do what one wants them to do. Yet in spite of this decline in intellectual vigor, or even perhaps because of it, Neo-Platonism remained, until the pagan schools of Athens were closed, the one system of religious philosophy that served as a refuge for the last defenders of paganism, who were caught in the onrush of Christianity but not swept away, to whom Christianity seemed "a fabulous and formless darkness mastering the loveliness of the world." [7]

Astrology and magic

Accompanying this turn of the Roman world to mysticism, whether in religion or in philosophy, was the infiltration of eastern magic and astrology and a corresponding decay of "tough-mindedness." Wandering magicians and astrologers were common on the highways. Some of the oriental cults adopted astrology as the basis of their theological systems. The whole atmosphere was peopled with angels and demons. Books of wonders catered to the popular taste for the miraculous, and the wonder-working pagan saint had already made his appearance.

Education

In the schools the emphasis on style and form, on an empty, polished rhetoric, betrayed the absence of vital subject matter. Romans flocked to the lectures of professors devoted to such profound subjects as the praise of the fly, the mosquito, or the parrot. Respect for authority in all fields was characteristic of the intellectual *élite*. Much earlier Petronius had complained in his *Satyricon:* "I believe that college makes complete fools of our young men, because they see and hear nothing of ordinary life there." Typical subjects assigned for declamation were: "pirates standing in chains on the beach, tyrants pen in hand ordering sons to cut off their fathers' heads, oracles in times of pestilence demanding the blood of three virgins or more, honey-balls of phrases, every word and act besprinkled with poppy-seed and sesame. People who are fed on this diet can no more be sensible than people who live

[7] Quoted in E. R. Dodds, *Select Passages Illustrating Neoplatonism*, p. 8.

in the kitchen can be savoury." [8] Later Roman art tells the same tale—
a decline in taste revealed by the vulgar craze for what was big and
grand and a deterioration in technique. Obviously many features of
what has been characterized as the medieval point of view were already
clearly evident in the later Roman empire.

It may have struck the student that, in this attempt to picture the
transformation that revolutionized the Roman empire in the third,
fourth, and fifth centuries, no attempt has been made to explain the *Why did the*
phenomenon. It is an absorbing question, which has tempted many *Roman empire*
scholars, and it is a matter of great importance, if it be assumed that *fall?*
it is possible to distinguish causes and results in history. For even though
the supposed causes for the decline of one civilization might not be
applicable to that of another, yet if we knew them for a certainty we
should have some clue to the prevention of decadence in our own and
future civilizations. But since we have not discovered as yet, and are
unlikely ever to discover, that which brings a civilization to what in
retrospect appears to be a brilliant climax, or what it is that holds a
society together and enables it to assimilate its past and go beyond that
past, how can we proceed to explain the reverse of these tendencies? At
every turn one is baffled by facts susceptible of different interpretations
and by the difficulty of distinguishing between causes and effects. No
government has ever succeeded in controlling either organic growth or
organic decay in human society. Civilizations change and pass; men are
always talking about the changes, but are seldom aware of the passing
until it is over. The pagans attributed it to destiny or fate, Christians
to providence or the will of God. The historian frankly says that he
does not understand; he can sometimes establish the facts, perhaps
even identify symptoms, but the how and the why of things eludes his
analysis.

[8] Quoted in Halliday, *op. cit.*, p. 196.

Chapter 2

THE CHRISTIAN CONQUEST OF THE ROMAN EMPIRE

THE SPREAD AND TRANSFORMATION OF CHRISTIANITY

The importance of Christianity

I
T SEEMS a very strange and mysterious thing that today most people in Europe and America who worship at all worship under the name of a religion that had its origin in the radical teachings of a young Jew who, hardly over thirty years of age, was crucified in Palestine 1900 years ago. There is no clearer example of the way in which the happenings of a distant past, or the life of one person, fundamentally condition the lives of an unknown posterity. More astounding still is the fact that this religion of Jewish origin has for a long time been carried by Europe and America to highly civilized peoples of Asia, and to primitive peoples within the vast continent of Africa and elsewhere, as the one and only true religion, for which all others are to be abandoned. The leaders of this Christian imperialism are swayed by the vision of a Christian world and a Christian peace similar to that Roman world and that Roman peace referred to in the preceding chapter.[1] In considering Christianity, therefore, we are considering one of the most important of all historical phenomena, no less important today than it was fifteen hundred years ago. For Christianity is not only a chapter in the decline of the Roman empire; it forms the very warp and woof of all the history of that western Europe which immediately followed upon Rome. The whole intricate complex of our present political, social, and even economic life is shot through and through with Christian rites and Christian teachings. The Christian churches still exercise a great, if waning, influence upon all aspects of our civilized existence. Because we incline to take for granted the things closest and most familiar to us, we seldom inquire seriously into the origins and history of this phenomenal religion.

[1] See p. 5.

The Roman Catholic Church is not only the oldest but, many historians would be willing to say, the greatest historical institution that we still possess. It preserves a creed, a ritual, and an organization the main features of which have been perpetuated with little fundamental change from the later Roman empire. Yet Catholic Christianity itself was the result of a transformation as significant as the sixteenth-century transformation of Catholicism that produced the Protestantism that prevails today in northern Europe and America. The primitive Christianity of Christ's disciples and the early Church was no more suited to the cosmopolitan civilization of the Roman empire than, to the minds of Martin Luther and John Calvin, the Christianity that they inherited was suited to their day. This early transformation occurred in the fourth, fifth, and sixth centuries, the very centuries when the Roman empire was suffering serious decline. Was there, then, any relationship between these two phenomena? Was Christianity one element in the destruction of Roman civilization, or was the declining Roman empire one element in the transformation of early Christianity?

The first great transformation of Christianity

(In its origins Christianity was less a new religion than a reform movement within the confines of Judaism) the religion of the Jews of both Palestine and the cities of the Mediterranean world. In the course of a long and tortuous history the Jews had elaborated a strictly monotheistic conception of a god, but he was none the less the national god of his specially chosen people. Jewish religious experience had been recorded in a body of Hebrew literature known to us as the Old Testament. It existed also in a Greek translation, called the Septuagint,[2] for the benefit of the Jews who had wandered away from their homeland. The long succession of conquerors, of whom the Romans were only the last, who had overridden the Jewish homeland had driven the Jewish people to the great hope and definite expectation that their God would some day release them from political bondage to foreign masters. It was thought that through the instrumentality of a messiah especially sent by God a new Jewish kingdom was to be set up, a new era of peace and plenty, of power and splendor, ushered in, which would end forever grief, subjection, and despair. Jehovah would bring his people into their rightful heritage at last.

The messianic hope in Judaism

It was this messianic hope that inspired Jesus. He looked to the new Kingdom of God to establish the final relationship of fatherhood and sonship between the Jewish God and the Jewish people, and a reign of brotherly love among men.) Moreover, he was convinced that this

[2] From the Greek word meaning seventy, because it was thought to be the work of seventy divinely inspired translators.

Jesus and
the Gospel

new day was about to dawn and that it was his duty to announce the Gospel, the good news of the speedy coming of the Kingdom of God. Yet it was to be established only after a day of reckoning, when those who were judged worthy to become citizens of the new Kingdom were to be separated from those judged unworthy. His message was therefore "Repent, for the Kingdom of God is at hand." It was a message meant especially for Jews. "There is no adequate reason to suppose that he thought of a Gentile mission, still less of a Gentile Christianity divorced from Judaism." [3]

Opinions differ as to whether Jesus believed himself to be the Messiah who was to deliver his people, the agent of God in establishing the new Kingdom, but many of his immediate followers took him for the Jewish Messiah. Thus when at Jerusalem he was first publicly pro-

The early
failure of
Christianity

claimed as the inaugurator of the expected new era, it was inevitable that he should be looked upon by the authorities as a dangerous and fanatical revolutionist, about to disrupt the well-established order of things. He was consequently arrested and crucified. The movement behind him did not die with him: his followers continued to believe, despite the fact that he had died without having undertaken to assume the rôle of the deliverer, that he was nevertheless the Messiah and that, moreover, he was not dead, but had risen from his tomb and ascended to heaven, whence he was to come a second time as the deliverer of his people. This firm and enthusiastic conviction gave purpose to the lives of his followers: they must prepare for this second coming of the Messiah to usher in at last the Kingdom of God. But the Jewish nation as a whole clung to its ancient beliefs and would not be convinced by the message of Jesus's followers, who thus developed into a sect clinging to their peculiar faith. As a Jewish reform movement and as a definite messianic cult within Judaism Christianity had failed.

The triumph
of Christianity

Four hundred years later history records a strangely different picture. By the end of the reign of the Emperor Theodosius in 395, Christianity had become a magnificent success and had swept aside all other religions in the whole Roman empire. It was recognized in Roman law as the one and only official state religion; all others were proscribed for all time. Moreover, it had perfected a masterful organization, modeled on the reorganized empire of Diocletian and Constantine, through which it was gradually absorbing the political functions of the declining Roman state. This organization was already elaborating a body of

[3] A. C. McGiffert, *A History of Christian Thought*, I, 8.

church law with which to govern. It had codified its religious belief into an abstruse and complicated system of theology, which admitted of little modification. The organization of this body of belief was in the hands of a group of clergy carefully set off from the laity by its costume and its privileges and powers, conferred by the already ancient ceremony of ordination. The clergy performed a series of mysterious, sacramental acts, prescribed by a fixed ritual, in which it was necessary for the individual to participate if he were to be saved from sin and gain eternal life. Into their hands were pouring from all sides vast quantities of landed wealth. So thoroughly had the organized Christian Church become a state within a state, so completely a part of the world in which it existed, that large numbers of Christian men and women would have nothing to do with it, but preferred to live the lives of monks, nuns, and hermits. Obviously this was no longer the Christianity that Jesus had preached in Palestine; four centuries of existence had already wrought a revolution.

The victory of Christianity in the Roman empire had come only after a long and bitter struggle with the Roman state. Towards Christianity the Roman government was forced to adopt an attitude of hostility quite unlike that which it had adopted towards other oriental religions of unofficial character. What made this attitude necessary was the exclusiveness peculiar to Christianity, a trait which it inherited from its Jewish background. Rome had no difficulty in coming to terms with other foreign religions, for polytheism readily admits new gods into its pantheon if only they are willing to be received. Oriental gods were inscribed on the Roman religious calendar and their festivals celebrated just as were the festivals of any older Roman deity. To the ordinary pagan mind it was absurd to entrust oneself to the whims of only one god. But Christianity was born of a monotheistic religion, and this monotheism it kept in modified form even after it had ceased to be simply a Jewish sect. There was only one true God, and in the Old Testament he had proved himself wholly intolerant of other gods. No compromise was possible with the variegated paganism of the Roman empire. It was not even to be tolerated; it must be destroyed. Those who held to it were only ignorant, misguided, and lost idolaters. Moreover, this earthly life was of no importance. Christians were only strangers here; heaven was their true home. They were citizens of the coming Kingdom of God. "Now this age and the future are enemies. The one speaks of adultery and corruption and avarice and deceit; the other bids these things farewell. . . . We reckon that it is better to hate the things

Christianity versus paganism

that are here, for they are small, short-lived, and corruptible, and to love the things that are there, for they are good and incorruptible." [4]

Christians as citizens

The Christian conducted himself in logical accordance with his belief. He could not participate in any of the activities of Roman society, not even games or festivals, if they involved recognition of pagan gods or pagan beliefs. Indeed, it was difficult for Christians to take on any of the services and duties of a citizen or to assume public office; hence they had to withdraw from society, thereby laying themselves open to the charge of being unsocial. Being obliged to meet in secret and at night, they were looked upon as a dangerous political group who in their private gatherings engaged in grossly immoral practices. Finally, it was impossible for Christians, being out-and-out pacifists, to serve in the army, and it was equally impossible for them to recognize in any shape or form the official cult of the worship of the emperor and the goddess Roma. This was, of course, a direct affront to the state religion, tantamount to treason, and no state has ever dealt gently with the traitor.

It is therefore not surprising that the Roman state undertook to exterminate a group so fundamentally hostile to it. Yet so long as the Christians remained relatively few in number they suffered from no uniform policy of persecution. Not indeed until 250 did the Emperor Decius undertake to destroy Christianity throughout the empire. Up to this date such persecutions as there were had been local and sporadic, often stimulated by popular fury against the Christians. After this date the emperors Valerian, Aurelian, Diocletian, and Galerius undertook to wipe out what they regarded as a further menace to a state already in desperate straits; their persecutions may be regarded as part of their reforming activities. But it was now too late to effect a wholesale eradication, and it is difficult at best for any government to succeed by persecution in suppressing for long a vigorous body of dissident opinion. The victims of persecution going to their deaths with fanatical and heroic enthusiasm for the new faith became martyrs who only added moral strength to the fervor of those who escaped. "The blood of the martyrs is the seed of the church." After each persecution the Church reformed her ranks and drew into her fold men dumbfounded by the courageous loyalty of those who had been put to death. "More than any other factor it [martyrdom] secured the ultimate triumph of the Church, for it rendered plain to all the fact that Christianity was the

The persecutions

[4] *Ibid.*, I, 79, quoting the author of Second Clement.

one remaining power in the world which could not be absorbed in the gigantic mechanism of the new servile state." [5]

Christianity had developed largely as an urban religion among those who labored and were "heavy laden," the "toiling, sweating masses of the ancient lowly," but it had also claimed large numbers from the urban middle classes and even some from the aristocracy. The great highway system of the Romans, the uniform public security, the widespread commerce, the prevalence of Latin in the west and Greek in the east had made possible an extraordinarily rapid growth of Christianity into far distant places. And yet, when the moment of official toleration finally came, the Christians probably did not number more than one-tenth of the total population of the empire. They were more firmly entrenched in the east than in the west, where the diffusion of Christianity lagged about a century behind its diffusion in the east. The edict of toleration came in 313, in the midst of the civil war following the abdication of Diocletian. It adopted the policy of the Cæsar Galerius in his edict of toleration of 311. The exact procedure in the promulgation of the edict is doubtful. It has been supposed that Constantine, in gratitude for his miraculous victory at the Milvian Bridge due to the intervention of the Christian God, granted toleration to the Christians in an edict published at Milan in 313. It seems rather that the co-emperors Constantine and Licinius at Milan together agreed upon a policy of toleration, which was put into effect by Licinius in an edict issued at Nicomedia and made general by Constantine when he became sole master of the state. At any rate, the fact that all the leading participants in this complicated struggle granted toleration one after the other makes it seem only too likely that they all were moved by political motives in an effort to rally the Christians to their support.

The edict of toleration

The new policy merely made Christianity one of the many legalized religions tolerated in the state. Certainly Constantine showed no undivided allegiance to it, and it was only on his deathbed that he was finally baptized into the Arian form of its faith, which previously he had chosen to regard as heretical. He saw clearly the futility of continued persecution and the expediency of toleration, his task being to reconcile the warring interests in the state and to utilize every possible source of strength and unity. He kept his official title as head of the old state religion, which preserved its official position, its temples, and its ceremonies, and he continued to be worshipped as the divine emperor. At his court bishops and priests of rival Christian sects mingled with

Constantine's attitude towards Christianity

[5] C. Dawson, *The Making of Europe*, p. 29.

pagan priests and pagan philosophers; the high offices of state were filled impartially by pagans and Christians. If he venerated the Star of Bethlehem, he honored also the "unconquerable Sun," which was stamped on his coins. As for his private life, the execution—not to say murder—of his own son and of his wife indicates that he was untouched by any spiritual influence of Christianity.

To the new faith Constantine granted special legal privileges such as were enjoyed by the pagan religions. Among the most important of these was that which provided that clergy "are altogether exempt from public obligations." This made it possible for the *curiales* to escape from their crushing burdens by entrance into the clergy. So great, in consequence, was "the ungodly rush for holy orders" that a subsequent law had to limit entrance into the clergy to lower social classes than the

Privileges to the Church

curiales. The Church was also permitted to receive legacies from the dying, a privilege which recognized its corporate existence. Under Constantine's sons (337–61) strict legislation against pagan sacrifice was passed. "Let superstition cease; let the madness of sacrifices be abolished." "It is our pleasure that in all places and in all cities the temples be henceforth closed, and, access having been forbidden to all, freedom to sin be denied the wicked. We will that all abstain from sacrifices; if any one should commit any such act, let him fall before the vengeance of the sword." [6] The persecution of paganism had now begun. Christianity, not satisfied with parity with other religions in the state, as indeed it could not logically be, was already displaying a fierce intolerance and looking toward the destruction of all its rivals.

The Emperor Julian

The years 361–63 marked the attempt of the philosopher-scholar-emperor Julian to relegate Christianity to oblivion and to resuscitate a dying paganism with the principles of Neo-Platonism. Julian was dubbed "the Apostate" by Christians, but he was no intolerant bigot. He saw in Christianity and the Christian Church elements of strength, such as its organized care of the poor and sick, which paganism could well imitate. But paganism could not now be resuscitated. The Christian Church met the threat to its existence by a more united stand. The next step, the actual proscription of the pagan cults, came with the emperors Gratian, Valentinian II, and Theodosius I towards the end of the fourth century. Gratian refused to assume the title of chief priest of the official Roman cult, as all previous emperors had done, and be-

The proscription of paganism

gan the confiscation of the property of the temples. The final proscription came from legislation of Theodosius in 392, although it cannot be said to have been strictly enforced. Pagan worship was henceforth to

[6] Ayer, *A Source Book for Ancient Church History*, p. 322.

be classed as treason. "If any one undertakes by way of sacrifice to slay a victim or to consult the smoking entrails, let him, as guilty of lese-majesty, receive the appropriate sentence." [7]

In 394 the last Olympian games were held. The systematic destruction of ancient sanctuaries in Syria and Egypt began. The Serapeum in Alexandria, which housed a library second only to the great Alexandrian library, was demolished and its manuscripts scattered or destroyed. Entrance into the temples was forbidden, their priests were driven out, and their doors closed. Destruction and plunder of pagan temples was a kind of pleasure in which fanatical mobs, led often enough by clergy and monks, were eager to participate. "He [John Chrysostom] got together some monks fired with divine zeal and despatched them armed with imperial edicts against the idols' shrines. . . . He persuaded certain faithful and wealthy women to make liberal contributions to pay the craftsmen and their assistants who were engaged in the work of destruction, pointing out to them how great would be the blessing their generosity would win. Thus the remaining shrines of the demons were utterly destroyed." [8] Such religious mob fury directed itself upon occasion against notable preservers of the pagan philosophic tradition, such as the learned Neo-Platonist of Alexandria, Hypatia, whom a Christian mob in Alexandria attacked. *Hypatia* "Dragging her from her carriage, they took her to the church called Cæsareum. There they completely stripped her and murdered her with tiles. When they had torn her in pieces, they took her mangled limbs to a place called Cinaron, where they burned them." [9] For about thirty years after Theodosius the war against paganism continued. Paganism as a distinct and separate religion may perhaps be said to have died, although, driven out of the cities, it found refuge in the countryside, where it lingered long—and whence, indeed, its very name is derived.[10]

In a very real sense, however, it never died at all. It was only trans- *Pagan in-* formed and absorbed into Christianity. It is this transformation, and *fluence on* the absorption of classical culture in its various manifestations into the *Christianity* very substance of Christianity which, perhaps more than anything else, explains why after its toleration Christianity swept on with such relentless force to become the undisputed heir of the whole complex of Mediterranean civilization. Christianity presents the paradox of a most exclusive and at the same time a most absorbent religion. It made no compromise on what it regarded as fundamentals, once it became quite

[7] *Ibid.*, p. 347.
[8] *Ibid.*, pp. 372–73.
[9] *Ibid.*, pp. 373–74.
[10] The Latin word *pagus* means a country district.

sure of what those fundamentals were. But in defending itself from what it regarded as contamination, it chose to use the very weapons of its enemies, by borrowing their strength. Jewish to begin with, it became in the process of time oriental, Greek, Roman, until at last it remained the sole embodiment of much that was best, and much that was not the best, in Græco-Roman civilization.

The chief enemies of Christianity

The more important enemies of Christianity were, specifically: first, the flourishing rival oriental cults; second, an enervated Græco-Roman polytheism; third, the classical systems of philosophy, chiefly Neo-Platonism; and, fourth, divisions within the ranks of the Christians themselves. In what particular ways, then, did Christianity overcome these particular enemies?

Christianity takes on features of an oriental mystery cult

The competing oriental mystery cults Christianity overcame by becoming itself an oriental mystery cult. This began to happen as soon as Christianity was preached beyond the confines of Judaism, in the Greek world of the eastern Mediterranean. The transformation is first marked in the Christianity of the apostle Paul. It was of course inevitable. The religious atmosphere of the Hellenistic world was permeated with the mystery cults. In preaching Christianity to these prospective converts a religious language had to be used which they could understand. The idea of a man-god-savior, come to relieve the world of its miseries, was already familiar to them. Jesus as a savior they could therefore understand; Jesus as a Jewish messiah could make little appeal. They were familiar with the idea of mystic unification with the hero of the cult, through definite ceremonial acts. Jesus as a new deity with a familiar history, with whom union was achieved by the sacramental rites of baptism and the Eucharist—ceremonies which non-Christian cults themselves possessed—was a fresh, original, and convincing figure. And, more important still, Jesus was believed, like many of the heroes of other cults, to have conquered death and gone to heaven. Identification and union with him through the ritualistic sacraments meant that the new initiate himself would share the same fate: he too would conquer death and become immortal, immortal in the spirit and, as some believed, resurrected in the flesh. While this transformation of Christianity was naturally slow, in its spread through the Roman empire it gradually freed itself from all necessary connection with Judaism and Jewish ceremonial law and became one of many religions of a similar type. Yet in the historical personality of Jesus and in the dogma of his special relationship as the son of a one and only God, Christianity had a decided advantage. It borrowed only what could be adapted to its own fundamental creed. It compromised only to satisfy the urgent religious needs of the great mass of men.

Pope Gregory the Great (590–604), in giving instructions to a group of monks about to set off to convert the pagan Saxons in England, said: "Remember that you must not interfere with any traditional belief or religious observance that can be harmonized with Christianity." Gregory was not here announcing a new policy of the Church; he was only commending an old and well-established practice. Yet in speaking of the relationship between Christianity and the oriental cults and Græco-Roman paganism one must be careful. Sometimes it is impossible to show that a given belief or practice was directly borrowed by Christianity. It is not always certain that it was not rather from Christianity that the other cults were borrowing; and there is always the further possibility that Christianity and the pagan cults developed in parallel fashion similar rites and practices, with little or no borrowing on either side. It does at any rate seem safe to say that the idea of Christianity as a cult in possession of powerful religious secrets, to which one was introduced only after initiation, derived from the mysteries. Such specialized priesthoods as that of Isis, with tonsure and white linen garb, certainly influenced the development of a special Christian priesthood. The highly formalized, symbolic, and mystic ritual centering about wonder-working sacramental rites likewise came in large part from the mysteries. Other specific examples of more or less certain borrowings are some features of hell, as it was finally elaborated in Christian dogma, the practice of sprinkling infants, the elevation of sacred objects in the course of the religious service, the procession of sacred images, the burning of incense, and the use of music.[11] The similarities between rites and beliefs of Mithraism and Christianity struck many ancient observers. Shepherds watched the wondrous birth of Mithras from a rock. Mithras ascended to heaven in the chariot of the Sun God. Mithraic initiates were bathed (baptized) in blood and made whiter than snow, and they were also confirmed. The use of Sunday instead of the Jewish and early Christian Sabbath as the sacred Lord's day was apparently derived from Mithraism. And certainly Christianity appropriated the date of the festival of the Sun God of Constantine's coins, December 25, as the date of the birth of Christ, whom indeed one Christian Father called the "New Sun."

In like manner Christianity overcame Græco-Roman polytheism by itself becoming in some degree polytheistic. Its polytheism consisted

Specific influences from oriental cults

Polytheism in Christianity

[11] For this paragraph see Laing, *Survivals of Roman Religion*.

in devotion to its martyrs and its ascetic heroes as saints. To be sure the theologians differentiated, and the Catholic Church still differentiates, between the worship of the Trinity and the veneration of saints; but it can hardly be supposed that the distinction ever was, or is now, carefully drawn by simple folk. The campaign in Romance countries today against excessive devotion to the saints, or often to the newest saint, to the neglect of God and Christ, reveals the difficulty that the Church has always had in making the distinction real. The common people of city and country among whom Christianity spread did not intend to be deprived of the many little services that their old gods had rendered them. Local Christian saints became endowed with the powers of local pagan gods. The aches and pains, the fears and hopes, that had formerly been cured or assuaged or satisfied by pagan gods were now taken care of by their Christian substitutes, whose special days of worship in some cases can be clearly shown to have been the days dedicated to their pagan predecessors. In some instances the Christian saints inherited the very temples of their predecessors. Many of the features of our celebration of the Christmas season—the giving of gifts, the burning of candles, the general high spirits and good feeling—came from the Roman Saturnalia, celebrated in the week following December 17. The Roman cult of the worship of ancestors was transferred to the saints; All Saints' Day (November 1) and All Souls' Day (November 2) perpetuate the Roman festival of the dead, the Parentalia. Corresponding to pagan mythology, a Christian mythology developed from the lives and miracles of the saints; indeed, miracles are absolutely essential for canonization. There developed also a special veneration of remains and relics of saints, which also had its pagan origin.

Nor did Christianity overlook the popular appeal of the great pagan goddesses, Venus, Diana, Magna Mater, and Isis. As its great goddess it adopted Mary, the Virgin Mother of Jesus. The Virgin acquired many of the titles that these pagan goddesses held. If Diana was "Queen of Heaven," the Virgin came to be "Queen of the Universe"; if Isis was the Powerful Goddess (*Dea Potens*), the Virgin was the Most Powerful Virgin (*Virgo Potentissima*). From the worship of Isis and her baby son Horus, it was a natural step to the worship of the Virgin and the Child Jesus. Their representations in art are so similar that it has even been claimed that actual representations of Isis and Horus were used as images of the Virgin and Child. The addition of the Virgin to the Christian cult was a wonderful human accommodation to the religious wants of great masses of people.

Many Roman practices of temple worship also influenced details of

Christian worship. When the students of the University of Paris line the walls of the Church of St. Genevieve with votive tablets to the patron saint of Paris or to the Virgin for having successfully brought them through their examinations, they are carrying on the Roman practice of setting up tablets in temples. Roman forms of prayer and adoration influenced Christian forms. One of the chief pagan influences on Christian belief and practice was the transformation of the ceremony preceding the actual sacrament of the Eucharist into a sacrifice at the altar. It came to be held by Christian theologians that in the ceremony of the Mass the priest was actually repeating the sacrifice of Christ on the cross. Every time that Mass was said the sacrifice of Christ to God for the sins of mankind was repeated. Christians, therefore, as well as pagans had the advantage of witnessing and profiting by a sacrifice which, if indeed very different in character from its archetype, was nevertheless just as real. Finally, the art of early Christianity was naturally greatly influenced by the symbolism and *motifs* of pagan art.

Pagan and Christian sacrifice

Against the attacks of the classical schools of philosophy Christianity defended itself by developing its own philosophy. This it was obliged to do unless it were to remain merely a religion for the unlettered, who demand only that a religion be comforting and are satisfied with simple explanations of deep mysteries, or with none at all. The Christian apologists who undertook the defense of Christianity against pagan attacks had to deal in the terms and methods of the attack. For the Greek intellectual of the cities of the eastern Mediterranean these could only be the terms and methods of Greek philosophy, especially of the Platonic school. That is, just as to the masses Christianity became a religion in many respects similar to their paganism, so to the educated classes Christian theology became a divine science similar in many respects to their philosophy. It was chiefly in the Greek east that this Christian theology developed, whence it was handed on to the west. In addition to the apologists, the men who in the beginning were chiefly responsible for giving an intellectual tone to Christianity and for defining its theological problems were Clement and his pupil Origen, who in the first half of the third century were heads of a theological school in Alexandria. For both these men Christianity was a superrational religion, whose fundamental tenets were to be accepted on faith. For the unsophisticated this simple faith was enough. But for a higher type of Christian, who saw into the deeper mysteries of the faith, things were not as they seemed, and the words of Scripture meant much more than they said. To get beyond the mere literal interpretation of the text into its hidden significance required all the talents of the logician trained in

Christianity and philosophy

Clement and Origen

Allegory

secular philosophy. The chief means, however, to the profounder and subtler interpretation was allegory, a time-honored device of those who would be easily and mystically wise, to whom the plain literal word is uncomfortable or embarrassing or inartistic, as indeed many passages in the Old Testament were to these men. The deeper meaning was the implied, not the expressed, meaning. The Christian philosopher was henceforth free to discover the real and authentic Christian truth behind the bare word of the text. Scripture was "a prolonged metaphor."

The Logos

Two examples of the application of terms of Greek philosophy to Christianity are to be seen in the identification of the Greek *Logos* with the person of Jesus, and the identification of the Greek philosophic god, a purely abstract idea, with the personal God of the Jew and the Christian. *Logos* is a word used in the vocabulary of Greek philosophy to mean simply the power of reason. It was used by the Stoics to indicate the divine forces present in the world, and by the Platonists for those beings or intermediate agents that connect the visible universe with the Platonic abstract god. In the fourth Gospel it is translated as "Word": "In the beginning was the Word, and the Word was with God, and the Word was God." Now the apologists, such as Justin Martyr in the second century, in order to give Christianity a philosophical tone and to give Jesus philosophical importance, identified him in his pre-earthly existence as Son of God with the philosophic *Logos*. The *Logos* itself was divine reason, begotten by God to be his agent in creating the world. From the divine *Logos* men have received whatever reason or truth they have. Moreover, the *Logos* became incarnate in the human figure of Jesus, the Son of God. It was in this conception of Jesus as the divine *Logos*, the Son of God, that Clement was chiefly interested; and the same is true of Origen, who calls Jesus not only *Logos* but also *Sophia* (wisdom), who as Son of God had no more beginning in time than God himself. This sort of thing is indeed a far cry from Jesus the Messiah or Jesus the hero of a mystery cult.

What Clement and Origen so ardently began was continued with unabated zeal century after century by the theologians of the east. It resulted inevitably in what was perhaps the greatest danger that ever threatened Christianity, a danger greater than any of its external foes —schism and heresy within its own ranks. The first of the great contro-

The Arian-Athanasian controversy

versies was begun early in the fourth century by two clerics of the church at Alexandria, the presbyter Arius and the bishop Athanasius. They drew not only the whole Eastern Church but even to some extent the Western Church into an argument that was prolonged for centuries. We have already seen that before the time of this controversy the theologians had identified with the *Logos* or divine reason the Son of God, who became incarnate in the person of Jesus. Now what was the relationship between God and this Son of God, the *Logos* that became Christ? Arius admitted that a *Logos* became incarnate in Christ, *The position of Arius* but he insisted that it was not the *Logos* which was the divinely begotten Son of God, not the divine reason, but a new, a separately created being, intermediary between God and man and possessed of a nature wholly different from God's. Arius was willing to call the *Logos* that did become incarnate in Jesus Christ the Son of God; but in insisting that its nature was not of God, but only from God, he denied to Jesus his complete union with God as the incarnation of a pre-existent *Logos*, a Son of God whose nature or essence was the very nature and essence of God. Jesus was thus denied a complete divinity, and God was preserved in all his isolated transcendence. Jesus simply was not God, but a wholly different creature, however unique. To Athanasius and his supporters all this seemed to deny the very fundamentals of Christianity as a mystic religion of salvation. Salvation man achieved by becoming one with the Savior, Jesus Christ, who was himself the incarnation of the *Logos*, the Son of God, begotten by God and of his very nature and essence. Jesus was deified by fusion with God; man was saved through oneness with the deified Jesus. Therefore Athanasius insisted that the *Logos* that became incarnate in Jesus was actually the divine *Logos*, the Son of God, of the very nature and substance of God the Father and no separate or subordinate creature. The *Logos* of Arius, then, was the most dangerous of heresies.

The issue was first decided at the first general council of the whole *The Council of Nicæa* Church ever called, the Council of Nicæa in 325. Here a statement of the orthodox position of the Church was agreed upon, which amounts to a complete victory for Athanasius. Nevertheless the controversy went on for another fifty years, with now an orthodox emperor at Constantinople exiling the Arian heretics and now a heretic emperor exiling the orthodox Athanasians. The issue was further complicated by the question of the relationship of the Holy Spirit to God the Father, some insisting that the Holy Spirit was a separately created being and not to be identified with the substance of the Father. A compromise formula was finally worked out by certain theologians of Cappadocia, who proposed the doctrine of the Trinity to explain the relationship between God the Father, Christ the Son, and the Holy Spirit. The Trinity was "one substance in three persons," "a common nature or substance or essence possessed by three individual things or persons." This became the accepted formula for both east and west, though it

The doctrine of the Trinity

was not always interpreted similarly. The final orthodox statement of the doctrine of the Trinity, the Nicene Creed of today, is commonly believed to be the work of the Council of Constantinople of 381. At any rate, a fixed statement was at length agreed upon. Ultimately, therefore, like Neo-Platonism and other pagan schools of philosophy, Christianity made use of the sacred number three. If the very abstruse dogma of the Trinity could not be understood, the theological formula that expressed it could at any rate be believed in as a mystical formula. Conversion to Arianism of the Germans who were by now pouring into the empire prolonged the controversy around the Trinity for centuries to come, with Arianism coming more and more to be regarded as a deadly infection in the body of the Church.

When the doctrine of the Trinity had at last been formally agreed upon, there still remained questions to be decided before Christianity could claim to possess a finished theology. For example, what was the

The controversy over the nature of Christ

nature of Jesus after the *Logos*, the Son of God, had become incarnate in him? What was left of his human nature? Did it disappear into the divine, so that Christ had but one theanthropic, divine-human nature, or did Christ so preserve his human nature that it remained uninfluenced by the incarnation of the divine, with the result that he had two separate natures, one divine and one human? This question followed logically upon the Council of Nicæa. The Alexandrian theologians insisted upon a single divine-human nature, for only by a completely deified Christ could man be assured of salvation. The first theologians to insist upon preserving intact Christ's human nature were those of Antioch, who wished to emphasize his supreme worth as an ethical being of heroic stature. Because this view was championed by Nestorius, Archbishop of Constantinople in the early fifth century, those who adhered to it came to be called Nestorians. Since, too, the sees of Alexandria and Constantinople were rivals for precedence, a good deal of political rivalry between them was involved in the dispute. A compro-

The Council of Chalcedon

mise formula was finally reached at the Council of Chalcedon, in 451, which made of Christ a complicated personality. "Jesus Christ, the same perfect in deity and perfect in humanity, God truly and man truly . . . of one substance with the Father in his deity and of one substance with us in his humanity . . . acknowledged in two natures without confusion, without change, without division, without separation; the distinction of the natures being by no means taken away because of the union, but rather the property of each nature being preserved and concurring in one person." [12]

[12] McGiffert, *op. cit.*, I, 285.

Although this compromise theory of Christ as one person with two natures became orthodox for both east and west, it did not wholly satisfy either party to the dispute. Those who insisted upon the theory of a single divine-human nature became a powerful sect, the Monophysites. They even organized churches of their own in Egypt, Palestine, Syria, and Armenia which still exist. Nestorian churches likewise still exist in Syria, Persia, and beyond. The whole east, indeed, continued passionately interested in theology. Nor was this interest confined to the rarefied intellectual plane of the logicians. Gregory of Nyssa says of Constantinople as early as the fourth century: "This city is full of mechanics and slaves who are all of them profound theologians and preach in the shops and the streets. If you want a man to change a piece of silver, he tells you in what way the Son differs from the Father; if you ask the price of a loaf of bread, you are told by way of reply that the Son is inferior to the Father; and if you inquire whether the bath is ready, the answer is that the Son was made of nothing."

The west was content to accept these theological definitions from the east. In fact, as we have seen in other respects, the westerner was less inclined to work out metaphysical puzzles than to consider the more utilitarian ethical and legal aspects of philosophy. In his mind also *The Romani-* Christianity was being worked over in his own fashion, until by the *zation of* end of the third century it had become well adapted to the Roman, or *Christianity* Latin, point of view. To be sure, from the very beginning Christianity could not escape from the legal implications of Judaism, with its lawgiving God, judging his chosen people according to their obedience to his law, and the interpretation of Christianity in this light always kept pace with the mystical interpretation.

But in the west, particularly in Tertullian in the second century and *Tertullian* Cyprian in the third, this interpretation found a typical Roman ex- *and Cyprian* pression. These two North Africans, Tertullian a priest at Carthage and Cyprian its bishop, together offer an eloquent contrast to the two Alexandrians, Arius and Athanasius. In fact Carthage was to Latin Christianity what Alexandria was to Greek Christianity. To these men, who stamped their ideas indelibly upon Latin Christianity, the Christian religion was essentially a legal and moral code given by God to his chosen people. God was no amalgamation of abstractions; he was a union of the absolute sovereign and the administrator of divine law, revealed by him to men. Christ his Son was his agent in revealing this law and his assistant in judging men by their obedience to it. Sin was nothing more than disobedience to the law. Such sin was guilt and therefore punishable. The original disobedience of Adam was the greatest sin, inherited by all his descendants, who were therefore all guilty, even before they had had an opportunity to commit sins of their own. Repentance and baptism freed the individual from previous guilt; hence baptism was to be postponed as long as possible to avoid punishment for sin committed after it. In Cyprian's mind there was only one subsequent chance to be cleansed: after public confession of sins and severe self-castigation. However, the rigor of his attitude was ultimately softened to meet the weakness of mortal flesh by the very human sacrament of penance. A code was suggested by Tertullian listing seven mortal sins and countless venial, more pardonable ones. Salvation, won by obedience to the divine code, meant freedom from punishment and the enjoyment of bliss commensurate with one's earthly merits. It is a grave Christ who still stares down from the apses of many of the oldest churches in the west, to remind his followers of the strict obedience due his law; while over many a church door the Last Judgment, carved in stone, does far more than merely suggest the dreadful consequences of disobedience.

Cutting across these main currents of development there were smaller but none the less dangerous eddies of heresy, within the Church or just outside of it, which at times even threatened to divert the whole stream. Among the more important of these were the sects of Gnostics, Montanists, Monarchians, Donatists, and Manicheans.

Gnosticism Gnosticism existed before Christianity, and also outside of Christianity during the Christian era; but it was the Gnostics who fitted Christianity into their general scheme of things who were looked upon by the Christians as especially dangerous, because of the remarkable similarity of their adaptation of religion and philosophy to the kind of adaptation that Christianity was making. The final difference was one mostly of emphasis. Gnosticism was in essence a mystic philosophy, which attempted to give to its mysticism an intellectual basis similar in general to Neo-Platonism. The world was a hopeless mixture of the material and spiritual, created by a demiurge. Man himself was a composite of matter and spirit, whose chief purpose it was to escape the material and find refuge in the spiritual being from which his spiritual nature had originally come. Christ was identified with a savior whom pre-Christian Gnosticism had conceived, although the prototype was a wholly spiritual being who never assumed human form. Union with Christ the Savior was the chief means of escape from the material; ascetic exercises were also of assistance to this end. The Gnostics severed all connection between Christianity and Judaism. The Jewish God they either rejected or identified with the creator of this impossible world, the demiurge. Likewise the Old Testament was either cast aside or associated only with the demiurge. Gnosticism, in brief, attempted to fit Christianity into a philosophy, whereas Christianity was adapting philosophy to religion.

Montanism, which, like Gnosticism, attained great strength in the second century, originated in Asia Minor. Its founder Montanus *Montanism* looked upon himself as a new prophet, the herald of a speedy second coming of Christ for which Christians must immediately prepare by gathering in one place. He was the first of a long line of such heralds of the imminent end of the world; his successors still appear frequently in our newspapers. The more serious significance of Montanism, however, lay in the fact that it constituted a protest against the constantly increasing formality in the ritual and organization of Christianity. As in the very early Church, the Holy Spirit working through the prophets by trances and visions was to announce the intention of God, a function disturbing to the constituted authorities of the Church. A spirit of extreme asceticism and a longing to win the crown of martyrdom as the highest good animated the Montanists in their return to the zeal of the early Church. It was this moral earnestness that won for them their most famous convert, Tertullian.

The Monarchian sect represented an extreme protest against the *The* treatment of Christ's personality made by the eastern theologians with *Monarchians* their complicated doctrines of the *Logos* and their elaborate attempts to work out a nice distinction between Father, Son, and Holy Spirit. They were fearful that philosophy with its complexities would destroy Christianity. For them the figure of Christ as supreme lord was enough. There was only one God, and Christ and the Holy Spirit were the same God as God the Father; they were merely made manifest in different ways. Obviously such a simple faith in Christ the Savior alone, held by many simple Christians, would be anathema to the theologians. Some Monarchians, on the other hand, known as Adoptionists, went so far as to insist that Christ was only an ordinary human being, but of such extraordinary perfection that at his baptism he was adopted by God as his Son and then given divine power. This view, entirely disregarding any *Logos* at all and aiming to preserve Christ as a human being of supreme value as a moral example, was, if possible, an even more dreadful heresy.

The Donatists were a group of rigorists named for one of their leaders, Donatus, Bishop of Carthage in the early fourth century. The *The* point at issue between them and the leaders of the Western Church *Donatists* was a point rather of discipline than of doctrine, narrowing down to the question whether the performance of the sacraments of the Church by priests of unworthy or improper personal life was valid. The issue was of great importance to the ordinary Christian, since the Church was coming to insist that sacraments such as baptism and the Eucharist were necessary to salvation; hence it was essential to be assured that the sacraments in which one participated were valid. The Donatists insisted that no valid sacrament could be performed by a priest of unworthy character—for example, one who had fallen away from Christianity during a time of persecution and later returned to the Church. They were opposed by men like St. Augustine, who insisted that the personal character of the officiant had nothing whatsoever to do with the efficacy of the sacrament. Sacraments were valid whenever performed strictly according to the prescribed ritual of the Church, by any priest of whatever character. This came to be the accepted teaching of the Church, and it was a very human attempt to remove any uncertainty from the minds of the faithful as to the validity of the ceremonies in which they participated.

The Manicheans

The Manicheans were followers of the prophet Mani, who began to preach his peculiar doctrines at Ctesiphon, in the valley of the Tigris and Euphrates, in 242. The spread of Manicheism throughout the Roman empire is further evidence of the orientalization of western culture; and indeed it may well be that it, rather than Mithraism, was the most formidable rival of Christianity in the third and fourth centuries. Fear of this rival is perhaps the explanation of the readiness with which the Church came to brand any distantly similar heresy as Manichean. The fact that, although bitterly persecuted everywhere it spread, it held for nine years the allegiance of the greatest of the Latin Church Fathers, St. Augustine, is some indication of its subtle appeal.

Manicheism offers a most pessimistic interpretation of this sorry and hopeless world of matter. The sooner the world is destroyed, the better —which, indeed, was the early Christian view. To perpetuate the human race is only to perpetuate evil. The earth was created out of the excrement of emissaries of the awful King of the Realm of Dark. Adam and Eve were likewise his creations. In fact, the whole history of the universe was interpreted as a struggle between the forces of Dark, which represent the evil, disorderly, material elements in life, and the forces of Light, which represent the good, peaceful, intelligent, spiritual elements. Fortunately, in the creation of Adam and Eve there were some light particles unavoidably included. These and the light particles in the earth shall be gradually separated from the evil dark matter by the children of Light. When once all Light is separated from the Dark, evil will therewith cease. Light joins Light in the realm of Light, presided over by the Father of Light, and matter is consigned to the kingdom of the Dark. Jesus in essence is wholly of Light, a divine being not born of woman nor actually crucified. He it was who first awoke Adam to an appreciation of the irreconcilable mixture that he was. "Jesus made him stand upright and taste of the Tree of Life. Then Adam looked up and wept, he lifted up his voice like a roaring lion, he tore his hair and beat his breast and said, 'Woe, woe to the creator of my body! Woe to him who has bound my soul to it, and to the rebels who have brought me to servitude.' " [13] Thus Manicheism, being fundamentally a dualistic religion, seems to be a form of Christianity. It attempted to incorporate some elements of Persian philosophy as well as some of Gnosticism. Its organization, too, it seems to have borrowed from the sect, somewhat akin to the Gnostics, of a certain Marcion, a rebel Christian of the second century, who set up his own church in Mesopotamia. The wandering Manichean clergy, the Elect, who eschewed marriage and property, were greater concentrations of light particles than the ordinary Manichean laymen, the Hearers, who supplied the Elect with their means of subsistence. Driven underground by severe persecution, Manicheism appeared in the course of later centuries in various forms not always identifiable with, but certainly influenced by, the original teachings of Mani—for example, in the doctrines of the Bogomiles of Bulgaria and the Cathari or Albigensians of southern France.

[13] Burkitt, *The Religion of the Manichees*, pp. 31–32.

Chapter 3

THE CHRISTIAN CONQUEST OF THE ROMAN EMPIRE

THE DEVELOPMENT OF CHURCH ORGANIZATION.
MONASTICISM. THE LATIN CHURCH FATHERS

The necessity for the organization of a church

TO WARD off the danger of dissolving into small warring sects, to assist in the battle against classical paganism, to protect itself in the face of official hostility and popular suspicion, to give succor to its followers in their isolation from the body of Roman society, to care for its poor, to instruct its neophytes and to administer its services, Christianity had perforce to perfect an organization. This it did with speed and skill, under the influence to some extent of the Jewish synagogue and pagan religious associations, but mostly under the influence of the political organization of the Roman state. So thoroughly was this enormous labor of organization accomplished that the Christian Church survived all the disorders that wrecked the empire in the west. Not only that, but it gathered unto itself the wreckage, preserved it, took over many of the functions of the state, brought the Germans within its organization, and became the chief stabilizing and civilizing influence in Europe. It is no exaggeration to say that the Christian Church in the west practically superseded the Roman state and became the one healthy living organism capable of survival and growth.

Early organization

This organized Church grew out of a real and desperate need. The magnificent conception of a catholic church bound together in one organization, one faith, one ritual could hardly have been realized by imagination alone, without the aid of time and circumstances. At first the many scattered, self-governing churches, held together only by wandering missionary apostles, were directed by local prophets possessing the gift of the Holy Spirit. Gradually within each of the independent churches there emerged local officers with Greek names:

the *presbyteros* or elder, the *episkopos* or overseer, and the *diakonos* or server. These names came to indicate specific ecclesiastical rank—priest, bishop, deacon—when, under the influence of pagan mystery cults, the distinction between laity and clergy began to appear.

The most important step in the early development of the Church was the establishment in every important city of the supreme local power of one bishop, who may be called the monarchical bishop. He outranked the other bishops, the presbyters, the deacons and the other *The* lesser officials such as acolytes, exorcists, and readers, who increased *monarchical* in number as the churches increased in size. In the whole history of *bishop* the Church, in fact, the bishop is the most important figure. As early as the beginning of the second century Bishop Ignatius of Antioch almost identified the Church with the bishop, making salvation dependent upon fellowship with the bishop. "We ought to regard the bishop as the Lord himself. It is good to know God and the bishop. He that honoureth the bishop is honoured of God. As many as are of God and of Jesus Christ are with the bishop. . . . The Spirit preached, saying, 'Do nothing without the bishop.' " In all the chief cities of the Roman provinces there arose the monarchical bishop. His diocese, a term borrowed from the civil diocese of the Roman government, approximated the smallest unit of Roman government, the *civitas*. When in the third and fourth centuries the diocese began to be further subdivided into rural parishes, no new bishops were created for the new churches, but the dignity of the bishop was heightened by assigning parishes to the subordinate grade of the priesthood. The bishop, practically unlimited in his ecclesiastical power, sat upon a throne, the *kathedra*, surrounded by a graduated hierarchy of lesser clergy, his counsellors and deputies in administration, who assisted him also in the services of the church. In the course of the fourth and fifth centuries the state granted him important judicial powers, not only in the administration of Church law and over the clergy but also in the settlement of civil disputes among the laity. Like a Roman judge of old, he tried suits and imposed penalties and executed judgments. He maintained the state of a prince, with a retinue of officials and servants. At first the rival of the provincial governor, he gradually supplanted him in influence. It was around the bishop and his church that the life of the waning Roman city came to center, while in the new German kingdoms of the west he was almost from the beginning the chief holder of authority.

It was the bishop also who became the chief means of fighting heresy in the Church. In order to combat what was generally felt to

*Irenæus and
the doctrine
of apostolic
succession*

be dangerous opinion, however, it was necessary to fix a norm of belief, to establish definitely what was the Christian belief and what was not—to determine what was orthodox and what heterodox. Irenæus, a bishop of Lyons in the latter part of the second century, perhaps contributed most to the solution of this problem. As the standard of belief he laid down the teachings of the twelve apostles and St. Paul, and established a canon of writings which he considered to be of apostolic origin. Since, however, there was great variety in the interpretation of these apostolic writings, it was necessary also to determine the one correct interpretation, the one true tradition. Irenæus held that the true interpreters of apostolic writings were the bishops, who were the successors by appointment of the apostles in the governance of the Church. Every episcopal church could trace its ancestry back to a foundation either by an apostle himself or by some agent appointed by an apostle. "We are able to enumerate those whom the apostles appointed bishops in the churches and to trace their succession down to our own time." [1] Through the apostles the bishops were therefore the direct spiritual descendants of Christ, who was thus made the founder of the Church. They were bishops by divine right, not mere products of the historical development of the Church. Who, then, could be better qualified to pronounce on the authenticity of the apostolic tradition than they, the very successors of the apostles? This doctrine of apostolic succession was a perfect solution for the vexing question of authority. It resided in the bishops. Who were declared heretics by the bishops were heretics; what was declared orthodox by the bishops was orthodox.

*Church
councils*

But the bishops themselves often could not agree as to the orthodox tradition. It was therefore necessary for them to meet in councils, to resolve their differences and reach some conclusion or compromise as to what was to be regarded as apostolic truth. At first these episcopal councils were provincial or regional. The Council of Nicæa, convoked by the Emperor Constantine in 325, was the first attempt to gather all the bishops in a universal council. Ecumenical councils henceforth determined orthodoxy, which then came to be the law of the Church. By the first century this canon law was already being reduced to codes. Thus the councils, local or general, became a fixed and necessary part of the machinery of the Church. They are interesting, moreover, as an early experiment in a kind of representative government. But could even these councils always reach a successful compromise? Was there no need of a still higher authority in the

[1] A. C. McGiffert, *A History of Christian Thought*, I, 160.

Church? Before we can answer those questions we must know more about the next step in the development of the hierarchy of the Church, that is, distinction in rank among the bishops themselves.

The growth of a hierarchy within the ranks of the bishops was the work mainly of the fourth and fifth centuries. With the acceptance of the doctrine of apostolic succession, inevitably the bishops of the oldest churches came to be regarded with especial reverence. And with local *The develop-* and provincial councils becoming more frequent, it was only natural *ment of an* that bishops of the larger cities, which had greater political and *ecclesiastical* economic importance, acquired superior authority. As early as the *hierarchy* Council of Nicæa the dignity of the metropolitan bishop, much later called the archbishop, was recognized and his consent required in choosing an ordinary bishop. His sphere of superior jurisdiction, his province, approximated the civil province. Moreover, by the end of the fourth century an attempt was made to create a larger unit, the exarchate, which corresponded to the civil diocese of the empire governed by a vicar—a term borrowed by the Church. At any rate, within the ranks of the metropolitans the higher dignity of patriarch arose. These were the bishops of the oldest and largest Christian communities, such as Alexandria, Rome, Antioch, and, for political reasons, Constantinople.

Thus by the fifth century the Church had an organization much like that of the state. The citizens of the city were now citizens of the Church. The magistrates of the city had their parallel in the chief local ecclesiastical clergy. The bishop's diocese was usually the territory of the *civitas*. Corresponding to the Roman provincial governor was the metropolitan bishop; corresponding to the vicar of the civil diocese was the patriarch. Almost as if from internal logic there slowly emerged, corresponding in his dominating position to the Roman emperor in the west, an ecclesiastical head at Rome, the pope (likewise, less slowly, in the east the Patriarch of Constantinople, who, however, was hardly more than the docile creature of the eastern emperor). The perfection of this organization gave to the Church a strength and unity, a catholicity, which a common belief alone could not give. Indeed, one might almost say that to a large extent the Church supplanted Christianity. As the monarchical Church took form, general councils after the fifth century gradually lost their importance; they had by then done their most important work in establishing the fundamentals of belief. The Church's next task was to preserve this dogma and to enforce it, a feat most easily accomplished by a hierarchy centralized under one supreme head.

The Bishop of Rome possessed all the advantages that gave pre-dominance to all the oldest episcopal churches. The fact that he was the sole prelate in the west who could claim this distinction gave him a unique advantage in his rise to primacy among, and finally to su-premacy over, the bishops of the other Latin churches. Until the founding of Constantinople the Roman Church reflected all the pres-tige of the capital of the empire. Henceforth, although it had to combat the rivalry of Constantinople, nevertheless, because of the belief that the Roman bishopric was the foundation of the apostle Peter (whose throne and tomb were in its church) and that the apostle Paul had visited the city and had been martyred near one of its gates, the Roman bishops continued to acquire increasing prestige. In the second century Irenæus had already written of the Roman Church: "With this church, on account of its more powerful leader-ship [*potiorem principalitatem*], every church, that is, the faithful who are from everywhere, must needs agree; since in it that tradition which is from the apostles has always been preserved by those who are from everywhere." [2] The fact that it was the largest and wealth-iest church in the west, that it was generous to needy churches, and that its opinion was generally conservative and popular tended to con-firm the peculiar authority with which the belief in its foundation by two apostles endowed it.

The primacy of the Bishop of Rome in the west

The Roman bishops, however, wanted something more than a position of superior dignity or primacy, something more than metro-politan and patriarchal rank, which made them only the equals of other metropolitans and patriarchs. They wished to rule the Church as its supreme head, and to be recognized as such by the whole Church. This was to substitute a new conception of the unity of the Church—unity in agreement with Rome—for the older conception of unity based on agreement among bishops who were all equal in rank as the divinely appointed successors of the apostles. Such a claim to primacy was therefore long regarded as effrontery by other bishops; it was never really accepted by the Eastern Church and only gradu-ally came to be accepted in the west.

Roman ambi-tion for su-premacy over the whole Church

From the third century on the bishops of Rome rested their claim to supremacy on the Petrine theory, based largely upon those im-pressive words of Christ recorded in Matthew xvi, 18–19: "Thou art Peter, and upon this rock I will build my church; and the gates of hell shall not prevail against it. And I will give unto thee the keys of the kingdom of heaven; and whatsoever thou shalt bind on earth

The Petrine theory

[2] Ayer, *A Source Book of Ancient Church History*, p. 113.

shall be bound in heaven; and whatsoever thou shalt loose on earth shall be loosed in heaven." From these verses and others in the Gospels it was argued that Peter was appointed by Christ to be his chief agent and successor, the ruler of his Church, with power unlimited on earth and in heaven. It was commonly accepted that Peter founded the bishopric of Rome; therefore the bishops of Rome succeeded to his position as chief of the apostles and were through him the successors of Christ and the rulers of the Church. The syllogism was complete and perfect.

On the face of it this appears to be a simple and powerful argument, and so it proved to be. It "is the fundamental basis of the whole papal structure." [3] To the critical there are difficulties in the way of accepting this particular interpretation of the original scriptural texts, the tradition that Peter founded the Roman Church, and the implications of the doctrine of apostolic succesion. The Catholic Church today insists that even if these matters could not be established as historical facts, they are at least to be accepted as dogmatic facts—that is, accepted on faith and on its authority.

By the fifth century the Roman doctrine had swept the west, though not without protest. The recognition by the western Council of Sardica, in 343 or 344, of the right of appeal from the decisions of local provincial councils to the Bishop of Rome materially strengthened the claims of Rome to act as supreme judge of the Church. Requests to Rome for opinions on disputed questions soon led to the assertion that what the Roman bishop declared to be the law of the Church was indeed such. Late in the fourth century Pope Siricius, in the earliest authentic papal decretal extant, says: "No priest of the Lord is free to ignore the statutes of the Apostolic See and the venerable definitions of the canons . . . they should remain inviolate." [4] In the first important collection of canon law, made early in the sixth century, the decisions of Church councils and the decretal letters of the popes from Siricius on were given much the same authority and the Bishop of Rome's decisions upon appeals made as valid as a council's.

The right of appeal to Rome

The first papal decretals

The Eastern Church struggled against the ascendancy of the Bishop of Rome. It had its own contenders for the honor of primacy in the patriarchs of Alexandria and Constantinople. Rome's policy was to ally itself with whichever of these patriarchs at the moment seemed weaker. It supported Alexandria against Constantinople until the

The opposition of the Eastern Church

[3] Shotwell and Loomis, *The See of Peter*, p. xxiii.
[4] Ayer, *op. cit.*, pp. 416–17.

middle of the fifth century, when it reversed its policy to support Constantinople and the eastern emperor against the growing strength of Alexandria. The Council of Chalcedon in 451 acknowledged the privileged position of Rome, but under imperial auspices also raised Constantinople to the same rank, and in the east even made Constantinople supreme.

Pope Leo I

The legates of Pope Leo I (440–61) protested against the passage of this canon in their absence; the pope refused to accept it, and the Roman Church never has accepted it. Leo I, the first great pope, held to an interpretation of the sixth canon of the Council of Nicæa, stating that "the Church of Rome always has possessed primacy." In a sense Leo completed the first phase of papal development: Rome's spiritual supremacy, based on the Petrine theory, was generally recognized throughout the west. It was he who first gave strong expression to that papal mysticism which unites the popes to the person of Peter, and attributes whatever they do or say to the Prince of the Apostles. "If anything is rightly done or rightly decreed by us, if anything is obtained from the mercy of God by daily supplications, it is his [Peter's] work and merits, whose power lives in his see and whose authority excels." [5] With Leo I, now that spiritual supremacy was established, began also the development towards temporal power and ultimately temporal supremacy. In 455 Valentinian III, emperor in the west, issued an edict making all western bishops subject to the pope, and commanded all imperial officials to compel the bishops to obedience. The popes were indeed moving into the palace of the emperors.

Christianity becomes a monopoly

With the perfection of the organization of the Church in the fourth and fifth centuries, the main features of the transformation of Christianity were complete: it had developed into a universal religion, embodying important features of the oriental mystery cults; it had developed and systematized a theology; it had grown into an organized body, controlled by a specialized clergy administering ritualized sacraments and services. As early as Cyprian it had been asserted that outside this Church there was no possibility of salvation. So intolerant had Christianity become that a man like St. Augustine was willing to have the force of the state used to crush heretics, in his case the Donatists. His attitude is logical from one point of view, no matter how distasteful to enlightened modern opinion: "Heresy is a crime more atrocious than forgery or murder. If a heretic dies in sin,

[5] *Ibid.*, pp. 477–78.

and if you might have saved him by using force, will not your tolerance be actual hatred? It is better to save with harshness than to destroy with gentleness." Christianity had become, in fact, a religious monopoly.

When Christianity became officially tolerated, then favored, and finally enforced, large numbers came into the Church for not very religious motives. Legislation that forced the people to embrace *Undesirable* Christianity naturally did not make sincere converts, and the dra- *elements in* gooning of converts by bishops brought many into the Church who *the Church* were unlikely to benefit it or be benefited by it. By this time Christianity was so strong that discontent, such as had been expressed in earlier times in heretical teachings, could be openly voiced by the most orthodox. Thus we find St. Basil complaining: "The laws of the church are in confusion, the ambition of men who have no fear of God rushes into high posts, and exalted office is now publicly known as the prize of impiety. The result is that the harder a man swears, the fitter men think him to be a bishop." [6]

With its position officially established, the Church quickly became a wealthy institution, surpassing as a landowner the great senatorial aristocracy of the later Roman empire. It too had its "patrimonies scattered all over the world," peopled by slaves and serfs whose labor contributed to its ever increasing riches. The emperors donated lavishly to the Church from the imperial treasury and private endowments poured in upon it. Some of this wealth was employed to care *Growing* for the poor and the sick, to maintain the clergy, and to build new *wealth and* churches. But there were complaints that churches were too grand: *display of* "Many build churches nowadays, their walls and pillars of glowing *the Church* marble, their ceilings glittering with gold, their altars studded with jewels. Yet to the choice of Christ's ministers no heed is paid." On the other hand, "it becomes the priest especially to adorn the temple of God with fitting splendor, so that the court of the Lord may be made glorious." [7] Wealth and display, however, were not in the spirit of the early Church, and they widened the gap between clergy and people. The changed attitude of the Church in condoning serfdom and slavery marked an acceptance of the ancient Roman social system. As early as the late fourth century Roman law had to prohibit legacy-hunting by the clergy. St. Jerome gives a deservedly familiar description of a certain type of Roman cleric:

[6] J. W. Thompson, *Economic and Social History of the Middle Ages (300–1300)*, p. 81.
[7] Jerome and Ambrose, in *ibid.*, p. 69.

"I speak of men of mine own [priestly] order, who covet the priesthood or diaconate only that they may have the more liberty to see women. All their care is for their clothing, their scents and odours, the close and even fitting of their shoes. The curling-iron has left its traces in their crisped locks; their fingers flash with rings, and they scarce venture to go a-tiptoe lest the puddles in the street should soil their feet. To see such men as these, you would deem them rather bridegrooms than clerics. Some spend the whole care of their lives in learning the names and houses and manners of the matrons."

Of "one man, the chief of this art," Jerome continues:

"If he sees a cushion or a tablecloth that takes his fancy, or any other household furniture, he praises, admires, handles it with his hands, complains that he lacks just such an one as this, and at last rather extorts than obtains it as a gift; for there is no woman that dares to offend the man who bears all the tittle-tattle of the town. This man is no friend of chastity or fasting; he judges his dinner by its savouries, and his general nickname is *The Fatted Fowl*, or *Puffing Billy*. . . . Whatever news be spread abroad, it was he who made or exaggerated the report. He changes his horses hourly; they are so sleek and fierce that you would take him for the blood-brother of Diomede." [8]

The rise of monasticism

These criticisms came from men who would abandon the kind of formalized religion that Christianity had become for many people; would abandon the Christian Church that had made its peace with Roman society; would indeed abandon that society altogether and seek salvation far away from the crowd, in the solitude of desert, swamp, forest, or mountain fastness. Certainly the rise and spread and popularity of monasticism can in part be explained as a protest against the change that had come over Christianity since its early days, a revolt against the semi-pagan, semi-Christian life of the Roman empire in the fourth century. The sharp contrast between the simple religion and simple life of the New Testament and the rigid theology and worldly life of the carefully graded and regimented clergy, not to mention the licentiousness of the world outside the Church, dismayed more sensitive souls, who fled to the desert to escape the temptations of the world and to find peace in solitude. Renunciation of property, home, and kindred became a new mode of self-sacrifice and

[8] G. G. Coulton, *Life in the Middle Ages*, IV, 16–17.

religious expression; poverty and austerity bestowed sanctity; hardship and loneliness could make amends for sin; mortification of the flesh ministered to the spiritual life. In this sense monasticism can be regarded as another reform movement, harking back to the earlier *The monastic* other-worldly ideals of Christianity. In place of the earlier martyrs *ideal* the hermit and the monk became the heroes of the Faith, the perfect embodiment of Christian attributes, and such they remained for a thousand years.

Even so, the ascetic ideal that so stirred the Christian world in the third and fourth centuries is not to be explained solely as a reaction to conditions within or without the Church. Asceticism seems to be natural to civilized man. It has become institutionalized in many re- *Universality* ligions besides Christianity. In pagan religion and pagan thought *of asceticism* there was an increasingly strong ascetic strain, so that it is by no means impossible that Christian asceticism was influenced by that of other religious and philosophic systems. Moreover, escape from the world offered an opportunity to put mysticism into practice, to win one's way to God through contemplation, which has already been noted as an element recurring in all popular religions and in much of the philosophical thought of the later Roman world.

Like almost all else in Christianity, the ascetic ideal originated in *Eastern origin* the east, whence it spread westward. It made its appearance in the *of monachism* third century in Egypt, and became general in the east in the fourth century. In the west it was only sporadic in the fifth, and not general until the sixth century. The asceticism of the early Christians had taken the simple form of prolonged prayer and fasting and, for women, of the cultivation of chastity. But in Egypt in the third century it became popular for the hermit, or anchorite, to separate himself from his environment, or even to abandon civilized society alto- *The hermits* gether, as did St. Anthony, the earliest of Christian anchorites of whom we have knowledge. It is difficult to sympathize with their mode of existence, yet to fail to do so is to fail to understand the attitude of twelve later centuries on the question of the highest Christian virtues. Their extreme form of anchoritism seems a kind of religious hysteria, even mania. To a world that idealizes its plumbing fixtures, a world that looks upon poverty with suspicion, their excessive austerities—dwelling with vermin and sitting amid filth, eating revolting food or starving for days—their tendency to glorify ignorance, their confounding of sensuousness with sensuality, their "counting beauty an enemy to holiness"—all this seems far removed from any sensible standard of values. Their competitive asceticism,

which made Macarius, "if he ever heard of any one having performed a work of asceticism, be all on fire to do the same," [9] we are
inclined to smile at as a form of exhibitionism. The bouts with the
devil or with demons, resulting in the inevitable victory of the saintly
recluse, even St. Jerome, himself an arch-champion of the monastic
life, castigated as "designed to magnify their heroes in the eyes of
the world and before all to extort money from it." [10]

But the victories of this fierce piety were sweet to the winners. St.
Jerome relates how, after terrific buffetings of the flesh for daring
to dwell in thought on the "fleshpots of Rome" and the enticements
of feminine companionship: "I would oftentimes plunge alone into
the desert. Wheresoever I could find hollow valleys, steep mountains,
beetling precipices, there I chose my place for prayer and there I punished my wretched flesh with labour; until (the Lord Himself is my
witness!) after many tears, after the straining of eyes to heaven, I
seemed at times to be among the angelic host, and sang in joyful
jubilation: 'We run after thee in the savour of thy good ointment.' " [11]

Once having made his appearance in lower Egypt, the hermit was
henceforth never to disappear completely from the scene. In Palestine and Syria such extreme types appeared as grazing saints, who
St. Simeon
Stylites
lived on herbs, and pillar saints. St. Simeon Stylites, who schooled
himself by wearing a spiked girdle in a dark cave and by spending
one summer as a rooted vegetable in a garden, began his career as a
pillar saint near Antioch in 423; he gradually raised himself to a
height of sixty feet above the ground, and spent thirty years on top
of his pillar. But the life of the anchorite was too hard for the ordinary ascetic, and even St. Anthony was obliged to give the hermits
who collected about him in great numbers an opportunity to enter
into some form of group life.

A return towards reason began in the fourth century, with the substitution of cenobitic or common group life in a monastery, under a
prescribed set of regulations, for the earlier form of hermit life.
Pachomius
and the
cenobitic life
This was begun by St. Pachomius near Thebes in southern Egypt in
the first half of the fourth century. He seems to have been a native
of lower Egypt, born of rich pagan parents, and is said to have been
a soldier in the army of Constantine. After his conversion he retired
to the desert to live the life of an anchorite. But he was soon disillusioned; he realized that men are social animals, and that, like

[9] Butler, *Benedictine Monachism*, pp. 13–14.
[10] Hannah, *Christian Monasticism*, p. 64.
[11] Coulton, *op. cit.*, IV, 7–8.

solitary imprisonment, the anchorites' life made them mad. Accordingly, in about 340 Pachomius retired with a few disciples to the island of Tabenna in the Nile, where he built a *koinobion*, or common establishment, in which cells are said to have been arranged after the plan of a Roman camp. He instituted a series of regulations, imitating the organization and discipline of the Roman legions, and enjoining absolute obedience, silence, manual labor, and religious exercises. Thus cloistered monastic group life supplanted and, by its rational system, eliminated the gravest abuses of anchoritism. According to Palladius, a contemporary historian who visited Egypt about 390, there were fourteen hundred monks in Tabenna and seven thousand in subsidiary houses.

Monachism, in its monastic or cenobitic form, as well as in its anchorite or eremitical form, soon spread from Egypt into the remaining provinces of the east. The work begun by St. Pachomius was continued in the fourth century by St. Basil, Bishop of Neo-Cæsarea in Cappadocia, who drew up a set of rules for his colony of monks. St. Basil was a rare combination of idealism and practicality. For the complete isolation of the anchorite he substituted monastic life; he abandoned the desert and established his communities near, though not in, towns. He suppressed self-flogging and degrading maceration of the flesh; the body was to be disciplined by work, not abused until it was incapable of work. The manual labor substituted for ascetic mortification was calculated to make the monasteries not only self-supporting but able to succor the poor and afflicted. Religious meditation was encouraged, as a complementary part of an active, vigorous life, but must offer no pretext for idleness. Monastic works were to be practical—farming, gardening, weaving, leather- and wood-working, stone-cutting, and building. The possession of personal property, except clothing, was forbidden. The monk's clothes were to be the garments of simplicity, humility, and poverty; his food was to be nourishing but not rich. Silence was strictly enjoined, except during open hours. Ribaldry was forbidden, but light laughter was the sign of a serene and happy heart. The Basilian rule became the standard for all eastern, and later for Slavic, monasteries, and so has remained unchanged to this day.

Monachism of the anchorite type was introduced into Italy by the great Athanasius,[12] friend of St. Anthony, during the second of the many exiles that he suffered in the course of his conflict with his Arian enemies. It met with an enthusiastic reception, and the life of

Spread of Egyptian monachism in the east

The Basilian rule

Spread of eastern monachism to the west

[12] See p. 38.

St. Anthony was translated into Latin. But from the beginning the Roman west, as we should have expected, showed rather more interest in the organized type of monastic life than in that of the solitary anchorite. St. Jerome translated the rule of St. Pachomius, and a Latin abridgment of St. Basil's rule was also made. As early as 410 St. John Cassian, who had lived in the Thebaid, founded the monastery of St. Victor at Marseilles, for which—and for the older monastery of Lérins on an island not far from Marseilles—he drew up his *Institutes* and *Collations*, monastic rules which had considerable early influence in the west.

St. Martin of Tours

The earliest real hero of western monasticism, however, had little influence upon the organization of monastic institutions. St. Martin, Bishop of Tours in the fourth century, founded near Tours the monastery of Marmoutier, which housed some eighty of his followers, many of whom carved out cells for themselves in the cliff of a hill overlooking the Loire. Most of St. Martin's life was spent in fighting the paganism that survived in Gaul, principally in the rural areas. Against the votaries of dying gods and goddesses among the country folk he instigated veritable crusades, importuning the peasants, invading cottages, destroying ancestral household gods, and demolishing rural fanes and the temples still standing in the towns. This "evangelization of the fields" was no peaceful missionary movement but a genuine invasion. Paganism shrank away into the depths of the forests and the moors, where in a fragmentary way its beliefs and practices persisted for centuries and became part of folk-lore and popular superstition. The life of St. Martin, written by Sulpicius Severus, was, like that of St. Anthony, widely read in Gaul, Italy, and Illyria and found its way even to the hermits in the deserts of Egypt and Cyrene. It contained all the tales of wonder and miracle that rapidly clustered around St. Martin's name, and it was for centuries the model for saints' biographies. The incident of his sharing his cloak with Christ disguised as a beggar became one of the best loved of all saints' legends.

Other western innovators

Here, then, at the very beginning, western monasticism produced its own typical hero in the man of action, "the soldier of the Cross." Another western innovation of great historical significance was due to St. Martin's contemporary, Bishop Eusebius of Vercelli, who forced the clergy attached to his cathedral to live according to rule. When he was followed in this practice by St. Augustine at Hippo, an important precedent was set. Hitherto all monks, not to say all hermits, had been laymen; henceforth a gradually larger proportion of monks became clergy. The west was subject, therefore, no less to the influence of its own monastic pioneers than to that of eastern monachism. So far as concerns the anchorite, neither the eastern climate nor western social and political conditions offered him much encouragement.

The early interest in organization and regulation was not successfully followed up. Before the end of the fourth century there were numerous establishments of monks in Rome and throughout Italy, but these monastic houses, if indeed they deserve to be called such, adopted what rules and regulations they pleased, which must frequently have amounted to none at all. The result was that the new movement fell into an early decay in the west. Fake monks issued from fake monasteries to roam freely to and fro and up and down the country. St. Jerome complained of a certain type of monk in Italy that "in them all is affectation; loose-sleeved, slipshod, coarsely clad, sighing and groaning, they visit virgins and backbite the clergy; and, whensoever a great festival is held, they eat and drink till they vomit." [13] Nor did St. Augustine spare the monks of North Africa, who were "so many hypocrites under the garb of monks, strolling about the provinces, nowhere sent, nowhere fixed . . . some hawking about limbs of martyrs, if indeed of martyrs . . . and all asking, all exacting, either the cost of their lucrative want, or the price of their pretended sanctity." [14] Obviously every kind of person, through every sort of motive, sordid and mean as well as fine and noble, was entering the monasteries.

Early degeneration of western monachism

Moreover, in spite of the enthusiasm of great churchmen like St. John Chrysostom, St. Ambrose, St. Jerome, and St. Augustine, who were no less eager to praise the good majority of monks than to blame the bad minority, monasticism in a number of ways was proving a disintegrating force in society. The Synod of Gangra in 362 justly complained of the break-up and impoverishment of families wrought by the movement, while the government, alarmed over the number of men withdrawn from shops and crafts, legislated to prevent men from evading military service by becoming monks. The monks were also far more fanatical than the secular clergy, and sometimes incited the populace to violence and riot against heretics and pagans. For the regulation that it needed to adapt it to the conditions of western life, western monasticism had to wait until the sixth century for St. Benedict.

The lives and works of the three greatest Latin Fathers of the

[13] Coulton, *op. cit.*, IV, 28.
[14] *Ibid.*, p. 37.

Church, Jerome (340–420), Ambrose (374–97), and Augustine (354–430), are all typical of the conflict between the old pagan tradition in literature and thought and the new victorious Christianity. With them the absorption of paganism by Christianity is so complete that not for a thousand years—not until the fourteenth and fifteenth centuries—could the literature and learning of the ancient world free itself from Christianity. The conflict came out in Jerome in a characteristically Christian fashion. Even as a hermit, Jerome says, he could not bear to give up his library; Cicero was sweet balm after his fasting, and Plautus was relief to a mind overconcerned with sin. In a vision he was caught up before the throne of God, and when he declared that he was a Christian, he was answered: "Thou liest; thou art no Christian, but a Ciceronian; where thy treasure is, there thy heart is also." [15] While Jerome could not keep his promise to give up his classics, he did devote his great learning to the service of the Church and produced for it a translation of the Scriptures into Latin.

Jerome

By this time the Old and New Testament canonical books had been agreed upon. Jerome went to Palestine, where he learned Hebrew in order to translate the Old Testament directly from the original instead of from the Greek of the Septuagint. Although he adopted some earlier Latin versions for parts of the work, the bulk of the translation he did himself. Jerome's Bible, known as the Vulgate, has remained to this day the authoritative translation for the Roman Church. It preserved to a remarkable degree the style and spirit of the originals, and its language and vocabulary had great influence on all subsequent literature, both theological and secular.

The Vulgate

Ambrose, after a distinguished career as a Roman provincial governor, was forced to accept the archbishopric of Milan even before he was baptized a Christian. Although no theologian to begin with, he acquired considerable learning from the eastern theologians and from his predecessors in the west. He was interested chiefly in ethics, and wrote *The Duties of the Clergy*, a handbook of Christian morals for laity as well as clergy, modeled upon Cicero's *De officiis* (*Concerning Duties*). He attempted to show the superiority of Christian morality to the Stoic morality of Cicero, but like Jerome he could not escape the influence of the classics, and ended by adopting a good deal of Cicero as the essence of Christian morality. Since his book was for centuries the one authoritative work on this subject, it was he who was chiefly responsible for the introduction of Stoic ethics into Christianity. As an ecclesiastical statesman he made Milan a dangerous

Ambrose

[15] *Ibid.*, p. 19.

rival to Rome and compelled Roman emperors to respect the power of the Church in its own sphere. He would not allow the Emperor Theodosius I to enter his church until he had made amends for a massacre of the citizens of Thessalonica. In matters within the jurisdiction of the Church he held that the emperor was subject to episcopal authority. "The emperor is within the Church, not over it. . . . In matters of faith bishops are wont to be the judges of Christian emperors, not emperors of bishops." [16]

This, in effect, was a summary of the position of the Church on the relationship between Church and state. It was only with the victory of Christianity and the growth of an organized church with its own law and its own administration that the distinction between temporal and spiritual authority became a serious problem. Classical paganism *The problem* was an official religion and the pagan priests were officials of the state; *of the relation* there could be no question of separation or conflict. Christianity also *of Church* was now a state religion; the emperors did not hesitate to legislate *and state* for it as they would for any other state institution. In the east the Church continued to remain subservient to the state. In the west it was no longer hostile to the state; on the contrary, it preached submission to it, co-operated with it, and demanded and accepted aid from it. But it would not be governed by the state. Gradually the Church became a state within the state, supreme in the realm of morals and religion, claiming its own authority and the right to govern its officials according to its own laws. More than that, it took unto itself or accepted from the state many purely temporal powers, political or judicial. This question of the proper relation between Church and state is still an unsolved problem; it has continued to agitate all Europe, and now America, to our own day.

Augustine is almost in himself the culmination of the early history of Christianity. He was the greatest of the Latin Fathers, the man with whom, more than any other, every serious thinker for over a thousand years, and every theologian down to our own time, has had to come to terms. By any possible criterion he was a great man. He *Augustine* was a prolific writer, but his two most important works are his *Confessions*, written after he was forty-five, to make available for others the experiences that led to his conversion to Christianity, and his *City of God* (*De Civitate Dei*), written after the sack of Rome by the Visigoths in 410, to prove that Christianity was not responsible for the evils that were overwhelming the Roman world.

St. Augustine's *Confessions* not only reveal a richly emotional and

[16] Quoted in C. Dawson, *The Making of Europe*, p. 44.

religious nature, but his efforts to solve the mystery of the world and of human existence mirror the larger conflict that was going on in the Roman world. As a youth of eighteen he was attracted by Cicero to the adventurous world of philosophic ideas, and assimilated by hard study the literary and philosophical culture of his generation. He had been taught by his Christian mother Monica the elements of her faith, but turned from what he regarded as its crudity and superstition to the gospel of Mani, then flourishing in his native North Africa. He remained a Manichean for nine years; then, after a brief period of moderate scepticism, he turned to Neo-Platonism. Neo-Platonism led speedily to the transforming psychological experience of conversion to Christianity, into which he was baptized by no less a person than St. Ambrose. In the impressive organization of the Church he found the authoritative confirmation of the answer given by Christian dogma to his problems. He returned to his home in North Africa and was made Bishop of Hippo; and there, after a life of stubborn fighting against Manichean and Donatist heretics, he died in 430, just as the Vandals were on the point of capturing his city.

In his *City of God* Augustine stands as the triumphant and last apologist for Christianity. His work is mainly a defense; yet in the course of it, under the influence of his years as a Manichean and of his acquaintance with Neo-Platonism as well as Christian dogma, he arrives at a kind of final interpretation of human existence and human history. He reduces it all to a conflict between the City of God (*Civitas Dei*) and the Earthly City (*Civitas Terrena*), the equivalent of the Manichean conflict between light and dark and the Neo-Platonic conflict between spirit and flesh. God's city is composed of all good and faithful Christians; the earthly city is composed of bad Christians and all non-Christians. The origin of the divine city is God; that of the earthly city, the disobedience and fall of a part of the angelic host long before the creation of the universe. The history of the two cities is nothing more than the long unfolding of the will of God—a grand and wholly novel conception, in philosophical language called the teleological interpretation of history. The only history of importance, then, is the history of the Jews, God's chosen people, whose prophets foretold the coming of Christ and his kingdom, and the history of the Christian religion and Church. All else is of no account.

Augustine inclines to identify the *Civitas Dei* with the organized Church of his day and the *Civitas Terrena* with the Roman empire.

The end of the conflict, towards which all human history is leading, is the Last Judgment, when the citizens of the true kingdom will be rewarded with its most precious gift, immortality, while the false kingdom will be destroyed and its citizens condemned to everlasting fire. All life, all history, has no other meaning than this. Therefore the Church, which is leading its faithful to this glorious end, is the world's supreme institution, and the chief purpose of the state is to assist the Church. Augustine did not take the final step in his argument and conclude that the ruler of the organized Church, the pope, is the only rightful ruler of the world. But later the popes took it, translated it into action, and in part succeeded in translating it into fact.

Meanwhile Augustine, its great architect, believed that the millennium had already dawned. Because in himself he was so many things—a practical ecclesiastic, a mystic, the inheritor of the Platonic Christianity of the east as well as of the western legal Christianity of Tertullian and Cyprian—Augustine could hardly construct a system free from inconsistencies. There was, for example, the stumbling-block of his doctrine of predestination—the notion that God chooses of his own good pleasure whom he will save and whom he will damn. But he supplied all his successors with one great program, no matter whether they could accept all its details. Finally, the fact that all the main currents of the classical world flowed together through Augustine was of tremendous advantage to a subsequent age, which was in need of a simplification of classical culture if that culture were to survive at all. In a very real sense, therefore, St. Augustine is a complete embodiment of the transformed Christianity of the third, fourth, and fifth centuries.

Augustine the embodiment of his time

Chapter 4

THE GERMAN CONQUEST OF THE ROMAN EMPIRE

TO THE END OF THE FOURTH CENTURY

The Indo-Europeans

THE early history of Europe is hardly more than the record of the spread of civilization among the fresh, vigorous, and primitive peoples who lived outside the Roman empire. These peoples were the Celts, the Germans, and the Slavs, offshoots of an Indo-European parent stock, from which also the Italian, Greek, Armenian, Iranian, and Hindu peoples had sprung. Scholars have been unable to agree as to the original homeland of the Indo-European peoples. Their presence in Europe seems to be the result of far-flung migrations westward, of indeterminable date but early enough for them to have come upon peoples of neolithic culture, whom they subjugated.

The Celts

The main body of the Celts was located at first in what today is southern Germany, in the valleys of the upper Danube, the Main, and the upper and middle Rhine. From this area they were in part ousted by the movement of Germanic peoples from what seems to have been their first European abode, in southern Scandinavia and along the southern shore of the Baltic Sea. The movement of the Germans southward and westward, beginning about 400 B.C., pushed the Celts into Gaul and into what we now call the British Isles. It drove them into Italy, where they made the first barbarian attack on Rome, into Greece, and even into Asia Minor, where they settled in Galatia. The Celts were thus scattered from the Black Sea to the Atlantic, but their main territories—the Po valley in northern Italy, the region south of the upper Danube, Gaul, and Britain—became parts of the Roman empire. Julius Cæsar by his conquest of Celtic Gaul in a real sense began the history of western Europe. The Celts lost their own identity in that of Rome, and it was through the Romanized and later Christianized Celts that the Germans too were brought into the Christian Mediterranean world. Only in Brittany, Wales, Ireland, and Scotland, where Roman and German influence penetrated the least, did specifically Celtic traits survive.

Just as the Celts were civilized by Rome, so to a lesser extent were the Germans; but whereas the Celts were conquered by a flourishing pagan Rome, the Germans came under the later influence of a decadent Rome already fast becoming Christian. In what we must assume was a steady if not wholly continuous movement southward and westward, the Germans for at least four hundred years had been moving *The earliest* towards the Rhine and the Danube. The Romans had hitherto been *German* far too preoccupied with their own internal problems and external ex- *migrations* pansion to be concerned with these far-away Germans, about whom they knew little and cared less.

The invasion of the Cimbri and Teutons into Gaul and Italy at the end of the second century B.C. had been of no lasting importance. Cæsar's conquest of Gaul in the first century B.C., on the contrary, brought the Romans face to face with the Germans as they had never been before. What he found out about them he recorded in his account of his Gallic campaigns, published in 51 B.C. They were, he learned, a seminomadic, pastoral, warlike people, devoted to "hunting *Cæsar's* and thoughts of war rather than to agriculture. They clothed them- *Germans* selves in reindeer skins, leaving a large part of the body bare, and fed on milk and cheese and flesh." They cultivated the virtues of hospitality, chastity, and cleanliness, bathing together "promiscuously in the streams." They were constantly on the move. Land was assigned by magistrates and chieftains to clans and groups of kinsmen as a whole, to be held for only one year, and no individual was allowed to possess "a particular piece of land as his own property with fixed boundaries." It was these simple people who, after centuries of roaming through forest and swamp, stood on the banks of the Rhine and the Danube, eager to cross over into the warmer and richer lands of the Roman provinces.

Now, therefore, at the moment when the Roman state was being established upon a new political foundation, the question of limiting or extending the northern frontiers had to be faced. Cæsar himself, although he had to drive back out of Gaul an advance guard of Germans that had settled there, and made two military demonstrations across the Rhine, certainly regarded the river as the northeastern frontier. It remained a cardinal point of Roman policy that the Germans were under no circumstances to be allowed to cross the Rhine

or the Danube, until the time came at last when the Romans compromised by permitting what they could no longer prevent. Cæsar's
successors, however, toyed with the idea of pushing the frontier beyond
the two rivers. This involved the actual conquest of wholly German
territory, and the first of his successors, Augustus, took what looked
like definite steps in that direction. It was indeed an altogether splendid prospect, which, had it been realized, would have changed fundamentally the course of European history. It would have meant bringing the large quadrilateral area enclosed between the Rhine, the

*The Roman
offensive
against the
Germans*

Danube, the Vistula, and the Baltic and North Seas into the Roman
empire. At any rate, whether to supply an adequate base from which
to conduct an offensive movement or only to protect adequately the
territory west of the river, Augustus organized the frontier of the
Rhine. The left bank from the Alps to the sea was divided into the
provinces of Upper and Lower Germany. Camps joined together by
roads were subsequently established along the river; those which attracted traders and settlers developed into towns that are still important. Mainz, at the junction of the Main with the Rhine, came to
be the key fortress. Below it along the river were fifteen additional
camps, the most important of which were Bingen, Bacharach, Ober-
wesel, Coblenz, at the confluence of the Moselle with the Rhine,
headquarters of the river-patrol, Andernach, Remagen, Bonn, Cologne, Xanten, Nijmegen, Utrecht, and Leiden. Above Mainz the
principal camps were Worms, Speyer, Strassburg, and much later
Basel. From the middle and lower Rhine Roman legions penetrated
the dark forests and crossed the huge swamps of barbarian Germany
on roads made of felled trees. Roman fleets skirted the coast of the
North Sea and made their way up the Weser and Elbe rivers. Roman
armies followed up the valleys of the Lippe, the Ruhr, and the Main
into the heart of the country.

Similarly, along the right bank of the Danube Augustus organized
the new provinces of Rhætia, Noricum, and Pannonia, in which the
chief camps were finally located at Augsburg, Lorch, Regensburg, and
Vienna. After the destruction of Varus's army by Germans under
Arminius (Hermann) in A.D. 9, in a battle in the heart of the Teu-
toburger Forest, which still so solemnly covers the heights between
Detmold and Paderborn, Augustus abandoned any hope he may have
had of conquering northern Germany. Germans still take pride in the
story of the fight, and from the summit of the ridge a gigantic statue
of Hermann, Germany's first national hero, looks down upon the
forest in which he ambushed the Roman legions. But despite this dis-

aster, it is perhaps safe to say that for the first two centuries of the empire the Romans continued to hold the offensive against the Germans.

At any rate, two important salients were established beyond the Rhine-Danube frontier. One was the so-called tithed lands (*agri decumates*), colonized by veterans. This was an extension of the province of Upper Germany reaching from Rheinbrohl, on the Rhine below the Main, southeastward across the Main for two hundred and twenty-eight miles to Pfahlbronn, and thence an extension of the province of Rhætia eastward for one hundred and eight miles to Eining on the Danube. To mark the limits of this expansion a stone wall was built along the Rhætian frontier, and along the frontier of Upper Germany a ditch and palisade connected seventy forts, built a half day's march from each other. This became in German folk legend the Devil's Wall (*Teufelsmauer*). Today, not far from Frankfort, surrounded by pine woods among the foothills of the Taunus Mountains, stands the Saalburg, a learned reconstruction by German professors of one of these forts. As the traveler approaches the main gate, he passes a temple of Mithras, whose worship the Roman legions carried into these central German wilds. Inside the fort he finds the perfectly formal and conventional arrangement of a Roman camp. Straight through the camp he goes, and out the rear gate. About a hundred yards down a narrow path through a dense growth of fir he comes to the ditch. The wooden palisade, over which the Roman legionary peered into the dim and unknown country inhabited by these restless new people, is gone. Secure in his fort, he could hardly suspect that the future was not with him, but with those blue-eyed, yellow-haired barbarian giants.

The tithed lands

The Saalburg

The other salient was on the lower Danube, far to the east, covering the area of modern Rumania. Conquered by the Emperor Trajan about A.D. 100, it was made into the province of Dacia and its frontiers fortified in the same way as those of the tithed lands. The destruction by Marcus Aurelius between 171 and 173 of the strong state of the Marcomanni and Quadi in Bohemia and Moravia meant the destruction of the one stable power thus far established in Germany. It is not at all unlikely that if Marcus Aurelius had lived longer a third salient would have been formed by a new province, to take in Bohemia, Moravia, and the valley of the Theiss in Hungary.

Dacia

Now that the Romans found themselves in first-hand contact with the Germans all along this extended frontier, the numerous and pretty constant campaigns in the interior of Germany and the peaceful

The Germania of Tacitus

business of the trader brought them fuller knowledge of German character, customs, and institutions. Their simple, unspoiled ways won the admiration of conservative Romans, who deplored the course into which their own people seemed to be slipping, and held up to them as examples of what they should strive to become again these rude children of the north. Such a Roman was the historian Tacitus, who in A.D. 98 published his *Germania,* a book about the Germans. Whether or not it was based on his own observations, at any rate Tacitus was in possession of reliable information secured from those who had had personal experience. The *Germania* gives us practically the only information we have, after Cæsar and before their wholesale migrations into the empire at the close of the fourth century, concerning the life and manners of the early Germans. It is therefore an invaluable historical source. Inasmuch as the German was the human mold into which was to be poured the intellectual heritage of Rome and the religious teachings of Christianity, and because it was he who made possible the building up of a new western European civilization, it is important to know what the German was to begin with. For this one must go back to Tacitus and then fill in the picture with what remains of early Anglo-Saxon and Norse sagas and the pale reflection of earlier heroic days in medieval German epics. The early Germans had no Homer.

The Germans
at home

Germany, according to Tacitus, is a country "covered over with wild forests or filthy swamps." [1] "It is suitable enough for grain . . . and though rich in flocks and herds, these are for the most part small, the cattle not even possessing their natural beauty nor spreading horns. The people take pride in possessing a large number of animals, these being their sole and most cherished wealth." They live together in villages and hamlets, "as a spring or a meadow or a grove strikes their fancy." Their houses are made of "undressed timber, giving no beauty or comfort. Some parts they plaster carefully with earth of such purity and brilliancy as to form a substitute for painting and designs in color. They are accustomed also to dig out subterranean caves, which they cover over with great heaps of manure as a refuge against the cold and a place for storing grain."

German
dress

The Germans "all have fierce blue eyes, reddish hair and large bodies, fit only for sudden exertion." "Generally their only clothing is a cloak fastened with a clasp, or if they haven't that, a thorn; this being their only garment, they pass whole days about the hearth or

---

[1] This and the following quotations from Tacitus are taken from *Translations and Reprints* of the University of Pennsylvania, vol. VI, no. 3.

near a fire. The richest of them are distinguished by wearing a tunic
. . . close-fitting and showing the shapes of their limbs. There are
those also who wear the skins of wild beasts, those nearest the Roman
border, in a careless manner, but those further back more elegantly,
as those do who have no better clothing obtained by commerce. They
select certain animals, and, stripping off their hides, sew on them
patches of spotted skins taken from those strange beasts that the
distant ocean and the unknown sea bring forth. The women wear the
same sort of dress as the men except that they wrap themselves in
linen garments, which they adorn with purple stripes, and do not
lengthen out the upper part of the tunic into sleeves, but leave the
arms bare the whole length. The upper part of their breasts is also
exposed."

The German family is monogamous, "excepting those few who *The German*
because of their high position rather than out of lust enter into more *family*
than one marriage engagement." The wife is admonished "by the
very initiating ceremonies of matrimony that she is becoming the
partner of her husband's labors and dangers, destined to suffer and
to share with him alike in peace and in war." Adultery is rare and
severely punished; the injured husband "cuts off the woman's hair in
the presence of her kinsfolk, drives her naked from his house, and
flogs her through the whole village." "In every household the children grow up naked and unkempt into that lusty frame and those
sturdy limbs that we admire. Each mother nurses her own children;
they are not handed over to servants and paid nurses."

The care of the "hearth and home and . . . of the fields is given
over to the women, the old men, and the various infirm members of
the family." When the German is not at war, he spends his time in
hunting and in idleness, "given over to sleep and eating. . . . The
masters lie buried in sloth, by that strange contradiction of nature *The Germans*
that causes the same men to love indolence and hate peace. . . . As *at leisure*
soon as they awaken from sleep, which they prolong till late in the
day, they bathe, usually in warm water, as their winter lasts a great
part of the year. After the bath they take food, each sitting in a
separate seat and having a table to himself. They proceed to their
business, or not less often to feasts, fully armed. It is no disgrace to
spend the whole day and night in drinking. Quarreling is frequent
enough, as is natural among drunken men, though their disputes are
rarely settled by mere wrangling, but oftener by bloodshed and
wounds. Yet it is at their feasts that they consult about reconciling
enemies, forming family alliances, electing chiefs, and even regarding

war and peace, as they think that at no other time is the mind more open to fair judgment or more inflamed to mighty deeds. . . . On the next day the matter is reconsidered, and a particular advantage is secured on each occasion. They take counsel when they are unable to practice deception; they decide when they cannot be misled."

German amusements　　In their games "naked youths who make profession of this exhibition leap and dance among swords and spears that threaten their lives. . . . They indulge in games of chance, strange as it may seem, even when sober, as one of their serious occupations, with such great recklessness in their gains and losses that when everything else is gone they stake their liberty and their own persons on the last and decisive throw. The loser goes into voluntary slavery." "No other race indulges more freely in entertainments and hospitality. It is considered a crime to turn any mortal man away from one's door. According to his means each one receives those who come with a well-furnished table. When his food has been all eaten up, he who had lately been the host becomes the guide and companion of his guest to the next house, which they enter uninvited. There is no distinction between guests; they are all received with like consideration."

But the German is primarily a warrior. Around the profession of arms his whole life centers, from the early age when "in a full assembly some one of the chiefs or the father or relatives of the youth invest him with shield and spear. This is the sign that the lad has reached the age of manhood; this is his first honor. Before this he was only a member of a household, hereafter he is a member of the tribe." A typical German institution, which later had a definite influence on the shaping of the feudal system (especially in the relationship of overlord to underlord, of suzerain to vassal), was the war *The* comitatus band, the *comitatus, das Gefolge,* the following. "Certain more experienced chiefs of approved merit" gather about themselves chosen youths who fight their battles and share in their renown and profit. "They look to the liberality of their chief for their war-horse and their deadly and victorious spear; the feasts and entertainments, however, furnished them on a homely but liberal scale, fall to their lot as mere pay. The means for this bounty are acquired through war and plunder. Nor could you persuade them to till the soil and await the yearly produce so easily as you could induce them to stir up an enemy and earn glorious wounds. Nay, they think it tame and stupid to acquire by their sweat what they can purchase by their blood." The relationship of the leader to his band is cemented by a personal oath. "It is in accordance with their most sacred oath of allegiance to defend and protect him, and to ascribe their bravest deeds to his renown." In battle chief and followers are rivals in courage, but neither must outshine the other. "For any one of the followers to have survived his chief and come unharmed out of a battle is life-long infamy and reproach."

The Germans performed all public and private business under arms. Their weapons were battle-axes of metal or stone, short swords called *seax* (from which the name Saxon probably came), daggers, spears, and bows. Their shields were "distinguished by the most carefully chosen colors." The warriors wore corselets of leather, sometimes plated with sheets of brass, but no other armor. Nobles were often mounted, but "on the whole their chief strength lies in their infantry, nude or lightly clad in a small cloak," who "rain missiles, *The Germans* each man having many and hurling them to a great distance." The *at war* Germans were happy warriors who entered battle singing. "The effect they particularly strive for is that of a harsh noise, a wild and confused roar, which they attain by putting their shields to their mouths so that the reverberation swells their deep full voices." "Certain figures and images taken from their sacred groves they carry into battle, but their greatest incitement to courage is that a division of horse or foot is not made up by chance or accidental association but is formed of families and clans, and their dear ones are close at hand, so that the wailings of the women and the cry of the children can be heard during the battle." "It is the greatest ignominy to have left one's shield on the field, and it is unlawful for a man so disgraced to be present at the sacred rites or to enter the assembly; so that many, after escaping from battle, have ended their shame with the halter."

The religion of the early Germans embraced the worship of gods as *German* forces of nature, inventors of the arts, protectors of human institutions, *religion* guardian spirits, and rulers over the afterworld—the whole colored, embroidered, and humanized by a strong, vigorous, and superb mythology. Thor, the Thunder God (whose name we still preserve in Thursday), wielding an axe or holding a banner, walked about or was driven in a car drawn by goats. He was the Defender of the World, the guardian of the land and of law and order. Woden (Wotan, Odin), whose day is Wednesday, "shifty, full of guile," skilled in magic and the inventor of poetry, was the Lord of Valhalla, whither dead warriors were carried from the battlefield by his handmaidens, the Valkyries, there to feast and fight everlastingly. His wife Frigga was the goddess of the sky, the protectress of marriage and the hearth, whose day is Friday. She has often been confused with Freya, the goddess of fertility, of love and beauty. Tyr seems to have been an earlier war god, like Mars; he was supplanted in popularity by Woden, but his name is still preserved in our Tuesday. The Norns were the three German Fates, guardian spirits, who brought men good or evil fortune and appeared to them in dreams to warn them of immediate danger.

There were many other gods and goddesses whose influence waxed and waned during the long, shadowy pre-Christian period. The Germans had both priests and priestesses. Indeed, women were thought to possess "a certain sanctity and prophetic gift." The priests proclaimed silence and kept order in the assemblies, but they formed no influential caste as the Celtic Druids did. The usual sanctuaries of the Germans were sacred groves and trees. "They hold it to be inconsistent with the sublimity of the celestials to confine the gods in walls made by hands, or to liken them to the form of any human countenance." There were, however, some temples, altars, images, and sacred pillars. The sacrificial victims were ordinarily animals, but there is some evidence of the persistence of human sacrifice among the Germans, as in Cæsar's time among the Gauls. They took omens from the flight of birds, and divined the future by casting twigs on a white cloth or listening to the neighing and snorting of sacred white horses.

In the early nineteenth century it became fashionable for historians obsessed by the liberal and national movements of their time, which they sought to buttress with historical precedent, to attribute a fantastic degree of democratic dignity and importance to the institutions of the early Germans. Constitutional monarchy, democratic republican government, the parliamentary and representative system, local self-government, trial by jury, "an independent and self-developing system of law"—all alike were enthusiastically discovered in the undeveloped embryo of primitive German institutions. So, too, the early Germans have been credited with great moral contributions to civilization, such as love of liberty, the sense of personal worth, and the sentiment of honor. There is, of course, no reason to suppose that the Germans possessed these virtues to any greater degree than any other people in a similar stage of development. They are the monopoly of no particular people, but the possession of all free peoples and the aspiration of those who have lost or have yet to win their liberty. In western Europe they have come out of centuries of human experience, in which the Germanic element has been fused with the very different Roman and Christian elements into a new synthesis.

At least two early Germanic institutions, however, were of considerable importance for subsequent history: German law and the German

The sentimental attitude towards early German institutions

village. German law at this early date was a large accumulation of customs, varying according to the tribe. It was, of course, unwritten, and was regarded by the individual German as a personal possession which *German law* he took with him wherever he went. It was therefore very different from Roman law, which was quite well fixed, in large part codified, and administered within a definite territory irrespective of persons. Since these German tribal customs were later written down under Roman influence, after the entrance into the Roman empire of large numbers of the tribes, it will be more convenient to consider them in greater detail later as part of the civilization of early Germanic society. Here it will be sufficient to note that the administration of the law was still largely in private hands, regulated by the principle of blood feud between groups of kinsmen or clans. An offense committed by a member of one clan against a member of another involved both groups in a state of enmity that imperiled the life of every individual until revenge or satisfaction was obtained. All members of a clan were thus liable for an offense committed by one of its members. Later on satisfaction could be made for all offenses, including murder, by fines regulated by custom. Tacitus remarks: "A German is required to adopt not only the feuds of his father or of a relative but also their friendships, though the enmities are not irreconcilable. For even homicide is expiated by the payment of a certain number of cattle and the whole family accept the satisfaction." It was for the Germans a long and difficult struggle to reach the point of regarding crime as an offense committed chiefly against the state and therefore punishable only by the state. For that matter, by no means all Americans have yet reached that point, but in a primitive tribal society such a thing as the state hardly exists.

One of the notable features of Tacitus's *Germania,* compared with Cæsar's brief comments on the Germans, is the emphasis that he puts on the settled agricultural life of the Germans in their villages, which *The German* must have developed mostly since Cæsar's time. The Germans took the *village* main features of their village community with them when they migrated into the provinces of the Roman empire. It is not easy from Tacitus alone to reconstruct a clear and complete picture of the early German village. In one place he says that "they lay out their villages not, as with us, in connected or closely joined houses, but each surrounds his dwelling with an open space." In another he says that the land is held "by the villages as communities, according to the number of the cultivators, and is then divided among the freemen according to their rank. . . . They cultivate fresh fields every year and there is still land to spare." Again, he speaks of slaves, from whom "the lord extracts a certain amount of grain or cloth or a certain number of cattle, as in the case of a tenant." We have already noted that the women and children and old men worked in the fields, while the master of the household hunted or fought or rested or caroused.

Tacitus's account must be filled in with details from written codes of law and other sources from a later period. Each village had an assembly composed of all its freemen, called a "moot," which reconciled local differences and interpreted village custom. The village was not necessarily isolated: there were adjacent villages each of which owned tracts of forest and pasture that were parts of a larger tribal holding; and villages sometimes communicated with each other over forest trails or by stream.

The early German land system

It is apparent, then, that we cannot merely say of the early German, as of the early Roman, that he was a free peasant warrior, cultivating his own lands or leaving them, like Cincinnatus, to go off to fight the battles of his tribe. While most Germans were freemen, obviously Cæsar's simple statement of their communal system of land ownership would no longer be adequate. By this time there was plainly a drift towards the formation of a small landlord class, a social aristocracy, with tenant farmers or even serfs to work the land. Richer men lived in larger isolated houses, surrounded by barns, stables, and the cottages of the tenantry, the whole sometimes enclosed by a stockade or even by stone walls. But the typical arrangement was the village, situated in a glade in the forest or on a river. It comprised meadows and woods, rudely cultivated fields, and a cluster of houses somewhere in the midst, protected by hedges, ditches, and the village dogs. The woods, the pasture, and the waste land were owned and used in common, whereas the farm land was held by individuals. But the rudimentary agricultural skill and the narrow resources of these early German villagers made anything like individual farm management impossible. Agriculture was a co-operative village enterprise, regulated by custom of such long standing as to be compulsory. Not every householder owned a yoke of the small, scrawny German oxen, or even a rude plow. Often all the oxen in the village would be required to turn the furrow in the stubborn sod, and oxen and plow would pass from field to field. To harvest the crops likewise required co-operation. The land was cultivated on a two-field system: one-half of the arable land was left fallow each year. But at best the crop was small, and the risk of loss from drought or heavy rains had to be reduced as much as possible. Hence, when a man's own crop had been gathered he turned in and helped the neighbors who had helped him. In Tacitus's time the wealth of the

Germans was still mostly in cattle, but by the time of their migrations into the empire they had developed from the pastoral into the agricultural stage of civilization. Once within the empire, they found the simple agrarian life to which the Roman empire had reverted not unlike their own, so that the German village contributed with the large late Roman estate in shaping the early European manor, the basis of the typical agricultural system of later times.

Above the village the next political unit was the hundred, a term *Political* that may hark back to the remote days when the Germans first settled *divisions* in central Europe. The original hundred may have been a band of a hundred warriors who, having fought together, settled down together. At any rate, the hundred became a territorial area and a political unit, corresponding somewhat to the later township. A combination of hundreds in turn formed the larger territory of a canton, or gau. The cantons, some of which were later coterminous with the county, together formed the territory of the tribe; this, when kingship developed among the Germans, was called *Reich* or kingdom. It must always be kept in mind that in Tacitus's time these political units were only beginning to emerge. There was still no political administration as such, and no political solidarity; the family, the clan, the tribe were the only cohesive forces in German society.

An early institution of importance was the public assembly of all free *The public* warriors of the tribe, which met to make decisions in matters affecting *assembly* the tribe as a whole, such as war or migration. On minor matters the chiefs alone consulted together. Even matters important enough to be referred to the tribe as a whole were first considered by the chiefs, and then presented to the assembly by the "king or a chief . . . each being heard according to his age, noble blood, reputation in warfare, and eloquence." "If an opinion is displeasing, they reject it by shouting; if they agree to it, they clash with their spears. The most complimentary form of assent is that which is expressed by means of their weapons." In this assembly the kings were chosen "on account of their ancestry" and generals "for their valor"; magistrates were also chosen, to "decide suits in the cantons and villages . . . with the assistance of a hundred associates." The general assembly, as well as the lesser assemblies of the canton and hundred and village, were also judicial assemblies where accusations were brought, trials held, and penalties assigned. "Traitors and deserters are hung to trees. Weaklings and cowards and those guilty of infamous crimes are cast into the mire of swamps, with a hurdle placed over their heads."

"The kings do not have free and unlimited power, and the generals lead by example rather than command, winning great admiration if they are energetic and fight in plain sight in front of the line." From Tacitus it is evident that all German tribes had by no means yet adopted kingship; most still had their elected chieftains and subchieftains, for tribe and canton and hundred, in addition to the special leader elected to undertake a specific campaign. In the main, German hereditary kingship developed during the critical period of the migrations, when the tribe or confederation, in a chronic state of war, found it necessary to adapt tribal organization to military expediency. The war leader necessarily had absolute authority during the war, but at its termination that authority lapsed. During a war or a migration a leader of prowess would often be re-elected. When he died, usually in harness, his son, if a true warrior, would ordinarily be elected to succeed him. In some such fashion by slow stages the old chieftainship was transformed, first into an elective kingship, then into a kingship in fact hereditary, though the formality of election was retained. Some of the German tribes already had hereditary kingship when they first made their appearance in history; others, when they entered the Roman empire, some as late as the sixth century, still elected their chieftains.

Between what the Romans called the barbarian, or simply alien or foreign, German and the cosmopolitan Roman citizen there existed in Tacitus's day vast differences. The Romans ruled a Mediterranean empire with a growingly complex administrative machine; the Germans were a heterogeneous mass of individual warring tribes with no political administration to speak of. The Romans possessed a rich and complex intellectual culture; the Germans had no intellectual culture at all. Roman religion had been weakened by sceptical philosophy; German religion was still the fresh and lively product of awful elemental forces. Roman society was a highly developed system of social classes, based upon economic and hereditary differences, in which the middle class was only then beginning to lose its predominance. German society was a loose association of tribes, clans, groups of kinsmen —in the main a large class of freemen, differentiated somewhat by the beginnings of stratification according to birth and wealth, but with no middle class at all. Roman industry and commerce were still active and Roman agriculture, at least outside of Italy, still fairly healthy. There was, properly speaking, no German industry or commerce, and in agriculture the German had made hardly more than a beginning. But the German, although still on a cultural level far beneath even that of Homer's Greeks, showed great capacity to absorb what the Roman world had to teach. His courage was fresh, his blood flowed fast, his body was strong. It was no tremendous calamity when the Germans began to drift over the frontier into the empire. Indeed, the Romans thought that they could use the Germans to advantage in solving some of their serious internal problems.

Beginning with the third century, the most critical in the history of the empire, the Romans were forced again to assume the defensive against the Germans because of their great influx. It is not easy to account in detail for this larger movement of what now appear to have been rather confederations of former independent tribes than small individual tribes themselves. The whole movement of the Germans was perhaps most like a constantly fluctuating but ever rising tide. Possibly the constantly increasing pressure of the Slavs upon the eastern German tribes forced them to migrate in search of new homes. Moreover, in general the land of the Germans was poor, vast areas were covered with forest and swamp, and their rudimentary agriculture ill sufficed to provide for an increasing population. They were also at the mercy of elemental dangers like flood, drought, famine, and forest fire, and it may be that such catastrophes drove them out. In any case, it was chiefly land-hunger—not mere want of room at home, but a food supply insufficient for an increasing population and inability to reduce the wilderness to cultivation—that made the Germans restless and truculent; that led the stronger tribes to dispossess the weaker; that made them look with envy upon the neatly tilled fields and quiet provincial life on the Roman side of the border in the valleys of the Rhine and Danube. *Factors influencing the migration of German tribal confederations*

Lombard legend records that the Lombards in their original home, perhaps Scandinavia, because of the increase in population divided themselves into three groups and drew lots to determine which of the three should migrate. The migration of any tribe or confederation inevitably threw others into confused movement, pushing them ahead, shoving them aside, drawing them in to occupy the vacated territory. The long wars of Marcus Aurelius with the Marcomanni and Quadi were apparently the result of such a thrust from migrating tribes to the east, which precipitated them upon the Roman frontier in Pannonia.

The identity of the barbarian people whose mighty trek was so deranging the whole eastern German world was for years unknown, until in the reign of the Emperor Caracalla (211–17) it became evident: the Goths, the first great German nation in history, loomed above the horizon. The period of German migrations on a large scale had now begun. Roman tradition and their own legends placed the original home of the Goths in Scandinavia. Thence they probably migrated across the Baltic *The migration of the Goths*

in the fourth century B.C., settled on the German mainland between
the Oder and the Vistula, and there remained until the middle of the
second century A.D. What compelled them to move again we do not
know; it may have been hostile neighbors or floods (both rivers are
notorious for their destructive spring floods), famine or pestilence.
Whatever the reason, they were off again, driving their cattle before
them; the women and children following the lumbering wains that
bore their rude household goods; the fighting men marching in the
van and guarding the wings of the column, with their great hunting
dogs stalking along beside them. The Goths naturally started up the
river valleys, then crossed the low watershed in western Russia between
the Baltic and the Black Sea, and slowly moved down the Dniester
until they came in sight of the Roman settlements in Dacia. This migration occupied more than a hundred years, during which they were
not always moving, nor yet ever settled for long in one place.

The hardships and perils of this long trek made an indelible impression upon the Gothic people, and gave rise to a body of legend and
saga, from which in the sixth century Jordanes, an historian of half-
Gothic ancestry, wrote a crude but vivid chronicle of Gothic history. He
tells of battles with tribes more savage than the Goths—not other Germans, but Slavs and Huns, at that time just beginning to push out of
Asia into Europe. He tells how once a great number of the Goths were
caught in a treacherous marsh and sucked down to death; and how,
hundreds of years later, the peasants of that region, in the moonlight
beaming through the mist hanging heavy over the swamps, could see
the forms of struggling men and women and horses and cattle, and
hear the wailing of the women, the crying of the children, the lowing
of the frightened cattle.

By the third quarter of the third century the Goths were in Dacia
and along the northern shores of the Black Sea. Once having reached
the sea, they built a fleet by means of which they passed through the
Bosporus and the Dardanelles into the Ægean Sea and attacked the
cities of Greece and Asia Minor and the islands of the Ægean.
Although, after crossing the Danube into Mœsia and Thrace, the
Goths were severely beaten at Naissus (modern Nish) in 268, the
Romans gave up all hope of recovering Dacia. The province was
abandoned by Aurelian in 275; the legions and all Roman civil officials
were withdrawn. The Goths, having at last found new homes where
they might dwell in comfort and peace, were glad to settle down and
give up both warfare and piracy in exchange for their new lands and,

The Visi-
goths settle
in Dacia

in addition, liberal subsidies in money paid them by the Romans to keep the peace.

In their first century as neighbors of the eastern or Greek half of the Roman empire the Goths split into two groups, which it is important to distinguish carefully. The West Goths, or Visigoths, occupied in Dacia territory which in the brief course of a century and a half had been so thoroughly Romanized that its inhabitants still speak a Latin language. North of the Black Sea the East Goths, or Ostrogoths, occupied an area once a flourishing center of Greek colonization and civilization, into which Sarmatian horsemen had meanwhile come from the plateaus of Iran. These had brought with them, or themselves invented, stirrups and spurs, which the Goths in turn adopted. This was an improvement of far-reaching importance, for it made possible the subsequent development of the military instrument most characteristic of warfare in Europe until the invention of gunpowder, namely, heavy-armed cavalry. "The mail-clad Sarmatian and Gothic horseman, armed with lance and sword, was the true ancestor and prototype of the medieval knight." [2]

The Ostrogoths north of the Black Sea

Both groups of Goths, coming under the influence of Græco-Roman civilization, may be said to have been partially Romanized. Still more important, during the same period they were converted to Christianity. That is—and this was of tremendous significance later—they were converted to Arianism, which at this time was no mere heresy but was the predominant form of Christianity in the east. The first missionary to the Goths, the fourth-century Ulfilas, was himself a Roman citizen, perhaps of Gothic descent. In connection with his work among the Visigoths he compiled an alphabet of his own and translated most of the Scriptures into Gothic, omitting those portions that he felt would supply martial inspiration unnecessary to so warlike a people. Ulfilas is thus responsible for the first written piece of Germanic literature, and his Bible is the foundation for all study of Gothic. From the Visigoths Arianism spread gradually among all the other eastern Germanic peoples, and came to be looked upon by them as a peculiarly German kind of Christianity. It can hardly be supposed that they understood much about the *Logos,* or even abandoned immediately their old Teutonic religion. But Christianity, the religion of a superior culture upon which they looked with naïve wonderment and awe, was for them a means of accommodation to a civilization of which they were anxious to become a part.

The Goths become Arian Christians

Ulfilas

[2] C. Dawson, *The Making of Europe,* p. 86.

The movements of the Goths had been responsible in part at least for setting loose other tribes in northeastern Germany; new tribal confederations were formed, and the thrust was felt as far west as the upper Danube and the Rhine. The confederation of the Alemanni *The Alemanni* formed first of all from the Swabian Semnones, living between the Elbe and the Oder, finally joined to themselves groups of Hermunduri and Swabians from southern Germany and threw themselves upon the tithed lands east of the Rhine and north of the Danube. Like Dacia, in the end this salient also had to be abandoned by Rome. The Bur- *Burgundians and Vandals* gundians at approximately the same time moved from their home between the Oder and the Vistula; they were joined on their march by the Siling Vandals of Silesia, and together they occupied the valley of the upper Main, whence they contested unsuccessfully with the Alemanni the possession of the northern part of the tithed lands. Another group of Vandals, the Asdings, moved into the valley of the Theiss River in Hungary. The expanding confederation of the Saxons, on the lower Weser and Elbe, pushed another northern German con- *The Salian Franks* federation, the Salian Franks, on to the Rhine, whence for the remain- der of the third century they made constant raids into Gaul and once even into Spain.

The Romans, forced back to the original Rhine-Danube frontier of Augustus, fortified their river camps with walls, reorganized by subdivision the frontier provinces, and under Diocletian under- *A century of peace on the frontier* took a thoroughgoing reorganization of the army. Nothing could pre- vent constant German raids, but the first great tumultuous period of migrations was now over and the pressure on the empire was eased. All along the frontier, from the Goths in distant Dacia, along the middle Danube, where the Vandals were quietly established, through the tithed lands, where the Alemanni were restrained from further incursions into Rhætia, Gaul, or Italy, all the way to the lower Rhine, where the Franks were still held in check after a fashion, a term of relative peace and repose ensued. Even internal Germany seemed to have become somewhat composed. German penetration of the empire, in one way or another, never for a moment ceased, but from the end of the third to the end of the fourth century relations between Romans and Germans continued in the main to be peaceful.

The German- ization of the empire The sort of Romanization of the Germans which had seemed possible in the first and second centuries of the empire was thwarted when the empire was forced, by the loss of the tithed lands and Dacia, to return to a purely defensive policy; conversely, there had already begun— and continued with growing strength afterwards—what might be called a Germanization of the empire. Tacitus in the *Germania* holds the German up for imitation by the degenerate Roman. It was hardly the sort of thing that he had in mind, but it is a fact that German modes became the vogue among Roman ladies of high society, who dyed their hair a fashionable German blonde or red or wore wigs of imported German hair. To most Romans the typical German physique could not but seem beautiful and admirable. Angels in early Christian art soon began to have blue eyes and golden hair. But in far more serious ways than by mere imitation, and long before the mass invasions of German peoples, the Germans had begun to make their way into the empire, where they became indispensable as colonists, citizens, soldiers, and statesmen. A "pacific invasion," promoted by the Roman state itself, preceded the later armed migrations. Indeed, in large part the earlier invasion explains the later: what the Germans could no longer get in peaceful fashion they easily learned they could take by force.

Even before Cæsar Germans had begun to cross over to the left bank of the Rhine, and they were actually encouraged to do so by him and his successors, after whose victories over them they were transplanted *Peaceful* by thousands into Rhenish Gaul. The Ubians formed the Germanic *penetration of* foundation for the city of Cologne, the Vangiones for Worms, the *the frontier* Nemetes for Speyer, the Triboci for Strassburg; subsequently the Alemanni moved into Alsace. All along the Rhine and the Danube frontier towns were established around the Roman forts, and they attracted traders, who penetrated into the interior of Germany. An active frontier life quickly grew up along both banks of the rivers. The frontier population became more and more homogeneous; Roman, Celt, and German in the course of centuries of intermarriage ceased to be easily distinguishable. The actual frontier became somewhat vague; whole tribes along and beyond the frontier were enlisted as allies (*fœderati*) of Rome and bound to protect it against their fellow Germans.

When plague, depopulation, and the movement of farmers to the cities brought on a crisis in Roman agriculture, which threatened to deplete the treasury by loss of taxes and also to diminish the best supply of recruits for the army, the Roman government adopted the policy of settling Germans as colonists within the empire, especially upon empty public lands, but also upon unused lands of private landowners. This policy seems to have been inaugurated by Marcus Aurelius during his wars with the Marcomanni and Quadi. In addition to relieving still *German* further the pressure on the frontier it was expected to solve Rome's *colonists in* great internal problem by using Germans to resuscitate a declining *the empire* agriculture.

Settlements might be voluntary or, as in the case of prisoners of war, involuntary, but the families thus settled on Roman soil were made perpetual tenant farmers, bound to their land, subject to the usual taxes, and obliged to perform military service if called upon. Such colonists naturally preserved their native customs, their family life, and their own primitive methods of farming. They formed German enclaves, dependent German village communities, among the Roman population. During the third century there was hardly a German tribe that did not furnish voluntary or involuntary colonists for the empire. Thousands of Goths were thus colonized by Claudius II, thousands of Franks and Alemanni by Aurelian, thousands of Bastarnæ and Franks by Probus, thousands of Carpi by Diocletian, thousands of Chamavi and Frisians by Constantius. By the fourth century the majority of German *coloni* were no longer compulsory settlers; they were voluntary immigrants who occupied waste lands, filled sparsely populated regions, or repeopled the depleted domains of the aristocracy. The *laeti* seem to have been a more definitely military type of colonists; they received allotments of farm lands on a distinctly military tenure. Such settlements naturally were most frequent in the border provinces, but we find plentiful evidence of their existence elsewhere.

The Roman had confessed his inability to do without the German as a farmer; Roman land had been peacefully opened to the barbarian, not only on the frontier but also in the interior. What was to be the outcome of such a policy? Could the Roman forever prevent the German from taking any land that he wanted, vacant or not? Could the growing number of foreigners be assimilated into the civilized Roman way of life, or would these primitive colonists contribute to a barbarization of Roman culture—which was indeed already threatening even without them?

The Roman army becomes German

No more could the Roman do without the German in the army. The gradual Germanization of the Roman army had actually begun, mostly in the cavalry, as early as Cæsar's time. The first recruits for the legions were drawn from immigrants already settled within the empire. There were German cohorts in Italy and even in Rome. Some Suevi fought in the front rank under Vespasian at the battle of Cremona in A.D. 69. The imperial German bodyguard, bivouacked in the palace on the Palatine, was proverbially loyal to the emperors. Chieftains of a tribe that had entered into alliance with Rome would join the Roman army with their warriors. These chiefs were at once tribal leaders and army captains, for the organization of the German *comitatus* was preserved under the armor of Roman legionaries. They and their men received regular pay and rations. The records abound with notices of such barbarian commanders and their barbarian troops; there were detachments of Batavians at Arras, of Franks at Rennes, of Suevi at Coutances, Le Mans, and Bayeux. In common speech the word *barbarus* came to mean a soldier, and by the beginning of the fourth century the Roman army was predominantly German. Most of Constantine's army at the Battle of the Milvian Bridge was composed of Germans, and his opponent Licinius had large numbers of Goths among his troops. The Germans naturally filled many of the lesser officerships in the army, and not a few German chieftains rose to high command. Arbogast, a Frank, was *magister militum,* or marshal, under Valentinian I, and was succeeded by another Frank, Bauto. Still another Frank, Richomer, first became count of the domestics to Gratian and later *magister militum* to Valens in the east. The emperors Theodosius and Gratian were especially partial to Germans. In the fifth century all the great commanders in the western empire were of barbarian extraction. A constitution of 441 shows that by the time of Theodosius II German brigades were so numerous in the army that a separate bureau of the treasury (*scrinium barbarorum*) was created to administer the payment of these troops. Roman citizenship was granted for service in the army.

Germans in high military and civil office

Germans also got well up in the civil service. In the fourth and fifth centuries at least nine consuls in the west were Germans, while in the latter century many counts of cities in Gaul and Italy were former German officers in the imperial armies. Not only land, therefore, but citizenship and honors and offices, military and civil, were open to the German, who was, of course, eager enough for these Roman emoluments. Indeed, the Germans might be said almost to have taken peaceful possession of the real basis of power in the state, before the time when whole tribes broke through the frontiers in search of lands, position, and honors such as they knew had been won by their earlier compatriots. In a sense, therefore, the defense of Rome against the later invasions—to the extent that there was any defense—was made largely by Germans already in the empire, defending in the Roman name their possessions and privileges against newcomers covetous of them.

Many of the highest German commanders were the equals in culture and manners of their Roman contemporaries. Symmachus, the most cultivated Roman of the fourth century, prized the friendship of the Franks Bauto and Richomer. Mixed marriages were not uncommon even in the third century. A lieutenant of Aurelian's married a Gothic

Germans in high social position

princess, and the Emperor Gallienus's second wife was a daughter of the king of the Marcomanni. In the fourth century Bauto married his daugher Eudoxia to Valentinian II. By that time, as the inscriptions show, such marriages were indeed so common that in some places, notably in the Rhine cities, the fusion of races had proceeded far. In the next century the poet Prudentius speaks of it as an accomplished fact; and in the sixth century we find Cassiodorus, the Latin secretary of Theodoric the Ostrogoth, writing of "old and honorable" Italian families of mixed Roman and German ancestry.

Obviously the Germans who so far had entered the empire, numerous as they were, had entered in groups small enough to be quickly Romanized. If the Germans could have continued for another two centuries under the conditions of the fourth century slowly and quietly to filter into the empire, the gradual fusion of races and institutions, all the necessary political and social adjustment, might have taken place without undue violence or gross injustice; a Roman-German-Christian civilization might have been peacefully established.

The final results of peaceful penetration

This might well have happened had not the precarious equilibrium established along the frontier in the third century been destroyed a century later by hordes of Asiatic nomads bursting upon eastern Europe. It became clearly impossible when the Germans in 375 began to pour across the frontier in great masses, as nations under national kings, transforming what had hitherto been a controlled and pacific infiltration into an unmanageable mass movement of portentous dimensions and vast momentum. However, we should perhaps not attach too much importance to any profound new cause that may be suggested for this change. In fact, the change itself was in size and degree rather than in kind. Looked at from the long point of view, what happened from 375 on was only the continuation of what began about 400 B.C.: the expansion of the Germanic peoples from their original homes around the Baltic to the warmer, more fertile, more highly civilized Mediterranean lands.

Of any basic racial antagonism between Roman and German, of Roman fear of a "German peril" or of German desire to conquer or destroy either the Roman political state or Roman civilization, there can be no thought. The idea that the Roman empire would perish never entered the mind of either Roman or German. Four centuries of pressure on the Rhine-Danube frontier had weakened the resistance of the Roman state, which had first been obliged to withdraw within the frontier, and then, owing to further internal decline, to introduce the Germans peacefully into the state. The German was well aware to what degree he was indispensable to the Roman. He had had centuries of opportunity to learn what was to be had southward in lands, booty, honors, and position and to learn also to respect and admire Roman power and appreciate the privilege of sharing in Roman civilization.

But the gradual decline of the Roman state made impossible further resistance to the wholesale invasions for which peaceful penetration had so well prepared the way. Now at last the Romans were faced with migrations of a new sort, too unwieldy to control, too huge to take in.

Chapter 5

THE GERMAN CONQUEST OF
THE ROMAN EMPIRE

FROM THE END OF THE FOURTH CENTURY TO THE
END OF THE SIXTH

The Huns reach Europe

T HE race of the Huns, fiercer than ferocity itself, flamed forth against the Goths." [1] "A race of men hitherto un-known had suddenly descended like a whirlwind from the lofty mountains, as if they had risen from some secret recess of the earth, and were ravaging and destroying everything which came in their way." [2] For hundreds of years these nomadic *Hiung-Hu*, as Chinese historians called them, had been moving westward from the borders of China, where as early as the third century B.C. the Great Wall had been built to protect the northern and western provinces of the Celestial Empire from their depredations. When once the raids of these yellow Asiatic horsemen upon the Chinese had been checked by the Han emperors, they swept across central Asia through the natural gateway between the Ural Mountains and the head of the Caspian Sea onto the steppes of southern Russia; there they met the Germans on their trek from the Baltic to the Mediterranean. The impact of the Huns upon the Germans was the direct occasion for the last phase of the Germanic penetration of the Roman empire, the heroic period of the migrations of enormous masses of rude nations under the leadership of their national kings throughout almost every province of the empire. The natives of far-away Egypt, when reports of this new danger reached them, built their huts of Nile mud within the vast confines and behind the massive walls of the temples of the Pharaohs.

[1] Jordanes, in J. F. Scott, A. Hyma, and A. H. Noyes, *Readings in Medieval History*, p. 30.
[2] Ammianus, *op. cit.*, p. 584.

Europe had known nothing like the Huns. Detachments of them
first appeared in the Crimea about A.D. 100, but the main body did
not arrive until the fourth century, and then slowly. Roman and German alike recoiled in horror from these hideous savages. They practically lived on horseback. "There is not a person in the whole nation
who cannot remain on his horse day and night. On horseback they
buy and sell, they take their meat and drink, and there they recline
on the narrow neck of their steed." They terrorized the Germans by
their sudden, unexpected appearances and their fierce aspect. They
were "small, foul and skinny," low-browed, high-cheeked, and scar-
faced. "Their swarthy aspect was fearful, and they had a sort of
shapeless lump, not a head, with pinholes rather than eyes." They
wore dirty leather tunics (until they rotted from their backs) and
helmets made from the skins of rats. They "live on the roots of such
herbs as they get in the fields, or on the half raw flesh of any animal,
which they merely warm rapidly by placing it between their own
thighs and the backs of their horses." They were homeless nomads, *The character*
wandering from place to place with their herds. They had no form *of the Huns*
of writing. From early childhood, when they were taught to ride on
the backs of sheep and shoot rats and birds, they were hunters. Sons
took over a deceased father's wives, and younger brothers took over
the widows of their elder brothers.

These savage hordes had first overwhelmed part of the Ostrogoths
north of the Black Sea, and pushed the rest on to join the frightened
Visigoths in Dacia, who were crowding down upon the Danube and
imploring permission to cross over into the eastern Roman empire.
The Huns moved on westward and entrenched themselves in the
valley of the Theiss River in modern Hungary. They established
and for seventy-five years ruled a motley kingdom in central and eastern Europe, composed of Mongolian Huns and German tribes,
Gepidæ, Ostrogoths, Rugii, Sciri, Heruli, Quadi, Suevi, and Thuringians. They collected annual tribute from the eastern emperors, *The Hunnic*
who were willing to pay to be freed from this scourge, and established *court in*
contacts with the new German kingdoms of the empire as well as *Hungary*
with the western emperors. Their court was a refuge for political
outcasts from the empire, their primitive state a harbor for oppressed
Roman provincials. Their German-Hun army was a threat not only
to the Germans on the Rhine-Danube frontier but to the empire as
well. During the course of these seventy-five years they inevitably
came under some German influence and the civilizing influences of
the Roman empire. Their last and greatest king, Attila, maintained

a court of some splendor. With his "dignified strut" he moved about the wooden buildings of his palace compound. Ambassadors were entertained in a large palace hall, at the head of which Attila himself sat. Cupbearers and numerous attendants plied the guests with food and drink, served on silver plate, though Attila himself clung to his wooden cup and the simpler ways of an earlier day. In the course of the evening "torches were lit and two barbarians, coming forward in front of Attila, sang songs they had composed, celebrating his victories and deeds of valor in war." [3] When his diplomatic duties were performed, he retired to a bed on a raised platform at some distance behind his presiding couch. It was "covered with linen sheets, and wrought coverlets for ornament, such as Greeks and Romans used to deck bridal beds." From the back of a horse to clean white linen sheets and embroidered coverlets in the span of seventy-five years or less was a rate of progress that might have given Attila pause for reflection as he closed his squint eyes for slumber.

Within the space of a hundred years after the crossing of the Visigoths into the empire the whole western half of it, with the exception of central Gaul and Italy, was occupied by new German kingdoms. *The location of the German tribes towards the end of the fourth century* To visualize this transformation it is necessary to locate on the Rhine-Danube frontier and in the German interior, at a moment subsequent to the Visigothic crossing, the tribes that were the chief participants in this occupation. Above the Visigoths on the lower Danube was a miscellaneous group of German tribes, which became subjects of the Hun empire when it centered in the valley of the Theiss. The remnant of the Ostrogoths that had crossed with the Visigoths into the empire was subsequently established, together with a group of Mongolian Alani, as allies of the empire in the Roman province of Pannonia. Above them on the Danube were groups of Quadi, Suevi, Asding Vandals, and remnants of the earlier Marcomanni, who, after the departure of most of the Suevi and Vandals, coalesced into the confederation of the Bavarians in the fifth century. Occupying the whole bend of the upper Rhine and Danube were the Alemanni. In the valley of the Main were the Burgundians and the Siling Vandals. Below them, occupying the whole right bank of the Rhine, was the confederation of Ripuarian Franks; and on the lower Rhine, settled partly within the empire as allies, was the confederation of the Salian Franks. Behind the Salian Franks and bordering on the North Sea were the Frisians. Beyond them, in the valley of the Weser, and

[3] J. H. Robinson, *Readings in European History*, I (1904), 49.

thence east to the Elbe and in Schleswig-Holstein and Denmark, were the Saxon confederation, the Angles, and the Jutes, all formidable pirates. Below the Saxons, west of the Elbe, was the confederation of the Thuringians. To the east of the Elbe there were still some Suevi and Vandals, and still farther east, in the upper valley of the Oder, were the Lombards, already pushing southward. The eastern German people—Goths, Vandals, Burgundians, and Lombards, threatening both the eastern and western halves of the empire—were all to establish comparatively short-lived kingdoms within it. They were all *Eastern and* Arian Christians. Of the western German peoples—Thuringians, *western* Angles, Saxons, Jutes, Frisians, Franks, Alemanni, and Bavarians, *Germans* threatening only the western half of the empire—all but the Thuringians and Frisians participated in the occupation of Roman soil; and of these only the Angles, Saxons, and Jutes cut themselves off directly from their German homeland. Those that entered the empire were still devoted to their pagan gods. Except for the Angles, Saxons, and Jutes in Britain, the history of all of them, as well as of the Visigoths, Burgundians, and Lombards, was destined to be swallowed up in the history of the Salian Franks.

When in 376 the request of the Visigoths for permission to settle in the empire was granted by the Roman Emperor Valens, a new Roman policy of allowing the immigration of whole German tribes was inaugurated. "They poured across the stream day and night, without ceasing, embarking in troops on board ships and rafts, and in canoes made of the hollow trunks of trees." [4] "The man who would wish to ascertain their number might as well . . . attempt to count the waves in the African Sea, or the grains of sand tossed about by the zephyrs." Actually their numbers, according to modern estimates, *The Visi-* are much less impressive, running all the way from thirty-five thou- *goths cross* sand to a million persons, and from eight thousand to two hundred *the Danube* thousand warriors. The Visigoths were allowed to settle in Thrace as allies of the Roman state, bound to give hostages and to give up their arms. The provision concerning the surrender of arms could not be enforced. The "treacherous covetousness" of the Roman officials drove them to desperation. For a time they endured the scanty food furnished them by the contractors, who profited by their misfortune. But when their wives and children were seized and sold as slaves they rebelled, and two years of desultory fighting culminated in 378 *The Battle of* in a disastrous defeat of the Roman infantry by Gothic cavalry at *Adrianople*

[4] Ammianus, *op. cit.*, p. 586.

Adrianople. The Goths had broken through the outer defenses and de-feated Rome within the limits of the empire. They were there to stay.

For the next few years, at a time when Christianity was achieving its final victory in the Roman empire, the Goths were comparatively quiet. After the death of the Emperor Valens in the Battle of Adri-anople the Roman general Theodosius had succeeded to the imperial throne in the east, and was finally able to arrange for the division of the empire after his death between his two young and utterly inca-pable sons, Arcadius and Honorius. The Goths, after futile attempts to take Adrianople and Constantinople, were pacified temporarily by Theodosius in 382 by a new agreement, which gave them land in Lower Mœsia and took them into the Roman army as paid merce-naries. They lost none of their tribal independence, and no attempt was made to interfere with their national characteristics, their law, or their Arian faith. It was during this period that they elected their first king, Alaric, under whom they had served as loyal troops in the armies of Theodosius against his western rivals. Alaric as a chieftain of the Visigoths had been used against the leading general of the west, Arbogast, a Frank, a significant and oft to be repeated situation.

The Visigoths
are settled
in Mœsia

The case was immediately repeated with Alaric now in the rôle of enemy after the death of Theodosius in 395. In the west the young Honorius was under the tutelage of the Vandal general Stilicho, a brave, intelligent, ambitious, and able man, with a far-sighted policy of amalgamating his fellow Germans with the Romans. He was at the moment the only hope of defense of the western empire against the impending German invasions. The Visigoths had become dissat-isfied with the terms of their previous agreement with the Romans. Their pay was long in arrears, Alaric resented not having received the position of *magister militum,* and they had suffered what they felt to be unjustified losses in Theodosius's last campaigns. In the east Arcadius was in the hands of officials unfriendly to the Goths, who were attacked as unsightly heretics now that Arians had been officially proscribed. In 395, therefore, they broke loose in search of a new place of settlement under their new king, Alaric. Their march led them to a futile attack on Constantinople and down into the Greek peninsula. Athens paid a heavy ransom, Corinth was sacked. Once past Sparta, they turned northward. Stilicho, who was busy with larger problems of state and anxious to settle the Visigothic problem, joined with Alaric in an alliance against Constantinople. But the al-liance was broken when the eastern government permitted the Visi-goths to settle in Epirus and granted Alaric the coveted position of

They rebel and
are settled in
Illyricum

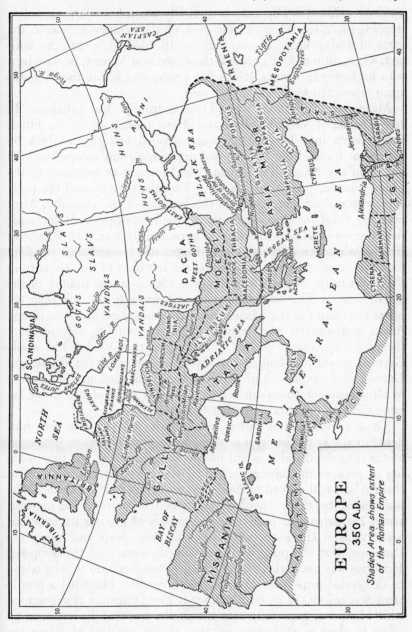

EUROPE
350 A.D.

Shaded Area shows extent
of the Roman Empire

magister militum in Illyricum in 399. Illyricum, however, was only a stopping-place for Alaric: at the turn of the century he was at the gates of Italy. There he was successfully blocked by Stilicho until 403, when, although he defeated the Romans at Verona, he withdrew with his Goths to Epirus. It was five years more before the Visigoths again attempted to locate farther west.

Meanwhile the whole Rhine-Danube frontier had collapsed. In 405 a horde of Vandals, Suevi and Alani, pushed on by the Huns, swept down into Italy. They were stopped and thrown back by Stilicho at Fiesole. But Stilicho had drawn too many troops from the guard on the Rhine. The defeated barbarians now migrated to the Main, whence, joined by the Siling Vandals, they crossed the probably frozen Rhine into Gaul on the last day of the year 406. After ravaging Gaul for three years they passed into Spain. At the same time the whole Rhine frontier was permanently lost. The Ripuarian Franks, who, then in the service of Rome, had resisted their crossing, took this occasion to occupy for good the left bank of the Rhine from the Main to the Meuse, where they bordered on the country of the Salian Franks. The Burgundians moved across to the left bank opposite the mouth of the Main. The Alemanni spread across to occupy Alsace and western Switzerland. There was nothing now to check the similar movement of the Germans across the Danube. The whole German world had bulged beyond the confines of the Rhine and Danube in an expansion of permanent and fundamental importance to all subsequent European history. The left bank of the Rhine became German once and for all at this moment.

The left bank of the Rhine becomes German

These events, among others, cost Stilicho his life. He was murdered in 408 at the instigation of Honorius, and his troops butchered by the misguided and fanatical people of Italy. There was then nothing to prevent the onward march of the Visigoths. In the general chaos Alaric had moved to Noricum, where after Stilicho's death he was joined by thirty thousand German troops from the imperial army. He demanded four thousand pounds of gold as payment for his services in Illyricum, and offered to make peace and move into Pannonia. But the puny and cowardly diplomacy of the Emperor Honorius was unequal to the situation. Rome was open to Alaric, and he descended into Italy. For the first time since Hannibal a hostile army was before the gates. Alaric made three attempts at negotiation with Honorius, personally safe within the walls of Ravenna, in an effort to reach a satisfactory solution of the problem of where the Visigoths were to settle and what was to be his reward. He then made

three attacks on Rome in which he collected considerable booty, scorn-
ing the threat of the Romans to fall upon him with all their numbers
with the remark, "The thicker the hay, the easier to mow." He finally
sacked the city for two or three days in 410—the city that had rifled
the world. But the Visigoths could not settle in Rome; its sack was
only an incident in their search for a permanent home. They moved
southward, with the evident intention of settling in the rich grain
fields of northern Africa. But a storm destroyed their ships as they
were about to embark at Messina, and this plan was given up immediately. Alaric died in southern Italy the next year from fever. We
are told that to bury him "his followers . . . diverted the river
Busento from its ordinary bed . . . and had a grave dug by captives
in the middle of the channel. Here they buried Alaric together with
many precious objects. Then they permitted the water to return once
more to its old bed."

The events of the thirty-five years preceding the Visigothic sack
of Rome could scarcely have left the intelligent Roman unmoved.
The moral shock was far greater than the military or political. St.
Jerome from his monastic retreat in Palestine set up rhetorical wails
for the "wretched empire," for "noble Mainz," for Strassburg and
for Toulouse. "Who could believe that Rome, built upon the conquest of the whole world, would fall to the ground? That the mother
herself would become the tomb of the peoples?" St. Augustine at
Hippo set about immediately to prove in the *City of God* that under
no circumstances could the sack of Rome be regarded as punishment
of the Romans by their abandoned heathen gods for taking up the
worship of the Christian God. Rome stood for all that was great and
lasting in human achievement, *urbs æterna*. The new Christian Roman empire was looked upon as the reflection of the Kingdom of
God, and Rome, already the city of the popes, was regarded as peculiarly his city. Its sack by German Christian heretics must have filled
many with consternation and despair.

Yet the historian, with his own easy dramatization of past events,
may well exaggerate the shock of the event to contemporaries. Such
things had been going on for centuries, and Rome had for a century
ceased to be the actual political capital. A Roman poet, leaving the
city six years after Alaric's sack, "sees only the crowded monuments
of her glory, and has his eyes dazzled by the radiance of her glittering fanes. . . . The temples of the gods are still standing in their
dazzling radiance under the serene Italian sky. The cheers of the
spectators in the circus reach his ears as his ship still lingers in the

Tiber. He feels a passionate regret at quitting 'this fair queen of the world,' so mighty, so merciful, so bounteous, whose visible splendor is only the faint symbol of her world-wide and godlike sway. Certainly there is here no querulous and faint-hearted lamentation over crushing and appalling disaster. The troubles of the time, referred to in a few vague phrases, are treated as merely vicissitudes of fortune, such as Rome has known before, and from which she has always risen with renewed vitality." [5]

In 412 the Visigoths moved into a much circumscribed Gaul with the intention of settling there permanently, and as allies of Honorius crushed one imperial usurper. By this time their new leader, Athaulf, had come to the conclusion that it was hopeless to try to subvert the Roman state. Like Stilicho he would work towards some kind of amalgamation of German and Roman. "Once," he said, "I sought eagerly to efface the name of Roman and to transform the Roman Empire into a Gothic empire. . . . But a long experience has taught me that the unbridled barbarism of the Goths is not compatible with law. Without law there is no state. I have therefore decided to play the part of restorer of the Roman name in its integrity by Gothic strength. I hope to be known to posterity as the restorer of Rome, since I can not supplant her."

The vicissitudes of policy at the court of Honorius, however, in 415 forced the Visigoths out of Gaul into Spain, whither a few years earlier Vandals, Suevi, and Alani had immigrated, to settle down as allies of the Roman state. The new Gothic allies were turned against them, and in three years so desperate had the situation become that Honorius intervened. As a reward for their loyalty, forty-two years after their crossing of the Danube, the Visigoths were now given *Settlement of* what they had always wanted, a place of settlement. They were quar-*the Visigoths* tered as troops with the landholders and on the imperial land of *in southern* south central Gaul, between the Garonne and the Loire, with Tou-*Gaul* louse as their capital. Two-thirds of the land and of the slaves and *coloni* were to be at their disposal, but their kings were given authority over the Goths only. The fiction of Roman sovereignty was given up eight years later, when in 426 complete sovereignty was granted to them.

From this region they expanded, especially under King Euric in the second half of the fifth century, to an impressive extent. They occupied southern Gaul between the Garonne and the Pyrenees, and

[5] S. Dill, *Roman Society in the Last Century of the Western Empire*, p. 258.

southeastern Gaul along the shores of the Mediterranean to Italy, thus cutting off the southward advance of the Burgundians down the Rhone valley to the sea. They returned to Spain, where they forced the Suevi—who, after the departure of the Vandals for North Africa, had spread over most of the peninsula—back into Galicia, and incorporated all Spain except this northwestern corner into their empire. Yet despite its extent this Visigothic state struck no real roots in Roman soil. They were only a small number of Goths scattered among the much larger Roman population. They adhered firmly to Arianism, for which they were regarded with horror by the orthodox clergy; to them, although they themselves were not persecuted by their Arian masters, no duty seemed more sacred than to plot against the Goths with orthodox outsiders. Their domains north of the Pyrenees were to fall an easy prey to the orthodox Franks, those south of the Pyrenees to the infidel Mohammedans.

By 429, when they crossed over from Spain to Africa, the Vandals had had twenty-three years of varied experience within the Roman empire. Together with Suevi and Alani they had plundered Gaul for three years. In Spain they had first settled down as allies of the empire, and then had been forced to contend with Rome's Visigothic allies. The Siling branch of the Vandals had been destroyed and the Suevi driven into the mountain fastnesses of Galicia, where the Asding Vandals and the few remaining Alani had been forced to join them. Under the constant pressure of the Visigoths, they saw in Africa a more promising hope of settlement than in Spain. North Africa, like Gaul when they first entered it, was torn by civil war. Moreover, the land was in religious turmoil because of the conflict between orthodox and Donatist Christians. The Moors of the Atlas had never been thoroughly quieted by Roman arms. Since the Punic Wars Africa had been a rich grain field, and no special invitation was needed by Gaiseric, the Asding king of the Vandals and Alani, to take advantage of this internal confusion and make these grain fields the property of Vandal landlords. The same prospect had dangled before the eyes of Alaric, and again before settling in Gaul the Visigoths had thought to cross over by the route that Gaiseric took. Abandoning Spain to the Suevi, and leaving as the sole reminder of Vandal power in Spain the name of the province of (V)andalusia, Gaiseric crossed the straits between Gibraltar and Morocco with eighty thousand men, women, and children. Within a year the Vandals were besieging St. Augustine's city of Hippo. By 435 they were settled in

The Vandals migrate from Spain to Africa

Numidia as allies of Rome. After taking Carthage in 439, for a few years they played again the old rôle of Carthage against Rome in the western Mediterranean. Within three years they were recognized as an independent power, centering around Carthage, though their power extended from Morocco to the Syrtis.

The Vandal state in Africa

The brief history of the Vandal state in Africa is almost solely the history of Gaiseric, small in stature, lame, cruel and rapacious, but one of the outstanding leaders of the period of the migrations. The Vandals took to the sea as pirates, bringing finally the Balearic Islands, Corsica, Sardinia, and Sicily under their sway. In Africa they dispossessed the large landholders and the orthodox clergy. In persecuting the orthodox clergy Gaiseric pursued a policy unique among German Arian rulers, which was only slightly mitigated under pressure from Rome and Constantinople. As in Gaul, conspiracies of orthodox exiles were a danger to the Arian state. No less to the Vandals than to the Romans, the Moorish tribesmen of the mountains to the south were a constant threat to peaceful development. In 455 the Vandals took advantage of the political disturbance occasioned by the murder of Valentinian III to plunder Rome for two weeks.

The Vandal sack of Rome

A Frenchman of the eighteenth century, with this event in mind, coined the word *vandalism* to refer to all ignorant and wanton destruction of beautiful things. By adopting the word into English, and even extending its meaning to include any willful damage to property, we have unjustly branded the Vandals as guilty of deeds that were no more characteristic of their attack on Rome than of the warfare of any other people of their time—or, for that matter, of later times. The fact is that upon the plea of Pope Leo I they actually spared the churches of the city, although they did carry away as hostages the widowed empress and her daughter. After Gaiseric's death in 477 the Vandal power in Africa speedily crumbled. They were a scanty landowning aristocracy, who quickly took on the vices of the conquered. At court they even preserved a spark of Roman culture. Only the chaos in the west and the preoccupation of the eastern emperors with greater concerns prolonged the life of their state into the sixth century.

The abandon-ment of Britain

At the same time that Rome was losing her southernmost provinces to the Vandals she was abandoning her northernmost province of Britain. Even before usurpers began to withdraw the Roman troops in Britain to fight their battles in Gaul, and before the chaos of the fifth century made it impossible to defend this outlying province, the Romanized and Christianized Celtic Britons had begun to "fear the Scottish darts, to tremble at the Pict, and to watch along all the shore for the Saxon who might come with any wind." [6] By the time of the complete abandonment of Britain to its own defense, which may be regarded as final by the middle of the fifth century, it had been thoroughly ravaged by the Picts and Scots. "These two races," wrote the native historian Gildas in the sixth century, "differ in part in their manners, but they agree in their lust for blood and in their habit of covering their hang-dog faces with hair, instead of covering with clothing those parts of their bodies that demand it." [7] In the face of "the foul hosts of Picts and Scots" landing from their coracles, and of attacks of the mysterious cannibal Attacotti, it is not inconceivable that the native British "agreed . . . to introduce those ferocious Saxons of unspeakable name, hateful to God and man, bringing as it were wolves into the fold." As early as the middle of the fourth century the keels of Low Dutch pirates from Frisia and Jutland began to grate upon the coast, and not long after 440 settlements of Angles, Saxons, and Jutes were made on the eastern coasts of Britain.

Invasion of the Angles, Saxons, and Jutes

For a century and a half the fate of Britain hung in the balance in the fight between the Christianized Celtic Britons and the German heathen. For a second time the land was thoroughly overrun. "The fire . . . fed by the hand of these sacrilegious ruffians in the east, was spread from sea to sea. It destroyed the neighboring cities and regions, and did not rest in its burning course until, having burnt up nearly the whole face of the island, it licked the western ocean with its red and cruel tongue. . . . All the 'colonies' were leveled to the ground by the frequent strokes of the battering-ram, and all the inhabitants with the overseers of the church, priests and people, were slaughtered, with swords flashing and flames crackling on every side. Terrible was it to see, in the midst of the streets, tops of towers torn from their lofty fittings, the stones of high walls, holy altars, fragments of bodies, covered with clotted blood, so that they seemed as if squeezed together in some ghastly wine-press. There was no burial for the dead, save in the ruins of their homes or in the bellies of beasts or birds." The Britons who escaped the destruction of Pict, Scot, Angle, Saxon, and Jute found refuge in Wales and Cornwall, or else "sought the regions beyond the sea [i.e., Brittany], and un-

---

[6] Claudian, quoted in Chambers, *England Before the Norman Conquest*, p. viii.
[7] Gildas, in *ibid.*, p. 79.

der the swelling sails chanted in place of the rowers' cry these words, 'Thou lettest us be eaten up like sheep, and hast scattered us amongst the heathen.' " [8]

The German kingdoms in Britain

Out of the darkness and struggle of the early sixth century emerges the half-historical, half-legendary figure of King Arthur as the defender of Celtic civilization. The oldest German kingdom in Britain seems to have been that of the Jutes, established in Kent at the southeastern corner of the island. Between them and the Britons in Cornwall, occupying all of the island south of the Thames and also a region northeast of the Thames, were the Saxon kingdoms, of which Wessex in the last quarter of the century rose to a position of importance. At the end of the century the growth of the Anglian kingdom of Northumbria under Æthilfrid foreshadowed its predominance in the seventh century, when it was overlord of all the German kingdoms in Britain. The eighth century brought to the front the conglomerate German kingdom of central England, Mercia, under Offa, who subdued Kent and built a great embankment along the Welsh border from Chester to the Severn's mouth, known to this day as Offa's Dyke, and was acknowledged as overlord of all England south of the Tees. Thus in three centuries the numerous earlier German kingdoms, after continuous fighting among themselves, were reduced to three, Wessex, Northumbria, and Mercia, each in its turn the most powerful, but each failing to unite England. At the end of the eighth century Viking ships landing at Lindisfarne —announced, contemporaries believed, by a rain of blood at York— ushered in a new period of barbarian, heathen attack.

To return to the continent. Roman territory in Gaul we have already seen greatly reduced by the settlement of the Salian Franks between the Scheldt and the Meuse as allies; by the events of 406, which brought Ripuarian Franks, Burgundians, and Alemanni across the Rhine; and by the expansion of the Visigoths to the Loire and along the northern shore of the Mediterranean to Italy. What was left to the Romans was, first, the area between the Loire and the Salian and Ripuarian Franks; second, the Rhone valley from the Alemanni in western Switzerland to the Mediterranean (until, that is, the Visigoths occupied the lower valley). Almost the whole Rhone valley then became the province of the Burgundians. Their first settlement on the left bank of the Rhine had been around Mainz and Worms; it is estimated that there were some eighty thousand of them. From this region they first attempted in 435 to move into

The Burgundians in the Rhone valley

[8] Quoted in Chambers, *op. cit.*, p. 86.

Belgium, but met a terrific defeat at the hands of Huns in the employ of the Romans. It is the neighborhood of Worms and this defeat by the Huns that furnish the setting for the tragic German epic poem of the *Nibelungenlied*. Eight years later the Burgundians were settled by Aëtius, the Roman governor of Gaul, in Savoy, between the Jura and the Saône. According to the practice of quartering soldiers, they were finally given two-thirds of the cultivable land, one-third of the slaves, and one-half of the buildings, gardens, forests, and meadows. They were called allies of Rome, but they were virtually an independent kingdom of Arian Christians. Their subsequent expansion included Besançon, Lyons, Vienne, and Vaison, and carried them almost to the Mediterranean. But the Burgundian state was never strong; it could not maintain its hold in Provence, and succumbed quickly to the advance of the Salian Franks.

The end of the period of invasions in Gaul is marked by the appearance of the Huns to the west of the Rhine in 451. What persuaded Attila, the "Scourge of God," to lead his united tribes of Huns and a large number of conquered Germans westward it is difficult to say. It is hard to believe that he came as the chivalrous defender of the emperor's sister Honoria in her marital difficulties, and to claim Gaul as her dowry after she had made what he considered a marriage proposal by sending him a ring and money. It is as difficult to believe that he attacked the Visigoths in Gaul to oblige his friend the Vandal King Gaiseric, who feared an attack of the Visigoths on Africa after he had cut off the ears and slit the nose of a Visigothic daughter-in-law and sent her home. After 450 the Huns received no more tribute from the emperors at Constantinople, and it is not inconceivable that Attila was interested in providing a substitute for this deficiency, and at the same time providing an outlet for the restless energies of those Germans within his realm whose kin had found a career within the empire. The Huns sacked Trier and Metz; Rheims was abandoned by its inhabitants; St. Genevieve is credited with having saved Paris, although the Huns actually passed the city by. Roused by the news that the Roman governor Aëtius was marching against him, Attila passed by Troyes, Châlons, and Sens and made for Orléans on the Loire. The strategy of Aëtius forced him back into the broad plains of Champagne. Somewhere near Troyes (the Mauriac Plain) a Roman-Salian Frank-Burgundian-Visigothic army faced a Hunnic-German army in a battle erroneously called the Battle of Châlons. On the morrow of the first encounter Attila, without having been actually defeated, vanished with his

The Huns in Gaul

The "Battle of Châlons"

horsemen beyond the Rhine. Roman and German had successfully made a united stand against invasion; henceforth, those already in possession of Gaul were to fight among themselves for the mastery of it.

In the spring of 452 Attila made a sudden descent from Pannonia into Italy. Aquileia was deserted by its frightened populace. It never recovered its importance: in their flight to the marshy islands at the northern end of the Adriatic its people, joined by others possessed of a like fear, are supposed to have furnished the beginnings for the growth of Venice. As if there were nothing else to interfere with a successful march on Rome—such things as the possibility of Aëtius's marching from Gaul into Italy, the presence of the eastern Emperor Marcion's troops in the Balkans, the Italian climate with its threat of disease and hunger—later legend has ascribed the withdrawal of the Huns to Pannonia to the embassy of Pope Leo I. When Attila faced this "old man of harmless simplicity, venerable in his grey hair and his majestic garb," and when in addition the apostles Peter and Paul appeared beside him, "clad like bishops" with "swords stretched out over his head," and threatened him with death if he did not obey the pope's command,[9] there was nothing for the trembling yellow heathen to do but return with his troops to his wooden palace in Pannonia and his wife Kreka and his linen sheets and embroidered coverlets. In the next year the great Hun died, we are told, in a drunken orgy in his Pannonian camp. His sons tried to partition his empire between them, but the subject Germans took this occasion to rebel and free themselves in a battle, far more important than that of 451 in Champagne, fought in 454 on the banks of the little river Nedao in Pannonia. The empire of the Huns was shattered, and the remaining Huns scattered to the east and disappeared. They were the first of a succession of Asiatic nomads to influence the development of Europe, soon to be succeeded by the Avars and the Bulgars.

Although not yet at the expense of German immigration, Italy too was in other ways submitting to German control, which prepared the way for the establishment in the peninsula of the authentic barbarian kingdom of the Ostrogoths. After the Visigothic migration through the peninsula and the death of the hopeless Honorius in 423, the chief tower of strength in the west, the defender of the last remnants of Roman territory, was Aëtius. But two years after Attila's descent into Italy he was murdered, like Stilicho, at the instigation

The Huns in Italy

The Huns vanish from Europe

Germans get control of the government of Italy

[9] Robinson, *op. cit.*, I, 50–51.

of a worthless emperor, Valentinian III. The murder of Valentinian himself in the next year opened the way for the sack of Rome by Gaiseric's Vandals in 455, which left the city gutted and prostrate. Only the most strenuous and heroic efforts could now raise Rome and Italy from the slough, whereas in fact the remains of Roman political power fell into the hands of German mercenary leaders. From 456 to 472 the Suevian general Ricimer, without assuming the imperial title himself, set up and deposed emperors at will, while on all sides in the west the barbarian kingdoms were expanding. He was succeeded by a Burgundian, Gundobald. But Gundobald was unable to prevent Julius Nepos, commander of the troops in Dalmatia, from setting himself up as western emperor in 474, with the aid of the Emperor Zeno at Constantinople. The new emperor himself was forced back to Dalmatia the next year by his own appointed *magister militum*, Orestes, a former officer in Attila's army. Orestes raised his young son Romulus, "the little Augustus," to occupy Nepos's position. Confronted with such confusion, the German mercenaries in the army, quartered on the Italian landholders, demanded what their fellow Germans had received in other parts of the empire, one-third of the land of Italy. When this was refused they crowned Odovacar, a Scirian chieftain and one of themselves, killed Orestes, and deposed the twelve-year-old Emperor Romulus in 476. So the line of Roman emperors in the west ended, as the line of Roman kings was supposed to have begun, with a little Romulus.

Theoretically Julius Nepos was still emperor of the west, and he was so recognized by the eastern empire until his death in 480. But he was not recognized by Odovacar, the actual ruler of Italy, who chose rather to govern what was left of the west as the regent (*patricius*) of the eastern Emperor Zeno. It may be said, therefore, that with the death of Nepos the empire was in theory reunited under the emperor at Constantinople. A new group of Germans had been settled on land throughout Italy. In charge of the administration of the western empire was a virtually independent barbarian king, Odovacar, commander of the mercenary troops in Italy. But except for this harassed and Germanized Italy and a small bit of Gaul between the Loire and the Somme, there was no western empire left: the last Roman emperor was gone and the first German emperor was over three hundred years away.

The establishment of the Ostrogothic kingdom in Italy is reminiscent to some extent of the Visigothic advance some hundred years earlier, while at the same time it has the external aspect of a Roman *The Ostrogoths in the fifth century* restoration from the east. The main body of the Ostrogoths had been a part of the Hunnic empire. After its collapse in 454 they were settled in northern Pannonia as allies of the eastern empire. It was a precarious and comfortless sort of liberty. The condition of the Danubian provinces was dreadful. Above the great bend of the river only the most meager remnants of Roman civilization still survived. The former Roman towns were ruined, and the population of both town and country was fearfully reduced in numbers and stricken with poverty. The land was filled with famished peasants, vagabonds, brigands, wandering bands of soldiery who preyed on the countryside, and fragments of broken barbarian German tribes—all the terrible aftermath of the retreat of the Huns. From Pannonia the Ostrogoths moved in 471 under the leadership of their King Theodoric, who had spent many years as a hostage in Constantinople, into the province formerly occupied by the Visigoths, Lower Mœsia. Here they experienced all the ancient evils of corrupt paymasters, hard quarters, and scanty food.

A five-year plundering expedition through Macedonia, Epirus, and Thessaly brought the eastern Emperor Zeno to terms; he granted Theodoric the title of *magister militum* and even a consulship, and the Goths were settled again below the Danube in Lower Mœsia. In view of the constant interruption of good relations with them, and in the face of a threatened attack from the west by Odovacar, Zeno thought to kill both his birds with one stone by entering into a formal treaty with Theodoric in 488. According to this the Ostrogoths were to take Italy from Odovacar, and Theodoric was to rule as *magister militum* and *patricius* of the eastern emperor.

The Ostro-gothic king-dom in Italy

As a Roman army, therefore, and indeed with Romans and a Roman general in it, two hundred thousand Ostrogoths set out in 488 and crossed the Adige into Italy in the spring of the next year. As Stilicho had met Alaric, so now Odovacar met Theodoric, except that this time both the German leaders were acting under Roman auspices. After a two and a half year siege of his stronghold of Ravenna, Odovacar was forced to agree to share the control of Italy with Theodoric. A few days later he was blotted out of the picture, when Theodoric murdered him and had all his troops in Italy and their families slaughtered with him.

Theodoric had already been elected king by his army, and in 497 he was recognized from Constantinople as vice-regent of the western empire, which was now essentially an Ostrogothic kingdom comprising at its widest extent Italy, Sicily, the Danube provinces, Dalmatia,

Illyricum, and Provence. In his relations with the other German kingdoms of the west, however, Theodoric appeared, by marriage alliances with the Franks, Burgundians, Thuringians, Heruli, and Vandals, to be drawing together again the severed threads of western unity, this time in German hands. The Ostrogoths were given the lands vacated by the slaughter of Odovacar's troops, and stationed as the defenders of the state throughout Italy.

Theodoric preserved intact the Roman administration; in fact, as will be shown later, he ruled as a Roman of the Romans. Although the Arian head of an Arian people, he pursued for the greater part of his reign an enlightened policy of religious toleration. "We can not," he is quoted as saying,[10] "order a religion, because no one is forced to believe against his will. . . . To pretend to rule over the spirits is to usurp the rights of the Divinity. The power of the greatest sovereigns *Theodoric's* is limited to exterior police. They have a right to punish only the dis- *policy of* turbers of the public order, which is placed under their guard, and *religious* the most dangerous heresy is that of a prince who separates from him *toleration* a part of his subjects simply because they do not believe what he does." In his protection of the Jews against the violence of orthodox Christians this barbarian heretic showed himself not only more enlightened than his orthodox contemporaries, but considerably more civilized than many of his successors down to the twentieth century.

But the Ostrogothic kingdom, like the Vandal, was a one-man state. The secret hostility of orthodox clergy and aristocracy during Theodoric's own lifetime prepared the way for orthodox intervention, and soon after his death in 526 the troops of the eastern empire landed on Italian shores. Not far from the church in Ravenna containing the brilliant mosaics of the Emperor Justinian, who destroyed the Ostrogothic state, stands the isolated tomb of Theodoric, covered with a huge monolithic dome. And in the *Nibelungenlied* he still survives as Dietrich von Bern, the invincible hero who conquered even Siegfried.

Before the destruction of the kingdom of Odovacar by Theodoric, the Salian Franks under their King Clovis had already absorbed the *German king-* last bit of the Roman empire in the west, in central Gaul. By the end *doms in the* of the fifth century, therefore, the western part of the empire existed *west at the end* only in theory. It had been supplanted by the separate German king- *of the fifth* doms and peoples: the Ostrogoths in Italy, the Vandals in North *century* Africa, the Visigoths in Spain and southern Gaul, the Burgundians in the Rhone valley, the Salian Franks in central and northern Gaul, the Angles, Saxons, and Jutes in Britain. The left bank of the Rhine above

[10] D. C. Munro and R. J. Sontag, *The Middle Ages*, p. 52.

the Salian Franks was occupied by the Ripuarian Franks and Alemanni.
The right bank of the Danube was occupied by Alemanni and a variety of smaller German peoples, Heruli, Rugii, Sciri, and Gepidæ,
who had established themselves here after the break-up of Attila's
empire, adding themselves to the already confused remnants of Marcomanni, Quadi, Suevi, and Vandals. Properly speaking, therefore, the
period of migrations was over. Only one new German people, the
Lombards, was still to be added to this medley of German stock. And
before the Lombard immigration into Italy in 568, all the German
states established on Roman soil, except the Visigoths in Spain and
the Anglo-Saxons in Britain, had been extinguished either by the reconquest of the eastern Emperor Justinian or by the advance of the
Salian Franks. Vandal Africa, Ostrogothic Italy, and for a short
period the southeastern corner of Visigothic Spain fell before the superior military forces of the eastern empire (events that may more
properly be considered in the following chapter). Visigothic Gaul, the
Burgundian kingdom, the Alemanni, and the Ripuarian Franks were
absorbed into the Frankish state. With the exception of Ripuarian
Franks and Alemanni these short-lived states were all composed of
what were originally eastern German peoples.

The transi-
tory character
of the German
kingdoms

The transitory character of these states is to be explained partly by
their comparatively small numbers, thousands of Germans settled
among millions of Romans and Roman provincials, by whom they
were quickly absorbed and only too easily influenced. Moreover, they
had never permanently grounded themselves as cultivators of the soil,
but lived as a military aristocracy, quartered as troops on the lands of
the state and of private native landowners. Finally, they were all
Arian Christians, and Arianism was now a heresy proscribed by Rome
and abhorred and detested by the orthodox clergy to a degree that
is difficult for us now to appreciate. In this connection it is important
to remember that the orthodox clergy included the bishops, who were
now themselves fast becoming the leaders and governors of society.
These ephemeral east-German kingdoms are therefore of no great
importance to us, except in so far as they illustrate a phase of the
decline of ancient civilization and typify the chaos out of which a new
western Europe had to be made.

The Lombards were the last east-German nation to establish themselves within the Roman empire. In the fifth century they had moved
from their homes on the upper Oder to the Danube, which they
reached before the end of the century. They had been admitted into
Noricum and western Pannonia by Justinian as allies against the

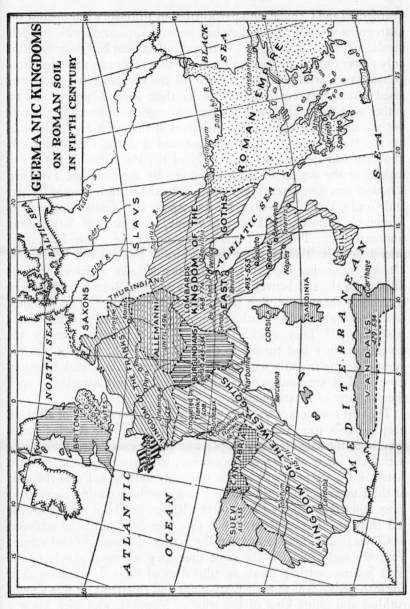

GERMANIC KINGDOMS
ON ROMAN SOIL
IN FIFTH CENTURY

The Lombards in Italy

Ostrogoths and Gepidæ, and participated in Justinian's war against the Ostrogoths in Italy. Thus they had become acquainted with the peninsula, and by destroying the Ostrogoths Justinian had destroyed the only power capable of keeping them out of it. Pushed on by the Mongolian Avars, who had rushed in to fill the vacuum left by the vanished Huns, they entered Italy under their King Alboin in 568 together with thirty thousand Saxons, no longer as allies of the empire but as conquerors, and pagan conquerors at that, of a land exhausted by the recent struggle between Justinian and the Ostrogoths. By 569 they had spread over the valley of the Po, reducing Pavia and making it the capital of their kingdom. By the time the Lombard conquest was completed there was left to the eastern empire Trieste and Grado, Venice, Ravenna, the Pentapolis (the coastal region from Rimini to Ancona), the Duchy of Rome, the Duchy of Naples, and southern Italy. The Lombards had occupied the whole Po valley, inland Venetia, Tuscany, and the duchies of Spoleto and Benevento. Unlike the earlier Germans, the Lombards seem to have made no division of the soil between themselves and the Roman landholders, contenting themselves with tribute from the produce. The soil they took over only at the death, exile, or disappearance of the Roman landholders.[11] They quickly became Arian Christians, but by the seventh century had turned to the orthodox faith, when it was too late to become friendly with the Roman Church. As a weak kingdom controlled by semi-independent dukes the Lombard state lasted until the conquest of Charlemagne.

The real founders of the new western Europe were none of all these peoples; they were the Salian Franks. Except for the Anglo-Saxons, they were the sole German people who really established themselves within the limits of the western empire; their kingdom in some form lasted in France until 987 and in Germany until 911. From the time of the Emperor Julian the Salian Franks, without cutting themselves loose from their kindred beyond the Rhine, had been settled on the left bank as allies of Rome. Such they remained until the accession of Clovis in 481, loyally fighting the battles of Rome in Gaul against Visigoths and Huns. At the same time they advanced slowly to the river Somme, settling down as cultivators of the soil, retaining their German gods, loyal to their petty kings and chieftains. It was Clovis, ruthless and astute king of the tribe of Sicambri, who with his war band of some five or six thousand men set out on a career of conquest in 486, in the course of which he adopted a policy towards the con-

The Salian Franks

Clovis

[11] J. B. Bury, *The Invasions of Europe by the Barbarians*, pp. 271–72.

quered that became the fixed policy of the Frankish rulers and was carried through to its end by Charlemagne. Clovis is therefore between Cæsar and Charlemagne the largest and most important political figure in western Europe.

It is evident that the movement of the Frankish peoples cannot be called a migration at all. Their movement was rather an expansion. The other German nations—Goths, Vandals, Burgundians—had moved entirely out of their ancient seats and, after years of wandering, settled in lands far distant from Germany in the midst of a Latin population. Contact with the homeland was permanently lost, and slowly each in turn became less German and more Roman. Not so with the Franks. They expanded from their homeland in the lower Rhine valley, adding one conquered territory after another to their dominion; but their center of gravity remained fixed, and unlike every other German invading nation they maintained their contacts with Germany and the German tribes that remained there long after Goth and Vandal, Burgundian and Lombard, had quit the land forever. In consequence, the Franks preserved their Germanic culture and vigor, whereas the other German nations were fused with the Latinized peoples among which they settled. From their farms on the lower Rhine, they expanded through the conquests of their kings and war bands. But at the same time careful colonization of the newly conquered territories by Frankish peasants provided concrete means of preserving and continuing what they had begun.

The special character of the Frankish conquest

The first addition that Clovis made to the Salian state was the conquest of the last remaining Roman territory in Gaul, between the Somme and the Loire, governed by Syagrius in so independent a fashion that he was called a king. He was attacked in 486 near Soissons, and his defeat marked the passing of the last vestige of Roman power in the west, exactly ten years after the last western Cæsar ceased to reign. There was no wholesale movement of Franks into this area, and for the local Roman population the event had only the significance of a change of masters. There was consequently no need to undertake a division of the land between Frank and Roman such as had taken place elsewhere in the German kingdoms. "The land tenure seems to have been disturbed as little as possible. Here and there in the heat of conquest there may have been cases of spoliation and violence. But there is no trace of the partition of estates such as was clearly enforced under the Burgundian and Visigothic kings. Clovis, coming into possession of the treasures of the Roman fisc, together with the booty which always falls to a victorious invader, had

Clovis conquers the last remnant of Roman Gaul

ample means of rewarding his leading followers; and he had the derelict lands which belonged to the imperial government in Gaul to distribute. Moreover, a population probably dwindling in the barbarian raids and inroads of a hundred years must have left great tracts open for new settlers. . . . Everything goes to show that long after the noises of the invasion had died away numbers of Gallo-Roman families were enjoying undisturbed the lands of their ancestors. It would be difficult to discover any sign of hate and bitterness between the two races." [12]

The second annexation to the Frankish state had important implications. It was the addition of the Alemanni, both within and without the empire, on the right and left banks of the Rhine, in modern Alsace, Baden, Württemberg, and northern and western Switzerland. In 496 the Alemanni from the upper Rhine and the Vosges began to press hard upon the Ripuarian Franks below them, who appealed to Clovis for support. In two campaigns he destroyed the independence of the Alemanni. By the inclusion of a people who in their expansion across the Rhine had likewise never lost contact with the German interior, Clovis strengthened the German character of his state. Moreover, in extending his power across the Rhine into the German interior, Clovis made it clear that the Franks had no intention of limiting themselves to Roman soil merely, but were ready to go beyond the old Roman frontier, to include German tribes that had been little touched by the civilization of the empire. Although it may not have been in Clovis's mind this early, such an expansion foreshadowed the inclusion of all or nearly all the continental German peoples outside the empire in the new Frankish monarchy. What the Romans had been unable to do by expansion beyond the Rhine

The importance of the conquest of the Alemanni

and the Danube in the first century A.D. the Franks, with the cooperation of the Church, were now making possible. This tendency to include German peoples both within and without the empire was furthered by the incorporation of the Ripuarian Franks on both sides of the Rhine into Clovis's kingdom; before his death in 511 he was elected king of the Ripuarians. Then too, if, as a chronological limit, Attila's incursion terminated the actual migration of new German peoples into Gaul, the addition of both Alemanni and Ripuarian Franks to the Frankish state made impossible any westward movement of hitherto unmigrated peoples, such as the Bavarians, Thuringians, Saxons, and Hessians. The Franks therefore stopped further migrations by actually turning the current in the other direction: the

[12] S. Dill, *Roman Society in Gaul in the Merovingian Age*, pp. 114–15.

Germans beyond the Rhine and the Danube had to think rather of *The conver-* preserving themselves from the rapidly expanding western Germans. *sion of*

A factor more important than any of these, and usually associated *Clovis's* with his campaign against the Alemanni, is the conversion of Clovis *Franks to* and his Franks from German paganism to the orthodox Christianity *Christianity* of the west. The Gallo-Roman bishops of the south, who were sustaining a difficult cause against the Arian faith of the Burgundian and Visigothic kings, had watched with keen interest the expansion of the Franks over the north. They saw that Clovis, although pagan and more barbarian than the Burgundians and Visigoths, had not dispossessed orthodox proprietors, had not molested the clergy, and, indeed, from the beginning had shown deference to the northern bishops. All the clergy of Gaul began to hope that the Franks might be converted to orthodox Christianity, especially after Clovis married Chlotilde, the orthodox niece of King Gundobald of Burgundy, and permitted their children to be baptized into the orthodox faith. From this conduct it seems only too probable that Clovis was waiting to make his final decision solely because, as he told the Bishop of Rheims, "The people that followeth me will not suffer it, that I forsake their gods." [13] But orthodox pride at his conversion, as indeed in the case of Constantine's so-called conversion, embellished this event with a similar pretty legend. In the thick of his battle with the Alemanni, when "the army of Clovis was being swept to utter ruin . . . he lifted up his eyes to heaven, and knew compunction in his heart, and, moved to tears," vowed that for a victory he would become a Christian. "And as he said this, lo, the Alemanni turned their backs and began to flee." Clovis and more than three thousand of his army were baptized at Rheims. "The streets were overshadowed with colored hangings, the churches adorned with white hangings, the baptistery was set in order, smoke of incense spread in clouds, perfumed tapers gleamed, the whole church about the place of baptism was filled with divine fragrance. And now the King first demanded to be baptized by the bishop. Like a new Constantine he moved forward to the water, to blot out the former leprosy, to wash away in this new stream the foul stains borne from old days. As he entered to be baptized, the saint of God spoke these words with eloquent lips: 'Meekly bow thy head, proud Sicamber; adore that which thou hast burned, burn that which thou hast adored.' "

The conversion of the Salian Franks to the orthodox Christianity of the Western Church contains in it the germ of a great deal of

[13] O. M. Dalton, *Gregory of Tours*, II, 69.

The great im-
portance of the
conversion
of the Franks

all subsequent western history. There is no point in giving Clovis credit for extraordinary foresight in choosing, for himself and his people, against Arianism. He had no choice between Arianism and orthodoxy; his choice was between the orthodox Christianity of Gaul and paganism. The eastern Germans had become Arians as a result of the activities of Arian missionaries, before they came into the empire, at a time when Arianism was predominant in the Eastern Church. That time was long since past. No Arian missionaries had worked among the Franks, and they had remained stubbornly pagan. The area into which they first moved, from the Rhine to the Loire, was quite untouched by Arianism. Clovis had had sense enough from the first not to antagonize the bishops of northern and central Gaul, the chief hope of his success; and it cannot be imagined that he would deliberately have gone out of his way to cut himself off from them and his Gallo-Roman subjects, or that, if he even thought of it, the vituperation of the orthodox clergy against the filthy heresy of Burgundian and Visigoth would not have brought him to his senses. But the conversion, which we may assume would have come at some time, did at this date smooth the way for expansion and assimilation by the Franks. It secured them the support of the large orthodox population, not alone of Gaul but of the entire west. It encouraged a sympathy and co-operation and fusion between Germans and Romans impossible for the Goths or Burgundians. It stimulated their conquest of the Burgundians and the Visigoths. It guaranteed the alliance of the Frankish crown with the bishops, the most important social group in Gaul and the bearers of the Christianized civilization of the ancient world, and pledged the crown to the protection of Christian missionaries in Gaul and Germany. It opened up relations with the papacy, and made possible the subsequent alliance of the Frankish kings with the papacy, which was to culminate in the Roman-Frankish ecclesiastical empire of Charles the Great in 800. It made possible the co-operation of Church and state in the furtherance of all

Clovis's policy
towards the
Frankish
Church

the works of civilization. At the same time it must not be thought that the Church of the Frankish state, or of any other early Germanic state now or at any time in the early history of western Europe, was an independent entity, free from the supervisory control and dictation of the state. Although Clovis was generous to the Church, especially to the Abbey of St. Martin at Tours, from the beginning he kept the clergy under his control. This is clear from a council of thirty-two bishops which he summoned in 511 at Orléans, to which he proposed certain measures and whose canons were submitted to him before publication. Among its provisions was one that forbade laymen to enter the ranks of the clergy without the authorization of the king.

Clovis no more than Constantine was transformed by his conversion from a raw barbarian into a mild-mannered Christian who turned the other cheek. It was murder and treachery that made him sole king of all the Salian Franks and king of the Ripuarians, and therefore king of all the Franks. Yet so strong was the Church's belief that Clovis was a divine instrument that the pious bishop-historian Gregory of Tours, the rude Tacitus of the Franks, condones his murders, bloodshed, and treachery on the ground that they were for the service of God. "Thus did God each day deliver his enemies into his hands and increase his realm, because he walked with a perfect heart before Him, and did that which was right in His sight."

Under the stimulation of the clergy Clovis's orthodoxy made him conveniently sensitive to the Arian heresy of his Visigothic and Burgundian neighbors to the south and southeast. Avitus, Bishop of Vienne, the most learned and influential prelate in Gaul, had written to him after his conversion, assuring him that the Church was interested in his future victories, and that every one of his battles would be a battle for the cross. "It irketh me," Clovis said to his men, "that these Arians hold a part of Gaul. Let us go forth, then, and with God's aid bring the land under our own sway." The Burgundians he forced into a status of dependence that prepared the way for their final incorporation into the Frankish state after his death. With the way prepared for him by orthodox bishops in Visigothic Gaul, who were disposed either to pursue a policy of nonresistance or to support him actively with troops, Clovis launched a campaign against the Visigoths, with the support of the guileless Burgundians. He met the Visigoths at Vouillé, south of Poitiers, "but when, as their habit is, the Goths turned to fly, King Clovis by God's aid obtained the victory." Clovis slew the Visigothic king, Alaric II, with his own hand, and "after wintering in Bordeaux carried off all Alaric's treasures from Toulouse and came to Angoulême. And the Lord showed him such favor that the walls fell down of themselves before his eyes; he drove out the Goths and subjected the city to his own rule. Then, his victory being complete, he returned to Tours and made many offerings to the holy shrine of the holy Martin." Thus the good Bishop Gregory, writing of the orthodox conqueror of the heretic. The Visigoths moved their capital to Toledo in Spain, keeping their hold in Gaul on Septimania, the region along the Mediterranean be-

The Frankish conquest of the Burgundians and the Visigoths

tween the Pyrenees and the Rhone. Theodoric, the Ostrogothic King of Italy, retained Provence in return for his assistance to the Visigoths.

Before his death Clovis had succeeded in uniting both Salian and Ripuarian Franks under one king; he had conquered what was left of the Roman empire in Gaul, and the Alemanni and the Visigoths north of the Pyrenees; and he had begun the conquest of the Burgundians. His territory included both banks of the Rhine and all Gaul except Brittany, Septimania, and Provence. As a kind of legitimization of his position he had been recognized by the eastern emperor as a proconsul, probably also as a *patricius*. With him the history of western Europe began again; the Roman foundation was still there, but something new had been built upon it.

The division of Clovis's kingdom

Treating his kingdom as private property, in accordance with German law, Clovis before his death divided this wide territory, inhabited by such different and mixed peoples, into four roughly equal parts, one for each of his four sons. This, however, was not intended to be, and in fact was not, a dismemberment of the Frankish state. The four kingdoms, each with its own chief place of residence—Metz, Orléans, Paris, Soissons—together formed the greater kingdom, though it was no longer a monarchy. In spite of strife among the brothers the work of expansion and conquest went on for another generation. By the time the kingdom was reunited for a short period under Clovis's youngest son, Chlotar I, from 558 to 561, it had expanded to the southeast to include Burgundy and Provence. In the

Further expansion of the kingdom

northeast the kingdom of the Thuringians had been destroyed, and into its northern half, the region of the Harz Mountains, the pagan Saxons had moved. Southern Thuringia was colonized by the Franks themselves. By this time the Bavarians also had been reduced to dependence. Thus the movement of the Franks into the interior of Germany was almost completed within the generation after Clovis. The first great period of Frankish expansion was over.

The second partition

When Chlotar I died in 561, for the second time the Frankish kingdom was partitioned among four sons. By this time, partly because of the precedent of 511, but much more because of historic differences inherited from the past and the great variation in the population in each of them, these divisions were tending more and more to separate into distinct political and social entities. The three grand divisions or realms that formed the Frankish kingdom, by the beginning of the seventh century, were Austrasia, Neustria, and Burgundy. Aquitaine was a dependency of Neustria. Roughly, Austrasia, the "east land," included northeastern Gaul and the Rhine and Danube lands as far as the Inn River. Neustria, the "new land," was northern Gaul from the Meuse to the Loire, corresponding to Clovis's first conquests after 486. Burgundy was approximately the former kingdom of the Burgundians. Aquitaine represented the territory wrenched from the Visigoths. In culture the two northern kingdoms were predominantly Germanic, the two southern predominantly

THE EXPANSION OF THE
SALIAN FRANKS
481 - 555

The Salian Franks in 481
The Conquests of Clovis
Conquests after Clovis to 555

Latin; but within these categories there was wide cultural variation and racial distinction. Austrasia was almost purely German, the Roman element being strongest principally around Rheims, Metz, and Toul. Neustria was less German than Austrasia, but less Roman than the two kingdoms to the south, the Roman population being densest around Paris, Orléans, and Tours. Burgundy was Germanized, but the Latin culture there was strong, and the majority of the population of Latin lineage. Aquitaine was like Burgundy, except that in Gascony south of the Garonne the Basque population of the Pyrenees had crept down from the mountains and were spreading over the plain.

Historians vary greatly in their opinions of both the nature and the degree of the German conquest. But some things commonly believed of the Germanic invasions are certainly not true. The Germans neither destroyed nor regenerated western civilization. They introduced neither equality nor liberty, for they had neither among themselves. They cherished no dream of conquering the Roman empire

The general
character of
the Germanic
migrations

and never knew that they had done so. The German incomers were more than mere war bands, but they were not always invaders, nor were they always predatory. The Germans were not ravenous barbarians, neither were they children of nature endowed with a singular genius for constructing a new world upon the ruins of an old. They were not hostile to Roman civilization. They did not ruin it, for the good reason that it was well-nigh in a state of dissolution when they entered the empire. So far from the Roman's being an enemy to the German, the Roman army offered a career for German fighting men; individuals, families, war bands, and whole tribes entered it to seek their fortunes.

The manner
of German
immigration

The invasions were not a sudden contact between peoples hitherto unknown to one another; on the contrary, they were a long-drawn-out process of penetration, much of it accomplished without violence. The overthrow, therefore, of the entire fabric of the western empire was neither immediate nor complete. The dissolution was prolonged by three circumstances, quite independent of any measures of the government or the civilian population in their own defense. In the first place, the number of the invaders was inadequate for permanent occupation for many years; second, the migratory and predatory nature of some of the invaders was unfavorable to fixed occupation; third, even when the imperial government had become incapable of resisting the Germans in a military capacity, its fiscal machinery was still employed either to divert German occupancy or to ameliorate the hardship of it by means of payments or stipends or plain bribes given to a chieftain and his men.

Here and there some disgruntled Roman proprietors refused to have any intercourse with the barbarians and sulked by themselves, living aloof upon their property. But such malcontents were not numerous. The immense majority of the Roman provincials rallied to the new condition of things, accepted it, and tried to adapt themselves to it. A change of rulers mattered little to the proprietary class so long as it was not deprived of its land and its social status. As for the great mass of the servile and slave population, which had long been exploited by the imperial fisc, it must have felt a sense of relief to know of the collapse of Rome's formidable tax machine. Indeed, a contemporary writer insists, "So far are the Germans from tolerating the evil taxation of the Romans, that not even the Romans who live under German rule are compelled to endure it, and hence the one wish of all the Romans in these parts is that they may escape from Roman domination."

The essential fact seems to be that the capacity for resistance had broken down in the Roman empire at the end of the fourth century, and when the great fabric at last began to crumble, it disintegrated rapidly. The government, the financial system, the army had ceased to function effectively. A half-independent landed aristocracy and an arrogant and selfish bureaucracy had displaced the old senatorial nobility. The mass of the Roman people, except in the towns, was reduced to serfdom, when not actually enslaved. Commerce had declined; industry was slack; agriculture had decayed. The population had diminished, especially in the border provinces. In fact, the provinces that suffered most from decrease of population, and in which the problem of waste or abandoned farms was most acute, were precisely those where the Germans settled in greatest number. These regions were northern and eastern Gaul, western and southern Germany, Britain, and northern Italy, from which much of the Roman population had fled to find safety within the central or more southern provinces. The Germans did not flow into a vacuum, but they did flow into half-evacuated provinces. It is significant that in all of these regions the Germans established relatively permanent kingdoms. In the other parts of the empire their kingdoms were fragile and short-lived. *The break-down of the empire*

The most immediate effect of the conquest was perhaps the infusion of the blood of a young and vigorous race into the stagnated and anemic blood of the Roman population of the western provinces. The German conquest was everywhere a drastic and sometimes a violent experience, which supremely tested the vitality of both men and institutions. It was a weeding and winnowing process that eliminated the weak. It imposed a new people, with new institutions, upon the old. For every migration, every conquest, stamps the features of one culture upon the features of another, and a mixture of institutions as well as of blood follows. The old and the new fuse to form something resembling both and different from either. Much less of things Roman perished than is usually supposed. The Church incorporated and preserved a great portion of the Roman heritage. The residue, although often reduced to broken and mutilated débris, was incorporated by the Germans into their institutions. *Fusion of German and Roman*

*The effect of
the migrations
on the Germans*

The long period of the migrations had also revolutionized the institutions of the German nations. Old Germany was dissolved in the crucible of the fifth century as effectually as Roman civilization was dissolved. Kingship lost its early elective character and became hereditary. The German kings of the period of the conquest were strong, brutal, and irresponsible rulers. Assassination was often the only redress against a bad king. The ancient Germanic assembly had degenerated to a merely military review in the spring, when the season for war opened. There is no evidence of any traditional constitutional powers or of the preservation of popular rights in any of the Germanic kingdoms. The old folkmoot, the old village moot, the old free warrior class, the old German nobility proud of its lineage— all of these things vanished during the migrations. The new German aristocracy was like that of the late Roman empire, a landed and proprietary nobility, while most of the former class of freemen had sunk into a status differing little from serfdom.

BYZANTINE
CIVILIZATION

Vestibule mosaic from Santa Sophia, recently uncovered from the coating of paint put on by the Moslems. The mosaic represents the Emperor Justinian (left) offering the church, and the Emperor Constantine offering the city of Constantinople, to the Virgin and her son. (BYZANTINE INSTITUTE.)

An ivory leaf of a diptych of the sixth century representing Justinian as Defender of the Faith

BETTMANN

Justinian and his suite, a mosaic from the Church of San Vitale in Ravenna (See p. 149)

BETTM.

MAXIMIANVS

Chapter 6

THE BYZANTINE EMPIRE

"E AST" and "west" have been employed in the preceding chapters to emphasize the differences between the Greek and Roman Mediterranean regions. Similar use has been made of the terms "eastern empire" and "western empire," as if there were indeed two empires. After the reorganization of the empire by Diocletian and Constantine and the partition by Theodosius in 395 the use of such terms seems especially justifiable. The end of a line of Roman emperors in the west has been assigned to 476 with the deposition of Romulus Augustulus—perhaps more properly with the death of Nepos in 480—and the accession to power of Odovacar. Historians once used the date 476 to mark the "fall" of the Roman empire. Hence the reader might naturally conclude that there were actually two Roman empires —a false conclusion if anything more than a loose geographical and cultural significance be given to the terms. In any political or constitutional sense denoting two independent halves of a formerly united state, there was never an eastern or a western empire. Even after the Germans had set up their own states and no western territory was governed solely by Roman officials, every Roman, and certainly the emperors at Constantinople, considered that the empire was still one. German kings were only vice-regents of the emperor, or at worst mere usurpers, and often enough they were proud to bear the title of *patricius* or consul, honored representatives of the eternal Roman state. This was the position taken by all legal and political writers and by the emperors at Constantinople until a German was crowned Roman emperor at Rome in 800. Even after this date the eastern emperors resented any diminution of their title. When envoys of the pope called the tenth-century Nicephorus merely "Emperor of the Greeks" and not also "Emperor of the Romans," he promptly put them into a Byzantine prison.

At Constantinople from the time of Constantine's foundation of the city there continued to reign a line of Roman emperors in unbroken

Significance of the terms "eastern" and "western empire"

117

*The continuity
of the Roman
empire in
the east*
succession until 1453—a matter of over a thousand years. After the experiments begun by Diocletian with administrative subdivisions of the empire, following the occupation of the west by the Germans, there was still no break, no "fall" of the Roman empire. All official titles remained the same, or were merely translated into Greek. This continuation of the empire has therefore sometimes been called the "later Roman empire." As a matter of fact, in spite of all pretensions this was not at all the Roman empire founded by Augustus, although its emperors considered themselves his successors. It was in fact the eastern, Greek half of the old empire, after the Germans had cut away the western half. For this reason it has sometimes been called the "eastern Roman empire" or simply the "Greek empire."

What we shall call the "Byzantine empire" had its cultural and political center in Constantinople, which was founded on the site of the Greek colony of Byzantium, established in 660 B.C. But "Byzantine" signifies more than is in this derivation: it is meant rather to suggest that, just as in the west there began to take form after the German migrations a new European civilization that was neither German nor Roman but a combination of both under the influence of Christianity, so too in the eastern half of the empire there developed an entirely new type of civilization, which deserves a new name. The essential elements of this new Byzantine civilization were not themselves new; only the combination of them was new. The accomplishments of the Hellenic Greeks in literature, art, philosophy, mathematics, and science formed the basic tradition on which Byzantium continued to live. The larger Greek world of Alexander's conquests, the combination of Greek and oriental that we call Hellenistic, was a second basic

*The
significance
of the term
"Byzantine"*
tradition of the Byzantine world. The empire was Greek and as such may be regarded as the third phase in the development of Greek civilization, following the Hellenic and the Hellenistic. Yet Constantinople faces the world of the orient, and was subject to the influences of Syria, Palestine, Egypt, and Persia. Persia in particular was beginning to cast off its Greek tutelage and to reassert its native tradition under the new Sassanid dynasty.

However, the most characteristic element in this Byzantine civilization was its Christianity, which became estranged from western Christianity by its Greek love for theological subtleties and was divided within itself by divergent Greek and oriental sects.[1] Moreover, Greek Basilian monasticism and the peculiar relationship of the Byzantine Church to the Byzantine state also helped to give a distinctive turn to

[1] See p. 41.

eastern Christianity. This eastern Mediterranean combination of the political tradition of the Roman and the intellectual and artistic tradition of the Hellenic and Hellenistic Greek with the renascent oriental tradition and the new Græco-oriental Christianity, the whole worked into a new synthesis under the most terrific external pressure, is what is meant by Byzantine. The contrasts between east and west gradually became stronger and led to a sharp rivalry or enmity and occasionally broke out in open hostility.

It was not until the sixth century that it became clear that a really new civilization was developing in Constantinople. The east had never suffered the severe economic depression of the west) Its cities continued *Factors in* to find the source of their vitality in commerce and industry, at a time *Byzantine* when the west was reverting to agrarianism. The location of Constan- *strength* tinople made it virtually impregnable. On three sides it is surrounded by water, and its northwest side was soon fortified by the famous long walls, eighteen leagues in length, from the Black Sea to the Propontis, built about A.D. 500 by the Emperor Anastasius and still standing. Hence only a combined attack by land and sea was really dangerous. As long as the city stood, the empire managed to stand.

The city soon became the great entrepôt for far-eastern and western trade. Under the close economic supervision exercised by the state the trade routes from central Asia to China and India ended in Constantinople. A strict monopolistic control over industry brought in, in addition to customs duties, a large steady income, which could support an army and a navy the like of which no western power knew. This army and navy long remained the basis of the power of the state. After the Battle of Adrianople in 378 the army consisted largely of heavy mail-clad cavalry. The Byzantine emperors learned from bitter experience the weakness of an army that was largely barbarian, and returned to the older Roman practice of recruiting from their own ruder subjects. With its army and navy and by the use of devious diplomacy Constantinople had kept the east free from settlement by Germans. Visigoths and Ostrogoths had moved on to the west; the Huns had been bought off. By the time of Justinian's accession in 527 the empire *The accession* was in a flourishing condition, with a treasury well filled with some *of Justinian* sixty-five to seventy million dollars. The new Byzantine east was about to enter upon its first golden age.

And yet the emperor of the east had his mind on the west. It is easy to say now that Justinian had done better to forget the west, to regard *Justinian's* it as irretrievably lost, and to concentrate his attention on the Danube, *western policy* where already new hordes of Slavic and Mongolian barbarians were threatening the frontier so insistently as to make clear that they could neither be easily bought off nor be moved on into an already occupied west. Or he had no doubt done better to devote more attention to his southeastern frontier, where with the accession of his able rival Chosroes I, the greatest of all the Sassanid dynasty, Persia was again becoming formidable.

But as a native Illyrian, trained in the Roman tradition, and as Roman emperor he was imbued with the idea of a single Roman state, reunited under one law and under the orthodox Christianity established by the Church councils. To him the German kingdoms of the west were only evidences of temporary imperial weakness: the German kings were barbarian usurpers who must be destroyed now that the empire had recovered its strength. "The Goths," he said, "having seized our Italy, have refused to give it back." Moreover, to an orthodox Christian prince the Arianism of Vandals, Visigoths, and Ostrogoths was anathema; it also must be destroyed. Persecuted orthodox clergy, mostly from Africa, stimulated Justinian to this task. The loyalty of the Roman population in North Africa, Spain, and Italy he felt, quite rightly, that he could count on, and the German armies he knew were no match for his superior forces.

The recovery of North Africa and part of Spain

In North Africa the weak, predatory Vandal state fell with incredible swiftness. In 532 Justinian disembarked his heavy cavalry on the North African shore while the Vandal fleet and part of the army were in Sardinia subduing a rebellion. His general Belisarius with fifteen thousand men marched on Carthage, where the orthodox native population rapturously welcomed him. In two battles he destroyed the Vandal kingdom, though it took much longer to subdue the Berber tribes. Vandal leaders were deported to the east; the soldiery and their wives were enslaved. The imperial fisc, the Church, the native population resumed possession of the lands of which they had been deprived. This part of North Africa was organized into the Exarchate of Africa. Farther west, Morocco was not brought under Byzantine control, although at Ceuta a position was occupied from which Visigothic Spain might be reconquered. No such attempt was made, however, until 554, after the desperate struggle for Italy, and then only with partial success. Southeastern Spain, including Seville, Málaga, Cartagena, and Cordova, did fall into Byzantine hands, but only for a short time; by 629 the Visigoths had recovered the lost territory.

The recovery of Italy

Meanwhile, from Sicily—which, together with Sardinia, Corsica, and the Balearic Islands, had been recovered from the Vandals—Belisarius had launched the attack on Ostrogothic Italy, even before the Vandal campaign was over. The murder of one of Theodoric's daughters, who as regent had been friendly to Justinian, furnished him his pretext. As in Africa, the whole Roman population was hostile to their barbarian masters. Naples, Rome, and Ravenna fell to Belisarius's troops, but when he was called home the Ostrogoths under new leadership renewed the campaign. Belisarius returned to wage desperate war in Italy. When he was recalled again to fight the Persians, the war was finished by the eunuch Narses. After the defeat of the Ostrogoths at Taginæ in 552 their last king, Totila, was slain and their power broken. In ten years more all resistance had been crushed, and the race of the Ostrogoths disappeared over the Alps. The Byzantine government of Italy was centered at Ravenna under an exarch.

This last war had ruined Italy, and especially Rome, as no German *The condition* invasion had ever ruined it. "The flocks remained alone in the pastures *of Italy* with no shepherd at hand. . . . You might see villas or fortified places, lately filled with people, in utter silence. The whole world seemed brought back to its ancient silence; no voice in the field, no whistling of the shepherds. The harvests were untouched; the vineyard with its fallen leaves and its shining grapes remained undisturbed while winter came on. There were no foot-steps of passers-by." [2] War, famine, and pestilence had enormously reduced the population. Many of the great families had been broken up. Peasants and townsmen were sunk in desperate poverty. Brigandage was rampant, and wolves infested the countryside and even invaded the towns. In the northeast the people of Padua, Aquileia, and other towns near the coast fled to the lagoons in the Adriatic, the refuge, since the invasions of Alaric and Attila, of increasing numbers of people. Venice was beginning to rise from the water. Rome ceased once and for all to be the ancient city of the Cæsars and became the dreary city of the popes; not until the fifteenth century was it to regain some of its ancient splendor.

Justinian never realized his program of re-establishing the western frontiers of the Roman empire. The Visigothic kingdom in Spain had barely been touched, and that only briefly. The Frankish kingdom, whose destruction was necessary to the restoration of Roman power, was left unmolested; the best that Justinian could do was to prevent the Franks and the Alemanni from taking advantage of his war with the Ostrogoths. His campaigns, except in Italy, were mere episodes;

[2] Paul the Deacon, quoted in J. W. Thompson, *Economic and Social History of the Middle Ages* (1928), p. 125.

they left little permanent mark, except perhaps his now ruined fortifications in North Africa, and this territory was destined soon to fall to the Mohammedans.

*The signifi-
cance of Jus-
tinian's west-
ern conquests*

By destroying the power of the Ostrogoths in Italy Justinian opened the way for the invasion of the Lombards, which considerably reduced the area of Byzantine control even in Italy.[3] Thereafter Italian unity, restored for a fleeting moment, was hopelessly broken, and Italy until 1870 was merely a geographical name. The peninsula was divided among three political authorities roughly as follows: the Lombard kingdom in northern Italy, with its outlying duchies of Benevento and Spoleto; Byzantine Italy, with its capital at Ravenna; the city and territory of Rome, which, though nominally subject to the Exarch of Ravenna, under the popes soon became at least *de facto* independent. This nominally tripartite division really represented an extreme territorial disorganization. Nevertheless Byzantium—despite the gradual encroachment of the Lombards upon imperial territory, and the rising papacy and later encroachments of the Mohammedans in Sicily and the south—maintained its hold in southern Italy for more than five hundred years; this was of great importance to Italy and to western Europe. From Byzantine territory in Italy there kept quietly trickling into the lower civilization of the west the varied influence of the advanced civilization of the east, an influence that slowly prepared the way for the Greek enthusiasm of the fifteenth century.

The Byzantine empire inherited the age-long conflict of Greece and Rome with Persia. For centuries Armenia and the provinces lying west of the Euphrates had oscillated between the two powers. The struggle was not merely for political mastery and territorial possession; it was for control of the commerce of the east and was embittered further by religious differences. Justinian did nothing to solve the Persian problem; he handed it on to his successors. In order to satisfy his dream of recovering the west, he imperiled the interests of the empire in the east. Instead of following up the victory over the Persians won by Belisarius at Dara in 530, he bought freedom to pursue his war on the Vandals by paying tribute to the Persian King Chosroes in 532. This was the beginning of humiliation after humiliation. Between 540 and 545 the Persians renewed the war, captured Dara, ravaged Syria, and occupied Antioch. Rather than abandon Italy, Justinian bought the Persians off in 545 and again in 562. He did, however, retain control over the Black Sea and the trade routes to the east.

*Justinian's
weak Persian
policy*

For the security of the Byzantine empire the maintenance of the

[3] See p. 106.

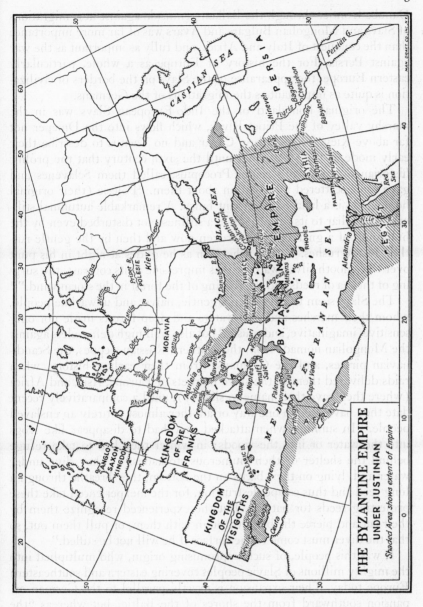

THE BYZANTINE EMPIRE
UNDER JUSTINIAN
Shaded Area shows extent of Empire

Danube frontier through the Balkan peninsula against new migrations of Slavs and Mongolian Bulgars and Avars was of far more importance than the conquest of Italy and Africa, and fully as important as the war against Persia. For the history of Europe as a whole, particularly eastern Europe, the appearance of the Slavs on the borders of civilization is quite as important as the migrations of the Germans.

The original homeland of the Indo-European Slavs was in the marshy valley of the Pripet River, which flows into the Dnieper not far above Kiev. They had no Cæsar and no Tacitus to describe their early mode of life; it was not until the sixth century that the prolific historian of Justinian's reign, Procopius, called them Sclavenes and gave some scattered information about them. "Polesie (their original homeland) is a land of exuberant fancy. A remarkable autumnal stillness is peculiar to its sea of marsh, a stillness not disturbed even by the humming of a gnat and only broken now and then by the gentle rustling of the rushes. To the fisherman as he glides at night in his punt over the smooth silver water it is as impressive as its contrast, the surging of the sea of reeds and the roaring of the forest in the storm-wind." [4]

The Slavs seem to have been a gentle, naïve, and unwarlike people, whom their marshes and still waters and deep forests made not only sensitive, imaginative, and musical but also well-nigh defenseless against the Mongolian nomads from the southern Russian steppes, the Scandinavian pirates, and the Germans. From their earliest history, when raids delivered them to the slave markets of Europe, Asia, and Africa (where they gave their name to slavery), until a comparatively recent date they have been in one way or another almost entirely an enslaved people. "In summer when attacked they had to disappear like frogs into the water or into the woods; in winter they had to take refuge behind the shelter of their numerous stockades." "They dive under water and, lying on their backs on the bottom, they breathe through a long reed and thus escape destruction, for the inexperienced take these projecting reeds for natural. But the experienced recognize them by their cut and pierce the body through with them, or pull them out, so that the diver must come to the surface if he will not be stifled."

It was this people, of such unpromising origin, who multiplied into the mighty millions of Slavic peoples covering eastern and southeastern Europe today. Their expansion is exactly parallel to the German expansion southward from the shores of the Baltic; but whereas "the Germanic migration was eruptive like a volcano, the Slavonic was a gradual percolation like that of a flood rolling slowly forward." From

[4] *Cambridge Medieval History*, II, 424.

their very nature and experience the Slavs could not expand by con- *Early Slav* quest, but they moved noiselessly into unclaimed territory or areas *expansion* vacated by the emigration of Germans. To the northeast of their original homeland stretched the empty regions of Russia; to the north, the valleys of the upper Niemen and the Dvina; to the northwest, the valleys of the Vistula and the old, now abandoned, German homeland of the Oder, extending west to the Elbe and the Saale; to the southwest, the northern slopes of the Carpathians and the abandoned homeland of the Marcomanni and the Quadi, modern Czechoslovakia; to the south, the steppes of southern Russia, for a while the home of the Ostrogoths but now filled by a regular succession of Mongolian nomads from Asia.

The Slavs north of the Black Sea became the subjects of Mongolian Bulgar horsemen, who drove them ahead in hordes into battle and on plundering raids into the Byzantine empire. By the beginning of the sixth century these raids of Bulgar and Slav were harassing the lower Danube frontier. Justinian first used the Mongolian Avars to attack *The Slavs on* them from the rear. Then, along the northern frontier from the *the Balkan* mouth of the Save to the mouths of the Danube, he erected eighty *frontier* fortresses, and within this barrier a line of six hundred lesser fortified places, straight across the Balkan provinces. The great masses of Slavs were thus kept from settling in the Balkan peninsula while Justinian lived; nevertheless, in spite of the network of fortresses along the frontier there were repeated invasions of Bulgars and Slavs. In 540 a great raid devastated the northern zone of provinces as far as the Adriatic. In 558 the Hunnic chieftain Zabergan led a horde of Huns and Slavs across the Danube on the ice; they traversed the gorges of the Hæmus Mountains and pushed through a breach recently made by an earthquake in the new walls of Constantinople. Meanwhile there was constant infiltration into the empire, similar to that of the Germans into the western provinces in the fourth century.

It was chiefly the incursions of the Avars that kept pushing Bulgars *The Avars* and Slavs together into the Balkan peninsula in the later sixth and seventh centuries, just as the Huns had pushed the Goths ahead of them. These same Avars also forcibly transplanted Slavs close to the German frontier from the head of the Adriatic straight north to the Baltic. At the height of its power the Avar empire, exceeding even that of the Huns, stretched from the Baltic to southern Greece, and from the eastern Alps into the heart of Russia. The Avars were yellow herdsmen, lording it over a servile agricultural Slavic people, whose wives and daughters they "harnessed . . . like beasts to their wagons, violating them systematically, destroying their family life, and indeed reducing their whole existence to the level of brutes."

Pushed by the Avars up against the Elbe and Saale rivers, facing Saxons, Thuringians, and Frankish colonists, were Slavs who subsequently came to be differentiated as Sorbs (Serbs), Liutizi, and Obodrites. Behind them were the Poles. Facing the Bavarians, in the valleys of the Regnitz and upper Main and north of the Danube, were the Czechs and Moravians. At the head of the Adriatic and in the eastern Alps and the valleys of the Drave and Save were the Croats and Slovenes. Into the Balkan provinces of the Byzantine empire, whose land was devastated and whose population was partly destroyed or enslaved, poured ever larger masses of Asiatic nomads and Slavs. The Slavs settled down as peasants, the nomads as herdsmen, and out of the subsequent amalgamation of these masses came the leading Balkan groups of Serbs and Bulgars. The formation of all the Slav nationalities, Serb and Bulgar, Pole and Czech, was of course the work of centuries.

The Slavic settlement of the Balkans and eastern Europe

In the Balkan peninsula the native Illyrians were pushed into the mountains of the west, where we call their descendants Albanians; the Greeks were pushed down to the seacoast. The Latin-speaking provincials of Roman Dacia were crowded into the uplands, where they subsequently fused with Mongolian nomads in the region of present-day Rumania: "the Roumanians are Romanized Altaians" (Mongolians). In the same way the yellow Bulgarian in the course of centuries lost his identity in the larger mass of the peasant Slavs; he gave up his language and customs, his blood was mixed with Slavic blood, and to all intents and purposes the Asiatic became a Slav. The other Asiatic nomads, the Avars, who settled down elsewhere with the Slavs, preserved their distinctive shepherd's existence; moreover, the headship of many Slavic villages was long held by them, and to the village head they gave their own name, *zupan*. Thus in the course of the sixth and seventh centuries the whole Balkan peninsula and all Europe east of the Germans, with the exception of the actual valley of the middle Danube, became completely Slav. When the Avar empire was at last totally destroyed by Charlemagne, these wider areas also were left in the undisputed possession of the Slavs.

Eastern and western Slavs

This expansion of the Slavs into the vacant regions of eastern and southeastern Europe is the setting for all subsequent history of this territory, and the fundamental explanation of much even of its recent and contemporary history. The Slavs who moved close to the western German world were subjected to the influence of its Latin-Christian-German civilization. Those who moved close to, or within the boundaries of, the Byzantine empire were subjected to the Greek-Christian-oriental civilization of the east. On the borderland, therefore, the Slav had to choose between the two. But for the Balkan and Russian Slavs the rôle of the Byzantine empire was settled; it was exactly like that of the Latin-Christian empire for the Germans. Their Christianity and their means to the development of a higher literary, artistic, and material culture all came from Byzantium.

More than for his conquests history will always be indebted to Justinian for his part in the preservation of Rome's greatest contribution to western civilization, her system of law and scientific jurisprudence. The body of civil law (*Corpus Iuris Civilis*) that was consolidated under Justinian was the fruit of very slow growth. It had begun as the customs of the Latin tribes of Italy, which in the course of Rome's long history had necessarily to be enlarged by Roman magistrates, the Roman senate, and Roman emperors. In this way a vast amount of what might be called statutory law was formulated. At the same time, however, a body of law was developed by the commentaries and opinions of what were at first private lawyers, who under the empire came to be officials, *iuris consulti*. Their peculiar position gave to their opinion on the facts of a case authority binding upon the judges, and their decisions came to be regarded as valid legal precedent, just as are the decisions of our judges. This body of extra opinion on the law was equivalent to common law.

Moreover, a notable feature of Roman law was due to the fact that with the expansion of the Roman state it became necessary to decide cases between Roman citizens and those who were not citizens, or between two persons neither of whom was a Roman citizen. In these instances the Roman jurisconsult was not minded solely to impose the body of Latin custom upon non-Latins, but to take into consideration the laws and customs of other peoples and to accommodate Roman law to them. The result of this accommodation was *ius gentium*, the law of nations. It was also influenced by the speculations of the Stoic philosophers on natural law—a common body of principles governing the life of all men as brother human beings; *ius gentium* came to be considered the embodiment of this natural law. Thus Roman law developed into a system that could be used for the whole Mediterranean world, regardless of nationality, irrespective of persons. This in itself was a unique intellectual and practical achievement.

The development of Roman law

After the first two centuries of the empire the creative writing of the jurisconsults ceased; Papian, Ulpian, and the others had done their work. But the body of statutory law naturally continued to grow. Moreover, with the acceptance of Christianity and the changed nature of the state in the later empire, the law had perforce to take a turn different from its old course under the late republic and early empire. A good deal of the older law was no longer applicable; there was much duplication and even contradiction; much needed to be brought up to date. Furthermore, in the confusion of the later empire there was danger that the large body of the works of the jurisconsults would be lost entirely.

Before Justinian, notably by Theodosius II in 438, attempts had been made to systematize and bring up to date the body of statutory law, but nothing had ever been done to systematize the body of precedent contained in the writings of the jurisconsults. Justinian took it *Justinian's* to be one of his first obligations as emperor to systematize both, and *codification* to produce authoritative texts of the whole body of law still ap- *of Roman law* plicable, to serve henceforth as the fixed standard for the courts and for study in the law schools. To carry out his wishes he relied upon his minister Tribonian. Within two years of Justinian's accession in 527 a commission of lawyers under Tribonian, making use of previous summaries, had arranged, systematized, and brought up to date in one volume all the statutory law of the emperors from Hadrian to Justinian. This was the Justinian Code proper, *Codex Justinianus.*

Tribonian's commission then set to work on the writings of the jurisconsults. In three years more they had ready one volume of one hundred and fifty thousand lines, condensed from two thousand rolls containing some three million lines, called the Digest (*Digesta*), or Pandects (*Pandecta*). Henceforth this was to be the one authoritative commentary. In 534 a revised code was published, after experience in the preparation of the Digest had shown some of the contents of the first edition to be obsolete. Finally, as a kind of introductory textbook on the principles of Roman law as contained in both the Code and the Digest, for the use of law students in the universities, the Institutes were published. As a supplement to the Code, but, unlike it, published for the most part in Greek, the Novels (*Novellæ Leges*) later embodied the legislation of Justinian and his immediate successors. Code, Digest, Institutes, and Novels together constitute the *Corpus Iuris Civilis*, the whole body of the civil law.

Even though the *Corpus* has been criticized for the haste with which it was compiled, and on the ground that it is too much a mere compilation and not enough a reasoned code of Roman law, no one has ever minimized the accomplishment nor, it seems, overestimated its importance to posterity. In it is preserved what might otherwise easily have been lost, the product of Rome's creative genius in the law. In it is preserved, too, a picture of the declining Roman empire and the reign of Justinian, in so far as that picture can be recovered from the legislative alterations of the emperors. In it is preserved what little softening effect Christianity had been able to work upon Roman law by the time of Justinian's reign. *The importance of Justinian's codification*

From the twelfth century on it supplied the basis for a large part of the development of the law of western Europe, which was later carried to such remote regions as South Africa, Ceylon, Guiana, and Louisiana. Incorporating as it does the absolute authority of the despotic late Roman emperors, it transmitted the legal theory of that authority to the new monarchs of western Europe in their conflict with a stubborn feudal aristocracy. It was therefore the medium for the transplantation from the orient to western Europe of the divine right of absolute monarchy. Emphasizing as it does the right of private ownership, it became in the fifteenth and sixteenth centuries the means of dispossessing the peasants of western Europe of rights and property used in common. It was incorporated into the canon law of the Church. The *ius gentium* was the starting point for the development of our still feeble code of international law. "To Politics, to Moral Philosophy, to Theology it contributed modes of thought, courses of reasoning and a technical language. In the western provinces of the Empire it supplied the only means of exactness of speech and, still more emphatically, the only means of exactness, subtlety and depth in thought." [5]

Justinian was resolved to see the empire reunited under a revised and authoritative law, but he was no less inclined to regard the Church of his empire as completely subject to his will, with its clergy subject to his appointment, its ecclesiastical affairs subject to his judication, and its dogma subject to his dictation. This is the policy referred to as Cæsaropapism: the emperor was not only Cæsar, the absolute head of the state, but also pope (*papa*), the absolute head of the Church. The policy had its source in the idea of the emperor as the divine representative of God on earth, the head of the divine administration of the Church as well as of the secular administration of the state, the possessor of full temporal and spiritual power. In the east it was transplanted from the pagan world to regulate affairs between the Christian state and the Christian Church. In the west there was the opposite tendency of the Bishop of Rome to regard himself as entitled to assume temporal power because possessed of spiritual authority. To the Byzantine emperor it was necessary to exercise spiritual *Cæsaropapism*

[5] *Ibid.*, II, 53.

power in order to maintain the unity of the Church and thus to maintain the Church as a powerful support for the throne.

To maintain the unity of the Eastern Church, let alone unity of Western and Eastern Church together, was no easy matter.[6] Certain ecclesiastical independents in the east refused to recognize as authoritative dogma the decisions of the councils of Nicæa and Chalcedon, and the two important sects of Nestorians and Monophysites had arisen by the end of the fifth century in Syria, Palestine, and Egypt.[7] Although these sects were based on doctrinal differences, they had political significance too; they represented the rise of the native element in those three countries against the domination from Byzantium of Greek Hellenistic culture. Monophysitism may be regarded, therefore, as the national religion of the Syrians and Egyptians, represented by their respective patriarchs of Antioch and Alexandria, and propagated in their vernacular languages, Syriac and Coptic. Accordingly, from the point of view of the Byzantine emperors it was no less a political than an ecclesiastical necessity to establish and maintain the unity of the Faith.

The importance of religious unity in the eastern empire

Their usual method was to establish by decree compromise doctrines of their own, and then attempt to force the Bishop of Rome to concur. In 492 the Emperor Zeno attempted by a decree (the *Henoticon*, or Act of Union) to reconcile the differences between the orthodox Church and the Monophysites over the question as to whether Jesus Christ had two distinct natures, divine and human, or only one divine-human nature. In it he avoids using the words "one nature" or "two natures" by announcing that Jesus Christ was "of the same nature with the Father in the Godhead and also of the same nature with us in manhood," and anathematizes "all who have held or hold now or at any time, whether in Chalcedon or in any other synod whatsoever, any different belief." [8]

Zeno's attempt at religious compromise

But the determination of new doctrine by imperial fiat did not satisfy the conscience of either the orthodox or the Monophysites. Justinian tried for a time a policy of unity based on co-operation with the Roman pope, whose support was often enough needed by the Byzantine emperors to hold their Italian provinces. But the support of Rome meant sacrificing the Monophysites, since it involved recognition of the authority of the Council of Chalcedon. It also complicated Justinian's home life, for his charming wife Theodora was a Monophysite and accordingly opposed to the persecution of the sect. In the end he yielded

Justinian's religious policy

[6] See p. 51.
[7] See p. 41.
[8] Vasiliev, *History of the Byzantine Empire*, I, 135.

to her; but meanwhile the new policy of unity had little effect, for Syria, Palestine, and Egypt remained disaffected. In pursuit of the more general policy of Christianizing the whole empire Justinian in 529 closed the pagan philosophical schools at Athens and confiscated their endowments. It was only a decadent Neo-Platonism that he was suppressing, but even in that he failed. The fugitive professors were welcomed at the court of the Persian emperor, and later they were permitted to return to Constantinople.

When the Emperor Heraclius had recovered Syria, Palestine, and Egypt from the Persians in the first half of the seventh century, he made another attempt to achieve by decree a compromise that might unite the orthodox and the Monophysites. His decree of 638, the *Ecthesis*, or Exposition of the Faith, expounded the imperial dogma of Monotheletism, according to which Christ had two natures (substances) but only one operation (energy) or will: the Monophysite insistence upon a single nature might perhaps be reconciled by granting a single will. But the new decree was no more successful than Zeno's *Henoticon* in bringing theological and political peace. Religious differences had already paved the way for the conquest of Syria and Palestine by the Arabs, and the conquest of Egypt was not far off. *Attempts at compromise in the seventh century*

In 648 the Emperor Constans II returned to the policy of unity with Rome, in his decree called *Typus*, or Type of Faith, forbidding "all orthodox subjects . . . to contend and quarrel with one another over one will and one operation (energy) or two operations (energies) and two wills." Finally, in 680 at the Sixth Ecumenical Council in Constantinople the imperial compromise dogma of Monotheletism was condemned, and it was specified that in addition to two natures Christ had "two natural wills and operations (energies), going together harmoniously for the salvation of the human race." [9] This permanently alienated Syria, Palestine, and Egypt, which had maintained their Monophysite churches under Mohammedan rule. (They maintain them to this day: there is in Egypt the Coptic Church, in Syria the Monophysite Church, in Palestine the Jacobite Church, and besides these an Armenian or Georgian Church.) And so the original contention among the patriarchs for superiority ended in each having his own church. *Failure of the policy of compromise*

The Sixth Ecumenical Council virtually ended the development of theology in the Eastern Church; henceforth, although there was no cessation of theological discussion, the Eastern Church rested content with what had been elaborated. This was conveniently summarized

[9] *Ibid.*, I, 272–73.

by the learned monk John of Damascus, who lived during the first half
of the eighth century. He called his summary the *Fount of Knowledge*.
In it he elaborated for the Greek Church, on the basis of the Scriptures
and the Greek Church Fathers, the theological drama of salvation.

John of Damascus

John's work remained henceforth authoritative for the Eastern Church,
and was never superseded. The considerable use of Aristotle in the
work, for the first time in a major theological treatise, marks John as
the first scholastic in the east. In the twelfth century his work was
translated into Latin and was looked upon with respect by the western
theologians, especially by the great summarizer of western theological
development, St. Thomas Aquinas. It is worth noting that the east
produced a summary of its theology five hundred years before the
west was ready with its own.

If in the east the Greek and oriental halves of the Church were unable to maintain peace between themselves, neither could the Greek
and Latin Churches, which ultimately came to have nothing to do

The attitude of the papacy towards Constantinople

with each other. The split between Rome and Constantinople grew out
of the rival ambitions of their two prelates for the supreme headship
of the Church Universal; the differences of theology and ecclesiastical
usage that crept between them; the political history of the Byzantine
empire in its relations with western Europe; finally, most of all and
more fundamentally, the disparity between western and Byzantine
civilization.

In the view of Rome, Constantinople was an upstart patriarchate
with no apostolic foundation or tradition, owing its prestige to the mere
fact that it was an imperial capital. Its patriarchs were no better than
menials of an absolute lord, and its pretensions to equality with Rome,
if not to superiority, merely a cover under which the eastern emperors
could tighten their power over society.

The west had received its theology from the east, but it had always
been ill at ease with eastern subtlety; Rome longed to have the deci-

Early conflict between Constantinople and Rome

sions of councils regarded as authoritative and final, and to cease the
endless process of theological refinement. It had early adopted the
Greek spirit to its own more practical point of view. Never for a moment had Rome acknowledged Constantinople as its equal in rank.
That now the eastern emperors should turn theologians was intolerable
to Rome.

When Zeno issued his *Henoticon*, the pope excommunicated the
Patriarch of Constantinople for his part in it. When Justinian established relations with the papacy Rome would go no further than to
admit that "the most blessed see of the Archbishop of Constantinople,

the new Rome, ranks second after the Most Holy Apostolic See of
old Rome." Justinian himself is reported to have said to Pope Agapetus,
"I shall either force you to agree with me or else I shall send you into
exile"; and indeed Pope Vigilius was forced to spend more than seven
years in Constantinople. When Heraclius suggested the compromise
of Monotheletism, Rome declared it a heresy. When Pope Martin
declared both his *Ecthesis* and Constans II's *Typus* heretical, he was
arrested, brought to Constantinople, and exiled to Cherson. After their
conquest of Italy the Byzantine emperors could treat the popes as they
treated their own patriarchs at home, but they found their spirit more
difficult to subdue. Peace established in 680 by the Council of Constantinople was broken again by the Trullan Council of 691. It was
soon re-established by Justinian II, but the controversy over the use
of images in the Church disrupted it again, and this time far more
seriously.

In the Greek Church the image of God or Christ, a martyr or a
saint, whether painted flat, set in mosaic, or carved, is called an icon.
Those opposed to the use of icons in the Church were called iconoclasts,
or image-breakers; those favoring their use were iconodules, or image-
slaves. The appearance of an iconoclastic movement in Byzantium in
the eighth century marked the recrudescence of an old protest against
the importation into the Church of pagan practices. This revival was *The issues in-*
precipitated by the growth of many superstitious practices connected *volved in the*
with the worship of images. (One Byzantine senator even wore a toga *iconoclastic*
embroidered with the whole life of Christ.) It was further stimulated *struggle*
by the caustic criticism of Jew and Mohammedan, who alike abhorred
the "graven image." It represents, too, a protest of oriental mysticism
within the Greek Church against the use of the material thing to represent the divine idea—the same kind of protest as that of the Monophysite, who could not tolerate the idea of a separate human nature for
the incarnate *Logos*. The emperors who led the iconoclastic movement
were from the Asiatic provinces of the empire, Isaurians, Syrians,
and Armenians. As a whole, therefore, this was a sophisticated reform
movement, aiming at the restoration of Christianity to its primitive
purity; such a serious protest was not made in the Western Church
until the time of Erasmus.

Like the later criticism of the humanists in the west, it was directed
in some of its phases against the cult of relics and such practices as the
use of candles and incense in ritual. Moreover, because of the support
given to these popular practices by the eastern monks, who were themselves makers of images, it amounted also to an attack upon monasti-

cism. In the opinion of the reforming emperors, monasticism, because of its growing popularity, was taking men needed in agriculture, industry, and the army and consigning them to a useless life of contemplation, as well as depriving the state of much-needed income from land given by the devout to the monasteries. Because, furthermore, the movement was led by the emperors themselves, it raised the whole question of the relation of Church and state. The iconodules employed the subterfuge of arguing the freedom of the Church to conceal their real opposition to the reform, which in the view of the emperors made them nothing but rebels. The issues were therefore of fundamental importance.

The iconoclastic campaign was launched by the Emperor Leo III in 725 or 726 by a decree against images. This was confirmed by another decree in 730. The campaign was continued by Constantine V (741–75), who also sponsored a severe persecution of monks and monasteries. In 753 or 754 he called a council which proclaimed that *The course of the iconoclastic struggle in the eighth century* "there shall be rejected and removed and cursed out of the Christian church every likeness which is made out of any material whatever by the evil art of painters," and anathematized those "who venture to represent the divine image of the *Logos* after the incarnation with material colors." [10] The terrific upheaval caused by this attempt to turn back the centuries was somewhat calmed by the milder iconoclasm of Leo IV.

Images, relics, and monasteries were all restored to favor by a Greek woman, the Empress Irene (780–802), who called the seventh and last ecumenical council of the Eastern Church at Nicæa in 787. This council not only restored images, but excommunicated those "who called the holy images idols, and who asserted that Christians resort to icons as if the latter were gods, or that the Catholic church had ever accepted idols."

The iconoclastic campaign was revived by Leo V, whose council in 815 restored the measures of the first iconoclastic council of Constantine V; it was continued by his two successors. It was finally ended in 843 when another woman, the regent Theodora, called another council to restore the use of images and other outlawed practices to their former place in the Church. The Greek population of the empire and the Greek monks had defeated the protestant zeal of the Asiatic reformers. Incidentally, the cause of Byzantine art was thereby saved; however, the use of sculptured icons was henceforth discontinued in favor of flat images only.

[10] *Ibid.*, I, 319.

The Roman Church never had any sympathy with the iconoclastic movement, and excommunicated the iconoclasts. In the midst of the struggle in the eighth century it turned from the Byzantine emperors to the Franks for support, and thus laid the foundation of its temporal power in former Byzantine territory in Italy.[10a] In 800 it cast its lot definitely with the west by crowning a Frankish king Roman emperor. To the Byzantine Cæsaropapists these were the ungrateful acts of rebellious barbarians. The patriarchs of Constantinople were instructed to detach Calabria, Sicily, Crete, and Illyricum from Roman control and to confiscate all papal territory in the east. The tension was further increased when in the third quarter of the ninth century Pope Nicholas I attempted to interfere in the election of the Patriarch of Constantinople and entered into unsuccessful competition with Constantinople to convert the Bulgarians. A council at Constantinople informed the pope that he was only a patriarch, with no authority over the whole Church, and his legates were arrested in Constantinople.

Further conflict between Rome and Constantinople

Minor differences hastened the breach between the two halves of the Church. The Greek Church permitted its lower clergy to marry. It used unleavened bread in the sacrament of the Eucharist, and allowed laymen to partake also of the wine. There were differences in Lenten observances and in the date of the celebration of Easter. A new theological dispute arose over the question of what theologians called the procession of the Holy Spirit. The Eastern Church insisted on the statement of the Nicene Creed that the Holy Spirit proceeded from the Father through the Son; the Western Church had come to insist that the Holy Spirit proceeded from the Father and the Son (*ex patre filioque*) jointly. The addition of the words "and the Son" (*filioque*) in the eyes of the Eastern Church made heretics of western Christians, whereas their omission in the eyes of the Western Church made heretics of eastern Christians.

In spite of the prohibition of the Latin ritual in the Greek provinces of southern Italy, Roman influence began to grow there in the late tenth and early eleventh centuries, under the auspices of a reform movement one of whose features was the strengthening of papal influence. Leo IX, the first great reforming pope, informed the Patriarch of Constantinople that he would not "seethe the kid in its mother's milk" but "scrub its mangy hide with biting vinegar and salt," and his legates at Constantinople treated the patriarch with such insolence that he refused to make any concessions or even to negotiate with them. Finally, in the summer of 1054 they laid on the altar of Justinian's

The final split between the Greek and Roman Churches

[10a] See p. 201.

great Church of Santa Sophia a bull of excommunication of the patriarch "and his followers, guilty of the above mentioned errors and insolences . . . along with all heretics, together with the devil and his angels." The Patriarch of Constantinople, Michael Cerularius, summoned a council in which the papal legates were excommunicated, together with all those who had come to "the God-guarded city like a thunder or a famine, or, better still, like wild boars, in order to overthrow truth." [11]

The final break had come, and therewith another step in the collapse of the Byzantine empire, inasmuch as ecclesiastical differences prevented the west, under the influence of the popes, from coming to the proper assistance of the east when help was needed later. The Eastern Church, already deprived of its oriental provinces and now severed from all connection with the west, developed into a national Greek or Byzantine Church, whose chief mission was to convert the Slavs in the Balkans and in Russia.

Nowhere is more illuminating and invaluable insight into the attitude of east and west to each other offered than in the report of Liutprand, Bishop of Cremona, of his embassy to the court of the great military Emperor Nicephorus Phocas (963–69). He had gone on behalf of the German King and Emperor Otto I, who wanted a Byzantine princess as wife for his son. The testy Liutprand was disgusted with his journey; he could neither understand nor sympathize with the ceremonial splendor of the Byzantine court, and he was no match for the devious ways of eastern diplomats, who never let slip an opportunity to twit him on the uncouth ways of his western masters. He was, accordingly, unable to write fairly, but he did not fail to make himself plain.

Liutprand of Cremona on Byzantium in the tenth century

His embassy was housed in a drafty, leaky, tumble-down palace where they all got sick. The food was inedible: "a fat goat . . . deliciously stuffed with garlic, onions and leeks, steeped in fish sauce"; a "disgusting and foul meal, which was washed down with oil, after the manner of drunkards, and moistened also with another exceedingly bad fish liquor." [12] Oh, the smell of garlic and onions, and the "filthy . . . oil and fish juice," and the Greek wine, or rather "brine, . . . mixed with pitch, resin and plaster"! Oh, the kisses, "very sweet and very loving," of Byzantine courtiers, "soft, effeminate, longsleeved, hooded, veiled, lying, neutral-gendered, idle creatures," and

[11] Vasiliev, *op. cit.*, I, 411.
[12] The quotations are from the translation in Henderson's *Historical Documents*, pp. 442 ff.

the "capon" Greek bishops, "sipping their bath water [wine] from a very small glass"! And their elegant parks filled with wild asses! "But why, I ask, wild asses? Our tame ones at Cremona are the same. Their color, shape and ears are the same; they are equally melodious when they begin to bray." Their only authentic wild ass was Nicephorus, the emperor, "a monstrosity of a man, a pygmy, fat-headed," with little eyes like a mole's, "disgusting with his short, broad, thick and half hoary beard; disgraced by a neck an inch long," with long, thick, bristly hair; "in color an Ethiopian; one whom it would not be pleasant to meet in the middle of the night; with extensive belly, lean of loin, very long of hip, considering his short stature, small of shank, proportionate as to his heels and feet; clad in a garment costly but too old, and foul-smelling and faded through age . . . bold of tongue, a fox by nature, in perjury and lying a Ulysses." And to think that when Nicephorus, "like a creeping monster," entered the Church of Santa Sophia, "the singers cried out in adulation, 'Behold the morning star approaches; *Eos* arises; he reflects in his glances the rays of the sun, he, the pale death of the Saracens, Nicephorus the ruler!'" "And accordingly they sang, 'Long life to the ruler Nicephorus! Adore him, ye people, cherish him, bend the neck to him alone!' How much more truly might they have sung, 'Come, thou burnt out coal, thou fool, old woman in thy walk, wood-devil in thy looks, thou peasant, thou frequenter of foul places, thou goat-foot, thou horn-head, thou double-limbed one, bristly, unruly, countrified, barbarian, harsh, hairy, a rebel, a Cappadocian!'"

It was in the presence of such a person that one had to take off one's hat. It was good to retort to Nicephorus, when he remarked that Constantine had left in Rome "nothing but vile minions, fishers namely, pedlars, bird catchers, bastards, plebeians and slaves," that indeed "world rulers, that is, emperors," were descended from the insolvent debtors, fugitive slaves and homicides who composed the Roman nobility, "whom we, namely, the Lombards, Saxons, Franks, Lotharingians, Bavarians, Swabians, Burgundians so despise that when angry we call our enemies nothing more scornful than Roman, comprehending in this one thing . . . whatever there is of contemptibility, of timidity, of avarice, of luxury, of lying—in a word, of viciousness." Constantinople was a "half starved, perjured, lying, wily, greedy, rapacious, avaricious, vainglorious city." "If I ever come back here again, may Nicephorus present me with a crown and a golden sceptre."

Details of the political history of Byzantium from the sixth century to the end of the eleventh have little interest for the student interested

The paradox of Byzantine political history

primarily in Europe and in Byzantium mostly for its influence on Europe. The strictures of older historians on the prevalence of palace intrigues, mutinies in the army, rioting mobs, party sedition, and deposition and murder of emperors are as valid as ever. But they gave these faults an exaggerated importance, while the true originality and refinement of Byzantine culture were overlooked. What is still more striking is the vitality of this civilization. In spite of all these evils, in spite of incessant outside attacks that seemed to threaten continually its very existence, it nevertheless endured for more than a thousand years. After every crisis it came back, preserving and developing its tradition, even after its territory had been gradually and greatly reduced.

At its widest extent under Justinian the empire embraced southeastern Spain, North Africa from Morocco to Egypt, Italy and Sicily, the whole Balkan peninsula to the Danube, Asia Minor, the islands of the Ægean, Syria, Palestine, and Egypt. Spain was soon lost to the Visigoths. Italy was divided with the Lombards. The Balkan peninsula, if not wholly lost to Mongolians and Slavs, was by the end of the seventh century at any rate repopulated by them.

The first great crisis in Byzantine history occurred at the beginning of the seventh century, when Persia renewed its attack; this seemed likely to cost the whole Asiatic half of the empire. In the years from 611 to 619 the Persians took Syria, Palestine, and Egypt, with its rich port of Alexandria and the wheat fields of the Nile valley. A political revolution in Constantinople brought to the throne Heraclius, son of the Exarch of Africa, who was emperor from 610 to 641. Heraclius saved the empire from the Persians. He drove them from Asia Minor and recovered Syria, Palestine, and Egypt. He advanced into the heart of the Persian empire, and in 627 near the ruins of Nineveh crushed the Persians and advanced upon their capital, Ctesiphon. The tremendous effort and expense of the war left both Persia and Byzantium exhausted, easy prey for the Moslem armies that were soon coming out of the Arabian peninsula.

The defeat of Persia

The expansion of the Mohammedan Arab empire caused Byzantium's second major crisis and created the hostility between the two that, while it might fluctuate in intensity, never henceforth ceased. Even before the death of Heraclius, while the Arabs were conquering Mesopotamia and Persia, they overran Syria and Palestine, which he had just recovered from the Persians, and shortly after his death in 641 they took Alexandria. Within a few years they completed the conquest of Egypt and marched westward across North Africa to attack

Early conquest of the Arabs

the Exarchate of Africa. By the beginning of the eighth century they had taken Carthage and Ceuta, and Byzantine Africa was gone. Meanwhile, having advanced to the Mediterranean, the Arabs had to protect their new possessions against the Byzantine fleet. They took Cyprus and Rhodes and entered the Propontis, where from Cyzicus they besieged Constantinople every summer. They could not take it, partly because of the Byzantine army's skillful use of Greek fire, "a sort of explosive compound, discharged by special tubes or siphons, which ignited when it struck an enemy's vessel, and burned even on water." *The early sieges of Constantinople*

In 677 the Arabs abandoned this attempt on Constantinople, but they returned in 717, having meanwhile forced their way through Asia Minor by land to Abydos. The city was now besieged from the European land side and by a fleet of some eighteen hundred vessels; but after a year's siege the Arabs had to give up again. The savior of the city was the first of the Isaurian emperors, the iconoclast Leo III. What would have happened if Constantinople had at this date fallen to the Mohammedans is an interesting speculation. Would the rest of the Byzantine empire likewise have fallen to the Arabs? Would they have attacked nascent western Europe from the rear and joined with their armies advancing northward from Spain? Would any such advances have proved permanent enough to change completely the course of European history? And if so, in view of the brilliance of Mohammedan civilization, would that have been such a calamity? These questions can never be answered, because in that early siege of 717–18 the city was not taken, whereby to that extent the fate of Byzantine, Slavonic, and western Europe civilization was settled.

In the course of the next hundred years the Arabs took Crete and most of Sicily, and began their attacks on Byzantine southern Italy. This was all of Italy that remained to Byzantium since the Lombards had taken the Exarchate of Ravenna in 751, which had then been turned over to the popes after the Frankish conquest. These losses to Islam and the repopulation of the Balkan peninsula by Mongolians and Slavs reduced the empire to Constantinople and its immediate hinterland in Europe, and outside of Europe to Asia Minor. It was accordingly now a state composed predominantly of a Greek-speaking population. Although the empire lost southern Italy, the Arabs never succeeded in overcoming it completely, and its Greek character was even reinforced by the immigration of Greeks from Egypt and North Africa fleeing before the Mohammedan advance. The flight from Greece and Asia Minor of the Greeks who took refuge there from the iconoclastic persecution of the eighth and ninth centuries contributed *The empire reduced to a Greek state* to the same result, while at the same time further weakening the empire.

During the period of the Macedonian dynasty (867–1057) the Byzantine empire recovered to some extent from two centuries of attack by Islam upon its outlying provinces. Syria was recovered in 968 by the Emperor Nicephorus, and was held until 1029. The recovery of Crete in 961 restored to the Greeks the control of the Ægean Sea. Against the Mohammedans in the western Mediterranean a campaign was begun which gave promise of restoring completely Byzantine

THE BYZANTINE EMPIRE
IN THE
TENTH & ELEVENTH CENTURIES

Lands of the Eastern
Emperors before 960
Lands conquered
between 960 and 1045
(965) Figures are dates of conquests

prestige in this area. They were driven out of the few towns they had seized on the west coast of southern Italy, and Byzantine influence was extended to include Naples, Amalfi, Gaetà, and the principalities of Salerno, Capua, and Benevento, which were a sort of borderland between the Byzantine empire and the German empire. Sicily, however, remained in the hands of the Moslems. Venice, which had recovered its independence from Byzantium in the ninth century, again became a loyal vassal of the empire, protecting the Adriatic with its fleet. In 992 it received the extensive trading privileges in Constantinople that formed the basis of its later prosperity.

In the Balkan peninsula Byzantine sway was once more pushed to the Danube. The Bulgarian kingdom, formed in the second half of the seventh century and completely Slavonized by the middle of the ninth, began in the time of its first tsar, Krum, in the early ninth century, to grow into a large Bulgar-Slav state, which continued until the death of its last tsar, Samuel, in 1018 to threaten Constantinople itself. The Emperor Basil II (976–1025), the "Bulgar-slayer," in most terrible fashion destroyed the Bulgarian state. "When Samuel beheld fourteen thousand Bulgarians blinded by Basil II and sent back to their homeland, he died from the shock received from this horrible sight." [13] Bulgaria then became a Byzantine province, and the Serbs and Croats to the west recognized the overlordship of Constantinople, thus completing the reacquisition of a territory that had seemed likely to become permanently alienated. The reconquered territory was organized into themes. The theme was the product of an administrative *The themes* reform begun as early as the time of Heraclius and completed by the eighth century; it had been made necessary by constant external attacks on all sides. A number of adjacent provinces were united in the new theme—there were thirty themes in the whole empire—and all civil and military authority, hitherto separated, was concentrated in the hands of a single governor, the strategos, appointed by and responsible to the emperor at Constantinople.

It was also during the period of the Macedonian dynasty that the work of Byzantium as civilizer of the Slavic peoples was begun. About 864 Tsar Boris of the Bulgarians was converted to Christianity under the auspices of the Greek Church, and under Tsar Simeon, who died in 927, an independent Bulgarian patriarchate was established. The *The conversion* Serbs were really converted about a century later, recognizing the su- *of the Slavs* periority of the Patriarch of Constantinople. In 988 or 989 Prince Vladimir of Russia was baptized and the transformation of the Russian Slavs into a Christian nation begun. A hundred years earlier the Greek Church had extended its interest even to the Slavs of Moravia, but here, even before the break with Rome, it was blocked by the hostility of the Bavarian Church, which coveted this region for its own. The same Greek brothers, Cyril and Methodius, who attempted the conversion of Moravia translated the Scripture into Slavonic and thus gave the Slavs a literary language and the Cyrillic alphabet still used by the eastern Slavs—the same work that Ulfilas had done for the Goths. All these events meant, of course, that Byzantine Christianity, including its monasticism, its theological literature, its art, spread into the Slav world of the Balkans and Russia, and Constantinople to these peoples became what Rome became to the Germanic peoples of the west.

[13] Vasiliev, *op. cit.*, I, 888.

The Norman conquest of southern Italy

In the latter half of the eleventh century the scene was considerably changed. In southern Italy, where venturesome bands of Normans had established themselves at the beginning of the century, Bari, the key to the whole region, was taken in 1071, and the rest of the Byzantine territory was quickly organized into the Norman Duchy of Apulia. The eyes of the shrewd Norman leader, Robert Guiscard, looked towards the east; by 1082 the Byzantine port of Durazzo in Dalmatia had opened its gates to him, thus opening up the road to Thessalonica and thence to Constantinople. Although Durazzo was recovered shortly before his death in 1085, southern Italy was now permanently lost to Byzantium. Venice, the faithful ally in the campaigns against the Normans at Durazzo, was repaid by further liberal trading privileges, which became the basis for a virtual monopoly of trade between east and west. To Venetian merchants was granted "the right of buying and selling all over the Empire . . . free of custom, port and other dues connected with trade. . . . In the capital itself the Venetians received a large quarter with many shops and stores, as well as three landing places . . . where the Venetian vessels could be freely loaded and unloaded." [14]

The first victories of the Seljuk Turks

The same year that witnessed the final loss of Byzantine Italy, 1071, witnessed also the defeat of the Byzantine army by a new and formidable enemy, the Seljuk Turks. (These Mongolian Turks from western Asia had moved into Persia, where they embraced Islam. They first served as mercenaries under the Caliph of Bagdad, commanded by their military chieftain, the sultan. The break-up of the caliphate facilitated their conquest of Persia in the middle of the eleventh century, and led them on to Bagdad, where the caliph, long since reduced to the position of mere head of a religion, was henceforth under the protection of the Seljuk sultans. Under Alp Arslan, sultan from 1063 to 1072, a Seljuk Turk state reaching from Afghanistan almost to Egypt began to take shape.

Their conquest of Asia Minor

When the Turks penetrated into central Asia Minor, the Greeks fell upon the local emirs that Alp Arslan planted there and drove them back beyond the Euphrates. Flushed with these victories, they marched on into Armenia with a motley army of one hundred thousand men (including some western Europeans, among them Ursel Baliol, ancestor of the kings of Scotland) and laid siege to Manzikert. The great army was annihilated by the Turks; the emperor, Romanus Diogenes, was captured, and released only upon his promise to pay the staggering ransom of one million pieces of gold and an annual

[14] *Ibid.*, II, 20.

tribute of three hundred and sixty thousand pieces. The destruction of this army opened the way for the Turks into the interior of Asia Minor, and led to the loss of the provinces that had furnished to Byzantine armies their best troops. The Seljuk state in Asia Minor, soon organized into the Sultanate of Rum, with its capital at Iconium, quickly expanded to the Black Sea on the north and to the Ægean on the west; the Hellenized native Christian population, except on the west coast, was largely supplanted by Mohammedan Mongolian Turks.

During the same period the Balkan peninsula was falling into the *The Patzinaks* hands of another Mongolian race, the Patzinaks, kindred to the Turks. Before them there had flowed into the steppes of southern Russia Huns, Bulgars, Avars, Magyars; behind them came the Cumans. The Patzinaks plundered the whole Balkan peninsula, and in alliance with the Seljuk Turks threatened the very existence of the empire by a combined attack on Constantinople. The years 1090–91 were a desperate time; "the Byzantine empire was drowning in the Turkish invasion." Alexius Comnenus (1081–1118), the first of the dynasty of the Comneni, who rose to the purple from their strong position as feudal landholders in Asia Minor, enlisted the aid of the Cumans and saved the city. Just as Rome attempted by the use of Germans to save herself from the Germans, so Byzantium by the use of Mongolian nomads would save herself from Mongolian nomads.

In his desperate plight Alexius sent also to western Europe for aid. His letter to Count Robert of Flanders was later modified for propaganda to stimulate crusading ardor in the west. "There is left almost *The appeal* nothing but Constantinople, which the enemies threaten to take away *to the west* from us in the very near future, unless speedy help from God and *for help* from the faithful Latin Christians reach us. . . . Therefore hasten with all your people, strain all your forces, lest such treasures fall into the hands of the Turks and Patzinaks. . . . Endeavor, so long as you have time, that the Christian Empire and, which is still more important, the Holy Sepulchre be not lost to you, and that you may have in heaven no doom, but reward. Amen!" [15] The answer of the west was the first crusade. Byzantium had lost its leadership, which was now taken over by the lusty children of the west.

During the five centuries from Justinian to the first crusade the Byzantine empire preserved and developed a civilization far superior to anything in the contemporary west. Its great superiority would justify much fuller treatment than this history of western Europe will

[15] *Ibid.*, II, 26.

The form of the Byzantine state

allow. The Byzantine state was a continuation of the orientalized autocratic monarchy of the later Roman empire, whose divine sanction came now from the new religion, Christianity. As the representative of God the emperor was head of the Church as well as of the state, the supreme dictator in all walks of life. The state itself was a divine institution, and its officers and their functions, even the very quarters housing them, were "sacred" or "holy" or "divine."

The palace of the emperors

On the outskirts of Constantinople, overlooking the Sea of Marmora, was the palace of the divine emperors, so brilliantly described by the French historian of Byzantium, Charles Diehl. "Precious marbles and glittering mosaics abounded. In the great saloon of the New Palace, constructed by Basil I, above the magnificent colonnade of green marble alternating with red onyx, were vast compositions, monuments of that secular art which the Byzantine masters practised far more commonly than one imagines, representing the sovereign enthroned among his victorious generals, and unfolding the glorious epic of his reign: 'the Herculean labours of the *Basileus*,' as a contemporary chronicler has it, 'his solicitude for his subjects, his deeds on the battlefield, and his God-awarded victories.' But above all the imperial bedchamber must, it seems, have been a marvel. Below the high ceiling, studded with golden stars, in the midst of which, in green mosaic, was a cross, the symbol of salvation, the whole of the vast chamber was magnificently decorated. In the mosaic floor a central medallion enclosed a peacock with spreading plumage, and in the corners were four eagles, the imperial bird, framed in green marble, with wings outstretched ready to take their flight. On the lower part of the walls the mosaic made, as it were, a border of flowers. Higher up, against a background of glowing gold, still other mosaics represented the entire imperial family in state costume: Basil crowned and seated on his throne, near him his wife Eudocia, and grouped around them, very much as they may be seen in the faded miniatures of a fine manuscript in the *Bibliothèque Nationale*, their sons and daughters, holding books on which were written pious verses from the Scriptures. They all raised their hands solemnly towards the redeeming cross; and long inscriptions carved on the walls invoked upon the dynasty God's blessing and the assurance of eternal life. The Pavilion of the Pearl, with its golden vault upheld by four columns of marble and its mosaic wainscot with hunting scenes, contained the summer bedchamber of the sovereigns, and opened through porticoes on two of its sides upon cool gardens. There was the winter bedchamber in the Carian Pavilion, so called from being constructed throughout of Carian marble, protected from the violent winds that blew from the Sea of Marmora; there was the Emperor's wardrobe, wainscotted in the white marble of Proconnesus, and covered with pictures of the saints. And, finest of all, there was the bedchamber of the Empress, a wonderful room whose marble pavement seemed like 'a meadow of enamelled flowers,' the walls of which, lined with porphyry, Thessalian breccia and white Carian, were such rare and happy combinations of colour that it was known as the Pavilion of Harmony. There was the Pavilion of Love also, and that of the Purple, wherein, according to custom and tradition, the imperial children must be born, and from which they derived their title of *Porphyrogenitus* [i.e., purple born]. And everywhere was the splendour of silver and ivory doors, purple curtains sliding on rods of silver, tapestries embroidered in gold with fantastic animals, great golden lamps swinging from the domes, precious furniture wonderfully incrusted with mother of pearl, ivory, and gold." [16]

In these sacred precincts court life was regulated by a ceremonial code, which Constantine VII had put into writing in the tenth century, *On the Ceremonies of the Byzantine Court*. It prescribed, for officials with high-sounding names, a ritual of stiff and formal grace. Henceforth in the courts of all monarchs with similar pretensions to absolute and divine authority—those Hapsburgs, Bourbons, Romanovs, and Hohenzollerns of departed glory—the titles and ceremonies of the Byzantine court were closely copied. *The Byzantine court*

Byzantium had an efficient army and navy, which looked with scorn on anything the west could produce, and even acted as instructor for the west. Its treasury collected very heavy taxes with such thoroughness that the provinces were often exasperated to the point of looking to any source for relief—this at a time when no direct taxes at all could be collected in the west. At a time when western Europe was governed, when it was governed by any law at all, by a medley of barbarian German codes and the remnants of the Theodosian Code, Byzantium had a unified system of law administered in regular courts by trained judges and jurists. Moreover, this law did not remain static in the form fixed by the Justinian Code; it was continually being adapted to changing conditions. It received a final unification about 890, as a result of the efforts of Basil I and Leo VI; this version is called the *Basilica,* and ever since has formed the basis of civil law for all Christian communities of the east, and for the Greek people to this day. While the west, therefore, after the confusion of successive centuries of barbarian attack and migration, was desperately struggling to settle down into an *Byzantine administration*

[16] C. Diehl, *Byzantine Portraits*, pp. 3–5.

ordered civilized existence, the Byzantine empire continued unbroken, though transformed to its own needs, the highly organized and centralized bureaucratic machinery of the absolute monarchy of the later Roman empire.

Constantinople The political, economic, and ecclesiastical administration of the whole empire was centered in Constantinople. At its height in the tenth century it may have numbered a million inhabitants; at any rate, there was no city in the west remotely to be compared with it. Here was the residence of the patriarch; here the triumph of Byzantine architecture, the imperial coronation Church of Santa Sophia, the Holy Wisdom; here the other churches, monasteries, palaces, baths, porticoes, and parks, which gave the city the architectural dignity so impressive to visitors from the west. Through its crowded streets passed diplomatic embassies of barbarian and civilized states, and stately religious processions of handsomely robed clergy. Into its harbor sailed the ships of merchants of many lands, east, west, north, south: Syrians, Alexandrians, Persians, Scandinavians, Venetians, Amalfitans, Greeks. Out of its harbor through the Bosporus into the Black Sea, through the Dardanelles into the Ægean, passed its own merchant marine under the protection of the imperial fleet. The city was the home of the bureaucracy—perhaps better called the hierarchy—of the court and of the chief ministries, a well-trained and well-educated body of civil servants, who formed also the social aristocracy of Constantinople. In the hippodrome the rival charioteers were cheered on by the two chief factions of Greens and Blues, the nearest approach in Constantinople to popular political parties. In the university learned professors trained students in the arts and professions. The colorful and cosmopolitan megalopolis, the "great city," as it was sometimes called in official documents, gave to Byzantine civilization an urban character at a time when the west, after the decay of Rome, was predominantly rural.

One of the most characteristic features of Byzantine civilization was the Greek Church. Perhaps no other feature is so distinctive as Byzantine art, which, indeed, is intimately associated with that Church. It is in the arts particularly that we discern most clearly the fusion of the Hellenic tradition with that of the orient to form a new organic whole. This new art was in large part symbolical of the mystery of eastern Christianity, and its chief monument must remain for all time the Church of Santa Sophia. The church was built at tremendous cost by Justinian within five years, by the labor of ten thousand men. Its archi-

Santa Sophia tects were two Ionian Greeks, Anthemius of Tralles and Isidor of Mi-

letus, but it is far different from any Greek temple. The Greek temple
was the center of public outdoor worship and was chiefly the home of
a god; its glories were external rather than internal, with its peristyles
and colored sculpture welcoming the weathering effects of sea breeze
and sun and rain—all these characteristic of a religion of external formalities rather than of a religion of inner conviction. We must seek
elsewhere for the source of the inspiration of Santa Sophia. Its glories
are all internal; it houses a worship essentially private, not public; its
appeal is to the inner world of the spirit, the source of which is oriental
Christianity. It has the balance, the harmony, the moderation, the perfect propriety of the Greek temple, but beyond these it gave scope to
the scientific and adventurous sides of the Greek genius as no other
building ever did.

Santa Sophia is a combination of oriental domed church with Roman
basilica. The chief engineering problem of the architects was the erection over a square area of a dome whose diameter should equal the
sides of the square. The Romans had built impressive domes, for example, in the Pantheon at Rome; but there the round dome merely
rested on the round walls of the temple itself. The dome of Santa
Sophia, on the contrary, was never intended to limit the size of the
church and determine the plan, but only to dominate the central area   *The dome*
of the cruciform structure. Accordingly, resting on the four piles at
the four corners of the central square there were erected four arches,
spanning the four sides of the square. Piles and arches thus formed
the framework upon which the dome should rest, the keystones of the
four arches forming the points of contact with the rim of the dome.
Between the keystones of the arches and reaching down to the points
where the arches rested on the piles were built four triangular curved
segments of masonry called pendentives, upon whose long upper sides
the rim of the dome rested between the keystones of the arches. The
central dome of Santa Sophia is one hundred and seventy-nine feet
above the floor, one hundred and seven feet in diameter, forty-six feet
deep.[17] So secure did the architects feel, so confident of their solution
of the engineering problem, that they dared to put in forty windows
around the base of the dome. It was perhaps in large part this final
touch of genius that wrought the miracle of Santa Sophia: the dome
seems to have no support, but to remain suspended in mid-air. Anthemius and Isidor had taught architects for all time how to build a dome.

[17] The corresponding dimensions of the dome of the Capitol are: height, 220
feet; diameter, 96 feet; depth, 40 feet.

Opening off the domed central square to east and west are two much lower half-domes, like apses, from each of which three smaller half-domes open.

The mosaics   A wealth of oriental color and imaginative ornament, combined with Syrian Christian symbolism, decorated this interior. The walls and domes were covered with that typical Byzantine equivalent of paint-

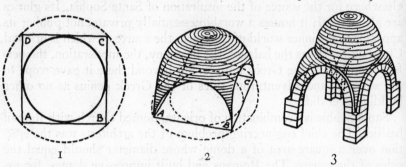

1   2   3

A Dome on Pendentives. ABCD is the square area over which a dome is to be erected. If the diameter of the dome is equal to one side of the square, the area will not be covered; if it is equal to the diagonal of the square, the dome will project beyond the sides (1). The latter diameter was sometimes used and the sides of the dome cut off vertically so that the square was exactly covered; but the result was an imperfect dome (2). To secure a perfect dome the Byzantine builders conceived the idea of slicing this imperfect dome off horizontally just above the arches made by the vertical cutting, thus securing a circular base upon which to erect a true dome (3). The triangular segments of the original dome are the pendentives.

From Helen Gardner, *Art Through the Ages*, p. 156, fig. 80. Harcourt, Brace and Company, New York.

ing, mosaics, small pieces of colored glass or stone fitted together in designs and images. Persian ornamentation in colored tiles and Græco-Roman floor mosaics are presumably the sources of Byzantine glass mosaics, applied, as had not previously been done, to walls and ceilings. The deep blue and shining gold backgrounds for the formal, stylized figures and the exuberant elaboration of oriental decorative *motifs* produced in varying lights an exquisitely new and resplendent interior, which the plain surfaces of multicolored marbles, the colored marble columns crowned with capitals of delicate grace and infinite variety, only served to enhance.

Every beholder has fallen under the spell of Santa Sophia. When it

Court of the Lions in the Alhambra. Note the rich detail and typical Islamic use of geometric motifs

Interior of the great Mosque of Cordova

The monogram page of The Book of Kells, *with the letters* XPI, *the sign for autem and the word* GENERATIO. *It is "the most elaborate specimen of calligraphy which was ever executed," "presumably surpassing, as a piece of decoration, anything to be met with in any other written book." Notice at the lower left, between the* X *and the* P, *"two rats nibbling the Eucharistic bread under the eyes of a pair of cats." (See p. 212)* [*Reproduced from "The Book of Kells" published by "The Studio," London and New York.*]

was still new, Procopius wrote: "It is singularly full of light and sunshine. You would declare that the place is not lighted by the sun from without, but that rays are produced within itself, such an abundance of light is poured into this church. . . . Who could tell of the beauty of the columns and marbles with which the church is adorned? One would think that one had come upon a meadow full of flowers in bloom. Who would not admire the purple tint of some and the green tint of others, the glowing red and the glittering white, and those too which nature, like a painter, has marked with the strongest contrasts of color?" [18] A contemporary of ours speaks of "the greatest domed church in the world, the perfect union of oriental plan and decoration with Greek organic structure. . . . When we look at the Byzantine church as a whole, with its polychrome adornment of mosaic and coloured marbles, its antique columns, its carved capitals, oriental in richness and variety, yet Hellenic in proportion and grace, above all the crowning miracle of the dome of Santa Sophia, in which architecture transcends its limitations and becomes impalpable and immaterial as the vault of the sky itself, we must admit that never has man succeeded more perfectly in moulding matter to become the vehicle and expression of the spirit." [19]

And now we may even hope that the only one of its glories that Santa Sophia lost when Constantinople fell at last will some day be restored to the world. Since 1453, when it became a Mohammedan mosque, its mosaics have been whitewashed, in accordance with the Mohammedan prohibition of the use of images. Now, however, the Turkish government has given permission to American scholars to remove the whitewash that for almost five hundred years has covered what may well be the most wonderful and beautiful mosaics in the world.

Byzantine architecture did not cease to develop with the production of Santa Sophia. It also adorned the walls of the simple Roman type of basilica with mosaics, as seen in the apses of several churches in Rome and throughout several at Ravenna. Under the influence of the classic tradition it began to adorn also the exterior of its churches, the best example being St. Mark's at Venice. In the Arab empire many a mosque was built in Byzantine style. Ravenna in the sixth century became thoroughly Byzantine in spirit. Its finest treasure is the domed octagonal Church of San Vitale, in the mosaics of which are preserved the only contemporary portraits of Justinian and Theodora. "Beneath her imperial mantle she appears stiff and tall; under the diadem that hides her forehead her delicate small face, of a narrow oval shape, and her

The spread of Byzantine architectural influence

[18] Palestine Pilgrims' Text Society, II, no. 2, pp. 8 and 11.
[19] C. Dawson, *The Making of Europe*, p. 120.

large, thin, straight nose, invest her with a sort of solemn gravity, almost with melancholy. One feature alone remains unaltered in this
faded portrait, and that is the beautiful black eyes that Procopius speaks
of, under the heavy, meeting eyebrows, which still illumine her face
and seem almost to engulf it." [20] "The costume she is wearing is of unparalleled magnificence. Clad in a long purple-violet mantle with a
broad border of gold embroidery flowing in glistening folds, she wears
on her aureoled head a lofty diadem of gold and precious stones; in and
out through her hair are wound twisted strands of gems and pearls,
while other jewels fall in sparkling streams upon her shoulders." [21]

St. Apollinare Nuovo and St. Apollinare in Classe at Ravenna are
simple Roman basilicas, with classical columns separating the nave from
the side aisles, but decorated with mosaics. Charlemagne copied San
Vitale in his palace church at Aachen, and this in turn was widely imitated, notably in the beautiful little church at Fulda. In the Norman
church at Monreale above Palermo, and on a smaller scale at nearby
Cefalù, the glory of Byzantine mosaics shines forth in almost incomparable splendor. St. Mark's at Venice is an example of the later Byzantine church, cruciform in plan, with five domes and embellished exterior. The typical early Italian churches, unless they are in the Lombard
tradition, belong to the earlier Byzantine tradition, with their barn-
like exteriors and their lavishly adorned interiors. The same indifference to external beauty appears in some of the Romanesque churches
of southern France. The best stained glass of Gothic churches seems but
an adaptation of Byzantine mosaics. Naturally the Byzantine style was
adopted by the southern Slavs and the Russians; by 1037 there was a
Church of Santa Sophia at Kiev.

In the other arts, as well as in architecture, Byzantium maintained
during the same period an unchallenged supremacy. In the sixth century under Justinian Byzantine art enjoyed its first golden age, and
in the ninth century after the end of the iconoclastic struggle, a second.
Into the west poured a constant stream of refined products of Byzantine
Minor arts   manufacture. Heavy silks, the products of state factories established
when the silk-worm was introduced into Byzantium during Justinian's
reign, were imported into Italy until the Italian cities began to make
their own silk. "Think of a silk on which are lions and stags, odd and
heraldic, and the only colors dark royal blue, turquoise and two shades
of green; or another in orange, tomato-red and white; or a third in
blue-black and purple; all alike in great lozenge designs with griffins

[20] Diehl, *op. cit.*, p. 53.
[21] *Ibid.*, p. 60.

and elephants and lions." There were embossed satins. There was jewelry with "two stones and only two predominant, the sea-blue sapphir-
ine and the dark green bloodstone, spotted with red." There was the
beautiful work of goldsmiths, such as the rare main altar of St. Ambrose's in Milan. There was intricate ivory carving, like the archiepiscopal throne preserved at Ravenna. There were embossed glassware, inlaid bronzes, enamels. "Imagine an onyx plate . . . in the center of
which is a gold circular cloisonné plaque. That plaque is not more than
an inch and a quarter in diameter, and yet the scene depicted on it is
the Last Supper. Just think what intricate work went into its making,
for the designing of every one of the figures at the table in a thin strip
of gold, the hollows filled with different-colored enamels!" [22]

There were also fresco painters, who covered the walls of the monasteries of Mt. Athos, the later center of Byzantine monasticism, and
of monasteries and churches elsewhere. Indeed, the long tradition of *Byzantine*
Byzantine painting, after influencing profoundly the beginnings of *painting*
painting in Italy, finally reached its own glorious culmination in the
sixteenth-century Cretan who settled in Spain and is known by his Spanish nickname, El Greco, one of the greatest of all painters. We find
Byzantine painting also in the illumination of beautiful manuscripts
and in the products of the painters of the imperial icon schools.

The iconoclastic struggle brought about a crisis in Byzantine art in
the ninth century. The opposition to the representation of the human
body turned it into new channels and to new subjects, such as animals,
hunting scenes, fruits, plant *motifs*. Many artists and craftsmen of the
old school emigrated to Italy, taking with them their tradition and
technique. When once iconoclasm was defeated, the artistic revival that
followed turned somewhat from the earlier Byzantine conventional-
ized style back to the Hellenistic tradition of naturalism. So strong was
Byzantine influence in Italy, however, that it was not until the fourteenth century that painters began to strike out into new fields, ignor-
ing the tradition of Byzantine fresco and mosaic.

In Byzantium there was no great conflict between pagan Greek lit- *Byzantine*
erature, science, and philosophy and Christian theology. The Greek *learning*
Church was not troubled, as the Western Church was, by conscientious scruples as to a Christian's right to enjoy the inheritance of the
old pagan world. Justinian's closing of the pagan philosophical schools
at Athens did not mean that the Greek intellectual tradition was
henceforth neglected: there was always a class in Byzantium, consist-

[22] Stanley Carson, quoted in J. F. Scott, A. Hyma, and A. H. Noyes, *Readings in
Medieval History*, pp. 370 ff.

ing mostly of officials, thoroughly schooled in it. Greek literature was studied intensively; by the copying of manuscripts it was preserved until it was taken up by the learned Mohammedan world and, from the thirteenth century on, by western Europe. Byzantium, however, did not succeed in handing on to the Slavic peoples, as to a limited extent Rome and the Western Church did succeed in passing on to the Germans, its classical inheritance. But to the Byzantine scholars who preserved Hellenism, even though they could develop it no further, the debt of the west is incalculable, for otherwise the later humanists would have had few Greek manuscripts to study.

Besides preserving and copying manuscripts, Byzantine scholars also compiled learned encyclopedias and lexicons, and there was a steady stream of historical writing of good quality, of saints' lives, and of medical works and legal and theological treatises. To Byzantium we owe our anthologies of Greek verse. Often the emperors themselves were learned men and engaged in scholarly activities, or were active promoters of learning. Constantine VII was such an emperor; in addition to a biography of Basil I he wrote *On the Administration of the Empire* and *On Themes,* and was responsible for the writing of *On the Ceremonies of the Byzantine Court.* The patriarchs of the Greek Church, such as Photius in the ninth century, often exercised a decisive influence on scholarship. Even before the foundation of the University of Constantinople in 1045, with its faculties of law and of philosophy, there had long been a school for higher studies.

The significance of Byzantium

From any viewpoint the pre-eminence of Byzantium during this period is incontrovertible. Its importance from the sixth to the end of the eleventh century in protecting Europe from the Persians, the Arabs, and the Turks, its rôle as civilizer of the Slavs, its contribution to our civilization in preserving the language, literature, philosophy, and science of the Greeks, cannot be overemphasized. On the other hand, it is now patent that the conservatism of its state and its church and the static character of its society left it inflexible and rigid, without those possibilities of development that western Europe in all its crudity contained.

Chapter 7

THE EMPIRE OF THE ARABS

THE long-continued struggle of the Byzantine empire with the Arabs might alone justify our tracing the remarkable rise of Arabian power from its origin. It would indeed be urgent if this book were a history of the great civilizations of the world. Since our interest in the Arabs largely concerns their influence on the development of the west, we shall consider their civilization in a general way in this chapter, and in more detail later on. When they encountered the civilization of western Europe they had rich treasures of science and philosophy quite unknown to the west. They accordingly contributed one of the basic elements in the composition of western culture.

The importance of the Arabs

Into the Fertile Crescent—the belt of land connecting the Nile valley, through Palestine, Syria, and the valleys of the Tigris and Euphrates, with the Persian Gulf—from earliest times there had poured out of the northern Arabian desert tribes of Semitic nomads. Sumerians, Babylonians, Assyrians, Chaldeans had in turn settled in Mesopotamia, founding empires and building civilizations upon the many layers of culture left by their predecessors. Into the western half of the Crescent had come Syrians, Phœnicians, and Jews. Egypt, Assyria, Persia, Macedonia, and Rome had in turn extended their imperial sway over that part of the Crescent bordering on the Arabian peninsula.

Arabia before Mohammed

But Arabia proper had never been conquered, and only the few tribes along the frontier had been touched by the superior Syrian or Mesopotamian civilization. On the other hand, caravan routes and Red Sea commerce gave the peninsula some contact with the outside world. The most important of the caravan routes, connecting Egypt, Palestine, and Syria by sea with India, ran north and south through the Hejaz, the western part of the Arabian peninsula. Its northern terminus was Teima, whence it ran southwards through Khaibar, Yathrib, Mecca, and Taif to Yemen, the southwestern corner of the peninsula. The extremely lucrative caravan trade had very early drawn to these points large numbers of Jews, who preserved their own religion and culture, even though they sometimes merged with the Arabs and adopted their tribal organization. In Yemen before Mohammed's day an important local state had developed, with a partly Jewish culture of its own. Christianity also had filtered in from Abyssinia. The Arab state of the Ghassanids, bordering on Syria, and that of the Lakhmites, bordering on Mesopotamia, had encouraged the development of a flourishing Arabic poetry. These states had disappeared, however, before the seventh century, and there was no organized Arabian state at the time of Mohammed's birth. But there is reason to believe that the general level of Arabic civilization was higher than has usually been estimated.

Arabian civilization before Mohammed

The typical Arab was not settled in an oasis or in a caravan city or on the frontier; he was a nomad. Al-Qutami, poet contemporary of Mohammed, well describes the nomadic mode of life:

> "You who admire the life of the city dwellers,
> What think you of us, the sons of the open desert?
> You may jog the streets on asses; we have our chargers,
> Clean-limbed, and our lances, strong and keen for plunder.
> When times are straitened, we raid the clans of Dabba;
> Then he whose time has come to die—he dies!
> Ay, it may happen to us to raid our brethren,
> When for our need no other foe comes handy." [1]

The nomadic Arab was governed by the life of the tribe and the clan and the smaller family, each group with its patriarchal chieftain or sheik. The principle of blood revenge, the retaliation of clan upon clan for injuries suffered by individual members of the clan, was prevalent among them. Even among the more highly civilized townspeople this clan tradition persisted. The nomad was known by his tribe, the townsman by his family. "Learn your genealogies," said Omar. The interior tribes, the Bedouins, were pastoral, living upon their flocks and herds. They were not entirely nomadic, however, for each clan from time immemorial possessed the particular right to some oasis. Their principal foodstuffs were dates from the trees in the oases, and the flesh and milk of their animals. The system of clans and the desert economy produced interminable tribal wars, broken only for the four months of the sacred spring season, when the great fairs at Mecca and Medina were held. Usually the feuds arose from conflicts over wells and oases,

[1] Quoted in C. C. Torrey, *The Jewish Foundation of Islam*, p. 29.

or from sheep- and camel-raiding. The hardy manner of life bred a love of freedom, a roving military spirit, courage, endurance, self-confidence, and a strong family pride.

Mecca, controlled by the tribe of the Kuraish, was the largest of the *Mecca* caravan cities of the Hejaz. Tribes of the interior resorting to it during the months of truce for the intertribal exchange of goods made it the commercial center of the Arabs: it was more economic opportunity than religion that originally drew them there. But Mecca was also a place of pilgrimage and possessed a shrine, the temple Kaaba (the cube), which is said to have housed the images of the chief gods of the tribes that visited the city, and certainly contained within its walls the sacred black stone miraculously sent down from heaven, a common object of veneration for the Arabs. Their religion, in spite of the aspirations of those poets who proclaimed the existence of a single god, was unadulterated polytheism, the tribes having their own patron deities, combined with an animism that peopled spring and grove, rock and tree, with spirits. Among this people, without political or religious organization, in the commercial atmosphere of the wealthy caravan city of Mecca, was conceived a monotheistic religion that has spread until today it embraces approximately two hundred millions of people, from Gibraltar to Japan.

Some nine years after the death of Chlotar I and about five years after the death of Justinian, around 570, there was born to the Hashimite clan of Mecca, one of the poorest clans of the tribe of Kuraish, the infant Mohammed. It is impossible to get a clear picture of the growth and development of the child, so distorted a picture has Mohammedan tradition left of the miraculous man. He was early left an orphan, and it was upon his grandfather and later his uncle that his rearing devolved. As he had been born into the tribe that controlled the city—a sort of merchant republic, where wealth confirmed the social status of *Mohammed's* the tribe—his early training was of a character to fit him for participa- *early life* tion in the caravan trade along the main route through the Hejaz. He learned to read and write enough to handle business accounts, and at twenty-five he was employed by a rich widow of his tribe, Khadija, to manage her business. He accompanied her caravans as far north as Teima, the distributing point for Egypt and Syria, but it is unlikely that he went farther. The successful young business man soon became the husband of his much older patroness, who was wholly devoted to him. Once established so securely, he was free to indulge his own religious interests.

It appears that as a very young man Mohammed developed into

the kind of lean-faced and flashing-eyed religious neurotic who could never be at home in his environment of practical affairs. He got into the way of going to the lonely regions outside Mecca to meditate on some means of relieving his personal discontent and refashioning the larger Arabic world nearer to his heart's desire. In Mecca and in other cities that he visited along the caravan route Jewish communities of considerable size preserved a well-ordered religion and a cohesive society based on long tradition, which in comparison with the disorganized society and religion of his own people might well have seemed to

Mohammed's religious development

him enviable. He must also through hearsay have come into contact with the new Christian religion that had well-nigh surrounded the Arabian peninsula and filtered into its northern and southern regions. Did Judaism or Christianity have any solution for the problems that were besetting him? To find out he must have more definite knowledge than he could acquire from external observation.

It seems probable that he went to one or more Jews in Mecca to be taught.[2] In this way he may even have learned enough Hebrew to pursue, with his teacher's aid, the study of the Hebrew Scriptures, or enough of the Aramaic current in the Jewish community to enable him to read some of its literature. In any case, most of what he knew of Judaism and Christianity he must have learned through conversation and oral instruction. He learned of the righteous and avenging only God of the Hebrews, Jahveh, who must have reminded him of the Allah of the earlier Arabic poets. He learned of the Christian Trinity, which he understood to be God the Father, Mary the Mother, and Jesus the Son of Mary, who was also the Spirit and the Word. He learned of the Hebrew Book, which the Christians had adopted, and of an additional Christian Book, which—or both of which—contained the revelations of this only God, made through his specially chosen prophets to his specially chosen people. He heard of a final Judgment Day, when God passed out the rewards of heaven and the punishments of hell to all mankind, arisen from their graves. Like his own Arabs, the Jews and the Christians also had their angels and their evil spirits. More than this, Mohammed became acquainted with Jewish homiletic literature, and Jewish law as enshrined in the Talmud. From his own observation, from conversation with people in Mecca who knew something of Judaism and Christianity, and from such instruction as he received Mohammed thus accumulated a large fund of information upon which to meditate.

Gradually his chaotic thoughts and feelings were clarified into an

[2] This is worked out in Torrey, *op. cit.*

ordered simplicity. At about the age of forty he began to preach enthusiastically to his family and friends, and on the streets of Mecca, the new synthetic religion that he had worked out. This religion, however, was not offered as the simple conclusions of a mere man, reached after long observation, instruction, and reflection. The long, hard straining after religious insight had made his hypersensitive constitution subject to nervous fits or seizures, which have been diagnosed by physicians in various ways, even as epilepsy. It is also possible that in his lonely hours in the desert he learned the trick of self-hypnosis. At any rate, in these abnormal psychological states his mind worked with such clarity that he seemed to be hearing words dictated to him by a higher power. These he identified as the words of Allah (God), dictated through his intermediary, the angel Gabriel. He concluded that he had been chosen as another of God's prophets, unto whom was being delivered a new revelation. There can be no question of Mohammed's sincerity in this belief. *Mohammed the prophet of Allah*

Mohammed's revelation came to him not as a single whole in any continuous stretch of inspiration, but bit by bit, from time to time, throughout the rest of his life. The revelations were influenced not only by his own reflections, but by the hostile reception of his message among the Meccans and the Jews, by his personal experiences with his opponents, and, after his removal to Yathrib, by political and military considerations and the necessities of legislating for a new religious community. It was Mohammed's convenient—and dangerous—conviction that Allah inspired him to pronounce judgment on all practical matters and crises as they arose. These revelations were not always consistent; Allah not infrequently inspired him to change his mind, or to make an exception of himself, or to enlarge later upon earlier revelations.

It is probable that Mohammed himself, when the wording of these divine inspirations became fixed in his mind, wrote them down in rhythmic and riming prose. They constitute, as collected, "a great literary work, admirable throughout in its discriminating use of words, the skilful structure of its sentences, and the surprising mastery of all the nuances of a highly developed grammatical science." [3] Amanuenses made copies to be distributed among his followers: the word of God as revealed through his prophet Mohammed was to be memorized day and night by the faithful. To lend the greatest interest and widest appeal to his revelation, Mohammed incorporated in it narratives from the Hebrew Scriptures and native Arabian legends and folk-lore, such as tales of Alexander the Great and the Seven Sleepers of Ephesus. *The Koran*

[3] Torrey, *op. cit.*, p. 36.

This was an especially delicate matter, for it was essential that such stories should seem original enough to pass as fresh revelation, and at the same time authentic enough not to seem mere perversion or falsification of the older stories. Mohammed succeeded so well that "we may well question to what extent they show shrewd calculation rather than child-like inconsequence."

During the prophet's life it was not necessary to collect his revelations into a book, and they were not given their present form until some twenty years after his death. This text, established by the Caliph Othman, has hardly been changed in any detail. It is the Koran (Arabic for "book" or "lection"). The Koran is not arranged in the order in which Mohammed is supposed to have delivered it; the 114 chapters, or *suras*, are arranged in order of length, the first chapter being the longest. The entire book, containing 77,639 words, is not so long as the New Testament. The Koran constitutes the sole authoritative basis for the new religion and for the civil and social regulation of the new community founded by Mohammed. But it was later supplemented by a body of tradition (the *hadith*) containing further sayings and doings of the prophet, interpreting passages that were not clear, and deducing from his early prescriptions a body of law and practice for a much larger and more complicated Mohammedan community. In the *hadith* the influence of Jewish tradition and law is predominant. Only in the simple Mohammedan religious service does there seem to be any borrowing from Christianity.

Islam

Mohammed called his new religion "Islam," meaning submission to God; the Moslem is he who professes Islam, that is, submits himself to God. In Mohammed's mind it was not so much a new religion as the perfection of an old one. Islam had first been revealed to the prophet Abraham and his family, the original founders of the Kaaba; and from Ishmael, Abraham's eldest son, was sprung the race of the Arabs. Jews and Christians had strayed away from the true religion, and were now to be brought back into the fold by the latest, and last, prophet of God. All history was reduced in Mohammed's mind to a series of special revelations to special prophets. The Koran enumerates twenty-five such prophets, including three earlier Arabians, the patriarchs of the Old Testament, and Jesus. With some of these God had made a special covenant, as with Adam, Noah, Abraham, Moses, Jesus, and finally Mohammed himself. The Koran was but a confirmation of earlier Hebrew and Christian Scriptures, and Islam but the perfection of Judaism and Christianity, which should unite all men. Islam, therefore, unlike Christianity, was from its beginning conceived as a world religion, the final revelation of God's truth, which must inevitably win the allegiance of all men.

None the less, Mohammed was rooted in his native soil, and Islam was more particularly a final revelation to the Arabs. Mohammed was the prophet of the Arabs, and the Koran was the Book of the Arabs. Therefore, while it incorporated teachings and practices common to both Jews and Christians, it must not divorce itself more than was necessary from old Arabian paganism. This was precisely the attitude of the later Christian leaders towards paganism. The Islam of the Koran, accordingly, was a masterly piece of eclecticism. To Christians it seemed hardly more than a heresy; for Jews—even though it was rejected by the Jewish people as a whole—it was easy of acceptance; while for the Arabs, although it involved a complete change in religion and some change in manner of life, it became a unifying religious enthusiasm. For millions of others, neither Christians nor Jews nor Arabs, including some to whom Christianity failed to appeal, its positive simplicity made it easy to accept. Mohammed's accomplishment speaks sufficiently for his practical wisdom.

The most conspicuous teaching of Islam is its unqualified monotheism. There is but one God, almighty and omniscient, Allah, who rules over men like a benevolent oriental despot. The worship of any other *The teachings* god in any form whatever is idolatry and abomination. The Christian *of Islam* Trinity was as abhorrent to Mohammed as the polytheism of his native Arabia, and the use of images in religious worship was anathema. Neither in painting nor in sculpture was the Moslem to picture any animal or plant, for fear that such an image of a living thing might itself become an object of worship and encroach upon the worship of the one and only God. Allah's revelations to man are contained in the infallible words of the Koran, conveyed to his last and greatest prophet Mohammed by the angelic messenger Gabriel. On the Day of Judgment all human beings shall arise in the flesh from the dead. In the words of the Koran,

> "The earth shall be shaken in a shock
> And the mountains shall be powdered in powder
> And become like flying dust."

Then the faithful will be rewarded with the eternal joys of heaven,

> "In gardens of delight . . .   *Heaven*
> Upon inwrought couches,

Reclining thereon face to face.
Youths ever young shall go unto them round about
With goblets and ewers and a cup of flowing wine—
Their heads shall not ache with it, neither shall they be confused—,
And fruits of their choice
And flesh of birds to their desire;
And damsels with bright eyes like hidden pearls,—
A reward for what they have wrought . . .
Amid thornless date-trees
And bananas laden with fruit
And shade outspread
And water flowing
And fruit abundant,
Never failing nor forbidden." [4]

Hell

But the condemned "shall be cast into scorching fire to be broiled. They shall be given to drink of a boiling fountain. They shall have no food but of dry thorns and thistles, which shall not fatten, neither shall they satisfy hunger. . . . They who believe not shall have garments of fire fitted unto them. Boiling water shall be poured on their heads, their bowels shall be dissolved thereby and also their skins, and they shall be beaten with maces of iron. So often as they shall endeavour to get out of hell because of the anguish of their torments, they shall be dragged back into the same; and their tormentors shall say unto them, 'Taste ye the pain of burning.' " [5]

Mohammedan observances

This was plainly a simple catalogue of beliefs, with no complicated system of salvation. Nor were the requirements of Mohammedan observance rigorous. The Moslem must bear witness that "there is no God but Allah, and Mohammed is the prophet of Allah." Five times a day, in answer to the muezzin's call from the minaret of the mosque, he must face Mecca (it was to have been Jerusalem, but Mohammed was disappointed in his hope of support from the Jews) and pray. The most severe requirement was that he fast during the day throughout the sacred month of Ramadan, probably in imitation of the Christian Lenten fast. He must give alms to the poor; the giving, at first voluntary, later became compulsory, corresponding to an income tax for poor relief and for the support of the caliphate. Finally, if it was at all possible, he must make a pilgrimage to Mecca at least once in his lifetime; this was a continuation of the earlier Arab practice of pilgrimage to

[4] J. H. Robinson, *Readings in European History*, I (1904), 118–19.
[5] Robinson, *History of Religions*, p. 184.

the Kaaba. There is no organized church in Islam, no priesthood, no pope; there are no sacraments. The leaders of the service in the mosque are laymen. There is no intermediary between the Moslem and Allah.

The Koran also contains regulations for the business, social, and family life of the Mohammedan community, all reminiscent of Hebrew legislation and often in imitation of it. These regulations were both a recognition of long-established practice among the Arabs and an attempt to raise its level. Mohammed was therefore a social as well as religious innovator. The Jewish distinction between clean and unclean food was imitated; no Moslem might eat blood or swine's flesh or the flesh of any creature found dead, or "whatever has been strangled, killed by a blow or fall or by goring; that of which wild beasts have eaten; and whatever has been slaughtered on heathen altars." [6] Intoxicating beverages were prohibited, and a later dictum pronounces a solemn curse on anyone "who drinks wine, or gives it to drink; sells it or buys it; carries it or has it brought to him; presses it out or has another press it out for him; takes possession of it or profits from its price." [7]

Gambling and usury were prohibited. Polygamy was recognized, but only the prophet himself was allowed to exceed the limit of four wives. Slavery was countenanced. The regulations controlling inheritance were liberalized to benefit female children, and the exposure of female infants was forbidden. Adultery was punished by flogging. Divorce, however, was made easy for the husband, who could divorce himself, but impossible for the wife. Altogether it may be that the low *Mohammedan* status of Arab women was slightly improved by Mohammedanism. The *law* Semitic principle, found in the Old Testament, of "an eye for an eye, a tooth for a tooth," was retained, but the right of blood revenge was curtailed. The ceremonial cleanliness of the Jew was transferred to the Arab: "the bathing of the convert to Islam and the Friday bath both likewise correspond to the baptism of [Israelite] proselytes and the Sabbath bath." [8] Circumcision, although not prescribed by the Koran, was continued by the Arabs. Mohammed was lenient towards debtors, but recommended the strictest honesty in carrying out private contracts. His general counsel concerning the relationship of human beings to one another can match the highest ethical teachings of any religion. "Be kind to your neighbor. Draw the veil over him. Avoid injury. Look upon him with an eye of kindness. If you see him doing evil, for-

[6] Torrey, *op. cit.*, p. 153.
[7] *Ibid.*, p. 154.
[8] *Legacy of Israel*, p. 162.

give him. If you see him doing good to you, proclaim your thankfulness." [9]

Mohammed's message was not received in Mecca with the enthusiasm for which he hoped, but he consoled himself with the knowledge that such has always been the native prophet's fate. The new preaching might well seem to the Meccans a mere doing over of beliefs and practices current among foreigners, of whom there were many all about them. Moreover, they could easily discern in it a threat to the importance of Mecca as a pagan religious, and therefore commercial, center for Arabia. The Jews in Mecca likewise remained aloof.

Within several years Mohammed had converted only his wife, his freedman and adopted son Zaid, his cousin Ali, and his friend Abu-Bekr. By preaching to pilgrims to Mecca he gained no great number of followers. From indifference the attitude of the Meccan commercial aristocracy turned to hostility, and Mohammed was practically boycotted for years. In the face of growing public disapproval some of his few converts fled to Abyssinia. After the death of his wife Khadija in 619 he looked about for a more promising location, where his claims might be regarded with more objectivity than in his native town. The city of Yathrib, to the north on the caravan route, was torn by internal feuds, and all factions seemed willing to submit to a neutral outsider.

The Hegira As they were willing to accept Mohammed, he began to send his few followers thither, and in September 622, with the last of them he moved there himself. Yathrib henceforth was Medina, "the city of the prophet" (*madinat an Nabi*). The migration to Yathrib, known as the Hegira (the English corruption of the Arabic *hijra*), marks a turning point in Mohammed's career, and was clearly recognized as such by the Mohammedans. The Mohammedan calendar dates from the Hegira; 622 is the year one of the Mohammedan era.

The transformation of Islam From the Hegira dates the transformation of Islam from a small group of religious enthusiasts into a larger political and religious community, and the transformation of Mohammed from a religious and social reformer into the political and religious despot of this larger community. His rejection by the Jews of Mecca, and more particularly by the larger number of Jews at Medina, embittered him and, following his rejection by the Arabs of Mecca, obliged him to look for support to the Bedouin Arabs of the desert. Islam began to take on a less universal and more strictly Arab aspect. The life of the Bedouins was characterized by blood feuds, continual raids on neighboring tribes, and the plundering of caravans. From the day that he left Mecca Mohammed

[9] *Legacy of Islam*, p. 308.

was determined upon revenge against the city for its unholy repudiation of his prophetic claims. Such a program, promising rich rewards in booty from attacks on Meccan caravans, naturally attracted the Bedouin tribes, as well as his own followers in Medina, who had little means of subsistence. When in addition Allah revealed to Mohammed that it was a holy obligation to attack infidels, and that those who died in such a cause were assured of the bliss of a cool and fragrant heaven, the elements of the *jihad*, or the holy war, were ready at hand. "Fight for Allah's cause against those who fight you; kill them wherever you find them and drive them from the place from which they have driven you; it is worse to tolerate their offense than to kill them . . . make war on them until there is no more offense and all men worship Allah alone." [10] It has always been easy for men to find a religious sanction for war, and Mohammed had the advantage of believing that he was the mouthpiece of God.

The Jews in Medina paid for their lack of sympathy and their treasonable support of Mecca by exile, confiscation of property, and in one instance by the slaughter of some six hundred of them and the enslavement of their wives and children. During the years 623 and 624 Allah instructed Mohammed to make raids upon six caravans to Mecca, and in the following year the Moslems captured the most important Meccan caravan. When the Meccans took up arms, they were badly beaten. *The capture of Mecca* Medina was now fast becoming the center of a large and predatory Islam. After it had successfully withstood a siege by Meccan forces, Mohammed decided that the time had come to attack Mecca itself. At the news that he was approaching with ten thousand men, the city capitulated; in January 630, Mohammed entered it as a conqueror. He treated the city leniently; a few of his personal enemies were done away with and the idols in the Kaaba were destroyed, but the temple itself was preserved and the ceremonies connected with it were incorporated into the religion of Islam.

Two years later Mohammed died. To the end he kept to the simple *Mohammed's death* way of life he had always led. At his death Arabia was still by no means united under the political and religious domination of Islam. Possibly one-third of the peninsula had come under his sway, but most of the Arabs had not yet even heard of the new faith.

From these small beginnings at Medina the Arab church-state spread with prodigious rapidity. Within fifty years after Mohammed's death it had conquered Persia, Egypt, Syria, and Palestine. Within one hun-

[10] O. J. Thatcher and E. H. McNeal, *Europe in the Middle Age* (1920), pp. 258–59.

dred years it had reached the frontiers of India to the east, and to the west had swept across North Africa through Spain and beyond the Pyrenees. The astonishing speed and magnitude of such conquests challenge explanation. The easy explanation has long been that Mohammed first succeeded in giving political cohesion to Arabia, and then so fired the Arabs with the burning zeal of religious fanaticism that almost *en masse* they dashed out of the peninsula with the fierce determination to convert the world by the sword, knowing that, if they died in the attempt, Islam guaranteed them the most precious of all booty, the fruits of paradise.

The facts are quite otherwise. In the first place, it is impossible at this early date to speak of Mohammedan fanaticism, except possibly in isolated instances. Mohammed himself in his conquest of Mecca displayed a fierce enough zeal; but in general no such militant intolerance as, for example, characterized the struggle of Christianity against paganism, characterized Mohammedan expansion. The fanaticism of Islam is that of much later converts, and even so Mohammedanism has normally been marked in practice by its tolerance. For all its expansion and conquest, from Mesopotamia to Spain, Judaism and Christianity by no means ceased to exist by its side. The only impositions made by the Arab conquerors upon unbelievers were a special poll tax and the prohibition of possession of arms. Facilitated by the fundamental similarity of Islam to those two religions, these disabilities and the prospect of official position and reward in a rapidly expanding state began to bring in converts in crowds. The Arab authorities were by no means pleased with this too easy and too great success. It was rather to their advantage to keep the number of the governing class small, although there were always Christians and Jews prominent in official and learned circles. Moreover, it made their political control easier to encourage religious differences among the governed, in accordance with the old Roman principle *divide et impera*.

In the second place, it is impossible to speak of Mohammed's creating any such thing as Arabian unity, nor can it be supposed that in any substantial way the nomadic Arab tribes were suddenly consolidated into a unified state after his death. Unified states are not organized in the desert. In fact, after Mohammed's death it was only by hard fighting, in the so-called Ridda Wars, that a recognition of the loose political overlordship of Medina over the other Arab tribes was secured. Even then there was not, and could not be, any interference with tribal organization. As for the early Arabian conquests, few of Mohammed's

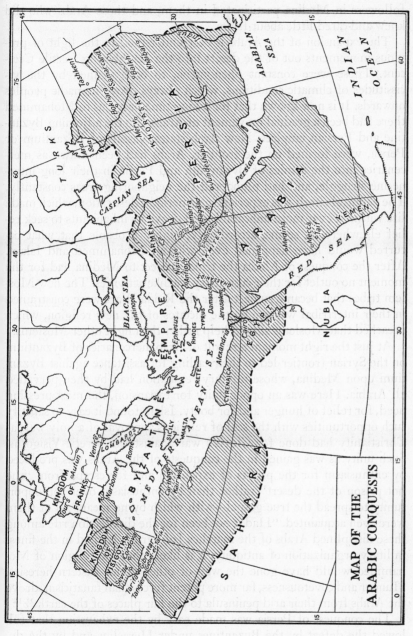

MAP OF THE
ARABIC CONQUESTS

followers in Medina participated in them, and those Arabs who did knew and cared little about Islam.

The expansion of the Arabs is best understood in the light of previous movements out of the desert into the neighboring Fertile Crescent. These were constant phenomena, to be explained by the vicissitudes of climatic conditions, which always drove nomadic peoples onwards. It is now known that for a long time previous to Mohammed there had been a gradual movement of Arabs into the adjoining Byzantine and Persian empires. New Arab states, vassals of Byzantium or Persia, were formed on the frontier. Arabs had been drawn as mercenaries into the armies of Byzantium and Persia in their long internecine struggle, and had plundered the neighboring areas constantly. The peninsula itself was experiencing a periodic desiccation, which made life within it ever more unbearable and drove its inhabitants to seek relief elsewhere. It seems, accordingly, highly probable that what occurred would have happened even without Mohammed and Islam. After the conquest of Mecca the tribes subject to Medina had for the moment no outlet for their customary warlike activities. The new Moslem tribes that became subject after the Ridda Wars were constrained in their intertribal warfare by the dictates of the new religion, which preached that Moslems should help rather than fight other Moslems.

At just the right moment a revolt of Arab mercenaries of Byzantium on the Syrian frontier led to their calling for assistance against Byzantium upon Medina, whose military reputation had by then pervaded all Arabia. Here was an opportunity for expansion, the most pressing need, for relief of hunger and for booty. Islam found it easy to sanctify such opportunities with the seal of religious approval of a holy war, as Christianity had done for Clovis's war against the heretic Visigoths. Such unity as was gained in the conquests of the Arabs was produced by enthusiasm for the profits of expansion and for escape from "the hot prison of the desert" rather than by enthusiasm over the opportunity to spread the true gospel—with which by no means all of them were even acquainted. "Had it not been for the disaffection rife among these disciplined Arabs of the marches [of Syria], trained in the finest military organization of antiquity, it is likely that the religion of Mohammed would have gone the way of other minor eastern heresies. Hunger and covetousness, far more potent forces than fanaticism, drove the Arabs from their arid peninsula to the fair places of the earth." [11]

The conquest of Persia was made easy by the exhaustion that followed the defeat by the Byzantines under Heraclius and by the do-

[11] *Legacy of Israel*, p. 150.

mestic intrigues of the nobility and the clergy against the crown. The Arabs defeated the Persians in three successive battles, and in 641 the Sassanid dynasty came to an end.

While one Arab army conquered Persia, another invaded Syria. It met with no resistance at all except from the Byzantine armies stationed there, and Byzantium was likewise too exhausted from the Persian war to put up an adequate defense. Moreover, in Syria and Palestine Semite welcomed Semite; the Arabs were relieving their kinsmen of the intolerable burden of Byzantine servitude. The empire's heavy taxation outraged Syria, Palestine, and Egypt; and its oppressive religious policy alienated the Monophysites and the Nestorians, and, when it was mitigated, by its concessions to heretics alienated the orthodox. For the lighter burden of taxation under the Arabs and for their religious toleration the people of these provinces were willing to exchange masters. Received with open arms by most of the cities of Syria, by 639 the Arabs had driven the imperial armies out of the country and had made favorable treaties with the large cities. Jerusalem had been captured after a long siege.

Arab conquest of Persia, Syria, Palestine, Egypt

There were important reasons for next undertaking the conquest of Egypt. It was a great Byzantine naval base, and unless the Arabs controlled it their fleet could not defend the Syrian coast towns against the Byzantine fleet. Furthermore, Mecca had become more and more dependent upon Egyptian wheat; the increasing number of pilgrims required more grain, to contain which enormous magazines were erected in the Holy City. The conquest of Egypt was accordingly begun in 646, and by 650 the Arabs had driven the Byzantines out and mastered the country as far south as Abyssinia and as far west as Lydia. From Egypt they had already taken to the sea, occupied Cyprus and Rhodes as early as 650, and were soon making serious attacks on lower Italy and Sicily.

The hoary tale that the Arabs destroyed the great Greek library at Alexandria is false; there was no great library to destroy. The larger library was severely damaged, if not destroyed, by fire during Cæsar's siege of the city in 48 B.C. The smaller—but still very large—library was destroyed in A.D. 389 by Christian monks. In Egypt, Syria, and Palestine Christianity was left undisturbed. Jerusalem even became a sacred city and a goal of pilgrimage for Moslems, as the place where the first Ommiad was proclaimed caliph and whence Mohammed ascended to heaven. The patriarchates became Monophysite, but privileges were extended to orthodox Christians, who were later even permitted to have their own patriarchs at Alexandria and Antioch.

The Arabs, after consolidating their power in Egypt by the rapid conversion of many of the natives to Islam, moved west, and within a short time had conquered and converted Cyrenaica and Tripoli. Their attack upon Byzantine Africa, the Exarchate of Carthage, was delayed by a furious siege of Constantinople between 673 and 677. When the siege was lifted, they resumed their attack upon Carthage. After a desperate resistance the city was captured in 695, but was lost in 697, and then retaken in 698. While they were attacking Carthage, the Arabs subdued and converted the Berbers, the warlike hill people of Morocco, who had never been conquered even by Rome; their subjugation was necessary if North Africa was to be secure. Christianity was left undisturbed in Africa also, so far as the Arab government was concerned, but within half a century the flight of the Roman and Greek population before the Mohammedan advance had practically obliterated results of long centuries of Roman and Byzantine work in this area.

It was the Berbers of North Africa, incorporated into the Moslem ranks, who forced the conquest of Visigothic Spain. The throne of the Visigoths, unlike that of the other German kingdoms, never became hereditary. When, late in the sixth century, the Visigothic king abjured his Arian faith for orthodox Christianity, he fell an easy victim to the combined efforts of the great nobles, most of whom had by this time become orthodox, and of the orthodox high clergy, to get the crown under their control. Church councils became as much political as religious bodies, which made the kings their creatures and really governed the realm. Their legislation shows that bigotry in Spain is no new thing. Heretics and Jews were mercilessly persecuted and suffered confiscation of property or exile. Most of the exiles found refuge in Africa, where their descendants fraternized with the Mohammedans when they appeared a century later, and contributed greatly to the Spanish campaign.

The campaign was launched in 710, when a band of four hundred horsemen under a Berber lieutenant named Tarif landed in Andalusia at the place ever since called Tarifa. In the following spring a far more famous captain, Tarik, crossed with a force reported to have consisted of three hundred Arabs and seven thousand Berbers. He captured the citadel on the great rock that guards the straits, where long stood the pillar to Hercules that gave the place its classical name, and renamed it Djebel Tarik, the Rock of Tarik, now corrupted to "Gibraltar." After a single battle north of Gibraltar had destroyed the Visigothic army, town after town, province after province, was overrun, until the Mohammedans had conquered all Spain except the mountainous districts of Galicia and Asturias in the northwest. Their seat of government, first fixed at Seville, was transferred to Cordova in 715.

By 725, seven years after their futile attempt to take Constantinople,[12] the Arabs had crossed the Pyrenees and penetrated as far into Frankish Gaul as Autun. In 732 their northward expansion was finally checked by the Frankish mayor of the palace, Charles Martel, in a battle ordinarily referred to as the "Battle of Tours," although it was fought somewhat nearer Poitiers. This battle has regularly been called one of the few truly decisive battles of the world, although it has been more correctly characterized as "the fortuitous puff of a movement already spent." Any further Mohammedan advance northwards would presumably have been checked anyway by revolts among the Berber tribes in North Africa, which stopped reserves from moving across into Spain. To be sure, the Mohammedans continued to harass southern Gaul and the valley of the Rhone for many years, and were not finally driven back across the Pyrenees until 759. On the other hand, we must allow great significance to the events of 732 and the years following in southern Gaul. For western Europe they meant the same thing that the failure of the Arab siege of Constantinople in 717–18 meant for eastern Europe: in each case a line of development already begun passed successfully a crisis that might have turned the course of history into quite other channels. The fact that the Arabs at almost the same time attacked Constantinople and advanced into Gaul makes it seem possible that they contemplated joining forces in central Europe, thus duplicating the feat of the Romans in girdling the Mediterranean.

The "Battle of Tours"

In western Asia after their conquest of Persia the Arabs spread across the hinterland beyond. The ancient cities dotting this vast and semi-arid territory—Merv, Bokhara, Samarcand, Tashkent, and Balkh— were conquered one by one, and by 724 the Mohammedans were at the Indus River and the western frontier of the Chinese empire. Here for many years the advance of Islam was arrested. But the seas were open, and just as the Arabs in Egypt learned to sail on the Mediterranean, so also they became a seafaring people in the Far East. They sailed along the Persian Gulf and across the Indian Ocean, and colonized Makran and the Malabar coast of India. Arab dhows began to appear in the China Sea, and Mohammedan colonies were settled in Hangchow, Canton, and other Chinese ports. Mohammedanism was spread in the east both from these trading colonies and by missionaries, and has continued to expand to the present time. Parts of China, Java, the Celebes, the Philippine Islands, and the Malay Peninsula are still strongly Moham-

Arab expansion eastward to India and China

12 See Chap. 5, p. 139.

medan, though they have never been part of the political empires of the Arabs or the later Turks.

In the eighth century the Arabs also penetrated south from upper Egypt into Nubia, and from Tripoli, Kairwan, and Fez into the Sahara; for the first time in history central Africa was brought into contact with the civilization of the Mediterranean. As successfully as in the east, Islam was spread in Africa by traders and missionaries. It reached both the east and west coasts, where, as in the Far East, it has maintained itself and continued to expand ever since. Christianity, once well rooted in northern Africa, has never since the Mohammedan invasions been able to retain even a modest foothold among the natives.

Islam in central Africa

The traditional Arab tribal organization and love of liberty had prevented the growth of anything like a single state in Arabia. Arabian characteristics helped Islam conquer a vast territory in a brief time, but prevented it from establishing a political empire equal to the demands made upon it. The centrifugal tendencies of Arab society were aggravated by Mohammed's failure to leave a male heir or to designate a successor or even a method of choosing one. His companions chose as first caliph (successor, or vicar) his friend and companion of the Hegira, later his father-in-law, Abu-Bekr, who died in 634, only two years after Mohammed's death. The second caliph was Omar (634–44), the son of a Meccan merchant and also a companion of the Hegira; the third, Othman (644–56), another Meccan of the Hegira and a member of the important Ommiad family. By this time a movement of opposition to the choice of caliphs from outside Mohammed's family had already sprung up. This movement also opposed the tendency to supplement the Koran with the *hadith*. These legitimists who would limit the caliphate to the family of Mohammed, and purists who would keep the Koran as the sole authority for the life of the Mohammedan community, were called the Shiites (from *shi'a*, a sect). Their opponents were the Sunnites (from *sunna*, traditions), who embodied in their principle of election to the caliphate the old Arabian patriarchal tradition, and upheld as valid the body of tradition growing up outside the Koran. The Shiites grouped themselves around Ali, the husband of Mohammed's daughter Fatima, who became caliph after the murder of Othman in 656.

The caliphate

Sunnites and Shiites

Ali's caliphate (656–61) was marked by continuous civil war, the opposition being led by the head of the Ommiad family, Muawiya, Governor of Syria, who proclaimed himself caliph at Jerusalem in 660. After the murder of Ali at Basra in 661 Muawiya was generally recognized as caliph, and the capital was moved from Medina to Damas-

The Ommiad caliphs at Damascus

cus. The line of Ommiad caliphs, following in hereditary succession, lasted until 750. The removal of the capital to Damascus marks a turn from the original Arab domination of Islam to the domination of the Syrian Arabs, and from a patriarchal to a dynastic state, modeled on Byzantium and emphasizing less the religious than the political character of the empire. The court at Damascus became a luxurious center of art and learning, and the Great Mosque the Santa Sophia of Islam. But the Ommiads were unable to suppress the opposition of the Shiites, or to allay dissatisfaction over the changed character of the Mohammedan state. The Shiites persisted obstinately in Egypt, Persia, and parts of Arabia. The unruly Berbers in North Africa successfully revolted in 724, during the caliphate of Hashim, and the Turkish provinces broke away. The whole opposition was concentrated under the Persian Shiites, who, under the leadership of a great-grandson of a cousin of Mohammed, Abu-l'Abbas, revolted and overthrew the Ommiads at Damascus in 750, killing the reigning caliph Merwan II and ninety princes of the house.

The new dynasty of the Abbasids moved the capital of the caliphate *The Abbasid* from Damascus to the newly built city of Bagdad, in the heart of Meso- *caliphs at* potamia. Islam thus finally lost completely its national Arab character. *Bagdad* It now entered into the ancient heritage of Persia, especially of Persia in its last phase, the Sassanian Persia that had so strongly influenced the later Roman empire and Byzantium. More even than at Damascus the caliphate at Bagdad became definitely an oriental despotism, resting on the Persian administrative system which it took over, and living in the midst of the luxury and extravagance characteristic of an oriental court.

The Abbasids were no more than the Ommiads equal to the task of maintaining a united empire. The only one of the Ommiads who escaped destruction in 750, Abd-ar-Rahman, grandson of Hashim, fled to Spain and established at Cordova in 756 a virtually independent hereditary emirate, which by 929 felt strong enough to declare itself *The rise of* an independent caliphate. In northwestern Africa a descendant of Ali, *the other* named Idris, set up an independent state with Fez as its capital. Mod- *caliphates* ern Tunis and Algeria came under the control of the Aghlabids, descendants of a native potentate, with their capital at Kairwan, whence they began their conquest of Malta and Sicily in the ninth century. Egypt was lost in 972 to the Fatimite dynasty, which had in 909 established itself in Tunis and founded Mahdia and which now founded Cairo as its new capital. The caliphs at Bagdad themselves came to be the creatures, first of their Persian viziers, later of their Turkish mercenary troops. In spite, however, of the formal surrender of temporal power to the sultans of the Seljuk Turks in the eleventh century, after their capture of Bagdad, the caliphs managed to prolong their dynasty until the Mongol conquest of 1258 finally destroyed the whole Abbasid family.

But after all, the miracle of Arab history is not to be found even in the new religion of Islam, still less in the phenomenal expansion of the Arab state. As for the character of that state, it is hardly more than an *Moslem, not* embodiment of the inherent political incapacity of the Arabs of the *Arab, civiliza-* peninsula, though to be sure it is an embodiment on a world-wide scale. *tion* The miracle is that in a comparatively short time throughout the length and breadth of the short-lived empire a Moslem civilization came into existence which for several centuries shared with Byzantine civilization the cultural leadership of mankind. It is to be noted that the term "Moslem" has just been used to characterize this civilization, not "Arab" or "Arabian" or "Arabic," inasmuch as the persons who were responsible for creating it, while they were for the most part Moslems, were not Arabs.

The Arabs first incorporated as part of their new empire areas that had originally been the cradle of occidental civilization, which recently had been parts of the Byzantine and Persian empires. To administer these areas the Arabs could do nothing but take over what they found of the Byzantine and Persian administrations and employ as governors trained and experienced natives; they had nothing of their own to offer in this field. The same thing is true in the domain of culture. Egypt, Palestine, Syria, and Persia were provinces of Hellenistic civilization, and Sassanid Persia had also developed a civilization of its own. Moreover, in Egypt, Palestine, and Syria, under the stimulus of Christianity a new literature and art had developed. Indeed, recent cultural developments in all these countries just before the Mohammedan conquest seemed to point to a new outburst of oriental activity. Culturally, therefore, the Arabs had nothing to offer these lands. They came rather to enjoy what they themselves did not possess; they destroyed very little. In politics and in culture they remained the inferiors of the conquered, and were in fact conquered by them, as always happens when a semi-civilized people moves into a civilized region. They were wise enough to put no obstacles in the way of the continuation of lines of development already begun. Development in art and science in particular they positively stimulated by a policy of active support. Furthermore, their religious tolerance and their liberal use of all the resources of the native population acted as a definite liberating force, in view of the wider scope offered to talent and experience in the new empire.

On the other hand, the Arabs had two things of value to contribute. One was their new religion, which was open and free to those who would accept it, and which demanded new forms of expression in the arts and a new accommodation with secular philosophy. The obligation of pilgrimage to Mecca made for a more mobile world; pilgrims brought ideas from Spain, India, and central Asia and carried ideas back home from the capitals of the empire. The other contribution of the Arabs was the unifying influence of their wonderful language, Arabic. Inasmuch as the Koran might not be translated, it was necessary for every scholar, every person of any importance, indeed anyone who would read the Koran at all, to know Arabic. Thus it quickly became an international language of prime importance, which it has ever since remained, and the standard means of literary expression for the whole Moslem world. The religion and the language of the Arabs, therefore, gave to a society hopelessly disunited politically a cultural unity far more important and permanent than any political unity probably could have been. *The new contributions of the Arabs*

Reinforcing the cultural unity of religion and language, the economic basis for the patronage of the Moslem artist, craftsman, and scholar was the exchange of manufactured goods within the empire, which was facilitated by the absence of tariff boundaries. Mohammedan merchants had established trade relations with China in Canton by the middle of the tenth century, and still earlier with Ceylon and the west coast of India. Down the east African coast they got as far as Madagascar. Scandinavian merchants carried Mohammedan coins by the thousands to Russia, Finland, Scandinavia, Iceland, and Germany. King Offa of Mercia in the eighth century imitated Moslem gold coins in England. Except for the Ægean Sea and the trade route from Venice to Constantinople, Moslem ships controlled the whole Mediterranean. Commercial relations were established with the interior of Africa. *Mohammedan commerce and industry*

Until the middle of the eleventh century exchange of goods with Christian Europe was looked upon with disfavor by both Christian and Moslem, and each engaged in piracy upon the other's ships. When, however, this barrier was once broken down by the Italian cities, a prosperous and almost uninterrupted trade developed between the Moslem countries and Europe. Acquaintance with the bill of exchange and the conception of the joint stock company came from contact with Mohammedan methods of trade.[13] This trade was of great importance not only for the growth of towns in the west, but because Moslem goods furnished suggestions to western artisans for improvement of their

[13] J. H. Kramers and A. H. Christie in *The Legacy of Islam*, p. 105.

craftsmanship. Venetian workmen learned so much from Mohammedan inlaid metal work that a special Venetian style developed, using the
technique and the oriental designs of Moslem workmen. Italian potters
acquired much of their advanced technical knowledge from Moslem
potters.

From Valencia the Moslems exported their famous luster pottery
widely in the west, and the manufacture and sale of textiles flourished.
Goods from Mosul were called muslin, goods from Damascus, damask.
From Bagdad came a heavy cloth called in the west baldachin—a name
still preserved in altar canopies. From the Attabiyah quarter of Bagdad
came silks whose Spanish imitations were called attabi, in France and
Italy tabis, in England tabby; and from the "brown and yellow Attabi
patterns of watered silks" the tabby cat gets her name. Gauze, cotton,
and satin are either Arabic words or Persian words introduced by the
Arabs. Carpets from the orient came into the west as early as the fourteenth century. From the Chinese the Moslems learned to make paper.
Its manufacture spread throughout Islam, and there are Mohammedan
paper manuscripts extant from as early as the ninth century.

Moslem
geography

The Moslem mariner knew the compass in 1282, and he perfected
the Greek astrolabe, which he handed on to the west. Extensive travel
was recorded in a voluminous geographical literature. When the Norman King of Sicily, Roger II (1101–54), wanted a written description
of all the known world, he naturally turned to a Moslem at his court,
Al-Idrisi, to produce it. Moslem scholars kept alive the theory of the
sphericity of the earth, without which the discovery of America would
hardly have been possible. From acquaintance with Moslem seafaring
and from trade with Moslem countries have come such terms as "admiral," "cable," "average," "shallop" or "sloop," "barque," "mon-
soon," "traffic," "tariff," "risk," "caliber," "magazine," and "check." [14]

Agriculture

The Arabs greatly promoted the sciences and arts of agriculture. In
Egypt their water works and canals enabled the farmers to irrigate the
higher ground, and much sterile land was made to yield rich harvests.
The increasing numbers of pilgrims to Mecca needed so much grain
that the Arabs reopened the ancient canal of the Ptolemies between the
Nile and the Red Sea to speed the passage of wheat to Mecca, and the
early Abbasid caliphs are said to have thought of digging a Suez canal.
Under the Spanish Ommiad dynasty an intricate system of irrigation
carried water from the mountains to the plains and opened immense
tracts of arid land. The Arabs terraced the slopes with vineyards. In
country that had been reduced to a depopulated and dry waste by the

[14] *Ibid.*, pp. 89, 93, 97, 98, 105.

Visigoths, villages multiplied and cities sprang up. Into western Europe from Mohammedan countries were introduced orange, lemon, peach, apricot, banana, spinach, artichoke, rice, sugar cane, cotton, saffron, rose, morning-glory, and many other flowers and plants,[15] and the silkworm with the mulberry tree. The following describes a garden of Cordova: "They spared no pains in the superfluity of fountains, hydraulic works and artificial lakes, in which fish were raised for the table. . . . There were also menageries of foreign animals, aviaries of rare birds. . . . Under the shade of cypresses cascades disappeared; among flowering shrubs there were winding walks, bowers of roses, seats cut out of the rock, and crypt-like grottoes hewn in the living stone. Nowhere was ornamental gardening better understood; for not only did the artist try to please the eye as it wandered over the pleasant gradation of vegetable color and form . . . he also boasted his success in the gratification of the sense of smell by the studied succession of perfumes from beds of flowers." [16]

In the extreme east Islam reached the borders of India, and from the Hindus Moslem scholars learned arithmetic, algebra, and trigonometry. From the Hellenistic Greeks they learned far more: geometry, astronomy, logic, and medicine, for example. Before this store of knowledge could be assimilated it had to be translated into Arabic from Sanskrit or Greek—or at second-hand from Syriac or Persian, into which, before the Mohammedan conquest, Christian Monophysite and Nestorian scholars had already begun to translate the works of Hellenistic science and learning. Some of them, driven from Syria and Palestine by the persecutions of Byzantine emperors, had withdrawn to Mesopotamia and Persia, where at Nisibis and Jundeshapur they established centers for translation from Greek and Sanskrit. Thus the scientific tradition had been kept alive in Persia until the Arabs conquered the country, and the means of carrying it on were already at hand in the linguistically expert Christian scholars. These heretics were thus the mediators between orthodox Byzantium with its heritage of pagan Greek culture and the infidel Arabs.

Christian heretics transmit Greek learning to the Moslems

It was, however, not until the period of the early Abbasids, especially under the great caliphs Harun-ar-Raschid (786–809) and Al-Mamun (813–33), that the whole corpus of Greek scientific and philosophical learning was translated into Arabic, mainly by Nestorian Christians. At

[15] *Legacy of Islam*, p. 104, and D. C. Munro and R. J. Sontag, *The Middle Ages* (1928), p. 217.
[16] Draper, quoted in J. F. Scott, A. Hyma, and A. H. Noyes, *Readings in Medieval History* (1933), p. 133.

Bagdad Al-Mamun founded a school of translators, and sent to Constantinople and India for copies of scientific manuscripts, which were sometimes collated in order to establish a sound text. Schools, often headed by Christians, were also established in connection with mosques.

The leading figure of the Bagdad school was the Nestorian Christian Hunayn ibn Ishaq (809–77), who with his son and nephew translated most of the important Greek scientific writings into Syriac and Arabic. Hunayn himself was especially interested in medicine and translated almost all the writings of the Greek physician Galen of the second century, and some of those of the Greek "father of medicine," Hippocrates, as well as Galen's commentaries on Hippocrates's works. He was no mean physician himself, and wrote especially on diseases of the eye. Incidentally, the treatises of Ali ibn Isa of Bagdad and Ammar of Mosul on ophthalmology were "the best textbooks on eye diseases until the first half of the eighteenth century." The efforts of Hunayn ibn Ishaq, therefore, brought to Arabic medicine the most important works of the Greek physicians, and it is only in his or his pupils' translations that some of Galen's works are preserved at all.

The medical tradition thus established was carried on with great zeal by Moslems and Jews, who in the course of the centuries made many additional contributions out of practical experience to Greek medical lore. The result was that the Moslem physician was incomparably superior to his contemporary in the west. Following closely upon Hunayn came Al-Razi, known to western Europe as Rhazes, a Persian, "undoubtedly the greatest physician of the Islamic world, and one of the great physicians of all time." He wrote more than two hundred works, more than half of them on medical subjects. His book *Smallpox and Measles* was printed as late as 1806. His greatest work is his *Comprehensive Book*, "perhaps the most extensive work ever written by a medical man," in twenty volumes, containing all Greek, Syriac, and early Arabic medical knowledge.

Medicine

A contemporary of Al-Razi, an Egyptian Jew known in western Europe as Isaac Judæus, in his *Guide for Physicians* offered the following advice: "Neglect not to visit and treat the poor, for there is no nobler work than this. Comfort the sufferer by the promise of healing, even when thou art not confident, for thus thou mayest assist his natural powers. Ask thy reward while the sickness is waxing or at its height, for, being cured, he will surely forget what thou didst for him." [17]

However, the greatest figure in the history of Arabic medicine, in so far as its influence on western medicine is concerned, is Avicenna (979–

[17] *Ibid.*, p. 326.

1037). He wrote a final summary of Greek and Arabic medicine in his Canon of Medicine, "the culmination and masterpiece of Arabic systematization," which was read down to the second half of the seventeenth century. In Spain the court physician Abulcasis of Cordova, who died about 1013, laid the foundations for the development of surgery. Haskins quotes from a Syrian physician, Thabit, to show "the contrast between oriental skill and the older Christian superstition": [18]

"They brought to me a knight with an abscess in his leg and a woman troubled with fever. I applied to the knight a little cataplasm; his abscess opened and took a favorable turn. As for the woman, I forbade her to eat certain foods and I lowered her temperature. I was there when a Frankish doctor arrived, who said, 'This man can't cure them!' Then, addressing the knight, he asked, 'Which do you prefer, to live with a single leg or to die with both of your legs?' 'I prefer,' replied the knight, 'to live with a single leg.' 'Then bring,' said the doctor, 'a strong knight with a sharp axe.' The knight and the axe were not slow in coming. I was present. The doctor stretched the leg of the patient on a block of wood, and then said to the knight, 'Cut off his leg with the axe, detach it with a single blow.' Under my eyes the knight gave a violent blow, but it did not cut the leg off. He gave the unfortunate man a second blow, which caused the marrow to fly from the bone, and the patient died immediately.

"As for the woman, the doctor examined her and said, 'She is a woman with a devil in her head, by which she is possessed. Shave her hair.' They did so, and she began to eat again, like her compatriots, garlic and mustard. Her fever grew worse. The doctor then said, 'The devil has gone into her head.' Seizing the razor, he cut into her head in the form of a cross, and excoriated the skin in the middle so deeply that the bones were uncovered. Then he rubbed her head with salt. The woman, in her turn, expired immediately. After asking them if my services were still needed, and after receiving a negative answer, I returned, having learned from their medicine matters of which I had previously been ignorant."

Many Greek works on alchemy were also translated into Syriac and Arabic. The father of Arabic alchemy was Jabir, a writer of the tenth century. The principles on which alchemy was based were known to Egyptian and Greek scholars; they consisted chiefly in the belief that all metals were the same in essence, and could accordingly be changed *Alchemy*

18 C. H. Haskins, *Renaissance of the Twelfth Century* (1927), pp. 326–27.

one into another. It must therefore be possible, if the proper means were found, to change the baser metals into silver and gold; to find the substance that would accomplish this, experimentation was necessary. Thus alchemy contributed the first chapter in the history of chemistry. It was only when alchemy was influenced by philosophic speculation that a mass of hocus-pocus was imbedded in it.

Science and mathematics

The one great original Moslem writer of the ninth century and one of the few pure Arabs to achieve intellectual distinction, Al-Kindi, did much work in physics. Two hundred and sixty-five works are credited to him, on such subjects as tides, music, optics, and the reflection of light. Indeed, "the glory of Moslem science was in the field of optics. Here the mathematical ability of Alhazen and Kamal-al-Din outshone that of Euclid and Ptolemy." [19] Moslem scholars translated the great work of the second-century Hellenistic astronomer Ptolemy, the *Almagest*, and by their own observations made many corrections and improvements, which prepared the way for the revolution in astronomy inaugurated by Copernicus about 1600. They also translated Euclid's *Elements of Geometry*. From India they adopted the system of numerals which, when introduced into western Europe, where they supplanted the clumsy Roman system, were called Arabic numerals. These new numerals included the cipher, or zero, which has been called one of the great inventions of the human mind, without which the later development of higher mathematics would hardly have been possible. On Hindu and Greek foundations Moslem mathematicians made tremendous progress in algebra, their two most distinguished algebraists being Al-Khwarizmi, of the ninth century, and the poet Omar Khayyám, who died in 1123. They "laid the foundations of analytical geometry; they were indisputably the founders of plane and spherical trigonometry, which, properly speaking, did not exist among the Greeks." [20] From the works of Moslem scientists and mathematicians come such Arabic terms as "alkali," "antimony," "alembic," "algebra," "alcohol," "alchemy," "zenith," "nadir," "amalgam," "cipher," "zero," "benzine," and knowledge of sal ammoniac, corrosive sublimate, aniline, silver nitrate, senna, aconite, rhubarb, nux vomica, and camphor. [21]

Philosophy and theology

Arabic philosophy was a strange compound of Plato, Aristotle, and Plotinus. Practically all Aristotle's logical and philosophical works were translated into Arabic, as well as some of Plato's and some of Neo-Platonic origin. Arabic intellectual culture, therefore, came to be a

---

[19] Max Meyerhof, in *Legacy of Islam*, p. 345.
[20] *Legacy of Islam*, p. 376.
[21] R. A. Newhall, *The Crusades* (1927), pp. 90–94.

composite of Semitic revealed religion, Greek philosophy, and Greek and Hindu science. It would seem almost impossible to combine into any one system such divergent sources, yet that is what Moslem philosophers in some fashion succeeded in doing. The work of translation was almost completed by the school of Hunayn in the ninth century.

The association of Christian and Moslem scholars introduced into Islam the same kind of theological problems that Christianity had contended with, though there was fortunately no need to speculate on the dual nature of Christ or on the Trinity. It was rather with such fundamental problems as the nature and power of God and his relationship to the universe and the nature of the soul and the intelligence that the Moslem philosopher concerned himself. The Arab Al-Kindi was chiefly responsible for the introduction of Neo-Platonism into Islam, and thus became, with St. Augustine, an important source of its influence on western thought. The tenth-century Turkish philosopher Al-Farabi wrote elaborate commentaries on Aristotle, and on as much of Plato as the Moslem scholar knew. In addition to his work in medicine, Avicenna wrote commentaries on the theories of his predecessors, which became the chief source for western knowledge of Arabic philosophy.

Finally came the inevitable conflict between faith in revealed religion and the reasoned speculations of secular philosophy. The leading liberal group of theologians were the Mutazilites, who spread throughout the Islamic world. They insisted that theology should be more than a matter of faith in revealed dogmas, that it should correspond as well to the teachings of secular philosophy, and that it should not prescribe as a matter of faith what was objectionable to reason. Although suppressed by the state, the liberal theologians were responsible for the attempt to achieve a synthesis of faith and reason, in which apparent contradictions should be wiped out. Such harmonizations were made as early as the tenth century. For the west the chief representative of this movement was the Spanish Moslem Averroës, who wrote a huge commentary on Aristotle's works, which when translated into Latin remained the western scholar's authority on Aristotle until the renaissance restored the original Greek text. Averroës's synthetic writings, which were thoroughly scholastic in their use of Aristotelian logic to effect theological and philosophical concord, were of vast importance to western scholastics when they were later faced with the same problem; and differences in religious creed did not keep them from using his methods and arguments! [22]

[22] A. Guillaume's chapter on "Philosophy and Theology" in *The Legacy of Islam*, pp. 239–83.

Arabic science and scholarship found a home in universities at Bagdad, Nishapur, Damascus, Jerusalem, Cairo, and Alexandria; these institutions were endowed mostly by the state, some centuries before
there were any universities in the west at all. It is evident that the
Arabic scholar was distinguished not so much for his original creative
work, although he was by no means unoriginal or uncreative, as by the
encyclopedic character of his learning. He preserved Hellenistic science
and thought and added to it from Hindu learning. He was then in a
position to hand on this whole heritage, when the west became ready
and eager for it in the twelfth century, at a time when his own civilization had already begun to decline. He handed on, too, what was just
as important, the love of learning for its own sake and an unquench-
able zeal in its pursuit. Thus it was that three centuries before the
renaissance the excoriated Infidel forged the first strong link in the
broken chain that was to bind together again eastern and western Europe. It would be hard to overestimate the magnitude of the debt that
Christian civilization owes to the Mohammedans.

The cultivation of the arts by the Moslems was no less intense, and
its results no less superior and fruitful, than their scholarship. On the
whole theirs was much less a religious art than the Byzantine. The
The mosque   things that Islam required of and forbade to its artists constituted both
an opportunity and a limitation. The opportunity of building and decorating mosques was limited by the prohibition, due to Islam's horror
of idolatry, of any representation of any human being, animal, or plant
—a prohibition that was not, to be sure, always rigorously observed.

For the simple needs of Mohammedan worship the mosque had to
provide a place for ablutions before worship, a place for prayer and for
public reading from the Koran, and a place from which to summon the
Moslem five times a day to his prayers. Because there were no clergy
to mediate between the Moslem and Allah and no sacraments around
which to build an elaborate ritual, the mosque differed greatly from
the Christian church. An arcaded entrance court with a fountain in the
center led to the mosque proper, whose chief furnishing was the pulpit.
A small niche in the wall towards Mecca told the worshippers which
way to face in their prostrations. Oriental color and intricate design in
woodwork, stucco, tile, and mosaic, featured by passages copied from
the Koran, contributed to an effect of quiet, elegance, and dignity. The
oriental-Byzantine dome marked the exterior, and from the graceful
minaret the muezzin announced the hours of prayer.

In the construction of the great mosques of Bagdad, Damascus, Sa-
marra, Jerusalem, Cairo, and Cordova architectural features were incor-

reconstruction of a Merovingian villa (after Garnier) (See p. 186)

The ordeal of hot iron (See p. 191)

Benedictio ferri ingne.

The ordeal of cold water (See p. 191)

In noīe loco dūatorus ei benedicam
ma mea dūo. Ds inadutoriū meū

The interior of the octagonal church at Aachen; the chandelier was presented to the church by Frederick Barbarossa.

Charles the Great's church at Aachen. The original octagonal church is the central domed structure. (See pp. 150, 252)

porated or invented whose influence on the development of architec- *Influence of*
ture in the west is only now beginning to be appreciated. The pointed *Moslem*
arch, the cusped window opening, sometimes filled with stone or stucco *architecture*
tracery, sometimes with "crudely colored glass," the use, instead of
classical columns to support the arcades, of brick piers surrounded by a
series of small circular or octagonal marble shafts, the use of alternating dark and white stone in the interior as well as on the façade, the
ornamental battlements, even the ribbed vault itself—all characteristic
features of Gothic architecture—may have originally come from Moslem architecture. Stone tracery decorating the exterior, such as that on
the façade of the cathedral at Strassburg, may have come from the
same source. The term "arabesque" reveals the source of that style
of decoration.[23] It is possible that the minaret of Cairo influenced the
renaissance campanili of Italy. Moslem fortresses in Syria and Egypt
taught western crusaders some features of fortification. In textiles,
ceramics, inlaid metal work, enamel, ivory, leather tooling, and book- *Minor arts*
binding Moslem artists did superior work. Guibert, an eleventh-century
abbot of Nogent, complains of the young ladies he sees with "their
shoes of cordovan morocco with twisted beaks." Early renaissance
painters did not hesitate to use Arabic letters to decorate the figure
of Christ and the sleeves of the Virgin.

Moslem literature is known to us chiefly through the glamorous
tales of the Arabian Nights, many of which are a faithful reflection of
the civilization of Bagdad, especially in the great times of Harun-ar- *Literature*
Raschid. We must also mention Edward Fitzgerald's translation of
the Rubáiyát of the great mathematician Omar Khayyám; although
in those immortal quatrains there is perhaps as much Fitzgerald as
Omar, they do perhaps fairly represent the splendors of Moslem
literature in its decline. Arabic poetry before Mohammed, although
still unwritten, had reached its peak in the expression of the moods
and activities of the nomads of the desert. The old nomadic spirit
breaks through the restraints of the new civilized city life in a poem
written possibly by the wife of the Syrian governor Muawiya, who
established the Ommiad caliphate at Damascus:

> "I prefer a tent where the wind blows around me
> To high palaces;
> And a cloak of wool
> To sorrowful ceremonial garments.

[23] M. S. Briggs on "Architecture," *ibid.*, pp. 176, 179.

"The crusts I ate in that tent
Were better than fine bread—
And O the wind's song on the hill-path
Drowns out your tambourines!

"Likewise to tame cats
I prefer watchdogs that bark—
And a desert horseman
To you, you fat barbarian!" [24]

Except for the drama and the epic, Mohammedan literature exploited to a nicety the usual literary forms, and Arabic was the first among languages in Europe to use perfect rime in its poetry. That its complex formality and conventionality in handling the theme of Platonic love, and its meters as well, influenced the earliest Provençal and Italian poetry cannot be questioned; the very word "troubadour" is apparently of Arabic origin. The new middle classes in western Europe took eagerly to collections of Arabic stories, which included animal tales brought from India. Early Spanish prose drew heavily on translations from the Arabic.[25] The Moslem historian, geographer, and writer of memoirs, no less than the poet and the story-teller, brought the west entertainment and instruction. In philology the Arabs worked out the grammar of their own complicated and growing language, and Jews even learned the rudiments of Hebrew from grammars written in Arabic.

Music   Arabic music, both in theory and in practice, exercised a decisive influence on the development of music in the west. It seems that from Islam came the first notions of time values assigned to notes, which permitted the writing of music for several voices singing together. The arabesque instrumental accompaniment of the melody may well, in its strict applications, have turned western musicians towards the consideration of harmony. The Arabic instruments with their fingerboards marked into frets to place the notes definitely may have helped to fix the standard musical scale for Europe. It was, of course, through Spain into Provence that Moslem musical influence reached Europe. "Perhaps the gaudy raiment of the occidental musicians, their long hair and painted faces, were due to oriental influences. The Morris dances (i.e., Moorish dances), with their hobby-horse and bells, are certainly reminiscent of the Arab minstrels." "Lute," "rebec,"

[24] Allen and Jones, *The Romanesque Lyric*, pp. 196–97.
[25] H. A. R. Gibb on "Literature," in *The Legacy of Islam*, p. 195.

"guitar," "tambourine," "fanfare" are words of Arabic origin, and the whole family of stringed instruments of the lute and guitar type, as well as bowed instruments of the rebec type, were importations into the west from Spain. Indeed, the roots of contemporary Spanish music are to be sought in the music of the Moors.[26]

Long before the crusades Europe had in Spain and Sicily direct contact with the civilization of Islam. Cordova and Seville were *Moslem Spain* western Bagdads. The Christians living under Moslem rule in Spain, called Mozarabs, were censured for preferring to listen to the tales and songs of their Mohammedan masters rather than to the discourses of Church Fathers; they remind us of St. Jerome in the desert, tempted by the forbidden fruit of the classics. The Christian Church in Spain even developed a special Mozarabic liturgy of its own. The civilization of Islam in Spain profoundly affected the life of the small Christian states to the south of the Pyrenees, and fostered in them the attitude of religious tolerance that made it possible for their princes later to fight the battles of Albigensian heretics in southern France against the papacy. When León, Castile, Aragon, and Navarre began to push the Moslem out of Spain, the multifarious contacts between the two civilizations increased. The tradition of Moslem workmanship became the foundation of Spanish art. Moslem Sicily no less than Byzantine southern Italy was the foundation of the brilliant Norman state in those countries. It was chiefly the stimulus of Islam that began before the renaissance to bring western Europe to maturity.

[26] H. G. Farmer on "Music," *ibid.*, pp. 372–75.

Chapter 8

THE CIVILIZATION OF EARLY WESTERN EUROPE

THE period from about A.D. 400 to 800 has traditionally been called "the dark ages." That any real civilization should come out of a decadent Roman society, which had been harassed for more than a century and a half by barbarians, would seem miraculous. Looking forward from the Augustan age, or backward from the thirteenth century, one surely finds no Virgil and no Thomas Aquinas; and if a period lacking such supermen, and lacking other evidences of a civilization at its peak, must be dark, then dark this period is. But one who tries to look into the depths of these centuries from no special point of view, but from every possible angle, will find in the efforts being made to save Europe from complete ruin, and even to build it up again anew, much evidence that the human spirit was alive. It was above all an age of pioneers who, because no education could be had outside the Church, and because there was no other civilizing institution, were for the most part churchmen. Popes and monks and bishops were forging the new instruments of a new culture. They were never without the support of the barbarian kings, while in the remnants of towns and in the country simple artisans and peasants were bearing their share of responsibility by the production of the material means to support life. The decline of ancient civilization was somehow checked, and under the auspices of the Church Roman and German institutions were fused to form a new civilization.

A formative period of pioneers

The transfer of political authority from the Roman government to the German kingdoms brought at first little actual change in political administration, little in the economic system, and none at all in social life and organization. During the long reign of Theodoric the Ostrogoth, for example, relatively few of the existing institutions in Italy were changed. The senate, the magistrates, the administrative system, the schools, the monuments, were still preserved. The Goths in theory preserved their own law for themselves, but in practice it

Ostrogothic and Lombard Italy

was so Romanized that within a few generations it would have wholly disappeared. For the rest of the population Roman law was preserved. The kingship, modeled upon imperial authority, was absolute, and at Ravenna were a prætorian prefect, a quæstor, a master of the offices, and bureaus and officials similar to those at Constantinople. The most illustrious of Theodoric's ministers, Cassiodorus and Boethius, were of the Roman nobility. Roman Italy, indeed, revived under the stimulus of the brilliant courts at Verona and Ravenna, which undertook patronage of the arts and the construction of aqueducts, roads, bridges, amphitheaters, and baths.

It was just this intense desire of Theodoric to preserve and revivify Roman civilization, keeping the Germans as a distinct class for the defense of the state, that, along with the difference in religion, proved to be the fatal weakness of Ostrogothic Italy. The emphasis of the later Lombard occupation was somewhat different; it attempted rather to accommodate the Roman to the German. Of all the German peoples, except those in Britain, the Lombards clung most tenaciously to their native institutions; Lombard law preserved its identity, and was long studied in the schools of Italy. But the strength of Roman life in the peninsula, especially in the cities, resisted accommodation with the German invaders, so that it took longer in northern and central Italy than elsewhere in the west to bring about a fusion of peoples and institutions.

In the other early kingdoms the picture is much the same. The provinces of the old empire, if not actually retained as administrative districts, were preserved as archbishoprics, and the *civitates* as bishoprics. Burgundian kings dated their reigns according to the consuls of the imperial government, and the coins of the Visigoths bore the images of the emperors. Roman law was maintained for the Roman subjects of Burgundian and Visigothic kings: in each kingdom there was published a code for Roman subjects, in Burgundy the Roman law of the Burgundians (*Lex romana Burgundiorum*), and for the Roman subjects of the Visigoths the *Breviarium* of Alaric II. The Germans preserved their own law, and ultimately the two laws were fused with local custom. Attempts were made to preserve the Roman financial administration. The social position of the large landholder was not touched.

The Burgundian and Visigothic kingdoms

It is in Merovingian Gaul, the Gaul of Clovis and his successors, that the preservation of the old Roman tradition and its intermixture with new German institutions can best be seen; here the fusion was most complete, and it was accomplished by the middle of the eighth

century. From Clovis on the Frankish kings were as absolute as kings
can be. They controlled the Church, and treated the kingdom as a
private patrimony to be divided among the male heirs. Though the
kingship was actually hereditary, there was a formal election, after
which the king was raised upon a shield in the old German way. He
wore his hair long as a sign of his royal office, while the other Franks
wore theirs short. He was called *princeps*, like an Augustus, Your
Glory (*Gloria vestra*), Your Sublimity, Your Serenity, like the oriental potentates of the later Roman empire, and court life was a pinch-
beck imitation of Roman imperial grandeur. Court officials bore Roman
titles, and the kings issued decrees, edicts, and constitutions, which
were based upon those in the Theodosian Code. The royal residences
were great rambling villas, close to a great forest, to enable the Merovingians to satisfy their lust for hunting; the ambulatory court was a
sacred palace (*sacrum palatium*); the treasury was the fisc (*fiscus*),
whose chief official was sometimes called in good Roman style a
chamberlain (*camerarius*) or treasurer (*thesaurius*).

*The govern-
ment of the
Franks*

The attempt was made to preserve the Roman tax administration
with custom and market dues, a poll tax paid by unfree subjects
(therefore not by Franks), and a land tax paid only by Gallo-Romans.
The later Roman practice of relying on the citizens for the performance of services to the state, such as keeping up roads and bridges, and
the obligation to furnish regular supplies upon demand, the old *sordida
munera*, were maintained by the Merovingians. Imperial lands became crown lands, and the produce of the mines belonged to the income of the kings. In so far as possible the monetary system of the
Romans was preserved. While the old civil province (the archdiocese
of the Church) disappeared, the *civitas*, as the diocese of a bishop, remained as a unit of administration in Gaul as elsewhere. The unofficial
Roman *pagus* became the unofficial, but not the administrative, district
of the tribe in the strictly German regions of the Frankish empire.

*Changes in the
Frankish state*

In spite of this residue of Roman titles, ceremonies, and usages,
however, the Merovingian state and administration took on with time
a definite character of its own, and was in no real sense a continuation
of the absolute bureaucratic monarchy of Rome. In the sixth and
seventh centuries Gaul still had some commercial contacts with the
orient, and the Mediterranean ports were still important, trade and
commerce being largely in the hands of Syrian and Jewish merchants.
But with the growth of Moslem sea power in the western Mediterranean, those contacts ended and almost all commerce became merely

local. Urban life disappeared within the walls of once populous cities; ancient buildings were abandoned and fell into ruin.

The Frankish kings henceforth reigned over an agricultural society, and their whole activity was conditioned by the life of the peasantry living on large estates controlled by a semi-independent aristocracy. It was impossible to maintain any regular system of direct taxation, and what was left of the Roman system gradually disappeared, except as it was preserved in local customs and manorial dues. The kings were obliged to live like any other landowners on the produce of their land, and since it was impracticable to bring this produce from royal domains scattered through the kingdom to any central point, the kings had to visit their means of livelihood. They were therefore constantly on the go, accompanied by an ambulatory court with no fixed capital. The king's livelihood was supplemented by income derived from the administration of justice, one-third of all fines going to the crown, and by requisitions in kind, gifts from subjects, and local services. These revenues were devoted principally to the personal expenses of king and court.

Practically the only survival of the old bureaucracy of the Romans *The officials* was the Merovingian referendary, the head of a bureau of scribes, *of the palace* composed exclusively of clergy, which prepared all royal documents. As this official traveled about with the king, it is from the dates and indications of place in these documents that historians have been able to trace the itineraries of the kings and to locate their chief estates. The other chief officials of the kingdom were private officials of the king's household, the mayor of the palace, the marshal, the butler, the chamberlains, the constables, and the count of the palace. Of these the chief was the mayor of the palace, under whose supervision was the administration of the royal estates, whose authority extended over all persons at court and at times to the appointment of counts and dukes, and who gradually rose to the position of a veritable prime minister. The king's own court at the palace, presided over in his absence by the count of the palace, had jurisdiction in cases of treason and cases involving high officials.

Local administration rested on the count, whose district, the county, *Local ad-* was the old Roman *civitas*. Appointed ordinarily by the king, he was *ministration* his local representative, in charge of collecting revenue due and trans- *and courts* mitting it to the royal treasury. His chief function was that of a judge, moving about on circuit through the county, assisted in his duties by a vicar and in each village by a lesser official called the hundred-man. The county was in fact subdivided into vicariates, and these into the old German units known as hundreds. All freemen were bound to attend the public sessions of the court, which in the villages were presided over by the hundred-men. In each case the count or vicar imposed and carried out the sentence, according to the verdict rendered by a group of men chosen from the locality to interpret the law of the district.

The count was paid no definite salary, as the monetary income of the crown did not warrant it. While on circuit he and his helpers were maintained by the local population, and he received one-third of the fines assessed besides the income from certain crown lands. Most of the counts in the sixth century were still Gallo-Romans, but as time went on more and more were chosen from the Franks. In the cities, now largely episcopal residences and centers of episcopal administration, the bishops exercised a quasi-political authority. In the sixth century and for some time later they were likewise mostly Gallo-Romans, and so the natural mediators between the local population and the German rulers; ecclesiastical courts were more lenient, and the churches offered the right of asylum. The naturally resulting clash between the count's administration and the bishop's frequently led to bitter conflict between the two.

In addition to the counts there were also dukes, especially on the frontier, where as special military commanders they raised troops and conducted campaigns. But more often the local count called to arms the freemen of his own district, and led them during a campaign. The army was no expense to the crown. Every free Frank was obligated to serve as a foot soldier and to furnish his own equipment. For every *The army* campaign the army was raised anew, by summons in spring or early summer. The gathering for review at an appointed place, from which they proceeded directly to war, was all that was left of the old-time German assembly of all the freemen of the tribe. Together with the obligation to attend court this military obligation imposed upon the free Frankish peasant no light burden.

The codification of Germanic law The law that the Germans brought with them into the empire was a body of unwritten custom. It was regarded as the inalienable possession of the individual German. Wherever he was, if he got into difficulties or needed the assistance of the law, it was his right to be tried or to negotiate according to his own tribal law. Within the empire the Germans found a society whose law was a written law, the same for all people of a given territory. The clash of these two antithetical systems of law led to the writing down in Latin (except in England) of the German custom. Anglo-Saxon law was codified in the vernacular between 597 and 614. Visigothic custom was codified under King Euric (466–85); and, as has already been noted, his son Alaric II published a special code for the Romans, since according to the German principle the Roman must live by his own law. Subsequently a new code was issued, which set up one common law for all Visigothic territory, an interesting example of the victory of the Roman territorial principle as well as of the fusion of Germanic and Roman institutions. In fact, all Germanic law ultimately became territorial.

The Burgundian codes compiled around 500 continued to be used into the ninth century. A Lombard code was published in the seventh century and modified a century later. The law of the Ripuarian Franks was codified in the early seventh century; that of the Alemanni, Bavarians, and Saxons, between the seventh and the ninth centuries. The law of the Salian Franks was probably set down at the instance of Clovis in the sixth century. But the Franks, being bound to respect the laws and customs of the peoples they conquered, while exacting military service of the Thuringians, Alemanni, and Bavarians, left them their own laws and their own tribal dukes; under the Merovingians there was no Frankish count beyond the Rhine. The law of the Frankish realm was therefore a medley of Roman and different barbarian codes, which finally fused into a body of local custom.

In their general characteristics the German codes are all remarkably similar. They are concerned primarily not with public but with private law; they attempt to regulate the relationship of person to person. This amounted in fact, in the interests of peace, to the regulation of *General* the blood feud. The chief aim of the codes is to substitute for acts of *features of* violence a specific fine for various offenses, part to be paid to the in- *the Ger-* jured family, and part to the king and his judicial officer, the count. *manic codes* Every crime had its price; for example, the price for murder was the wergild (man-money). In a few instances the codes recognized the right of the state to intervene and punish in some other fashion, by death by war-axe or sword or hanging, or by outlawry.

The code of the Salian Franks [1] reveals many interesting features of their rough, primitive, and highly stratified agricultural society. Throughout a very careful distinction is made between Roman and Frank; there is no social fusion at this early date. There are different fines for stealing a "sucking pig" and a "pig that can live without its mother"; for stealing a "bull which rules the herd and has never been *The code* yoked," a "bull used for the cows of three villages in common," and *of the Sa-* a "bull belonging to the king." Theft or housebreaking by slaves *lian Franks*

[1] E. F. Henderson, *Historical Documents*, pp. 176 ff.

might likewise be punished by fine, or by one hundred and twenty blows, or even by castration. If a free Frank committed rape, he was fined; if a serf carried off a free woman, he was to be sentenced to death. It cost a Roman culprit more to plunder a Salian Frank than a Frank to plunder a Roman. Specific fines are enumerated for striking another "with a poisoned arrow," or "on the head so that the brain appears, and the three bones which lie above the brain appear," or "between the ribs or in the stomach so that the wound appears and reaches to the entrails."

The wergild of a woman "after she can have no more children" was one-third less than for one who was pregnant, or a "free woman after she has begun bearing children." The wergild of a man in the service of the king was three times higher than that of an ordinary free Frank or barbarian living under Salian law, but slaying "a Roman who eats in the king's palace" was only half as expensive as killing a man in the service of the king. If the "Roman shall not have been a landed proprietor and table companion of the king," his wergild is one-third lower than if he were. Although under no circumstances could land be inherited by a woman, the wergild of a free Frank woman was six hundred *solidi*, whereas that of a free Frank man was two hundred, of a Roman landowner one hundred, of a Roman renter sixty-two and a half. In the code of the Ripuarian Franks the wergild of a king's follower was six hundred *solidi*, of a free Frank two hundred, of a German of another tribe one hundred, of a Gallo-Roman one hundred. The importance of churchmen among the Ripuarians appears in the fact that a subdeacon's wergild was four hundred, a priest's six hundred, a bishop's seven hundred, the equivalent of a herd of four hundred and fifty oxen or one hundred and fifty horses. Despite all the efforts of the kings to suppress blood feuds between clans and make acts of violence public crimes rather than private offenses, the old-time feuds nevertheless continued for centuries.

Many of the methods used to determine the guilt or innocence of the accused were old pagan German practices, adopted by the Christian Church in German lands. If testimony of witnesses was lacking, or in the absence of other indubitable evidence, and because also of the complication of having different systems of law in force at the same time and place, resort was often had to God, in the implicit belief that he would never permit the innocent to be punished or the guilty to escape. In Roman law the plaintiff must prove the truth of his accusation, just as we still hold the accused innocent—at least in legal theory—until proved guilty. German law, on the contrary, in some cases required the defendant to establish his innocence. It was therefore the first duty of the court to decide whether plaintiff or defendant should undertake to prove the truth of his cause.

One of the commonest methods of appeal to God was compurgation, which gave the defendant a decided advantage. The accused swore to the truth of his story, usually on relics of the saints, and brought forth a group of oath-helpers, or compurgators, to swear that in their opinion his oath was good. Originally the compurgators were members of the family, then simply neighbors or other persons; their number varied according to the importance of the charge and the accused person. The Merovingian Queen Fredegund used three bishops and three hundred nobles as compurgators to establish the paternity of her child. The theory of compurgation, of course, was that God would punish the perjurer, as indeed the state did if the compurgator were found to be lying. But it proved to be too easy a way to escape punishment, and lost favor when the study of Roman law was revived in the twelfth century.

Compurgation

The person chosen to undergo the ordeal of hot water was obliged to retrieve some small object from a kettle of boiling water. If after a short period, usually three days, his hand and arm were found to be healing properly, God had established the truth of his assertions. Obviously the case was actually decided by the persons who determined whether God had caused the injury to heal properly or not. In some cases there was no need to wait. Gregory of Tours reports that in a dispute between an orthodox Christian believer and an Arian heretic, when resort was had to the ordeal of hot water, an orthodox deacon reached into the boiling pot and drew out a ring and "suffered no harm, protesting rather that at the bottom the kettle was cold while at the top it was pleasantly warm." [2] The Arian was emboldened in like manner to establish his innocence, but "as soon as his hand had been thrust in, all the flesh was boiled off the bones clear up to the elbow." In the ordeal of cold water the person under examination was thrown bound into some body of water. "And . . . whoever after the invocation of God . . . seeks to hide the truth by a lie, cannot be submerged in the water above which the voice of the Lord God had thundered; for the pure nature of the water recognizes as impure, and therefore rejects as inconsistent with itself, such human nature as has once been regenerated by the waters of baptism and is again infected by falsehood." Other ordeals were the red-hot iron, the glowing plowshares, and the fire, and there were still others. In the ordeal

The ordeals and trial by battle

[2] The quotations are from *Translations and Reprints*, IV, 11 ff.

of the cross both contestants held their arms straight out from their sides, and God justified him who held out his arms the longer time. Trial by battle was perhaps the most popular of all the ordeals; like the ordeal of the cross it required the participation of both plaintiff and defendant, and it furnished spectators the best show. Women and clergy were represented by champions.

While the essential barbarity of all these practices was of course in fact tempered by the good sense of those in charge, who themselves virtually made the decisions, they gradually and inevitably became unpopular. When William Rufus, son of William the Conqueror, saw a band of criminals escape punishment by the use of the ordeal, he vowed that, God or no God, he would try them with the more effective means of royal justice. A French bishop is said to have replied to a monk who remarked that with the relics of a certain saint he would enter a roaring furnace, that with the bones of such a saint he wouldn't wade through a teacup of hot water. The revival of Roman law completed what common sense had begun. It was the Church itself that first lost confidence in these methods of determining God's will. In the early thirteenth century clergy were forbidden to employ ordeals in ecclesiastical courts, and trial by battle. The Church was followed by the monarchs of the new European states, armed in most cases with Roman law. Yet compurgation, ordeals, and trial by battle survived in statute-books until the early nineteenth century.

The Franks, although they adopted some Roman usages, in the main continued their German mode of life, leaving the Gallo-Roman population likewise to its own old ways. They lived in the country and *The Merovin-* spent most of their days hunting. In these early years of the Frankish *gian court* monarchy the veneer of Christianity was equally thin on both classes of the population. At court and in the upper classes drunkenness, sexual excess, murder, and gluttony were perhaps more general than in most periods. The untamed ferocity of Queen Fredegund we shall have occasion to speak of in the next chapter. King Charibert married a nun, and Dagobert I had three wives at the same time.

The Merovin- The chief difficulty was no doubt the fact that the early Frankish *gian clergy* Church had not learned to control itself. It was learning fast enough to control its environment. In their cities bishops were acquiring judicial and taxing rights leading to local independence; some of them were distinguished by their careful management of their estates and as builders of public works. They were active in all state affairs, for the episcopate as a whole had already undergone considerable secularization. King Chilperic was hard on the bishops. "To one he imputed levity, to a second arrogance, to a third excess, to a fourth loose living; one bishop he would call a vain fool, another pompous. . . . He would often say: 'See how poor our treasury is! Look how the churches have drained our riches away! Of a verity, none ruleth at all save the bishops. Our royal office is lost and gone; it hath passed to the bishops in their cities.' " [3]

A better witness is the famous bishop, Gregory of Tours. He is himself an indication that not all bishops were bad, but some of his portraits throw a glaring light on the life of Merovingian Gaul. Salonius of Embrun and Sagittarius of Gap were a precious pair of bishops. They went about "armed not with the heavenly cross but with the helm and mail shirt of the world, and are said to have slain many of the foe with their own hands." "They passed most of their nights in feasting and drinking, so that while the clergy were celebrating matins in the cathedral church, they were calling for fresh cups and keeping up their libations. No word was there of God upon their lips, nor did they remember the order of the services. Not till the return of dawn did they rise up from the banquet; then they put on soft garments, and all bedrowsed and sunk in wine, slept on until the third hour of the day; nor did there fail them women with whom to be defiled. When they arose, they took a bath, and lay down to feast anew; leaving the table at evening, they were soon greedy for their supper again, which lasted . . . until the morning light. Thus they did day after day." Bishop Eunius of Vannes "was overmuch addicted to wine, and often was so grossly drunken that he could not stir a step." As late as the eighth century Boniface complained to the pope of the Frankish clergy: "Religion is trodden under foot. Benefices are given to greedy laymen or unchaste and publican clerics. All their crimes do not prevent their attaining the priesthood; at last, rising in rank as they increase in sin, they become bishops, and those of them who can boast that they are not adulterers or fornicators, are drunkards, given to the chase, and soldiers who do not shrink from shedding Christian blood." [4]

With the foundation of the German kingdoms new problems confronted the papacy, and the steps taken in their solution were of fundamental importance to the later history of Europe. The gradual rise of the bishops of Rome to a position of primacy in the Western Church has already been seen. One of the important developments was the recognition of their right to hear appeals in questions of canon law. The

[3] O. M. Dalton, *Gregory of Tours*, II, 279.
[4] C. Dawson, *The Making of Europe*, p. 212.

inevitable outcome of such a development, if long enough continued, must be the recognition of the pope as the spiritual head of the west and the regimentation of all local metropolitans, bishops, and subsidiary clergy in a centralized organization headed by the pope as monarch with unlimited disciplinary and spiritual authority. There can be little doubt that this grand prospect, a characteristically Roman inheritance, was shaping itself in the minds of the Roman bishops at an early time. But a spiritual empire can no more than any other be built in a day, and the popes hardly began to realize the vision until the eleventh century. Meanwhile the Church in the new German kingdoms stood squarely in the way of any papal advance. We should rather say, "the German churches," for essentially they were state churches, with clergy either appointed or confirmed by the king, who called together their councils and approved their decrees. For the popes to exercise any control at all over these churches it was necessary either to subvert the authority of the German kings, to control them, or to co-operate with them. In this early period the most they were actually able to do was to co-operate; but the papal program was none the less fixed; it was to remove the local clergy from the control of the state and subject them to the jurisdiction of Rome.

The Church in the Germanic kingdoms

Meanwhile a necessary preliminary step for the popes was to secure economic strength enough to support their spiritual claims, or, even more, to acquire a measure of temporal authority sufficient to treat on equal terms with other temporal rulers; in short, to found an ecclesiastical state in Italy of which the popes should be the rulers. Such economic and political ambitions did not, of course, aim solely at enhancing the importance of the Bishop of Rome in the spiritual and temporal affairs of Italy and western Europe; they also enabled the papacy to engage more actively in the spread of Christianity and in the support of Christian institutions.

Long before they actually achieved the position of temporal rulers in Italy, the popes had achieved *de facto* independence in the city of Rome. When Rome ceased to be the political capital of the empire, it was natural that the bishop, who was moreover the chief prelate of the Western Church, should assume authority. The protection of the city against invading barbarians was undertaken with notable success by Leo I in his dealings with Attila the Hun and with Gaiseric the Vandal. When in 476 the line of Roman emperors ceased entirely in the west, not only was the position of the popes in Rome strengthened but their European prestige was also correspondingly enhanced. Odovacar and Theodoric interfered little with them. The Byzantine reconquest was

The beginnings of the temporal power of the papacy

a period of humiliation, for the popes were then treated like the patriarchs of Constantinople; they were subject to the Byzantine duke at Rome, and, when not appointed from Constantinople, were obliged to notify the emperor of their election. The Lombard conquest was a great opportunity for the papacy to emancipate itself from Byzantine control. In the face of the Lombard advance, the exarch at Ravenna, never supported adequately from Constantinople because of the greater necessity of defending the frontier elsewhere, could no longer protect the Roman duchy adequately, not to say maintain a strict control over its government. The popes were therefore obliged to assume the governmental functions of Byzantium in the city and duchy. They were not, however, strong enough to protect Rome from the Lombards without relying upon such Byzantine military support as they could still get, while at the same time in their anxiety to escape Byzantine tutelage they sometimes found it politic to ally themselves with the Lombards. It is this triangle of forces that explains the devious diplomacy pursued by the papacy, until it reached an entirely new solution of its difficulties in the middle of the eighth century.

At the critical moment of the Lombard invasion Gregory I, the Great (590–604), one of the most capable and important of all the popes, came to the throne of St. Peter. He was born in Rome about *Gregory* 540, of an old and rich senatorial family, long attached to the Church *the Great* and identified with the city government. When only thirty years of age he was appointed Prefect of Rome. When he fell heir to the considerable fortune of his family, he founded six monasteries in Sicily and that of St. Andrew in Rome. He then resigned his official position, gave to the poor the rest of his wealth, even his jewels and expensive robes and furniture, and, refusing the abbacy of his own Roman monastery, himself became a simple monk there. But he was too valuable a man to be let alone, and Pope Benedict I forced him to return to the world by making him, first, one of the regionary deacons of Rome, and then papal legate to Constantinople. On his return to Rome he again entered St. Andrew's, this time as abbot; the rigor of his discipline became famous. At the death of Pope Pelagius II (590), the clergy, the Roman senate, and the people insisted upon Gregory's election to the papacy. Though he earnestly protested and never ceased to deplore his forced abandonment of his beloved monastery, he was elected and consecrated on September 3, 590, the first monk to become pope.

As pope Gregory was the richest man in Italy, the owner and busi- *The Patri-* ness manager of the very large landed estates known as the Patrimony *mony of* of St. Peter. From the time of Constantine, when legacies to the *St. Peter*

Church became possible, the Bishop of Rome had profited greatly from the generosity of the faithful. These territories, centering about Rome, were spread over much of the peninsula, and were located also in Sicily, Sardinia, Illyricum, North Africa, and southern Gaul. They have been estimated to have been from thirteen hundred and sixty to eighteen hundred square miles in extent, populated by slaves and serfs, and to have brought in an income in money and kind of over one and one-half million dollars. In his administration of this property Gregory showed himself to be a far-sighted, kindly, and practical overseer. If he did not originate, he certainly established, the administrative system of the papacy, inherited in its essentials from the proprietary régime of the late Roman empire. Gregory found time to watch details in both the collection of the revenues and their disbursement. A good business man, he watched markets, and shipped Sicilian wheat to Constantinople in time of scarcity, Sardinian timber to woodless Egypt, copper from Sardinia and iron from Bruttium to the Byzantine arsenals and shipyards. The many heavy demands upon the papal income indeed required skillful management. The papal treasury supported not only the Roman clergy, churches, schools, orphanages, hospitals, and monasteries, but many clergy and Church establishments elsewhere in Italy. The care of the poor, always a burden, was just then a heavier drain upon the treasury because of the many refugees driven to Rome before the Lombard attack.

Gregory and the Lombards

The invading Lombards had seized the papal lands in northern Italy, and their conquests down the center of the peninsula menaced not only the papal lands in middle Italy but Rome itself. Moreover, the Lombards were Arian heretics. Such a threat to the position of the Roman bishop obliged Gregory to remain on good terms with Byzantium. He was active in combating Lombard Arianism; he spent much money in ransoming Italian prisoners; and it was he, rather than the Byzantine Duke of Rome, who, by the use of money and diplomacy, saved Rome from capture by the Lombard King Agilulf and the Lombard Duke of Spoleto. Gregory was acting as, if he actually was not, the secular ruler of the Roman duchy. In comparison with him the imperial duke, despite his title of *gloriosissimus*, was so insignificant that Gregory referred to him as a "useless and pettifogging thing."

Gregory and Byzantium

Gregory not only maintained intact, but notably strengthened, the primacy of the Roman pope in the Church. When John the Faster, Patriarch of Constantinople, inserted as part of his title the words "ecumenical patriarch," Gregory took this as a slight upon the position of Rome and wrote to John to protest against his "execrable and profane

assumption," his "usurpation of proud and foolish titles." "As regards
the church of Constantinople," he wrote, "who can doubt that it is subject to the Apostolic See?" He was never able to get the patriarch to
drop the offensive words, but, as if himself to display proper modesty
in titles, he adopted as part of his title "servant of the servants of God"

ITALY
IN A.D. 590

IMPERIAL DOMINIONS
LOMBARD TERRITORY

(*servus servorum Dei*), which was subsequently adopted by all popes.
Although he did, after some delay, notify the emperor of his election
to the papacy, he resented any kind of imperial pressure. When the
Emperor Maurice struck at the abuses of monasticism, Gregory un-
hesitatingly denounced him, and when Maurice was murdered in a
rebellion which brought the "utterly incompetent, licentious, and sanguinary" Phocas to the throne, Gregory's joy was unrestrained.

"Gregory never for an instant denied, or made any pretense of deny-

ing, that the Pope was the Primate and chief of Christian bishops." [5]
To him this meant that the Roman see as "the head of all the
churches" was to govern the whole Church. The decrees of councils
had no validity without the confirmation of Rome. The Roman bishop

*Gregory's
conception of
the primacy of
the papacy*

could hear appeals against the decisions of the Patriarch of Constantinople, and his court could reverse them. "If any fault is discovered
in a bishop," Gregory wrote, "I know of no one who is not subject to
the Apostolic See." Yet in spite of his many letters censuring western
bishops for their faults, he had no success in weakening the hold of the
Visigothic and Frankish kings on their respective churches. Indeed,
when things were going well he had no desire to interfere in the local
administration of a bishop: "When no fault requires it to be otherwise,
all bishops according to the principle of humility are equal." His un-
swerving maintenance of papal claims, however, set an example which
could never be forgotten.

*Gregory as a
Church Father*

Gregory's writings have earned him a place with Ambrose, Jerome,
and Augustine among the Fathers of the Latin Church. His eight hundred and twenty-three letters reveal him in his many-sided activity.
During the few rare moments of leisure left him by his exacting duties
and his ill health he could unbend with childlike simplicity to welcome
into the papal palace a wandering minstrel with an ape. We find him
also sending out filings from the chairs of St. Peter and St. Paul in little crosses as miraculous aids to the recovery of health. His *Pastoral
Rule* long continued in use as a sensible and practical guide for the
duties of a bishop. His *Homilies* on Ezekiel and the Gospels display
his earnest, austere, and always intensely human spirit. In his *Dialogues* he indulged his love for the miraculous in his accounts of saints
and monks in their invariably successful combats with Satan and his
demons. His most important and influential work was his *Moralia,*
wherein, ostensibly writing a commentary on the Book of Job, by extensive use of allegory he manages to expound all that he thinks worth
expounding of the theology of the Church and Christian morality. For
many centuries the *Moralia* remained an authoritative textbook of
theology for the west.

The qualifications that won for Gregory his place as a Church
Father were not those of a learned and original thinker offering new

*Gregory's
theology*

solutions to theological problems. With his simple, practical, and rather
credulous mind he brought together, from the teachings of the earlier
Fathers and from the actual practice of the Church of his day, and set
down, plainly and emphatically, in a Latin that laid no claim to classical

[5] F. H. Dudden, *Gregory the Great* (1905), II, 224.

purity or literary excellence, those doctrines and beliefs that appealed to his own generation. He was what we call a popularizer, in a society that had great need of just that sort of work.

In the two centuries that had elapsed since Augustine's summary of Christian belief his doctrines had undergone some modification in the west. His doctrine of absolute predestination and that of original sin had already been rejected by his contemporary, Pelagius. The British monk allowed the individual complete freedom of will in choosing the good or evil way of life, and made salvation dependent upon the individual's choice of these alternatives, with the assistance of no mysterious grace of God, but only of the knowledge of God's will as revealed by Christ in the Scriptures.

Such a complete rejection of Augustine, however, was unacceptable to western theologians and ecclesiastics, because it slighted the rôle of the Church as God's agent in dispensing divine grace. At the Council of Orange in 529 Augustine was rehabilitated, in a way that was more appealing to the western mind. The general question of predestination was avoided, except to insist that God predestined no one to evil. On the question whether God was solely responsible for man's salvation, or whether man himself shared the responsibility, the council compromised. Man could not save himself without God's grace, which, imparted to him first in the sacrament of baptism, with subsequent increments finally restored the mature man to a condition of free will that enabled him henceforth to choose for himself whether he would follow good or evil. Thus the moral responsibility of the individual was preserved, as well as his dependence on the Church for imparting the grace of God. Augustine's position, thus modified, although not always clearly understood by Gregory, was adopted by him and officially given the authority of orthodox dogma.

In the *Moralia* Gregory also laid great stress on the current beliefs in regard to purgatory, which he established permanently as Catholic doctrine. One could never know, he insisted, whether the penance per- *Doctrines* formed by any individual was really enough to atone for his sin; man must always fear that his penance was in fact insufficient. For those who died without having done satisfactory penance for less serious sins there was therefore a place, purgatory, in which they must undergo further purification and suffering before admission to heaven.

Gregory likewise gave the weight of his authority to the doctrine that in the ceremony of the Mass, by the consecration of the bread and wine and its transubstantiation into the actual body and blood of Christ, the priest was repeating the original sacrifice of Christ on the cross. He repeated it to atone for the sins of those present at the ceremony, or for those for whom the Mass was especially ordered—either the living or the dead, the duration of whose stay in purgatory could be shortened by Masses thus said in their behalf. The sacrament was accordingly made an integral part of penance. To the popular belief in the ever-present activity of angels and demons and to popular devotion to the saints who interceded with Christ, Gregory lent the dignity of papal authority.

It was this readiness to gather from all sources the elements of belief, and this convenient simplification and summarizing of them, which made Gregory the typical expression of the modified, one might almost say barbarized, Christianity of the west. He has been credited also with a reformation of the music of the ritual, still called Gregorian chant, but this is a doubtful matter. His devotion, as a former monk, to the institution of monasticism, his complete adherence to monastic practices, his absorption of the monastic outlook were all important in the history of the union of the papacy and the monastery, which will be considered in more detail, later.

The Lombards in the seventh century

The seventh century was an interlude between two periods of aggression by the Lombards, during which they codified their law, abandoned Arianism in favor of the orthodox Church in their own territory, and framed their administrative institutions. Their fusion with the Italian population was well begun; their language was already more Italian than German in character; court life at Pavia was much superior to that at the Frankish court. During the same period Greek influence was predominant in Rome, where there were two monasteries following the Basilian rule. What is more important, in the thirty years between 685 and 714 seven of the popes were either Greeks or Hellenized Syrians.

The predicament of the papacy in the eighth century

The pontificate of Gregory II (715–31) and the reign of the Lombard King Liutprand (712–44) brought an end to this state of affairs. Under Liutprand began an offensive against Byzantine territory in Italy that looked like an attempt once and for all to unite Italy, including Rome, into a Lombard kingdom. When in 726 the iconoclastic struggle broke out in the east, relations between Rome and Constantinople were seriously strained. The papacy, having already lost its lands in Illyricum to the Slavs and its lands in North Africa and southern Gaul to the Arabs, now lost its income from its lands in Sicily, Calabria, and the Duchy of Naples to Leo the Isaurian, the eastern emperor, and found itself in conflict with the Byzantine empire, upon which it had to depend for military support against the Lombards, whose advance endangered what was left of its lands in central and north-central Italy. At this moment the papacy conceived the plan of establishing itself as an independent temporal power in Italy, to take the place of the purely decorative imperial government in the city and Duchy of Rome, and if possible to acquire all territory in north-central Italy taken from Byzantium by the Lombards. In the first step of open revolt Gregory II succeeded in preventing an imperial levy of taxes in Italy, and, with the help of the Lombards, in keeping out of Rome a Byzantine army sent to enforce obedience. This Lombard-papal alliance lasted until the death of Gregory II. Liutprand went so far as to turn over to the pope lands conquered within the Roman duchy but not belonging to the papacy.

However, the establishment of a papal state in Italy was in fact endangered more by the Lombards than by the Byzantine empire. Any alliance with the Lombards could only be of a temporary and opportunistic character, for their constant defeat of imperial forces made them the real enemy. Clearly conscious of this, Gregory III (731–41) took the momentous step of turning to the Frankish mayor of the palace, Charles Martel, for assistance against the Lombards, offering him a protectorate over the city of Rome in return for aid. But three papal missions were received coldly, and the proposed alliance was not finally cemented until the pontificate of Gregory III's successor, Stephen II, and the reign of Martel's son Pepin the Short.

In 751 the Frankish mayors of the palace, having decided to dethrone the Merovingian dynasty and themselves assume the crown, sought authorization for this perfectly illegal act. The pope, even had he not been planning a similar revolt against the Byzantine empire in Italy, had good reason to grant this authorization, if only because the implied recognition of papal authority constituted a valuable precedent. At this same moment the Lombards under their King Aistulf drove *The papacy* the Byzantines out of Ravenna and conquered the whole exarchate; *allied with* they were now for the first time undisputed masters of all north and *the Franks* north-central Italy. In the next year Aistulf started out to complete Lombard expansion by conquering Rome itself. In desperation Pope Stephen II turned to King Pepin for aid, in return for the favor of papal sanction of the dethronement and imprisonment of the last Merovingian king. The pope decided to go to the Frankish court in person, where under royal escort he arrived in January 754 at the royal villa of Ponthion near Metz. As a public sign of papal approval he reanointed Pepin as king. In return he seems to have received the promise of the gift of all the land that the Lombards had taken from the empire, and, in addition, of the protection of the Franks in holding this territory. Stephen II was now on the road to the realization of the papal program.

The Donation of Pepin

In two campaigns against Aistulf the Franks made good their promise; in 756, after the second campaign, a Frankish envoy at the head of a small army marched to Rome and laid the keys of the conquered cities and the actual deed of donation upon St. Peter's tomb. This "Donation of Pepin" was a grant of all the territory of the exarchate as a temporal possession, over which the pope had the rights of sovereignty of an Italian prince. It was a goodly state, extending from Ravenna down the Adriatic coast to Sinigaglia and across the Apennines to Narni. Together with the Duchy of Rome, already *de facto* the pope's, it was the most powerful territorial state in Italy. The Lombard kingdom was effectually blocked in its attempts to unify Italy, and as long as the Papal States lasted (until 1870) unification was precluded. Though the final step of formally denouncing allegiance to Byzantium was not yet openly taken, two centuries of tortuous diplomacy had set the papacy free from any dependence upon the east. Henceforth its lot was cast solely with the west.

The claim of the popes to supplant the Byzantine empire in Rome and the Roman duchy is understandable, since they had ruled it actually for so long, but it is difficult, in spite of the ease with which monarchs manufacture claims upon territory which does not belong to them, to see the basis for their claiming the whole territory of the Byzantine exarchate. It is not at all impossible that the popes themselves realized the insubstantial basis upon which this claim rested, and the need of confirmation, in order to facilitate their negotiations with the Franks. At any rate, there was drawn up, most probably "in the papal chancellery during the third quarter of the eighth century," a document alleged to be a donation of the Emperor Constantine to Pope Sylvester I.

The Donation of Constantine

The document relates that Constantine, while still a pagan, was healed of leprosy by the pope and thereupon professed Christianity. In gratitude he decided to vacate Rome, removing the imperial capital to Constantinople. As his legacy to Sylvester he left "our imperial Lateran palace . . . likewise all provinces, places and districts of the city of Rome and Italy, and of the regions of the west; and, bequeathing them to the power and sway of him and the pontiffs, his successors, we do . . . determine and decree that the same be placed at his disposal, and do lawfully grant it as a permanent possession to the holy Roman Church. . . . The sacred see of blessed Peter shall be glori-

ously exalted above our empire and earthly throne. . . . And the
pontiff who for the time being presides over that most holy Roman
Church shall be the highest and chief of all priests in the whole
world. . . . he shall have rule as well over the four principal sees,
Antioch, Alexandria, Constantinople, and Jerusalem." [6] Such a grant
of temporal and spiritual supremacy was basis enough for any claim the
popes might care to make. "To an ever-growing proportion of the
students of this period, the historical setting in which alone it can be
made to fit is that of Stephen's visit to the Franks, or of the years which
closely followed it." [7] This forged Donation of Constantine, which
may therefore have played a decisive part in first establishing papal
temporal authority, was quoted often by popes and papal partisans in
their subsequent struggles for temporal power. For seven hundred
years it was generally believed to be authentic.

In the same century that witnessed the reinvigoration of the papacy
under Gregory the Great, one of his countrymen, Benedict of Nursia,
was initiating a revolution in western monasticism. It has already been *St. Benedict*
seen [8] that monasticism in the west had in the fifth century suffered a
considerable decline because it was unregulated, and because it vainly
tried to conform to the more extreme types of eastern asceticism. It
was the great service of St. Benedict that he corrected both of these
defects.

Benedict, the son of rich and aristocratic parents, was born in Umbria
about 480. He was sent to Rome for schooling, but the profligacy of
the city dismayed him and he fled, like the eastern hermits, to a wild
solitude near Subiaco in the Sabine Hills. Here, living in a grotto, he
suffered from religious hysteria, was tortured by hallucinations and
dreams, and for a time gave himself over to extreme physical privation.
As his fame as a man of God spread, others flocked to him. To escape
the annoyance of neighboring hermit bands Benedict resolved to remove his communities from near Rome, and sent out two of his followers to discover a more desirable place. They returned with word
that in an excellent sequestered location halfway between Rome and
Naples, on a hill near Cassino (Monte Cassino), was an ancient temple
of Apollo, still frequented by the local peasantry. Benedict took this *Benedict*
information as a sign from heaven, and upon this site he built a monas- *founds Monte*
tery out of the stones of the ancient pagan temple—the mother monas- *Cassino and*
tery of the Benedictine Order. (The founding of Monte Cassino is *draws up*
his rule

[6] Quoted from R. G. D. Laffan, *Select Documents of European History*, I, 4–5.
[7] *Cambridge Medieval History*, II, 586.
[8] See p. 59.

reminiscent of the building of the papal palace of the Vatican on the site of a temple of Mithras.)

As one thoroughly conversant with the rules previously drawn up for monastic communities, as a man who through his own experience and observation realized full well the extremes, dangers, and abuses of contemporary monasticism, Benedict decided to draw up a rule for his monks at Monte Cassino which would avoid all extremes and correct existing abuses. The traditional date of the rule is 529, the very year when Justinian closed the pagan schools of philosophy at Athens and published his code. Benedict's code is perhaps no less important than Justinian's, some of whose spirit he incorporated into his own. Monte Cassino was to be a community of cenobites: no place was left for the ascetic exercises of the solitary hermit, and moderation rather than austerity was its keynote. Moreover, it was to be a community of monks fixed by the vow of stability to the one spot of Monte Cassino; a monk was not to be permitted to go wandering about the country as he pleased. The monk took a vow of obedience in all things to the will of the abbot, who, like a Roman paterfamilias, had practically unlimited authority, and was even permitted to use the rod on a refractory monk.

The daily life of the monks   The chief concern of the monk was his own salvation, and his main function was to praise God and pray, in unison with his brother monks met together in the choir of the church. During the winter they rose at about half past three for vigils, sang lauds at five o'clock and prime at sunrise. Tierce was sung at a quarter past eight, sext at midday, nones at half past two, vespers before sunset, and compline at bedtime, shortly after sundown. The intervening hours were spent in meditation, reading, and manual labor, for "idleness is the enemy of the soul," according to the rule. There was but one meal in winter, simple but adequate, with wine but without meat, and time was allowed for an afternoon nap in summer. In summer the schedule was more rigid, with more time for work and less for sleep at night, but with an extra meal. There was no provision for recreation, and throughout this routine an unbroken silence reigned! The monks slept in separate beds in common dormitories. "They shall sleep clothed, and girt with belts or with ropes; and they shall not have their knives at their sides while they sleep, lest perchance in a dream they shall wound the sleepers." [9] "The use of baths shall be offered to the sick as often as it is necessary; to the healthy, and especially to youths, it shall not be so readily conceded." The monk was to own no property, "neither a book, nor tab-

[9] Henderson, *op. cit.*, p. 285. He publishes the whole rule.

lets, nor a pen—nothing at all." Clothes were to be "given to the brothers according to the places where they shall dwell, or the temperature of the air. For in cold regions more is required, but in warm, less." For the simple laymen, peasants in part, who were drawn into Benedict's community, while this was by no means an easy life, it was certainly no more difficult than most of them would otherwise have had.

Benedict passed the remainder of his life quietly with his monks in their lofty retreat, where their successors still welcome the stranger. When the Lombards sacked the place in 581 or 589, the community moved temporarily to Rome. The change from country to city brought *Changes in* about changes fundamental to the history of the Order. Originally the *and spread of* Benedictines were only laymen, not clergy, but now they began to take *the Benedic-* holy orders and become priests; and in the course of time it became *tine system* a fixed principle that Benedictine monks should be ordained. The natural result was that gradually manual labor was diminished and much more time was devoted to chanting in the choir. In the Benedictine house of today the work in the kitchen and in the fields is performed not by the monks themselves, but by servants called lay brothers.

The move to Rome also brought the Benedictines into touch with the papacy at the moment when Gregory the Great, who indeed may himself have been a Benedictine, came to the papal throne. Immediately the two institutions, the papacy and monasticism, joined hands; the monks fought the battles of Rome in western Europe, and the popes became the special patrons and protectors of the monks. In addition to its own inherent moderation and sensibleness, it was the support given to it by the popes that made of the Benedictine rule the standard rule for all western monasticism. By the time of Charlemagne Benedictine monks had swept the field. Yet there was not until much later a Benedictine Order of monasteries; each house prided itself on its autonomy and remained as free as the mother house at Monte Cassino.

The gradual regimentation of the monks of the west under the Benedictine rule clarified the split between the regular clergy, the monks, who lived according to a definite rule (*regula*), and the secular clergy, who lived in, not away from, the world (*sæculum*), the priest, bishop, and archbishop. Between these groups there never ceased to exist a sharp rivalry. In a sense the monk in his whole way of life was *Rivalry be-* a standing protest against the active political and social life of the secu- *tween regular* lar clergy. He may almost be said to have introduced a double standard *and secular* of morality among the clergy. As the object of veneration on the part *clergy* of the faithful, he soon began to profit by their generosity. What the monk was not permitted to own in person could be owned by the monastery as a whole, and monasteries became the owners of exceedingly large landed estates, accumulated to some extent at the expense of the episcopate, which no longer received the major share of legacies to the Church. Competition between the two groups for the favor of the laity was accordingly inevitable. Furthermore, the monks resented the attempts of bishops to subject them to their control by interfering in elections of abbots, by visiting monasteries to check up on discipline, and by otherwise interfering in their local affairs. To escape the jurisdiction of the local bishop monasteries turned to Rome to secure exemption from episcopal control. Since the popes for their own reasons were interested in breaking the independence of the local bishop, and glad to have within the diocese an institution which could stand up to him, they were generous in granting such exemptions.

It was no part of Benedict's original plan that his community should be a seat of learning such as the typical Benedictine monastery later became. To be sure, his monks were to be literate, able to read the Scriptures and sacred literature, and boys brought to the monastery had to be supplied with this minimum of learning. The tradition of the monastery as a center of literary culture, aiming to preserve and disseminate the literature of the past, was established rather by Benedict's younger contemporary Cassiodorus, who, although he seems not to have been known to Benedict, at least knew the Benedictine rule.

Cassiodorus makes his monastery a center of learning

Before retiring to devote himself to the cause of learning, Cassiodorus had had a long and distinguished public career, chiefly in the service of Theodoric, King of the Ostrogoths. He had also written a history of the Goths. After his retirement to his ancestral estates at Squillace in Apulia he was able to fulfill his hope of establishing some kind of institution for the preservation, study, and duplication of copies of Christian and classical literature. Cassiodorus realized his plans through the establishment at Squillace of a monastery, which he called Vivarium, from the fish ponds (*vivaria*) on its grounds. Here he spent the remainder of his long life with his monks, guiding them in their work. During this time he collected from Italy and North Africa Greek and Latin manuscripts of such wide variety and scope that his monks had a considerable library to work with. These manuscripts they were to collate and copy, and copy correctly, fighting "against the devil's illicit temptations with pen and ink." "Of all the works that can be accomplished by manual labor none pleases me so much as the work of the copyists—if only they will copy correctly." Thus Cassiodorus and his monks not only preserved many works which would otherwise have been lost, but set a standard and example for the Benedictine monks to follow. Henceforth until the twelfth century, with the exception of some episcopal schools, the monastery was the sole repository of learning and education. "There is nothing extant of ancient literature . . . that has not been copied and preserved for us by monks," for manuscripts earlier than the sixth century are very few. The crotchety old senator, who sent a lute-player to the Frankish King Clovis in the hope of softening his wildness, saw one of the needs of his day, and promptly filled it. When over ninety he was still worrying about the spelling of his monks, and wrote for them a work on orthography.

In spite, therefore, of his profession of abandoning the world, the monk returned to it and rendered it untold services in the name of service to God. If his ideal of personal salvation was purely selfish it was nevertheless the highest ideal recognized by the society of which he was a part; and his method of realizing it, thanks to St. Benedict and Cassiodorus, obliged him to compensate society for what he had taken away. His work as student, teacher, scholar, copyist, and author alone is enough to justify, if justification be needed, his profession. The good monk, as the highest exemplification of the Christian life, *The services* was a constant inspiration to the common people, to the nobility, and *of monasti-* to the secular clergy as well. The monastery was a haven for the way- *cism to society* farer: "all guests who come shall be received as though they were Christ." It was an almshouse for all who asked at the monastery portal. The monks were practically the only physicians and the monasteries the only hospitals that there were.

"If men know how to farm and to drain and till the land scientifically; if they know how colleges may be built and large households maintained without confusion; if they have learned to value economy, punctuality, and dispatch; nay more, if the minor obligations of social life, the unwritten laws of natural respect, good breeding, and politeness, have grown up amongst men, these were all derived from the monasteries. . . . The court, the great lord and landowner, the universities, the city company, the merchant with his ledger, the farmer, the architect, the artist, the musician and the author owe just so much to the monk as is the difference between the rude untutored efforts of the savage and the disciplined and developed powers of cultivated genius, energy, taste and imagination. Nor were all forms of manual labor, in a lower degree, without their obligations to monasticism. The stone-mason, the jeweller, the worker in brass and iron, the carver of wood, the joiner, the glass-maker, the weaver and embroiderer, the maltster, the brewer and the baker, even the hedger, the ditcher and the gardener, learned each the lesson of his peculiar craft from these societies of well-bred and educated men, who took their turn at the trowel or the dung-cart, and were deft and skilful alike in the kitchen, the brew-house and the bake-house, in the workshop and in the field, as they were in illuminating manuscripts, in choral music, in staining a glass window, or erecting a campanile." [10]

We need hardly say that monks and monasteries were not always of the best. Inevitably such an institution attracted men with the most diverse motives, including those who sought no more than an easy escape from the responsibilities of life. It is never easy to maintain in any group of men over a long period of time their original enthusiasm and steady devotion to a high level of achievement. The history of monasticism was bound to be the history of periodic decay. But, almost without exception, from within those same monastic ranks where decay had set in came once more the regenerative forces of reformation.

Gregory the Great sends Benedictine monks to convert the Anglo-Saxons

The first notable example of co-operation between the papacy and monasticism was Gregory the Great's conversion of the Anglo-Saxons in Britain. Earlier Christianity in Britain had not been wiped out by the German conquest in the middle of the fifth century, but the older Celtic Britons, pushed back into the western part of the island, while they had preserved their religion, were cut off from the continent and from Rome. Their Church had accordingly acquired certain characteristics peculiar to itself, and had, moreover, as yet no opportunity to influence the heathen conquerors. The Church in Gaul had likewise remained inactive. It is certainly indicative of the two chief sources of pioneer energy in the west that a pope should use a Benedictine prior to do what others closer home had failed to do. It is no less significant that, in undertaking to spread Christianity and with it the heritage of Roman civilization, the pope and the monks together were furthering the special interests of both parties in the project. Gregory's mission to the Anglo-Saxons, headed by St. Augustine, Prior of St. Andrew's in Rome, landed on Kentish shores in 597. King Ethelbert of Kent was quickly converted, and at Canterbury Augustine built Christ Church, the mother church of all England. Here also a group of Benedictine monks were settled, so that with Christianity the mission introduced the Benedictine rule into England, its first foreign area of expansion. Within less than a century the work of converting England, though it

[10] Quoted from J. S. Brewer by Butler, *Benedictine Monachism*, pp. 320–21.

was accompanied by occasional pagan reaction and warfare between the different small Anglo-Saxon kingdoms, was completed.

In the course of time the Benedictine monks and the Roman clergy got the co-operation of the British Church, which had at first been stubborn in maintaining its own character in opposition to the foreign intruders. The conversion of the Anglo-Saxons therefore became a common Christian undertaking. Indeed, in Northumbria and north-central England most of the work was done by monks and bishops from Lindisfarne, a colony of the Irish monastery on the island of Iona. The Church in England, however, was gradually reorganized on the Roman model; it recognized the primacy of the pope and his right to hear appeals. The last attempt to settle important differences between the local British and Irish clergy and the Roman faction came at the Synod of Whitby in 664, where the chief point of dispute, the date of celebrating Easter, was decided in favor of Rome. The Irish monks, to be sure, withdrawing to Iona and the monasteries affiliated with it, did not adopt the reform until 716, while the Welsh and British held out still longer. *The native British Church*

This movement towards Rome in English Christianity was furthered when the pope sent to Canterbury as archbishop in 669 Theodore of Tarsus, a Byzantine Greek. By increasing the number of English bishops and establishing his own authority over them, by calling councils of all the bishops of the separate kingdoms to draw up common regulations, Theodore perfected the centralized episcopal organization of the English Church and brought it more definitely within the federation of western churches headed by Rome. It can hardly be doubted that in so doing he contributed more than the Anglo-Saxon kings had been able to do to ultimate English unity. The introduction from Rome of Christianity and Benedictine monasticism, both of which aided in the resuscitation of an almost forgotten Roman tradition in Britain, together with fresh impulses from Ireland, made the Englishmen of the eighth century the leaders of western European civilization. *Theodore of Tarsus*

Ireland, indeed, in the late sixth and seventh centuries was a source of civilizing influence on England and the continent hardly less fruitful than Rome itself. In the "golden age of Irish culture," it was quite superior to anything else in the west. Its foundations were rooted in a Celtic society which was the outgrowth of the first Celtic wave that swept across Europe, not later than the sixth century B.C. Ireland was the one country of western Europe known to antiquity that the Romans had not conquered even in part, and it was consequently untouched by *The golden age of Ireland* any Roman influence. The Irish druid and the Irish bard went their own ways in prayer and song. The island had achieved no political unity; the characteristic social unit was the clan, engaged in constant warfare with neighboring clans. Irish pirates, under the name of Scots (for most of Ireland was then known as Scotia, only the north being called Erin), early in the fifth century made formidable raids upon Britain in its last years as a Roman province; and the influx of Scots from Ireland into Caledonia was so great that their name, lost in Ireland, was preserved in Scotland.

St. Patrick

In one of these raids, about 400, a young Briton named Succat, the son of a Christian Roman decurion in a garrison near Dumbarton, was taken captive to Ireland. After six years he escaped to Gaul, where he was educated, perhaps at Lérins, "the favorite center towards which Greek, Syrian and Egyptian monasticism tended." Obeying an inward urge, he determined to return to Ireland, the land of his captivity. Though Christianity was certainly known to some degree in Ireland before this time, the real conversion of a large part of the Irish from druidism was the achievement of this young Briton, whom we know as St. Patrick.

Irish mo-
nasticism

Ireland was organized on a tribal basis, each clan having its own chieftain, or "king." Thus when a chieftain became a Christian his clansmen usually followed him. And since the missionaries were monks, monasteries were built along with churches. They were supported by and recruited from the tribe. Abbots filled the place of the bishops of the continental Church; Irish bishops were of less account, and there were no actual dioceses. The monasticism introduced into Ireland by St. Patrick was the eastern type, as practiced at Lérins and in Cassian's house at Marseilles. Irish monasteries in the sixth century were found also in close contact with Celtic houses in western England, whose inspiration was likewise wholly eastern. These houses, with small huts for one or two monks, small oratories, common refectory and kitchen, were similar to the Egyptian ones. The monks practiced the ascetic austerities of eastern hermits, prostrations, praying with their arms extended like a cross, and praying and sleeping in cold streams and springs. Of St. Patrick it was said that not even cold weather kept him from "sleeping at night in pools." Like the eastern monk, the Irish monk desired to live a hermit's life; his only wish was "for a hut to dwell in, a little hut, hidden where none had trod."

The fusion of old Irish culture with Christianity in its eastern monastic form and with the late Roman literary tradition introduced from the monasteries of southern Gaul, where both Latin and Greek

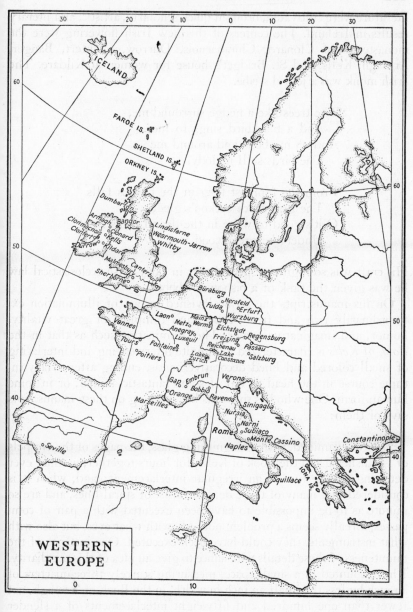

WESTERN
EUROPE

The Irish scribe

literature were cultivated, brought quick scholarly, artistic, and literary results in Ireland. The centers of this new Irish flowering were the monasteries of Clonard, Clonmacnois, Durrow, Clonfert, Bangor, Armagh, Kells, and St. Bridget's house for women at Kildare. The Irish monk was a joyful scribe.

> "The trees like a hedge surround me,
>   And a blackbird sings to me,
> And on my book and around me
>   The birds spill melody.

> "From the topmost twig in the bushes falls
>   The gray-frock cuckoo's glee;
> O it's good to write in the dear Lord's sight
>   Under the greenwood tree." [11]

His craft was so highly respected that in early Irish ecclesiastical law he was given the rank of a bishop or abbot.

Illumination of manuscripts

On his manuscripts the scribe lavished an art of illumination extraordinarily rich and fresh, subtle and complex, of great vitality, humor, and imaginative fervor. The illumination such as that in the *Book of Kells* is characterized by infinite interweaving and interlacing of small colored and lined decorative bands, ending after a labyrinthine course in the head or tail of some fantastic animal, or in some human form. One who has spent his life working on these manuscripts says of them:

"I have examined, with a magnifying glass, the pages of the Gospels of Lindisfarne and the Book of Kells, for hours together, without ever detecting a false line or an irregular interlacement; and, when it is considered that many of these details consist of spiral lines, and are so minute as to be impossible to have been executed with a pair of compasses, it really seems a problem not only with what eyes, but also with what instruments, they could have been executed. One instance of the minuteness of these details will suffice to give an idea of this peculiarity. I have counted in a small space, measuring scarcely three-quarters of an inch by less than half an inch in width, in the Book of Armagh, not fewer than one hundred and fifty-eight interlacements of a slender ribbon-pattern, formed of white lines edged by black ones upon a black ground. No wonder that an artist in Dublin, lately applied to by Mr.

[11] Allen and Jones, *The Romanesque Lyric*, p. 186.

rossbow of the fifteenth century decorated with plaques of e (See p. 317)

An heraldic badge of recognition (fourteenth century, Spanish)

mplete suit of Gothic armor with a defense (Italian, about 1400) (See 16)

Besieging a town in the fifteenth century

Golden Bull of the Emperor Charles IV (1356)
(See pp. 918–19)

The king distributing grants and charters (mir-
ture painting, 1430)

The walls of Carcassonne (See p. 500)

Chambers to copy one of the pages of the Book of Kells, excused himself from the labour on the ground that it was a tradition that the lines
had been traced by angels." [12]

The sixth, seventh, and eighth centuries in Ireland likewise wit- *Irish vernacu-*
nessed the culmination of a poetry in the Gaelic vernacular some five *lar literature*
hundred years before such outbursts in France and Germany. There
are at least five hundred titles of stories and poems written in the
seventh and eighth centuries, all redolent of the Celtic world of adventure on land and sea and of the glamorous world of faëry, and
many expressive also of deep and intimate human feeling.

What the Irish monasteries represented in this whole cultural development is well expressed by an American enthusiast. They "were
schools, all the way from kindergarten to university, hospitals, hotels,
publishing houses, libraries, law-courts, art academies, and conserva-
tories of music. They were houses of refuge, places of pilgrimage,
marts for barter and exchange, centers of culture, social foci, newspaper
offices, and distilleries. A score of other public and practical things
were they: garrison, granary, orphan asylum, frontier fort, postoffice,
savings bank, and general store for surrounding agricultural districts.
We carelessly imagine the early monasteries as charnel houses of cant
and ritual—whereas they were the best-oiled machines for the advancement of science, the living accelerators of human thinking, precedent to the University of Paris." [13]

Like all healthy civilizations the Irish was expansive. The combination of Irish *Wanderlust*, the desire to find a quiet hermitage, and
missionary zeal sent the Irish monk out in all directions. Colonies of
Irish hermits were to be found in all the northern islands, the Faroes,
Orkneys, and Shetlands. They discovered Iceland long before the
Norsemen. They crossed in their coracles to Scotland, Britain, and the
continent, singing

"Heia, fellows! Echo, resounding, sends back our heia!
So that our emulous prow may cut the waves like a dolphin,
Row till the timbers groan and the ship leap under your muscles—
Backward our whitened path flows in a lengthening furrow."

In the sixth and seventh centuries the whole nation seemed to become
missionary, pilgrim, and traveler. One of the pioneers was St. Co-

[12] J. O. Westwood in Gougaud, *Christianity in Celtic Lands,* p. 379.
[13] Allen and Jones, *op. cit.,* p. 164.

The expansion of Irish influence into northern England and Scotland

lumba, "the dove of the Church," who in 563 with twelve companions founded a monastery on the island of Iona. This was the home monastery of the missionaries who converted the Picts in Scotland and founded Lindisfarne, the center for the conversion of Northumbria. They were one with the surviving British Church in their date for the celebration of Easter, their peculiar tonsure, and their manner of celebrating baptism and consecrating bishops. With it they co-operated to bring about the overthrow of Anglo-Saxon heathendom in the seventh century, "by a vigorous encircling movement from North and South at once, the religion of Columba . . . coming from Scotland and the religion of Gregory and Augustine coming from Rome." More even than that, these same Irish monks were also scholars, poets, and copyists and illuminators of manuscripts.

To the continent Irish Christianity, and with it Irish civilization, was carried first of all by St. Columban and his companions, notably St. Gall, during Gregory the Great's pontificate. These two were edu-

The expansion of Irish influence to the continent

cated and trained at Bangor, "then at the height of its fame and, with its thousands of students from abroad and at home, a beacon light of learning surely, and of piety perhaps." They brought with them into a Gaul of half-tamed barbarism their austere monastic religion, conveniently summarized in Columban's rule, and a new discipline for sinners. This last was a system of private penance, requiring private confession to the priest, private penitential exercises assigned according to a fixed tariff, and the individual's final reconciliation with God through the priest. This new ecclesiastical code, all unknown to the system of public penance in the Western Church, offered a new means of disciplining the undisciplined German, so excellent that it was ultimately adopted by Rome for the whole Church.

Columban and his companions were settled finally in Burgundy, where King Guntram granted him a site for a monastery on the ruins of an old Roman camp at Anegray. The community became so popular that new Irish houses were soon founded at Luxeuil and Fontaines. From Luxeuil alone it has been estimated that directly or indirectly fifty new monasteries were founded; and monasteries without an Irish origin are known to have later fabricated one for themselves. "It is certain," says a later chronicler, "that by virtue of its [Luxeuil's] authority, almost the whole of the land of the Franks has been for the first time properly filled with regular institutions."

As the Irish monasteries were large agricultural houses, their monks were active in helping to stamp out the paganism of the countryside, which was now transformed into allegiance to Christian saints. The

Irish monks, too, were children of nature, on friendly terms with the beasts of the field. Columban's biographer says of him: "And do not wonder that the beasts and birds thus obeyed the command of the man of God. For we have learned from Chamnoald, royal chaplain at Laon, who was his attendant and disciple, that he has often seen Columban wandering about in the wilderness fasting and praying, and calling the wild beasts and birds. These came immediately at his command and he stroked them with his hand. The beasts and birds joyfully played, frisking about him, just as cats frisk about their mistresses. Chamnoald said he had often seen him call the little animal, which men commonly name a *squiruis*, from the tops of high trees and take it in his hand and put it on his neck and let it go into and come out from his bosom." [14]

For twenty years Columban labored at Luxeuil. His hold over the peasantry was strong, but by his unsparing denunciation of the vices of the Austrasian [15] court he aroused the hostility of the whole ruling caste. Nor were the Frankish bishops—the native majority, that is, not those recruited from the new Irish foundations—pleased to see the Irish ignore the continental practice of an abbot's getting permission from the bishop of the diocese to found a monastery. Columban was with difficulty forced to leave Luxeuil for home. But circumstances permitted him to return to the Rhine, whence he moved to Switzerland. After laboring for a short time around lakes Zurich and Constance, he finally crossed the Alps, leaving behind his old companion, St. Gall. On the spot where his oratory stood was subsequently built *St. Gall* the great monastery of St. Gall. In Italy Columban was cordially received by the Lombard King Agilulf, who assisted him in founding Bobbio, another of the great Irish monasteries of the continent, which became the repository for an unusually large number of priceless manuscripts. Here Columban spent his last days.

St. Columban was the first of a long line of Irish monks and scholars who for centuries penetrated the continent. Southern Germany was dotted with Irish houses, notably at Würzburg, Regensburg, and Reichenau. Columban's rule, however, did not long preserve *Irish mon-* a separate existence. Some monasteries attempted a curious combina- *asteries on* tion of its drastic prescriptions with the more moderate Benedictine *the continent* rule; but by 700 the latter had crowded out its Irish rival, bringing with it a recognition of papal overlordship. Nevertheless, even after accepting the Benedictine rule, the Irish houses never forgot their

[14] C. 30 of the *Life of Columban* in *Translations and Reprints*, II, 18.
[15] See p. 192.

Celtic origin, and continued to be known as *Schottenklöster* (Irish monasteries). Irish scribes in continental houses, too, can always be recognized by the personal notes they added to their manuscripts: "Let some of the best wine be given to the scribe"; "Let no reader blame that script, for my hand is cramped through excess of labor"; "I am very cold"; and, comfort of all ages, "Time for dinner." [16] Old Irish monks for long sent greetings back home with returning younger monks:

> "Since, if but Christ could give me back the past,
> And that first strength of days,
> And this white head of mine were dark again,
> I too might go your ways." [17]

The weight of Irish influence on the continent is incalculable. It penetrated even into the still unchristianized regions of central Europe. Together with the brilliant accomplishments of the Irish at home, it makes the "dark ages" a patent ineptitude. For three hundred years the light of Ireland flamed, shedding its rays upon Scotland, England, and the continent, until diminished in the darkness of the Norse invasions.

The Anglo-Saxon mission to the continent

The co-operation of the papacy and Benedictine monasticism which had sponsored the Roman mission to Britain was continued by an Anglo-Saxon mission to the continent. The success of that earlier co-operation at the end of the sixth century, and the vitality of English Christianity, may be measured by the fact that as early as the first half of the eighth century Anglo-Saxon monks were ready to bear the standard of Rome and Monte Cassino beyond the Rhine. The Irish monks were not subservient to the pope, and did not concern themselves directly with promoting ecclesiastical organization. Theirs was a severe, highly individualistic enthusiasm, which limited itself to evangelization. The Anglo-Saxon Benedictines, having prevailed against the old Celtic Church in England and learned the advantages of organization and co-operation with Rome, were ready to take up the work where the Irish left off. To some extent they had been preceded across the Rhine also by Frankish bishops. Rupert of Worms and Emmeram of Poitiers, with a Frank Corbinian, completed the much earlier work of St. Severinus in Bavaria and founded churches in Salzburg, Regensburg,

[16] Gougaud, *op. cit.*, pp. 362–63.
[17] Helen Waddell, *Medieval Latin Lyrics* (1929), p. 75.

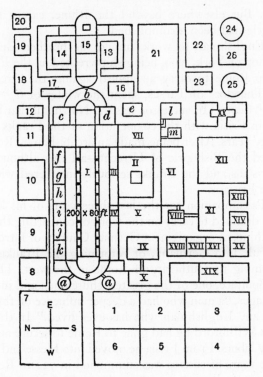

A Projected Ground Plan for the Abbey of St. Gall c. 430 x 300 ft.

I Abbey church	VI Refectory	7 ?
a Campanili	VII Living room and	8 Kitchen for noble guests
b Vestibule	dormitory	9 Inn for noble guests
c Library	VIII Kitchen	10 Outer school
d Sacristy	IX Inn for pilgrims	11 Abbot's hall
e Building for prepara-	X } Bakery and brew-	12 Servants' house
tion of host	XI } ery	13 Inner school
f Refectory	XII Artisan's workshop	14 Hospital
g Guest chamber	XIII } Crushing and hand	15 Church
h Magister's study	XIV } mills	16 Students' kitchen
i Magister's bedroom	XV Malt-house	17 Hospital kitchen
j } Porter's rooms	XVI Threshing-floor	18 Building for blood-
k }	XVII Wood-turners' shop	letting
l Necessarium	XVIII Cooper's shop	19 Doctor's house
m Bathroom and wash-	XIX Stable	20 Herb garden
house	XX Barn	21 Churchyard and or-
p Porch for pilgrims and	1 Sheep stalls	chard
servants	2 Goats' stalls	22 Kitchen garden
II Cloister court	3 Cowshed	23 Gardener's house
III Chapter house	4 Breeding-stud	24 Goose-pen
IV Anteroom	5 Pigsties	25 Hen-pen
V Cellar and pantry	6 Servants' house	26 Poultry-keeper's house

and Freising. But elsewhere beyond the Rhine, except among the Alemanni, little had been accomplished.

The first Englishman to work among the heathen Germans was Wilfred, Bishop of York, who, being shipwrecked on the Frisian coast on his way to Rome to carry an appeal against the Archbishop of Canterbury, Theodore of Tarsus, spent the winter of 677–78 among the heathen Frisians. His successor was the Northumbrian Willibrord, who worked in Frisia with the co-operation of the Franks and Rome for nearly fifty years. After being made an archbishop by Rome, Willibrord founded the Bishopric of Utrecht—all this although war between the Frisians and the Franks seriously interfered with the conversion of the Frisians.

Willibrord's companion for the last three years of his life was the man who was destined to carry on the work of converting the Germans beyond the Rhine, of organizing a German Church, of introducing the Benedictine rule into Germany, of reforming the Frankish Church, and of confirming the authority of Rome in the west. This was the Benedictine Boniface, one of the greatest churchmen and monks of the early middle ages, "a man who had a deeper influence on the history of Europe than any Englishman who has ever lived." In the course of his work with Willibrord he had gone to Rome to secure authority for *St. Boniface* his missionary labors. From Frisia he moved into Hesse and Thuringia, and after five years of success was summoned in 722 to Rome, where he took an oath of allegiance to the pope, and was consecrated bishop for his converts, "the races in the parts of Germany and on the east side of the Rhine who live in error in the shadow of death." In Hesse and Thuringia many Benedictine monasteries and nunneries were founded as training schools for converts and centers for further expansion, notably Hersfeld and Fulda, two of the most important centers of learning in Germany. After ten years' more labor he was made archbishop, and after a third visit to Rome organized the Bavarian Church into the four episcopal sees of Salzburg, Passau, Regensburg, and Freising. His work in Hesse and Thuringia was completed by the organization of the bishoprics of Büraburg, Würzburg, Erfurt, and Eichstädt.

As papal legate Boniface undertook also the reform of the Frankish Church. In a series of councils the Frankish bishops were obligated to respect his authority as archbishop and papal legate, to respect and obey the precepts of Rome, to hold regular councils, and to correct abuses and wipe out survivals of pagan practices. In 747 he was appointed Archbishop of Mainz, titular head of his newly created German Church and superior of all the Rhine bishops. He it was, probably, who co-operated with Stephen II in bringing about the alliance between the Frankish monarchy and the papacy in the years following 751; he may even have anointed Pepin king in 752. As an old man of seventy-three, with failing eyesight, he turned back to the enthusiasm of his youth, the conversion of the pagan Frisians, by whom he suffered martyrdom in 754. Through St. Boniface's hands ran all the threads of the history of the first half of the eighth century, and from those threads was spun Europe's future.

Boniface's compatriot and contemporary Bede was the last of a meager line of scholars, historians, and poets who through this formative period of the early middle ages kept burning—sometimes feebly enough—the light of the ancient world. Boethius heads the list, which runs on through Isidore of Seville, Venantius Fortunatus, and Gregory of Tours to Aldhelm and Bede. All parts of western Europe *Scholarship* touched by the German invasions are represented here, and two of these men are themselves Germans, but it is only natural to find as yet no representative from beyond the Rhine. It is equally significant that of these men three were bishops, one a monk, and one both monk and bishop. The only layman is the first on the list, Boethius; after him there were hardly any lay writers for seven or eight centuries. Latin was almost the sole written language, but it was so modified by time and so corrupted by the influence of the Latin spoken by the illiterate masses of western Europe that its writers, who could still read, when they could no longer write, classical Latin, often felt constrained to apologize. Only the last on the list, Bede, was interested in making learning available in his native language, Anglo-Saxon. At the same time, however, it must be remembered that poetry in the vernacular got an earlier start, not only in Ireland but also in England, where Anglo-Saxon literature had its auspicious beginnings in the epic of the hero Beowulf and the poetry of Cædmon, both written earlier than the time of Bede.

The Church during these centuries had gradually become the sole *Donatus* avenue to education, and the only refuge where leisure and training could be found for literary and scholarly pursuits. The language of the Western Church was everywhere Latin. The sort of instruction in Latin that its clergy needed had been furnished by the schools in the later empire. It was systematized in such manuals and textbooks of grammar, rhetoric, prosody, composition, oratory, and literature as those of Donatus and Priscian. The Church could do no better for its own purposes than to borrow such textbooks and methods of instruction. By far the most popular were the works of Donatus, who actually became one of the most important and influential of all Latin writers. We know from Jerome that he was the leading grammarian of Rome in the fourth century, and his teacher. He wrote commentaries on Virgil and Terence, and, by far the most important, a longer and a shorter Latin grammar, all based on the best Greek and Latin sources. In the eleventh century a Benedictine monk protested that "monks cared little for the rule of Benedict in comparison with the rule of Donatus." In the twelfth century the only Greek work in the library of Christ Church at Canterbury was a translation of Donatus. When printing began in the fifteenth century Donatus was still so popular that between 1472 and 1476 there were four editions of his commentary on Terence. Hardly less important than Donatus's own work was the enormous number of commentaries on it, belonging to every century from the fifth to the fifteenth. He was one of the grammarians upon whom St. Boniface based his two books on grammar and meter. The end of it all was that his name became a common noun. First it meant a textbook of grammar; for example, in the thirteenth century an Englishman wrote a Greek grammar which he called *Donatus Græcorum,* and later Colet speaks of "certain introductions to Latin speech called Donates." In the statutes of Winchester College, founded in 1386, Latin grammar was officially referred to as *antiquus Donatus.* The word then came to mean an introductory treatise on any subject; so we find an English bishop writing a "Donat into the Christian religion." Finally it passed into popular speech meaning simply "lesson," and is so used by Chaucer and in *Piers Plowman.*

The Church felt the need of the full power of the Latin language to express itself and combat paganism and heresy. So, as in the details of its cult and calendar, it compromised. Inevitably the question arose, was it not dangerous to find one's models in pagan literature? There *The conflict* were always those—for the most part monks—who were horrified at *between pagan* the danger of pollution from the obscenities of non-Christian literature, *and Chris-* a literature that celebrated many false gods, condoned many vices, ex-*tian letters* pressed many damnable ideas, and in general proceeded from a spirit wholly antithetical to Christianity. There was even some feeling that it was bad form for a Christian to write Latin too well. One commentator said that the Holy Ghost knew more Latin grammar than Donatus; and Gregory the Great, so far from apologizing for his style, well expressed the feeling of most students of Latin since his day when he wrote: "I have scorned to observe all art of style. . . . I avoid not the disorder of barbarisms; I despise a conformity to constructions and moods and cases of prepositions. For I deem it exceedingly inept to fetter the words of the Heavenly Oracle to the rules of Donatus." Even St. Jerome, as we have seen, was troubled by the fear that he was more Ciceronian than Christian. And, indeed, they could hardly escape it; the monks in their libraries continued to use the sign of scratching their ears like dogs when they wanted a copy of Ovid's *Art of Love,* and they hid Virgil under their pillows. "How shall I be rid of these things? At mass, in the very act of contrition, the old stories flaunt before my mind the shameless loves, the sight of old heroes going into battle." [18] Gregory the Great wrote to the Bishop of Vienne: "It has come to our notice that you, my dear Brother, have been holding conferences on ancient literature. . . . This information we received with reluctance and vehemently rejected. . . . For the same lips cannot sound the praises of Jupiter and the praises of Christ. How serious an impropriety it is for a bishop to sing what is ill suited even for a religious layman, do you yourself reflect." Others reflected, and came to a different conclusion. Indeed, Augustine not only spoke for himself, but well expressed what came to be the general policy of the Church, when he said: "To study poets and philosophers with a view to making the wit more keen and better suited to penetrate the mystery of the Divine Word is to spoil the Egyptians of their treasure in order to build the tabernacle of God."

Certainly in this matter the Church was reasonable and sensible and liberal. We, at any rate, have every reason to be grateful. For the methods of studying literature adopted by the Church contributed, no less than the practice in the monasteries of copying manuscripts, to keeping the tradition of ancient civilization alive. Distorted though it might be to fit the requirements of Christian use, misunderstood by ignorance, misinterpreted into allegory or plain nonsense, nevertheless ancient literature continued to be read. Comparetti in his great book, *Vergil in the Middle Ages,* speaks eloquently of the modern world reaching out its hand in the renaissance to clasp the hand of the ancient world across the intervening darkness. But he forgets the hand that even in the dark never quite lost its hold on that of the ancient world, and so was ready, when the time came, to place that hand in the waiting hand of later humanists.

Although Boethius has not been considered so far, he belonged in fact to the same century as Gregory the Great and was a colleague of Cassiodorus, in the service of the Ostrogothic King Theodoric. Few men have contributed so much to the intellectual sustenance of pos- *Boethius*

---

[18] Quoted in Helen Waddell, *The Wandering Scholars,* p. xv.

terity as Boethius did. Like Cassiodorus, fearing the loss of much of the learning of the past, he wished to do what he could to prevent it. "I am glad," he wrote, "to assume the remaining task of educating our present society in the spirit of Greek philosophy. Wherefore this is verily a part of my consular duty, since it has always been a Roman habit to take whatever was beautiful or praiseworthy throughout the world and to add to its lustre by imitation." [19] He was distinguished by a knowledge of Greek in a generation that was fast losing its Greek. He conceived the huge project of translating Aristotle and Plato into Latin. He got only so far as to translate a part of Aristotle's logical works, and an introduction of the Neo-Platonist Porphyry to Aristotle's *Categories,* to which he added commentaries of his own. But even in so doing he supplied all that was known of Aristotle in the west for six centuries.

As an orthodox Christian thinker, he attacked, in several theological *Tractates,* the chief heretical opinions that were disturbing his generation; for, while accepting the principle of a revealed faith, he was not averse to using his own reason to buttress it. Indeed, in his use of Aristotelian logic for this purpose he was himself "the first scholastic," supplying to later schoolmen, along with the Latin philosophical vocabulary that he worked out in his commentaries on Aristotle, both a method and the prospect of reconciling, "if possible, faith and reason." His works on arithmetic and geometry were about all the west knew of these subjects until the introduction of Arabic mathematics. His work on music was equally authoritative, and was used as a textbook at Oxford until the eighteenth century. He is best known, however, for his *Consolation of Philosophy,* which he wrote in prison, having been condemned to death by Theodoric, who was suspicious of his political opinions) In prose and verse he takes up in closely reasoned and unsentimental fashion those fundamental questions of existence which must concern an intelligent man. This work long remained the most popular among philosophical treatises, even after his other works had been supplanted by the republication of the Greek philosophers; it was translated into all the vernacular tongues, and is still read today. An American scholar has even pleaded for his canonization, if only because "a certain saintliness attends a scholar who lost so fine a library and who yet could transport so much of it, inside, to his dungeon-cell." [20]

[19] Quoted in E. K. Rand, *Founders of the Middle Ages* (1928), p. 158.
[20] *Ibid.,* p. 180.

From about 600 to 636 Isidore was Bishop of Seville. He held to *Isidore*
all the conservative opinions of his day, and his Christianity was most *of Seville*
orthodox. "We are not permitted," he says, "to form any belief of
our own will, or to choose a belief that someone else has accepted as
his own. We have God's apostles as authorities, who did not themselves choose anything of what they should believe, but they faithfully transmitted to the nations the teaching received from Christ.
And so, even if an angel from heaven shall preach otherwise, let him
be anathema." He thoroughly approved of monasticism: "It is always
advantageous for those who are well and strong to become infirm, lest
through the vigor of their health they be defiled by illicit passions and
the desire for luxury." [21] He advises the monk to "beware of reading
the books of gentiles and heretics. It is better for him to be ignorant
of their pernicious doctrines than through making acquaintance with
them to be enmeshed in error." [22]

Yet in his own work Isidore did not hesitate to go beyond these
limitations. His chief work was an encyclopedia which he called
Etymologiæ sive Origines (*Etymologies or Origins*) because of his
fondness for explaining what things were by derivation—often dubi-
ous—from what they were called. In it he aimed to preserve all the
information, sacred and profane, that was available to him, "about all
that ought to be known." He ranges from God, angels, and saints,
through races, kingdoms, citizens, men, languages, the liberal arts,
fabulous monsters, agriculture, botany and shipbuilding materials, to
dress, food, drink, and furniture. The book, like many scholarly books,
is largely a compilation from older authorities. In his naïveté and his
credulous love of the fabulous Isidore was a part of his generation,
and not so far removed from one of his great Roman authorities, the
Pliny of the *Natural History;* to read Pliny on the swan or the dolphin is only less amusing than to read Isidore. None the less, Isidore,
like Boethius and Cassiodorus, was engaged in the serious and noble
task of preserving as much as he could of the learning of the past. He
was so successful that for about three centuries his encyclopedia was
the main work of reference, of which every important monastic library must have a copy.

Venantius Fortunatus was an Italian who had come to Gaul to visit *Venantius*
the tomb of St. Martin at Tours out of gratitude for a miraculous *Fortunatus*
cure. He was taken up by the Austrasian court, where he became court

[21] Brehaut, *Isidore of Seville*, p. 70.
[22] M. L. W. Laistner, *Thought and Letters in Western Europe*, pp. 90–91.

poet and orator and made friends with many of the Gallo-Roman
nobles and bishops, in whose honor he wrote verses. To his friend
Gogo, for example, he wrote:

> "Nectar and wine and food and scholar's wit,
> Such is the fashion, Gogo, of thy house.
> Cicero art thou, and Apicius too,
> But now I cry you mercy: no more goose!" [23]

Finally he settled down at Poitiers, where he ended his comfortable
life as bishop in 609. Here in the monastery of the Holy Cross the
Thuringian Princess Radegunde, having escaped the fury of her
Merovingian husband, lived a life of exemplary holiness. She befriended Fortunatus, who became thoroughly devoted to her and celebrated in verse her holiness, kindness, and beauty. "He is a troubadour
with as deep a devotion as ever knight had for his lady." [24]

Fortunatus is better known, however, as a hymn writer, continuing
the tradition of Prudentius and Ambrose. Two of his hymns, "The
Banners of the King Advance" (*Vexilla regis prodeunt*), "one of the
first creations of purely medieval feeling," [25] and "Extol, Oh Speech"
(*Pange, lingua*), have been incorporated into the ritual of the Church.
They celebrate the mystic symbolism of the Cross, and are full of
tender compassion for the crucified Savior. Two of the stanzas of
Pange, lingua run as follows:

> "crux fidelis, inter omnes arbor una nobilis
> (nulla talem silva profert flore fronde germine),
> dulce lignum, dulce clavo dulce pondus sustinens!

> "flecte ramos, arbor alta, tensa laxa viscera,
> et rigor lentescat ille quem dedit nativitas,
> ut superni membra regis mite tendas stipite."

> "Faithful Cross! above all other,
> One and only noble Tree!
> None in foliage, none in blossom,
> None in fruit thy peer may be;

[23] Waddell, *Medieval Latin Lyrics*, p. 65. Apicius was a Roman epicure.
[24] Allen and Jones, *op. cit.*, p. 142.
[25] Raby, *Christian Latin Poetry*, p. 89.

Sweetest wood, and sweetest iron!
Sweetest weight is hung on thee.

"Bend, O lofty Tree, thy branches,
Thy too rigid sinews bend;
And awhile the stubborn hardness,
Which thy birth bestow'd, suspend;
And the limbs of heav'n's high Monarch
Gently on thine arms extend!" [26]

Gregory of Tours, the friend who urged Venantius Fortunatus to collect his poems, has already been seen fighting Arian heretics and glorifying those who fought them. His family had almost monop- *Gregory* olized the see of Tours before he became bishop in 573. While he did *of Tours* not confine himself to the writing of history, it is his *History of the Franks* that has put posterity in his debt; he was the only distinguished historian in the west between Ammianus Marcellinus and Bede. Gregory was not proud of his Latin; at the beginning of his work he says: "I beg indulgence of those who may read what I write, if haply in letter or in syllable I transgress the laws of Grammar, an art in which I am ill versed." The *History of the Franks* was, however, by no means so modest in scope; Frankish history began with the creation. For material on Roman history Gregory used a work, *Seven Books against the Pagans,* which Augustine had suggested to his friend Orosius to write, to prove his thesis that Christianity had not brought calamity *His* History to the Roman world. Gregory carries his history down to 591, three *of the Franks* years before his death. It is not what we should regard as perfect history, but were it not for Gregory, we should know practically nothing about the early history of the Franks.

From him, however, we get more than a glimpse of Merovingian society; we are aware of a vigorous personality writing. Of King Chilperic, whom he calls "the Nero and Herod of our time," he writes: "He gave himself over to gluttony, and his god was his belly. No man, he would declare, was cleverer than he. . . . The mind can conceive no hurt or debauchery that this man did not practice. He was ever on the watch for new ways of torturing people; when he found a man guilty, he ordered the eyes to be torn out of his head. . . . Never a soul did he love in singleness of heart, by none was he himself loved." [27] No more in his portraits of the bishops of Gaul did

[26] *Ibid.,* p. 91.
[27] Dalton, *op. cit.,* II, 279.

he spare his colleagues, and the picture he leaves of his credulous, stubborn, hard-working, sincere self is an ingratiating thing.

Out of the English monasteries in the late seventh and early eighth centuries came the first two German scholars to carry the torch of the learning of Christian Rome. The first of these, the West-Saxon Aldhelm, was trained in the Irish monastery of Malmesbury and at Canterbury, and became Bishop of Sherborne in 705. Although "in prose he seems incapable of writing a readily intelligible sentence," yet because of his wide acquaintance with the Roman poets, with the writings of the Latin Fathers, and with men like Gregory the Great and Isidore, it has been said of him that "no country in western Europe during the seventh century could show his equal in intellectual achievement." [28]

Aldhelm

The glory of early English scholarship, however, was the man generally called the Venerable Bede. He worked quietly in his cell in the Benedictine monastery of Wearmouth-Jarrow. "It has ever been my delight," he says, "to learn or teach or write," and during his whole life, from 672 or 673 to 735, he never ceased to do any of these things. The range of his subject matter was large: metrics, figures of speech, spelling, chronology, the physical universe. From his work on chronology came our custom of reckoning dates from the birth of Christ, B.C. and A.D., rather than forward from the creation of the world.

The Venerable Bede

But he is best known as a commentator on Scripture and as the author of the *Ecclesiastical History of England*. Tremendously learned, and acquainted with Greek, he drew heavily from the Latin Fathers in his exposition of Scripture. Bede was a genuine scholar, indefatigable in collecting material, both oral and written, and scrupulous in citing his authorities. Nor was he gullible in his use of them; he went so far as to point out that Jerome had made mistakes in the Vulgate. That part of the *Ecclesiastical History* not dependent upon previous writers reaches from the mission of St. Augustine down to 731. "The result is by universal consent a masterpiece . . . not merely the history of the growth of a church, but of the formation of a people." [29] It has never ceased to be an authoritative work. Bede's wide reading and intensive study of the art of writing gave him a style not only free from the crudities of Gregory of Tours but almost classical in perfection, "the finest prose style that the earlier Middle Ages can display." His translation of the fourth Gospel into Anglo-Saxon

[28] Laistner, *op. cit.*, p. 121.
[29] *Ibid.*, p. 129.

was a work hardly less important, for it laid the foundations of learning in the vernacular, and may well have furnished the idea that the English Benedictine missionaries carried with them to Germany.

Between the late seventh and early ninth century there was also put into writing the oldest English epic, *Beowulf*. Its picture of the life of the early Angles, Saxons, and Jutes does much to compensate for the lack of contemporary historical record of their migration across the North Sea from their homelands in the marshes and fens of Jutland and Frisia. Beowulf's heroic exploits constituted the saga of the English folk until their history began to be written in the seventh century.

Beowulf

Chapter 9

THE FRANKISH STATE UNDER THE CAROLINGIANS

EINHARD, the close friend and secretary of Charles the Great, began his excellent biography of the emperor thus:

Einhard on the last Merovingians

"The Merovingian family, from which the Franks used to choose their kings, is commonly said to have lasted until the time of Childeric, who was deposed, shaved, and thrust into the cloister by command of the Roman Pontiff Stephen. But although, to all outward appearance, it ended with him, it had long since been devoid of vital strength, and conspicuous only from bearing the empty epithet Royal; the real power and authority in the kingdom lay in the hands of the chief officer of the court, the so-called Mayor of the Palace, and he was at the head of affairs. There was nothing left the King to do but to be content with his name of King, his flowing hair and long beard; to sit on his throne and play the ruler; to give ear to the ambassadors that came from all quarters, and to dismiss them, as if on his own responsibility, in words that were, in fact, suggested to him, or even imposed upon him. He had nothing that he could call his own beyond this vain title of King, and the precarious support allowed by the Mayor of the Palace in his discretion, except a single country-seat, that brought him but a very small income. There was a dwelling house upon this, and a small number of servants attached to it, sufficient to perform the necessary offices. When he had to go abroad, he used to ride in a cart, drawn by a yoke of oxen, driven, peasant-fashion, by a ploughman; he rode in this way to the palace and to the general assembly of the people, that met once a year for the welfare of the kingdom, and he returned home in like manner. The Mayor of the Palace took charge of the government, and of everything that had to be planned or executed at home or abroad." [1]

[1] From translation of S. E. Turner.

It would be difficult to improve upon this short summary of the political development of the Frankish state in the seventh and first half of the eighth centuries, but however well it describes what happened, it does not explain the developments. One must study the *Aristocracy* beginnings of a social and economic transformation that has condi- *and serfdom* tioned all western European history to date. This transformation was twofold: the concentration of wealth in land in the hands of a relatively small number of owners, who constituted an official governing class, which became an hereditary aristocracy; and the depression of the majority of the population into the position of serfs and dependents. The domination of the mayors of the palace meant the victory of men who represented at first the interests of the new aristocracy. And yet to call this aristocracy new is hardly accurate. Only to the extent that the aristocracy of the west was German, and that it was augmented from the ranks of the clergy in the persons of bishops and abbots, may it be said to have been new. For the concentration of large landed estates in the hands of privileged owners was, as we have seen, a development within the later Roman empire. Likewise the status of the serf-peasant was new only in so far as Roman and German freemen became serfs, for serfdom in the Roman empire was at least as old as Constantine. In fact, the social pattern already developing among the Germans when they entered the empire fitted nicely into the Roman.

The growth of a wealthy, landed, semi-independent aristocracy, which sapped the strength of the monarchy and interposed itself between the king and the people, was specifically promoted by three practices that tended to substitute for the public relationship of citizen to state a dependent personal and economic relationship between private individuals. These practices were commendation, the benefice, and immunity. The landless or luckless man, poor or weak or hope- *Commen-* lessly in debt, with no prospects for the future and without means of *dation* protecting himself through his own kin, commended himself personally to the service of the great landowner, count, duke, or official at court, or even the king, thereby becoming his vassal (*vassus*), faithful one (*fidelis*), or—as the king's vassal was usually called—his antrustion. A Frankish formula of commendation of the seventh century follows: "You [the lord] should aid and succor me as well with food as with clothing, according as I shall be able to serve you and deserve it. And so long as I shall live I ought to provide service and honor to you, suitably to my free condition, and I shall not during the time of my life have the ability to withdraw from your power or guardianship; but must remain during the days of my life under your power or defence." [2]

The old German clan organization had broken down, but the new state was as yet impotent to guarantee the enjoyment of life and property; what neither clan nor state could do the private individual had no choice but to do, or get done, for himself. Every man's social prestige and influence then inevitably came to depend upon the number of vassals or faithful retainers he had. This practice of commendation reminds us not merely of the old German institution of the chief and his war band (*comitatus*), but of the situation Cæsar describes in Gallic society in the first century B.C. As under more settled circumstances the *comitatus* lost its military character and became rather a civil body of retainers or table companions of the king or lord, the result obviously approximated the later status established by the practice of commendation, likewise the conditions Cæsar describes in earlier Gaul, when the great majority of the common people were serfs.

From one point of view the benefice may be described as the commendation of land. The small landowner, wishing to escape the responsibilities of ownership, upkeep, debt, and taxes, turned over to some wealthy and influential person title to his land, on condition that he be permitted to remain on it and live from its produce: he held it in usufruct, for his own lifetime, or for that of his children, or for any definite time specified in the agreement. After the period specified complete ownership passed to the second person. The land that a person who surrendered title got back for his own use from the title-holder was a benefice (*beneficium*). This practice on a large scale could only lead to the concentration of property under a few owners. Moreover, in the course of time the holder of a benefice, being a mere tenant, might easily be reduced to a dependent or even servile condition. In a society none too well organized there were frequent opportunities for the powerful and unscrupulous lord to force his small neighbors to turn over title to their lands to him and to receive them back from him as benefices. Many persons, too, transformed their land into a benefice of their bishopric or of a neighboring monastery, a pious evidence of devotion to the Church and an approved method of insuring eternal salvation. The system of benefices cannot, however, be quite so simply described. Often an ecclesiastical or secular lord, as an inducement to a landowner to deed him his title, would grant him an additional benefice out of his own land, to be held likewise in usufruct. The lord thus provided for the cultivation of land he already

The benefice

[2] *Translations and Reprints*, IV, no. 3, p. 3.

owned but was in no position to use, while at the same time he was in the long run increasing his own property. Meanwhile the man receiving the additional benefice enjoyed the income from more land than he originally held. Finally, kings, bishops and abbots, big landowners, in order not only to build up a large personal following and to utilize all their land, but to reward their servants and pay their officials, granted benefices wholly from their own lands, to be held for a limited time under specific conditions.

Obviously all this transferring of titles, this using of land without owning it and owning it without using it, in the course of time was sure to occasion endless dispute and even the use of force. For when the state could not enforce these private agreements, the private individual had no choice but to let his rights go by default or take it upon himself to enforce them. Nor was it by any means only the holder of the benefice who was likely to suffer. There was an inevitable tendency, conditions or no conditions, to retain a benefice and pass it on in the family, and it required a watchful owner to keep it from slipping from him and his heirs. This danger was perhaps particularly great with benefices granted as payment or due reward for services rendered. Furthermore, for the king there was the special danger, when benefices went to royal officials, such as counts, that benefice and office would become inseparably fused. When, as actually happened in seventh-century Gaul, the king was obliged to promise that he would appoint his counts only from the county in which they lived, the danger was very real that the office would come to be the hereditary possession of a local family, the perquisite of the owner of specific lands. *The dangers of the benefice*

There was also danger in the practice, which developed in the eighth century, of stipulating, in granting benefices, the performance by the benefice-holder of military service on horseback. It is hardly to be supposed that benefices had not previously been granted upon such conditions, nor was cavalry an entirely new thing in the west in the eighth century; but the typical German army was an infantry of all German freemen, for almost all of whom service on horseback was very expensive, if not impossible. The Church suffered particularly in this matter, for Charles Martel hit upon the expedient, supposedly to meet the attack of Arab and Berber horsemen, of forcing the Church to grant benefices to men who would serve him as cavalrymen, so that the Church was forced to aid in building up the military power of the state. To what extent this particular precedent was adopted by other landowners it is difficult to say, but it is true that the granting of *Benefices in return for military service* benefices to be held on military tenure became in time a general practice.

Immunity

The custom of granting what were called immunities likewise resulted in putting more power into the hands of large landowners. The royal or crown lands, the fisc proper, were governed by private officials of the king as his private patrimony; no public official, such as the count, entered them. When lands were granted out of the fisc to bishops or abbots, or to secular persons, it was natural for them to insist that this immunity of royal lands from public jurisdiction be preserved for them and that these lands pass from the king's private jurisdiction directly into the private jurisdiction of the secular or ecclesiastical recipient. But immunity went further than this. In view of the difficulty of setting up an efficient administration for the whole state, the Merovingian kings found it convenient to grant, first to ecclesiastics, later also to laymen, similar immunity for land already owned or subsequently to be acquired by them. Such a grant of immunity to a bishop reads: "in the vills [villas] of the church of that lord, which in recent times, or in ours, or by the gift of anyone, he is seen to have, or which, in the future, godly piety shall wish to amplify in the right of that holy place, no public judge shall at any time presume to enter for the hearing of causes or for the exaction of payments, but the prelate himself or his successors . . . shall be able to rule over this under the name of a complete corporation." [3] It was chiefly churchmen who got such immunities, which were looked upon as a special indication of royal piety. By the exclusion of royal officials from immune lands the lord of the immunity acquired private jurisdiction. He was a judge, he collected taxes and dues and requisitioned services; in a word, he enjoyed complete local independence, bound only by his general obligation to the crown. Again the crown was giving away powers it legally possessed but was unable to exercise.

Feudalism

Taken together, commendation, benefices, and immunities embody a situation in which power and prestige were slipping from the hands of the monarch into the hands of private persons. This process of decentralization, when completed—when, that is, monarchy had become little more than a name—is called feudalism. If this tendency, as we see it in Merovingian Gaul, had not been temporarily checked, it would have brought about a feudal Europe much sooner than it actually did.

The struggle between the Merovingian crown and the aristocracy became for the first time clear-cut in the midst of the civil wars fol-

[3] *Ibid.*, p. 12.

lowing upon the partition of the realm among the four sons of
Chlotar II in 561. These wars were ostensibly a struggle between two
women driven by a poisonous hatred of each other. Chlotar's eldest
son, Sigibert, King of Austrasia, had married the Visigothic princess
Brunhild, with Venantius Fortunatus present to celebrate the wedding
in a poem. "She was a girl of graceful form, fair to look upon, honourable and comely, prudent in judgment and amiable of address,"
says Gregory of Tours. Not to be outdone by his brother, Chilperic,
the second son and King of Neustria, married the second "pearl of
Spain," Brunhild's elder sister Galswintha. In order to marry her,
however, he was obliged to put away a beautiful but cunning and cruel
mistress, Fredegund. Galswintha was soon afterwards found murdered, and nothing we know of Fredegund makes it difficult to believe that she was responsible. Chilperic thereupon married his former
mistress. Brunhild swore eternal vengeance against Chilperic and his
queen, and war between Neustria and Austrasia did not cease until
both the women were dead. Fredegund's methods of getting rid of
her enemies were simple and direct; she usually sent servile clerics
with poisoned daggers to murder them. Sigibert of Austrasia was
murdered at her instigation, Chilperic's son Merovech was murdered
by her emissaries, and she had the refractory Bishop of Rouen murdered at the high altar. She even tried to get rid of her daughter
Rigunth. "Rigunth put her arm into the chest to take out more things,
when her mother seized the lid and forced it down upon her neck.
She bore upon it with all her strength, until the edge of the chest
beneath pressed the girl's throat so hard that her eyes seemed about
to start from her head." Fredegund died in 597 without having had
the pleasure of murdering Brunhild, who was always a little too much
for her.

Brunhild, in fact, was too much for almost everybody. The Frankish
nobles encouraged civil war in order to weaken the crown and
strengthen themselves; and in Austrasia Brunhild waged lifelong battle against the nobles, who particularly hated her as a foreign woman
striving desperately to maintain against them the prerogatives of the
crown. She had to struggle to keep the crown for her son Childebert
after the death of Sigibert, and she made it possible for him to inherit
Burgundy from his uncle. When Childebert died, Brunhild secured
Austrasia for one of his sons and Burgundy for the other. When the
Austrasian nobles drove her into Burgundy, she sent one grandson
to fight against the other; and when they had both died, Brunhild
managed to hold both Austrasia and Burgundy for her little great-

Brunhild and Fredegund

Brunhild and the Austrasian nobility

grandson Sigibert II. Finally in 614 nobles of both kingdoms invited
the Neustrian King Chlotar II in to aid them against this lone woman.
Her great-grandsons were strangled. "Brunhild herself was tortured
for three days, set upon a camel as a mark of derision, and then tied
by her hair, one arm, and one foot, to the tail of a vicious horse, which
was then lashed to fury." [4] Chlotar II became king of all the Franks,
united once more.

The real victory, however, belonged to the nobles. That is clear
from the concessions that clerical and secular nobles combined to force
from Chlotar in his edict of 614. The king promised that, with certain
limitations, he would permit the free election of bishops according to
the regulations of canon law. He also extended jurisdiction of Church
courts over the clergy, and engaged himself to respect legacies made
by private persons to the Church. To the nobles he promised to suppress all unjust taxes, and to choose his counts from the districts which
they were to administer. In other words, Chlotar promised to relax
the strict control that the Merovingians had hitherto exercised over
the Church, to confirm its claim to be judge of its own affairs, and to
permit it to accumulate landed wealth untrammeled. As the Church
was less firm in its support of the Merovingian dynasty, concessions
had to be made to retain its support. By promising to choose his counts
from their own locality Chlotar was turning over this royal office to
local landed magnates. As the aristocracy was abandoning the crown,
the reins of government had to be shared with them. At about the
same time the hereditary character of succession to the office of mayor
of the palace was recognized; even the organs of central administration
were slipping from the king's control.

*The do-
nothing
Merovingians*

Chlotar's successor Dagobert (629–39) was the last Merovingian
of any account. After him began the line of do-nothing kings (*rois
fainéants*), youngsters of enfeebled physical constitution who married young and died young and lived the impotent and useless lives
described by Einhard. The history of the Frankish state henceforth
depended upon the Carolingian mayors of the palace. The royal line
of the Merovingians (the name came from Meroveus, its half-
legendary founder) faded away before that of the Carolingians
(named from its greatest representative, Carolus Magnus, or Charles
the Great).

*The first
Carolingian
mayors of
the palace*

The Carolingian family originated in Austrasia, the thoroughly
German part of the Frankish realm, when the son of St. Arnulf,
Bishop of Metz, married the daughter of the great magnate, Count

[4] *Cambridge Medieval History*, II, 123.

Pepin of Landen, whose private domains are said to have comprised all of modern Belgium. Both these ancestors of the house played an important part in the tardy victory of the Austrasian nobles over the indomitable Queen Brunhild. Later they were also the chief counsellors of King Dagobert, and Pepin was his mayor of the palace. The aims of the family were starkly revealed when Pepin's son Grimwald, who had fought hard to succeed his father as mayor of the palace, attempted to put the Merovingian king safely away in a monastery and have his own son Childebert reign in his stead. The attempt, however, was premature by a century, and it cost both Grimwald and his son their lives. The Church resented not having been taken into confidence, and the aristocracy was alarmed at the attempt of one of their own number to establish his dynasty on the ruins of the crumbling Merovingians. They preferred to keep the monarch as their tool.

For a while a wave of belated loyalty to the Merovingian house actually revived its prestige. Under this cover the mayor of the palace of Neustria, Ebroin, sought to unite the offices of mayor in the three kingdoms in his own person. His high-handed practices led to a new civil war, of which the Bishop of Autun, Leodegar (St. Leger), "an adventurous, sanguinary, rapacious feudal chieftain," and Pepin of *Pepin of* Heristal, grandson of old Pepin of Landen, were the chief instigators. *Heristal* Although Ebroin was for a moment successful, with his murder in 681 the brief Merovingian revival and the ascendancy of the Neustrian mayor of the palace alike came to an end. Instead, by a later victory over the Neustrians at Tertry in 687 Pepin of Heristal succeeded in establishing himself in the position of mayor of the palace for the whole Frankish realm.

He began to work against the decentralizing efforts of the Frankish nobles, for the Carolingian mayors, although elevated to power as representatives of the aristocracy, as a matter of fact aimed to check its encroachment upon the central authority and usurpation of government. They took up where Clovis had left off the task of which not one of his successors had proved worthy, and continued it to its splendid culmination in Charles the Great. At the moment of Pepin of Heristal's victory the Frankish kingdom was on the verge of dissolution. The Bretons and Aquitanians had cast off the Frankish yoke; the Gascon duke had expelled the Frankish counts and made himself independent; the Lyonnais, the valley of the Rhone, where Burgundian tradition was strong, had recognized no king since 674. Thuringians, Bavarians, and Alemanni had rebelled against Frankish domination and were rallying around dukes backed by the local aristocracy. The Frisians north of the Rhine were dangerous. In long and fierce campaigns into Alemannia, Bavaria, and Aquitaine Pepin struggled to restore political unity, and by beginning the conquest of Frisia blazed the trail for Willibrord and Boniface.

Pepin's work was interrupted after his death in 714 by a short struggle over the question of his successor. His wife tried to keep her husband's office for her young grandsons, but could not withstand his illegitimate son Charles. This man, whom we call Charles Martel (i.e., the Hammer), from his continual poundings against the Mohammedans in southern Gaul, was the greatest man among the Franks between Clovis and Charles the Great, and the true founder of the Carolingian state. Although he refused the pope's pleas to abandon his Lombard ally Liutprand, who had helped him against the Saracens, he was glad to have the help of the papacy in supporting Boniface's work in converting the Germans beyond the Rhine and organizing their Church.

Charles Martel

Boniface was quick to recognize the need for his support: "I am able," he wrote to the pope, "neither to rule the people of the church nor to defend the priests and deacons, the monks or nuns, and I am not powerful enough to hinder the very rites of the pagans and the sacrileges of idols in Germany, without the patronage of the Prince of the Franks, without his order and the dread of him." Martel accordingly deserves a share of the glory of Boniface's work. Although he laid a heavy hand upon the lands of the Church in order to meet the constant danger from the Mohammedans, thus earning the unsparing condemnation of later clerical chroniclers, and although, too, he filled many episcopal sees with his roistering followers, his campaigns against the Saracens were as much to the Church's interest as to any layman's, and there was no reason why the Church should not share the responsibility and the cost. By using Church lands as benefices to pay men to fight on horseback he built the strong army necessary not only to hold off the Saracens but to crush the subversive local movements for independence within the Frankish state. His famous victory at Tours in 732 [5] over the Saracens, although it was long the fashion to overestimate its significance, with his subsequent campaigns against them did help partially to remove that danger and give him time to spend his efforts elsewhere.

His policy towards the Church

Martel succeeded his father Pepin as single mayor of the palace for the whole Frankish realm, and continued his efforts to crush the

[5] See p. 169.

decentralizing forces prevalent on all sides. This meant a fight against *Martel's do-* the locally entrenched nobility. Martel's particular method was to re- *mestic policy* move local counts and dukes and to substitute for them Austrasians whose loyalty he could depend upon. This policy was carried through with special thoroughness in Burgundy, and when the Alemanni were subdued, they lost their duke too. Aquitaine after a period of almost complete independence was forced to recognize Frankish overlord-ship, and two campaigns against the Bavarians brought the same re-sult. Martel continued the conquest of the Frisians begun by his fa-ther, and conducted five campaigns against the Saxons. The crumbling Frankish state was consolidated once again. For the last few years of his life Martel did not even bother with the formality of Merovingian kingship, but ruled the Franks simply as mayor of the palace.

For a short while after Martel's death in 741 his two sons Carlman and Pepin the Short shared the government. Carlman's withdrawal from public life in 747 to enter a monastery cleared the way for Pepin to end the anomalous relationship between the Carolingian mayors and the Merovingian kings. No doubt as a measure to reconcile the Frankish Church to a dynastic change, some of the lands taken from the clergy by Martel were restored by Pepin. Inasmuch as many of the benefices held by nobles of the Church could no longer be recalled, he further compensated the Church by liberal grants from the lands of his own family, the crown lands of the Merovingian kings having *Pepin the* been almost completely dissipated long before this time. Pepin was *Short crowned* elected king by the Frankish nobles between November 2, 751, and *King of* January 23, 752, at Soissons, and was probably anointed by Boniface *the Franks* himself.

It has already been seen [6] how he sought papal authorization for this dynastic revolution, and why the papacy was anxious to sanction it, and how Pope Stephen II came to Gaul in 754 to reanoint Pepin king—the first western king ever to be consecrated by a pope—and received as his reward military aid against the Lombards and the Donation of Pepin. We can now see that this alliance between the Frankish kingdom and the papacy was more than the result of the difficulties already noted in the pope's relations with Constantinople and with the Lombards in Italy; it was also the outcome of the early alliance between Clovis and the Gallo-Roman episcopate and of the close relationship between the Carolingian mayors and the Anglo-Saxon missionaries. The shift from Merovingian to Carolingian was

[6] See p. 201.

not only the dramatic end of numerous past developments but also the starting point for a new line of western development.

For the history of the Frankish state in particular the alliance with the papacy marks also the establishment of lordship over the Lombards and of a protectorate over the papacy. In Gaul Pepin drove the Saracens beyond the Pyrenees in 759 and added Septimania to the realm. Campaigns in Aquitaine, in Bavaria, and against the Saxons maintained the authority of the Franks and defended their boundaries, preserving the accomplishments of father and grandfather by further consolidating the unity of the kingdom. Pepin also supported Boniface's reform of the whole Frankish Church. Such reform was badly needed. Boniface complained that for eighty years no synods had been held. The bishoprics had suffered from Martel's partial secularization; many, and many parishes too, had long been vacant. The clergy were licentious, the priests vagabond and drunken. Many churches had been despoiled by robbers, or by predatory nobles who seized their endowments. The improvement begun by Boniface and seconded by Pepin made it possible for the Church to resume its spiritual and cultural leadership. Pepin himself hoped, "if later God shall grant us days of peace and leisure . . . then to restore in all their scope the standards of the saints."

Pepin and the Church

For a few years after the death of Pepin the Short in 768 the Frankish kingdom was again divided, now between his two sons Charles and Carloman. The death of the latter reunited the state in 771, and so it remained until Charles's death in 814. Charles's long reign marked an epoch in the history of Europe. After a long preliminary formative period, during which Roman and German peoples, languages, and institutions were fusing, and such important western institutions as the papacy and monasticism were taking on definite form, Charles seemed to co-ordinate and re-form them all into the appearance of an organic whole. Behind Charles was the Frankish policy of expansion to include all the Germans in Europe, which he pursued to its completion, bringing the borders of his empire to touch those of the Slavs, and of the Byzantine and Arab empires. Behind him was the Frankish policy of co-operation and alliance with the papacy, which led him to the re-establishment of a Roman empire in the west centralized in his own person. Behind him was the policy of Church reform inaugurated by Boniface, which he so far promoted that through the clergy a genuine intellectual revival took place in the west. Indeed, the permanent foundations for a united Roman-German-Christian Europe appeared to be laid during these years.

Charles the Great

Einhard gives an ingratiating picture of Charles. He was typically German in personal appearance, "large and strong, and of lofty stature [over six feet]; . . . the upper part of his head was round, his eyes very large and animated, nose a little long, hair fair, and *Einhard's* face laughing and merry; . . . his neck was thick and somewhat short *description* and his belly rather prominent." "His voice [was] clear, but not so *of Charles* strong as his size led one to expect. . . . At the last he even limped a little with one foot. . . . Physicians . . . were almost hateful to him, because they wanted him to give up roasts, to which he was accustomed, and to eat boiled meat instead. In accordance with the national custom, he took frequent exercise on horseback and in the chase . . . and often practiced swimming, in which he was such an adept that none could surpass him. . . . He used to wear the national, that is to say, the Frank, dress—next his skin a linen shirt and linen breeches, and above these a tunic fringed with silk; while hose fastened by bands covered his lower limbs, and shoes his feet, and he protected his shoulders and chest in winter by a close fitting coat of otter or marten skins. Over all he flung a blue cloak. . . . He was temperate in eating and particularly so in drinking . . . but he could not easily abstain from food, and often complained that fasts injured his health. . . . He was so moderate in the use of wine . . . that he rarely allowed himself more than three cups in the course of a meal. . . . He had the gift of ready and fluent speech and . . . was such a master of Latin that he could speak it as well as his native tongue; but he could understand Greek better than he could speak it. . . . He took lessons in grammar . . . and other branches of learning. He also tried to write, and used to keep tablets and blanks in bed under his pillow, that at leisure hours he might accustom his hand to form the letters; however, as he did not begin his efforts in due season, but later in life, they met with ill success." [7] In the great wooden hall of one of his villas, surrounded by Frankish nobles, most of them with the typical Frankish moustache, and all similarly dressed, Charles was still the German king flanked by the companions of his war band.

Charles's reign is in large part a chronicle of wars: wars to extend the frontiers, wars to establish and defend the frontiers, wars to convert the heathen to Christianity. It was successful warfare that earned him his appellation "the Great." No less than fifty-four campaigns are recorded, directed either by Charles in person or by his sons or other *Charles's wars* lieutenants: five against the Lombards, eighteen against the Saxons,

[7] Quoted from the translation of S. E. Turner.

three against the Frisians and Danes, one in Thuringia, one in Bavaria, four against the Avars, four against the Slavs, two against the Gascons, seven against the Mohammedans in Spain, five against the Mohammedans in southern Italy, two against the Byzantines, and two against the Bretons. Of the remarkable year 790 a chronicler commented: "This year was without war."

The relations of the Franks with the Lombards and the papacy had been determined by the events of 751 and the years following. By inheritance Charles was overlord of the Lombards and protector of the Papal States, with the title of *patricius* already bestowed upon his father Pepin. At the beginning of his reign it seemed as if this relationship might be disturbed, for, without intending any hostility to Rome, Charles contracted a marriage with the daughter of the Lombard king. Pope Stephen III was furious and dismayed: ". . . this marriage is the inspiration of the devil; the Lombards are a stinking people, the source of all leprosy, a people not recognized among civilized peoples." He forbade the marriage and pronounced a curse upon him who disobeyed. Charles, unmoved by this ultimatum, married the Lombard princess—the first of a long series of wives and concubines. But when, after a year, he sent her home to her father, normal relations were restored with Rome; and the new pope Hadrian I held as fast to the alliance, his biographer says, as to a diamond.

Charles and the Lombards

When the Lombard king renewed his attack upon papal possessions and threatened Rome, Charles answered the papal appeal for help by descending into Italy over the Mt. Cenis. The Lombard capital, Pavia, was besieged for nine months, all Lombardy was overrun, and subsequently the Lombard duchies of Benevento and Spoleto were conquered. Charles made himself king of the Lombards, and the Lombard kingdom was absorbed into the Frankish, which was fast becoming an empire, for its territory now bordered on the Byzantine empire in southern Italy. Additional campaigns brought Venice, Istria, the Dalmatian coast, and the island of Corsica within the empire.

Charles and Rome

During the siege of Pavia in 774 Charles left for Rome to celebrate Easter, the first Frankish monarch to enter the Eternal City. He was received with a pompous welcome, concluded by his mounting the steps of St. Peter's as a pilgrim, on his hands and knees, to embrace Pope Hadrian. While in Rome Charles confirmed the Donation of Pepin, though not quite to the extent, it would seem, that Hadrian's biographer would have us believe.

Yet if Charles did recognize the Papal State in Italy, he made it quite clear that as *patricius* of the Romans and protector of the Holy

See he regarded himself as the actual sovereign of this territory, to whose orders the popes must hearken in governing it. He ordered the pope as he would any other bishop in his realm. To his mind the pope was distinguished only by the tradition of his see, and yet he was not in all respects willing to grant even complete spiritual autonomy to the successor of St. Peter. "It is the king's business," he wrote in one of his letters to the pope, "to defend the Holy Church of God outwardly with arms and inwardly to maintain the Catholic Faith, and it is the business of the Holy Father to support the royal work with his prayers. . . . Always follow the canons in your exercise of authority, let your life be a pattern of holiness, and let your mouth never be opened except to give holy exhortations." And he gave these instructions to one of his legates to the pope: "Take heed to warn him of the holy life that he ought to lead, of the kindness with which he should govern the church, and especially of the fidelity which he should manifest in observing the sacred canons . . . engage him to eradicate simony, and to reform the other abuses, of which, as thou knowest, I have often complained." Charles's whole conception of the papacy must have seemed to the popes disappointingly spiritual and other-worldly; obviously, in turning from Constantinople to Gaul, the popes had merely exchanged a Byzantine for a Frankish master.

The second German nation finally to be incorporated into the Frankish state was Bavaria. While long recognizing the overlordship of the Franks, it had always retained an autonomy under its own dukes which amounted to virtual independence. The Bavarian Church as organized by Boniface had preserved a similar autonomy. The pope was accordingly as anxious as Charles to terminate this state of affairs. Bavaria lost its independence by stages. Duke Tassilo, after contesting his allegiance, was forced by armed invasion to turn over Bavaria to Charles and become his vassal. As a disloyal vassal he was arrested, deposed from his duchy, and confined to the Rhine monastery of Lorsch, where his memory is still enthusiastically preserved. Later he renounced all claims for himself and his family, and Bavaria was incorporated into the Frankish empire, whose boundaries on the lower Danube now touched the Avars. *Charles and Bavaria*

The third, and for later history the most important, German nation to be conquered by Charles was Saxony. A German historian has observed that its conquest meant for Germany what Cæsar's conquest of Gaul meant for western Europe. "No war ever undertaken by the Frank nation was carried on with such persistence and bitterness, or cost so much labour, because the Saxons, like almost all the tribes of *Charles and the Saxons*

Germany, were a fierce people, given to the worship of devils and hostile to our religion, and did not consider it dishonourable to transgress and violate all law, human and divine." That is Einhard speaking. It was not only to terminate centuries of fierce border warfare that Charles began this conquest, but also specifically to force Christianity upon this last pagan German nation. "A fiercer, more dogged struggle than their conquest never was." For over thirty years the Franks poured troops into Saxony, often led by Charles in person. At the moment when victory seemed assured, a stubborn pagan reaction would undo all previous gains. The most extreme measures were resorted to, such as beheading forty-five hundred Saxons at Verden, and finally deporting thousands into Frankish territory and colonizing their land by Franks.

As quickly as possible after victory the Church was organized in Saxony. Probably as early as 782 Charles in one of his edicts gave the Saxons their choice of Christianity or death, and punished minor infractions of Church discipline with death. "If any one of the race of Saxons . . . shall have wished to hide himself unbaptized, and shall have scorned to come to baptism, and shall have wished to remain a pagan, let him be punished by death. . . . If any one, out of contempt for Christianity, shall have despised the holy Lenten fast and shall have eaten flesh, let him be punished by death." The first bishopric in Saxony was organized by Willehad, the English Bishop of Worms, at Bremen, whence Christianity was to spread to the Scandinavian north. Within a short time other bishoprics arose at Verden, Minden, Halberstadt, Hildesheim, Paderborn, Münster, and Osnabrück.

The conquest begun by arms was completed by Christianity, and the Christianization begun by conquest had still to be completed by force. The Saxons resented it and were slow to forget it. For centuries the Saxon bishops complained of the paganism of their flocks. Alcuin, the great English scholar at Charles's court, bitterly condemned his methods. "Let but the same pains be taken," he wrote, "to preach the easy yoke and light burden of Christ to the stiff-necked people of the Saxons as are put forth to collect the tithes from them, and mayhap the Saxons would no longer be found to refuse baptism with abhorrence." At any rate, the Saxons were brought within the community of western European civilization, and Frankish frontiers now touched the heathen Danes and faced the heathen Slavs across the Elbe and the Saale.

With the conquest of Lombardy, Bavaria, and Saxony the Frankish expansion begun by Clovis was complete; of Germanic peoples only *The marches* the Anglo-Saxons and the Scandinavians remained outside of this new empire. Beyond the actual boundaries of German territory, however, further campaigns established a circle of marches (German *Mark*) to protect the frontier from outside incursions. The smallest of the marches was in the isthmus between Saxons and Danes, the Danish mark, established to prevent the Danes from giving aid to the Saxons, from which the later Kingdom of Denmark derived its name. In the territory east of the Saxons, inhabited by Slavic tribes whom the Franks indiscriminately called Wends, Charles organized a march, with its seat at Magdeburg, which, as the first and oldest Slavic march, came to be known as the Old March (*Altmark*). Other marches on the eastern frontier were the Thuringian and the Bohemian, or Moravian, with its administrative center at Regensburg in Bavaria. After the Bavarian campaign a Frankish army had continued eastward as far as modern Hungary, where it destroyed the already declining Avar state and opened this territory to later Christianization. To protect Bavaria and Italy from further attacks of the Avars Charles formed the East March (*Ostmark*) on the lower Danube, and the March of Friuli to protect Italy especially. These five eastern marches were in fact not organized merely for protection; they were also, like the early territories of the United States, the first steps of advancing colonization. There was, however, this important difference, that the German peoples were reaching out for lands that had once been their own homes, which since their emigration westward had been filled up by immigrants of other races from the east. It was centuries before German colonization among the Slavs made any headway, but after the destruction of the Avars a beginning was made in the *Ostmark* and among the Slavs along the upper Drave and Save rivers. These first few settlements—mostly by Bavarians—were the beginning of German Austria, whose very name means "the eastern realm."

The Spanish march in the south and the March of Brittany in the west completed Charles's ring. After Aquitaine was conquered by Pepin the Short it still needed protection from the Mohammedans in Spain. Charles took advantage of a rebellion threatening the Ommiad *Charles in Spain* Emir of Cordova to cross the Pyrenees, but his first campaign ended in disaster. As the Frankish army was returning north after failing to take Saragossa on the Ebro, it was attacked in a defile of the Pyrenees known as Roncevalles by the Christian Basques (Gascons), whom Charles had not spared on his march southward. "As the army was advancing in the long lines of march necessitated by the narrowness of the road, the Gascons, who lay in ambush on the top of a very high mountain, attacked the rear of the baggage-train and the rear-guard in charge of it, and hurled them down to the bottom of the valley. . . . . Roland, Governor of the March of Brittany . . . fell in this engagement." With this disaster the history of French literature may almost be said to have begun, for the Spanish expedition and the heroic death of Roland grew into a patriotic legend which later became the first notable work of French literature, the epic *Chanson de Roland*. Later campaigns established Frankish overlordship beyond the Pyrenees almost to the Ebro and finally organized the Spanish march. The first step in pushing the Mohammedans out of Spain had been taken.

Charles crowned Roman emperor

The culmination of Charles's career was no doubt his coronation as "Emperor of the Romans" by Pope Leo III on December 25, 800. The event as described in one of our main sources seems simple enough. "At mass on the most holy festival of our Lord's birth, when the King arose from kneeling in prayer . . . Pope Leo placed a crown upon his head, and all the Roman people cried aloud: 'To Charles, Augustus, crowned of God, great and pacific Emperor of the Romans, life and victory!' After the applause he was adored by the Pope after the manner of the princes of old, and, instead of patrician, he was called Emperor and Augustus." [8] Einhard implies, however, that Charles's pleasure was not unmixed. "Charles . . . came to Rome to reform the disordered state of the church, and there passed the whole of the winter. It was then that he received the title of Emperor and Augustus; from which at first he was so averse that he declared that he would not have entered the church that day, although it was a great festival, had he been able to foresee the Pope's intention."

For many months Pope Leo had been in great trouble. As early as April 799, he had been so thoroughly manhandled by enemies in his advisory council that he betook himself in haste all the way to Paderborn in northwestern Germany to implore Charles's protection. His enemies followed him even there, to accuse him of adultery and perjury. He was finally returned to Rome under strong escort, there to await his fate at the hands of a council. Charles himself arrived in Rome on November 29. In order to avoid the appearance of a court's pronouncing sentence upon the successor of St. Peter, on December 23 the pope was permitted to clear himself on oath of the charges against him. Two days later came the coronation ceremony. Now what was there for Charles to be surprised about, granted that we

---

[8] R. G. D. Laffan, *Select Documents of European History*, I, 6.

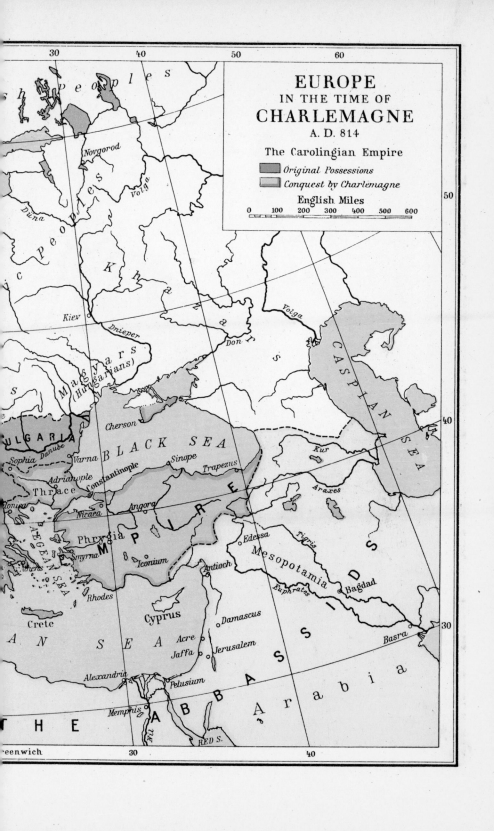

EUROPE
IN THE TIME OF
CHARLEMAGNE
A. D. 814

The Carolingian Empire

Original Possessions
Conquest by Charlemagne

English Miles

0   100   200   300   400   500   600

may take Einhard's word for it that he was? Or was Einhard merely trying to show the true modesty of his hero? Or perhaps trying to make clear to the Byzantine emperor that Charles was not primarily responsible? In any case it is inconceivable that Charles was wholly unaware of what was to happen, that Leo III, in view of his own predicament, would have dared to take so momentous a step without consulting him. Charles may have disliked the particular time chosen for the ceremony or the manner in which it was performed. It is perhaps most plausible, in view of his general conception of the papacy, that he was not overjoyed to receive the imperial crown from the hands of a pope. Furthermore, although Einhard says that it was only at first that he was averse to his new titles, yet it seems significant that in his division of the realm in 806 he entirely disregarded the imperial title. And when in 813 he had his son Louis crown himself emperor, he plainly either no longer set much store by the pope's coronation, or set so much store by it that he wished to avoid the dangerous—as they seemed to him—implications of it for his son. There is good reason to suppose that Charles would have argued that no pope, but only God, could crown the emperor.

At any rate, the importance of the fact can scarcely be disputed: for the first time a German had been crowned Roman emperor, and crowned by a pope. To be sure, there was in reality no longer a Roman empire. Charles as Roman emperor, the Frankish state as the western Roman empire—it was all a curious anachronism. And yet the tradition of western Europe organized as a whole under Rome was still so strong that, when it was actually reunited by a German, it seemed to contemporaries a return to the golden age. For all that, it is perhaps not too much to say that the ceremony of the coronation was, if not an indication of the fusion of Roman, Christian, and German elements in western society, at least a symbol of that fusion, still to come, always hoped for, which had indeed already gone beyond a mere beginning. At the least, a new empire of some sort had in fact been founded, which in various forms lasted until Napoleon gave it its quietus in 1806. Moreover, it had been set up under papal auspices. This, to be sure, was of no immediate consequence, for under Charles's strict control the popes could make no use of the precedent. None the less, it was an invaluable aid to them in their advance towards a position of leadership in Europe, for the time was coming when they were to speak of their creating the empire, of their translating it from the head of the emperor of the east to the head of the Frankish king of

Significance of the revival of empire

the west, of their consequent superiority over the emperor, of the impossibility, indeed, of there being any empire or emperor at all without papal approval and papal coronation.

Meanwhile a new secular lord had been raised to the headship of western Europe. Henceforth there were two heads, papal and imperial, and a vast deal of time, thought, sweat, and blood was wasted in later centuries in a futile effort to decide which was subordinate to the other. Under Charles there could be no question about that. The title of emperor, in making him legal sovereign of Rome and the Papal States, merely confirmed him in powers he already exercised. Upon his government of the Frankish state the new title had no effect at all, except that he made it the occasion of exacting from his subjects and vassals a new oath of allegiance to him as emperor.

Charles and Byzantium

Whatever he may have thought, Charles was extremely careful to come to terms with the eastern empire over his assumption of the title of Roman emperor. The pope's part in his coronation amounted to a public proclamation that henceforth the papacy severed itself from Byzantine control. To Byzantium the only Roman emperor was the emperor of Constantinople, who still claimed to be ruler of the west, as if nothing had happened since the days of Constantine. The pope was therefore a rebel, and Charles was a rebel. It was even feared that this new western emperor might march on Constantinople to dethrone the real Roman emperor (at this moment the Empress Irene) and seize the real Roman government by force. In some circles in the west it was argued that, since "the title of Emperor had then come to an end among the Greeks, who were under the rule of a woman," it was only fitting that the unused title should be assumed by Charles. Charles himself well enough realized that his being crowned Roman emperor was no reason to expect that after Irene there would be no more Roman emperors in the east. He therefore conceived the project of marrying Irene and thus uniting "the eastern and western provinces," which would have been an even stranger resurrection of Rome. Irene herself was willing, but her deposition and exile in 802 prevented the realization of these plans. By 812 Charles was recognized as emperor by the Byzantine Emperor Michael I, after he gave up his claims to Venice, Istria, and the Dalmatian coast. The theory was that the situation which existed after the division of the Roman empire in 395 by Theodosius was being restored; there was still only one Roman empire but there were again two emperors. Such sporting with historical facts reveals the state of mind of both east and west in the ninth century. The name of Rome had not lost its magic; it still represented the ideal of a political entity embracing the whole of Christendom, or at least the Christendom of the west. That was the most important thing about December 25, 800.

Between his comment on Charles's fondness for the roast that his huntsmen used to bring in on the spit and the remark that he was moderate in the use of wine Einhard tells us that Charles enjoyed the books of St. Augustine, "especially the one entitled *The City of God*." Without some rise in the general level of culture in the west Charles could not, and even so had he been a monarch of lesser stature he would not, have made such strenuous efforts to realize the ideal of the City of God on earth. His large conception of his duties set him apart not only from his remoter Merovingian predecessors but even from his own father and grandfather. His government was in aim a theocracy, that is, a government based upon divine precepts, under the direct inspiration of God. He was God's anointed agent for the realization of God's purpose, and consecration and coronation by God's priests gave him a holy character. In his edicts he made no distinction between political matters and moral or religious matters, because there was no such distinction in his mind; they were all alike part of the business of government. The oath of fidelity to him as emperor he took to mean, among other things, "that each one shall strive with all his mind and strength on his own account to serve God according to the commandments." *Charles's conception of theocracy*

Charles had no doubt about the importance of having an educated, efficient, and loyal clergy to help accomplish his high purposes, but never for one moment did he let anyone else doubt that he was the one supreme ruler of the Church of his empire. Like the Byzantine emperor, he was "the representative of God who has to protect and govern all the members of the church, the Lord and Father, King and Priest, Leader and Guide of all Christians." He accordingly legislated on every possible ecclesiastical subject, on Church property, Church discipline, education, the ritual, ecclesiastical punishments, church building, Church organization. His legislation touched all ranks of the clergy, both secular and regular. He was responsible for the organization of the archbishoprics of his realm. He interfered in dogmatic questions, and went so far on one occasion as to try to dictate to the pope what he should believe, namely, what he himself believed. He controlled the personnel of the clergy and all appointments to important Church offices, and he presided over councils. He told the parish priests what to preach and the congregations how to sing. He wished to keep his clergy out of secular affairs, and to that *Charles and the Church* end guaranteed to the Church an adequate income by making the payment of tithes obligatory.

But in spite of all his efforts he was often displeased at the conduct of his clergy, and in particular broke out in bitter reproof of their land-grabbing zeal. "What does renouncing the world mean, more than that the clergy do not fight and are not publicly married? Has that man relinquished the world who is daily laboring to increase his possessions in every manner and by every artifice, by sweet persuasions about the blessedness of heaven and by terrible threats about the punishments of hell, who uses the name of God or of some saint to bespoil simple and less learned folk, whether rich or poor, of their property, to deprive the lawful heirs of their inheritance, and thus to drive many through sheer destitution to a life of robbery and crime which they otherwise would never have embraced?" On the other hand, it was to this same clergy, whom he rebuked so bitterly for their worldly interests, that Charles turned to secure competent government officials, because he had nowhere else to turn. His policy, therefore, while it did produce some important results, was doomed—as is generally the case with the high intentions of rulers as expressed in legislation—to fall far short of its aim.

Charles's system of government was in the main a continuation of the Merovingian, with certain modifications intended to lighten the burden of the Frankish freeman and to centralize and improve the administration. The government was of course still that of an agricultural society; its economic basis was land—the king's land, no distinction being made at this early date between government revenue and the king's private income. The almost exhausted estates of the Merovingian kings were replenished by the family lands of the Carolingians, and the importance that was put on the administration of these lands is made clear by the elaborate instructions contained in Charles's Decree concerning Villas (*Capitulare de Villis*), given in the first year of his reign as sole king to the stewards of his many estates. Its seventy sections give a detailed picture of the time. "Each steward on each of our domains shall always have for the sake of ornament swans, peacocks, pheasants, ducks, pigeons, partridges and turtle doves. . . . For our women's work, they are to be given at the proper time . . . linen, wool, woad, vermilion, madder, wool-combs, teasels, soap, grease, vessels. . . . In each of our estates the chambers shall be provided with counterpanes, cushions, blankets, pillows, bedclothes, coverings for the tables and benches; vessels of brass, lead, iron and wood; andirons, chains, pot-hooks, adzes, axes,

Charles's government

Capitulare de Villis

angles, knives, and all other kinds of tools, so that it shall never be necessary to . . . borrow them from a neighbor." In only one section does Charlemagne mention fairs or markets; the bailiffs are enjoined to see that "our serfs do not wander off to visit markets and fairs." The inventory of one of his estates does not even mention money. Nearly everything necessary for living was locally produced. "Each steward shall make an annual account of all our income . . . of the pigs; of the forests, of the fields; of the bridges and boats; of vineyards . . . of the hay, firewood, torches, planks and other kinds of lumber . . . of the vegetables . . . of the wool, flax and hemp; of the fruits of the trees, of the nut trees, of the grafted trees; of the gardens, of the beets; of the fish-ponds; of hides, skins and horns; of honey, wax, fat, tallow, and soap; of mulberry wine, cooked wine, mead, vinegar, beer; of new and old grain; of hens and eggs; of geese; of the number of smiths and workers in metal, sword-makers and shoemakers; of bins and boxes and measures; of colts and fillies." The steward had a regular staff of officials under him: mayors, foresters, cellarers, toll collectors, masters of the serfs, and, as we might expect in a good German household, "masters who ought to make good beer." The detailed method of administration contained in the *Capitulare de Villis* became the standard system for the growing number of large estates in the empire.

By Charles's time the Roman system of taxation had completely *Services* fallen away, except for local survivals in private hands. The citizen no longer paid taxes to the state; he performed services for it instead. Hospitality had to be extended to the court, which was on the move most of the time, and to officials traveling on public business. For such few public works as were undertaken forced labor was used. But the chief services, and the most burdensome, were judicial and military. The old obligation still rested upon every Frankish freeman to attend the courts summoned by the count or his representatives. He was also obliged, when summoned by the count, to present himself fully armed and equipped for military service. Charles's constant campaigns, often into far removed regions, might well make such an obligation ruinous for the ordinary small farmer, and even constant attendance upon court sessions was onerous enough. It is therefore easy to understand why freemen on the verge of subsistence voluntarily gave up their freedom to become serfs, delegating their judicial and military obligations to others who could better afford to perform them. This condition Charles attempted to alleviate by legislation.

Courts in the counties for the consideration of the most serious crimes were limited to three a year, and courts for less serious crimes freemen were relieved from attending at all. In place of the Merovingian *rachimburgi,* who had been chosen from the attending freemen to pronounce upon the law, was set up a group of seven judges (*scabini*), chosen for life by the count from the more important people of the locality, to act as official assessors of punishment. Charles also provided that summons to military service should henceforth be made for specific regions rather than for the empire as a whole, and he made

military service dependent upon property ownership. Those owning, for example, three hides of land were obliged to come fully equipped. Freemen owning less land, or none, were to co-operate in small groups, according to a fixed plan, in equipping one of their number for military duty on the basis of a certain unit of land for one man. The very measures of relief, however, by helping to remove the ordinary freeman from participation in political affairs and encouraging him to turn over his functions to the wealthy landowner, actually tended to favor the shift of ever larger numbers of freemen into serfdom. For the man who had no status in court and did not fight was in fact hardly better than a serf. The continued development of the system of commendation, of granting benefices in return for military service, and of issuing privileges of immunity further reinforced this parallel growth of a noble fighting class and a servile peasant class.

Under Charles the laws of such German tribes as still had no written law were codified. Bavarian law had been codified between 744 and 748, and Charles added codes for the Frisians, Saxons, Angles, and Verini, and for the Chamavi, a subgroup of the Ripuarian Franks. Charles did nothing to disturb the old basis of German law; each group within the empire preserved its own law. Such law, however, made no provision for the immediate problems that arose in the formation of the empire, nor for the larger problems of administration. To take care of these Charles, as king and emperor, sometimes with the advice of small groups of nobles, issued his own special edicts or capitularies. No semblance of the participation of all freemen in deliberations and decisions, as in the old German assemblies, remained. Yet the constant legislation of the monarch on public policy created a body of public law that tended to offset the particularism of the tribal codes and to concentrate attention on matters of general importance.

The king continued to be represented throughout the realm by his personal appointees, the counts, who ordinarily held office for life.

The Carolingian count held the same large position in the county in judicial, military, and financial affairs as his Merovingian predecessor. Moreover, the system of counties was introduced into Italy, Bavaria, and Saxony. On the other hand, the office of duke, representing not local but tribal interests, was eliminated. So was the office of mayor of the palace, by which the Carolingians had risen to power. Within the county the count had as assistants vice-counts (viscounts) and hundred-men (*centenarii*) or vicars. Much more systematically than in the Merovingian epoch the counties were subdivided into hundreds or vicariates. For the new marches of the frontier a new official was created, a kind of military governor, the count of the march (German *Markgraf*, English margrave, French marquis), who combined with the duties of count, extended over a much larger area than the ordinary county, the duty of defending the frontier.

Charles had good reason to fear that the office of count, which was naturally filled from one of the strongest of the local families, might become hereditary, and the county become in fact the count's private jurisdiction. To supervise the counts and check their frequent abuses of power Charles created a new official, the *missus dominicus*, or royal messenger. The empire was divided into districts, each consisting of a number of counties, over which the *missi*, usually two, a layman and a bishop or abbot, made yearly circuits. They were intended also to serve as a direct link between the people and the emperor, to whom they submitted regular reports. In his *General Capitulary about the Missi*, of 802, Charles ordered them "to investigate and to report to him any inequality or injustice that might appear in the law as then constituted . . . to inquire diligently into every case where any man complained that he had been dealt with unjustly by anyone, and in the fear of God to render justice to all, to the holy churches of God, to the poor, to widows and orphans and to the whole people; . . . they are not to be hindered in the doing of justice by the flattery or bribery of anyone, by their partiality for their own friends or by the fear of powerful men." The *missi* held their own courts, and supervised the administration of the counts and their subordinates, of the bishops and abbots, and of the officers of the royal domain. They were even given the authority in extreme cases to remove for cause royal officials. They were protected by a triple wergild, and armed resistance to them was punishable by death. When loyal and honest the *missi* were an effective aid to efficient centralized administration. But from the beginning Charles feared that

The missi dominici

they too might become identified with local interests, and provided that their circuits be changed every year, to prevent collusion between *missi* and counts.

The extension of the system of counties and their more systematic subdivision, and the creation of two new classes of officials, margraves and *missi*, were the most important steps in Charles's attempt to reform the administration he inherited from his predecessors. He himself was constantly on the move during his long reign. Even while he was at home in Gaul, he was generally traveling from one royal estate to another, the itinerant court moving with him. His empire cannot even be said to have had a capital. His favorite residence, and the closest approach he ever made to a permanent one, was Aachen, located in the heart of the crown lands and near the natural hot springs that he loved. There still stands the palace church of which he was so proud, and there he was buried.

Einhard says of Charles: "He most zealously cultivated the liberal arts, held those who taught them in great esteem, and conferred great honours upon them. He took lessons in grammar of the deacon Peter of Pisa, at that time an aged man. Another deacon, Albin of Britain, surnamed Alcuin, a man of Saxon extraction, who was the greatest scholar of the day, was his teacher in other branches of learning." But Charles devoted to the intellectual life of his empire even

The Caro-lingian renaissance

more careful attention than to his own education. The result was a revival of interest in education and scholarship, literature and philosophy, so notable as to be called the Carolingian renaissance. If by the term "renaissance" we understood a return to the classical purity of the Latin language, after its neglect by such men as Gregory the Great and Gregory of Tours, and the writing of new works under the influence of the classical forms of prose and poetry, then we can indeed find here a renaissance of limited scope. To classical influence was also added the great influence of the Christian Latin Fathers, whose works now began to be more fully appreciated by western scholars. The great emphasis placed on education, the original work done in philosophy, the large amount of new poetry were certainly tokens of a genuine revival. It reached, in fact, beyond the limits of Charles's own reign far into the ninth century, despite the political chaos that followed his death.

Alcuin and the palace school

The center of the revival was the palace school, developed by Charles into an institution whose influence radiated into the monasteries of Gaul and Germany and even into the bishoprics. The school was attended not only by Charles himself, but by the children of

government officials and nobility, and by any promising children presented to Charles. The scholars who directed it, the men forming
the intellectual circle about Charles, were still for the most part
not Franks, but other Germans, and almost all churchmen. The
leader of the palace school and the most important figure in the
Carolingian renaissance was the Northumbrian Alcuin, who was
pupil and then teacher at the cathedral school of York, which succeeded Yarrow as the chief intellectual center of England. Charles
had invited Alcuin to court at Parma in 781, and henceforth, except
for short visits home, he remained at court until the last few years of
his life, which he spent as abbot of the famous monastery of St.
Martin at Tours. His textbooks, in the form of dialogues on grammar, spelling, rhetoric, and dialectics, were the standard of his time.
From Italy Charles brought the Lombard called Paul the Deacon,
whose *History of the Lombards* is of considerable importance, especially for its preservation of Lombard folk legends. From Italy came
also the grammarian Peter of Pisa, and Paulinus, later Patriarch of
Aquileia. From Spain came the Visigothic exile Theodulf, the outstanding poet of the court circle. There were also Charles's biographer Einhard, himself a product of the palace school, and the Frank
Angilbert, who as Abbot of St. Riquier later distinguished himself
as the collector of some two hundred manuscripts. These men formed
a congenial academic circle around Charles. They liked to call themselves by the names of classical writers or Biblical heroes (Charles
himself was David).

Theodulf in his poetry gives an intimate picture of the circle:
"Here we meet Alcuin, always surrounded by young men, for whom,
as well as for himself, he always replies as befits one clad in authority
and years, ever ready to speak on theology and to utter edifying
maxims, and withal showing himself a good trencherman. 'And father
Albinus [Alcuin] would sit, ever about to utter pious words and
freely to partake of food with lips and hand.' Einhard, little in stature,
but great in mind, bustles hither and thither, like an ant. . . . Over
all, unruffled in regal dignity, Charles presides, as he deals out huge
portions to his guests. . . . Nor must we forget that 'mountain of
flesh,' the peer of Falstaff, Knight Wibod, fuming at Theodulf's
poems and lumbering forward heavily when summoned to the
royal presence. 'Haply the large-limbed hero Wibod may hear this
and shake his fat head three or four times. And scowling he may
threaten with looks and voice, and overwhelm me in my absence with
his threats. If perchance the king's most gracious majesty should

summon him, he would go with bent and shaking knees. And his swollen belly would march before his chest, a Vulcan in his gait, a Jupiter in voice.' " [9]

One of the most noteworthy reforms of the Carolingian renaissance was the return to good texts. Jerome's Vulgate, for example, which had suffered many and various corruptions in Italy, Spain, Ireland, and England, was restored to the purity of the original text. Likewise the liturgy of the Church in Gaul had deviated from the correct Roman practice. With the co-operation of the papacy the standard liturgy for the Western Church, the Roman Missal, was given its present form during Charles's lifetime or immediately afterwards. He also sent to Monte Cassino for an authoritative copy of St. Benedict's rule, which became the only rule for all monasteries. Another standard text, a collection of homilies based upon the Fathers, he had Paul the Deacon make for the use of priests who were unable to prepare their own sermons. In the copying rooms (*scriptoria*) of the monasteries an important reform in handwriting was carried through. In the course of the Merovingian period the script of the earliest classical manuscripts, called uncial or majuscule, written in large or capital letters, had degenerated into a running script called cursive, which was almost illegible. The new Carolingian script, called minuscule, which used neat and elegant small letters, quickly replaced all others. It is found in most fine manuscripts, and it was to the Carolingian minuscule that the scholars of the Italian Renaissance returned.

It must not be supposed that the palace school of which we have spoken was the only school. In a letter to Baugulf, Abbot of Fulda, Charles writes as follows: "Instruction in the exercise of letters should be vouchsafed to those who with God's help are able to learn, each according to his capacity; . . . we exhort you not only not to neglect the study of letters but even with the most humble God-approved earnestness to vie in learning, so that you may prevail more easily and rightly in penetrating the mysteries of sacred literature." [10] In the monasteries and cathedrals schooling was available; and Theodulf, when Bishop of Orléans, ordered his parish priests to provide for schooling in the villages. Men trained under Alcuin were patrons of learning when they became abbots or bishops.

In the troublous times after Charlemagne's death schools inevitably suffered, but the scholarly activity started in the monasteries by the

Texts and manuscripts

Monastic schools and libraries

[9] M. C. W. Laistner, *Thought and Letters in Western Europe*, pp. 282–83.
[10] *Ibid.*, pp. 153–54.

Carolingian reform carried on in spite of everything. Large libraries were assembled in many monasteries, certain of which became centers for copying and distributing important manuscripts. Fulda, the foundation of Boniface, where Einhard was trained, preserved such treasures as Suetonius, Tacitus, Columella, and Ammianus Marcellinus. The incomplete catalogue of Lorsch lists six hundred volumes, and Bobbio by the tenth century had some six or seven hundred volumes. Reichenau, St. Gall, and Monte Cassino also had notably fine libraries. After the Carolingian period no important classical writers were lost, and it is mainly to manuscripts written in this period that classical scholars have to turn for good texts. The *scriptoria* of some cathedral churches, notably Cologne, shared in this preservation and dissemination of ancient literature and learning. The copying of a book was an important event. The Bishop of Regensburg wrote at the end of a manuscript: "I, Baturicus, Bishop at Ratisbon, in the name of God had this book copied for the salvation of my soul. It was written in seven days and revised on the eighth in the same place, in the seventh year of my episcopate and the year 823 of our Lord's Incarnation. Moreover, it was copied by Ellenhard and Dignus, while Hilduin supervised the correctness of the writing. Pray for us." [11]

Einhard's correspondent, Lupus, Abbot of Ferrières, is one of the most attractive of the literary abbots in the period immediately following Charlemagne. He was a very learned man and the writer of the best Latin since Bede, and he was an indefatigable collector of manuscripts. He wrote to all the important libraries, even to England *Lupus of* and to Rome, for manuscripts, either to compare with his own in *Ferrières* order to establish a better text or to fill in gaps in his library. He was extremely careful about letting manuscripts get out of his hands, for fear that they should not be returned or should be lost or stolen on the way. Active as he was in the political and ecclesiastical life of his day, he spared no effort to make his house a good place for study.

Among new works produced by Carolingian scholars were extensive commentaries on the Scriptures consisting of excerpts from the *Carolingian* Fathers, glossaries on Biblical texts—often bilingual, in Latin and the *scholarship* vernacular, a practice that may have been introduced by the mission of Boniface—and collections of extracts from classical writers, with pagan words and allusions suitably revised for Christian readers. Rabanus Maurus, Abbot of Fulda from 823 to 842 and later Archbishop of Mainz, wrote an encyclopedia, *De Rerum Naturis,* based

[11] *Ibid.*, p. 190.

largely on Isidore's *Etymologies,* which it supplanted in popularity. His career as scholar, abbot of the leading German monastery, and archbishop of the leading German see won for him the title of "first teacher of Germany."

Einhard's invaluable biography of Charles, so frequently quoted above, is the best biography of the period. For his model he took the Roman biographer of the Cæsars, Suetonius, from whom he borrowed his general arrangement and many words and phrases wherewith to clothe Charles in the dignity of the ancient Roman empire. Paul the Deacon's *History of the Lombards* has already been referred to. The chief historian for the thirty years following Charles's death is the emperor's illegitimate grandson, Nithard, one of the few laymen to write history during the whole period of the middle ages.

The many annals written in various monasteries supplement such special works. While they were naturally written from a local point of view, they were sometimes officially inspired from court, and any general history of the period must draw heavily upon them. Annals as a form of historical writing began to develop in Roman times out of the practice of making brief annotations on the margins of chronological tables. Hence came the practice of recording events by years, the marginalia being separated entirely from the tables and gradually assuming the form of a more or less connected narrative. The monastic annals in particular doubtless owed much also to the tables of dates for the celebration of Easter brought to the continent by Anglo-Saxon monks. Very few western Europeans at this time had any real knowledge of Greek, but where there is evidence of acquaintance with it, it is almost surely to be traced to some Irish scholar or Irish influence. For the emigration of Irishmen to the continent, driven out in some cases by the attacks of the Norsemen, continued until the end of the ninth century.

When not devoted to problems of education, Carolingian thought was primarily concerned with theological problems, of which two were of especial consequence. No scholar since the Council of Orange in 529 [12] had read Augustine thoroughly enough to question the *The doctrine* modification of his doctrine of predestination there made and con-
of predes- firmed by Gregory the Great. In the middle of the ninth century
tination Gottschalk, a Saxon educated at Fulda, after intensive study of Augustine revived his doctrine of predestination in all its rigorous purity: men were elected by God to be saved or to be damned, and they could do nothing about it. The resurrection of Augustine's doctrine

[12] See p. 199.

was so unwelcome to the Western Church that Gottschalk was condemned, unfrocked, beaten, and finally, it seems, sentenced to solitary confinement in a monastery, where he held to Augustine to the very end. Two of his contemporaries, monks of Corbie, Ratbertus and Ratrammus, became involved in a dispute as to whether the bread and wine consecrated during the ceremony of the Mass were transformed (transubstantiated) into the actual body and blood of Christ. Such had long been the common belief, but now for the first— *Transub-* though far from the last—time it became the subject of formal aca- *stantiation* demic dispute. Ratbertus held to the common faith in transubstantiation, though he did not actually use the term; while Ratrammus held that the bread and wine were no more than symbols of Christ's spiritual body, and that the sacrament was a symbolic act, not the actual eating of Christ's flesh and drinking of his blood. The dispute was isolated and had no immediate consequences, but in later centuries it continued to plague the Church.

The one original philosopher of the period was John the Scot, usually called Scotus Erigena, an Irishman who came to the con- *Scotus* tinent some time before 850 and died after 877; he was the friend *Erigena* of Charles's grandson, the Emperor Charles the Bald, who maintained a lively intellectual circle at his court. John was a learned man, one of the very few of his time who had a good command of Greek; he was well read in the Greek theologians, and knew at first hand one of Plato's dialogues, not to mention Boethius's translations of Aristotle. An important part of his own work was the translation of Greek philosophical tracts into Latin, especially the works of a writer erroneously called Dionysius the Areopagite because he was long supposed to be the man of that name converted by St. Paul at Athens.[13] The real author of these tracts, a Greek of the late fifth century whom we can only call Pseudo-Dionysius, was a thoroughgoing Neo-Platonic mystic, well acquainted with the writings of Plotinus and his successors. In his Latin translation Scotus Erigena made available for western scholars the most popular works of eastern mysticism, thus continuing Augustine's rôle of mediator between Neo-Platonism and Christianity.

Scotus Erigena's own system of philosophy, which he held to be identical with theology, was accordingly strongly influenced by Neo-Platonic mysticism. In his work *Concerning the Division of Nature* (*De Divisione Naturæ*), however, he did not simply piece together the opinions of older writers; he was himself a truly original thinker, the

[13] Acts xvii, 34.

only one between Boethius and the scholars of the late eleventh century. He traces the evolution of the present world of ideas and matter from the transcendent and remote abstract God of the Neo-Platonists and back again to mystical contemplation and union with that God, a vast evolution of the many out of the one and back into the one. His philosophy, while not developed essentially as a Christian system—for example, to him heaven and hell were contrasting states of mind rather than actual places—was nevertheless identified with the Christian scheme of salvation. Perhaps Scotus Erigena was most original in that, while recognizing the validity of authority in thought and accepting the authority of the Scriptures, he insisted upon the equal validity of reason, as he showed in his attack upon Gottschalk's revival of Augustine's doctrine of predestination. "Authority," he wrote, "sometimes proceeds from reason, but reason never from authority. For all authority which is not approved by true reason seems weak. But true reason, since it is established in its own strength, needs to be strengthened by the assent of no authority." [14] Again: "Do not be alarmed, for now we must follow reason which investigates the truth of things and, overpowered by no authority and in no way shackled, sets forth and proclaims openly what it has studiously examined and laboriously discovered." This was disagreeably close to heresy, and was abhorrent to the good Deacon of Lyons who attacked him for failing to cite authority from the Fathers, "as if daring to define with his own presumption what should be held and followed."

Carolingian poetry

Four large volumes of Latin poetry have survived from the Carolingian period, the reading of which to one scholar "is perhaps as if one's hand had reached out half unconsciously for a book of poems and had picked up a table of logarithms instead." [15] These poems, some of inordinate length, are for the most part studiously based on the verse of Virgil and Ovid, varying in subject matter from the military victories of Charles and expositions of Christian doctrine to descriptions of monastic life. It is all clerical verse and none of it poetry of a very high order, yet it contains many fine expressions of human feeling and of appreciation for the world of nature. Alcuin wrote of a departed student:

"I fear the dark sea breaks above his head,
    Caught in the whirlpool, dead beneath the waves.

[14] H. O. Taylor, *The Medieval Mind*, I, 231.
[15] P. S. Allen and H. M. Jones, *The Romanesque Lyric*, p. 214.

Sorrow for me, if that ill god of wine
    Hath drowned him deep where young things find their graves.

"But if he lives yet, surely he will come,
    Back to the kindly nest, from the fierce crows.
Cuckoo, what took you from the nesting place?
    But will he come again? That no man knows." [16]

The same Theodulf who described Charles's court in his verse had also a true appreciation of beauty, whether in natural scenery or in works of art. "He could lovingly describe a finely written or illuminated manuscript, a painting, or a plastic decoration, or in a couplet bring before our vision the essential features of a landscape." Alluding to a visit to the monastery of Lorsch, he says: "O martyr [the poem is written on the tomb of a saint], thou hast set thy lordly shrine in a wooded country region, and thy hall shines bright in an empty waste. . . . As in haste I came from the city of the Wangiones [Worms] and sought this spot, I saw the snow falling from a cloud. I crossed in a skiff from bank to bank of the fish-laden Rhine, that I might more swiftly reach the saint's house." [17]

Rabanus Maurus, the great Abbot of Fulda, wrote good verse himself, but his pupil Walafrid Strabo, later Abbot of Reichenau, *Walafrid* was a better poet. Walafrid is known for the dedication of a book *Strabo* on gardening to Grimold, Abbot of St. Gall, in which he pictures the abbot in his garden with his pupils,

"In the green darkness of the apple trees,
    Just where the peach tree casts its broken shade.
And they would gather you the shining fruit
With the soft down upon it; all your boys,
Your little laughing boys, your happy school,
And bring huge apples clasped in their two hands." [18]

As a pupil at Fulda, Walafrid was lonesome for his native Reichenau, and cold.

"Fool that I was, a scholar I would be,
    For learning's sake I left my own country,

[16] Helen Waddell, *Medieval Latin Lyrics* (1929), p. 79.
[17] Laistner, *op. cit.*, pp. 281, 328.
[18] Waddell, *op. cit.*, p. 115.

No luck have I and no man cares for me,
Exiled and strange.

" 'Tis bitter frost and I am poorly happed;
I cannot warm my hands, my feet are chapped;
My very face shudders when I go out
To brave the cold.

"Even in the house it is as cold as snow,
My frozen bed's no pleasure to me now,
I'm never warm enough in it to go
To quiet sleep." [19]

To a departed friend he writes:

"Now while the moonlight down pure air is shining,
Thou art perhaps beneath its glorious rays,
Under that white torch in the sky, divining
As in a glass thy friend of other days.

"Perhaps thou thinkest how its single splendor
Binds in one body our divided hearts.
Divided? Rather say by friendship tender
Bound with a bond of trust that never parts.

"And if thine eyes should still deny thee greeting
Of thy friend's form and face, at least believe,
To such as we have been, even light so fleeting
Is yet a pledge of love, and do not grieve.

"Thy faithful friend transmits to thee his verses;
As a fixed chain running 'twixt me and thee.
So may our love be, while my prayer rehearses
Hope that the years may treat thee tenderly." [20]

Gottschalk, whom Rabanus Maurus persecuted for his defense of predestination, also wrote a few verses of deep religious feeling, and, out of the depths of a weary heart, one moving poem to a young friend.

[19] *Ibid.*, p. 111.
[20] Allen and Jones, *op. cit.*, p. 150.

Sedulius Scotus was another Irish emigrant of the ninth century, *Sedulius* who taught at the episcopal school at Liége, wrote a book on gov- *Scotus* ernment, and wrote charming verse. "That he continually grumbles is only to be expected of a classical scholar and of his nation, and to do him justice he made his grumblings comical. He did not like the east wind, nor leaks in his roof, nor draughts; and . . . he did not like the local beer, which was, he said, a beast of prey in a philosopher's inwards. But he was as hearty in his gratitude as in his grumbling, and as sincere in his repentance as he was joyous in his sinning." [21] To his patron, Bishop Hartgar of Liége, he wrote:

"I am a writer, I, Musicus, Orpheus the second,
    And the ox that treads out the corn, and your well-wisher I;
I am your champion armed with the weapons of wisdom and logic.
    Muse, tell my lord bishop and father his servant is dry." [22]

At Angers the bibulous monk Adam was celebrated for his surpassing feats in wine-drinking:

"He'll sup   no cup   politely like another man;
He passes   mere glasses   for a larger drinking can,
He'll ask   a cask   and, lifting it gigantically,
He'll drink   and swink   surpassing mere mortality!" [23]

Einhard writes of Charles that "he also had the old rude songs that celebrated the deeds and wars of the ancient kings written out for transmission to posterity." Of these songs in German none have survived, and of the important German heroic poetry written during the period nothing remains except a few fragments, the most im- portant of which is the *Lay of Hildebrand* (*Hildebrandslied*), an *Vernacular* episode in the struggle between Odovacar and Theodoric. The *literature* *Savior* (*Heliand*), written in old Saxon, handles its Biblical subject matter in good old German fashion. "Jesus Himself has the char- acteristics of a Teutonic ruler; His disciples are nobly born . . . and are actually designated as 'bold warriors.' The setting of the Sermon on the Mount is such that it unmistakably recalls a heroic assembly, with the king addressing his faithful followers and sub- jects. . . . The marriage feast at Canaan . . . a cheerful carousal in the best heroic style." [24]

[21] Waddell, *op. cit.*, p. 320.
[22] *Ibid.*, p. 121.
[23] Allen and Jones, *op. cit.*, p. 239.
[24] Laistner, *op. cit.*, p. 315.

In the monasteries, notably at Fulda, Reichenau, and St. Gall, translations into the different German dialects were made of material designed to help in the work of conversion, such as the Lord's Prayer and formulas of confession of faith upon baptism. But no considerable translation of standard Christian classics was undertaken on the continent.

Alfred
the Great

In England, however, Alfred the Great (870–901), along with the tremendous task of defending England against the Danes, undertook to foster in this way the intellectual growth of his people. He himself contributed translations of Gregory the Great's *Pastoral Rule*, and somewhat freer translations of Orosius's *Seven Books against the Pagans*, some of Augustine's *Soliloquies*, and Boethius's *Consolation of Philosophy*. In his preface to Gregory's *Pastoral Rule* he says: ". . . it seems better to me . . . that we too turn some books which are most needful for all persons to know into the tongue which we can all understand; and that you act, as we very easily can with God's aid, if we have quiet, to the end that all the youth now in England of free men, who have the wealth to be able to apply themselves to it, be set to learning so long as they are of no use for anything else, until the time when they can read English writing well." [25] At the same time there were translated also Gregory the Great's *Dialogues* and Bede's *Ecclesiastical History*. In the last years of Alfred's reign, if not earlier, was begun the *Anglo-Saxon Chronicle*, "next to Bede the most important source for English history before the Norman Conquest." [26]

Around the great figure of Charles there quickly grew up a mass of legend. Before the end of the ninth century the monk Notker of St. Gall had already transformed him into something of a myth.

The Chanson
de Roland

In the *Chanson de Roland* he became the crusader against the Infidel. A veritable cycle of romance developed about him and his peers, as about Arthur and Alexander the Great. It is this development of the romantic figure of Charles in French vernacular literature that has given the French name Charlemagne to the very German Emperor Karl.

[25] *Ibid.*, p. 319.
[26] *Ibid.*, p. 317.

Chapter 10

THE COLLAPSE OF THE CAROLINGIAN EMPIRE

"THE steel of the heathen glistened." "A hundred and twenty ships of the Northmen ravaged all the country on both sides of the Seine and advanced to Paris without meeting any opposition." "The Saracens . . . slaughtered all the Christians whom they found outside the walls of Rome." "Michael, bishop of Regensburg . . . gathered his troops and joined the other Bavarian nobles in resisting an invasion of the Hungarians." "The cities are depopulated, the monasteries ruined and burned, the country reduced to solitude." "Every man does what seems good in his own eyes." "The strong oppress the weak; the world is full of violence against the poor and of the plunder of ecclesiastical goods." "Men devour one another like the fishes in the sea."

These are a few random glimpses of the Europe that followed upon Charles the Great. No sooner had western Europe apparently laid a new foundation for steady development than that foundation crumbled, and Europe had to begin all over again. Four hundred years of slow, confused evolution seemed to have led to nothing but chaos. Indeed, the parallel between the ninth and early tenth centuries and the later fourth and fifth is dishearteningly close.

With Charles's death in 814 began a period of almost two centuries of attacks from all sides by heathen Norsemen, heathen Magyars, and infidel Saracen pirates. Furthermore, fratricidal civil wars within the empire led to the complete breakdown of such central government as Charles had succeeded in organizing. All this postponed for centuries the cultural maturity of Europe. On the other hand, Europe had at least acquired sufficient strength to assimilate the Norse and Magyar invaders, who contributed to the European community not only new territory but new vigor and greater variety and a wider outlook. Economically and socially the ninth

The period after Charles the Great

263

and tenth centuries were a continuation of the feudal developments of the Merovingian epoch, which had been only temporarily and superficially checked by the Carolingians. Charles as Roman emperor and the Carolingian empire as the western Roman empire corresponded to no historical reality. The loose collection of German peoples that made up his empire could not possibly in so short a time abandon their own long and fiercely cherished traditions for what in Charles's successors was little more than the idea of empire. Europe had first to develop not as a unit but as a group of communities. To be sure, the ideal of unity never died; it could always be revivified by a strong man. But the only actual European unity was the unity of Christianity and the Church.

The early Norsemen

The appearance of Viking boats on all the shores and on most of the rivers of Europe threatened to give an even stronger Teutonic impress to the civilization of the west. The Danes, the Swedes, and the Norwegians, dwelling in the same Scandinavia where their descendants live today, were known as Norsemen or Northmen, or, in their double-prowed, brightly painted ships on the high seas, as Vikings. Racially they were Teutonic, but historically they must be sharply distinguished from the earlier Germans. Scandinavia was barely known to Europe before the ninth century, and then only vaguely, from the reports of a few adventurous traders or from an occasional piratical foray made by Norsemen upon the Frisian or English coast. They were still heathen barbarians, with the primitive Teutonic forms of government, society, and religion.

The dense forests of beech and oak that covered the Danish peninsula; the wide morasses, shallow, stony soil, and steep mountain ranges of Norway; the maze of lakes, swamps, and boulder-strewn uplands—remains of the great ice age—in Sweden, made these lands inhospitable except along the coast. Dwelling along the coves and bays or at the heads of the deep fiords that indent the coast, the Norsemen were not only adventurous and warlike, but had become a hardy seafaring and fisher folk, masters of the art of shipbuilding. With them war took the form of piracy, instead of raids by land. Moreover, while the Germans migrated as whole peoples through the Roman empire, the Vikings attacked in single bands under individual leaders. Finally, unlike the Germans, who had been in contact with Roman civilization and Christianity for centuries before they entered the Roman empire, they had dwelt for unknown time in complete isolation. Europe never had a chance to discover the Norsemen; the Norsemen discovered Europe.

The area of Norse expansion was immense, comparable in extent *The extent* to that of the Arabs. They practically surrounded Europe, and *of Norse* steered their small boats into the unknown waters of the Arctic Ocean *expansion* and the North Atlantic. They colonized the Orkney, Faroe, Hebrides, and Shetland islands, and the Isle of Man. They settled Iceland and discovered Greenland and North America. They established a kingdom in Dublin, which lasted until 1014, conquered part of England and northern France, and settled in Frisia. They invaded Spain, attacked Morocco, and raided ports of the Riviera and Italy. They penetrated Finland and the plains of northern Russia and sailed north around Scandinavia to the White Sea. They founded colonies at Novgorod and Kiev, reached the Caspian and the Black Seas, and furnished guardsmen for the Byzantine emperors in Constantinople. They came into contact with Eskimos and Lapps, with Greeks and Arabs; they made themselves equally at home in Iceland and in Sicily. Enormous quantities of English, Frankish, Byzantine, Arabic, and Egyptian coins, plate, and jewelry have been unearthed from Scandinavian graves.

The Swedes crossed the Baltic and forced their way through Russia to the Black Sea; this was the "eastern route." The Danes, although they made some settlements at the mouths of German rivers, mostly followed the coast down as far as Brittany and even beyond, or else crossed over to the opposite shore of England; theirs was the "middle passage." The Norwegians, with many Danes, for the most part followed the "outer passage" around the head of Scotland, where they brought the northern islands into their grasp and thence pushed on to Ireland, Iceland, and Greenland. The history of the Norsemen is scattered in miscellaneous sources in the many countries that they invaded and colonized and in their own sagas. Their enterprises were so widespread and their invasions lasted so long that nothing like a general account of them could have been attempted by any medieval historian. Even in England and France, which perhaps suffered most at their hands and were most affected by them, no sustained account of their inroads was ever written.

The traditional idea that the Norsemen were no more than *The Norsemen* marauders and pirates is erroneous. Actually they were eager also *as traders* for legitimate trade. They had commercial relations with the Frisians and Saxons before the Frankish conquest, which indeed the Norsemen took as a grievance because it interfered with their commerce with these two peoples. Norse merchants, however, were still bringing furs and ivory to Dorestadt in Frisia and Haddeby in Schleswig as late as the reign of Louis the Pious. When St. Ansgar went as a missionary to Sweden in 818 he traveled with merchants of Dorestadt to Birka (now Björkö), then an important Swedish port on an island near the later Stockholm, where he found "many rich merchants and a large amount of goods."

Political influences

But not even the necessity of feeding an expanding population, love of piracy, desire for trade, the ambition of younger sons to make a career for themselves suffice wholly to explain the great Viking expansion. Political events at home also stimulated it. As among the early Germans, chieftainship was followed by kingship, and the rise of a monarch led to the exodus of many a jarl too proud to submit to a stronger chieftain. In 872, in a fierce naval battle fought at Hafrsfiord, Harold Fairhaired subjugated all the rival jarls along the Norwegian coast and created an early Scandinavian state. The defeated jarls sought refuge in the northern islands. In Denmark and Sweden too the ninth century witnessed the beginnings of monarchy, under Gorm the Old in Denmark and Eric in Sweden. It is also possible that religious motives contributed at least to Danish depredations. The Frankish conquest of the Saxons, who in the last stages of their resistance were helped by their Danish fellow pagans, may have led the Danes to fear Charlemagne's vengeance. If so, their attacks upon Frankish territory were in some sense defensive, and their notorious spoliation of monasteries prompted by religious fanaticism as well as by simple avarice.

The Swedes in Russia

The Swedish Vikings who in the ninth century crossed the Baltic and worked up the rivers into the interior of Russia were probably called by the Slavs the "Rus," from the Finnish word for Swedes, *Ruotsi*. Russia was accordingly the land of the Swedes, and it is with these Swedish merchant-pirates that the recorded history of Russia begins. "Russia of the ninth century consisted of many important commercial cities, situated partly on the Dnieper and its tributaries, partly in the far north on Lake Ilmen, and partly in the east on the upper Volga. Each of these cities possessed a large territory populated by different Slavonic tribes and had its own self-government, with a popular assembly, a council of the eldest and elected magistrates. For the purpose of defending its flourishing trade the population of each town invited a special body of trained and well-armed warriors, commanded by a prince. To this prince each city intrusted also the task of collecting tribute from the population and of fulfilling some administrative and judicial duties. These princes with their retinues were called in Russia Varangians."

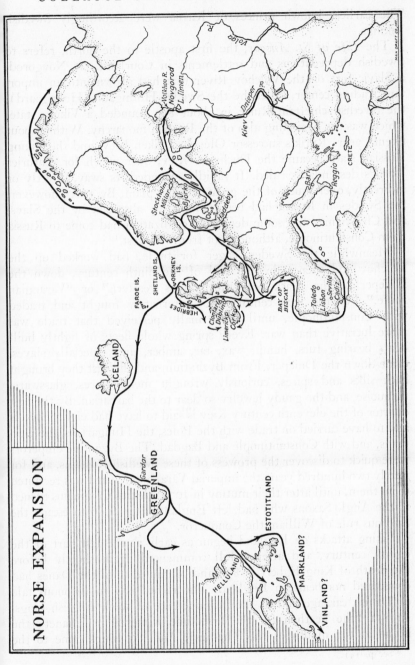

The earliest known princes of Russia were accordingly Swedish Vikings.

The *Life of St. Ansgar*, the first apostle to the north, refers to Swedish depredations and settlements in Courland. At Novgorod, a Slavic fort on the Volchov River that had grown into an important trading center, called by the Swedes Holmgadr (Holmgaard), the Swedish chieftain Rurik in about 862 founded a Viking state, which was the beginning also of the Russian monarchy. Within about twenty years Rurik's successor Olég had taken Kiev, and the Viking Russian state became the Duchy of Kiev, over which for centuries Rurik's descendants ruled. It rapidly extended its sway, directly or indirectly, over much of the great Russian plain. By 1000, however, the Swedes in Russia had been completely absorbed by the Slavs, and Christianity and some degree of civilization had come to Russia from Constantinople, although not from the west.[1]

Relations with Constantinople
Meanwhile the Swedes, eager for trade, had worked up the Volchov and thence, by the end of the ninth century, down the Dnieper to the Black Sea—the famous "eastern" or "Varangian route." For the next century they alternately fought and traded with Constantinople, until they finally perceived that trade was more lucrative than war. Every spring whole fleets of lightly built boats bearing furs, hemp, wax, tar, amber, and especially slaves, came down the Dnieper. From Byzantium and the east they brought back silks and spices, curiously wrought metal wares, glassware, turquoise, and the gaudy jewelry so dear to the barbarian. By the first quarter of the eleventh century Kiev is said to have had eight markets and to have carried on trade with the Poles, the Hungarians, the Germans, and with Constantinople and Bagdad. The Byzantine emperors were quick to discover the prowess of these Swedish Russians, and for nearly two hundred years the imperial Varangian Guard was recruited from them, until after their mutiny in 1079 Alexius Comnenus turned to the Anglo-Saxons who had left England after 1066 to escape the rigorous rule of William the Conqueror.

The Danes in England
Viking attacks on England began as early as the last part of the eighth century, and after a lull commenced again shortly before the death of King Egbert in 839 and continued until the Danes had conquered northeastern England. The record is a monotonous tale of Danish carnage and of the incompetence of weak English kings. In 851 "the heathen for the first time wintered in Thanet [the island at the mouth of the Thames]. And 350 ships came to the

[1] See p. 141.

mouth of the Thames and the crews landed and took Canterbury and London by storm, and then went into Surrey." Under Ethelred (866–71) the Danes took York, invaded Mercia, and passed the winter at Thetford. "The Danes got the victory," runs the record, "and slew the king and subdued all the land and destroyed all the churches and monasteries."

In 871 they invaded Wessex, the West-Saxon kingdom, where for the first time they met their match. England had found a *Alfred the* leader in Alfred the Great (871–900), who now, after the loss of *Great and* London, became the one hope of English independence. After long *the Danelaw* and hard years of dogged defense Alfred in 885 made an agreement with the Danish chieftain Guthrum by which he surrendered to the Danes a part of Northumbria and Mercia and East Anglia, exclusive of London—the larger part of England, in fact, which became known as the Danelaw. The Danes professed allegiance to Alfred and had no one king of their own, but they were none the less independent in fact. Constant accessions of other Danes driven from Denmark by the kings of Norway early in the tenth century strengthened the Danelaw, now ruled by a fierce military aristocracy. In the heart of the Danelaw the English were expelled entirely, and even agricultural labor became Danish. Although Guthrum had professed Christianity for himself and his people, it was a warlike civilization that was maintained in eastern England.

Nevertheless, Alfred the Great's heroic resistance had united the English people as the Church had never succeeded in doing, and his statesmanlike compromise with the Danes had saved the rest of England from conquest. Starting now where he left off, his successors proceeded to reconquer the Danelaw. As the English armies advanced northwards new burghs—forts which were also administrative centers—were erected, and in some cases they later became towns. The reconquest of the Danelaw was completed by Athelstan *Reconquest* (925–40), who even carried the offensive against a motley army *of the* of Scots, Irish, and Danes into southern Scotland, thus forestalling *Danelaw* a Danish reconquest from that quarter. Again an English king, Edgar the Peaceable (959–75), ruled over all England.

Yet the weak English monarchy was able neither to control an incipient feudalism in England nor to prevent a second Danish *The Danegeld* invasion. When this began in 980, led by the pagan Danish King Sven Forkedbeard, King Athelred began the practice of paying the Danes to stay away. The payments were called the Danegeld (*Geld*, German for money). The inevitable result was that henceforth the

Danes appeared regularly, and from 991 on the years alternated between frightful Danish attacks and the payment of the Danegeld. In 1016 a Danish king finally sat upon the English throne, Sven's great son Knut, the Canute of English legend, who reigned till 1035. Meanwhile Sven had conquered Norway as well as England, so that Knut was King of England and Norway and Denmark. England was thus cut loose from her continental moorings, and became part of a northern Scandinavian empire that had only recently been converted to Christianity. The Danegeld continued to be collected, being used now to hire Danish fleets for English service. London was the commercial capital of Knut's empire. "The shipping of London, anchored below the wooden town which clustered within its Roman walls, must have been a magnificent sight: 'small but entirely seaworthy vessels, manned by the best seamen in the world. . . . This Saxon and Danish shipping . . . lay here at London shore—bright with banner and shield and dragon-prow.' " [2] After the short reigns of two of Knut's sons the English throne reverted in 1042 to the house of Alfred the Great, in the person of Edward the Confessor, founder of Westminster Abbey. Even under him the Danegeld continued to be collected to 1051, but now only as a direct tax for the support of the crown.

The Norwegians in Ireland

The Norwegians, the "white pagans," first appeared in Ireland in 795, but their ravages did not become serious until 823. The chronic internecine strife of the Irish clans prevented any serious resistance, and the only wonder is that the whole island was not conquered. For the most part the invaders were content with establishing themselves in the bays and estuaries of the coast, as at Dublin, Limerick, Cork, Waterford, and Wexford. "There was not a point without a fleet." But they plundered the interior of the island, especially the monasteries, and damaged the whole monastic culture of Ireland. This provoked a new emigration of Irish monks, hundreds of fugitives fleeing to the monasteries of France, Flanders, and Germany—among them perhaps Sedulius Scotus and Scotus Erigena, who went to the continent at about this time.[3]

Just when the Irish were beginning to resist the Norwegians successfully, the "black pagans," the Danes, appeared in 852. Even though they were more formidable than their predecessors, they never succeeded in conquering the whole island. In the ensuing struggle between Norwegians and Danes the Norwegians maintained

[2] Chambers, *England Before the Norman Conquest*, p. xi.
[3] See pp. 257 and 261.

the superiority of their "kingdom" of Dublin. This was an important member, both politically and commercially, of the far-flung but never politically united Norse empire. After the heroic Irish chieftain Brian of Munster finally recaptured Dublin in 1014, the Vikings ceased to be formidable. But they were not driven from Ireland; they intermarried freely with the Celtic natives, and their contact with Irish literature bore results in the later development of Icelandic literature.

In following the "outer passage" the Norwegians conquered *The* and colonized the Orkney, Shetland, Faroe, and Hebrides islands *Norwegians* and the Isle of Man. Their attack on the west coast of Scotland *in Iceland* seriously weakened the power of the Picts. Whether they heard in Ireland of a great island lying far away in the North Atlantic—for it is certain that Irish monks had at least reached Iceland—or whether, as a saga relates, a Norwegian ship was driven there by a storm, at any rate the Norse came upon Iceland about the year 861. Colonization began in 874, when Ingolfr Arnarson was driven out of his homeland and settled there. Iceland then rapidly became a new Norway, organized, like the old Norway, as a federation of tiny villages nestling at the heads of the fiords or extending up the valleys. By the year 1000 Iceland had adopted Christianity. In 1930 it celebrated the thousandth anniversary of the first meeting of the Icelandic parliament. Here in the new home of hardy and stubborn refugees the traditions of the Viking chieftains, the stories of Norse gods and goddesses, in fact the whole moral and material civilization of the old Vikings, were preserved in Icelandic literature, in the prose and poetry of the Eddas, in the ballads of the scalds, and in the great prose epics called sagas. "It is indeed one of the miracles of history that this desolate island, settled by pirates and adventurers who revolted against the social restraint even of Viking Norway, should have produced a high culture and a literature which is of its kind the greatest in mediæval Europe." [4]

From Iceland the Norse pushed still farther west. According to the sagas an Icelander named Gunnbjörn was cast by storm upon one of the islands off the eastern coast of Greenland. His news of *Discovery* land farther west stirred Erik the Red in 986 to attempt to found *of Greenland* a colony in Greenland. His son Leif Erikson continued the effort, *and North* and then sailed on westward. Authorities dispute whether what *America* the Vikings called Vinland was Nova Scotia or Cape Cod or Rhode Island (Nova Scotia was probably known as Markland, Newfound-

---

[4] C. Dawson, *The Making of Europe*, p. 252.

land as Helluland, Cape Cod as Vinland), but there is little doubt that by the year 1000 the Norse had discovered and explored the northeast coast of North America. Greenland shortly became a prosperous colony, with settlers flocking in, mostly from Iceland but some also even from Norway. In 1126 the Bishopric of Gardar was established. The Greenlanders maintained a lively commerce with Norway, exporting fish and furs and whale oil.

The Vikings in western Europe

During the first half of the ninth century the forays of the Norsemen on the European continent were summer expeditions from which the marauders returned home in the autumn with their booty. By the middle of the century they had begun to winter abroad. For this purpose they always fortified a camp, preferably upon a conveniently located island, from which they raided the regions round about. For some years their depredations were confined to the coast; then, as military resistance to them proved ineffectual, they grew bolder and penetrated deeper and deeper into the interior. The seaboard, repeatedly plundered, became exhausted, and the local population fled for safety into the interior, followed by the invaders. The Norsemen invariably attacked the monasteries, which they discovered were rich in cattle, horses, and all sorts of portable stuff, especially coin, bullion, and plate. The final stage was reached when they began to settle in territory that they had once plundered.

The whole western fringe of Europe from Denmark to Gibraltar was curiously exposed to Viking raids by rivers. The Rhine opened up the valleys of the Meuse and the Moselle, and led to Cologne. The Somme led to Amiens, the Seine to Rouen and Paris. The Norsemen soon found their way around Brittany, and from there up the Loire to Tours and Orléans. After the first fierce visitation they left Frisia to itself, with its chief commercial center, Dorestadt, destroyed. Henceforth their principal centers were on the Scheldt, the lower Seine, and the Loire. From 840 on the annals are filled with their exploits.

In 843 for the first time they pushed up the Seine beyond Rouen; they attacked Paris in 845, 851, and 861. From the island of Noirmoutier in the estuary of the Loire they pillaged the rich abbeys of Touraine, notably St. Martin of Tours. In 853 they burned Nantes, at the mouth of the Loire. High water saved Tours from attack that year, but the monastery of Marmoutier across the river was entirely destroyed; one hundred and sixteen of its inmates were massacred and the abbot succumbed to torture rather than reveal the hiding-place of the abbey's treasure. Indeed, scarcely a monastery in western Europe near the coast or on a navigable river escaped the Vikings. They harried Aquitaine, and ascended the Garonne as far as Toulouse. Around 840 and again around 860 they invaded Spain; they attacked Lisbon, Cádiz, Toledo, Cordova, and Seville, and even took some captives in Morocco. On the second of these expeditions they plowed into the Mediterranean, plundered the Balearic Islands, visited Pisa and Luna in Italy, and attacked the southern coast of France. Here they established themselves at the mouth of the Rhone and pillaged as far up the river as Arles. At approximately the same time the Swedes were attacking Constantinople, which they had reached through Russia. The Vikings in their little boats had almost succeeded in surrounding Europe.

Political chaos within the Carolingian empire made impossible a successful defense of the land. The rebellious nobility refused to support the king against the Norsemen for fear of strengthening his power; they preferred, and likewise urged the king, to pay the Danegeld. Since they could collect more money as Danegeld from *Danegeld* their domains than they had to pay to the king's officials, it was also *in France* a profitable business for them. Between 845 and 926, twelve or thirteen general Danegelds were paid to the Vikings by the king, not to mention numerous local payments by the nobles. The total probably amounted to more than one hundred thousand pounds in silver. The Danegeld was in fact an extraordinary direct tax for the defense of the realm, levied on real property of noble and peasant, merchant and priest, and also, apparently, on income from landed property of merchants and clergy. Unlike the Danegeld in England, it was not collected after the Viking incursions had ceased, but it may well have tended to confirm the right of the lord to tax his peasantry with a *taille* whenever he saw fit to declare an emergency. The nobles also took advantage of the demand for coined money to exercise their right, whether legal or illegally assumed, of private mintage. For all this some compensation to public welfare was perhaps to be found in the fact that the large sums of coined money paid to the Norsemen stimulated trade, inasmuch as some of it had to be spent in France.

The effect of Harold Fairhaired's great victory in Norway in 872, in driving many of his defeated rivals to seek new homes in the northern islands, has already been seen. It had a like effect

Viking attacks
on France

elsewhere. By Alfred's Treaty of Wedmore with the Danes in 878 preceding his final peace of 885 [5] England was largely spared any further incursions. Guthrum's achievement in England, however, aroused the ambition of other chieftains to make similar conquests in France. In 879 the famous "grand army" entered the Scheldt and established quarters at Ghent, whence they ravaged Courtrai, Tournai, Cambrai, Arras, Amiens, the whole valley of the Somme, and Corbie and other monasteries. The next year they crossed the Somme and threatened Beauvais. The brilliant victory of Louis III of France at Saucourt in 881 checked them for a moment, but Flanders continued to suffer from Norse depredations until King Arnulf stormed and destroyed their encampment at Louvain in 891.

The Vikings had found it no less easy to penetrate Frisia by the Rhine and the Meuse; they got as far as Aachen and threatened Cologne. In 882 the Emperor Charles the Fat, when he might have captured their camp near Maestricht, resorted to negotiation. The Norse chieftain was granted Frisia as a German Danelaw, on condition that he become a Christian and recognize the overlordship of the German king, and two other chiefs received large gifts of money. "The humiliated army," says a contemporary, "was filled with shame to be under the command of such a prince." Far to the south Périgueux and Poitiers were sacked; the valley of the Garonne was again devastated, Bordeaux twice captured, and Toulouse looted.

The siege
of Paris

But the supreme object of attack was the valley of the Seine and Paris. In November 885, forty thousand Norsemen with seven hundred vessels laid siege to Paris. For ten months the people held out, under the leadership of Gozelin, Bishop of Paris, and Odo, Count of Paris. In September 886, Charles the Fat tardily arrived from Italy, only to conclude a wretched peace; the besiegers were paid seven hundred pounds of silver to abandon the siege of Paris, but were authorized to ravage Burgundy until March of the next year. After making Odo Duke of the Franks—that is, of so-called Francia—Charles the Fat after this single visit quitted France forever. Nevertheless, the failure of the Vikings after this long siege to take Paris arrested their progress, impaired their prestige, and raised Paris to a pre-eminent position. The Carolingian capital at Laon now had a rival, and from the counts of Paris the kings of France were destined to come.

While their failure to take Paris did not put an end to their raids, the Vikings were henceforth more interested in establishing

[5] See p. 269.

themselves permanently on French soil. As early as 885 it was obvious that the channel coast of France was to become a Norse dominion. They made Rouen their capital and continued to settle down. After the Norsemen had failed to capture Chartres in the summer of 911 they and Charles the Simple of France, who realized that there was no longer any hope of dislodging them from the channel coast, were ready to come to terms. Charles promptly concluded with their chieftain, Hrolf (Rollo), the peace of St.-Claire-sur-Epte. This treaty, similar to Alfred the Great's treaty with the Dane Guthrum, recognized what might be called the French Norselaw (Normandy), "the coastland from the river Epte to the boundaries of Brittany"; it also provided that Hrolf was to become a Christian and, as Duke of Normandy, a vassal of Charles the Simple for his duchy. This latter provision caused some trouble, for the chronicler reports that the new vassal Hrolf refused to bestow the required kiss upon his liege lord Charles's foot. " 'Never,' said he, 'will I bend my knees before anyone, nor will I kiss the foot of any Frank.' Moved, however, by their prayers he ordered one of his warriors to kiss the king's foot. The latter promptly seized the king's foot, carried it to his mouth and kissed it standing, thus throwing the king onto his back. At that there was a roar of laughter and a great disturbance amongst the spectators." [6] *The foundation of Normandy*

Officially the Norsemen gained a great deal of territory by the treaty, but as they had already practically dispossessed the old Frankish lords in the ceded territory, the treaty actually did little more than confirm an accomplished fact. Indeed, as the ceded territory had belonged to the Duchy of Francia, not to the crown lands, and as Hrolf became a vassal of Charles the Simple, the king did not even suffer any loss in power. Rather he had gained a powerful vassal to play off against another powerful and unruly vassal, the Count of Paris, and had barred Paris from the sea. The Frankish lords were thus the only real losers. For the common people the establishment of the Norsemen in Normandy meant simply a change of overlord. No more of the people were dispossessed, although those still remaining had already suffered so severely that they had little left to lose.

For the next twenty years Duke Hrolf made earnest efforts to encourage repopulation, reclaimed land, repaired monasteries, and built towns. The Norsemen were unpleasant invaders but good colonists. Wherever they settled, but especially in Russia, England, *The importance of the Normans*

[6] R. G. D. Laffan, *Select Documents of European History*, I, 14.

and France, they speedily adopted the language, manners, and institutions of the people among whom they settled. Within a hundred years after the grant of Normandy these Norsemen had become Norman-French, and fervent and staunch champions of Christianity. While in itself this was perhaps no more extraordinary than the accomplishment of the settlers of Iceland, in importance to the future of European civilization no Norse emigrants could rival the Normans. They retained much of their ancestral vigor. Within one hundred and fifty years after the settlement in France they had launched out again and established themselves in England and in southern Italy and Sicily, and a little later the crusades carried them to the eastern shores of the Mediterranean. They were destined to make out of Anglo-Saxon-Danish England a new England, and out of Byzantine-Moslem Sicily and southern Italy to bring to life a brilliant, cosmopolitan, tolerant civilization unparalleled in the west. Everywhere they went they carried their genius for government—they were the greatest governors since the Romans —and their surpassing ability as architects and builders. It is of their church building that Henry Adams says, "What they began, they completed." [7] But his statement applies equally well to all their undertakings.

The Christianization of Scandinavia

During all this time, and for over a century more, the three Scandinavian kingdoms of Sweden, Norway, and Denmark were taking shape. The Norwegian kingdom formed by Harold Fairhaired's defeat of his rivals in 872 did not hold together after his death, which was followed by a century of civil war. No more did the Danish-Norwegian empire of the Dane Sven, over which until 1035 his son Knut reigned in England; Norway and Denmark continued to fight for hegemony. Our chief interest in Scandinavia centers around its conquest by Christianity, which likewise proved to be a slow process. The first attempt to convert the Danes was made by Willibrord early in the eighth century. A century later Ebbo, who became Archbishop of Rheims, was a missionary in Jutland during his earlier years. St. Ansgar, the Archbishop of Hamburg and later Bishop of Bremen, labored in both Denmark and Sweden. Soon after his death Hamburg was joined to Bremen to form the Archbishopric of Hamburg-Bremen, the center of training for missionary work in Scandinavia. The Anglo-Saxon Church was also in the field, and was disposed to contest the primacy of the archbishops of Hamburg-Bremen.

[7] *Mont-Saint-Michel and Chartres* (1913), p. 52.

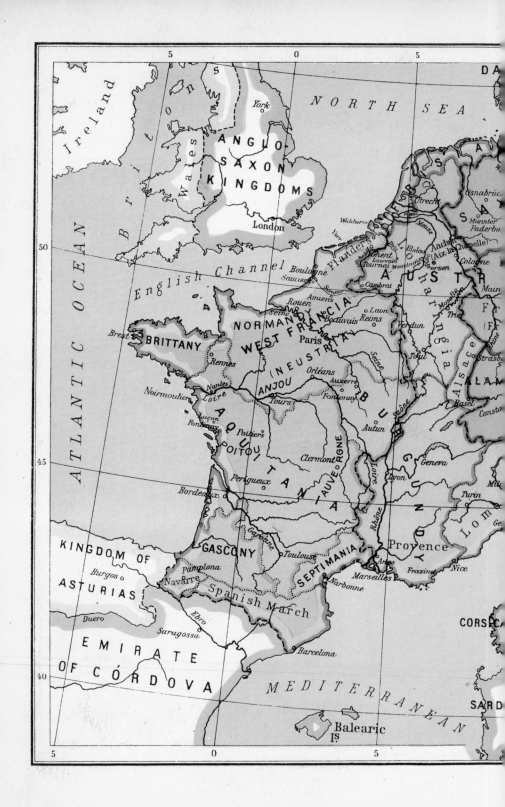

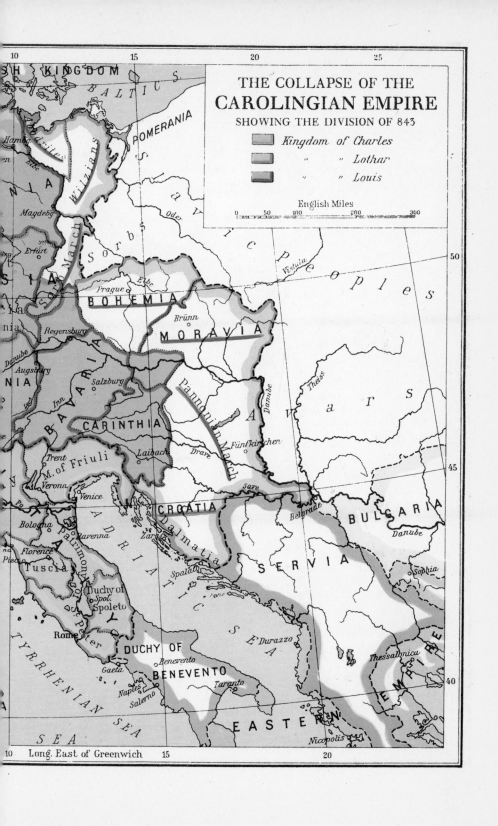

THE COLLAPSE OF THE
CAROLINGIAN EMPIRE
SHOWING THE DIVISION OF 843

Kingdom of Charles
  "   "   Lothar
  "   "   Louis

English Miles

0   50   100   200   300

Gorm the Old was the last pagan king of Denmark. His son Harold Bluetooth was baptized about 960. St. Olaf of Norway in the early eleventh century converted his people at the point of the sword. Not until the middle of the eleventh century did Christianity begin to take any kind of hold in Sweden. The paganism of the Norse, like that of the Saxons, and indeed like paganism everywhere, died hard; in fact it never wholly died, for, like other pagan divinities, the Norse gods survived in part in the cult of the saints.

As if the Vikings were not affliction enough for one century, *The Saracens* southern and eastern Europe were at the same time beset by Moslem pirates and Magyar horsemen. From the region of modern Tunis pirate subjects of the emirs of Kairwan began to attack Byzantine Sicily in 827, and within about fifty years converted the island into a Mohammedan stronghold. During the course of the occupation Moslems from Crete, North Africa, Spain, and the Balearic Islands joined with the Sicilian pirates in destroying the shipping of the western Mediterranean. They entrenched themselves like Vikings along the coast all the way from Fraxinet in Provence to Reggio and Bari in southern Italy. From their stronghold at Fraxinet they ravaged the Rhone valley, descended into western Lombardy, and even interfered with trade over the Alpine passes.

In 843 they plundered the very suburbs of Rome. The popes were hard put to it to organize resistance against them; at least one pope, Leo IV in 849, led his troops into battle against them. It was only gradually that the eastern empire was able to clear the Saracens out of southern Italy, thus preserving for a little longer the last Byzantine outpost in the west. Moslem forays continued to harass the region around Naples until their encampment on the river Garigliano was destroyed in 915. When in 972 Fraxinet was destroyed by the Christian magnates of the region, Moslem piracy was still more seriously crippled. But it continued until well into the eleventh century strong enough to close the western Mediterranean to commerce with the east and North Africa, until it was at last destroyed by the lusty young mercantile cities of Genoa and Pisa, which in their time had also suffered Moslem sacks. From Sicily the Byzantine empire could not dislodge the Saracens at all; they remained for two centuries, until the Normans drove them out.

At the western end of Lake Geneva Moslems from Fraxinet *The Magyars* had met and fought with Magyars from western Asia. The Magyars were Mongolian nomads, akin to the Finns, Bulgars, and Turks, and to the earlier Huns and Avars. They had followed in the wake of the Avars across the steppes of southern Russia, and occupied their territory in the plains of the middle Danube after Charles the Great had wiped the Avars out in this region. Thence in the late ninth century, at the moment when Norse attacks were beginning to let up in western Europe, the wild Magyar horsemen, armed with bow and arrow, began a series of fierce incursions into northern Italy and Provence, through all western Germany, and even across the Rhine into Lorraine.

It was the first two members of a new dynasty of Saxon kings in Germany who brought to an end sixty-five years of devastation, humiliation, and payment of tribute. Henry I, by defeating the Magyars in 933 on the Unstrut River in Saxony, saved Saxony and Thuringia from further attacks. In 955 his son Otto the Great, with the help of Udalrich, Bishop of Augsburg, drove them out of Germany for good in a great battle on the Lech River, not far from Augsburg. The Magyars withdrew to the territory of modern Hungary and ceased their raids on western Europe. From Germany, especially from Bavaria, Christian missionaries started out immediately. The first King of Hungary, St. Stephen, adopted Christianity, and as early as 1000 the first Hungarian bishopric was founded under the auspices of the pope. In an incredibly short time a new nation had been added to Europe. The Finns, Bulgars, and Magyars are the only people of Mongolian extraction who kept their foothold in Europe and became Europeans; and of these three by far the earliest, the most successful, and the most important were the Hungarians.

Disunion in the ninth century

If for almost two centuries after Charlemagne's death Europe could do no better than it did to defend itself against invasion, something must have happened to the strong central power that he had established. The fact is that by 886 there was no central power left at all. The empire had broken up into five separate kingdoms, and even in these the authority of the king was little more than nominal, each kingdom tending further to split up into half-independent duchies or counties. Within what had been the empire, therefore, the ninth century experienced the same conflict between the forces of unity and disunity, between centralization and localism, that had marked the seventh century. The earlier struggle had been won by the Carolingian mayors of the palace, but this time the local forces of disunion won a complete victory. The theocratic, monarchical power of Charles was shredded into bits by the government officials and local magnates whom he had strenuously and somewhat successfully attempted to control. His empire collapsed so rapidly after his death that we are forced to conclude that it was the strength of his personality alone that held it together while he lived.

Charles's successors were by no means simply the victims of circumstances. The Carolingian line tended to run out much as the Merovingian line had; in place of "the Hammer" and "the Great," the later Carolingians earned for themselves such epithets as "the Pious," "the Bald," "the Fat," "the Stammerer," "the Simple." Finally, the limits of Charles's own vision contributed to the debacle. In spite of what must certainly have been perceived to be the advantages of over a hundred years without any prolonged partition of the realm, even Charles—not to mention his son Louis—was unable to conceive of any better method of settlement than the disastrous old practice of dividing the realm among his sons. It was only the fortuitous death of his brother that enabled even Louis the Pious to succeed to the whole empire in 814. *Successors of Charles the Great*

That he was not of the stuff of his father was made clear early in his reign, when he permitted a papal election to be held in 816 without his having been consulted and in the same year submitted meekly to a second coronation by the new pope, although his father had had him crowned during his lifetime without benefit of clergy. Thus the precedent of December 25, 800, was confirmed: emperors must be crowned by popes. In the very next year Louis began, in morbid fear for his life, to provide for the succession: the empire was divided among his three sons, Lothair, Ludwig, and Pepin. But the idea of imperial unity, staunchly defended by the Church, was still strong enough to prevent a simple partition. The Roman principle of indivisibility found expression in the provision that Lothair, the eldest son, should receive the title of emperor and rule with his father over all the empire except Aquitaine and Bavaria, where his brothers were to reign as sub-kings, Ludwig in Bavaria and Pepin in Aquitaine.

The younger brothers chafed over this division of 817, but all three were reunited by the appearance in 823 of a new heir to the throne, Charles the Bald. He was the son of Louis's second wife, the beautiful Judith, daughter of Count Welf of Alemannia.[8] To make a place for his favorite son Louis had to cancel the partition

---

[8] The Welf dynasty is still preserved in the royal family of England.

of 817 and divide the kingdom among four heirs instead of three, which he did first in 829.

For the rest of his life he had no peace, being obliged to contend with the rebellion of the sons of his first wife, whom every new partition, enlarging Charles the Bald's inheritance, only made more furious. The sons were joined by malcontents among the nobles and in the Church, who were attracted by the hope of enlarging their holdings and breaking down the central authority. For a moment in 830 Louis lost his authority entirely; and when in a new rebellion in 833 his whole army deserted him, he was forced to abdicate. But Lothair's shameful treatment of his father brought about a revulsion of feeling, which restored Louis to the throne. Henceforth he managed to maintain himself to the end, though only by keeping up a constant fight with his sons. The situation was not much simplified by Pepin's death in 838, and still less by the death of Louis in 840 on an island in the Rhine, on the way to crush one more revolt.

Civil war

After Louis's death the brothers fell at once to fighting among themselves. The two younger brothers, Ludwig and Charles, allied against Lothair, who claimed the imperial title and was fighting to some extent for imperial unity, which won him the support and favor of the Church. The fratricidal struggle came to an early climax in a battle fought in the broad plain around Fontenay near Auxerre in June 841. "In this battle," says Nithard in his contemporary *History of the Wars of the Sons of Louis the Pious*, "every man fought to increase his domains." It was a huge cavalry engagement; Lothair rode into the fray standing erect in the saddle, the reins in his teeth, swinging his sword with telling effect.

"Hell laughed at broken trust, brother from brother torn,
 And war cried out upon the fearful battle fray;
 And brother brother killed, and kindred slew their kin,
 And fathers to their sons no mercy dared to pay.

.   .   .   .

The peasants call it Fontenay where fountains played,
 Fountains of blood that wrought the ruin of the Franks,
 And on those fields and woods and marshland horror stayed." [9]

[9] From Angilbert's contemporary poem on Fontenay, P. S. Allen and H. M. Jones, *The Romanesque Lyric*, p. 228.

The Battle of Fontenay ended slightly to the advantage of the younger brothers. Neither side was strong enough to renew hostilities. In the lull that followed Ludwig and Charles met at Strassburg in 842 and confirmed their alliance against Lothair by a famous oath. In it the personal ties binding fighter to leader and brother to brother took the place of any formal political tie between subject and king. Each noble in both armies swore as a vassal loyally to sustain his lord, "as became the honor of a noble." Then Ludwig took the following oath to Charles in front of Charles's men: "I will defend my brother Charles with my aid and in everything, as *The Strass-* one's duty is in right to defend one's brother, on condition that he *burg Oath* shall do as much for me, and I will make no agreement with my brother Lothair which shall, with my consent, be to the prejudice of my brother Charles." [10] Charles then repeated the oath in front of Ludwig's men. In order to be understood by Charles's men, Ludwig took his oath in the language they spoke, a dialect verging from Latin into French, and Charles for a similar reason took his oath in German. Of the two versions of the oath, fortunately preserved by Nithard, the one that is not German is of particular importance as the earliest extant specimen of a language that it seems more correct to call early French than late Latin. [11] The Latin of the Church, the only language common to all western Europe, was as yet known to few men outside the clergy.

After the Battle of Fontenay and the Strassburg Oath Lothair *The Treaty* had no hope of overcoming the strong combination of his brothers. *of Verdun* He therefore agreed, upon the intervention of the bishops, to negotiate a peace. The result was the Treaty of Verdun of 843, the first formal step in the dissolution of Charles's empire. By it the realm was divided into three parts. Lothair took the title of emperor and was granted a long, amorphous middle kingdom including Rome and the northern half of Italy. Its western boundary in general followed the Rhone, the Saône, and the Meuse from the Mediterranean almost to the North Sea, but turned west to include Aachen, Charles's favorite residence, and most of modern Belgium.

[10] *Cambridge Medieval History*, IV, 25–26.

[11] The student may be interested to know that when Ludwig swore, "I will make no agreement with my brother Lothair which shall, with my consent, be to the prejudice of my brother Charles," he said, "ab Ludher nul plaid nunquam prindrai, qui, meon vol, cist meon fradre Karle in damno sit"; and that when Charles repeated the oath in German, he said, "mit Ludheren in nohheiniu thing ne gegango, the, ninan uuillon, imo ce scudhan uuerdhen."

The eastern boundary followed the Rhine rather closely until the river turns west towards the North Sea, where it continued northeast to include modern Holland. Ludwig, called the German, took the rest of the empire to the east, the East-Frankish kingdom, and Charles the region to the west, the West-Frankish kingdom.

Although Lothair was emperor, Ludwig and Charles were none the less independent kings; yet their close relationship and the help and counsel they were to give to each other were supposed to preserve the community of empire. None of the boundaries corresponded to the linguistic boundary between the Romance-, or French-, speaking western part and the German-speaking eastern part of the empire. Obviously Lothair's conglomerate middle kingdom corresponded to no national frontiers, even had there been at this early date any "nations" in the modern sense—peoples with national self-consciousness, demanding to be enclosed within their own exclusive boundaries.

What the brothers seem to have done was first to estimate the resources of the empire in crown lands and in monasteries and bishoprics which made regular payments to the crown, and then, with consideration for geographical contiguity, to divide these imperial resources among themselves. This in itself goes far to explain the decline of the central power; a large body of crown lands, already depleted by grants to secure support, was now split into three parts, and the economic basis for a strong central power thus destroyed. Nevertheless the Treaty of Verdun marks the beginning of what the map of Europe was to become. The West-Frankish kingdom was the beginning of France, the East-Frankish kingdom of Germany; the middle kingdom was the beginning of little but trouble.

The prompt dissolution of Lothair's middle kingdom outside of Italy after his death in 855 did nothing but complicate the rivalry for political power within the limits of the Carolingian empire. His realm was divided among his three sons. Louis II got Italy and with it his father's title of emperor. Charles got the southern half of the middle kingdom outside of Italy, extending from Lake Geneva to the Mediterranean, the so-called Kingdom of Provence; Lothair II got the northern half, the area between the Scheldt and Meuse and the Rhine. This was called "Lotharii Regnum," or Lothair's Kingdom, which became in Latin Lotharingia, in German Lothringen, in French Lorraine. When Lothair II died in 869, his two uncles, Charles the Bald and Ludwig the German, rushed in to annex Lorraine, but compromised the next year in the Treaty of

Mersen, which assigned the territory of modern Holland to Ludwig, *The Treaty* that of modern Belgium to Charles, and divided Lorraine between *of Mersen* them.

The eastern half of Lorraine from the time of the barbarian migrations had been inhabited by Germans who never learned Latin, while the western half was inhabited by Franks who did. The eastern and western Frankish kingdoms now faced each other across a fateful border. Never since have the successors of Charles and Ludwig been content to have only one half of Lorraine. Ludwig's successors took the western, more French-speaking half in 879 and held it until 911, when Charles's successors recovered it, and appropriated with it the German eastern half. The Germans recovered the whole in 926. And from that day to this the fight has gone on along the west bank of the Rhine.

Ludwig the German divided his realm among three sons in 876, but after the death of two of them it was reunited in 882 under Charles the Fat, who also held Italy and the title of emperor. When, therefore, in 884 the nobles of the West-Frankish-kingdom passed over a young grandson of Charles the Bald and offered the realm to Charles the Fat, the whole empire of Charles the Great was for a short time reunited under his great-grandson. But to such a pass had the Carolingian line come that Charles the Fat's disgraceful bargaining with the Norsemen at the siege of Paris and his utter incapacity led to his being deposed in general disgust at an assembly at Tribur in 887. The nobles of France turned to elect as their king the hero of the siege of Paris, Count Odo of Paris. The Germans still stuck to the Carolingian line, and chose an illegimate nephew of Charles the Fat, Arnulf of Carinthia, who had won his spurs on the eastern frontier.

At the same time local magnates were establishing kingdoms of their own. As early as 879 Count Boso of Arles declared himself King of Burgundy, by which he meant the territory of Provence. In 888 one Rudolph, who had a dash of Carolingian blood in his *Further sub-* veins, count in the territory between the Jura Mountains and Lake *division of* Geneva, declared himself King of Upper, or Transjurane, Bur- *the empire* gundy. The imperial title sank so low as to be held by Duke Guido of Spoleto, head of one of two local dynasties struggling for the kingship of Italy. Such an emperor was not even known outside of Italy. On the other hand, although Arnulf secured the title in 891 and was recognized by the new kings, his position in Germany was so insecure that he promptly got out of Italy, which was left to independence, or anarchy. Thus in the space of two generations the mighty empire of Charles the Great had dissolved into five independent kingdoms. The epitaph of the Carolingian empire can be read in the lament of the poet Florus: "Once we had a king, now we have kinglets. Once there was an empire, now there are fragments called kingdoms."

Yet these new five kingdoms represent only part of the political dissolution that had taken place. Dukes, margraves, counts, viscounts, and imperial officials had by this time combined their lands and their offices into one hereditary dominion. The election of Arnulf of Carinthia as King of Germany, even though he was of Carolingian descent, marks the emergence of the strong man of the moment. The first dukes of the Franks and of Burgundy, the first counts of Paris, Anjou, and Flanders, are only a few of many examples of the new, self-made men of the inchoate feudal age.

The beginnings *of feudal* *principalities*   The real founder of the house of France and the remote ancestor of the Capetian kings was a hardy borderer called Robert the Strong, of uncertain lineage, whose lands in Neustria, centering about Paris, were continually raided by the Bretons. It was his son Odo who was elected King of France in 888. The earliest Count of Anjou was a brave hunter named Torquatus, who dwelt in the tract of forest wedged in between the lower Loire and the angle of Brittany, a region then harried by the Norsemen. Baldwin, the first Count of Flanders, a man of obscure lineage but great prowess, acquired popularity and power there by protecting the lower classes against the exploitation of the great abbots, as well as by defending the land against the Norsemen. In Germany the dukes of Saxony and Bavaria rose again to power, after having been put down by the Carolingians, by defending their people against Slavs and Hungarians. In Franconia and Alemannia, or Swabia, also tribal dukes arose.

"But disintegration did not stop there. The bishops and the greater immunists established their independence of the counts, and even the lesser proprietors, the vassals of the various grandees, exercised a free authority which was little trammelled by that of their overlords. In short, anarchy set in. The public authority, whether of king or count, was not quite in abeyance, but it was inefficient to check the private government and the endless private wars of the struggling atoms into which the empire had dissolved. The chief force making for order which was left was the tie of vassalage. This, although not yet crystallized into true feudalism, yet provided a framework and local centres around which the anarchic military, or knightly in later language, class of landowners grouped themselves, and unknowingly recreated the government of the state in a localized and particularist form. While the tie of the subject to the sovereign slipped gradually all but out of sight, and the tie of the royal vassals, who did not live at court, to the king, grew feebler and feebler, the tie of a vassal to his private lord, reinforced by local connection and economic and social dependence, grew stronger and became the main bond of society." [12]

The new local potentates were generally confirmed in their usurpation of public power by the mass of the population, the peasantry, who were, in view of the chronic state of barbarian attack and civil war, in crying need of protection that the king or emperor was powerless to give. If they did not approve of the new master, there was little they could do about it. The fortified strongholds of the new lords, at first wooden blockhouses surrounded by stockades, and only later stone castles, became the central point of administrative, economic, and social activity, as well as the one effective means of protection. The peasant was "no longer to be slaughtered, no longer to be led captive with his family, in herds, with his neck in a pitchfork. He ventures to plough and to sow and to rely upon his crops; in case of danger he knows that he can find an asylum for himself and for his grain and cattle in the circle of palisades at the base of the fortress. By degrees necessity establishes a tacit contract between the military chieftain of the donjon and the early settlers of the open country, and this becomes a recognized custom. They work for him, cultivate his ground, do his carting, pay him quittances, so much for house, so much per head for cattle, so much to inherit or to sell." As for "the vagabonds, the wretched, who in the universal disorder and devastation seek refuge under his guardianship, their condition is harder; the soil belongs to him, because without him it would be uninhabitable; if he assigns them a plot of ground, if he permits them merely to encamp on it, if he sets them to work or furnishes them with seeds, it is on conditions which he prescribes. They are to become his serfs. . . . People accordingly lived, or rather began to live, under the rude, iron-gloved hand which used them roughly but which afforded them protection. The seignior, sovereign and proprietor, maintains for himself under this double title the moors,

The early castle and the peasant

[12] C. W. Previté-Orton, *Outlines of Medieval History*, pp. 150–51.

the river, the forest, all the game; it is no great evil, since the country is nearly a desert, and he devotes his leisure to exterminating large wild beasts. He, alone possessing the resources, is the only one that is able to construct the mill, the oven, and the wine-press; to establish the ferry . . . or purchase a bull; and to indemnify himself he taxes for these or forces their use. If he is intelligent and a good manager of men, if he seeks to derive the greatest profit from his ground, he gradually relaxes, or allows to become relaxed, the meshes of the net in which his villeins and serfs work unprofitably because they are too tightly drawn. Habit, necessity, a voluntary or forced conformity, have their effect; seigniors, villeins, serfs, . . . in the end adapted to their condition, bound together by a common interest, form together a society, a veritable corporation. The seigniory, the county, the duchy becomes a patrimony, which is loved through a blind instinct and to which all are devoted." [13]

Bishops and kings

With the collapse of the institutions of the empire into the chaotic localism of feudalism, the Church evolved a conception of its importance as a unifying agency in the west and formulated a program for the realization of its largest ambitions. For the theocratic government of Charles the Great the Church was ready to substitute its own theocracy as the chief directing force in western society, with the great difference that now kings and emperors and all secular lords were to be governed by the Church instead, as Charles had conceived, of their directing the Church as an organ of the state. Among the Frankish clergy such a theory of government was formulated, chiefly by Hincmar, the learned Archbishop of Rheims. It is, he says, the evil prompting of the devil that suggests to kings that the ecclesiastical affairs of bishops are properly in their control. He told Charles the Bald in 868 that it is the bishops who by their consecration make kings, just as the popes make emperors. "It is rather through the spiritual unction and benediction of the bishops than from any earthly power that you hold the royal dignity. The bishops are superior in that they consecrate kings but cannot be consecrated by them." Nor were these idle words. When Charles the Bald was threatened with deposition by the Archbishop of Sens, he wrote: "From this consecration I ought to be deposed by none, at least not without the hearing and judgment of the bishops by whose ministry I have been consecrated king, for they are the Thrones of God, on whom God sits and by whom He passes judgment. To their paternal correction and chastising judgment I have always been ready to submit

[13] H. A. Taine, *Ancient Regime*, pp. 7–9.

and do at present submit myself." [14] In the West-Frankish kingdom the archbishops of Rheims were the chief mainstays of the later Carolingians, while in the East-Frankish kingdom such masterful prelates as Hatto of Mainz and Salomo of Constance virtually governed the state in the late ninth and early tenth centuries.

The Pseudo-Isidorian decretals

A far more important support for the theocratic claims of the Church than the pronouncements of bishops came in a series of decretals published in the middle of the ninth century, apparently in the neighborhood of Tours. The immediate occasion for their publication seems to have been the desire of certain Frankish bishops to escape the jurisdiction of officious archbishops like Hincmar, by establishing the right of appeal to the pope at Rome. The decretals therefore guarantee to the pope unqualified jurisdiction over the whole Church and limit the power of the archbishops, while at the same time strengthening that of the bishops. The pope was made the supreme arbiter of the Church and its only essential legislator. The archbishops were subjected to him, and their courts deprived of any exclusive original jurisdiction. No archbishop was to call a synod without the consent of Rome. But the decretals go much further than this attempt to break the power of the archbishops; they aim to free the bishops likewise from any control by the state. Cases involving them could be taken out of lay courts. Laymen were to be excluded from episcopal synods. Nor was even this enough. The power of the Church was declared to be above that of the state. "All the rulers of earth are bound to obey the bishop and to bow the neck before him." The state was an unholy thing, the Church holy, and such control as Charlemagne exercised over it was rank usurpation.[15] It would seem that practical conclusions were being drawn from the implications of Augustine's *City of God*.

The decretals contained also the forged Donation of Constantine. They were themselves in large part forged to represent the decretals of popes reigning before Constantine and the decisions of councils before his time, and were attributed to a fictitious canonist, Isidore Mercator. They were not proved to be a forgery until the fifteenth century. Meanwhile they became part of the canon law of the Church, and were a tremendous aid to the popes in pushing their claims to spiritual and temporal supremacy. To subsequent popes like Gregory VII and Innocent III their program was a veritable gospel, which came near being realized.

[14] *Cambridge Medieval History*, III, 443 ff.; Dawson, *op. cit.*, p. 262.
[15] A. C. Flick, *Rise of the Medieval Church* (1909), pp. 337–38.

Even in the ninth century the Forged Decretals had able champions. Pope Gregory IV sharply reprimanded certain bishops who neglected to hearken to his summons because of the orders of the emperor: "Why speak to me of the orders of the Emperor? Are not the orders of the Pope of equal weight? And is not authority over souls, which belongs to the Pope, above imperial rule which is of this world?" But it was Nicholas I, pope only from 858 to 867, who impressed himself most on contemporaries. "Since the days of Gregory I to our time sat no high priest on the throne of St. Peter to be compared to Nicholas. He tamed kings and tyrants and ruled the world like a sovereign." Nicholas was indeed the ideal pope of the Forged Decretals. He took it upon himself to decide who was to be Patriarch of Constantinople, forbidding the Byzantine emperor to interfere, with the remark that "the day of King-priests and Emperor-pontiffs is past." Kings and emperors were only ordinary Christians, amenable to the pope's authority, which was supreme because the See of Rome "confers upon the pope judiciary power over the whole church and the pope himself cannot be judged by anyone."

Nicholas was more than articulate. He forced Lothair II to bow to him in the matter of his divorced wife Theutberga, and in unparalleled fashion he deposed the bishops and archbishops who had helped Lothair get rid of her. He came into conflict also with the great Hincmar, who himself dictated to his own bishops and kings. Hincmar had ventured to discipline a bishop who had acted on his own authority in dismissing a criminal priest without consulting the archbishop. The bishop appealed over the archbishop's head to Nicholas I, who in spite of Hincmar's protests eagerly took up the case, declared the bishop innocent, and reinstated him, citing the Forged Decretals to prove his authority. Hincmar called these "a mouse trap to catch the archbishop," [16] and expressed his opinion of Nicholas's conduct: "A criminal was reinstated by the Pope, not by ordinary canonical rule, but by an arbitrary act of power, in a summary way, without inquiry and against the consent of his natural judges." Archbishops who controlled kings were themselves controlled by Nicholas I.

*The subjection
of the Church
to the new
feudalism*

The strong popes of the ninth century, who had managed to keep the shadowy imperial title within their grip, were succeeded by the creatures of the tenth century, who plunged the papacy into depths it had never reached before and was hardly to reach again. The papacy became first the plaything of rival factions within the papal *Curia* itself, and finally the tool of a local Roman family. Stephen III

[16] D. C. Munro and R. J. Sontag, *The Middle Ages* (1928), p. 145.

in 896 was a party to the extraordinary mock trial of his predecessor
Formosus, who was exhumed from his eight-months-old grave, dressed
in his pontifical vestments, and propped up on his throne for trial.
He was condemned, his robes were torn from him, the three fingers
with which he gave the papal blessing were chopped off, and his body
was thrown into the Tiber. For the first half of the tenth century
the popes were the lovers, the sons, the grandsons, the victims of
two women, Theodora and her daughter Marozia, members of a
family of the Roman aristocracy. What thus happened to the papacy
is in fact what was happening to archbishoprics, bishoprics, parishes,
and monasteries all over western Europe. They were all alike being
subjected to the new local lords whom the confusion of the ninth
century had brought to the surface; caught, that is, in the feudal
system. At the moment when the Church was proclaiming its independence of the state it was in fact being subjected, more than ever
before, to the masters of a new society.

Chapter 11

FEUDALISM

THOSE historical periods which appear on the surface to be most chaotic are usually found, when scrutinized more closely, to contain the germs of the reorganization that will remove the sources of disorder and decay. The terrific disorder and confusion of the ninth and tenth centuries were brought about in large part by the very forces that finally in some measure triumphed over them. The landed aristocracy and the public officials who sapped the strength of the central government themselves assumed the obligation of protecting Europe from barbarian attacks, and organized a system of economic, political, and social relationships that replaced both the discredited empire and the ineffective kingdoms into which it dissolved. This new system was feudalism. The ninth and tenth centuries therefore witnessed not only the destruction of the empire of Charles the Great but also the creation of a substitute for it. The period roughly bounded by the dates 800 and 1300 is properly the feudal age, an intermediary age between the last attempt at European empire and the rise of the national monarchies of western Europe.

Feudalism replaces empire

Feudalism was primarily a system of government—the typical medieval system of government—whose chief characteristic was the exercise by large landowners of sovereign rights formerly exercised by the monarch; the inseparable association, in other words, of landownership with powers of government. In many cases the acquisition of sovereign rights by local landowners was an outright seizure of royal functions along with the income pertaining to them, a usurpation which weak monarchs were obliged either tacitly or in formal documentary grants to recognize. In other cases, since the kings were unable to set up and control an efficient administration themselves, they were obliged to resort to the next best expedient, by entrusting political rights to private individuals who were able and anxious to exercise them. In still other cases the need for some kind of assumption of political authority arose

Feudalism as private government

locally in the demand for protection against outside attack, whether from Norse or Magyar or Saracen or Slav, or from unscrupulous land-owners anxious at all odds to take advantage of the general confusion to enlarge their own domains at the expense of others.

Whether, then, by illegal usurpation or by formal gift from the crown or because of local needs, monarchy as a type of centralized royal government was replaced by innumerable local governments. In many cases the new lords were the very persons who had formerly governed their localities as officials of the king: the dukes, counts and viscounts, margraves, *missi dominici*, who found it easy and necessary to continue to exercise their old authority in their new capacity. Government thus became a private affair; the prerogatives of office were owned as private property was owned and inherited as private property was inherited. In the old relationship between king and subjects the king's place was now taken by the local lord. The unit of government was no longer the kingdom, divided into the smaller administrative units of duchies, counties, and marches, but the counties, duchies, and marches themselves.

With a particular piece of land went a particular official position; the two were inseparable, and were handed down together as the family in-heritance. According to the medieval view the landowner was the natural governor. This tradition has remained strong in all European landed aristocracies, and is especially characteristic of the British aris-tocracy, in which, not only in theory but in practice, political function to a considerable extent depends upon landownership and inheritance. Feudalism as a system of government may accordingly be defined as private assumption of public authority. If the reader finds it hard to understand how it could have arisen or how it operated, let him con-sider the history of the Boston & Maine Railroad in New Hampshire, or of the Southern Pacific in California; or the system that has pre-vailed in the bituminous coal fields of Pennsylvania and West Vir-ginia, for example, where the miner, carrying to his home, a house rented from the coal company, groceries bought in a store owned by the company, meets a policeman employed by the company.

Feudalism was, however, more than a system of private government; it was also the system of land tenure upon which that government was based. A man held and used land belonging to another man, by some kind of contract establishing a sort of perpetual lease. The holder of land was required as part of his contract to assist the lord in performing his duties of government. His chief obligations of this sort were to assist in the administration of justice by attending his lord's court and

Feudal land tenure

to assist him in his police functions of maintaining law and order by serving him as a soldier or by supplying him with soldiers. The latter obligation amounted to making of feudalism also a military system, the means by which landowners carried on their private wars.

Feudalism as systematized personal dependence

The third main feature of feudalism was the personal bond that governed the relationship between the lord who granted and the vassal who received land. The governing landowners of feudal society entered into a network of mutual relationships with one another, based upon definite agreements which involved one man's becoming "the man" of his more powerful, or even in some cases less powerful, neighbor, surrendering himself into his service and throwing himself upon his protection. Entering into a state of vassalage involved no loss of social prestige; the lords and vassals belonged to the same class of landed nobility, most lords were also vassals, and the greatest lord was still, at least in theory, the king's vassal.[1] The definite mutual obligations involved in the relationship of lord and vassal were cemented by a ceremonial oath of loyalty sworn by the vassal to the lord. Feudal government and feudal tenure of land thus came to rest, at least in theory, upon loyalty not to the state but to an individual.

Fusion of elements in feudalism

Feudalism as a whole was accordingly a combination of private government, a particular system of landholding, and personal dependence, the last two entailing also a military system. In its more general aspects it came to connote, too, the whole manner of life of the aristocracy, regulated in theory by the knightly code of chivalry. Finally, when the code of chivalry was espoused by the Church and entrance into knighthood partook of the character of a Christian sacrament, the life of the knight became a specialized type of Christian life and feudalism an aspect of medieval Christianity. Feudalism is, therefore, one more embodiment of the truth that has been repeatedly emphasized in regard to western European civilization as a whole: it was a compound of Roman, Christian, and German elements, molded into a new form by contemporary conditions of life.

It has already been seen that certain features of the feudal system were present in western Europe as early as the late Roman empire; that certain others were present in primitive German society; and that when the Germans moved into the Roman world, similar institutions in each society tended to coalesce, or at least to borrow one from the other.[2] Already, too, something has been said of the general tendency towards

---

[1] It will be recalled that the Viking chieftain Hrolf became Duke of Normandy and the vassal of Charles the Simple for his duchy (see p. 275).

[2] See pp. 229–30.

feudalism in early western Europe, which the Carolingians were able to do no more than hold in check. Finally, in the century following Charlemagne's death we have seen it resume its growth with tremendous acceleration. Feudalism was therefore at least as long in taking shape as modern capitalism—fully five hundred years. We must now gather together the scattered references previously made to the forerunners of feudalism and to its early stages, in order to get a clearer picture of its origins and slow growth.

The sources of the element of personal dependence in the relationship of vassal to lord can be traced far back into late Roman and early German society. The ancient Roman institution of patronage (*patrocinium*), whereby the wealthy and influential man surrounded himself as patron (*patronus*) with a group of dependent followers, called clients (*clientes*), who sought his aid and support, was notably extended in the confusion of the later empire. A landless man, whether a casual free laborer or a small landowner who through foreclosure or confiscation for arrears of taxes had lost his land, would offer a local landed proprietor his services in return for shelter and support for his family. Such service might be labor on the lord's acres (in which case the man and his family and descendants would belong, together with the slaves and tenants (*coloni*), to a dependent class of peasants), or military service in the private militia maintained by many of the Roman senatorial nobility, or any other service that the client had to offer or his patron saw fit to demand. Moreover, weaker and smaller landowners sought the patronage of powerful neighbors "to escape the land-tax, gain a lawsuit, secure protection against an injustice, or obtain the means of perpetrating one." This was no more in principle than the now familiar case of men who are willing or obliged to perform various kinds of services in order to gain the support of those with influence.

The Celtic chieftains of Gaul had each a body of clients who lived upon his bounty, executed his orders in the rude clan government, and fought for him. The word *vassus* itself, from which "vassal" is derived, is Celtic in origin. The striking primitive German institution of personal dependence between warriors has already been described as the *comitatus*.[3] The particular feature of the *comitatus* that seems to have influenced the feudal relationship of vassal to lord was the ceremonial oath of personal allegiance to the head of the war band. It is plain that in both the Roman *patrocinium* and the German *comitatus* two features of the developed feudal system were present: the personal dependence

[3] See p. 70.

Patrocinium

of the weaker man on the stronger and the rendering of service, often military, in return for protection and support.

Feudal land tenure can also be traced back into later Roman society, where its chief antecedent was the *precarium*. Strictly speaking, the *precarium* was a grant of land by the owner to one who had made a formal request or prayer (*precarium*) to him for a piece of land to cultivate. In theory this grant was free of all cost to the petitioner. On the other hand, the grantor executed no formal deed, but retained title to the land, which he merely lent out for use and could recall at any time. This constituted precarious tenure, or, in the terminology of today, tenancy at will. But the theory did not correspond to the facts. The *precarium* was in practice a lease of land for rent, of which the owner assured himself by retaining the right to evict his tenant in case the rent were not paid. Ordinarily, if the rent was paid regularly, there was no difficulty in the tenant's retaining the use of the land, or even in handing it on to his children.

Precarious tenures were also established in ways other than a grant in response to a formal request. The small independent owner, harassed by debt, might find himself obliged by his creditor, or might find it convenient, to turn over to him the title to his land, retaining the use of it on payment of some kind of rent, but remaining subject in theory to eviction at any time by the new owner. Or again, a small owner, even if free of debt, might well in those troublous times feel the need of a powerful neighbor's protection, which he could purchase by surrendering title to his land and paying rent as a tenant. In all these cases there was no formal contract, and the occupant had no redress if the owner evicted him. Actually the tenant was reasonably safe from molestation, and eviction seldom occurred, for the proprietor increased his domain in some of these ways, or at least provided for more complete exploitation of land that he already owned by letting it out as *precaria* to new tenants.

The Church in the later Roman empire made special use of the *precarium*, either in the form of grants to specific requests or by the receipt of titles to lands to be occupied by the givers as *precaria*. To bring its own lands under cultivation the *precarium* proved especially useful, inasmuch as the canons of the Church forbade the complete alienation of Church property. Turning over the title to one's land to the Church and receiving it back as a *precarium* came to be looked upon, and was encouraged by the Church, as a meritorious and pious act, which assured the giver of the prayers of the Church.

Moreover, to encourage such transfers of titles both secular and

ecclesiastical lords, in return for the receipt of titles, enlarged the holdings of the giver by grants on precarious tenure out of their own lands.
This made the *precarium* of greater mutual advantage to lord and
tenant, the former enlarging the amount of property to which he held
title and from which he received rents, the latter enlarging the amount
of land that he actually occupied and used and thus increasing his income. The whole practice of *precarium* of course led inevitably to the
formation of larger estates. There was no necessary connection between
the personal dependence of the *patrocinium* and the dependent land
tenure of the *precarium,* but it is easy to see how the two might become
inseparable. When the holder of a *precarium* for any reason entered
into the personal service of his lord, thus becoming his client as well
as his tenant, then a long step had been taken towards actual feudalism.
In the early *comitatus,* before the Germans entered the empire, there
was no more question of land than in the Roman *patrocinium;* booty
was the reward of members of the war band.

The general drift of the common people towards a status of personal
dependence, whether or not based on land tenure, was naturally augmented during the period of the German invasions, when the Germans *Commendation*
were trying to adjust themselves to a new mode of life, and during the
civil wars of the sixth and seventh centuries, when the crying need of
the lower classes was for protection. The particular developments during the Merovingian period have been described elsewhere;[4] here we
need only study their relationship to earlier Roman practices. The
Roman *patrocinium* shaded into the practice of commendation, which
was also influenced by the old German *comitatus.* The kings assembled
their groups of antrustions and thanes, and the great landed magnates
their bodies of vassals and faithful men (*fideles*), as previously the
Roman patron had acquired his body of clients. Now the personal bond
tended more often to be cemented by the ceremonial act of homage,
probably Germanic in origin, which involved the promise of loyalty. *Homage*
As a result, it seems, of the intervention of the Church, which found the *and fealty*
ceremony of homage too important to do without religious sanction, it
became customary for the vassal to swear on the Scriptures or on saints'
relics an additional oath of fealty (a special term, derived from an old
French form of the Latin *fidelitas,* meaning specifically the feudal
fidelity of vassal to lord).

The *precarium* spread apace, chiefly through the agency of the
Church (the feminine form *precaria* was now the commoner name).
It came to be rather more specific in character, being granted, for ex- *The benefice*

[4] See pp. 229 ff.

ample, for a fixed term of years (usually five) or for the lifetime of the grantee or of his children. The natural urge to make tenancy no less hereditary than title, accordingly, was recognized in the *precaria*. But aside from the definition of the time limit the obligations of both parties remained a matter of custom rather than of any kind of law. Gradually the new term *precaria*, which had replaced *precarium*, was itself replaced in the course of the eighth century by another Latin term, *beneficium*. There was no difference between the later *precaria* and the benefice. Both were essentially leases of land for a definite period of time in return for rent or services; both could be revoked if the lord felt that the original terms of the grant had been violated. Actually, arbitrary action was at least to some extent restricted by custom, and in any case, in order to make his revocation good, the lord had to be in a position to use force on a recalcitrant vassal.

Vassalage and benefice

There was still no necessary connection between vassalage and the possession of a benefice. A vassal might or might not hold a benefice; if he did not, he was supported and sheltered at the lord's court. The holder of a benefice might or might not be a vassal. But certainly the connection between vassalage and benefice was much more frequent than that between *patrocinium* and *precarium* in the late Roman period. The benefice was about the only means of properly rewarding vassals and paying officials, but it could be used only by those very wealthy in land—kings, great nobles, and the Church. When the vassal got a benefice, the elements of personal dependence and dependent land tenure were definitely associated. When the Merovingian kings took for counts and dukes their own vassals, and paid them by giving them benefices, the additional element of public office entered clearly into the association. This practice, along with that of choosing officials from the local landed aristocracy, contributed to the gradual feudalization of public office—that is, to the inseparability of public office and landholding.

Into this fusion of various elements two more elements entered: first, the retention by landowners, both secular and ecclesiastical, of private jurisdiction over their peasants, which the German kings had not been able to break and indeed were obliged to recognize; second, the granting of immunities [5] to clergy and lay nobles by the kings themselves. The possible concurrence of these various elements would be exemplified by the case of a vassal made a count and given as salary a benefice carrying with it immunity; or by the case of a landowner who was made a duke and obliged to become a vassal for his duchy, and granted as salary a benefice carrying with it immunity; or by the

[5] See p. 232.

case of a bishop rewarded with a gift out of crown lands on beneficial
tenure and an immunity covering the new benefice and the lands of
his bishopric as well.

It was apparently during Charles Martel's government that military
service came to be more generally demanded of holders of benefices.
By this time military service as part of the client's obligation to his
patron or the vassal's to his lord was a long-established custom. It was *Benefice and*
the one occupation of the members of the *comitatus.* Nor was the custom *military*
of military service in return for a grant of land new in the eighth cen- *service*
tury. The Roman state had settled numerous Germans within the
empire and on the frontier as military colonists, and German tribes
were originally settled on Roman soil as *fœderati,* i.e., allies required
to render military service. The growing importance of the mounted,
mail-clad warrior, demonstrated by the necessities of defense against
mounted Mongolian nomads and the cavalry of the Saracens, made
the obligation of every German freeman to serve as a foot soldier seem
less important, inasmuch as the ordinary German freeman could not
be expected to assume the additional expense of service on horseback.

Granted the necessity of cavalry, the burden of war became so heavy
that only a landowner could perform military service for a government that provided neither equipment nor pay. To develop cavalry,
then, some kind of subsidy had to be found; and Charles Martel, confronted with the inadequacy of his own private lands for this purpose,
forced the Church to grant a large part of its lands as benefices to individuals who in return were to render military service on horseback
to the state. The gradual change from infantry to cavalry thus obliged
lay as well as ecclesiastical lords to grant benefices with the stipulation
of mounted service. The armies of the Carolingians ceased to be the
old *Landwehr,* the whole body of freemen, each under the leadership
of his own count, and became the body of wealthy landowners leading
their own mounted vassals into battle. Charles the Great's attempt
to permit small landowners to band together to equip one mounted
warrior has already been seen.[6] In time it became the general practice
in granting benefices to vassals for king or Church or nobles to require
mounted service. Military power thus became localized in the small
private armies of wealthy and powerful lords, lay or ecclesiastical, and
military service inseparably attached to vassalage and landholding, as
it had not been before. It was not long before the tradition was established that only a noble might fight on horseback. The new system also
brought into the ranks of the landed nobility a host of upstart adven-

[6] See p. 250.

turers, whose chief title to nobility, it has been remarked, was that they rode a noble beast, the horse.

The fate of the Carolingian monarchs depended upon their ability to keep all these feudal tendencies in check. In particular this required a strong hand on benefice-holders, to insure that the conditions of the original grants were fulfilled, or if not, that the benefices were recalled and granted to loyal men. The failure of beneficed landowners, for example, to perform their military service was punished by confiscation of their estates. It was necessary likewise to keep close watch on government officials, to see to it that they acted on behalf of the state and not in their own interests. Above all, the tendency to hand down benefice and office together in the family had to be checked when it threatened the power of the state.

Benefices under the Carolingians

The strong Carolingian monarchs did these difficult things well. But even so they were fighting a losing battle. Through the capitularies of Charlemagne can be seen what was actually going on beneath the surface. Pepin the Short in 768 ordered that "whoever holds a benefice from us shall be careful and diligent in its management; otherwise he shall lose the benefice, but retain his own property." His son, however, had to order that "no man shall lay waste a benefice in order to improve his own property." Again, Charlemagne said: "We have heard that counts and other men who hold benefices from us have improved their own property at the expense of the benefices, and have made the serfs on the benefices labor on their own land, so that our benefices are waste and those dwelling on them in many places suffer great evils." The same magnates who were laying waste royal benefices because the king was too strong to please them were driving small landholders to the wall because they were weak. "Poor men complain that they are despoiled of their property, and they make this complaint equally against bishops and abbots and their agents and against counts and their subordinates." [7]

Capitulary of Kiersey

The situation in the ninth and tenth centuries, when under the weak Carolingians the complete collapse of the central government gave free rein to feudal tendencies, has already been described. In 847 Lothair, Ludwig, and Charles the Bald were constrained to decree that every freeman in their kingdoms must have a lord, that no man should leave his lord without good cause, and that except in extraordinary circumstances every freeman should follow his lord to war. In 877 in the Capitulary of Kiersey Charles the Bald recognized the

[7] These examples are taken from O. J. Thatcher and E. H. McNeal, *op. cit.*, pp. 357 ff.

hereditary principle by providing that a count should be succeeded by his son, thus signalizing the completion of the feudalization of public office. He further recognized the same principle with regard to bene-fices: "Similarly also shall this be done concerning our vassals. And we will and command that as well the bishops as the abbots and counts and any others of our faithful also shall study to preserve this toward their men." [8]

When every man had to have a lord, when every official was a land-owner, when offices and benefices were hereditary, the feudal system was at least in principle complete. At the same time a significant change in terminology took place. To denote the hereditary benefice the word *The fief* "fief" (*feudum*), of Germanic origin, was gradually substituted for the Roman word "benefice"; the fief, that is, was the benefice become hereditary. If now we note further that the royal figureheads of the ninth century began to bestow lavishly sovereign rights beyond those entailed by grants of immunity, such as rights to establish and regulate markets, to collect tolls, to coin money, and to exploit forests, it is plain to see how deeply the decentralized régime of feudalism was striking its roots.

In the ninth, tenth, and eleventh centuries the general prevalence of feudal conditions and the common character of the mutual obliga-tions between lords and vassals warrant the term "feudal system." And yet the system in feudalism should not be overemphasized. Feudalism *Diversity of* took root and developed most thoroughly in France, whence it spread *feudalism* into Germany and Italy. But feudalism in Germany or Italy was not quite the same thing as feudalism in France; perfect accuracy would require separate descriptions of the feudal systems of France and Ger-many and Italy. Furthermore, within these general regions local feudal practices varied greatly, and a thoroughgoing treatise would have to take account of these differences. Then, too, not all men nor all lands were brought under feudal ties; in France, Germany, and Italy there were landowners who were not vassals of any lord, whose lands—called allods—were not held as fiefs. Feudalism of a different form is to be found, not where it was the outgrowth of centuries of slow change, but in those regions to which it was later transplanted outright from western Europe, usually by the Normans, e. g., in England after 1066, in southern Italy and Sicily after the Norman conquest, and in Syria and Palestine after its conquest by the crusaders. It is also to be remembered that feudalism in practice was far different from feudalism as drawn up by lawyers in local codes, after centuries of existence. Here, how-

[8] *Translations and Reprints*, IV, no. 3, p. 14.

ever, we can attempt to describe only its more common features, without detailing local variations.

Feudal theory ❧   Although feudalism destroyed the power of monarchy, nevertheless in theory it saved a place for the king whose power it had destroyed. When all real political power was in local hands, it was mere feudal theory that made the king the ultimate fount of law and justice. When, too, political power rested on landownership, and when the kings as landowners were less powerful than other nobles in their kingdoms, it was only the emptiest kind of pretense to say that all land was held in fief from the king as chief lord. None the less, the kings were in feudal theory still the final source of all political rights and all land tenure. In fact, of course, they were only as powerful as personality, intelligence, lands, and vassals made them; in other words, they too were feudal lords, on the same plane as the whole nobility. On the other hand, feudal theory was more realistic in preserving, no matter how insignificant he was, the sacrosanct character of the king's person, which had been inherited from antiquity. It is an impressive fact that throughout the middle ages, certainly as disorderly a period as any in history, assassination was all but unknown. If now the kings should ever succeed in converting their theoretical powers into actual powers, then feudalism would be destroyed. Feudal theory, therefore, in its very fundamentals provided for the destruction of feudalism.

Subin-feudation   According to the explanation of later feudal lawyers, the king had parceled out his kingdom into fiefs, which were held from him by his vassals, the great lords, variously called princes, dukes, margraves, earls, or counts. These chief vassals of the crown in turn, by the practice of subinfeudation—that is, by dividing their fiefs into smaller fiefs and regranting them to vassals—acquired a group of vassals of their own. The vassals of the great vassals of the king were the king's own rear vassals (French, *arrière-vassaux*), i.e., vassals behind the king's vassal, who was their mesne lord, i.e., middle lord. Their fiefs, held in theory indirectly from the crown, were called rear fiefs (French, *arrière-fiefs*). The practice of subinfeudation went on logically through the lesser nobility—viscounts, barons, and castellans—until it ended with the knight who held a fief only large enough to support himself and enable him to fulfill his duties as a vassal. Except for the king, therefore, who held his kingdom of God, all the lords were in turn vassals of other lords; and except for the humble knight whose fief was indivisible, all vassals had vassals of their own. Although these various noble titles might indicate difference in prestige, they indicated no difference in social status. The duke and the baron were both nobles, each the peer of the other. In fact, it must again be emphasized, there was no complete and logical development of the feudal hierarchy; such logic as the outline appears to have on paper is the later logic of the legal mind. The feudal hierarchy was built up by force and by circumstance, by human weakness and human ingenuity. Great lords imposed themselves upon society and lesser lords had to find their places as best they could.

The vassal was bound to his lord first by the ceremony of homage and then by the oath of fealty, in themselves quite separate but both symbolic of his personal dependence. A local chronicler describes as follows vassals rendering homage and swearing fealty to the Count of Flanders in 1127. "First, they did their homage thus. The count asked if he was willing to become completely his man, and the other replied, 'I am willing'; and with clasped hands, surrounded by the hands of the count, they were bound together by a kiss. Secondly, he who had done homage gave his fealty to the representative of the count in these words: 'I promise on my faith that I will in future be faithful to Count William, and will observe my homage to him completely against all persons in good faith and without deceit'; and thirdly, he took his oath to this upon the relics of the saints." In some cases further security was demanded by both lord and vassal. After the Count of Champagne had rendered his homage to King Philip Augustus of France in 1198, certain of his vassals guaranteed that he would fulfill his duty as a vassal, and that, in case he did not and then failed to make amends within a month, they would surrender themselves to the king to be held as prisoners until he did make amends; and vassals of the king entered into a similar engagement to guarantee his performance of his duty as overlord. To make the bond doubly—or rather, triply—secure, king and count further agreed to permit their lands to fall under the interdict of the Church in case either failed in his duty. When personal oaths and even such guarantees as these failed, the only resort was to force.

The ceremony of homage and the oath of fealty

When, as often happened, a man held fiefs from several lords at the same time, he had to render homage and swear fealty to each. If, however, as also often happened, two of his lords chanced to be enemies, it was difficult for a vassal to be loyal to both. Such difficulties gave rise to distinctions between kinds of homages, the distinction, for example, between liege or pure homage and simple or ordinary homage. A vassal would choose one of his lords as his liege lord, to whom his obligations were more binding than to any other lord, and whom usually he was obligated to serve personally as his liege man. Since, however, it

Liege homage and simple homage

became customary to render several liege homages to as many lords, this distinction lost its usefulness; a vassal then had to resort to such expedients as serving his lords according to priority, determined by the date of his having become the vassal of each, or simply according to the importance of his various fiefs.

The situation that might arise is well illustrated by the predicament of John of Toul: "I, John of Toul, make known that I am the liege man of the Lady Beatrice, Countess of Troyes, and of her son Theobald, Count of Champagne, against every creature, living or dead, saving my allegiance to Lord Enjorand of Coucy, Lord John of Arcis, and the Count of Grandpré. If it should happen that the Count of Grandpré should be at war with the Countess and Count of Champagne in his own quarrel, I will aid the Count of Grandpré in my own person, and will send to the Count and the Countess of Champagne the knights whose service I owe to them for the fief which I hold of them. But if the Count of Grandpré shall make war on the Countess and the Count of Champagne on behalf of his friends and not in his own quarrel, I will aid in my own person the Countess and Count of Champagne, and will send one knight to the Count of Grandpré for the service which I owe him for the fief which I hold of him, but I will not go myself into the territory of the Count of Grandpré to make war on him." John thus gave himself a certain amount of leeway, but in each case made it possible for himself to be fighting against his own vassals, if not also against one of his lords. What he intended to do if Lord Enjorand of Coucy and Lord John of Arcis fell out with each other, or if either fell out with the Count of Champagne or the Count of Grandpré, we may well wonder.

Such complications betray the extreme irregularity of the feudal system in practice, and—along with broken vows and guarantees dishonored—also explain much of feudal warfare. Another typical example on a larger scale will be found in the accompanying map of the *Fiefs of the* fiefs of the same Count of Champagne. By various means—by conquest, *counts of* marriage, inheritance, or purchase—the counts had brought together *Champagne* a vast agglomeration of twenty-six fiefs. Nor was their territory a compact whole; the lands of the King of France divided it into two parts. The count was the king's vassal for most of his fiefs, but he was at the same time the vassal of eight other lords—one abbot, three bishops, two archbishops, the Duke of Burgundy, and the German emperor. From the regranting of these fiefs to his own vassals the Count of Champagne had due him around 1172 the military service of over two thousand knights. In view of the fact that many of his vassals were also

vassals of the same lords as he was, he inevitably met some of them as a
fellow vassal at the court of their common lord. Now a man who was
the vassal of nine lords and the lord of literally hundreds of vassals,
of whom he was in many cases not only lord but also fellow vassal,

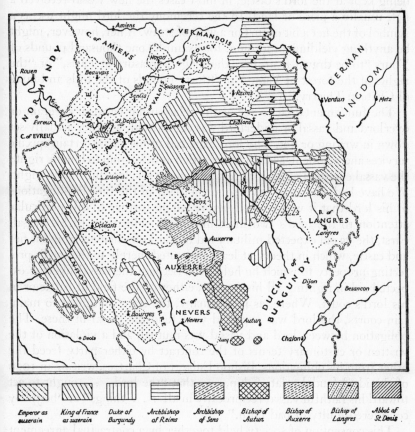

FIEFS AND SUZERAINS OF THE COUNTS OF CHAMPAGNE

would have to be a rare person indeed to keep clear of trouble. The
system that permitted, or even encouraged, such conflicting claims,
with the resulting friction of concurrent and rival jurisdictions, leading
to all sorts of legal and political entanglements, inevitably became so
complicated that it finally jammed and would no longer work. But
this was a long process.

"Afterward, with a little rod which the count held in his hand, he

Investiture

gave investitures to all who by this agreement had given their security and homage and accompanying oath." This was the final ceremony, the formal investiture of the new vassal with his fief. While in the developed feudal system not all vassals necessarily had fiefs, some being kept at the lord's castle, in most cases the new vassal received a fief, usually a piece of land. In the ceremony the lord might use as a symbol of the fief a bit of turf or a wisp of straw. A fief, however, might be anything yielding an income: for example, one thousand pounds of Tours "to be drawn from his [the king's] treasury at Paris," or "the rights of the forest of Vassy," or "thirty pounds of the tolls and taxes of Château-Thierry."

Contractual nature of the feudal relationship

The fundamental character of the relationship between suzerain or overlord and vassal or underlord was contractual, whether actually set down in writing or not. The lord expected of his vassal certain specific services and payments, which he regarded as belonging to him by right; the vassal expected of his lord certain definite services due him by right. We have had, and shall have, so much to say of the vassal's obligations to his lord that it will be well before we go further to call particular attention to the lord's two most important obligations to his vassal.

The lord's obligation to the vassal

First, the vassal expected military aid to ward off enemies from his fief and castle, which in theory at least amounted merely to the lord's protecting property to which he held title. Second, the vassal likewise expected aid in righting all his wrongs, either on the field of battle or in his lord's court. Where, as in Germany, the state continued to maintain courts, the lord was expected to defend his vassal in these. The obligation between lord and vassal was mutual, and a violation of the written or customary terms of the contract by either party freed the other from his obligations. Bishop Fulbert of Chartres, writing in 1020 of the ideal feudal relationship, says that "the lord . . . ought to act toward his faithful vassal reciprocally in all . . . things" or "be justly considered guilty of bad faith." [9]

This conception of society held together by a contractual agreement between lord and vassal did not die with feudalism. When monarchy succeeded in destroying the feudal system, the idea of a contract was transferred to the relationship between the king and his subjects and this became the basis for revolutionary theory, and finally for revolution in fact. It was argued that, in view of the contractual nature inherent in the state, once king or prince had failed to live up to the terms of his contract with his subjects it was their right and duty to revolt and set up a new government. The theory was used to justify

[9] *Ibid.*, pp. 23–24.

papal deposition of kings.[10] It was used by sixteenth-century political theorists to protect Protestant minorities from tyrannical princes and kings. It was used by the Englishman John Locke to justify the Glorious Revolution of 1688. It was an axiom of revolutionary political opinion in eighteenth-century France, being popularized by Rousseau. It played its part in forming a revolutionary sentiment among the American colonies. The origin of the United States, therefore, goes back to feudal principles of government.

Most fiefs were held on military tenure, which required the vassal to answer his lord's summons to battle, bringing with him the precise number of his own vassals called for by the contract under which he received his fief. As the lords often tried to keep their armies in the field during the whole spring and summer, by the twelfth century custom had limited a vassal's ordinary term of service to forty days. In later times military service was often compounded by a money payment, called in England scutage or shield money, wherewith mercenary soldiers could be hired. Feudal custom continued to restrict military service under the kings, even after they had regained much of their lost power, and so severely as to offer a great temptation to employ mercenary troops instead. In the thirteenth century the following regulations were promulgated by the French King Louis IX. "The towns and all vassals of the king are bound to appear before him when he shall summon them, and to serve at their own expense for forty days and nights, with as many knights as each one owes, and he is able to extract from them these services when he wishes and when he has need for them. And if the king wishes to keep them more than forty days at their own expense, they are not bound to remain if they do not wish it. And if the king wishes to keep them at his expense for the defence of the realm, they are bound to remain. And if the king wishes to lead them outside of the kingdom, they need not go unless they wish to, for they have already served their forty days and forty nights." Some fiefs required also a fixed amount of castle guard.

Military service

As an inheritance from the late Roman empire, when the state relied upon private citizens to furnish food and lodging to its officials on duty, the feudal lord enjoyed the right of entertainment, often called by its French name *droit de gîte*. When traveling through the fiefs of his vassals, he was entitled to food and lodging for himself and his whole escort. If the lord's train was large and if he traveled often, this might become a costly and intolerable burden for the vassal. In the course of time the *droit de gîte* was limited by custom, as to both frequency of

Droit de gîte

[10] See p. 386.

visits and number of escort entitled to entertainment, and lords—the
king included—when traveling were expected to live as far as possible
from their own manors, that is, manors not given out as fiefs.

Court service

The second of the vassal's chief civil obligations was to attend his
lord's court and assist in the administration of justice. No feudal lord
exercised his judicial functions alone; in the trial of a vassal his other
vassals sat with him as associate justices. It was a cardinal maxim of
feudal justice that no noble could be tried except by his peers, or fellow
vassals. If a vassal refused to answer the summons to court or to appear
for trial, the other vassals of the lord might be called upon to take the
field with him to enforce the summons or judgment. Under Louis VI
of France an entire court once rode to the fief of the recalcitrant lord,
and, seated on their horses in a circle around him, tried him then and
there.

Feudal aids

The vassal was also expected upon occasion to contribute money.
The payments were not looked upon in any sense as taxes; on the contrary, with the growth of a self-conscious nobility, which rendered
services regarded as noble, it came to be considered wholly incompatible
with its dignity to pay taxes (a reluctance not unknown in later times).
The payments were thought of rather as one more service, just as military service and court service were looked upon as forms of aid. They
varied in amount with the size of the fief and the importance of the
overlord, and varied also for different regions. They were meant to
help the lord in expensive emergencies, but their number and amount
were fixed by custom. The normal practice is represented in King
John's promise in Magna Carta: "No scutage or aid shall be exacted in our kingdom, unless by the common consent of the realm,
except for the ransom of our body, the knighting of our oldest son,
and the marriage of our oldest daughter; and these shall be levied at
reasonable rates." Special payments were sometimes made also to help
the lord meet the expense of a crusade.

Relief

There was, however, one more ordinary payment of money, so important as to have a separate name, the relief. This harked back to the
days when a benefice was not ordinarily hereditary, and was in theory
the price of the lord's consent, upon a vassal's death, to the inheritance
of his fief. Now that the fief was in fact, by custom and practice, hereditary, the relief was really an inheritance tax, besides being a formal
recognition by the son or heir that title to the fief remained in the lord's
hands. Relief was also paid by vassals when the lord was succeeded by
his son or heir. It was, finally, exacted also when a vassal sold his fief,
as the price of the lord's consent, which was required for such a trans-

fer; in this case, it amounted to a tax on transfer of real estate. The easy abuse of the relief made it one of the earliest feudal dues to be converted into a fixed money payment. The required sums, though not uniform, were always heavy, sometimes the entire revenue of the fief for a year.

Underneath the three forms of relief, for all their resemblance to certain modern taxes, lay one simple and consistent feudal theory. By the death of the lord or the death of the vassal or the disposal of a fief the vassal's tie of personal dependence upon his lord, expressed in homage and fealty, was broken, and new homage had to be rendered, new fealty sworn, to the old lord by the new vassal or by the old vassal to the new lord. Vassalage endured only for the lifetime of the original vassal and the original lord; upon the death of either it had to be renewed. Relief, therefore, meant the renewal of homage and fealty by the vassal and the reinvestiture of the fief by the lord.

Other rights of the lord were intended to protect his interest in the fief after the death of the vassal. In case the heir was a minor, the suzerain was usually the legal guardian; this was the right of wardship. *Wardship* He administered the fief until the heir reached his majority, meanwhile enjoying the income from it. Frequently enough, upon reaching his majority the new vassal found that his inheritance had been consumed by the lord. On the other hand, a vassal might console himself with the thought that, if his children should be left orphans, his lord would properly care for them. In the case of a minor heir or heiress it was to the lord's interest to see that the young vassal was married to a *Marriage* person who was not hostile to him, and who preferably might increase by inheritance the size of his fiefs.

It was equally important to the lord to see that the widow of a vassal married a suitable man. Later the right to control the marriage of a vassal's widow or children was customarily waived upon payment of a fee. English exchequer rolls contain entries illustrating both the exercise of the right and the acceptance of payments in lieu of it. "Thomas de Colville renders an account of 100 marks for having the custody of the sons of Roger Torpel and their land until they come of age." "Bartholomew de Muleton renders an account of 100 marks for having the custody of the land and heiress of Lambert of Ibtoft, and for marrying the wife of the same Lambert to whomsoever he wishes where she shall not be disparaged, and that he may be able to confer her [the heiress] upon whom he wishes." Robeisa de Doura paid the English exchequer for "license to marry where she wishes, so long as she does not marry herself to any of the enemies of the king." "Alice, Countess of Warwick, renders account of £1000 and 10 palfreys, to be allowed to remain a widow as long as she pleases and not to be forced to marry by the king." "Hawisa, the widow of William FitzRobert, renders account of 130 marks and 4 palfreys, that she may have peace from Peter of Borough, to whom the king has given permission to marry her, and that she may not be compelled to marry." Similarly, Mathilda, Countess of Nevers, promises the King of France that she will not marry "except by his will and grace." In case a vassal died without heirs, the fief reverted, or escheated, to the lord, to be regranted to a new vassal or disposed of as he should see fit.

Forfeiture

The contractual nature of the feudal relationship appears again in the lord's final prerogative, the right of forfeiture, i.e., the right to confiscate a fief for violation of contract. [11] This was balanced by the vassal's right to repudiate his lord for failure to furnish proper protection. Forfeiture of fief was the most severe penalty in the feudal code, and could be imposed only by a regular feudal court of the lord's vassals. It was the penalty, for example, for failure to answer a summons to court or to appear for trial. The decision of a feudal court forfeiting a fief and the actual loss of the fief, however, were two different things. The fief was actually lost only when the lord could command sufficient force to take it away; in other words, to make the forfeiture good the lord must be very strong or the vassal very weak. Repudiation of homage and fealty, on the other hand, depended solely on the vassal's own judgment of wrongs suffered; but, here again, the vassal who would repudiate his lord needed to possess no mean strength. The enforcement of all such decisions rested wholly on the use of force, and they were consequently responsible for much private feudal warfare. The confiscation in 1204 by King Philip Augustus of France of the French fiefs of King John of England and the Emperor Frederick Barbarossa's confiscation in 1181 of Saxony, the fief of Duke Henry the Lion, [12] are the most notable instances of large-scale confiscation in all medieval history.

The three estates

Society in the typical medieval form was composed of rigid social classes, called estates, each performing its own proper functions. The first estate was the clergy. The function of the second estate, the nobility, was government, including the defense of society. The third estate consisted of the rest of mankind, whose duty it was to labor, in order that the other two classes might properly perform their functions.

---

[11] The rights of wardship, marriage, escheat, and forfeiture are sometimes called the feudal incidents.

[12] See pp. 396 and 485.

ps in fields near Regensburg (See p. 334)

BETTMANN

German manor house with its outbuildings

four-ox plow for turning heavy soil

Romanesque royal palace at Goslar, dating from the eleventh century (See p. 374)

Frederick Barbarossa with his two sons, King Henry VI and Duke Frederick of Swabia (from a miniature, about 1180)

Feudalism was the system that regulated relationships among members of the second estate, or rather, inasmuch as many of the higher clergy were also lords and vassals, among members of the first and second estates. If it had not been tolerably well suited to the needs of the age, we may suppose that it would not have developed as it did. Feudal government functioned no more perfectly than any other system of government. Like every form of human government to date, it rested ultimately on force. Mutual obligations and services, sentiments of loyalty and honor, even religious sanction, were often mere high-sounding phrases. Ordinarily they did not suffice, in the absence of strong central government, to restrain the rampant individualism of the feudal lord.

War, always the greatest curse of all humanity, was the greatest curse of feudal society. To a particularly large extent feudal society was governed by private interests. Private interests were converted by the feudal system into private rights. If the system failed to protect the rights of a lord or a vassal, then the system itself guaranteed him the right to wage war to defend his rights. It is therefore quite true that to make private war for proper cause was a feudal right. One may go further and agree that "medieval wars are, as a rule, wars of rights; they are seldom wars of unprovoked, never wars of absolutely un-justifiable, aggression . . . they alleged a legal claim or a legal griev-ance, and in the majority of cases really legal claims and really legal grievances." [13] But how much is this distinction really worth? If one party was wholly or partly right, the other must have been wholly or partly wrong; it is hard to see how a feudal war could have been better than half right and half wrong. If one man fought to defend his mani-fest feudal right, some other man must have been willing to fight to make good a manifest violation of feudal justice. The truth seems to be that feudal institutions were weak at best. When they failed to secure what a man regarded as his right, he went to war if he dared. If a man was disposed to defy feudal right in his own interest, he also went to war if he dared. Feudal right was not unlike what is still called interna-tional law. At its best it controlled to some extent, at its worst it failed to control, the hostility latent between individuals, just as international law sometimes controls, sometimes fails to control, the hostility latent between nations.

The common ambition of the feudal lord was to increase the bounds of his authority by increasing the extent of his holdings, and especially

Right of private warfare

[13] Quoted from Stubbs by J. W. Thompson, *Economic and Social History of the Middle Ages*, p. 706.

to fill in and round out his holdings to form a compact territory. It was possible to accomplish both these aims peacefully by assuming new

obligations as a vassal to new lords, until the ambitions of rival lords or rival vassals clashed and broke out into war. Numerous wars were provoked also by the complications arising from the network of jurisdictions and the conflicting loyalties involved in a vassal's obligations to different lords. These local wars, sometimes fought by no more than a couple of dozen knights on either side, might amount to no more than family feuds, fierce enough, but not lasting beyond a summer's campaign. But a war might easily spread if lords began a quarrel, or if the lords of hostile nobles came to the support of their vassals. Even a pitched battle, so long as feudal cavalry still flourished, was a hand-to-hand conflict between small numbers of nobles, nothing like the scientific mass killings of modern warfare. The prevalence of private war in the middle ages has perhaps been exaggerated. It is sometimes difficult to distinguish between war and mere brigandage. It was the robber baron, not the feudal noble in private warfare, who waylaid merchants and pilgrims and extracted money from bishops and abbots. Genuine private war, when it did not look to the killing or capture of the enemy's army or the capture of his castle, sought to destroy his source of livelihood, the fields cultivated by his peasantry, if not indeed the peasantry itself. Although the peasants were not yet offered the privilege of serving in the army as infantry, none the less, like the common people of all ages, they bore the brunt of war and suffered most from its ravages.

For all this it would be wrong to say that feudalism was a failure. Arising spontaneously to meet the need of law and order in a disorderly

age, it served roughly the purposes of that rough age. As a kind of stopgap system of government it served likewise the purposes of the future, until such time as western society could be reorganized again by its kings and princes. Under its auspices slowly some order came out of anarchy, some justice out of force, some law out of custom, some honor out of fealty. It nourished a colorful, live, eager, intellectually curious civilization—a civilization, moreover, of great significance for the future, inasmuch as it contained many of the seeds of modern principles of liberty and modern democratic institutions. The feudal courts of kings and nobles developed trial by jury and such fundamental concepts of common law as the right to be deprived of neither life nor property without due process of law. The leeway provided by the feudal system for individual initiative and the large measure of freedom reserved to the individual, although confined to an aristocracy, did tend to emphasize the individual worth of at least a favored few. It seems strange, indeed, to speak of the later birth of individualism, in view of the immoderate individualism of feudal times. Feudal decentralization and localism brought forth a marvelous variety in western European civilization; and a good deal of the color that Europe still retains is due to this part of its history.

From feudalism two main lines of development were possible. Developing further along the line of its origin and its practice, it could result in the formation of numerous small sovereign territorial states. This, if not theoretically logical, was at any rate certainly a consistent *Developments* outcome, and this was the course it actually took in Germany. On the *from* other hand, feudalism could develop along the lines of its theory into *feudalism* absolute monarchy. Its confused and conflicting claims and jurisdictions offered the king, in theory still the lord of all lords and vassals alike, constant occasion to intervene, always to the advantage of the crown. Given enough time, enough strength, and enough intelligence, a succession of kings could create out of the feudal welter a national state belonging to and governed by the king. This is what happened in France. It is important to note that these two wholly different end products of feudalism have their most essential feature in common: in both alike feudal suzerainty was converted into independent sovereignty.

The chief architectural expression of feudal society was the castle, *The feudal* which, like feudalism itself, arose from the need for protection. Built *castle* on easily defensible hilltops, preferably behind the natural protection of a stream, or on artificial mounds surrounded by walls and moat, castles faced each other haughtily across the open countryside, each proclaiming the independence of its lord and his constant readiness to defend himself by force. "They throw up a little hill of earth as high as they can; they surround it by a fosse of considerable width and awful depth. On the inside edge of the fosse they set a palisade of squared logs of wood, closely bound together, which is as strong as a wall. If it is possible they strengthen this palisade by towers built at various points. On the top of the little hill they build a house, or rather a citadel whence a man can see on all sides. No one can reach its door except by a bridge, which, thrown across the fosse and resting on coupled pillars, starts from the lowest part of the fosse and gradually rises until it reaches the top of the little hill and the door of the house, from which the master can control the whole of it." [14] Such was the early "castle,"

---

[14] Quoted in Joan Evans, *Medieval France*, p. 43.

or timber blockhouse, of the ninth century. The rooms were narrow and dark, the windows were slits covered with glazed linen (window glass was unknown even in church architecture until comparatively late in the middle ages).

The early wooden blockhouse was gradually transformed by succeeding generations into the stone donjon or keep, a tower that was fortress and residence and storehouse all in one, piled up in successive stories like a diminutive skyscraper. In time new buildings were erected around the courtyard within the outside walls that protected the donjon; a private house for the lord's family, quarters for the household and for guests, a private chapel, stables, and storehouses. The donjon always remained as the indispensable fortress. Not until late in the twelfth century were engineers, stonecutters, and masons sufficiently skilled to attempt great stone buildings. Even then frequently only the lower courses were stone, surmounted by timbered or half-timbered upper stories. From then on into the thirteenth century the great castles were rising, like Château Gaillard, up the Seine from Rouen, which its builder, Richard I of England, boasted could be held even if its walls were made of butter; like Château Coucy, north of Paris, which lasted unharmed until it was destroyed by the Germans in 1917–18; or like—perhaps the most famous of all medieval castles —the Wartburg at Eisenach in Germany.

These gigantic structures, incorporating lessons learned by the crusaders from Byzantine fortifications, were really not castles but series of castles. The donjon was only the largest of several entrance towers, each with its own portcullis gate, drawbridge across an interior moat, and inner court. Around the whole castle ran a thick, high outer wall and a huge moat, difficult to cross whether dry or filled with water. Bastion towers at the angles of the wall and lesser towers between enabled defending archers to enfilade the outer wall with their arrows. The towers were often machicolated, that is, furnished with outside galleries supported by corbels, from which the defenders could beat off an enemy attempting to use scaling ladders or destroy his siege machines below, dropping down hot oil, molten lead, or rocks. The projecting battlement along the top of the wall protected the defenders while shooting and in moving from point to point. Here too there might be openings downward serving the same purpose as the machicolations of the tower.

Some of these castles were enormous, and contained within their walls veritable small communities. The walls might be from eight to twenty-five feet thick and enclose an area of fifteen acres.[15] Château Gaillard, and the great Krak des Chevaliers of the crusaders in Syria contained each as much masonry as the Great Pyramid. When in the thirteenth century the Byzantine principle of concentric fortresses (a series of fortresses actually built one within the other) was incorporated into the castles of the west, the main line of development in feudal architecture was over.

The castle was not the lord's only home, but it was the headquarters *Uses of the* of his fief, where he held court, audited the accounts of his tax collectors, *castle in* kept his records, and formally received important visitors. He had *peacetime* private quarters in the castle, of course, but frequently resided in one of his manor houses. In any case he had his own household and officials, chancellor, constable, seneschal, and butler. In the castle were the head-quarters of the provost, or bailiff, who administered the local affairs of the fief, in large fiefs under the supervision of the visiting seneschal. The lord's wife had to be a supervisor no less expert than the lord him-self, with a detailed knowledge of every aspect of the life of the fief, including agriculture. Ordinarily she had to keep running smoothly *The lord's* the domestic arrangements of the household, which involved the actual *wife* production of almost everything that was used, including presents of robes or chasubles for the clergy and cloths for the altar. In her lord's absence she had to manage the whole fief. If the castle was attacked, she directed the defense, and many a lord's wife mounted the walls in person. At a time when physicians were few and far between, she was doctor and nurse, and she was responsible for visiting the sick and poor among the tenantry of the fief.

Life in the castle underwent a gradual refinement in the course of *Life in* the middle ages in respect to food, dress, furnishings, and manners. To *the castle* us, however, with our overemphasis on material comfort, it must seem at best to have been rough and hard and uncomfortable, and painfully simple.

"Food was plentiful but of limited variety, and plain cooking pre-vailed until the Crusades brought in spices and condiments from the Levant." The usual vegetables were cabbages, turnips, carrots, onions, beans, and peas; the only plentiful fruits were apples and pears, though plums and cherries were not uncommon. Meat and fish were staple articles of diet. Milk in Europe is only now beginning to be regarded as a possible beverage; almost all milk was made into cheese, except

[15] The castle of the dukes of Bavaria at Burghausen runs atop the ridge of a hill for over two-thirds of a mile, and has six courtyards.

that reserved to make butter. Coffee and tea were unknown; the usual drinks were ale and wine. Vineyards, it is worth noting, extended much farther north in Europe—and still did only a century ago—than they now do. Olives were grown everywhere in the south. Fruit juices and honey were the only means of sweetening before the importation of sugar, which long remained a great luxury and was even used as a drug.

"Cooking was over charcoal or on a spit and with pots in the fireplace. The furniture was scant and primitive, plank tables on trestles, plank forms or settees, few chairs but rather stools, and many chests around the walls harboring clothing and bedding. Until the Crusades introduced rugs and tapestries floors and walls were bare and chilly. Rushes or willow wands or straw covered the floor in winter until it became so noisome from the filth of hunting dogs and the bones cast to them at meal time that the litter was removed. Woolen garments were universal, summer and winter; indeed, the interior of these castles was so drafty and so chilly that heavy clothing was necessary even in summer. Undergarments were introduced during the thirteenth century, again owing to the introduction of silk and cotton goods during the Crusades. But such material was expensive. Night garments were unknown. . . . The bed was high above the floor and hung with curtains to prevent drafts. Kings and queens were no better off in this particular than the richest of their subjects. . . . It is a popular error to believe that the upper classes were indifferent to cleanliness. . . . Every castle courtyard had a well and if possible running water was often introduced. Lead piping was used in the Middle Ages. As there were bath tubs, so there were latrines in the better castles." [16]

Amusements   There cannot have been much leisure in the medieval castle, certainly not for the women. There were guests to entertain, perhaps the lord with his suite, or the bishop making the rounds of his diocese, or an abbot en route to Rome. An itinerant merchant with his wares, a pilgrim with his tales of distant lands, strolling acrobats with perhaps a dancing bear, a minstrel with new songs afforded occasional diversion. When fairs became the fashion, the whole family might take a week off to attend one. When night fell the castle was all the more isolated on its wooded height. Eating and drinking in the main hall, especially when there were guests, were prolonged far into the night by the dim light of candles or burning rushes. Medieval folk were prodigious and inelegant eaters, washing down huge quantities of food with huge

[16] The quotations are from Thompson, *ibid.*, pp. 720–21.

quantities of wine.[17] Everybody cut his meat with his dagger and ate with his fingers. The use of forks, which seem to have been introduced from Constantinople in the eleventh century, spread from Venice over the rest of Italy and slowly through western Europe and England, but for a long time it was scorned as a finicky refinement. There were always backgammon and dice for amusement, though the Church frowned upon dice, because the players indulged in a lively and picturesque profanity that leaned heavily on the Virgin and the saints. And yet not all medieval nobles were merely hard-riding, hard-drinking, and hard-swearing gentry. Many of them came to be genuine patrons and cultivators of the arts, refined and cultured gentlemen, and still more of them acquired at least a thin veneer of culture.

Almost every medieval noble was an indefatigable hunter. When *Hunting* he was not in his lord's service in the field or at court, hunting was his chief pastime in all his daylight hours. If he went to visit neighbors or kinsmen, he expected to hunt. If he was at home, business had to be of the greatest importance to interfere with hunting. The medieval kings were hunting kings. The *Anglo-Saxon Chronicle* tells us that William the Conqueror "loved the tall deer as if he had been their father," and his son William Rufus was killed while hunting. The German Emperor Henry I got his surname the Fowler from the story that the envoys sent to inform him of his election found him hunting, and scared the birds away, to his great annoyance. Hunting was more than a sport: it was an art. Every noble must know how to kill, handle, and cut game. The time came when of all things he was perhaps proudest of his falcons, whose training, care, and use he studied and labored to perfect. But hunting was still more than a sport and an art. It was a cult, almost a religion, the special and cherished privilege of the nobility. The game and forest laws were burdensome and cruel to the peasantry; valuable land was specifically reserved for hunting, and the penalties for poaching were severe. All hunting rights belonged exclusively to the lord, including the right to set up warrens. Peasants complained in a manorial court that their wheat had been devoured "year by year by the rabbits of the Bishop of Chichester," or that one hundred acres of arable land

---

[17] Coulton (*Life in the Middle Ages*, III, 150–51) gives a menu for a bishop's installation banquet in 1478. Among the meats served were venison, rabbit, swan, pheasant, peacock, curlew, plover, lark, pike, carp, bream, perch, crayfish, and sturgeon. He refers also to a banquet of a prior of St. Augustine's Canterbury, in 1309 where 6000 guests ate "53 quarters of wheat, 58 quarters of malt, 11 tuns of wine, 36 oxen, 100 hogs, 200 little pigs, 200 sheep, 1000 geese, 873 capons, hens and pullets, 24 swans, 600 rabbits, 16 shields of brawn, 9600 eggs, with game, spice and almonds to the price of more than £1000 modern."

lay "annihilated by the destruction of the rabbits." The raising of destructive pigeons, prized both as food and for their manure, was likewise a monopoly of the lord; only he might put up a dovecote. These conditions, together with the whole feudal attitude towards hunting, persisted down to modern times in countries that passed through feudalism, perhaps most notably in England.

Armor   In the middle ages, as in our own, the cost of military preparedness was the heaviest item in the social economy. Even after the huge castles were finished, there remained the constant expense of maintaining the knight's personal military equipment. Every knight had to have his own charger, a horse strong enough to carry both its own armor and its heavily armored rider, several spare mounts for himself, and from three to ten other mounts for his esquires and hostlers, besides pack horses. The nobles were accordingly much interested in horse breeding, and imported many horses from Barbary and Byzantium. The lord's armor, another expensive part of his equipment, was at first only a shirt of mail reaching to the hips, and later to the knees, and a conical helmet having an extension called the nasal to protect his nose but leaving his face unprotected. Later complete sets of armor were made, with hoods, leggings, mittens, and gloves; underneath was worn the gambeson, a coat of leather or quilted cloth. Over the mail special plates were fastened for elbow and kneecap and shins. Over his armor the knight wore an embroidered cloak. The conical helmet was later rounded, and covered the head completely, with slits left only for seeing and breathing. An incidental result of this development of the helmet was the great development, from the middle of the twelfth century on, of armorial bearings, to identify the knights hidden beneath their armor.

As every modern improvement in projectiles or in armor plate forces improvements in the other, so the medieval armorer was constantly forced to improve his technique. When the crossbow came into use in the twelfth century, the knight began to wear a small iron plate over his chest, underneath or over his coat of mail. Finally, in the late thirteenth century skillfully jointed plate mail came in, with which both rider and horse were soon effectively protected against even the crossbow. The knight in full panoply of plate armor, however, is the knight of the fourteenth and fifteenth centuries. As further defense the knight carried a shield, oval or kite-shaped or triangular, which, as it became less and less necessary, gradually grew smaller. The standard weapon was the lance, but he also carried a sword, and for fighting at close quarters a dagger or poniard.

The crossbow was the most effective weapon of infantry at the height *Warfare* of the feudal period, though preceded by the pike of the Flemings and Brabanters. It was not a gentleman's weapon, but was employed by mercenaries, who, unlike feudal cavalry, could be used for distant and protracted campaigns, and were generally employed in the armies of the twelfth century. The crossbow might be mounted on the walls of a castle or carried by infantry in the field. Its missile was the quarrel, a sharpened iron bolt. When the bow of the weapon was made of steel, so strong that it had to be bent by a special contrivance, the moulinet, it was a terrible weapon. In 1139 the pope forbade its use except against the Infidel, but it remained in vogue nevertheless, especially among mercenaries. The favorite weapon of English foot soldiers from the thirteenth century on was always the long bow, with its gray goose-feathered arrows. There are many accounts of its astonishing accuracy; it could shoot very much faster than the crossbow, though not so far. It is the real hero of many English ballads, and the secret of the success of small English armies against the French throughout the fourteenth century.

The combined use of cavalry and infantry, tactics learned only after bitter experience, proved in time so effective that even before the discovery of gunpowder the knight in heavy armor was speedily becoming an anachronism. He survived, however, in tournaments into the fifteenth century. As if there were not enough actual war, the nobility eagerly took up the mock combat of the tournament, where parties of knights clashed, or the joust, where single knights tried to unseat each other. The imitation was in fact not so far from the real thing, and at least the early tournaments, which seem to have originated in France in the eleventh century, took their toll of maimed and killed. In time they became ceremonious affairs, hedged about with elaborate rules, and finally in the sixteenth century mere pageantry. Similarly, as armor became less useful it became more decorative. The art of the armorer reached splendid and amazing heights of delicate and beautiful workmanship, and his creations were worn on all ceremonial occasions not only by nobles and kings but by bishops and archbishops far into the sixteenth century.

The battering-ram, the catapult, the movable tower were the chief *Sieges* offensive weapons in sieges. They were essentially unchanged since Roman times, but until the crusaders saw them operated by the Byzantines they were not in general use in the west. After his visit to the Holy Land, Duke Henry the Lion of Saxony astonished Germany by using them. They were first employed in large numbers at

the siege of Milan by Frederick Barbarossa. As during the World
War the great guns had their pet names, so had the medieval
battering-ram or moving tower (similarly we know from many poems
that Joyeuse was Charlemagne's sword, and Roland's Durandel).

Under ordinary circumstances a besieging army, for all its machines
and all its methods of mining walls, was unable to take a strong stone
castle; the castle could only be starved into submission. Until the use
of gunpowder became general the advantage was ordinarily with the
defense. The great stone castle was the bulwark of local independence. It chiefly accounts for "the long survival of small states placed
among greedy and powerful neighbors, and the extraordinary power
of resistance shown by rebellious nobles or cities of very moderate
strength in dealing with their suzerains. These features persisted until
the invention and improvement of artillery made the fall of strongholds a matter of days instead of months. In the fourteenth century
the change begins, in the fifteenth it is fully developed, in the sixteenth the feudal fastness has become an anachronism." [18] Today
feudal castles are crumbling vine-covered ruins or, if they have been
cared for or restored, historical museums or the modernized homes
of the well-to-do.

The nobility　　In the course of time the upstart feudal landowners of early western Europe, bound to each other by ties of vassalage, took on the characteristics and attitudes of a noble, aristocratic, and exclusive caste.
When lands, titles, and offices had passed down in the same family for
generations, the blood of that family possessed a distinctive and
unique quality; such blood flowing through a man's veins was enough
to set him off from the ordinary run of mankind as one nobly born.
It was only the nobility who enjoyed the privilege of fighting astride
the noble horse with noble weapons and of riding him to hunt in the
forests. It was only the nobility who were capable of feeling and ex-
emplifying the noble virtues of honor, loyalty, and fidelity embodied
in the relationship of lord and vassal. It was only the noble who was
qualified to render service; that too was a privilege, which exempted
him from the servitude of paying taxes. And it was the noble only who
was fit to govern. In the Church it was uncommon for any man not
nobly born to rise as high as a bishopric.

It would be strange had there not arisen in feudal society some system of training the young noble to hunt and fight on horseback, to
render service to his lord, and to govern his inferiors; some system of
inculcating in him the ideals and virtues that bound him to the privi-

[18] C. W. C. Oman, *The Art of War in the Middle Ages*, p. 553.

leged class of which he was born a member. Such a system was chivalry, which we might define as the institution or profession of knighthood. It would be strange, too, if in the development of such an
institution the Church had not come to exert a large influence. Since
chivalry may be said to have been the attempt of the medieval aristocracy to formulate and to realize its highest ideal, the institution that
undertook to pronounce the proper aims of a good life could not possibly be left out. Chivalry, while undoubtedly influenced in some of its
aspects by the Mohammedan world, was essentially the creation of
feudal society. The very word is a literal description of a great part
of feudal civilization. "Chivalry" is etymologically the same word as
"cavalry," both coming from the Latin *caballus* (horse); and the medieval knight in his most characteristic activities was not sitting in a
chair or standing on his feet—he was sitting astride his horse.

Knighthood probably originated in the German ceremony, described by Tacitus, of conducting the young warrior with his arms into
a full assembly of the freemen of the tribe, thus making him a full-
fledged member of the tribe. The early medieval ceremony of dub-
bing a knight, before it was influenced by the Church, was a simple
matter of the accolade, a blow with the flat of the sword on the back
of the neck, the formal sign of entrance into the loose international
fraternity of knights. The ceremony might be performed by any other
knight at any place. It was ordinarily preceded by careful training at
the court of the king or of some distinguished noble or official. This
training emphasized hunting in all forms and the profession of arms,
and afforded much practice in the use of arms and some actual experience in battle. It also taught such few social graces as good breeding
at that time required. The early German courts provided some training also in governmental duties. But the knight of the middle ages
down to about 1000 was schooled chiefly in the confusion and disorder
and anarchy of nascent feudalism and barbarian attacks by Norsemen,
Magyars, Slavs, and Saracens. In this hard school he learned to be a
law unto himself, to get wealth and land, to make a career, to found
a family, to ride roughshod over the rights of others. "Psychologically
he is no more interesting than a modern machine gun, or any other
engine of indiscriminate slaughter." [19]

As early as the tenth century unbridled private warfare was clearly
recognized by the better elements in society as a menace that must
be abolished or curtailed. There was no central government strong
enough to control it, and the general run of feudal nobles were profit-

[19] F. J. C. Hearnshaw in *Chivalry* (E. Prestage, ed.), p. 6.

ing too much by it to want to check it. The task was therefore left to the Church, itself deeply involved in feudalism through its bishops, who as lords or vassals were suffering, and their lands and peasantry with them, in the chronic strife. The movement began in southern France with the proclamation by local synods of the Peace of God (*Pax Dei*). This was an attempt to prevent all violence and oppression under ecclesiastical penalty, on the ground that they were contrary to the spirit of Christianity. "Anathema," the Synod of Charroux angrily exclaims in 989, "against those who break into churches. . . . . Anathema against those who rob the poor. . . . Anathema against those who injure clergymen." In the following years the Bishop of Puy extended the classes who were to be exempt from molestation: "No one shall seize or rob merchants." [20]

The Peace of God

The movement was taken up to some extent by lay lords, who formed associations to maintain peace, binding themselves by oaths like the following: "I will not invade in any way churches, or the crypts of churches, unless it be to seize malefactors who have broken the peace or committed homicide; I will not assault clerks or monks not bearing secular arms. I will carry off neither ox nor cow nor any other beast of burden. I will do nothing to cause men to lose their possessions on account of their lord's war, and I will not beat them to make them give up their property. From the first day of May until All Souls' Day I will seize neither horse nor mare nor foal from the pastures. I will neither destroy nor burn houses, nor root up nor cut down the vines under pretext of war." [21]

But the Peace of God was not widely sustained by civil authority, and the Church was forced to supplement the exemption of certain classes of the population by the exemption of the whole population for certain periods of time. This idea was incorporated in the Truce of God (*Truga Dei*), born in the early eleventh century. At first, on pain of excommunication it forbade private warfare during the period from "vespers on Wednesday to sunrise on Monday." Then it proceeded to specify even longer periods of time: from Christmas to Epiphany (January 6), from the third Sunday before Lent to the Sunday after Easter or even to St. John's Day (June 24), and from the Assumption of the Virgin (August 15) to St. Martin's Day (November 11). Thus the Truce of God protected the peasant during the seasons of plowing, sowing, and harvesting. The wandering merchant was abroad during the same seasons, traveling from fair to fair. In only the coldest

The Truce of God

[20] Thatcher and McNeal, *Sources*, pp. 412–13.
[21] Quoted in Evans, *op. cit.*, pp. 56–57.

and the hottest months could the nobles now lawfully indulge in this favorite sport.

When these checks upon private warfare were reinforced by the growing power of the kings and the great feudal lords, to whose interests also it was a serious menace, the plague was brought under some control. Upon the knights who had saved Europe from the barbarian invasions of the ninth and tenth centuries there was impressed the larger consideration that their obligations extended beyond themselves to the protection of the Church and the poor and helpless, the *The protection* peasant, the widow, the orphan, and the pilgrim. It was not a lesson *of the* easily learned by "tremendous bullies, terrific in wrath, overflowing *defenseless* with animal courage and martial fury, men good at the battle-cry and with the battle-axe."

If some other outlet could be found for the military energy of the nobility, another step would be taken toward the elimination of private warfare. This the Church realized but found difficult to do, inasmuch *War for* as it professed the service of the Prince of Peace. But would not a war to *the Faith* vanquish the enemy within or without the Faith or to extend the Faith to new peoples be a holy war? The rise of Islam had for the first time given this question great practical importance. Surely it was God's work to fight the Infidel, the noblest self-sacrifice to die for the Faith. Christianity must promise, as Islam did, to those who gave their lives in its defense every blessing that it had to offer. Such war the Church undertook to sanctify: the crusader for the Faith against the Infidel was the noblest embodiment of Christian chivalry.

In the eleventh century the attack was launched against the Infidel in Spain, and large numbers of the French nobility responded to the call. By the end of the century the Turks had taken possession of the Holy Land, and the Church was summoning the nobility of all western Europe to go to the rescue. And go they did, at intervals for the next two hundred years. The crusades undoubtedly relieved the situation at home, although the crusaders were no blessing to the Christian folk through whose lands they passed on their holy errand. The famous crusading orders of Spain and of the crusaders' Kingdom of Jerusalem, the Hospitalers, the Templars, and the Teutonic Knights, united the profession of monk with that of knight in the defense of Christendom. Thus was completed through the agency of the Church the transformation of the ideal of knighthood: far from the negative duty of refraining from despoiling the Church and attacking its clergy, "the knight was held to the positive duty of furthering its interests with his arms."

"The knight was the champion of God and the ladies." At the same time that he was being enrolled in the service of the Church, the knight was being drawn into the service of his lady. This was none of the Church's doing, for the Church, following St. Paul's lead, had no high regard for woman. She was the devil's temptress, alluring men to commit sins of the flesh, and was to be avoided so far as possible. Celibacy was the highest human state and chastity one of man's chief virtues. Neither did early medieval society have much respect for

The noble beats his wife

women. They married very young, and aside from their importance as breeders, were important as wives chiefly for their dowry of land. A man "married a fief," with the necessary encumbrance of a wife, who could easily be kept in hand at home.

But the position of women improved as the castle became a court where feminine graces might shine, and most of all when the Virgin, the Mother of God and the Queen of Heaven, took powerful hold on human hearts. The knight became her especially devoted servitor, and in medieval tales she often substitutes for him in tournaments when he is delayed because of devotion to her. However, he had also to have an earthly goddess. Medieval poets held that the knight's lady must not be his wife nor a maiden he married for love, for marriage was strictly incompatible with love; any other lady, any other man's wife, would do. Once having won his lady's love, he must serve her under all circumstances, no matter what her commands. The trouvères of northern France, the troubadours of the south, the minnesingers of

Germany developed this cult of the lady into a highly formalized ritual of courtly love. This ritual every true knight must know in detail, and there were even some courts of love established for its practice. Chivalry therefore came to be also the cult and practice of gallantry, which, while at its worst it might elevate "adultery to the rank of a social obligation," [22] was nevertheless genuinely concerned with the idealization of woman and her protection. "The process of placing women upon a pedestal had begun, and whatever we may think of the ultimate value of such an elevation . . . it was at least better than placing them, as the Fathers of the Church had inclined to do, in the bottomless pit." [23]

Training for knighthood in later medieval times was accordingly something very different from the rough, simple training of earlier days. The knight was still as much as ever huntsman, warrior, and feudal governor, but he was also the defender of the Faith and the champion of womankind. At seven a vassal's young son might be sent to the court of his father's lord to serve seven years as page or varlet, under the care of the women of the household. Here his duties were those of a servant, since the knight must learn to serve before being served. He received religious instruction and learned the "rudiments of love"; *Training* he was trained in grace of carriage and in courtesy and deportment, *of page* especially in the proper way to enter and leave a room in which his *and squire* superiors were and in the proper forms for addressing them. He learned to keep his hands and nails and his whole person clean. At fourteen he became a squire under the direction of the men of the household, while still continuing his menial duties. He was thoroughly trained in horsemanship and in the art of war, not to mention sports, chiefly hunting and hawking. Music and poetry, chess and backgammon, might be added to his social accomplishments. Chaucer in his *Canterbury Tales* gives us a charming picture of the "youthful squire" at twenty-one, ready for knighthood:

> "A lover and a lusty bachelor
> With locks well curled, as if they'd laid in press,
> Some twenty years of age he was, I guess.
>
> . . . .
>
> Prinked out he was, as if he were a mead,
> All full of fresh-cut flowers white and red.

[22] *Chivalry* (Prestage, ed.), p. 31.
[23] E. Power, in *The Legacy of the Middle Ages*, p. 406.

Singing he was, or fluting all the day;
He was as fresh as is the month of May.

. . . .

He could make songs and words thereto indite,
Joust, and dance too, as well as sketch and write.
So hot he loved that, while night told her tale,
He slept no more than does a nightingale." [24]

The ritual of
knighthood

The ceremonial knighting of the squire was sometimes no more than the simple girding on of the sword followed by the accolade, which sufficed to make him a knight of the sword. But more often it was the richly symbolical ceremony developed by the Church, which was tantamount to a sacrament of ordination into the status of knighthood. For the true knight had a vocation no less genuine and in its own degree no less divine than the true priest's or the true monk's. The candidate was first given a ritual bath, which made him a knight of the bath as distinguished from a knight of the sword, a sort of baptism purifying him from sin. He was then clothed in a white linen tunic symbolic of his purity, a scarlet robe to remind him of his duty if need be to shed his blood for the Church, and black hose to symbolize death. He must fast for the twenty-four hours preceding his initiation, and spend the night watching upon his arms before the high altar of the church in prayer to Our Lady. The following morning he must confess his sins, attend Mass, and make his communion. After the service the bishop laid his naked two-edged sword upon the altar and blessed it; then, after administering the vows of knighthood and imparting instruction in its duties, he girded his sword about him as he knelt. After the accolade the new knight donned his armor, mounted his horse, and was off to prove his powers.

"A truly perfect, gentle knight" was bound "to fear God and maintain the Christian religion; to serve the King faithfully and valorously; to protect the weak and defenceless; to refrain from the wanton giving of offence; to live for honour and glory, despising pecuniary reward; to fight for the general welfare of all; to obey those placed in authority; to guard the honour of the knightly order; to shun unfairness, meanness and deceit; to keep faith and speak the truth; to persevere to the end in all enterprises begun; to respect the honour of women; to refuse no challenge from an equal and never to turn the back upon a foe." [25]

[24] Translation of J. U. Nicolson (*The Canterbury Tales, Complete*, 1935).
[25] *Chivalry* (Prestage, ed.), p. 24.

This was a difficult program. It would be idle to say that many men achieved it, and false to deny that many approached it. Knighthood made a man technically a gentleman, but it might leave him a bully or a ruffian, or make him a snob. None the less, in striving to inculcate some of the noblest of human virtues it was without question a potent civilizing influence on medieval society. Long after the system out of which it grew, and of which it was the idealization, had lost its vitality, it remained in fashion, like feudal armor, becoming more and more decorative and less and less useful. Finally, after its code had become fantastic and its demeanor arrogant, when it had lost the virtues but still retained the vices of caste, it was laughed away by the great Ariosto and other poets of the renaissance and by the greater Cervantes. Yet who has laughed at Don Quixote, the last of the knights, without loving him? The influence of chivalry was not lost; it may possibly even have increased. It persisted as the code of honor and standard of conduct of an aristocracy that was losing its political privileges and itself becoming a mere decoration for the courts of kings. Still more important, it seeped down into the middle classes, even before the bourgeoisie could win or purchase the titles of knighthood. Today, however much modified, it still determines in large part our conception of the gentleman, who need no longer be noble in blood, but must be noble in spirit; who need no longer ride his horse into battle, but must be brave in thought and deed. Loyalty, kindness, decency, humility, compassion, and generosity will never be outworn virtues. Indeed, the complete ideal of chivalry remains yet to be realized.

Chapter 12

MANORIALISM

MANORIALISM, the characteristic medieval system of cultivating the soil by the labor of a village community, from the political and economic points of view is definitely a part of feudalism. The manor, or rather the manorial village—for there was sometimes more than one village on a large manor—was the local unit of feudal government. It was in the manorial village through the manorial court that the lord as landowner enforced his political and property rights over his subjects, the peasantry. It was the heavy toil and the heavy rents of the peasantry on the manor that formed the economic foundation upon which the superstructure of aristocratic feudalism was built. Granted—which is doubtful—that in consequence of the full development of the Industrial Revolution agriculture has begun to lose some of its importance as the one indispensable basis of society, certainly it never ceased to be the basis of medieval society. The leisured classes could hunt and fight and build castles and churches because the peasants were there to support them by their toil on the land. Some understanding of the manorial system is therefore essential to an understanding of the middle ages. More than that, however, a description of manorial life will serve as a description of the life of most country people of western Europe almost down to our own times. For the manor has by no means yet disappeared from Europe. The strips of its arable fields, pretty much unchanged, still lend beauty here and there to the European countryside. Countless farmers still start out in the morning for their farms from villages that have had the same boundaries ever since they were medieval manors.

*Manorial
origins*

The origins of the manorial régime were as old as those of the feudal régime and, like them, partly Roman and partly German; indeed, the two institutions developed together and were the product of the same forces. The tendency towards the emergence of a landed aristocracy and a servile peasantry in the late Roman empire was

326

furthered by the confusion attendant upon the settlement of the Germans within the empire, by the disorder of the Merovingian period, and by the anarchy and peril of the ninth century.

Some manors were historically descended from Roman villas, others from free German village communities that had been brought into dependence upon a lord by their need of protection or by main force. The typical manor seems to have been such a German village, which lost its freedom and yet preserved a body of customary rights. The status of the Roman villa owned by a patrician and cultivated by slaves and tenants was influenced by the German village whose land was owned and cultivated in common by a group of freemen. The status of the German village in turn was influenced by the private ownership of the Roman villa. Finally, the spread of Christianity from the cities into the countryside favored the development of the manorial system, for the Church by its parishes attached itself to the large estates. The parish was often identical with the manor, and the relationship of the lord of the manor to the church of the manor merely continued the relationship of the Roman lord to the pagan temple. This medieval relationship survives in the right of nomination to a living possessed by many English noblemen, i.e., the right of the landowner to choose the clergyman of a church on his land. Manorialism, accordingly, was the same kind of fusion of pagan and Christian, Roman and German elements that we have found every medieval institution to be.

These diverse influences working unequally throughout western *Manorial* Europe could not be expected to produce a manorial system identical *diversity* everywhere. Detailed research on individual manors has, indeed, led some scholars to question whether there was ever any such thing as the typical, traditional manor. Manorialism by no means struck root everywhere: mountainous regions were no place for the manor; and land reclaimed from the sea, as in the Low Countries, or from the marsh, and land cleared in the forest were never subjected to the full manorial régime. The use to which the land was put also made a difference; for example, olive and grape culture were never manorial. But in general, where there was an abundance of good arable land, there the manor was to be found. Like feudal practice, manorial practice varied from country to country and from manor to manor. There never was a general rule; some of the most common features of the English manor are not to be found in Normandy, Languedoc, Provence, or Dauphiné. For all that, the institution was sufficiently prevalent in the west, and possessed enough common features, to make it reasonably accurate for our purposes to speak of western European manorialism. If by that term we mean also the general status and the whole manner of life of the peasants, then we are still better justified. For while their status always varied locally and in the course of the medieval period changed completely, the peasants found much the same lot everywhere: the same toilsome struggle with Mother Earth that the farmer's life has always been; the same rough, sturdy, joyous partaking of the fruits of labor, when there were fruits; the same bitter complaints but withal the same patient resignation when there were no fruits.

Medieval and modern agriculture

The medieval manor was far removed from anything in contemporary American agriculture. The American farmer is a free man, at least politically; the medieval peasant was ordinarily a serf. The majority of American farmers own their own farms—or did until recently —averaging somewhere between one hundred and two hundred acres; the medieval peasant seldom owned land, but was the tenant, ordinarily of thirty acres, of his lord's land. The American farmer lives with his family alone on his farm, but good roads, automobiles, the telephone, the postal service give him easy access to his neighbors; the medieval peasant lived in the isolation of a small village at a crossroads, which he rarely left except to go out to work in the fields. There was hardly such a thing as a good road, and even had there been, he would not have been permitted to go anywhere on it. Year in and year out he saw hardly anyone except his few neighbors or the rare traveler or pilgrim. The American farmer works with the aid of horses or machines; the medieval peasant had to do his work himself, with the help only of his family and a slow-moving yoke of oxen. The American farmer plows and sows and cultivates and harvests when and how he pleases; within the limits of nature he is his own boss and need consult no one but himself. In the enforced cultivation of demesne land, the soil held in reserve by the lord for his own use, the medieval peasant was subject to the orders of the lord or his officials, while in his share of the cultivation of the land held in common by the peasants of the village he was bound by rules prescribed by village custom. The ominously growing class of American tenant farmers, even the sharecroppers of the South, are still, compared to the peasants on the manor, free men. All this probably amounts to saying that the American farmer has not yet ceased to recall his pioneer forefathers, that the American farm is still the product of frontier conditions. If that be so, it is highly significant that whenever pioneer conditions existed in medieval Europe—as in the just-mentioned case of reclaimed or newly cleared land—the peasants stoutly, and generally with some success, resisted manorial organization.

The condition of the peasants on the manor was determined by two *Personal status* factors, their personal status and the tenure of their land. The peasant *of peasants* might be born a serf, for serfdom was hereditary. Children of a marriage between a serf and a freewoman would generally be serfs, although in some cases such a marriage raised the husband's status; local custom was decisive in this matter. There were also two classes of freemen whom it was difficult to distinguish from serfs. First, if a man was willing or compelled to hold a piece of land on condition of performing the services and making the payments that would be exacted of a serf, he was soon reduced thereby to a condition of virtual serfdom. Second, there always remained beneath the nobility a large number of freemen, the number varying according to the locality; some were small landowners, others held land by rent but not on servile tenure. If the latter, sometimes called free villeins, were obliged to cultivate their fields as members of a village, it became difficult to keep them separated from the majority of the community, who were serfs. Furthermore, the gradations within the class of actual serfs were infinite, depending upon the different amounts and kinds of services required by the particular tenure of their land. Servile status and the servile mode of life together accounted for the great majority of the population of western Europe during the middle ages. Strictly speaking, then, the peasant class was composed of a variety of special grades, always in the earlier middle ages tending downward to the level of the serf. Nor did the Roman institution of slavery ever cease entirely to exist. In most regions it declined until it was of small consequence, but the depression of increasingly large numbers of freemen into serfdom fully compensated for the decline.

In the definition of thirteenth-century feudal lawyers the serf is *The serf* scarcely to be differentiated from a slave. Legally he was the lord's chattel, and not much better than livestock. He could, in theory, own no property. In practice it was not uncommon for a serf to be sold like a slave, in some instances for less than the price of a good horse. The law did, however, give him personality, in that he could appear in court against another serf, though not against a freeman, not to mention his lord. The most irksome limitation of the serf's freedom was that he was prohibited from doing what he pleased with his person. He was forbidden to leave one manor for another of his own accord, or to move to a town; if he did either, the lord had the right of pursuit. The latter prohibition was the more important, for flight to the towns offered serfs their best chance of escape. This is only to say that the ordinary serf was unalterably bound to the land that he tilled. Under a ruthless lord this might well be an intolerable subjection; in any case it was a severe obstacle to bettering his condition. What did most to mitigate the serf's lot as defined by feudal lawyers was not the few legal reservations they admitted in his favor, but local custom of centuries' standing. It was ordinarily well established by custom that, if the serf could not leave the land, neither could the land be taken from the serf. If the manor was sold or if particular plots were sold, the serf stayed with the land he tilled. Such a guarantee of his livelihood, with freedom from fear of capricious ejection, more than compensated the serf for the fact that he was not free to leave his manor, which ordinarily was both impossible and undesirable for him to do anyway. The American farmer of today with a mortgage on his farm has no such security of tenure, and the workman in the factory no such security of employment. The serf's life was terrible enough, but he was at least protected from the misery and demoralization of unemployment.

Marriage and children of serfs

Another important limitation to the serf's freedom had to do with marriage. To marry he had to get his lord's authorization, for which he paid a fee, called on English manors merchet. In the case of marriage within the lord's domain there was little difficulty, and the fee was not very high. But in the case of marriage outside the domain, the lord—generally the lord of the female serf, as the wife commonly followed her husband home—often refused consent, preferring to marry his serf within his own manors. In the course of time, however, as it was often imprudent, if not actually impossible, to prevent the marriage of serfs from different domains, and as the Church objected to the separation of husband and wife, some solution had to be found to this difficulty. One was for one lord to trade the serf who was getting married for an unmarried serf belonging to the other lord. Another possibility of satisfying whichever lord was to lose his serf was the exaction from the serf of a fee, called in France *formariage*, for the right to marry outside. We know of a certain German manor where an outside serf marrying a woman of the manor paid a fee also to the lord of the woman; the fee was "a brass pan . . . of such capacity that the bride should be able to sit in it without undue compression." [1] In all such marriages it was not unusual for the two lords to enter into an agreement to divide between them the children that should be born.

Finally, forced marriages of serfs were prevalent, although here again there seems to have been an alternative fee or fine, whereby the serf could have his way against his lord's preference. So on December 11, 1279, "Thomas Robins of Oldburg came on summons and was

[1] G. G. Coulton, *The Medieval Village*, p. 51.

commanded to take Agatha of Halesowen to wife; he said he would rather be fined." [2] All these restrictions of course applied likewise to the marriage of a serf's children. Nor in other respects was he any freer to dispose of his children than of himself, for they were just as much his lord's property as he was. A serf could not send his son off to be educated for the Church, or to town to learn a trade, without getting his lord's consent and paying a fee. And he was subject to fine in the manorial court if he failed to recall his son from school at his lord's command.

According to strict feudal principle the serf was taxable at the lord's discretion (in French, *taillable à merci*). In practice, however, local custom fixed definitely the payments due the lord of the manor in money or in kind. Besides, every sensible lord realized that to have a contented peasantry it was neither prudent nor safe to resort to arbitrary exactions. Moreover, the Church was careful to warn the nobility. "The great must make themselves loved by the small. They must be careful not to inspire hate. The humble must not be scorned; if they can aid us, they can also do us harm. You know that many serfs have killed their masters or have burnt their houses." The number and kind of servile payments varied greatly from country to country, from district to district, even from manor to manor. The head or capitation tax was a general tax payable annually. It was by no means heavy, a few pence or so many pounds of butter or wax, but it was generally detested as an outward sign of servitude. Then there were taxes classifiable as tallage. Originally, at least in France, the taille was an arbitrary assessment, not extremely high, upon the person of the serf. But it was gradually modified into a direct tax upon the property that custom permitted the peasant to accumulate. There was, further, a host of customary payments in kind, which had originated as voluntary gifts, made at the chief festivals of the year, especially Christmas and Easter; these obviously were akin to the feudal aids due from the vassal to his lord. Similarly corresponding to feudal relief was an inheritance tax, called heriot, collected almost without exception when a serf's sons inherited the tenure of his lands in the village; it usually consisted of the best piece of furniture or the best head of livestock.

In addition to these manorial dues the peasant was expected to pay tithes to the Church; and the Church, on the theory that he had presumably not paid all his tithes, took as mortuary tax the second-best piece of furniture or head of livestock. For a very poor family heriot and mortuary tax together nearly cleaned out the cottage and the

The serf's taxes

[2] Quoted in *ibid.*, p. 82.

stable. Finally, special fees were collected for the use of those kinds of manorial land that were not divided up among the tenant peasantry, such as pasture, woodland, and waste land.

The banalities   Akin to these were the fees collected by the lord for the use of certain of his properties on the manor. Since the peasant was obliged to use them whether he would or no, they were in effect monopolies, although in origin they may have been only the means of providing for the peasant what he could not provide for himself. These fees were called banalities. The lord owned the mill, the bake-oven, the wine press, the brewhouse, sometimes even the village well and the village bull. Often these monopolies were not administered directly by his agents but were farmed out for rent. Every serf on the manor was required to bring his grain to the lord's mill, his flour to the lord's oven, his grapes to the lord's wine press, his barley to the lord's brewhouse, his cows to the lord's bull, and for each of these services there was a fee. The records of the manorial courts are full of attempts of the peasants to avoid these monopolies, especially when, as in the case of grinding grain or baking bread, the work could easily be done at home.

On one English manor it was ordained that "all the tenants shall grind their grain . . . at the customary mill and not elsewhere, if they can be served there, and they shall not use handmills for the future under pain each of them 6s. 8d." [3] "At the bakehouse are a baker and two bake-maidens; from each oven-full they shall take eight loaves, each of the value of eight halfpence, be the grain dear or cheap; two shall go to the lord abbot, two to the baker, and two each to the maids." [4] But "what rendered these monopolies so odious was not so much the fixed tariff, or the prohibition against crushing one's own grain with a hand-mill or between two stones and baking this meal at home, as the compulsion to carry the corn for long distances, over abominable roads, and then to wait two or even three days at the door of a mill where the pool had run dry; or again, of accepting ill-ground meal, burned or half-baked bread, and of enduring all sorts of tricks and vexations from the millers or bakers." [5]

The lord collected tolls for use of bridges and roads. If his domain was favorably enough situated to support a market, the rents from stalls and the fees for settling the inevitable disputes were the lord's. Finally, the lord often enjoyed a monopoly of the sale of wine in the village for a fixed period at definite times of the year, and the peasant

[3] Hone, *The Manor and Manorial Records*, p. 179.
[4] Coulton, *The Medieval Village*, p. 56.
[5] *Ibid.*, p. 58.

was required to take a certain amount whether he wanted to or not. Instances are recorded where, "if a man refused to take the prescribed quantity of wine, it was poured into his cottage under the threshold or through the hen-hole; or it was put into a pig-trough." And on a German manor, "if the tenant have not drunk his . . . two gallons . . . , then the lord shall pour a four-gallon measure over the man's roof; if the wine runs down the tenant must pay for it; if it runs upwards he shall pay nothing." [6]

All that we have so far said of the manor concerns primarily the personal status of the peasants. Important as this is, it is in a sense only incidental. The fundamental interest of both lord and peasant was the exploitation of the land. It was this, and this only, in the last analysis, that furnished peasants and lord their livelihood.

The land of the manor

A small proprietor might hold only a few manors, perhaps only one; a large and wealthy proprietor might possess many. The ordinary manor must have had from nine hundred to two thousand acres of arable land, with at least as much again of meadow, pasture, woodland, and waste land, besides the lord's demesne. The sum total of all his manors constituted the lord's domain. In most cases the manors of the domain were not adjacent; sometimes they were many miles apart. All lords were interested, for the sake of convenience and economy of administration, in consolidating their holdings by trading or selling outlying manors for others nearer home, just as the vassal was interested in consolidating his fiefs.

The three field system

The arable land of the manor was usually divided into three fields. One of these was sown in autumn with wheat or rye, which was reaped early in the following summer. The second was sown in spring with barley, rye, oats, beans, and peas and reaped in late summer. The third field was allowed to lie fallow. Crops were rotated so that the field sown in the fall of one year lay fallow in the next, the field planted in the spring was replanted in the fall, and the fallow field of one year was planted in the spring of the next. In the third year the original field for autumn planting, having lain fallow a year, was planted again in the spring, the original field for spring planting lay fallow, and the fallow field of the first year was planted in the fall. In the fourth year the rotation was back where it started.

This three field system was by no means universal. It was an innovation of the middle ages, and first appeared in the eighth century. Antiquity knew only the alternation between tilled and fallow ground. There is much evidence for the perpetuation of this two field system,

[6] *Ibid.*, p. 60.

and some evidence of attempts to work out a four field system. But the advantages of the three field system proved decisive and led to its gradual extension. Its chief advantage was that more land could be cultivated with less plowing. All fallow land was plowed twice in June. Three hundred acres of arable land cultivated according to the two field system would take for the year four hundred and fifty acres of plowing (two times one hundred and fifty for the fallow field plus one hundred and fifty for the field cultivated); for this labor crops would be harvested from one hundred and fifty acres. The same amount of land cultivated according to the three field system would take four hundred acres of plowing (two times one hundred for the fallow field plus one hundred each for the two fields cultivated), and crops would be harvested from two hundred acres. For three hundred acres, then, there would be fifty acres more of crops for fifty acres less of plowing.

Co-operative labor in open fields

The fields were open, not fenced or hedged. They were plowed, sown, and harvested by the co-operation of the peasants of the village. No single villager could plow or harvest unassisted; even if the peasant had a plow of his own he had not enough oxen to draw it. The stubborn glebe was hard to cut with the rude plow of the time, a forked tree trunk, with the angle stud sharpened, perhaps with a sharp iron shoe at the end, but without share or moldboard. Unlike the strong, heavy modern oxen, medieval oxen were thin and light animals hardly larger than heifers. The plow team was often made up of all the available oxen in the hamlet, ten or more yoke hitched to the tongue of the plow. The same co-operation was required at harvest time. Rye, wheat, and oats when ripe must be garnered at once lest the heads lose their grains; and men, women, and children all worked in the fields. When the harvest was over, the whole field was thrown open to the householders of the village as a common pasture.

The strip system

Within the large fields a certain number of strips were held by each peasant. Nothing separated one peasant's strips from another's except a ribbon of unplowed turf or a balk of two furrows thrown up one against the other to make a ridge. The strip in the open fields averaged forty rods in length and four rods in width, or one hundred and sixty square rods, the standard English and American acre. Forty rods is a furlong (a furrow long), two hundred and twenty yards; this was the average length that oxen could go before having to stop to rest. The rod was the old measurement of the ox goad, long enough for the usual team of eight oxen, i.e., sixteen and a half feet; the width of the strip was therefore four ox goads. The ordinary strip corre-

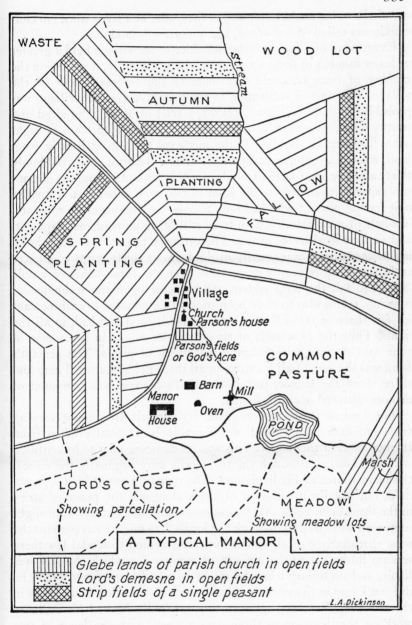

WASTE

WOOD LOT

stream

AUTUMN

PLANTING

FALLOW

SPRING
PLANTING

Village
✝ Church
Parson's house

Parson's fields
or God's Acre

COMMON
PASTURE

Barn   Mill
Manor   Oven
House

POND

Marsh

LORD'S CLOSE

Showing parcellation

MEADOW

Showing meadow lots

A TYPICAL MANOR

Glebe lands of parish church in open fields
Lord's demesne in open fields
Strip fields of a single peasant

L.A. Dickinson

sponded to what could be plowed in the course of a day's work (in German it was called *Morgenland*, i.e., a morning's land).

Every head of a family or householder in the village held a greater or lesser number of these strips, depending originally, it seems, on the number of oxen he could contribute to the common labor of the village. The unit of cultivation in the primitive German village was probably the hide (German, *Hufe*), a tract of about a hundred and twenty acres, which could ordinarily be handled by a team of eight oxen. The average holding of the medieval peasant, at least in England, was the virgate, or yardland, a variable measure, most commonly thirty acres, or one-fourth of a hide; for this amount of land the peasant was expected to contribute the labor of two oxen. There was a smaller unit for the peasant who had only one ox, i.e., the oxgang, or bovate, one-half of a yardland. There were still other units of measurement, and various local terms in use. The ordinary peasant's average holding of thirty acres was usually in the form of thirty strips of an acre each, scattered as evenly as possible over the three fields of arable land. Indeed, the strip system, while based upon the technique of plowing, seems also to have been meant to guarantee to each peasant his fair share of the different kinds of land, good and bad, in all the fields. Thus the plowlands of an old manor might in the course of time split up into a bewildering patchwork of pieces. The peasant's farm was the sum of all his strips in all three fields, scattered here and there about the manor, just as the lord's domain was composed of manors scattered over the district.

The lord's demesne

The lord of the manor reserved for himself an amount varying from one-sixth to one-third of the arable land, usually taken from the best land of the manor. This was his demesne (not to be confused with his domain, although the two words were originally the same), the main source of his livelihood. The demesne might be a separate field, but usually it consisted of strips alongside the peasants' strips in the three open fields. All the peasant's other obligations were slight compared with his duty to work the lord's demesne. It was perhaps the most characteristic of all servile duties. According to feudal law there was no limitation to the amount of services for which the serf was liable, and no telling when he might be asked to perform them; he did not know in the evening what he was to be called upon to do in the morning. Yet here again custom gradually limited his ordinary work on the demesne to three days a week, with the labor of two oxen. This was called week work; it sufficed for the normal demands of plowing, sowing, cultivating, and harvesting. In addition, when

Week work and boon work

the work was especially heavy, as at harvest time, the peasant could be called upon for extra work, called boon work. He was also responsible for cartage, bringing in firewood to the manor house, hay to the barns, and the harvest to the granaries. Another sort of forced labor was the *corvée*, a prescribed amount of work making roads, repairing bridges, digging ditches, and cleaning out moats. The serf's wife and children might be called upon for work as servants in and about the manor house. In everything the lord's land and the lord's work came first. It certainly claimed over half the serf's working time. In what time was left he had to support himself and his family.

It took more than arable land to make the manor a self-sufficing economic unit. Swine and sheep and oxen and cattle, as well as human beings, had to be fed. There must be wood and peat for fuel and wood for all kinds of repairs. Every manor had its pastures and meadows, its wood lot or forest, and its waste land. The right to the use of these every householder in the village enjoyed in common. Their common *Nonarable land* use may well date back to an earlier day when such tracts were actually owned in common by the village. It is even the opinion of some scholars that the early German village owned in common the arable land too; otherwise it is difficult to account for certain village rights. At any rate, over pasture and meadow, waste and forest, the peasant village retained common use after having lost to the lord common ownership. For the exploitation of these lands not much labor was required, except cutting timber and firewood and getting in the hay from the meadows. Hay is a precarious crop and must be got under cover in a hurry, as soon as it is dry, for fear of rain and mildew. Before the grass grew high, the meadow was divided by lines of stakes into squares or strips, according to the number of cattle each peasant possessed. After the hay was cut the meadow was thrown open to common pasture. In addition to the common pasture itself, meadowland as well as arable land after the harvest was thrown open to pasture, and the pasture was still further supplemented by the young grass on the fallow land. The meadowland, which supported the stock over the winter, was worth relatively far more than the arable land.

Only the best stock was carried through the winter. Old oxen, hogs, and sheep were killed, and the meat was salted or smoked. The best meat went to the cellars of the manor house. Hay frequently gave out *Livestock* before spring and the animals had to be fed on straw or tree loppings. Hence it often happened that the cattle in the spring were so weakened by starvation that they could barely walk to pasture when the young grass began to appear. The cattle were poor enough anyway. The cows were light and gave very little milk; one record states that three cows produced only three and a half pounds of butter a week. Wolves were a pest, especially to sheep. Hogs could shift for themselves in summer and for part of the winter; they fed on the refuse of the village and on acorns and beechnuts in the woods, and the tusked boars were able to defend the herd from wolves. But at best they were "long, flat-sided, coarse-boned, lop-eared omnivorous animals, whose agility was more valuable than their early maturity." Even poor stock, however, were vitally important, if only because of the necessity of fertilizer for the raising of all crops.

The manor nearly self-sufficient

The chief virtue of the manor was that it was largely, though not completely, self-sufficient. It produced almost all necessary food and most other necessities of life. The growth of markets, despite the fact that the early medieval manor was not run for profit, is proof that the manor often produced surpluses of grain, hides, and wool. In winter the wool was dyed and woven into cloth by the women; the hides were tanned and made into shoes, saddles, and harness by the men. Every manor had to have a wheelwright, a carpenter, and a blacksmith. All luxuries, of course, such as spices and pepper, had to be imported, and some necessary things, such as salt, iron, millstones, tar, canvas, metal, and earthenware of various kinds.

Manorial officials

Besides the lord's own officials, the steward and bailiff, there were several manorial officials selected by the village. There was a general supervisor, or reeve. The hayward, whose duty it was to see that the meadow was not invaded by wandering cattle, must be "a vigorous and austere man," going around "early and late, spying upon the woods, the farmyard, the meadows and fields" to see that all was well. The plowman must be "no melancholy or wrathful man, but merry, joyful, given to song, that the oxen may take their delight in his chants and melodies. . . . Let him love them, and sleep with them at night; let him tickle them, curry them, rub them down, and keep them well at all points," for "it is well to rub the oxen twice daily with a wisp of straw, that they may lick themselves with more affection." The dairymaid was to "be chaste and honest and faithful, laborious in her dairy duties, wise and neat-handed; not lavish but of a thrifty nature." [7] Then there were the cowherds, swineherds, shepherds, and aletasters. While at work on the lord's demesne the peasants could lawfully be beaten, and one peasant would be assigned the duty of holding a club over his fellows to keep them at their work.

[7] These examples are quoted from Coulton, *The Medieval Village*, p. 308.

The peasants' seasonal labors were regulated by saints' days. Spring *Manorial* plowing must be begun after Easter and planting be over by Whitsun- *custom* tide. Harvesting began with St. John's Day or Midsummer Day (June 24) and must be over by Assumption (August 15); in this time also fell the haying season. Fruits were gathered between Assumption and St. Michael's Day (September 23), and the root crops between then and St. Martin's Day (November 11).

Weights and measures and payments in kind were controlled by inveterate, and to us curious, custom. Peasants on an English manor had to collect "one hose of moderate size full of nuts well cleaned of their husks." When they had mowed hay for a day they might carry "so much grass or straw as they can bind in a single bundle and lift upon their sickle (or scythe) handle, so that the handle touch not the ground. And if perchance the handle break, then he shall lose his straw or grass and be at the lord abbot's mercy and pay a fine, coming to the best accord that he can with the abbot." "Another medieval measure was 'as far as a tame hen can go at a single flight, which is reckoned at three hundred of a man's paces.' " "A prisoner is to be kept in prison until he has been there long enough to consume two bushels of corn. A tithe-gosling may be refused if he be not old enough to pluck grass for himself without relapsing into an undignified sitting position; a tithe-hen rejected by the lord as sickly must be accepted if, when frightened, she can clear the garden fence or jump upon a stool. . . . The huntsman may pursue a stag into the lake of Lorsch 'as far as a red shield can be seen'; peasants are bound to follow up a hue and cry 'as far as a white horse can be seen'; the miller must not let the water in his dam mount so high above the stake as to prevent a bee from standing on the top and drinking without wetting its wings." [8] In a German village a man living outside of the immediate boundaries "shall stand on the ridge of his roof, shall pass his right arm under his left and grasp his hair in his right hand; then shall he take a sickle by the point in his left hand, and as far as he can cast, so far shall his hens go; and when they go further to other folks' harm, he shall fine with threepence for every third fowl." It has already been seen that in the cultivation of his strips in the open fields the peasant was bound by village custom; the necessity for co-operative labor left nothing to his own initiative.

We have remarked that the lord might prefer to live in one of his *The manor* manor houses rather than in his castle, and a less wealthy lord might *house* have no castle. Or the manor house might be the residence of the

[8] *Ibid.*, pp. 48–49.

lord's bailiff or steward. In any case it was the center for the local administration of the manor. In contrast with the huts of the peasants it was a display of wealth and luxury, though it would seem to us today hardly less rude and comfortless than the castle. It stood on the best site in the village, if possible on a knoll, to provide view and drainage and some protection; it might also be fortified. It had "three stories. . . . The cellar was a spacious place where were great woven baskets, wide-mouthed jars and barrels, and other domestic utensils. The first floor contained a great living-room, with a huge fireplace, pantries, cupboards, the bedchamber of the lord and his wife, near to which was a lavatory and servants' rooms, and a room or dormitory for the boys. The reception hall . . . was also used as a chapel. The kitchens were on two levels; on the lower pigs were roasted, geese, capons and other birds killed and prepared for eating. On the other floor of the kitchen other provisions were cooked. . . . The furniture of the manorhouse was scanty. Glass windows were rare; a table put on trestles, a few forms or stools or a long bench stuffed with straw or wool, with one or two chairs and a chest or two of linen, formed the hall furniture. A brass pot or two for boiling and two or three brass dishes, a few wooden platters and trenchers, or more rarely of pewter, and an iron or leather candlestick, a kitchen knife or two, a box or bowl for salt, and a brass ewer or basin, formed the movables of the house. The dormitory contained a rude bed and but rarely sheets and blankets, for the gown of the day was generally the coverlet at night." [9] Everything that has been said in the preceding chapter of life in the medieval castle might here be repeated of life in the manor house.

Parish church and priest's house

Not far from the manor house stood the parish church and the priest's house. The church and the manor house were the only real edifices in the hamlet, although in early days they were only timber structures. The priest had either his own field apart from the fields of the community or strips of land along with the tenures of the serfs. In either case his land had to be worked for him by the peasantry, although sometimes, if he was of peasant stock himself and on good terms with his parishioners, he might lend a hand in the planting and harvesting of his patches.

The peasant's home

The huddled manorial villages varied in population from twelve or fifteen families to as many as fifty or sixty. In such a small group, life was circumscribed, monotonous, and ingrown. The peasantry lived in wattled cottages without windows, with thatched roofs and floors of earth. The cottages were without chimneys; a hole in the roof let

[9] Thorold Rogers, *Work and Wages.*

army gathering supposedly for a crusade to the Holy Land (a contemporary miniature painting)

la-Ta-Hussan, one of the best preserved Crusaders' castles in Syria

A peasant wedding feast (from a painting by Peter Breughel the Elder)

A dancing bear

Sowing, harrowing, and chasing crows before the château (miniature from the Duc de Berry's Book of Hours) (See p. 1024)

out the smoke from a small fire in the center of the clay floor. The same hole let in rain and snow, so that the floor was often damp and slippery. No artificial light was used; candles were a luxury for the church and the manor house, and the danger of fire was too great for a flaming pine knot. Anyway, what could a peasant do after dark, since he could neither read nor write? He went to bed with the sun and was up with the sun. The furniture was scant and of the crudest sort. The bed was a box with a mattress filled with straw or dry leaves; the table was a few planks set on wooden trestles; a couple of three-legged stools, a chest, an iron pot, and some pieces of earthenware

A late French manor house

completed the furnishings. In summer the peasant's wife cooked out of doors at a crude fireplace, with the pot hanging over the fire from a crossbar supported by tripods. She had no oven, since the lord's oven baked for the whole village. The peasant shared his dwelling with his cats, dogs, and chickens and its thatched roof covered the stable as well.

Around the peasant's hut was the garden, which supplied him with fresh vegetables. Fresh meat was rare; meat ordinarily meant "salted meat and fish often half cured and half putrid." His bread was usually black or brown bread made from rye flour or a mixture of wheat and rye; rye bread "abode longer in the stomach and was not so soon digested with their labour." The peasant "is very glad when he can get black bread and milk and butter." Porridge and cheese filled out his meals. Only on special occasions might there be wine or beer for him. "Peasants must not eat fowls, but onions and cheese; nor rolls or white bread, but coarse bread: for base and coarse foods are to be given to base persons and delicate foods to noble folk." [10] Because of the difficulty of rushing food over poor roads into regions suffering from poor or no crops, famine was a curse second only to war in the middle ages.

Politically and economically, as observed before, manorialism was the complement of feudalism. Socially the two systems were as far apart as could be. Feudalism was the way of life of a free, hereditary, landowning class of nobles with the characteristic marks of caste.

The half-timbered house and barn of a prosperous German peasant

Manorialism was the way of life of a servile, hereditary class of ignoble tillers of the soil. While the two classes lived together on the manor, they met only in politics and business, never socially. To the nobility the peasantry were an almost untouchable caste. Although the Church might preach the equality of man in the sight of God, it was itself responsible for the conventional medieval theory that society was fashioned by God into the three distinct estates, the clergy, the nobles, and the nobodies whose duty it was to support their betters by their labor. The history of the last thousand years might be written as the chronicle of the gradual rise of the third estate. In the United States there is today theoretically no other estate. With the growth of medieval towns it began to gain ground, represented by merchants and artisans, from whom the bourgeoisie later developed. Throughout the middle ages, however, the third estate was composed predominantly of the peasants. The threefold division of society, being a divine institution, was final and admitted of no improvement. The best peasant was the peasant most contented with the lot to which it had pleased God to call him.

[10] Quoted in Coulton, *The Medieval Village*, p. 316.

Most medieval literature, whether written for the nobility or the *The peasant* bourgeoisie, deigns to take notice of the peasant only to scorn him. *in medieval* "Peasants are those who can be called cattle." "They have such hard *literature* heads and stupid brains that nothing can penetrate them." "They have one squint eye and the other is blind. They have a shifty look. They have one good foot and the other twisted." "The serf is born of ass's dung." "He was large and marvelously ugly and hideous. He had a huge head blacker than coal, the space of a palm between his eyes, large cheeks, a great flat nose, large lips redder than live coals, long, hideous and yellow teeth. His clothing and shoes were of cowhide, and a large cape enveloped him. He leaned on a great club." "He had enormous arms and massive limbs . . . his shoulders were large, his chest deep, his hair bristling, and his face black as coal. He went for six months without bathing: none but rain water ever touched his face." "The devil did not want the peasants in hell because they smelled too badly." "Go make them pay . . . they ought to pay well. Go take their houses; take both cows and calves, for the peasants are felons. . . . I do not know of a meaner people than the peasant." "They do not take cheerfully their need and poverty, and are dishonest and envious and backbiting and proud and full of envy and vice. Indeed, the peasant thinks that if he can get anything from the rich man, by whatever means, it is no sin." "The rustic is best when he weeps, worst when he is merry." "What part of speech is peasant? A noun. What sort of noun? Jewish. Wherefore? Because he is as silly and ugly as a Jew. . . . What gender? The asinine gender; for in all his deeds and works he is ever like unto an ass. . . . The backs of all peasants are bowed like the back of an ox. . . . The peasant grieves that the clerks make free with his wife and live on his labours." [11]

Under no circumstances could the life of the medieval serf be *Peasant life* called pleasant. Numerous fees and payments, obligatory services, and his own heavy labor left him little if anything more than the scantiest means of existence. His food was at best barely adequate, his cottage comfortless, the village hygiene abominable. By no means all medieval literature is such stuff as was quoted in the last paragraph. An Anglo-Saxon writer makes a peasant say: "I work very hard. I go out in the dawning, driving the oxen to the field, and I yoke them to the plough. Be the winter never so stark, I dare not stay at home for fear of my lord; but every day I must plough a full acre or more. . . . I have

[11] The quotations are from Coulton's *Medieval Village*, Luchaire's *Social France at the Time of Philip Augustus*, and Evans's *Medieval France*.

a boy who drives the oxen with a goad, who is now hoarse from cold and shoutings . . . it is very hard work." [12] Again: "They endure the severest tempests, snows, rains, tornadoes; they till the earth with their hands, with great pain and hunger. They lead a thoroughly wretched life, poor, suffering and beggarly." [13] "The peasants gnaw and browse upon their bread in great sweat of their brow, in great travail." "All the peasant amasses in a year by stubborn work the knight, the noble, devours in an hour. Not content with his pay as soldier, not content with his revenues and with the annual tax levied upon his subjects, he further despoils them by illicit taxes and heavy exactions. The poor are exhausted, the fruit of their years of pain is extracted from them." [14] "The truth is, that these lords and tyrants continually steal from those who have little or nothing (to wit, peasants and diggers of the earth) and seize and take from them that little which they have. For the poor men's goods are continually taken away, while rich men daily heap up other men's goods." [15] Perhaps no more eloquent description can be cited than that of the peasant family in the fields in the Creed of Piers Plowman:

"And as I went my way, weeping for sorrow,
I saw a poor man o'er the plow bending.
His coat was of a clout that cary was called,
His hood was full of holes and his hair sticking out,
His shoes were patched and clouted full thick,
His toes peeped out as he the ground trod,
His hose o'erhung his gaiters on every side,
All befouled with mud, as he the plow followed.
Two mittens had he, scanty, and made all of rags,
And the fingers were worn out and filled full of mud.
This wight was bemired in the mud almost to the ankle;
Four oxen were before him, that feeble had become,
One might reckon rib, so rueful were they.
His wife walked by him with a long goad,
In a cutted skirt cutted full high,
Wrapped in a winnowing-sheet to keep her from the weather;
Barefoot on the bare ice, so that the blood followed.
And at the field's end lay a little bowl

---

[12] E. Power, *Medieval People*, p. 11.
[13] Luchaire, *op. cit.*, p. 393.
[14] Evans, *op. cit.*, p. 55.
[15] Coulton, *The Medieval Village*, p. 21.

And therein lay a little child wrapped in rags,
And twain of two years old upon another side;
And all of them sang a song that sorrow was to hear.
They cried all a cry, a sorrowful note,
And the poor man sighed sore, and said, 'Children, be still.' " [16]

The manorial courts, which every member of the village community *Manorial* was bound to attend, have been mentioned above. They were held in *courts* the parish church or in the hall of the manor house or outdoors underneath a spreading tree. Here the property rights of the lord and the customary rights of the villagers were enforced. The peasants were called upon to help decide what was the custom of the place and to act as assessors of damages in case of proved infractions of custom; judgments were rendered in their name as well as the lord's. When later the custom of the manor was written down in village custumals, it was difficult to go beyond the pages written by lawyers in the interest of the lord. In fact, pronouncing judgments in the name of the village soon came to be hardly more than a mere form. The fines collected in court went to the lord and constituted a considerable part of his income.

Such records as we have from manorial courts are especially valuable for the light that they throw on the daily life of the peasants. They seem to have got into all the regular sorts of trouble. We should *Value of* expect a good deal of private violence in an age of so much public *manorial court* violence. Beton, Richard Walker's handmaid, was fined for assault *records* upon Jane, wife of Thomas Merriman, "smiting her even to the effusion of blood." Thomas Milner was fined "for that he shot two arrows by night at Lawrence Hunter," and John Smith for "drawing his knife to smite the curate." The American who reads in his newspaper that the police had to be called in to separate the players or to save the umpire will be interested to learn that on the English manor of Alcey "it was enjoined upon all tenants . . . that none should play at ball," and that at Southwick John, William, and Robert were fined "because they played at ball, through which grievous contention and contumely arose between the lord prior's tenants." The old legal principle *caveat emptor* (let the buyer be on his guard) apparently did not protect Belasis, who was haled to court "for bad ale, and moreover because the ale which she sent . . . was of no strength, as was proved in court"; nor an Alice, who was called upon to explain why the fish that she sold were rotten.

[16] Quoted in E. M. Hulme, *History of the British People*, pp. 121–22.

Many offenses grew directly out of the various obligations of the peasants to the lord or out of the obligations of community life in the village. Walter was called to account for filching a perch out of the lord's fishpond. John Hunting and his wife Cecilia got into difficulties with the widow Margaret because "their animals trampled and destroyed her cabbages," and a whole day was allowed the village to "inquire and present" whether John Hunting and Cecilia "beat Margaret the widow or not." And John's son stole apples from the lord's orchard.

The medieval tongue was as unruly as the medieval hand. John of Banniburg got into trouble for calling Adam of Marton "false,

A wrestling bout

perjured and a rustic." In one court the women were told "to restrain their tongues and not scold or curse any man," and in another not to "quarrel or swear at anyone at all." A fine was collected from "Agnes of Ingleby for transgression against William Sparrow and Gillian his wife, calling the said Gillian a whore." But if Agnes had had better evidence the fine would have been collected from the other lady, for on English manors there was a fine, called leyrwite, for incontinence. Margaret Calvert was less fortunate than Gillian Sparrow, for we find: "Margaret Calvert for leyr with the chaplain, 12s.," and "the same lady, the same chaplain and the same price recorded again in 1368." "We may hobnob . . . with John Jentilman, Adam Graundorge (i.e., Barleycorn), William Littlefair, John Cherryman and John Merriman; Gilbert Uncouth and Roger Mouse, Henry Almsman, Thomas Marmaduke, Walter Mustard, John Fairjohn, Roger Litilannatson, John Stoutlook . . . Stephen Satyne; and most medieval of all, Robert Litany, Alan Paternoster, Robert Benedicite. . . . Who would not join in dance and sunburnt mirth with Agnes

Redhead . . . Cicely Wilkinsdaughter, Maud Malkynsmaydin . . . Margaret Ferrywoman, Agnes Bonamy, Margaret Merry and Watsdaughter . . . ? Yet . . . let us not indiscreetly press any of these ladies to tell us what may have been her own special title to immortality." [17]

The hardships of the peasant's life, real as they were, nevertheless must not be exaggerated. Until the twelfth century he knew no other life; he was inured to toil and used to getting along on little, and his wants were simple and few. The immemorial and intimate contact with the soil which was the source of his misery was also the source of his consolation. By no means all manorial lords were cruel exploiters, though undoubtedly too many were. The medieval peasant, who had not only Sundays but saints' days off, actually had more holidays than the modern workingman. He might go to the near-by market, which was held weekly, fortnightly, or monthly. When fairs became popular in the twelfth century, he could take his whole family to one.

Peasant amusements

If a strolling conjurer or a band of acrobats or a man with a dancing bear was given a night's lodging at the manor, all the villagers were likely to see the performance, sometimes in the big hall of the manor house, sometimes in the church. For the parish church was not only a house of worship but, when there was no parish house, also a meeting place for social gatherings, the thunderings of the clergy to the contrary. The peasants danced in the porch of the church itself, and in the cemetery—always, the monastic chroniclers would have us believe, with the devil as dancing master. They sang "wicked songs with a choir of dancing women," "evil and wanton songs and such like lures of the devil." An English priest was kept awake all night by peasants dancing in the churchyard and singing a song with the refrain "Sweetheart have pity." He could not get the tune out of his head, and next morning at Mass he found himself singing, instead of the Latin service, the refrain "Sweetheart have pity." Or the parish might hold an ale for the benefit of the church, in the church or parish house, where cups were furnished dedicated to the saints.

On some English manors the lords held ales at regular times during the year, for which the peasants paid a small fee. "On Saturday the married men and youths come after dinner and are served three times with ale; on Sunday the husbands and wives come with their pennies, and they can come back again the next day if they will; the

---

[17] Coulton, *The Medieval Village*, p. 103, from which most of the above examples are taken; also Hone, *The Manor and Manorial Records*, and *Translations and Reprints*, vol. III, no. 5.

young men must pay a penny a head if they come on Sunday, but on the Monday they can come and drink for nothing, provided they do not sit on the bench; any one of them caught sitting down must pay his penny as before. These rights, they say, belong to the serfs born on the manor and their offspring; but a stranger who serves anyone in the manor or is abiding there shall have no share in the right." [18] The lord sometimes feasted his peasants after the spring sowing or at harvest or at church festivals. On an English manor at Christmas "the tenants cut and carried in the logs for a yule-fire; each brought his faggot of brushwood, lest the cook should serve his portion raw, and each has his own dish and mug, and a napkin of some kind, 'if he wanted to eat off a cloth.' There was plenty of bread and broth, with two kinds of meat and various savoury messes. At East Pennard the farmer had a right to four places at the yule-feast, and each man was entitled to have a fine white loaf and a good helping of meat, and to sit drinking after dinner in the manorial hall." [19]

The custumal of a monastic estate in the Black Forest gives us a vivid picture of a vintage festival. When the peasants "have unladen the wine, they shall be brought into the monastery and shall have meat and drink in abundance. A great tub shall be set up there and filled with wine that they have brought, and a stoup shall be set therein, and each shall drink for himself. And the cellarman shall lock up the cellar, and the cook his kitchen (for safety's sake); and if so be that the peasants wax drunken and smite the cellarman or the cook, they shall pay no fine for this deed; and they shall drink so that two of them cannot bear the third back to the wagon." [20]

The emancipation of the serf

One of the most important facts in the history of the middle ages, and indeed of all mankind, is the gradual emancipation of the peasant from serfdom. It was a phenomenon even greater than the emancipation of negro slaves in the late eighteenth and the nineteenth centuries, or the emancipation of the Russian serfs by Alexander III. Emancipation did not come from the leadership of the Church, for canon law regarded serfs as property. In some instances the clergy did preach against serfdom, but leading theologians sponsored the institution and advocated keeping the serf ignorant, submissive, and strong-bodied. Peasant insurrections occurred more frequently on Church lands, not because the clergy were necessarily harder of heart, but because the peasants suffered more from the pace and pressure of the Church's

[18] Coulton, *The Medieval Village,* p. 29.
[19] *Ibid.,* pp. 29–30.
[20] *Ibid.,* p. 27.

administration, which was usually more intelligent and efficient, especially monastic administration. When emancipation was once well under way, the peasants were naturally the more exasperated by the refusal of the conservative Church to budge, though it was always the monasteries that bore the brunt of their resentment. If emancipation owed so little to Christianity, it owed no more to philanthropic or humanitarian motives on the part of the nobility. Such motives account for individual instances of manumitting serfs, but on the whole they played an exceedingly small part. The emancipation of the serfs was won by the serfs themselves.

Serfdom was a halfway stage between ancient slavery and the *Changes* modern status of the free peasant landowner. Tenant farming might *before the* be regarded as a stage intermediate between serfdom and complete *eleventh* independence, though it has perhaps less often been a step forward from *century* serfdom than a retrogression—certainly it was so in the Roman world— from earlier freedom. Even before the mass movements of the eleventh century changes had begun to take place that affected profoundly the status of the serfs. The curtailment of private warfare and the growing authority of the greater feudatories over the lesser brought increased peace and prosperity to the countryside. The revival of commerce and industry in old and new towns, with improved roads and bridges, brought more prosperity and created a market for peasant products. The new demand in the towns for the agricultural surplus of the country began even to make it possible for a serf to accumulate enough money to buy his freedom. Furthermore, together with the marked increase in population everywhere in Europe, it stimulated the clearing of forests and the draining of swamp lands. Thus a new career on the frontier was open to pioneers; but to make such a life tempting inducements had to be offered, and no inducement could be stronger, or cheaper, than to offer serfs an opportunity to become free settlers. As the change proceeded from a predominantly agricultural economy towards an industrial and financial economy, manorial proprietors came to see that it was more convenient, or to realize that it was necessary, to accept fixed payments in money from tenants in lieu of services and produce from serfs. They discovered, too, that it was in fact more profitable to hire free day laborers, who worked with better spirit and produced more than serfs.

All these changes the serfs quickly learned to take advantage of. *Ways of escape* They offered an increasing number of lawful ways to gain freedom. *from serfdom* At least one other way to emancipation aside from the possibility of manumission by their lord had always been open to serfs: with their lord's consent they could take holy orders, and often did. Two illegal but effective ways of asserting themselves the serfs also made full use of. A serf could run away. It was becoming easier to escape to town, and easier to find employment in industry and business there; once safe in a town, a serf was likely to remain a lost serf. Or he could escape to some new settlement, or even go no farther than to the near-by manor of some other lord whose serfs were better treated. Secondly, the serfs could revolt or threaten to revolt. The fire of peasant discontent was always smoldering, and in every century actually broke out in revolt more frequently than we have been able to indicate. These revolts were ruthlessly crushed, but they nevertheless had their effect. In some instances, in imitation of the towns, villages banded together as communes and forced charters of liberty and a kind of self-government from their lords. In other cases entire villages bought their freedom. Sometimes whole villages seem to have migrated. The time slowly but inexorably came when to keep his serfs at all the lord had to free them. Finally, the great military and colonizing expeditions of the eleventh century, such as the Norman conquest of lower Italy and Sicily and England and the so-called Spanish crusades, were joined by countless runaway serfs. Many became mercenary soldiers, for the growing preference for mercenary over feudal troops offered the sturdier peasants an ideal way of escape. A good example of the peaceful exodus of serfs *en masse* is furnished by the Flemish colonies established in eastern Germany, beginning with the twelfth century. Beginning with the end of the eleventh century the crusades—especially the first crusade—attracted more thousands of serfs. For, besides offering every advantage of freedom that any other way of escape could offer, with adventure and glory thrown in, they guaranteed safe entrance into paradise—no slight inducement.

Mass movements of the eleventh century

The decline of serfdom

The abandonment of the requirement of week work on the lord's demesne in many parts of France, the Low Countries, and Italy marks an important stage in the serf's emancipation. Serfdom lasted longer in Germany and England than in France or Italy; in Normandy it had entirely disappeared by the eleventh century. In most parts of western Europe it lingered on into the thirteenth century, steadily declining; by the end of the middle ages it had pretty well disappeared in most localities. The free peasant sometimes became an agricultural laborer, but more often a tenant farmer paying rent; at least in France he was beginning to buy land and become a peasant proprietor. Once on the road to freedom and some measure of prosperity, the peasant took ill all obstacles in his way to greater freedom and greater prosperity.

In England the Black Death of 1348 and the effects of the Hundred Years' War furthered the emancipation of the serfs; but England had to pay some of the penalty that other countries paid where serfdom lingered too long. In the fourteenth and fifteenth centuries in England, Flanders, and Bohemia, and in Germany as late as the early sixteenth century, the peasants, stimulated by the new evangelical religious fervor, which preached a primitive sort of communism and revenge on the wealthy and worldly Church, broke out in a succession of armed rebellions.

Chapter 13

THE REVIVAL OF THE EMPIRE

*The inade-
quacy of
feudalism*

B
Y APPROXIMATELY 950, as the result of the invasions, migrations, and settlement of barbarian peoples, western Europe had experienced some five centuries and a half of incessant turmoil, broken only by a brief interlude under the three great Carolingians. Its reaction to this prolonged strain had been the feudal and manorial systems. Now that the period of dislocation and resettlement of new peoples was at length over, it remained to be seen whether feudalism and manorialism were capable of supplying the peace, order, security, and wealth necessary for a superior type of civilization. It may be said at once that alone they certainly could not have done so. Without the ubiquitous and pervasive influence of the Church to restrain the quick impulses that were at all times so close to the surface, without its inspiration to men to express themselves in art and writing, and without the education it offered—the only education to be had—it is difficult to see how manorialism alone, without the development of towns, could have furnished an economic foundation adequate for a life of any complexity and refinement. Nor was feudalism ingenious enough of itself to work out methods of controlling its libertine individualism. The restraining hand of the monarch was required to temper its zeal and direct it into channels of greater usefulness. Medieval civilization at its height in the twelfth and thirteenth centuries was the result of three factors: the authority and stimulation of the Church, the growth of towns to supplement the agricultural economy of manorialism, and the control of feudalism by the kings. Let us now consider the story of these kings, first of all in Germany.

Germany in the tenth, eleventh, and twelfth centuries was the most powerful state in Europe. The foundations of this strength were laid between 919 and 1024 by her first dynasty, the Saxon, or Ottonian. The second dynasty, the Salian, or Franconian (1024–1125), brought

352

Germany to a brief triumph in the middle of the eleventh century, followed by the first stage of her decline. Under the Hohenstaufens *German* (1138–1254) she rose again to flashing heights, only to succumb to *dynasties* speedy and thoroughgoing collapse. Her place in Europe was taken by France, never to be regained—if it ever was—until 1871. The history of Germany's rise to power and influence is the history of a successful battle with feudalism; the history of its decline is the history of victorious feudalism and a triumphant papacy.

Feudalism, after striking roots deep in France in the ninth and tenth centuries, spread more slowly into Germany. Here its character was modified in a way most significant for later history when it encountered an obstacle that did not exist in France. The ancient tribal subdi- *The tribal* visions of the Germans—Bavarians, Alemannians, or Swabians, Fran- *duchies* conians, Thuringians, Saxons, and Frisians—were as important as they had always been. Indeed, for a thousand years, filled with attempts to break down in one way or another this loyalty of the German to his tribal subnationality, they have remained almost as important down to our own time. The Bavarian or the Saxon has tended always to think of himself first as a Bavarian or a Saxon, not as simply a German (in 1914 there were Bavarian peasants who went cheerfully to war, supposing that they were going to fight their ancient enemies the Prussians). The present German government is striving desperately to break down this old feeling; perhaps it will succeed where all its predecessors have failed.

The Carolingian empire first succeeded in getting together these tribal confederations, and the East-Frankish kingdom continued to emphasize their common German character. The only fruit of over a century of effort was a great revival of tribal patriotism towards the end of the ninth century. In most of the tribes the tribal or stem dukes (German *Stamm*, tribe), who had been suppressed by Charles the Great, reappeared. In Saxony the Liudolfinger family achieved their *The stem* position by protecting the country from the Danes and the Slavs. They *dukes* extended their sway over Thuringia also by suppressing a Thuringian family that aspired to the rank of duke. In Bavaria the Arnulfingers likewise won the honor by fighting off the Magyars. In Franconia two families, Conradiners and Babenbergers, fought for the ducal position, until the victory of the Conradiners banished the Babenbergers to the East Mark, where finally they won a greater position than they had lost at home. In Swabia the struggle for the dukedom was equally fierce, but it is not so easily traced. Only among the Frisians did the tribal duke fail to make his appearance. Lorraine, which was divided by the Treaty of Mersen in 870, was not, properly speaking, a tribal duchy, but it had preserved the memory of its old unity and was struggling to become one.

Conrad I

When in 911 the eastern branch of the Carolingians died out, the Germans, rather than turn to the western or French branch, reverted to their ancient practice of electing a king. By choosing Conrad (911–18), Duke of Franconia, they recognized that the strongest force in Germany at the moment was the tribal duchy. The possible dissolution of the German state into completely independent duchies confronted

The king and the dukes

the kings with a simple but difficult problem. Would they be content to have their former fellow dukes recognize their royalty as a vague kind of overlordship, thus in effect organizing a confederation of tribal duchies under the meaningless headship of a king? Or would they fight the dukes, try to destroy the duchies, and attempt to crush the tribal spirit, in order to make themselves real kings of a German nation? It is difficult to formulate an answer that holds for all the kings of medieval Germany. Conrad I fought the dukes tooth and nail with no success, and then upon his death in 918 recommended that the crown be given to his most ardent opponent, Duke Henry of Saxony, who was elected in 919 by Franconian and Saxon nobles alone.

Policy of Henry I

Henry I (919–36), commonly called Henry the Fowler, pursued a policy of "live and let live" with regard to the dukes. He contented himself with their recognition of his overlordship, made no attempt to interfere with them within their duchies, and in the instance at least of Bavaria abandoned the Church to the duke's not very tender mercies. Nevertheless, as King of Germany and Duke of Saxony he made it possible for his son and successor, Otto the Great, as king and emperor to make the German monarchy the strongest state in Europe. Towards the only other strong force in Germany, and the only possible rival of the dukes, the Church, Henry's attitude was cool, if not actually unfriendly. When the archbishops suggested that he ought to be properly crowned and anointed by them as befitted a king, he put them off with the remark that he was not worthy of such a consecration. Either he felt that his election and his dukedom lent sufficient prestige to his kingship, or else he wished to have nothing to do with a Church that had so warmly supported his predecessor in his campaign against the dukes. Throughout his reign he remained cool to the German bishops and archbishops: he would govern without their help.

The Duchy of Saxony

In fact, Henry's chief attention was devoted to his duchy. For one thing, it needed protection from the Wends east of the Elbe and the Saale. In the winter of 928 he led the Saxons across the frozen marshes of the Havel River, stormed the Wendish town of Branibor (the later Brandenburg), and drove thence up the Elbe to Meissen. These towns became the centers of two new marches, which later, along with a third, Lausitz, guarded the middle valley of the Elbe. Here begins the history of the great margravate of Brandenburg, the forerunner of Prussia. Five years later he retook from the Danes the ancient territory of Charles the Great between the Schlei and the Eider rivers, the Dane Mark, which, subsequently colonized by Germans, gave Germany command of the mouth of the Elbe. Moreover, the Danish King Gorm the Old was forced to pay tribute and receive Christian missionaries. With this ancient German occupation of the narrow neck of the Danish peninsula began the thorny problem of Schleswig-Holstein, which has been settled a good many times since then, most recently in 1919–20.

Henry had likewise to protect Saxony from the Magyars. The tributaries of the Elbe made it easy for them to descend into Saxony; and the fact that the Saxons still dwelt, in the early German manner, in scattered villages in forest clearings or river valleys, not in walled towns, made them an easy prey for the Magyar horsemen. To make matters worse, Saxon freemen, like the early Germans, still fought on foot with their short swords, wearing their straw hats. To cope with the Magyars, therefore, Henry had to build fortifications and train a sufficient body of horsemen. During a nine years' truce which he bought in 924 by paying an annual tribute he began in earnest to put Saxony in readiness. Strongholds were set up in Thuringia and eastern Saxony; convents, monasteries, episcopal centers, royal villas, and country estates were surrounded with palisades of heavy logs set vertically in the ground, with timbered towers at the corners. Some of these, like Naumburg, Nordhausen, Merseburg, and Quedlinburg, later attracted traders and finally became cities, as had the Saxon episcopal sees founded by Charlemagne. Into these new strongholds (German, *Burgwarde*) were moved permanent detachments of armed servitors from Henry's own immense domains in Saxony. Every year, we are told, one-ninth of the Saxon male population capable of field service was moved into the *Burgwarde* to be trained for cavalry service. When the truce with the Magyars expired in 933, Henry defied them, the story goes, by throwing a dead dog into their camp. They were defeated near the Unstrutt River not far from Merseburg; henceforth Saxony was free from their depredations. As for the rest of Germany, Henry was quite willing to leave to each duke the responsibility of protecting his own duchy.

Protection of Saxony against the Magyars

In Lorraine, on the contrary, Henry I interfered most decisively. In 911 Lorraine had refused to recognize the new German king, Conrad I, but had acknowledged the western, or French, Carolingians as overlords. Between 923 and 925 Henry brought both halves of Lorraine, united as a new duchy, back within the German frontier, where the country was to remain until the seventeenth century. The addition of this old Carolingian homeland, where Charles the Great loved to spend most of his time, united to Germany the only large group of Germans not already in the new kingdom. Lorraine was important not only because it was rich land but because at the moment it was intellectually the liveliest spot in western Europe, where a monastic reform movement of serious import was beginning to gain ground.

It is not surprising that the German dukes and lesser nobility were willing to leave the crown with the family of so tolerant and capable a king. When Henry I died in 936, although the formality of an election was gone through, Otto I (936–73) in fact succeeded his father by hereditary right. Nor was any attempt made to revive the vicious old German custom of dividing the kingdom among the king's sons. When, therefore, Henry I was succeeded by his son and grandson and great-grandson in direct descent and then, after a struggle with rivals, by another great-grandson, it began to look as if the elective principle, after more than a century of the Saxon dynasty, had been superseded at last by hereditary kingship. From the first moment of his reign young Otto made it clear that he was looking farther beyond the boundaries of his Saxon duchy than his father had. Unlike him, he did not refuse to be crowned and anointed by the Rhenish archbishops. He went to Aachen to be crowned, as if to proclaim that the new Saxon king meant to follow in the footsteps of Charles the Great.

At the banquet following the ceremonies the German dukes Eberhard of Franconia, Herman of Swabia, Arnulf of Bavaria, and Giselbert of Lorraine served as honorary officials of his household, as chamberlain, seneschal, cupbearer, and marshal. This was a typically feudal symbol, as the event proved, of Otto's conception of the German kingdom that was to be. The great dukes were to be loyal vassals, servitors of the crown, their duchies were to be royal fiefs, and fealty and service to the king were to be demanded of them all.

If the harmony that prevailed between Otto and the dukes at his coronation banquet had continued throughout his reign, it is quite conceivable that he would have been content to follow his father's policy towards them. But he soon learned from bitter experience the measure of their antipathy to the monarchy. The first three years of his reign were a constant struggle to put down rebellions; and another rebellion in 941 actually aimed, if rumor may be believed, at his life. Otto's first thought was to control the duchies by parceling them out among members of his family. Bavaria went to a brother, Swabia to a son, Lorraine to a son-in-law; Franconia and Saxony he kept for a while in his own hands. But another revolt in 953–55, in which his son and son-in-law joined, convinced him that there was no solution here: members of his family identified themselves too easily with the old local traditions and interests of their new duchies.

As a matter of fact, unless Otto were willing to revert to his father's policy towards the dukes, forgoing the attempt to build a strong and united German nation, there was only one way out of his difficulties. This way he now saw and promptly took. The new policy was alliance with the Church—that is, with its secular branch, represented by the bishops and archbishops—against their common enemy, tribal feudalism. From the very beginning of his reign Otto had in fact to some extent realized the necessity of counterbalancing by the influence of the Church the influence not only of the dukes but also that of the lesser nobility, particularly the counts. From the first he had insisted on taking control of the Church and Church property out of the hands of the dukes. There is some evidence, too, that he attempted to use a new official in the duchy, the count palatine (German, *Pfalzgraf*), who was to have charge of crown lands within the duchy and as a special kind of *missus* represent the king in his dealings with the duke. *Alliance of king and Church*

What the king needed was an army at his command and an administration amenable to his will. He had neither, but only such use as he could get out of feudal troops and a feudal administration. Even to make a beginning he needed to strengthen enormously the economic resources of the crown, for without a larger income he could accomplish little. Some small beginnings had already been made along these lines. With nothing like a royal system of taxation and with the income from the courts largely passing into the hands of the counts, the crown's chief source of revenue was the crown lands. By the end of the Carolingian period in Germany most of these had been distributed in grants. Conrad I brought in the Franconian lands of his family, and Henry I the lands of the Liudolfinger family in Saxony; and confiscation of the property of dukes and other rebellious nobles further replenished the crown's depleted holdings. All this indeed amounted to a great expansion of crown lands, which alone would account for much of the strength of the Saxon line. *The needs of the king*

But the crown lands, scattered over the whole realm, furnished no convenient center from which the Saxon kings could operate, nor, since it was impossible to exploit them systematically and fully, did they bring in nearly so much income as they should have. Their chief use, in fact, was no better than to support the court as it moved about. There was in addition a large body of sovereign rights, not yet clearly defined but already beginning to be called regalian—such rights as administering justice, coining money, levying tolls, setting up markets, exploiting forests and other natural resources—which, although many of them also had been granted away, still likewise remained potential sources of income. But they too could not be utilized without an adequate administration. For a king determined to consolidate and enlarge the royal power, a king possessing lands and rights but no way of administering them, the only way to get them into use in his interest was to turn them over to someone who could and would pay for their use by loyal service. The secular nobles were already dangerous enough to the crown. However, there were the ecclesiastical nobles, the archbishops and bishops.

The attitude of the Church

The Church was at one with the king in his desire to thwart the ambitions of the dukes and counts. Some of the dukes had been none too lenient in confiscating Church property, and they strove to put their own men into the most important Church offices. There was accordingly every chance that, if left unchecked, they would succeed in subjecting the Church within their duchies to their own control. The Church was anxious to co-operate with the crown in avoiding such a possibility. At the same time no tenth-century bishop would support the crown out of mere sentiment; he must be paid. In fact, the bishop was essentially of the same mind as any other feudal lord, being ordinarily himself a member of the feudal nobility. He was interested in the same kind of local independence and in the same accumulation of land and sovereign rights. For lands and rights he was willing to contribute his ability and resources to strengthening the crown at the expense of his dangerous rivals, the lay nobility.

The Church the foundation of the monarchy

From the point of view of Otto I and his successors, alliance with the Church was worth trying. The clergy were the best educated and best trained men in the Germany of their day. The bishops were recognized as the best administrators in feudal society. They had the advantage of coming from the most important noble families, but—what was even more to the point—their office was not hereditary. In increasing their power the kings were not contributing to the power of local feudal families, although in the end they found that they had contributed to the same result by building up ecclesiastical principalities. But for the present every increase in the power of the Church within a duchy meant a corresponding limitation of the present or possible future power of the duke and the lesser nobles. If at the same time the king could control the personnel of the episcopate and see that only good, efficient, and loyal bishops sat on episcopal thrones, then to strengthen the Church seemed still less dangerous. At any rate, any reliance that the king could place on the bishops made him that much more independent of the nobility. So the alliance was made by Otto I and continued by every German king until the bishops and archbishops of Germany had attained the position of independent princes who no longer needed or wanted the king. It began with the lavish bestowal on bishops and archbishops of grants of crown lands, immunities, and sovereign rights; before long the kings were granting them the jurisdiction of a count within their territories, or even beyond. It continued over centuries until there was nothing left to grant. As long as the king could keep control of the bishops, they were the chief support of the monarchy, and the alliance of crown and Church was a success for both. When he lost control over them, the German monarchy lost its chief support and collapsed.

What Otto I and his successors established was their own system of ecclesiastical feudalism, of which the king was the actual, not merely the theoretical, head. They did with the Church what the dukes of Normandy and the Norman kings of England [1] did with the secular nobility: kept it tied to the crown. Bishops and archbishops in Germany were in effect appointed by the king. To be sure, the formalities of canon law providing for the election of a bishop by the clergy and people were complied with, but the candidate elected was usually the king's nominee. Indeed, the right of free election was a special privilege granted by the king. Frequently the king's nominees came from the royal chancellery or chapel, where they had been trained in state affairs and become personally known to the king. In time the relationship between king and bishop became strictly feudal: the bishop as vassal performed homage and took the oath of fealty to the king as lord. He received his lands and privileges and his spiritual office as a fief from the hands of the king in an actual ceremony of investiture. Before the twelfth century no clear distinction was made between his lands and privileges and his spiritual functions. The investiture was with ring and staff, properly the symbols of his spiritual functions, the ring symbolizing the bishop's marriage to the Church and the staff or crozier his position as shepherd of his flock. According to canon law

Appointment and investiture of bishops

[1] See Chapter 15.

these two symbols were to be turned over to the newly elected bishop by his archbishop, but the actual practice was for ring and staff to be carried to court immediately upon the death of a bishop and for the king to confer them on his newly elected successor. In this way it was made clear that an episcopal office was a royal office; to all intents and purposes the German Church was a state Church.

Services of the bishops to the crown

The services that the bishops rendered the crown were largely the ordinary feudal services of a vassal. The one most important service was their military aid, which filled perhaps the king's greatest single need. The armies of the Ottonians were composed mostly of episcopal contingents, contributed by each bishop according to his means. It was not unusual for a bishop to lead his troops in person. Bishop Michael of Regensburg lost an ear fighting against the Magyars, and if Udalrich of Augsburg did not actually fight, he certainly paced the walls of his city directing the defense against them. The art of war became an essential episcopal accomplishment. Bishops were held to attendance at court when the court was near, and on important occasions were held to attendance no matter where it was. The kings claimed the feudal *droit de gîte* from the Church. When in the course of its perambulations the court had to leave the royal manors, it resorted to monasteries, or preferably to episcopal towns, for food, lodging, and entertainment. But the kings relied upon the bishops for many necessary services for which they could never have trusted feudal nobles at all. Bishops administered royal lands. They were the tutors of princes and the counsellors of kings. The chief officials of the chancellery and chapel were bishops, the Archbishop of Mainz ordinarily being ex-officio archchancellor and archchaplain. Bishops acted as regents and were left in complete charge of the government when the king was absent in Italy. For what we would call diplomatic service the kings used bishops. They even entrusted rebels to them for custody.

A secularized Church

Under these circumstances the German Church became almost thoroughly secularized. German bishops acquired such a reputation that other kings envied the German kings their hard-fighting episcopal warriors; and later writers remarked that, if there was one thing certain, it was that a German bishop could not be pious. Megingaud,

Megingaud of Eichstätt

Bishop of Eichstätt in the reign of Henry II (whose kinsman he was), being about to start out on a journey to Rome, secured permission from his chapter to swear one hundred times, but this meager supply was so soon exhausted that he had to send back for several supplementary hundreds. Especially during Lent he suffered from what he called "the impatience of his belly," so, as an incentive to his chapter to speed through the services, he had placed before them in the middle of the choir a good-sized fish; the prolonged Easter Mass he simplified by starting different parts of the service at the same time. Another story told of Megingaud gives an interesting side light on at least one bishop's interpretation of the king's *droit de gîte*. A royal messenger who stopped at Eichstätt demanding food, when as a matter of fact he had plenty with him, got a whipping, even though a meal had to be interrupted to supply it. The pages of the chroniclers of the tenth and eleventh centuries are full of biographies and portraits of bishops.

Meinwerk, a bosom friend of Henry II, was appointed Bishop of *Meinwerk* Paderborn, not for his learning or piety, but for his practical abilities *of Paderborn* and because the emperor expected the see to be enriched by gifts from his rich patrimony. On one occasion Henry II, a practical jokester, asked Meinwerk to say Mass for his father and mother, after he and his chaplain had erased from the missal the first syllable of the words *famulis* and *famulabus*. They then enjoyed hearing him pray for the souls of he- and she-mules instead of the souls of the men and women of the household. Meinwerk, who was insatiable in the accumulation of property, was an exacting but kindly administrator. He sometimes went about disguised as a peddler. When he found, in testing the loyalty of his serfs to their steward, that they made no attempt to prevent damage to the grain by the bishop's men, he had them flogged; the next time the bishop's men had difficulty in getting into the manor at all. When he found the garden of the well-dressed wife of one of his stewards full of weeds, he had her stripped of her fine clothes and rolled about the garden until the tall growth was flattened down.

The career of Otto I's younger brother Bruno is perhaps most rep- *Bruno of* resentative of the alliance between Church and state, and at the same *Cologne* time typical of the tenth-century Church at its best. Bruno felt himself "begotten for the state," in whose service he wore himself out at the early age of forty. While he was Archbishop of Cologne and archchancellor of the realm, an illegitimate son of Otto was Archbishop of Mainz and another kinsman of Trier, so that all three of the very important Rhenish archbishoprics belonged to members of the family. When Otto was faced with the revolt of 953–55, in which the Duke of Lorraine participated, he simply made Bruno Duke of Lorraine for a while. As a side line Bruno acted as a kind of regent for the young Carolingians of France, whose uncle he was, and as mediator in the quarrels between them and the rising Capetian house, to which he was also related. After the king he was the most important man in the kingdom, and yet he was devoted to his clerical office, and not attracted to politics at all. As one of the most learned men of his time he was the active leader of an intellectual revival, carried on in many instances by his pupils from the cathedral school at Cologne. Bruno's life may well serve as a warning not to misunderstand the implications of the fact that the German Church in the tenth and eleventh centuries became a secular institution. Whatever it became, there can be no doubt that it was serving the best interests of civilization in its day. What, indeed, were secular activities? What was land administration but carrying out the behest "Feed my sheep," and what was service to the king and the state if not rendering unto Cæsar the things that were Cæsar's?

The Lechfeld *ends the Magyar menace*

To Otto I must be given the credit for putting a final stop to the invasion of any part of Germany by the Magyars. Not only were they in themselves dangerous and destructive but they were being used as allies by Otto's enemies, both lay and ecclesiastical. In a last swift movement up the Danube they reached a spot on the River Lech not far from Augsburg, where in 955 they were stopped and beaten once for all by an army mustered from all the duchies. Henceforth Germany had to deal with them only as a people settled in the lower Danube valley, whom we now call Hungarians, though they still call themselves Magyars. Charles the Great's Ostmark was re-established, and Bavarian colonists moved into it. Before long missionaries began to work in Hungary, and by 1000 the Hungarians had set up a Christian monarchy under their king, St. Stephen, with their own archbishopric at Gran. The Hungarians remained loyal sons of the Church; and, although they have always resisted German interference and maintained their own language, they inevitably became through German influence a European people.

The frontiers

The spread of Christianity and with it German influence made notable progress on the north and northeastern frontiers under Otto's auspices. In the Dane Mark three new bishoprics were founded under the Archbishopric of Hamburg-Bremen. The Slavic frontier along the Elbe and Saale was completely reorganized into five new marches, which were covered with *Burgwarde*. The northernmost of these, the Saxon *Nordmark*, was entrusted to Herman Billung, to whom Otto also granted the ducal title in Saxony—a strange capitulation to tribal sentiment. Herman was the first of a strong line of Billunger dukes, who as heads of a proud, stubborn, and independent people were a constant thorn in the flesh of the German kings, not to mention the archbishops of Hamburg-Bremen. An entirely new ecclesiastical organization was set up on the eastern frontier: six new bishoprics, including one at Brandenburg, were created and put under a new archbishopric at Magdeburg.

This formidable preparation for an eastward movement of Germans, however, proved to be premature, for the Wends were not so easily intimidated. They took advantage of the confusion following the death of Otto II to rise in a revolt that wiped out the German organization; and again in 1018, after the Germans had made another start, they rebelled and crushed the German-Christian threat to their own religion and independence. Relations between Germans and Slavs on the eastern frontier were much like those between the American colonists and the Indians as the American frontier gradually moved westward. Far to the southwest Otto I exercised a virtual protectorate over Burgundy. Thus on all the frontiers Otto I's policy displayed the same energy and skill as in his internal administration.

Finally, Otto I revived once more the idea of one great European state, which to the men of the middle ages could mean only the revival of the Roman empire. In the chaos of the break-up of Charlemagne's empire and the birth of feudalism such dreams of unity had lost whatever reality he had succeeded in giving them. Arnulf of Carinthia [2] had been the last Carolingian to occupy a position in Europe that could possibly have been called imperial; since 924 no one had even claimed the title of emperor. Otto first interfered in Italy in 951 to keep the King of Burgundy and the dukes of Swabia and Bavaria from creeping over the Alpine passes into northern Italy. Chivalrous contemporary historians explained his interest in Italy as the result of an appeal from Adelheid, the beautiful widow of one of the Burgundian contenders for the Italian throne, to save her from the matrimonial clutches of Berengar, Marquis of Ivrea, then King of the Lombards. Otto saved her by the simple device of marrying her himself, and then with no more ceremony took the title of King of the Lombards and returned to Germany without coronation or consecration, leaving Berengar as his vassal for northern Italy. *The revival of empire*

No one could meddle in Italian affairs without becoming involved with the papacy, and in 961 Otto returned at the request of the young Pope John XII. He was crying for protection against Berengar, who had designs on the Papal States. It was the usual story: the Franks had first come into Italy to protect the popes' possessions from their Italian enemies. Otto reached Rome on January 31, 962, and was crowned Roman emperor early in February, with his sword bearer standing beside him for protection. In return for renewing the Dona- *Otto and the papacy*

[2] See p. 283.

tions of Pepin and Charlemagne, he forced from the pope the recognition of his right to approve elections to the papacy. He then left to take care of Berengar. John XII, however, had counted on no such unqualified assertion of German control over his office, and after Otto's departure he conspired with Berengar to undo what had been done. Otto returned in 963, forced from the Romans a promise never to elect a pope without the emperor's consent, and summoned a local synod, which deposed John XII and elected a new pope, Leo VIII. But, again after Otto's departure, John XII drove Leo VIII out of the city and resumed the papal throne. When the career of John, "the most profligate if not the most guilty of all who have worn the tiara," was "speedily closed by the sword of an injured husband," the Romans, who shared his resentment of the strong German hand, without bothering to consult Otto, elected in his place Benedict V. Otto returned again in the summer of 964, called another synod, which deposed Benedict V and replaced Leo VIII upon St. Peter's throne, and once more returned to Germany. Leo's successor, John XIII, was elected with the proper co-operation of the emperor, but a rebellion in Rome drove him out of the city. Otto went back in 966, this time wreaked a terrible vengeance on the authors of the rebellion, and restored John XIII. Henceforth his authority was uncontested in Rome.

Significance of the imperial revival

962 was a momentous year for Germany, for Italy, and for the papacy. Unless the popes could get the upper hand of the new German emperors, they had jumped from the frying pan into the fire, for Otto's conception of his duty to the papacy was quite as rigorous as Charlemagne's had been. It was clear that restoration of the empire under his auspices meant German sovereignty over the city of Rome and over the Papal States, and the German emperor's control of the pope as rigid as the German king's control of his bishops. The German king had now donned the robes of Charlemagne and assumed the title of Lombard king and Roman emperor; henceforth the history of medieval Germany, for better or for worse, was indissolubly bound up with Italy and the papacy. And there can hardly be much doubt that what Otto did in Italy strengthened his position in Germany. His son was crowned Roman emperor as well as German king long before Otto's death. In fact, of course, the new empire was even less a Roman empire than Charlemagne's had been; it had lost France and the Spanish march and gained only some German territory from the Slavs on the east. It extended from Lorraine roughly to the Oder River and to Hungary, and from the North and Baltic Seas to southern Italy, where a little Byzantine territory was still left. Later, because (for one

thing) it was associated with the protection of the papacy, it came to be called the Holy Roman empire.

The last three kings of the Saxon house mainly followed the lines *Otto II* laid down by Otto the Great. Otto II (973–83) provided for still better protection of the Bohemian frontier by organizing northern Bavaria as a march and entrusting it to one of the Babenbergers. Thereby he aimed also to decrease the power of the dukes of Bavaria, who were deprived as well of the *Ostmark,* which was entrusted to another Babenberger, and of the marches of Carinthia and Friuli (or Verona), which were made into the new Duchy of Carinthia. Nor did Otto II neglect his imperial rôle; the last three years of his life were spent in an unsuccessful effort to carry the banner of empire still farther into southern Italy against the Byzantines, and to drive the Saracens back to Sicily.

In the case of Otto III (983–1002) the ideal of empire triumphed *Otto III* over the reality. His mother was the extremely capable Byzantine Princess Theophano, whom Otto I had had no little difficulty in winning as his son's bride. Together with Otto I's widow Adelheid and old Archbishop Willigis of Mainz she ruled Germany during Otto III's minority. The boy was, then, brought up by his mother and grandmother, advised and aided by an archbishop. Moreover, in Italy he came under the influence of the man reputed to be the most learned man of his day, his tutor, the Frenchman Gerbert, a pupil of the monastery of Aurillac. His religious upbringing made him throughout his life an admirer of the new monastic reformers, such as St. Nilus in southern Italy and St. Romuald near Ravenna, and he was devoted to St. Adalbert, the apostle to the heathen Prussians. As soon as Otto reached his majority in 996, he made his young cousin Bruno Pope Gregory V, the first German pope and an enthusiastic reformer. Upon Gregory's premature death Otto raised Gerbert to the papal throne as Sylvester II. His great ambition was to realize the dream of a resurrected Roman empire under the joint guidance of himself and Sylvester II as pope of a reformed Church. From his mother Otto had imbibed the authentic Roman tradition as enshrined in the Græco-oriental form at Constantinople. He built himself an imperial palace on the Aventine in Rome, which was to be his capital, not merely one of the towns of his empire. He introduced all the ceremonial etiquette of Byzantium; German bishops and Italian bishops were, as officers of the court, henceforth to be called logothetes, and the whole nomenclature of officialdom was to be similarly Byzantine. But the Rome that he so dearly loved rejected him, and the Germany that he was neglecting was in ferment when he died at the age of twenty-two. Two years before, the story goes, he descended into the tomb of the great Charles at Aachen and from round the neck of his mighty predecessor, still sitting upright upon his throne clad in the desiccated robes of empire, removed the golden cross. They carried the dead young emperor back from Rome across the Alps, to rest in the Germany that he had known so little, beside Charles the Great in the old church at Aachen.

Henry II

The last of the Saxon line was Henry II (1002–24), Duke of Bavaria, Otto's second cousin. Because of Otto's neglect of Germany it cost his successor a struggle to establish himself as king. He had a still harder struggle to establish himself in Italy, but with the efficient aid of Leo of Vercelli, a "bishop of the empire," as he called himself, he won the Lombard kingship and was crowned emperor at Rome in 1014. Henry II, however, returned to the policy of Otto I and Otto II by devoting himself primarily to the interests of Germany. He further strengthened the alliance between Church and crown, and indeed did so well by the Church that he became St. Henry and his queen became St. Kunigunde. As his monument—and in a sense a monument to the loyalty of the German bishops to their king—he chose to found a new bishopric at Bamberg, which he endowed richly. In its cathedral, one of the glories of medieval architecture, he is buried with his queen; they stand in stone at the portal, and inside their coronation robes still hang.

The Saxon renaissance

The chief contemporary historian of Henry II's reign was a Saxon bishop, Thietmar of Merseburg. It was characteristic of the literary activity of the Ottonian revival that most of it was by or about bishops. From the many good biographies of important prelates and local histories of important bishoprics a large part of the history of the period is written. It is noteworthy in particular how much—not all of it concerning the Church—comes from Saxony itself. Widukind, a monk of the monastery of Corvey, in his *Three Books of Saxon History* is so enthusiastic over the military successes of Henry I and Otto I that he neglects both the pope and the imperial coronation of Otto I. Roswitha, a nun of the Saxon convent of Gandersheim, celebrated Otto's deeds in a poem, and was also Germany's first dramatist, for she tried to combat what she considered the pernicious popularity of Terence by writing comedies based on the lives of illustrious virgins and saints.

At Otto I's court there was no institution corresponding to Charles the Great's palace school, but he was surrounded by a learned, cosmopolitan circle of Italians, Greeks, Irishmen, and one Spaniard. The stimulation and training that his younger brother Bruno got in this atmosphere served him well in his later efforts to make Cologne a center of learning. Theophano brought in her train Greek artists and workmen, whose influence can be traced in manuscript illumination and in architecture in a bishopric as remote as Paderborn. After the establishment of the empire Italian influence grew stronger. Bishop Bernward of Hildesheim, a lover and patron of the arts and a companion of Otto III in Italy, cast the first bronze doors in Germany and had a column made of scenes from the life of Christ similar to Trajan's column. The doors and the column at Hildesheim and the beautiful painted wooden ceiling of his Church of St. Michael (a transplantation of the Italian basilica into northern Germany, which one scholar called the most beautiful church in the world) can still be seen.

Even as the Saxon kings were creating the framework for a strong German state and restoring the tradition of the Roman empire in its peculiar German form, there were already at work the forces that were to destroy both the German monarchy and the empire in Italy. It has already been observed that the chief disruptive force in Germany was feudalism. Perhaps as much could be said for Italy, although in Lombardy in the eleventh and twelfth centuries the vigorous new growth of towns, which, like feudal lords, sought to achieve independence, proved another obstacle to the German emperors. Even so, if there had been no further complications they might have been able to cope successfully with both feudalism and the towns. But there was the Church. The papacy, which in 961 had invited Otto's protection against Berengar, later, to protect itself from Otto's successors, allied itself both with German feudalism in its struggles against the German king and with the Italian towns in their struggles against the German emperor. Moreover, in trying to carry through a reform of the whole Church, which implied the realization once and for all of its dreams of monarchical control over the Church as well as temporal supremacy over the state, the papacy carried on for over two centuries a bitter struggle against the German monarchy, which in the end was fatal to both. *Dangers to Germany and the empire*

The reform movement began in the monasteries. By the tenth century the monks were well aware of the serious need of reform in their ranks. A century earlier conditions had been bad enough for Louis the Pious to encourage Benedict of Aniâne in a reform of the Benedictine houses. The general anarchy of the ninth century had undermined monastic discipline and cost the monasteries a great deal of their property, which was lost to invaders like the Norsemen and to upstart *The need for monastic reform* feudal nobles. Like the secular Church they had become so completely subjected to the rising feudal system that they were regarded by nobles and kings as their private property. In many cases lay abbots were put in charge, who managed the monastery as a business for its owner. Mercenary traffic in monasteries and monastic property was notoriously flagrant. All over western Europe protests arose from monastic reformers against this state of affairs. Men like Saints Nilus and Romuald in Italy at the end of the tenth century, in Lorraine reformers of the type of Richard, Abbot of St. Vannes in Verdun, and in Flanders Poppo at Liége and Gerhard at Brogne denounced the ways into which monks and monasteries had fallen. These reform movements in Italy and Lorraine, however, were engulfed by the powerful wave that spread from the Benedictine monastery of Cluny in Burgundy. Cluny, indeed, was synonymous with reform, and so great was its influence that the whole reform movement has somewhat incorrectly been called the Cluniac reform.

The Cluniac Order   The monastery of Cluny was founded in 910 (approximately when the Vikings settled in Normandy and the Carolingian line died out in Germany) by William, Count of Auvergne and Duke of Aquitaine. From its very foundation it was meant to be free of all entanglements with feudalism. Its founder resigned control over it, and papal and royal privileges alike freed it from the control of any bishop and made it subject directly and only to the pope. Hence from its very beginnings it was a model of independence of the state and the secular branch of the Church. By assuming control over old monasteries and founding new ones Cluny expanded rapidly, and early developed a new type of monastic organization. St. Benedict had provided for no general organization of the monasteries following his rule; every Benedictine house was in spiritual affairs autonomous and had its own abbot. There was never but one abbot of the Cluniac system, the abbot of the mother house at Cluny. All other houses were priories headed by priors appointed from Cluny, who held regular meetings at Cluny presided over by the abbot. The abbot maintained the discipline of the system by regular visitations of Cluniac priories. The Cluniac system was thus highly centralized, a model for the institutions of popes and kings. The spread of the order was rapid and wide: from Burgundy into France and Spain, into Lorraine and England, into Germany and Italy. At its height in the twelfth century Cluny is estimated to have ruled over some three hundred priories.

Like most reformers, the Cluniacs claimed to advocate nothing new but simply a return to older and purer standards, which for them meant a return to Benedict's rule. Again like most reformers, they felt free to make improvements on these standards, which they did by emphasizing as the monk's proper occupation not so much manual labor (which Benedict had prescribed) and scholarly works, as chanting the praises of God for an increased number of hours for their own salvation and that of those for whom they were interceding. Chastity was particularly insisted upon. The reformers further demanded a return to the prescriptions of canon law in regard to the celibacy of the clergy, the method of clerical election and induction into Church offices, and the holding and management of Church property. Abbots were to be elected by the monks themselves, and care was to be taken to secure better young men as novices. Property lost to laymen was to be recovered and further efforts made to increase monastic wealth; and all monastic property was to be owned and managed by the monasteries themselves, free of any control by lay or other ecclesiastical persons.

If the Cluniac movement had remained what it first was, simply a monastic reform, it would have nothing like its actual importance. But it became in time much more than it began by being. First of all, Cluniac monks, especially in Lorraine, were appointed bishops. Henceforth their attention was perforce directed to the reform of the secular clergy, who were expected to comply with the superior standards of reformed monasticism. Here indeed was dynamite. For one thing, the movement inaugurated and led by Cluny began to attract a type of reformer whose aims were more radical than the original Cluniac program. For instance, Humbert, a Cluniac monk from Lorraine, who became one of the ablest and most enthusiastic of the cardinals supporting the reform program of Pope Gregory VII, published a famous pamphlet, *Three Books against the Simoniacs,* in which he argued that no Church property should in any way be owned or held or used by lay persons.

Second, some of the items of the Cluniac program itself had implications, when applied to the secular clergy, that they hardly had so long as they were restricted to the regular clergy. To demand, for example, that the secular priesthood should be celibate was to revolutionize the life of the parish clergy of western Europe, who were commonly married or lived openly with their "priestesses." To return to the prescriptions of canon law concerning the choosing of priests and bishops was to overturn the long-accepted relationship between the lord or the king and the clergy. Parish priests were chosen by the lord of the manor, bishops and archbishops were appointed by the great lords or by the king. Especially for the relationship between Church and state in Germany such a demand was revolutionary. It threatened to deprive the German kings of the very basis of their strength, their alliance with the Church, by making the Church free of them. The demand that bishops and archbishops should be invested with the spiritual symbols of their office, the ring and the staff,[3] by the proper ecclesiastical authority and not by the king, weakened the feudal tie between Church and state. The demand that Church property and acquired political rights should be held in full ownership by the Church, not on feudal tenure from the king, deprived the crown of essential income and services. All these accumulated divergences from the canon law, not to mention the outright buying and selling of Church offices and ordinations, the reformers branded as simony, and simony they said was heresy.

The reformers had no easier time of it than zealots ever have had in persuading men to forsake well-established or profitable or enjoyable practices. Some abbots were mutilated and murdered when they tried to reform their houses. The parish clergy, outraged at what seemed to them the inhuman demand for celibacy, turned synods into *The papacy* pandemonium when the subject was mentioned. The German Church *takes over the* as a whole was loath to break its alliance with the state and to become *Cluniac reform* embroiled with the German kings. Nor could the German kings be expected to disadvantage themselves by granting independence to the Church. Obviously the reformers must look elsewhere for the kind of support that would bear down with authority on a recalcitrant clergy and a hostile state. That place was Rome. Could the reformers get the papacy and use its spiritual prestige and its temporal power to force Church and state into line? For a moment in Otto III's short reign it looked as if they might. By the middle of the eleventh century they had succeeded. When the Cluniac reform program was adopted by the papacy it became a European movement of serious import. From 1046 to 1085, first as the power behind the throne and after 1073 as Pope Gregory VII, the monk Hildebrand was the leader of the movement; hence this stage of the Cluniac reform is called the Hildebrandine or Gregorian reform.

Gregory VII and the reforming popes before and after him were of course sincerely interested in the reform program for its own sake; *Implications* but there is no denying that they also realized its implications in rela-*of the reform* tion to the long efforts of the popes to make themselves spiritually *program for* supreme over the whole Church. Furthermore, it is difficult to suppose *the papacy and* that they did not early recognize that to carry out such a program *the empire*

[3] See p. 359.

would involve them in conflict with the state. Reform would inevitably raise the question of which was the superior power, the king or the pope, and lead directly to an attempt by the papacy to establish temporal supremacy not only over the German empire but over as much of Europe as possible. The Cluniac program of return to canon law necessarily included return to the Pseudo-Isidorian Decretals and to the Donation of Constantine.[4] These two "pious frauds" in themselves constituted a program for the pope's spiritual supremacy in the Church and temporal supremacy over the state; popes and reformers now began to quote them.

The reform program was in origin, and in theory remained, an attempt to free the Church from the trammels of feudalism and monarchy. But the reforming popes were interested in far more than the independence of the Church; they aimed to make the independent Church wholly dependent upon themselves. It was not merely that they hoped to achieve this result by reform; the recognition of papal supremacy, whatever the Cluniac program may have been, became an indispensable part of the Gregorian program. In other words, the popes saw in leadership of the reform a chance to do with the Church what the monarchs were striving to do with the state: destroy its feudalism and centralize its government. It is important to note that the great obstacle to the achievement of this end was monarchy, the same obstacle that stood in the way to achievement of the first purpose of the reform program. For the popes it was not merely temporal supremacy that required control over the German emperors who presumed to exercise control over them; as long as kings were responsible for the feudal subordination of the Church to the state, there could be no spiritual supremacy for the papacy within the Church either.

With the death of Henry II in 1024 the Saxon dynasty died out. The old practice of election was used to choose the first of the Salian or Franconian line, Conrad II (1024-39). He was one of the strongest and most far-sighted of all the German kings. He was aware of the limitations of Ottonian policy towards the Church, and was careful to keep a strong hold on the bishops and not to deplete further the crown lands (now increased by his own family holdings) by extensive new grants to the Church. He was personally interested in only two churches, the monastery church of Limburg near Speyer and the great church at Speyer itself, where all the kings of his line are buried. In fact, most of his grants of crown lands were made in an effort to build up from the ranks of nonnoble retainers a loyal body of servitors,

Conrad II

[4] See p. 202.

called ministerials (Latin, *ministeriales*), who could be used in place
of churchmen in royal administration and who could be expected to
be more singly devoted to the interests of the crown. Under Conrad,
too, regalian rights, for example market rights, began to be exploited

by the king rather than granted to others. He inaugurated another
new policy by looking for support against the dukes not only to the
Church but to the lesser German nobility, whom he won over by
recognizing the hereditability of their fiefs. In so doing, however, while
he may have temporarily strengthened his own position and weakened the position of the dukes, yet in the long run he was encouraging
the splitting up of Germany into small feudal bits. It was during Conrad's reign that, after the death of its King Rudolph, the Kingdom of
Burgundy, which had been a protectorate, was reincorporated into the
German empire. Burgundy was of great importance to the empire,
inasmuch as it brought the Alpine passes of Mont Cenis and Mont

Genèvre into German hands and thus kept the French out of Italy. Finally, Conrad did not regrant dukedoms falling vacant to other local families but turned them over to his young son Henry, who, when he succeeded his father in 1039, was duke of all the duchies except Lorraine and Saxony.

It has been customary to characterize Henry III (1039–56) as the *Henry III* strongest of the German emperors, chiefly because of his control over the duchies and because he made the papacy a German institution in 1046 by deposing three rival popes and inaugurating a succession of five German popes. But it must be remembered that he owed his power over the duchies to his father, in spite of whose example he had before his death regranted the duchies into private hands. And in turning the papacy over to Germans he was turning it over in fact to Cluniac reformers. What he bequeathed to his son was a Germany seething with discontent, a nobility on the point of rebellion, and in Italy the papacy under the thumb of the reforming Hildebrand and his allies. Leo IX (1049–54), Cluniac Bishop of Toul before his accession to the papacy, was the first pope to impose on the Church in western Europe the full weight of his apostolic authority in the interest of the reform, which he did by crossing the Alps to preside over reforming synods in France, Lorraine, and Germany.

It is indeed an ironic fact that those men who stood to lose most from the reform program, the German emperors, were the very men who made its success possible. Otto III, who first appointed reforming popes, was a mystical young enthusiast, but Henry III seems to have been a hard-headed and capable ruler. However, religious motives influenced the medieval mind powerfully, the king's mind as well as the peasant's. If Henry III had been guided only by self-interest, it would have been easy for him to ascertain that the Gregorian reform was by no means to his advantage. Yet he was personally devoted to it; he gave up simony in the strict sense by declining to sell episcopal appointments, and he himself preached from the pulpit in support of the Cluniac Truce of God.[5] Neither the dukes nor the other higher nobility nor the German bishops approved of his reforming proclivities. He alienated them further by gathering about him a large group of ministerials, but on the other hand he apparently dropped his father's plans to cultivate the allegiance of the lesser nobility to the crown and to exploit directly the regalian rights. He returned to the Ottonian policy of generosity to the bishops, making them his chief advisers and administrators, and thereby incurred the greater hostility

[5] See p. 320.

of the dukes. He left his throne in 1056 to a youngster of six, Henry IV, under the regency of his mother, Agnes of Aquitaine, herself a sympathetic supporter of reform in the Church. The possible union of the rebellious German nobility with the reforming papacy made this a perilous moment for German monarchy.

The regency for Henry IV

During the nine years of minority of young Henry (1056–65) all parties to the threatening conflict between Church and state labored to strengthen their positions. In Germany the nobility, both lay and ecclesiastical, made bold to appropriate royal property and sovereign rights on a generous scale. In 1062 a group of them, headed by Anno, the wily Archbishop of Cologne, took the young king from his mother at Kaiserswerth and made off with him to Cologne. The conspirators, joined by the handsome Archbishop of Hamburg-Bremen, Adalbert, soon proceeded to divide among themselves one of the chief resources of the crown, the royal monasteries. Although they succeeded only in part, it was evident how the regency was whetting episcopal and noble appetites.

It was only after Henry had reached his majority in 1065 that he was able to free himself from tutelage and adopt a policy of his own. This was in the main the old Ottonian policy, as modified by Conrad II. The young king used the Church as a major source of revenue,

The early years of Henry IV

and unlike his father trafficked right and left in all Church offices, to the outraged dismay of some reformers who appealed to Rome against him. He relied less upon the higher nobility for service than upon unknown men of obscure origin, ministerials from Swabia; for this he was hated. He was hated the more because he was determined to regain for the crown the property and privileges that had been expropriated during his minority. It seems quite likely, too, that he had larger plans for consolidating the monarchy, plans somewhat similar to those adopted so successfully by the Capetian kings of France. If so, it might well be argued that the wisest, if neither the greatest nor the most successful, of medieval German kings was Henry IV.

At any rate he was one of the most unfortunate and one of the most remarkable; as Cicero said of another sorely tried king, his enemies defeated him in such a way that he kept on being king. His idea was to establish in the region of the Harz Mountains in southern Saxony and northern Thuringia a compact royal domain, centering around the royal villa at Goslar, similar to the Capetian Île de France,[6] from which the kings might gradually extend their territory and make their kingship prevail. But such a policy necessarily aroused the opposition

[6] See p. 471.

of the Saxons and Thuringians, who of all German peoples had been least assimilated into the German nation. In Saxony especially the late regency had been costly to the crown; forests and heaths, the property of the crown, had been freely used by the Saxon peasantry for timber and fuel and pasturage. Henry's determination to reassert the royal prerogative over these lands, to forbid their private exploitation, and to render them productive of revenue for the crown by the sale of licenses for lumbering, pasturage, fishing, and mill sites, to the Saxon peasantry seemed arbitrary tyranny. Furthermore, to quell possible rebellion and protect the newly recovered land and resources, Henry continued his father's policy of building on the crown lands in Saxony and Thuringia castles, which he garrisoned with his faithful Swabian ministerials, whom the Saxons detested as foreign oppressors in the employ of a tyrant king. "Castles," an annalist exaggerates, "began to bristle on every hilltop in Saxony and Thuringia." By 1073 Henry IV had gone so far in this direction as to drive the Saxons to rebellion.

In the same year Hildebrand ascended the papal throne as Gregory VII. The papacy had, meanwhile, taken far-reaching steps to emancipate itself from German control and to prepare for rigorous enforcement of the whole reform program. In 1054 it finally severed all relations with the Greek Church.[7] In 1059 Pope Nicholas II convened *The papal* a special synod to eliminate once and for all the interference of Ro- *electoral* man nobles and German emperors in papal elections. It was provided *law of 1059* that henceforth the election of a pope (whenever possible from the Roman clergy) was to be solely in the hands of the cardinal clergy of Rome—the clergy, that is, attached to certain particular and especially revered Roman churches. The cardinal-bishops of these churches were to deliberate and negotiate and then call in the cardinal-presbyters and cardinal-deacons to help choose the candidate. When the candidate was selected, the remaining Roman clergy and the Roman people were to be given opportunity to approve of the cardinals' choice, thus formally completing the election as prescribed by canon law. As further protection from interference by factions of the Roman nobility, which had done more than any other influence to debauch the papacy, it was provided that election might be held outside the city.

Since most of the Roman cardinals by this time belonged to the reform party, the new electoral law in effect assured henceforth the election of reforming popes. The synod, not daring to ignore Henry IV altogether, included in its proceedings a provision that nothing in the above decrees should be to the damage of "the honor and reverence

[7] See pp. 135–36.

due to our beloved son Henry." This was an implicit recognition of the emperor's right of confirmation, but Henry's successors would have specifically to request the renewal of this right for themselves. If circumstances prevented the consecration and enthronization of the newly elected pope at Rome, which ordinarily took place only after the emperor's confirmation had been secured, the new pope by virtue of the mere fact of his election might exercise all the prerogatives of his office. This made imperial confirmation quite unnecessary, and Nicholas II's successor Alexander II in fact became pope without any reference to Dowager Queen Agnes. The first reaction in Germany to the new papal electoral decree was plain: a synod of German clergy voted before his death in 1061 to depose Nicholas II. But the opposition was short-lived, and by 1064 the young king's disloyal advisers, the archbishops Anno and Adalbert, had come to terms with Alexander II. The reformers had begun logically at the top with the business of freeing all ecclesiastical elections from lay interference.

In the same year, 1059, the papacy took another step to anticipate, almost to invite, conflict with the German empire, by making an alliance with the Normans of southern Italy. At the beginning of the eleventh century southern Italy was prey to a three-cornered fight between the Byzantine empire, struggling to maintain its last foothold in Italy, rebellious Lombard nobles, and Saracen pirates from Sicily.

Alliance of the papacy with the Normans

Venturesome Norman nobles, returning home in 1016 from a pilgrimage to Palestine, tarried to visit the chief shrines of southern Italy. There they saw possibilities of fame and fortune in selling their services to whoever would pay them best. Word reached Normandy of this rich and populous land where a poor knight might make his fortune with his horse and his sword, and soon a stream of Normans was flowing into southern Italy. The wresting of Apulia and Calabria from the Byzantine empire was led by the numerous sons of Tancred of Hauteville, chief among whom was Robert Guiscard, called the Crafty, a man of "towering stature, flashing eye and bellowing strength." [8] By 1053 the Normans' self-interest was obvious, and their conquest had gone so far that the papacy, alarmed at the prospect of a strong Norman state to the south, undertook to suppress them by force. But Leo IX was badly defeated in battle at Civitate and even held prisoner for a while. After this failure the reformers in the *Curia*, led by Hildebrand, discovered in the Normans possible allies against the Roman nobles and the German emperor. So Nicholas II, in return for a feudal oath of homage and fealty from the two Norman chiefs Richard of

[8] Haskins, *The Normans in European History*, p. 201.

Aversa and Robert Guiscard, invested them with their conquests as papal fiefs. Robert in his oath called himself "by the grace of God and St. Peter duke of Apulia and Calabria and, with their help, hereafter of Sicily." [9] Now this was an interesting step in the progress of papal temporal power, and for the German monarchy a humiliation. For the pope was usurping the claims of the German emperors to the sovereignty of southern Italy, which they had asserted from the beginning of the empire and had sought to make good by many campaigns. The Normans first came to the aid of the reforming papacy by helping to seat Alexander II in Rome in 1061.

Elsewhere in Italy the papacy was looking for more allies. In the house of Beatrice, Marquess of Tuscany, it found its most loyal support. In Milan and other Lombard towns it favored a popular movement called the Pataria, "the ragpickers," which aimed not only to get rid of the simoniacs and loose livers among the upper clergy (for the most part Germans or German appointees), but also to deprive the rich townsmen and the nobility of some of their property. The popes were thus willing to get temporary aid even from social revolution, which could hardly prove of lasting benefit to such an institution as the papacy. During these years synods were held yearly in Rome during Lent, to which were invited the leading reforming spirits among the clergy. Appeals to Rome were listened to with great attention and the practice of appeal encouraged; interference in local ecclesiastical administration grew more frequent. Recalcitrant bishops and archbishops were summoned to Rome to humble themselves before the pope. Excommunication, suspension, and even deposition from office were visited with greater freedom upon disobedient clergy. At this time the popes also developed the system of using legates having the full authority of the papacy for special missions, and in particular to enforce reforming decrees on local synods.

Other papal allies

When in 1073 Hildebrand, who chose as pope the name of Gregory I, the Great, came to the throne of St. Peter, he was a man in his fifties, with over twenty-five years' experience in the service of papal interests and as a reformer. He was ready to speak out boldly from the day that a tumultuous mob raised him to the leadership of the Church. In origin he was seemingly a Tuscan peasant, a little, homely, pale-faced man, with a weak voice but with eyes that revealed the passionate intensity of his nature and the cold steel-like quality of his will. The famous Italian hermit, Peter Damiani, one of the most enthusiastic of the reformers, called him a "holy Satan" and "the fluttering tyrant,

Gregory VII

[9] *Ibid.*, p. 204.

who showed pity with the love of a Nero, caressed by boxing the ears, and stroked with the eagle's talons." One of his favorite verses of Scripture was Jeremiah's "Cursed be the man who withholds his sword from blood."

Gregory VII was the chief champion between Nicholas I and Innocent III of the spiritual supremacy of the pope as monarch of the Church and his temporal supremacy over the monarchs of this world. No pope has been more completely hypnotized by the ineffable dignity of his office, and none perhaps has ever felt himself so completely identified with St. Peter. He was not only the successor of Peter, the first pope, as head of the Christian Church on earth, but the successor of Peter, the disciple of Christ, as the divinely chosen instrument of God to enforce righteousness upon sinful man. Righteousness meant obedience to God, and obedience to God Gregory identified with obedience to the pope. He could stand almost anything but disobedience, which he called simply "idolatry and therefore a rank form of unbelief." One of the commonest salutations in his letters is the bestowal of apostolic benediction upon the recipient, "if he shall be obedient." He gave the clergy sufficient opportunity to practice the virtue of obedience, for—to say nothing of his great reform program—there was no detail of ecclesiastical discipline anywhere in western Europe too insignificant for his attention. He lectured the clergy as a stern and unrelenting father. To enforce his will he employed to the full every means of centralized administration that the popes had slowly elaborated. He sent legates in all directions, on every kind of mission, and scolded them roundly when they did not report promptly and fully. He urged the clergy to look to him as the source of justice, to appeal all their troubles to Rome; he demanded with frequency that they come to Rome in person. When faced with rank disobedience he spared neither suspension nor deposition nor excommunication.

The Dicta-
tus Papæ

In the *Dictatus Papæ* (the Pope's Dictate) Gregory VII concluded, after consulting earlier collections of canons and decretals, that "the Roman church has never erred; nor will it err to all eternity"; that the pope "himself may be judged by no one," but that to him "should be referred the more important cases of every church"; and that "a sentence passed by him may be retracted by no one." "No synod shall be called a general one without his order"; "in a council, his legate, even if of a lower grade, is above all bishops, and can pass sentence of deposition against them"; "he may depose and reinstate (and transfer) bishops without assembling a synod." [10] Nor did Gregory's re-

[10] Henderson, *op. cit.*, pp. 366–67.

lentless logic stop here. The *Dictatus* goes on to declare that the pope "may absolve subjects from their fealty to wicked men"; that "of the pope alone all princes shall kiss the feet"; that "it may be permitted to him to depose emperors" and that "he alone may use the imperial insignia."

The government of the world is accordingly a vast theocracy; the Church has absorbed the state, and the whole earth is nothing else than St. Augustine's City of God. There was nothing new about theocracy: Charles the Great conceived of his empire as a theocracy, in which the emperor was God's representative, and in which the Church, whose one concern was religion, was one of the instruments of the state. Gregory concludes that the only emperor is the pope. His conception of the government of the world was feudal. If we may fill in the outlines of his draft, God is the great overlord of all, who rules through Christ, who rules through St. Peter, who rules through the pope. The pope is a subvassal of God and Christ through his lord St. Peter, and emperors and kings and princes are the vassals of the pope, and hold their domains as fiefs from him. All this was no more than a dream in Gregory's mind. But he was ready and eager to take steps to make his dream come true—the first pope of whom that can be said.

Papal theocracy

One such step he had already taken, for he had been instrumental in 1059 in arranging the bargain whereby the Norman principalities of southern Italy became fiefs of the pope. To French crusaders on their way to fight the Infidels in Spain he announced that "Spain was from ancient times subject to St. Peter in full sovereignty and . . . belongs of right to no mortal, but solely to the Apostolic See." He thanked the Duke of Bohemia for "the hundred marks of silver of your standard weight, which you sent to St. Peter under the form of tribute." He informed the King of Hungary that "Hungary was long since offered and devotedly surrendered to St. Peter by King Stephen as the full property of the Holy Roman Church under its complete jurisdiction and control. . . . The scepter of the kingdom which you hold is a fief of the apostolic and not of the royal majesty." He suggested to the King of Denmark that he commit himself and his kingdom "with loyal devotion to the Prince of the Apostles and . . . have the support of his authority." Corsica, its inhabitants learned from him, "belongs by right of legal proprietorship to no mortal person and to no power but that of the Holy Roman Church." In one letter he refers to the "King of Dalmatia, whom the apostolic authority has constituted." He claimed tribute from France, and tried to get William

the Conqueror to turn over England to him as a fief! To King Demetrius of Russia, who was not even a member of his Church, he
actually wrote that "in the name of St. Peter" he had "transferred
the government" of Russia to Demetrius's son.[11] No pope had ever
made such extreme claims to temporal sovereignty nor exercised that
sovereignty so largely. Gregory was consumed by the passion to rule,
by no means only for his own sake. It is no accident that it was he who
first dreamed of leading Europe on a crusade to the Holy Land, upon
which he was ready to lay down his life as a martyr for his Faith.

So much for Gregory VII's theories and ambitions. Meanwhile his
immediate objective, upon which the success of his whole policy ultimately hinged, must be to make the German king and the German
Church comply with his program of reform. The pope was not disposed to rely upon his spiritual authority alone. Resistance in the
Church he was ready to meet by urging the nobility to expel the unreformed clergy and the people to refuse to receive their spiritual min-
istrations. Resistance from the king he was ready to meet by withdrawing the support of the Church and encouraging rebellion—which
indeed, as long as the papacy continued to fight the empire, remained
one of its chief weapons. It was a handy weapon, too, for until feudalism could be put down there was always sure to be a group of discontented nobles anxious to thwart the king.

Gregory launched his reform program in earnest at the Lenten
synod of 1075. In addition to decrees against simoniacal and unchaste
clergy, whom the people were urged to reject, lay investiture was for
the first time prohibited. Three German bishops and one archbishop
The outbreak   who had been guilty of disobedience and five of Henry's counsellors
of the strug-   were threatened with excommunication if they did not quickly make
gle between   their peace with the pope. Having just successfully quelled the Saxon
Gregory VII   rebellion of 1073–75, Henry IV was in no mood to take these orders
and Henry IV   seriously, and he no longer felt it necessary to avoid trouble with the
pope. He did not put away his excommunicated counsellors and he
went on investing German bishops with their sees. Moreover, he put
his own candidates into the Archbishopric of Milan, the crucial see
for the control of northern Italy, and into the bishoprics of Fermo and
Spoleto—which were actually in papal territory. By now Gregory's
eyes were opened as to the real character of his "beloved son," to
whom on December 8 he dispatched a letter extending greetings and
apostolic benediction, "but with the understanding that he obeys the
Apostolic See as becomes a Christian king." Referring to his disregard

[11] The quotations are from Emerton, *The Correspondence of Pope Gregory VII.*

of the decree against lay investiture, he wrote: "This edict . . . is to be heartily accepted and obeyed, not only by you and your subjects but by all princes and people who confess and worship Christ." The legates entrusted with the letter were instructed to threaten Henry with excommunication and deposition if he did not submit.

Henry was so outraged over this ultimatum that he took an even rasher step to answer it. He summoned a council of German bishops on January 24, 1076, at Worms. They almost all came, and in an angry mood, not so much over the question of lay investiture, about which some were doubtful, as over the arbitrary way in which the pope was ordering them about, excommunicating them, and interfering in local church affairs. They addressed a joint letter to "Brother Hildebrand," not to Pope Gregory, which concluded: "Wherefore henceforth we renounce all obedience unto thee—which indeed we never promised to thee. And since, as thou didst publicly proclaim, none of us has been to thee a bishop, so thou henceforth will be Pope to none of us." Henry added a letter of his own, beginning, "Henry, king not through usurpation but through the holy ordination of God, to Hildebrand, at present not pope but false monk," and ending with the deposition of Gregory: "Thou therefore, damned . . . by the judgment of all our bishops and by our own, descend and relinquish the apostolic chair which thou has usurped. Let another ascend the throne of St. Peter, who shall not practice violence under the cloak of religion, but shall teach the sound doctrine of St. Peter. I, Henry, king by the grace of God, do say unto thee, together with all our bishops, Descend, descend, to be damned throughout the ages."

The legates who read these letters to the Lenten synod of 1076 in Rome would have been murdered then and there, had it not been for the personal intervention of the pope. Gregory was not in the least deterred by them. The synod excommunicated and suspended from office the Archbishop of Mainz, suspended from office all the bishops who "voluntarily joined his schism," and threatened with suspension all the other bishops who signed the letter unless they quickly made their peace with Rome. Then, in an edict addressed to St. Peter, Gregory VII gave his answer to the letter of Henry IV. "I deprive King Henry . . . , who has rebelled against thy Church with unheard-of audacity, of the government over the whole kingdom of Germany and Italy, and I release all Christian men from the allegiance which they have sworn or may swear to him, and I forbid anyone to serve him as king. . . . I bind him in the bonds of anathema in thy stead, and I bind him thus as commissioned by thee, that the nations may know and be

The deposition of Henry IV

convinced that thou art Peter and that upon thy rock the son of the living God has built his Church and the gates of hell shall not prevail against it." So Henry was deposed and excommunicated, and the German monarchy, so far as he was concerned, was dissolved. This was something new in papal procedure, but Gregory's conscience was clear. "Since," he wrote, "we could not bring him back to the way of salvation by gentle means, we tried . . . to do so by severity, and if . . . he should not be afraid even of the severest penalty, our soul should at least be free from the charge of negligence or timidity."

Rebellion against Henry IV

Gregory VII could hardly be suspected of negligence or timidity, and he did bring Henry IV "back to the way of salvation," so his letter of excommunication and deposition must be considered a success. It threw Germany into violent confusion, destroyed the unity of the German Church, and sent the more timid bishops scampering to make their peace with Gregory. By sanctifying rebellion against the king it encouraged every element of personal or party disaffection. The movement against Henry developed with such speed and spread so widely that he was powerless to cope with it. A meeting of German princes in October at Tribur, attended by two papal legates, compelled him to eat his words. He promised "to observe in all things the obedience due to the apostolic see and to . . . Pope Gregory"; "I will," he added, "either refute . . . or failing this I will at length willingly undergo a suitable penance" for "certain very grave charges . . . concerning attempts which I am supposed to have made against the same see and against thy reverence." In a new edict he retracted his condemnation of Gregory: " . . . if we have presumed to act too severely against him, we will atone for it by rendering fitting satisfaction." Until this was done the king was to be kept in loose confinement at Speyer. Moreover, the princes agreed among themselves that, if Henry had not removed the excommunication from his head by the following February 22, they would refuse to recognize him any longer as king. Finally, they planned another meeting for February at Augsburg, at which they invited Gregory to preside, where, if it were decided that Henry IV was not fit to reign, a new king was to be elected.

This was all good news for Gregory, who wanted nothing more than to be recognized as mediator in German affairs. He allowed himself ample time by setting out for Germany in December, but he was not quick enough to catch the king. For Henry IV the news was as bad as could be. He was unwilling to face his hostile subjects before the bar of the papacy at Augsburg, so he resolved to appear before the pope in Italy as a humble penitent. Quite secretly, accompanied

only by his devoted wife Bertha and their young son and a few faithful retainers, Henry slipped away from Speyer into Burgundy. It was
one of the coldest winters on record. The passage of the Mont Cenis
was made only with the greatest difficulty; Bertha and her ladies had
to be set on skins and dragged down over the ice, and the horses with
their legs bound were dragged on their backs in the same fashion.
Once in the plains Henry was greeted enthusiastically by the Italians,
who offered him military assistance. But the king disgusted them by
declining, and went his way to Canossa, a well-fortified castle of Mathilda, Countess of Tuscany, southeast of Parma, whither the pope had
withdrawn in consternation. A visit in Italy from Henry IV was no
part of his plans. What would the king do?

What he did Gregory described in a letter written to the German
princes at the end of January 1077. "There [at Canossa] on three successive days, standing before the castle gate, laying aside all royal
insignia, barefooted and in coarse attire, he ceased not with many tears
to beseech the apostolic help and comfort, until all who were present
or who heard the story were so moved by pity and compassion that
they pleaded his cause with prayers and tears." Gregory was in a
dilemma. He could scarcely refuse absolution to a penitent sinner.
And he could not penetrate behind the veil of Henry's demeanor to
determine whether his repentance was sincere or not. Yet to restore
Henry to communion with the Church was to remove the chief obstacle to his regaining favor in Germany, and so to miss the opportunity to co-operate with the German princes in judging him. It might
even preclude the triumphal journey to Augsburg. But the pope had
no real choice in the matter. He made what he could of the situation
after he had removed the excommunication by obliging Henry to take
an oath to "give satisfaction . . . in regard to the discontent and discord" of the German clergy and nobles, and not to hinder in any way
Gregory's journey to Germany.

But Gregory never got to Germany; he never received the safe conduct that he asked for. The king had accordingly won a strategic victory
by preventing the union of his enemies—it is hard to say at what cost
of personal and public humiliation. Contemporaries made little of
what happened at Canossa; it was no serious humiliation to reconcile
oneself to God through the Church. On the other hand, the pope had
made good his excommunication of a German king, who had been
forced to make a perilous journey and bow his neck before him; to
this extent the spiritual power had triumphed over the temporal. Posterity has chosen quite unhistorically to take Canossa as a symbol of

the subjection of the state to the Church. Perhaps the best known example is Bismarck's defiance in the course of his contest with the Catholic Church: "We are not going to Canossa." We must not forget, as Bismarck did, that Henry IV's main reason for going to Canossa had been to keep Gregory VII out of Germany.

Rebellion continues in Germany

It must be remembered, also, that Henry IV was not driven to that desperate journey until the disloyal feudal nobles of Germany saw an opportunity to turn against him with some hope of success. The significance of this appears in that they were not deterred by the reconciliation from proceeding against him on their own account. They reverted to their ancient right of electing the German king; in March 1077, with the approval of two papal legates, they elected Rudolph, Duke of Swabia—from whom they exacted a promise not to attempt to make the throne hereditary. Rudolph was never able to make much headway against Henry, but Gregory immediately took advantage of the situation by resuming his beloved rôle of mediator. He insisted that the final choice between the candidates belonged to the pope— this was something entirely new—and prescribed the conditions upon which he would recognize a king, chief among which was a vassal's homage and oath of fealty to the pope, who would bestow Germany and Italy upon the king as papal fiefs. This time Gregory took three years to make up his mind, when the three days of Canossa would have been more than enough, thus doing what he could to prolong civil war in Germany.

In 1080 Gregory announced his decision between Henry and Rudolph by excommunicating and deposing Henry for the second time. This edict he addressed not only to St. Peter but also to St. Paul. "I take from him all royal power and state. I forbid all Christians to obey him as king, and I release all who have made or shall make oath

The second deposition of Henry IV

to him as king from the obligation of their oath. . . . For as Henry is justly cast down from the royal dignity for his insolence, his disobedience and his deceit, so Rudolph, for his humility, his obedience and his truthfulness is granted the power and the dignity of kingship. . . . And so may the whole world know and understand that if you [i.e., St. Peter and St. Paul] are able to bind and loose in Heaven, you are able also on earth to grant and to take away from everyone, according to his deserts, empires, kingdoms, principalities, dukedoms, marquisates, earldoms, and the property of all men."

Gregory VII had overreached himself at last. The second excommunication had no effect in Germany comparable to the effect of the first. Although after Rudolph's death in battle in 1080 a handful of

German princes elected another king, Herman of Salm, he was never *Henry's*
more than a shadow who could be completely disregarded. Henry IV *triumph*
was free to act, and act he did. A council of German clergy at Mainz
deposed Gregory again, evening that score. This time they were
joined with the clergy of northern Italy at Brixen to elect as his successor Guibert, Archbishop of Ravenna. In 1081 Henry led an army
into Italy, but not until 1084 was he able to take possession of Rome,
install his antipope Guibert, and have himself crowned Roman emperor
at last, twenty-eight years after he became German king.

Gregory, deserted by thirteen of his cardinals, meanwhile had fled *The end of*
to the Castle of St. Angelo, whence he frantically called upon his Nor- *Gregory VII*
man vassals for help. By the time they arrived Henry had made for
Germany. The Roman populace feared the wrath of Robert Guiscard
for turning the city over to the Germans. And well they might. The
pope's vassal, furious over the failure of his campaign in the Balkans
against Henry's allies, the Venetians and the Byzantines,[12] sacked the
Eternal City as no barbarian Visigoth or Vandal had ever sacked it.
The city was looted and one-third of it reduced to ashes. Gregory was
no longer safe in the midst of the suffering and infuriated Roman people, and the Normans did him a kindness by taking him back south
with them to Monte Cassino. For the remaining months of his life the
great pope ate out his heart while the edifice of a lifetime began tragically to crumble around him. But he never lost courage; he sent out
appeals east and west for help, and even held one more reforming
synod at Salerno. There he died in May 1085. His last words were:
"I have loved justice and hated iniquity, therefore I die an exile."
Gregory VII failed to accomplish his aims, because they could not be
accomplished. But after him the German monarchy and empire were
never again what they had been before him; and the papacy he raised
to new heights of spiritual and temporal power, which foreshadowed
the world state of Innocent III.

The investiture struggle did not cease with the death of Gregory
VII, but it did change character. His successors dropped his extraordinary claim to be the feudal lord of secular princes, and contented
themselves with a vigorous enforcement of reform. Much of their
energy was diverted to launching the crusades. In a simpler form the
struggle continued over the question of the propriety of the ceremony
of lay investiture. To some degree the more general question of the *The investi-*
relationship between Church and state was made a public matter by *ture struggle*
many pamphleteers on both sides; for the first time in medieval Eu- *continues*

[12] See p. 142.

rope we may speak of such a thing as public opinion. Henry IV employed a jurist of Ravenna, Peter Crassus, to defend his cause in terms of Roman law, which marked the formal entrance of Roman law into the public life of medieval Europe. Manegold of Lautenbach, in support of the papacy, clearly formulated the revolutionary conception of the state as the embodiment of a contract between ruler and ruled, the terms of which are equally binding on both sides. "When he who is chosen to defend the good and to hold the evil in check himself begins to cherish wickedness, to stand out against good men, to exercise most cruelly over his subjects the tyranny which he was bound to combat, is it not clear that he justly forfeits the dignity conceded to him and that the people stand free of his rule and subjection, since it is evident that he was the first to violate the compact on account of which he was made ruler?" [13] Champions of the state remind us of Charlemagne's advice to the popes by admonishing them to stick to their business of preaching and teaching the heathen. "We have," one writer says, "the prophetic writings and the apostolic gospels in which all the commands of God are contained, and of these we have a fuller knowledge than he [the pope]." This is uncommonly interesting, for the emphasis on the Scriptures as God's word and the claim to be able to interpret them without human aid smacks strongly of what four hundred years later the Church was condemning as the heresy of Protestantism.

Gregory VII's successors
After several years of conflict between Henry IV's antipope Guibert and Gregory VII's properly elected successor there followed a succession of three French popes, Urban II (1088–99), Paschal II (1099–1118), and Calixtus II (1119–24), the first two of whom were Cluniac monks. Against Henry IV, whose final triumph over Gregory VII had not removed his second excommunication and deposition, the fight was continued by the usual method of supporting rebellion in Germany. When young Conrad revolted against his father in 1093 he was supported by Urban II and welcomed to Italy, where he took an oath of fealty to the pope. The same policy was pursued by Paschal II when Henry IV's second son, the future Henry V, revolted against his father in 1104. Italy was practically lost to Germany in the last years of Henry IV's reign; and in Germany too, although immediately after 1085 Henry's position was strong, he kept his hold with increasing difficulty and at times led a life little better than a fugitive's. In 1105 the German feudal princes elected young Henry V king in his father's place, but the old king never lost the loyalty of the towns and re-

[13] Quoted in McIlwain, *The Growth of Political Thought in the West*, pp. 209–10.

mained a force to contend with until his death at Liége in 1106. Not until 1111 did the Church permit his body to be buried in consecrated ground, in a tomb beneath the choir of the cathedral at Speyer.

By this time interest in the investiture struggle had begun to pale beside the fire of enthusiasm aroused by the first crusade. Both parties were interested in compromise and peace, and in both England and France satisfactory compromises had already been worked out. In both these countries the reform program had been pushed, but Gregory VII had been careful not to drive William the Conqueror and Philip I of France into the arms of Henry IV. In the English Church William had been cleaning house with the co-operation of his moderate Archbishop of Canterbury, Lanfranc, either removing Anglo-Saxon bishops outright or taking advantage of vacancies to supplant them with Normans. He supported every move calculated to increase the efficiency of the Church, but he was no more willing than the German kings to lose control of the Church; he rejected all claims which infringed upon the king's power. Bishops and abbots he treated as vassals of the king; he invested them with ring and staff, and regularly managed episcopal elections.

His son and successor, William Rufus, roused the ire of the reformers by riding roughshod over the rights of the Church. From 1085 to 1095 he would recognize no pope in England, and he deliberately kept the See of Canterbury vacant, declaring that he would be his own archbishop. Finally Anselm, the abbot of the Norman Abbey of Bec, was made Archbishop of Canterbury, but he was virtually forced out of England in 1097 because of his allegiance to the papacy and his predilection for reform. He was invited back by the next king, Henry I, only to be driven back to the continent in 1103 because of his stubborn refusal to do homage to the king and to consecrate bishops whom Henry had invested. The matter was negotiated during his absence from England; he therefore returned in 1106, and in 1107 a formal settlement of the investiture question was reached. The king was no longer to invest with ring and staff, but no consecration of a bishop or an abbot was to be refused because he had done homage to the king. The king maintained his influence by stipulating that he was to be present at all episcopal elections, and should concede to the newly elected bishops their temporal possessions and rights only after receiving their homage. The crown accordingly lost nothing essential by giving up the right of lay investiture. However, the Church took advantage of the disorders of the following reign of Stephen to secure a larger measure of independence, so that the great Henry II found

Settlement of the investiture question in England

it impossible completely to regain the hold of the first Norman kings on the Church.

In France the pitifully weak condition of the monarchy under Philip I (1060–1108) made impossible any great resistance to the reform program. Gregory VII had nothing but contempt for Philip, "who is . . . a tyrant rather than a king," "the worst of plunderers," *The French settlement* who wastes "churches by adultery, plunder, perjury and fraud of many kinds, for which we have often reproved him." Gregory threatened him with deposition and excommunicated him three times during his reign. His wife Bertrada was no better, for she sold Church offices to the highest bidder in order to pay her creditors. The popes through legates and in person had little difficulty in carrying to success their campaign against simony and marriage of clergy. By the end of Philip I's reign the question of investiture had reached a satisfactory settlement, essentially the same as the English one. Bishops and abbots were to be elected according to the provisions of canon law. There was to be no lay investiture with ring and staff, but the king or noble concerned was to grant the *regalia* after an oath of fealty. The king retained the right to interfere in clerical elections, and at all times he had the right to authorize and postpone as well as to confirm them. In France as in England, then, the papacy gained only the partial victory of getting rid of the noxious ceremony of lay investiture. It did not succeed in freeing the French Church from secular control, and indeed the French Church had no desire to dispense with the protection of nobles and king.

The settlement of the investiture struggle in Germany was incorporated in the Concordat of Worms, a compromise reached at a meeting of German princes and clergy and papal legates in 1122. It had *The German settlement* been preceded eleven years before by an agreement at Rome between Henry V and Paschal II, which was of no practical importance but highly interesting in theory because for once, whether in good faith or not, the question at issue was logically settled. This earlier "solution" was a counsel of perfection or a counsel of despair, perhaps both. The pope ordered the clergy to give up all *regalia,* "cities, duchies, marches, counties, mints, tolls, markets . . . manors, armed forces and castles," which they had received from the kings since the time of Charlemagne, and to "remain free with their offerings and hereditary possessions, which clearly did not belong to the kingdom." Since the clergy were to have no rights and no property that came to them from the king, the king was to abandon all the control over them symbolized by lay investiture. But no bishop nor abbot wished to make such a tremendous sacrifice of his worldly goods, and no noble wished to be deprived of the fiefs that he held of the Church and to see the power of the kings immeasurably strengthened by the return of the vast amount of property and rights that they had granted to the Church. The settlement was ineffective from the start. Then Henry V forced from Paschal II full recognition of his right to invest the German clergy with ring and staff. This settlement, as impossible as the first one, since it ignored all the results of the past half century and more of reform, was repudiated by Paschal as soon as Henry's departure from Italy released him from coercion.

The Concordat of Worms recognized clearly the double nature, spiritual and temporal, of the office of bishop. In Germany elections of bishops were to conform to canon law, which meant in practice election by the cathedral clergy; but elections were to be held in the presence of the king or his representative. In case of a disputed election the king, after consulting the archbishop and bishops of the province, was to give "his assent and aid to the more discreet party," thus virtually putting all disputed elections into the king's hands. After election the bishop was to receive his *regalia* from the king by investiture with the scepter, following his doing homage and taking the oath of fealty as the king's vassal. The bishop thus invested with the *regalia* was thereupon to be consecrated by his archbishop and invested with his spiritual functions (*spiritualia*) by means of ring and staff. The king thus resigned the long-established right of lay investiture, but the fact that investiture with *regalia* preceded investiture with *spiritualia* preserved his control of the personnel of the episcopate; for, should he refuse to invest with the *regalia*, it would be practically impossible for the newly elected bishop to maintain himself. In Italy and Burgundy, however, the king lost his hold, for here investiture with the *regalia* was to follow within six months after consecration and investiture with ring and staff. In any case the old Ottonian system was destroyed by the one fact that no longer could the kings appoint the bishops. Since the electoral cathedral chapters were filled largely by the sons of the local nobility, the ultimate effect of the Concordat was to turn over to these families control of the episcopate. To be sure, the king could refuse to invest with the *regalia*, but as time went on German kings had to be increasingly tactful to the nobility. The Concordat of Worms was thus to some degree a victory also for the German feudal princes.

The whole long struggle of Henry IV and Henry V with the papacy had been very costly to the prestige and power of the German monarchy. The loyalty of the German Church had in part been broken and

The Concordat of Worms

transferred to the popes. The constant encouragement that the struggle offered to rebellion and civil war threw Germany into a state of turmoil from which only the feudal princes, not the monarchy, could profit. The Ottonian system of alliance between crown and Church fell into disuse. Now the king was forced to take the feudal nobility into consideration upon all occasions; and the Church, since the king was less able to defend it, was forced to identify itself with the particularistic interests of the nobles and to seek further support from Rome. During the struggle with the papacy the kings had been forced to buy support by further generous grants of crown lands and sovereign rights to clergy and secular nobility alike. For the moment the future of the German monarchy looked dark.

For the papacy, on the other hand, the struggle was profitable in prestige and power. Although it cannot be said to have enforced anywhere its whole reform program, yet against simony and towards celibacy, or at least chastity, in the clergy it did make some headway. Lay investiture it succeeded in abolishing. If it had not succeeded in freeing the Church from the state, it had at least made progress in establishing its own supremacy within the Church. The papacy still had a long and difficult road to travel before reaching its medieval height, but it had invalidated the claim of kings to be God's consecrated agents and had proclaimed with assurance its own claim to temporal supremacy.

Chapter 14

THE APEX AND THE DECLINE OF THE HOLY ROMAN EMPIRE

THE German empire as restored by Otto the Great consisted of the German kingdom with its satellite states of Denmark, Poland, Bohemia and Hungary, the Burgundian kingdom, and the Italian or Lombard kingdom. It exercised sovereignty over the Papal States, including Rome, largely controlled elections to the *The Holy* papacy, and laid claim to all southern Italy. It was the largest and most *Roman* powerful state in Europe, and it could claim through Charlemagne *empire* the inheritance of the Roman empire. Yet during the period of the Saxon and Salian emperors, except for the few fruitless years of Otto III's reign, it had no great pretentions to universal sovereignty. It was the Hohenstaufen emperors Frederick I and Frederick II who, partly under the inspiration of a revival of Roman law, first became fully conscious of the wide implications of the imperial tradition. It was Frederick I who, in order to claim for his empire the same sacred origin and mission that the Holy Roman Church claimed, called it the Holy Roman empire: the universal empire was ordained by God to balance and complement the Universal Church. It ended in disintegration. Interpreted in the light of the course of events, its final history can be considered as the struggle of the Hohenstaufen emperors with the papacy. Interpreted by what lay behind events, it appears as the struggle between two conceptions of sovereignty and unity, one political, the other spiritual. This was an issue of far vaster import than the issues over which Henry IV and Gregory VII had fought, and its antagonists were mightier than even they. For now both sides, not one side alone, were ready to claim the whole world.

The Hohenstaufen period was characterized by the last stage of *The Hohen-* feudal decentralization in Germany and by the collapse of German *staufen period* power in Italy, two phenomena which we shall find were by no means unrelated. There were, however, compensations. During the same

391

period, although not under imperial auspices, the first substantial advances were made by the peasants of northern Germany in colonizing eastern Holstein, Mecklenburg-Schwerin, Brandenburg, and Pomerania. Indeed, before the end of the period the Teutonic Knights [1] had begun to thrust their advance guard along the southern shores of the Baltic to prepare the way for colonization still farther eastward, while Cistercian and Premonstratensian monks [2] were supplementing the work of German colonists on the older frontier. It was a time of great growth and development in town life. It was a new epoch in the history of German literature. Stimulated by the French ideals of chivalry and the poetry and song of the French trouvère and troubadour, German minnesingers, epic poets, and romancers burst into song in the vernacular. At the end of the twelfth and the beginning of the thirteenth century medieval German civilization attained its climax.

Until well on into the thirteenth century the Hohenstaufen emperors had to fight tooth and nail their strongest rivals in Germany, the Welf family. For the first time perhaps in German history it is permissible to speak of a division of the nobility, both lay and clerical, into two opposing parties, the one headed by the Welfs, who represented the particularistic ambitions of the feudal nobility, the other led by the Hohenstaufen kings and emperors, champions of a centralized monarchy and a powerful empire, both of which should keep feudalism in check. So it was Welf against Hohenstaufen, or rather, as the Hohenstaufen party was more commonly named after their village of Waiblingen in Swabia, Welf against Waibling. In the early thirteenth century these names were transplanted to Italy to refer to the ties there ranged behind the rival Welf and Hohenstaufen kings in Germany. English has adopted the Italian forms of the words, Ghibelline for the imperial party, Guelf for the anti-imperial papal party. In Italy the two names persisted, with various connotations in various places, as names for rival factions in the towns, long after the German empire had ceased to be of any moment.

The mighty figure of the Cistercian monk St. Bernard overshadows all the kings and popes of the second quarter of the twelfth century.[3] Beside him the successors of Henry V, Lothair and Conrad III, were mere dwarfs. All their policies had to be reversed by their successor, Frederick Barbarossa, who had to take up anew the task of restoring the prestige of both crown and empire. At the death of Henry V in 1125 the reform party in the German Church, led by the archbishops

Welf and Waibling

---

[1] See pp. 937 ff.   [3] See p. 613.
[2] See pp. 612-13.

of Mainz and Cologne and supported by the papacy, was determined that the anticlerical policy of the Salian house should not be continued by Henry's nearest heir, his nephew, the Hohenstaufen Duke Frederick of Swabia. This determination coincided with the desire of the nobility not to see the German crown continue to be hereditary. The two groups combined to reassert clerical influence and to vindicate the ancient right of the nobles to elect their king, and by the clever manipulation of the Archbishop of Mainz succeeded in defeating Frederick's candidacy and electing Lothair (1125–37), Duke of Saxony.

Lothair was a loyal son of the Church, who as duke had never *Lothair* thwarted the bishops and archbishops and as king never intended to do so. He was the first German king to ask for papal approval of his election, and for most of his reign was guided by the advice of the man whom he made Archbishop of Magdeburg, Norbert, the founder of the new monastic Order of Premonstratensians. His policy towards feudalism was similar to the "live and let live" policy of Henry the Fowler two hundred years earlier. By marrying his only child to the Welf Duke of Bavaria, Henry the Proud, whose lands in Saxony were already large, he practically presented him with a second duchy, thereby raising the Welf family to a position of dangerous importance. His two Italian campaigns brought him the imperial crown but had no effect on the turbulent rivalry of the north Italian towns, factional strife in Rome, or the onward march of Norman power in southern Italy.

Lothair would have liked to bequeath the crown to Duke Henry. But again a combination of the clerical party and the nobility, who now feared the greatly increased power of the Welf duke quite as much as the royal power, vindicated the electoral right of the princes by electing Conrad (1138–52), Duke of Swabia, first of the Hohenstaufen kings. Immediately the struggle between Welfs and Hohenstaufens broke out. For refusal to do homage to Conrad III Henry the Proud lost *Conrad III* both his new Saxon and his old Bavarian duchies, the former being given to Albert the Bear, Margrave of the *Nordmark*, the latter to Leopold, the Babenberg Duke of Austria. The fight to regain the duchies, successfully begun by Henry the Proud, was continued after his death in 1139 by the supporters of his young son, Henry the Lion. By 1141 Albert the Bear had lost Saxony to Henry the Lion, and against Leopold's successor in Bavaria the Welf party waged incessant war. Elsewhere in Germany Conrad was powerless to control the petty wars of the feudal nobles. Yet in spite of the situation at home, being even more devoted and subservient to the interests of the Church than his predecessor, he quit Germany in 1147 to participate in the disastrous second crusade. After his return he was even more helpless. He was obliged to give up the idea of an Italian campaign; indeed, he never went to Italy at all and was the first German king since Henry the Fowler not to bear the title of Roman emperor. Italy was beginning to forget German sovereignty.

Eastern advance of colonization

Offsetting the weakness of the monarchy, however, nobles along the Saxon frontier slowly pushed colonization forward. Count Adolf of Holstein sent Westphalians, Dutch, and Frisians into eastern Holstein and founded the city of Lübeck. Albert the Bear, to whom the territory of Brandenburg was bequeathed by its Slavic prince, began to call himself Margrave of Brandenburg. He co-operated energetically with bishops and abbots in the Christianization and Germanization of the land. Duke Henry the Lion of Saxony began to build up a principality east of the Elbe, with complete disregard of the metropolitan rights of the archbishops of Hamburg-Bremen; he appointed bishops and used them as his own officials. "Here," he remarked, "I am Lord; here neither emperor nor archbishop has anything to say." The crusade of 1147 against the Slavs, the German counterpart of the second crusade to the east, although responsible for the burning of Lübeck, did on the whole aid the work of the border nobles.

When Conrad III died in 1152, even the feudal nobles recognized the necessity of choosing a king who could compose the internal strife in Germany and revive the prestige of the empire. Conrad III had thought that this could best be accomplished by passing over his eldest son and electing his nephew Frederick, Duke of Swabia. Frederick was not only a Hohenstaufen: on his mother's side he was a cousin of Henry the Lion, the king's chief rival. Moreover, he was a very likable prince, who should get along harmoniously with the German nobility. He had a bright sunny countenance and a full reddish-blond beard

Frederick Barbarossa makes peace with the Welfs

which earned for him the name of *Rotbart*, or Barbarossa. He was elected unanimously in 1152, and set about immediately to make peace with the Welfs. Henry the Lion was recognized as practically independent in his new territory across the Elbe, his right to the Duchy of Saxony, which he had recovered, was recognized, and in addition the Duchy of Bavaria, of which Conrad III had deprived his father, was restored to him. To placate the Babenbergers for their loss of Bavaria the March of Austria (the *Ostmark*) was completely cut off from Bavaria and given to them as a practically independent duchy; this was the formal beginning of Austria. To the Welfs also went imperial fiefs in Tuscany, Spoleto, and the hereditary lands of Countess Mathilda of Tuscany, which Lothair III had secured after negotiation with the pope. With the leading family of the nobility his friends instead of his enemies, Frederick seemed to be in a position to rebuild the German monarchy.

Frederick made strenuous efforts to consolidate and increase the crown lands, notably by the purchase from the elder branch of the Welf family of their lands in Swabia and Italy. These he administered through an enlarged corps of ministerials. It was impossible to regain the regalian rights that had long since been granted to nobles, but it was possible to exploit those that were left. Frederick as king was as keenly aware of his sovereign rights as any feudal lord of his, and as fully determined to assert them. The royal court of justice became once more a thing to be feared and respected. His marriage to Beatrice, heiress of the County of Burgundy, besides bringing him additional land and vassals, restored to the crown a region that had been well-nigh lost to local feudal nobility. Frederick was the only German king who really ruled the Kingdom of Burgundy. *Increase of crown lands*

After the subservience of Lothair and Conrad III to the Church, Frederick returned with a vengeance to the old Ottonian policy of alliance with the episcopate. He insisted upon every one of the rights guaranteed to the crown by the Concordat of Worms. Reforming bishops sympathetic with the centralizing policy of Rome he managed to have replaced as quickly as possible by hard-headed, hard-fighting, political bishops of the old German school, who never deserted him. Out of this new old-style episcopate, drawn as often as of old from the training school of the chancellery, came such brilliant figures as, among others, Rainald of Dassel, Archbishop of Cologne, who combined with his love for a good fight and his patronage of wandering scholar-poets the most devoted allegiance to monarchy and empire. Until the day he died in the service of the state he spurred Frederick on to a defense of his rights beyond the point to which Frederick would have gone alone. In Christian of Buch, Archbishop of Mainz, Frederick had a like-minded and equally zealous supporter. *Frederick's policy towards the Church*

The new balance of power between crown and nobility and Church worked well for the first twenty-five years of Frederick's reign, bringing a peace long unknown to Germany and furnishing generally adequate support for Frederick's Italian campaigns. But in time it became evident that the predominance accorded to Henry the Lion had been a mistake. His strong-arm methods of establishing his position in Saxony and his independent colonial territory were greatly resented by the prelates and nobles of Saxony. His far-sighted founding of towns in his two duchies, such as Schwerin, Brunswick, and Munich, and his re- *Frederick's final quarrel with Henry the Lion* building of Lübeck, which all enjoyed a large degree of municipal autonomy, added envy to the hatred of the local princes. Time and again Frederick had to calm the storm brewing in Saxony. As long as Henry did his duty in the Italian campaigns, the king was inclined to support him. But in 1176, at a time of desperate need in the most critical of his Italian campaigns, he met Henry the Lion at Chiavenna and on bended knee had to beg him for troops. Henry, thinking that his moment had come at last, answered that he would help only if Frederick presented him with Goslar. The king heatedly spurned the suggestion.

The ruin of Henry

Upon his return to Germany after complete defeat Frederick was in the mood to listen to the complaints lodged against Henry the Lion by nobles anxious to share in the distribution of his property that would follow confiscation. Without closing the door to Henry if he cared to come to terms, Frederick permitted suits to be brought against him for violation of the king's peace and for treason in both territorial and royal courts. When Henry chose utterly to ignore all summons to appear, he was deprived, as a contumacious vassal, of all his fiefs and left only his private lands of Brunswick and Lüneburg. When in 1187, seven years later, the king appeared in Saxony to enforce these decisions, the whole nobility flocked to him. This time it was the Lion who on bended knee begged pardon. He was sentenced to three years' exile, which he spent in Normandy. After his return to Brunswick he lived the life of a simple noble, farming his acres and looking after his tenantry. But he found time also to pore over old German chronicles, and played his part in the renaissance of German literature by gathering about him a circle of poets writing in the vernacular to celebrate the virtues of chivalry.

The significance of the distribution of the Welf lands

The distribution of the fiefs of the now ruined Welf family completed the destruction of the only two tribal duchies that the German kings had not already got under some control. The dioceses of Cologne and Paderborn were separated from the Duchy of Saxony and made into the new Duchy of Westphalia, of which the Archbishop of Cologne was made duke. What was left of Saxony was bestowed upon Bernhard of Anhalt, the youngest son of Albert the Bear, to whom Saxony had been granted by Conrad III after it was taken from Henry the Lion's father. Bavaria was again diminished by cutting off from its southeastern frontier the March of Styria, which was made into a duchy; the rest was given to the Wittelsbach family, who held it until 1918.

Smaller nobles and churchmen likewise participated in the spoil. In fact, the crushing of the Welfs was as much a victory for feudalism as for the German crown. The lesser princes could no more tolerate a powerful princely family than a strong king, and they supported Frederick Barbarossa against Henry the Lion because the duke seemed to them more formidable than the king. The Germany of the tenth century, composed of a few large and powerful tribal duchies, had become by the thirteenth century a Germany composed of a multitude of smaller feudal territories headed by petty dukes, counts, landgraves, burgraves, margraves, counts palatine, and ministerials, of a multitude of feudal ecclesiastical principalities headed by bishops, archbishops, and abbots, and of an increasing number of free cities. To complete the break-up of Germany it remained only for the kings to grant out what they still had left of regalian rights, and that was soon to come.

The ruin of Henry the Lion was only a temporary victory for Barbarossa. He gained nothing of permanent value from it except the personal support and loyalty of the smaller princes who profited by it. The strength of the German crown had almost been reduced to such personal support and loyalty, however ephemeral it might be. And yet the victory seemed great and impressive, and Frederick Barbarossa's prestige at the moment in Germany and throughout Europe was enormous. *Frederick Barbarossa at the height of his prestige*

At the great gathering of German princes at Mainz in 1184 to celebrate the knighting of his two eldest sons, envoys were present from all important European states, and knights by tens of thousands. The banquet was held in a huge wooden structure built for the occasion. The wine flowed as generously as the near-by Rhine, and two big houses stocked from floor to ceiling with chickens, ducks, and geese helped to appease the medieval appetites of the guests. The emperor himself, although he was over sixty years old, joined in the round of tournaments. French minstrels combined with German minnesingers to sound the praises of Frederick, the new Arthur, the new Cæsar, the new Alexander.

The same year 1184 was the year after Frederick had concluded peace with the Lombard League and the very year in which his nineteen-year-old son Henry was betrothed to the thirty-year-old Constance, heiress presumptive to the throne of the Norman kings of southern Italy and Sicily. The peace and the betrothal were the chief results of Frederick's thirty years' attempt to make the German empire in Italy more than a name. Despite the efforts of the Saxon and Salian emperors there had never been any real consolidation of imperial power in Italy. Since the eleventh century imperial claims in the south *The situation in Italy in the eleventh century* had been completely ignored by the Normans, and the few earlier attempts to assert the empire's influence there had met with no success. The papacy, once it had won (with German help) its own independence, never ceased to oppose the predominance of German or any other power in Italy. To the popes the empire meant no more than the protection of their independence and assistance in carrying out their European program. Only in north-central and northern Italy had German power succeeded at all in entrenching itself. There were numerous crown lands, especially in western Lombardy, but there was nothing like direct administration. When the German kings were not in Italy, bishops whose loyalty was fostered by generous grants of regalian rights, together with Italian margraves, preserved some respect for German authority. When the kings were in Italy, they exercised more direct control, holding courts and enjoying some revenue from their lands; but at best this control was only intermittent.

In the first half of the twelfth century northern and north-central Italy became virtually independent of any kind of imperial control. The Concordat of Worms made it impossible for the emperors any longer to control the personnel of the Italian episcopate. Lothair had not concerned himself much with Italy, and Conrad III had never bothered to go there at all. This period of imperial indifference coincided with a profound change that was taking place in the episcopal towns of the Po valley. It was here that first of all in western Europe town life began to revive, stimulated by renewed commerce with eastern Mediterranean lands and by local industry. By the beginning of the twelfth century Lombard merchants and manufacturers were strong enough to throw off the restrictions of government by bishops and archbishops and to set up their own municipal governments, self-governing communes headed usually by consuls. In so doing they took over from *Lombard* bishops and nobles the administration of regalian rights formally *towns in* granted by German emperors, without bothering to have these sover- *the twelfth* eign rights regranted to their own new governments. To the legal *century* mind all this meant a flagrant usurpation of imperial prerogatives by upstart townsmen recently risen from serfdom, and Frederick Barbarossa found it intolerable.

Milan was the chief offender among the Lombard towns. The opposition of neighboring towns to her attempt to absorb them into a larger Milanese city-state seemed to offer him some support. Frederick, however, was interested in more than the usurpation of regalian rights by Italian towns. As the successor of Constantine and Justinian he aimed to inaugurate the same kind of direct administration in Italy as the ancient Roman emperors had enjoyed, as Charlemagne had created with his counts and his *missi,* and as the Normans had lately established in Normandy, England, and southern Italy and Sicily. To do so meant to destroy the liberties of the Lombard towns and to threaten the independence of the papacy. It was a large task that Frederick had set himself when he first came to Italy in 1154. Should his opponents—the Lombard towns, the papacy, and the Normans—unite to oppose him, the struggle would call for an effort such as Germany had never yet put forth to realize the dream of empire.

Frederick arrived in Italy on the first of his six campaigns with an agreement already made with the papacy to help destroy the new Roman republic, as its partisans called it, which had declared itself independent of the popes; to help prevent the Byzantine empire from regaining a foothold in Italy; and to co-operate against the Normans, who were dangerous vassals of the papacy and dangerous enemies of the empire. In return for all this he was to receive the imperial crown. On his way to Rome Frederick encountered difficulties with the Lombard towns. Milan stoutly resisted him, and he was persuaded by Milan's rivals, Pavia especially, to destroy Milan's subject town of Tortona as a warning to the rest of Lombardy. *Frederick's first Italian campaign*

The first meeting of king and pope was unhappy. The new pope, Hadrian IV, was Nicholas Breakspere, the son of a poor English priest, the only Englishman ever to become pope. He was the first pope since 1085 worthy to succeed Gregory VII, and he had to deal with an emperor who proved more formidable even than Gregory VII had found Henry IV. Frederick was willing to kneel and kiss the pope's foot, but he would not hold the pope's bridle and stirrup as he dismounted: he did not regard himself as the pope's vassal. Hadrian would not give him the kiss of peace until he had performed the ceremony: "Thou hast denied me the service which out of reverence for the apostles Peter and Paul thy predecessors have always paid to mine up to the present time, and until thou hast satisfied me I will not give thee the kiss of peace." They argued for two days, after which Barbarossa, convinced by his advisers that the ceremony was only an old custom, gave in. He was crowned emperor in June 1155. He had to suppress an uprising of the Roman populace; but aside from having Arnold of Brescia,[4] the hero of the Roman republic, hanged, he did nothing to crush the commune. Nor did he move against the Normans. He was forced to return home through hostile territory, while Milan began to rebuild Tortona.

Hadrian IV, having got so little of what he had bargained for, lost

[4] See p. 621.

little time in coming to terms with William I, the Norman King of
Sicily. In return for recognizing his kingdom as a papal fief and turning
over to him the long-disputed right to control elections to bishoprics in
his domains, the pope received the liege homage of the king and the
promise of considerable money as tribute. This was simply to ignore
ancient imperial claims to southern Italy, and constituted a definite
break with Frederick. Two of Frederick's Italian enemies had joined
hands.

Frederick's
quarrel with
the papal
legates at
Besançon

The ill feeling roused by the pope's treaty with the Normans was
intensified by a famous incident that occurred in October 1157, at
Besançon, whither Frederick had gone to receive the homage of Burgundy after his marriage to Beatrice. Papal legates appeared, headed
by Cardinal Roland, the future Pope Alexander III, bearing a strong
letter of protest from Hadrian IV against the attack on the Swedish
Archbishop of Lund on his way home from a visit to Rome, by some
Burgundian knights. Frederick sat on the throne at the head of the
palace hall, flanked on either hand by high Church dignitaries and
great nobles, among them Otto of Wittelsbach. Into the imperial presence walked Roland, clad in the reddish-purple robes of his office. At
ten paces from the throne he paused and made majestic salutation. To
one side, between the emperor and the papal envoy, stood Frederick's
beloved archbishop, Rainald of Dassel. From his vestments Roland
produced the papal parchment and began slowly to read the stately
Latin words, pausing at the end of each sentence for Rainald to translate into German. There was thunder in the air and lightning in the
emperor's eyes, and the impetuous Otto nervously fingered the hilt of
his two-handed sword. "Thou shouldst not forget, my most glorious
son," Roland was reading, "how graciously the Holy Roman Church
lately conferred upon thee the imperial crown. . . . Nay, we should
rejoice to confer even greater *beneficia* upon thee, if that were possible."
Roland got no further, for Rainald's translation of *beneficia* was
"fiefs." With a cry "Haro!" Otto of Wittelsbach whipped out his
sword and lunged at him. But Frederick was even quicker to leap, and
threw his imperial mantle over the papal chancellor. The legates were
quickly sent back to Rome under escort.

Both pope and emperor immediately appealed for support to the
German Church. Frederick's manifesto was hot with rage. The statement that the empire had been conferred on him as a fief by the pope he
branded as "a false and lying statement." "We hold this kingdom and
empire through the election of the princes from God alone. . . .
Therefore whoever says that we hold the imperial crown as a benefice

from the pope resists the divine institution and is a liar." Frederick's appeal won the fullest support from a Church that he was doing his best to protect from falling wholly into the clutches of Rome. When Hadrian saw that there was no possibility of stirring up a party in Germany hostile to the emperor, he thought best to explain his indiscretion, and wrote Frederick that by conferring the imperial crown he meant only that he had placed it on Frederick's head, and that by *beneficium* he really meant not "benefice" or "fief" but only what the Latin word originally meant, a "good deed," which certainly the coronation had been. Frederick accepted Hadrian's explanation, but it settled none of the issues of an old conflict between two irreconcilable ideals.

With the intention first of subduing the Lombard towns, particularly Milan, and then of establishing relations on a new basis between the empire and Italy, Frederick returned to Italy in the summer of 1158 with ten thousand German troops, to stay, it turned out, four long years. A successful siege of Milan led to an agreement which with some limitations guaranteed her autonomy but deprived her of her predominance in Lombardy. Frederick immediately called together at Roncaglia a commission consisting of four professors of the Roman law from the University of Bologna and representatives of twenty-eight towns, to define the emperor's regalian rights in Italy and how they should be administered. The fact that professors of Roman law were present is interesting not so much because they influenced the decisions of the commission as because their presence reveals the direction in which Frederick's mind was turning. To wish to have determined on a legal basis just what his rights were was wholly typical of him. The conclusion of the commission amounted to a complete restatement of the rights exercised in Italy by former German emperors and, together with new provisions for administering them, a complete denial of the communal revolutions that had taken place in the Lombard towns.

The second Italian campaign

The Diet of Roncaglia

The leading rights recognized as regalian were "the right to appoint dukes, marquises, counts and consuls; to coin money; to levy tolls; to collect the *fodrum* [a tax in provisions for the support of the emperor and his army when passing through the territory]; to collect customs and harbor dues; to furnish safe-conducts; to control mills, fish-ponds, bridges, and all the waterways; to demand an annual tax not only from the land but also from each person." [5] "Whoever could prove by lawful documents that he was in possession of any of these rights by royal gift was allowed to remain in permanent possession thereof." Otherwise they were to be administered for the empire by "the podestàs, con-

[5] Thatcher and McNeal, *A Source Book of Medieval History*, p. 189.

suls and other magistrates," whom Frederick was henceforth to appoint in every city "with the assent" of the people. We are further informed "that Frederick appointed over each district a judge, chosen not from the city concerned but from his court or from other cities." These decisions Frederick ordered the jurists at Bologna to incorporate into the Justinian Code.

For the Italian towns the Diet of Roncaglia was ominous not merely because the emperor was authorized to deprive them of all regalian rights for which they could show no documentary grant, but still more because under the cloak of administration of those rights he was empowered to impose upon them officials appointed by himself, who would make short work of the self-government that they had struggled to win. Such a program was foredoomed to failure; it presumed to deny too many facts. The townsmen resented it hotly and had no intention of complying. Moreover, because it was intended to apply likewise to papal territory, it was opposed from the start by the papacy. After the alliance between his enemies the papacy and the Normans, the emperor now seemed to be inviting his enemies the papacy and the Lombard towns to combine to resist him. In fact, before his death Hadrian IV was refusing to negotiate with Frederick and even thinking of excommunicating him, and had made an agreement with Milan, Brescia, and Piacenza not to make peace with the emperor without common consent.

Frederick crushes the resistance of the Lombard towns

The resistance of some communes to the surrender of the *regalia* led Frederick to take violent measures against them in the next few years. After a barbarous siege of six months Crema surrendered and was razed to the ground, only the lives of the inhabitants being spared. Piacenza and Brescia lost their fortifications. Upon Milan the emperor wreaked frightful vengeance: after a siege of more than a year the starving city surrendered unconditionally and was reduced to ashes. The townspeople were settled in the open country as the emperor's peasants and held to manorial services. Lombardy was cowed by this campaign of terror. Frederick made an alliance with the naval powers of Genoa and Pisa, and Rainald of Dassel succeeded in bringing central Italy into line. Frederick announced that "he would use his army and his victorious eagle for new undertakings and for a complete restoration of the empire"; that is, he was thinking of forcing all Italy to comply with the decisions of the Diet of Roncaglia. Negotiations had already been opened with the Roman commune: a restored Roman empire must certainly possess Rome. In 1162 the emperor marched south to complete his plans by campaigns against Rome and the Norman King William I.

Meanwhile the international situation had been complicated by Hadrian IV's death in 1159. Two groups of cardinals elected two popes to succeed him: the anti-imperial cardinals elected Cardinal Roland of Siena as Alexander III, and the imperial cardinals elected Cardinal Octavian, a Roman nobleman and the leader of the German party in Rome, as Victor IV. Frederick hastened to settle the schism by summoning all western Europe to a council at Pavia. "Although," he told the council, "in my office and dignity of Emperor I can convoke councils, especially in moments of peril for the church, as did Constantine, Theodosius, Justinian and in later times the emperors Charlemagne and Otto, yet we leave it to your prudence and power to decide in this matter." The council, attended for the most part only by clergy from imperial territory, recognized Victor IV and excommunicated the absent Alexander, who had refused to be judged by it. Alexander III answered by excommunicating Victor IV and Frederick and his chief advisers, and by releasing Frederick's subjects from their allegiance. Thus began an eighteen-year struggle between Alexander and Frederick. *Papal schism*

Sicily, the Spanish kingdoms, France, and England feared too much the increase in power of the German empire to recognize an imperial pope; and when after the death of Victor IV a new imperial pope was elected, his support in Europe was even less than Victor's had been. Frederick's fourth Italian campaign in 1166 was directed straight at Rome. It is worth noting that for the first time he had to reinforce his German troops with mercenaries from Brabant. The march on Rome itself was a brilliant success; Frederick's sovereignty over the city was recognized, the new antipope was installed in St. Peter's as Paschal III, and Frederick was again crowned emperor. But the schism was not ended, for Alexander III managed to escape. The next year a plague ravaged both the city of Rome and the imperial army, and the campaign melted away. Frederick's chief advisers, including Rainald of Dassel, lost their lives. The emperor was forced to make his way back to Germany through hostile northern Italy, a lonely fugitive disguised as a peasant. *Frederick's fourth Italian campaign*

Opposition to the emperor in northern Italy had begun to organize itself before the disaster of 1167. Venice, with the example of Milan before her, had concluded alliances with Sicily and Byzantium, and had gained the adherence of Verona, Vicenza, and Padua in 1164 to

*The forma-
tion of the
Lombard
League*

form the League of Verona, against which Frederick had had poor success in his third Italian campaign of that year. Following this example, and with the help of Venice and Alexander III, the Lombard towns began to form a league in the course of Frederick's Roman campaign. Beginning with Cremona, Mantua, Brescia, and Bergamo, it soon included Milan, whose restoration had been begun immediately after its destruction. Before the end of 1166 the Lombard League had joined with the League of Verona, now numbering eight cities, and soon embraced twenty-two cities. The League set up its own federal authority to maintain peace between member cities and to provide a common army. The new imperial officials vanished from the towns. Close relations were established with Alexander III. A new town, named Alessandria in honor of the pope, was founded by the League out of village communities between Tortona and Asti and fortified for defense and offense against the emperor. It was through this determined and organized opposition that Frederick had to find his way home after the disaster at Rome.

*Frederick's
fifth Ital-
ian campaign*

Frederick's fifth campaign in Italy (1174–78) was directed first of all at Alessandria, but he could not take it, even after a siege of more than six months. With the necessity for compromise becoming clear in his mind, the emperor offered liberal terms to the Lombard League, only to see them violated after being accepted. The issue, then, would have to be decided by war, for which Frederick, mindful of his failure at Alessandria, sent to Germany for reinforcements (it was at this point that Henry the Lion refused his assistance). The

*The Battle
of Legnano*

battle that followed in 1176 at Legnano was a complete victory for the Lombard League. It is of particular interest from a military point of view as the first major defeat in medieval history of feudal cavalry by infantry. It convinced Barbarossa that his policy in Lombardy was a mistake. He offered the League terms even more liberal than those that it finally secured. When, however, these terms were rejected by Milan and the League dissolved into a fight among its members, he determined at least to divide his enemies.

He made overtures to Alexander III at Anagni for a settlement of the outstanding differences between them, the main principles of

*Peace with
the pope
at Venice*

which were agreed upon with surprising ease. At a congress at Venice in 1177 the preliminary negotiations were brought to a successful conclusion. Frederick agreed to abandon his third antipope and recognize Alexander III; the pope agreed to remove the ban of excommunication from the emperor. With the Lombard League Frederick arranged for a truce of six years, and with William II, the Norman

WESTERN ROMAN EMPIRE

Western Roman Empire
(Roman Empire of the German Nation)

English Miles
0   100   200   300   00

KINGDOM

OF SWEDEN

DENMARK

Lund

BALTIC SEA

Estnonians

Livonians

Lithuanians

Düna

Minsk

RUSSIA

Bornholm

Rügen

Danzig

Prussians

Pinsk

Dnieper

Tchernigov

Pomerania

Stettin

Mazovia

Pripet

North Mark

Posen

Vistula

Plock

Oder

Kiev

Brandenburg

Mark of Lusatia

Elbe

M. of Meissen

M.of Meissen

DUCHY

OF POLAND

Silesia

Breslau

Chrobatia

Cracow

Hulisc

Dniester

Dnieper

Petschenegs (Patzinaks)

Dniester

k. of

Prague

Bohemia

Regensburg

M. of

Moravia

Brünn

Mark of

Austria

Presburg

K. OF

HUNGARY

Pruth

Danube

Jordan

Augsburg

Danube

D. of

Bavaria

Salzburg

Stuhlweissenbg.

Theiss

Transylvania

Cherson

Villach

D. of Carinthia

Trent

Verona

Zagrab
(Agram)

Drave

Save

BLACK SEA

Venice

K. OF

CROATIA

Belgrade

Varna

Amastris

Ravenna

Venetian Possessions

Zara

Spalato

SERVIA

Nissa

Romagna

Spoleto

Fermo

Rayusa

Triadilza
(Sofia)

Skopia

BULGARIA

Philippopolis

Adrianople

Constantinople

State

Rome

the Church

Benevento

Dyrrhachium
(Durazzo)

Brindisi

Macedonia

Thrace

Monte Casino

Lombards

Salonica

Thessalonica

Nicaea

Gaëta

Aversa

Naples

Sal.

Salerno

Castoria

Adramyttium

EMPIRE

S

Calabria

EASTERN

Larissa

AEGEAN SEA

Smyrna

Attalea

Palermo

Reggio

Sicily

Cephalenia

Corinth

Peloponnesus

Athens

R A N E A N   S E A

Crete

king, for a truce of fifteen years. Outstanding disputes over property in central Italy were postponed for future discussion, but Frederick remained in possession of the valuable lands of Mathilda, former Countess of Tuscany. With the settlement completed, Frederick was received by Alexander III in the square of St. Mark's, where they were formally reconciled. One cannot help being reminded of Canossa, but Venice was perhaps a lesser humiliation for the empire. To be sure, another emperor was obliged to abandon his scheme of reducing the papacy to subservience. But Frederick had succeeded in coming to terms with one of his enemies; the towns of the Lombard League, another enemy, were at each other's throats; and he was on the point of establishing friendly relations with his third enemy, Sicily. On his way back to Germany he had himself crowned King of Burgundy at Arles, the kingdom being now called that of Arles, and he celebrated his homecoming by compassing the destruction of Henry the Lion. His ambitions had suffered much, but the empire very little, for it was at least recognized as an independent institution alongside the papacy.

Upon the expiration in 1183 of the six years' truce with the Lombard League a final settlement was reached in the Peace of Constance. While the peace meant for the emperor a final abandonment of the program sponsored by the Diet of Roncaglia and a full recognition of the historical development of the Lombard towns, for the empire it was in no sense an abdication of its position in northern Italy. That monument of the League's pride and of its alliance with Alexander III, Alessandria, was refounded as an imperial fortress, renamed Cæsarea, to guard imperial crown lands in western Lombardy. Other cities were to have the right to fortify themselves. The Lombard towns recovered all *regalia* within their walls, but outside the walls retained only *regalia* for which they already possessed or should subsequently purchase an imperial grant. Towns that had previously enjoyed self-government were to regain the right, but after election by the town all consuls were to be invested with their office by the emperor and become his vassals by taking the oath of fealty.

Right of appeal to the emperor's court was granted for all cases of any importance, and courts of appeal had subsequently to be set up in the Italian cities. All persons between the ages of fifteen and seventy were to take an oath of fealty to the emperor. The *fodrum*, the contribution of the towns to the expenses of all the emperor's Italian campaigns, was retained. The Lombard League was expressly recognized as an organization authorized to renew itself indefinitely. In a sense the Lombard towns had won for themselves a position similar to that

The Peace of Constance with the Lombard League

of the German nobility, quasi-independence under the loose feudal sovereignty of the emperor. The concessions made by Frederick in the Peace of Constance were counterbalanced by successes elswhere in Italy. He never lost his hold on the Tuscan lands of Countess Mathilda, which had been regained with the destruction of Henry the Lion and which, strongly organized as they were, together with the Romagna provided a solid core of home territory in central Italy from which he could move northward or southward.

The Norman marriage

Frederick's greatest triumph in the opinion of his contemporaries was the betrothal in 1184 of his eldest son Henry to Constance, heiress to the throne of William II, King of Southern Italy and Sicily, or as it came to be called, the Kingdom of the Two Sicilies. For now by simple inheritance the son, if not the father, might hope to see joined to the rest of the empire the highly organized, richly endowed maritime state of the Normans. In 1186 the marriage of the German prince and the Norman princess was celebrated with great festivity in Milan. In Roman fashion, without bothering about the pope (who refused to crown him), Frederick raised Henry to the position of co-emperor with the title of Cæsar. For the papacy this marriage was a major disaster. The union of the German empire with the Norman-Italian kingdom would be a threat to its independence such as it had never before, even in its worst days, had to meet. Alexander III had been succeeded by a series of weak popes. If ever a pope of the caliber of Gregory VII should come again, the old battle between the two world institutions, papacy and empire, would begin all over. For there was now more to fight about than ever before.

The old emperor took one last bold step to put himself at the head of European affairs. The leadership of the crusading movement had always belonged to the papacy, but in 1188 he took the cross to head the third crusade.[6] It was masterfully organized and conducted up to the time of his death. When in the Balkan peninsula the opposition of the Byzantine emperor put obstacles in his way, Frederick considered attempting the conquest of the Greek east, until the crusaders were permitted to pass. And then in 1190 Frederick Barbarossa was drowned while bathing in the Seleph River in Cilicia. He remained enshrined as a hero in the hearts of the German people. In the days of tyranny and anarchy that followed the fall of the Hohenstaufens he became a legendary figure; he was *the* emperor, *der alte Kaiser*.[7] In the German legend of the just and powerful emperor who should one

Frederick's death on the third crusade

[6] See p. 538.
[7] See the poem of Rückert (1813), *Der alte Barbarossa, der Kaiser Friederich.*

day return he eventually displaced his grandson Frederick II, the hero of the earlier form of the legend. So through long centuries he slept an enchanted sleep, the old red-bearded Kaiser of knightly mien, some said in a cavern high up in the mountains near Berchtesgaden in Bavaria, others said in a cavern in the steep hill of Kyffhäuser in Thuringia, at the southern edge of the Harz Mountains. When the time came, he would awake and descend, to bring back unity and strength and peace to Germany. In the nineteenth century in the heat of the German struggle for unification he was quickly transformed into the great national hero. Monuments were erected to him, the greatest on the Kyffhäuser, and pious bands of German patriots made pilgrimages to Asia Minor to seek his final resting place.

During the short reign of Barbarossa's son Henry VI (1190–97) *Henry VI* both in idea and in fact the Holy Roman empire may be said to have reached its medieval height. Personally the young king was quite unlike his father; he possessed none of the Hohenstaufen good nature, none of his father's knightly character, and little of his physical robustness. Small, pale-faced, and large-browed, he was the learned and yet practical man of affairs, no hero of romance but a shrewd diplomat who knew how to wring the largest advantage from the smallest means. His was a glorious inheritance, and his single-minded purpose was to make the empire "still greater and more powerful than it had been under his predecessors." The chief means to this end was obviously to insure that he should come into the inheritance of his wife Constance in southern Italy and Sicily.

The century that followed the death of Robert Guiscard [8] in 1085 had seen extraordinary achievements in the Mediterranean kingdom of the Normans, which made it politically and culturally the most advanced state in western Europe. The conquest of Sicily begun by Robert *The unifica-* in 1061 was completed by his brother Count Roger, who forced the *tion of south-* last Saracen stronghold on the island to surrender in 1091. Four years *ern Italy and* after his death in 1101 his great son Roger II for the first time formed *Sicily under* one independent domain of the conglomerate territory of Capua, Cala- *the Normans* bria, Apulia, and Sicily, and on Christmas Day of 1130 was crowned in his rich new capital of Palermo with the pope's consent and "by the grace of God, King of Sicily, Apulia, and Calabria." Meanwhile Count Roger had secured control of the Church in his dominion for himself and his heirs by getting himself recognized as hereditary papal legate, an unusual privilege subsequently confirmed in 1128 and 1156.[9] The

[8] See p. 376.
[9] See p. 400.

northern frontier of the Normans in Italy from Gaetà on the west to the Tronto River on the east was recognized at the price of acknowledging the feudal overlordship of the pope.

The founder of this "first modern state" has been called the "first modern king." Roger II faced a task of extreme difficulty. The human and cultural ingredients of this territory were infinitely complex. In southern Italy the population was Latin, Lombard, and Greek. In Calabria Greek was spoken, and Greek Orthodox Christianity was the religion of Church and monastery. Sicily had long been a Saracen land. That same gift of adapting themselves to local tradition that the Normans exhibited in Normandy and England they displayed here even more strikingly. Realizing full well their own numerical inferiority, they did not compromise their position by attempting too thoroughly to impose on the native population their own institutions. Perceiving clearly the advantage to themselves of preserving the differences and the antagonisms of the various elements of the population, they undertook no program of standardization or cultural leveling. Their own adherence to western Christianity did not blind them to the superiority of the civil administration of the Greeks in southern Italy and of the financial administration of the Saracens in Sicily. They pursued an enlightened policy of tolerance rare to that age. Neither Jew nor Greek nor Saracen was molested in his religion. Local rights and usages were respected. The superior traditions of art and learning of the Greek and Mohammedan worlds were amalgamated under their patronage to produce the most dazzling results.[10]

Conglomerate and cosmopolitan though it was, the Norman state was held firmly together by the political administration of a professional bureaucracy of specialists, recruited from the nonfeudal classes and headed by and responsible to the king alone. Roger II and his successors William I (1154–66) and William II (1166–89) were no mere feudal overlords; they were absolute kings by divine right, in the style of the Byzantine emperors, with their powers similarly grounded in Roman law. Moreover, the whole luxurious atmosphere of the court, with its harem and eunuchs, was oriental. The king governed not through vassals who inherited their positions but through a central *curia*, or court (*curia regis*), composed of appointed officials, each responsible for a special department. Together the body of head ministers formed a cabinet. The chief minister was the admiral (Arabic, *al amir*, "the ruler"), who was in charge also of the navy; he and his subordinates were usually Greeks. The department of finance was the

Norman tolerance

Norman government

[10] See p. 718.

divan (Persian, *divan*, "council"), headed by the grand chamberlain, who was assisted by the chancellor and the constable, with a large staff of Saracen subordinates. The judicial department was supervised by the grand justiciar and manned by Greek logothetes and jurists. Roger II even had an English chancellor.

Local administration employed local Norman families, but was carefully linked with the *curia*, being supervised by royal justiciars for justice, royal chamberlains for finance, and *catepans* and *strategoi* (Greek for "generals") for general administration. The army was half feudal Norman and half Saracen. Documents of all departments were issued in Greek and Arabic as well as Latin and in form imitated both Byzantine and papal models. The income of the state was larger than that of any western state; in addition to revenue from royal lands the kings profited from state silk factories and the well-organized system of tariffs and tolls and harbor dues, collected from local merchants and from Genoese, Pisan, Venetian, and other foreign traders, who made the Norman ports centers of Mediterranean commerce. "The Sicilian state stood well in advance of its contemporaries in all that goes to make a modern type of government. Its kings legislated at a time when law-making was rare; they had a large income in money when other sovereigns lived from feudal dues and the produce of their domains; they had a well established bureaucracy when elsewhere both central and local government had been completely feudalized; they had a splendid capital when other courts were still ambulatory." [11]

Such, then, was the splendid realm, so different from Germany, whose acquisition promised in 1190 to make the empire a Mediterranean power. It was an alluring prospect for Henry VI, but from the first it was plain that there was no easy way of uniting the two realms. In the Norman kingdom a party opposed to the Hohenstaufen inheritance and supported by the papacy raised Tancred of Lecce to the throne of his stepbrother William II, who died in 1189. When Richard the Lionhearted, whose sister was William II's widow, stopped in Sicily on his way to the Holy Land as one of the leaders of Barbarossa's third crusade, he made an alliance with Tancred against the Hohenstaufens. Now the English royal house was connected by marriage with the Hohenstaufens' traditional German enemies, the Welfs, and so the alliance was extended to include them. The Welfs, still under the leadership of Henry the Lion after his return in 1190 from his exile, were becoming reconciled with the Saxon nobility and were ready to make any promising attempt to

International alliance against Henry VI

[11] Haskins, *The Normans in European History*, p. 233.

regain their lost position in Germany. Finally, the alliance of papacy, Sicily, England, and Welfs was still further strengthened by the adherence of the nobility of the lower Rhine, headed by the Archbishop of Cologne. Cologne had close commercial relations with England, and was pursuing the same territorial policy that the Welfs had pursued in Saxony, which made the Hohenstaufen king seem the great enemy.

Henry VI and Richard the Lionhearted

This formidable international combination Henry VI had broken by 1194. His Italian campaign of 1191 brought him the imperial crown, but his campaign against Tancred was a failure. In the next year he had the extraordinary good fortune to get hold of his chief enemy, Richard the Lionhearted, who was arrested near Vienna on his way back from the third crusade by Duke Leopold of Austria, even though he was a holy pilgrim, and turned over to the emperor. With great shrewdness Henry used this miracle of good luck to dissolve the alliance against him. Philip Augustus of France and Richard's brother John, who had joined Philip in a campaign against English territory in France, were so anxious to get possession of Richard that they were willing to pay handsomely for his person or for the prolongation of his arrest. By procrastination and by slowly raising his demands on Richard, Henry VI forced peace on Richard's allies, the lower Rhenish nobility. He held Richard to a ransom of one hundred thousand silver marks, obliged him to become the German emperor's vassal for England, and required military service of him against the Welfs and against Sicily. This brought the Welfs to terms. For fifty thousand marks more Henry released Richard from his obligation to assist in the projected expedition against the Normans, rightly preferring his money to his services. Then, making everything perfect, Tancred died in 1194. The campaign against the Normans turned into a triumphant military procession through southern Italy, across the Strait of Messina, and on along the northern Sicilian coast to Palermo. On Christmas Day of 1194, in the cathedral where he now lies, Henry VI, German king and Roman emperor, was crowned King of Sicily, Apulia, and Calabria.

Henry VI becomes King of Sicily

Henry VI was not a man to rest content with even so mighty a victory as this. He was bent on making the Holy Roman empire, which now included Sicily and southern Italy with central and northern Italy and Germany, hereditary in the Hohenstaufen house. In 1194 Constance had given birth to a son, Frederick II, in the presence of a notable group of churchmen in a tent in the public square of Jesi. Henry's plan was to have the infant crowned by the pope as

His plans to make the empire hereditary

the next emperor without the formality of any German or Sicilian election. But opposition in Germany, led by the Archbishop of Cologne, whose right it was to conduct the formal, if not also real, election and to consecrate the German king, combined with the pope's refusal to proceed immediately with the coronation of young Frederick as emperor, frustrated this plan. At the age of two, however, the child was elected by the German princes King of the Romans,[12] the title given to an emperor after his election and before his coronation by the pope. This Henry VI may have considered better for the moment than no claim at all, and in any event Frederick was his legitimate heir to the Norman kingdom.

The conquest of the Norman kingdom brought into the horizon of Henry's calculations aims pursued by the Norman kings since the days of Robert Guiscard, among them the further conquest of Byzantine territory. He had a grandiose scheme to bring Hohenstaufens by marriage to the throne of the Byzantine emperors, and although that came to nothing, he did manage to collect tribute from Constantinople; and the kings of Little Armenia and of Cyprus received their crowns from him as his vassals. He had claims to the Kingdom of Aragon, which he did no more than encourage the Genoese to press, and Philip Augustus of France he would have liked to make his vassal. The tribute paid to the Norman kings by the Mohammedan princes of North Africa continued to be paid to him. While he could not make good his feudal lordship over Denmark, on the eastern frontier he kept Bohemia and Hungary still dependent. Never had Germany been a world power of such magnitude. Then at last, like his father, Henry VI planned to confirm his position by taking the lead in the crusading movement. He began preparations for a crusade even better organized than his father's, which was to open the way for the German empire to the east. But in the midst of his plans he died suddenly at Palermo in September 1197, at the age of thirty-two. His death has been called by a German historian "the most fearful catastrophe of German history in the Middle Ages."

The great position of Henry VI in Europe

His death

Within a year after the death of Henry VI the old rivalry of Welf and Hohenstaufen in Germany had broken out afresh more sharply than ever. The election of the infant Frederick II was ignored, and in 1198 the leaders of both houses were elected king by their respective parties. The choice of the Hohenstaufen party in southern Germany was Henry VI's brother Philip, Duke of Swabia, a "sweet young man,"

Civil war and foreign alliances in Germany

[12] Napoleon revived the title after the end of the empire when he had his son called King of Rome.

as a poet called him, who, unlike Henry, combined in his person all the amiable qualities of his father. The choice of the Welf party in northern and northwestern Germany was Otto of Brunswick, the fierce, stubborn, and proud son of Henry the Lion. For fourteen years ruinous civil war raged in Germany, equal in destructiveness to the wars of the sons of Louis the Pious and similar in effect. The German lay and ecclesiastical nobles, by bargaining with both sides for grants of royal lands and royal rights in return for support and by changing sides with dexterity, managed finally to make themselves independent of the German king. Gradually the civil war took on an international character. Otto IV's mother was the sister of Richard the Lionhearted, whose use of English money and English diplomacy to support a Welf king in Germany was his way of requiting the Hohenstaufens for the treatment that he had suffered at the hands of Henry VI. In these circumstances it was inevitable that Philip of Swabia should turn for support to Richard's chief enemy, Philip Augustus of France. Thus a French-Hohenstaufen alliance directed against England and the Welfs divided central and western Europe into two hostile groups.

Italy after the death of Henry VI

In central and northern Italy Henry VI's death was followed by a strong wave of hostility to the Germans, the natural result of the Hohenstaufen policy in Italy. In Sicily the years after 1197 were chaotic. Constance labored to hold the kingdom for young Frederick II, which she was able to do only by sacrificing to the pope the royal control over the Sicilian Church that had been won by Roger II. At her death in 1198 she left her son under the guardianship of the new pope, Innocent III, and a regency of ecclesiastics. But the regents were so occupied in maintaining themselves against German lieutenants of Henry VI and Norman descendants of Tancred, who challenged their control of the government, that the boy Frederick II was left to grow up without much guidance, like any Sicilian lad in the streets and market places of Palermo.

Innocent III's first steps

When the cardinals in 1198 chose the youngest of their number, Lothair of Segni, as pope, they could not know that they had elected by all odds the greatest of medieval popes, Innocent III.[13] With the papal territory isolated as it had never been, the new pope's immediate problem was to preserve its independence by preventing the reunion of Sicily with the empire. But Innocent III was not the man to overlook the prospect of permanently crippling the power of the empire, perhaps even of reducing it to complete dependence upon the papacy. Chance had put the opportunity in his hands, and he was anxious to

[13] For Innocent's career as a whole, see pp. 645 ff.

use it. He enlarged the Papal States by conquering southern Tuscany, the Duchy of Spoleto, and the March of Ancona, thus consolidating papal territory into a zone extending from western sea to eastern sea and separating imperial Italy from the papal fief—for such in theory the Norman kingdom still was—of southern Italy and Sicily.

It was greatly to the interest of the papacy to prolong civil war in Germany, and it was in large part owing to Innocent's interference that the war continued as long as it did. He used the tactics employed by Gregory VII between 1077 and 1080; that is, he assumed the right to decide between the candidates for the throne and then postponed his decision, although his choice of a Hohenstaufen was as unlikely as Gregory VII's choice of Henry IV. For Innocent's first decision, not made until 1200, Otto of Brunswick paid a heavy price. He was obliged to recognize the independence of the Papal States in Italy and to free the German Church from royal control. The king resigned all the rights reserved to the crown in the Concordat of Worms of 1122. Henceforth bishops were to be elected by a majority of the canons in the cathedral chapter, by the same procedure as in papal elections. The king was to give up his right to the movable property of a prelate at his death (the *ius spolii*, German *Spolienrecht*) and the right to the income of an ecclesiastical benefice during a vacancy (*ius regale, Regalienrecht*). No limitations were to be put on appeals to Rome. The German crown was at last to be deprived of its strongest support; the German Church was to be free; the issues of the investiture struggle were at last decided in the pope's favor. In the years following, by the use of every means, legitimate or questionable, Innocent set the eyes of the German clergy towards Rome as never before, which of course was what he meant by the freedom of the Church. *Innocent III recognizes Otto IV*

Despite all that Innocent III could do, Otto IV's cause in Germany after 1204 was lost; the Hohenstaufen lands were too vast, and the influence and popularity of Philip of Swabia too great. The pope, as quick to change sides as the German princes and determined to back the winner, entered with Philip into negotiations looking towards his recognition and coronation as emperor. Arrangements were complete when in 1208 Philip was murdered by a personal enemy—one of the few cases of assassination in the middle ages. The German princes, tired of civil war and not wishing to introduce Innocent's young ward, Frederick II, into German politics, in 1209 turned back to Otto IV, married him to a Hohenstaufen princess, and re-elected him king. After renewing his earlier pledges with regard to Italy and the German Church, Otto IV was welcomed to Rome in the same year by *Innocent III recognizes Philip of Swabia* *Otto IV becomes emperor* a jubilant pope. But the pope was not jubilant for long. Promises or no promises, Otto IV, representing the union of Welfs and Hohenstaufens, could hardly abandon the old imperial policy. No sooner had he been crowned emperor than he became as Hohenstaufen in his aims as Barbarossa or Henry VI. He reclaimed the Tuscan lands of Mathilda, which he had previously abandoned to Innocent III, and actually launched a campaign to deprive Frederick II of his inheritance and reunite Sicily and southern Italy to the empire.

Innocent III turns to Frederick II

It must have been in great perturbation that Innocent III turned to his last chance, the young King of Sicily, Frederick II; to be sure, he was only sixteen years old, but he was half Hohenstaufen. By 1211 the pope had contrived with Philip Augustus of France and with disaffected German princes to get Frederick re-elected King of the Romans in Germany. The news of his election reached him in Palermo as Otto IV was about to finish his Sicilian campaign and he was waiting to escape by ship to Africa. Frederick always looked upon this good fortune as miraculous. He started northward immediately, coming to terms with Innocent III on the way (and good terms they were for the papacy). After an adventurous and dramatic journey he was welcomed in Germany and recrowned at Aachen in December 1212, as King of the Romans. The final settlement of the issue between him and Otto IV was reached on French soil at the Battle of Bouvines in 1214, where the French-Hohenstaufen alliance defeated the English-Welf alliance.[14] All Welf hopes were now blasted, and henceforth there was no serious resistance to Frederick in Germany. In the Golden Bull of Eger in 1213 he abandoned the German Church to the papacy in almost the same words as Otto IV had used, and made terms with Innocent III which amounted to a complete victory for the pope. His ward was on the imperial throne; Germany and Sicily were not to be reunited; the German Church had been freed from the German king and made subject to the pope—the same thing that had been accomplished in the Norman kingdom fifteen years before. With vast satisfaction Innocent III had Frederick II confirmed and Otto IV deposed and excommunicated at his Fourth Lateran Council of 1215.

The character of Frederick II

The next year the great Innocent III died. Frederick had no such luck as his father and grandfather had had. He never knew what it was to deal with a weak pope, for throughout the rest of his life it was his fortune to encounter a succession of three outstanding pontiffs, Honorious III (1216–27), Gregory IX (1227–41), and In-

---

[14] For the significance of Bouvines in French history, see p. 488.

THE HOLY ROMAN EMPIRE
UNDER THE
HOHENSTAUFENS

—— Boundary of the
Holy Roman Empire.

nocent IV (1243-54). And yet none of them would have agreed with Innocent III that the choice of Frederick II could possibly be a way out of any difficulties, however great. For they, in their determination to secure the political and spiritual victories of their great predecessor and to carry on his policies, found themselves engaged in a fight to the end with the man who—by one of the supreme ironies of history— had made his entrance on the imperial stage as the protégé of Pope Innocent III.

Frederick II was incomparably the most gifted, the best educated, and the most complex among European monarchs of the middle ages; indeed, he is one of the great figures of history. To us he seems the more complex and the more fascinating because for our knowledge of him we must rely so largely on his enemies that we can make him out only dimly through "the mist of calumny and legend" that "the undying hatred of the papacy threw around his name." [15] Like St. Francis of Assisi and Roger Bacon, his contemporaries, and like Dante, who followed him, he was one of the great transitional figures of the thirteenth century, who summed up in their own persons the best and worst features of their age, and prefigured what was to come. "Statesman and philosopher, politician and soldier, general and jurist, poet and diplomat, architect, zoologist, mathematician, the master of six or it might be nine languages, who collected ancient works of art, directed a school of sculpture, made independent researches in natural science, and organized states, this supremely versatile man was the Genius of the Renaissance on the throne of Emperors." [16] One of his contemporaries called him *stupor mundi*, the amazement of the world. Frederick was by birth only half German, his mother being half Norman and half Italian. In character and temperament and gifts he was much less than half German; of all the emperors, he and Otto III, who also had a foreign mother and a foreign upbringing, are the only ones who were by nature not so much northern as Mediterranean or Latin. Then the accidents of his early life all tended to make Frederick still more the Sicilian. Finally, circumstances conspired to force him to play his tragic part on the mighty stage of the thirteenth century chiefly as King of Sicily. It was as King of Sicily that he found himself in the false position of a feudal vassal disloyal to his lawful lord. It was as King of Sicily that the popes feared and hated and fought him.

[15] Bryce, *The Holy Roman Empire*, p. 208.
[16] Kantorowicz, *Frederick II*, p. 669. For the cultural significance of Frederick's reign, see p. 718.

Frederick inherited the German tradition of universal feudal em- *The condition* pire and the Norman tradition of centralized, nonfeudal, absolute *of the empire* monarchy. It was his task to combine these traditions into one system *at Frederick's* to be applied to the whole empire. But this was an impossible task. *accession* In Germany for so many decades political power had been slipping into the hands of feudal princes, lay and ecclesiastical, that to regain it for the crown would have required nothing less than a revolution. In northern and north-central Italy the communes had taken advantage of the confusion of recent years to usurp powers never granted to them by the Treaty of Constance of 1183. In central Italy the popes had acquired a temporal dominion greater than ever before, which they were anxious to expand. In southern Italy and Sicily after the death of Henry VI and the death the next year of Constance chaos had prevailed; such depredations had been committed even on crown property that the prosperous merchant families of Palermo had to take turns caring for the boy Frederick because he had no income.

The new king, who was crowned emperor at Rome in 1220, was *Frederick's* enough of a realist in politics to recognize that it was futile to attempt *Italian* to reduce the whole empire to the same system of administration at *policy* the start. The one possible foundation for rebuilding Hohenstaufen power was now southern Italy and Sicily. There, in spite of general disorganization, strong methods could still recapture for the crown the political and economic power built up by the Norman kings. Thence the system might be extended northwards to include all Italy in a united state, with Rome once more its capital. Frederick enjoyed his greatest success at home. Elsewhere in Italy he underestimated the resistance both of the Lombard towns and of the papacy, united always against him, but the degree of his success even in these regions was remarkable.

His greatest enemy was the papacy. Entrenched in central Italy, the popes were as determined as ever to free themselves from the crushing embrace of the Hohenstaufen to the south and to the north. To destroy the Hohenstaufens root and branch they were ready to use every weapon in their armory, spiritual or temporal, untroubled by subtle distinctions as to moral justification. Not only were they astute politicians, cleverly manipulating all the forces of opposition to Frederick, but they had the great advantage of having at their service an ecclesiastical organization covering central and western Europe. Frederick probably never originally desired to establish in principle or in fact the lordship of the emperor over the pope. He was interested only in securing for the universal empire a position of equal right beside the Universal Church; with this position guaranteed, he desired peace and co-operation. But because of the danger to their political position in Italy the popes would never grant him peace and co-operation; they demanded submission, and for the most part they were the aggressors in a conflict with him to get it. And so Frederick was driven to challenge them on their own ground and to claim the supremacy over them that they claimed over him.

Frederick's German policy

As for Germany, Frederick realized that he was powerless to destroy the power of the feudal princes and that he could only leave Germany to her fate. He can hardly be considered a German king at all; after 1220 he returned to Germany only once. All that he hoped for was by confirming the princes in their sovereign rights and even by increasing them to secure their support, especially military support, for his Italian plans. In any case he thought of Germany only as one province of the empire, joined to its core in southern Italy and Sicily by the intermediary link of northern and central Italy.

The privilege of 1220 to the German ecclesiastical princes

Before leaving for his imperial coronation in Rome in 1220 Frederick provided for the continuation of the empire by securing the election of his son Henry as German king and next emperor. To win the support of the ecclesiastical princes for the election he was obliged to grant them in a privilege of 1220 far-reaching concessions with regard to the exercise of sovereign rights. Already in the Golden Bull of Eger of 1213 he had given up his right to control the personnel of the German Church, and now he gave the independently elected bishops, archbishops, and abbots still more independence in their "territories." The king gave up the right to establish new toll stations and mints in ecclesiastical territories; he abandoned to the prelates all that was left of his rights in the courts; he gave up the *ius spolii;* he promised to regard as outlawed any person excommunicated by a bishop. Moreover, he took steps to protect the bishops against the towns within their territories, which were trying to win a larger measure of independence. Serfs who tried to escape from Church lands to imperial cities were not to be admitted. No new fortifications or towns were to be built in ecclesiastical territory.

In particular these concessions in regard to the towns were important not merely because they marked the further dissolution of royal control in the territories of the ambitious churchmen, who were by now well-nigh independent. They were important as one last example of the fatal blindness of all the German emperors that prevented their perceiving, as the Capetian kings of France perceived, that in the struggle against feudalism, which was inevitable if a strong nation were to arise, the new and growing towns were their natural and powerful allies. They could not even learn from the experience of Henry IV in his last days, when the towns remained true to him after he had been abandoned by the Church, by the nobility, and by his own sons. Even Frederick II, who of them all might most reasonably be expected to have sensed the situation, continued the old losing game of staking his hopes on the secular and ecclesiastical princes, who, once they had got from him what they wanted, were sure to abandon him.

When young Henry reached his majority in 1228, he pursued a policy quite the opposite of his father's, for he was more interested in being German king than Roman emperor. In his search for some support more stable than the fickle loyalty of feudal princes, he seems to have had a glimpse of what his father could not see, for he definitely favored the new towns. But the princes would have none of this. They could no longer be controlled, and they forced from Frederick II in 1231 a privilege which did for the secular princes what the privilege of 1220 had done for the ecclesiastical princes. They were granted complete control of the administration of justice, the establishment of mints, and the use of roads and streams. Measures were taken to close the towns to their runaway serfs. For the first time this document speaks of "territorial lords." The partition of Germany, however, was not to stop with the independence of the great princes, for the privilege provided that all new administrative ordinances made by them and all new taxation should be valid only after consultation with the secular and ecclesiastical lords of their territory. The latter were already beginning to strive for the same kind of independence that the great princes had just won. Taken together, these two privileges may be said to complete constitutionally the feudal dismemberment of Germany. It remained only to work out gradations in the hierarchy of German feudalism, to develop fully the system of local territorial sovereignty, and to systematize co-operation between the princes in matters of common interest. The power of the German king was gone.

The privilege of 1231 to the German secular princes

The privilege of 1231, confirmed by Frederick II in 1232, was so distasteful to Henry that two years later he openly revolted against his father and allied himself with the Lombard League. This treason brought Frederick back on his last visit to Germany in 1235. Henry was forced to submit and put under arrest; he died in prison in Apulia in 1244. He was succeeded by his eldest brother Conrad as German king and emperor elect. Frederick took further steps to pacify Germany, which temporarily even strengthened his own position. He

Frederick's last visit to Germany

made final peace with the Welfs by recognizing their private lands of Brunswick-Wolfenbüttel as a new German duchy, held in fief of the emperor. He was able to take Austria and Styria from the Babenbergers and keep them in his own hands for the time. At an imperial assembly in Mainz measures were taken to limit the feudal right of private warfare and to maintain internal peace. These measures are of interest not because they accomplished anything but for two quite incidental reasons: they were promulgated in the first official document to use German instead of Latin; and to supervise their enforcement Frederick made a feeble gesture towards real government by appointing a grand imperial justiciar in Sicilian style. This done, he quit Germany for ever in 1237, to return to his greater Italian plans, leaving her to her squabbling princes.

Following the example of his father and grandfather, Frederick II had expected to take the leadership of the crusading movement, now seriously neglected. He was peculiarly unfortunate in having given the popes a hold over him, for in his early days, when he was first Innocent III's ward and then Honorius III's dutiful protégé, he had twice taken the cross, once at his coronation at Aachen and again in Rome. However, the situation both in Germany and in southern Italy and Sicily required his first attention. The only preparation he made for his crusade was to marry as his second wife the heiress of the Latin Kingdom of Jerusalem, Isabella of Brienne, and assume the title of King of Jerusalem. In 1225 Frederick promised Honorius III, who was accusing him of breaking his vow, to go by 1227; if he did not, he should be liable to excommunication. In that year he sailed from Brindisi but fell seriously ill, and upon the advice of his physicians returned to Pozzuoli to regain his health.

Frederick's crusade

The events that followed were ironical enough to make good tragedy or good comedy. Frederick was promptly excommunicated by Gregory IX, who chose to interpret his return as deliberate trickery. Frederick, however, having no intention of letting his excommunication stand in the way of his crusade, as soon as he was ready continued on his way. This forced the pope, the leader of the Christian Church, into the position of opposing the crusade, since he could hardly overlook Frederick's sacrilege in presuming to lead it under the ban of excommunication. The crusade Frederick had never conceived of as a military expedition; he preferred to acquire the Kingdom of Jerusalem by friendly negotiation with the Sultan of Egypt, Al Kamil.[17]

[17] For details see p. 548.

The astonishing success of his negotiations in Gregory IX's eyes only aggravated his three previous offenses of not going before he did, of going when he did, and of choosing to negotiate with the Infidel instead of destroying him. The pope therefore rewarded him by putting his Kingdom of Jerusalem under interdict, and by spreading stories that he ordered up Christian women to dance before the sultan before being turned over to the pleasure of the Moslems.

These events marked the beginning of the almost continuous war with the popes that filled the rest of Frederick II's life. During his absence in the east in 1228 and 1229 Gregory made war on his domains in southern Italy with the first army of papal mercenaries that we know of, the "soldiers of the Keys." At the same time, however, while the pope was having some success there, imperial troops attempted to recover part of the territory recently lost to the Papal States. When Frederick returned in wrath from the east, he speedily drove the papal troops out of his kingdom, but rather than continue the war offensively against the Papal States he offered to negotiate with Gregory IX for peace. The result of the long-drawn-out negotiations at Ceperano was that Frederick was absolved from his excommunication at the cost of concessions limiting his control over the Sicilian Church. But at least he was free to go on with his plans for the consolidation of Sicily and Italy. *The beginning of Frederick's war with the papacy*

As early as the months following his coronation as emperor in 1220 Frederick had begun the complete reorganization of his southern kingdom. Like the Normans in England after 1066, he made a clean sweep by royal decree of all titles to property and royal privileges, in order to rebuild as he pleased. The work was completed in 1231 by the Constitution of Melfi, undoubtedly the most conspicuous and constructive single piece of statecraft that the middle ages knew. Its keynote is a centralized, bureaucratic absolutism by divine right, suggestive of the benevolent despotism of the enlightened monarchs of the eighteenth century. Yet even in the thirteenth century this was not a complete innovation, for a large number of the actual provisions of the constitution were merely a restoration of measures of the great Roger II. *The Constitution of Melfi*

Stronger than before was the influence of Roman law, which appears in the determination to abolish all vestiges of local feudal privilege in the state, in the large measure of concern with every phase of the state's life, and in the ready willingness to replace antiquated survivals by new regulations dictated by reason, necessity, and nature.

"In no wise," said Frederick, "do we detract from the reverence due to earlier Rulers, when we beget new laws to meet the peculiar needs of the new time, and find new medicines for new ills." The state was to be governed by a peculiar sacred justice, of which the emperor's will was the expression. It was, for instance, sacrilege "to discuss the Emperor's judgments, decrees and statutes." To buy office in the state was simony, a deadly sin. It was sacrilege "to debate whether that man is worthy whom the emperor has chosen and appointed." It was in full accord with such ideas of the sacred character of the state that "the crime of heresy, the heresy of any and every accused sect, under whatever name the sectaries are known, shall be accounted a crime against the state, as it is in the ancient Roman laws." On the other hand, antiquated methods of trial by battle and ordeal were abolished as contrary to nature and reason. "How could a man believe that the natural heat of glowing iron will become cool or cold without an adequate cause . . . or that, because of a seared conscience, the element of cold water will refuse to accept the accused?" "These judgments of God by ordeal which men call 'truth revealing' might better be styled 'truth-concealing.' " [18]

Government and policy in Sicily

In detail the administration provided for by the Constitution of Melfi was an extreme elaboration of the earlier Norman administration by trained, appointed, and paid officials. Frederick had founded the University of Naples, the first large state university in Europe, as a training school, particularly in Roman law, for future officials. The army was largely a mercenary army, of which a corps of Saracens, quartered together in Lucera in southern Italy, was the nucleus. Great emphasis was placed upon the fleet, not only for war but to protect trade. The organization of the finances, imitated elsewhere in Europe, astounded contemporaries. Irregular feudal dues were commuted into fixed payments, whenever possible, and in critical situations direct taxation was resorted to. On the frontiers and in all the seaports a highly developed system of import and export taxes was in force. The huge landed possessions of the emperor were carefully cultivated, often by Cistercian monks. The state enjoyed a virtual monopoly of the grain trade, the exchange of money, the baths, the slaughterhouses, weights and measures, salt, steel, and iron, and the manufacture of silk and textiles. Altogether Frederick II had an income with which that of no other state could compare. It was this income that made it possible for him to have paid troops ready to combat his only rival in income,

[18] Quotations from Kantorowicz, *op. cit.*, pp. 244 ff.

the pope. Frederick's economic policy was that system of rigid control of commerce exercised by the medieval towns called mercantilism. The privileges of other Italian cities, such as Genoa and Pisa, in Sicilian ports were abolished.

In general Frederick was laboring to create what one is tempted to call a modern national state in Sicily. The young men of the kingdom were to be given a strictly Sicilian education by being obliged to attend the University of Naples, and the blood of the Sicilian race was to be kept pure by the restriction of marriage with outsiders. "When the men of Sicily ally themselves with the daughters of foreigners, the purity of the race becomes besmirched, while evil and sensual weakness increases, the purity of the people is contaminated by the speech and habits of others, and the seed of the stranger defiles the hearth of our faithful subjects." Perhaps this familiar doctrine was rather more absurd in Greek-Punic-Roman-Saracen-Norman Sicily than it has ever been in any other land, especially coming from this half-German foreigner, whose Sicilian ancestors were only Normans, the latest comers in fifteen hundred years of colonization and immigration.

Before his crusade Frederick had failed in one attempt to force the Lombard towns to observe the terms of the Treaty of Constance. Shortly after his return, he failed in a second attempt. These failures offended his pride and outraged his principles of government. He could never give up the towns for lost, as he did the German princes, and accordingly compromise with their efforts for independence. They were Italian, they were rebels against the empire, and so they must be crushed. After his second visit to Germany Frederick took up the war against them in earnest, and after a smashing victory at Cortenuova in 1237 had them at his feet. In the face, however, of his insistence upon unconditional surrender, individual towns held out, and the fruits of his victory were considerably limited by his inability to proceed rapidly with their reduction. *Frederick subdues the Lombard towns*

Elated by his victory, Frederick, like a triumphant Roman emperor, sent the captured Milanese *carroccio*, the standard-bearing wagon, with flags and trumpets as spoils of war to the Romans. At the same time he announced far-reaching plans calculated to stimulate their loyalty. "Our heart," he wrote, "has ever burned with the desire to reinstate in the position of their ancient dignity the Founder of the Roman Empire and the Foundress, Rome herself," in the hope "that in our auspicious days the honour of the blood of Romulus may revive, *Frederick's Roman policy*

the imperial Roman speech be heard again in its glory, the ancient
Roman dignity renewed and an inseparable bond by our grace be tied
between the Roman Empire and the Roman people themselves." The
new Italy was to be divided into provinces administered by Roman
governors. "We shall no longer delay the execution of the plan we
have evolved: that to the honour and glory of Rome distinguished
Romans shall preside over the business of State and shall be resplendent in dignity."

This was far too much for Gregory IX. It not only threatened his
control of the city of Rome, which had always been a peculiarly sensitive point in papal policy; it threatened the extinction of the Papal
States in Italy. Moreover, his claim that the pope "should possess
supreme power over the affairs and persons of the entire world" had
The second ex- been rudely ignored when Frederick refused even to tolerate him as
communication mediator in his quarrel with the Lombard towns, well aware that
of Frederick papal mediation was always inclined to be anti-imperial. Frederick
had further offended him by marrying his natural son Enzio to the
heiress of Sardinia, which the popes regarded as a papal fief, and making him King of Sardinia. Gregory IX therefore again declared war
by his second excommunication of Frederick II, on Palm Sunday of
1239.

An extravagant propaganda was immediately launched by both imperial and papal chancelleries to influence public opinion. Gregory
Papal and called Frederick "this scorpion spewing poison from the sting of his
imperial re- tail." He was, moreover, a blasphemer and a heretic: "This King of
crimination the Pestilence has proclaimed that, to use his own words, all the
world has been deceived by three deceivers, Jesus Christ, Moses and
Mohammed, of whom two died in honour, but Christ upon the Cross.
And further he has proclaimed aloud (or rather he has lyingly declared) that all be fools who believe that God could be born of a
Virgin . . . and Frederick maintains that no man should believe
aught but what may be proved by the power and reason of nature."
He was accused of seeking to found a new religion, of considering
himself a sort of divinity. Behind so much smoke there must have
been some fire; Frederick was, for example, at least highly indiscreet
to refer, and to allow his partisans to refer, to his birthplace Jesi as
Bethlehem. At any rate, whatever the facts may have been, the pope's
frantic accusations helped to inflame men's minds to a new heat of
passion. "The time was one of intellectual upheaval and unrest;
heresies were rife; the air was full of new doctrines. To this troubled
or rebellious spirit Frederick, himself perhaps influenced by Muslim

speculation, and certainly no dutiful son of the Church, made his appeal." [19]

He stressed the Lombard question. "Because by God's grace all has prospered with us and we are pursuing the Lombards, our rebels, to the death, this apostolic priest who wishes them to live heaves a sigh and seeks himself to obstruct our good fortune." But he went much further than that. He "appealed to law, to the indelible rights of Cæsar; he claimed the right of reforming the Church against the will of the hierarchy, compared himself to Elijah rooting out the prophets of Baal, and denounced his foe as the Antichrist of the New Testament, since it was God's representative on earth whom he was resisting." [20] And yet he would not in fact claim for the empire more than the moon's place in the same heaven with the sun of the papacy. "But, O marvel of unheard of arrogance! The Sun would fain steal from the Moon her colour and rob her of her light! The priest would bait Augustus, and with his apostolic greatness would obscure the radiance of our majesty, whom God has set upon the pinnacles of Empire. . . . There he sits in the seat of the Pharisees and of false doctrines, anointed by his comrades with the oil of civil unrighteousness. . . . Insolently he tries to stultify the order of things decreed in heaven, and perchance believes that the laws of nature will be governed by his heated will. He seeks to darken the radiance of our majesty by perverting truth to lies."

To the cardinals Frederick appealed, "Call ye back our roaring lion from his purpose," and proposed that they summon a council to settle the questions at issue and reform the Church along the lines of apostolic poverty. The call to reform was no doubt only a weapon against the papacy, although Frederick did keep in touch with the reforming Franciscans. To all the princes in Europe he called: "Ye princes, ye beloved princes, reproach not us alone, reproach also the church which is the community of the faithful; for her head is weak, the leader in her midst is as a roaring lion, her prophet a madman, her bridegroom an infidel, her priest a defiler of the Most High, who acts unrighteously and contemns the law." In fact, Frederick proposed a league of the monarchs of Europe to protect themselves against the attacks of the papacy: "Neither the first are we, nor yet the last, whom priestly power opposes and seeks to hurl from the seats of the mighty. And the fault is yours who give ear to these hypocrites of holiness whose arrogance would fain believe that into their

[19] Bryce, *op. cit.*, p. 209.
[20] *Ibid.*, p. 210.

gullet all the Jordan floweth." "They begin with us, but be assure of this, they will end with the other princes and kings, whose migh they will no longer fear when once we are overcome." [21]

Arguing that "the Italian towns would be unmindful of their own advantage if they preferred the luxury of freedom to the repose of peace and justice," Frederick at once took steps to complete the amalgamation of northern and central Italy into the administration of the empire. Except for the towns that still resisted him and for part of the Papal States, the whole territory was organized on the Sicilian system into a number of general vicariates headed by general vicars, divided into provinces headed by vicars. In each city was an imperial podesta; not even the cities that had been constantly loyal were permitted to have native podestas. Rather than use Germans or North Italians as his governors Frederick chose to use Apulians, and for the most important offices his own relatives. The whole administration of northern Italy was thus fused with that of southern Italy into one system dominated by the emperor. This, had it proved permanent, would have been an important step in the unification of Italy; even as it was, it did in some respects lay the foundations for the later northern Italian despotisms.

Reorganization of northern and central Italy

The prospect of the conquest of the Papal States by this machine terrified Gregory IX into summoning the clergy of western Europe to a council at Rome in 1241. There was little doubt that the emperor would there be deposed; hence it was so important for Frederick that the council should not meet that he took the unheard-of step of commanding the admiral of his fleet to attack the Genoese ships bearing the foreign prelates to Rome. The exploit was remarkably successful; the Genoese ships were attacked off the island of Elba, three of them sunk, and the rest captured. One hundred prelates, including three papal legates and two cardinals and the generals of the leading monastic orders, were Frederick's prisoners. It was a rude assault upon the independence of the Church, which pretty generally scandalized western Europe, but at any rate the council of deposition was postponed. Meanwhile Frederick gathered forces for an advance on Rome. In the Duchy of Spoleto and the March of Ancona and in papal territory in Tuscany the authority of Gregory IX collapsed, and these areas were joined to the empire. Frederick stood at the peak of his success. As Henry IV had done in 1084 and Barbarossa in 1167, he was about to take the Eternal City itself, "to revive the ancient festivals and the triumphant laurels, to show the victorious eagles honour due."

Frederick captures a Church council

[21] The quotations are from Kantorowicz's biography of Frederick II.

The shock was too much for Gregory IX, who was a very old man. He died, and by dying snatched the victory from his enemy's hands.

During the twenty-two months between the death of Gregory IX and the accession of Innocent IV in 1243 the emperor labored incessantly to bring about the election of a friendly pope. He thought that he had succeeded, but he was doomed to bitter disappointment. Gregory IX had been an honest and forthright enemy, with whom it had been possible to come to terms. His successor, the Genoese Innocent IV, a brilliant jurist who had been a professor at the University of Bologna, was a man of guile "with a heart of ice." *Innocent IV*

Moved by no concern for the spiritual proprieties of his office, he devoted all the resources of the Church with great energy and ingenious skill to the destruction of the empire. After the failure of negotiations, in which Frederick made surprising concessions for the sake of peace but which the pope seems to have regarded only as a means of gaining time, Innocent escaped from Italy to conduct his campaign from abroad. In 1244 he went to Lyons, and immediately summoned a council for the next year to depose the emperor. This council Frederick could not possibly prevent. It met, and approved Innocent's solemn deposition of the emperor for perjury, breach of the peace, sacrilege, heresy, entrusting his wives to the care of eunuchs, and a further long list of alleged atrocities. *The deposition of Frederick*

Frederick received the news of his deposition with affected surprise and genuine disdain. He is reported to have ordered his treasure chests brought to him and out of one of them to have taken his imperial crown and placed it on his head. "Does it look as if I had lost my crown?" he asked his courtiers. "I have been the anvil long enough, now I shall be the hammer." "We shall pursue after them [the papal party] with greater zeal and fury, we shall the more mightily display our powers to compass their destruction, we shall wield the sword of vengeance more cruelly against them . . . and the hate that consumes us will be slaked only by their annihilation."

The last five years of the struggle were desperate. Innocent unleashed his legates and the Franciscan and Dominican monks against the emperor. He went so far as to proclaim a crusade against the Hohenstaufens, whom he branded as worse than Infidels; the same privileges should be the reward for taking the cross against Frederick II as for going to the Holy Land. He carried the fight against the emperor into Germany. The old papal stratagem of setting up an antiking (Frederick had never resorted to creating an antipope) was used. Landgrave Henry of Thuringia was given twenty-five thousand *Innocent IV's policy in Germany*

silver marks by the pope to accept the German crown from a packed
electoral assembly of German princes, and with six thousand marks
more papal agents bought a victory for Henry over Frederick's son
Conrad. After the death of Henry, Innocent's clerical supporters
elected another antiking, Count William of Holland, who, however,
was never much more than a figurehead. In the German Church
Innocent wrought havoc. Imperial supporters in episcopal sees were
deposed without reference to the cathedral chapters, and new bishops
were appointed by the pope. Threats, excommunications, interdicts,
and the use of force drove the German clergy with but few exceptions
out of the camp of the emperor and into the camp of the pope. And
yet, despite this general defection in the German Church, the first of
its kind, the Hohenstaufen cause was by no means ruined in Germany.

*The end of
Frederick II*

In Italy the papal party resorted to a conspiracy to murder the
emperor and his leading supporters, and it is not impossible that
Innocent IV himself at the last moment knew of these plans. The
conspiracy was discovered in time and put down in cold blood, although
Frederick barely escaped being poisoned by his own physician. He
was forced to arrest and blinded his great chancellor, Peter of Vinea,
whose Latin periods had for so long rivaled in style those of the papal
chancellery, for gross malversation in the administration of justice.
He lost his son Enzio, who was taken prisoner by the Bolognese.
But in spite of a severe defeat outside of Parma and temporary losses
elsewhere, the emperor maintained and even strengthened his position
in northern and central Italy with the aid of such outrageous tyrants
as Ezzelino of Romano and Margrave Hubert of Pelavicini. In the
midst of plans for a fourth marriage to insure the permanence of his
dynasty, to carry his fight through to final victory, Frederick II died
of dysentery in southern Italy in 1250.

The popes carried on the struggle until the Hohenstaufen house
was extinguished. Frederick left the empire to his son Conrad IV,
with his natural son Manfred, of "snow-white skin and pink cheeks
and eyes like stars," as his regent in Sicily. After a short but successful
career in Sicily Conrad IV died in southern Italy in 1254, leaving
his young son and heir Conradino in charge of his grandfather, the

*The end of
the Hohen-
staufens*

Duke of Bavaria. Before his death in the same year Innocent IV had
been negotiating with Henry III of England, with the aim of establishing Henry's son Edmund as papal vassal for the Norman kingdom
in place of the Hohenstaufens. In the following year, however, Manfred succeeded in regaining control of the Sicilian kingdom, and in
fact nearly recovered the strong position that his father had held in

all Italy. In 1261 a Frenchman came to the papal throne, Urban IV, and he was succeeded in 1264 by another Frenchman, Clement IV. Together they succeeded in perfecting the plan of bringing Charles of Anjou, brother of the French King Louis IX, into Italy to destroy the remnants of the Hohenstaufens and take over the Sicilian kingdom as a papal fief.

The inordinately ambitious French prince invaded Manfred's kingdom in 1266, and entered into the inheritance of the Hohenstaufens by defeating Manfred near Benevento in a battle in which Manfred himself was slain. The aggressive greed of the French régime, however, led to a Ghibelline reaction throughout Italy; and Conradino, the last of the Hohenstaufens, was called from Germany to take over his inheritance. The imperial army was defeated by the French near Tagliacozzo in 1268, and Conradino was captured. To make sure the end of the Hohenstaufens, the fifteen-year-old boy was taken to Naples and beheaded, with at least the approval of Pope Clement IV. By such means was the struggle between empire and papacy finally decided in favor of the popes. Such was the heritage that Frederick Barbarossa bequeathed to his descendants when he won the Sicilian heiress as his son's bride.

The year 1268 may be taken as marking the end of the Holy Roman empire. Imperial echoes continued to resound in Italian history, especially in the lofty Ghibelline sentiments of Dante Alighieri,[22] but henceforth few German emperors thought seriously of reviving the Hohenstaufen program in Italy. They were content to liquidate their imperial rights there for a substantial consideration, leaving Italy to herself, a confusion of petty despotisms, warring communes, feudal principalities, and Papal States, with a French kingdom in the south. But in spite of political chaos Italy was building, on the foundations laid by the Hohenstaufens, the beginnings of the spiritual unity that appeared in the Italian renaissance. As for the papacy, at the cost of blighting its spiritual outlook it had won a great temporal victory in destroying German power in Italy. But the means it had employed had offended the sensibilities of all Christians concerned with the spiritual mission of the Church, and aroused the opposition of the French and English kings and the lasting suspicion of the German people, especially in the cities. It was no accident that Frederick II became the first hero of the legend of the emperor who should return to establish peace and justice and reform the Church. In particular, the introduction by the popes of the French into Italy was but the

The end of the Holy Roman empire

22 See p. 788.

prelude to the introduction by French kings of the popes into France.[23]

The extinction of the Hohenstaufens likewise marks the end of an epoch in German history. The days of the strong German kings were over; the days of the territorial princes had come. Feudalism had won a complete victory in Germany; or, put in another way, the Germans had failed to solve the problem of political unity. To be sure, the Holy Roman empire continued for centuries to exist in theory, incorporated in imperial titles and ceremonies reflecting the glories of the past. But it became at last little better than a laughingstock, "neither holy nor Roman nor empire," in Voltaire's famous epigram; and when Napoleon finally did away with the whole pretense in 1806 he was only giving the dead decent, though belated, burial. In 1273 the first Hapsburg emperor was elected; thereafter such reality as the empire retained was the reality of the growing power of Austria and the Hapsburgs, for which it was only another name.

Feudalism triumphant in Germany

It has for generations been the contention of one school of German historians that the chief explanation for the failure of the German kings at home was their waste of time, energy, resources, and blood in the pursuit of the fantastic dream of Italian and world domination. Had they confined their attention to Germany they could have prevented its partition; thus the shame of German impotence in succeeding centuries would have been avoided, and the unification of Germany that came in the nineteenth century would have come five hundred, seven hundred, years sooner. On the face of it this argument seems plausible, and it is certainly sound in political theory, but it is nevertheless in large part the product of the wishful thinking of modern German nationalists. It is easy to see where the domestic policy of the emperors was wrong; their costliest blunder—their failure to sense the importance of the growth of German towns—has already been seen.

The significance of the medieval empire

Again, without insisting that their whole foreign policy was a mistake, one can see how they could have carried it through to greater success abroad with less danger to their position at home. For instance, Frederick Barbarossa should have realized that his enemies, the Lombard towns and the papacy, were natural enemies of each other, and that it was to his interest and within his power to keep them so, instead of driving them into each other's arms. To do so, however, he would have had to acknowledge to himself that he was not strong enough to conquer all his enemies and retain all his rights, and so had better by concession to his lesser foes secure their co-operation against his greatest foe, the papacy, which was likewise their foe. But that was what

[23] See p. 959.

Frederick Barbarossa could not or would not do; his empire must be universal.

With that word we come to the root of the difficulty. The tradition of international unity embodied in the Roman and Carolingian empires was too binding, the invitation to assume a protectorate over the papacy too flattering, the actual increase in material resources too convincing, to allow the German kings to stay at home. In their position (as the French kings were not) and with their opportunities (which the French kings had not) it is doubtful that any medieval kings could have done differently. They did not do for Germany what the French kings did for France. On the other hand, to the extent that they brought a measure of peace and security to Italy, thereby promoting the growth of the Italian towns, and to the extent that they facilitated the exchange of ideas and goods between Germany and more highly civilized Italy, they were rendering important service to European civilization. Their liberation of the papacy from the control of Roman factions, thus making possible its development as an international institution, was a contribution to European development, whether for better or for worse, the importance of which is beyond calculation. If these services were rendered at the cost to Germany of territorial and administrative unity, who today, now that the supreme virtues of nationalism have become somewhat suspect, shall say that the cost to Europe was too high?

Chapter 15

THE DEVELOPMENT OF THE ENGLISH
STATE (1066–1272) *

The Battle of Hastings, 1066

*A*S DUSK fell on October 14, 1066, after a daylong battle, and Harold Godwinson lay dead among his huscarls, a revolutionary change in English history began. The Battle of Hastings made Duke William of Normandy King of England. For five more years he had to crush sporadic uprisings, repel Danish invasions, and even turn the northern shires of his new kingdom into a desolate waste, but he had destroyed the Anglo-Saxon kingdom at Hastings. William and the mercenaries whom he had gathered from all northwestern Europe by promise of plunder were the governors of the new Norman Kingdom of England.

Anglo-Saxon political history, 400–1066

William conquered a people whose ancestors, six centuries earlier, had brought little more than a tribal organization, a language, and a decadent religion across the North Sea to destroy a Roman province. In England their tribes, fractions of tribes, and war bands had become petty kingdoms. These kingdoms occupied the lands abandoned by the Romanized Britons whose descendants, the Welsh, were slowly pushed back into the mountainous west of the island. While kingdom fought against kingdom in vain attempts to secure supremacy, the Christianity brought from Rome by St. Augustine swept away the old paganism and introduced the learning and organization of the Church. After Viking raids had sacked the wealthy and cultured monasteries of Bede and destroyed all but the southernmost of the kingdoms, Alfred the Great in Wessex reorganized his forces and compelled the invaders to consent to a formal division of England. His descendants were able to conquer this second Normandy and make the former Roman province a single state. During the century preceding William's

---

* The author of this chapter is Dr. Glenn W. Gray.

conquest this state had been for a generation absorbed in the great Scandinavian empire of Knut. Then during Edward the Confessor's pious reign it became in effect the property of powerful earls. Upon Edward's death in 1066 the greatest of these, Harold Godwinson, made himself king. After a two-hundred-mile march from London to York he destroyed an army of Danish invaders at Stamford Bridge —only, less than three weaks later, to be slain by William's archers at Hastings.

In the six centuries intervening between the Anglo-Saxon and Norman conquests a local government had been constructed in England that was efficient enough to survive the Norman conquest and to be used throughout the middle ages. The kingdom as united in the tenth century by the kings of Wessex was composed of thirty-four shires or counties,[1] each under the joint supervision of a bishop, an earl, and a sheriff. The bishop, although appointed by the king, represented the Church; the earl represented nascent Anglo-Saxon feudalism; the sheriff represented in part the earl, in part the king. The government of the shire was carried on by its county court, which met semiannually in Anglo-Saxon times and at intervals of either four or six weeks under the Normans. The shire court, attended by all landowners, was primarily a judicial body, although it had some administrative functions. The law administered was of the ordinary Germanic type: the attendants were the judges, the bishop and the sheriff were only presiding officials, and proof was made by ordeal or compurgation. All Anglo-Saxon courts tried cases both civil and criminal, both secular and ecclesiastical, besides being regularly used to witness business transactions. The shire, largely through the sheriff, was also a fiscal and military unit for the central government.

Local government: the shire

Each shire was divided into smaller units called hundreds. The hundred court, also attended by the landowners of its area, met every four weeks under the presidency of the sheriff or his deputy. Its procedure was similar to that of the shire court, but it handled less important cases and transacted the business of less important persons. The inhabitants of the hundred were organized for police purposes into groups called tithings. Each hundred was divided into hides of approximately one hundred and twenty acres for military purposes and for assessment of the Danegeld, the one great tax known to the

The hundred

---

[1] The total of forty shires in present-day England results from the addition of Cumberland and Westmorland, annexed from Scotland by William Rufus, the creation of Lancashire, Rutland, and Durham from parts of other counties, and by the incorporation of Monmouth from Wales.

Anglo-Saxon kingdoms. The vill or parish was also a subdivision of the hundred for governmental purposes.

Towns

There were few towns of importance in Anglo-Saxon England. London, whose merchants were powerful enough at times to influence the government, was by far the greatest; Bristol in the west and York in the north were less important centers. The capital, in so far as there was one, was Winchester, the old home of the kings of Wessex. Many burghs had been established as centers of defense in the early tenth century, some of which were favorably enough situated to prosper and become thriving mercantile centers in later years. Even the inhabitants of London, however, in 1066 regularly kept their own cows and chickens and gathered the harvest quite as did the country folk. England was rural.

The class system

The old Germanic class system of warrior, farmer, and slave had become a complex maze of personal rights and legal relationships by 1066; subclasses had evolved, and subclasses of subclasses, each with varying rights before the law. Even the legal-minded Normans soon lost patience with these Anglo-Saxon technicalities and roughly swept the whole people into one or the other of the two great classes of the feudal age, freemen or serfs.

Central government: the king

Although the Norman kings found many attributes of Anglo-Saxon royalty worthy of retention, they recognized the inherent weaknesses of the central government that allowed William's invasion such easy success. The small household of the Anglo-Saxon kings was a blurred copy of that of the Carolingian monarchy, composed of seneschal, butler, chamberlain, steward, chancellor, and minor servants. However, the English chancellors, who supervised all the secretarial work and kept the seal of Edward the Confessor, commanded a small staff of clerical workers who possessed a better technic than their continental contemporaries.

The witan

A more numerous body of advisers called the witan could be summoned by the king, but both its powers and its membership were undefined. Composed of the wise or the great men of the kingdom, the witan had sometimes chosen and deposed kings, but at other times had been limited to the function of witnessing royal acts. It was a court for the greatest personages and the most important cases, but had no appellate jurisdiction over local courts. The king's revenue consisted of the rental or produce of his own lands, of the Danegeld, of two-thirds of the fines imposed by local courts, of the

Public finance

right to food from each district (by 1066 this had been mostly commuted to a money return), and of such supplementary income as tolls and the profits from treasure-trove and stranded whales.

The Anglo-Saxon kings possessed certain judicial rights, called pleas of the crown, which were theoretically valid throughout the kingdom, although they were probably effective only in the south.[2] In fact law as enforced in Wessex, in Mercia, and in the Danelaw had so little in common that Norman chroniclers recognized that the land was divided among these three territorial laws, each of which, moreover, varied from locality to locality. The custom of Kent with its Jutish antecedents was powerful enough to maintain its individuality for centuries against the king's law. Anglo-Saxon kings, however, were accustomed to legislate, with the advice of the witan, for the entire kingdom. *The judicial system*

The military system of the Anglo-Saxon state was based upon old Germanic custom, which imposed upon all able-bodied landholders the duty to serve whenever called. This national army or militia was called the fyrd; the shipfyrd manned the navy. Harold's army at Hastings was composed largely of the fyrd of the southeastern counties. William was able to cross the channel without dispute because the shipfyrd had tired of waiting and disbanded to gather the harvest. During the eleventh century the Anglo-Saxon kings had additional naval and land forces, called huscarls. Edward the Confessor disbanded most of the naval force in 1050; the remainder, after defeating the Vikings at Stamford Bridge, fell around Harold's dragon standard at Hastings. *The military system*

During the six centuries that elapsed between the Anglo-Saxon and the Norman conquests of England purely Germanic institutions had been allowed to develop without external influence for two centuries, then for another two centuries had been modified by the Roman institutions introduced with Christianity. These modified institutions had then been further altered by contact with the Norsemen. By 1066 southern England had reached a stage in governmental evolution very like that attained in France a century earlier, while central and northern England still remained comparable to the France of Charlemagne. Hastings is justly considered one of the decisive battles of world history because it gave control of England to rulers in close touch with western Europe—and, moreover, to rulers so able that in two generations they remodeled English public institutions until they were a full century in advance of their counterparts on the continent. *The significance of the Battle of Hastings*

William the Conqueror introduced into England the best govern-

---

[2] In the eleventh century the pleas of the crown were breach of the king's peace or protection which he had especially given to a person or place, housebreaking, ambush, the receiving of outlaws, neglect of summons to the fyrd, and treason to one's lord.

ment that he knew. Although illegitimate, he had inherited Normandy in 1035 when he was only eight years old. He began twelve years later to govern it himself; he then suppressed its turbulent baronage and made himself the most powerful vassal of the French king. Under his firm and efficient control the little duchy's prosperity, culture, and population increased until surplus Norman energy was expending itself as far away as Sicily. The government that William devised for England was the feudalism of western Europe with the modifications suggested to him by his experience as Duke of Normandy. Harold's resistance and the frequent uprisings in the five years that followed the Battle of Hastings furnished William pretext enough to claim that all land of the kingdom was forfeit. Upon this assumption he acted; thenceforward every hide of English land was considered to be owned either directly or indirectly by the king.

William gradually used this land to reward his followers, granting it to them by one of the four forms of feudal tenure. Somewhat less than half he gave to the great barons and knights who had aided in the conquest. This was held subject to the ordinary feudal dues and incidents [3] and by military tenure. Military tenure, or, as it was frequently called, knight service, required the vassal to provide for forty days annually the service of from one to sixty knights, depending upon the value of his fief. By military tenure William secured about one hundred and seventy great tenants-in-chief, frequently called his barons or magnates, and many less powerful vassals. The land formerly held by the Church, in value about a quarter of the kingdom, was for the most part restored and held by frankalmoin, or free alms, a tenure employed by the Church exclusively. It was not subject to the feudal dues and incidents, although the Norman kings were powerful enough to secure regularly homage, court attendance, and something corresponding to the relief; the ordinary return consisted of prayers and Masses for the grantor, his family, and his descendants. A relatively small portion of the kingdom was restored on payment of ransom to its former owners, mostly small holders and townsmen. Much of this land returned a service of money and was held by free socage or, in the towns, burgage tenure.[4] The fourth type of feudal tenure created by the Normans was tenure by sergeanty. This returned most of the ordinary dues and incidents, but some form of service other than military, ecclesiastical, or financial. William used it to provide for the countless

[3] See p. 308, n. 11.
[4] In many cases holders of lands by socage tenure rendered some agricultural service in addition to the money payment.

miscellaneous needs of a great king. Land was granted by sergeanty for so many arrows or coats of mail a year, for carrying the royal banner, for scalding the royal swine. The king's butler, his marshal, and his cook held land by sergeanty. One holder cared for the king's mistresses, while another had the job of holding the king's head if he were seasick crossing the channel. Finally, William retained about one-sixth of the kingdom in his own hands.

By thus disposing of England William rewarded all his followers for services already rendered, and also provided for his own future needs. As a feudal suzerain he could summon approximately five thousand armed knights into the field at a time when the army of his Capetian overlord Philip I fled before the garrison of a single small castle. In addition to the uncertain feudal aids and incidents he possessed a regular income in money from his socagers and burgesses. Hundreds of his officials and servants were paid in advance; even his women and his deer were systematically provided for. All over the realm his serfs were laboring upon his manors while Philip and his servants were living in pitiful fashion or at best eating their way from abbey to abbey. Only a royal navy was lacking, and arrangements were later made whereby the seaports provided ships at need. Finally, the clergy, both regular and secular, were busy providing by prayers and Masses for the salvation of the Conqueror's soul in the world to come. *William's position as feudal suzerain*

Not for nothing had William been Duke of Normandy and a vassal of the King of France for thirty years before he conquered England. With feudalism he introduced many safeguards for royal authority. Some of these safeguards were themselves feudal in character. Compact fiefs of land were granted to the great barons only upon the frontiers. Mesne [5] tenants were sworn to premier allegiance to the king rather than to their immediate overlords. The majority of castles were royal, and all were theoretically the king's upon demand. No castle, again except in the marches of Wales and Scotland, might be erected without royal license. Private war, except in Wales, was successfully forbidden by William, although no French king before Louis IX went so far as to prohibit it in his domains. The coinage in England remained a royal prerogative. Other safeguards William borrowed from Anglo-Saxon custom. The Danegeld, the shire farm,[6] *Limitations imposed upon English feudalism*

[5] See p. 300.
[6] This consisted of a fixed annual payment promised by a sheriff in return for the profit of the royal manors and the smaller judicial fines from the local courts of the shire.

and judicial fines furnished a steadily increasing nonfeudal revenue. The Anglo-Saxon fyrd provided the Norman kings with a nonfeudal army which, since the people soon decided that one royal thief was far preferable to five thousand predatory knights, proved an invaluable deterrent to feudal rebellion. The judicial system of shire and hundred courts which gave the king direct access to all freemen was retained, although many hundred courts became feudalized. The sheriffs, very like the vicomtes that William had used in Normandy, were given absolute charge of the shire governments to the exclusion of earls and bishops; at the same time that their authority was increased it was controlled by the monarchs as never in the past.

Domesday
Book

In the last years of his life the Conqueror ordered the compilation of a great survey of his new English kingdom. He sent his clerks to all the shire courts, where groups of older men from every hundred and vill were ordered to meet them. These groups, called sworn inquests,[7] were put under oath and questioned. Thus William learned "the name of the manor, who held it in the time of King Edward, who holds it now; the number of hides; the number of plows on the demesne, the number of those of the men; the number of villeins; the number of cottars; the number of serfs; the number of freemen; the number of sokemen; the amount of forest; the amount of meadow; the number of pastures; the number of mills; the number of fishponds; how it has been increased or diminished; how much it was all worth then; and how much now; how much each freeman and sokeman held and holds there. All this three times over, namely in the time of King Edward, and when King William gave it, and as it now is, and if more can be had than now is." [8] The answers compiled by the clerks in two parchment volumes constitute the *Domesday Book,* now one of England's greatest treasures. Few men of that time could have conceived of such a project and fewer still could have executed it.

William
and the
Church

William, with the aid of his great lawyer Archbishop of Canterbury, the Italian Benedictine Lanfranc, was no less efficient in dealing with the Church. No papal commands were to be valid, no royal officials were to be excommunicated, without royal consent. No pope was recognized by the English Church without William's approval. Recog-

[7] The sworn inquest was one of the old institutions used with great advantage by the kings of England. The first known provision for its use is found in the Code of Theodosius (438). There is evidence of its use thereafter in Italy, then by the Carolingian monarchs, and finally by the counts of Anjou. William may have learned of it from either of the latter two sources

[8] Domesday inquest for Ely. Translation from Adams and Stephens, *Select Documents of English Constitutional History.*

nition of Gregory VII's demand for papal overlordship of England was firmly refused. William not only appointed bishops and abbots, but invested them with their spiritual as well as their temporal powers. The great churchmen were incorporated within the feudal system; they were required to attend the *curia regis*, and in many cases to render military service for their dioceses and abbeys. At the same time the nonpolitical reforms of the Cluniac program were encouraged. Foreign churchmen replaced easy-going Anglo-Saxon bishops and abbots; monastic discipline and clerical celibacy were demanded. Secular and ecclesiastical courts were separated; general synods were encouraged and a period of building magnificent cathedrals was begun. From the fact that, for refusing to chant in the French manner, Thurston, Abbot of Glastonbury, hunted his obstinate Anglo-Saxon monks through their own church with knights and archers till the steps of the altar were covered with blood, it appears that the English Church under William was being reformed as thoroughly as the English state.[9]

Little is known of the details of William's administration. His officials were of the same type as those of his Anglo-Saxon predecessors, but his chancellor and chamberlain-treasurer must have been of far greater importance. One new official, the justiciar, was created to act as viceroy whenever the king crossed the channel to Normandy; in the following century he was retained as permanent head of the financial and judicial departments. The *curia regis*, a feudal council composed of the king's tenants-in-chief and greater officials, replaced the Anglo-Saxon witan. It met regularly three times a year, but could be convoked upon any special occasion. It was at a great meeting of this kind at Salisbury in 1086 that the Conqueror imposed the oath of premier loyalty to himself upon his mesne tenants. The *curia* acted as an advisory body for the king and also tried cases involving tenants-in-chief, in which judgment was made not by the king but by the *curia* itself. At times the king's commands, embodied in writs,[10] ordered members of his *curia* to perform administrative or judicial work in a particular shire, as had the *missus* of the Carolingian state.

The curia regis

William of Malmesbury, one of the greatest of English chroniclers,

[9] See p. 387.
[10] A writ consisted of a royal command usually drafted in the chancery and sent to the parties concerned. Writs had been frequently used by the later Anglo-Saxon kings. They might be grants of lands or privileges, orders to officials, or commands sent to the sheriffs for public proclamation and observance. The last were in reality legislative and of the same type as the capitularies earlier issued by the Carolingian monarchs. A charter was a specialized form of writ.

says of William: "He was of just stature, extraordinary corpulence, fierce countenance: his forehead bare of hair; of such strength of arm that it was often a matter of surprise that no one was able to draw his bow which he himself could bend when his horse was on full gallop: he was majestic whether sitting or standing, although the protuberance of his belly deformed his royal person: of excellent health so that he was never confined with any dangerous disorder except at the last: so given to the pleasures of the chase, that, . . . ejecting the inhabitants, he let a space of many miles grow desolate, that when at liberty from other avocations he might there pursue his pleasures."

William's character

It may be added that he was choleric and mendacious and avaricious. His crushing taxation, in conjunction with the exactions of greedy Norman landlords, played a major part in submerging the great mass of Anglo-Saxon freemen into serfdom. He was one of the greatest military captains of his age, who from a duchy owing eight hundred knights conquered a kingdom able to return five thousand. In a world in which feudalism meant poverty-stricken and powerless central governments, vassals greater than their suzerains, the endless petty alliances and counter alliances strong enough only to burn a town or loot an absent neighbor, William created a feudal state that brought order and peace, law and commerce, and a strong central government capable of endless growth. To be sure, he was fortunate both in conquering a backward state where institutions of the past like the fyrd and effective nonfeudal local government survived, and in his opportunity to create a government unhampered by past commitments; but his own ability, typically Norman, to take from the old the useful and to amend the new for his own greater profit, created the English state.

Differences between English and continental feudalism

Early feudalism upon the continent was a slackening of the bonds of central government, a constantly increasing weakness of the state, and a corresponding increase of localism. That localism was creating the petty states in Germany and Italy which were to continue into the nineteenth century and which were not crushed in France or Spain until the end of the middle ages. William himself was a product of it. In England, however, the Danelaw and Wessex are forgotten names because the feudalism created by William at the end of the eleventh century was from its beginning strong monarchy and effective central government. It permitted the growth of modern political institutions in England generations in advance of elsewhere in Europe.

William's death

In 1087, while at war with his suzerain, King Philip I of France, William was injured fatally by his horse as he watched his army burn the city of Mantes. His sons raced to secure their legacies and his barons joyfully to riot and pillage while his unburied corpse decayed. There has since been no monarch of England who was not his descendant.

The Conqueror's second son, William II (1087–1100), called *William Rufus*, who inherited England, had his father's strength without his piety or restraint. His financial exactions far exceeded those of the previous reign: the yield of the Danegeld was trebled, the king's feudal rights were extortionately used, and crushing levies were laid upon the Church. Since knowledge of the Red King is almost entirely derived from monastic chroniclers, little good is known of him. In illness and fear of death he appointed the saintly Anselm Archbishop of Canterbury; when he recovered he quarreled with him, until Anselm went into a self-imposed exile. William Rufus acquired Normandy from his elder brother, Robert, in part by sharp dealing, in part by conquest, and in entirety by lending his careless brother enough money to go upon the first crusade. In 1100 he was preparing to acquire Poitou by mortgage when an arrow from an unknown hand ended his career. There was no investigation.

Henry I (1100–35), who succeeded to the English throne,[11] *Henry I* governed with the same firmness and purpose as his predecessors, but where Rufus had been rash and passionate his younger brother was prudent and stubborn. His reign the chroniclers describe as one in which a maiden with a purse of gold could travel unmolested throughout the kingdom, unmolested, that is, save by the king. Henry disarmed opposition to his coronation by a formal promise, since called the Coronation Charter of Henry I, to abandon the exactions of Rufus and return to the good practices of the Conqueror; but after election he disregarded the majority of these campaign promises.

In his reign the machinery of government developed rapidly. The demand of the Norman kings for efficient service, their close supervision of their territories, the new demands they made upon them, all led to increase in number and specialization in function among *Curia and* the staff surrounding the monarch, which as a group was called the *household* royal household. Many of its members were rewarded in part by gifts *under* of land, thus becoming vassals of the king, while others, rewarded by *Henry I* high ecclesiastical office, became bishops and abbots. Both methods of payment enrolled their recipients within the feudal order, and as

---

[11] After continual bickering with his elder brother, he conquered Normandy and captured Robert at the Battle of Tinchebrai in 1106. Robert was imprisoned for the remaining twenty-eight years of his life by his cautious brother.

tenants-in-chief made the more important of them members of the king's feudal *curia*. Neither method of payment was entirely satisfactory, any more than it was in Germany. Holders of land annexed to an office attempted to make the office hereditary with the land, thus removing it from the king's control. The appointment of officials to ecclesiastical office subjected them at least in part to a second master, the pope. The Norman and Angevin rulers met the first danger by depriving feudalized offices of power, and the second by the compromises that followed the investiture struggle—until they discovered a new method of payment with none of the above disadvantages and with great advantages of its own. They soon began to pay their officials by the fees received from the public. This cost the king nothing and made the officials greedy to increase the king's business, in order to increase their own salaries.

The great and small councils

The old *curia* of William the Conqueror, composed of all tenants-in-chief, still met quite regularly, although it probably grew smaller as tenants-in-chief with smaller fiefs ceased to attend unless they had personal business. At the same time, since the royal officials were more numerous and since their duties kept them constantly with the king, Henry I began using them as a group to perform exactly the same functions as the older *curia*, and gave them exactly the same powers. Thereafter there were two councils in England: the greater council of tenants-in-chief, which met when summoned, and the ever-present small council of officials, which, since its members were tenants-in-chief, was absorbed in the great council whenever the latter met.[12] From this small council, whether it be regarded as the more important members of the king's household or as the officials of the feudal *curia*, are descended the administrative and judicial departments of the governments of all English-speaking peoples today. The specialization that began under Henry I progressed during his reign only to the extent of creating an official class, a bureaucracy specializing in government as a whole; for the members of the chancery were still officials of the exchequer, and members of either continued to serve as judges whenever needed.

The chancery

The first great expansion naturally occurred in the secretarial staff. Since the Norman kings governed two lands, maintained far more intimate relations with foreign rulers than their predecessors, required the compilation of great series of accounts like the *Domesday Book*, and were continually increasing the use of writs and charters, they

[12] Cf. p. 510.

required more than the chancellor and the chapel clerks of Edward the Confessor. Their chancellors became heads of a great department called the chancery, which performed all the secretarial work of the government. The chancellors also kept the king's seal, soon to be known as the Great Seal of England, without which no document of state was valid. A clerkship in the chancery soon became one of the main roads to high preferment.

The financial department necessary to strong kings was appearing *Public* at the same time. Henry's revenues were first of all those provided *revenues* by ordinary feudal law: aids, reliefs, fines for marriage, wardships, escheats, and forfeitures. He also began the practice of accepting a money payment, called scutage, in place of the military service owed him by his vassals.[13] He had, moreover, the proceeds of certain taxes such as Danegeld and, probably, customs duties called lastage and scavage. In Henry's reign began the practice of exempting the royal towns from the Danegeld while imposing upon them far heavier fines, later called tallage. Henry possessed, in addition to the ordinary revenue from his own manors and towns (which was regularly farmed or rented in return for a lump sum to the sheriffs of the various shires), the right to exact fine or tallage from those manors and towns. The ordinary fines from the local courts of shire and hundred were also farmed to the sheriffs, except where the hundred court had become feudalized. The returns from pleas of the crown, however, and the *mudrum* fine inaugurated by the Conqueror for the killing of a Norman belonged to the king. Other royal revenues were derived from vacant dioceses and abbeys, the *regale* and *ius spolii*[14] of the continent, from the sums paid for charters, such as those authorizing the formation of town gilds, and from the sums, euphemistically called gifts (*dona*), taken from wealthy Jews, moneyers, and prelates. Finally, the king possessed a miscellany of minor financial rights, such as treasure-trove, wreck,[15] and purveyance. The Anglo-Saxon treasury consisting of a chest under the king's bed was no longer enough.

During the reign of Henry I a financial department with three *The develop-* subdepartments was elaborated. At the old capital, Winchester, the *ment of the exchequer* king's treasure was stored in the treasury. At London a department

[13] This at first was advantageous to both parties, but at a period of rising prices the Angevin rulers under whom it became quite customary had difficulty in securing the money equivalent of forty days' service. Both Normans and Angevins regularly employed mercenaries, usually Flemings and Welsh.

[14] See p. 413.

[15] See p. 574.

called the receipt, or lower exchequer, received and tested, by count or weight or assay,[16] incoming coin. Wooden sticks called tallies, notched to show values and then split through the notches so that each party would have a record, were cut in the receipt, one half being given the payer and the other half sent to the upper exchequer.[17] Soon after, if not during, Henry I's reign an official of the treasury and lower exchequer began to keep careful record of all money disbursed. Also at London sat the financial section of the *curia*, called both the account and the upper exchequer, composed of the justiciar, the treasurer or chamberlain, the chancellor, and other officials who were soon to be designated barons of the exchequer. Here twice each year the receivers of the king's revenues came to audit their accounts. On a long table covered with a cloth divided by lines into squares representing pounds, shillings, and pence (it was from this squared or chequered cloth that the name "exchequer" was taken) were laid counters representing payments due. On the basis of tallies and other evidence showing the amounts already paid in, similar counters were placed in squares opposite those that showed amounts due. In this way the most illiterate collector could see at a glance what was paid and what was due. All disputes were judged then and there by the great officials of the upper exchequer. Everything was carefully recorded by a chancellor's clerk and filed away in the pipe roll for the year.[18] It was not easy to cheat Henry I.

Five legal systems in use in England

Less concrete but quite as important were the developments in law during his reign. Like the continental states, England for centuries was subject to several competing jurisdictions. Anglo-Saxon law was still enforced in the shire and hundred courts, and, although the Normans had deprived it of its jurisdiction over the ownership of real property, it was still the law for the great majority of persons and things. The Normans had introduced their feudal law, which in the courts of

[16] Although shillings, marks, and pounds were used as money of account at this time the only English coin was the silver penny. The need to test its quality can be judged from Henry's ordering, after one investigation, ninety moneyers emasculated.

[17] The use of tallies was not discontinued until 1826. When in 1834 the old tallies were destroyed, at the closing of the receipt, the overheated chimney flues caused the parliament buildings to burn down.

[18] The only pipe roll that survives from the reign of Henry I is the one for 1130. The rolls from the second year of his grandson Henry II are continuous. English medieval public documents were frequently called rolls from the chancery practice of sewing the foot of one sheet of parchment to the head of the next in a continuous series, which was then rolled and stored. Some records, however, were sewn together at the top in files. The term "pipe" probably referred to the separate sheets of parchment.

overlords ruled in questions of fiefs, vassals, and feudal obligations. The various attempts made during the reign of Henry I to formulate the law of England were largely odd combinations of Anglo-Saxon and feudal law. A third legal system, the canon law of the Church courts, began under the last Norman kings to seize jurisdiction. In the great *Corpus Iuris Canonici* being created at the time [19] the Church possessed a code more rational and complete than either Anglo-Saxon or feudal law. Its claims to jurisdiction over all questions involving churchmen, heresy, last wills and testaments, morals, and breach of faith were so sweeping that they needed only to be conceded to make other laws superfluous. A fourth competitor appeared in the first half of the twelfth century as the merchants, shipmen, and townsmen slowly began to develop in their fairs and markets a law of their own, the law merchant,[20] which covered all types of business transactions from guarantee and negotiable instruments to insurance. Finally, following its earlier revival in Italy, the civil law of the Roman empire was being studied in England before the Norman period ended. In the *Corpus Iuris Civilis* [21] it possessed a code far more complete than even the canon law. This advantage, and the fact that it was the favorite law of kings because it exalted the position of the monarch, enabled it on the continent to supplant all its competitors.

Into this chaos of conflicting jurisdictions the English kings introduced a sixth competitor which borrowed from, improved upon, and eventually destroyed the others. None but able rulers could have conceived of a national law in the twelfth century at all, and Henry I and his Angevin successors, who did conceive of it, were interested primarily in its revenue-producing aspects. It was possible, moreover, only because each of the older systems had weaknesses that rendered it vulnerable to attack. Anglo-Saxon law was archaic and written in a language almost unknown to the French-speaking governing classes, and it was the law of a conquered people disdained by their conquerors. Feudal law was limited in scope and applicable only to the small feudal class of the population, and was wholly foreign to the Anglo-Saxons. Canon law in twelfth-century England had only begun to create the administrative and judicial machinery necessary to make a legal system effective, and it always depended upon the state for police purposes. Its international character and its complex legal con-

The weaknesses of the systems

[19] See p. 655.
[20] See p. 568.
[21] See pp. 740 ff. for a description of the Roman or civil law.

ceptions were disadvantages in dealing with a society primarily rural and feudal. The law merchant was hampered by lack of a central authority quite as much as by its limited jurisdiction and the slight numbers and importance of the class with which it dealt. The civil law was successful upon the continent because it entered into competition only later and with previous types of law, but in twelfth-century England, even when known, it was far too complex for popular use. Its conceptions had been refined by the development of seven centuries to suit a society of urban communities very different from the medieval world.

*The com-
mon law*

Henry I and Henry II, with the aid of the bureaucracy that they together created, were able to superimpose upon these legal systems, which chiefly dealt with persons as members of classes—Anglo-Saxons, vassals, Christians, merchants—a system that dealt with all persons dwelling in a definite area, regardless of class, equally and alike as subjects of the king. This new king's law, which borrowed whatever it needed from other systems and adapted it to English medieval conditions, became the common law in use today. Only its merest beginnings can be traced back to the reign of Henry I. The great royal lawmakers were Henry II and Edward I. Nevertheless Henry I, who was sometimes called the Lion of Justice, laid much of its foundation. The kings of England in the twelfth and thirteenth centuries had no more theories of kingship than the people (theories were for churchmen), but on one point all were agreed: it was the king's duty to preserve order and see that justice was done. In Henry I's reign a resident royal justice or justices appeared in the shires, whose functions were apparently quite as much to watch the conduct of the sheriff and record the pleas of the crown as to determine suits. The chaotic character of the king's law, its preoccupation with revenue, and its capacity for growth can all be seen in the list of pleas of the crown claimed by Henry's judges. "Breach of the king's peace given by his hand or writ; danegeld, contempt of his writ or precepts; death or injury done to his servants; treason and breach of fealty; every theft punishable with death; murder; counterfeiting his coin; arson; housebreaking; ambush; neglecting a summons to the fyrd; receiving outlaws; premeditated assault; robbing; street breach; taking the king's land or money; treasure trove; shipwreck; waif of the sea; rape; forests; reliefs of barons; fighting in the king's house or household; breach of peace in the army; neglecting to repair castles or bridges; neglecting a summons to the army; receiving an excommunicate or outlaw; breach of surety; unjust judgment; default of justice; perverting the king's law." [22] Writs directing sheriffs and members of the *curia* to try specific cases in local courts became more frequent, likewise the use of the sworn statement of neighbors, i.e., the sworn inquest, to discover facts. Finally, Henry I occasionally commissioned groups from his *curia* to make special trips to a county or to several counties, to try cases, investigate thoroughly the conduct of the local officials, discover if royal prerogatives had been infringed upon, and hear complaints.[23] These men would answer a complaint in one county just as they did a similar complaint in another county, and thus commenced to make one law for all England.

At the beginning of his reign Henry found himself involved by Anselm, Archbishop of Canterbury, in the investiture struggle, which was formally settled in 1107.[24] Thereafter as before Henry had no difficulty in rewarding faithful officials by lucrative Church preferments. Although a precedent for appeals to the pope had been made Henry otherwise maintained successfully his father's policy towards Rome. The only feudal revolt in England during Henry's reign was one purposely provoked by the king soon after his accession.[25] Henry deliberately baited his most powerful vassal to revolt, defeated him, and confiscated his estates. *Henry I and the Church*

In 1135, when sixty-seven years old, Henry ate too many lampreys and died. His prudence, avarice, stubbornness, and ability to select able servants [26] made him one of the great kings of England. The nineteen years following his death, however, were a cruel interlude, for Henry's plan for his daughter Matilda's succession was defeated by his nephew Stephen of Blois (1135-54).[27] He was a brave and chivalrous man at arms, nothing more. His adherents fought those of Matilda while *Stephen*

[22] *Leges Henrici Primi* Section 10. Translation from Maitland, *The Constitutional History of England*, pp. 107-8.

[23] Cf. Charles the Great's *missi* and St. Louis's *enquêteurs*.

[24] See p. 387.

[25] Cf. the numerous feudal revolts upon the continent.

[26] The nature and paucity of our sources make it difficult not to exaggerate the personal contributions of medieval monarchs. The chroniclers delineate clearly few other persons than the kings, and these they judge with a clerical bias. Yet it is probable that many or most royal contributions consisted of choosing and supporting able officials whose actual work remains hidden. The development of the exchequer in the reign of Henry I, for example, was largely the work of Roger of Salisbury, a Norman priest first employed by Henry because of the speed with which he could celebrate the Mass. Roger's relatives continued to dominate that department for nearly a century after his death. Just as Ranulf Flambard, Bishop of Durham, probably gave William Rufus the ideas for many of his financial exactions, so there were numberless medieval experts lost behind more public figures.

[27] Henry had nineteen children of whom some record has survived. Of the three who were legitimate his two sons had died childless. See p. 478.

the baronage in general fought for aggrandizement and for joy. Torture, murder, rape, and arson became commonplace.

"When the traitors perceived that he was a mild man, and a soft, and a good, and that he did not enforce justice, they all did wonder. They had done homage to him, and sworn oaths, but they no faith kept, all became forsworn, and broke their allegiance, for every rich man built his castles, and defended them against him, and they filled the land full of castles. They greatly oppressed the wretched people by making them work at these castles, and when the castles were finished they filled them with devils and evil men. They then took those whom they suspected to have any goods, by night and by day, seizing both men and women and they put them in prison for their gold and silver and tortured them with pains unspeakable for never were any martyrs tormented as these were. They hung some up by their feet, and smoked them with foul smoke; some by their thumbs or by their head, and they hung burning things on their feet. They put a knotted string about their heads and twisted it until it went into the brain. They put them into dungeons wherein were adders and snakes and toads, and thus wore them out . . . and I cannot and may not tell of all the wounds, and all the tortures that they inflicted upon the wretched men of this land, and this state of things lasted the nineteen years that Stephen was king. . . . Then was corn dear, and flesh, and cheese, and butter, for there was none in the land—the wretched men starved with hunger—some lived on alms who had been erewhile rich; some fled the country . . . and it was said openly that Christ and His saints slept." [28]

England was an unhappy land, but in those years England learned both what a strong king was worth and what continental feudalism was like.

Henry II

The anarchy of private war was brought to an end by the son of Matilda, Henry II, who by a treaty with Stephen became, upon the latter's death in 1154, the first Angevin King of England. Henry Plantagenet (1154–89) at twenty-one years was the ruler of a vast continental empire that included Normandy by inheritance and conquest, Anjou and Maine from his father, Geoffrey of Anjou, and Poitou and Aquitaine by marriage. He immediately became one of the greatest of English kings. Folk tales of Anjou told that among his ancestors was a demoness; that, if true, would explain the devil of sorts that

[28] *Anglo-Saxon Chronicle* for 1137, ed. Plummer.

certainly possessed him. He was short, stocky, red-headed, and freckled, a bundle of devouring energy, quite without religion and morals, and subject to wild fits of rage, in which he would weep, curse, and roll upon the ground. Yet he had a passion for order and efficiency, and was a patron of scholarship and literature. "Faithless father of a faithless brood," he quarreled constantly with his sons and battled with Eleanor of Aquitaine, his wife, who was, however, a match for him until he imprisoned her.[29] He fought his feudal nobility, the Church, and the kings of France. He ruled from Ireland to the Pyrenees, and his claims extended from the Orkneys to the Mediterranean. Biting his nails to the quick at religious services or riding so recklessly through his lands that the King of France declared that he must have wings, or, defeated and dying, turning his head to the wall and moaning, "Shame! Shame on a beaten king!" Henry II lives vividly for us in pages of the chroniclers as do few men of his time.

The magnitude of the new ruler's first task can be estimated from the eleven hundred and fifteen—according to the chronicler—unlicensed castles in his kingdom.[30] While engaged in either demolishing these or bringing them under royal control, Henry II rapidly reestablished the government of his grandfather, Henry I. More than that, he broadened its scope and increased its efficiency until England soon became a treasure house for the Angevin empire, which it was to remain for half a century. Exemptions from the Danegeld during Stephen's reign and his reckless granting of royal manors to pay barons for their support had so depleted the public revenue that careful accounting and a great increase in incidental or casual payments was necessary.

The exchequer quickly became still more specialized, as the withdrawal of such curial officials as the chancellor left it more and more in the hands of its own professional staff. Towards the end of Henry's reign his treasurer, Richard Fitz Nigel, Bishop of London and nephew of Roger of Salisbury, wrote the *Dialogus de Scaccario* (*Dialogue on the Exchequer*) as a manual of procedure, and so bequeathed to the future a unique account of medieval public finance. Henry II collected scutage regularly, and collected with it a fine from those whom he permitted to pay it. Aids and tallages from shires and towns supplemented older sources of revenue, but the income from writs and fines of judicial process was especially increased. For crusading purposes, Henry levied the first English tax on personal property, the sixpence in the

The exchequer and public revenues

[29] See pp. 479–80.
[30] After the ninth century there was no such thing as licensing castles on the continent.

pound of 1166, and in 1188 the Saladin tithe of ten per cent on both property and income.[31] At the end of his reign he had a balance in the treasury equal to at least three years' regular income.

It is impossible to overestimate the importance of the judicial reforms introduced by Henry II. One cannot conceive of the law of today in the British empire or in the United States without the basic elements woven into it by Henry II. He gathered around him a staff learned in both canon and civil law, such men as his justiciars Richard Luci and Ranulf de Glanville, and with their aid built the common law upon the foundations laid by Henry I. Although the conception of law as something that could be made rather than discovered was still to come, the instructions sent to officials, by which changes were put into effect, were in reality legislation. Henry thus legislated with the advice of his small *curia*, but he did not alter greatly the rights and duties of his subjects: rather he furnished them with new procedures for the enforcement of old rights and duties. Since the great majority of his reforms were inaugurated by instructions, probably in many cases oral, the changes he introduced and the extent to which his reforms encroached upon the jurisdiction of competing systems of law could only be guessed were it not that one of his officials, perhaps Glanville, described the king's law as it was in effect at the close of his master's reign. The *Treatise on the Laws and Customs of the English Kingdom*, a manual for the use of judges, was one of the first attempts made in the new states of medieval Europe to explain just what the law was and how to put it into effect.

The importance of Henry II's judicial reforms

Writs were nothing new; Henry II merely extended their use and made them available to the general public. By sending writs to their officials former kings had supervised the administration of justice, and even, for a stiff price, used their machinery to determine private suits. Henry provided his chancery with approximately fifty different writs ordering judicial action, which could be purchased for a moderate fee by any person; that is, the chancery now dealt not only in writs made to order, but in ready-made writs as well. Many of the new writs commanded a royal official to try a lawsuit, the writ specifying the nature of the suit. One form of writ was used to collect a debt; others to secure an inheritance of real estate or a dower. A man unjustly held as a serf could get a writ to recover his freedom; a landlord one to capture his escaped serf. Since procedure in each type of case varied, each of such writs was the first step in a particular legal process called a "form of action." The common law expanded with the increase in the number of

Writs and forms of action

[31] See p. 555.

forms of action, as the king or chancellor offered new writs for public use. Not all writs, however, were designed to begin lawsuits: others proved to be necessary in the course of a trial or to provide for execution of judgment when rendered. There were writs ordering the sheriff to seize persons or property, or directing him to give possession of property to a successful litigant. Of still another type was the writ of prohibition which forbade an ecclesiastical court to try a particular case. In most of the new writs the novel, and the only really revolutionary, feature was that the ordinary private individual could make use of the king's writ.

Five of the new writs, however, provided for a new and revolutionary method of deciding cases. A representative one, the writ of novel disseisin, could be purchased from the chancery by any man recently and forcibly dispossessed of his freehold estate. The writ directed the sheriff of the shire in which the land was situated to repossess the plaintiff, take bond for appearance from both parties, and bring writ and parties, together with twelve men who knew the facts of the case, before the king's justices. The twelve were there asked under oath if the plaintiff's statement were true, and in accordance with their answer the king's justices gave judgment and imposed fines. A new method of trial had been created, yet it was no more than an adaptation of the sworn inquest used by the Conqueror and his successors. But Henry II made use of this machinery more frequently than his predecessors and for many purposes: for example, to make assessments when they were necessary for the Saladin tithe and to determine individual responsibility under the Assize of Arms.[32] By encouraging the public to use it to settle their disputes he enlarged the scope of the king's law, which alone could use the new process, and laid the foundation for trial by jury.[33] *The origin of the trial jury*

All these reforms rapidly extended the jurisdiction of the king's law. Henry's order that no one be disturbed in the possession of his freehold estate without the king's writ prevented the strong man from lawlessly seizing property. At the same time it gave the king's law wide jurisdiction over real property, which at times brought it into conflict with the feudal courts. The writ of right to determine ownership of land was particularly used in such a way as to deprive lords of the right to try the cases of their vassals. Under this new jurisdiction the judge gradu-

[32] See p. 455.
[33] In Henry II's reign the men who knew the facts were called, from the law providing for their service, an assize. Assize, however, had several meanings according to its context, including a law, the group of men placed under oath to state the truth, and a court. The word "jury" came into use early in the next century in other forms of action.

ally formulated several rules governing landownership, which widened the difference between English and continental custom. One, forbidding the bequeathing of land by will, was probably directed at the deathbed repentances that gave land to the Church. Another, providing that land held by military tenure must be inherited by primogeniture, while unsuccessful as an attempt to prevent the splitting of fiefs, was important later in the formulation of the English rule that only the eldest son of a noble becomes a noble. Others provided for a rather broad right to alienate land, and provided an opportunity, hitherto unknown in the middle ages, to register land titles by an official record.

At the same time the royal judges increased the scope of the king's criminal law by broadening the definition of the king's peace. This in Anglo-Saxon times had originally meant the king's right to a heavy fine for violence done in his presence or to individuals given his special protection, and had been extended to cover similar cases in his palaces and on a few of the great highways of the kingdom. The Norman kings demanded forfeiture of property for breaches of the king's peace and extended it to include the entire kingdom. The king's peace, however, still lapsed upon the death of a king, which allowed a period of anarchy until the coronation of his successor.[34]

The old method for the detection of crime, which depended upon the injured party or his relatives to make complaint, was ineffective when there was great disparity in rank between the offender and his victim, or when the parties chose to settle out of court. Its ineffectiveness can be measured from the English practice, both at this time and later, of suspending a convicted criminal's sentence if he could successfully appeal against—that is, prosecute as a private individual—a certain number of persons whom he knew to be criminals.[35]

In two laws, the Assize of Clarendon in 1166 and the Assize of Northampton ten years later, Henry II ordered the sheriffs to bring before his judges on their rounds of the shires groups of men who were familiar with all the affairs of all the vills and hundreds of the shire. Under oath these men were required to report every case of homicide, arson, robbery, theft, harboring of thieves, or forgery[36] that had occurred in their neighborhoods since the last visit of the king's justices,

---

[34] This practice continued until the death of Henry III in 1272. Since his heir, Edward, was in Palestine on a crusade, the council decided that the period of anarchy would be too long and immediately proclaimed the peace of Edward I.

[35] Trial was by battle, with hanging the penalty for losing.

[36] These, together with wounding, rape, and treason, were the greater pleas of the crown accounted for separately by the sheriffs. They were in the process of development into felonies, while mere breach of the king's peace was becoming a misdemeanor or tort.

and also to name the persons whom they considered responsible in each case. To be sure, Henry II was not looking beyond the better maintenance of public order, save in the direction of greater revenue—a goal of which he never for a moment lost sight—which would naturally follow a higher proportion of crimes detected and prosecuted. But what he actually did by this reform was to produce from the old sworn inquest, from which he derived the beginnings of the trial jury, the grand jury as well.

For all these new procedures new courts were required. Of these the most striking, the court of general eyre, originated in Henry I's occasional practice of sending members of his *curia* out on an eyre (journey) to try cases in a shire. This Henry II did regularly, and began to extend their commissions to cover everything of interest to the king. Every local official had to report to the judges of the general eyre, while sworn inquests from every subdivision of the county made similar reports as a check on the officials. Every lawsuit involving the shire pending in any court was transferred to the eyre. Every franchise was submitted for verification; even the quality of every keg of ale in the county was tested. In later times a single session of the general eyre might last a whole year. Since it was in fact quite as much a royal device for collecting money as a law court, everything was a pretext for fines. In the next century the people of Cornwall, hearing that the justices of the eyre were coming, took refuge in the hills and forests until they had departed. Indeed, popular resentment was responsible for the later custom of the general eyre's not visiting any shire oftener than once in seven years. *The court of general eyre*

Less interesting but of greater permanent importance was the court of the assizes, which was invented by Henry II. This court, composed of royal judges who visited each shire several times yearly to try cases of novel disseisin and similar forms of action, was the first circuit court of the English-speaking peoples. The requirement in the assizes of Clarendon and Northampton that the sheriffs draft grand juries from each hundred and vill soon combined with their older function of visiting each hundred and vill semiannually to see that every adult male took an oath of allegiance to the king and swore to keep the peace. This combination of duties led to the rapid development of a local king's court called the sheriff's tourn, held twice a year in every hundred to settle minor cases. The king's justice was costly, but it was the best to be had in England; [37] the result was that the new procedures brought *Other new courts*

[37] It possessed such a reputation for impartiality that in 1177 the kings of Castile and Navarre sent a dispute between them to be judged by Henry and his *curia*.

such a press of judicial work upon the *curia* that Henry II in 1178 delegated five men to do nothing except try lawsuits. They were to develop into the court of common pleas, the first of the three great central courts of the common law that dominated English judicature until 1875.

*Henry II
and Thomas
à Becket*

Relations between Church and state during the reign turned largely upon Henry's struggle with Archbishop Thomas à Becket. In view of the unprecedented liberties secured by the Church during Stephen's reign, Henry's efforts to re-establish the sound government of his grandfather urgently required a restatement of the respective powers of the two jurisdictions. After waiting eight years for the opportunity to appoint his own Archbishop of Canterbury, he discovered that his appointee, Thomas à Becket, whom he had raised from obscurity to the position of boon companion and chancellor, was determined not only to retain every shred of power possessed by the Church but wherever possible to increase it. After minor quarrels Henry had an authoritative statement of earlier customs drafted, the Constitutions of Clarendon of 1164, and secured their acceptance by the higher clergy, including the archbishop, who, however, immediately afterwards repudiated them. The six-year controversy that followed between archbishop and king culminated in the murder of Becket before his own altar at Canterbury. He was killed by four of Henry's knights stung by their master's question, in one of his mad rages, if those who ate his bread were going to continue to allow him to be bearded by this upstart priest.

*The conse-
quences of
Becket's
murder*

Henry cleared himself on oath to the pope of complicity in the murder and went on an expedition to Ireland until the first wild excitement died, but it cost him far more than the humiliating personal penance that he was compelled to undergo. He had not only to consent to the sole right of the Church to punish its clergy—benefit of clergy, as it soon came to be called—but he had to recognize the right of appeal to papal courts. During the fifteen years following 1170 the decretals of popes Alexander III and Lucius III introduced canon law into England to an extent never before tolerated, and for generations the common law suffered from the results of that one fatal outburst of Henry II's temper. Yet his defeat was by no means complete. The fourteen remaining clauses of the Constitutions of Clarendon remained as he wished them. Although courts of the canon law developed rapidly, the invention of the writ of prohibition and the rule forbidding the devise of land limited their jurisdiction. Henry and his council were successful in preventing direct taxation of the English Church by the papacy, and the king continued to enjoy the *dona* and the *ius regale* [38] and to reward officials of the state by appointing them to Church offices.

Miracles began immediately at Becket's tomb, and he was canonized only two years after his death to become "the holy blisful martir" of Chaucer's *Canterbury Tales*. Neither of the great antagonists was victorious, for the king had greater control over the Church at the death of Henry II than at the death of Stephen, yet less than at the death of Henry I. The controversy was to continue.

Henry II's passionate and efficient versatility can be seen from a mere list of a few of his countless activities. He led military expeditions everywhere between Ireland and Toulouse, beginning the English conquest of Ireland and making the King of Scotland his vassal. He found time to reform thoroughly the Anglo-Saxon fyrd by his Assize of Arms, which required all freemen to possess arms according to their wealth.[39] From the *cartæ* of 1166 he discovered whether any of his tenants-in-chief had enfeoffed more knights than necessary to render the service owed the king and thenceforth demanded scutage from them all. He also made a general investigation of relations between tenants-in-chief and their vassals and one of knight service in Normandy. After an investigation by sworn inquests of the sheriffs of England he dismissed nearly all of them. He revised and made more effective the administration of the royal forests, and ordered the building of county jails. He erected dikes for flood control in Anjou. He regulated both the quality and the price of English bread and beer. Henry II was like few medieval kings in preferring power to either pleasure or display. He worked furiously and died at the age of fifty-six. More will be said of him in the next chapter in connection with his contest with Philip Augustus. But it was his work in England that made him a great king, although he himself doubtless considered his continental empire far more important.

Henry II's versatility

He was succeeded in 1189 by his eldest surviving son, Richard the Lionhearted, who spent less than six months of his ten-year reign in England. To provide money for his part in the third crusade, his ransom from captivity, and his wars with Philip Augustus he sold everything salable in England, sometimes more than once. A more efficient form of land tax, the carucage, assessed upon the plowland of one hundred acres, replaced the Danegeld. To raise money to pay his enormous ransom a tax on personal property and income was again

The financial exactions of Richard I

---

[38] The *ius spolii*, discontinued by Stephen, was not revived.

[39] The exporting and pledging of such weapons were forbidden. The assize was applied to Henry's continental possessions and copied by Philip Augustus; see p. 496.

levied; and, in addition to customary forms of taxation, property in wool and gold and silver plate was confiscated. The great period in England for the granting of municipal charters began when Richard sold them to finance his wars. After a nation-wide pogrom had not only massacred a great number of Jews but destroyed the evidence of debts due them, a separate department of the exchequer was established to protect the debts, since English law made the king sole heir of all Jews.

Despite rapacious taxation, the sale of offices, and the king's long and habitual absence, the bureaucracy created by Henry II continued to do the work of government efficiently. For the first time since the departure of the Roman legions a governmental machine capable of functioning without the constant presence of a king existed in England. Two new officials were developed: the coroner, then a royal local justice who apparently tried pleas of the crown and served as a check upon the sheriff, and the conservator of the peace, who eventually became the justice of the peace.[40] The rolls of the *curia* and the records of land titles were begun; the sheriff's power to pack juries, that is, assizes, was limited; and wines, weights, and measures were regulated. But all this was the work of the *curia*. Richard I was a formidable warrior and a good troubadour.

The efficiency of the new government

He was succeeded by his younger brother John (1199–1216), called both Lackland and Softsword, who, for his time, was neither outrageously tyrannical, cruel, mendacious nor avaricious; he merely possessed all the more unpleasant aspects of contemporary practice in those respects while lacking in more commendable qualities. It was his fortune, when he had already acquired a rather shoddy reputation, to inherit the Angevin empire at a moment when its resources had been strained for a generation and to find himself confronting two of the ablest figures of the medieval world, Philip Augustus at Paris and Innocent III at Rome—formidable antagonists for even the strongest king. Philip Augustus had intrigued and fought with indifferent success against both Henry II and Richard the Lionhearted; but John's most desperate efforts were unable to prevent his conquest of Normandy, Brittany, Maine, Anjou, Touraine, and part of Poitou.[41] Henry II had been able to regain many of the prerogatives lost to the Church by Stephen, and even to wrest some profit from his fatal controversy with Thomas à Becket, but John was utterly humbled by Innocent III.[42]

John

---

[40] See p. 952.
[41] See p. 485.
[42] See pp. 647–48.

It was an already twice-defeated king that faced an indignant people at Runnymede in 1215 for his third and greatest defeat.

From his accession John's difficulties had required financial exactions as great as those of his brother. At the same time the restrictions imposed upon the baronage by the judicial and administrative reforms of Henry II were beginning to be more keenly felt, and the hitherto unchecked encroachments of royal authority plainly presaged for all classes still greater exactions and restrictions. English barons, churchmen, and townsmen were able to combine and force John on June 15, 1215, to affix his seal to the charter that has been called the cornerstone of English liberties. Magna Carta consisted of sixty-three chapters granting rights to each of the classes that combined to secure it and imposing limitations upon the king. The Church won the promise of freedom of election, together with a general statement that it should be free and possess its liberties inviolate. Feudal exactions connected *Magna Carta* with matters like reliefs and aids were to be discontinued. Two chapters provided that scutage should not be levied without the counsel of the great *curia*. These were a forerunner of the later doctrine that no taxation could be imposed by the mere order of the king. A few chapters were for the special benefit of townsmen. The new judicial machinery was treated in two ways: there were some attempts to protect the old feudalism, such as the chapter forbidding the use of the writ of right in such a way as to cost a lord his court over his vassal, but the majority of the clauses dealing with the common law were attempts to make that law even more effective and just. Excessive costs and excessive fines, for example, were to be discontinued; only men learned in the law were to be made judges; Henry II's new court of common pleas was to be held in one fixed place. Magna Carta did not contain, despite the later common belief, any promise of habeas corpus, or of trial by jury, nor any assurance of no taxation without the consent of Parliament. But it did contain such chapters as the following, perhaps the most familiar things in it:

"No free man shall be taken or imprisoned or dispossessed, or outlawed or banished, or in any way destroyed, nor will we go upon him, nor send upon him, except by the legal judgment of his peers or by the law of the land.

"To no one will we sell, to no one will we deny, or delay right or justice." [43]

[43] Magna Carta, Chapters 39 and 40. Translation from Adams and Stephens, *op. cit.*

Moreover, its true greatness is not to be found in any chapter or combination of chapters. Magna Carta is justly considered the cornerstone of the English constitution because it established the principle that the king is subject to, not above, the law. It marked the beginning of the end for absolutism tempered only by rebellion, and the beginning of the successful effort of the English people, almost alone of all European peoples, to work out a satisfactory form of limited monarchy. John's great rival and conqueror, Philip Augustus, has no successor in France today. The Holy Roman emperors are long since gone. But thanks in no small part to the work begun so early in Magna Carta, the pitiable John's successors still reign in London.

Until near the close of John's reign the bureaucracy continued to function well. The method of paying officials from the fees they received provided more than the stimulus necessary to continue the growth of the functions of the royal government. The great seal had come to such an extent to represent the government, as distinguished *Development* from the king, that John had his own, the privy seal, to validate his *of the gov-* own commands and to authorize the use of the great seal.[44] The ex-*ernment in* chequer became so completely a department of state that the king's *John's reign* wardrobe and chamber were separately organized as petty departments for the king's private needs and, in addition, to serve as a sort of war department. It was John's officials who commenced to multiply the great series of public records that make England unique among medieval states. No fewer than eight new series of rolls from exchequer and chancery were begun.[45] Among the developments in legal process during his reign was one that, by making it possible for the defendant in a criminal suit brought by a private individual to have his defense judged by a sworn inquest, introduced trial by jury in criminal cases.

The grant of Magna Carta by no means ended the quarrel between John and his subjects. With no expectation that John would keep his

[44] The normal evolution for any department in medieval government, as in the case of the great seal, was for the king first to delegate some personal servant to perform a specialized duty, and for this servant then to acquire helpers, his subordinates, and at the same time to increase his functions. At this stage the former servant would have become a domestic or household official. The next step was taken as the new functions removed the former servant from personal contact with the king and thus from the latter's immediate control. As this happened the household official became a public official and the head of a department of state, and the king had to appoint a new servant to care for his personal wants. The new servant of course would try to repeat the same process.

[45] The records happen to be complete enough to let us infer that John had three baths, granted that he took the free one he had a right to, between April 16 and August 3, 1212.

promises the barons attempted, in Chapter 61 of the charter, to provide means of enforcement. This first attempt to create machinery to limit *Civil war* the monarchy authorized them to choose twenty-five of their number, *and the* who should have authority, if necessary to secure redress for the viola- *death of* tion of any of its provisions, to organize armed rebellion against the *John* king. Since neither this "committee for rebellion," composed of his bitterest enemies, nor John himself acted honestly, civil war broke out almost immediately. Innocent III attempted to aid John, and a party of the barons invited Prince Louis, son of Philip Augustus and husband of John's niece Blanche of Castile, to assume the English crown.[46] Louis landed in England, occupied London, and met at first with some success. John fought back with vigor, but his greatest service to his supporters was to fill himself too full of fresh peaches and new cider and die of the colic.

His son, Henry III (1216–72), was only nine years old at his accession, but his regents defeated Louis, suppressed the baronial revolt, and re-established the normal functioning of the departments of state. The new king's character can well be judged from Dante's description *Henry III* of him in purgatory as "of simple life and plain." He was a good man, excessively pious and exceedingly devoted to his family. But he was also excessively vain of his own ability—which was, in matters of state, slight. Throughout his reign the struggle of the barons to limit royal authority continued. At first it centered around the enforcement of Magna Carta, which was confirmed seven times during the reign. The clauses dealing with the royal forests were issued as a separate Charter of the Forests after 1217; and the Great Charter itself did not acquire its permanent form, that contained in the statute books, until the reissue of 1225. It is noteworthy that all the reissues allowed greater royal authority than the original accepted by John.

As it gradually became apparent that observance of the charters was not enough to procure efficient government from Henry III, the barons began the attempt to control the royal officials, which was to continue throughout the rest of the middle ages.[47] In 1244 they demanded that the more important officials be appointed by the great council and that four of themselves be made permanent members of the small council. *Continued* In 1258 they were powerful enough to establish by the Provisions of *attempts* Oxford a committee of fifteen barons with power to supervise the king's *to limit the monarchy*

[46] For Philip Augustus's hopes in this direction, see p. 488.

[47] One result of the attempt in Henry III's reign was a reform of the chancellorship, which placed that office upon a salary rather than a fee basis. Another reform abolished the justiciarship, previously the premier office under the king. For a comparable struggle in France see pp. 476–77, 493–94.

government. Six years of domestic strife followed, culminating in outright civil war. The leader of the barons was Simon de Montfort, the younger son of the French Simon de Montfort who had achieved dishonorable distinction as the head of the Albigensian crusade.[48] With increasing popular support Simon finally succeeded in procuring the adoption of a further plan of reform. Three men chosen by the king and the great council were to select the nine members of the small council with whose approval the king was to appoint the great officers of state and without whose approval he was to do nothing. But this plan died with the defeat and death in battle of Simon de Montfort in 1265, leaving the great baronial leader to be remembered rather for his part in the development of a parliament than for his plan to establish a limited monarchy. So continued the series of fruitless attempts by the barons, beginning with Chapter 61 of the Great Charter, to find some way of making sure that royal promises would be kept.

.The barons were anything but disinterested: they were jealous of all their feudal and other rights; they were jealous of foreigners come to seek their fortunes from the king's favor; they wished to hold the more lucrative positions themselves. They were, moreover, now beginning to aim not at limiting the powers of the central government so much as at controlling that government themselves. Precedents for the method that finally proved successful, the method of parliaments, were being laid down during Henry III's reign, but they belong more properly to the history of later years.

Developments in the common law
    The growth of the common law continued. Within a few years the cleavage, already apparent in John's reign, between the rest of the *curia* and those members of it who specialized in law led to the creation of the second of the central courts, the court of king's bench. The new court was superior in jurisdiction to the court of common pleas and dealt primarily with pleas of the crown, leaving suits between private individuals to the older court. A new local court to try less serious criminal cases was also created, called the court of gaol delivery; its commission authorized a number of judges to empty a county jail by freeing, bailing, or hanging the inmates. The obedience of the English clergy to the decree of the Fourth Lateran Council forbidding clerical participation in trials by ordeal necessitated a new method of trial. After some hesitation trial by jury, modeled upon the assizes of Henry II, was adopted and became customary, although pressure was necessary and relics of older procedures did not disappear until the nineteenth century. The action of trespass, which covered damage to persons

[48] See p. 500.

and chattels as well as to land, was developed as a breach of the king's peace and soon became the most popular of all forms of action. The chancery and the judges invented new writs so rapidly that the barons in the Provisions of Oxford forbade the chancellor to add further to their number. By the end of Henry III's reign the thirty or forty main types of forms of action, with their several hundred varieties, had for all practical purposes destroyed both Anglo-Saxon and feudal law. This was the last period in which the common law grew by the unrestrained invention of new writs; henceforth it invaded new fields by the extension of old writs and by statutes.

The thirteenth century also closed the period of great judges who were learned in both canon law and the civil, or Roman, law as well as in their own common law. A new type of judge and lawyer, trained solely in the king's courts, gradually replaced their less specialized but more widely learned predecessors. Bracton, author of *De Legibus et Consuetudinibus Angliæ* (*On the Laws and Customs of England*), one of the masterpieces of English legal literature, was almost the last of the older generation of jurists. In his work he both inaugurated the common-law custom of citing precedents and incorporated most of the few borrowings from the civil law still necessary to make the king's common law a coherent and organized whole.

In public finance likewise there were significant developments under Henry III. In general the financial clauses of Magna Carta were observed and the great council's consent regularly obtained for any levy of scutage, aids, and other taxes. The tax on personal property was levied more successfully and more frequently and for less extraordinary purposes, but a poll tax graduated according to rank was a failure. The machinery of assessment, collection, and accounting was made more efficient. People of the locality were sworn in as assessors, and the practice was adopted of exempting from taxation the poorest classes and the tools of a man's trade. Henry's financial troubles were augmented by a general rise in prices, but they were due primarily to his own carelessness and extravagance, mostly for the benefit of his favorites. Indeed, his continual requests for money were one of the primary causes of the barons' zeal to limit royal authority.

Developments in public finance

When Henry III died in 1272 the peoples of the continent, in their search for a form of government strong enough to suppress the anarchy of feudalism, were groping towards a solution in absolute monarchy. England, except for the reign of Stephen unacquainted with the worst evils of the feudal system, had possessed for more than a century a monarchy for practical purposes absolute, and from 1215 on, had entered the next stage of political evolution, the search for a satisfactory form of limited monarchy.

The results of two centuries of strong monarchy

In the two centuries following the Norman conquest the English absolute monarchy had established a system of national taxation that included taxation of real and personal property and that had attempted before 1272 to levy both poll and income taxes. It had experimented with feudal, professional, and national military service. From the undifferentiated *curia* of the Conqueror it had constructed a skilled and professional civil service, divided into its great secretarial, financial, legal, and other lesser departments. It had created in the common law the only national system of jurisprudence that has been built in western or central Europe since the days of Rome. In addition it had commenced, unknowingly, a still greater work. The commissions issued to the circuit courts—assizes, gaol delivery, and general eyre—regularly included knights of the county among the judges. Sworn inquests and juries forced the middle-class landowners to keep familiar with the work of government. The coroners, conservators of the peace, sheriffs' assistants, and escheators [49] were regularly members of the same class. When Henry III died the English were being taught self-government.

In the two centuries between 1066 and 1272 three great kings, William the Conqueror, Henry I, and Henry II, produced the elaborate administrative and judicial machinery necessary to a modern state. The Conqueror established in England the best government he could conceive, feudalism confined by elaborate checks. Within that government as within a builder's scaffolding Henry I and his grandson created a far more complex and efficient mechanism that almost of itself commenced to destroy the feudalism within which it had been erected. The effectiveness of this new machinery in the hands of a vicious or a weak monarch was dangerous enough to force the articulate classes of medieval England—the baronage, the clergy, and the townsmen—to attempt to control it. Moreover, the oppressive Norman and Angevin kings, strong and weak alike, welded Anglo-Saxons and Vikings and Normans into the English race and compelled that race to begin the task of governing itself, and not the less successfully because such was never the royal intention.

Recapitulation

[49] Local officials entrusted with guarding the king's feudal right of escheat.

Chapter 16

FRANCE UNDER THE CAPETIAN KINGS
(987–1204)

THE great theme of European political history in the middle
ages, once government had become feudalistic, was the
attempt of the monarchs to reassert their lost authority and
to reduce the evil of continuous war. No progress was possible while
the peasantry and the Church, in fact all society, were at the mercy of
the unrestrained license of rapacious bullies. The kings, therefore, and *The conflict*
the Church and the greater feudal nobles in so far as they co-operated *between*
with the kings, were forerunners of a better day, as well as guardians *monarchy*
and feudalism
of their own interests, when they undertook to master the turbulent *the same in*
elements in their domains. They were thus making it possible for the *France as in*
peaceful pursuits of the peasant and priest, the merchant and artisan, *Germany and*
the poet, the scholar, and the artist to bless life with the products of *England*
their industry and genius. The German emperors failed in this large
undertaking. The English kings succeeded far better.

If now we recapitulate the last three chapters, it is because the best
introduction to the history of the conflict between monarchy and feudalism in France is to compare it with the same conflict in Germany and
England, and to note to what extent these histories are really interwoven. In choosing for the present to keep to this theme we are post-
poning for later consideration [1] the chief glory of France in the middle
ages, its religious, literary, and artistic culture. And yet it is no accident of chronology that at a time when the University of Paris was
the intellectual center of Europe, when the French Gothic cathedral
was the model for most European churches, when French literature
and the French language were pre-eminent among European vernacular languages and literatures, the French monarchy reached its
medieval height in the person of Louis IX. Louis was as typical a

---

[1] See Chapters 23 and 24.

product of French medieval culture as Notre Dame de Paris or the *Romance of the Rose.*

It was noted above that feudalism could equally well follow either of two diametrically opposed lines of development.[2] Originating as it did to satisfy the barest necessities of government, although it usurped in fact the powers that monarchy had become impotent to exercise, it still did not in theory deprive the king of his traditional rights. Theoretically the king was the head of the feudal system, the suzerain of all *The outcome* vassals. The development of feudalism then resolved itself into a *of the conflict* struggle for power between the king-suzerain and his vassals. The *in these* logical outcome of such a struggle could only be either a victory for the *countries* vassals, which meant a victory for decentralization and localism, or, if the monarchy should ever regain strength enough to translate its theoretical rights back into actual power, a victory for the king-suzerain, which meant a victory for centralization and nationalism. Germany is the best example of the first outcome; France is the best example of the second.

Germany at the death of Frederick II in 1250 was in its form of government at about the point where France began in the tenth century. France in 1328, with all due allowance for vast differences, was already on the way to becoming what Germany did not become until five hundred years later. Until 1272 England and France followed parallel paths, the chief difference being that England was approximately a hundred years ahead of France in developing the institutions of a strong monarchy. After 1272, or perhaps more accurately after 1204,[3] England and France went different ways in government: France proceeded in the direction of absolute monarchy, where the king ruled by divine right; England in the direction of limited monarchy, where the king reigned indeed, but ruled only in conjunction with Parliament. Up to 1270 the victory of the French monarchy over feudalism was not so much victory for the traditional powers of the king as victory for the king as suzerain of all French vassals. The reader must remember, however, that the historian is always prone to distort when he tries to simplify, and tempted to exaggerate when he would be emphatic. The fact is, of course, that French feudalism was not wholly destroyed until the French Revolution—if it had been, there might have been no revolution—and that French localism in culture and sentiment is still by no means dead.

Why did Germany go in one direction and France in the opposite

[2] See p. 311.
[3] See p. 486.

direction? Why was England in political development a century ahead of France? To give a complete answer to these questions is impossible, and even to suggest one is difficult enough. The source of political power in the medieval state was wealth, intelligence, and character. There had to be wealth to create and maintain an army and an administration; there had to be intelligence to direct and control them; there had to be character to balance the particular interests of the ruler with the general interests of society, if government was to be either good or popular.

That the constitutional development of England from 1066 to 1204 was a century in advance of France was owing largely to two facts. In the first place, England after 1066 was a conquered state, and after 1154 was part of an empire reaching from Scotland to the Pyrenees, with Normandy as its center. The Norman dukes were able to introduce revolutionary changes in English government and land tenure, *Reasons for the* which at once made the king the wealthiest man in the state and the *earlier develop-* manipulator of its political machinery. The intelligence and adapta- *ment of strong* bility—if not the genius—of such kings as William the Conqueror, *monarchy in* Henry I, and Henry II supplemented this revolution by organizing *England* in the exchequer an efficient financial administration and by organizing a new judicial system and a competent civil service. Itinerant justices and royal writs brought the central administration into touch with the older local institutions of shire and hundred; they permitted the crown, without destroying these institutions, to interfere in local affairs; and, above all, they won for the central government popular confidence and gratitude.

In the second place, from 1066 on Normandy was a part of the English state, and from 1154 on the English king's continental domain was enlarged by the possessions of the counts of Anjou, and the dukes of Aquitaine. Perhaps we should rather say that from 1066 on England was a part of the Norman state, and from 1154 on a part of the Anglo-Norman-French realm of the Angevin kings. Beginning with William the Conqueror, the English kings were Norman or French in blood and speech and manners; they were lords of French fiefs and vassals of the French king. At least Henry II and Richard were far more concerned with their continental possessions than with England, and in fact spent very little time at all in England. A glance at the map of France at the end of the twelfth century will show them holding two-thirds of the country, and will suffice to explain their ascendancy over the puny and relatively powerless French kings, who were in constant danger of being swallowed up by their powerful vassals, in particular by their most formidable vassal, the King of England. Naturally England profited from belonging to the state of which its king was the head. From Normandy especially came many suggestions for the improvement of its government. It is suggestive, too, that there were interchanges of ideas and men between Norman and Angevin England and Norman southern Italy and Sicily. After 1204 England lost its ascendancy because, first, it lost most of its continental domain to the French, and because after Henry II its kings had neither the intelligence nor the character to keep from treading too heavily on the toes of the English barons, nor the strength to suppress the feudal reaction that they thus provoked.

Monarchy in Germany not hereditary

If England overshadowed France until 1204, until 1197 the Holy Roman empire overshadowed both (and at least for a few years under Innocent III the papacy overshadowed them all). The speedy collapse of the empire after 1197, notwithstanding the heroic efforts of Frederick II to hold it together, and the final victory of the German princelings over the king were only the result of weaknesses that had always existed in the German state underneath the superficial display of imposing strength. First among the circumstances that made for the victory of feudalism in Germany is the fact that the German monarchy never succeeded in making itself hereditary, but had to recognize the old right of the nobles to elect the king. Some German kings strove to secure the succession by having their sons elected and consecrated during their lifetime, but others were not lucky enough to have sons to succeed them. Of the three German dynasties studied above, each was established by election. Electors can demand favors in return for their votes, and the favors that feudal electors demanded were rights pertaining to their local independence. Moreover, when kingship lacks the sanction of the hereditary principle, it is easier to organize opposition and set up antikings, as the papacy well knew and constantly did. The failure to establish succession by primogeniture also left room for the rebellious claims of legitimate or illegitimate sons not chosen to succeed, who were often instigated to rebel by discontented nobles, in whose hands the right of election remained a powerful weapon.[4]

Lack of a compact royal domain in Germany

Another weakness in the German monarchy was the scattered location of the crown lands, its chief source of wealth, all over Germany and Italy. In order to maintain themselves and to carry out their policies, the kings of every dynasty were obliged to buy support by granting away most of the crown lands before the dynasty was ended.

[4] The Norman kings of England complied with the Anglo-Saxon tradition of elective kingship until Henry II.

Along with the crown lands went one other possible source of income, the exploitation of regalian rights; but by the close of the Hohenstaufen period there were as few crown rights as crown lands that had not been alienated. Although the crown lands were replenished at the beginning of each dynasty, the fact that they were so widely scattered made the organization of a royal administration for their direct exploitation difficult at best. For the most part the German kings found in them another reason to infeudate their lands and rights to nobles, ministerials, and the Church—which in the long run amounted to giving them away. The lack of royal administration made it impossible for the crown to profit directly from additions to German territory, such as Lorraine, Burgundy, and parts of Italy; similarly, by leaving the expansion of the eastern frontier to the nobles alone the crown secured absolutely no advantage from it. The German kings never had any central point where they could entrench themselves and from which they could expand; the German monarchy had no capital. German kings were in possession of rights that they could not exploit and lands that they could neither administer nor keep.

Besides these two fundamental causes of the failure of monarchy in medieval Germany, there were others only less important. The *Other reasons* strength of the tribal duchies was a constant danger to the central *for the weak-* government not only in itself but because it early forced the kings into *ness of Ger-* alliance with the Church. Generosity to the Church in the end merely *man monarchy* impoverished the crown and created still more feudal principalities. Then, when the control of the Church that the kings secured in return for their generosity involved them in the investiture struggle with the popes of the Hildebrandine reform party, they lost the control of these ecclesiastical principalities. Much has already been said of the costly mistake—no matter how inevitable—that the German kings made in sacrificing the interests of the German monarchy to the dream of the Holy Roman empire. But it is worth repeating that this imperial policy involved them, in the century after the investiture struggle, in another and deadlier struggle with the papacy, which proved fatal alike to the empire and to the German monarchy. Finally, the German kings, obliged to compromise with the nobility, with the German Church, and with the papacy, never succeeded in making the monarchy represent the interests of the common people. For one thing, they failed to achieve peace and security for the peasantry, and they failed to do their part to alleviate serfdom. Second, they antagonized the Lombard towns and abandoned the growing German towns to the mercies of secular and ecclesiastical feudal lords, so that the towns won their freedom in spite of, not by the help of, the kings, whose strongest support they should have been.

These general circumstances of English and German history make it easier to understand the peculiar political development of France during the same period. From 987 until 1328 the kings of France were Capetians, the direct descendants of Hugh Capet, Count of Paris, who in 987 was elected "king of the Aquitanians, of the Bretons, of the Danes (Normans), of the Goths, of the Spaniards and Gascons, and of the Gauls." From the beginning each succeeding Capetian labored to circumvent the right of the French nobles to elect the king by having his eldest son elected and consecrated king during his own lifetime and by associating his son with him in the government. This was the practice of co-optation adopted by the Roman emperors of the second century. By continuing this practice for about two hundred years the French kings thoroughly established the right of the eldest son to succeed his father. Philip Augustus (1180–1223), observ- ing the rebellion of young Henry against his father, Henry II of England, wisely decided that the danger from a disloyal son already crowned king was greater than the danger of a break in the succession. He therefore took the chance of forgoing co-optation, and his eldest son succeeded him without any difficulties. The Capetians were lucky,

The Capetian monarchy he- reditary from the beginning

until 1316, in always having a son for the succession. They were often lucky enough to have only one son to succeed them, thus being under no necessity of doling out crown property to younger sons, or the alternative danger of leaving discontented sons prone to rebellion, or even both. They were fortunate enough to have healthy sons, who might grow fat and bald and stupid, but who generally had long reigns and begat sons early enough to avoid the danger of regencies for minors. When regencies appeared unavoidable, they were careful to provide for them before their own death. The incalculable advantage of a regular, direct succession of eleven eldest sons for a period of three hundred years, filled mostly with long reigns, was one of the great sources of strength of the Capetian house. More than that, Louis IX in the thirteenth century was so prolific that he furnished ancestors not only for the Capetians until 1328, but after them for the Valois and Bourbon dynasties until 1848.

Accession of Hugh Capet

Hugh Capet came to the throne in 987, after a century of conflict between the French nobility and the later Carolingians. The date 987 has no significance except to mark the beginning of the uninterrupted succession of Capetian kings; for three Capetians had held the throne before Hugh, and his kingship was hardly different from theirs or

rom that of the later Carolingians. The ninth and tenth centuries, it
vill be remembered, were marked by the break-up of the Carolingian
:mpire and the emergence of feudalism. The struggle of Hugh's
ancestors against the later Carolingians was the struggle, in conjunction
vith other nobles more powerful than either Capetians or Carolingians,
of feudal lords against their lawful king. The election in 888 of the
irst Capetian, Odo, as king was the victory of a feudal lord, Margrave
of Neustria and Count of Paris, who had won his spurs defending his
ands from the Norsemen while the Carolingian kings were content
o buy them off. But the Carolingian tradition was too strong to be
out aside all at once, and it was, moreover, supported by the Church,
always legitimist in its policy. Consequently, at Odo's death in 898
he Carolingian Charles the Simple regained the throne. It was he
vho virtually put an end to the invasions of the Norsemen by settling
hem at the mouth of the Seine in 911, thereby securing for the
'rench crown a dangerous vassal more powerful than itself.

While the western half of the Carolingian empire was rapidly dis-
olving into marches, duchies, and counties created to defend the
tate, the impotent Carolingians continued with few interruptions to
vear the crown. Nobody paid much attention to them; their posses-
ions were restricted to such a small fragment of territory about Laon
hat they were almost obliged to travel about, staying with their
riends, when they were not being dragged around in captivity by
oowerful nobles. During the reign of Otto the Great they were prac-
ically under German tutelage, and without German protection would
orobably have lost the throne sooner than they did. All that the
Germans were interested in was keeping the French Carolingians out
of their homeland in Lorraine. In 987, after the death of King Louis V,
he last male Carolingian was his uncle Charles, Duke of Lower
Lorraine. The French Church and nobility had no desire to see a
German vassal on the throne, and no more did the German regents
or Otto III care to see the German Duke of Lorraine become King of
'rance. Thus the last Carolingian suddenly lost the two main supports
of his house. Led by the Archbishop of Rheims, the French nobility
urned to the head of the house that had been calculating for some
ime on permanently occupying the throne. Hugh Capet was crowned
oy the archbishop and anointed with the sacred oil believed to have
oeen brought down from heaven by a dove for the baptism of Clovis,
he first Christian King of the Franks.

The King of France in 987 was three persons in one. He was
king of an ill-defined region called France, he was feudal lord of his

*French king-
ship in the
tenth century*

own domain, and he was at least in theory recognized by the other
great feudal lords of France as their suzerain. The title of king
amounted to little in actual wealth or power. Its chief value was the
moral preponderance that it gave its holder as inheritor of the monarchical tradition established by the long line of his Carolingian and
Merovingian predecessors. Certainly the Carolingians left the Capetians little else: the crown property consisted of a little land and a
few royal residences. Theoretically the king was still the chief defender of the realm, the chief officer of police, and the fountain of
justice. He was the defender of the widow and the orphan, and of
all the poor and oppressed who could not protect themselves. He was
the protector of property and the suppressor of all disorder and license.
But feudalism had, of course, in one way or another deprived the
king of the actual exercise of any of these powers. It was the feudal
noble who defended his own locality, maintained such law and order
as there was, and administered such justice as could be had. Royal
sovereignty was an idea, not a reality.

In France as in Germany it was in the Church that the memory of
the strength and protection of the Roman and Carolingian monarchies was best preserved. In the ceremony of coronation and conse-
*Coronation
and conse-
cration*
cration an indelible sanctity was imparted to the king, which in time
inspired a mystical sort of devotion. After his election the king was
crowned and given the scepter by the Archbishop of Rheims in an
elaborate and impressive rite. Then he was clothed in the robes of
a priest and parts of his body were anointed with holy oil, whereby
he went into holy orders of a special kind reserved for the king, en-
dowing him with the authority of a priest. Not only did he thus become king by divine right and the grace of God, but it was not long
before Church chroniclers, as in the case of Robert the Pious, began
to ascribe to the king the power of working miracles. No other feudal
lord was thus distinguished, and in spite of everything, so long as the
Church existed the monarchy could never quite lose this sanctity in
the minds of the people. In the course of the coronation ceremonies
the king took the coronation oath, which, in addition to the general
obligation to preserve peace, maintain justice, and succor the oppressed,
especially imposed on him the obligation loyally to defend the Church.
This oath the Church never allowed the kings to neglect. It made
Church and state allies in mutual defense against their common enemy,
the lawless feudal nobility. Not until the French Revolution did the
Church cease to be one of the chief supports of the French monarchy.

The Capetian kings were indebted to the Church for more than this sort of moral support. From it they derived much of the actual power that they possessed. As patrons and defenders of the Church they had some access to its immense wealth both within and without their own feudal domain. They enjoyed many of the same rights as the German kings from Otto I to Henry IV: the right to nominate candidates for election to vacant bishoprics and archbishoprics, to bestow on churchmen their temporal rights and possessions, to appoint to certain vacant benefices, the right to the income of a bishopric during a vacancy (which the king could easily prolong), and the *ius spolii*.[5] In southern France, Brittany, and Normandy, where local lords dominated the Church, the king exercised no such control. But in the four archbishoprics of Rheims, Sens, Tours, and Bourges, and in some twenty bishoprics the Capetians enjoyed these rights. Furthermore, in addition to monasteries founded by the Merovingian or Carolingian kings and monasteries in their own feudal domain (together called royal monasteries), the early Capetians enjoyed rights of patronage to thirty-two of the five hundred and twenty-seven monastic foundations in France at the end of the tenth century, and shared rights of patronage to sixteen more. The king was himself abbot of the monastery of St. Martin at Tours, of St. Denis outside of Paris, of St. Germain des Prés in Paris, and of St. Corneille at Compiègne. Thus, although the Capetians enjoyed no such control over the French Church as the German kings had over the German Church, theirs was by no means inconsiderable. It was surely enough to have made the investiture struggle an important issue for them, had they been sufficiently alert to concern themselves with it in time. As it was, they put few obstacles in the way of the success of the Cluniac reform movement in France.[6]

Relations of the early Capetians with the Church

The chief resource of the Capetians, however, was always their own feudal domain—the land that they had possessed as counts of Paris—which may be called the royal domain, inasmuch as no careful distinction was made between public property and the private property of the king. At Hugh Capet's accession in 987 the Capetian domain was the Île de France, a small, compact area of four thousand, two hundred and fifty square miles, the average size of a modern French department, extending from Paris on the Seine (where the early Capetians had only a tower) in a narrow strip to Orléans on the Loire, and including the districts of Étampes, Arpajon, Poissy, Senlis, and the port of Montreuil. Orléans was the most frequented residence of the early Capetian kings. Actually this domain was much smaller than that of

The Capetians as feudal lords

[5] See p. 413.
[6] For the settlement of the investiture in France, see p. 388.

many other French nobles; indeed, one reason for Hugh Capet's elevation to the throne may have been that as a landowner he did not seem especially formidable. The Capetians were extremely fortunate in the central location of their domain. Because it lay between the Seine and Loire, on the future highway of the great overland trade route from the Mediterranean via the Rhone to the English channel it made its owners possessors of the heart of France. The fact that it was also a compact domain, unlike the German crown lands, was an inestimable advantage from the start. Administration was greatly simplified, and the Capetians were entrenched in an inalienable homeland At the beginning of their rule, however, they were no more than any other feudal lords in France or elsewhere complete masters of their domain. Much of it they did not exploit directly, but had enfeoffed to vassals who were quite independent. From their castles controlling the main highways these vassals descended with their retainers to pillage travelers, pilgrims, peasants, merchants, and churchmen. The petty feudal lords nibbled at the power of the great just as these encroached upon the king.

Finally, because they were kings the Capetians were also suzerains of all the independent feudal lords of what was called the Kingdom of France. As overlords they were entitled to all the rights and privileges conferred by feudal law. Due them from their vassals were homage and fealty for the fiefs that made up the kingdom. They could summon their vassals for counsel, or summon them to constitute a court of justice for the trial of other vassals. As guarantors of the feudal contract they could hear complaints from rear vassals over the heads of their lords, or interfere locally to maintain justice. They had the right to collect feudal relief and all the usual feudal aids. They were entitled to the customary military service from their vassals, though they could not summon rear vassals for service without the consent of their immediate lords. They enjoyed the right of wardship over minor heirs and of consent to the marriage of widows and their daughters, or of daughters inheriting a fief. They enjoyed the right of escheat. But it has been seen that the act of homage and the oath of fealty were not always followed by the loyal fulfillment of the feudal contract. The overlord, like any other lord, was just as powerful as his arm was strong. Since the Capetians were relatively small landowners and not exceptionally powerful even in their own domain, they were for long quite impotent in the face of vassals whose domains were much larger than theirs. Nevertheless, they were kings, and their

The Capetians as feudal suzerains

royal prerogatives remained rights in feudal law. And there might come a day when royal theory could be translated into fact.

The early Capetians were not men of extraordinary wisdom or strength. Yet even if they had been, they could scarcely have seen more clearly where to begin and how to proceed to make themselves kings of France in fact as well as in name. To be sure, because as feudal kings they were so many things in one, any advancement along one line would inevitably redound to their advantage along other lines. Progress in mastering their own domain would enhance their authority as feudal suzerains, which would in turn exalt their position as kings. Their first policy—or necessity—was to keep their heads above water. In 987 this was no more than the task of the other great lords of France, the dukes of Normandy and Burgundy and Aquitaine, the counts of Brittany, Flanders, Champagne, Blois, Anjou, Poitou, and Toulouse. Although perhaps none of these alone could have destroyed the Capetians, any strong combination of them could easily have wiped them out; but because the Capetians at first did only what all other feudal lords were doing, they suffered no serious interference from their rivals. Obviously they must begin by gaining new vassals, by asserting their authority over subvassals, by rounding out their domain, increasing it as much as possible but at all costs keeping it intact. They must clean house and make themselves respected at home before they could demand respect abroad. If meanwhile they could retain the kingship, they would at least be losing no ground and would be in a position to profit from any luck that might come their way. *The cautious policy of the early Capetians*

Early French history is largely local or provincial, and that of the Capetians is no more interesting than that of the other great feudal houses. In fact, it is less interesting, for until the accession of Philip Augustus in 1180 the Capetian kings were petty enough compared with the dukes of Normandy and the counts of Blois and Anjou who were conquering England and making themselves its kings. While the sons of Tancred of Hauteville were establishing a Norman kingdom in southern Italy and Sicily, while a Flemish noble was King of the Crusaders' Kingdom of Jerusalem, while other French nobles were answering the call to war against the Infidel in Spain and the east, while the brothers of the Duke of Burgundy were establishing a Portuguese dynasty, the Capetians were at home, struggling unsuccessfully against obesity and the domination of their wives and household officers. They took little part in those great movements that were transforming western Europe in the eleventh and early twelfth *The relative insignificance of the early Capetians* centuries, the building of the new Romanesque churches, the Cluniac reform, the attempts to establish the Peace of God and the Truce of God, the investiture struggle, the new intellectual life stirring in the schools of Paris and in the new vernacular literature. Whether through farsighted prudence or just weakness or lack of imagination, whether confident of the future or merely indifferent to it, they stayed at home, watering their own gardens and mending their own fences.

The importance of hereditary succession

The fact that the first six Capetian kings together reigned for one hundred and ninety-three years was their good fortune.[7] On the other hand, their success in making the throne hereditary by primogeniture was no mean accomplishment. Although under a weak king the monarchy might cease to grow, its power was still not reduced. Yet even during this early period some small additions were made to the royal domain. Henry I added Melun and Sens. Philip I acquired the district of Gâtinais between Sens and Orléans, Corbie in Picardy, and part of the district of Vexin on the Norman border; and the impecunious Lord of Bourges, to get money to go on a crusade, sold the city to him for fifteen hundred silver marks.

Subjugation of vassals within the domain by Louis VI

The greatest accomplishment of the Capetians during this early period was their signal success in achieving what was necessarily the first objective of a sound policy, the thorough suppression of independent vassals within their domain. This was the work of Louis VI, called the Fat, who by the end of his reign could hardly get around, though he never got too fat to fight. Travel was unsafe in any direction out of Paris because of the castles of lawless vassals, who infested the highways like common brigands. "It was unsafe to venture upon the road without either obtaining their consent or securing a considerable escort." The road from Paris to Melun was endangered by Corbeil; that to Dreux or Chartres and Nantes by half a dozen formidable fortresses. Between Paris and Orléans were the castles of Montlhery, Châteaufort, La Ferte-Alais, and Le Puiset.

The most distinguished of these brigands was perhaps Thomas of Marle. "After a youth spent in debauchery and in robbing unfortunate pilgrims bound for the Holy Land, Thomas had come to take a positive delight in murder. His cruelty . . . 'so far exceeded previous experience that men who were notoriously cruel killed cattle, apparently, with more regret than he shewed in slaying men.' He slaughtered without cause for the sheer pleasure of it, and he exhibited great ingenuity in devising horrible deaths for his victims.

[7] Hugh Capet (987–96); Robert II, the Pious (996–1031); Henry I (1031–60); Philip I (1060–1108); Louis VI, the Fat (1108–37); Louis VII (1137–80).

Sometimes, it was said, he would hang a man by his thumbs or some other part of the body, and shower blows upon him till he died. Guibert of Nogent declares that he was present one day when Thomas of Marle had the eyes of ten of his victims torn out, with the result that they immediately expired. On another occasion he asked a peasant who had angered him why he did not walk faster, and on the man [sic] answering that he was unable to do so— 'Wait a moment,' cried Thomas; 'I'll make you bestir yourself!' and leaping from his horse he drew his sword and cut off both the peasant's feet at a single blow. The poor wretch died; and Guibert, who tells the story, adds: 'No one can imagine the number of those who perished in his dungeons, from starvation, from torture, from filth.'" [8] Louis VI destroyed two of his castles in 1115, but it was not until 1130 that he was captured, mortally wounded, and died, "to the great relief of the whole district."

Another of these devils, Hugh, Lord of Le Puiset, Louis suppressed by burning his castles, confiscating his holdings, and forcing him to go on a pilgrimage to the Holy Land. A third, Hugh of Crécy, he forced to give up his lands and enter a monastery, "to meditate on the difference between massacring a few common peasants and murdering a baron." By unremitting combat against such gentry Louis succeeded in bringing comparative peace to his domain, winning thereby the gratitude of peasants and clergy, who had been the chief sufferers.

This accomplishment made it possible for Louis VI and his successor Louis VII to look beyond their immediate domain to the enforcement of their suzerain rights. They were urged thereto by their clerical advisers, who kept reminding them of the king's duty to maintain peace and justice throughout the realm. Unruly vassals were summoned before their lord's court, and if they failed to appear the king often went after them. "What a disgrace it would be for the majesty of the Crown," Louis VI exclaimed, "if we were to hold back for fear of a bandit." Louis VII learned from his father. When the Count of Nevers harassed the monastery of Vézelay, Louis wrote to the monks: "I have sent my messengers to summon the count. As to what he will answer or what he will do I know nothing as yet; but you may rest assured that if he has as much land as the King of England in our kingdom, I should not allow his violence to go unpunished." The count appeared and made his peace.

Appeals to Louis VII from outside the domain

Appeals to the king as overlord from vassals of far-removed regions

[8] Halphen, in *Cambridge Medieval History*, V, 593–94.

became notably more frequent during the reign of Louis VII. The townsmen of Toulouse wrote him: "Very dear lord, do not take it amiss that we write to you so often. After God, we appeal to you as to our good master, our protector, our liberator. Upon your power, next to the divine power, we fix all our hopes." Ermengarde, Viscountess of Narbonne, wrote Louis in spirited language: "We are profoundly distressed, my fellow-countrymen and I, to see this country of ours—owing to your absence, not to say your fault—in danger of being subjected to the authority of a foreigner who has not the smallest right to rule over us. Do not be angry, dear lord, at the boldness of my words; it is because I am a vassal, especially devoted to your crown, that it grieves me to see the lightest slur cast on your dignity. . . . I entreat you of your valour to intervene, and appear among us with a strong army. The audacity of your foes must be punished, and the hopes of your friends fulfilled." Even from outside the boundaries of the kingdom came offers of vassalage in return for help. One lord from imperial Burgundy wrote to Louis VII: "Come into this country, where your presence is as necessary to the churches as it is to me. Do not fear the expense; I will repay you all that you spend; I will do homage to you for all my castles, which are subject to no suzerain; in a word, all that I possess shall be at your disposal." [9]

Changes in administration under Louis VI and Louis VII

While the authority of the Capetians was being established within their domain and its prestige increased without, some small advances were made in the administration of the domain and in the organization of the household, or central government. These were necessitated by the tendency of feudalism to make all offices hereditary, thus depriving the king of control over both local and central officials. The first Capetians were no more masters in their own household than they were masters in the royal domain. The chancellor was always a churchman; the other court offices—seneschal, constable, chamberlain, and butler—rapidly tended to become hereditary. Lesser court officials intruded themselves into the administration; even royal cooks and scullions affixed their seals to documents. General assemblies of vassals to assist the king in making decisions of state and in administering justice met less frequently. Important decisions were made and carried out rather by domestics of the household and intimates of the palace, who, because of the inertia of the monarchs, were usurping the administration of public business and keeping important offices within their families.

[9] Quotations from Halphen, *op. cit.*, p. 616.

By the time of Louis VI the situation had become alarming. The notorious Garlande family succeeded in getting hold of the positions of chancellor, seneschal, and butler; and one of them, Stephen, who was called by one bishop "an illiterate gambler and libertine," was both chancellor and seneschal, besides holding the clerical positions of Archdeacon of Notre Dame at Paris, Dean of St. Genevieve of Paris, Dean of St. Samson and of St. Avitus at Orléans, and Dean of the Cathedral of Orléans. St. Bernard was horrified: "Who without surprise and horror can see this man serving both God and Mammon— at one moment clad in armour at the head of armed troops, and at the next robed in alb and stole, chanting the gospel in a church?" When Louis VI awoke to the danger, he deprived this family of political influence, and subsequently the offices of seneschal and chancellor were kept vacant for years at a time.

To take the place of these noble officials at court, Louis VI and Louis VII began to put their trust in men of lower birth, chiefly from their own domain, in loyal clergy, and even in the citizens of the new towns. Suger, the "little, frail, intelligent, practical, hard-working" Abbot of St. Denis, who, after the dismissal of the Garlandes, served both Louis VI and Louis VII until his death in 1157, was typical of the new royal servant. He was not blind to the temptations of public office. "There is nothing more dangerous," he said, "than to change the personnel of government without due thought. Those who are discharged carry off with them as much as they can, and those who take their place are so fearful of receiving the same treatment as their predecessors that they proceed, without loss of time, to steal a fortune." [10] The *villici* or stewards, who managed the crown properties, and the vicars, who administered petty justice on them, also tended to become hereditary officials independent of the crown. Consequently, under Henry I a new official was created, the *prévôt*, who combined the administration of justice with the collection of taxes in the domain.[11]

Small accretions to the domain and innovations in local and central administration, however, were no more noteworthy than similar accomplishments of other French nobles. Compared with the progress made by the contemporary kings of England in administration, finance, and judiciary, the best that the early Capetians could do was insignificant. Moreover, at the very moment when the Capetians were

[10] Quoted *ibid.*, p. 623.
[11] The *prévôt* was the equivalent of the Anglo-Saxon shire reeve and the Norman *vicomte*.

*Relations
between the
Capetians and
the Norman
kings of
England*

beginning to gain some prestige as kings and feudal overlords on the continent, their very existence was threatened by these English kings, who acquired in France an empire that reduced the Capetian kings along with the rest of the French nobility to the rank of petty princelets. The conquest of England by Duke William of Normandy in 1066 and the accession of Count Henry of Anjou to the English throne in 1154 are the most important facts in early French history.

From their first establishment in Normandy in 911 the Norman dukes had been none too amenable vassals of the late Carolingian and early Capetian kings. The conquest of England in 1066 united England and Normandy in one realm, which, whether jointly administered or not, at once became the chief danger to the French throne. The fact that the Norman kings of England were vassals of the Capetians for the Duchy of Normandy did nothing to mitigate the hostility between vassal and suzerain. The Norman kings did not take their vassalage seriously, and the Capetians were powerless to enforce the rights of a suzerain. Border warfare between the two was almost constant. William the Conqueror was fatally wounded while attacking Mantes, below Paris. His son William Rufus intermittently continued the conflict. Henry I built up a formidable coalition against Louis VI, who was beaten and almost captured at Brennerville. One of the regular means of carrying on the struggle, employed from the beginning, was for each king to encourage the rebellion of the other's vassals and make alliances with them. Perhaps nowhere else is the hollowness of feudal oaths better exemplified. The kings' use of feudalism was to destroy feudalism.

The previous chapter mentioned the fact that Henry I of England attempted to secure the succession of his daughter Matilda, whom he had married in 1128 to Geoffrey, heir to the County of Anjou.[12] Geoffrey was then a boy of only fifteen, who succeeded his father as count in 1129. In extending their domain the counts of Anjou had been even more successful than the kings of France. To Anjou they had added Maine and Touraine. Then, after 1135, while Matilda was struggling unsuccessfully in England against Stephen of Blois, her young husband conquered Normandy, of which their son Henry was made duke in 1150. When Geoffrey died the next year, young Henry, succeeding to Anjou, Maine, and Touraine, became the head of a powerful state quite overshadowing the Kingdom of France. Three years later he became King of England.

Yet even this was not the end of Angevin good fortune. At the

[12] See p. 447.

point of death in 1137 Duke William X of Aquitaine, in order to *Eleanor of* preserve his fast-diminishing duchy, entrusted his daughter Eleanor, *Aquitaine* his sole heir, to Louis VI to be married suitably. The French king *marries* lost no time in marrying the heiress to the most suitable possible *Louis VII* husband, his son, who succeeded him as Louis VII in the same year. Eleanor was only fifteen, a gay, warm-blooded child of the south, used to a court where nobles composed and sang their own vernacular poetry. She had little taste for the humorless and colorless northern court, where abbots like Suger put in a moderate word, or like St. Bernard thundered moral exhortations. Besides, as she put it, she thought she had married a king, but found she had married a monk.

When Louis VII, urged on by St. Bernard and the pope, and conscience-stricken over the death of some thirteen hundred persons caused by the burning of a church at Vitry in the course of a campaign against the Count of Champagne, decided to go on the second crusade, Eleanor went along, anxious for a bit of adventure. Louis VII loved her passionately, but he was intensely jealous of her. He could not quite tolerate her conduct on the crusade. Later stories charged her with improper relations "now with a Saracen slave of great beauty; now with Raymond of Poitiers, her uncle, the handsomest man of his time; now with Saladin himself." At any rate, probably because of her infidelity, king and queen were permanently estranged when they passed through Rome on their way back from Palestine in 1149. All the efforts of Pope Eugenius III to reconcile them (he went so far as to make them sleep together) were unavailing. When, after returning home, Eleanor gave birth to a second daughter instead of the hoped-for heir to the throne, Louis got a divorce on grounds of consanguinity from a council of French clergy on March 21, 1152. It is perhaps the most famous divorce of all history. Louis VII with his eyes wide open gave up not only his charming wife but her magnificent dowry of Aquitaine. Or else Eleanor gave up Louis.

Eleanor was not a woman to remain unmarried for long. On her way back home from Beaugency, where the divorce was granted, she was constantly besieged by ardent suitors. "She started at once for Poitiers, knowing how unsafe she was in any territory but her own. . . . Her first night was at Blois, or should have been; but she was told, on arriving, that Count Thibaut of Blois, undeterred by King Louis's experience, was making plans to detain her, with perfectly honourable views of marriage; and . . . she was obliged to depart at once, in the night, for Tours. A night journey on horseback from Blois to Tours in the middle of March can have been no pleasure-trip, even in 1152; but, on arriving at Tours in the morning, Eleanor found that her lovers were still so dangerously near that she set forward at once on the road to Poitiers. As she approached her own territory she learned that Geoffrey of Anjou . . . was waiting for her at the border, with views of marriage as strictly honourable as those of all the others. She was driven to take another road, and at last got safe to Poitiers." [13]

Eleanor marries Henry of Anjou

Eleanor had already met Geoffrey's elder brother, Henry of Anjou, at the French court. He was "heavy, bull-necked, sensual, with a square jaw, freckled face, reddish hair, and fiery eyes that blazed in sudden paroxysms of anger . . . a rough, passionate, uneasy man." [14] But she seems to have fallen in love with the vigorous young warrior some years her junior. On May 18, 1152, she married him, to the humiliation and astonishment of Louis VII, who actually seems not to have seriously considered the probability that she might remarry. Her dowry, added to Normandy, Maine, Anjou, and Touraine, made her new husband lord of more than half of France and reduced her first husband to insignificance. In 1153 Henry set out to conquer England, the kingdom of his grandfather Henry I, and by December of 1154 he was King Henry II of England. Eleanor, Queen of France for fifteen years, was Queen of England for thirty-five and dowager queen for fifteen more. To Henry she bore five sons. As an old woman of eighty she was trying to teach one of them how to manage his continental possessions. She has been called "the greatest of all Frenchwomen."

Angevin power at its height

Henry II increased his continental empire by the acquisition of Brittany and by the purchase of the County of La Marche. During his reign and the reigns of his sons Richard and John the counties of Angoulême and Périgord and the Viscounty of Limoges were occupied at various times, and Berry, Auvergne, and the Toulousain contested for with the Capetians. Henry II's ambition for his house was boundless: he hoped to extend his empire to the Mediterranean and to the Alps, and Eleanor bore him children enough to aid in carrying out his plans. One daughter was married to the King of Castile, another to William II of Sicily, a third to the Saxon duke, Henry the Lion. In the south an alliance was made with the Count of Barcelona, and Richard married Berangaria of Navarre and later received the homage of the counts of Toulouse. A marriage was contemplated between John and the heiress of Savoy. Richard did homage to Henry VI for the Kingdom of Arles and Burgundy, and

---

[13] Adams, *Mont-Saint-Michel and Chartres*, p. 211.
[14] Haskins, *The Normans in European History*, p. 92. Cf. pp. 448–49.

wanted the crown of the Kingdom of Jerusalem, which his father had refused. He even dreamed of becoming Byzantine emperor and, after the death of Henry VI, Holy Roman emperor.

Thus, during the period when Frederick Barbarossa, Henry VI, and Frederick II were attempting to incorporate Italy and Sicily into the German empire, the Angevin kings of England, not content with defending their French empire, were attempting to extend it in France and even beyond, to match the Holy Roman empire. The Hohenstaufen emperors were defeated by the formidable opposition of the papacy. The Angevin kings were defeated by the opposition of the relatively weak Capetians, against whom they proved unable to hold even what was lawfully theirs. One would have allowed the Capetians slight chance to withstand Angevin power, a danger far greater than they had ever had to face. Henry II was master of almost two-thirds of France; Louis VII was master of half the remaining third. *Angevins versus Capetians*

The English kings' vassalage to the French kings for their continental lands could make little difference so long as the Capetians were in no position to enforce the obligations of vassals far more powerful than they. Nevertheless, for three hundred years after 1154 the French kings maintained a dogged determination to destroy the Angevin empire on the continent. That they succeeded was probably owing primarily to their good fortune in heirs: to oppose Henry II's unworthy successors, his son John and his grandson Henry III, were the two greatest kings of the Capetian line, Philip Augustus and Louis IX, the second of these with an extraordinary woman, Blanche of Castile, for a mother. They did succeed, at the cost of two long wars, each lasting about a century. By the end of the first Hundred Years' War, waged by the Capetians, the English had lost their French fiefs north of the Loire. At the end of the second, fought by the Valois kings, they had left of their empire in France only the city of Calais. In the course of these three centuries the French state was unified, the French monarchy established, the French nation formed. And in point of fact the same things happened in England.

When Philip Augustus succeeded his paralytic father Louis VII as King of France, he was a boy of fourteen. From earliest youth men felt that he was destined to be a great king. There is a story that, when he was fifteen or sixteen years old, one of the barons, seeing him idly chewing a stem of grass, remarked that he would give a good horse to know what the king was thinking about. When another ventured to ask him, Philip replied that he was wondering if God would ever restore France to the glory that had been hers in the reign of Charles the Great. Philip Augustus was no heroic figure. As a boy he was nervous and flighty, easily moved to anger, the victim of wild and morbid fears. After his return from the third crusade in 1191 he became bald, lost the sight of one eye, and was so nervously over-

Royal Domain
Lands of the House of Blois
Boundary of the Kingdom
Boundary of Henry II's Dominions

FRANCE
IN 1189

wrought and physically worn out that two years later he could not consummate his marriage with Ingeborg of Denmark. And yet he never forgot his goal. Patient, calculating, and practical, by taking advantage of every turn in the wind he managed in his long reign of forty-four years to get half of their territory in France away from the Angevins and to make of himself the real creator of the French monarchy and founder of France. His opponents were personally no match for him. Richard was the impetuous and ever boyish hero of western chivalry, a valiant warrior and a capable diplomat, but the faithless son of a great father, boasting of his faithlessness, and inheriting from his mother Eleanor the high spirits capable of understanding southern France if not England. John, possibly a victim of periodic psychosis, was "false to his father, false to his brother Richard . . . false to all, man or woman, who ever trusted him . . . petty, mean, and cowardly, small even in his blasphemies, swearing by the feet or the teeth of God, when Henry II had habitually sworn by his eyes, and William the Conqueror by his splendor—*par la resplendor De!*" [15] Philip Augustus, on the contrary, had no use for blasphemy, although he swore "by the lance of St. James." St. Louis did not swear at all.

The long-drawn-out border warfare between England and France took a new turn when Henry II attempted to extend to Normandy, and to a lesser extent to his other French fiefs, the strong government that he created in England. The resentment of the barons expressed itself in support of the rebellions of Henry's sons on the continent. For Philip Augustus this was an ideal situation, and he kept the Angevin empire in turmoil by supporting the rebellions of young Henry, Geoffrey, Richard, and John, though always under the guise of maintaining his legal rights as suzerain of the Angevin fiefs in France. Henry II was cited several times before the court of the French king but never appeared, and in 1187 Philip went through the empty formality of declaring him a contumacious vassal. Just before Henry II's tragic death in 1189 he was forced to make a peace with Philip, ceding him part of Berry and part of Auvergne.

The conflict of Philip Augustus with Henry II

For a moment Anglo-French rivalry was forgotten in the demand of public opinion that Richard and Philip take the cross to reconquer the Kingdom of Jerusalem from Saladin. Richard as Count of Poitou was the first prince in western Europe to go on the new crusade. He was soon followed by Frederick Barbarossa and Philip Augustus. But Richard and Philip did not for long forget their rivalry at home in the holy task of fighting the Infidel in Palestine. The French king, so soon as he heard of the death of the Count of Flanders, whose daughter he had married and whose death he hoped to turn to his profit, left the Holy Land for home in August 1191, after a four months' stay. He promised Richard before he left that, so far from attacking his French fiefs, he would protect them, as their suzerain, just as he protected his own dear city of Paris. Once at home, however, he entered into a deal with John against Richard, by which he

The conflict of Philip Augustus and Richard I

[15] *Ibid.*, p. 122.

gained certain strongholds in Anjou and Touraine, and moreover began to attack Normandy. Together Philip and John rejoiced over Richard's captivity on the way home from the Holy Land,[16] and did what they could to prolong it. At the same time Philip was working out a plan to place his son on the English throne. He married Ingeborg of Denmark in order to come into the heritage of the great Knut and obtain the Danish fleet for the conquest of England.

When Richard was released in 1194 Philip wrote to John, "The devil is loose," and prepared to defend his newly acquired possessions. Five years of frontier warfare followed Richard's return. Richard, "breathing vengeance and slaughter" and, it was reported, refusing the Sacrament in order not to be obliged to forgive his enemy, used Saracen cavalry and Syrian artillery in his army, and at a cost of fifty thousand pounds Angevin built the imposing Château Gaillard to defend the Seine valley above Rouen.[17] In 1194 he suddenly attacked Philip near Fréteval in the Orléanais; Philip barely escaped, though he lost his plate, his baggage, the seal of the realm, and the registers of the treasury. A chronicler records that Richard pursued Philip so hotly that his horse went blind. In general the war, broken by truces, went in Richard's favor, and it seemed likely that he would triumph over Philip. But the pope succeeded in 1199 in imposing a five years' truce; and Richard's death in the same year, in the pursuit of a rebellious noble of Aquitaine, delivered Philip Augustus from the only foe who could stand up to him after Henry II's death.

The foreign policies of states generally remain the same despite changes in the personnel of government. John, the King of England, was inevitably the enemy of the French king, the former ally of John, the rebellious brother of the King of England. His succession to the

King John and Arthur of Brittany English throne was contested by his twelve-year-old nephew, Arthur of Brittany, who was supported by the barons of Brittany, Anjou, Maine, and Touraine, and of course by Philip. With the advice of his experienced mother, Eleanor, John managed without difficulty to secure the royal throne of England and the ducal throne of Normandy. Young Arthur turned to Philip, did homage for Brittany, Anjou, Maine, Touraine, and Poitou, and was betrothed to Philip's daughter Marie. In May 1200, however, serious difficulties with Innocent III forced Philip to consent to the Peace of Goulet, by which John was recognized as lord of Brittany and Anjou in return

[16] See p. 410.
[17] See p. 312.

for ceding to Philip the region about Évreux, a part of the Norman Vexin, and of Berry. John was to do homage for his continental fiefs, pay twenty thousand marks sterling as feudal relief, and give Blanche of Castile, his niece, in marriage to the heir to the French throne.

Such a clear-cut recognition of French overlordship was the entering wedge with which Philip altogether legally prepared to ruin the Angevin empire. Hugh of Lusignan, Count of La Marche, was engaged to marry Isabelle, the fourteen-year-old heiress of the County of Angoulême. To prevent the union of La Marche and Angoulême, and because he was attracted to the youngster, John in August 1200 suddenly married Isabelle in the absence of her betrothed. When the *Philip* Lusignan family was not compensated for this matrimonial robbery, *Augustus* they complained in proper feudal fashion against their lord John to *confiscates* their common overlord, the King of France. For two years Philip *John's French* Augustus did nothing, watching meanwhile the struggle between *fiefs* John and Arthur and gathering together his resources to act on the complaint. Then he summoned John in 1202 to appear before his lord's court to answer the charge of his fellow vassal. John paid no more attention to this summons than had his father, Henry II, to a similar summons fifteen years before. Thereupon, on April 28, 1202, in a court of the vassals of the French king he was declared to be a contumacious vassal, and to have forfeited all the fiefs that he held of the King of France.

The novelty of this decision was that Philip Augustus meant to enforce it. He planned to conquer the Angevin empire in alliance with Arthur of Brittany and his supporters; but in 1203 he received unexpected assistance from John, who murdered his young nephew, probably with his own hands. The revulsion of feeling against John was so great that he abandoned the continent to Philip. By 1204 not only Brittany, Anjou, Maine, and Touraine but also Normandy, the heart of the Angevin empire and the fairest and most advanced region of northwestern Europe, had been added to the Capetian domain. Poitou Philip could not take, but its conquest was completed by his son Louis VIII. All the feeble efforts made after John's death by Henry III to recover the lost empire were thwarted by Blanche of Castile and St. Louis. Only Aquitaine, south of the Loire, remained to the English. St. Louis, rather than take advantage of English weakness to conquer this territory also, preferred to sign with Henry III in 1259 the Peace of Paris, which recognized French possession of *The Peace* Normandy, Maine, Anjou, Touraine, and Poitou, and confirmed the *of Paris*

English king's vassalage for his holdings south of the Loire. Another Hundred Years' War was still to be fought over this region.[18]

Significance of the loss of the Angevin empire in France

It is difficult to overestimate the importance of the fall of the Angevin empire to both France and England. The Capetians had much more than doubled their domain. They were now in possession of the valleys of both the Seine and the Loire, Paris was secure at last, and with the acquisition of the important port of La Rochelle the Kingdom of France had become a maritime power. The sudden expansion of their domain supplied the Capetians now for the first time with sufficient resources to enforce their legal rights as suzerains and sovereigns of France. The acquisition of the Duchy of Normandy gave them the efficient and highly developed machinery of English government there, upon which they could model a similar royal administration for France. England was cut off more from the continent, for it was now less easy to reach her territories south of the Loire. She was left to herself to develop as a nation. From 1066 to 1204 the larger history of England is at least as much a part of French history as of English. After 1204 it is all English history, and England gradually became more independent of the rest of western Europe than any continental nation could possibly be. The unstable and incompetent John, he who eleven years later was forced to confirm Magna Carta, in spite of himself certainly became one of the founders of England's national greatness.

Welf-Angevin alliance versus Hohenstaufen-Capetian

The victories of 1202–04 did not by any means preclude an attempt by John to regain his lost possessions, and Philip had to be prepared for any emergency. It has already been seen how in the later days of Frederick Barbarossa English influence had been extended into Germany by the marriage between the Welf and Angevin families, and how this marriage had been countered by a Hohenstaufen-Capetian alliance.[19] This pair of alliances had been strengthened somewhat when after the death of Henry VI in 1197 the Welf-Hohenstaufen conflict in Germany broke out anew. After 1204 the Welf-Angevin alliance was refashioned and enlarged in an attempt once and for all to crush the Hohenstaufens and humble the Capetians. John and Otto IV of Brunswick were joined by two important vassals of the French crown, the Count of Boulogne and the Count of Flanders, who resented certain measures of their now strong overlord, Philip Augustus. In 1212 the Hohenstaufen-Capetian alliance was likewise renewed when Crown Prince Louis of France met Frederick II at Vaucouleurs.

[18] See Chapter 26.
[19] See pp. 409–10,

FRANCE
AT THE CLOSE OF THE
REIGN OF PHILIP AUGUSTUS

Royal Domain at Accession of Philip

Acquired from the Plantagenets,
   during his reign.

Acquired from other vassals,
   during his reign.

Plantagenet Lands (1223).

Other Vassal Lands.

In the same year, when Innocent III deposed John for his persecution of the English Church, Philip saw the long-awaited chance to realize his old dream. The next year the pope actually urged the French king and his vassals as their religious duty to put Philip's son Louis on John's throne. But by the time Philip Augustus had gathered together an army and navy for the conquest of England, John had come to terms with the pope, who now forbade on pain of excommunication the very campaign that he had just been urging.

Battle of Bouvines

The final settlement between the two alliances took place the next year in Flanders. In 1214 the troops of the Anglo-Flemish-German alliance on their march towards Paris were met by Philip near Bouvines,[20] with a fine cavalry of his own creation and an infantry composed largely of bourgeois militia, the whole directed by Guerin, Bishop of Senlis. The enemy could not withstand the attack of the new French army; Otto IV fled and Philip took a fine lot of prisoners, including the Duke of Brabant and the Count of Flanders. The battle was a splendid affirmation of the invigorated French monarchy, backed by its own army, its faithful towns, and its loyal clergy. It secured to France her new Angevin possessions; it eliminated the possibility of German interference; and finally, it was a notable victory for the French crown over rebellious and traitorous vassals. That Philip Augustus, ten years after his defeat of John, should now overwhelm an international coalition not only assured the supremacy of the Capetians in France: it marked the beginning of French predominance in Europe over England and the Holy Roman empire.

[20] See p. 414.

Chapter 17

FRANCE UNDER THE CAPETIAN KINGS
(1204–1328)

SOME kind of internal strengthening of the Capetian monarchy must have been going on before 1204 for Philip Augustus to be able to do what his predecessors could not. After 1204 it was inevitable that the acquisition of so much new territory must accrue to the power and prestige of the crown. The expansion of the Capetian domain was accompanied by the slow elaboration of a constitution—not a written document outlining the framework of government, but an accepted group of governmental institutions. The early development of the medieval French constitution was the development of a feudal monarchy, that is, the emergence of the king as feudal overlord, constantly limited by the rights of his vassals, but at once careful to take advantage of all rights properly his. As time went on, in a way not always easy to distinguish, more and more emphasis was put on the powers of the king as king, rather than on his prerogatives as feudal overlord; the kings were regaining the position held by Charles the Great, before feudalism destroyed the powers of monarchy. Without a body of central and local institutions, monarchical rather than feudal in character (even though they often grew from feudal roots), this growth of royal power would have been difficult in any event, and certainly would not have been enough to break the power of French feudalism.

The development of the French constitution

In general the development of monarchical institutions in France was similiar to their earlier development in England. The king as defender of the realm and protector of the oppressed must possess an army independent of feudal ties. As supreme judicial magistrate he must possess an administration capable of supervising and limiting the institutions of feudal justice. He must be equally free of feudal obligations in the choice of all his chief officials. To make his power felt locally he must have a staff of subordinate officials appointed and removable by him, and paid in money, not with feudal grants. To do all these things the king must have an adequate income, which necessitated the organization of an efficient financial administration. Before the accession of Philip Augustus the king had had to rely upon the support of the Church and the petty nobility against the great nobles. From Philip Augustus on the kings found a new and invaluable source of support in the rich bourgeoisie of the towns. From his reign dates the uninterrupted growth of the monarchical institutions which, by the end of the reign of his grandson Louis IX in 1270, had wrecked the feudal foundations of France and cleared the ground for the development of strong, centralized, absolute monarchy. When the last Capetian king died in 1328, this was the heritage that he transmitted to the first Valois king.

The Scripta de Feodis

The way in which Philip Augustus and his successors manipulated the feudal system in France to their own advantage by perfectly legal means deserves emphasis. Like William the Conqueror, sponsor of the Domesday survey, and like Henry II in England, Philip was interested in getting precise and detailed information as to his specific feudal rights in the kingdom. In the archives left from his reign (he was the first French king to provide for their systematic preservation) are the documentary results of one hundred and thirty-two inquests made between 1195 and 1220. The *Scripta de Feodis* (*Documents Concerning Fiefs*) lists, on information furnished by his local officials, the king's fortresses, the feudal obligations of the bishops of the domain, thirty-two dukes and counts, sixty barons, seventy-five castellans (administrators of a castle with the surrounding territory), a host of lesser nobles, and thirty-nine towns, together with the military service due from them in time of war.

Utilizing feudal suzerainty

Philip was determined to be no man's vassal for any fief, and on several occasions when he found himself such he simply bought himself free of homage and fealty. Successful attempts were made by him and his successors to increase the number of the king's vassals, to transform ordinary into liege homage, to make sub- or rear vassals immediate and direct vassals, and to prevent possible direct vassals from becoming subvassals.[1] When, for example, in 1213 Philip granted Brittany to Pierre de Dreux, he not only demanded liege homage but obliged him to swear that he would receive homage and fealty from the Bretons only on condition that they should in no wise impair his fidelity to the king, and that, moreover, if he failed in his duty,

---

[1] Or, in the phraseology used in England, to increase the tenants-in-chief at the expense of the mesne tenants.

his own vassals should aid the king against him until he was brought to terms. To prevent the diminution of fiefs held directly of the king and the increase of subvassals, Philip forbade in 1209 that, in case a fief were divided among heirs, one heir only should remain the king's vassal, the others becoming the chief heir's vassals and thus the king's subvassals: all were to remain chief vassals of the king. The number of direct vassals could be increased perhaps most easily by purchase; thus St. Louis bought direct overlordship of the counties of Chartres, Blois, and Sancerre, and of the Viscounty of Châteaudun from the Count of Champagne. Binding guarantees of many sorts were demanded of the king's vassals for the fulfillment of their feudal contracts.[2]

Beginning with Philip Augustus the French kings were in a position to collect feudal relief or in lieu of it to appropriate good portions of fiefs changing hands. They bought fiefs from collateral heirs when there were no direct ones. They took advantage of their rights of wardship to extend their authority into new areas, by providing rich widows or other heiresses with husbands from ambitious kinsmen of the royal family. Champagne became a virtual protectorate of Philip when the widow of Count Thibaud III put herself in his care. The widowed Countess of Eu he forced to pay a relief of fifteen thousand marks and to accept a royal official to help administer the fief until the relief was paid. In their own marriages the kings looked to eventual succession to important fiefs. Philip Augustus added Artois to the royal domain by his marriage to Isabelle of Hainault, niece of the Count of Flanders. The kings were now in a position regularly to levy and collect all the ordinary feudal aids. They were even able to demand the *droit de gîte*, although, like other feudal dues, it was often commuted into cash. In spite of its limitations the duty of military service furnished the king with a good army, or, when a money payment was substituted, with the means to buy one. The ability to enforce attendance at court enabled the king to found his whole policy on the consent of his vassals, not to mention enhancing his authority. *Utilizing feudal rights*

The development of a local administration for the royal domain and of a central administration to control the local and take care of the enlarged business of state was the principal means of breaking down feudal independence and anarchy in the realm and of strengthening the sovereign's prerogatives. The chief local official in the domain of the earlier Capetians was the *prévôt*. Since the *prévôts* were paid by grants of fiefs in their districts, or *prévôtés*, as were the *Development of local administration*

[2] See p. 301.

central officials, their positions tended to become hereditary, thus escaping from the king's control; and their administration was often so rapacious as to bring forth much complaint. Philip Augustus, after local investigation of their administration, in which he heard many complaints of bishops and abbots, decided, even before he went on the crusade of 1190, to institute a new local official to control the *prévôts* and to act as the king's representative in matters of finance and justice and in military affairs. One thinks immediately of Charles the Great's *missi*, appointed to control the administration of the counts; but it is more likely that, besides the actual need for a new local official, it was the precedent of government in Normandy that influenced Philip.

At any rate, he chose for the new representative of the crown the same name, *bailli*, that Henry I had used. In his directions for the governance of the realm during his absence on the crusade Philip included instructions for the *baillis*. In general, the duties were a combination of those of the English itinerant justice with those of the English sheriff. The *baillis* collected the revenues from the royal domain, acted as the king's local judges, and saw to the enforcement of his rights as feudal lord. Their tenure of office was not feudal; they were appointed and removable by the king, and were paid a definite salary. Specific and numerous limitations were put upon their authority, to keep them from identifying themselves with local interests. Originally their administrative district (the *bailliage*) was not carefully circumscribed and was often named from the personal name of the *bailli*, but with time the domain was formally divided into *bailliages* with their own designations. As the domain expanded under Philip Augustus, the number of *baillis* and *bailliages* likewise increased. After large districts of southern France were added to the royal domain,[3] the *bailli* was introduced there also, but under a different name, the seneschal, head of a district called the *sénéchaussée*. The seneschal was assisted by subordinate officials called *viguiers* and *bailes*, corresponding to the *prévôts* in the north. Here, of course, was the germ of a hierarchy of local officials. Many of the seneschals, far removed from Paris and therefore the more difficult to control in days of wretched transportation, were developing into local tyrants by the middle of the reign of St. Louis. One of them remarked that he would give a hundred silver marks never to hear the king or queen spoken of.

Baillis and seneschals

[3] See p. 502.

With the new administration so soon getting out of hand, St. Louis instituted a series of inquests, like Henry II's inquest of sheriffs in 1170, to determine the degree to which the seneschals were violating local custom in the interest of the crown or in their own interest. The result was the creation of new officials to supervise the supervisors. Over both *baillis* and seneschals were placed *enquêteurs* (investigators or inquisitors), who were, at least under St. Louis, for the most part Franciscan monks, as independent of local interests as men could be. The inquests led also to the publication of a new ordinance regulating the *baillis,* which aimed to limit further their excessive zeal and to make it easier for complaints against their administration to be lodged with the crown.

Such an administration, dependent upon the personal favor of the crown for its livelihood and its advancement, was a most effective means of forwarding the local interests of the monarchy everywhere *Importance of* in the domain and of checking the independence of feudal lords within *the* baillis and without the domain. The *baillis* in particular pushed the rights of their king as far as possible. They interfered with the local administration of feudal justice, in order to transfer its administration to the king, either directly by assuming jurisdiction, or indirectly by encouraging appeals to the king. They policed the highways. They were quick to seize upon every opportunity to increase the domain and extend the king's suzerainty outside the kingdom; they were eager to apply to the limit every new extension of royal authority emanating from the court. On the other hand, inasmuch as the king honestly attempted to safeguard local custom and to control his administration and supervise the activity of his agents, he won a reputation for fairness, honesty, and decency which augmented the moral prestige bestowed upon him by his coronation.

The expansion of the state and the increase in the feudal authority of the king led to the parallel development of a central administration to handle the vast amount of new business brought to court. The transferring of the business of the court from feudal retainers *Development* to specialists in a particular branch of government marks the same *of central* change already seen in local administration, from feudal to essen- *administration* tially royal government. It has been noted already that the places *at court* of the old domestic officials—the seneschal, butler, chamberlain, and constable—because of their feudal tendency to become hereditary, were kept vacant or turned over to clergy or to lesser nobles without influential attachments. Philip Augustus suppressed the seneschal's office in 1191, and kept the chancellorship vacant after 1185. Henceforth the other domestic officers were relieved of purely domestic concerns and became the great officers of the realm.

The remaining domestic organization crystallized into that of the *hôtel;* little about it is known until the reign of St. Louis, but it came to be separated into the departments of the pantry, the wine cellar, the kitchen, the fruitery, the stable, and the chamber, which included the department of archives. Besides the chief officers, there were always at court the so-called knights of the king (*chevaliers du roi*), from whom diplomats, *baillis,* and lesser officials were chosen, and a large number of clergy, from whom were chosen the chief advisers of the king. These men were all paid with special prebends or benefices of the Church, with fiefs of money, or with a definite income from some *prévôté* or from the treasury of the chamber in the Louvre. On occasions of special moment this court was enlarged by summoning nobles and bishops, and now even important bourgeois, of the realm to participate in important decisions of state or to act as a court of justice. This enlarged court represented the body of vassals giving counsel and assisting in the administration of feudal justice. The advice of the nobles of the realm in all important matters gave the kings a limited popular sanction for their measures of government, which paved the way for their legislating later with the advice not of the nobility as a whole but only of a selected few, the king's private council (*conseil du roi*). As yet, however, there was no such institution. These large and irregular assemblies of feudal vassals were themselves the beginning of a future States-General, the French equivalent of the English Parliament.

The early parlement

It was necessary occasionally to appoint special groups or commissions from the *curia regis* to consider some particular matter, such as a special case in law or finance, which the whole court was either too unwieldy or unfamiliar with the details to consider. Especially the multiplication of cases of first instance as well as of appeals called for more organization and specialization in the administration of justice. By the time of St. Louis there were some thirty counsellors, also called masters, at court, trained jurists, to whom more and more judicial business was wholly entrusted. Paris was the natural seat of these new judges, who began to adopt a written procedure, thus making necessary some fixed place for archives. This royal court of justice came to be called in the fourteenth century the *Parlement de Paris.* But, strictly speaking, in the thirteenth century the *parlement* was the king's court sitting in judicial session; it was still a branch of, not separate from, the *curia regis*. The masters did not necessarily sit alone, but often sat with persons of no legal training who had reason to be present at the session.

Much the same things may be said of the French equivalent of the English exchequer, the *chambre des comptes* (chamber of accounts). The name does not appear until the beginning of the fourteenth century, at the time of the great financial reforms; but long before then, even before the tentative beginnings of the *Parlement de Paris*, there were special financial sessions of the *curia regis* to receive the accounts of the *baillis* and audit receipts and expenditures. It is interesting to notice how in France as well as in England these special royal organs of justice and finance emerged from the old feudal court. They are important not so much as mere governmental machinery as because they exemplify the growth of new institutions out of the inadequacy of the old, to meet the needs of a changing and more complex society. *The chambre des comptes*

To support the crown and the new administration after the annexations of 1204 there was a large increase in income. In addition to the English lands north of the Loire Philip Augustus acquired Artois and Vermandois and the city of Montreuil-sur-Mer in the north. Boulogne and in the south Auvergne he confiscated from rebellious vassals. In all, he quadrupled the Capetian domain. From the manors, forests, and fishing rights of the domain came a large part of the royal income. Customs, tolls, fines assessed in the courts, fees of the chancellery, and profits from the royal mints were added to this. The commutation of the *droit de gîte*, feudal aids, and military service into money and the collection of relief meant a good increase in cash. The income from vacant benefices in the Church brought in revenue, even from outside the domain. Special levies on Jews, who were harshly exploited, and on Lombard bankers, fees for the liberation of serfs, fees for the recognition of new communes, aids, and forced loans extracted from the towns all helped to transform the revenue of the crown from insecure feudal income, much of it paid in kind, into fixed royal income paid in money. *Royal income*

It is important, however, to note that the French kings of this period could not levy direct taxes. The opening wedge for a direct tax on property was the regular collection of feudal aids. The wedge was driven in farther when in 1146 the nobles accepted the taxation of those who did not go on a crusade; but the tax was resented, and Louis VII had to promise not to make it permanent. In 1166 both Louis VII and Henry II tried to collect a direct tax based on property *Progress towards direct taxation* for the support of the Christians in the east, but it is not likely that it was levied. In 1188 Philip Augustus and Henry II levied the famous Saladin tithe, a tenth of all the movable property and of one year's income of all clerics, nobles, townsmen, and peasants who did not go on the crusade to reconquer the Kingdom of Jerusalem from Saladin. But the protests of the Church against such a tax, even in that holy cause, were so numerous that Philip Augustus had to abandon it after a year. Only fifty years later, however, St. Louis, supported by the papacy, regularly levied such aids for his crusade to the east, for the crusade against the Hohenstaufens, and for the crusade against the Albigensians. The kings of France were still far enough from the time when, secure in their power, they could levy direct taxes without opposition, but they were plainly already moving in that direction.

The military service due from his vassals, despite its limitations, supplied the French king with a fairly adequate army, especially after the annexations of 1204. Fees collected for exemption from military service furnished the means to pay mercenary troops. Already under Louis VII infantrymen from Brabant had been hired. In order to have crossbowmen and archers ready, special fiefs of *Military re-* land or revenue were granted to them by the crown. It seems prob-*sources of* able that Philip Augustus wanted to revive the old Germanic prin-*the crown* ciple of the duty of every freeman to render military service. There is evidence for his attempting to enforce an ordinance similar to the English Assize of Arms of 1181,[4] on the abbeys, towns, and *prévôtés* of the domain. From a document of 1194, the *Prisée des Sergents* (*Estimate of Sergeants*), which lists certain towns and villages and ecclesiastical communities that were obliged to furnish and pay a certain number of sergeants, or in lieu of them to pay a certain tax, it has been estimated that Philip Augustus had at his service during the whole year some two thousand sergeants. The addition of the bourgeois militia to the military resources of the crown was an incalculable advantage, well demonstrated at the Battle of Bouvines in 1214. But these developments were as yet only petty beginnings of a standing army; French armies were still largely made up of feudal cavalry.

Philip It must already have become clear that the rise of towns in France *Augustus* was one of the chief elements in the growth of royal power.[5] Here *and the* the contrast with the relation of the German kings to their towns is *new towns* striking. As early as the reign of Philip I, at the end of the eleventh

---

[4] See p. 455.
[5] For the medieval town, see Chapters 19 and 20.

century, the development of towns had gone as far as the attempt
to set up autonomous town governments or communes. Philip I was
quite unaware of the significance of this movement. His son Louis
VI could never come to terms with it; at times he supported the
efforts of merchants to establish communes, at times he opposed them.
But town liberties first made their appearance in his reign. His son
Louis VII, Philip Augustus's father, regularly supported the formation
of communes in ecclesiastical territories outside the domain, as a
means of weakening the Church; but he was not convinced that this
policy was good for the domain proper. Philip Augustus was the
first Capetian to support enthusiastically the formation of quasi-
independent communes anywhere; he granted no less than seventy-
eight communal charters. But it must not be supposed that the assumption of control over this new nonfeudal phenomenon was inspired by
any high-minded devotion to the principle of liberty. The chief motive of the Capetians, like that of the Angevins in supporting the
communes in Normandy and the Loire country, seems to have been
military. Charters were most easily secured by towns strategically
located on the frontiers of the domain and by those that had militias
ready for service. The kings were shrewd, too, in tapping the growing concentration of wealth in the new towns. The towns accordingly
paid for their royal charters of liberty with money and military support.
The alliance thus formed between bourgeoisie and crown was real by
the time of Philip Augustus. For the peace and protection on which
alone trade and industry thrive, and which at the moment only a
strong monarchy could supply, the towns were willing to share
their wealth, their soldiers, the counsel of their leading citizens, even
their independence, with the crown.

Philip Augustus drew six bourgeois of Paris into the government *Paris*
before he left for the Holy Land. Paris was already fast becoming
the glory of France and of Europe. The main departments of government were being concentrated there; the royal court was settled
there for a great part of the time. Philip Augustus freed its great
university from the clutches of his *Prévôt* of Paris. He straightened
and paved important streets, and surrounded the city with a wall
ten feet thick and twenty-eight feet high. He began the palace of the
Louvre.

By the end of the reign of Louis IX in 1270 the communal *St. Louis*
movement had spent itself, and a new and more vigorous control *and the towns*
was set up by the monarchy over its "good towns." St. Louis confirmed many old charters, but granted only one new one—to the

town of Aigues Mortes on the Mediterranean, which he built as a port from which to start on his crusade in 1248 and on his crusade in 1270 to Tunis. Like the *municipia* of the Roman empire, the towns were none too successful in the preservation of order or in the management of their finances. The monopolistic control of town government by a rich merchant oligarchy led to frequent revolts of the underprivileged small merchants, tradesmen, and artisans, while the ability of the oligarchy to escape paying its fair share of local taxes frequently brought the towns to bankruptcy. At this point Louis IX stepped in. The towns were ordered to submit their accounts to the *curia regis*. In 1262 Louis ordered that the communes present their accounts every year at Paris, and that every year their right to exist as municipalities must be renewed. Such measures gave the crown some idea of the financial resources of its towns. The king then began to put further pressure on them. Mayors were imposed on the towns, and royal officials introduced, even in towns outside the domain. By this time the towns were complaining that their bankruptcy was owing to their exploitation by the king. And yet, although under Louis IX the French communes lost no small measure of their independence, the advantages to them of a strong central government always held their allegiance to the crown.

The crown and the Church

Throughout this period the Capetians maintained firmly their alliance with the French Church. But it is characteristic of the new strength of the monarchy that from Philip Augustus on the kings were quick to defend their temporal rights against the so-called liberties of the Church. There was frequent conflict, as elsewhere in Europe, between the jurisdiction claimed by canon law for the Church and the secular law of the state. In general, the Church in France fought a losing battle. In matters temporal the clergy were held amenable to the king's court. The manifestoes of Frederick II against the Church found a short-lived echo in protests of the French nobility, who even organized a league to defend themselves against the clergy. Towns began to assert control over the clergy within their walls. With the papacy the Capetians had more difficulty than with the French Church. In the conflict between Frederick II and the papacy St. Louis strove to preserve an honorable neutrality. Until the last years of his reign, when he became miserably subservient to the political program of the papacy in Italy, he protested against the interference of the papacy in the affairs of the French Church; but towards the end the popes began to appoint their own candidates to French benefices without interference from the crown. Nevertheless, it was ominous for the future relations of the crown to the papacy that St. Louis's counsellors wrote to the pope in 1247 that, in case it became necessary for him or for the kingdom, it was the king's right to take as his own all the treasures of the Church and all her temporal possessions.

Louis VIII completed the annexation of Poitou and he also ac- *Minor addi-* quired, besides some cities in the north, the County of Perche. Louis *tions to the* IX added the County of Mâcon, in Burgundy. But the largest addi- *domain* tion to the Capetian domain after the confiscation of the Angevin fiefs was in the south: Languedoc and the Toulousain, the County of Toulouse, were acquired as the result of the crusade against the Albigensian heretics.[6] With this Philip Augustus would at first have nothing to do, and it was only under Louis IX that these regions were finally incorporated into the domain. Ever since the accession of the Capetians the southern provinces had had no close relation to the rest of France. Guienne and Gascony (Aquitaine) belonged to England. Authority in the south, the *Midi,* was divided between the house of Barcelona and the house of St. Gilles. The former was represented by the King of Aragon, a foreign prince who held the County of Montpellier, and by a cadet branch established in the County of Provence. The house of St. Gilles governed the rich County of Toulouse with its attendant fiefs, among them Narbonne, the Albigeois, Nîmes, Béziers, and Carcassonne. The political independence of the south was accentuated by the sharp differences in culture between it and the north of France. In the sunny land of Languedoc and Provence the ancient Latin heritage had been preserved with greater purity than anywhere else in Europe. The only serious misfortune that had befallen the country was the Moslem domination of the lower Rhone valley between 888 and 972, after which recovery from the ravages of the Saracens had been speedy. A talented people, a marvelous climate, a rich and fertile land, accessibility to the commerce of the Mediterranean, and intelligent and just rulers had combined to produce a superior civilization. The earliest French vernacular literature made its appearance in Provence in the songs of the troubadours, and in the south Romanesque architecture was at its best. Princes and people were urbane and tolerant.

In Provence and lower Languedoc the Albigensian heresy was *The Albigen-* espoused not only by great masses of the population, but by many of *sian heretics* the nobility, anxious to confiscate the lands of the orthodox Church. Montpellier, Narbonne, Toulouse, Marseilles, Agen, and Montauban were dense centers of the heretics, who, because they were particularly

[6] For the doctrines of the Albigensians, or Cathari, see pp. 625–27.

numerous in the diocese of Albi, came to be known as Albigenses.
Their number before the Albigensian crusade is doubtful; the Church
tended to exaggerate the number in order to justify its proscription,
while opponents of the Church's policy perhaps underestimated the
number in order to make the proscription and persecution seem more
odious. At any rate, the Church made religious toleration an equal
crime with heresy, and warred not only against heretics and Jews but
against every feudal noble who tolerated new and dissident religious
ideas within his domain. The papacy was greatly alarmed by the
widespread diffusion of the heresy. Neither admonition nor censure
was effective among a population that denied the fundamental authority and teachings of the Church, and the clergy got little support
from the nobility of Languedoc and Provence. Papal legates were
as impotent as the local bishops. By the end of the twelfth century
the most civilized portion of Europe, Mediterranean France, was
beginning to slip from the domination of the Church.

*The Albigen-
sian crusade*

At last, after forty years of persuasion had failed, Pope Innocent
III resolved to suppress the heretics by force. In 1208 he called for a
crusade to extirpate the Albigenses, promising their land to the crusaders. The French barons of the north were quick to respond: the
Duke of Burgundy and the counts of Montfort, Nevers, Auxerre,
and Saint-Pol, among many others, swarmed into the *Midi* with
their armies, bent upon plunder and conquest. Philip Augustus maintained a firm neutrality; at the moment he was fearful of an English
campaign of revenge for 1204 and had no desire to waste his efforts in
the south. Nor had he any desire to see an orthodox Catholic principality established in the south stronger than the heretical counts of
Toulouse, unless the orthodox prince were a Capetian. He also resented papal interference in France and the pope's assumption of the
right to confer upon the crusaders French fiefs taken from heretics.
In fact, he wrote to Innocent III that his advisers had informed him
that under no circumstances did the popes have any such right; if
the Count of Toulouse were a heretic, he would first have to be convicted of heresy, whereupon the French king should be notified of
his conviction and directed to confiscate his land as a fief of the king.

The actual crusade, begun in June 1209, was a fearful slaughter.
The crusaders captured Béziers and massacred its inhabitants, and
Carcassonne succumbed to siege. The notorious Simon de Monfort,
a small seigneur from the neighborhood of Paris, was the only person
who displayed the necessary qualities of military direction. He was
made Viscount of the captured territory of Béziers and Carcassonne by

the crusading army, with both the clergy and a papal legate present.

The religious crusade soon degenerated into a destructive war of *The aftermath* conquest, waged not only against heretics but against all the feudal *of the crusade* princes of the south. When Peter II of Aragon, as lord of Raymond VI, the great Count of Toulouse, came to the support of his vassal in 1213, he was defeated, and Raymond fled to the protection of the English in Gascony, while the crusaders overran his lands. Contrary to the pope's wishes, the Fourth Lateran Council of 1215 deposed Raymond VI from his county, deprived him of his estates, and exiled him. It gave the County of Toulouse, the Duchy of Narbonne, and the viscounties of Béziers and Carcassonne to Simon de Montfort, who divided the lands as fiefs among his vassals. Raymond VII, the son of Raymond VI, was left all the region not conquered by the crusaders, the Marquisate of Provence, Beaucaire, and Nîmes. In the next year Philip Augustus received the homage of Simon de Montfort for his new territories, although at times he treated him as a mere agent of the king.

Young Raymond VII, to whom his father entrusted the task of regaining the lost lands of his house, was able to take advantage of the dissension that soon broke out among the crusaders because of Simon's irresponsibility and violence. Béziers and Toulouse were recovered, and Simon was killed in a vain siege of Toulouse in 1218. His son, Amaury de Montfort, proved incapable of continuing a successful campaign against Raymond VII. Unless the whole enterprise in the south were to come to naught, the intervention of some strong military power was necessary.

Rather than see the Count of Champagne assume the leadership, Philip Augustus permitted his son Louis to lead a horrible expedition southwards. But after it failed to regain Toulouse, the nobles in the army soon tired of fighting a losing battle and were disposed to leave Amaury to his own devices. By 1223, the year of Philip's death, Amaury had lost most of his father's conquests, and the heretics had raised their heads again. Louis VIII at once assumed the leadership of a new crusade to exterminate the Albigensians and destroy the house of Toulouse. Pope Honorius III would not hear of the sub- *Intervention* mission of Raymond VII; he was excommunicated and his lands *of Philip* assigned to the French crown. Amaury de Montfort ceded to Louis *Augustus and* VIII all his rights in the south. *Louis VIII*

Although outwardly Raymond VII's position might have seemed strong, actually his authority had been seriously impaired. There had been appalling destruction of life and property; thousands had been driven to exile; commerce, industry, and agriculture had been destroyed; the land was filled with invaders. When Louis VIII appeared armed with a royal ordinance condemning all heretics to the flames and all their supporters to death—"the first French law which sanctioned fire as a punishment for heresy"—everyone rushed to make his peace with the king before the actual destruction began. After demolishing the walls of Avignon, although it was in imperial territory, on his march south, Louis occupied Raymond VII's lands in Provence. An assembly at Pamiers decreed that all lands confiscated or to be confiscated from heretics should belong to the king. At the time of Louis's death in 1226 Toulouse still held out, but royal officials had been introduced into Beaucaire and Carcassonne.

Louis IX
acquires
Languedoc

The death of Louis VIII gave a short lease on life to the house of Toulouse, but in 1229 Raymond VII, in the Treaty of Paris, made his peace with Louis IX. The king was to keep the *sénéchaussées* of Beaucaire-Nîmes and Carcassonne-Béziers, almost all the rest of Languedoc between the eastern end of the Pyrenees and the Rhone, and the County of Quercy and land between it and Albi. Although Raymond made a later effort, in alliance with Henry III of England, to regain some of his lost territory, he was unsuccessful. Throughout the new royal territory in the south an uncompromising persecution, aided by the Inquisition, a new instrument of terror manned by Dominican monks, rooted out the last vestiges of the Albigensian heresy in the *Midi*. Together, two popes and three French kings had succeeded in practically ruining a civilization.

Acquisition of
the Toulousain

Before the death of Raymond VII the way had already been cleared for the absorption of the last of his lands, the County of Toulouse, into the royal domain. Louis IX's brother, Alphonse of Poitiers, had married Raymond's daughter Jeanne, on the understanding that at Raymond's death his territories were to pass to his daughter, or rather to her husband, and that, if these two died without issue, they should fall to the French crown. In 1249 Alphonse came into his inheritance. Being in character somewhat like his brother St. Louis, he was able to remedy to some degree the disasters that the county had suffered and to restrain the callous zeal of the Inquisition. When he died in 1271 without heirs, the Toulousain escheated almost intact to the French crown. So in less than a century Philip Augustus quadrupled the domain of the French monarchy in the north, and his son and grandson, Louis VIII and Louis IX, aided by religious fanaticism, doubled the domain in the south. Standing upon his own soil, the King of France could now look out on the stormy

English channel and on the deep, sparkling blue of the Mediterranean.

Louis VIII seems to have feared that, unlike most of his Capetian ancestors, he had too many sons. To preclude the danger of revolts, he abandoned what had hitherto been a cardinal principle of Capetian policy. Instead of handing down the domain intact to the eldest son, he apportioned one-third of it into appanages, and assigned them to his three younger sons. The second son received Artois; Anjou and *Royal* Maine went to his third son, Charles; and Poitou and Auvergne to *appanages* the youngest, Alphonse. Louis IX respected his father's wishes, but gave his own younger sons only very small appanages. The establishment of collateral lines of the royal family in important parts of the domain did not impede the growth of monarchical power in the thirteenth and early fourteenth centuries. Charles by marriage added Provence to Anjou and Maine, and was engrossed in the conquest of southern Italy and Sicily from the Hohenstaufens.[7] Alphonse, it was just noted, in addition to his appanage came into possession of the lands of Raymond of Toulouse, where he was absorbed in imitating the good administration of his brother the king. But in the later fourteenth and fifteenth centuries the creation of appanages for younger sons proved so dangerous to the very existence of the French monarchy that the newer precedent was abandoned in favor of the old.[8] It may well seem strange that Louis VIII failed to realize how much of his inherited power was due to the fact that his ancestors had not done just what he did.

For the first ten years of Louis IX's reign, until 1236, he was under the strict care, and France under the regency, of his Spanish mother. Blanche of Castile was a great woman and a formidable person; she would have been a match for Eleanor of Aquitaine. Despite the complaints of the French nobles that she was bringing up her son to despise them, and that France should not be governed by a woman anyway, certainly not by a foreign woman, she kept a firm hand on the government and thwarted all attempts at feudal revolt. She ac- *Blanche of* quired an ascendancy over her son that always made him somewhat *Castile* afraid of her, and made her jealous of his attractive wife, Margaret of Provence. Blanche "would not suffer, in so far as she could help it, that her son should be in his wife's company, except at night when he went to sleep with her." In the palace at Pontoise Louis and Margaret used to talk to each other on a spiral staircase that connected their

[7] See p. 429.
[8] See pp. 884–85; 894 ff.

apartments. When Queen Blanche was heard coming towards either's room, servants beat a warning on the door, so that the king or queen might scamper back in time to receive Her Majesty. "Once the king was by his wife's side, and she was in great peril of death, being hurt for a child that she had borne. Queen Blanche came thither, and took her son by the hand, and said: 'Come away; you have nothing to do here!' " [9] When Louis, in the Holy Land, heard of his mother's death, "he made such lamentation that for two days, no one could speak to him." Blanche reared her son in all the Christian virtues. To the Church he was the model of a Christian gentleman and a Christian king. And in fact Louis was just that; he was the perfect embodiment of medieval Christianity. He was the one king of the middle ages who honestly attempted, and in large part succeeded in his attempt, to make Christianity a code of public as well as private morality. The Church hastened to canonize him in 1297.

An inimitable account of Louis comes from the pen of his intimate friend and counsellor, his seneschal for Champagne and his honest biographer, John, Lord of Joinville. Joinville by no means approved of all of Louis's pious practices. He was mildly reproved for his answer to the king's question whether he preferred to be a leper or to have committed a mortal sin: "I, who never lied to him, made answer that I would rather have committed thirty mortal sins than be a leper." To another question, whether he washed the feet of the poor on Holy Thursday, he replied: "Sir, it would make me sick! The feet of these villains will I not wash!" And he thanked God that he was not with his master on the crusade to Tunis. On the other hand, he agreed with the king about the evil of blasphemy and cursing. During the twenty-two years he was in the king's company, he says, "I never heard him swear by God nor His Mother nor His saints"; as for cursing by the name of the devil, "In the house of Joinville whosoever speaks such a word receives a buffet or pummel, and bad language is nearly outrooted."

John of Joinville, biographer of St. Louis

In Joinville's portrait of his king we see the pious knight, the valiant crusader,[10] the firm, upright, decent monarch who wants peace, although not at any price. St. Louis was the humble and unquestioning son of the Church, but he stood up to his bishops and for most of his reign defended his own temporal control over the Church against both French prelates and the pope. After he was drawn into the crusading movement, he became more and more concerned with

St. Louis

[9] *Memoires of Joinville* (Everyman's Library), p. 288.
[10] For Louis's crusades, see pp. 549–50.

his own salvation and that of his people, and more ascetic in his habits. After his return from his first venture in the east "he lived in such devotion that never did he wear fur of beaver or grey squirrel, nor scarlet, nor gilded stirrups and spurs. His clothing was of camlet and blue cloth; the fur of his coverlets and clothing was deer's hide, or the skin from the hare's legs, or lambskin." In appearance and attitude he was more monk than king, and the Parisians came to call him Brother Louis (*Frater Ludovicus*). He tried to keep his brother Charles of Anjou from playing at dice, and the nobles from holding tournaments. He was temperate in eating and drinking, and watered his wine. While he disapproved of extravagance in raiment, he told his noble counsellors: "You ought to clothe yourselves well and suitably, so that your wives may love you the better, and your people hold you in the greater honour." Minstrels played for him after his meals, and he heard them through before he heard grace, but if the monks suggested that they read to him from some book, he lost patience. "You shall not read it to me; for there is no book so good after eating as to talk freely, that is to say, so to talk that every one says what best pleases him."

For all his virtues, St. Louis belonged wholly to his own time. He died a martyr to the Faith on his crusade to Tunis. On the other hand, his unbending zeal for orthodox Christianity led him to recommend that the Christian layman, as the only method of settling a dispute with a Jew, should draw his sword and pierce the Jew's stomach "as far as the sword will enter." St. Louis added to the architectural treasures of France with countless abbeys, convents, chapels, and hospitals, many of them the expression of his large compassion for the poor, the hungry, the maimed, the blind, and for all unfortunates. His greatest monument is doubtless the exquisite Sainte Chapelle at Paris, as perfect today as when he built it, of stone and iridescent stained glass, as a precious reliquary for Christ's crown of thorns. "And like the scribe who, writing his book, illuminates it with gold and azure, so did the said king illuminate his realm with the fair abbeys that he built and the great number of almshouses." Under Louis Paris and France could rest awhile in peace and glory, at the height of their medieval greatness.

Although St. Louis was still the feudal king *par excellence*, it is clear that his rights as feudal lord, now thoroughly exploited, had raised his status to the point where he could in fact exercise the sovereign powers which in theory he inherited as king. There was no longer any question of the king's royal—not feudal—function in the

The administration of justice

administration of justice through the *Parlement de Paris*. The number of cases appealed from lower feudal courts was increasing rapidly. Louis did not hesitate to interfere when his vassals plainly denied justice to a rear vassal. The lawyers at court, still only slightly influenced by Roman law, were eager to set up a special category of cases called royal, which only the king's justice could handle. Such were cases of treason, cases involving protection of highroads, and cases involving maintenance of the "king's peace," a vague and expansible term. The inclusion of the communes, even outside the domain, within the sphere of royal justice by the creation of a special class of "bourgeois of the king" helped to supply a wider national basis for the royal court.

But Louis's interest in seeing justice done went far beyond sponsoring the *Parlement de Paris*. He was personally, and quite informally, accessible to pleaders. Joinville relates that "ofttimes it happened that he would go after his mass, and seat himself in the wood of Vincennes, and lean against an oak, and make us sit round him. And all those who had any cause in hand came and spoke to him, without hindrance of usher or of any other person." "Sometimes have I seen him, in summer, go do justice among his people in the garden of Paris, clothed in a tunic of camlet, a surcoat of tartan without sleeves, and a mantle of black taffeta about his neck, his hair well combed, no cap, and a hat of white peacock's feathers upon his head. And he would cause a carpet to be laid down, so that we might sit round him, and all the people who had any cause to bring before him stood around." His genuine concern for the weak and the afflicted, for the widow and the orphan, enhanced his position as protector of the lowly. So did his freeing of thousands of serfs on the royal demesne, even though the crown did raise money by the fees paid for their liberation.

Ordinances of the king

It is especially noteworthy that Louis IX was the first King of France to take it upon himself to issue ordinances for the whole realm without the previous consent of his vassals. Such an assumption of legislative power was the consummation of a gradual departure from the feudal practice of the lord's taking counsel with his vassals before making important decisions of state. At first the king legislated for his own domain, but outside of it only by special agreement with his vassals. Then on certain questions he began to issue ordinances for the whole realm, signed by a representative group of vassals, but held to be equally binding on vassals not signing. Finally, in the interest of the "general good," after having won the confidence of his nobles, he undertook to legislate in his own name. This stage was reached under

Louis IX, although his successors by no means ruled by ordinance alone.

Louis's ordinances were even more novel in content than in form. He aroused great antagonism by forbidding private warfare, the lifeblood of the feudal system, as well as the carrying of arms. He even made honest attempts to enforce this striking reform, but it remained long after his day rather a pious aspiration than a reality. Another ordinance outlawed trial by battle in the domain before royal judges. In this Louis had been anticipated by the Church in 1215, and by Frederick II in Italy and Sicily. The attempt to substitute formal legal procedure according to a written code for bloody combat was at least a civilized undertaking, which tended to encourage appeals to royal justice, and was also influential as a precedent beyond the domain. A third ordinance aimed at clearing the way for the extension throughout France of money coined in the royal mints. Though private feudal coinage was not prohibited, royal money was to circulate everywhere, and where there was no local coinage was to have preference over any other.

The guiding principle of Louis IX's foreign policy, if we omit consideration of his crusades, was peace. He can quite properly be called a pacifist: differences with foreign powers he preferred to settle by compromise. In the Peace of Paris of 1259 with Henry III he was content with liege homage for England's retention of Guienne and Gascony. The year before he had settled with King James of Aragon conflicting feudal claims in southern France arising out of the Albigensian crusade: Louis gave up old Carolingian claims to Catalonia and Roussillon and James gave up his claims to Languedoc, with the exception of Montpellier, whose suzerainty he retained. Louis was called upon by foreigners to arbitrate their differences, so confident were they of his probity. The chief instance of this was his arbitration of the dispute between Henry III and the barons of England over the validity of the Provisions of Oxford, which he decided in favor of the king. St. Louis succeeded in making the monarchy so popular among the nonfeudal classes in France that its character was fast becoming national rather than feudal. Inhabitants of the kingdom began to think of themselves as subjects of the king rather than as vassals of a lord. In his person the cult of monarchy by divine right awoke an early response. All France united in mourning his death in 1270.

St. Louis as pacifist and arbitrator

St. Louis's son Philip III (1270-85), "the carbuncle sprung from that most precious gem of Christ, St. Louis," attempted to use the new strength of the monarchy to encroach upon Aragon, but the effort was

futile and cost him his life. On the other hand, by the peaceful means
of betrothing his son to the heiress of the King of Navarre, who was
also heiress of that old rival of the Capetian kings, the Count of
Champagne, he added Navarre and Champagne to the royal domain.
Philip IV, his son, added also some French-speaking territory on the

Legend:
- — · — Boundary of French Kingdom
- ▤ Royal Domain
- ▨ Lands of English Kings (Treaties of 1259-19)
- ▧ Lands of Alfonse of Poitiers (Incorporated with the Domain 1271)
- ▦ Lands of Charles of Anjou
- ▩ Lands of Robert of Artois
- ⬚ Other great fiefs

FRANCE
IN 1270

northern and eastern frontier that had belonged to the empire: Toul,
the Free County of Burgundy (Franche-Comté), formerly a part of
the Hohenstaufen Kingdom of Burgundy or Arles, and Lyons.

The character of Philip IV, the Fair, during whose dramatic reign [11]
(1285-1314) the new aspects of the French monarchy became quite
clear, remains an enigma. One of his enemies compared him to "the
eagle owl, the finest of birds, and yet worth nothing at all. He is the

[11] For Philip's struggle with the papacy, see pp. 955 ff.

handsomest man in the world, yet all he can do is to stare at people without saying a word." [12] He must be judged by the group of clever and unscrupulous lawyers from the south of France, trained in Roman law, who were his intimate advisers. To one of them, Peter Flote, he is reported to have said, in parody of Christ's words: "Thou art Peter, and upon this rock I will build my council." Another, Peter du Bois, set no limit to his exaltation of the king's might: the Church should surrender all temporal power to him; he should stand at the head of all Europe; he should be entrusted with the recovery of the lost Crusaders' Kingdom of Jerusalem. But whether Philip dominated these devoted servants of absolutism or they him cannot be known.

The new financial needs of a state expanding on all sides, externally *Philip's* and internally, drove Philip to seek new sources of revenue. Thereby *financial* he earned an evil name among his subjects, for never had France been *policies* so taxed. Feudal contributions hitherto irregular became so regular as scarcely to be differentiated from direct taxes. Taxes of a tenth on Church property and income and the collection of a year's revenue from new holders of ecclesiastical benefices were resorted to often after the king's victory over the pope on this issue. Payments for exemption from military service were carefully assessed on a property basis, and collected upon every pretext. The feudal aids were likewise exacted upon every possible occasion. Forced loans were squeezed out of the towns. Customs duties were increased. New taxes called *maltôtes*, levied first on "every commercial transaction, became a tax levied on such essential things as wheat, wine, and salt, whether sold or owned."

From 1295 on Philip steadily debased the royal currency. Not content with these measures, he drove the Jews out of the realm in 1306, and in 1311 expelled the Italian bankers, confiscating the property of all these agents of the new commercial order and collecting all debts due them. In these violent measures he could rely upon popular hatred of the new bankers to support him. Moreover, it is doubtless true that Philip IV, with the burdens of a larger and more complicated state, had no choice but to draw upon the newly created wealth of the commercial and industrial classes, who could protest only that his methods were newfangled and that his demands infringed upon old feudal rights. Philip even dared to use the papacy to destroy the Order of Knights Templars, largely to get their enormous wealth. Finally he found himself forced to consult with representatives of the chief classes of the state before resorting to new taxation.

In the development of French political institutions—what we have

[12] Quoted in *Cambridge Medieval History*, VII, 310.

called the French constitution—nothing of absolute novelty occurred during the last years of Capetian rule. The tendency towards bureaucratic absolutism and the specialization of administrative functions, already plainly at work in the reign of St. Louis, grew unhindered and rather rapidly in the reign of Philip IV. The old differentiation between the fully assembled court of the king (*curia regis*) and the great officials of the household now crystallized into two definite councils, the great or full council (*grand conseil* or *plein conseil*), composed of important persons whom the king summoned to meet on irregular occasions, and the small or secret council (*étroit conseil* or *conseil secret*), the group of special advisers holding important offices of the household and always on hand. Later these two united to form the king's council (*conseil du roi*). The financial affairs of the king's private household were now entrusted to a special penny chamber (*chambre aux deniers*). The Templars, who had formed a sort of government bank, were replaced by special royal treasurers in the Louvre; to supervise them, by the end of Philip IV's reign a special permanent board of hard-worked officials on salary, called the chamber of accounts (*chambre des comptes*), had been formed. The preparing, copying, registering, and sealing of private correspondence and memoranda of the king were entrusted to a group of officials called simply the chamber; public correspondence and documents were taken care of by an organized chancellery, at whose head, after 1315, there was again a chancellor. These new financial and secretarial arrangements indicate the growing tendency to differentiate between the king as a private person and the king as the embodiment of the state.

Further developments in the central administration

Councils and chambers

The Parlement de Paris

The same specialization can be traced in the organization of the *Parlement de Paris* during Philip IV's reign, although it did not become exclusively a professional body until Philip V (1316–22) finally excluded ecclesiastics from it entirely. In the great chamber or chamber of the pleas (*grand' chambre* or *chambre des plaids*) all pleadings were held and all decisions rendered. The chamber of petitions (*chambre des requêtes*) heard requests that the royal court assume jurisdiction in a case. In the chamber of inquests (*chambre des enquêtes*) all questions dealing with local investigations of the administration of justice were handled. The local administration of *baillis* and seneschals underwent no important changes during this period, but the *enquêteurs* degenerated from the correctors of local abuses that St. Louis's *enquêteurs* had been into moneygrubbers for the king.

The only development of the French constitution under the last Capetians that might fairly be called an innovation was Philip IV's summoning of his great vassals and his rear vassals, both lay and ecclesiastical, together with representatives of the French communes, in 1302, to consult with him regarding measures to be taken in his conflict with Pope Boniface VIII. This has been called the first meeting of the States-General, the nearest approach to a national legislative assembly, corresponding to the English Parliament, that France achieved before the Revolution. In 1308 Philip called together a similar body to consult with him on measures to be taken against the Templars, and in 1314 he summoned a third assembly to grant him money for his war with Flanders. As in the case of the early development of the English Parliament,[13] we must not be deceived by what appears to be a radical innovation. It had always been the duty of vassals to render counsel to their lord, and from the earliest days of the feudal system they had been convened for this purpose.

Frequent mention has been made of the feudal lord's court, particularly in its judicial aspect, and in this chapter of the king's court, out of which the central administration of the realm grew. There was no question of the right of assembly, and the three assemblies convoked by Philip IV were no concession wrung from the king by the nobles or the people. Those who attended were obliged as vassals of the king to answer his summons; so far had royal authority progressed that they had no alternative but to obey. The innovations of 1302 were twofold. First, Philip IV summoned not only his direct vassals but also his indirect or rear vassals, after gaining the permission of their lords to do so. His bitter conflict with the pope made him anxious to appeal to as many of his vassals as he could assemble, in order to capitalize on the advantage of a single appeal to a group that might be said to represent the whole nation, rather than to mere representatives of the different social classes. Second, in order that the assembly might really seem to represent the whole nation, he included bourgeois representatives of the towns, i.e., members of the third estate. And yet, while it is true that under the feudal system the third estate had no standing, the first States-General was in this respect an innovation in theory rather than in fact. In the course of the twelfth and thirteenth centuries the towns, both within and without the royal domain, had become essentially vassals of the crown, as a result of royal charters recognizing their communes. They might almost be said to have entered the feudal system, for as corporate vassals they were held to the same obligations as any other vassal. Among these was the obligation to render counsel to their lord the king, and

[13] See pp. 833 ff.

before 1302 their representatives had often met in separate assemblies therefor.

French
States-General
and English
Parliament

In England out of the same beginnings Parliament developed into a genuine partner in government, with which the king was constrained to share his authority. In France the States-General (the name did not come into use until later), except on rare occasions, never became anything better than a new and somewhat suspect instrument of the royal will. To be sure, that the last Capetians felt confident enough of their position to call together and to direct their whole body of vassals is evidence of their new strength, and their ability to do so with success is evidence of their popularity. The precedent established by Philip IV in 1302 was followed frequently by Philip V, and down to 1614, when it was forgotten until 1789. It seems, then, that the French kings grew so strong that they ceased to feel the need of calling representatives of their people to consultation. From the beginning it is important to note for what sort of purpose Philip IV summoned the States-General, and what sort of business it transacted. The king only desired support for some particular measure upon which he was resolved; when that support was had there was nothing for the representatives of the nation to do except to go home.

Why did the *curia regis* in England and in France develop in contrary directions? The difference is hardly to be explained by dissimilarities in the character of the representation in Parliament and in the States-General, though there were such; there was, for example, no element in the States-General corresponding to the English knights of the shire. Probably the explanation lies rather in the fact that the English constitution developed so much earlier than the French. No matter how strong the position of the Norman kings and of Henry II in England may have been, their incompetent successors in the thirteenth century, when they had to deal with the beginnings of Parliament, could have been more competent than they were and still been by no means so strongly entrenched in their position as Philip IV was in his in 1302. By that time Magna Carta was almost a century old, and it was almost half a century since a parliament of English barons had openly, and successfully, defied King Henry III. In French history there never was a Magna Carta. The early Capetians, who in the main were not strong kings, never offended their vassals—whether from wisdom or because they dared not—as did the Angevins in England. And then, when the reaction came in England, while the English crown was in the hands of such poor creatures as John and Henry III, France was governed by Philip Augustus and

Louis IX, two of the greatest and strongest and best kings that France, or any other land, ever had. Finally, the divergent trends of the English Parliament and the French States-General are to be explained in part by later differences in the circumstances attending the meetings of the two bodies.[14]

In spite of what has just been said, the tremendous development of the monarchy under Philip IV did bring about a sort of feudal reaction in the last year of his reign. Leagues of nobles in Burgundy, Champagne, Vermandois, and other localities demanded that the feudal privileges of the days of St. Louis be restored. Feudalism in France had, then, degenerated so rapidly since his time (to no small degree because of precedents set by him) that to the subjects of Philip IV he seemed to have been a good feudal king. Louis X (1314–16) met their demands by special provincial charters of liberties for their respective domains, not by one like Magna Carta for the nobility as a whole. While these charters continued for centuries to be hailed by their holders as warrants of their provincial liberties, they contained nothing that was important enough, or that demanded enough respect from the crown, to handicap Louis X's successors. His short reign was notable for one other thing: he resumed St. Louis's policy of freeing "from personal bondage every French serf." *Feudal protest in France*

Provincial charters

When Louis X died, in 1316, for the first time in three hundred and twenty-nine years a Capetian king left no son to succeed him. The crown went to his brother, Philip of Poitiers, who was crowned Philip V in 1317, after an assembly had concluded that "a woman does not succeed to the throne of France." At his death in 1322 the situation was repeated and the crown went to his brother, Charles IV; he, after three marriages had failed to furnish him a son, died in 1328. Thus the direct line of the Capetians came to an inglorious end. The crown then passed to Charles IV's nearest male heir, his cousin Philip of Valois, the first of the Valois line. French lawyers subsequently discovered that the early law of the Salian Franks had barred women from inheriting property; by stretching this provision to include the throne they tried to make it seem that the new principle that only a male could inherit the throne was of long standing. *The last Capetians*

Philip V carried on the tradition of his ancestors. In 1317 he did for France what Henry II and Edward I had done for England in the Assize of Arms and the Statute of Winchester. The inhabitants of all towns and castellanies were directed to provide themselves with arms befitting their rank, and to submit to the orders of "good and *French monarchy in 1328*

[14] See pp. 846–47.

sufficient captains," who were grouped together in larger districts under captains general. Nonnoble as well as noble subjects were now armed and officered by men devoted to the interests of the crown. Philip also attempted, without success, to establish uniform coinage and a common standard of weights and measures for the whole kingdom. Thus the fifty-eight years following the death of St. Louis witnessed the completion of the constitution of the medieval French monarchy. The king who in 987 had been a relatively powerless victim of the feudal system had now succeeded, by carefully exploiting the rights which that system gave him, in getting the upper hand of his former masters or equals, and in recovering the ancient prerogatives of kings who ruled by divine right. He had even begun to travel the road towards absolutism, escorted by an elaborate and relatively efficient centralized bureaucracy of paid officials. The question that fourteen-year-old Philip Augustus asked himself, as he chewed his blade of grass, had been answered: God had restored France to the greatness that was hers in the reign of Charles the Great. And God was ably seconded therein by the kings of France, most notably by Philip Augustus.

Chapter 18

WESTERN EUROPE ENCROACHES ON ISLAM. THE CRUSADES

HISTORIANS have long associated the missionary activities of Christianity with the imperialistic activities of western nations. An unappreciative reception of the one true Gospel *Christianity* by non-Christian peoples has led to the intervention of the secular *and* state. On the other hand, successful missionaries have brought in their *imperialism* wake the trader and then the flag, so that the result has been the same. Or again, Christianity has been introduced by the state to confirm its hold upon new areas. This intimate relationship between political and religious expansion is older than the peculiar combination of religious enthusiasm and practical politics that made up the mass movements to Syria and Palestine called the crusades. Out of the crusades, however, came the first plans for the peaceful conversion of non-European peoples to Catholic Christianity. From that day to our own, missionary activity has taken on an ever wider scope, until it has become coterminous with the expansion of western European civilization.

Yet we do not think of the Christian missionary movement of today as a crusade. Its long history of converting distant peoples has so *The crusading* tempered its zeal and modified its program that it has lost some of *temperament* its earlier ardor, and in some instances has become the enemy of the very imperialism on which it formerly thrived. The emotional enthusiasm of the authentic crusade has been transferred in modern times to the solution of economic, social, and political problems. "Crusader" now means the vociferous reformer or his equally clamorous opponent: the prohibitionist or the antiprohibitionist, the pacifist or the professional patriot, the communist or the anarchist. But not only does the modern crusader preserve the emotional fervor of his medieval predecessor; the movement that he heads makes the same use of propaganda and appeal to group action.

As early as the thirteenth century a crusade had come to be not

515

what it was at the end of the eleventh—a mass movement of warriors and noncombatants, ostensibly under the leadership of the pope, to recover the Holy Land from the Infidel. Their great success in arousing western Europe for this cause led the popes to divert latent enthusiasm into channels of more immediate advantage: that is, into crusades not just against the enemies of the Faith, but against the enemies of the papacy. They organized crusades in Italy against the Hohenstaufens; and the impossibility of bringing the Albigensian heretics to terms led to the organization of a diabolical crusade against them. When once the popes assumed the attitude that has misled so many men—that in a good cause they could do no wrong—their supremacy in an organization believed to be of divine origin re-enforced their doctrine that all opposition was unholy and that any suppression of it constituted a "holy war."

The crusading movement that dominated western Europe decreasingly from the end of the eleventh to the end of the thirteenth century was primarily a resumption of the offensive against Islam. In the century after Mohammed's death the Arabs had with phenomenal rapidity pushed their boundaries in the east to Constantinople and in
the west into southern France. At both limits they were successfully stopped, and in northern Spain Charlemagne opposed them by establishing the Spanish march. The ninth and early tenth centuries then witnessed a new Moslem offensive that brought them possession of Sicily, Sardinia, and the Balearic Islands, from which they controlled the sea and pillaged the coasts of southern France and western Italy.[1] Local feudal lords, the popes, and the Byzantine emperors drove them from their strongholds on the mainland in the course of the tenth century; but at the beginning of the eleventh they still retained the islands, controlled the sea, monopolized all commerce between western Europe and Africa, endangered all commerce with the east, and threatened the coasts of southern France and western Italy. In the Spanish peninsula the little Christian states of León, Castile, Navarre, Aragon, and Barcelona, which had replaced the Spanish march, just managed to hold their own against the Caliphate of Cordova, which in the tenth century was enjoying its period of greatest brilliance.

By the beginning of the eleventh century western Europe had recovered sufficiently from the dissolution of the Carolingian empire and the formation of feudal Europe to turn its attention to something other than internal troubles. The Saxon emperors had restored some

[1] See p. 277.

order and refounded a kind of Roman empire in medieval guise. The Cluniac reform bred a new and contagious ascetic fervor, and led to attempts to restrain warfare by means of the Peace of God and the Truce of God. The eleventh century confirmed these tentative beginnings of ordered and civilized society. The monastic reform movement expanded into wider circles; its program was adopted and modified by the papacy. The first stirrings of a revival of commerce and industry were being felt. In France the energy of the nobles burst its local bounds, and the Normans conquered England in 1066 with the pope's blessing. This consecration of conquest may be said to mark the beginning of the crusades.

Already, however, the offensive against Islam in the west had begun. By the end of the eleventh century the Normans had taken *The offensive* Sicily, with papal benediction and with the co-operation of Genoa and *in the western* Pisa. Before this conquest Genoa and Pisa had driven the Moslems *Mediterranean* from Sardinia, with the help of the papacy; and in 1087 they carried the offensive to Africa, where they captured the chief port, Tunis. With Sardinia and Sicily in Christian hands and with Italian and Norman navies patrolling the western Mediterranean Moslem control of the sea was at an end. The route to the east was open as never before to the ambitious merchants of Genoa, Pisa, and Amalfi.

Meanwhile, under the same general auspices, the campaign against Islam in Spain had progressed notably. After the great days of Abder-Rahman III (929–61) the Caliphate of Cordova declined, suffering from revolts of insubordinate generals and officials. By a revolt in *Spain in the* 1009 the caliph was overthrown, and in 1034 the caliphate no longer *tenth century* existed. It was supplanted by twenty-three local kingdoms, or emirates, called the kingdoms of the Taifas. In such a dismembered condition Spanish Islam was ripe for attack. The brunt of the offensive devolved upon Castile, which was joined with León around 1050, and upon Aragon, which was later joined with the County of Barcelona. Navarre, hemmed in by these two, never had much chance to expand southward.

The danger to the independence of these small northern kingdoms from a reunion of the Mohammedan principalities was felt also by the nobles of southern France. If this small Christian bulwark in Spain were destroyed, there was nothing to prevent the Moslems from reentering southern France. Moreover, the princely families north and south of the Pyrenees were closely connected by matrimonial alliances. To the nobles of northern France Spain offered as promising a field for adventure and profit as southern Italy or England. Cluniac monasteries had spread their crusading zeal into Spain. The pilgrim road to the shrine of St. James at Compostella was lined with Cluniac houses, facilitating communication across the Pyrenees. All the conditions that concurred to send crusades to the east were here present in Spain. The reformed and reforming papacy was as well aware of all these conditions as of its general responsibility for the defense of the Faith. Besides, as Gregory VII reminded the French nobles about to invade Spain, the peninsula actually belonged to St. Peter.

The Spanish crusades

Beginning in the eleventh century there was a succession of expeditions of French knights to assist the Spanish kings. In the first, summoned in 1063 by Pope Alexander II, southern Italians joined with Normans, Aquitanians, and nobles from Champagne. An army from southern France supported Alfonso VI of Castile in the first large advance southwards. His capture of Toledo in 1085 led to the establishment of a dependent Moslem prince as King of Valencia and opened the way into Murcia. The kings of the Taifas hastened to submit to Castile by treaty or by paying tribute, and Moslem domination in Spain appeared to be doomed.

The Almorávides

At that moment the Spanish Moslems summoned aid from northwestern Africa, where from Senegal to Algeria a new Mohammedan state had been formed by the Berber Almorávides under Yusuf ibn Tashfin. Landing at Algeciras, Yusuf marched northward to Zallacca, where in 1086 he defeated a Spanish-French army under Alfonso VI. This defeat called forth another French crusade, sponsored by Pope Urban II, the father of the crusades to the east. For a few years, while Yusuf and his son Ali were engrossed in reducing the Moslem princes in Spain to obedience, the Mohammedan advance was halted. Its resumption with the taking of Seville, Valencia, and Saragossa threatened Barcelona and called forth a new crusade from France. In 1118, with French help, the King of Aragon recovered Saragossa—the biggest success so far for the Christians. By this time the first crusade to the east was twenty years past. When Castilian kings were asked for aid in Syria and Palestine, they could reply, "We are always on crusade here, and so we do our share."

The Seljuk Turks in the eleventh century

The course of events in Asia Minor in the eleventh century was roughly parallel to that in Spain. After the Battle of Manzikert (1071) [2] the advance of the Seljuk Turks continued into western Asia Minor, Syria, and Palestine. Within a few years they were in possession of Nicæa, whither they moved the capital of the Sultanate of Rum. The nomads then took to the sea and captured the Greek

[2] See p. 142.

islands of Chios, Lesbos, Samos, and Rhodes. By 1085 not only most of Asia Minor but also Antioch and all Syria were lost to the Byzantine empire. The Turks had taken Jerusalem from the Fatimite caliphs of Egypt, with whom they were disputing the rest of Palestine. At the death of the Sultan Malik Shah in 1092, however, the

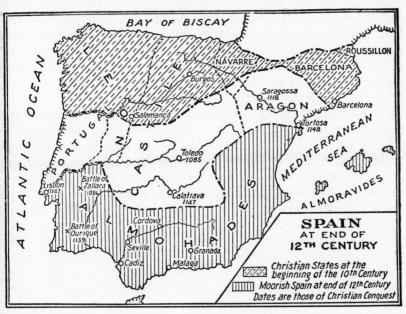

SPAIN
AT END OF
12TH CENTURY

///// Christian States at the beginning of the 10th Century

||||| Moorish Spain at end of 12th Century

Dates are those of Christian Conquest

Seljuk empire fell apart. The Sultanate of Rum in Asia Minor became practically an independent state, and the Turkish governors of the Syrian cities conducted themselves as they pleased. Jerusalem was recovered by the Egyptian caliph in 1098.

Just as the break-up of the Caliphate of Cordova after 1034 seemed to invite a new Christian offensive, so after 1092 the moment seemed propitious to the Byzantine emperor, Alexius Comnenus, to begin the recovery of his lost possessions. The power of Islam in the east, already weakened by the strife between the Sunnite [3] Turks and the Shiite caliphs at Cairo, was now paralyzed by the complete dissolution of the great empire of the Seljuk sultans. But the once mighty Byzantine empire, after its exhausting struggle for existence in the previous twenty years, was in no better position to undertake the attack on Islam alone than the little Christian principalities of Spain had been a century earlier. Once before a Byzantine emperor had appealed to

Alexius Comnenus appeals to the west

[3] See p. 170.

the west, through Pope Gregory VII, for the aid of mercenary troops. Now in 1095, after individual appeals to western nobles, Alexius Comnenus sent envoys to a council that Pope Urban II was holding at Piacenza, to implore help. Could not the crusade against Islam in the west be extended to the east?

Pilgrimages

Western Europe had long been concerned with the fate of Syria and Palestine, as the scene of the foundation of their faith and the land where the Lord Jesus and the Blessed Virgin Mary and many saints had lived. As early as the days of Constantine a pilgrimage to the Holy Land, though not a religious obligation, like the Mohammedan's pilgrimage to Mecca, was becoming the ambition of every Christian who could possibly hope to make the trip. Some pilgrims wrote accounts of their experiences, and guidebooks for pilgrims appeared very early. Pilgrimage to a shrine preserving the relics of a saint or housing some miracle-working image soon began to be imposed upon sinners as penance. It might be merely to some local shrine, or a more serious sin might entail the obligation to go a greater distance, for example, to the shrine of St. James at Compostella in Spain or to the scenes of the martyrdom of St. Peter and St. Paul at Rome. Longest, hardest, and always most meritorious was the pilgrimage to Jerusalem and other sacred places in the Holy Land. The great prevalence of pilgrimages, however, was not due wholly to either the piety or the sinfulness of medieval Christians. A pilgrimage was the best excuse to travel, and the cheapest way, for every Christian owed hospitality to a pilgrim. Young men, before resigning themselves to the hardships of a monk's life, betook themselves to Jerusalem if they could. The pilgrim's road might be long and arduous, but it was likely to be a merry one. Minstrels traveled its way; there were new sights, new faces, new stories, new songs; there might well be adventures. Indeed, St. Boniface protested much earlier that too many pilgrims were adventurers or vagabonds at best, or peddlers, or even fugitives from justice.

Neither the conquest of Syria and Palestine by the Arabs in the seventh century nor the later conquests of the Seljuk Turks interfered seriously with pilgrimages to the Holy Land. Although there were inevitably minor disturbances owing to personal fanaticism, under Mohammedan tolerance the number and size of pilgrimages actually increased. We are told of six in the eighth century, twelve in the ninth, sixteen in the tenth, and one hundred and seventeen in the eleventh. The largest mass pilgrimage before the first crusade, led by Gunther, Bishop of Bamberg, included at least seven thousand Ger-

Pilgrimages after the Mohammedan conquests

mans.[4] They went unarmed, but they were able to take care of themselves when attacked in Syria by a group of plundering Bedouins, thanks to Gunther. The Bedouin chieftain was no match for the Christian bishop. When, in the course of a conference, the chieftain took off his turban and threw it about Gunther's neck as a kind of lasso, the good bishop, in righteous indignation at this bold profanation of a man of God, knocked the Bedouin unconscious.

There is little evidence that people in western Europe were greatly exercised over the capture of Antioch and Jerusalem by the Turks. There was no reason to suppose that it would make much difference. But when all the arts of propaganda and rhetoric were turned loose upon them, they became aroused. They would rescue the holy places and the holy relics of the birth and infancy of their faith from the pollution of infidel hands; they would clear the pilgrim routes of the pollution of infidel feet. It has been said that the crusades at the start were pilgrims' progress as well as holy war.

The whole complex of motives that led to the crusades was embodied in Pope Urban II. The Spanish crusades he had sponsored not only as pope but as a Frenchman. He was a Cluniac monk, well acquainted with the ascetic spirit in the monasteries, now being quickened by the foundation of new orders, and with the heightened religious sensibility of the people of western Europe. He had been a devoted minister of Gregory VII, and remembered how, when Gregory received the appeal of the Byzantine emperor for help, he had thought most of all of the opportunity to reunite the Greek and Roman Churches after the final separation of 1054 [5]—with, of course, the pope once more the head of all Christendom. The crusade became a cardinal feature of the foreign policy of the papacy, and such it remained for over four hundred years. In 1095 Urban II thought not so much of rescuing the Byzantine empire from the Turks as of leading western Europe on a holy mission. The west was to act for itself, not merely in the interests of a schismatic emperor. There can be little doubt that the popes always conceived of the leadership of the crusading movement as one means of furthering their own political and ecclesiastical ends. The opportunity to order kings, to command the material resources of both clergy and secular princes, was one that the popes could no more resist than the German kings could resist the glamour of the imperial title. Finally, Urban II was en-

Urban II and papal policy

[4] For a complete and interesting account of this pilgrimage see Joranson, in *Essays Presented to D. C. Munro.*

[5] See p. 135.

gaged in the desperate investiture struggle. Did he perhaps think by the glorious distraction of a crusade to the east to facilitate his victory in the west?

Eagerness for the recovery of Syria and Palestine was first aroused by Urban II at the Council of Clermont in 1095, held soon after the council at Piacenza where he received the envoys of the Emperor Alexius Comnenus. His subtle speech, which has been called the most effective ever delivered, shows clearly that he well knew that he must appeal to something more tangible than religious fervor. As a Frenchman speaking to Frenchmen, he appealed to their vanity and to their glorious history. "Oh, race of Franks, race from across the mountains, race chosen and beloved by God—as shines forth in very many of your works—, set apart from all nations by the situation of your country as well as by your Catholic faith and the honor of the Holy Church . . . let the deeds of your ancestors move you and incite your minds to manly achievements; likewise, the glory and greatness of King Charles the Great and his son Louis and of your other kings, who have destroyed the kingdoms of the pagans and have extended in these lands the territory of the Holy Church."

Urban II at the Council of Clermont

As for the accursed and bastard race of Turks, "they destroy the altars, after having defiled them with their uncleanness. They circumcise the Christians, and the blood of the circumcision they either spread upon the altars or pour into the vases of the baptismal font. When they wish to torture people by a base death, they perforate their navels, and, dragging forth the end of the intestines, bind it to a stake; then with flogging they lead the victim around until his viscera have gushed forth, and he falls prostrate upon the ground."

Then with a more realistic note, the speaker went on to emphasize the great opportunity for worldly advancement. "Let none of your possessions detain you, no solicitude for your family affairs, since this land which you inhabit, shut in on all sides by the sea and surrounded by mountain peaks, is too narrow for your large population; nor does it abound in wealth; and it furnishes scarcely food enough for its cultivators. . . . Enter upon the road to the Holy Sepulchre; wrest that land from the wicked race and subject it to yourselves. That land which, as the Scripture says, 'floweth with milk and honey' was given by God into the possession of the children of Israel. Jerusalem is the navel of the world; the land is fruitful above others, like another paradise of delights."

No part of the pope's speech is of greater interest than his fierce diatribe against feudal society. He looked to the crusade also as a means of alleviating Europe's dreadful curse, the madness of private war. "You, girt about with the badge of knighthood, are arrogant with great pride; you rage against your brothers and cut each other in pieces. . . . You, the oppressors of children, plunderers of widows; you, guilty of homicide, of sacrilege, robbers of another's rights; you who await the pay of thieves for the shedding of Christian blood—as vultures smell fetid corpses, so do you sense battles from afar and rush to them eagerly. . . . If, forsooth, you wish to be mindful of your souls, either lay down the girdle of such knighthood or advance boldly, as knights of Christ, and rush as quickly as you can to the defence of the Eastern Church." [6]

Urban's large audience responded eagerly. "It is the will of God," they shouted, and kept this as their battle cry. They rushed forward to take the crusader's oath and sewed the sign of the cross on their garments. But the religious fervor of such a crowd was a different thing from the enthusiasm of the princes, upon whom the military success of the expedition depended. To the French nobles who led the first crusade war against the Infidel meant the same kind of opportunity for winning fame and fortune as the Norman conquest of England, southern Italy, and Sicily and the crusades in Spain. For great numbers of them, to be sure, the religious appeal was effective enough, but it was effective because it sanctified their ambition and greed. Urban II, however, did not stop with that. He promised that the journey to Jerusalem "should take the place of all penance" and accordingly insure eternal life. Later, as the crusading ardor itself waned, privileges to crusaders were increased. Their property was to be under the protection of the Church and subject to no lawsuits; their debts were to be free of interest. The religious enthusiasm of the moment, great and sincere as it was, could not last long enough to transform these doughty warriors into devoted servants of the Church or of any better master than themselves. Whatever else they may have done, the crusades made painfully clear how little Christianity, aside from its purely formal aspects, had touched the lives of the people of the west, and how hollow and superficial the pretensions of western chivalry were. The crusades were a phase of the political and economic expansion of western Europe, the medieval chapter in the history of imperialism.

The limitations of the religious appeal

The hysteria so artfully worked up at the Council of Clermont was augmented by further journeys of Urban II in France, and by the impassioned preaching of men like Peter the Hermit, who roused

The peasants' crusade

[6] The quotations are from Krey, *The First Crusade*, pp. 30 ff.

peasants and townsmen to participate in an affair for which they were totally unfitted. The stampede among the peasantry, who, even without their half-crazed devotion, would have welcomed any release from their circumscribed and oppressive life on the manor, emptied whole villages. In April 1096, mobs from northeastern France and western Germany poured up the Rhine valley, pillaging farmsteads and sacking Jewries as they went. After a march down the Danube through Hungary and the eastern part of the Balkan peninsula, equally hazardous to the native population and to themselves, these wretched bands at last reached Constantinople. They swarmed all over the city, looting and pillaging almost with impunity. This was hardly what Alexius Comnenus had expected in answer to his plea for help. The only thing to do with these hordes was to speed them on their way. They were hastily shipped across the Bosporus to Asia Minor, where most of them were promptly massacred by the Turks. Among the few who escaped was Peter the Hermit.

This first detachment from the west was a great enough disappointment to the emperor, and he had little reason to be any better pleased with the four main armies that arrived in Constantinople in the following winter and spring. Not one of the monarchs of the west answered the call of Urban II—neither William Rufus of England, nor Philip I of France, nor Henry IV of Germany. The response came largely from French nobles, knights, and adventurers. The French character thus imparted to the movement from the first was never lost: the crusades always bore the imprint of French civilization. Among the leading feudatories of France who took the cross were Count Robert of Flanders, Duke Robert of Normandy, who mortgaged his duchy to his brother William Rufus to raise the money to go, Count Hugh of Vermandois, brother of Philip I, and Count Stephen of Blois, the future King of England. None of these was, however, destined to play a distinguished part. The men who emerged as leaders were Godfrey of Bouillon, Duke of Lower Lorraine, his brother Baldwin, Raymond of St. Gilles, Count of Toulouse, the papal legate, Bishop Ademar of Puy, and Bohemund, son of the Norman Robert Guiscard of southern Italy. With Bohemund came his nephew Tancred. For all that has been and is yet to be said of the shabbiness of the crusades, it was nevertheless not so easy for these men to leave their homes on such a journey. To guard their possessions and to rear their children they had often enough to leave their wives behind, protected only by the walls of their castles, by their native wit, and by girdles of chastity.

The leaders of the first crusade

The crusaders' host was no army unified under one command; it was a collection of bands of vassals pledged to their respective lords. *The crusaders' army* There was little common purpose, except somehow to get to Jerusalem and rescue the Holy Land. Among the lords there were many cross-purposes, personal ambitions, and rivalries that often threatened to wreck the whole undertaking. The main groups from northern France, Lorraine, southern France, and southern Italy were ultimately joined by representatives from all Europe. "The Welshman left his hunting; the Scot his fellowship with lice; the Dane his drinking party; the Norwegian his raw fish." [7] Perhaps some twelve to fifteen thousand armed men finally reached Syria. With them went as many noncombatants: women and children, infants born en route, the sick and infirm, monks, clerks, priests. Nobody knew much about the land through which they must travel; none took care to provide the necessities for such a journey. The enemy was largely an unknown quantity; many felt that it was unnecessary to know his methods of fighting, so invincible was the western knight. The crusaders made their way to Constantinople by land, living off the countryside, to which they were a scourge no less terrible than the peasants had been. The Archbishop of Bulgaria wrote of their passage through his land: "My lips are compressed; first of all, the passage of the Franks [as the western crusaders were called in the east] or their invasion, as I know not how one may call it, has so affected and seized all of us that we do not even feel ourselves. We have drunk enough the bitter cup of invasion." [8]

The Byzantines felt that a horde of barbarians had descended upon them. Western Europe had by no means yet reached anything like the level of culture represented either by the Byzantine empire or by Islam in Syria and Palestine. The westerner was in truth entering into a land of wonders, of which he had but dimly dreamed, and which he was ill qualified to understand or appreciate. The cultivated Greek or Moslem looked down upon these boors from the west with scorn, and his disdain was not softened by any humility on the crusaders' part. One of them, in an audience granted by Alexius Comnenus, took the liberty during the tiresome ceremonial of sitting on the imperial throne. Count Baldwin upbraided him, but could not convert him to respect for court etiquette. To him the emperor was only "this rustic that keeps his seat, while . . . valiant captains are standing round him." This is the same attitude as that expressed in Liutprand's tenth-

Antagonism between east and west

[7] Quoted by Munro, *The Kingdom of the Crusaders*, p. 40.
[8] Quoted by Vasiliev, *History of the Byzantine Empire*, II, 53.

century account of his mission to Constantinople.[9] Meanwhile, still unrelieved by the understanding that comes from acquaintance, it had developed into something like mutual hatred. The stronger man felt his inferiority; the superior man felt his weakness.

Byzantine fear of the crusaders

But there was more behind this hatred than difference in the level of culture. Alexius Comnenus had already had experience with the peasant hordes of Peter the Hermit. What he had asked for was the aid of western mercenary troops; crusades like these were no idea of his. He was quick to recognize that his aims and those of the westerners were fundamentally divergent. He wished to recover Asia Minor from the Turks; they wished to reconquer and keep Syria and Palestine for themselves. The prospect of aggressive Latin states in the eastern Mediterranean was disagreeable to the emperor; he feared for his very throne. This crusading army had no less a person in it than Bohemund, son of that Robert Guiscard who not long since had attempted a march on Constantinople from Durazzo.[10] Anna Comnena, Alexius's daughter, who wrote vividly of the sojourn of the crusaders in Constantinople, saw the situation clearly. "The more astute, especially men like Bohemund and those of like mind, had another secret reason, namely, the hope that while on their travels they might by some means be able to seize the capital itself, finding a pretext for this." Alexius was careful to give instructions to his son "to take thought of accumulating enough to fill the open mouths of the barbarians, who breathe out hatred upon us, in case there rises up the force of a numerous army hurling lightnings angrily against us, at the same time that many of our enemies encircling our city rebel." [11] The Byzantines were equally well aware of the ambition of the Roman Church to bring the Greek Church under its control; the two had been separated only since 1054. Finally, the greed of Venice and other Italian mercantile towns for a larger share of trade with the east, which they could get only at the cost of Byzantium's own trade, was plain to the Greek emperors. They were quite right to fear the crusaders, who indeed eventually destroyed all but a remnant of the Byzantine empire.

The crusaders' oath to Alexius Comnenus

Alexius Comnenus was determined that the leaders of the crusading bands should at least take an oath of fealty to him, and swear to restore all lands they might conquer that had previously belonged to the empire. This proposal was perhaps made with the stipulation that

[9] See p. 136.
[10] See p. 142.
[11] Quoted by Vasiliev, *op. cit.*, II, 50.

the reconquered lands should be held by the crusaders as fiefs, and on condition that the emperor should assist in the reconquest. At any rate, after considerable difficulty the oath was taken by all the western leaders, who were then transported to Asia Minor. Of course such an oath, an absurdity from the beginning, soon proved to be quite meaningless. The crusaders went their own way, and the Byzantine empire for most of the time remained their enemy.

Accompanied by Greek troops, the crusaders first captured the *The march* Turkish capital at Nicæa in June 1097. They turned the city over to *to Syria* Alexius, as had been agreed; but they were infuriated when they were not permitted to plunder it, and some of them were outraged at the emperor's parsimony when he tried to mollify them with gifts. The capital of the Sultanate of Rum was moved back to Iconium. After clearing the way of Turks by a battle at Dorylæum in July, the crusaders pushed on over desolate roads to Syria with great but foolhardy courage, in much distress from hunger and thirst. "There most of our cavalry ceased to exist, because (thereafter) many of these became foot-soldiers. For want of horses many of our men used oxen in place of cavalry horses, and because of the very great need goats, sheep and dogs served as beasts of burden." [12] On the way they lost one of their leaders, Baldwin, who, at the invitation of the Christian *The Latin* Armenian ruler of Edessa, took possession of the city, married an *County of* Armenian princess, and was adopted by the ruler as his son. There *Edessa* he settled down to enjoy the fruits of his labor: for him the crusade was over. The County of Edessa was the first of the Latin states in the east; it became the bulwark of Syria against Turkish raids from Asia Minor.

In Syria the crusaders met nothing more formidable than the local opposition of Turkish governors left in possession of the cities at the break-up of the Seljuk empire. Before they finally captured Antioch, one hundred and sixty-five Syrian towns and fortresses fell into their hands. In the course of their seven months' siege of Antioch they *The capture* were aided by supplies and siege equipment brought by a Genoese *of Antioch* fleet, which continued to co-operate with them as they moved down the coast. By this time "the poor began to leave, and many rich who feared poverty." Finally, with the aid of a traitor within the gates Bohemund's troops entered the city on June 3, 1098. But while "engaged in counting and identifying their spoils," after they "had desisted from the siege of the citadel and, listening to the pagan danc-

---

[12] Quoted by Munro, *op. cit.*, p. 47.

ing girls, feasted in splendor and magnificence," [13] they were shut up in the city for twenty-six days by the Turkish Governor of Mosul. Had he arrived four days sooner, "it is not improbable that the crusading movement would have been extinguished at the gates of Antioch." [14]

In the course of the siege Stephen of Blois escaped and started for home. On his way he met Alexius Comnenus coming to relieve the city, and told him of the situation; thereupon the emperor abandoned the crusaders to their fate. But fate was kind. Stirred by what many believed to be the miraculous discovery of the lance that had pierced the Savior's side, the crusaders, bearing the lance before them, beat off the siege. Antioch was saved and the crusade assured of success, although it was another year before the remains of the army stood before the walls of Jerusalem.

Meanwhile Bohemund had determined that Antioch belonged to him, not to Alexius or to any of his colleagues. After much quarreling among the leaders he was left in possession of the city, and the *Bohemund* Principality of Antioch, the second of the states of the crusaders, was *founds the* founded. Bohemund did not then go on to Jerusalem. Instead, he *Principality* launched a campaign of conquest at the expense of the Byzantine *of Antioch* empire in southeastern Asia Minor. Not long afterwards, leaving his nephew Tancred in Antioch, he went back to Italy to organize an attack, like his father's, on Byzantium from the west across the Balkan peninsula. The Genoese were richly repaid for their services, "with the church of St. John . . . together with the warehouse and cistern and thirty houses which are in the square beside the said church, with all their appurtenances, free of all claims and customs."

Led by Raymond of Toulouse, the rest of the crusaders marched down the Syrian coast without opposition, and appeared before Jerusalem early in June 1099. With the aid of the Genoese fleet, now stationed at Jerusalem's port of Joppa, they took the city from its Egyptian garrison on July 15, 1099. With a pathological fury the Christians prepared a holocaust for their God. "When the hour approached on which our Lord Jesus Christ deigned to suffer on the Cross for us . . . one of our knights, named Lethold, clambered up the wall of the city. . . . Our men followed, killing and slaying even *The capture* to the Temple of Solomon, where the slaughter was so great that *of Jerusalem* our men waded in blood up to their ankles. . . . The battle raged throughout the day, so that the Temple was covered with their [the

[13] Quoted *ibid.*, p. 50.
[14] Stevenson, in *Cambridge Medieval History*, V, 292.

Saracens'] blood. When the pagans had been overcome, our men seized great numbers, both men and women, either killing them or keeping them captive, as they wished. . . . Afterward the army scattered throughout the city and took possession of the gold and silver, the horses and mules, and the houses filled with goods of all kinds. Later all of our people went to the Sepulchre of our Lord, rejoicing and weeping for joy, and they rendered up the offering that they owed. In the morning some of our men cautiously ascended to the roof of the Temple and attacked the Saracens, both men and women, beheading them with naked swords; the remainder sought death by jumping down into the Temple."

Another chronicler reports that "the amount of blood that they shed on that day is incredible. . . . Wonderful sights were to be seen. Some of our men (and this was more merciful) cut off the heads of their enemies; other shot them with arrows, so that they fell from the towers; others tortured them longer by casting them into the flames. Piles of heads, hands and feet were to be seen in the streets of the city. It was necessary to pick one's way over the bodies of men and horses. But these were small matters compared to what happened at the Temple of Solomon, a place where religious services are ordinarily chanted . . . men rode in blood up to their knees and bridle reins. Indeed, it was a just and splendid judgment of God that this place should be filled with the blood of the unbelievers, since it had suffered so long from their blasphemies. The city was filled with corpses and blood." After the sack of the city the leaders "ordered all the Saracen dead to be cast outside because of the great stench, since the whole city was filled with their corpses; and so the living Saracens dragged the dead before the exits of the gates and arranged them in heaps, as if they were houses. No one ever saw or heard of such slaughter of pagan people, for funeral pyres were formed from them like pyramids, and no one knows their number except God alone." [15] An attempt by the Egyptian caliph to recover Jerusalem was thwarted by the crusaders in August near Ascalon. After that a large number of them returned home.

When the Christians had achieved what was destined to be their only great success in Syria and Palestine, the question was, how to make these acquisitions permanent. Obviously, possession of the coast towns was necessary to assure the constant flow of pilgrims and supplies indispensable for the security of the new principalities. The only ships available for such a conquest were the navies of the Italian *Co-operation with Italian cities to take the coastal towns*

[15] From Krey, *op. cit.*, pp. 256 ff.

towns of Genoa, Pisa, and Venice. The shrewd merchants who controlled these towns were not the men to sell their services cheaply. The Venetians, appearing at Joppa in 1100, "bargained to aid the crusading hosts from June 24 to August 15, 1100, on condition that they should have a church and a market place in every city, both on the seashore and in the interior, which the Christians held or might conquer. If any cities were captured jointly by the Crusaders and the Venetians, the latter should have one-third of the booty in each city. If Tripolis should be taken, the booty should be divided, and the Venetians should have the whole city in return for a small annual payment. . . . In addition, the Venetians should be exempted from all taxes in all cities in the possession of Jerusalem." [16] Tripolis was taken in 1109 by the son of Raymond of Toulouse and his nephew but without the help of the Venetians. When Tyre was taken in 1124 the Venetians were promised one-third of the city and its surrounding territory, a trading quarter in Jerusalem, exemption from customs and tolls in all territory belonging to Jerusalem, and special judicial privileges in Tyre. With Genoese help Arsuf and Cæsarea were taken in 1101, the Genoese being promised a section in each city and one third of the booty. In addition Acre, Sidon, Beirut, Haifa, Ascalon, Tortosa, Jubayl, and Laodicea were captured. Elim on the Red Sea was taken and held until 1170. After many of these sieges promises made to the townspeople that they might depart in safety were violated. Instead, the inhabitants were massacred, and the ripping open of dead bodies to recover the gold the victims were supposed to have swallowed was common.

Of the three Italian towns mentioned, Pisa took the least part in the conquests. Amalfi had already established colonies in Syrian sea ports before the beginning of the crusades. While Christian control of these places was important for the maintenance of the crusaders' states, nevertheless, in their exploiting of the east the commercial colonies were quite free from any control by the crusaders' governments. They were responsible only to their home governments, and aided the Latin princes only when and as they pleased. In fact, they proved to be a hindrance to the stability of the Christian states, for with the coast towns once in Christian hands, the astute Italian merchants were more interested in peace with the Infidels than in any holy war.

The political organization set up by the crusaders in the east could only be a reproduction of the feudal monarchy that they had known

[16] Munro, *op. cit.*, pp. 67–68.

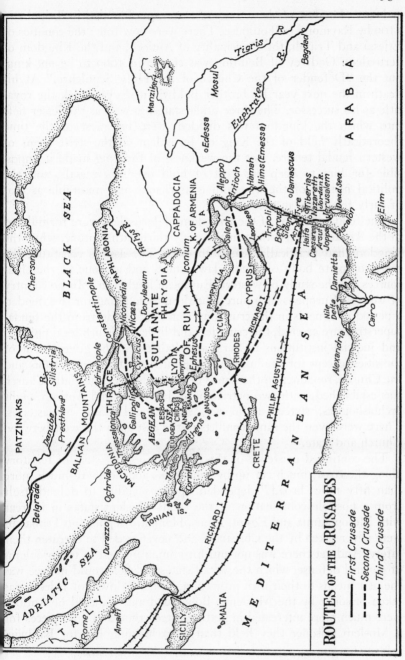

ROUTES OF THE CRUSADES

—— First Crusade
－－－ Second Crusade
┼┼┼ Third Crusade

at home. The last of the crusaders' states was founded in Tripolis in 1109 by Raymond of Toulouse. There were now four: the counties of Edessa and Tripoli, the Principality of Antioch, and the Kingdom of Jerusalem. Godfrey of Bouillon was chosen in 1099 to be not king, but the "Defender of the Church of the Holy Sepulchre." At his death in the next year his brother Baldwin of Edessa took the royal title as his successor. The three other states, as well as the lesser fiefs into which the kingdom was divided, were for most of the time theoretically held of the King of Jerusalem on the strict terms of western feudal tenure. But the weakness of the king made it impossible for him to keep any sort of hold over his vassals, and the political history of the kingdom is as chaotic and miserable as that of early feudalism in the west.

The Latin Kingdom of Jerusalem

The feudal customs of the Kingdom of Jerusalem were formulated in the Assizes of Jerusalem in the early thirteenth century, when the kingdom had practically ceased to exist. The assizes constitute the most complete body of feudal law extant, and are one of the chief sources for the study of western European feudalism. "In no country of western Europe is such pure feudalism to be found for so extended a period of time as in the crusading states." [17] Aside from the feudal superstructure erected, the crusaders did little to disturb local political and judicial institutions in Syria and Palestine. The government of the cities, except for the immunities granted to Italian merchants and the Church, remained in the hands of local officials. The Latin Church was established, with two patriarchs at Jerusalem and Antioch, eight archbishoprics, sixteen bishoprics, and several Latin monasteries. There were even the same conflicts in the east as in the west between Church and state.

The Assizes of Jerusalem

The continued existence of this "long straggling strip of territory along the coast, much cut up by mountains and nowhere much more than fifty miles broad," depended upon its ability to defend itself from a possible combination of the small Moslem states in its rear with Mesopotamia and Egypt. Hims, Hamah, Aleppo, and Damascus were never taken by the Christians, and never ceased to threaten their safety. And yet there was not much common interest in the problems of general defense, which the vassal states and fiefs could not see was the best means to their own protection. When Baldwin of Edessa was taken prisoner by the Moslems, Bohemund and Tancred of Antioch were much more interested in getting fifteen thousand gold pieces for a Moslem prisoner they held than in exchanging her for Baldwin.

[17] La Monte, *Feudal Monarchy in the Latin Kingdom of Jerusalem*, p. 243.

Peter's Gate at Assisi

defenders' passage on the walls of Rothenburg

The market place at Hildesheim. The house of Butchers' Gild is in background

The Town Hall at Perugia

The Gothic Rathaus (Town Hall) at Münster

Medieval houses of Gothic half-timber construction at Hildesheim

As in the west, the nobles were generally at war with one another, and they did not hesitate to make alliances with Turkish rulers and generals against their Christian neighbors.

The kings of Jerusalem could not rely upon feudal service, and, even had they been able to do so, there were altogether only seven hundred knights and five thousand foot soldiers to muster. They supplemented their feudal army by a small standing army, maintained *The defense of* by fiefs of money or goods in kind, and enrolled native archers, *the kingdom* engineers, and cavalry as mercenaries. A stream of pilgrims from the west for Easter and Christmas, composed in part of men who wanted a little military experience against the Moslems, periodically swelled their forces. The chief defense of the kingdom was always the magnificent castles, built at tremendous cost and effort, which utilized all the engineering resources and skill of the Byzantines and the Saracens. The famous Krak of the Knights (*Krak des Chevaliers*) commanded the caravan route from Hims or Hamah to Tripolis or Tortosa. Kerak and Montreal beyond the Jordan dominated the caravan route from Egypt to Damascus and the pilgrim route from Damascus to Medina and Mecca. Scandalion stood on the coastal route between Tyre and Acre. Yet these castles were in the hands of semi-independent vassals or of the wholly independent military orders, not in the hands of the king. For a time they successfully defended the crusaders' states, but the frequent plundering of caravans did much to exacerbate the naturally strained relations between Christians and Moslems.

The Kingdom of Jerusalem found its most reliable soldiers in that strange combination of chivalry and monasticism, the military orders of the Templars and the Hospitalers. It is remarkable how the institution of monasticism always came forward to defend the interests of the Church at critical moments. In this instance it is the more remarkable in that for the first time monks fought the battles of this world in armor instead of remaining isolated within the cloister to fight the spirit's battles with the devil.

The Knights Templars owed their origin to a French knight, Hugh *The Knights* of Payens, who about the year 1119 joined with him a few other *Templars* knights to act as guides and protectors of pilgrims on the way to the Holy Land and as warriors in its defense. They took their name from the quarters given them by the King of Jerusalem near the Temple of Solomon. In 1128 their organization was confirmed by the Council of Troyes and by Pope Honorius III. St. Bernard drew up a rule for them, based on the rule of his own reformed order, the Cistercians.[18]

[18] See p. 613.

He also wrote a special treatise, "In Praise of the New Chivalry," in which he said of the new order: "Never is an idle word or useless deed or immoderate laughter or a murmur, if it be but whispered, allowed to go unpunished. Draughts and dice they detest. Hunting they hold in abomination, and take no pleasure in the frivolous pastime of hawking. Soothsayers, jesters and story-tellers, ribald songs and stage plays they eschew as insane follies. They cut close the hair, knowing, as the apostle says, that 'it is a shame for a man to have long hair.' They never dress gaily, and wash but seldom. Shaggy by reason of their uncombed hair, they are also begrimed with dust, and swarthy from the weight of their armour and the heat of the sun. They strive earnestly to possess strong and swift horses, but not garnished with ornaments or decked with trappings, thinking of battle and victory, not of pomp and show." [19] The Knights Templars wore a white outer robe decorated with a red cross.

The Hospitalers and the Teutonic Knights

The Knights of the Hospital of St. John of Jerusalem, generally called simply the Hospitalers, came from the founding by merchants from Amalfi of a hospital for the comfort of pilgrims; this was even before the Seljuk Turks took the Holy City. After the capture of Jerusalem by the crusaders the Hospitalers engaged in actual nursing of the sick and wounded. About the time of the founding of the Templars they added the task of fighting in defense of the holy places to their other duties, and thenceforth became primarily a military order. The Teutonic Knights, or Order of the Knights of the Hospital of St. Mary of the Teutons in Jerusalem, exclusively a German order, had their beginning about the same time as the Hospitalers; they were originally associated with them, but soon after the loss of Jerusalem to the Turks in 1187 they became a wholly distinct military order. The Hospitalers wore a black robe with a white cross, the Teutonic Knights a white robe with a black cross.

The organization and development of the military orders

The military orders took the regular monastic vows, though not necessarily for life, and dedicated themselves to a life of fighting. They were organized in three distinct ranks: the knights proper, who could be recruited only from the nobility; the chaplains; and the serving brothers, corresponding to the lay brothers in ordinary monasteries, who need not be noble but must be free-born, and who served as squires to the knights and as servants in the hospitals. The houses of these orders were not confined to the Holy Land; they were established as recruiting stations in the seaports of western Europe and throughout the land. The orders perfected a centralized

[19] Munro, *op. cit.*, p. 99.

organization of commanderies, priories, and local chapters and utilized a system of representation for the election of officers, who could be chosen only from the knights proper. They were by no means neglected by the generosity of those of the faithful who did not themselves take the cross, and so, like the other monastic orders, they grew wealthy in land. Moreover, the Teutonic Knights and the Templars acquired large trading privileges and soon were doing a thriving business. The Templars especially took advantage of the new and growing need for banking services, in part due to the crusades, and became the leading bankers of Europe (they have already been seen serving the French monarchy in this capacity).

With the loss of the Holy Land to the Moslems the military orders lost their *raison d'être*. Under such circumstances it was inevitable that they should deteriorate, or at any rate greatly change, in character. Ultimately they suffered various fates.[20] Even as defenders of the Holy Land they were no unmitigated blessing, although, especially in the earlier years of the Kingdom of Jerusalem, they were indispensable. They fought with one another in intense rivalry, often in alliance with Moslem princes. Since they were responsible not to the King of Jerusalem but only to the pope—to whom they were ultimately responsible, in so far as they acknowledged any authority outside their own organization—they found it easy to act with complete independence, and took full advantage of their privileged position.

Jerusalem remained in Christian hands until 1187. From the outset the disunity of the Moslems did more than castles and soldiers to preserve the small military aristocracy of Christians from the consequences of their folly: their internecine strife, their intriguing with Greeks and Moslems against one another, the rivalries of the military orders and of merchants from different Italian cities. But the intermittent harrying of the eastern borders of the Kingdom of Jerusalem finally provoked the Moslems to seek strength in union. The first steps were taken by Zangi, the atabek, or lieutenant, of the Governor of Mosul; he took Aleppo and Hamah from their Moslem rulers, and then in 1144 destroyed the oldest of the Latin states in the east, the County of Edessa, by virtually wiping out the city of Edessa.

The fall of Edessa

When the news of this disaster reached the west, the pope asked St. Bernard to undertake the preaching of a new crusade. "You have

---

[20] For the Templars, see pp. 509, 959; for the Teutonic Knights, pp. 937 ff. In Spain similar conditions called for the Spanish military orders of Calatrava (1164), Aviz (1166), St. James of Compostella (1175), and Alcantara (1183).

commanded," wrote the abbot; "I have obeyed. Because of my preaching towns and castles are empty of inhabitants, seven women can
scarcely find one man." His preaching was so effective that this time
two kings were induced to take the cross, Louis VII of France [21] and
Conrad III of Germany. There is a story that Conrad was persuaded
to go, although he had made up his mind not to, by listening to St.
Bernard's appeal in Latin, a language that he could not understand.

*The second
crusade*

By the spring of 1147 the two kings were leading their armies along
the old crusaders' road down the Danube to Constantinople. The German army went ahead, to avoid friction with their Christian brethren,
and pillaged and robbed and stripped the country so thoroughly that
the French, following them, suffered greatly from lack of provisions.
The Byzantine Emperor Manuel, with a well-grounded suspicion
of crusaders, ordered the fortifications of Byzantium strengthened.
And, indeed, Louis VII was in touch with Byzantium's old enemy,
Roger II of Sicily, who, while the crusade was in progress, seized
Greek islands in the Adriatic and invaded Greece, sacking Thebes,
Corinth, and Athens.

After repeating the mistake of choosing the land rather than the
sea route to the east, the two kings avoided few of the other mistakes
of the first crusade. Most of the German army was destroyed in Asia
Minor, and the French army suffered almost as badly. "The description of the faults of the Frank as a soldier which Maurice wrote
in 580 and Leo the Wise repeated in 900 might still be utilized almost word for word in describing the Crusaders of 1150." [22] With
fragments of their armies the two kings finally reached the Holy
Land by sea the next year. Here they received a strange welcome
from the Christian princes, who seemed to feel no need of allies or
assistance. An agreement was made to attack Damascus. Then, as
Conrad III wrote, "when we had gone to Damascus and . . . pitched
our camps before the gate of the city, it was certainly near being
taken. But certain ones . . . treasonably asserted that the city was
impregnable on that side, and hastily led us to another position where
no water could be supplied for the troops and where access was impossible to anyone. And thus all, equally indignant and grieved, returned, leaving the undertaking uncompleted. Nevertheless, they all
promised unanimously that they would make an expedition against
Ascalon, and they set the place and time. Having arrived there according to agreement, we found scarcely anyone. In vain we waited

[21] See p. 479.
[22] Oman, *The Art of War in the Middle Ages*, p. 250.

eight days for the troops. Deceived a second time, we turned to our own affairs." [23]

Conrad went home, stopping on the way at Constantinople, where he made an alliance with Manuel against the Normans. Louis VII, who was having his troubles with Eleanor, and whom his chief minister, the Abbot Suger, was urgently entreating to return, left for home by way of Rome.[24] The crusade had accomplished absolutely nothing except the needless destruction of thousands of human lives. St. Bernard's dismay put his faith to the test: "We have fallen on evil days, in which the Lord, provoked by our sins, has judged the world, with justice indeed, but not with his wonted mercy. . . . The sons of the Church have been overthrown in the desert, slain with the sword, or destroyed by famine. . . . The judgments of the Lord are righteous, but this one is an abyss so deep that I must call him blessed who is not scandalized therein." [25]

Moslem recovery, once begun, continued without interruption. In 1154 the capture of Damascus by Zangi's son Nureddin brought all the Moslem cities of Syria under one hand. Both Nureddin and the King of Jerusalem recognized that the issue between Christian and Moslem depended upon which of the two should seize possession of Egypt, where the Fatimite caliphs were tottering. In 1164 Nureddin sent a Turkish army under Shirkuh to Egypt to support one of the rival political factions there. In time Shirkuh made himself vizier, and when he died he was succeeded by his nephew Saladin, who had long been associated with the Moslem revival. Saladin was destined to *The rise of* complete the union of the Mohammedan east; he now devoted his *Saladin* efforts to the pacification of Egypt. When the last Fatimite caliph died in 1171, he took control of the country; three years later, at the death of Nureddin, he restored Egypt to the orthodox caliphs at Bagdad and became sultan at Cairo. By 1183 he had brought the Moslem cities of Syria and Mesopotamia under his control, and ruled from the Euphrates to the Nile as "King of all Oriental Kings." The little Christian states were at last surrounded by a united Islam.

"When God gave me the land of Egypt," Saladin said, "I was sure that he meant Palestine for me also." So far from the Christian princes making any last attempt to unite in the face of their doom, they let the Kingdom of Jerusalem be torn by the pettiest kind of bickering over the succession to the throne. The inevitable war was

[23] *Translations and Reprints*, I, no. 4, p. 14.
[24] See p. 479.
[25] Quoted in Munro, *op. cit.*, p. 136.

*Reginald of
Châtillon*

precipitated by the exploits of a French adventurer, Reginald of
Châtillon, who had come to the east with Louis VII. He had taught
the Patriarch of Antioch to mind his own business by having him
"scourged and then bound naked on the highest tower [of the city],
after smearing honey on his bald head and the wounds made by the
scourge." He had led an expedition against Cyprus and had almost
succeeded in capturing Mecca and Medina. Now he was vassal of the
King of Jerusalem for the fief beyond the Jordan, containing the
castles of Kerak and Montreal. Violating a truce of the king with
Saladin, he plundered an Egyptian caravan supposed to be escorting
Saladin's sister. The sultan vowed to kill him with his own hands if
he ever got hold of him.

Saladin did just that in 1187, after annihilating a Christian army
near Nazareth. Within a few months the kings of Jerusalem had left
of their kingdom the lone city of Tyre. Jerusalem itself Saladin
forced to surrender, on rather lenient terms. When the Infidels recovered the city that the Christians had "filled with corpses and

*The fall of
Jerusalem*

blood" in 1099, there was no slaughter. When the rich Christians,
after ransoming themselves from slavery, displayed almost complete
indifference to ransoming the poorer Christians, and after the patriarch, the head of the Christian Church in the Holy City, had hustled
away with his own wealth and the plate and treasure of the churches,
Saladin released at least three thousand persons without ransom and
liberated all the aged. Christian refugees from the city on their flight
northward were "refused admittance to Tripolis (still in Christian
hands), and were robbed by their fellow Christians of the property
which Saladin had allowed them to carry away." [26] Even the crusaders
had to admit that this Mohammedan possessed every quality of a
Christian knight.

The fall of Jerusalem called forth the third crusade. Despite the
pope's attempts to assume control, it was perhaps even more a kings'
affair than the second crusade had been, and only somewhat less

*The third
crusade*

futile. After Frederick Barbarossa failed in his attempt to lead a
united Europe to the east, he led his own well-organized and carefully provisioned German army over the land route through Hungary
and the Balkans. They spent the winter of 1189–90 in Thrace, while
"the whole city of Constantinople shivered with fright, thinking that
its destruction and the extermination of its population were near."
Through Asia Minor the German army advanced, suffering greatly

[26] *Ibid.,* p. 168.

but without serious mishap, until Frederick was drowned in Cilicia.[27] Many of the German knights then turned back; the rest were led on by Barbarossa's younger son, Duke Frederick of Swabia, to be joined by the English and French troops before Acre—the first two armies to have taken the sea route to the east.

Richard Lionhearted and Philip Augustus, neither of whom would have left the other at home to go on any crusade, naturally could not accomplish anything by working together. They quarreled almost continually from the time they left home. "The two kings and peoples did less together than they would have done apart, and each set but light store by the other." On his way Richard stopped at Messina to attempt to thwart the Emperor Henry VI's plan to conquer southern Italy and Sicily; [28] he then stopped to take Cyprus from a Byzantine usurper (he later presented it to the impoverished King of Jerusalem). He hove in sight of Acre in June 1191, where he found Philip Augustus already arrived. After a siege of over a year and a half by Guy of Lusignan, the King of Jerusalem, Acre—or St. Jean d'Acre— fell on July 12. This time no slaughter of the Moslems was at first *The crusaders recover Acre* contemplated; but "when the ransom was not paid promptly, Richard . . . ordered twenty-seven hundred of his hostages to be led out and slaughtered in cold blood before the eyes of the other Moslems. . . . And his Christian chronicler added, 'Nor was there any delay. The king's followers leapt forward eager to fulfill the commands, and thankful to the Divine Grace that permitted them to take such vengeance.' " [29]

The capture of Acre and Joppa and Ascalon was the meager result of the expedition of three royal armies to the east. Philip Augustus returned home as soon as he found a plausible excuse, although he left troops behind him. Richard, in spite of many single-handed feats of valor, which made him the darling of romance, failed to take Jerusalem. After pushing Saladin hard in battle, he concluded a three-year truce with him in 1192. He could not forget that Philip Augustus was already back in France, where he himself should be. He then set out on a long journey home, interrupted by shipwreck and then by his capture by Henry VI, who held him for ransom.[30]

By the terms of the truce the King of Jerusalem retained the strip

---

[27] See p. 406.
[28] See p. 409.
[29] Munro, *op. cit.*, p. 168.
[30] See p. 410.

of coast from Joppa to Acre, and Christians were to be free of hindrance in visiting Jerusalem—a concession that Saladin would have granted at any time without bloodshed. Saladin died in 1193, without having realized his dream of driving the Latin princes from the east: besides what remained of the Kingdom of Jerusalem, Antioch and Tripoli were still Christian principalities. But he had recovered Jerusalem, which, except for a few years under Frederick II, was to be in Christian hands no more, until 1917.

The fourth crusade

Neither the failure of the third crusade nor the cutting short of Henry VI's plans to invade the east [31] had any effect on the policy of such a pope as Innocent III. He was determined to recover for the papacy the direction of the crusading movement. He cannot have realized that his success in flogging distressed western Christendom into a new effort to win the Holy Land would only provide an opportunity for the enemies of the Byzantine empire to join in a piratical raid on Constantinople. This expedition, usually dignified by the inappropriate name of fourth crusade, was the one successful western invasion of the east after the capture of Jerusalem in 1099. For the knights who participated in it, it was the booty-collecting and career-making exploit *par excellence* of the middle ages. For the clergy of the Roman Church it was an opportunity to rob the Greek Church of wealth and property and to pilfer its treasure of sacred relics. And when we come to the participation of the Venetians in the pious venture, we enter into the sordid atmosphere of modern imperialism. The fourth crusade throws a glaring light on several facets of western European society at the beginning of the thirteenth century.

Innocent III summons the crusade

Innocent III's appeal to the princes of western Europe is reminiscent of the eloquence of Urban II at Clermont. "Our enemies," he says, "insult us and say, 'Where is your God who can free from our hands neither Himself nor you? We have polluted your sanctuaries, put forth our hands against the objects of your adoration, and violently attacked the Holy Land. In spite of you we keep in our hands your fathers' cradle of superstition. . . . What has all this valor which you sent against us accomplished? Where is your God? Let Him rise and help you! Let Him show how he protects you and Himself!' " And Innocent adds, "Indeed, that which they say is partly the very truth." [32] This time, however, no kings answered the call: Philip Augustus and John of England were busy warring against each other, and Germany was torn with civil war. Again, as in answer

[31] See p. 411.
[32] Quoted in Vasiliev, *op. cit.*, II, 111–12.

to Urban II's summons, the chief response came from French nobles
and knights, notably the counts of Champagne, Blois, and Flanders;
but there were also English, German, and Sicilian troops. Along with

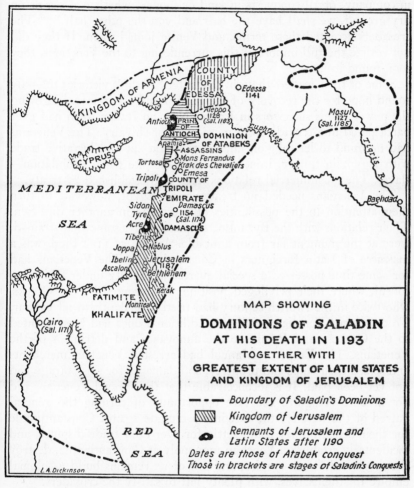

MAP SHOWING

DOMINIONS OF SALADIN

AT HIS DEATH IN 1193

TOGETHER WITH

GREATEST EXTENT OF LATIN STATES
AND KINGDOM OF JERUSALEM

– – – Boundary of Saladin's Dominions

▨ Kingdom of Jerusalem

⬤ Remnants of Jerusalem and
Latin States after 1190

Dates are those of Atabek conquest
Those in brackets are stages of Saladin's Conquests

L. A. Dickinson

all the others, fortunately for us, went an honest knight from Champagne, Geoffrey of Villehardouin, who has left us a full and naïve
account of the whole amazing business.

The leaders, having decided to follow the example of the third *Venice joins*
crusade in avoiding the difficulties and dangers of the land route, *the crusade*
began negotiations with Venice for food and transport. This the
Venetians offered for eighty-five thousand marks. "And this will we

do, moreover," blind Henry Dandolo, the astute old Doge of Venice, told the envoys of the crusaders: "For the love of God we will add to the fleet fifty armed galleys, on condition that, so long as we act in company, of all conquests in land or money, whether at sea or on dry ground, we shall have the half and you the other half." [33] The crusaders accepted these terms, and Venice joined them. If they did not realize the full import of this surrendering to the Venetians, they soon found it out.

Some of their leaders thought that after Saladin's victories the only sound hope for the recovery of the Holy Land lay in first destroying the power of his successors in Egypt. Now no Italian town had ever participated in a crusade from mere piety or chivalry. The Venetians had no mind to let religion imperil their ancient and lucrative trade with Egypt in timber, iron, arms, and—despite papal prohibition—slaves. These commercial relations were well established by treaty.

The Venetians needed no treaties with Egypt, however, to turn their attention to the possibilities of a crusade in another direction. Their relations with the Byzantine empire, always somewhat strained, were at the moment far from amicable. As late as 1182 there was a *Venice and* massacre of Latin foreigners in Constantinople. The Venetians had *Byzantium* for some time possessed a special quarter in the city under their own consul, where their privileged position was resented by the Greeks, who twice in the twelfth century had tried to shake them off by war. To counteract Venetian privileges, additional ones had been granted to the Genoese and Pisans, to the annoyance and detriment of the Venetians. The Emperor Manuel had arrested Venetian merchants and seized their ships and property, and damages for this outrage had not yet been paid. It is inconceivable that the shrewd Venetians did not at once recognize the rare opportunity of turning the general hatred of the west for the east into a crusade against Constantinople for their benefit. They could settle for ever their trade disputes, and incidentally establish a Venetian monopoly at Constantinople, destroy the moribund Greek empire, and out of its remains build a colonial empire for themselves, with plenty left to satisfy the crusaders.

The crusade was ready to start from Venice, but the crusaders could not carry out their part of the hard bargain: of the eighty-five thousand marks due, thirty-four thousand, according to Villehardouin, still remained to be paid. The Venetians may never have expected to be paid in full; perhaps they preferred not to be. At any rate, the doge was ready with a plan for liquidating the debt. The town of

[33] Villehardouin, *The Fourth Crusade* (Everyman's Edition), p. 6.

Zara on the Dalmatian coast stood in the way of Venetian control of the Adriatic. It had formerly belonged to Venice, but a revolt had turned the city over to the Christian King of Hungary. This was Dandolo's plan: "Let us . . . ask them to help us reconquer it, and we will remit the payment of the debt of thirty-four thousand marks of silver, until such time as it shall please God to allow us to gain the moneys by conquest, we and they together." Though not without protest, the crusaders nevertheless agreed, their resources being nearly exhausted.

The destruction of Zara by the crusaders

Pope Innocent III was furious at the idea of attacking a Christian city that was itself prepared to join the crusade, and that belonged to a Christian king who had himself taken the cross. But he could not stop the gorgeous fleet that sailed forth from the lagoons of Venice. "The Doge had with him fifty galleys, all at his own charges. The galley in which he himself sailed was all vermilion, and there was a pavilion of red satin stretched above his head. And there were before him four trumpets of silver that trumpeted, and cymbals that made joy and merriment. . . . Never before had . . . so fine a fleet been seen. And then the pilgrims caused all the priests and clerks there present to get up into the castles of the ships and sing the *Veni Creator Spiritus*, and all, both the great and the small folk, wept for great joy and happiness. . . . It seemed as if the whole sea swarmed with ants, and the ships burned on the water, and the water itself were aflame with the great joy that they had." [34] And Villehardouin cannot help exclaiming, as he recalls the loading of the ships, "Oh God! what fine war-horses!"

Zara was taken and destroyed in November 1202. Innocent III now excommunicated the crusaders *en masse*. "Instead of reaching the Promised Land, you thirsted for the blood of your brethren. . . . The inhabitants of Zara hang crucifixes upon the walls. In spite of the Crucified you have stormed the city and forced it to surrender." Notwithstanding, he proceeded to release the crusaders from the ban, and did not forbid them to associate with the still excommunicated Venetians. Thus began the fourth crusade.

Meanwhile, new developments gave to the muddled aims of the participants a direction hitherto lacking. The Byzantine Emperor Isaac II, Angelus, had been dethroned and blinded by his brother Alexius III in 1195. Some years later Isaac II's son, also named Alexius, sent to his brother-in-law, Philip of Swabia, for help to restore his father to the throne. Philip was then engaged in a bitter

[34] *Ibid.*, p. xxiv.

The inter-
vention of
Philip
of Swabia

struggle with Otto of Brunswick for the German throne; [35] but he delegated an embassy to the crusaders at Zara appealing to them to sail to Byzantium and restore young Alexius and his father before proceeding with the crusade. Extravagant promises were made: the Greek Church was to be united with the Roman; Alexius was to pay the Venetians the balance of the crusaders' debt, furnish them money and provisions and ten thousand men for conquering Egypt, and also supply five hundred men as a permanent guard in the Holy Land. Again there were many protests, but again the crusaders agreed. What had happened? Was the German king trying to use the crusade as a weapon in his warfare against the papacy? Was another German emperor dreaming the old imperial dream of subjecting the Byzantine empire to the Holy Roman empire? Was it German intrigue as well as Venetian guile that diverted the crusade to Constantinople? We cannot tell.

The crusade
turns aside to
Constantinople

We know only that in May 1203, the Venetians and the crusaders, with Alexius, set sail for Byzantium from Corfu, which they took for Alexius from the Byzantine emperor. "And the day was fine and clear, and the wind soft and favourable, and they unfurled all their sails to the breeze. . . . Never was yet seen so fair a sight. And well might it appear that such a fleet would conquer and gain lands, for, as far as the eye could reach, there was no space without sails and ships and vessels, so that the hearts of men rejoiced greatly." In a month they were before Constantinople. "Now you may know that those who had never before seen Constantinople looked upon it very earnestly, for they never thought there could be in all the world so rich a city; and they marked the high walls and strong towers that enclosed it round about, and the rich palaces, and mighty churches—of which there were so many that no one would have believed it who had not seen it with his eyes—, and the height and the length of that city which above all others was sovereign. And be it known to you that no man there was of such hardiness but his flesh trembled; and it was no wonder, for never was so great an enterprise undertaken by any people since the creation of the world." [36] By the end of another month Isaac and Alexius were again on the Byzantine throne. Constantinople for the first time in history had fallen, though the Varangians had defended it bravely. [37]

In the face of the resentment of all patriotic Greeks at this inroad

[35] See p. 411.
[36] Villehardouin, *op. cit.*, p. 31.
[37] See p. 268.

of barbarians, Isaac and Alexius were slow to carry out their agreement with the crusaders. When one hundred thousand marks were paid, the Venetians took eighty-four thousand as their half of the booty and as payment of the balance of the crusaders' debt to them. Alexius seemed loath to give more. At the end of 1203 a rebellion in Constantinople overthrew Isaac and Alexius and put on the throne the son-in-law of Alexius III, Alexius V, Ducas. Then Isaac died and Alexius was strangled, and the crusaders saw themselves suddenly robbed of all hope of completing their crusade. Perhaps we should better say they—or at any rate the Venetians—realized that the time had come for their final reckoning with the Byzantine empire: they were bound by no agreements with Alexius V. Before the beginning of the second siege the Venetians drove another shrewd bargain with the rest of the army over the division of the booty and conquered lands, the election of the new emperor, and the organization of the Latin Church in the east. On April 13, 1204, Constantinople fell for the second time. The following three days' pillage and destruction by the crusaders and the Venetians are one of the most wanton crimes in all history. The contemporary Byzantine historian Nicetas saw and heard what happened: "The images . . . were trodden under foot. . . . The divine body and blood of Christ were spilled upon the ground or thrown about. They snatched the precious reliquaries, thrust into their bosoms the ornaments which these contained, and used the broken remnants for pans and drinking cups. . . . Nor can the violation of the Great Church [Santa Sophia] be listened to with equanimity. For the sacred altar, formed of all kinds of precious materials . . . was broken into bits and distributed among the soldiers, as was all the other sacred wealth of so great and infinite splendor. . . . Mules and saddled horses (to carry away the booty) were led to the very sanctuary of the temple. Some of these, which were unable to keep their footing on the splendid and slippery pavement, were stabbed when they fell, so that the sacred pavement was polluted with blood and filth. Nay more, a certain harlot . . . sat in the patriarch's seat, singing an obscene song and dancing frequently. . . . In the alleys, in the streets, in the temples, complaints, weeping, lamentations, grief, the groaning of men, the shrieks of women, wounds, rape, captivity, the separation of those most closely united." When the Abbot Martin, a "holy robber," finished with the church of Pantokrator, "he was hastening to his vessel, . . . stuffed full. . . . Those who knew and loved him saw him from their ships as they were themselves hastening to the booty, and inquired joyfully

The second siege of Constantinople

The sack of Constantinople

whether he had stolen anything, or with what he was so loaded down as he walked. With a joyful countenance, as always . . . he said, 'we have done well.' To which they replied, 'Thanks be to God.' " [38]

Villehardouin reports: "The booty gained was so great that none could tell you of it. Gold and silver and vessels and precious stones and samite and cloth of silk and robes, vair and grey, and ermine and every choicest thing found upon the earth . . . never, since the world was created, had so much booty been won in any city." Innocent III was at first inclined to regard the success of the venture as a miracle, until he learned what had happened. Then he wrote: "These defenders of Christ, who should have turned their swords only against infidels, have bathed in Christian blood. They have respected neither religion nor age nor sex. They have committed in open day adultery, fornication and incest. Matrons and virgins, even those vowed to God, were delivered to the ignominious brutality of the soldiers." [39] The ransacking of libraries and destruction of manuscripts and works of art were an irreparable loss. The few plays of Sophocles and Euripides that we now possess are only the salvage of this atrocious demolition. Much of the booty found its way to the west: the four bronze horses standing today above the portal of St. Mark's at Venice were plundered from the Hippodrome. "Greatly did they rejoice and give thanks because of the victory God had vouchsafed to them—for those who before had been poor were now in wealth and luxury. Thus they celebrated Palm Sunday and the Easter Day following in the joy and honour that God alone bestowed upon them."

The Venetian colonial empire

From 1204 there was no Byzantine empire at Constantinople until 1261. In the partition of territory Venice took three-eighths of the city, including Santa Sophia; she also took the city of Adrianople and a highway by sea from Constantinople to the Adriatic, taking in Gallipoli, the Ægean islands of Naxos, Andros, Eubœa, and Crete and the Ionian Islands. The Venetian colonial empire was brilliantly founded, and Venice was raised to the height of her extraordinary career. From the rest of the European territory of the Byzantine empire, and from the extreme northwestern corner of Asia Minor, was constituted the

The Latin Empire of Constantinople

Latin Empire of Constantinople, sometimes called Romania, with Count Baldwin of Flanders as its first emperor. The empire was organized by feudal custom, which was subsequently codified in the Assizes of Romania. Throughout the Balkan peninsula numerous principalities were founded by the crusading leaders, all in theory, of

[38] *Translations and Reprints*, III, no. 1, pp. 15 ff.
[39] Quoted in *Cambridge Medieval History*, IV, 420.

course, fiefs of the emperor at Constantinople. There was a Kingdom of Thessalonica, a Duchy of Philippopolis, a Duchy of Athens and Thebes, a Principality of Achaia. Feudal castles went up on the mountains of Greece, and pagan Greek temples turned into Greek Christian churches were now converted into Latin churches. The Latin Church was established in the empire, with a Venetian at its head as Patriarch of Constantinople, and the property of the Greek Church was confiscated. But the Greeks would never accept the Latin Church, so no effective union of the two churches was ever brought about.

The Latin Empire of Constantinople was even shorter-lived than the Kingdom of Jerusalem, and its political history even more trivial. Of the three small Greek states left, it was the one in Asia Minor grandly called the Empire of Nicæa that was destined to restore the empire in Byzantium. It rallied to itself the humiliated Greek patriots and the dispossessed Greek Church, and soon ruled all of northwestern Asia Minor that remained Christian. But the old empire never recovered from the events of 1204 and the half century following; and the new empire, after its restoration by the Palæologus family, was ultimately no match for the coming invasion of Ottoman Turks. With all its other sins, the fourth crusade contributed to the final fall of Constantinople in 1453 and the subsequent European conquests of the Ottoman Turks, the consequences of which have been so disastrous for southeastern Europe right down to the present. It is only fair to add that the earlier crusades may well have forestalled an invasion of Europe by the Seljuk Turks three centuries earlier, but the total effect of the crusades on Europe was nevertheless probably a net loss, not a gain. *The restoration of the Byzantine empire*

The fourth crusade also delivered a serious blow to the whole crusading movement. For one thing, by setting up a new Latin state in the east it divided the interest and the resources of the west between Constantinople and Jerusalem. The pleas of the petty emperors at Constantinople for help soon became almost as pitiful as those of the kings of Jerusalem. Most of all, its outcome deeply shocked good men, and revealed the crass motives of many of those who had been leading and profiting by the crusades and the incompetence of the rest. Yet crusading continued, always increasing in futility and absurdity. In 1212 bands of children from France and Germany started to march to the sea; they were confident that it would recede before them to make a path to the Holy Land, which they would then take without a blow. The French children were stopped, but thousands of *The children's crusade and the fifth crusade*

German children actually reached Genoa. There they were separated; some were ultimately sent home from Brindisi, but others, it seems, were sold into slavery by merchants of Marseilles. After the fourth crusade those who thought seriously about another concluded that the best hope of success lay in attacking Egypt first, and from there the Holy Land. The fifth crusade did capture Damietta in 1219, but the city was quickly lost.

Frederick II's
(the sixth)
crusade

Frederick II's crusade, the sixth, differed from all those before and after in three respects. It was led by a man who had not only brains but an intelligent and sympathetic understanding of the world in which he lived—the first man since Roman times who could fairly be called a citizen of the world. Second, it involved no fighting, no slaughter, no pillaging and robbing. Finally, this crusade was the only one that easily and quickly attained its objective. We have already noted the uncommon circumstances attending the beginning of Frederick's crusade.[40] His success in negotiating as lawful heir to the Kingdom of Jerusalem with Al Kamil, Sultan of Egypt, was no less extraordinary. The excommunicated crusader made such good use of his knowledge of the Arabic language and culture that in 1229 he made a treaty with the sultan that put all the accomplishments of all the military campaigns of all the French, English, and German kings to shame. Jerusalem, Bethlehem, and Nazareth were to be his, with the exception of the area in Jerusalem containing the Mosque of Omar, where the Mohammedans were to have the right to pray. Moreover, a corridor of land connecting Jerusalem with the strip of coast that constituted what was left of the Kingdom of Jerusalem was ceded to Frederick. The treaty provided for a truce of ten years, after which it was renewed for five years. Without the co-operation of the Christian Patriarch of Jerusalem Frederick himself placed the crown of the kingdom upon his head in the Church of the Holy Sepulcher, and hurried home to the war that the pope had begun against him during his absence.[41]

Already the position of both Christians and Moslems in the east was threatened by a new incursion of Mongol tribes from central Asia on a scale unprecedented since the invasion of the Huns. For many years before 1206 the unification of the heterogeneous mass of Mongol tribes had been going on under a leader whom we call Jenghiz Khan (in that year he took the title of khan, or ruler). One small part of the amazing conquests of Jenghiz was the empire of the Sel-

[40] See p. 420.
[41] See p. 421.

juk Turks, which collapsed after the death of Malik Shah in 1092. The Sultan of Egypt took advantage of the Turks' defeat to invite them into Syria and Palestine to aid him against both his Christian and his Moslem foes. In 1244 they took Jerusalem, which then for the second and last time until 1917 passed from Christian back to Moslem hands.

Meanwhile Jenghiz, who it has been said was responsible for the death of five million people, had died in 1227. His successor, Ogdai, had conquered northern China, and his nephew Batu had led the western Mongols into Europe. By 1240 they had reached the Dnieper and destroyed Kiev. "Princes, bishops, nuns and children were slain with savage cruelty. It is impossible to describe the barbarities that prolonged the death of the unfortunate inhabitants. None remained to weep or to tell the tale of disaster." [42] They moved on into eastern Europe in two columns, the northern against Poland and the southern against Hungary. In 1241 the whole of Silesia was devastated, while Batu destroyed an Hungarian army, took Pesth and Gran, and sent expeditions into the Balkans. There seemed to be nothing to prevent the Mongols from overrunning central and western Europe. Europe, torn by the struggle between empire and papacy and absorbed in local affairs, made only the feeblest efforts to rise to the emergency. In fact, it was saved only by the death of Ogdai in that year, which compelled Batu and the other Mongol chieftains to go back to Karakorum in Mongolia for the election of a new khan. The Mongols later returned to Poland and Silesia, took Cracow and Beuthen, and drove away great numbers of slaves, but contented themselves with imposing their suzerainty on Russia.[43] *The Mongols in northeastern Europe*

The fall of Jerusalem in 1244 stirred St. Louis to take the cross. The faithful Joinville, who went with him, tells how he himself left clad as a pilgrim, "on foot, barefoot, not to reenter the castle till my return. . . . And never would I turn my eyes towards Joinville for fear my heart should melt within me at thought of the fair castle I was leaving behind, and my two children." The expedition sailed with great enthusiasm from Aigues Mortes in August 1248, for Egypt. They landed at Damietta, where the king was foremost among his knights in bravery. He "leapt into the sea, which was up to his armpits. So he went, with his shield hung to his neck and his helmet on his head and his lance in his hand, till he came to his people, who were on the shore. When he reached the land and looked *The crusade (the seventh) of St. Louis*

---

[42] *Cambridge Medieval History*, IV, 637.
[43] See pp. 950–51.

upon the Saracens, he asked what people they were, and they told him they were Saracens; and he put his lance to his shoulder, and his shield before him, and would have run in upon the Saracens if the right worthy men who were about him would have suffered it."

It was, however, all to no purpose that the finest traditions of Christian knighthood and all the religious fervor of the original crusading impulse were embodied in St. Louis. His crusade was a quarrelsome, badly managed, and foolhardy expedition. After the capture of Damietta the crusaders, advancing across the delta of the Nile towards Cairo, were surrounded by the Turks and forced to surrender, the king himself being among the many prisoners. After paying a heavy ransom and giving up Damietta, he was permitted to leave Egypt with his army in 1250 for Palestine. Thence, after accomplishing little more than the fortification of the few remaining Christian ports, he returned to France in 1254. Sixteen years later he set out, an enfeebled and weak old man, on a crusade to Tunis, and died before Carthage soon after landing.

The fate of the remaining Christian states in Syria and Palestine was now merely a question whether they would fall to the Mongols or to the Khwarazmian Turkish sultans of Egypt, who had taken the throne from Saladin's successors in 1250, or their mercenary soldiers, the Mamalukes. From Persia Hulagu, nephew of Jenghiz Khan, launched a campagin against Bagdad, which in 1258 finally destroyed the Abbasid caliphate.[44] After the fall of Bagdad the caliphate was moved to Cairo, and Hulagu fell on Syria, where he captured Aleppo, Damascus, and Antioch. Once again a Mongol khan died at a moment auspicious for his enemies, for Hulagu was now called back to central Asia for the election of a new khan. Led by his general Ketbogha, the Mongols in 1260 met the Egyptians under their Turkish sultan and his Mamaluke general, Baibars, at 'Ain Jalut, in Palestine; there they suffered their first decisive defeat, which drove them back into Mesopotamia. This wholly Moslem victory may have been responsible for keeping the Mongols from invading Europe through Asia Minor.

The Mongols in Syria

The end of the crusaders' states

Baibars assassinated his sultan on the triumphal march back to Cairo, took the Egyptian throne, and began to eradicate the remaining Christian states. In 1271 he captured the Krak of the Hospitalers,[45] and before his death Antioch and much of the coast were in his hands. His successors, after thwarting another Mongol invasion, com-

[44] See p. 171.
[45] See p. 533.

pleted what he had begun. Tripolis fell next, and in 1291 Acre, the last stronghold of the Christians on the mainland, was taken after an heroic resistance. This time the Moslems, commanded now by no Saladin but by Turks, did a job worthy of the crusaders: they massacred sixty thousand prisoners and filled the port with the débris of the fortifications. Thus ended two centuries of effort to maintain the states of the crusaders in Syria and Palestine. But the end of the crusades was still far off; indeed, the crusading spirit was soon to find in the defense of Europe from the Ottoman Turks greater work than it had ever had in Palestine.

The loss in the thirteenth century of the few insubstantial conquests of the crusaders in the east was more than balanced by the substantial gains of the crusade in Spain. What had happened to the Caliphate of Cordova in the eleventh century was repeated in the twelfth when the Almorávides lost control of their subject princes. Their possessions in northwest Africa they lost in 1125 to the puritanical sect of the Almohades, or Unitarians, from the Atlas Mountains, whom revolting Moslem princes in Spain then summoned to their aid in 1146. In a comparatively short time these fierce Berber fanatics had unified the Moslems in Spain and begun a persecution of Christians and Jews foreign to customary Moslem policy. Even unreformed Moslems they regarded as little better than infidels. The advance of the Almohades and conflict among the Christian states cooperated to cripple the Christian offensive until the beginning of the thirteenth century. Then in 1212 Alfonso VIII of Castile appealed to all the sovereigns of Spain and to the pope, whose summons to a crusade was answered by many foreign knights. The army thus recruited Alfonso led to a great victory over the Almohades at Las Navas de Tolosa, northeast of Cordova, which opened the way to the south. The battle was the beginning of a series of victories that carried the Kingdom of Castile to the sea. Cordova was taken in 1236, and within the next twenty-five years Murcia, Seville, and Cádiz. Meanwhile the Kingdom of Aragon, a Mediterranean power ever since its union with the County of Barcelona in 1137, had conquered the Balearic Islands and captured Valencia, and in 1266 joined with Castile to complete the conquest of the Kingdom of Murcia. By then nothing was left the Moslems in Spain but the southeastern corner of the peninsula, which as the Kingdom of Granada remained in their hands until 1492.

The conquest of Spain presented many new problems to the Spanish monarchs. As the frontier moved southward the land had to be recolonized, mostly with Mozarabs and with Mudejares, Moslems who be-

The Spanish crusade in the thirteenth century

came subjects of Christian sovereigns. But to this day the central plateau of Spain is a sparsely populated, treeless plain, known as the *Despoblado* (the uninhabited country). A large Jewish population had also to be assimilated. Both Moslems and Jews were taken into the enlarged Christian states without loss of the rights they had enjoyed

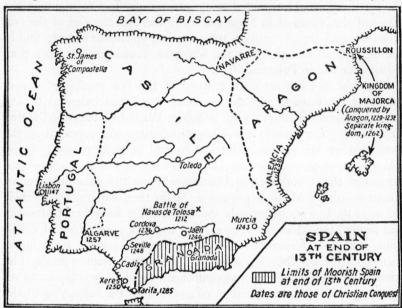

SPAIN
AT END OF
13TH CENTURY
Limits of Moorish Spain
at end of 13th Century
Dates are those of Christian Conquest

under the generally tolerant Moslem governments. The long wars against the Infidel bred in the Spanish people that intense Catholicism for which they have ever since been noted, but in general the Church played no greater part in Spanish life than elsewhere in western Europe. The individual states of Castile, Navarre, and Aragon, with Portugal, which by 1250 had developed from a Castilian fief held by a Burgundian into a kingdom with almost its present boundaries, developed politically along similar lines, though in other respects (for example, the liberation of serfs) quite independently. The political problem in Spain was the same as in the rest of Europe: Could the anarchic tendencies of feudalism be subdued by strong monarchy? In Castile and especially in Aragon the towns flourished, and assumed part of the obligation of quelling feudal disorder by their leagues, the *hermandades* or *comunidades*. In León, which was united with Castile in 1037, representatives of the towns appeared in the *Cortes*, the Spanish equivalent of the States-General or Parliament, as early as 1188—actually earlier than in England and France—and in the *Cortes* of Castile they may have been present even earlier. It was only after the conquest of the Moslems in the thirteenth century that Moslem civilization had upon the development of Spain its full effect, which has given to Spanish literature, architecture, and music their characteristic quality.

To summarize the results of the crusades to the east: From the foundation of the Latin County of Edessa in 1097 to the fall of Acre in 1291 Europeans were domiciled in the east for almost two centuries. The lower Latin culture of the west, unless it had been represented by *The crusaders* a large majority of the population, could have made no impression *at home in* upon the higher Byzantine and Saracen civilizations. The only place *the east* where the small Latin Christian minority left its mark was the less civilized Kingdom of Armenia in southeastern Asia Minor, which to a surprising degree took on features of the feudalism and Christianity introduced by the crusaders. Elsewhere, the westerner who chose to stay in the east, living among people of various races and diverse creeds, could not remain the same man he was when he left his homeland. Surrounded by heretics and Infidels who enjoined refinements of life of which he had never dreamed, he lost some of his naïve confidence in his own superiority and with it most of his barbarous intolerance. He had to learn to live decently and at peace with these Infidels and heretics, whom he found not unlike himself, except that they had so much to teach him and so little to learn from him.

Religion could not stand in the way of peaceful diplomatic and commercial relations between Christian and Moslem states and individuals. The difference between Mohammed and Christ could not keep men who enjoyed hunting from protecting each other in their sport and teaching each other their tricks. The eastern varieties of Christianity—Jacobite, Nestorian, Greek Orthodox—shook the confidence of intelligent westerners in the uniqueness of their own form, and made them, as rulers and as individuals, tolerant of the Moslem too. There was no religious persecution as such in the crusaders' states. Mohammedans had their own mosques, or joined with Christians in using the same churches. Christian saints performed miracles for both Moslems and Christians. Moslems were converted to Christianity, and Christians to Islam. Intermarriage was common in all classes of society, although the offspring of such unions were looked at somewhat askance by the most orthodox. The newcomer inevitably took to the clothes, the food, and the drink of his neighbors, and called in their doctors when he was sick.[46] The Latin princes could not resist the temp-

[46] For Moslem medicine, see p. 176.

tation to play the oriental potentate in their little courts. To facilitate trade with Mohammedans they minted coins inscribed with a verse from the Koran, and, when the popes protested against such impiety, substituted the Bible for the Koran but continued to use Arabic letters. A cultural cleavage grew up between some of the Latins permanently resident in the east and their brethren from home, who came only for long enough to make a pilgrimage to the holy places or to fulfill a crusader's vow.

The influence of the crusades on the west

So much for the crusaders in the east. What, then, was the effect of the crusades on the west? During the twelfth and thirteenth centuries western Europe reached the peak of its medieval development. Historians once explained the transformation that led to this climax as the result of the crusades. Today scholars are reluctant to speak dogmatically of any positive results of the crusades. One reason for their reluctance is the fact that before the beginning of the crusading movement western Europe had experienced social and economic changes fully adequate to account for what happened in the twelfth and thirteenth centuries. We may grant that the crusades hastened the maturity of these developments, but they were in no sense determinative: without them western Europe would still have become much what it did become. Another difficulty is that in Spain and Sicily long before the first crusade western Europe was in close contact with Moslem culture, so that in discussing the influence of the crusades to Syria and Palestine one must first make sure that the influence did not come rather from Sicily or Spain. Perhaps we should discard all such traditional historical labels as "the crusades" and speak rather of the interaction of Islam and Christianity in the middle ages. All that is said here, therefore, of the influence of Mohammedan culture on the west must be read in the light of our earlier chapter on the empire of the Arabs.

Influence on the Church

We can hardly doubt that the papacy would inevitably have risen to the height it reached under Innocent III, whether under him or some other pope, even had not Urban II inspired the first crusade and assumed the leadership of the movement. And it is doubtful to just what extent the popes ever had actual control of it. In any case, it is a question whether it did not do more to discredit the papacy than to strengthen it. The tithe levied upon the clergy in the thirteenth century for the ostensible support of a crusade gave the popes a new source of income which they were slow to give up, but which when abused brought heavy protest from the clergy themselves. The sharper wits of western Europe were not hoodwinked by the use the papacy made of crusading ardor for its own political purposes. The liberality with which indulgences were given to crusaders, exempting them from the performance of all penance, was soon extended to others who were not crusaders, was abused for financial profit, and contributed to a relaxation of the priest's control over his parishioners and to disrespect and criticism from sincere Christians. The new military orders, a product of the crusades, exerted their influence in large part outside the field of the Church. The greatest product of the crusades in the domain of religion, the missionary movement of St. Francis of Assisi, which it has been said saved the medieval Church, was inaugurated as a protest against crusading methods. It was also stimulated by the desire to convert the Great Khan of the Mongols, which led to important projects for establishing a school for the study of oriental languages at the University of Paris. But the failure of religious enthusiasm alone to maintain a Christian state in the east must have led the more intelligent Christians to question the practical value of any such attempt. Nevertheless, in spite of all that has just been said, the whole crusading movement must have deepened the devotion of countless devout Christians and quickened the piety of others less devout—especially if they stayed at home, as most Christians did.

The crusades seem to have exerted some influence on the development of strong monarchy by weakening the feudal nobility. Inasmuch as they were largely a French enterprise, whatever such effect they may have had we should expect to appear chiefly in France. For one thing, they were costly. Joinville confesses: "While I was abroad in the king's service before, I was so impoverished that I did not think I would ever recover from it. I saw clearly that, if I went on another crusade, it would be the total destruction of my property." The nobles sold and mortgaged property, and sold privileges to communes and to communities of serfs, to get money to go on a crusade. The kings, on the other hand, were able not only to meet the same urgent need of money more easily but even to turn it somewhat to the advantage of the monarchy. It gave Philip Augustus in France and Henry II in England a pretext for imposing the first direct tax in medieval Europe, the Saladin tithe of 1188.[47] Later the increase in the cost of living, when certain eastern luxuries became necessities in the west, seems to have pinched the nobles particularly hard. The loss of life among the nobility was also heavy, although it is not easy to point to instances where the dying out of a noble family led directly to the escheat of their fiefs to the crown. Finally, the participation of different peoples in the same crusade, notably in the second and third, may have done something—

Political influence of the crusades

[47] See p. 450.

in an age blessed with no newspapers, when travel was difficult and expensive and dangerous—to make the common people for the first time aware of their mutual differences. We may perhaps justly see in the decision to have the French and German contingents in the second crusade march separately to Constantinople the beginning of a national self-consciousness. If there was any such tendency, it was of course bound to operate against feudalism in favor of national monarchy.

In speaking of the results of the crusades for western Europe we are probably on the surest ground when we come to their social and economic effects. They certainly hastened to some extent the liberation of the common people of town and country. Impecunious nobles sold privileges earlier than would otherwise have been necessary. Many serfs found in the crusades an opportunity to break from their bondage, and the growth of the towns and the development of their industries offered many others an easier escape from the manor. It has been suggested, too, that the notable change in the status of women during the crusading period may have come about in part as a result of the larger responsibilities that they were obliged to assume in managing their husbands' lands while they were away.

Social influence

Many features of daily life in the west were changed by the fresh contact with the Greek and Saracen east. The west came to know and demand eastern foods and products, and to ape eastern ways. Long, flowing robes and full beards seem to have been fashions adopted from the east. "Sesame and carob, maize and rice, lemons and melons, apricots," and the shallots with which housewives have ever since rubbed their salad bowls, may have come this way into Europe. One writer lists among the manufactures or fashions either introduced or made popular by the crusades: "Cottons; muslins from Mosul; baldachins of Bagdad; damasks and damascenes from Damascus; . . . dimities and diapers from Byzantium; . . . rugs and carpets and tapestries from the Near East and Central Asia; lacquers; new colours, such as carmine and lilac (the words are both Arabic); dyes and drugs and spices and scents, such as alum and aloes, cloves and incense, indigo and sandalwood; articles of dress and of fashion, such as . . . powders and glass mirrors; works of art in pottery, glass, gold, silver and enamel; and even the rosary itself, which is said to have come from the Buddhists of India by way of Syria to western Europe." [48] The demand for sugar became so great that it began to be grown extensively in southern Europe.

The increase in the power and prestige of the bourgeoisie during the

[48] Barker, in *Legacy of Islam*, pp. 60–61.

period of the crusades, while quite as much a social phenomenon as the *Economic* change in the position of the serfs, is best regarded as the inevitable *influences* result of the economic changes of the same period. There can be no doubt that the crusades hastened the urbanization of western Europe. It has been seen how Venice, Genoa, Pisa, and to a lesser extent Amalfi shared in and profited by them. Marseilles and the Catalonian towns did likewise. The Latin states in the east offered a limited market for the western goods now beginning to be manufactured in abundance; and the west, once acquainted with the articles of eastern commerce, became an almost unlimited market for eastern wares. The impulse given to the development of the Italian towns carried across the Alps to German, French, and Flemish towns. The fourth crusade gave the west naval control of the Mediterranean, and eliminated Constantinople as middleman in trade between east and west. Henceforth Venetian and Genoese ships plied the Black Sea and sought to tap the resources of southern Russia and central Asia. To transport troops and supplies to the east on a large scale bigger ships had to be built; and northern nations, particularly England, became acquainted with the advanced naval practice of the Italians and the Saracens. The compass and the astrolabe may have been introduced through the contact of the crusaders with Saracen mariners.

To carry on trade with the Moslems the crusaders had to mint gold coins; and it was eastern commerce that brought gold coinage—the Sicilian ducat, the Florentine florin, the Venetian sequin—into fashion in Italy. The crusades and the commerce they promoted created a similar demand for banking services. Some means had to be found to avoid carrying about the large sums of money needed for a crusade, or the sums necessary to pay large trade balances. To meet this demand the Templars and the Italian banking families came forward with letters of credit, whose use they learned from the Saracens. After all this it may not be amiss to repeat the warning: towns had already begun to grow and trade and industry to revive in western Europe before the crusades, and they would have continued to do so, perhaps less rapidly, perhaps somewhat differently, had there never been any crusades at all.

The crusades were naturally not without influence on western mili- *Influence* tary science. The crusaders seem to have brought back knowledge of *on arts and* the concentric type of large, heavily fortified castle, and new ideas of *sciences* siege tactics. The portcullis, the crossbow, heavier armor for both knight and horse, Greek fire, and the use of carrier pigeons have been cited as importations from the east. Nor did the arts of peace fail to profit. The first Europeans to see a windmill were probably crusaders. Heraldry in all its phases seems definitely to be an eastern importation, associated with the use of family names as a better means of identification. Ecclesiastical architecture was enriched by the round churches (the most accessible is the beautiful Temple Church in London) built in imitation of the Church of the Holy Sepulcher at Jerusalem. What the crusaders were perhaps most sure to bring back was a big collection of oriental tales, which influenced western poets to use the same romantic atmosphere. The writing of history received splendid encouragement from the chronicles of the crusades and from the personal memoirs, written in the vernacular, of Villehardouin and Joinville. The Assizes of Jerusalem and the Assizes of Romania are an invaluable legacy for the study of feudalism. In general, the direct influence of Greek and Saracen culture does not seem to have been great. There is, however, evidence of direct translation from the Greek of some of Aristotle's works after the fourth crusade; and the obvious superiority of Moslem medicine led to the importation of some Mohammedan doctors, notably at Montpellier.

Influence on travel and exploration

Of one thing about the crusades we may be certain. They expanded the geographical knowledge of the west and enlarged its intellectual horizon. Maps of the Mediterranean basin, itineraries of pilgrims, accounts of travelers to the court of the Mongolian khan—most famous of whom was Marco Polo, at the end of the thirteenth century—all came directly or indirectly from the crusades. The effect of the travels of hundreds of thousands of western Europeans in the east over a period of two hundred years is not easy to estimate. More than that, by accustoming men to the idea of travel the crusaders contributed to its increase up and down the water and land highways of Europe, to shrine and market and fair, and must thereby have done something to break down provincialism. The traveler can scarcely help learning, if he is capable of learning at all.

The unfulfilled task of the crusaders was left for later generations to attempt. In the east the battle had to be continued against the Ottoman Turks. In the west Portuguese navigators going down the coast of Africa thought of themselves as continuing the crusade against the Moslems in Spain by turning the flank of Islam with an attack from the rear. The new interest in finding an easy sea route to the Far East continued unabated after the early hopes of converting the Mongols to Christianity were disappointed by their conversion to Mohammedanism. There is more than a slight connection between Urban II and Christopher Columbus, and the establishment of the first American settlements was not altogether different from that of the Kingdom of Jerusalem. If today the French and British hold mandates in Syria and Palestine, that is in part because not even twentieth-century imperialism is wholly unrelated to the crusades that first took them there over eight hundred years ago.

Chapter 19

THE REVIVAL OF TRADE AND INDUSTRY

I N HIS Prologue to the *Canterbury Tales* Chaucer introduces us
to an English merchant of the fourteenth century:

> "There was a merchant with forked beard, and girt
> In motley gown, and high on horse he sat,
> Upon his head a Flemish beaver hat;
> His boots were fastened rather elegantly.
> He spoke his notions out right pompously,
> Stressing the times when he had won, not lost.
> At money-changing he could make a crown.
> This worthy man kept all his wits well set;
> There was no one could say he was in debt,
> So well he governed all his trade affairs
> With bargains and with borrowings and with shares."

*Towns and
trade in the
fourteenth
century*

Then in the Sailor's Tale we meet a French merchant of St. Denis, who
was rich, "for which men held him wise." He attended the fair at
Bruges, where he went "fast and busily about his trade, and bought,
and borrowed gold." After his return to St. Denis he went on to Paris:

> "Since goods were very dear
> He needs must get more cash at his command,
> For he was bound by his own note of hand
> To pay some twenty thousand crowns anon."

In Paris he got his loan, paid off his note "to certain Lombards," and

> "Now home he goes as merry as a jay.
> For well he knew he stood in such array

That now he needs must make, with nothing lost,
A thousand francs above his total cost." [1]

In the fourteenth century there was nothing new in the idea that a rich man must be a wise man. And by that time the French merchant visiting the center of Flemish wool manufacture at Bruges, and then off to Paris, the financial center of France, to borrow money to pay a note to Italian bankers was a familiar figure. But there was still something novel there: for only a comparatively short time had much been heard of merchants, fairs, profits, notes, and bankers in the western world.

It has already been necessary to consider the towns, to an extent. The northern Italian towns, organized in the Lombard League, have been seen successfully resisting the Hohenstaufen emperors. We have seen the French kings in the twelfth century encouraging the growth of towns for what they could get out of them, and the German emperors failing to do so. The crusades could not have been understood without some knowledge of the commercial ambitions of Venice, Genoa, and Pisa. This and the following chapter will bring these things together by explaining in greater detail the emergence from the agricultural and feudal society of the early middle ages of the towns that were to transform western Europe. In other words, how, beside the peasant and the knight, there arose the merchant and the artisan. They will describe those features most typical of the town that favored the further growth of industry and commerce and capitalism.

A merchant implies merchandise, just as commerce involves manufacture and industry. Where we find a merchant, we shall also find a banker, without whose help the merchant cannot ordinarily meet the financial demands of business. The modern is often told that he is living in a new industrial and capitalistic society, whose ruling motive is greed for profits. Be that as it may, there is nothing new in industry and capitalism *per se*. Merchant, trader, manufacturer, banker, artisan, workingman began to co-operate after some fashion seven or eight hundred years ago. To be sure, the commerce, the industry, the towns were then vastly different from those of the twentieth century. Whether we have progressed, or merely moved, this much is certain: the commercial and industrial capitalism that we have known (we had best say nothing of the financial capitalism developed recently out of the older form) is the outcome of an economic and social evolution that began with the revival of trade and industry in the medieval town. Special

The medieval origin of industry and capitalism

[1] *The Canterbury Tales* (tr. J. U. Nicolson).

developments at critical moments in its long history have modified its course and accelerated its movement, but they have not changed its direction. This fact alone should make us beware—if we have not already learned to be suspicious—of all such convenient terms as "modern" and "medieval." Some of the features supposedly most characteristic of the modern world developed so early and so far as to be typical also of the middle ages.

The agrarian economy of early western Europe

The most characteristic feature of the society of the classical Mediterranean world was the self-governing city-state, which even with the Roman empire never wholly lost its autonomy. With the decline of the Græco-Roman city-state went the decay of Græco-Roman civilization. A combination of circumstances led to the impoverishment of the Roman municipalities in Italy and throughout the west after the second century.[2] Society became predominantly agricultural, and localized on the large estate. The Germanic invasions of the fourth and succeeding centuries only accelerated the already well-advanced shift from an urban to an agrarian economy. The majority of the population of western Europe settled down as serfs or quasi serfs upon the almost self-sufficient manor, producing the food they used and making the tools they needed. There was little or no agricultural surplus, and, if there had been, little market for it in towns. Moreover, with no effective government it was next to impossible to transport goods safely any distance. What little exchange of goods there was took place at local markets, by means of barter rather than cash. Population was relatively stationary. Large regions of western Europe were still covered with forest, brush, or swamp.

Commerce in the Merovingian and Carolingian periods

Even so, some few luxuries, such as silk, spices, and frankincense, continued to be precariously imported from the east through Marseilles and other Mediterranean ports, at enormous expense, for the clergy and the Church services. Papyrus was also imported for writing material. For these goods wine and oil were exchanged. This trade was almost entirely in the hands of orientals—Jews and Syrians: the Christian merchant had practically vanished in the west. The conquests of Islam from the seventh to the tenth century in the western Mediterranean—northern Africa, Spain, Sicily, Sardinia, Corsica, and the Balearic Islands—no doubt did something to perpetuate the economic stagnation of the west and to make revival more difficult. Still, they did not sever connections between Constantinople and Italy. Venice never ceased to act as middleman between east and west; and the towns of Byzantine southern Italy—Bari, Tarento, Naples,

[2] See p. 14.

and especially Amalfi—maintained commercial relations with the Greek homeland.

That the west did not recover sooner from the prolonged depression of late Roman times is sufficiently explained by its difficulties in restoring even a primitive kind of order after the fearful dislocations of the breakdown of Roman society and the Germanic migrations. The Merovingian was a period of the utmost confusion: the growth of the landed aristocracy and the depression of large numbers of freemen into serfdom did nothing to establish the orderly conditions under which alone wealth can easily accumulate. The west had little to buy with, and very little to sell. In such circumstances it made little difference whether the Byzantine market was open or not, or in whose hands the western Mediterranean was. Businessmen have seldom let religion stand in the way of the making of a profit. As soon as it became possible, trade was brisk enough between the pope's Christians and the Greek Christians and the Moslem Infidels. The Carolingian period did little to hasten that time. The reconstruction of the early Carolingians was almost wholly political, and was achieved only at the cost of a heavy military outlay. Even at that, it did not build up either a political or a military organization strong enough to withstand the terrific onslaughts of Norsemen, Saracens, and Magyars in the ninth and tenth centuries. Once again western Europe had to face the question of survival. The answer was feudalism. But while feudalism succeeded in beating off these enemies or in finding room for them, it produced its own new obstacle to economic revival in the feudal lord, bent on private war.

Under all these circumstances it is surprising that Europe recovered as soon as it did from the primitive economy of the early middle ages. The revival begun in the eleventh century lasted throughout the twelfth and thirteenth before quieting down into a steadier course. It is characterized by three features, mutually interdependent, each of which was both cause and effect of the other two, the total result being a social and economic revolution. The first was the large-scale resumption of commerce with Byzantium and Islam, and through them with the Middle and Far East. The second was the growth of western industry, manufacturing for foreign as well as local markets. The third was the extension of agriculture by groups of pioneers sent out to clear forests and drain marsh and swamp. Together these movements produced three new social classes, all urban: the bourgeoisie, composed of manufacturers, merchants, and small traders; a new class of workmen, the skilled artisans; and the unorganized proletariat of unskilled labor. Together they revived old Roman towns and founded countless new

The character of the economic revival in the eleventh century

ones. They contributed more than anything else to the liberation of the serfs and to a tremendous increase in population.

The commercial revival was ushered in by the Italian towns. As early as the eleventh century Venice was a rich and prosperous city, a virtually independent oligarchy of merchant plutocrats. Her first object was to clear the Adriatic of Slav pirates and reduce all possible rivals to economic dependence. When Ancona and Ravenna, Aquileia and Pola had been brought to terms, Venice, to prevent the Normans in southern Italy from bottling up the Adriatic, became the natural ally of the Byzantine empire. Her assistance in thwarting Robert Guiscard's attempted march on Constantinople [3] secured for her in 1082 a monopoly for the empire of all exports and imports to and from the west, an *The revival* auspicious beginning that was completed by the crusades. What Venice *of trade by* was doing in the Adriatic Genoa and Pisa were doing in the Tyrrhenian *Venice, Genoa,* Sea and the western Mediterranean. The Moslems were driven from *and Pisa* Sardinia and Corsica, which were valuable for their timber and minerals. By co-operating with the Normans in the conquest of Sicily the two cities captured for a while the Sicilian market, and settled their own colonies at Messina, Syracuse, and Palermo. In 1087 the capture of Mahdia in Tunis won them important trading privileges on the North African coast. What little they left undone was completed by the Kingdom of Aragon, which, having become a maritime power in 1137 by acquiring the County of Barcelona, a hundred years later conquered the Balearic Islands. At the time of the first crusade, however, the whole western Mediterranean was largely monopolized by Genoa and Pisa.

The crusades gave the three Italian cities control also of the Ægean and the eastern Mediterranean; they were established in the coastal cities of Syria and Palestine, at many points in the interior, and likewise throughout much of the Byzantine empire. By the beginning of the thirteenth century they had a virtual monopoly of all Mediterranean trade, and had become deadly rivals. In the twelfth century Genoa had begun to get the upper hand of Pisa. She had privileged merchant colonies at Barcelona, Montpellier, Narbonne, Marseilles, Arles, St. Gilles, Albenga, and Savona. She claimed a monopoly in the trade of St. Gilles because of aid given its count, Raymond of Toulouse, in the capture of Tripolis in 1109; she dictated terms of trade to Narbonne, Montpellier, and Savona. During the same century the Genoese captured the market at Ceuta, across the straits from Gibraltar, and pushed on down the Atlantic coast to get at Fez and Morocco. Besides

[3] See p. 142.

lding a road between two cities (Flemish miniature, fifteenth century)

e Druggist's Shop

The Butcher Shop

*A window in the Wiesenkirche at Soest, representing a thoroughly German Last Supper, with boar's h
Westphalian ham, and beer on the table*

The Normans Cross to Pevensey   Part of the Norman Army at Hastings

*Two scenes from the famous Bayeux Tapestry, a piece of embroidery describing the Norman Conque
of England, and practically contemporary with the events it describes. It was probably made f
Odo, the Bishop of Bayeux, a half-brother of William the Conqueror (see p. 432)*

Mahdia both Genoese and Pisans were trading with Bougie, Tunis, Sfax, Gabes, and Tripoli on the North African coast.

For assisting the Palæologus family to recover Constantinople in 1261 the Genoese were rewarded with extensive trading privileges in the Black Sea, where they competed with the Venetians. When the Syrian towns were lost to the crusaders, the Italians moved to Cyprus *Trade with* and up the coast to Aias, or Laiazzo, in Armenia, whence they pene- *the Near and* trated north to Sivas and east to Tabriz. Towards the end of the thir- *Far East* teenth century the Polos of Venice traveled as far as Peking, whence the famous Marco came back by way of the Indian Ocean and the Persian Gulf. In the fourteenth century, when Chinese wares reached the Crimea, Trebizond, and Tabriz, both Genoese and Venetians were to be found in all three places, whence they could also tap trade from the Near East. The Italians brought back the spices—cinnamon, ginger, pepper, cardamon, cloves, nutmeg—with which the European had learned to tickle his palate and—more important—to disguise the taste and smell of his stale meat.

"To satisfy these imperative gastronomic requirements Arabia, India, Ceylon, the Moluccas and China had to be called on. . . ." [4] They brought back medicines, such as camphor, cassia, and rhubarb, as well as incense, balm, and scents. The textile industry of the west depended on the east for such staples as cotton and silk, for dyestuffs such as indigo, and for alum, a necessity in the treatment of cloth before dyeing. Then there were "ivory from Ethiopia, pearls from Ceylon and the Persian gulf, and all the precious stones, doubly precious in western eyes for their exquisite beauty and the miraculous virtues which were attributed to them," [5] not to mention again all the articles of furniture, clothing, and food—notably sugar—the introduction of which we have already seen was a result of the crusades.[6] Before the end of the thirteenth century Genoese sailors had gone out through Gibraltar into the Atlantic to look for a shorter route to the Far East. In the ninth century the Normans had almost circumnavigated Europe; the Italians in the thirteenth seemed about to circumnavigate the globe.

Even before the large expansion of Italian commerce that began in *Trade through* the eleventh century western Europe had had some contact with the *and from* east. Normandy, northeastern England, Ireland, the islands off Scot- *northern* land, Iceland, Norway, Sweden, Denmark, and Russia, although with- *Europe* out any political unity, formed, nevertheless, a kind of economic whole.

[4] Halphen, in *Medieval France*, p. 193.
[5] *Ibid*.
[6] See p. 556.

Goods came through from Byzantium and the Moslem east by the Varangian route [7] from the Black Sea up the Russian rivers and down to the Baltic, and thence to the North Sea. In Flanders this stream of trade met the flow of raw products coming from the north; lumber, tar, pitch, resin, hides, furs, fish, and amber. The Vikings probably used much of the Danegeld to pay for eastern wares. At the end of the eleventh century the incursions of the Tartar Petchenegs into southern Russia blocked the Varangian route, but as the Norsemen settled down into some kind of political stability they developed all the more their own natural resources. In the course of the twelfth century the merchants of northern Germany began to drive Scandinavian shipping off the North and Baltic Seas in anticipation of the great days of the Hanseatic League in the thirteenth and fourteenth centuries.[8] Western Europe was thus stimulated commercially from the north by way of Flanders as well as from the south by way of Venice, Genoa, and Pisa.

Western industry and exports

It is a commonplace of international trade that to buy one must also sell; in exchange for eastern imports the west had to export either raw products or manufactured goods. The importation of the products of eastern industry furnished models and an incentive to western craftsmanship, and the profits of eastern trade began to furnish capital for the development of western industry. Whether from native or imported raw materials, in many lines the west began to make goods formerly imported from the east—textiles, tapestries, carpets, furniture, enamels, and glass. Western products soon equaled the eastern in excellence; finally they surpassed them and drove them off the western market.

The lifeblood of western industry was the revived trade in wines and the new trade in textiles. As early as the twelfth century Europe had begun to specialize in textiles. The chief centers were Flanders, northern France, and northern Italy, and the great specialty was wool. From the raw wool imported from England or from Champagne and Artois the Flemish and north French towns wove cloth for all northern Europe. It has been estimated that by the end of the fourteenth century half the population of Flanders were weavers, fullers, or dyers. Ghent, Bruges, Douai, Louvain, Ypres, Tournai, Arras, Lille, St. Omer, Cambrai, Valenciennes, Abbéville, Amiens, Beauvais, St. Quentin, Rheims, and Châlons were the important centers. The chief Italian centers were Milan, Verona, Modena, Bologna, and Florence. It became a specialty of the Italian towns, particularly of Florence, to dress

[7] See p. 268.
[8] See p. 928.

and finish for the market the rough, unfinished woolens of Flanders. At the beginning of the fourteenth century Florence had some three hundred shops working one hundred thousand pieces of woolen cloth annually; a little later thirty thousand workmen, a third of her population, were dependent on this industry. Southern Italy, Venice, Florence, and Lucca were centers for the manufacture of silk, Tuscany for cottons and fustian. Gold brocades were made at Genoa and Lucca and at Montpellier, which was noted also for a beautiful crimson woolen. Champagne and the Meuse and Rhine countries specialized in linen.

Wines and textiles, however, were not the only commodities. Dinant, on the Meuse, became famous for its copperware, Nuremberg for its wooden wares, Poitou for arms and armor. Lumber, furs, hides, stone, metals, cereals, salt and other minerals were exported raw, or finished for the foreign market. Western Europe was manufacturing more than it consumed; commerce and industry were breaking all local bonds.

Imports from the North and Baltic Seas through Flanders and Flemish and north French woolens were exchanged for Mediterranean *The Cham-* imports and Italian manufactures at the Champagne fairs. Already well *pagne fairs* established in the twelfth century, these functioned as a clearing house for international trade down to the beginning of the fourteenth century. For this purpose Champagne was ideally situated. Italian merchants coming along the Provençal coast or over the pass of Mont Cenis met merchants going up the Rhone from Marseilles, Montpellier, Arles, and Nîmes. Italians using the St. Bernard pass went through Lausanne and Besançon to Langres. From the west the Loire and the Seine, from the north the Meuse, the Moselle, and the Rhine all gave easy access to Champagne. This fertile plain was ruled for three centuries by able counts, who effectively promoted the commercial interests of their territory. The importance of the Champagne fairs was so great that a foreign merchant who defaulted obligations contracted there could be forced to honor his commitments by the threat of barring all his fellow citizens from the fairs. Elsewhere fairs were held in perhaps a single great hall, but in the Champagne towns spacious halls and storehouses were scattered over the entire city. A regular routine was developed for the conduct of the fairs, to obviate confusion and to give the count's financial agents time to make sure that all the proper payments reached his coffers. The fairs, usually seven weeks long, were run in a cycle that filled almost the entire year. Lagny opened its fair in January. Then followed in order the fairs of Bar, the first fair of Provins, the first of Troyes, the second at Provins, and finally the second at Troyes, which closed the week before Christmas. Then within a few weeks it was again time for the fair at Lagny.

About a week before the fair opened merchants arrived to unpack their goods and arrange their exhibits. Each day the fair was opened and closed by the ringing of a bell, and business was permitted only between bells. During the first ten days of the fair, the *foire de draps,* only textiles were sold. The next ten days were devoted to hides and furs. After the third fair, for *avoir de poids,* or things sold by weight, two weeks were allowed for merchants to make their inventories, pay their dues to the count's officials for the privilege of having attended the fair, and obtain the seal of the fair upon important contracts. In the great throngs of merchants were men from all Europe. A list of the articles sold is a list of the wares of medieval Europe: silks and spices from the orient, woolens from Flanders and Italy, linens from Champagne and the Rhine, furs from Russia and Scandinavia and Africa, iron and leather goods from Germany and Spain, wines from France and Spain. Philip IV of France, in his efforts to get control of Flanders, put a heavy tax on Flemish goods bound for the Champagne fairs, but this action, intended to strike at the Flemish, was in fact a great blow to the fairs. The final blow was the inauguration in 1317 by the Venetians of a direct route by sea from the Mediterranean to Flanders and England.

Other fairs

The Champagne fairs were only the most important of countless fairs held all over western Europe in the twelfth and thirteenth centuries. There were the four great fairs in England, at St. Giles, St. Ives, Stourbridge, and Bartholomew; the four leading Flemish fairs were held at Thourout, Bruges, Ypres, and Lille; at Paris there was the famous and very old fair of Lendit. To the prelate or noble authorized by the crown to set up a fair a rich income accrued from the rents of booths and stalls, taxes on goods bought and sold, and fees and fines. These came from the special police courts before which the private police haled all violators of the peace of the fair.

There was also a more important special court of the fair called in England the piepowder court (from *pieds poudrés,* dusty feet), for the summary settlement of commercial disputes between merchants, who had no time to wait for the sittings of the ordinary courts.

The law merchant

This court was governed by the law merchant (*ius mercatorum*), a body of custom that had evolved without relation to other systems of law into a sort of private international code. Merchants acted as judges, determining the law in each case and assessing the punishment for its violation. The law merchant was enforced not only in the special courts

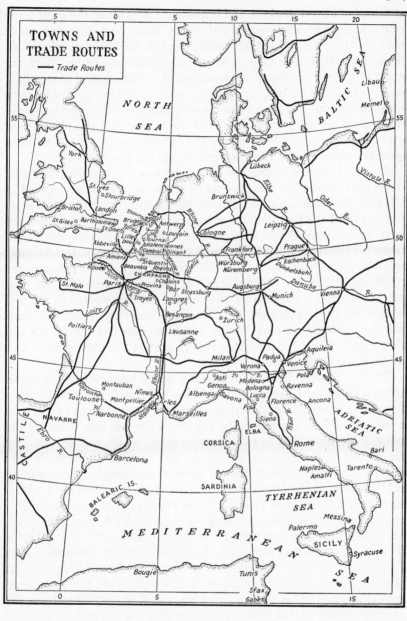

TOWNS AND TRADE ROUTES

— Trade Routes

at fairs, but also at markets, and important towns along the great trade routes had permanent commercial courts. Based on earlier customs of trade in the eastern Mediterranean, the law merchant developed especially in the Italian cities from the eleventh century on. With the expansion of their industry and trade and the establishment of merchant colonies in foreign ports, the Italians insisted upon being tried by their own commercial law under the consuls they took along with them— whence, of course, our modern consular service and the principle of extraterritoriality. At the Champagne fairs the commercial custom of southern and northern Europe blended into the law merchant.

A special branch of the law merchant was the maritime law that developed out of the old customs of sea-borne commerce codified at Rhodes. Disputes were adjudicated by the merchants themselves on the strand of the port, and, to avoid delay, between one tide and the next. These customs were then put into writing, to form the three chief codes for the three great trade areas, the Mediterranean, the Atlantic, and the North and Baltic Seas. For the western Mediterranean the consulate of the sea, written down at Barcelona around 1340, was predominant; for the Atlantic the rolls of Oléron, written in the first half of the twelfth century, were standard, and they formed the basis for the maritime code of Wisby, which prevailed in the North and Baltic Seas. These codes still survive in part in the distinct branch of modern law known as admiralty law.

The tradition of the fair

The fair was much more than a place where business could be transacted with security and freedom. Many fairs were connected with a festival in honor of some local saint, at which the throngs of pilgrims were game for all merchants. In any case a fair was sure to attract the countryside for a day or two of amusement, which was provided by wandering animal trainers, minstrels, and jongleurs—minstrels who degenerated into a combination of minstrel and juggler. The opening proclamation of the fair at Bartholomew warned visitors not to "presume to break the Lord's Day . . . in sitting, tippling or drinking in any tavern, inn, alehouse, tippling house or cook's house, or in doing any other thing that may tend to the breach thereof." [9] The utility of the fair is not yet outworn. Large European fairs, of which the one at Leipzig is perhaps most widely known, still perform as regularly as of old the same services to business. In this country the annual or semi-annual marts, such as the furniture mart in Chicago, differ from the old fairs chiefly in that they are held entirely indoors and are devoted exclusively to business. Nor has the social and recreational side of the

[9] Quoted in Lipson, *Economic History of England*, I, 215.

old fairs gone out of fashion. Though our occasional expositions and world's fairs have taken on a serious educational character that the medieval fairs did not possess, most of our town and county fairs, and to only a lesser extent our state fairs, have gone so far in the direction of amusement that they have largely degenerated into exhibitions and side shows. Yet even there the merchant is still conspicuous, advertising and selling his wares to tired and dusty crowds, milling about from booth to booth and from wonder to wonder.

Since many feudal lords were privileged to coin money, no business *The origin* could have been done at the fairs without the services of money *of banking* changers, who stood ready to exchange all good coins in circulation into any money their customers wanted. As the money changer had a strong box, men would deposit their money with him for safe-keeping, and borrow money from him, giving valuable goods as security. Thus the money changer became money keeper and money lender. When he found that he had more money on deposit than he needed for the daily requirements of business, he began to put out at interest the unused balance that did not belong to him, just as he lent the money that was properly his. The money lender had now become a banker. The bill of exchange, first used in Italy as a means to avoid the transportation of precious metals, was later introduced through Europe by the papal fiscal agents. The theory of the bill of exchange is simple: if Marco of Milan owes money to Giovanni of Turin, and if Pietro in Turin owes Francesco in Milan, no money need be sent between the two cities, for Marco will pay his fellow townsman Francesco, Pietro will pay Giovanni, and the accounts will all be clear. The device of the check was also adopted: a merchant who had money on deposit with a money lender could pay a creditor by sending the money lender an order to make the payment; the latter then simply made the proper entries in the two accounts, and again no money had changed hands. The same fertility of invention that developed the operations of banking soon devised insurance for shipments by land or water; the hazards of business were then spread in such a way that the risk of no single merchant was more than he could afford to take.

Caprice did not dictate the choice of four Italian names to illustrate *The Jews* the operation of the bill of exchange. The Italian cities produced the *and the* first Christian bankers in Europe. Their capital came originally from *Lombards* the profits of the overseas and overland trade whose needs they served. The bankers of Venice, Genoa, Florence, Siena, Lucca, indiscriminately called Lombards in northern Europe, largely displaced the Jewish pioneers in the field, as men began to distinguish between usury and a legitimate rate of interest,[10] and as the religious fervor of the crusades expressed itself in laws intended to cripple the activities of the Jews. In countries where the Jews were expelled *en masse*, as they were from England and France and later from Spain, it was all the easier for the Italians to replace them. The Italians, moreover, were naturally favored by the papacy, which employed them extensively in the collection and transmission of its enormous revenues. The popes favored the great banking houses of Florence, although the most famous single bank of the middle ages was probably the Genoese Bank of St. George. Many of the great Florentine banking houses, notably the Bardi and the Peruzzi, dated from the thirteenth century. These bankers were direct prototypes of our great modern international bankers, for they not only financed industry and commerce, but by advancing money and furnishing financial advice met the needs of indigent popes and clergy, princes and kings. Some of them had branches all the way from England and Flanders to the eastern Mediterranean. Rates of interest in the middle ages were high. Fifteen per cent or more was charged on commercial and industrial loans, while small personal loans, as they still do, brought an excessive rate of interest, perhaps eighty or even one hundred per cent. To remedy this situation the Church stepped in. The Franciscans in Italy opened pawnshops, where poor people could obtain loans on personal property at more reasonable rates. The three golden balls of the modern pawnbroker's sign are borrowed from the business device of the Medici of Florence, who were bankers before they became princes.

Navigation　　Caravans of merchants traveling by land, flotillas of merchant barges on the rivers, ships on the Mediterranean, Baltic, and North Seas began to reappear in western Europe in the eleventh century. In spite of enormous difficulties many technical improvements were made in transportation, as the conditions under which it was carried on began to improve. Though travel by sea had its dangers, they were probably less than the dangers of travel by land; at any rate, there was greater improvement in navigation than in travel by land during the middle ages. In the thirteenth century ships were still sailing along the coast, just as Greek and Roman ships had done, always in sight of land; for though the danger of shipwreck was great, to be lost at sea was worse. Joinville advised that no one undertake a voyage to the Holy Land who had not cleared himself of sin; for one could never be sure at night that one would not be at the bottom of the sea in the morning.

[10] See p. 597.

Not until the compass came into general use, in the fourteenth century, did ships sail directly across the Mediterranean. Then the supply of nautical information also increased, and sailors had better charts and could get information on such vital matters as the prevailing winds. By 1500, of course, navigators were sailing the open seas. Nevertheless, throughout the middle ages merchant ships made only seasonal voyages, at those times of year when the weather was clement.

Ships increased in size and seaworthiness. William the Conqueror crossed to England in boats of about thirty tons, carrying fifty to sixty *Medieval* men. By the time of Edward III the average English ship was about *ships* two hundred tons, the largest perhaps three hundred. The crews averaged sixty-five men for each one hundred tons, and a ship carried about half as many archers and soldiers. The Mediterranean ships were larger than those used in the North and Baltic Seas, possibly because the northern harbors were shallower. During the crusades Venetian galleys are said to have carried five hundred tons of cargo "under hatches, besides a large cargo upon their decks." Including the crew, such ships might carry eight hundred or even one thousand persons, although these figures alone would give us a misleading idea of their size. The passengers were badly crowded: an ordinary passenger might be given a space on deck, marked off with chalk, the length of a man and the width of a cot, where he was supposed to sleep and sit. One Venetian ship provided for St. Louis was one hundred and eight feet long and carried a crew of one hundred and ten. The largest ships had several cabins in the bow and stern and two decks almost six feet apart. Columbus's *Santa Maria* was probably about two hundred tons, with a crew of about sixty. The Mediterranean galley was usually propelled by oars, and used sails only when running before the wind. For the tremendous labor of rowing some galleys carried as many as two hundred oarsmen. Galley slaves were most cruelly treated; sometimes they were chained to their benches. And yet one medieval traveler reported that merchants "sometimes became voluntary galley slaves in order that they might ply their trade in harbors."

Pirates were almost as numerous at sea as robbers on land, so that *Piracy and* ships usually sailed in fleets for protection against attack, sometimes *the law of* with convoys of armed ships. The maritime cities, though indignant *shipwreck* enough if their own fleets were attacked by pirates, did not prevent pirates from attacking the fleets of rival cities. As commerce grew, however, it was found necessary to suppress piracy; at least the maritime cities were forced to make the attempt in territory in which they aimed to establish a monopoly of trade. Venice was successful in suppressing piracy in the Adriatic;[11] Genoa and Pisa made similar attempts in the western Mediterranean; the Hanseatic League and the Teutonic Order cleared the North and Baltic Seas of many marauders.

The danger of shipwreck, always serious, was made worse by the law of wreck, which provided that goods washed ashore or abandoned in a stranded vessel were the property of the owner of the shore. Peasants or local fishermen, probably with the connivance of their lords, would place lights in misleading positions on shore to cause unsuspecting mariners to wreck their boats. Though the injustice of this law was acknowledged, it was difficult to curb the practice, which persisted for centuries. Henry I of England decreed that if any person escaped alive from a stranded vessel it was not legally a wreck. A later law provided that pilots who, in the pay of lords on the coast, deliberately wrecked their vessels were to be hanged, and that the lord who connived with wreckers or pilots was to be burned in his own house. The members of the Hanseatic League agreed that goods shipwrecked in the territories of member cities should be returned to the owners. But it was no less difficult to suppress piracy and wrecking than it was to suppress robbery on land; and the injured city usually had no recourse but to attempt reprisals on citizens of the offending state, just as the United States once waged war on the Barbary pirates of North Africa, who had carried the tradition of piracy down into the nineteenth century.

The extent and importance of maritime shipping

Nevertheless, in spite of storms, shipwreck, and pirates, as long as there were no tolls at sea and ships could carry heavy cargoes, shipping flourished increasingly. At the beginning of the fifteenth century Venice had a merchant fleet and navy combined of thirty-three hundred vessels, with crews numbering thirty-six thousand men. The business of loading and unloading vessels was organized with modern-seeming efficiency. The famous Arsenal, which so impressed Dante,[12] was "like a great street on either hand with the sea in the middle." Warehouses, each with its particular kinds of goods, lined the water front. A galley making ready for a voyage was towed from one warehouse to the next and filled "from both sides with everything that might be required, and when the galley reached the end of the pier she was equipped from end to end." For safety ships had lines to indicate maximum load marked on their hulls, and inspectors made sure that this load was not exceeded. Ships were even specially built to carry horses; the horses were led into the ship through a door in the stern, which was then

[11] See p. 564.
[12] "Inferno," xxi, 7.

closed and calked, "being underwater when the ship was at sea." At its best, however, medieval transportation by sea was so difficult and dangerous that it was very costly. A premium was put on the carriage of articles valuable in proportion to their bulk. On precious cargoes like spices freight was so high that they were twice as expensive in Flanders as in Venice, and a bulky commodity like English wool cost much more in Florence than in England.

Since a single boat could carry as much freight as five hundred pack *River trans-*
horses, inland commerce moved as much as possible by water, even *portation*
before the invention of the lock in the fourteenth or fifteenth century encouraged the building of canals to connect river systems. This is as true in Europe today as it ever was, for European railroads were never permitted, as the American were, deliberately to ruin the waterways in order to make transportation more expensive. Barges and boats became so common on the rivers that gilds of keelmen were formed in all the important river towns of France, Germany, and Italy. But tolls were annoyingly frequent, sometimes only six miles apart, and even then the nobles who levied the tolls often failed to keep the rivers navigable. The merchants of the river cities therefore frequently formed associations to take over the toll rights and to attend to dredging and marking the channel, maintaining towpaths, and building docks.

The obstacles to overland travel were many and for long seemed *Medieval*
insuperable. The great Roman roads, built of stone and running directly *roads*
between the most important points, had gone to pieces from long centuries of neglect. Medieval roads were little more than cross-country trails, and since they were neither graded nor drained they were either muddy or dusty, and in any case full of holes. Bad spots were crudely repaired with rushes or fagots or boughs of trees. Bridges were infrequent and unsafe, and the traveler often had to ford rivers or cross on rude ferries. Efforts were made, of course, to keep roads in passable condition. Landowners along the highways were supposed to keep up their stretch of road, and the tolls they levied were meant to be used for that purpose. But though tolls were frequent, being levied at bridges, for merely traveling on certain roads, or even for protection while crossing the lands of some noble, little of the money was actually spent on the roads. In many territories the nobles actually claimed all goods that might fall off in transit on their own stretch of road—an interesting analogy to the law of shipwreck. Even an honest lord's desire to improve his roads suffered from the fact that unless his neighbors all did the same his single efforts could not be of great consequence.

Nevertheless, as time went on the importance of good roads was more clearly recognized. To say nothing of national or local governments, even the Church interested itself in the problem. The building and maintenance of roads was declared to be a pious act, no less commendable than to give alms or undertake a pilgrimage and equally deserving of indulgences. Cistercian monks in out-of-the-way districts turned their industrious hands to this work, and among medieval religious orders there was even a special Order of Bridge Brothers, the *Fratres Pontis*.

Conditions of overland travel

As a result of these conditions medieval merchants were long obliged to use horses or mules to carry their wares; the humblest merchants, the chapmen, carried their goods on their backs. Carts were probably first used in Italy, where the cities endeavored to keep the roads in fair shape. The earliest rude carts used in France and Germany were heavily built, and had small wheels to keep their balance better. But for a long time carts were mostly used only for local transport to markets or fairs. Henry I of England tried to enforce the building of roads wide enough to permit two waggons to pass and sixteen armed knights to ride abreast. Meanwhile merchants were paying for the upkeep of roads that were not kept up, and then, because they had to add the toll charges to the price of their goods, reducing the number of possible purchasers. A later English statute provided that roads between market towns should be clear of trees and shrubs for two hundred feet on either side, so that robbers could at least not lurk so close to the roadside. Robber barons, mercenary soldiers, ordinary criminals, and in the late middle ages impoverished knights infested the highways. Though the political authorities did what they could to maintain order, in general merchants had to protect themselves. The cities sometimes paid nobles who held land along the roads to suppress robbers. A great merchant might hire men to guard his wares in transit, but ordinary merchants traveled together for mutual protection. Sometimes they formed special traveling associations, or entrusted their caravans to companies organized to assume all the risks of the road. Inns were at first infrequent and none too safe, and here again we find the Church meeting the need by establishing in lonely or dangerous places shelters and hospices offering hospitality to all comers. As commerce and travel increased, private enterprise provided additional inns, to which in later times merchants usually resorted, leaving the monasteries to entertain the poor, whom they were glad to aid, and the rich, whom they were glad to cultivate.

Speed of travel

Travel was at best painfully slow, and in terms of time Europe was incomparably larger than nowadays. There was, however, postal service in Italy as early as the twelfth century and in Germany in the thirteenth, and the courier service was probably as fast as any such service until the coming of steam. The news of Frederick Barbarossa's death in Asia Minor reached Germany in four months; news of the capture of Richard I in Dalmatia reached England in one month. The trip from Canterbury to Rome was ordinarily made in seven weeks. The couriers of the Italian banks made their trips to the Champagne fairs in three weeks or a little more. The messengers that brought Louis XI of France word of his father's death covered three hundred and thirty miles in less than two days, although to do it they rode their horses to death. A fair average for travel was eighteen or twenty miles a day.

The thirteenth century saw old trade routes changed and new ones opened, old monopolies broken and new ones secured. The Albigensian crusades, though they destroyed much of the prosperous commerce of Languedoc, had given the kings of France access to the Mediterranean. The ravages of war were quickly repaired by the administration of St. Louis, and Marseilles and Barcelona entered into the Levantine trade. In Prussia the Teutonic Knights pushed German trade eastward along the Baltic coast and founded the ports of Libau, Memel, and Reval.[13] The Mongol destruction of Kiev in 1240 again cut the Varangian route from the Black Sea to the Baltic, and Novgorod profited by establishing trade connections with the new ports of Esthonia and Kurland and so with north Germany. The Mongol destruction of Bagdad in 1258 re- *Changes in* routed commerce with the Far East from its old ports on the Medi- *trade routes* terranean to Trebizond on the Black Sea. In that region the Genoese *in the* after overthrowing the Venetian monopoly at Constantinople in 1261 *thirteenth* entered into competition with Venice. On the other hand, Venice ac- *century* quired a stronger hold in Egypt and a larger control of the former Syrian trade, which was in part driven to Cyprus in 1291 by the Egyptian conquest of Palestine and Syria. After the conquest of Sicily by Aragon in 1282 [14] the Aragonese cities rapidly developed a great commerce in the Mediterranean. Castile by the capture of Seville in 1242 and Cádiz in 1262 had already reached the sea, and likewise became a commercial and maritime power.

This great medieval revival of commerce and industry spread inland from the coast towns, which it first favored, and stimulated all central *Changes in* and western Europe with new life, even down to local manorial and *agriculture* monastic markets. It had the following important general effects upon agriculture. The old markets were no longer adequate to meet the demand; the towns were calling for agricultural products, and even

[13] See pp. 937 ff.
[14] See p. 1007.

more distant markets were beckoning: for the first time since the prosperous days of the Roman empire there was demand for a surplus. A surplus could be raised either by improving the yield through better methods of agriculture or by bringing more land under cultivation. When plenty of land is available, as it was in medieval Europe and has been in America, the latter alternative is always easier. From about 1100 on forests were extensively cleared in the valleys of the Elbe, the Meuse, and the Loire, in Normandy, Picardy, and Roussillon. In Flanders and Poitou, in the lower Elbe valley, northern Hanover, and Holstein marshes were drained and land reclaimed from the sea by dikes.

Calls came from Flanders, Burgundy, Hesse, Brandenburg, Carinthia, northern Italy, and Tuscany for pioneers to do this arduous work. The monks, notably the Cistercians, set their lay brothers to work as agricultural colonists. But it was impossible to entice large numbers of new settlers from older regions without offering some inducement far more tempting than the prevalent type of servile land tenure. The type of contract offered to colonists can best be illustrated by reference to the French pioneers called *hôtes*. Generally the *hôte* was freed from all servile charges and all arbitrary dues. The rent of his land was fixed; his *corvées* were fixed or abolished; the fines he was liable to were reduced. He was usually freed from all military service, except for actual defense. Finally, he was given the free disposition of his holding. Thus he became practically a free renter. Such an obvious betterment of all the conditions of life was a powerful influence for the general amelioration of the servile status. Lords at home had to choose between seeing their manors depopulated and offering similar terms. Lords of new lands had to compete to attract settlers. Whole communities of serfs were transplanted to newly opened lands.[15] Thus did the frontier join with the free towns to seal the doom of serfdom. With the increase in the area of cultivable land came the desired agricultural surplus and a natural increase in population, which all co-operated with the revival of trade and industry to hasten the transformation of western Europe.

[15] See p. 586.

Chapter 20

THE URBAN REVOLUTION. THE GILDS

THE economic and social revolution of the eleventh, twelfth, *The origins* and thirteenth centuries led to the concentration of popu- *of medieval* lation in the old Roman or in entirely new towns, which *towns* immediately demanded a privileged status in feudal society. The origin of these new urban centers with their special privileges has long been an engaging mystery. The enigma has been in large part due to the paucity of documents relating to the beginnings of towns. Was the medieval town the direct descendant of the Roman town? Did it arise out of the manor, or around the monastery or the cathedral or the castle? Does it go back to primitive Germanic associations called gilds, or to the early establishment of local markets? Each of these possibilities, and others as well, has had its defenders; but it is now clear that there is no one explanation, or that in any case it is certainly none of these. The origins of individual towns are as differ-ent as their subsequent history. Nevertheless it is possible, for the purpose of generalizing, to pass over exceptions and to explain the medieval town as originating either from the remnants of the old Roman town or from the episcopal church, the monastery, or the castle.

That there was any direct connection between the institutions of the *municipia* in the Roman empire and the new medieval towns it is impossible to prove, except perhaps in Italy, where at Ravenna and Rome the old Roman *collegia* [1] may have passed into medieval gilds. If this did happen, there or elsewhere, it was a purely local phenomenon, of no general importance. On the other hand, many old Roman towns in Italy did continue to exist, even though they were in general completely transformed. There is surely some sig-nificance in the fact that *città*, Italian for "city," is the Latin *civitas*, while the French *ville* is the Latin *villa*, meaning "country estate."

[1] See p. 16.

579

What actually happened to the most important of the Roman city-states, or *civitates*, was that they became dioceses of the Church, their urban centers becoming the seat of the bishop's church, the cathedral, and headquarters for the administration of the diocese.[2]

Episcopal towns

These episcopal centers were by no means towns in our understanding of the term—communities of traders and artisans. They included little except what was indispensable for the ceremonies of the Church, the management of the diocese, and the support of the cathedral clergy: that is to say, a market, granges, and warehouses to store the produce of the bishop's manors, possibly a school, a few vassals of the bishop employed in an administrative and military capacity, servitors, petty artisans, and peasants. The episcopal town was a fortified, half-ecclesiastical, half-agricultural community. New episcopal centers, founded outside old Roman towns in the course of the early middle ages, were no different. The history of the episcopate from the late Roman empire down to the eleventh century is the record of the success of the bishops in gradually winning temporal as well as spiritual control of their towns. They were granted, like other feudal lords, privileges of immunity and justice, and rights of market, mint, and toll.

Monastic centers

The spread of monasticism in the west led here and there, often right in episcopal cities, to the growth of large agricultural establishments, which needed the labor of artisans as well as of peasants. The occasional founding of a monastery in an episcopal town divided authority over the inhabitants between the two ecclesiastical institutions, but only intensified the clerical aspect of the place. Until the end of the middle ages the town supported a large number of clergy belonging to the numerous churches and monasteries within its walls. The fortification of monasteries in the open country made them centers of refuge in times of trouble. The monasteries were granted the same privileges and rights as the bishops, while the protection of the Peace of God probably made settlement on their estates more attractive than on secular property.

The burgs

More important for the growth of towns than either episcopal headquarters or monasteries were the forts and castles of the nobles. These were not yet the great stone structures of the thirteenth century and later, but only rude, palisaded wooden blockhouses, often erected in a hurry to meet some crisis of invasion In contemporary documents they are often called burg, which meant merely a fortified place, rather than castle (Latin, *castellum*); and sometimes *urbs*,

[2] See p. 185.

classical Latin for "city," is applied to them. Countless burgs were built by dukes, counts, and margraves in the ninth and early tenth centuries for protection against Norsemen, Magyars, Slavs, and Saracens, especially in Saxony and on the eastern German frontier and in England, where many boroughs (burgs) served for defense against the Danes.[3] The burg was not only the military but also the administrative center for the immediate locality, often in charge of a castellan, who ruled practically as an independent lord.

Before the large-scale revival of commerce in the eleventh century the walled episcopal center or the fortified monastery or the burg was scarcely a town, but it was certainly the nucleus of many a town. *The nucleus of the town* It could not fail to attract a new and larger community of serfs. The denser population of this social group, the confined area in which it dwelt, and the protection it enjoyed stimulated home industries. The serf who worked on the land in spring, summer, and fall, in winter busied himself with wood turning, leather working, weaving, or making pottery; more and more the community came to rely upon the countryside round about for foodstuffs. The products of these simple crafts were sold across the threshold of the worker's cottage or at the local market. To this growing community of serfs and artisans the revival of commerce brought itinerant peddlers and then more considerable merchants, with distant wares to sell to the bishop or abbot, to the noble or his wife or his vassals. These merchants needed the lord's protection and facilities for transport and storage; moreover, they were looking for markets in which to buy as well as to sell. Here was a new kind of man, a freeman coming from God only knew where, living by trade alone. As soon as one of them settled in the community, then for the first time there was a local merchant or trader. And now there was enough need for the services of butcher, baker, brewer, vintner, or weaver to occupy a man's whole time. Genuine local industries developed, which, once started under favorable conditions, were interactive and cumulative in their effect.

The development of the town from such a nucleus can be traced in contemporary documents. The new agglomerations of merchants, traders, artisans, and serfs outside the walls of the burg were called faubourgs (from the Latin *foris burgum*, "outside the burg") or suburbs (Latin *suburbia*, "close to the urbs"). The new faubourgs and

[3] The student of American history need only compare with these burgs the similar wooden forts set up by the government for protection against the Indians as the frontier moved westward. In their importance in contributing to the growth of frontier communities, so easily traced in American annals, we may be sure that these differed not at all from medieval burgs.

suburbs soon had to have their walls for protection, and, as they increased in population and overflowed their earlier bounds, often had to be rewalled. Some of them completely encircled the old burg. The new character of the inhabitants of the faubourgs was also recognized by a new name, burgesses or burghers (Latin, *burgenses*). A new social class was in process of formation, the middle class or third estate proper, the *bourgeoisie*. The same thing happened to some monasteries and episcopal towns. It did not, of course, happen to all burgs. It came about, naturally, in such centers of feudal society as were easily defensible and located at strategic points on highways of trade or at places convenient for the exploitation of a local market. Paris expanded from *la Cité* on a little island in the Seine to both banks. At Cologne a colony of merchants occupied the ground between the walls of the old Roman and episcopal town and the Rhine. Constance, on the highway from northern Italy to France, began as a Roman fort, became an episcopal town of ten acres, annexed a colony of merchants, and had expanded to an area of eighty acres by the end of the eleventh century and by 1300 to two hundred and sixteen.[4]

The names of towns often betray their origin or the source of their prosperity. Some began as burgs—Magdeburg, Merseburg, Burghausen. Bischofshausen was the bishop's house; Bury St. Edmunds was the burg of St. Edmund's monastery. Towns naturally grew up at bridges, like Cambridge, Pontoise (bridge over the Oise), and Pont l'Évêque (the bishop's bridge), or at fords, like Oxford in England and Frankfort in Germany. Other spots predestined for towns were an important crossroads, a natural harbor or the mouth of a river, and the head of a navigable river, where goods had to be transshipped.

The new urban communities of burghers could not be contented in a society regulated by feudal and manorial custom. From the early time when professional merchants began to travel the highways they were recognized as a unique group, governed by their own customs and entitled to the special protection of princes and kings. They had long managed their own affairs, settled their own disputes, organized caravans for trade, and protected themselves when feudal lords could not or would not protect them. They had never been touched by the legal disabilities of serfdom. They could tolerate no personal limitation, no restriction of the freedom of movement that their very business demanded. So long as they were only a small and itinerant

---

[4] Stephenson, *Borough and Town*, p. 25.

class such exemptions presented no great difficulty. But a considerable group of traders and artisans permanently settled on the land confronted feudal society with a serious problem. The merchants expected to retain all their privileges, which they sought to have confirmed for themselves and extended to include their local colleagues, and then enlarged to take in the whole nonagricultural community. The burghers grew painfully conscious of the restrictions on their whole manner of life entailed by a body of custom that had grown up in a society wholly agricultural. Since they did not cultivate the soil, why should they—indeed, how could they—be liable for the personal services and customary dues paid to the lord by his peasantry? Since they were not vassals for fiefs, what had they to do with feudal dues and military service? Since their world was governed by their own law merchant, why should they be subjected to feudal law? The more advanced of the new groups soon held that they should govern themselves, judge themselves, tax themselves, defend themselves; in other words, that they ought to have complete local autonomy.

Accompanying, therefore, the economic and social revolution, as an essential part of it, went a political revolution, the establishment of a group of legally privileged towns within the framework of feudal society. It was a movement of extreme complexity and variety, difficult to summarize, but for a general understanding it may be compared with the emergence of the independent or quasi-independent feudal nobility in the ninth and tenth centuries. Just as feudal independence was often the result of downright usurpation of royal powers, which the kings had no choice but to recognize as a *fait accompli*, so in many cases, as in northern Italy, the burghers won their privileges by quietly assuming the management of their own affairs and then having their usurpation legally confirmed by a charter or peace treaty.[5] Or again, as kings and nobles, in order to raise an army, exploit their lands, or get political support, transferred lands and privileges to vassals, so farsighted kings, princes, bishops, and abbots sought to reap whatever profits could be got from a movement that they could not control by freely granting urban charters of privilege. Many were so enthusiastic over the possibility of turning the movement to their own advantage that they literally carved new towns out of the forests and open fields and deliberately attempted to attract settlers to them by liberal grants of privileges. At the risk of a contradiction in terms, therefore, we may say that a

Privileged towns

[5] E.g., the Peace of Constance of 1183; see p. 405.

new bourgeois feudalism arose out of the old feudalism in much the same way as the old noble feudalism had freed itself from the restraints of the monarchy.

The zone of privileged towns

The growth of privileged towns was naturally greatest in regions most affected by the revival of commerce and industry—in northern and north-central Italy, southern and northern France, the Rhineland, and Flanders. The height of the movement was reached in the twelfth century. While it extended to all parts of western Europe, in Germany east of the Rhine it lagged about a hundred years behind. Town independence was most successful in countries where the central government was weakest. In Italy the towns took advantage of the struggle between emperor and pope to establish themselves as independent merchant republics, medieval counterparts of the ancient city-states. In Germany feudal decentralization and anarchy resulted in a similar group of virtually independent towns. In France and England, on the other hand, strong monarchy restricted the ambitions of the bourgeoisie to various degrees of local autonomy, and in Flanders a similar limitation was imposed upon them by the counts.

Everywhere the object of the towns was the same: freedom from serfdom and all its entanglements. The townsman was to have freedom of movement, freedom of trade, and freedom to marry, without any interference from the lord, and his children were to inherit all his liberties. Town charters not only granted these privileges, but, to help attract settlers, commonly provided that any serf who had taken refuge in a town should, after residing there unmolested for a year and a day, be regarded as a freeman, quit of all the claims his former lord had upon him. "City air makes a man free"; so runs an old German proverb (*Die Stadtluft macht frei*). The townsman also had complete freedom in the disposition of his land and property; he could sell, exchange, and bequeath without interference, and all feudal charges were reduced to a fixed rent in cash. The taille, military service, the *corvée*, the *droit de gîte*, the banalities were abolished, or at least curtailed or commuted to a fixed payment. Tolls and customs were abolished or reduced. To spare the townsman trouble it was provided that trials be held in local courts and that fines and punishments be reduced to a fixed tariff.

Customary town privileges

Most towns never secured more than these "elementary urban liberties," although the largest and wealthiest, not content with these, secured a somewhat greater degree of autonomy. But "ultimate control of municipal magistrates, supreme judicial authority,

powers of taxation, and military command regularly remained with *Town*
the lord or his suzerain." [6] Many towns, however, won recognition *government*
of the municipal government, headed by elected consuls in northern
Italy and Provence, by *échevins* or *jurées* in northern France and
Flanders, and by aldermen in England. "Everywhere the chosen
magistrates, by themselves or through appointees, administered justice; collected tolls; held charge of walls, gates, streets, and other
public works; laid taxes; and saw to the payment of the lord's dues.
At first no specifically municipal buildings existed. . . . It was left
for a later age to produce *hôtels de ville*, belfries, and elaborate official paraphernalia." [7]

Usually the towns acquired their privileges slowly, over a long
period of time, their successes being interrupted by temporary, or
checked by permanent, reverses. The prelates of the Church were
notably slow in coming to terms; in many episcopal and monastic
towns, in fact, especially in northern Italy and along the Rhine, the
burghers had to resort to violence to secure their demands. Often a
community was able to take advantage of the lord's lack of money to
buy its charter of liberty.[8] No matter what degree of autonomy a
town achieved, in the course of time the body of townsmen was recognized as a collective legal personality. Everywhere the new communities were at first conceived in conventional feudal terms as vassals, even if of a special kind. As vassals they entered the privileged
ranks of society, entitled to the rights specified in their charters, and
obligated by responsibilities which they discharged by services and
payments for their self-government or the quashing of ancient feudal
and manorial rights.

The earlier charters of privilege were secured by the organized *Communes*
effort of the towns. Charters were granted either to co-operative associations long existent, confirming *de facto* rights already exercised,
or to organizations formed for the particular purpose of fighting for
a charter. Such an association was often called a commune, and towns
liberated thereby—usually only after resort to violence—many historians have called communes. But these communes were no different from any towns with a charter, or with a recognized body of
rights but without a charter, so the term has little historical significance. The example of the communes, however, was an effective
stimulus to simpler rural communities. For instance, seventeen vil-

[6] Stephenson, *op. cit.*, p. 46.
[7] *Ibid.*
[8] See p. 555.

lages of the Bishop of Laon organized a commune, or sworn confederation, with Anizy-le-Château as its center, to secure a privileged status. In order to prevent the escape of multitudes of serfs to the towns which would make them free, lords and kings were compelled to recognize the demands of these rural towns for privileges. The charter granted by the Archbishop of Rheims in 1182 to Beaumont-en-Argonne was given in the course of the following years to some five hundred communities within and without France. Regular families of towns were thus established. The example of communities of pioneers like the French *hôtes* also must be reckoned with that of the towns as an encouragement to older agricultural communities to try for a larger measure of liberty.

The advantages to feudal lords of having towns on their lands, especially the increase in income from the newly produced wealth, *New towns* led to what has been called "a veritable craze for urban development." Lords tried to make old rural communities into towns or to found new towns. In many instances the circumstances were not unlike the well-known features of a modern real estate boom, and the motive often was the same hope of increased land values without much labor or expense.

A privilege granted to the rural community of Lorris by Louis VI of France became extremely popular with other communities and other lords. "First of all . . . the man who elects to reside at Lorris is to pay only six *deniers* for his house and *arpent* of land. If he lives there peaceably for a year and a day, he is henceforth free and cannot be claimed by a previous master. He is to be quit of all *taille* and forced exactions; of all military service, save for one day within the immediate vicinity; of all watching service and *corvées*, except that those men who own horses and carts have to carry the king's wine once a year to Orleans. Whenever he pleases, the man of Lorris can sell his possessions and go elsewhere. He cannot be tried outside the town, and there only according to specified rules of procedure. Fines and punishments are strictly limited. No one shall be molested while coming to or going from the market of Lorris, unless he has committed some offence on the same day. Various restrictions of tolls, customs, and other dues are established." [9]

Montauban, in southern France, was founded in 1144 by the Count of Toulouse. Munich, Brunswick, and Lübeck are only the most important of the towns founded by Henry the Lion. In the late middle ages the Teutonic Knights founded at least eighty-five

[9] Stephenson, *op. cit.*, p. 29.

owns in northeastern Germany, whose rights and customs were generally modeled upon the privileges of Magdeburg. The house of Zähringen in southeastern Germany produced notable founders of towns; Conrad of Zähringen's foundation of Freiburg im Breisgau in 1120 was "the first great success in urban colonization beyond the Rhine." Needless to say, many attempts were born of too much enthusiasm tempered by too little good sense and foresight, so that the projected towns failed to materialize. New towns made to order, in contrast with old towns that had grown slowly, were laid out with almost the regularity of a modern real estate development.

The towns, whether newly founded or finally recognized, were *New urban* faced with a host of new problems. They had to devise instruments *problems* of local self-government. They must defend their newly won liberties with walls and militias, and pay for them by taxation. Since alone they could not do all this, they took to uniting in town leagues. Such unions for mutual protection have already been seen in the Lombard League of northern Italy, the Spanish leagues, and the Rhenish, Swabian, and Hanseatic leagues. In monarchical states such as France and England there was no place for such leagues. The towns were also seriously concerned with the question of food supply, which they tried to solve in part by bringing under their jurisdiction the surrounding countryside. Most serious of all, however, were the problem of regulating trade and industry within the town and trade with other towns, and the numerous new social problems presented by the maldistribution of wealth—which, as always and everywhere, began almost as soon as its accumulation.

Of these the chief concern was the regulation of trade and industry *Regulation of* within the walls. In the middle ages the question whether it was *trade and* necessary and proper to curb the activities of the individual in the in *industry* terests of his social group was not, as with us, matter for argument. "The medieval burghers were not convinced that man's self-love is God's providence, or that the economic interests of the individual and society must necessarily and invariably coincide." [10] Another historian says: "The economists of that period had not grasped the fact that the cleverness shown in buying an article cheap and selling the same thing, without any further expenditure of labour, dear, if done on a sufficiently large scale, constitutes a claim to the honours of knighthood or a peerage." [11]

The greed of capitalism was effectively curbed until the later mid-

[10] Lipson, *Economic History of England*, I, 266.
[11] Salzman, *Medieval English Industries*, p. 324.

dle ages. This perhaps amounts only to saying that it was curbed so long as there was not much opportunity for it to exist. Many towns were still half agricultural, and the capital needed for local trade and industry was small and the profits limited. One should be careful not to attribute too large a measure of social-mindedness to medieval businessmen. For while they often displayed genuine concern for the welfare of the town upon which they depended for a living, the control of economic life was nevertheless exercised by specially organized groups, the gilds, whose whole policy was monopolistic: namely, to exclude from the local market so far as possible, and when not possible at any rate to penalize, both the outside trader and the independent trader inside who was not a member of the gild. Their social attitude, to be sure, was to some extent influenced by the teachings of the Church; but their aim was to use the town market peacefully, profitably, and pleasantly for themselves alone. The economic regulation of the merchant gilds and the craft gilds together might be compared to what we should have under the joint regulation of the economic life of our cities by the chambers of commerce and the labor unions of skilled workmen. Wholesale trade at the fairs was free from all concern with the local market, and demanded so much more capital that it escaped the control of the gilds. From this source organized capitalism as we know it might well emerge. In the very means, however, by which the medieval towns controlled industry and commerce there was plainly present from the first the germ of monopoly, and monopoly has ever been the dream of unrestricted capitalism.

The origin of gilds

The origin of the merchant and craft gilds is even more difficult to determine than the source of the town corporations. Besides these two main types of federation there were many religious confraternities, not always easily distinguishable from the gilds proper, and from which the gilds themselves may in some cases have arisen. Presumably, however, like the town itself, the gild ordinarily began as a voluntary organization of individuals engaged in the same pursuit, and formed for mutual protection and advantage. The merchant gild was sometimes responsible for securing the town charter, which was issued in its name, and which recognized it as a privileged body.

The merchant gilds were the first to appear, in the late eleventh and early twelfth centuries. They were composed of all merchants and traders within the town, including at first the artisans, who in earlier medieval times were also traders. As industry in the larger towns began to specialize in various crafts, the earlier merchant gild split up into as many craft gilds as the town could support, each composed of all the citizens following the same trade. Such splitting off of special craft gilds tended to weaken the original merchant gilds, which, except in towns too small for special craft organizations, generally disappeared. Both types of gild sought recognition as privileged, self-governing associations. They sought, that is, just what the towns had sought, special immunity from outside interference; and they achieved it with the same varying degrees of success.

Although the gilds must be distinguished from the organization of the town itself, the merchant gilds at least were almost identical with the town corporation, inasmuch as the leading men of the gild were sure to be the leading men of the town. The craft gilds were usually subordinate to both merchant gild and town. But even the craft gilds, being authorized to do the work of municipal officials in supervising their own crafts within the city, should be regarded as a part, however subordinate, of the municipal administration; they, and the merchant gilds much more, were quasi-public institutions, and their private ordinances were in reality municipal ordinances. But the situation varied from town to town, and was never simple. There were residents who were not burghers, burghers who were not gildsmen, and gildsmen who were not burghers.

The chief purposes of both types of gild were to preserve their monopoly of the town market against any outsider; to maintain *Gild* equality among their members by restraining the initiative of the *monopolies* more enterprising; to guarantee the consumer wares of good and uniform quality; and to establish a system of industrial education. Before the monopolies were well organized, membership was not exclusive; on the contrary, it was important to get as many members as possible. The merchant gild's monopoly of trade within the town was protected by exemption from all tolls and customs. Foreign merchants and natives not members of the gild were at a disadvantage in that they were obliged to pay these fees, allowed to sell only to members of the gild, and forbidden to buy certain commodities at all. No foreigner was permitted to practice a trade in a town without becoming a member of his craft gild: the idea of the closed shop is thus no modern invention.

The degree of monopoly varied from town to town. The merchant gild at Southampton decreed that "no one of the city . . . shall buy anything to sell again in the same city unless he is of the gild merchant or of the franchise" (i.e., a citizen). Further, "no private man nor stranger shall bargain for or buy any kind of merchandise coming into the city before a burgess of the gild merchant, so long as the gildsman is present and wishes to bargain for and buy this merchandise." The gild of leather dressers in London prescribed that "no stranger shall work in the said trade, or keep house for the same in the city, if he be not an apprentice [of the gild] or a man admitted to the franchise of the said city." The attitude of the medieval English town towards the foreigner is made plain by the necessity of a regulation of 1421 at Coventry "that no man throw ne cast at noo straunge man, ne skorn hym." [12] Echoes of this ancient attitude can be heard today in such slogans as "Trade at home" and "Buy American." No doubt most people who parrot these words honestly believe that they have at heart the welfare of the community and the country; but the spirit behind the words is the spirit of monopoly.

Equality within the gilds

The attempts of the gilds to maintain equality among their members by guaranteeing equal opportunities to buy and sell in the local market took the form of regulations concerning technical processes, hours of labor, wages, number of workmen to be employed, prices, and trade practices of all sorts. Every effort was made to nip the capitalistic spirit in the bud. One regulation common in the merchant gilds guaranteed to every member the right to participate in any purchase made by any other gildsman; that is, it was considered unfair for any one member to derive advantage from a particular bargain. Attempts to corner the market were vigorously opposed and punished. The employment of improved methods of manufacture, due to new inventions or to the use of water power, was frowned upon unless all producers shared alike in the benefits. No one might employ his workmen longer than another, nor pay higher wages. The number of men employed was regulated in order to keep the production of all gild shops approximately equal. All members must charge the same price for the same goods. What might happen to a merchant who cut prices is illustrated by the complaint of an English herring merchant that "because he sold his merchandise at a less price than other merchants of the town of Yaxley . . . they assaulted him, beat him and ill-treated him and left him there for dead, so that he despaired of his life." [13] No man might try to get another's customers or entice his workmen away. Advertising of many kinds was forbidden. This kind of close supervision of trade and industry, which today is called planned economy and is branded

[12] *Ibid.*, p. 333.
[13] Quoted by Lipson, *op. cit.*, I, 246.

as communism, was obviously designed to benefit not so much the consumers as the producers organized in the gilds.

On the other hand, medieval manuscripts are full of evidence of a need for supervision in the general public's interest. Many of the spurriers of London, we learn, "are wandering about all day, without working at their trade, and then, when they have become drunk and frantic, they take to their work, to the annoyance of the sick *Objectionable* and all their neighborhood, as well by reason of the broils that arise *craftsmen* between them and the strange folks who are dwelling among them. And then they blow up their fires so vigorously that their forges begin all at once to blaze, to the great peril of themselves and of all the neighborhood around. And then, too, all the neighbors are much in dread of the sparks which so vigorously issue forth in all directions from the mouths of the chimneys in their forges." [14]

The Church found plenty to inveigh against. St. Antonino of Florence speaks of sailors, "risking their lives, sharing immense labors, commonly the worst of men and the most blasphemous, praying only when the storms are upon them, promising repentance in a fear that is wholly servile, and when the danger is past . . . returning to their vomit, troubling neither about God nor holy things." Painters drew still hotter fire. They painted "pictures that provoked to lust, not because of their exquisite beauty, but because of the direct suggestion of evil shown in their arrangement of nude figures; . . . pictures that were heretical, such as 'the monstrous representation of the Holy Trinity as a man with three heads'; or 'the Annunciation in which the child Jesus is shown descending into the Virgin's womb, as though He had not been formed of the substance of her virginal body'; or 'Jesus as a child learning His letters from a book, for He was never taught of men'; or 'midwives sitting near the manger for the Mother who remained a virgin'; or . . . 'the foolish introduction of comic elements into the pictures of the Saints, a monkey, or a dog in pursuit of hares, or such like, especially by illuminators.'" St. Antonino rebuked painters also for "their working on feast days, or their overcharging, or 'most of all the use of bad paints which lose their color, and the habit artists have of never completing what they have begun.'" [15]

It became apparent that if the gilds were to be protected in their *Gild inspec-* monopoly of the market they must not only fix fair prices but guar- *tion of goods* antee the quality of their goods and prevent all kinds of dishonest

[14] *Translations and Reprints,* II, no. 1, p. 22.
[15] Jarrett, *Social Theories of the Middle Ages,* pp. 178–79.

dealing. The inspection by gild wardens of the whole process of manufacture was one of their most important functions. The merchant gilds seem originally to have been responsible for the quality of goods; but after the rise of the craft gilds each did its own inspecting, always by authority of the municipality or state. The miller, the baker, and the brewer in particular were notorious for their fraudulent practices. Chaucer's miller, whose nose was decorated with a wart tufted with hairs "red as the bristles of an old sow's ears . . . could steal corn and full thrice charge his fees." A London baker "did skilfully and artfully cause a certain hole to be made upon a table. . . . And when his neighbours and others, who were wont to bake their bread at his oven came with their dough . . . [he] used to put their dough upon the said table and over the hole. . . . One of his household . . . [was] seated beneath the hole, and carefully opening it, piecemeal and bit by bit craftily withdrew some of the dough." [16] The buyer of upholstery " 'seeth withoute and knoweth not the stuf within,' down pillows being stuffed 'with thistill downe and cattes tailles' (the vegetable variety, I imagine) and 'materas stuffed with here (hair) and flokkes [tufts of wool] and sold for flokkes.' " [17] Night work was generally forbidden, because for one thing it offered larger opportunities for fraud. The spurriers of London forbade it because "then they introduce false iron, and iron that has cracked, for tin, and also they put gilt on false copper and cracked." [18]

Apprentices, journeymen, and masters

Each craft gild had three classes of members: the masters, the journeymen, and the apprentices. Only the first two ever had anything to do with electing officers and managing the gild, and in the later middle ages the journeymen lost their vote in elections. The institution of apprenticeship was the gild's system of educating the youth for his craft; how good a system it was can be judged by that superior medieval craftsmanship which was always so close to fine artistry. A boy was received as apprentice by the master upon definite terms and upon payment of a fee, for a period varying for the different crafts from two to the more usual seven years. He was given board, clothes, and lodging in the master's house. The contract of apprenticeship often provided for the boy's education in ordinary elementary subjects, and it was the master's duty to watch over the development of his character as well as to teach him his trade. An

[16] H. T. Riley, *Memorials of London*, p. 163. Cf. Lipson, *op. cit.*, I, 297, n. 2.
[17] Salzman, *op. cit.*, p. 309.
[18] *Translations and Reprints*, II, no. 1, p. 22.

English master barber promised to give his apprentice "suitable clothing, shoeing, board, bedding and chastisement"; one apprentice complains of his master for not "well-using him in beating him."

At the end of the period of apprenticeship, spent in the master's house and shop working under close supervision at his side, the apprentice became a journeyman. He was then available for hire by

Medieval masons in the windows of the cathedral at Chartres

the day (French *journée*, "day" or "day's work"), and was entitled to keep his wages; but normally he still lived with the master, or at least under his supervision. The close personal relationship between master and apprentice was thus continued between master and journeyman. It was a rigorous system. "If any serving man shall conduct himself in any other manner than properly towards his master, and act rebelliously towards him, no one of the said trade shall set him to work until he shall have made amends before the mayor and aldermen." One gets a notion of the extraordinary vitality of the system from the account in Carl Schurz's autobiography of his stay in the master locksmith's house in Cologne, where only the senior journeyman was sometimes allowed to speak at meals without having first been spoken to by the master. The apprentice system originated in the latter part of the twelfth century; Schurz was writing of 1839.

By carefully saving his money the journeyman might reasonably expect in time to accumulate enough capital to set himself up as a master with his own shop. Entrance into master's rank followed an examination, which sometimes required the journeyman to present a masterpiece, and always included an oath to fulfill all the obligations and regulations of the gild. A master's shop was usually on the ground floor of his house. At first he made goods only to order, usually from his own raw materials, though a buyer might furnish them. All of the dealings between the master and his customers—placing orders, paying bills, making complaints—were just as immediate and personal as those between the master and his workmen.

Social functions of the gilds

The gilds were also religious associations, benefit societies, and social clubs. They celebrated together, with colorful processions, pageants, or original plays, the numerous feast days of the Church and especially the festivals of their patron saints. When the mystery plays were transferred from the Church, where they originated, to the market place, the gilds took charge of the productions. Their drinking parties, held in their own gildhalls, were impressive and serious affairs. The gild took care of its sick and poor members. "If a gildsman is ill and in the city, wine shall be sent to him, two loaves of bread and a gallon of wine, and a dish from the kitchen; and two approved men of the gild shall go to visit him, and look after his condition." Gildsmen attended the funerals of deceased members and tried to care for their families. They kept candles burning in the chapel of their patron saint, and often hired special chaplains to say Masses for the repose of the souls of their dead colleagues. Members were expected to be generally helpful to each other, as for example, to co-operate in getting an unfortunate member out of jail. As an organization they often assumed responsibility for a member's debts. They were expected to settle their disputes in their own tribunals, without going to court. They were bound to respect each other's persons: ". . . if any brother of the aforesaid fraternity and craft despise another, calling him knave or whoreson or stupid or any other misname, he shall pay."

Capitalism in the gilds

For the needs of a single town the anticapitalistic gild system might well suffice. Through their control of the production, distribution, and exchange of goods the gilds could avoid the evils of unemployment, strikes, lockouts, the intrusion of the middleman, speculation, and the accumulation of excessively large fortunes. But for interregional or international wholesale trade by land or sea the gild system was wholly inadequate; and it was from this source that the germs of capitalism emerged to permeate and destroy the gilds from within, and replace them by a new type of organization.

The ordinary merchant or artisan in the gilds could not participate in the export trade by himself. Savings had to be pooled in new types of organization, such as family companies, partnerships, joint-stock companies, and regulated companies, in order to exploit this new kind of commerce. When the craft gilds began to produce for the export trade, the individual artisan found himself slowly losing his independence. He could not assume the risks of producing for a foreign market subject to incalculable fluctuations in demand, of manufacturing for sales hoped for abroad instead of filling orders at home. A rich fellow gildsman stood ready to furnish raw materials and pay him a wage for working them up into the finished product, which he took off his hands for cash and exported for his own profit. The exporter was ready also to supply the tools of the trade, and in time the poorer masters, unable to stand the pace, had nothing left but their hands: they had slipped into the ranks of wage earners.

The gilds themselves fell more exclusively into the control of the richer members, who aimed to restrict them to their own families. The term of apprenticeship was made longer. The requirements for mastership were raised so that the ordinary journeyman could no longer hope to become a master; he had to pay high fees, give elaborate banquets, and supply himself with rich liveries. Distinctions between greater and lesser gilds began to appear.[19] In vain the journeymen tried to organize special associations of their own, and to strike in order to better their conditions. In vain related crafts tried to organize in larger gilds. They could not withstand the merchant-industrialist-capitalist boring from within. Free artisans as early as the fourteenth century were becoming groups of wage earners, in some instances already working in primitive factories. The class distinction between employer and employee gradually displaced the old personal relationship between master, journeyman, and apprentice. The history of the gild system is the sad story of the enslavement of the crafts.

This social transformation in the later middle ages found upon the continent, if not in England, its counterpart in political struggles

[19] For example, in Florence there were seven greater gilds: (1) the importers and finishers and dyers of French cloth; (2) the money changers and brokers, represented such families as the Frescobaldi, Bardi, and Peruzzi; (3) the notaries and judges; (4) the wool manufacturers, the wealthiest and most influential of all the gilds, with twelve hundred houses, at its height; (5) the silk manufacturers; (6) the doctors and the wholesale druggists; (7) the furriers. The lesser gilds were the builders and stonecutters, ironworkers, carpenters, locksmiths, manufacturers of armor and swords, leather dressers, harness makers, linen drapers, shoemakers, wine merchants, oil merchants, bakers, butchers, and innkeepers.

in the towns. Most town governments were to a greater or lesser extent in the control of just such a merchant oligarchy as ruled Venice with conspicuous success. The rich merchants used their political prerogatives to their own economic advantage by crushing not only new attempts at organization, but all forms of opposition and even discussion among the crafts. In all industrial towns, particularly in Flanders and Italy, the craft gilds and the unorganized workmen sought to get some voice in a government which was often both inefficient and dishonest. In 1378 at Florence and in 1382 at Ghent and Paris formidable insurrections occurred. Nor were these isolated instances; before and after them revolts of the medieval workingman against the abuses of nascent capitalism were widespread. The soap makers and dyers of Florence in 1342 protested that "the wool merchants had power to pay the work of those under them not in ready money but in installments, and with postponements that lasted even up to five years. The wool merchants fixed at their pleasure the price of the work of dyeing, nor were the men able to object if brought before the consuls, who were wool merchants themselves. They begged that they might be permitted to form an association on equality with the Greater Guilds."

Occasionally the crafts were successful in winning some share in the government, notably in Flanders, but seldom for long, while in many instances their success only served to exacerbate internal dissension. In France the crown intervened to establish order and a more even justice. But in Germany and Italy the rich classes retained this hold on the government; and on the whole the attempts of the workingmen, who were sometimes moved by vague communistic sentiments, were dismal and pathetic failures.

The Church, whose founder said that "it is easier for a camel to go through the eye of a needle than for a rich man to enter into the Kingdom of God," could not in theory countenance the new capitalistic tendencies of medieval society. An early Church Father had written: "He that buys a thing in order that he may sell it, entire and unchanged, at a profit is the trader who is cast out of God's Temple." Moreover, the Church, which had attained its power and influence in a predominantly agricultural society, seemed instinctively to realize that the growing preoccupation of the upper classes with this world's goods threatened that power and influence by substituting for the old, approved spiritual ideals new worldly ideals which the Church had no part in shaping. Through the canon law and through its theologians and moralists the Church therefore tried

chapter room

The fountain chapel from across
the garden

The monks' refectory

Views of the Cistercian
monastery at Maulbronn

The carved stalls of the
monks in the choir of the
church

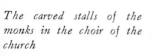

The refectory of the lay
brothers

The Romanesque cloister of the Benedictine Abbey of Maria Laach

The monks' cellarer samples the brew

Monks from the tombs of the dukes of Burgundy (See p. 1027)

A monastic scribe

to direct the spirit of business into wholly ethical channels. It insisted upon a "just price," which would cover raw materials, wages, and profit enough to maintain a man and his family suitably. But no more: men in business to make money and for nothing else were mortal sinners. Everything beyond a man's genuine needs belonged to the poor: charity was a cardinal virtue, avarice a cardinal sin.

The Church, whose founder also bade men "lend, hoping for nothing again," likewise was bound to condemn usury, which was originally defined as taking interest for a loan of money. Of course it succeeded no better in this than in its attempt to prevent excessive profits and the accumulation of money from business. There are always many ways for respectable men, while obeying the letter, to violate the spirit of a law. The borrower might promise to pay a thousand florins without interest, having actually received only nine hundred. Or he could agree to pay by a certain date or suffer a specified penalty, and then, as soon as the limit had expired, pay principal and penalty together. The popes themselves could not do without loans from the Italian bankers, for which they paid interest. They advised widows to invest in good securities, which would hardly have been good had they paid no interest. And what could they do when prelates pledged the sacred relics of a saint as security for a loan? At length canon law began to accommodate theory to facts. If the lender himself suffered loss, either because the money was not repaid promptly or because, not having it in hand, he was prevented from making a profit that would have been legitimate, then it was permissible to charge interest. Or if he lent money with as good a chance of losing it as of making a profit on it, then interest was legitimate. Such loopholes an agile conscience could easily enlarge and escape all penalties.

The Church's attitude towards usury

An Italian preacher of the fourteenth century observed that "nowadays the old fashion is changed; for those who once avoided to give such men [i.e., usurers and profiteers] the kiss of peace in church are now ready to kiss their feet . . . and they whose bodies were wont to be buried in the field or the garden are now entombed in churches before the High Altar." [20] And yet the Church never quite gave up the notion attributed to St. Jerome, that it was hard for the merchant to please God. It did not approve usury, though it modified its definition by admitting many exceptions. The merchant was not necessarily a sinner, "but this business is full of perils and deceits, and seems sometimes inseparable from usury." At the very end of

[20] Coulton, *The Medieval Scene*, p. 130.

the middle ages a German abbot could write: "Whoever buys corn, meat and wine in order to drive up their price and to amass money at the cost of others is, according to the law of the Church, no better than a common criminal. In a well-governed community all arbitrary raising of prices in the case of articles of food and clothing is peremptorily stopped . . . in every community care should be taken that all the members be provided for, and not only a small number be allowed to grow rich and revel in luxury to the hurt and prejudice of the many." [21] Such an attitude towards business is again possessing some men's minds. The state is beginning to take by income taxes, inheritance taxes, and taxes on excess profits what the medieval Church preferred should never be accumulated.

Medieval towns today

The physical aspect of the medieval town remains to be noted. The traveler in Europe today finds it easy, despite all the corrupting influences of tourists, to recapture the air of the medieval town, from its streets and from its architectural remains. To enter France by way of St. Malo is to go a long way back towards the middle ages; there stands the town intact within its walls. San Gimignano is still crowded with its medieval skyscrapers, the towers of its quarreling noble families; and upon the narrow streets of Florence still look down the frowning fortress-homes of her early merchant and banking princes. Modern trade routes have happily passed by Troyes and Provins, close though they are to Paris, leaving them still their medieval walls and churches, their dark, narrow alleys lined with tall houses almost falling into each other. The gradual expansion of the town by the inclusion of new suburbs, which necessitated tearing down old walls and building new, can be traced especially well in Vienna, Paris, Munich, and Nuremberg. In the first three the walls have been replaced by modern boulevards, but inside them the old town still retains much or all of its ground plan. At Nuremberg the railroad station stands in the middle of the city, just outside the latest walls; a good part of those walls are still standing, skirted by the great moat, now filled with trees and flowers. Every medieval town, great or small, that has survived at all seems somehow to have preserved its individuality.

The appearance of the medieval town

Outside the main gate of the town were the public gallows, with generally a corpse or two still swinging, pecked at by crows, and on iron spikes over the gate were stuck the weathering heads of other criminals. A deep moat, dry or wet, girded the main wall, into which

[21] Quoted by Adair in Hearnshaw, *Medieval Contributions to Modern Civilization*, pp. 246-47.

towers were built at intervals, sometimes only three hundred feet apart. The entrances were reached by drawbridges across the moat and were protected by great gates. From gate to gate across the town ran streets wide enough to permit the passage of carts bringing produce from the country. Around the town inside the wall ran a street designed to give quick access to any point on the wall. The rest of the streets were usually crooked and always narrow, perhaps ten feet in width or even less, and darkened by the projecting upper stories of the houses, which made them seem even narrower than they were. There were no sidewalks until long after streets began to be paved. The first paved streets were in Italy. Paris had none until Philip Augustus paved the roadway in front of the Louvre in 1184. Once paving was begun, the rivalry of the cities soon led them all to pave their chief streets. During the fourteenth century Lübeck, Strassburg, Prague, Nuremberg, and Frankfort began paving, and by the end of the fifteenth century all the principal German cities had streets paved with stone. Refuse was thrown into the streets, so that the pedestrian might at any moment be drenched by the contents of a pail of garbage thrown without warning from some upper window. Rain and the numerous pigs and dogs roaming at large were trusted to clean the streets. With sanitation so primitive, and with wells usually the only water supply for cities not on rivers, plagues and epidemics were frequent, and even the normal death rate was very high compared with modern cities. Public and private baths were introduced late; indeed, the Church was always somewhat suspicious of too much care of the body, and set no great store by cleanliness. At night, except for an occasional light before a shrine, the streets were dark. Robbers were numerous enough to make it unsafe to go about unescorted after nightfall, when the honest householder usually battened his windows with thick wooden planks and fastened his doors with chain and lock against thieves and hoodlums.

In the center of the town was the public square or market place, *The life of* faced by the principal church and the town hall. In the middle of *the streets* the square was the town fountain, usually adorned with a piece of humorous sculpture. On market and festival days the streets were crowded with people who scarcely knew how to be drab in dress. In Paris one might encounter "the beggars who sat at the church doors and by the bridges, the peasants who came in from the country to buy and sell, the artisans and craftsmen in their open shops, the hawkers and merchants, jongleurs and mountebanks, monks and friars, canons of the cathedral and professors of the university, students and schoolboys; couriers with their white wands, heralds in tabards, knights in armour; nobles riding out to hawk or hunt outside the city, ladies taking the air in litters, judges in their scarlet riding to the Law Courts, pilgrims going to Ste. Geneviève, prisoners, gyved and bound, being driven to the Grand Châtelet; and, secure within his turreted fortifications, the King in the Louvre. Paris was then, as now, an epitome of the life of France." [22] In London you might follow the stroller and be tempted at every step:

> "Then to the Chepe I began me drawne,
> Where mutch people I saw for to stande;
> One ofred me velvet, sylke and lawne,
> An other he taketh me by the hande,
> 'Here is Parys thred, the fynest in the land';
> I never was used to such thyngs indede . . .
> Then went I forth by London stone,
> Throughout all Canwyke streete;
> Drapers mutch cloth me offred anone . . .
> Then I hyed me into Est-Chepe;
> One cryes rybbes of befe, and many a pye;
> Pewter pottes they clattered on a heape;
> There was harpe, fyfe, and mynstrelsye . . .
> The taverner took mee by the sleve,
> 'Sir,' sayth he, 'wyll you our wyne assay?' " [23]

If you accepted his invitation, you would meet

> "Cis the sempstress (who) sat on the bench,
> Walt the gamekeeper and his wife—drunk;
> Tom the tinker and two of his 'prentices,
> Hick the hackneyman, Hogg the needler,
> Clarice of Cock Lane and the parish clerk;
> Parson Piers of Pray-to-God and Pernel the Flemish woman,
> Daw the ditcher and a dozen more of them;
> A fiddler, a ratter and a Cheapside scavenger,
> A ropemaker, a lackey, and Rose the retailer,
> A watchman and a hermit and the Tyburn hangman;
> Godfrey the garlic-seller and Griffin the Welshman." [24]

[22] Joan Evans, *Medieval France*, p. 75.
[23] From "London Lykpenny," a ballad sometimes attributed to John Lydgate.
[24] Quoted from *Piers Plowman* by Salzman in *English Life in the Middle Ages*, p. 77.

It might well be a Sunday, too, for despite the lamentations and prohibitions of the clergy markets were often held on Sunday. In London on holidays "the boys and young men would play at tilting, wrestling, football or other games of ball, not only in the fields but in the streets, though as time went on efforts were made to suppress street games; wrestling was forbidden in St. Paul's churchyard; 'bars,' or 'prisoner's base,' and games that involved the annoyance of passers-by were prohibited in Westminster when parliament was sitting, and football was constantly denounced, with good reason, as it was not an orderly game with a fixed number of players, definite rules and regular goals, but a wild struggle between opposing parties to force the ball through the streets from one end of the town to the other, frequently resulting in broken legs. Bowls and quoits, played down the streets, doubtless relieved life of its monotony, but also occasionally relieved an unwary pedestrian of his life altogether, and were, therefore, not encouraged in towns. In the winter, when the marshes were covered with ice, the young men would fasten to their feet rough skates made of the leg-bones of animals, and, propelling themselves with iron-shod poles, shoot across the ice, tilting at one another, to the breaking of many heads and limbs." [25]

Within the strictly limited area enclosed by the town walls land was valuable and rents correspondingly high. To get the greatest return possible from their property landlords built as high as they could. The city government, to prevent too great crowding and perhaps to insure that no private building should be as tall as the town hall or the cathedral, often limited the height of buildings. Amsterdam forbade the erection of any building higher than the third story of the Rathaus. It was the duty of the Archdeacon of Rheims to look daily from the portholes in the eaves of the cathedral while a new building was being erected, to make sure that it did not rise higher than the eaves of the cathedral. Houses in Venice might not exceed seventy feet in height. Many persons might own a large house co-operatively, each holding a few rooms. Overcrowding was as bad as in modern city tenements; as many as sixteen people sometimes lived in three rooms. With almost all private buildings and many public ones constructed wholly of wood, fires were tragically frequent. The town sometimes rented space on the walls or in the moats for gardens or cottages, and the towers in the walls were used for granaries and stables. *Living quarters*

The wife of the prosperous burgher had her hands full, managing

[25] *Ibid.*, pp. 82–83.

a large establishment. One young woman of Paris at the end of the fourteenth century had a complete manual of household economy prepared for her by her aged husband. From this invaluable work she learned to take no servants "until you first know where their last place was, and send some of your people to get their character, to wit, whether they talked or drank too much, [and] how long they were in the place. . . ." When she went out she had only to follow instructions: "Bear your head upright and your eyelids low and without fluttering, and look straight in front of you about four rods ahead, without looking round at any man or woman to the right or to the left, nor looking up, nor glancing from place to place, nor stopping to speak to anyone on the road." [26] She would learn how to rid the house of fleas, flies, and mosquitoes. Most important of all, she would know how to prepare food that her husband liked, and she would never fail in those little wifely attentions that nourish a husband's love.

On his travels, "in rain and wind, in snow and hail, now drenched now dry, now sweating now shivering, ill-fed, ill-lodged, ill-warmed and ill-bedded," the merchant husband is "upheld by the hope that he has of his wife's care of him on his return, and of the ease, the joys and the pleasures which she will do to him, or cause to be done to him in her presence: to have his shoes removed before a good fire, his feet washed and to have fresh shoes and stockings; to be given good food and drink; to be well served and well looked after, well bedded in white sheets and nightcaps, well covered with good furs, and assuaged with other joys and amusements, privities, loves and secrets, concerning which I am silent; and on the next day fresh shirts and garments. Certes, fair sister, such service maketh a man love and desire to return to his home and to see his goodwife and to be distant with other women." [27]

Not all women, however, stayed at home. They played no small part in industry. They controlled the brewing trade in England, and were admitted to the gild of barber-surgeons. In other large industrial centers, notably in Florence, they were conspicuous in the textile trade as weavers.

Urban population in the middle ages was never what we should call large, nor were there many large cities. We can only estimate, in the absence of anything like modern census statistics, and estimates vary considerably. It is estimated that at the end of the twelfth century

---

[26] Power, *Medieval People*, p. 92.
[27] *Ibid.*, p. 96.

Palermo had a population of about five hundred thousand. In the thirteenth century Florence, Venice, and Milan had possibly a hundred thousand. During the same century Paris grew from one hundred thousand to two hundred and forty thousand. At the same time Douai, Lille, and Ypres had from sixty to eighty and London from forty to forty-five thousand. In the first half of the fourteenth century Genoa, Barcelona, and Cologne had about fifty thousand, Bologna, Padua, Strassburg, Lübeck, and Hamburg from twenty to forty, Nuremberg about twenty, and York, Bristol, Antwerp, Frankfort, Augsburg, Zurich, and Basel from six to twenty thousand. By the end of the middle ages Venice had expanded to about one hundred and ninety thousand. England doubled her population from 1086 to 1340—from one million, two hundred thousand to two million, three hundred and thirty-five thousand. Of a population of only sixty millions or so in all western Europe in the second quarter of the fourteenth century it has been estimated that one-tenth lived in towns, the greater number of which had from eight hundred to six thousand people.

Many towns, except in Lombardy and Flanders, for a long time— sometimes for centuries—retained within their boundaries areas surviving from earlier feudal or ecclesiastical dominion, whose population was exempt from municipal jurisdiction. Even Paris had such enclaves as late as the reign of Louis XIV. Some towns were a regular mosaic of fiefs: in Marseilles the bishop and the Abbey of St. Victor shared jurisdiction with the municipality; in Poitou, the count-duke of Poitou and the bishop. Nevertheless, the burgher's devotion to his town was generally even more intense than the loyalty of the Roman to his *municipium*. Admission to citizenship was an honor not to be taken lightly. Some towns admitted foreigners—any outsiders —to citizenship, others would not. In any case, a prospective citizen had to be proved; property, residence, and good character were often prerequisites, and there were fees to pay. In return for the privileges of citizenship, such as using the town's pastures, fishing in the town's waters, riding the town's ferries, protection in trade from alien competition, access to the local markets, freedom from servile charges, the protection of the municipal court in all difficulties, he had to swear to observe municipal regulations and perform all the duties of military and civic service. *Town citizenship*

Medieval town politics was likely to be hotter than municipal politics today. Besides the class conflicts and armed revolts already referred to, towns were often divided on external issues, particularly in Italy, where the Guelf and Ghibelline factions in most of the cities were bitter foes. Italian towns were also beset by more local organizations than towns elsewhere. In addition to the gilds themselves, noble and wealthy families were united in close special groups (*consorzerie*); the gilds combined into larger groups and sometimes allied with the unorganized workmen. Cutting across all these were the organizations of the separate districts or wards of the city. Internal struggles were so constant and intense that finally most Italian towns resorted to the practice—obviously a step away from sound municipal government towards dictatorship—of calling in from some other city a supreme magistrate, the podesta, who brought with him a whole retinue to take over many of the functions previously exercised by local officials.

Town rivalry

Medieval towns sometimes united to meet a serious common danger, as the Lombard towns did to resist Frederick Barbarossa. They would co-operate enough to maintain the public order necessary for good business. But often they were commercial rivals and political enemies. Like internal politics, external rivalry was especially fierce in Italy. The larger towns sought to reduce their smaller neighbors to economic dependence, and fought with their great rivals to monopolize trade routes on land, river, or sea. This rivalry, however, went far beyond trade and politics; cities competed in every phase of municipal activity. To this day the resident of Milan or Venice thinks of himself first as a Milanese or a Venetian, not as an Italian. If Florence built a fine new church, Siena would have to build a bigger and better; and beside Siena's great cathedral still stands the fragment of the vast new church, which the resources of a city many times greater would not have sufficed to complete. We see the same thing in far-away Beauvais, where the loftiest Gothic church ever projected was begun, but completed only as far as choir and transepts.

Economic and social importance of the urban revolution

The new towns did far more than change the physical aspect of western Europe, whose only walls had hitherto been castle and monastery walls. They introduced two new classes into medieval society, the bourgeoisie of merchants, industrialists, bankers, and capitalists, and the working class of skilled artisans and unskilled laborers. From the last we can even see a proletariat beginning to develop in the late medieval towns. Ever since the emergence of these two classes, a major part of economic and social history and an increasing share of political history has been concerned with their growth and development; "progress" has been largely dependent on them. Because of them a modern agricultural society, even the most backward, is vastly different from the medieval agricultural society. The towns played an important part in undermining the feudal and manorial systems. Landed property was no longer the only title to rank and power when fortunes could be made in trade and industry, and when soldiers, officials, relatives, and friends could be paid in cash more conveniently than rewarded with fiefs. The town was a haven of freedom for the serf. Moreover, its economic needs led to a more specialized and intensive type of agriculture, which likewise helped the serf on the farm to break his bonds. The town, not the castle or the monastery, was the market for the agricultural surplus, and the proprietor who sold for cash in town was bound to commute the old servile duties of his peasants to fixed payments in money.

In many ways the towns contributed to the growth of absolute national monarchy. The kings came to rely upon the bourgeoisie *Its political* for a good part of their officialdom, and drew the burghers into *effects* Parliament or the States-General or the *Cortes*. The burgher demanding law and order to protect his business found in the king his natural ally against feudal insubordination and anarchy. The money to pay for the central bureaucracy and for mercenary and standing armies, the real support of absolutism, came in large measure from the towns. Without them, indeed, the whole political development characteristic of the later middle ages is inconceivable. The economic experience of the towns redounded to the advantage of the nation: their money and their systems of weights and measures became in many instances national money and national weights and measures. Or, we are tempted to say, in some cases it redounded to the disadvantage of the nation. The self-righteous and exclusive protectionism that made every town a little polity unto itself by setting up customs duties as a barrier to trade became the mercantile policy of the national state, and protective customs became our protective tariffs. The economy of the medieval town was thus intermediate between the economy of the earlier medieval manor and the national economy of the modern state. The emergence, with mercantilism, of capitalism started a development that has not yet ceased, and from which perhaps we are only now beginning to look backwards —or forwards—in the direction of earlier medieval—or shall we say earlier Christian?—concern with human values.

Culturally the development of towns meant an acceleration of all the social processes of growth and change. Ideas, following goods *Its cultural* and merchants, traveled faster from town to town than from manor *effects* to manor or from monastery to monastery. Accumulated wealth in the hands of burghers made it possible for towns to attempt improvements. Expansion of trade and industry and concentration of population posed new problems demanding new solutions, which in turn afforded valuable experience in social experimentation. The wealth of the burgher brought new patronage for the arts; the technical needs of his business, a new demand for specialized education; his own person, his house, and his town, new subjects for adornment. The whole manner of life of the rich burgher, concentrated on making or keeping a fortune and enjoying the pleasant things of this life, was fundamentally different from the spirit of earlier centuries, when, aside from war and religion, there was little to enjoy. Now that a man might lead, or hope to lead, a full and active, pleasurable and profitable earthly life, asceticism lost most of its charm, and even heaven some of its attraction. The great institution that preached the ascetic life and kept open the road to heaven was doomed in any event to suffer at least some loss of influence.

Chapter 21

THE MEDIEVAL REFORMATION

HISTORIANS have termed the intellectual and artistic revival of the twelfth and thirteenth centuries the "medieval renaissance," partly as a protest against the pretentious claims of students carried away by their enthusiasm for the later Italian renaissance, and partly to emphasize the fact that the cultural history of western Europe is one continuous stream of growth. If that continuity is true in general, it is true in particular of the movements of religious discontent and protest during the middle ages, which it is equally proper to call the medieval reformation. This reformation did not destroy the religious unity of western Europe; it aimed to do so only to a limited extent. But it was for the moment extremely dangerous; and, although it was crushed, it did weaken that unity permanently, despite all outward appearances to the contrary. The body of critical opinion formed in its course was the beginning of an avalanche whose descent was stemmed by the Church only temporarily.

The "medieval reformation" is a term meant to include several distinct but interrelated phenomena. By it we mean a whole series of monastic reforms within and without the framework of the Benedictine-Cluniac system; we mean a revolutionary development in monasticism, the founding of the new mendicant orders of Franciscans and Dominicans; we mean the large growth of heretical opinion, crystallizing into widespread organizations that attacked both the dogma and the priesthood of the Church; we mean the appearance of a cynical and light-hearted indifference to the Church in some circles of the new universities; finally, we mean the zealous measures whereby national monarchies and towns began consciously to restrict the sphere of jurisdiction and activity of the Church. The first three of these phenomena are the subject of this chapter. The fourth and

The medieval and the Protestant reformations

607

fifth will be considered in connection with the medieval renaissance and with the history of the Church in the later middle ages.[1]

If from the religious point of view the mainsprings of the Protestant reformation of the sixteenth century were a return to the unqualified authority of the literal words of one book and only one, the Bible, an attempt to recover the personality and imitate the life of the founder of Christianity, a longing for some inwardly satisfying personal religion to replace the cult of priests and sacraments, and a desire to return to the simplicity and poverty of the early Church, in every one of these respects the medieval reformation of the twelfth and thirteenth centuries was also distinguished. If in its economic aspect the later reformation was an adjustment to the demands of a flourishing commercial capitalism, then in part the earlier reformation was a bewildered protest against inchoate capitalism. Finally, if monarchs and princes of the sixteenth century championed Protestantism because they recognized the opportunity to subordinate the new religion to the state, it was because long centuries of similar attempts on the part of their medieval forebears had demonstrated the difficulty of subjugating the old, established, international religion. The Protestant reformation had its real beginnings in the twelfth and thirteenth centuries.

Reform of the Church controlled by the Church

It may seem an anomaly that just when the body of medieval protest reached its height the medieval papacy attained its zenith. This it did under Innocent III, who clearly established its spiritual supremacy within the Church, and for a moment its temporal supremacy over the state. That such a combination of circumstances was possible is to be explained partly by the stringent methods used by the Church to eradicate "heresy," and partly by the shrewd way in which the papacy gathered into its protecting arms those sons of the Church who were or who threatened to become dangerous, if they could possibly be won to its embrace. The Church, however, could have found no support for its stringency and no employment for its shrewdness if it had not always demonstrated the superiority of its organization, appealed to rulers everywhere as an ally in the maintenance of law and order, and convinced all classes of the validity of its interpretation of life and therefore of its right to compel, if necessary, adherence to its system of belief and practice. The medieval reformation was accordingly accompanied by a steady elaboration of the organization, law, and dogma of the Church, which became an absolute ecclesiastical monarchy, living according to its own canon law and enforc-

[1] See pp. 746 ff.; 992.

ing a system of belief that was hardening into an unchangeable theology.

In a sense this development of organization, law, and belief can be considered a part of the reformation itself; the Church was strong enough to answer criticism by choosing its own methods of reforming itself. But this was in large part an answer that ignored or obfuscated the very criticism that it pretended to heed. Accordingly, although hostile and subversive opinion was driven temporarily underground, the Church remained as vulnerable as before to the same kind of attack. When in the fourteenth and fifteenth centuries the challenge was taken up by new reformers, the Church received not only the same criticism of old abuses, which had meanwhile grown worse, but serious new complaints, arising out of the methods of government that it had perfected to nullify earlier criticism.

The monastic reform of the eleventh and twelfth centuries was by no means unconnected with earlier reform movements or with the enthusiasm aroused by the investiture struggle and the crusades. It left untouched no aspect of monastic life, and introduced innovations in organization of great subsequent importance. In general, it tended to emphasize the type of ascetic life associated with the hermit or anchorite, which had never appealed greatly to the west. New groups *New* of cloistered anchorites or hermits were founded in Italy and France, *anchorite* many of them inspired directly by those offshoots of Greek monasti- *monasteries* cism, the hermit colonies of Calabria. The anchorite foundation of St. Romuald early in the eleventh century at Camaldoli, near Florence, developed after his death into the hermit order of the Camaldolesi, which was confirmed by the papacy in 1072. There was a similar hermit foundation of St. John Gualbert at near-by Vallombrosa. A foundation at La Cava, near Naples, has been likened to Mount Athos; [2] oddly enough, its offshoot at Monreale became in the twelfth century the cathedral chapter of the resplendent archiepiscopal church of the Norman kings. In 1080 at Muret, near Limoges, the son of a local viscount founded a hermit community, on the Calabrian model, which was to own nothing—not even churches— and live entirely on alms. The austerity of the original community was modified after its removal to Grammont, whence it expanded outside of France as the Order of Grammont.

The most important of the new hermit orders was the Carthusian, *The* whose first house, in a most desolate region of the western Alps up *Carthusians* from Grenoble, was "built almost above the clouds and very near to

[2] Mount Athos became the later center of Byzantine monasticism. See p. 57.

God." Its German founder, Bruno of Cologne (1030–1101), had had a painful experience as chancellor of an archbishop of Rheims who was supposed to have remarked that "it would be good to be archbishop of Rheims if one did not have to say mass." Bruno refused to take the office when his archbishop was deposed, and retired in disgust from the secular clergy to found a community of hermits, La Grande Chartreuse, named from the neighboring village of Cartusia. The Carthusian monks lived together in one monastery but in individual cells, each with its own adjoining garden. In his cell the monk prepared his meatless diet on each of the four weekdays when he was not fasting on bread, salt, and water. There, except for the few occasions when the monks met together for services in the church, he repeated the service in solitude, sought his God in mystic contemplation, and copied manuscripts. On Sundays he enjoyed a meal with his fellows. The order acquired a reputation for excessive severity. "There men, whom you see live on the rocks, are harder than the rocks themselves; they have no pity on themselves, or on those who dwell with them. Their site is fearful, but their order is yet more fearful." The visitor today still feels something of the austerity that fills Matthew Arnold's "Stanzas from the Grande Chartreuse":

> "The silent courts, where night and day
> Into their stone-carved basins cold
> The splashing icy fountains play—
> The humid corridors behold!
> Where, ghost-like in the deepening night,
> Cowled forms brush by in gleaming white.

> "The chapel, where no organ's peal
> Invests the stern and naked prayer—
> With penitential cries they kneel
> And wrestle; rising then, with bare
> And white uplifted faces stand,
> Passing the Host from hand to hand;

> "Each takes, and then his visage wan
> Is buried in his cowl once more.
> The cells!—the suffering Son of Man
> Upon the wall— The knee-worn floor—
> And where they sleep, that wooden bed,
> Which shall their coffin be, when dead!"

The order spread into Italy, where its houses were known as *certose;* the most famous *certosa,* at Pavia, became the sumptuous tomb of the Visconti family of Milan. The houses in England, known as charterhouses, were especially revered by Henry II. Always the Carthusians boasted of their discipline, which never relaxed and therefore never needed reforming. Between the time of their return to France after their first expulsion during the French Revolution and their second expulsion in 1903 they became more widely known for the yellow or green liqueur made by their lay brothers from young pine buds than for their piety, and today they should be shocked to know that chartreuse green is a fashionable color. Bruno himself found life even at the Grande Chartreuse not rigid enough, and betook himself to Calabria to join a hermit community there, where the climate at least was less severe. He rejoiced in it, too, and in the beauty of his environment. "How can I do justice to the mildness and softness of the air," he wrote, "and to the plain, wide and pleasing, which extends far among the mountains, where there are green fields and flower-strewn meadows? Or what words can adequately picture the more distant view of hills rising gently on all sides; of shaded valleys, of the numerous rivers, brooks and springs? And there is no lack of well watered gardens nor of various fruitful trees." [3]

Another aim of the monastic reform was to transform the cathedral chapters—the groups of clergy, called canons, attached to cathedrals (sometimes also to the larger churches)—into semimonastic communities. Originally canons lived as independently perhaps as bishops or priests; they might own their houses or other private property. In the eleventh century they were holding benefices called *The Augus-* prebends; that is, they were supported by definite shares in the prop- *tinian canons* erty and income of the church to which they were attached. As early as the fourth century, however, Bishop Eusebius of Vercelli and St. Augustine at Hippo had sought to compel their clergy to live together as a community under regular discipline.[4] In the eighth century Chrodegang, Bishop of Metz, drew up a rule for the canons of his cathedral. Those living according to a rule came subsequently to be called regular canons, and those living independently secular canons; both groups were of course in orders (monks, it will be remembered, did not necessarily or even ordinarily take orders). The rule of Chrodegang, though subsequently amended, was neither

[3] Quoted by Davison, *Forerunners of St. Francis,* p. 44.
[4] See p. 58.

universally adopted nor very satisfactory where it was adopted, so that by the eleventh century canons were in still more serious need of reform. A new rule was compounded from a letter of St. Augustine to a community of nuns, his description of the community life of his cathedral clergy, and other writings attributed to him. This rule of St. Augustine was widely adopted, with local variations, and was urged upon all canons; those accepting it were known as Augustinian canons or canons regular. In 1139 the papacy ruled that all regular canons must adopt the Augustinian rule, which was in general less stringent than the Benedictine rule and provided for the same kind of local autonomy.

The Premon-stratensians

The most conspicuous group of regular canons in the twelfth and early thirteenth centuries was the order founded in 1119 by another German, Norbert of Xanten, in a marshy region in the forest of Coucy outside Laon. The spot chosen, which Norbert claimed was pointed out to him by an angel, was called Prémontré ("designated in advance"), from the Latin form of which (*præmonstratum*) comes the English name of the order, Premonstratensian. Norbert had already had an important public career at the court of the German Emperor Henry II and a stormy career as a stern preacher of apostolic poverty and simplicity. In his rule he combined with the Augustinian certain features of the Cistercian. He set his monks to reforming the secular priesthood by attaching themselves to churches as canons. He himself finally accepted the Archbishopric of Magdeburg; there his reforming zeal made him so unpopular that he had to leave the city for a while. Norbert also sent his monks out to work in and with the world. He introduced them into northeastern Germany as missionaries and agricultural pioneers among the Slavs. Within ten years after his death in 1144 there were at least seventy Premonstratensian houses, and they subsequently spread over all Europe.

Double monasteries

St. Benedict's sister, Scholastica, had offered a Benedictine system of government to women who wished to enter conventual life. Some few attempts had been made by Irish abbots to institute double houses for monks and nuns, but they never proved successful. To make more adequate provision for nuns was accordingly the third purpose of monastic reform. Both the Augustinian canons and the Premonstratensians at first admitted women to double monasteries, in which the nuns devoted themselves exclusively to prayer and the monks directed the spiritual life of the nuns and the temporal affairs of the house. In both instances, however, the experiment had to be abandoned. A more successful attempt was made in 1131 by Gilbert, rector of Sempringham in Lincolnshire, whose Order of Sempringham brought nuns and Augustinian canons together under an abbess within the walls of a single monastery. A similar order was founded in France in 1100 on Benedictine principles by the Breton Robert Arbrissel at Fontevrault, in Anjou; within a few years it covered western France with branches.

All these new orders illustrate how the wealth and worldliness of the secular church constantly aroused new protests, which took monastic form; how, in other words, the medieval conscience, though easily placated, was ever ready to torture itself anew. But none of them, either because they were confined to a particular locality or because of their special character, could have any great influence in bringing about a revival of discipline in the older Benedictine and Cluniac houses, which must be one of the chief aims of monastic reform. So soon as the beginning of the twelfth century the reforming ardor of the great Cluniac movement of the tenth century had spent itself. The wealth that poured in to endow the reform undermined its zeal, and the order that had insisted with some exceptions upon a return to the original vigor of St. Benedict's rule in time was countenancing just such relaxation of discipline in matters of food, dress, and manual labor as its rigorous founders had protested against. The Abbot of Cluny and Cluniac priors were expending their ample surplus of income on lavish architecture, expensive church furniture, and luxurious ritual. The time was ripe for the second and, as it turned out, final great wave of Benedictine reform. *Cluniac decline*

The Cistercian Order was founded in 1098 at Cîteaux (the Latin Cistercium), in Burgundy. Its founder, St. Robert, had been abbot of a Benedictine house at Molesme, from which he moved with a small group of brothers when he found it impossible to reform his own house. The order received its constitution, the Charter of Charity (*carta caritatis*), from its third abbot, the English Stephen Harding. But the chief embodiment, for his own and for all time, of the pure Cistercian spirit was neither the founder nor the chief legislator, but a handsome young Burgundian nobleman, who entered Cîteaux with a band of thirty followers in 1112 and three years later became abbot of the daughter house at Clairvaux. This man, until his death in 1153 the most prominent figure of his day in Europe, was St. Bernard. *The Cistercians*

We have already seen St. Bernard at the French court under Louis VI and Louis VII, and at the German court of Conrad III. *St. Bernard*

We have seen him preaching the second crusade, the greatest disappointment of his life. He drew up a rule for the Knights Templars. He settled a papal schism in 1130, and preached against the heretics of southern France. A great friend and supporter of Norbert, the founder of the Premonstratensians, he acted as protector of that order after Norbert's death. We shall see him again defending the orthodoxy of the Church against the questionings of Abélard and Abélard's pupil, Arnold of Brescia.[5] There was no movement of any account for almost forty years in which he did not have a hand.

Ostensibly, judged by his public career, St. Bernard was as far as possible from the typical cloistered Cistercian. Nevertheless, for all his preoccupation with the affairs of this world, his life at Clairvaux, where he preached and taught his monks and wrote many dissertations and letters, makes it clear that public life was not his own preference. He had ruined his health by ascetic practices during his novitiate, and "his whole body was meagre and emaciated." The one tendency of his mind was towards a rarefied mysticism combined with a deep personal adoration of Christ and the Blessed Virgin. And yet even this very depth and genuineness of religious feeling conspired to keep him at the center of the stage of European affairs. Above all he was a bitter and voluble critic of society, sparing least of all the Church, from pope to parish priest, from the greatest abbot to the meanest monk. The whole burden of his complaint was: "Who will grant me before I die to see the Church of God as it was in the days of old?" Of the concentration of ecclesiastical power at Rome he wrote: "The ambitious, the grasping, the simoniacal, the sacrilegious, the adulterous, the incestuous, and all such like monsters of humanity flock to Rome, in order either to obtain or to keep ecclesiastical honours at the hands of the pope." A good bishop, he said, was a rare bird. He hated to see "an abbot with a train of sixty horses or more; on seeing such pass by, thou wouldst say that they are not fathers of monasteries but lords of castles, not rulers of souls but princes of provinces."

It was doubtless only natural that St. Bernard should reserve his choicest excoriation for the degenerate Cluniac monks. In a letter to a Cluniac prior he wrote: "When thou wilt buy a frock, thou goest from city to city, scourest the markets, searchest the fairs from booth to booth, scannest the merchants' shops, turnest over each man's store, unrollest vast bales of cloth, touchest with thy fingers, bringest close to thine eyes, holdest up to the sunlight, and rejectest whatsoever is

St. Bernard's criticism of the Church

⁵ See p. 621.

seen to be too coarse or too slight; on the other hand, whatsoever taketh thee with its purity and gloss, that thou seekest to buy forthwith at any price." [6]

With equal vigor he castigated the Cluniac monks for their devotion to their bellies. "Who, in those first days when the monastic Order began, would have believed that monks would ever come to such sloth? . . . Dish after dish is set on the table; and instead of the mere flesh-meat from which men abstain, they receive twofold in mighty fishes. Though thou have eaten thy fill of the first course, yet when thou comest to the second thou shalt seem not even to have tasted the first; for all is dressed with such care and art in the kitchen that, though thou hast swallowed four or five dishes, the first are no hindrance to the last, nor doth satiety lessen thine appetite. . . . For (to say nothing of the rest) who may tell of the eggs alone, in how many ways they are tossed and vexed, how busily they are turned and turned again, beaten to froth or hard-boiled or minced, now fried and now baked, now stuffed and now mixed, or again brought up one by one? . . . What shall I say of water-drinking, when watered wine is on no account admitted? All of us, forsooth, in virtue of our monkish profession, have infirm stomachs, and are justified in not neglecting the Apostle's salutary advice as to drinking wine; yet (I know not why) we omit that word 'little' wherewith he begins. . . ." [7]

St. Bernard's denunciation of the Cluniac monks

When it came to the glorious Romanesque architecture of the Cluniac houses, Bernard could not contain himself for puritanical fury:

"I say naught of the vast height of your churches, their immoderate length, their superfluous breadth, the costly polishings, the curious carvings and paintings which attract the worshipper's gaze and hinder his attention. . . . At the very sight of these costly yet marvellous vanities men are more kindled to offer gifts than to pray. . . . Their eyes are feasted with relics cased with gold, and their purse-strings are loosed. They are shown a most comely image of some saint, whom they think all the more saintly that he is the more gaudily painted. Men run to kiss him, and are invited to give; there is more admiration for his comeliness than veneration for his sanctity. Hence the church is adorned with gemmed crowns of light—nay, with lustres like cart-wheels, girt all round with lamps, but no less brilliant with the precious stones that stud them. Moreover, we see candelabra standing like trees of massive bronze, fashioned with

[6] Coulton, *Life in the Middle Ages*, IV, 171.
[7] *Ibid.*

marvellous subtlety of art, and glistening no less brightly with gems than with the lights they carry. . . . The church is resplendent in her walls, beggarly in her poor; she clothes her stones in gold, and leaves her sons naked; the rich man's eye is fed at the expense of the indigent. . . . Do we not revere at least the images of the Saints, which swarm even in the inlaid pavements whereon we tread? Men spit oftentimes in an Angel's face; often, again, the countenance of some saint is ground under the heel of a passer-by. And if he spare not these sacred images, why not even the fair colours? . . . What avail these comely forms in places where they are defiled with customary dust?"

At this point Bernard shows how closely he had studied Romanesque sculpture. "In the cloister, under the eyes of the Brethren who read there, what profit is there in those ridiculous monsters, in the marvellous and deformed comeliness, the comely deformity? To what purpose are those unclean apes, those fierce lions, those fighting knights, those hunters winding their horns? Many bodies are there seen under one head, or again, many heads to a single body. There is a four-footed beast with a serpent's tail; there, a fish with a beast's head. Here again the forepart of a horse trails half a goat behind it, or a horned beast bears the hinder quarters of a horse. . . . We are more tempted to read in the marble than in our books, and to spend the whole day in wondering at these things rather than in meditating the law of God. For God's sake, if men are not ashamed of these follies, why at least do they not shrink from the expense?" [8]

The Cistercians as reformed Benedictines

The Cistercians, in their protest against Cluniac laxity, went even beyond the prescriptions of the original Benedictine rule, which they made more stringent. For the flowing Cluniac dress they substituted simple vestments, white instead of the traditional Benedictine black. They restored the manual labor, which Cluny had largely abandoned, required by the Benedictine rule. Their diet was strictly vegetarian. St. Bernard wrote: "Pepper, ginger, and spices delight the palate, but salt with hunger is sufficient condiment to one who lives soberly and prudently: the food one spurns when indolent, one takes with a relish after a day's toil. Cabbage, beans, and coarse bread are unappetizing to an idle person, but are delicacies to the labourer, for idleness produces distaste, but exercise, hunger. Watchings, fastings, and manual labour are tiring, certainly, but compared with eternal burnings are mere trifles; and solitude is far easier to bear than outer darkness. Nor is

[8] See p. 810.

silence a trial when one considers the punishment meted throughout eternity to him who used vain words or dealt in lies. A couch of boards is as nothing when compared with weeping and gnashing of teeth; and he who keeps the night watch conscientiously knows not if his bed be hard or soft." [9]

Cistercian churches must eschew all such vanities as St. Bernard denounced: stained glass and elaborate and distracting ornamentation or sculpture. The service must be simple, the vestments plain: no gold altar plate, only simple, painted wooden crosses instead of bejeweled ones, and candlesticks of plain iron. There should be no stone towers; wooden bell towers, if any, should be of moderate height. The Cistercians were to live absolutely on their own, accepting no income and none of the positions pertaining to the secular branch of the Church.

In organization the Cistercian Order reacted against the centralization of the Cluniac system.[10] The Abbot of Cîteaux enjoyed a kind of primacy throughout the order: he had the right of visitation of all the houses, but he could introduce no innovations without the consent of the monks of the local house. Each mother house—one of the four main houses from which the others branched—retained the right of visiting or inspecting its filial houses annually. Once a year at Cîteaux there was a meeting of the general chapter of the order, composed of the Abbot of Cîteaux, the heads of the four oldest mother houses, and five abbots from each of the four filiations. The Abbot of Cîteaux was responsible to this general chapter, by which he could be deposed after sufficient warning. The Cistercian government was thus both aristocratic and federal. Subject to the limitations mentioned, each house preserved a large measure of the old Benedictine autonomy, electing its own abbot and being governed only by the spiritual dictates of the mother house. *Cistercian organization*

Cistercian monks did not themselves perform the labor necessary to keep up their estates. Most of it came in time to be done by a special group called lay brothers, who took the usual monastic vows and followed a simplified religious routine, but were never allowed to learn to read or write or to become full-fledged monks sitting in choir and singing the whole service. They were admitted to the order as agricultural laborers and artisans, in order to leave the monks free to devote all their attention to religious services. Cistercian estates were dotted with granges, where the lay brothers got their tools in the morning and stored their harvest at the end of the day. There *Lay brothers*

[9] Quoted by Davison, *op. cit.*, p. 64.
[10] See p. 368.

was no lack of work, for most Cistercian houses were situated off the beaten path, on unreclaimed land. In northeastern Germany, where their houses still preserve their original character of large farms, they were the leading pioneers. The Cistercians made important practical contributions to society: their agriculture, pomology, cattle breeding, sheep raising, and methods of reclaiming swamp and clearing forest were the most advanced of the time, and nobles and kings employed them to administer their estates.

The decay of the Benedictine orders

The order grew tremendously. At St. Bernard's death it numbered three hundred and forty-three houses, and before the end of the thirteenth century more than twice as many. With growth came prosperity, and with prosperity wealth. The order compromised with its earlier severity, and even entered the world of trade; in England, for example, the Cistercians became producers of wool on a large scale. There is bitter irony, in view of St. Bernard's strictures of Cluniac architecture, in the fact that they became especially notable as architects; indeed, they have been ranked among the great builders of all time. So the Cistercians suffered the same fate that overtook the original Benedictines and the reformed Cluniacs, the inevitable end of all idealists when they get organization and endowment wherewith to put their ideals into practice. The fact is that after about 1200, when the repercussions of two centuries of monastic reform had subsided, monasticism of the old Benedictine type, rooted in a primitive agricultural society, was found no longer adequate to absorb the critical spirit within the Church. Its very nature was antithetical to the rising towns, which it took pains to avoid. In its search for the "bliss of solitude" it could only abhor strife and dispute with heretics. The older Benedictine ideal was doomed to be supplanted by a new type of monasticism, better suited to a society from which escape no longer seemed so tempting and which in its new towns was confronting the Church with new problems that it must solve in order to preserve itself.

The older houses, of course, lived on, carried along by the force of tradition and accumulated wealth, progressively deteriorating until they became so flagrant an anachronism that they were wiped out by the governments that adopted the tenets of the Protestant reformation, although elsewhere they persist down to our own day and in our very midst. It is instructive to meet no later than in the fourteenth century Chaucer's jolly Benedictine monk, who "loved his venery," and had "full many a blooded horse in stable" but not much use for the rule of St. Benedict.

"By reason it was old and somewhat strict,
This said monk let such old things slowly pace
And followed new-world manners in their place.
He cared not for that text a clean-plucked hen
Which holds that hunters are not holy men.

Greyhounds he had, as swift as bird in flight.
Since riding and the hunting of the hare
Were all his love, for no cost would he spare.
I saw his sleeves were purfled at the hand
With fur of grey, the finest in the land;
Also to fasten hood beneath his chin
He had of good wrought gold a curious pin:
A love-knot in the larger end there was.
His head was bald and shone like any glass,
And smooth as one anointed was his face.
Fat was this lord, he stood in goodly case.
His bulging eyes he rolled about, and hot
They gleamed and red, like fire beneath a pot;
His boots were soft; his horse of great estate.
Now certainly he was a fine prelate:
He was not pale as some poor wasted ghost.
A fat swan loved he best of any roast.
His palfrey was as brown as is a berry." [11]

It has just been noted that as a general thing the monastic reforms *The Church* of the late eleventh and early twelfth centuries kept away from the *and the towns* new towns, which seemed to represent the antithesis of everything that they stood for. The new concentration of population nevertheless forced upon the Church, which had hitherto had to adapt itself primarily to an agricultural society, the necessity of adaptation to the religious needs of the towns. It seems that, not unnaturally, the Church was slow to make this change. The organization of new parishes and the training of new priests by no means kept pace with the growth of urban population. Town populations as a whole were therefore insufficiently instructed in the tenets of the faith. Moreover, the towns, concerned with industry and commerce, which are always essentially cosmopolitan and irreligious, offered a market for the exchange of ideas as well as goods, and engendered a spirit more receptive than the conservative countryside to new opinions. The towns

[11] *The Canterbury Tales* (tr. Nicolson), pp. 6–7.

would thus in any case have been readier to give ear to the criticism and teaching of those who wandered, innocently or purposefully, from orthodox paths in the field of religion. In the towns there was always an audience and a following for the increasingly numerous champions, drawn more from lay than from ecclesiastical circles, of what the Church called heresy, which has been defined as "obstinate adherence to opinions arbitrarily chosen in defiance of accepted ecclesiastical teaching and interpretation."

New economic, social, and political conditions in the towns created in time a body of discontent that seemed able to find no more effective expression than a religious fervor impatient of restraint and critical of ecclesiastical authority. The growth of towns multiplied the number of the poor, and at least in the larger towns there were always many people not organized in gilds and anxious to find some sort of corporate life in religious organizations. The control of town corporations by the wealthier gilds produced in the lesser gilds a spirit of criticism and revolt against authority of any kind. Finally, in their long struggles for emancipation the towns were so often pitted against the Church itself, as landowner and feudal lord, that they acquired a natural hostility to the jurisdiction of the Church, which was generally opposed to, when it did not actually compete with, the local self-government of which they were so proud.

Heretics of the early twelfth century

As a matter of fact, although it is true that in general the monastic reform movement of the twelfth century concentrated on other interests, two of its outstanding leaders took a prominent part in combating heresy. Norbert and his Premonstratensian canons recovered Antwerp for the Faith at a time when the city is said to have had only one priest. It had gone over almost in a body to the following of one Tanchelm, who was denouncing the moral shortcomings of the priesthood and the pompous assumption of ecclesiastical rank. His campaign must have been somewhat related to the attempts of the Gregorian reform to cleanse the priesthood by urging nonattendance upon the services of unchaste or simoniacal priests. Tanchelm preached what Gregory VII approached, the old Donatist heresy that the sacraments were not valid when performed by unworthy priests.[12] He taught also that all hieratic ranks from pope down to deacon were vain, and urged that no tithes be paid to an organization such as the Church had become. In 1115 he was "knocked in the head by a pious priest."

St. Bernard was active for a short time at Albi, far away in southern France, in opposition to the teachings of Henry of Lausanne, who

[12] See p. 43.

at least as early as 1116 was preaching with success merely against the worldliness of the clergy. Subsequently Henry came under the influence of Peter of Bruys, an uncompromising opponent of the organization, ceremonial, and dogma of the Church. Peter was in fact a very early "Protestant." He preached salvation by faith and personal character rather than by good works and attendance at religious ceremonies: God would judge each person according to his own righteousness and faith. Churches were superfluous and should be destroyed: the Church was "the united congregation of the faithful." Against the doctrine of the Eucharist [13] Peter was especially vehement: "O people, believe not the bishops, the priests, and the clerks, who, as in much else, seek to deceive you as to the office of the altar, where they lyingly pretend to make the body of Christ and give it to you for the salvation of your souls. They plainly lie, for the body of Christ was but once made by Christ in the supper before the Passion, and but once given to the disciples. Since then it has never been made again." [14] Peter, whose followers were called Petrobrusians, was preaching a religion of simple purity and of a personal relationship with God that needed no church as mediator. He was burned as a heretic at St. Gilles in 1126. Henry of Lausanne followed Peter's lead in preaching against the Eucharist, against supporting with tithes and offerings a priesthood which he hated, and even against going to church. He was also a stern moralist, who would prohibit second marriage and disapproved of "any conjugal relation." He is believed to have died after ten years' imprisonment.

St. Bernard pursued two other liberal thinkers of the twelfth century, Pierre Abélard [15] and his pupil Arnold of Brescia. At least so far as Arnold was concerned, Bernard's feelings were reciprocated; Arnold called him "a seeker after vainglory, jealous of those who won fame in religion or heresy." After a Lateran council in 1139 had failed to silence him the Council of Sens in 1141 condemned him together with Abélard, and ordered him imprisoned and his books burned. Bernard succeeded in having him expelled from France in 1142. When Arnold was found at Zurich, Bernard wrote the Bishop of Constance about him. "His mouth is full of maledictions and bitterness; his feet are agile for shedding blood. Evil is in his words, and he ignores the way of peace. The enemy of Christ, the disturber of peace, he changes unity into discord. His tongue is a sharp sword,

Arnold of Brescia

[13] See p. 679.
[14] Lea, *History of the Inquisition in the Middle Ages*, I, 68.
[15] See p. 697.

his words are more sweet than oil, but in reality they are death, and he seeks ever the favor of the rich and powerful."[16] Arnold left Zurich to join a papal legate in Bohemia and Moravia, where he was again tracked down by Bernard. "What an agreeable present it would be for our Mother Church," wrote Bernard to the legate, "to receive from your hands this vessel which has so long outraged her. It is permissible to attempt it." At the end of 1145 or the beginning of 1146 Arnold appeared in Rome in the midst of a political revolution. The movement aimed to abolish the pope's control of the city; it was in fact only one of many revolutions of cities against their bishops. Here Arnold remained for nine years, an ardent champion of urban liberties, until in 1155 he was abandoned by those whom he had served, tried and condemned by the Church, and hanged and burned by Frederick Barbarossa at the behest of Pope Hadrian IV.[17]

Arnold's opinions

The opinions that cost Arnold his life were anything but abstruse. They had been formally recognized by Paschal II in his famous privilege to Henry V in 1111,[18] and were grounded in Scripture. The Church, in Arnold's opinion, had in the course of many centuries deviated widely from the early apostolic Church: it was rich where the other was poor; it exercised temporal power where the other was absorbed in the single task of saving men's souls. The Church was a spiritual institution and, if it would not give them up, should be deprived of its excessive wealth and its temporal powers. One need not go beyond Scripture to support this position, but it is possible that in Brescia Arnold was influenced by the radical Patarenes of Milan and elsewhere.[19] Certain it is that he was a devoted follower of his master Abélard; Bernard notes that "he had held to Peter Abelard, all of whose errors, attacked and condemned by the church, he undertook to defend with enthusiasm and energy, with him and for him."

Like the Patarenes in Milan, he was associated with the maintenance of a republican commune against the bishop of the city. In Rome Arnold was also haunted by the dim tradition of the imperial city, center of a world empire. At any rate, the best place to carry out his program was surely the very center of Christendom, where pope and *Curia* were engaged in the unholy business of governing a city and a state, and the best means of reducing the papacy to its proper spiritual functions was through the organization of the revolutionary

[16] Quoted by Davison, *op. cit.*, p. 123.
[17] See p. 399.
[18] See p. 388.
[19] See p. 377.

commune. The College of Cardinals seemed to Arnold "by reason of the pride and avarice of its members, their hypocrisy and manifold sins, not the Church of God, but the house of buying and selling and the den of thieves, who played the part of the scribes and pharisees toward the Christian people. He said the Pope was no pope, because he was not an apostolic man and a shepherd of souls, but a man of blood who maintained his authority by killing and burning; a tormentor of churches; an oppressor of the innocent, who did nothing in the world but feed on flesh and fill his coffers and empty those of others. Nor was he apostolic, because he did not imitate the doctrine nor the life of the Apostles, and therefore no reverence nor obedience was due him. Further, 'nothing in the government of the city pertains to the supreme pontiff; ecclesiastical jurisdiction ought to be enough for him.' " [20]

Arnold's program exempted no part of the clergy. "The sacred laws, he said, did not sanction clerical possessions; the monks and priests had no right over the land; nor should the abbots relegate to themselves temporal power which belonged to the princes on the earth; government was the prerogative of the elected representatives of the people alone. Offerings and tithes should be tendered only for the needs of the body, not for their own pleasure. He condemned without restriction the luxurious lives of the priests, the delicacy of their viands, the splendour of their vestments, their lascivious joys, and the relaxed manners of the monasteries." [21]

Arnold was therefore guilty, in the eyes of Hadrian IV, of something more like treason than heresy. His program was of course utterly impracticable, but no more so than Paschal II's privilege of 1111. He was among the boldest and most disinterested of medieval reformers. It was told that Frederick Barbarossa regretted his part in putting him to death, and there were loyal churchmen who deplored that his blood was on the pope's hands. Arnold's ideals, however, did not die with him. The associations of Arnoldists in Italy after his death were only one of the fruits of his preaching. Brescia has set up a statue to commemorate her son, one of the earliest of many men to give his life to the cause of a free church. History has made us wise enough to know now that the only way whereby the Church could have avoided the disaster that overtook it in the Protestant reformation was the way pointed not by Innocent III but by Arnold of Brescia.

[20] Davison, *op. cit.*, pp. 145–46.
[21] *Ibid.*, p. 114.

There were other preachers of the apostolic life in the twelfth century. In Brittany, soon after Tanchelm's career in Antwerp, an unbalanced and illiterate hermit, Éon de l'Étoile, proclaimed himself the Son of God and set about pillaging churches and distributing the booty to the poor. In Périgord an illiterate peasant named Pons won a considerable following to return to the life of the apostles and early Christian poverty. In the neighborhood of Cologne a group called Apostolics lived according to their interpretation of the practices of the early Church and the words of Christ himself. "You," they told the Provost of Steinfeld, "add house to house and field to field. You seek your own and the things of this world. Even those who are held most perfect among you, the monks and the regular canons, though they do not hold property as individuals, but possess it in common, have all things. . . . You love this world and are at peace with this world because you are of this world. . . . We are the Church, because we alone walk in the footsteps of Christ and follow truly the apostolic life. We seek not the things which are of this world; we possess nothing, neither houses nor lands nor any money, just as Christ possessed nothing and allowed his disciples to possess nothing." [22]

In the Lombard towns towards the end of the twelfth century members of the underprivileged classes, especially laborers in woolen textiles, formed a lay brotherhood called the *Humiliati*, i.e., the Poor and Humble. They wore a special garb, lived at home a life of apostolic simplicity and poverty, preached against the secularization of the Church, and advocated a return to a life of labor according to Gospel precepts. The fate of the society is an interesting example of the papacy's neat way of pulling aching teeth that might bite. Foreseeing the danger of forcing such a widespread movement into open heresy, Innocent III diverted it into monastic channels. In 1201 he confirmed a rule for the *Humiliati*, who were henceforth to have three ranks of membership: laymen following the rule, to be called tertiaries, a second order of monks and nuns, and a first order of priests and canons. Some of the *Humiliati*, however, chose not to be hobbled by recognition and organization: they would not be confirmed within the pope's tidy order, but refused to take oaths, declined to become involved in lawsuits, and maintained their homes and families as before. These were branded as false and heretical, and later were identified with the heretical Waldensians, the Poor Men of Lyons.

The fundamental similarity of these heretical or half-heretical

[22] Quoted in *ibid.*, p. 226.

minor sects is obvious enough. To prove their influence upon one another is difficult, although its assumption is only natural and wholly plausible. But it is indisputable that they were influenced by the two major heretical sects of the twelfth century, the Cathari, now usually called, as they were in southern France, Albigensians, and the Waldensians, for the reception of whose doctrines they themselves prepared fertile ground. A mighty flood of heresy threatened to submerge the Church at the end of the twelfth century.

In the case of the Albigensians, unlike the lesser heretical sects, it is possible to trace the direct descent of their doctrines from Christian heresies of the third and fourth centuries. It is fascinating to speculate *Origin and* why these ancient heresies, when intermingled in their teachings, *spread of* made such a powerful appeal to western Europe. The circumstances *the Cathari* of life against which they were a reaction must have been similar in the two periods. The chief ancient ingredient of Catharism was Manicheism, tempered, however, in its spread by Gnostic and Adoptionist influences.[23] Armenian Adoptionists, influenced by Manichean and Gnostic ideas, had moved into Thrace some time in the eighth or ninth century, and from there to the lower Danube, where they carried on missionary work among the Bulgarians. The resultant sect of the Bogomiles in Bulgaria spread to Hungary, Bosnia, and Dalmatia, whence it radiated to Apulia, to Lombardy, and to southern Germany. As early as the tenth century the Cathari were organized in France, and by the eleventh century in the Rhineland and Flanders. For a long time the Church confounded them with other heretical sects, merely branding them all alike as Manicheans; in France they were often called simply Bulgars. At their height they had "well organized communities in a thousand towns" and bishops in Lombardy and Tuscany and at Toulouse, Carcassonne, and Cologne.

Their doctrines seem to have been first carried across the Alps by Italian students attending schools in Rheims, Paris, Orléans, and Chartres, or by Lombard merchants going to the Champagne fairs and Flanders. The Cathari were active missionaries, often establishing schools, where they taught crafts as well as religion. Because of the scandalous condition of the clergy in southern France they became especially popular there, as their Albigensian name indicates, and so strong that they held their own councils and threatened orthodox Christianity with virtual extinction. Even in northern Italy Innocent III had trouble enough merely to keep them out of public office. Their extinction in southern France by the Albigensian crusade has

[23] For these sects see pp. 42–44.

already been recounted.[24] Elsewhere they were exterminated by the Inquisition.

The doctrines of the Albigensians are known to us chiefly through their persecutors; and the fact that they had no general organization, so that there existed among them countless variations of belief, makes it doubly difficult to speak with accuracy for the sect as a whole. Of conventional Christianity they retained very little. Their doctrine was not even monotheistic. Catholic Christianity explains evil as a falling away from divine grace: Satan, originally an angel, through pride, ambition, and disobedience fell from heaven and divine grace to become the master of all the forces of evil; but, no matter how pernicious and persistent, no matter how successful for the moment, Satan and his demons are always in the end only tools of the omnipotent God. The Albigensians, on the contrary, explained the existence of evil by recognizing, in opposition to the Good God, an Evil God. The Good God of things spiritual, the Manichean God of Light, they identified with the God of the New Testament; the Jehovah of the Old Testament they rejected as the Evil God, the Manichean God of Darkness, and rejected together with him all the Old Testament. Life on earth they interpreted, much like orthodox Christians, as a conflict between good and evil, matter and spirit, the Good and the Evil God. They predicted the ultimate victory of the Good God, who would finally gather together in heaven his spiritual beings in spiritual bodies. Meanwhile Satan, the Evil God, presided over this world of matter, including the physical bodies of its human inhabitants.

The dualism of Albigensian doctrine

From these premises the Albigensians made some startling deductions. Since the Church, in the persons of its clergy, abounding in wealth and preoccupied with temporal affairs, was obviously identified with this world of matter, they would have nothing at all to do with its organization or ritual or doctrine. It was nothing more than the servant of the Evil God of matter, "the Synagogue of Satan." They were the only true church of the spirit, theirs the only road to eternal bliss. They therefore looked forward to and preached the extinction of the orthodox Church, as a tool of Satan that led only to perdition. The term "Cathari" is Greek, meaning "the Pure": the good life on earth, the Cathari taught, consists of gradual purification from evil matter. One means of achieving purity was to abstain from marriage, which was only a union of evil bodies to produce more evil bodies: if celibacy was good for priests and monks, it was good for everybody. To this extent the sect can fairly be considered antisocial. To eat any-

Albigensian beliefs and practices

[24] See p. 500.

thing that was the ultimate product of sexual union was to take more evil matter into one's already evil body. Hence they eschewed meat, milk, cheese, and eggs, eating only vegetables and—through some inconsistency—fish. They had disturbing ideas about capital punishment and war; they were out-and-out pacifists, acknowledging no right ever to go to war; soldiers, preachers of crusades, judges who sentenced men to death they lumped together as common murderers. They refused to take any oath. The state could therefore no more tolerate them than could the organized Church.

The Cathari were doubtless wise not to demand the full degree of asceticism from all members. The sect was conveniently divided into two classes, the believers (Latin, *credentes*) and the perfect (*perfecti*). All that was required of a believer was to renounce the orthodox *The believers* Church, to support and venerate the *perfecti*, and to receive before *and the perfect* death the *consolamentum*, the sacrament of consolation that admitted him into the class of *perfecti*. Until the *consolamentum* was administered the simple believer was permitted to marry, to eat meat, and in general to do as he saw fit, all without fear of hell or worry about purgatory, both of which the Albigensians rejected. The soul of one who died unconsoled entered into the body of the animal most like him, from which through endless cycles it must make its way up again to another opportunity to receive the *consolamentum*. On the other hand, once the *consolamentum* had been received the rigid standards of the faith must be adhered to, and so difficult were they that suicide was often urged upon the *perfecti*, in order to avoid any relapse into evil and thus to make salvation sure. This distinction within the sect, behind a front of imposing austerity, between the perfect and the mere believers—corresponding in a general way to the distinction between clergy and laity—was obviously a supremely practical bit of doctrine. Together with the tempting prospect of confiscating the property of the wicked organized Church, it goes far to explain the popularity of the sect. The concentrated ferocity with which Church and state combined to wipe the Cathari off the face of the earth in the Albigensian crusade is easy to understand. How, one wonders, would they fare today?

Quite distinct to begin with from the heretical Albigensians, the *Origin of the* Waldensians were interested only in a simple return to the apostolic *Waldensians* life of the Gospels. They were named from their founder, Peter Waldo, a rich merchant of Lyons, who in 1173 experienced conversion, gave up his wealth to the poor, and founded a purely lay order called the Poor Men of Lyons. "They never have settled homes, but two by two they travel about with bare feet, clothed in wool, possessing nothing as individuals, but holding all things in common." The Poor Men were preachers of the literal Gospel in the vernacular tongue, from vernacular translations of the New Testament. There was nothing whatever heretical in their teaching, but to the established hierarchy it was unthinkable that a group of laymen should wander about, preaching the Gospel without authority and incidentally inveighing against the immoral and worldly character of the clergy. Waldo himself never intended to found a sect outside the Church. In 1179 he went to Rome to attend the third Lateran council and to obtain from Alexander III confirmation for his order. Being too wise to drive the Poor Men into opposition, the pope approved of their vow of poverty and gave them permission to preach, provided they first got the consent of the proper ecclesiastical authority.

The spread of the Waldensians

The order spread widely after Waldo's return to Lyons, but its members tended to ignore the stipulation that they secure local authority to preach. The Church, dropping its efforts at conciliation, grouped the Waldensians with the Cathari and the Patarenes of northern Italy in condemnation at the Council of Verona in 1184, and they were banished from Lyons by the ecclesiastical authorities. But condemnation and banishment could not check their growth; they spread into southern France and Spain, into Lombardy, the Rhineland, Bohemia, and Hungary. As they spread they came into contact with genuinely heretical movements—with Arnoldists and *Humiliati* in Italy, with Petrobrusians and Cathari in France, perhaps with the Apostolics around Cologne. They were influenced by these groups, and these groups by them. Persecution, by driving the Waldensians underground, made their whole position more radical. Quite naturally they began to teach that ordination was unnecessary for preaching, that any good man could preach the Gospel and take charge of a religious service (an anticipation of the "priesthood of all believers" of the sixteenth-century Protestants), and that they were in fact the only true successors of the apostles. They learned the Gospels by heart and boasted—if so modest a claim may be called boasting—that they knew more about the Scriptures than most of the clergy. They fastened a firm hold on the hearts of peasants and of simple workingmen in the towns.

Gradually a split developed in the ranks of the Waldensians. Those in France tended to become reconciled to the Church. Elsewhere, notably in Lombardy, the radical Waldensians advanced to bolder positions. They broke with the whole organization of the Church, with

...ricus de Alemania lecturing at the University of Bologna (miniature, second half of the fourteenth ...ury)

...e scribe at work in ...scriptorium

The façade of the Cathedral of Amiens

its ritual, and with many of its beliefs. They organized their own *The Walden-*
Church and their own simple religious services; they appointed their *sian tradition*
own preachers and met together in their own councils; in Germany
and Italy they organized an impressive educational system. The persecution of the thirteenth century, while it succeeded in either diverting
their enthusiasm into more orthodox channels or forcing them to meet
secretly, did not, as in the case of the Cathari, succeed in destroying
the Waldensians. In northern Italy, where they joined with the
Humiliati, they were ineradicable, and their Church in Italy today is
a flourishing institution. The Waldenses of Piedmont through centuries of persecution preserved their identity. French Protestant
leaders of the sixteenth century visited them, and they were one source
of the radical forms of the Hussite following in Bohemia and probably of sixteenth-century Anabaptism. The Waldensian Church may
fairly be called the oldest Protestant church in existence.

To look now for a moment in the opposite direction, back to the
mother of all our churches, we find the Waldensian spirit active there
too. The Waldensian leader in Aragon, Durand of Huesca, after
reconciling himself with the Church, formed an order called Poor
Catholics, whose rule was approved by Innocent III. This order, composed of priests trained in theology in order to combat heretics, took
a vow of poverty, and supported pacifism and the refusal to take an
oath. It spread from Aragon into southern France and as far as Milan
before it was practically wiped out in the fury of the Albigensian
crusade. But surely it is no long step from Durand's order to the two
mendicant orders of Franciscans and Dominicans, if indeed we may not
regard it as a definite prototype of the Dominicans.

The Franciscans originally represented the same protest against the
wealthy and secularized Church as all the monastic reforms and all
the heretical movements discussed above. St. Francis of Assisi (1182–
1226) emerged from the same kind of environment as Peter Waldo
of Lyons. He also was a rich merchant's son whom the life of a young .
man about town did not satisfy. After conversion he abandoned his *St. Francis*
inheritance, married My Lady Poverty (*Madonna Povertà*), donned *of Assisi*
the rags of a beggar, and, filled with the loving spirit of his new Lord
Jesus Christ, set out, in the true—and rare—spirit of Christian chivalry
upon the great adventure of following in his steps. His mission he
conceived to be to preach the gospel of salvation to the lowly and the
heathen, and to administer in all humility to the needs of the poor and
the sick—in a word, to all the helpless outcasts, lepers not excluded,
whose number the new conditions of urban life had done so much to

increase. When his example gained him followers, for whom he had to draw up some code of living, the best he could do was to turn to the New Testament. "He called his twelve disciples together, and gave them power and authority over all devils, and to cure diseases. And he sent them to preach the kingdom of God, and to heal the sick. And he said unto them, Take nothing for your journey, neither staves, nor scrip, neither bread, neither money; neither have two coats apiece. And whatsoever house ye enter into, there abide, and thence depart. And whosoever will not receive you, when you go out of that city shake off the very dust from your feet for a testimony against them. And they departed and went through the towns, preaching the gospel and healing everywhere." [25] "Then said Jesus unto his disciples, If any man will come after me, let him deny himself, and take up his cross and follow me. For whosoever will save his life shall lose it, and whosoever will lose his life for my sake shall find it. For what is a man profited if he shall gain the whole world and lose his own soul?" [26]

St. Francis felt himself to be the directly chosen vessel of God. In his testament he says: "When the Lord gave me some brothers, no one showed me what I ought to do, but the Most High himself revealed to me that I ought to live according to the model of the Holy Gospel." When one of his brethren asked, "Whence comes it, then, that it should be thee whom the world desires to follow?" he answered: "Thou wishest to know why it is I whom men follow? Thou wishest to know? It is because the eyes of the Most High have willed it thus; he continually watches the good and the wicked, and as his most holy eyes have not found among sinners any smaller man, nor any more insufficient and more sinful, therefore he has chosen me to accomplish the marvellous work which God has undertaken; he chose me because he could find no one more worthless, and he wished here to confound the nobility and grandeur, the strength, the beauty, and the learning of this world." [27] St. Francis was completely possessed by a compassionate and mystical love for the person of Christ, and before his death felt himself to have received in miraculous fashion the same five wounds, the stigmata, that Christ received upon the cross. "As he had imitated Christ in the deeds of his life, so it behoved him to be conformed unto Him in the afflictions and sorrows of His Passion."

[25] Luke ix, 1–6.
[26] Matthew xvi, 24–26.
[27] Sabatier, *St. Francis of Assisi*, p. 185.

The Franciscan friars in their coarse brown robes rapidly replaced the monks of the older orders in the affections of plain men and women. That they did so must be accounted for by the fact that they *Friars* exemplified in their conduct not only a higher idealism than either the *and* older or the reformed Benedictine houses, but also a practical, demo- *monks* cratic idealism of a sort better suited to the needs of a society in transition. The word "friar," from the Latin *frater*, chosen as the name for all the new mendicant orders, is important in itself. St. Francis's friars were, at least to begin with, so different from monks that in his mind it would have been a misnomer to call them monks at all. The monk was concerned primarily with his own salvation through ascetic practices, in some spot far from easy communication with an evil and dangerous world. Because they grew out of a rural society, the necessity of self-support started the older houses on the way to becoming immense agricultural establishments, but their great services to agriculture were incidental to their main purpose. Their services to art and scholarship were likewise by-products of monasticism. Monks lived according to a definite rule, and as time went on took orders in large numbers. With the growth of the institution of lay brothers they tended to become an aristocratic caste, and to lose whatever touch they may have had with the common people. They were pledged to poverty, but they had failed to achieve it, thanks to the convenient and necessary distinction between the private ownership forbidden a monk and the community ownership allowed the monastery.

Like the Waldensians, the Franciscans began as a lay order, and *St. Francis's* such St. Francis would have liked them to remain. They were dis- *conception* tinctly an evangelical order, transfigured by the peculiar and extraor- *of his order* dinary genius of their founder. With individual exceptions, they were not concerned with the rigid ascetic practices of monasticism in its original purity. Their salvation they conceived in terms of bringing salvation to others by preaching and teaching in the language of the people. Historically perhaps the most important part of their work was as foreign missionaries and the immense amount they did of what we should call social service. The Franciscan friars, in direct contrast to the new monastic orders of the preceding century, were predominantly a town order, for it was in the towns that the need for their work was greatest. St. Francis conceived of their being utterly free to accomplish their mission, unconfined within the walls of an institution and unfettered by the words of a rule. His first rule was only a quotation of difficult Gospel precepts, and he was impatient at the mention of any other. "My brothers, my brothers, the Lord called me in the way of simplicity and humility, and showed me in truth this way for myself and for those who wish to believe and imitate me. And therefore I desire that you will not name any rule to me, neither the rule of St. Benedict, nor that of St. Augustine or St. Bernard, or any other rule or model of living except that which was mercifully shown and given me by the Lord." [28]

He felt as little need of learning as of a rule: it was better for the brethren to be saints than to read about saints. "My brothers who are led by the curiosity of knowledge will find their hands empty in the day of tribulation. I would wish them rather to be strengthened by virtues, that when the time of tribulation comes they may have the Lord with them in their straits—for such a time will come when they will throw their good-for-nothing books into holes and corners." [29] When a brother asked permission to get a psalter, St. Francis answered: "When you have your psalter, you will want a breviary, and when you have a breviary you will seat yourself in a pulpit like a great prelate. . . . He who would be Brother Minor [St. Francis called his friars *Fratres Minores*, lesser brothers] ought to have nothing but his clothing." [30]

Franciscan poverty

St. Francis's ideas on the subject of private property were truly revolutionary. Not only were the friars to own no property individually, but they were to hold no corporate property: no houses, no churches, no land—absolutely nothing. Accordingly, the friars had either to work for their living or beg for it, and it was from their reliance on begging that they—and kindred orders—came to be called mendicant friars, or simply mendicants. In his testament St. Francis says: "I worked with my hands and would continue to do, and I will also that all other friars work at some honorable trade. Let those who have none learn one, not for the purpose of receiving the price of their toil, but for their good example and to flee idleness. And when they do not give us the price of the work, let us resort to the table of the Lord, begging our bread from door to door." [31] To the Bishop of Assisi he remarked: "My lord, if we should have possessions, we should need arms to protect ourselves. For thence [i.e., from property] arise disputes and lawsuits, and for this cause the love of God and of our neighbor is wont oft-times to be hindered, wherefore we be minded to possess naught of worldly goods in this world." [32] His own

[28] Quoted by Taylor, *The Mediæval Mind*, I, 435, n. 1.
[29] *Ibid.*, pp. 444–45.
[30] Quoted by Sabatier, *op. cit.*, pp. 249–50.
[31] *Ibid.*, p. 338.
[32] Quoted by Scudder, *The Franciscan Adventure*, p. 69.

personal standards, quite foreign to our way of thinking, were exceptionally difficult. One of his biographers reports that "he suffered to see any poorer than himself, not from desire for vainglory but from affectionate compassion." And he himself admitted: "Always I have taken less than I needed, lest I should defraud other poor folk of their portion; for to do the contrary would have been theft." There cannot have been many complete Christians since Christ. If St. Francis of Assisi was not the best and the noblest, he is certainly the most widely known and the greatest. And if he was not the best and the noblest, who was a better and a nobler?

"Of more than middle height, Francis had a delicate and kindly face, black eyes, a soft and sonorous voice. There was in his whole person a delicacy and grace which made him infinitely lovely." [33] *The personality of* Although he has been the victim of an uncommonly pious and exaggerated legend, few who have become at all acquainted with him *St. Francis* have failed to be attracted. The source of this attraction must be in part wonder that there could be a person of such completeness and oneness. The combination of guileless simplicity, genuine humility, endless patience, remarkable physical and moral courage, clear intelligence, infinite love for his fellow creatures, whether lowly humans or birds of the air or beasts of the field, and serene joyousness amounted to genius of a most rare kind.

"Let the brothers take care not to appear sad or gloomy," he wrote, "like hypocrites, but joyful in the Lord, merry and becomingly courteous." "Keep thou this sadness between thee and thy God . . . but before me and others study always to have joy, for it befits not the servant of God to show before his brother or another the sadness of a troubled face." His friars were to be "God's troubadours," with hearts as full of music as his own. "Drunken with the love and pity of Christ, the blessed Francis would sometimes act like this, for the sweetest melody of spirit within him, often boiling outward, gave sound in French, and the strain of the divine whisper which his ear had taken secretly broke forth in a glad French song. He would pick up a stick and, holding it over his left arm, would with another stick in his right hand make as if drawing a bow across a violin (*viellam*), and with fitting gestures would sing in French of the Lord Jesus Christ." [34] No one else, without seeming silly or grotesque or unbalanced, could preach to the birds, kiss the sores of lepers, or address the fire in a cauterizing iron about to be applied to his face as

[33] Sabatier, *op. cit.*, p. 182.
[34] Taylor, *op. cit.*, I, 448.

"Brother Fire, noble and useful among other creatures, be courteous to me in this hour, since I have loved and will love thee for the love of Him who made thee." Into his "Canticle of the Sun," written shortly before his death, he put his whole self.

"O most high, almighty, good Lord God, to thee belong praise, glory, honor, and all blessing!

Praised be my Lord God with all his creatures, and specially our brother the sun, who brings us the day and who brings us the light; fair is he and shines with a very great splendor: O Lord, he signifies to us thee!

Praised be my Lord for our sister the moon, and for the stars, the which he has set clear and lovely in heaven.

Praised be my Lord for our brother the wind, and for air and cloud, calms and all weather by the which thou upholdest life in all creatures.

Praised be my Lord for our sister water, who is very serviceable unto us and humble and precious and clean.

Praised be my Lord for our brother fire, through whom thou givest us light in the darkness; and he is bright and pleasant and very mighty and strong.

Praised be my Lord for our mother the earth, the which doth sustain us and keep us, and bringeth forth divers fruits and flowers of many colors, and grass.

Praised be my Lord for all those who pardon one another for his love's sake, and who endure weakness and tribulation; blessed are they who peaceably shall endure, for thou, O most Highest, shalt give them a crown.

Praised be my Lord for our sister, the death of the body, from which no man escapeth. Woe to him who dieth in mortal sin! Blessed are they who are found walking by thy most holy will, for the second death shall have no power to do them harm.

Praise ye and bless the Lord, and give thanks unto him and serve him with great humility." [35]

The papacy's transformation of the Franciscans

St. Francis died a sorely tried and disappointed man. Long before his death, with the entrance into his order of unexpected thousands of men and with the bounteous offers of countless supporters, it had become clear that it was impossible to practice his simple idealism on so large a scale. The papacy, moreover, having had almost a cen-

[35] Sabatier, *op. cit.*, pp. 305–6.

tury's experience with the dangers of evangelical movements, was not minded to let the Franciscans run loose: the Gospel taken undiluted so easily led men to heresy. Innocent III was cool in his original confirmation of St. Francis's plan in 1210, but he and his successors soon saw that, if once this contagious movement could be brought within the organization and control of the Church, it would act as the great absorber of all critical tendencies, a weapon in the fight against heresy, latent or overt, such as the papacy had not yet had. In the frescoes on the walls of the Church of St. Francis at Assisi one of the most striking of Giotto's great series of scenes from the saint's life portrays the dream of Innocent III, who in a vision beheld the whole tottering edifice of the Lateran upheld by the shoulder of this lone man. The fate of the Franciscan Order is the most brilliant and tragic example of the success with which the papacy disarmed the critics who alone might have saved it from its enemies. Until the Protestant reformation no force so great was unloosed, none of such promise.

Because St. Francis was unalterably opposed to any formal organization of his order—"I will not," he said, "become an executioner to strike and punish as political governors must"—he was urged to give up his official leadership in 1220. Since he could not or would not write a rule to suit the papacy, Honorius III helped him in 1223 to draw up one conformable to papal ideas of what the Franciscans should be. The papacy was particularly anxious to grant privileges that would put the friars at its service, but on this point St. Francis in his testament was adamantine. "I absolutely interdict all the Brothers, in whatever place they may be found, from asking any bull from the court of Rome. . . . Let the Brothers take great care not to receive churches, habitations, and all that men build for them." Plainly there was only one thing to do: set aside the testament. St. Francis was canonized in 1228, two years after his death. In 1230 Gregory IX declared that his will had no binding force. Then began a series of compromises on the question of the possession and use of money and property, which, when continued by his successor, Innocent IV, rendered all St. Francis's own regulations about personal and corporate property void. The Franciscans borrowed the elaborate form of government of the Dominicans. By 1266 the ruin had been so well wrought that all early lives of St. Francis were ordered destroyed, that it might be less easy for men to learn too much about the man he had once been. The order lost its lay character when men in orders were admitted. It lost its simplicity when it was insisted that for efficient preaching university training was necessary. When the friars accordingly made for the universities, there was a new need for houses and means of support.

The decline of the Franciscan Order actually began, as we have just seen, before the death of its founder. If, however, it is worth while to distinguish between its transformation into a tool of the papacy and its loss of effectiveness even as such, we might say that the beginning of the final decline was marked by the acceptance of privileges from the papacy conferring the right to preach and hear confessions without the consent of the local ecclesiastical authorities. By thus entering into competition with the parish priesthood the Franciscans won their cordial hatred. Finally the order split into two factions, the moderates or conventuals, who favored the change from earlier days, and the observants or spirituals, who remained faithful to St. Francis. They fought and persecuted each other. By the beginning of the fourteenth century spirituals were burnt at the stake, and teaching the simple fact that Christ and the apostles lived in poverty was pronounced a heresy by the pope.[36] Thus, within a hundred years St. Francis turned out to be what Innocent III originally suspected that he might easily become—if indeed he was not such already—a heretic. When one of the faithful Franciscans saw the great basilica built over the tomb of St. Francis at Assisi, he is reported to have remarked, "Now the only thing you lack is women," and it was not long before, in common report, the friars had these, too. And so the Franciscans went the same way, and for the same reasons, as all the earlier monastic orders, and like them soon became the butt of popular ridicule and scorn.

And yet we dare not say that the Franciscan Order, had things gone otherwise, would have succeeded: such things never go otherwise. The Franciscan ideal was for St. Francis alone, or at the most for a few choice spirits like him. On the other hand, the momentum of the movement has carried it down to our own time, and before the friars became a target for lampoons they exercised no mean influence upon many aspects of medieval civilization. Together with the Dominicans they were—paradoxically enough—the leading figures in science and philosophy at the universities. They inspired a new personal note in medieval religion, which found expression in both Latin and ver nacular poetry and in the supreme art of the Florentine painter

The decline of the Franciscans

[36] See p. 960.

Giotto. These phases of Franciscan history it seems better to consider later.[37]

The Dominican friars, founded by St. Dominic (1170–1221) in 1206 and confirmed by Pope Honorius III in 1216, were officially called Friars Preachers. Their founder was a noble Castilian, who came to southern France in the service of his bishop in 1205 and remained there for ten years. From experience in discussions with the Cathari, from observation of the character of both upper and lower clergy in southern France, and from contact with the uppish Cistercian monks used by the papacy to combat heresy, he came to the conclusion that the only intelligent way to fight heresy was to combat the ignorance of both clergy and laity. To this end he founded an order of preachers to be trained in theology and in preaching in the vernacular tongues and to hold themselves ready to be sent anywhere. Dominicans flocked to the universities, to capture the chairs of theology and philosophy and thus control opinion from the centers of learning. The constitutions of the order subordinate all else to study. "All the hours in church shall be shortened, lest the friars lose devotion and their study be at all impeded"; the superior of every convent may "grant dispensations whenever he may deem it expedient, especially in regard to what may hinder study or preaching or the profit of souls." No doubt from the example of the Franciscans, in order to make his brothers more popular, St. Dominic forbade even corporate ownership of property. The Dominicans were therefore the second mendicant order. They went the same way as the first; soon they had their own houses and common property, and Dominicans were even permitted to have private incomes.

The Dominicans

St. Dominic's personality left no such imprint even upon his generation as St. Francis's did, although he was canonized in 1234. His genius lay in devising for his friars an organization that was adopted by the Franciscans, after their founder's death, and influenced all subsequent monastic organization and reorganization. The main principle of the early Benedictine system was local autonomy. The Cluniac organization was a reaction towards centralization in the mother house of Cluny. The Cistercians formed a federal government of abbots under the mother house of Cîteaux. The Dominicans were, strictly speaking, Augustinian canons, but St. Dominic introduced striking modifications in the so-called Augustinian rule. The

Dominican organization

[37] See pp. 714, 758, 1025–26.

essential feature of Dominican organization was election by majority vote of delegates to representative bodies. Dominican houses, each of which elected its own conventual prior, were grouped together into provinces. The province was governed through a provincial chapter, consisting of the conventual priors and one elected representative from each house, meeting annually. The provincial chapter elected a provincial prior, visitors for the province, and a group of four administrators to govern the province until the next chapter meeting. The general chapter of the whole order, which elected the master general, was composed of the provincial priors and elected representatives from each province. Within it a special body of definitors, composed sometimes of elected representatives of the provinces, sometimes of the provincial priors, was the ultimate source of authority. "It is arguable that the English Parliament, beginning its new career under the auspices first of Simon de Montfort,[38] St. Dominic's godchild, and then of Edward I, whose confessor and friends were Dominicans, owed some of its features to this Dominican influence." [39]

The Dominicans, like the Franciscans, had an auxiliary order of nuns. They also maintained close contact, as some of the newer orders of the twelfth century had begun to do, with laymen by the organization of a third order, the Tertiaries. These were not held to the vow of personal and corporate poverty, but did obligate themselves to live a pious life according to a fixed rule, which at least in the case of the Franciscan Tertiaries involved abstention from military service and refusal to take oaths. As the mendicant orders represented the last important monastic reform of the middle ages, so their organization marked the completion of development in monastic government.

The In-
quisition

St. Dominic was often called "Hammer of Heretics" and his friars "Hounds of God," who drove lost sheep back into the fold. His order performed well the service for which it was organized. To the same end it was utilized by the papacy in a way that St. Dominic did not contemplate, to direct a new institution, the Inquisition, whose purpose was to bring heretics by more stringent means than preaching and teaching back into the Church, or, in case this proved impossible, to prevent their heresy from contaminating others. In this work Franciscans were often associated with the Dominicans. Before the organization of the Inquisition, or Holy Office, the responsibility for

---

[38] See p. 837.
[39] B. Jarrett, in *Encyclopedia of the Social Sciences*, V, 210.

detecting and punishing heresy rested with local bishops and their courts. The natural result was that there was no common opinion as to what actually constituted heresy, no uniformity of zeal in persecuting it, and no regularity in methods of punishment; often enough infuriated mobs brought about the death of reputed heretics. How successful this method was in checking heresy the events of the twelfth century proved. When in the early years of the thirteenth century the Church found itself in actual danger from the formidable spread of Albigensianism, after Cistercians used as papal missionaries in southern France had failed to bring the heretics around, Innocent III, as we have seen, resorted to the novel and brutal method of organizing a crusade against them. Innocent III and his successors, however, were quite well aware that the use of military force alone could not dispose of the Albigenses. Force must be followed up by some entirely new method of ferreting out and dealing with heretics still alive and unrepentant.

The new method was formally inaugurated by Gregory IX in 1233, when as representatives of the papacy permanent local delegate-judges were appointed to organize special inquisitions for heresy. Originally they were to co-operate with the bishops, but ensuing friction between bishops and inquisitors soon led to the dropping of the former. The inquisitors, being then for the most part mendicant friars, transformed the Inquisition into a monastic institution. As such it proved an effective instrument in papal hands to reduce western Christendom to religious conformity. At times it was used by the popes also as a weapon against their political enemies, the Ghibellines, just as Frederick II's henchmen relied upon heretics in their struggle with the pope. For the rest of the middle ages the Inquisition was directed, after Albigensianism was finally destroyed, against the newer types of evangelical and purely personal religion and against sorcery and witchcraft. It was active in France, Germany, Italy, Sicily, Sardinia, Aragon, and Bohemia. When introduced into Castile and Portugal at the end of the middle ages by Ferdinand and Isabella, it proved an effective weapon against political enemies. In Italy it was revived in the sixteenth century to combat Protestantism. England and Scandinavia were spared its acquaintance.

When the inquisitor appeared, all heretics were summoned to present themselves within a certain time, usually thirty days, called "the period of Grace." Those who appeared and renounced their false *The pro-* beliefs were punished with comparatively light penance. After this *cedure of the* period the faithful were called upon to denounce all heretics to the *Inquisition* inquisitor, who, if necessary, could call upon the civil authorities to bring them before him. Only two witnesses were needed to make an accusation, which did not have to agree at all points; and the witnesses might themselves be heretics, perjurors, excommunicated persons, or murderers. The aim of the inquisitor at the formal interrogation was to wring a confession from the accused and bring him back into the Church after proper punishment. Postponement of trial and consequent prolongation of imprisonment with insufficient food were means used to persuade the accused of his guilt. The trial, held in the presence of two members of the clergy and of lawyers whose duty it was to watch for irregularities, was likely to be technical, inasmuch as inquisitors were instructed to distinguish between affirmative and negative heresy, perfected and imperfect heretics, and the lightly, the vehemently, and the violently suspect. The whole process was recorded by notaries. It is easy to guess how many people had the courage to appear as witnesses for the accused. The accused was allowed no lawyer, nor was he confronted with his accusers or even informed of their names, for fear revenge might be taken on them. He could discount their evidence only by reciting a list of his enemies; if in so doing he named any of the witnesses against him, the inquisitors were obliged to discredit the testimony of that witness.

If there was no voluntary confession, the Inquisition after 1252 was empowered by the papacy to use torture in accordance with the provisions of Roman law. The three chief forms of torture were the rack, the strappado, and the burning coals. The rack was "a triangular frame, on which the prisoner was stretched and bound, so that he could not move. Cords were attached to his arms and legs and then connected with a windlass, which when turned dislocated the joints of the wrists and ankles." When the strappado or vertical rack was used, "the prisoner with his hands tied behind his back was raised by a rope attached to a pulley and windlass to the top of a gallows, or to the ceiling of the torture chamber; he was then let fall with a jerk to within a few inches of the ground. This was repeated several times. The cruel torturers sometimes tied weights to the victim's feet to increase the shock of the fall." When burning coals were used, "first a good fire was started; then the victim was stretched out on the ground, his feet manacled, and turned toward the flame. Grease, fat, or some other combustible substance was rubbed upon them, so that they were horribly burned. From time to time a screen was placed between the victim's feet and the brazier, that the Inquisitor might have an opportunity to resume his interrogatory." If there was still no confession, the accused was held guilty until he could explain away the accusation, "a practically impossible undertaking. For if two witnesses, considered of good repute by the Inquisitor, agreed in accusing the prisoner, his fate was at once settled; whether he confessed or not, he was declared a heretic." [40]

The confessed or declared heretic might either abjure or persist in his belief. If he abjured he was subject to punishments ranging from a heavy penance, such as a pilgrimage, to imprisonment. If he failed to abjure he was turned over to the civil authorities to be burned at the stake, the customary punishment for those convicted of heresy, inasmuch as canon law forbade the clergy to shed blood. Although the heretic was handed over with the formal but not wholly ingenuous prayer that death or mutilation might be prevented, Innocent IV's bull of 1252 provided that, if the state did not punish with the stake, the officials responsible should be excommunicated as abettors of heresy. For a person once brought before the Inquisition to escape punishment of any sort was practically impossible, and its severity tended to increase with time. Burning at the stake, however, was always the exceptional punishment, although that may prove only that few men can hold out against torture. Bernard Gui, the Inquisitor of Toulouse, condemned six hundred and twenty heretics between 1308 and 1322. Of these one hundred and twenty-four were either dead or fugitives; of the remaining four hundred and ninety-six, forty were burned at the stake. The property of convicted heretics was confiscated by the state, although it was sometimes shared with the Church —a circumstance that doubtless explains some of the ardor of the state in co-operating with the Inquisition.

The Inquisition has an evil reputation, and justly so. Nevertheless, if the shrieks of the torture chamber and the odor of burning flesh cause us to shudder with nausea and shame over human brutality *The In-* committed in the name of Christianity, it is well to remember that *quisition in* the medieval Church was the child of a cruel age and no crueler than *retrospect* any Christian state. It is well to remember that Protestantism in the sixteenth century had its own little inquisition. It is well to remember that witches were tried and burned in Massachusetts. Political heresy, if it goes so far as treason, is still punishable by death; in the middle ages public opinion condemned with equal horror "an opinion chosen by human sense, contrary to Holy Scripture, openly taught, pertinaciously defended." Innocent III spoke for his time when he said that, inasmuch as "the civil law punishes traitors . . . all the more should

[40] Quotations from Vancandard, *The Inquisition*, pp. 152 ff.

we excommunicate and confiscate the property of those who are traitors to the faith of Jesus Christ; for it is infinitely greater sin to offend the divine majesty than to attack the majesty of the sovereign." Public opinion went even beyond that, as papal policy later did, and sanctioned the death penalty.

Much else in the procedure of the Inquisition that offends our sense of decency and fair play seemed to contemporaries, familiar (as we are not) with canon law, quite sensible and fair. Perhaps we should withhold criticism until national and international scandals cease to arise from the procedure of American courts. In regard to the one most terrible feature of the Inquisition, which is certainly more responsible for its ill fame than all its other sins put together, the use of torture, a special word of caution is necessary. Torture was a recognized method of interrogation in Roman law (it was the regular method of examining slaves); and it was under the influence of Roman law, which was just then being more intensely studied and more extensively copied in the west, that the Inquisition adopted torture as part of its method. Until all officials realize that torture is a good way to get what they want but a poor way to get the truth, it will doubtless continue to be used to extract "confessions." At any rate, no American who is not bitterly indignant at the use of the "third degree" by our police should waste any indignation on the Inquisition.

Chapter 22

THE TRIUMPH OF THE CHURCH

EVERY so often in the history of mankind there has come a time when a people or an ideal seems to reach a fullness of development beyond which it is impossible to go. Institutions, ideas, artistic forms acquire a kind of perfection peculiar to the age, and their mutual influence and interpenetration produce a synthesis of thought and action that earlier and later periods cannot' show. During such a period it usually happens that some one individual who has absorbed the sum total of the cultural influences of his time focuses them so exactly in himself that the perfection of the age is forever associated with him. The fifth century B.C. is so closely identified with Pericles in Athens that we call it the Periclean age; for a like reason the early years of the Roman empire we call the Augustan age. For the middle ages the thirteenth century must be regarded as the period of synthesis and perfection, whose best embodiment is the greatest of medieval popes, Innocent III.

The triumph of the Church embodied in Innocent III

The last chapter showed the world of ideas and affairs in the second quarter of the twelfth century centered about the person of St. Bernard. From 1198 to 1216, the few years of Innocent's pontificate, the whole western European world seemed to revolve even more completely about him, for he had not only influence but power. He was born in 1161 at Anagni of the noble family of the Conti, from which came eight popes. We have already seen him on numerous occasions. He was the great manipulator of the events that settled the fate of the Holy Roman empire.[1] He stood behind the lines in the conflict between the Capetian kings of France and the Angevin kings of England, whose issue was finally settled during his pontificate. He was the original leader of the malodorous fourth crusade, which broke the power of the Byzantine empire. He was pope when the great crisis in western Christianity precipitated by the growth of heresy came to a

[1] See pp. 413–14.

head; he confirmed the new order of the Franciscans, participated in the organization of the Dominicans, and inaugurated the Albigensian crusade. Philip of Swabia and Otto of Brunswick and Frederick II, Richard and John and Philip Augustus, Henry Dandolo, Raymond VI of Toulouse and Simon de Montfort, St. Francis and St. Dominic —all are inseparably associated with his name.

The history of the idea of papal theocracy

To consider Innocent III more closely from the point of view of the unique institution of which he was the head, we need first a brief résumé of matters already discussed above. From the Roman empire the middle ages inherited the idea of a world state. This inheritance came originally through the Church, for which St. Augustine developed his grandiose conception of the City of God. The world state was conceived in the form, likewise inherited from Rome, of absolute monarchy, embodied in a centralized bureaucracy. Within the Church it was especially the bishops of Rome who were devoted to this ideal. From an early date they began to transform it into reality by making good their spiritual supremacy over other bishops, relying upon the imposing Petrine theory combined with the forged Pseudo-Isidorian decretals. The popes, as the only likely successors of the Roman emperors in Italy, also at an early date began to cherish dreams of temporal power and supremacy, towards which they made a start by the acquisition of the Papal States, with the documentary support of the forged Donation of Constantine. Thus the Church transformed the Roman idea of world dominion into the idea of a Christian theocracy, governing the world through the Church, ruled by the pope.

This idea was challenged first by Charles the Great's short-lived revival of the Roman empire as an imperial theocracy. Although for a brief moment in the ninth century there was one vigorous theocrat on the papal throne, Nicholas I, in general the papacy and the whole Church became hopelessly subject to the same feudal system that disrupted the Carolingian empire. The second German revival of the imperial tradition in the Holy Roman empire renewed the conflict between these two international institutions. The popes embarked upon the great Cluniac-Gregorian reform, which aimed to free the international Church from the feudal state, to subject the Church to the papacy, and to reassert the claims of papal theocracy. Gregory VII and the following popes succeeded to some extent in imposing their temporal overlordship on Europe and on the Church their spiritual control, but at Innocent III's accession to the papal throne at the age of thirty-seven the program of papal theocracy ruling Church and state alike still remained to be realized. The greatest of the successors of Nicholas I and Gregory VII was able for a few brief years to come closer to carrying out this program in full than any pope before or after him.

Innocent III was, if anything, bolder than any of his predecessors in asserting the rights of the successor of St. Peter. In his first sermon after election, indeed in the very announcement of his election to the princes of Europe, he said: "For to me it is said in the Prophets, 'I have this day set thee over nations and over the kingdoms, to root out and pull down and to destroy and to throw down, to build and to plant.' To me it is said in the Apostles, 'I will give unto thee the keys of the kingdom of heaven; and whatsoever thou shalt loose on earth shall be loosed in heaven.' The successor of Peter is the Vicar of Christ: he has been established as a mediator between God and man, below God but beyond man; less than God but more than man; who shall judge all and be judged by no one." [2] Innocent was particularly fond of expressing the relationship between papal and royal power by the popular medieval simile of sun and moon. "As God, the creator of the universe, set two great lights in the firmament of heaven, the greater light to rule the day and the lesser light to rule the night [Gen. i, 15, 16], so He set two great dignities in the firmament of the universal church, . . . the greater to rule the day, that is, souls, and the lesser to rule the night, that is, bodies. These dignities are the papal authority and the royal power. And just as the moon gets her light from the sun, and is inferior to the sun in quality, quantity, position and effect, so the royal power gets the splendor of its dignity from the papal authority." [3] The reader may recall that Frederick II used the same simile, but insisted that the sun should keep out of the moon's orbit. [4]

Innocent III's claim to papal supremacy

Again Innocent wrote: "The *sacerdotium* [priestly power] is the sun, the *regnum* [royal power] is the moon. Kings rule over their respective kingdoms, but Peter rules over the whole earth. The *sacerdotium* came by divine creation, the *regnum* by man's cunning." "Princes have power in earth, priests over the soul. As much as the soul is worthier than the body, so much worthier is the priesthood than the monarchy." "The Lord Jesus Christ has set up one ruler over all things as his universal vicar, and as all things in heaven, earth and

[2] Packard, *Europe and the Church Under Innocent III*, p. 15.
[3] Thatcher and McNeal, *op. cit.*, p. 208.
[4] See p. 425.

hell bow the knee to Christ, so should all obey Christ's vicar, that there be one flock and one shepherd." "No King can reign rightly unless he devoutly serve Christ's vicar."

Gregory VII and the popes before and after him in the eleventh century had begun to translate theocratic theory into fact by asserting the pope's rights as feudal overlord of the kings and princes of Europe. Between 1059 and 1144 they had succeeded in the cases—in order of time—of the Norman King of southern Italy and Sicily, the King of Aragon, the Prince of Kiev, the King of Croatia, the Count of Provence, the Count of Melgueil, the Count of Barcelona, and the King of Portugal. Gregory VII laid claim to Hungary and to all of Spain that had been conquered from the Moslems. In the twelfth century Hadrian IV claimed authority over England and Ireland by reason of the Donation of Constantine, and is said to have invested Henry II with Ireland as a papal fief by sending him a gold ring. There is some doubtful evidence to show that Henry II, in the throes of embarrassment over the murder of Thomas à Becket, in 1173 formally recognized himself—for the moment—to be the faithful vassal of the pope for his whole kingdom. To this already impressive list of successes Innocent III added the Holy Roman empire, England, Poland, Norway, Sweden, Denmark, Bohemia, Bulgaria, Serbia, Armenia, the Kingdom of Jerusalem, the Latin Empire of Constantinople, and the Duchy of Athens; and he was not too proud to accept the allegiance of towns—for example, Montpellier and Châteauroux —or even of the castle of Levada in Spain.

Innocent's dealings with the empire we have already considered in sufficient detail.[5] He not only freed the German Church from the state, but vindicated the pope's right to investigate all candidates for the German throne as well as his rights of general supervision over the empire. When in 1201 he decided the disputed succession in favor of Otto IV of Brunswick, he stated his position in no unmistakable terms: "It is the business of the pope to look after the interests of the Roman empire, since the empire derives its origin, and its final authority from the papacy; its origin, because it was originally transferred from Greece by and for the sake of the papacy, the popes making the transfer in order that the church might be better protected; its final authority, because the emperor is raised to his position by the pope, who blesses him, crowns him and invests him with the empire."[6] By the transfer of the empire from Greece Innocent meant the coronation

[5] See pp. 413–14.
[6] Thatcher and McNeal, *op. cit.*, p. 220.

of Charles the Great by Leo III in 800, which now at length received its official papal interpretation as signifying the transfer of the Roman imperial crown from the head of the Byzantine emperor to the head of the King of the Franks. What Charles the Great would have thought of that may easily be surmised.[7]

In 1199 Innocent III succeeded in imposing a truce upon Philip Augustus of France and Richard I of England. Four years later he tried to repeat his success by intervening in the quarrel between Philip and John, but this time he was told firmly by the French king that relations between a lord and his vassal were none of the pope's business. To this particular point Innocent agreed, but he took pains to point out to Philip that the King of France had no power to limit the illimitable jurisdiction given by God to the popes: the quarrel of Philip and John was a war; war inevitably led to the commission of sin; sin endangered the soul; where the question of sin was involved the pope had sole jurisdiction. It was therefore the pope's right and duty to decide in this case which king had sinned in violating the rights of the other. Innocent therefore ordered both Philip and John to send representatives to Rome to submit their respective cases to his judgment, and ordered his legates to proceed with excommunication in case either king proved refractory. In fact, however, the pope, being unwilling to push his point to the length of compromising his policy in Germany by forcing Philip Augustus into the arms of Philip of Swabia, felt compelled to drop the matter. *Innocent's intervention in the quarrel between Philip Augustus and John*

Over John of England, on the other hand, Innocent III won a triumph so astounding as to make Gregory VII's so-called victory over Henry IV at Canossa seem almost trifling, although, to be sure, he was far more fortunate in his antagonist than Gregory had been. The controversy began in 1206 over a disputed election to the Archbishopric of Canterbury. Both the royal party in the electoral chapter and the antiroyal party appealed to the pope, who pronounced the whole procedure illegal and won over the delegates in Rome to the election of the English cardinal, Stephen Langton. John was furious, exiled the Canterbury chapter, confiscated the property and revenues of the see, and threatened the whole English Church with similar treatment. Within two years he brought down an interdict on England, which lasted for five years. At first he took advantage of this to lay hands on the wealth of the English Church and drive large numbers of the English upper clergy to the continent. In 1209 Innocent added to the interdict the personal excommunication of John, and two years later *Innocent's triumph over John*

[7] See p. 245.

practically deposed him by releasing all Englishmen from their oath of allegiance. He then began negotiations with Philip Augustus to organize a political crusade to put a Capetian prince on the English throne. When these negotiations reached the point of actual preparations for an invasion of England, John, having the best reasons to be fearful of the loyalty of his English subjects, abjectly capitulated on all points in 1213. He promised the papal legate to recognize Langton as Archbishop of Canterbury, to restore his confiscations, and to recall the exiles. Far more important, John recognized England and Ireland as fiefs of the papacy, for which he and his successors were to do liege homage to Innocent III and his successors, and pay an annual tribute of one thousand marks sterling in lieu of service and of the annual Peter's pence.[8]

For the rest of John's reign a papal legate resident in England was the king's firm ally, but had no more to do with the government than that. After John's death the legate was one of the three regents for the young King Henry III; but in 1221 the second legate withdrew, and no successor was appointed. As his feudal overlord Innocent did his best to protect John against the rising tide of baronial opposition by ordering English nobles to honor and obey and serve their king. But it was impossible to protect John from himself. After he was driven to agree to Magna Carta, the pope pronounced it null and void, "a shame for England": it had been wrung from his vassal by force and without his overlord the pope's consent, and, moreover, it impaired the value of England as a papal fief. On pain of excommunication the king was forbidden to observe its terms and the nobles to demand its enforcement. When thereby he merely inspired fresh revolt, the pope excommunicated the rebels, including his own appointee to the See of Canterbury, Stephen Langton, who with other leaders among the clergy had played an important part in securing the charter. Thereupon the English barons themselves offered the crown to the son of Philip Augustus, the same Prince Louis whom a few years before Innocent III had been arranging to seat on the throne, but whom he now resolutely opposed.[9] The death of king and pope in the same year, 1216, cut all the tangled knots. The great pope's victory was, of course, in the long run a hollow triumph. In the longer run it was probably a costly triumph too, for it not only confirmed the English people in their hostility to irresponsible autocrats on the English

---

[8] See p. 658.

[9] For Innocent III's dealings with Philip Augustus in this matter, see p. 488.

throne, but aroused in them a hostility to irresponsible autocrats on the papal throne.

Everywhere Innocent III proceeded with the same vigor in trying *Innocent's* to compel kings to observe the principles of Christian morality or to *dealings* acknowledge his feudal overlordship. From the day of his accession *with other* until he finally gained his point in 1213, he fought Philip Augustus, *princes* using the interdict, among other weapons, to force him to restore to her conjugal rights his Danish wife Ingeborg, whom Philip had repudiated the day after their marriage. He put Castile and León under interdict when their princes refused to recognize his abrogation of their marriages. He laid an interdict on Norway, and urged the kings of Denmark and Sweden to get rid of "that limb of the devil," King Sverre. Peter II, King of Aragon, came to Rome in 1204 to do homage for his kingdom; subsequently Innocent announced that Peter's successors were to ask the popes for their crown, but that the Archbishop of Tarragona would be authorized to receive their homage and crown them. In recognizing the right of the Duke of Bohemia to call himself king, "out of consideration of your obedience"—in other words, to reward him for supporting Otto IV of Brunswick, the papal candidate for the German throne—Innocent cautioned him to "shun the vice of ingratitude." "Show that you have deserved our favor which we have so graciously shown you, and try also to retain it. See to it that you are solemnly crowned by Otto as soon as possible." In recognizing the King of Bulgaria, who had taken an oath of vassalage, Innocent informed him that a papal legate was bringing his scepter and diadem, and that he might coin money if he wished. Henceforth the archbishops of Tirnova were to crown the Bulgarian kings after their oath of vassalage.

Although Philip Augustus would have nothing to do with Innocent's Albigensian crusade, the crusade was put through, ostensibly a papal expedition in charge of papal legates. There is perhaps no equal in the middle ages to the humiliation that Raymond VI of Toulouse was forced to undergo at St. Gilles in 1209, and it was to Innocent III that he surrendered himself and his son and all their domains in 1214.[10] Simon de Montfort held Béziers and Carcassonne as fiefs of the pope, and had to await his final certification of his new state in southern France. The temporal power of the papacy stood for a few years at its apogee.

Under Innocent III, likewise, the spiritual supremacy of the papacy

[10] See pp. 500-1.

within the Church was at length achieved to the full limits of Petrine theory, and recognized by the rest of the Church. This, in terms of canon law, meant the pope was in possession of *plenitudo potestatis*, that is, fullness of power, which made him an absolute monarch with unlimited administrative, judicial, and financial powers. The complete theory of *plenitudo potestatis* was not worked out by canon lawyers until later, nor was the organization whereby the papacy exercised these rights perfected until the fourteenth century; but under Innocent III the theory and practice were already in working order.

Full administrative authority meant that archbishops and bishops, in fact all ecclesiastical officials, were the pope's agents, appointed by him. The whole bureaucracy of the Church was by no means yet in the pope's hands, but Innocent demanded and exercised the right to investigate the persons of all elected clergy and the legality of elections and to correct all irregularities. It was his sole right to depose higher clergy, to transfer them from one see to another, and to appoint in case of resignation. The right of devolution, formulated by the Lateran Council of 1179, which provided that failure to fill a vacancy within six months made it incumbent upon the official immediately superior in the hierarchy to fill it by appointment, gave the pope one means of appointing archbishops. In the case of clergy dying in Rome Innocent III claimed the right to appoint their successors. He began the practice of appointing officials of the papal *Curia* to benefices situated anywhere in Europe, an easy way of judiciously scattering papal agents throughout all the national branches of the Church. The system of papal legates, or *missi*, invested with all the pope's own powers, was developed into an effective instrument of centralization. The possession of full judicial power not only made the pope supreme judge over the Church and the papal court the canon law court of last resort; it made his court also the supreme court of appeal for clergy who had failed to secure justice in any civil court. Innocent III's chancery was the most efficient in all Europe. The pope's financial power gave him access, in ways to be described, to all the local wealth of the Church for all such purposes as he approved. Innocent, himself a trained lawyer, well knew how to draw full advantage from his old prerogatives and to create opportunities for the exercise of new ones. In his letters, numbering approximately six thousand, he reveals, like Gregory VII, all the born administrator's unlimited patience and all his loving and meticulous care for each detail.

In 1215, the year before his death, Innocent III convoked in the Church of St. John Lateran at Rome the fourth Lateran council. In legislating for the whole Church the popes—even Innocent III—always considered themselves liable to error and subject to correction. The only practical way whereby the Church could exercise control over the sovereign pontiff was the general or ecumenical council. The medieval popes revived the practice of calling councils, but the medieval council, unlike the early Church councils, was in fact no deliberative assembly at all, but hardly more than a rubber stamp for the pope. In the course of a long evolution the popes had succeeded to the place formerly occupied by the Roman emperors, for example, by Constantine at the Council of Nicæa. They not only summoned councils (ordinarily at Rome), but determined what business was to be transacted, presided over the formal meetings, and confirmed decisions made or canons adopted. As in our Congress, most of the work was done not in full and formal assemblies, but by special commissions meeting in the papal palace, where they could more easily be guided to the right decision. The canons of the councils were scarcely more than decretals of the popes. Not until the fifteenth century was there an attempt to make the general council a real legislative body for the whole Church and a genuine instrument for the control of the papacy.[11] Until then the fourth Lateran council may be taken as wholly typical.

It was composed of four hundred and twelve bishops, some eight hundred abbots and priors, and representatives of clergy who could not attend and of all the leading secular princes of Europe and the Crusaders' States. Nothing better exemplified Innocent III's supremacy in Europe than his domination of this council, composed of the most important men in Europe, which settled far-reaching matters of politics as well as strictly ecclesiastical affairs. The council loyally confirmed the acts and policies of Innocent III's whole pontificate. It confirmed the deposition of Otto IV of Brunswick and of Raymond VI of Toulouse in favor of Frederick II and Simon de Montfort; it condemned the English rebels against the pope's vassal, King John, and confirmed the suspension of Archbishop Stephen Langton. It ratified the principle of confiscation of the property of all heretics and deposition of all princes who refused to co-operate with the Church in their extermination. The measures it adopted to ferret out heresy may be regarded as preliminary steps towards the establishment by Gregory IX of the more efficient Inquisition. The council relegated Jews to a subordinate position in the society of western Europe: they could exist only on sufferance of the Church, were obliged to wear a distinctive dress and to keep off the streets on festival days, and were denied the

The fourth Lateran council

[11] See pp. 976 ff.

right to hold public office. The council resonantly proclaimed the Church's independence of the state. Clergy once appointed or elected the lay authorities were to let strictly alone. Clergy were forbidden henceforth to participate in trials by battle and in ordeals. They were to be exempt from taxation; they might contribute voluntarily to the needs of the state, but only in case the contributions of the laity did not suffice, and then only with the consent of the bishops and clergy, confirmed by the pope. "This was in effect to leave to the Pope, who was omnipotent, the exclusive right to tax the church." "Legislation harmful to the church and its interests" was declared "ipso facto null and void," a canon that "really epitomizes the Middle Ages . . . a permanent challenge to every secular state in Europe and a perpetual source of inspiration for the Church." [12]

Transubstantiation and penance

Of all the transactions of the fourth Lateran council the most far-reaching historically was the adoption of two canons, one proclaiming a doctrine, the other prescribing a discipline. The doctrine defined was transubstantiation, long a matter of dispute among theologians.[13] The council resolved that in the sacrament of the Eucharist the body and blood of Christ "are really contained in the sacrament of the altar under the species of bread and wine, the bread being transubstantiated into the body and the wine into the blood by the power of God." This decision made every priest at every altar the agent in the performance of a stupendous miracle, which ever since has remained the core of the ritual of the Church. The new discipline imposed upon every Christian was to confess his sins at least once a year to his parish priest, to perform the penance assigned, and then to partake of the sacrament of the Eucharist at least once a year, preferably at Easter. It requires a distinct effort of the imagination for us now to realize the import of such a prescription. Every single individual within the jurisdiction of the Church who was at all concerned over his salvation must henceforth submit an oral record of his sins to his priest and undergo punishment therefor. The Church had attained a point of prestige where it felt that with one stroke of the pen it could subject the consciences of western European Christendom to its supervision and control.

At the final moment of the council's sessions Innocent III, undismayed by the outcome of his last venture in that line, the fourth crusade, proclaimed a new crusade for the following summer, and, that nothing might interfere with its glorious consummation, ordered a general peace of four years' duration. It was as if he expected by

[12] Packard, *op. cit.*, p. 98.
[13] See pp. 257, 692.

pontifical fiat to bring to pass a great miracle. Such bold confidence in the inevitable fruition of the papal program, as representing the Christian ideal at its highest, such resolute refusal to look at facts, takes one's breath away; it could only be utterly sublime or utterly ridiculous, unless it could be both together.

To explain the predominant position held by the Church in western Europe during the pontificate of Innocent III and for most of the thirteenth century is no mean task, but it must be attempted if the essential character of the middle ages is to be made clear. Something has already been said about the varieties of religious practice that the Church was willing to tolerate and the discipline that she administered when religious expression threatened to become disruptive, and we shall have to return to this theme. In the following chapters we shall consider the ability of the Church to meet the intellectual and artistic demands of the time. Now part of its success must no doubt be explained by this ability to adapt itself to a considerable variety of religious feeling and to satisfy other than purely religious needs, but these considerations are properly only auxiliary.

Reasons for the success of the Church

In the main, the success of the Church represented the victory of law and organization at a time when in Europe outside the Church there was nothing but a variegated complex of unwritten custom, when monarchical and territorial states were only just beginning to emerge from the welter of feudalism. By this time the Church had succeeded in elaborating a method of translating its interpretation of life into practice. To be more specific, the victory of the Church was due primarily to its system of canon law, to its monarchical organization, and to its system of sacraments. Having had to meet no competition in the religious field since the early centuries, except for the outburst of heresy in the twelfth century, it enjoyed a religious monopoly unknown since the sixteenth century. For most of the time, until it found itself at odds with the new national territorial states of the later middle ages over the question of the respective jurisdictions of canon and secular law, and until it was seriously challenged by the emancipated spirit of the towns, it had to deal with nothing more formidable than the ingrained paganism of the peoples of western Europe. This, like the natural paganism of all human beings, resisted the rigorous kind of discipline imposed by organized religion; but the Church, being reasonable and taking seriously St. Paul's injunction to be "all things to all men," knew well how to compromise on the best terms to be had.

The medieval Church was an international state, transcending the

territorial limits and the particular policies of all other states. It had
its own law and its own judicial system, its own lands and its own
financial system. Its administration was in the hands of the ecclesiastical hierarchy, subordinated to the pope. The ostensible purpose of this
international, ecclesiastical, absolute monarchy was the establishment
of the City of God on earth and the preparation of all mortals for
their home in the greater city beyond this life. In their desperate battle
to free the Church from the smothering embrace of feudalism and at
the same time to organize it under a central administration the popes
set an example for the secular monarchs and princes of Europe. For
a moment in the thirteenth century they seemed to have achieved also
their greater aim of establishing the Church as a theocratic superstate,
governing the whole world. Of this aspect of the Church's development it is to be hoped that we have by now said enough.

The constitution of this church-state was—or rather is, since it still
governs the Roman Catholic clergy and the social and spiritual lives
of all good Catholics everywhere—its canon law. Beside the Scriptures,
the sources of canon law were the canons of Church councils and the
decretals (decrees or ordinances) of the popes. It was perfected only
in the course of many centuries, but collections and codifications of
canon law began very early. The first important one was the work of a
Scythian monk, Dionysius Exiguus, of the sixth century,[14] which remained authoritative until the Western Church split up into its various
feudal and national divisions. Henceforth there appeared various local
collections of conciliar decrees and papal decretals, including the half-
spurious Pseudo-Isidorian collection of the ninth century. The reformers of the eleventh century, in their zeal to get back to the fundamentals of Church discipline, were suspicious of these local collections,
of which there were some forty after the Pseudo-Isidorian. The collections were not even consistent, to say nothing of meeting the needs
of the universal Church that the reformers hoped to see take shape
under the pope's hand.

The discovery in the eleventh century of the Digest of Justinian's
Code [15] provided the reformers with a solution for many new and
unsolved problems. The revival of the study of Roman law encouraged hope of a similar codification of canon law, and the theologians
worked out a method of resolving the conflicting traditions of the
different collections.[16] About 1140 at Bologna, the center for the

[14] See p. 51.
[15] See p. 128.
[16] See pp. 701–2.

study of Roman law, the monk Gratian compiled a code called by him *Concordia discordantium canonum* (harmony of conflicting canons), but ordinarily called the *Decretum*. Although it originated as a private compilation, its popularity in the universities as a textbook for the study of canon law and its approval by the pope quickly made it official. In 1234 Gregory IX codified canons of councils and decretals of popes issued since Gratian's codification, and in 1298 Boniface VIII did the same for the period from 1234 to 1298. In 1317 another collection was published, bringing to completion the official issue of medieval canons and decretals.

At the end of the middle ages another private collection was made of decretals of John XXII (1316–34) previously omitted, and of a series running from 1298 to 1484 that had not been included. Gratian's *Decretum* and the three collections of 1234, 1298, and 1317 and the final collection just mentioned constitute the *corpus iuris canonici*, the body of canon law, corresponding to the *corpus iuris civilis*, the Justinian Code of Roman law. A final corrected edition of canon law, published in 1582, after the Church had taken its stand on the Protestant reformation, remained unchanged until 1918, when a new code was issued, based in large part upon work done in the middle ages.

Before Roman or civil law had any appreciable effect upon secular legislation in the west, before there was any sort of body of written law for the various western states and principalities, the Church accordingly had a well-integrated and complex legal code, influenced to a large extent by Roman law, which in some respects it even carried to new developments. The procedure of canon law courts, borrowed almost exclusively from Roman law, had great influence on secular procedure.

Canon law formally recognized the *plenitudo potestatis* of the *The jurisdiction of canon law* Roman pontiffs, and in its regulation of relations between members of the ecclesiastical hierarchy incorporated all the papal principles and practices. It undertook to protect clergy and Church property from all attacks by laymen. Every clerk—that is, every man who had been tonsured, whether he was in orders or not—enjoyed benefit of clergy, the right in all criminal and civil cases to be tried only by canon law courts. The Church sought through its law to enforce obedience to its system of belief. It was its exclusive right to try all cases of heresy, schism, apostasy, and simony, and it claimed for its own all cases arising out of its system of sacraments. In this connection its jurisdiction over the sacrament of marriage was all-important, since cases involving adultery, legitimation of children, separation, or dowry came into its courts. It claimed cognizance of all contracts made under oath and of last wills and testaments. In all these respects canon law exercised and still exercises an important influence upon the development of secular law, especially upon the law of contract, of wills, of marriage, and upon criminal law, wherein it was much concerned with tempering the punishment according to the motive and the circumstances of the offense.

The Church was always ready to invoke canon law in cases where the secular law did not act; if the state did not punish perjury, blasphemy, sacrilege, sorcery, usury, bodily injury, and sins of the flesh, the Church imposed the penalties of secular law, besides assessing the proper punishment according to canon law. To widows and orphans and all the oppressed it extended the protection of its law whenever secular law failed to render justice. The Church would have liked to use canon law also to enforce observance of its principles of morality, by bringing all cases classifiable as sin within its jurisdiction; but soon after its codification canon law came into conflict with secular law, which was just as anxious to bring as much as possible of the life of the individual under its jurisdiction. This conflict filled the whole later middle ages, and in fact has not yet ceased, although the Church has been steadily forced to give way.

Excommunication and interdict

The Church used the ordinary punishments of secular law, but avoided capital punishment and any shedding of blood. It made special use of what it called medicinal penalties, the chief of which were excommunication and interdict, which were intended to bring the sinner back repentant to full enjoyment of the privileges of the Church. Excommunication, which could be pronounced by bishops and archbishops as well as by the pope, came to be differentiated into minor and major. Minor excommunication entailed exclusion from the sacraments and ritual of the Church. Major excommunication exiled an individual from the whole body of the faithful and deprived him of all the privileges of a Christian: he could not attend Church services, he lost whatever benefices he held of the Church, he could not appear except as defendant in Church courts, he could not be buried in consecrated ground. In both cases the soul of the individual was temporarily condemned to hell, and he was deprived of the companionship of his fellow Christians, inasmuch as association with an excommunicated person was punishable by excommunication. The state often supplemented excommunication by outlawry, which made it especially deadly. The pronouncement of major excommunication in the extravagant language of a curse was known as anathema.

Interdict was laid on churches or groups of people or geographical areas rather than on persons. In its utmost rigor it forbade all public functions of the Church, but it was often mitigated by the exception of some of the sacraments. Because it discriminated against large numbers of innocent people in order to punish guilty and refractory princes, it could arouse tremendous resentment, which would frequently bring the offender to terms. The excommunication of a ruler in the eyes of canon law automatically deprived him of the right to govern; his subjects were not only released from the duty of obeying him, but were sometimes actually enjoined to disobey him. As long as the fear of hell was real, excommunication and interdict were powerful weapons; and in any case they were extremely inconvenient in practice, in that they subjected the individual to all the malignity of horrified public opinion. Like the crusades, excommunication and interdict were used to further the economic and political interests of the Church. It is not a bad way of testing from time to time the hold that the Church kept on western society to watch the degree of seriousness with which its sentences of excommunication and interdict were taken.

The bureaucratic machinery through which papal absolutism functioned was not perfected until the fourteenth century, when—oddly enough—the papacy was not at Rome but at Avignon,[17] but a great deal of progress was made in the thirteenth century. To assist in his innumerable spiritual, administrative, financial, and judicial functions the pope had his court, or *Curia*, like any secular monarch. In the *Curia*, largely composed of clerks, scribes, and notaries, the leading positions were held by cardinals. Originally, as we have seen, the cardinals were the subdeacons, deacons, priests, and bishops of certain Roman churches, who in 1059 were constituted a papal electoral college, a position that immensely enhanced their importance. After 1179 a two-thirds vote by written ballot—later a majority—of the College of Cardinals elected the pope, usually a cardinal himself. The method of election in conclave, as the electoral assembly of cardinals came to be called, was prescribed in detail in the thirteenth century. At that time cardinals were given precedence over archbishops, and the College of Cardinals became known as the Sacred College. By this time the cardinalate was already an international body, to which appointments were made from beyond the Alps as well as from local bishops and archbishops.

By the thirteenth century there were three fully developed depart-

The College of Cardinals

[17] See pp. 968 ff.

Departments
of the papal
Curia

ments of the *Curia:* the chancery, the penitentiary, and the camera. Each of these, as in a king's *curia,* had some jurisdiction as a court. The pope acted as supreme judge, in cases of great moment alone, but ordinarily presiding over a council of cardinals, called a consistory. The fact that the pope and the *Curia* were the supreme court of appeal for canon law courts—a position which the popes did everything they could to strengthen—brought an immense quantity of judicial business to Rome. Aside from its judicial functions, the chancery, headed by the chancellor, prepared all necessary documents and bulls (Latin *bulla,* "seal"). It has been called "the most technical and also the most efficient administrative machine which had ever existed." It was a matter of prime importance that on the papal seal there should be "seventy-three dots around the circumference, twenty-five around the head of St. Paul, twenty-six around the head of St. Peter, twenty-five to compose his hair and twenty-eight his beard"; Innocent III once rejected a document reputed to be his because it lacked one dot. The penitentiary was responsible for the administration of excommunications and interdicts, or indulgences, or absolution from sins from which only the pope could absolve (e.g., assault upon a cleric), and of such dispensations from the provisions of canon law as were necessary to give it proper flexibility. The camera (Latin for "chamber"), headed by the chamberlain, was the papal equivalent of the English exchequer and the French *chambre des comptes;* it had charge of the collection, transportation, and expenditure of all papal revenue.

Papal revenue

By the end of the thirteenth century papal revenue was considerable, and it increased in the fourteenth. The popes collected revenue from papal estates, from legacies, and from gifts made by pilgrims in the churches of Rome. As temporal rulers of the Papal States they collected such taxes and dues as had not been feudalized. From monasteries exempted by the pope from episcopal jurisdiction and from kings and princes who had become papal vassals they collected the census. From England, the Scandinavian states, Poland, and other areas they collected Peter's pence. Innocent III began the practice of taxing the clergy for the benefit of the crusades; his example quickly led to regular papal taxation of the clergy for other purposes, and even some of the money collected for the crusades found its way into papal coffers. The popes also collected subsidies, the equivalent of feudal aids, from the clergy. Their right of confirmation and appointment to benefices, practically established by Innocent III's individual appointments and fortified before the end of the thirteenth century by appointments to whole classes of benefices, was utilized to collect fees

Clergy confirmed or appointed by the pope paid a fee called services (Latin, *servitia*), amounting to one-third of one year's income of the benefice. Those who did not pay services paid annates, theoretically the first year's income of the new benefice, though actually it never amounted to more than a fraction of that amount. Prelates whose positions obliged them to visit Rome paid a visitation tax.

The popes exercised the *ius spolii* [18] upon the movable goods of clergy dying intestate in Rome. Papal legates, papal nuncios, and popes when traveling were entitled to the equivalent of the feudal *droit de gîte*, called procurations, from the clergy. From the sale of indulgences [19] to be used for the crusades and from money paid to purchase release from crusading vows without loss of indulgence the papacy drew a large income. Part of the fees collected by the chancery for drawing up documents and by the penitentiary for absolutions and dispensations went into the camera. Fines and fees of course came in from the normal administration of papal justice. For taxes and fees collected at the source the camera devised a system employing local collectors and special collectors sent out from Rome. For the transportation and storing of coin the popes relied upon the Templars and the Italian bankers. In spite of all this taxation the popes never had enough money to finance all their activities, and from the later twelfth century on were forever borrowing money from the Italian bankers.

Europe was divided into ecclesiastical provinces, each governed by an archbishop, who until Charles the Great's reign had been called the metropolitan. The titles of patriarch and primate remained in use in the west, but practically they were only honorary. Just as the pope was always Bishop of Rome, so the archbishop was bishop of the particular diocese in which his cathedral was situated, and had all the ordinary rights and duties of a bishop. As archbishop he consecrated suffragan bishops, presented them with ring and staff, and presided over the annual provincial council convoked to publicize papal decretals, act as a special court, or legislate on the affairs of the province. He presided over a court to hear appeals from the courts of the bishops. The popes were always bent on keeping the archbishops from setting themselves up as an intermediate authority between them and the bishops. They did everything possible to get the appointment of all archbishops into their own hands. From an early date they compelled the archbishop to come to Rome for his pallium (a strip of white woolen cloth worn over the shoulders of an archbishop while

Archbishops

[18] See p. 413.
[19] See p. 679.

officiating at the altar), to take a special oath of allegiance to the pope, and to make repeated visits to Rome.

But something more was necessary for firm control of the vast subsidiary organization of archbishops and bishops. For this purpose *Papal legates* the popes appointed legates to keep an eye on the local administration and to bring to bear on local synods the weight of apostolic authority. Legates were also employed as special ambassadors to kings and princes. Some legates were cardinals sent out from Rome, especially for some particular occasion; others from the local clergy were given permanent appointments as resident supervisors for the pope.

Bishops Each province was subdivided into dioceses, governed by bishops. Altogether—including archbishops also as bishops of a particular diocese—the bishops were always the mainstay of the Church. At least in the earlier middle ages a large part of the whole burden of civilization rested on their shoulders. Before monarchies and towns and universities opened up careers for young men of ability, the episcopate attracted, mostly from the nobility, the best talent of medieval society. Even after the compromises that settled the investiture struggle kings and princes never ceased to exercise a direct influence on the personnel of the episcopate. By the thirteenth century bishops were ostensibly elected by the cathedral chapters, just as popes were elected by the College of Cardinals; but among the canons who composed the chapter were always many younger sons of noble families, who were amenable to all kinds of influence.

In any case, the episcopate remained by and large an aristocratic office; and the bishop, because of his rank and wealth or his ability and training—generally on both accounts—was always a public figure of the first importance. Before monarchs and princes succeeded in developing a professionally trained bureaucracy, bishops were everywhere to be found in charge of the chief departments of state and acting as trusted advisers of kings. It proved to be difficult for the papacy to intrude upon episcopal preserves. The popes never succeeded in securing the right of appointment, although they did make good their right to confirm all elections. They also to a large degree broke the state's control of the episcopate by obliging bishops to take a special oath of allegiance to the pope and to come to Rome as often as possible for councils or on special visits. The popes tended to support bishops against their archbishops in order to keep the latter in hand, while the bishops themselves they kept in line through legates and by cooperating with the cathedral chapters against the bishops.

As great landowners the bishops played an important part in the

The Romanesque Cathedral at Worms

The Romanesque group at Pisa: the baptistery, cathedral, and campanile

Nave, choir, and apse, covered with mosaics, of the
Norman Cathedral of Monreale in Sicily (See p. 150)

The Romanesque rib-vaulted nave of
Stephen's built by William the Conque
at Caen (See p. 814)

The Romanesque nave and Gothic apse of the church at Mont-Saint-Michel

feudal system. The bishop's domain was called *mensa episcopalis*
(episcopal table). For a long time the *mensa* belonged jointly to
bishop and chapter, but by the beginning of the eleventh century the
chapter had its own *mensa*. The bishop's *mensa* included in the town
an area surrounding the cathedral and land in various parts of the
diocese or in neighboring dioceses. These lands were in part administered by the bishop directly, and in part held as fiefs and administered
by his vassals. The lands directly administered were the bishop's
demesne, comparable to the *patrimonium* of the popes in the days of
Gregory the Great. They were in charge of agents called mayors or
provosts. In his relation to the serfs on his estates the bishop differed
in no way from lay landholders. As vassal and as overlord he was likewise responsible for and entitled to all the services of any feudal vassal
and any feudal lord. In addition to the actual fiefs granted out from
his *mensa* there were benefices of certain collegiate churches (churches
with endowment enough to support a chapter of canons) and certain
monasteries and priories which the bishop treated as fiefs. Besides
these he had the bestowal of many salaried clerical offices and of the
lay offices of his household, which amounted to fiefs and for which the
holders did homage to him. Among his vassals a bishop might number
the greatest feudal lords in the land. At one time the Bishop of Mende
had for vassals the King of Aragon and the Count of Rodez; among
the vassals of the Archbishop of Paris were the King of France and
the Duke of Burgundy.

Among feudal services for which the bishop was liable military
service was not excepted. Henry I of France explained to the pope
that his bishops and abbots were too busy helping him put down a
rebellion to attend a council at Rheims. An unwilling bishop would
sometimes protest when called upon to defend his suzerain by arms,
but it was poor policy to refuse. So far from refusing, bishops often
performed their military service in person, and a few actually fell in
battle. Not to mention Archbishop Turpin, a great warrior in the
Chanson de Roland, six French bishops went as fighting men on the
third crusade. The Archbishop of Auch was made an admiral by
Richard Lionhearted; and Simon de Sully, Bishop of Bourges, led an
army in the Albigensian crusade. Hugh of Noyers, Bishop of Auxerre,
was so formidable a soldier that his military ambition was punished by
his suzerain. Occasionally a bishop's military zeal became actually
criminal. Matthew, Bishop of Toul around 1200, lived in reckless
immorality, dismissed most of his clergy and oppressed the rest,
plundered the country like any robber baron, and defied Innocent III

and Thibaud, Duke of Lorraine, until he ended his life on Thibaud's sword.

Whatever else he was—and he was much else—the bishop was first and foremost the governor of his diocese. At least once a year he held a synod of the diocese for the same purposes as the annual provincial council presided over by the archbishop. When present the bishop presided over his court, which was ordinarily the canon law court of first instance, except for cases reserved from the start for decision by the pope. The examination and appointment of all cathedral clergy and parish priests in the diocese, unless the papacy's encroachment had been successful, was ultimately the bishop's responsibility. In the many cases where the right of presentment to these offices, whether prebends or parishes, remained in the hands of those who had furnished the endowments for them, it was the bishop's duty to examine candidates and reject the ineligible. He was responsible for the administration and the discipline of all regular and secular clergy in his diocese, except in such monasteries as had been exempted from episcopal control by papal privileges. This obligation he discharged by visitations—inquests held on the spot in the monastery and parish—the expenses of which were paid by the local clergy. In this way all misdemeanors and any dereliction of duty on the part of laity as well as clergy could be detected by a scrupulous and efficient bishop.

The cathedral, it must be remembered, served also as the church for one of the parishes of the city; and the bishop, like any priest, was the shepherd of his own little flock, for the welfare of whose souls he was responsible. This duty, obviously, he could not possibly attend to in person. He had to leave the regular administration of the sacraments to the cathedral chapter, and limit his personal participation to great festive occasions when he happened to be in the city. There have probably been few bishops who did not love to deck themselves with all the splendid trappings of their office. The cathedral itself, in which stood the episcopal throne, was the special object of the bishop's care. The enthusiasm with which architect-bishops exhausted their own and their dioceses' resources in order to build the finest possible houses of God was contagious, and often developed into out-and-out rivalry between neighboring bishops. To a cathedral of any importance there was attached a school, where young clerics and lay pupils studied under the immediate direction of the canons and the general supervision of the bishop.

The diocese was in turn subdivided into rural deaneries, each headed usually by the oldest priest of the district, sometimes called rural dean, sometimes archpriest. As local representative of the bishop *Archpriests* the archpriest's chief function was to keep relations smooth between *and arch-* the bishop and the parish clergy by enforcing the bishop's regulations *deacons* and the decrees of the diocesan synods. He acted as intermediary in presenting to the bishop candidates for ordination, adjusted minor differences among the parish clergy, and—what made him especially disliked—if he was a conscientious soul reported any scandalous conduct of either clergy or laity to the archdeacon.

This official—there were usually several archdeacons to a diocese— was the intermediary between the bishop and the archpriests and parish clergy. He was a member of the cathedral chapter to whom, because of the bishop's necessary preoccupation with secular affairs, so much business was entrusted that in time he came to enjoy an independent quasi-episcopal jurisdiction of his own. It was an archdeacon who often made the visitations to the parishes and monasteries of the diocese, collected taxes from the clergy, and punished those who strayed from the straight and narrow path. He often held courts of first instance, and at times presided over the bishop's court, himself drawing up all the necessary legal documents. He examined the fitness of clerics proposed for office, supervised the administration of the revenues of the diocese, and kept his eyes open to everything that went on. A strict archdeacon was a stumblingblock to all those who looked upon a position in the Church as a comfortable sinecure, but one less strict could be persuaded not to see what his fellow canons of the chapter did not want him to see. The archdeacons managed to get so much power and to acquire so much influence in the diocese that the bishops came to look upon them as dangerous rivals in authority and conspired to undermine their position. Rather than simply quash the office they created a new official, the vicar-general, to represent them in the diocese, taking care that he also should not acquire too much independent jurisdiction. The archdeaconate subsequently fell into decay, but only after no little resistance and a none too friendly struggle with the episcopate.

The archdeacon of the clergy of the bishop's or archbishop's city *The cathedral* was often dean of the cathedral chapter of canons. The chapter by the *chapter* thirteenth century enjoyed a position of virtual independence and had its own organization; its members were appointed by the bishop, but generally after consultation with the chapter. Its independence was partly due to the fact, already mentioned, that by that time it had long had its own share of the property of the diocese. Each cathedral canon enjoyed the income from his benefice or prebend, and in addition got his share of the common fund divided annually among members of the chapter. Some prebends consisted of parishes in the diocese, in which case the canon might fulfill the function of priest for the parish and maintain a substitute, called a vicar-choral, at the cathedral. The independence of the chapter was also due in part to the necessity of entrusting to it so much of the business of the cathedral and the diocese, which the bishop, engaged in larger affairs, often outside the diocese, could not possibly manage.

Organization and duties of the chapter

From its members the chapter elected the dean, who was in charge of the diocese during the bishop's absence, and regularly presided at its meetings, held in the chapter house adjoining the cathedral. If the canons were regular, their monastic buildings, including a cloister, were built next to the cathedral, in whose choir they sang their regular monastic offices. Whether regular or secular, they occupied the choir stalls at services, assisted the bishop in celebrating Mass and in his other public functions, and accompanied him in procession. They assisted him also in administering canon law. The chapter acted as the bishop's council in the government of the diocese—a council which he would often have been glad to do without, but which, in matters likely to put a permanent obligation upon the diocese or diocesan property, he was obliged to consult. After a bishop's death the chapter administered the diocese until they could elect his successor. Besides the dean there were other officials of the chapter. There was, of course, a treasurer. A chancellor was in permanent charge of the cathedral school. The fourth Lateran council required that every cathedral support a master to teach the rudiments of Latin, and if possible a theologian also. A precentor had special charge of the cathedral services. The organization of chapters differed somewhat according to their size and importance. The chapter of Notre Dame at Paris, for example, in the second half of the twelfth century had seven officials: a dean, a chancellor, a cantor, a subcantor, and three archdeacons. In addition to ordinary canons some chapters included chantry priests, endowed by special organizations or individuals to chant Masses for the dead in the numerous chapels of the cathedral.

Demoralization of some chapters

For all their independence, the chapters could not keep the bishops and archbishops entirely out of their affairs. The bishop frequently asserted his right of visitation to inquire into the business affairs and the personnel of the chapter. From the records of such visitations it is evident that some chapters were seriously in need of correction. In the thirteenth century an archbishop of Rouen reports that canons "wander about the church and talk in the church with women during the celebration of divine service. . . . The psalms are run through too rapidly without due pauses. . . . The clergy leave the choir without reason before the end of the service. . . . The chapter revenues are mismanaged." Members of the chapter were accused of "incontinence, theft, manslaughter, tavern-hunting, drunkenness and dicing," and one Master John of giving "out of his money to merchants to share in their gain."

In the next century a bishop of Exeter wrote to the dean of the chapter that he had learned "that certain Vicars and other Ministers of our Cathedral church . . . fear not to exercise irreverently and damnably certain disorders, laughings, gigglings and other breaches of discipline during the solemn services of the church; which is shameful to relate and horrible to hear. To specify some out of the cases, those who stand at the upper stalls of the choir and have lights within their reach at matins, knowingly and purposely throw drippings or snuffings from the candles upon the heads or the hair of such as stand at the lower stalls, with the purpose of exciting laughter and perhaps of generating discord, or at least rancour of heart and silent hatred among the ministers (which God forfend!). . . . Some whose heart is in the market-place, street or bed, though their body be in the choir, seeking for their own part to hasten through God's work negligently and fraudulently or to draw others as accomplices into the same fault —these (I say) will sometimes cry aloud . . . to the very official himself or to others, commanding and enjoining them to make haste." Other canons "during the solemnity of mass have rashly presumed, putting the fear of God behind them, after the pernicious example of certain [other] churches, to assemble together within the church itself and play certain and noxious games, unbecoming to clerical honesty; nay, rather to conduct detestable mockeries of Divine Service: wherein they have in many fashions defiled the Vestments and other Ornaments of the Church . . . by whose gestures, or laughter and derisive gigglings, not only are the congregation . . . distracted from their due devotion, but they are also dissolved in disorderly laughter and unlawful pleasures, the Divine worship is mocked, and the Service wickedly impeded." [20]

The lowest subdivision of the Church was the parish, a district *The parish* whose inhabitants worshiped in one church. The division of western Europe into parishes was a long process, but by the beginning of the thirteenth century it was practically complete. The number of parishes in a town naturally depended upon population. The rural parish was

[20] The translations are from Coulton's *Life in the Middle Ages*, I, 95 ff.

usually coterminous with the manorial village. No reform movement in the Church had succeeded in depriving the lord of the manor, as patron of the local church founded by him or by his ancestors, of his right of advowson, i.e., the right to present candidates for the parish priesthood. The parishes of his diocese were therefore not at the disposal of the bishop, but remained in the hands of some secular or ecclesiastical lord or perhaps a monastery. "The advowson of a church was looked upon as a matter of private property, which could be granted, sold, divided, or unjustly occupied in exactly the same way as any other property." Especially in the late middle ages parishes were often served not by priests but by vicars, who were paid small wages, while the patron appropriated the largest part of the revenue of the parish for his own use. Appointments to parish priesthoods were often used as scholarships for university training. As much might have been said a moment ago of the prebends of cathedral chapters, when it was remarked that a parish priesthood occasionally served as a prebend. It could also be used as a means of paying some official of the lord of the manor.

The parish priest

Parish priests without exception came from the common people. Many were of servile birth, but, having attracted attention by ability somewhat above the humble average, had been given their freedom (no serf could be a priest) and finally taken holy orders. In many cases they were simply forced on the parish by the patron. Rural priests served small manorial villages of serfs and peasants, above whose level they naturally did not always rise very far. Often they possessed the merest rudiments of education, or could scarcely read at all, so that they had to recite the services by rote, sometimes making absurd blunders, of which their hearers were as blissfully unaware as they were, since the whole service, except for the sermon, was in Latin. Reports of visitations and of examinations of candidates for holy orders and the decrees of diocesan synods reveal these conditions. We are fortunate in knowing something of one candidate's examination. He was tested first on a portion of the service of the Mass beginning *Te igitur clementissime Pater . . . supplices rogamus ac petimus* ("We most humbly pray and beseech you, most merciful Father"). When the archdeacon asked him what was the case of *Te*, he didn't know. "Well," said the archdeacon, "look closely. What word governs it?" He looked closely enough to see *Pater*, and answered, "Pater, for He governs all things." After that it was a small matter that he did not know what *clementissime* meant. Later, when asked for the meaning of *annuam* (anniversary), he replied, "Annual." "What does that mean?" demanded the archdeacon. "Many times." "How many times?" "Every day." He was asked to conjugate *fio*, which he must have surprised his torturer by doing after a fashion; but when he was asked, as millions of schoolboys have been asked since, if it has a passive, "No," he replied, "for it is neuter." Latin has of course always been regarded by some as an abominable language, but examiners have always been criminally charitable (they have to be), and the candidate passed. No doubt there was something behind the synodal regulation: "No one should give or promise to the archdeacon . . . anything in order to be ordained a priest."

Parish priests frequently had wives or concubines. Parishioners were *Marriage* rather indulgent on this point, not understanding how it was possible *of clergy* to get along without a woman. The Church was less indulgent. Official opposition to the marriage of clergy began early, owing in part to the ideal of chastity derived from St. Paul, in part to the feeling that it was not seemly that any Church revenue should go to supporting the families of clergy. The first definite prohibition of marriage by councils of the fourth century applied only to the higher clergy, and this is still essentially the custom in the Greek Church. In 385 a decretal of Pope Siricius extended the prohibition to priests and deacons. While the ideals of the regular clergy were not without effect on the practice of the secular clergy, little was done to enforce this prohibition until the stringent measures taken by Gregory VII, under the influence of St. Peter Damiani. By the thirteenth century open marriage was all but gone in France and Italy and was dying out in England and Germany. Concubinage, however, was a different matter. The English chronicler Matthew Paris observed that "when the pope deprived the clergy of sons . . . the devil sent them nephews." Innocent III ruled that concubinage was simple fornication, so that for a time marriage was a deadlier sin for a priest than unchastity. In 1545, when the Council of Trent finally made celibacy practically an article of faith, the question was still so far from dead that a strong party advocated the contrary procedure of once more legalizing marriage for all clergy.

Parish priests were not always able to resist the temptations of the *Peccadillos of* tavern. Reports of visitations note that "the chaplain frequents tav- *parish priests* erns," or that "the curate drinks wine without water." Synods did their best to keep the clergy out of local drinking bouts, for drink often made pugnacious parish priests so belligerent that they had to be censured for fighting, and sometimes they actually set upon their parishioners in church. Needless to say, there were two sides to a picture of that kind: both priests and parishioners no doubt generally gave as good as they got. We know of one priest who cited two parishioners before the bishop's court "for striking him on the head, the arms and the legs and throwing him on the ground." Or the priests would get to playing ball or quoits or dice, and in their excitement leave some of their clothes behind in the tavern. Inviting parishioners to dine was frowned upon; if it was done, they were "to eat friendlily without noise, scandal, or many and superfluous courses." Parish priests had also to be watched to keep them from making a little money on the side. Some lent money at interest. Some rented out church lands. Others fattened pigs for the market, or bred rams, cows, or horses, or sold hemp, grain, wood, wine, or cider. Still others speculated in the grain harvest. A few even had ships at sea. Of one parish priest it was noted that he was so absorbed in his secular affairs that he was inclined to syncopate the services, and to introduce into his reading all sorts of profane babblings.

Selling the sacraments

Synodal decrees cried out against the practice of some priests of making money by selling the sacraments. "We have heard," one bishop exclaims, "and greatly grieve to have done so, that some priests exact money from the laity for the administration of penance and other sacraments, and that some for the sake of filthy lucre impose penances which bring in money to them." "The curates after baptism claim the vestments of the baptized, in order to sell them or apply them to secular usages." "Like crows and vultures swooping down from afar upon cadavers, so flock together the priests in bands at funerals. Very often, to the great scandal of the people, they dispute among themselves who is to celebrate the obsequies. They even defer the burial until the money has been turned over to them." Priests turned to fraudulent use their services in the making of wills. "Certain priests make agreements with the friends of the departed, in order to receive a quarter or a fifth of his heritage in exchange for the promise of leaving to them [the friends] the rest of his goods and of leaving the last desires of the departed one unexecuted."

The good priests

It is always a temptation to dwell on the abuses that creep into any human institution organized on a large scale, because they are amusing or shocking or picturesque. Granted that they are a proper part of the complete picture, it must be remembered that they are the more glaring precisely because they are the exception rather than the rule. Indeed, if they were not the exception, we should not know so much about them. The very sources of our information reveal at the same time the vigilance and persistence with which the ecclesiastical authorities tried to cope with human frailties in an undisciplined age. Moreover, many bad priests seemed bad only because the standards set for the secular priesthood were very high. This, and the fact that even so they were not so high as the standards of the regular clergy, subjected the occasional failure of the parish priesthood to live up to them to comment all the more vitriolic. Most priests must always have been honest, simple, hard-working, sincere men, serving God and their fellow men to the best of their ability. In the last chapter we borrowed Chaucer's portrait of the degenerate Benedictine monk. Let us now quote his portrait of the "good man of religion":

> "A country parson, poor, I warrant you,
> But rich he was in holy thought and work.
> He was a learned man also, a clerk,
> Who Christ's own gospel truly sought to preach.
>
> . . . .
>
> Wide was his parish, houses far asunder,
> But never did he fail, for rain or thunder,
> In sickness, or in sin, or any state,
> To visit to the farthest, small and great,
> Going afoot, and in his hand a stave.
>
> . . . .
>
> There is nowhere a better priest, I trow,
> He had no thirst for pomp or reverence,
> Nor made himself a special, spiced conscience,
> But Christ's own lore, and His apostles' twelve
> He taught, but first he followed it himself." [21]

The income of the parish priest came partly from the parish land, *The tithes* located, like the peasant's, in strips in open fields, partly from offerings made in church and from customary fees for marriages, burials, and baptisms, and especially from tithes, the "tenth part of all fruits and profits justly acquired, owed to God in recognition for His supreme dominion over man and to be paid to the ministers of the Church." The payment of tithes was first regularized by Charles the Great. Canon law recognized two kinds, the prædial tithe, paid from the produce of the land, and the personal tithe, paid from the profits of trade and business. Prædial tithes were in turn classified as greater and lesser: the greater came from grain, wine, and wool; the lesser

[21] Nicolson's translation.

from livestock, cheese, fruits, honey and wax, flax, hemp, and fallen wood. Actually a large amount of the tithes was appropriated by patrons or in other ways got into lay hands. Canon law provided that one-fourth should go to the bishop, one-fourth to the poor, one-fourth to maintenance of the church property, and one-fourth to the local priest.

Tithes were no more popular than any other taxes, and the clergy were constantly urged to preach about them. Many were the tricks used by parishioners to reduce their tithes. They would sell part of their harvest first and then pay tithes on the rest, or pay on what was left after the secular lord had his dues, or deduct before payment the cost of production. But the bishops were firm: ". . . expenses are by no means to be deducted first"; ". . . men straying blindly in damnable error stumble into the destruction of their own souls, paying first the tenth sheaf of their crops for the harvesters' wages and thus by a false calculation rendering only the eleventh sheaf as a tithe, contending that they may fairly pay their laborers' harvest wages from their crops before tithing, and thus setting at naught the precepts of the Old Testament and the New." Difficulties over tithes between peasant and priest were by no means always verbal. In one instance some irate parishioners, resenting the practice of paying in cheese their tithes of milk, carried their pails into the church and dumped the milk before the altar. On the theory that all Christians had at some time neglected to pay all the tithes due, which was mortal sin, the Church collected a mortuary tax on the property of deceased persons. Often this tax was the next best piece of furniture or head of cattle after the lord had taken his heriot, and its collection was sometimes flagrantly abused. Tithes, therefore, were a land tax, an income tax, and a death duty of no mean weight.

Duties of the parish priest   The duties of the parish priest were heavy. Aside from the regular administration of the sacraments he was chiefly occupied with funerals, marriages, and the visitation of the sick. If at a funeral there was too much loud weeping and extravagant demonstration, he was expected to stop the ceremony until the atmosphere grew calmer. If the Eucharist was to be administered to the sick, the priest, clad in his vestments, carried in both hands the sacrament covered with a cloth, preceded down the street by a clerk holding a taper and ringing a bell, to warn the parishioners that "the King of Glory under the veil of Bread was being carried in their midst." If it was necessary to go some distance, the priest would ride, with lamp and bell hung around the horse's neck. He was required to be careful about marriages, since bishops had ruled that "marriage should be celebrated with great discretion and reverence, in proper places and at proper times, with all modesty and mature consideration"; it should be celebrated at the door of the parish church, not "in taverns nor during feastings and drinkings nor in secret and suspect places." The priest was supposed to supervise the morals of his parish, keeping close watch for prostitution, adultery, abortions, and the exposure of infants. It was his duty to report usurers, incendiaries, and murderers, violators of churches and cemeteries, falsifiers of papal documents and heretics, not to mention lesser lawbreakers, and to serve citations before the bishop's court. The priest was even responsible for the care of lepers in his parish.

Sundays, saints' days, the great festivals of the Church, and especially the feast of the patron saint were the big days in the parish. On the most important of them the women would hang their best lace, embroidery, and tapestry from the windows, and the streets would be decorated with banners and streamers—customs that still survive in Italy. The folk crowded early into church. Inasmuch as Christians have been known to dispute over seats in church when there are plenty, it is not surprising to learn that they disputed when seats were few, and most of those reserved for the high-born. "We have heard," a bishop says, "that many quarrels have arisen amongst members of the same parish, two or three of whom have laid claim to one seat. For the future no one is to claim any sitting in the church as his own, with the exception of the noble people and the patrons of churches." Most of the floor of the church was an open space covered with rushes, which were renewed two or three times a year—none too often, as is suggested by an entry in one warden's account of "three rat-traps." The distinguishing feature of the interior of the parish church was its strong color. Glaring down from the space above the chancel arch might well be a painting of the Last Judgment, with blood and fire and devils done "in such pitiless realism that when they come to light nowadays, even sympathetic restorers are often fain to cover them again under decent whitewash." The side walls were often covered with scenes from the lives of saints in warm blues, greens, red, and gold. The woodwork was all colored to blend with the stained glass in the windows, and when stone churches replaced wood, stone interiors were painted, too.

The parish church

Bishops had to reprove persons who brought their dogs or falcons with them into church or otherwise "made a tumult" during service. But that was only one of many abuses to which church property was subject. It was especially difficult to keep churches and cemeteries from be-

Abuses of church property

ing used for secular purposes, for they were the natural—indeed, the only—center for the social life of the parish. Bishops' orders and decrees of synods directed that "all cemeteries . . . be enclosed securely and that no animal . . . be allowed pasturage on the grass that grew in them." The people "use the ecclesiastical ornaments in lay processions, dance in the cemeteries and in the churches; they sing profane songs there and chansons, get drunk, fight, wound each other and celebrate blasphemous fêtes." "Secular judges, bailiffs, officers and secular lieutenants are under no circumstances to hear their cases, trials and litigation between the laity in the churches or in the cemeteries." Nor did medieval Christians regard Christ's casting out "all them that bought and sold in the temple" as a precedent. In spite of proclamations forbidding "the sale of any or every kind of merchandise in our church," it was a common observation that "pedlars come into the church porch on feast days and there sell their goods," and "a common market of vendibles is held in the churchyard and on Sundays and holy days." "It is precisely Sunday, the day of rest, that the scribes stretch out their stands for making wills, the barbers set up their tents for shaving and cutting hair, and the merchants set up their stalls."

The church service   The church service was the occasion for important announcements —of marriage banns, of a coming confirmation day, of excommunication or threat of excommunication. The congregation had its opportunity to take part; we know, for example, that Brother Milford confessed publicly to his sorrow that he had slandered his neighbor, and that Margaret Reed admitted calling Martha Hawkett "a horse godmother and a water witch." The bishops urged the clergy "not to be dumb dogs, but with salutary bark to drive away the disease of spiritual wolves from the flock" with preaching; and collections of sermons and stories were prepared for their use. The Roman Catholic service, however, has never centered around the sermon; its core has always been the miracle of the sacrifice of the Mass. In their sermons the parish priests did their best by the articles of faith, the cardinal sins and virtues, the sacraments, and the lives and miracles of the saints, but as preachers they were not distinguished.

They could not hope to rival the Franciscans and Dominicans, who, to their great annoyance, came into the villages, climbed up the steeples to ring the bells, spread out their relics for display, heard confessions, and preached in the churches, market places, and streets. The friars never hesitated to come to the point and tell their audiences what they thought. One Dominican, preaching on a subject often expounded—but, so far as is known, wholly without effect—says:

"Women are as well created for the Kingdom of Heaven as men, and they need it also as much as men, and many more of them would come into the Kingdom of Heaven but for this one snare. Fie! ye wicked devils! How many thousand poor women's souls would now be in heaven but for the single snare which ye have laid so cunningly for them! Ye women, ye have bowels of compassion, and ye go to church more readily than men, and come to hear preaching and to earn indulgences more readily than men; and many of you would be saved but for this one snare, which is called vain glory and empty honour. In order that ye may compass men's praise ye spend all your labour on your garments—on your veils and your kirtles. Many of you pay as much to the sempstress as the cost of the cloth itself; it must have shields on the shoulders, it must be flounced and tucked all round the hem; it is not enough for you to show your pride in your very buttonholes, but you must also send your feet to hell by special torments, ye trot this way and that way with your fine stitchings; and so many ye make, and with so much pains, that no man may rehearse it all. At the least excuse ye weary yourselves with your garments; all that wherewith ye busy yourselves is nought but vanity. Ye busy yourselves with your veils, ye twitch them hither, ye twitch them thither; ye gild them here and there with gold thread, and spend thereon all your time and trouble. Ye will spend a good six months' work on a single veil, which is sinful great travail,—and all that men may praise thy dress: 'Ah, God! How fair! Was ever so fair a garment?' " [22]

After the service it was the custom for the clerk of the parish to go about, entering the houses and aspersing the residents with holy water. Chaucer's clerk,

> "This Absalom, who was so light and gay,
> Went with a censer on the holy day,
> Censing the wives like an enthusiast;
> And on them many a loving look he cast." [23]

However important its vast organization and its great code of law in explaining the all-pervading power of the Church in the middle

[22] Coulton, *Life in the Middle Ages*, III, 64.
[23] Nicolson's translation.

ages, the fact remains that these could not have existed had they not been built around a system of religious belief and practice that had fastened hold on the hearts and consciences of an overwhelming majority of the people of western Europe. It is doubtless sad and certainly true that for most people life is a burden almost too heavy to bear. Human intelligence leaves life's remote origins so mysterious, its purpose so inscrutable, its course so hazardous that men are driven to seek some way of escape in order to make it tolerable at all. Most men have sought such solace in supernatural religion; they have placed their trust in gods. Then the mysteriousness, the purposelessness, the danger of life vanish, and the ritual that grows up with the accepted explanation and justification of life offers a constant emotional release from everyday strain and the comfort that comes from immediate contact with the divine. Our contemporary western world offers more or less free choice of a great variety of religious explanations, predominantly Christian. In the classical Mediterranean world there was a similar variety of pagan cults. The most striking feature of medieval Europe was that there was but one religious explanation available, from which no serious deviation was tolerated. That religion we call Christianity, but we must never forget how obstinately classical and barbarian paganism survived, and how many of its elements were incorporated into the new cult. If by Christianity we mean the teachings of Christ and nothing else, we are almost bound to call the new religion paganized Christianity—if it was not, as some have claimed, rather Christianized paganism.

Those qualified to concern themselves with the subtleties of theology are necessarily only the learned. The majority of mankind is willing to accept from the theologians their explanations of the meaning of life, and to rely on simple acts of devotion to satisfy religious needs. The religion that can appeal to both learned and unlearned by a complicated theological system and a simple and attractive ceremonial, if at the same time it avoids the excesses of fanaticism by a reasonable compromise with the weaknesses of the flesh, can hardly fail of success. Medieval Christianity was such a religion.

The essentials of medieval theology were taken from St. Augustine's system as modified by Pope Gregory the Great.[24] For many centuries western theologians were too busy with acquainting themselves with the writings of these men and the other Church Fathers to make any contributions of their own. Not until the late eleventh century did western theology again become original. Meanwhile the

[24] See pp. 198 ff.

Church as a practical institution administering salvation to a variety of peoples had had to make various adaptations to the varied customs of those to whom it ministered. So many divergencies grew up that tradition conflicted with tradition, practice with practice, and tradition with practice. When the theologians set themselves to resolving the differences, they likewise differed among themselves. An early attempt to harmonize tradition and practice was made by Peter Lombard, a professor at the University of Paris in the second half of the twelfth century, whose book, the *Sentences,* became a popular textbook on theology in the universities. But it was not until the thirteenth century, when the administration of the Church was well centralized under the papacy and canon law well developed, that a more or less unified system of theology and a common ritual were achieved. In the absence of papal pronouncements on any except a very few doctrines, different theological schools continued to exist until the Council of Trent in 1545 finally put an end to the variety and confusion of the middle ages. Only on the main points were medieval theologians agreed, and then only after long centuries of argument and practical compromise.

Medieval theology offered for this world only a counsel of despair. The one purpose of life here below is to prepare man for the enjoyment after death of eternal life, to be spent in the perfect bliss *Original* of paradise with God, his angels, and his saints. This is the one way *sin and* of escape from the petty, sordid, and evil routine of daily life, the *salvation* one reward for following faithfully the teachings of the Church. Relying on the revelation of the Old and New Testaments as interpreted by the Church Fathers, the theologians explained that the world had not always been in its present sorry state. In the earthly paradise prepared for him with his creation the first man, by God's help, or, as the theologians put it, by God's grace, lived in a state of perfection, possessed of free will and always striving for and willing the good. But Adam fell from this perfect state when he committed the first sin, whereby he lost the grace of God and his own free will and became the slave of the devil, doomed to eternal death and perdition. Moreover, in begetting children he passed on his sin to his descendants, and they to their descendants. All mankind is thus from the very day of birth tainted with original sin, and would have been irrevocably damned but for the Son of God, Jesus Christ, the incarnate *Logos.* He sacrificed himself upon the cross to atone for the sins of mankind. Thus God redeemed mankind from its doom, extended to it once more in compassion his grace, and restored to it the hope of attaining the perfection that Adam had enjoyed before his fall. Man was utterly helpless to save himself; salvation could come only through God's grace, which was not imparted to any man who did not have faith in redemption by Christ.

Now St. Augustine held that faith itself was imparted by God, of his own good pleasure and for no other reason, to certain individuals predestined to salvation, the rest being predestined to damnation. Mankind was therefore the creature of an inscrutable and arbitrary divine providence. This doctrine medieval theologians found harsh *Predestination* and unpalatable. The organized Church was developing in practice *and fore-* a system whereby the individual could, by the performance of good *knowledge* works, acquire merit in the sight of God that would stand him in good stead at the Last Judgment. The doctrine of predestination made good works quite unnecessary and futile: salvation was by faith only, and faith was predestined. The theologians therefore undertook to restore to man at least part of his lost free will by insisting that God in the beginning, because of the quality of his vision and knowledge, scrutinized the lives of all men in the long centuries that were to come, foresaw and foreknew that some of their own accord would choose the good rather than the evil, and included these in his original decree of predestination to salvation—"the terrible decree," as John Calvin later called it. Man was thus made partial master of his own destiny, in that his faith and his good works in prospect had influenced God: he must co-operate with God by achieving in fact that faith and those good works. Nevertheless, salvation remained impossible without the grace of God.

The medieval theologians were ready to indicate the one way in which God's grace could be secured. God imparted his grace to man through the medium of the Church, the hierarchy of ordained clergy headed by the pope, the Vicar of Christ and successor of St. Peter. The Church, founded by Christ, had instituted certain ceremonies *Theory of the* whereby grace was infused into men. These ceremonies were the sac- *sacraments* raments, defined as the visible signs of invisible grace. It came, however, to be the prevailing doctrine that the sacraments not only were the signs or symbols of God's grace but actually caused grace to exist in the participant. The medieval system of salvation thus became for the ordinary man quite simple and somewhat mechanical: grace was essential for salvation; it was imparted by the Church through the sacraments; participation in the sacraments was open to every properly qualified Christian; every Christian could qualify by following the prescriptions of the Church. Good works of all kinds, some of them imposed by the sacraments, acquired for the doer merit in the sight of God, and were therefore also important. God, the Church, and the individual co-operated in making certain a blissful sequel to this impossible world.

Any sacrament correctly administered according to prescribed ritual by a properly ordained priest was valid; its efficacy in no wise depended upon the character of the officiating priest. The reader may recall the dispute on this point in the early days of the Church between the Donatist heretics and St. Augustine.[25] Augustine's opinion had prevailed, that "between an apostle and a drunken man there is a great difference, but between the baptism of Christ which an apostle gives and that which a drunken man gives there is no difference." This was not only a most convenient doctrine from the human point of view, but the only logical position. Otherwise a sacrament might be considered valid at first, and later turn out to have been vitiated by some defect in the character of the officiating priest not known at the time of administration. Neither, according to the commonly held opinion, had the disposition of the recipient of a sacrament anything to do with its efficacy. To be sure, some theologians did hold that one must be sincerely repentant and truly believe if the sacrament were to impart grace, while others insisted upon the necessity of at least a "good disposition," or at the very least absence of a "bad disposition"; but it was generally held that the mere act of performing the sacrament was enough to cause grace to exist in any person willing to have the sacrament administered to him at all. If it is obvious that two such opinions tended to lay emphasis not on the matter but on the form, not on the spirit but on the ceremony, it is none the less hard to see how the Church, granted its premises, could have reached any other conclusion.

The seven sacraments were baptism, confirmation, penance, the *The seven* Eucharist, or Lord's Supper, extreme unction, marriage, and holy *sacraments* orders. The number was not officially restricted to the mystic seven until the Council of Florence in the fifteenth century. Peter Lombard in his *Sentences* listed seven essential sacraments, and the wide use of his book gave sanction to the number, but there was no general agreement. Like the organization and the law of the Church, the sacramental system was of slow growth. It was not always imposed from above by authority, but grew out of the requirements and local customs of the people; in many instances the theologians and the papacy simply set their seal upon popular demand.

[25] See pp. 43–44.

Baptism   Baptism by infusion had at an early date replaced immersion. Baptism washed away the guilt of original sin. Infants were accordingly baptized as soon as convenient, to preclude the possibility of their being consigned to limbo if they should die with the stain of original sin still upon them. Baptism also washed away all the individual's sins to date, and regenerated with grace his whole life. It did not, however, eradicate the natural human tendency to sin, so that means had to be

Confirmation   provided for the forgiveness of subsequent sins. Originally confirmation, administered by bishops only, immediately followed baptism; but as the Church spread over the countryside it became impossible for a bishop always to be present at baptism, so that the two ceremonies were soon separated. Moreover, since it was not always convenient or possible to bring an infant to the episcopal city to be confirmed, and as bishops were necessarily irregular in making the rounds of the parishes, confirmation gradually came to be postponed to later years, finally to the age of twelve. By the laying on of hands and the anointing of the forehead with oil the bishop gave his sign or confirmation to baptism, and therewith imparted a second installment of grace, sufficient to make the youth a perfect Christian and a full-fledged member of the Church.

Penance   But alas, although grace should now have been sufficient, it was still not effective. If it was natural that the child should sin after baptism, it was inevitable that the adult should sin after confirmation. To take care of all sins committed since baptism the sacrament of penance was devised. It was originally a public ceremony: in the presence of the assembled congregation the penitent confessed his major sins, whereupon he was excluded from church services until a later ceremony of reconciliation, also public. The system of private penance introduced by the Irish monks,[26] which they possibly borrowed from eastern monasticism, was so plainly superior that it gradually superseded public penance and became the established practice of the Church.

It was the prevalent opinion that if the sacrament were to be effective, the penitent must be contrite, that is, sincerely sorry for his sins and resolved to do better; later theologians held that it was necessary only to be attrite, that is, repentant in fact, although from an imperfect motive, such as fear of hell. The contrite, or at least attrite, sinner made a secret confession of his major sins and of their attendant circumstances to the priest in the confessional, where the priest could not see and might not even recognize him. The priest was bound to the strictest secrecy; to divulge information gained in the confessional

[26] See p. 214.

meant lifelong imprisonment in a monastery doing penance. When the confession was completed, the priest by virtue of the power of the keys [27] absolved the sinner from the eternal guilt of his sin, thus without further ado freeing him from the terrors of punishment in hell.

But to satisfy God's justice the sinner must still undergo a certain amount of temporal punishment, either here on earth or in the flames of purgatory, commensurate to the number and the gravity of his sins. To provide a means of escape from this punishment the priest, immediately after pronouncing absolution, assigned penance of the proper severity. Penance, which might consist of a certain number of prayers, so many rounds of the stations of the cross, a period of fasting, almsgiving, or even a pilgrimage to some near or distant shrine, was assigned according to fixed schedules called penitentials.

If the priest had assigned just enough or more than enough penance, all was well as soon as the penance had been faithfully performed. But suppose he had not assigned enough? Then the sinner, for all his confession, absolution, and penance, would still be obliged to suffer in purgatory long enough to atone in full for his sins. Fortunately, theologians are never for long at a loss. To meet this emergency the medieval theologians discovered the "treasury of merits." Christ, they explained, and all the saints and many good people during their lives had accumulated many more merits than they needed for their salvation. This surplus, stored in a treasury to which the pope had access, could be distributed in the form of indulgences to the less fortunate Christians who did need them. Indulgences could be had *Indulgences* not only to meet the danger of unassigned penance that might be due, but also to cover all or part of the assigned penance for a given length of time. They were originally granted to reward virtuous deeds, but gradually came to be sold for money. To simple minds unacquainted with theological subtleties indulgences might be a bit hard to understand, but they seemed an easy way to purchase sure salvation. Eternal punishment was taken care of by confession and absolution, temporal punishment by penance and indulgences. Circumspect persons by means of indulgences guarded against untold years of punishment in purgatory.

The sacrament of the Eucharist concludes the ceremony of the *The Eucharist* Mass. At the most solemn moment in the service the priest, after careful preparations at the altar, pronounces over the bread and wine the words "For this is my body. . . . For this is the chalice of my blood." By virtue of these words he performs a miracle: he causes the

[27] See pp. 50–51.

bread and wine without changing their form or appearance to change their substance, that is, he transubstantiates them into the actual body and blood of Christ. The Mass is closely related to absolution and penance, for the Church interprets it as a repetition without blood of the bloody sacrifice of Christ upon the cross for the sins of the world, having accordingly the efficacy of the original sacrifice. Masses can be said for the unrequited sins of the dead as well as of the living, thus achieving the same result as indulgences secured before death. The sacrament of the Eucharist consists in eating the actual body and drinking the actual blood of Christ in the form of the bread or wafer and the wine. At first both bread and wine were given to the laity, but because of the danger of spilling the wine, now the precious blood of Christ, and inasmuch as the theologians held that Christ's body and blood were present equally in both bread and wine, it became the rule for the laity to receive only the bread and for the priest to take the wine on behalf of all the faithful assembled. (This is called taking the sacrament in one kind.)

The extraordinary character of this sacrament and of the service that precedes it, so redolent of pagan sacrifice and of pagan mystery cults,[28] makes it the most impressive and the most important of the sacraments, the very core of the public service of the Church. Properly to understand its awful character one must watch it carefully and reverently performed in a Catholic church of good taste. With the fumes of incense, the lights of many candles, the music of organ and choir, the solemn intonation of the Latin by priests in rich attire, all in the somber colored light of the dim and spacious interior of a Gothic church, it should not be difficult for any, even the least sympathetic, person to sense something of the wonder and love that it has inspired and still inspires.

Extreme unction

The sacrament of extreme unction, the anointing of the body with oil consecrated by the bishop, is administered at the point of death. It is meant to assist physical recovery if that be still possible, or to prepare the Christian for death by relieving him of all uncertainty as to his salvation. In the words of the Council of Trent, it "wipes away offenses, if there are any still to be expiated, as also the remains of sin; and raises up and strengthens the soul of the sick person by arousing in him great faith in the divine mercy, supported by which he bears more lightly the inconveniences and labors of illness and more easily resists the temptations of the devil who lies in wait for his heel; and

[28] See p. 37.

sometimes attains health when expedient for the welfare of his soul." [29]

The remaining two sacraments, unlike these five, were not intended for all Christians. While the Church at first preferred virginity to marriage, it could not afford to let an institution of such social im- *Marriage* portance as marriage escape its control. And without children, where would the Church be? Obviously marriage must be tolerated; if it must be tolerated, it should be controlled; the best of all ways to control it was to sanctify it. Not until the sixteenth century, however, was it necessary for marriage to be performed by a priest in order to be valid, and the sacrament did not even become general until the tenth century.

The provisions of early canon law with reference to betrothal followed Roman law, according to which marriage was a civil, not a religious, ceremony, the priestly benediction being without legal significance. Although the Church permitted separation, it came to regard marriage as indissoluble because it symbolized the marriage of Christ to his Church. Its attitude towards divorce, however, was slow in crystallizing. In the early Church, divorce and remarriage were permitted, though general opinion favored separation with the hope of reconciliation. Even so late as the Council of Tours, in 1061, bishops were allowed to grant divorce with the right to remarry. The change came with the growth of papal power and of the hierarchy, with the formulation of canon law, and with the legislation of the Church concerning degrees of relationship. In 1066 new prohibited degrees were substituted for those of Roman law: uncles could not marry nieces nor aunts nephews, and the marriage of cousins was forbidden. Even "spiritual affinity" became a bar to marriage; that is, godfathers and godmothers were considered to be related as if by blood. In the upper classes such rigid legislation offered more occasions for the popes to exercise their powers of special dispensation, for the Church often found it advisable—and profitable—to approve dynastic alliances within the prohibited degrees or to separate politically influential persons already married. As for the lower classes, the ingrown and inbred character of the medieval village made it inevitable that some of these restrictions should subsequently be relaxed.

The sacrament of holy orders, or ordination, administered only by *Holy orders* the bishops, gave to the priest the indelible character that set him forever apart from ordinary men, so long as he was not formally de-

[29] Quoted by McGiffert, *A History of Christian Thought*, II, 327.

graded from the priesthood by proper ecclesiastical authority. It gave him the full jurisdiction of his office, including the power of the keys, by virtue of which he could forgive sins. It gave him the power to perform the miracle of transubstantiation at the altar. In general it gave him the power to dispense the grace of God through all the sacraments, and thereby made him indispensable to the salvation of every Christian.

The religion of the people

The formal structure of the theological drama of salvation had necessarily slight appeal for simple folk. They were interested only in the high points: the Creation and the fall of Adam, the birth and the crucifixion of Christ, the Last Judgment, the horrors of hell, the in-

Dressing for the Last Judgment, Cathedral of Basel

effable bliss of heaven. The sacramental system they regarded from the practical point of view as the one sure way of attaining this eternal bliss. The masses of the people had always had their own religion, largely of their own making, which owed more to pagan cults and less to classical philosophy than the religion of the theologians. It gave expression to simpler and warmer and more elemental religious feeling than the subtleties and austerities of theology. The popular religion of the middle ages was built upon the cult of the saints and martyrs and the miraculous power of their relics, and above all upon the veneration of the Blessed Virgin Mary, the Mother of Christ.

Relics

Like the custom of pilgrimages, the veneration of relics was borrowed by popular Christianity from paganism. Early in the fourth century St. Helena, Roman empress and mother of the Emperor Constantine, made a pilgrimage to Jerusalem, where she was believed to have discovered the fragments of the true cross. By the sixth century worship of relics and belief in miracles wrought by their means were the most influential factors in the religious life of the people. The religious revival of the eleventh century and the crusades gave new impetus to the quest for relics, which became a positive mania. German bishops in Italy robbed and cheated Italian bishops and even robbed graves to get relics. The dead bodies of holy men who seemed likely to be canonized were attacked by the populace for pieces of their clothing or of their bodies, and monasteries and churches fought bitterly for the possession of the bodies of such men. Wonder-working relics brought wealth and popularity to a church: it became a goal for local or even far-distant pilgrimages and the object of the generosity of the faithful. The same relics brought wealth and prosperity to the community: the crowds of pilgrims were good for business. Inevitably there grew up a considerable traffic in fictitious relics. The sack of Constantinople in 1204 flooded the west with genuine and spurious remains of martyrs and saints. No church could properly be founded without some, and gifts of relics from one churchman to another were the most highly prized of all gifts. Whole walls in some churches— St. Gereon and St. Ursula at Cologne, for example—were covered with the bones of martyrs and saints. One can still find everything from specimens of the Virgin's milk to one of St. Peter's knuckles.

The high value placed on relics is indicated by Richard I's paying Saladin, after his recovery of Jerusalem in 1187, fifty thousand bezants to redeem the relics of the Church of the Holy Sepulcher. In 1241 the Venetians paid the King of Jerusalem twenty thousand gold pieces for a newly found piece of the true cross. Oaths were taken upon relics in court; they were used to cure disease, to avert the evil eye, to stop a plague among cattle, to insure good harvests. The mania for relics, against which the more spiritual minds in the Church protested in vain, was a tremendous stimulus to all the arts. Caskets and other reliquaries for the sacred remains are among the most beautiful examples of medieval work in gold, silver, enamel, and ivory. Whole churches were built to house relics, like the beautiful Sainte Chapelle in Paris, which St. Louis built as a magnificent reliquary for a thorn from the crown of thorns.[30]

[30] In the late fifteenth century Frederick the Wise of Saxony built a church at Wittenberg to house the five thousand and five relics he had collected. On these indulgences had been granted equivalent to fourteen hundred and forty-three years of purgatory, and to make absolutely sure of his salvation Frederick had ten thousand Masses said yearly in the churches of Saxony. (P. Smith, *Martin Luther*, p. 33.)

The only asset a church could have that might be even greater than valuable relics was a local saint. In the twelfth century the papacy asserted its sole right to enroll new saints, and established a special court to investigate and decide claims to canonization. The candidate for sainthood must previously have been declared "blessed," and it must be proved that after beatification his intercession had wrought at least two miracles. Nowadays at least fifty years must have elapsed between death and canonization; but in the middle ages, as we noted in the cases of St. Francis, St. Dominic, and St. Louis, canonization often followed much more promptly after death. Even so it was often too slow for popular sentiment, which had completed a local canonization, quite valid for the purposes of popular religion, long before official canonization at Rome.

According to theology, all that the saints could do was to intercede with God in behalf of those who presented their petitions to them in prayer; but in popular opinion prayer made directly to the image of the saint in the chapel dedicated to him in the church was answered directly by the saint, often in miraculous fashion. One may still see in Italian churches notices posted to warn the petitioner that unless he first prays to God at the high altar no saint will deign to receive his prayer. Like the lesser gods of antiquity, the saints performed all manner of little services that one would hesitate to ask of the members of the Trinity. They were, again like the pagan gods, all specialists. One appeals to St. Anthony of Padua for help in finding something lost, to St. Agnes for help in securing a husband. Local patron saints were the general guardians of the welfare of the whole community. If the saints seemed to ignore petitions after proper offerings had been made at their shrines, their images were sometimes taken from the churches by disappointed and angry followers and given a severe beating. The lives and miracles of saints were the popular mythology of the middle ages.

The most universal appeals for help went to the Blessed Virgin Mary, probably more than to the Holy Trinity and all the saints together. Who, after all, could have more influence with Christ than his beautiful and all-compassionate Mother, who knew not how to deny any petition from any source? Her cult was of early origin,[31] but it did not attain great proportions until the eleventh century, that century so phenomenal for intense and varied religious expression. One of the most obvious explanations of her popularity is the fact that

[31] See p. 36.

the Church, with its imposing hierarchy, its enormous spiritual and temporal power, its formidable authority to save or to damn, its preaching of the terrors of hell, its majestic doctrine of an omnipotent and avenging God, awed and frightened men. They feared God, but

Our Lady of the beautiful window in the Cathedral of Chartres

they did not love him. Christ, the mediator between sinful men and the wrathful God, as the Son of God still partook too much, even in human flesh, of God's formidable nature to be entirely lovable. Men preferred Christ as the baby at his Mother's breast.

Mary, all lovable and lovely, humanized Christianity by her divine sympathy. No perplexing theological dogmas invested her figure. She was the Queen of Heaven, but she was not awful to contemplate, nor far from men; she was the Mother of God, but she was human. She was the friend of all, from the highest to the lowest; no burden of the heart was too great to bring to her in prayer, nothing too trivial for her attention. If the Virgin shared all men's sorrows, all men shared hers, and gloried in her glory. They rejoiced with her in the birth of her Son; they wept with her over his tragic death. They wrote deeply moving poems picturing her grief at the foot of the cross; they wrote lyrics of the pretty young mother beside the cradle. Her worship inspired the secular cult of the lady in chivalry. The whole world of art was inspired by her.

Chapter 23

THE MEDIEVAL RENAISSANCE

PHILOSOPHY, SCIENCE, EDUCATION

THE term "renaissance" has long been used by historians to *The term* refer to the revival of art and learning in Italy in the four- *"renaissance"* teenth century, which spread across the Alps in the fifteenth century and ran out its course in the sixteenth. The meaning of the term, the "rebirth of art and learning," implicitly assumes that there had been nothing of the sort since the great days of the Roman empire. No intelligent person who has read thus far need be told that such an assumption is mistaken. Like the reformation,[1] the renaissance, at least among American historians of the middle ages, has been pushed back two hundred years to the twelfth century.[2] It would be possible to make out a case for a renaissance in the eleventh century, and we have already spoken of the Carolingian renaissance of the ninth century and the Ottonian of the tenth.[3] It begins to look as if the middle ages were one grand succession of renaissances. In this instance, as in so many others, the historian would no doubt do well to discard a traditional terminology which new knowledge has rendered inaccurate if not absurd, for there was of course no such series of renaissances. The millennium between Gregory the Great and Martin Luther was no different from any other time so far as intellectual and artistic interest, capacity, and performance are concerned. Intelligent and sensitive men and women were as curious about the unknown, as anxious to solve the riddle of man and the universe, as eager to have beautiful things about them, as they have ever been. The difference comes in the degree, or perhaps rather in the quality, of their success.

[1] See p. 607.
[2] This has probably been owing, more than to anything else, to one book, C. H. Haskins's *Twelfth Century Renaissance.*
[3] See pp. 252, 366.

Culture, in so far as it needs to be differentiated from civilization, we might define, borrowing from Matthew Arnold, as the refinement of mind and spirit that comes from intimate acquaintance with and enjoyment of the best that mankind has produced in the realms of thought and the arts. It is often argued that what we call culture is possible only in a society able to support a leisured class with time and means and disposition to cultivate this best and to patronize those who are able to create it. If this be true, medieval culture, supported by an aristocracy of clergy and nobility, was made possible by the labor of the peasants on the manor, which supported the aristocracy. The social support of medieval culture, then, was the serf, and its economic foundation was agriculture. The term "civilization" has a wider connotation. It might be defined as the relative level of attainment above mere animal existence, in all phases of human activity that make up the life of a society. Culture would then be the superior intellectual and artistic products of a civilization, and the acquisition of culture a part of civilization. For civilization is essentially the process of disciplining the untamed thoughts and emotions and actions of the human animal. As means to this discipline every society creates or borrows a certain number of institutions adapted to its own peculiar needs.

Culture and civilization

When the Roman civilizing of western Europe was interrupted by the decay of the empire and the migrations and invasions of primitive Germanic peoples, the Church made the task its own. It quickly adapted itself to a primitive agricultural society composed in the main of rather wild children, and was itself somewhat barbarized in the process, but it did preserve the tradition of Latin culture. Because of its tradition, its organization, its wealth, and its ability to draw the most gifted young men into its service, the Church was able until the end of the middle ages either to produce all that might be called culture or to control its production. Medieval culture, whatever its basis, was essentially ecclesiastical in character. So brief a summary of course makes everything seem much simpler than it was. The supplanting of one civilization by another is a long and complicated process of many centuries, as witness the supplanting of Celtic civilization by Roman civilization in western Europe. Nor is it ever really complete. The Christian Church, in assuming the burden of disciplining the Roman or the Roman-German or the purely German paganism of western and northern Europe, was entering upon a task not even yet fully accomplished. We are all still pagan in part; the clergy never tire of the theme of the new paganism; paganism is always

The Church the agent of culture

new, always modern. Nevertheless, if ever there was a time when Christianity dominated civilization and permeated culture, that time was the period from Gregory the Great to Dante.

The conflict between western European paganism and Christianity can be traced in the competition between the vernacular languages and Latin as the medium of literary expression. The Anglo-Saxon *Beowulf*, the German *Heliand*, and the earlier redactions of the *Niebelungenlied*, early Irish poetry, the Icelandic eddas, and the Norse sagas are all representative of a pagan world untouched, or little touched, by the influence of Christianity. This earlier vernacular literature was swallowed up in the floodtide of Latin, which not only was the language of the Church, but became the language of literature, learning, politics, law, and business. Meanwhile, in the countryside the Church was fighting a constant battle with the remnants of pagan religion—pagan festivals, pagan magic—which she conquered by becoming herself half pagan and half magical. The origins of feudalism were not Christian, but the Church sanctified the oath between lord and vassal, summoned western knighthood into her service in the crusades, and converted the ceremony of knighthood into a virtual sacrament. When vernacular literature reappeared in the twelfth century with the *chansons de geste*, it celebrated the virtues of Christian chivalry. In southern France during the eleventh century troubadours began to celebrate in the vernacular a cult of love wholly unrelated to Christianity, which in its extreme form made a virtue of adultery. At the same time, the trouvères of northern France were relating the valorous deeds of the Celtic heroes of Wales and Brittany. The Church was able to refine the cult of love by the cult of the Virgin, and to transform pagan knights cultivating married ladies into Christian heroes relieving the poor and the oppressed, succoring maidens in distress, fighting for the cross, and seeking the Holy Grail.

The Christianization of medieval paganism

In the twelfth and thirteenth centuries western Europe became acquainted with a new world of the intellect, whose origin was Greek and Mohammedan. No sooner had the Church accommodated this pagan learning to Christian theology than it was confronted in the thirteenth century with a new secular spirit. With the revival of commerce and industry and the growth of towns a new class of merchants and industrialists arose to join nobles and clergy as patrons of art and learning, and a new class of artisans arose to join the serfs in supporting society by their labor. We have seen how the Church tried likewise to tame this spirit, but with only indifferent success,[4] for

The new secular spirit

[4] See pp. 596–97.

this time the pagan and secular spirit tamed the Church to its own purposes; it made a formal obeisance to the old ideals in order to be left free to continue its own ways.

The fourteenth and fifteenth centuries mark a great transition. So long as life remained hard, primitive, and dangerous, the Church was able to persuade society of the validity of its point of view and its discipline. It was able to enforce an ideal of behavior conducive to the realization of what it took to be the purpose of life, that is, preparation for an eternal life after death. To be sure, life was still bare enough, as it remains to this day for most people, but at least the secular state and the secular law were making it less dangerous, and the development of commerce and industry were making it less primitive and more comfortable. The Church failed to keep its hold on society. Gradually the old ecclesiastical culture of an agricultural society was transformed into a secular culture rooted in the new capitalism. Those who were outraged at the Church's failure to rise to the occasion began to preach religious reform, which eventuated in the Protestant reformation of the sixteenth century. The rising national states and capitalism co-operated with classical art and pagan learning to bring in a new day.

The medieval renaissance, western Europe's coming of age, properly began with the Carolingian revival, which imposed a higher standard of education on the clergy and preserved the Latin classics and the writings of the Latin Church Fathers. From the ninth century to the eleventh its accomplishments were constantly threatened but never lost. Meanwhile external circumstances were gradually preparing the way for the utilization of this ancient heritage. After its birth pangs feudalism settled down to some kind of order. The

The eleventh-century background of the twelfth-century renaissance

Norman conquest of England in 1066 not only laid the foundations for the strong Norman-Angevin kingdom of the twelfth century, but enriched English culture by all sorts of fertilizing influences from the continent—in particular the Norman genius for architecture already developing in Normandy—while at the same time it facilitated the transmission of Celtic legend and romance to the continent. The Norman conquest of southern Italy and Sicily afforded a unique opportunity for the amalgamation of Greek, Latin, Saracen, and Christian cultures. The Christian advance in Spain in the eleventh century opened the way into western Europe for Arabic science and philosophy, and for the influence of Arabic literature and music, the full significance of which scholars are not even yet in a position to estimate.[5] The quickening of religious life in the eleventh century, marked by the Cluniac reform and by the growing custom of pilgrimages culminating in the first crusade at the end of the century, laid the foundations for Romanesque architecture, created subjects for the vernacular *chansons de geste,* and widened the whole intellectual horizon of western Europe by getting people to moving.

The papacy of Gregory VII was beginning to feel the need of trained scholars and lawyers, and to bring churchmen from all over western Europe on frequent trips to Rome. The investiture struggle between Church and state, empire and papacy, stimulated controversy and produced a large and important literature.[6] In Italy Monte Cassino was an important center for ecclesiastical studies, Salerno for medicine, Bologna for Roman law. The beginnings of the revival of commerce and industry had already brought the first new contacts with Greek culture. The eleventh century was a great period of preparation for something greater to follow.

That European scholarship was maturing in the eleventh century is indicated by the fact that some scholars were beginning to appeal to reason. What scholars meant by the use of reason, now and for *Aristotelian* the rest of the middle ages, was the use of dialectics, the formal syl- *logic* logistic logic that had been perfected by Aristotle in a series of treatises. Of these treatises Boethius had made available to the west in Latin translation the *Categories* and *On Interpretation,* and had also translated an introduction to the *Categories* by the Neo-Platonist Porphyry and written Aristotelian commentaries of his own. Until the middle of the twelfth century these few works were the substance of the west's knowledge of logic; for seven hundred years it owed such intellectual discipline as it got almost entirely to one man.

The first westerner who seems to have taken full advantage of Boethius's labors was Gerbert of Aurillac, whom we have already met *Gerbert of* as Pope Sylvester II.[7] Soon after his death Notker, a monk of St. *Aurillac* Gall, was translating logical treatises of Aristotle into German. Gerbert is the link between the Ottonian renaissance of the tenth century and the dialectical and classical revival in the French schools of the eleventh, which was carried out to some extent by men who had been his pupils at the cathedral school at Rheims between 972 and 982.

[5] For example, it is altogether possible that some day it will be demonstrated that the background of the Provençal troubadours was Arabic culture.

[6] See pp. 385–86.

[7] See p. 365.

For all his emphasis on dialectics Gerbert was a man of universal interests, who absorbed all the learning available to his generation. To enrich the library of his school at Rheims he sought far and wide for copies of works that were still missing. His teaching of rhetoric was based on the Latin poets: ". . . he read and explained the poets Virgil, Statius and Terence, the satirists Juvenal and Persius, and Horace; also Lucan the historiographer." From his study of mathematics in Spain he knew the Arabic numerals, though not the zero, for part of his legendary reputation as a sorcerer seems to have been derived from his expert handling of the abacus. He interested himself in investigations of the nature of steam, and invented an organ in which steam was forced through graduated pipes. Astronomy "he explained by means of admirable instruments." Indeed, Gerbert's learning represents the sum total of western scientific knowledge prior to the diffusion of Arabic science. Compared with science as it then flourished in Arabic centers, it is not very impressive. The fact that his learning was nevertheless regarded with awe is evidence how much the west had yet to learn. When he became pope, legend had it that he sold his soul to the devil for the honor. Honor he richly deserved, for he learned all that it was possible for him to know in the midst of a crowded career as monk, abbot, teacher, tutor and counsellor to the Emperor Otto III, archbishop, and pope.

The work of Gerbert at Rheims was carried on by his pupil Fulbert in the cathedral school at Chartres in the first quarter of the eleventh

The dispute of Berengar of Tours and Lanfranc of Bec on transubstantiation

century. Here the emphasis was put on the Latin classics, and the enthusiastic revival of their study was destined to bear fruit in the next century. Gerbert's influence extended also to the monastic school at Fleury-sur-Loire and to the famous old school of St. Martin at Tours, over which Alcuin had once presided. Here Berengar, one of Fulbert's pupils, was among the first medieval scholars to insist that more was required of an intelligent man than simply to accept on faith the dogmas of the Church and the opinions of the Church Fathers: it was essential to comprehend these dogmas and opinions by reason. "It is a part of courage," he argued, "to have recourse to dialectic in all things, for recourse to dialectic is recourse to reason, and he who does not avail himself of reason abandons his chief honor, since by virtue of reason he was made in the image of God." When authority and reason conflict, one must follow reason, inasmuch as no authority can supersede reason in a mind capable of discovering truth. Berengar did not hesitate to criticize Boethius, Priscian, and Donatus. In applying reason to the popular belief in transubstantia-

The façade of Notre Dame, Paris

The Butter Tower of the Cathedral at Rouen

The Gothic façade of the Cathedral of Coutances (thirteenth century)

Flying buttresses to nave vaulting of the Cathedral at Amiens

The flying buttresses to the apse on the Chur[ch] St. Francis at Bologna

The main portal of the Cathedral at Chartres (twelfth century)

tion he could not understand how, when the bread and the wine of the Eucharist continued to look and taste and smell as if they were still bread and wine, they could actually have been changed by consecration into the body and the blood of Christ; and in his book. *On the Eucharist* he concluded that as a matter of fact, since these accidents of color, flavor, and smell remained unchanged after consecration, neither had their substance been changed. Therefore no transubstantiation had taken place, and Berengar found himself occupying the position of Ratramnus in the ninth century.[8]

His conception of the importance of logic and his views on transubstantiation were opposed by Lanfranc, abbot of the Norman monastery of Bec, who was made Archbishop of Canterbury by William the Conqueror. Lanfranc too had been an ardent disciple of dialectics, but abandoned logic in favor of authority, probably because he could not meet Berengar's arguments on their own ground. Nevertheless it was with a syllogism that he crushed his opponent. The Fathers defined a heretic as one who disagreed with the Church; Berengar had attacked the Faith, the Fathers, and the popes; therefore he was a heretic. Although Berengar had said that a brave man should prefer to die rather than surrender his reason to authority, at the crucial moment he changed his mind: he could not bear to be a heretic. He was therefore forced to subscribe to the statement that "the bread and wine which are placed on the altar after the consecration are not only a sacrament but also the true body and blood of our Lord Jesus Christ, and sensibly, not merely sacramentally but in verity, are handled and broken by the hands of the priests and bruised by the teeth of believers."

It should be emphasized that the dialecticians, in setting up reason against authority, did not claim that in case of conflict it was possible to substitute their syllogisms for the articles of faith and the revelation of God in Scripture. Their fundamental idea was that there can be no genuine conflict between revealed truth and rational truth: truth is one. But they did believe that it was possible to make revealed truth intelligible not only to those willing to accept it on faith but *Reason* also to unbelievers; and the best of them set no limits to this intel- *and faith* ligibility except the impossibility of hoping ever to exhaust the full meaning of revelation. When, however, reason failed to make clear revealed truth or defined dogma, then these must be accepted on faith. As one dialectician put it, ". . . no Christian ought in any way to dispute the truth of what the Catholic Church believes in its heart

8 See p. 257.

and confesses with its mouth. But always holding the same faith un-
questioningly . . . he ought himself as far as he is able to seek the
reason for it. If he can understand it, let him thank God. If he cannot, let him not raise his head in opposition but bow in reverence." [9]

No outstanding scholar of the middle ages openly got beyond
this attitude. Nevertheless, in emphasizing intelligibility the logicians
were in fact emphasizing the power of human reason. By demanding
that the intelligent man never abandon his attempt to understand
they must often have led themselves and their students to trust reason
more than revelation. They must thus have driven many to doubt and
not a few to disbelief. Naturally such results were never broadcast,
but we know enough to guess the rest. The monk of St. Emmeram
in Regensburg was not alone in his cry for help: "Where is the hope
you held hitherto in Scripture? Can you not prove that there is no
rational ground for the testimony of Scripture, or for the existence of
the created world? Does not experience show you that the Scripture
says one thing and human conduct another? Is the age-long refusal of
men to follow Scripture unjustified? . . . Oh, if thou existest Almighty, and if thou art anywhere, as I have often read in many
books, show, I pray, who thou art and what thou canst do." [10] The
dialecticians called upon men to think,

> "And if they think, they fasten
> Their hands upon their hearts."

The eleventh-century revival of logic raised another question inherited from Boethius, the origin of which, however, went back to
Plato's theory of ideas. [11] Plato had conceived of reality as consisting
in a hierarchy of general ideas or forms, chief of which was the idea
of the good. There was no reality in a particular thing except as it
partook of the nature of its general idea: there was, for example, no
such thing as a good man except as he partook of the general idea
of goodness. Generalities, abstractions, concepts preceded particular
things, to which they gave reality. The question now raised was
whether these general terms or ideas had real existence of their own
or whether, as Aristotle thought, they were a mere intellectual convenience, reality entering only into individual things. Those who held
to the latter view were called nominalists (from Latin *nomina*,

*Nominalist
versus realist*

---

[9] Anselm, quoted by McGiffert, *A History of Christian Thought*, II, 186.
[10] MacDonald, *Authority and Reason in the Early Middle Ages*, pp. 101–2.
[11] See p. 23.

"names"), since the extreme statement of their position defined the general concept as a mere name, a word whose only reality consisted in the disturbance of the atmosphere caused by its utterance. Opposed to them were the realists, who adhered to the Platonic position that only general concepts were real: they formed the body of truth originally conceived in the divine mind, and particulars were real only in so far as they embodied general ideas. The nominalist would say, then, that no such thing as scholarship exists, but only things to be learned, whereas the realist would argue that there are things to be learned only in so far as they partake of the nature of learnability. The nominalist would say that there is no such thing as felinity, there are only cats; the realist, that a cat is a cat only in that it has felinity.

Let no one suppose that this controversy was mere quibbling about words. The realist threatened to swallow up the individual in an abstraction. The nominalist threatened the existence of a body of truth derived from divine revelation. If, for example, there really is no such thing as humanity, how justify our punishment for the sin of Adam, an individual with whom we have only the vaguest connection? But if Adam was largely an embodiment of the same humanity that we embody, then perhaps humanity in us is justly punished for its defect in him. The social corollaries of each position are clear enough. If there really are such things as universals to which our concepts correspond—the Church, Germany, Paris—then there is logically a binding force to commitments made in the names of those universals by particular individuals. But if the state is only the name of a concept, then there is no better reason than expediency why one group of politicians in power should not repudiate bonds issued by other politicians in the name of the nonexistent state. The extreme form of either realism or nominalism is a *reductio ad absurdum*. It is possible for the concept of the Catholic Church or the Protestant Church to attain such reality that we hold our Catholic neighbors personally responsible for the horrors of the Inquisition, or our Protestant neighbors for the outrages committed by Cromwell's men in Ireland. It is perhaps fair to say that the social philosophy of realism tends to be conservative of both good and bad, whereas nominalism tends to promote change, which may easily be change for the worse. Nor let anyone suppose that the controversy has been settled. In contemporary society the old question is still with us in new form, in the bitter quarrel between individualism and collectivism. In its original form it was discussed for two hundred years, and is still capable of engaging the attention of thoughtful men. "He who has given his

The impor- tance of the controversy between realism and nominalism

answer to it has implicitly constructed his theory of the universe." [12]

It was naturally the theological implications of realism and nominalism that medieval scholars were quickest to see. Extreme realism tends to assert that all lesser universals are merged in one great absolute universal; it thus becomes pantheistic, and pantheism is heresy. Nominalism finds it difficult to avoid the heresy of materialism. The

The dispute of Roscellin and Anselm on the Trinity

controversy in the eleventh century quickly led to a dispute on the doctrine of the Trinity between Roscellin of Compiègne and Anselm of Bec. Roscellin, a thoroughgoing nominalist, understood that there was a Father, a Son, and a Holy Spirit, but as for the Trinity as distinct from these three persons, it was only a convenient term, corresponding to nothing existing in reality. Anselm, an unqualified realist, charged him with believing in three gods. "Either he wishes to confess three gods or he does not understand what he says. If he confesses three gods, he is not a Christian; if he says what he does not understand, he is not to be trusted." And in general, Anselm continued, "those dialecticians, or rather dialectical heretics, of our time, who think that universal substances are nothing but words . . . should be wholly excluded from the discussion of spiritual questions. . . . For how can he who does not yet understand that many men are in species one man comprehend how in that most lofty and mysterious nature a plurality of persons, each of whom singly is perfect God, are one God?" In other words, on the question of the Trinity strict nominalism led straight to heresy.

Anselm was a firm believer in the use of dialectics to explain the

Anselm of Bec

tenets of the Christian faith. He took for his own St. Augustine's motto: "Nor do I seek to know that I may believe, but believe that I may know" (*neque enim quæro intelligere ut credam, sed credo ut intelligam*). In his first theological treatise he undertook to prove the existence of God by logic alone, without the aid of authority. Having accomplished this feat in good Platonic fashion, he was still not satisfied, for he felt that he had used too many arguments, and so in a second work, he tells us, he resolved "to seek within myself whether I might not discover one argument which needed nothing else than itself alone for its proof; and which by itself might suffice to show that truly God exists." The result has remained forever famous as the ontological argument for the existence of God.

It may be worth while to quote Anselm's own words, if only as a specimen of scholastic reasoning of the sort that has made it so easy for the modern man to overlook the fact that these scholastic phi-

[12] Rashdall, *The Universities of Europe in the Middle Ages*, I, 38.

losophers were, after all, interested in questions of the first importance to anyone who thinks about life at all. "Even the fool is convinced that there is something, at any rate in the understanding, than
which nothing greater can be conceived, for when he hears this he
understands it, and whatever is understood is in the understanding.
And certainly that than which a greater can not be conceived can not
exist in the understanding alone. For if it be in the understanding
alone, it is possible to conceive it as existing in reality, which is greater.
If, therefore, that than which a greater can not be conceived is in the
understanding alone, that very thing than which a greater can not be
conceived is one than which a greater can be conceived. But this as-
suredly can not be. Without a doubt, therefore, there exists something, both in the understanding and in reality, than which a greater
can not be conceived." In another notable treatise, designed to explain
why it was necessary for God to become man in Christ (*Cur Deus
Homo?*), Anselm succeeded in giving western theology its first clear
statement of the theory of the atonement. A man who proved the
existence of God by one argument was an inexhaustible inspiration
to his successors in dealing with less essential doctrines.

The peak of the early dialectical movement, based primarily on
the few works of Aristotle then accessible, was reached with Pierre
Abélard (1079–1142). This handsome and gifted young Breton of   *Abélard's*
noble birth, having forsaken the adventures of knighthood for those   *early career*
of learning, arrived in Paris when not yet twenty years old to study
with William of Champeaux, who taught in the cathedral school of
Notre Dame. William was a staunch realist, but, Abélard tells us
in his autobiography, "I brought him great grief, because I undertook
to refute certain of his opinions, not infrequently attacking him in disputation, and now and then in these debates I was adjudged victor.' [13]
Abélard set up his own school at Melun, but because, he says, "my
fame in the art of dialectics began to spread abroad, so that little by
little the renown, not alone of those who had been my fellow students but of our very teacher himself, grew dim and was like to die
out altogether," he moved to Corbeil. After an illness he was back
again in Paris combating William, and "in the course of our many
arguments on various matters I compelled him by most potent reasoning, first to alter his former opinion on the subject of the universals,
and finally to abandon it altogether."

[13] This and the following quotations are from the translation by H. A. Bellows
of the *Historia Calamitatum* (*The Story of My Misfortunes*), one of the most
interesting autobiographies ever written.

With this victory behind him Abélard proceeded from dialectics to theology. He went to Laon to study with Anselm, a pupil of the famous Anselm of Bec, of whom, however, he formed a poor opinion. "If any one came to him impelled by doubt on any subject, he went away more doubtful still. . . . When he kindled a fire, he filled his house with smoke and illumined it not at all. He was a tree which seemed noble to those who gazed upon its leaves from afar, but to those who came nearer and examined it more closely was revealed its barrenness." Abélard boasted to fellow students that any intelligent person ought to be able to read the Scriptures for himself and lecture upon them, and, when challenged to do so, did it, he says, with great success. But his position in Laon had become untenable, and he returned to Paris to lecture in the cathedral school to growing crowds of students. He was always the idol of his students, among whom were such men as Arnold of Brescia, Peter Lombard, and Pope Alexander III. The fact that he drew such crowds in Paris suggests the need which the University of Paris was organized to meet. "By this time," he confesses, "I had come to regard myself as the only philosopher remaining in the whole world." "Pride," he might have read in the Proverbs, "goeth before destruction, and an haughty spirit before a fall."

Abélard and Héloïse

It was his love affair with Héloïse that brought him down. She was the niece of Canon Fulbert of Notre Dame, a girl "of no mean beauty," with an "abundant knowledge of letters." "It was this young girl whom I, after carefully considering all those qualities which are wont to attract lovers, determined to unite with myself in the bonds of love, and indeed the thing seemed to me very easy to be done. So distinguished was my name, and I possessed such advantages of youth and comeliness, that no matter what woman I might favor with my love, I dreaded rejection of none." Abélard went to live in Fulbert's house as Héloïse's tutor. "Our speech was more of love than of the books which lay open before us; our kisses far outnumbered our reasoned words. . . . I wrote poems. They dealt with love, not with the secrets of philosophy," and they were sung far and wide. After Héloïse gave birth to a son, to make peace with Fulbert Abélard offered to marry her, provided the marriage were kept secret. Despite her protestations that she would not ruin his career by becoming his wife, they were married. When Fulbert broke his word by spreading the news, Héloïse denied it, and entered a nunnery at Argenteuil, near Paris. Outraged at what they thought was Abélard's attempt to get her out of the way, Fulbert and his kinsmen broke into his quarters while he was asleep. "Then they had vengeance on me with a most cruel and most shameful punishment, such as astounded the whole world, for they cut off those parts of my body with which I had done that which was the cause of their sorrow."

If it surprises us to learn that Abélard's reputation suffered little if at all from this ordeal, it is a reflection on us rather than on the twelfth century. Medieval Christianity, not only in its ideals, as we find them portrayed by Dante, but in its practice, as we see in this case, exemplified Christ's own compassion and charity for sins of the flesh. Abélard had sinned grievously and suffered a dreadful punishment (as had also his assailants); he had repented and been forgiven. By that the men of the middle ages meant not only that they believed that God had forgiven him, as we also piously profess, but that they forgave him too: the whole matter had passed out of their hands through the hands of the Church into God's hands, where they thought it belonged, and where they were content to leave it. The sins for which Abélard would have been mercilessly condemned, could the Church and the society of his time have known them as well as his confessor must have and as we know them from himself, were the deadly sins of pride and egotism and selfishness.

After his calamity and the loss of Héloïse he took refuge as a monk in the monastery of St. Denis. But "the abbey . . . was utterly worldly and in its life quite scandalous," and since Abélard was not the man to keep quiet, he soon found himself unwelcome. He sought relief and comfort by returning to Paris to resume his teaching, but a book he wrote on the Trinity brought him into conflict with conservative theologians, who in a council compelled him to cast his book into the flames with his own hand and shut him up in a monastery at Soissons. When released he returned to St. Denis, but this time, when on the authority of the Venerable Bede he presumed to question the identity of the patron saint of the monastery, he was treated with such severity that he escaped to appeal to the civil authorities. He was finally permitted to build himself a hermitage near Troyes, where the usual crowd of students soon gathered about him. When Norbert of Prémontré and Bernard of Clairvaux began to organize a campaign against him, he accepted an offer to become Abbot of St. Gildas in Brittany, where the "vile and untameable way of life" of the monks was "notorious almost everywhere." It was here that he wrote his autobiography. After an unsuccessful ten-year struggle with his monks, whom he accused, among other crimes, of trying to poison him, he returned once more to Paris.

Abélard's monastic career

The closing years of Abélard's life were dominated, as indeed was all western Europe, by St. Bernard. He, with the theologians of the school of the monastery of St. Victor at Paris, was the leader of a conservative party opposed to the whole dialectical method. Mystics whose souls sought God through love alone, who cherished as the most sublime of all experience the ecstatic "swoon into the absolute," could not but detest the chilling blight of the syllogism and the pretentious intellectual audacity that would explain the mysteries of faith by reason. St. Bernard openly expressed his horror of Abélard: "He, the 'scrutinizer of Majesty and fabricator of heresies,' is trying to make void the merit of Christian faith, when he deems himself able by human reason to comprehend God altogether. He ascends to the heavens and descends even to the abyss. Nothing may hide from him in the depths of hell or in the heights above. . . . He sees nothing as an enigma, nothing as in a glass darkly, but looks at everything face to face." [14] Abélard's tolerance of Greek philosophy was just as abhorrent to him. When Abélard professed to believe that there was truth in Plato, that Plato might even know more about the Trinity than Moses, to Bernard this merely proved not so much that Plato was half Christian as that Abélard was more than half pagan. Abélard found, as Arnold of Brescia found,[15] that St. Bernard was an uncompromising opponent. In 1141 he was brought before a council at Sens to answer many charges of false teaching. He might well have defended himself successfully, for even St. Bernard was afraid of so formidable an antagonist, but his proud spirit was broken. He was found guilty, his students said by a drunken council, and condemned to the penalty of silence, for him a penalty of intolerable severity. Bernard took care to have him condemned also at Rome. On his way thither to appeal his case to the pope Abélard was forced by illness to stop at the Abbey of Cluny, near which he died on April 21, 1142.

His body was taken back to his hermitage at Troyes, to which meanwhile he had moved Héloïse and her nuns. Her passionate appeal for some token of their former love he had answered with the cool advice of a brother in Christ and with hymns for her and her sisters to sing. But he had remained true to her memory, and the world that knows little and cares less about Abélard the supreme dialectician has remained true to the memory of the lovers Abélard and Héloïse—more, let us hope, for her sake than for his. At her death many years later she was laid by his side in the same tomb. In 1817

[14] Quoted by Randall, *The Making of the Modern Mind*, p. 94.
[15] See pp. 621–22.

the two bodies were removed to the cemetery of Père Lachaise in Paris, the last refuge of so many great and unhappy men and women.

Abélard's general attitude towards the relation between authority and reason was the reverse of Anselm's: he sought rather to know in order that he might believe (*intelligo ut credam*). He sympathized wholly with his students in their search for rational and philosophical explanations, "asking rather for reasons they could understand than for mere words, saying that it was futile to utter words which the intellect could not possibly follow, that nothing could be believed unless it could first be understood, and that it was absurd for anyone to preach to others a thing which neither he himself nor those whom he sought to teach could comprehend." His answer to the question at issue between realist and nominalist, gleaned from Aristotle, was a sort of compromise, which has been called conceptualism. Universals, he held, are not the only realities, neither are they mere names. Reality is inherent in the world of differentiated particulars, but these have common attributes which the mind conceives after observation and reflection. The name given to these attributes is a concept existing in the mind, and as such is real, even if not possessed of the intrinsic reality that makes particulars real. Thus you and I are real persons and different from each other, but we have attributes that make us very like all other persons at all times and in all places. To group these attributes together under the common term "humanity" is not to give to humanity an objective reality, by virtue of our share of which we are human, but only to establish an intellectual concept valid and real as far as it goes. This common-sense position, whatever may be its logical and philosophical validity, was adopted by the orthodox schoolmen of the thirteenth century, and may be regarded as the official position of the Church.

Abélard's position in the nominalist-realist controversy: conceptualism

In the preface to a work called *Yes and No* (*Sic et Non*) Abélard clearly reveals his general attitude: "We decided to collect the diverse statements of the holy fathers . . . raising an issue from their apparent repugnancy, which might incite the reader to search out the truth of the matter. . . . For the first key to wisdom is called interrogation, diligent and unceasing. . . . By doubting we are led to inquiry; and from inquiry we perceive the truth."

The Sic et Non

In this work Abélard listed certain questions fundamental to theology, on each of which he cited from the Church Fathers contradictory opinions. If, then, an affirmative and a negative answer could be derived from equally good authority, it was plainly impossible to rely on any authority except correct authority. This made it necessary to posit an authority higher than that of the Church Fathers themselves. Such an authority was the revelation of God in the Scriptures. There at last was an authority that no medieval philosopher would have presumed to question. Certainly Abélard, who was always more dialectician than philosopher, had no desire to question it. He would not, he said, become a philosopher if that meant contradicting St. Paul; he would not even become another Aristotle if that meant parting from Christ. Nevertheless, in the *Sic et Non* he made clear what the canonists were already conscious of, the conflicting nature of tradition, and thus pointed out to future theologians their chief task, namely, to reconcile conflicting tradition by means of dialectic. Peter Lombard in his *Four Books of Sentences* did just that: after quoting authority for and against a question, he proceeded to resolve the conflict by the use of logic. The same method was adopted by Gratian in his codification of canon law. Together these men helped to fix the method of the later scholastics, whereby a scholar who was worth anything at all could prove that he was right, not only by citing authorities to support him but by proving that authorities opposed to him were either wrong or only appeared to be opposed to him.

During Abélard's lifetime a series of events was taking place in the intellectual world which, besides making it more difficult than ever to harmonize the conflicting traditions of the Church, opened up an entirely new prospect to western scholars. We have already seen that during the early middle ages Byzantine and Mohammedan scholarship was far superior to anything the Latin west could show. Byzantine scholars preserved ancient Greek literature and did important new work in theology. Saracen scholars were interested chiefly in philosophy, mathematics, and science, in which fields they translated the *The west dis-* chief Greek works and wrote important commentaries and made sig-
covers Greek nificant advances on their own account.[16] In the early twelfth century,
and Arabic assisted by the progress of events in southern Italy, Sicily, and Spain,
learning the western European scholar gave further evidence of his growing maturity by his sudden realization that, compared with the knowledge of Byzantium and Islam, his own was only a child's knowledge. There was available the accumulated wisdom of Greece, Byzantium, and Islam, if only he could get at it, and get at it he must if he were not to remain in childish ignorance. The chief barrier in his way was ignorance of the languages in which these treasures were stored. The knowledge of Greek had well-nigh disappeared in the west, while

[16] See pp. 175 ff.

written Arabic was a new language not yet subject to grammatical rules, besides being the language of the Infidel. Now Greek and Arabic became immediately indispensable tools. The west, however, was too avid to wait until it could learn to use these tools: it sought to have the new learning promptly translated into the familiar Latin language. But it was not easy to find persons qualified to do the translation. Arabic naturally gave more trouble than Greek. Some help could be expected from men in Italy who were obliged to learn Greek or Arabic by the necessities of trade. In the Norman Kingdom of Southern Italy and Sicily a knowledge of Greek, Arabic, and Latin was a political necessity. Western scholars knowing no Arabic went to southern France and Spain in search of translations, only to find there scholars who knew Arabic but not necessarily enough Latin, so that the most ingenious linguistic combinations had to be devised to produce a final translation from Arabic into Latin.

With an enthusiasm that amounted to a mania the work of translation was begun in the second quarter of the twelfth century at the Norman court in Sicily, in Spain, especially at Toledo, and in southern France. By the end of the century most of the important works of Greek philosophy and science—but not Greek literature—and of Mohammedan philosophy and science, together with some of Byzantine theology, were available in Latin translations. Just so soon as the west had access to the new learning, a significant change began to manifest itself in the relationship between eastern and western culture. If before the thirteenth century the east was by all odds superior, that superiority ended after its learning had passed on to the west. Henceforth the current tended to run in the contrary direction, and translations began to be made in the east from Latin into Greek and Hebrew. The fresher intellectual vigor of the west, nourished from the east, joined to its greater economic resourcefulness, likewise fed by the east, carried off the victory, which it has ever since maintained.

We know the names of some of these translators and the spirit in which they worked. The most important of them, the Italian Gerard of Cremona—who spent most of his life in Toledo—before his death at the age of seventy-three had translated at least seventy-one Arabic works into Latin. English, French, German, Italian, Spanish, and Jewish scholars all participated in the exciting treasure hunt. Plato of Tivoli prefaces one of his translations thus: "The Latins . . . have not a single author [in astronomy]; for books they have only follies, dreams and old wives' fables. This is the reason that moved me, Plato

Latin translators and translations from Greek and Arabic

of Tivoli, to enrich our tongue with that which it lacked the most, by drawing upon the treasures of an unknown language." But naturally the translations concern us now more than the translators.

First of all, there were new tools of logic to sharpen the western scholar's wits. In addition to the old logic, Aristotle's *Categories* and *On Interpretation,* there was now made available the new logic, his *Prior and Posterior Analytics, Topics,* and *Sophistical Refutations.* At the same time the rest of his scientific and philosophical treatises, constituting a complete summary of Hellenic science, were translated, notably the *Physics, Metaphysics,* and *On Animals.* His *Ethics, Poetics,* and *Rhetoric* were translated directly from the Greek, unlike the works just mentioned, which were translated from Arabic versions. Thus Aristotle was not only more firmly than ever established as master of logic for the west: his authority in all fields of knowledge was second only to the authority of the Scriptures and the Church; he was "the philosopher," whom Dante called "the master of those who know." With the new Aristotle came the commentaries of Averroës, the great Arabic authority on Aristotle. Of Plato's *Dialogues* the *Meno* and the *Phædo* were added to an older Latin version of part of the *Timæus.* Anyone who would comprehend medieval thought must still know his Aristotle and Plato. From Byzantine theology and hagiography the most notable contribution was a translation of a summary of Greek theology, *The Fount of Knowledge,* by John of Damascus.[17]

But perhaps more important than any of these in the history of western learning were the new translations of Greek and Arabic mathematical and scientific works. For at this time, on these foundations, began the history of that experimental science which is the particular glory and boast of the western world. Arabic numerals, including the zero, were introduced, although they had still to wage a long and stubborn fight to oust the abacus. The algebra and trigonometry of Al-Khwarizmi came to stay for centuries, and Euclid's *Elements of Geometry* came to plague students even longer. Ptolemy's *Almagest,* a summary of the wrong school of Greek astronomy, fixed for the western world the concept of a geocentric universe until Copernicus destroyed it in the sixteenth century. Outranking astronomy proper in interest were Arabic works on astrology, the chief of which, Albumazar's *Introduction to Astrology,* paved the way for the acceptance of astrology by the Church, and for the important

[17] See p. 132.

part it has played ever since in the daily life of man. Translations of Arabic works on alchemy seem to have had no great influence until the fourteenth and fifteenth centuries. In addition to works on optics and perspective and physics in general, the whole corpus of Greek medicine, the works of Hippocrates and Galen, now became available, together with a comprehensive summary of Arabic medicine, Avicenna's *Canon of Medicine*. With large omissions, to be sure, medieval Europe had now inherited no inconsiderable portion of the legacy of four great cultures, Hellenic, Hellenistic, Byzantine, and Arabic.

Just as the early middle ages had to digest the works of the Latin Church Fathers and such classical science as was contained in Pliny's *Natural History*, so the later middle ages had now to assimilate Greek and Arabic learning. The scholar's first task was to read and understand, no mean undertaking when one considers the huge bulk of the new learning and the fact that the best translations were no better than barely adequate. Once all this new material was mastered, it was still another matter to relate it to what the western scholar had hitherto regarded as the truth. *Christianity and the new learning*

By the beginning of the thirteenth century, when the work of translation was practically complete, the Church had already worked out what it took to be the definitive formulation of truth. This was the truth as revealed by God in the Scriptures, preserved in the tradition of the Fathers, and enforced by the system of canon law. The formula was to be found in Peter Lombard's *Sentences* and Gratian's *Decretum*. The pope was charged with the duty of enforcing it. The whole body of new learning now introduced into the west was not Christian at all, but pagan. So far from concerning itself with explaining the mysterious truths of Christianity, it denied certain fundamental tenets of Christian belief, such as personal immortality and the existence of a provident personal god, governing according to his will the world that he had created out of nothing and would in the end destroy, and yet interested in every individual human being. To dabble in unchristian speculation was certainly dangerous; how dangerous the Church had learned from the Albigensian heresy and was at the very moment beginning to teach the Albigensian heretics. Were it not better to rest content with the old learning? Why endanger it with the new? To the eternal credit of the Church and of Christian scholars a liberal rather than a narrow view of the whole situation was taken. Latin literature, learning, and education had been absorbed by the Fathers to the strengthening, not the weakening, of Christianity: the same could be done with Greek and Moslem philosophy and science. All that was necessary was the unquestioning recognition of the pre-eminence of Christian truth.

The work of reconciling what was essentially irreconcilable was undertaken with blithe self-confidence. The result was what is called scholasticism, which we may define as the organization of all knowledge —or, as the medieval scholar would have put it, all science—into one coherent system subordinate to theology. The method of reconciling contradictions, eliminating errors, and bringing the whole into line with God's purpose for the universe, confided to the Scriptures and the Church, was the application of Aristotelian logic as worked out by the logicians of the eleventh and early twelfth centuries.

Scholasticism   In earlier times scholars had a little Aristotle to apply to a limited store of learning. Now they had all Aristotle's logic to apply to a large new body of Greek and Arabic science and philosophy. It was a vast and difficult task that they were attempting, whose magnitude would stagger the most courageous mind and has compelled scholars of later times to dismiss it as impossible. Whereas the contemporary scholar is driven willy-nilly to confine himself to one subject, and to a limited field within that subject, the medieval scholar took all knowledge as his province, and must prepare himself to answer all questions. Since most of the new knowledge came from Aristotle, the new task was to a large extent to Christianize Aristotle. But since much of it came from Plato through Neo-Platonism, which was inherent in much of Arabic philosophy, it was necessary to bring the mysticism of Neo-Platonism into accord with the intellectualism of Aristotle. And since some of it came from the mystic theology of the Byzantines, this had to be harmonized with western theology. All this the scholastic philosophers did to the apparent satisfaction of most of their contemporaries. The characteristic products of their pens were great summaries of knowledge (Latin *summa*, "sum total"). These took the form of a commentary on Peter Lombard's *Sentences*, or a summary of theology (*summa theologiæ*), or an encyclopedia—a mirror, as medieval scholars called it—of doctrine or science (*speculum doctrinale* or *speculum naturale*), or a history of the world from its very creation.

These monumental works of the human mind compel the most unsympathetic student's admiration. "They have an architectonic and imaginative glory of their own, building all the wisdom of the ages bit by bit into the massive walls, cementing the whole together with a beautiful and faultless logic, rising in the towers to a hymn of praise to the Truth that is God." [18] Henry Adams's great work, *Mont-Saint-Michel and Chartres*, begins with Gothic architecture, but then passes on to the architecture whereby the whole medieval world of unseen reality was built, and so ends with Abélard and St. Thomas Aquinas.

Nevertheless, the fact remains that the attempt to rationalize the old Christianity and the new secular learning into a synthetic, coherent whole was dangerous. It was dangerous not merely because it opened the way into fields of thought where Christianity had no jurisdiction, but still more because it led straight to the realization that the attempt in itself was foredoomed to failure. Traditional Christianity and science were not compatible. As early as the twelfth century Adelard of Bath, an English translator from the Arabic and a writer on scientific subjects, says to his nephew: "It is hard to discuss with you, for I have learned one thing from the Arabs under the guidance of reason; you follow another halter, caught by the appearance of authority; for what is authority but a halter?" [19] Christianity was a supernatural revelation, utterly irrational, to be accepted on faith or not at all; science was a matter of reason and experience. Or, as it was sometimes put on the authority of Aristotle, there were two kinds of truth, divergent and unrelated, the truth of religion and the truth of science.

Reason versus faith

Acquaintance with Arabic commentaries on Aristotle, chiefly those of Averroës, in the early thirteenth century produced a group of radical thinkers at the University of Paris called the Averroists, chief of whom was Siger of Brabant, who openly held opinions contrary to Christianity. There were other enthusiastic rationalists, of one of whom, Simon of Tournai, it is reported that, after having magnificently demonstrated the truth of the Trinity, he announced that he could just as incontrovertibly demonstrate its falsity. Amalric of Bena was forced to retract opinions of a pantheistic character; David of Dinant was sentenced to be burned at the stake for similar opinions.

The Church tried repeatedly to prohibit the reading of Averroës and of Aristotle's nonlogical works, but all to no avail. The danger, however, stood revealed with the necessity of removing it by purging secular knowledge. And yet the very men who undertook this task, chief of whom were Albert the Great and Thomas Aquinas, themselves exposed the breach between religion and science. When Albert says that of course God's will rules the universe, but rules it by cer-

---

[18] Randall, *op. cit.*, p. 102.
[19] Quoted by Haskins, *Studies in Mediæval Science*, p. 40.

tain natural causes, he is trying to harmonize religion and science; but when he goes on to say that, while he would not presume to expound the inscrutable will of God, he does intend to investigate these natural causes, the scientist, not the theologian, is speaking. From that position it was easy to forget God entirely. When Thomas Aquinas distinguishes between revealed theology and natural theology or philosophy, he professes with the utmost emphasis the superiority of the former, but he is chiefly concerned with the latter. After that distinction it was easy to forget revealed theology.

Soon men interested chiefly in what we call science began to talk of the necessity of experimentation, or at least of basing knowledge upon experience. By relegating the revealed truth of Christianity to the sacrosanct domain of faith, the scholastic philosophers were clearing the way for an exclusive concern with science. At the same time, by laying aside the book of Christian revelation, the Bible, for Peter Lombard and Aristotle, they were preparing the way, once their own synthetic harmonies were proved illusory, for a return to the Scriptures. Thus the European stage was set for the Protestant reformation and for the open conflict between religion and science that followed it, which has continued to our own day. For reasons diametrically opposed to theirs St. Bernard four hundred years before them agreed with the men of the renaissance "that the scholastic method was false and mischievous, and that the longer it was followed, the greater was its mischief." [20] And what St. Bernard rejected because it was not faith the modern world rejects because it is not science.

Albertus Magnus

The man who did most to make the new translations of Aristotle intelligible and began the labor of Christianizing him was the prolific German scholar usually called by his Latin name, Albertus Magnus, Albert the Great, perhaps the only scholar—oddly enough —whom posterity has thought worthy to join the procession of Alexander, Gregory, Charles, and all the other Greats. He was born a Swabian count in 1193, when almost all of Aristotle had been translated. After joining the Dominicans he pursued an active career as teacher and scholar in various German towns, especially at Cologne, and at the University of Paris. In addition he somehow found time for practical tasks: he was provincial of his order and Bishop of Regensburg, although we are told that he did not fancy the life of a German bishop because it demanded such constant use of the sword. He outlived his most famous pupil, Thomas Aquinas, and before his death in 1280 had published no fewer than twenty-one folio volumes.

[20] Adams, *Mont-Saint-Michel and Chartres*, p. 315.

In Albert, after long centuries of training, a German became at last the intellectual master of the west. He took as his special task the writing of commentaries on all the works that Aristotle ever wrote, and of new works on subjects that Aristotle had planned to treat, or should have included to complete his scheme of knowledge. Actually Albert's writings are not so much commentaries on the text of Aristotle as, like Avicenna's, paraphrases of Aristotle, wherein, however, all that is specifically unchristian is expunged or explained away. The titles of many of his works, accordingly, duplicate those of Aristotle—*Physics, Concerning the Soul, Concerning Meteors, Concerning Heaven and Earth, The Causes and Creation of the Universe, The Causes and Properties of the Elements and Planets*—not to mention extensive works on geography, botany, and zoology. So universal were his interests and so wide his learning in other Greek philosophers and in Jewish and Arabic thought that he became for the thirteenth century the authority *par excellence*. He was known as the Universal Doctor, quoted beside Aristotle himself, and even by so grudging a critic as the Englishman Roger Bacon granted a place in the front rank. Not only was he the chief influence in the life of his pupil Thomas Aquinas, but by his acquaintance with and sympathy for the writings of the Greek mystics he became, through his pupil Ulrich of Strassburg, the founder of the important school of German mystics in the Rhineland in the fourteenth and fifteenth centuries.

Albert was no mere reworker of ancient material. Acquaintance with the new world of Greek and Arabic science made him aware of the necessity of testing this very science by experience, personal observation, and experiment. No one who knows him can say, as it has been so long the custom to say, that the medieval scholar was only the credulous slave of authority. On the contrary, not even under the staggering mass of new learning that the thirteenth-century scholar had to master did Albert lose contact with the actual world about him. All his critical faculties were rather stimulated to a kind of activity that may properly be called scientific, or even experimental. *Albert's scientific attitude*

He was always testing authority by experience. "This," he says in one instance, "has not been sufficiently proved by certain experience, like the other facts which are written here, but is found in the writings of the ancients." Or again: "We pass over what the ancients have written on this topic because their statements do not agree with experience." Some of his sources he brands as mere stories, "read in story-books rather than proved philosophically by experience," or as only assertions "not based on experience" by "men of no great authority." "These philosophers," he remarks, "tell many lies, and I think this is one of their lies." In his book on animals he says that he is going to tell "what he knows by reason and what he sees by experience of the nature of animals." He advises falconers not to pay too much attention to Frederick II's advice in his book on falcons, for "experience is the best teacher in all matters of this sort." He cannot believe that ostriches eat iron, because when he offered them iron they would not take it. In his book on plants he says: "We satisfy the curiosity of our students rather than philosophy, for philosophy cannot deal with particulars." In fact, he defines natural science "as not simply receiving what one is told, but the investigation of causes in natural phenomena." [21]

In the thirteenth century what more could fairly be expected? If for all that Albert and his colleagues still seem to us credulous, theirs is the credulity of minds not yet thoroughly disciplined. Some of the theories of contemporary scientists may appear to be only twentieth-century superstitions to scholars of 2500; for that matter, there are eminent scientists of today who seem to some people to have confused science with theology. If to his great service in rendering Aristotle intelligible to the west we add the contributions based on his own observation and experience found in all his works on natural science, it is difficult to overestimate the importance of Albertus Magnus to the philosophy and science of the Europe that was to come.

Thomas Aquinas

The work of Albert's pupil Thomas Aquinas was in a sense clearly marked out for him by the accomplishment of his teacher, by the heretical tendencies of the Averroists in Paris, and by the protests of the Obscurantists. Much as Albert had done, there was still much to do. His paraphrases of Aristotle's various works needed to be organized into a comprehensive system of knowledge. Moreover, it was becoming clear that, to say nothing of the need for better translations of Aristotle direct from the Greek, there was need for a commentary from the Christian point of view on the actual texts of his works, analogous to the commentaries of Averroës, such as Albert had not undertaken. Meanwhile the Averroists were following Aristotle and Averroës so slavishly that they ignored certain fundamental teachings of Christianity. This danger the Obscurantists would meet by limiting the field of scholarship to the truth of divine revelation and Christian tradition, barring all dealings with the newly discovered Greek and Arabic philosophy.

[21] The quotations are from Thorndike, *A History of Magic and Experimental Science*, II, c. 59.

Thomas was born in Frederick II's Kingdom of Southern Italy and Sicily, at Aquino, near Monte Cassino, where he studied as a youth. "His father, Count of Aquino, claimed descent from the imperial line of Swabia; his mother, from the Norman princes of Sicily; so that in him the two most energetic strains of Europe met." After attending the University of Naples, rather than enter Frederick's service he joined the new Dominican Order, and betook himself to Cologne to study with Albertus Magnus. He followed him to Paris, where he took his degree and was teaching at the university as a full professor by the time he was twenty-five. Later he was in great demand as a teacher in Italy; he acted as adviser to the papacy, and spent his last days in Naples reorganizing the university for Charles of Anjou. He died around his fiftieth year, in 1274, leaving seventeen folio volumes of works.

Thomas Aquinas refused to listen, as his teacher had refused to listen, to the protests of the Obscurantists against the study of Aristotle and Arabic science. His general attitude towards secular learning in relation to Christian dogma was therefore liberal. It must be possible, he held, for faith and reason to agree; that was, in fact, the great Christian tradition. In particular it must be possible to show that secular learning in its Greek and Arabic forms was not inconsonant with the truths of Christianity, and that the interpretations of the Averroists were based on faulty or incomplete understanding of Aristotle. To demonstrate the strict compatibility between divine and human knowledge Thomas adopted the already suggested distinction between revealed theology and natural theology, or philosophy. Revealed theology comes from God, who is first cause and prime mover of all things, the very embodiment of all truth, whose will governs the universe and man. Natural theology, or philosophy, is the product of reason acting upon the evidence of the senses. Its chief purpose is to make plain God's dealings with the world of men and things governed by him. Theology and philosophy are equally valid, each in its own sphere; they are not independent, nor do they contradict each other; they are interdependent and supplement each other. Spiritual wisdom from above, accepted when necessary by faith, illumines the wisdom from below; rational wisdom from below strives to attain intellectual comprehension of the truth revealed from God. Never on earth can these two fuse; only in heaven, inhabited by angels, saints, and the souls of the saved, can the ultimate bliss of man be achieved, where the intellectual vision blended with faith shall behold, believe, understand, and love, and so become part of the daz-

Theology and philosophy as conceived by Thomas Aquinas

zling radiance that is God. Here we find traditional Christianity and uncompromising Aristotelian rationalism bound together by the mysticism of Neo-Platonism as Christianized by St. Augustine. All earlier modes of thought and feeling were grasped by the capacious mind of St. Thomas Aquinas, and wrought by his logic into one mighty system of order and balance.

The two works in which Aquinas most fully elaborated his system are the *Summa contra Gentiles* (*Summary against the Gentiles*), directed against the Averroists, and the *Summa Theologiæ* (*Summary of Theology*). The *Summary of Theology*, the most popular of all such works ever produced, quickly supplanted Peter Lombard's *Sentences*, and is still an authoritative statement of Catholic doctrine. Its first and third parts treat of the whole Christian drama of salvation, with due emphasis on the sacramental system; the second part is the most elaborate treatment of ethics that Christianity had thus far produced. In it Thomas makes clear his method:

The Summa
Theologiæ

"As other sciences do not argue in support of their principles, but from these principles go on to prove other things, so this doctrine does not argue in support of its principles, which are the articles of faith, but from them goes on to prove something else. . . . In this doctrine it is particularly fitting to argue from authority, for its principles are given by revelation, and hence should be believed as the authority of those to whom the revelation was made. Neither does this detract from the dignity of the doctrine, for although an argument from authority based on human reason is very weak, an argument from authority based on divine revelation is most efficacious." [22]

It must, however, be repeated that, aside from this particular attitude towards revelation, Aquinas in his use of Aristotle or any other human authority is never uncritically blind. He emphasizes again and again the necessity for good authority, and justifies his use of it on the ground that anybody who presumes to write on any subject must, if he is worthy of his hire, first find out what other distinguished authors have said on the same subject. What more can any good scholar or scientist do today?

The three parts of the *Summa Theologiæ* are divided into thirty-eight sections, in which St. Thomas poses six hundred and thirty-one questions. By quotation from authority and by the use of the syllogism he then supplies an answer to each. This is followed by a series

[22] Quoted in McGiffert, *op. cit.*, II, 277.

of quotations and syllogisms setting forth the contrary opinion. A harmonizing conclusion is then worked out, chiefly on the authority of St. Augustine or Aristotle, and further objections to this final conclusion are then disposed of in the same way. In the *Summa Theologiæ* St. Thomas answers some ten thousand objections to his conclusions. The student, if he thinks he has a philosophy, may like to see whether he is intellectually ingenious enough to think up ten thousand objections to it, and then honestly dispose of them to his satisfaction.

In the *Summa contra Gentiles* St. Thomas works out the relationship between revealed theology and philosophy. His success in discrediting the Averroists was a favorite subject of medieval art. His supreme achievement in erecting a mighty edifice of the Faith in the *Summa Theologiæ* won for him the title of the Angelic Doctor. But his triumph was not immediate. The Franciscans were long forbidden to read his works, and even among his fellow Dominicans, not to say among the secular clergy, there was much criticism of his bold rationalism. In the end his good sense, his good manners, his clear style based on clear thought, and his orderly exposition made him the one authoritative teacher. In 1328 he was made a saint; as the pope put it, every article that he wrote was a miracle. For all that, Thomas Aquinas was no more than his teacher Albertus Magnus a mere theologian. Like all medieval scholars, he was universal in his interests. After his death the Dominicans at Paris wrote to the Dominicans at Naples that they would like to have the manuscript that he had begun on mechanical engineering. He was responsible for stimulating the translation of Aristotle directly from the Greek, and may have used the new translations for his own commentaries. What Innocent III meant in thirteenth-century politics Thomas Aquinas meant for thirteenth-century scholarship; and more, for the great pope's work was less enduring than the great scholar's. Huxley, the eminent scientist and agnostic, wrote of him six hundred years later: "His marvelous grasp and subtlety of intellect seem to me to be almost without parallel."

By distinguishing between theology and philosophy the two Dominican friars, Albert and Thomas, cleared the ground for the development of western philosophy, and, together with other scholars, created the technical vocabulary necessary for it, "powerful, precise language, the remnants of which, blunted, dulled and broadened by long and varied usage, are still the center of the philosophic idiom." [23]

The works of Thomas Aquinas

[23] McKeon, *Selections from Medieval Philosophers*, II, xviii.

While the Dominicans were pointing the way in philosophy, their rivals the Franciscans in similar fashion were pointing to a new development in science. To say nothing of the anomaly of finding Franciscans so soon after their founder's death interested in such things, it is still more paradoxical that their philosophical background was Neo-Platonism as transformed by St. Augustine. Being interested rather in adapting Aristotle to Platonism than the reverse, they were inclined to emphasize the mystical approach to an understanding of God and his relation to the world of particulars. On the continent the French Franciscan Alexander of Hales, who died in 1245, in his *Summa Universæ Theologiæ (Summary of Universal Theology)* had been the first scholar to utilize the new Aristotelian learning in a comprehensive work. The general of the Franciscan Order, the Italian John of Fidanza, better known as St. Bonaventura, who died in the same year as Thomas Aquinas, was continually objecting to Thomas's partiality for Aristotle over St. Augustine.

As further evidence of the renewed interest in science we may briefly note the Encyclopedists, the thirteenth-century successors of *The Encyclo-pedists* Isidore of Seville and Rabanus Maurus.[24] In a work called *On the Nature of Things*, written at the beginning of the century by Alexander of Neckam, an English abbot of the Augustinian Order, we find "perhaps the earliest references to the mariner's compass and to glass mirrors." The English Franciscan Bartholomew later in the century wrote a book *On the Properties of Things*, in the course of which, while ostensibly making clear scriptural allusions, he so far forgets himself as to discourse charmingly on the nature of the cat. The most notable of the Encyclopedists, however, was the French Dominican, Vincent of Beauvais, a contemporary of Thomas Aquinas. His *Speculum Maius (Larger Mirror)*, in some six thousand folio pages, included much of the new scientific material brought in from Spain. In addition to the older sources of encyclopedic learning, Pliny and Isidore, he cites Aristotle, Albumazar, Avicenna, and Averroës, as well as Albertus Magnus. For a picture of the state of western scientific learning in the thirteenth century one can hardly do better than turn to Vincent, whose long popular work supplied information to medieval sculptors and furnished Chaucer a good deal of his medical lore.

The Franciscans at the University of Oxford were strictly concerned with scientific problems, and launched a critical movement of great import against contemporary scholarship. They talked about and

24 See pp. 255–56.

practiced an "experimental science" of whose implications they were only dimly aware, although they did emphasize its utility in conquering the world of nature for man. The scientific preoccupations of the Oxford school are a good illustration of the way in which, by their search for an understanding of God in his government of the universe, medieval scholars were led directly to an investigation of the universe itself. The leaders of the school were especially interested in mathematics. "The effect of the application of mathematics was so to turn the search for God in things to the elucidation of things that the inquiry for God was to inspire the first systematic experimental investigation of things." The two outstanding members of the school were Robert Grosseteste, who became Bishop of Lincoln and died in 1253, and Roger Bacon.

It is now recognized that Grosseteste, as Bacon acknowledged, was responsible for the critical bent of the whole school. For authority he *Robert* turned not to Peter Lombard but back to the original sources of *Grosseteste* Christianity in the Scriptures, the writings of the apostolic period, and the earliest Fathers of the Church. Thereby he helped to prepare the way for the later Christian humanism that did its part in undermining the foundations of traditional faith.[25] Grosseteste stressed the importance of consulting documents in the original language, or at least in reliable direct translation. He himself knew Greek and translated many works, including those of the mystic Pseudo-Dionysius and of the Byzantine theologian John of Damascus and many of Aristotle. There seems, however, to be no evidence for his knowing Hebrew. In addition to mathematics and philology Grosseteste had an absorbing interest in astronomy and in physical problems of every sort, optics, perspective, color, heat, and sound. These interests he passed on to his pupils, chief of whom was Roger Bacon.

Of Bacon's life not much is certain; he was a Franciscan, who studied at both Oxford and Paris and died in 1292. He seems to have been repeatedly censured by his order and finally imprisoned for suspected novelties in his teaching, although at one time in his life his writings were sought by the pope himself. No more than any other thirteenth-century writer did he question the validity of Christian revelation or the authority of the Scriptures or the Church. At all times he agreed with *Roger Bacon's* his contemporaries that all knowledge, including strictly scientific *criticism* knowledge, must contribute to the glory of the queen of sciences, theology. Moreover, the originality that has long been attributed to him has been rather severely impugned of late. Nevertheless, it must be ad-

[25] See pp. 1016–17.

mitted that in Bacon's chief writings, the *Opus Maius* (the *Greater Treatise*), the *Opus Minus* (the *Lesser Treatise*), and the *Opus Tertium* (the *Third Treatise*), there is a fierce zeal for the advancement of knowledge, a harsh criticism of contemporary scholars and their methods, a staunch pleading for a new experimental science, which are certainly novel in emphasis and mark Roger Bacon as a queer and contradictory sort of genius, who, despite the confusion of his thought, was struggling for a new method and thereby heralded a far-distant dawn.

"There are," he said, "four principal stumbling blocks to comprehending truth, which hinder well-nigh every scholar: the example of frail and unworthy authority, long-established custom, the sense of the ignorant crowd, and the hiding of one's own ignorance under the show of wisdom." Among the "seven . . . vices of the chief study, which is theology," he counted theologians' ignorance of what is most germane to their studies. "I refer to the grammar of the foreign tongues from which all theology comes. Of even more value are mathematics, optics, moral science, experimental science and alchemy." If that seems even to us a strange list for a theologian's use, what must it have seemed to theologians of Bacon's own time? "The text of Scripture is horribly corrupt in the Vulgate copy at Paris," he remarks, but anyway "they study and lecture on the Sentences of the Lombard instead of the text of Scripture; . . . any one who would lecture on Scripture has to beg for a room and hour to be set him." He speaks of boy theologians at Paris, and deplores the lack of decent teachers; he boasts that he could impart more real geometry in a fortnight than ordinary teachers of mathematics do in ten or even twenty years. Contemporary writings on medicine were just as bad; they contained thirty-six "great and radical defects with infinite ramifications." Like too many scholars, Bacon was possessed of an unpleasant vanity, which when coupled with his honest despair over most of what he saw about him, made him sparing of his precious praise for anybody or anything. He did not, however, stop with criticism; he wrote grammars of Greek and Hebrew, and planned one for Arabic.

Beyond even such genuine sciences as mathematics and optics "is one more perfect than all, which all serve and which in a wonderful way certifies them all: this is called the experimental science, which neglects arguments, since they do not make certain, however strong they may be, unless at the same time there is present the *experientia* of the conclusions. Experimental science teaches *experiri*, that is, to test by observation and experiment the lofty conclusions of all sciences." "There

Bacon and experimental science

are two modes of arriving at knowledge, to wit, argument and *experimentum*. Argument draws a conclusion and forces us to concede it, but does not make it certain or remove doubt, so that the mind may rest in the perception of truth, unless the mind find truth by the way of experience." "Because, although we know through three means, authority, reason and *experientia*, yet authority is not wise unless its reason be given, nor does it give knowledge, but belief. . . . Nor can reason distinguish sophistry from demonstration unless we know that the conclusion is attested by facts." [26]

The fact that Bacon conceived of experiment as a separate science rather than as a method applicable to any science is of no importance. We know that he was not the first medieval scholar to recognize the importance of experience to test authority. For that matter, neither was Albertus Magnus the first; in the eleventh century an English prior sought to determine the difference in time between Italy and England by comparing the time at which he noticed an eclipse in Italy with the time at which it was noted at home. But Roger Bacon does appear to have been the first to glimpse the unlimited possibilities of science specifically applied to the conquest of nature for man's use. Nor was he a mere theorist: he undoubtedly performed some experiments himself. His writings on optics were authoritative for centuries, and he may well have had a compound system of lenses in the form of a primitive microscope or telescope. He shared his master Grosseteste's interest in astronomy, which in time took the practical turn of advocating a reform of the calendar. He has been called the first systematic geographer of the middle ages, who definitely influenced the theories underlying subsequent exploration. He was much interested in mechanics, and writes of "machines for navigating . . . without rowers, so that great ships suited to river or ocean, guided by one man, may be borne with greater speed than if they were full of men. Likewise cars may be made so that without a draught animal they may be moved with unthinkable speed. . . . And flying machines are possible, so that a man may sit in the middle turning some device by which artificial wings may beat in the air in the manner of a flying bird." He possessed in cipher a description of the composition and manufacture of a gunpowder, which he may have discovered for himself (much of his information he preferred to secrete in cipher).

But whatever else Roger Bacon may have done, it was enough—and in any event his greatest achievement—to have insisted that theology

[26] Quotations from Taylor, *The Medieval Mind*, II, 532 *et passim*.

needs a wide and deep foundation of knowledge of the world in which men live; that observation and experiment are the basis of science; and that science should be useful to man and subservient to the principles of morality. That last point, almost any medieval scholar would have said, is the most important of all. And indeed, who can look out upon the world today without asking himself how great a blessing science will turn out to be if it is subservient to no principles but its own, and ceasing to be merely man's servant threatens to become his master, because man is not morally equipped to use wisely what he is scientifically equipped to discover and invent? Just how far wrong on that point, one wonders, were Roger Bacon and the men of his time?

Science at Frederick II's court

Medieval science seemed to flourish best where there was Norman blood. While the Franciscans were working in England, the second important scientific center was the court of Frederick II in southern Italy and Sicily. Already in the twelfth century King Roger had been especially interested in geography; he had experienced travelers summoned to his court from all quarters whose information he had embodied in a silver map and in a volume of description that he had the Moslem Edrisi compile to go with it. During the same century a Greek translator at the Sicilian court observed the volcanic action of Mt. Etna at close quarters. Roger's successors encouraged translations from Greek mathematical and astronomical treatises. The official court philosophers or astrologers at Frederick II's court were Michael Scot and Master Theodore. Michael was born in Scotland, studied in Spain, translated works of Aristotle and Averroës's commentaries, came to Italy (where for a while he was patronized by the papacy), and then entered Frederick's service. For him he not only acted as official interpreter of the stars, but wrote on many scientific subjects, including zoology, meteorology, and volcanic action in the Lipari Islands. Master Theodore, who brought eastern learning to the Sicilian court, is reputed to have been sent to Frederick by the Sultan of Egypt; he acted as one of Frederick's Arabic secretaries, prepared prescriptions for the imperial household, and wrote on hygiene and the care of falcons and dogs. With Frederick's court the mathematician Leonard of Pisa, the outstanding Italian scientist of the thirteenth century, was in close touch, and the emperor was equally liberal in encouraging Mohammedan and Jewish scholars. All this activity was dominated by the eager and curious mind of Stupor Mundi, the astounding emperor himself. He sent inquiries to Asia Minor, Egypt, Arabia, Morocco, and Spain touching on important religious, philosophical, and scientific questions. To Michael Scot he wrote:

"My dearest master, we have often and in divers ways listened to questions and solutions from one and another concerning the heavenly bodies, that is the sun, moon and fixed stars, the elements, the soul of the world, peoples pagan and Christian, and other creatures above and on the earth, such as plants and metals; yet we have heard nothing respecting those secrets which pertain to the delight of the spirit and the wisdom thereof, such as paradise, purgatory, hell, and the foundations and marvels of the earth. Wherefore we pray you, by your love of knowledge and the reverence you bear our crown, explain to us the foundations of the earth, that is to say, how it is established over the abyss and how the abyss stands beneath the earth, and whether there is anything else than air and water which supports the earth, and whether it stands of itself or rests on the heavens beneath it. Also how many heavens there are and who are their rulers and principal inhabitants, and exactly how far one heaven is from another, and by how much one is greater than another, and what is beyond the last heaven if there are several; and in which heaven God is in the person of His divine majesty and saints, and what these continually do before God." [27]

Frederick II had a superior and well-trained mind with a definite bent for experiment. His reputation as a performer of extraordinary *Frederick* experiments quickly developed into a legend, of which Haskins cites *as scientist* numerous examples.

"There is the story of the man whom Frederick shut up in a wine-cask to prove that the soul died with the body, and the two men whom he disemboweled in order to show the respective effects of sleep and exercise on digestion. There were the children whom he caused to be brought up in silence, in order to settle the question 'whether they would speak Hebrew, which was the first language, or Greek or Latin or Arabic, or at least the language of their parents; but he labored in vain, for the children all died.' There was the diver Nicholas, surnamed the Fish, hero of Schiller's *Der Taucher,* whom he sent repeatedly to explore the watery fastnesses of Scylla and Charybdis, and the memory of whose exploits was handed on by the Friars Minor of Messina, not to mention the 'other superstitions and curiosities and maledictions and incredulities and perversities and abuses' which the friar of Parma had set down in another chronicle now lost. Such again was the story of the great pike brought to the Elector Palatine in 1497, in its gills a copper ring placed there by Frederick to test the longevity of fish, and still bearing the inscription in Greek, 'I am that fish which

[27] Haskins, *op. cit.,* p. 262.

Emperor Frederick II placed in this lake with his own hand the fifth day of October, 1230.' On another occasion Frederick is said to have sent messengers to Norway in order to verify the existence of a spring which turned to stone garments and other objects immersed therein. According to Albertus Magnus, Frederick had a magnet which instead of attracting iron was drawn to it." [28]

When the emperor heard that in Egypt the eggs of ostriches were hatched in the sun, he tried out the same method on hen's eggs in Apulia. His traveling menagerie delighted Italy and Germany. He was responsible for the first western work on veterinary medicine, written by one of his officials, Giordano Ruffo, on the diseases of the horse. Before taking his army east on his crusade he had Adam of Cremona write a work on the hygiene of a crusading army. Before he left he had to recuperate at the medicinal springs at Pozzuoli, about which he was extremely curious. And when he finally got started, he took along with him a master of dialectic. About his own diet and person he was scrupulous; "his Sunday bath was the cause of much scandal to good Christians."

Frederick as author   Frederick II was not only investigator and experimenter but also an author in his own right. His book *On the Art of Hunting with Falcons* was no mere practical treatise but a definite contribution to zoology, much of whose information has not yet been superseded. He wrote as one who had acquired his knowledge at first hand by observation and experiment, and at great expense. No medieval scholar would have presumed to ignore Aristotle, but Frederick is one of the considerable number who made bold to criticize him in details. "We have followed Aristotle," he writes, "where necessary, but we have learned from experience that he appears frequently to deviate from the truth, especially in writing of the nature of certain birds. We have therefore not followed this Prince of philosophers in everything . . . for Aristotle seldom or never hunted with birds, while we have ever loved and practiced hawking." The scientific traditions of his father's court were maintained by Manfred for the few years of his power. In many ways Frederick stands out as much more strictly scientific in his attitude than Roger Bacon. He is the only emperor whom Dante, that passionate Ghibelline, could bear to consign to hell, but there he had to go for following the Epicureans in denying the immortality of the soul. Perhaps now, after all that we have been saying about science, we should conclude with a word of warning, lest the student be deceived by these

[28] *Ibid.*

striking anticipations of the future by a few great men, which were still immeasurably far from making the twelfth and thirteenth centuries an era of what we today should call scientific method. But what immediately follows should be sufficient warning in itself.

Astronomy, which before the introduction of Arabic astronomy and astrology was concerned primarily with the Church calendar, merged with astrology as the Church gradually abandoned the hostility towards astrology that it had acquired during the late classical period. It was *Astrology* now willing to accept the influence of the stars on human affairs just so long as it did not interfere with the will of God and the free will of man. That might seem to be a difficult trio of influences and wills to reconcile, but St. Thomas Aquinas did it nicely, though only by denying to astrology its most popular function. "The majority of men," he says, "are governed by their passions, which are dependent upon bodily appetites: in these the influence of the stars is clearly felt. . . . Astrologers consequently, are able to foretell the truth in the majority of cases, especially when they undertake general predictions. . . . [But] nothing prevents a man from resisting the dictates of his lower faculties. . . . If any one employs the observation of the stars for predicting fortuitous events, or such as happen by chance, or even for predicting with certainty a man's future actions, he does so falsely. In this sort of prophecy the activity of demons is called into play." [29] In the thirteenth century Italian universities had professors of astrology. For at least three centuries after that it maintained its authority little if at all impaired. Nor can the medieval astronomer be charged with inventing it; he had it on the good authority of Aristotle and of later Græco-Roman and Mohammedan learning. Some aspects of modern science may well appear to the eyes of the future as astrology appears to us. Or rather, to most of us: for there are plenty of troubled souls today who still turn to it for enlightenment; indeed, if the number of individuals who today make their living as astrologers could be known, it would doubtless shock the few astronomers who gaze through huge telescopes into limitless space, seeking no answer and finding none to the riddle of human existence.

Alchemy, which stood in the same relation to chemistry as astrology *Alchemy* to astronomy, was likewise an inheritance from the past, but contained *and magic* a smaller proportion of sheer nonsense. Just how absurd, in fact, should the alchemist's dream of transmuting baser metals into gold seem to scientists who, after laughing at alchemy for a few centuries, are now beginning to make successful experiments in transforming one element

[29] Quoted by Wedel, *The Mediæval Attitude toward Astrology*, p. 69.

into another, which we have so long believed on their authority cannot be done? Where, after all, is the line to be drawn between the observations of the astrologer and the astronomer, between the experiments of the alchemist and the chemist? Like the common magician, with whom the Church would never make peace, the astrologer and alchemist prided themselves on being able to do things, to help people through difficulties; theirs was pure and applied science in one. As for magic, it was so uniformly associated with experiment that Thorndike suggests that medieval natural science may well have borrowed the very idea of experimentation from the magicians. Certainly magic, if an apparent contradiction in terms be allowed, became more scientific during the middle ages. Nowadays it has learned to parrot the language of science so well that in its most popular form, fake medical lore, especially when it reaches us by the magical means of the radio, we lap it up, being just as determined as all our forefathers have been to believe all the magic we can.

Frederick II reduced the University of Salerno to a state medical school, and ordered that at the University of Naples three years of logic should precede the study of medicine. Like all other sciences, medicine was studied by the scholastic method from texts of Hippocrates, Galen, and Avicenna. But what authority can long keep the alert physician from experiment? Before dissection of the human body was possible medieval physicians dissected animals. At Bologna, where *Medicine* public dissection of the human body was first practiced, there was a surgical school as early as the end of the twelfth century. Thence its

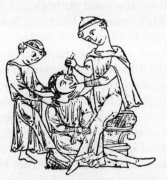

"Couching" for a cataract

traditions were carried across the Alps to Montpellier. Standard works on anatomy and surgery were produced in the fourteenth century. In fact, if we may believe an old story, there was one monk in the monastery of St. Gall in the tenth century who could not be fooled on an analysis of urine. Medieval doctors used a narcotic inhalation for anesthesia. The modern hospital profits from the experience of the medieval hospital, of which it is the direct outgrowth. Experience with leprosy and the plague led to public regulations to prevent the spread of what were already recognized to be contagious diseases, which could be handled only by isolation. The modern quarantine, in practice as well as in name, we owe to the middle ages.

The middle ages understood the use of the lens. Roger Bacon described it as a "useful instrument for the old who have impaired eyesight"; and about 1300 someone wrote: "When the reader who looks at the writing of any book, however difficult it may seem to read to the naked eye, uses a lens, the letters appear greater, so that even the old can read with ease." Medieval scientists developed the technique of distillation, by which they produced pure alcohol; they produced also many acids and alkalis and some explosive agents, including gunpowder. They knew almost every remedy in the pharmacopœia of the days before modern chemistry. Everywhere—in the home, on the farm, in the workshop, at sea—improvements and inventions were introduced: chimney flues, windowpanes, clocks, windmills, the rudder, the mariner's compass, and in the late middle ages the printing press [30] and the spinning wheel. Their greatest handicap was poor technique; lacking instruments of precision, themselves the result of great accumulation of scientific knowledge, they did all they could with such tools as they had. *Inventions*

We may smile at the shortcomings and failures of medieval scientists if we do not forget our debt to them. If they had done no more than preserve the heritage of Græco-Roman science they would have done enough to earn the lasting gratitude of all scholars. It is safe to say in particular that without their translations some important Arabic scientific works would certainly have been lost to Europe, for the Church never put the seal of its unqualified approval upon Arabic learning as it more or less did, without inquiring too carefully into the contents, upon anything written in Greek or Latin. It is to the middle ages that we owe our system of arithmetical notation, based upon the Arabic zero. Medieval scientists inherited many of their errors from their predecessors, so that if we wish to indulge in the pleasure of laughing at them, as has long been the fashion, we should laugh also at the Greeks and the Romans and the Arabs, which has not been so fashionable. For example, what perhaps seems to us their most glaring error, their geocentric *The significance of medieval science*

[30] See pp. 1033 ff.

astronomy, was not their original error at all: the choice between the right system and Ptolemy's wrong system was made for them in ancient times. Even so, none of them believed that the earth was flat. The sifting of the true from the false in our inheritance is for us an extremely slow and difficult process, never quite complete, and it was so for the men of the middle ages. Finally, when we consider the entrenched forces of religious conservatism against which, more than their predecessors or their successors, medieval scientists had to contend, we can only marvel that they were able to make the beginning that they did. An American scholar says of them:

"Crude, naïve beginners they were in many respects, yet they show an interest in nature and its problems; they are drawing the line between science and religion; they make some progress in mathematics, geography, physics and chemistry; they not only talk about experimental method, they actually make some inventions and discoveries of use in the future advance of science. Moreover, they feel themselves that they are making progress. They do not hesitate to disagree with their ancient authorities, when they know something better. . . . Magic still lingers, but the march of modern science has begun." [31]

Most of the controversy engendered by the expansion of western Europe's knowledge in the twelfth century took place within a new institution called into being by that same new knowledge, the university. Of all the institutions handed down to us from the middle ages, the Catholic Church alone excepted, this is perhaps the one that has changed the least, at any rate in so far as organization is concerned. The university (Latin, *universitas*, which originally meant the whole body of teachers and students), headed by a chancellor (*cancellarius*) and divided into colleges (*collegia*), administered by deans (*decani*) or rectors, in which a faculty presents a definite curriculum at fixed hours to a group of students who take academic degrees, goes back at least to the twelfth and early thirteenth centuries. We have, of course, inherited much more than this and, for good or for evil, added still more.

Other influences than the new learning favored the growth of the earliest universities. The heresy of the twelfth century seemed to call for some kind of institution where large numbers of students could be trained to defend the organization and dogma of the Church. By this time the Church had developed into a huge centralized organization, which needed lawyers for its courts, and for its chancelleries men

Factors in the rise of the universities

[31] Thorndike, *op. cit.*, II, 979.

The intricate fan vaulting of late English Gothic in the chapel of Henry VII at Westminster Abbey

The severe nave of the Cathedral of Meissen

The nave of Chartres from the choir to the façade

The nave of Coutances looking towards the apse

Perpendicular Gothic at Lincoln

U &

York Minster

trained in the intricacies of correspondence and of drawing up proper documents. By this time, too, feudal nobles of the larger principalities and feudal kings had gone so far in organizing their states as to need a new group of civil servants trained especially in the law and in the use of the Latin language. The fast-growing towns had the same needs. To meet these needs the scholarship of the twelfth century proved to be well adapted. Peter Lombard in his *Sentences* had written a suitable textbook for the study of theology. Gratian with his *Decretum* had produced a convenient compendium for the study of canon law. The discovery of the *Corpus Iuris Civilis* led to a revival of the study of Roman law,[32] in which the new civil servants of centralized absolute monarchy could be trained. The new translations of Greek and Moslem medical works opened up to laymen a profession hitherto manned chiefly by monks. The new Aristotle and the new science gave fresh impetus and hope to the career of the scholar.

Before the actual emergence of the universities as distinct corporations education had been largely supplied by monastic and cathedral schools. To be sure, some simple religious instruction had been given in the villages by parish priests or clerks. The workshops of the masters in the gilds furnished education in the trades, and a few rudiments besides. Feudal courts provided a definite type of secular education for the boy and the girl from the castle. But generally formal training in the ABC's was limited to those who intended to enter the Church in one capacity or another. For the ordinary nobleman it was no more necessary than for the peasant and the workman. Hence it was that such educated civil servants as were needed in the earlier middle ages had to be drawn from the clergy, the only literate class. While the monastery and cathedral schools were well able to take care of the training of candidates for the regular or secular clergy and of the few laymen who wanted an education, they were in no position to meet the demands of crowds of students for education in the new professions and the new philosophy. Moreover, with mighty waves of reform sweeping over them in the eleventh and early twelfth centuries, the monasteries had tended to concern themselves somewhat less with education *per se* and rather more with the harder way of salvation. Consequently, during the same period it fell to the schools attached to the cathedrals to supplant them, and they rose correspondingly in importance. The most notable of the cathedral schools during this period were at Canterbury, Laon, Rheims, Paris, Chartres, and Toledo. When the new learning invaded the cathedral schools in the twelfth century, a very

Education before the universities

[32] See p. 741.

few of them developed into universities. The rest were eclipsed by the new universities as centers of higher learning, and in elementary education by the grammar schools of the towns and gilds.

The trivium and quadrivium

The curriculum of the earlier monastic and cathedral schools was inherited from Rome through Martianus Capella and Boethius. The former distinguished seven liberal arts—grammar, rhetoric, logic, arithmetic, geometry, astronomy, and music—which were then divided by Boethius into the trivium (i.e., the triple road to knowledge) of grammar, rhetoric, and logic and the scientific quadrivium of the other arts. This remained the standard classification of the liberal arts throughout the scholastic period, and we see it carved in stone on the cathedrals. That does not mean, of course, that a full curriculum in liberal arts was offered by all monastic and cathedral schools; many had to restrict themselves to the mere rudiments of education, while others contented themselves with music, Scripture, theology, the lives of the saints, and homiletic literature suitable for the training of monks and priests. Latin grammar and rhetoric, indispensable in an age when educated men had to write and speak Latin like their native tongue, were studied in the textbooks of Donatus and Priscian,[33] which were filled with examples taken from classical authors, also to some extent by reading a few of these authors. Training in logic rested chiefly on Aristotle's *Categories* and *Concerning Interpretation*. The quadrivium was dominated by Boethius, who may well be called the schoolmaster of the early middle ages. Arithmetic was taught from a textbook of his, figuring being done with roman numerals and the abacus. Geometry and music likewise depended for their textbooks on works of Boethius. For astronomy there was Pliny the Elder's *Natural History* and the summaries found in the earlier encyclopedias of Isidore of Seville and Rabanus Maurus.[34] Even when supplemented by some of the works of Bede, Alcuin, and a few others, the intellectual fare of the earlier schools was scant enough.

Textbooks and courses in the universities

At the risk of repetition it is worth emphasizing the extent to which the twelfth-century renaissance enlarged the resources available for the study of liberal arts in the cathedral schools and the new universities, and furnished material for new professional courses. Donatus and Priscian remained the basic texts for grammar and rhetoric, although by some pious souls, and even at Paris in the fourteenth century, it was thought better to substitute the *Doctrinale* of Alexander of Ville Dieu, whose examples were taken from Christian rather than pagan authors.

[33] See p. 219.
[34] See p. 255.

In the universities rhetoric was somewhat professionalized by the *dictatores*, masters of the *ars dictaminis*, who gave secretarial courses on writing letters for all occasions, including that most important occasion of asking for money, and on how to draw up the ordinary official documents with which a notary must be familiar. For logic not two but all of Aristotle's logical works were now available, with their Arabic commentators, as well as three of Plato's finely spun *Dialogues, Timæus, Meno*, and *Phædo*. For the degree of master of arts not much more was yet needed than a thorough knowledge of the chief works of Aristotle, a requirement, however, which present-day candidates for that degree may well ponder. As for the quadrivium, arithmetic was now studied in Moslem treatises, and the new Arabic numerals were in use. For geometry Euclid was available, and there were new Arabic treatises on algebra and trigonometry. For astronomy there were Ptolemy's *Almagest* and Moslem astronomical tables. In music great strides were made in the singing schools, especially in the Netherlands in the fourteenth century, possibly under the influence of Moslem music, but mostly by practical experience. In addition to training in the old liberal arts, the universities began to offer professional training. Courses in canon and civil law, based on Gratian's *Decretum* and the *Corpus Iuris Civilis*, led to the degree of doctor of laws. Courses in theology used Peter Lombard's *Sentences*, until that work was supplanted by Thomas Aquinas's *Summary of Theology*. Medicine was studied from the

Advice on a case of mumps

works of Hippocrates and especially Galen, and from Avicenna's *Canon of Medicine*. For astrology, except in Italy, and for alchemy there were no organized courses, but plenty of material was to be found in Arabic treatises, and there was a growing opportunity for professional court astrologers. There were no courses in art and literature. Art was a practical matter; the middle ages were perhaps too busy creating it to stop to talk about it. Although in the cathedral schools of Chartres and Orléans, as we shall see, there was ardent enthusiasm for the Latin classics, as subjects for study they were crushed out by the relentless victory of logic in the universities. The curriculum of the medieval universities was what the middle ages considered severely practical.

The oldest of the universities were those at Salerno, Bologna, Paris, and Oxford, though at just what date each of them was embodied in a definite corporation it is impossible to say. The origins of Salerno as a medical center go back to the tenth century, to the Moslem tradition in southern Italy. The origins of Bologna go back to Irnerius, a great teacher of Roman law in the late eleventh century; in 1158 Frederick Barbarossa gave it special recognition. The origins of Paris go back to Abélard, another great teacher, this time of dialectics; it received its first privileges from Philip Augustus in 1200. The origins of Oxford are more obscure; it was certainly later than the others, possibly the outgrowth of a migration of English students from Paris. Cambridge was formed as a result of a secession of students from Oxford in 1209. Until 1837 Oxford and Cambridge were the only English universities. About half the new foundations on the continent in the later middle ages were similarly the result of secession by disgruntled students and faculty; thus Padua seceded from Bologna and Leipzig from Prague. For Italian and Spanish universities Bologna furnished the pattern of organization, and was acknowledged by Modena, Reggio, Vicenza, Naples, and Salamanca as their mother. For northern and eastern Europe Paris was the mother university. In Germany universities were founded some centuries later than elsewhere in Europe, one more fact indicating the general retardation of German culture; German students in the twelfth and thirteenth centuries were compelled to go to France for higher education. When they did come, the German universities were imperial or princely foundations, with some endowed professorships whose holders were exempted from the customary dependence upon the fees of students. The Emperor Charles IV founded the University of Prague in 1347; and Heidelberg, the first university in what is now Germany, was founded in 1385 by Ruprecht I, Elector Palatine of the Rhine. By the end of the middle ages there were some eighty universities in Europe.

As is still the case in Europe, it was the great teacher and scholar that made a university distinguished, and students moved from one university to another, as they still do in Germany, in search of the best instruction. Although they could not boast of their athletic teams, the

The earliest universities

University publicity

universities were even franker than ours in advertising their wares. The masters of the University of Toulouse in 1229 notified all the universities of the world that "the Moses of our undertaking was the lord cardinal legate in the kingdom of France. . . . He decreed that both masters and students should receive plenary indulgence for all their sins. . . . Lectures and disputations are held more frequently and longer than at Paris." If the last sentence seems to the modern student publicity of doubtful value, in what follows there is surely something to appeal to every taste. Toulouse was "a second land of promise, flowing with milk and honey, where the herds are prolific, trees grow with fruit, Bacchus reigns in the vineyards and Ceres has personal charge of the fields. . . . The theologicans instruct the students in the pulpits and the people at the crossroads, logicians instruct Aristotle's recruits in the liberal arts, grammarians fashion the tongues of stammerers into the semblance of speech, masters of music soothe the popular ear with the instrument of the honeyed throat, lawyers extol Justinian, and at their side masters of medicine preach Galen. The books on natural science which have been prohibited at Paris may be here studied by those who desire to scrutinize the innermost secrets of nature's recesses." [35] Charles of Anjou informed the doctors and students of Paris in 1272 that the newly reorganized University of Naples "has just been opened with modern improvements, with assurance of suitable protection, and appropriate favors to help its development. . . . This very city . . . is praised for the purity of its air, its incomparable and healthful location, its richness in all products of the soil, its convenience for communication by sea with other parts of Italy. Wherefore (to all beginners and graduates) let them come, in so far as they are able, to this University, as (they might come) to a great feast which is adorned by the presence of illustrious guests and which overflows with an abundance and variety of refreshing food." [36]

Some universities, for example Bologna and Paris, were originally *The University* organized as gilds, distinguished from other gilds only in that they *of Bologna* worked with young men instead of with wool or leather. The first gild (*universitas*) at Bologna was composed of mature students already trained in the arts, who had come there to be trained in law in the quickest, cheapest, and most efficient way possible. They organized for protection against high room rents and high food prices. They were at equal pains to get their money's worth for the fees they paid their teachers; on this subject, indeed, they seem to have had queer notions.

[35] Sellery and Krey, *Medieval Foundations of Western Civilization*, p. 249.
[36] *American Historical Review*, XXXVII, 515.

"A professor might not be absent without leave, even a single day, and if he desired to leave town he had to make a deposit to ensure his return. If he failed to secure an audience of five for a regular lecture, he was fined as if absent—a poor lecture indeed which could not secure five hearers! He must begin with the bell and quit within one minute after the next bell. He was not allowed to skip a chapter in his commentary, or postpone a difficulty to the end of the hour, and he was obliged to cover ground systematically, so much in each specific term of the year. No one might spend the whole year on introduction and bibliography!" [37]

The poor professor might have only one day off for his honeymoon. Under such circumstances the masters did the only thing they could do: they organized a gild of their own in self-defense against this relentless pursuit of knowledge. The amalgamation of the students' gild and the masters' gild produced the University of Bologna as we know it today. Not only were the Italian universities dominated by the students, who employed their own instructors, but, unlike universities beyond the Alps, they were secular rather than ecclesiastical institutions, students and faculties alike being generally neither clergy nor clerks.

The University of Paris   The University of Paris was so definitely an outgrowth of the episcopal school of the Cathedral of Notre Dame that, even after it achieved its own organization and spread out from the shadow of the cathedral across the Little Bridge to form the Latin Quarter on the left bank of the Seine, the chancellor of the cathedral chapter still reserved the right to grant the *licentia docendi*, or license to teach. To Paris, unlike Bologna, young students flocked to study liberal arts. When Abélard set himself up as a teacher, we are told that twenty, even thirty, thousand students poured into the city. With so large a group of younger students to be supervised it is not surprising that the first gild at Paris was not a gild of students but a gild of masters. It included the members of the four faculties into which the university came to be divided, of arts, canon law, medicine, and theology, each headed by a dean. When the teaching of civil law at Paris was forbidden by the pope after 1219, the university, while it was always notable as a school of liberal arts, became known primarily as the chief theological school of the west. Here the theology of the Latin Church was summarized and defined by Albertus Magnus and Thomas Aquinas and their coworkers. The masters of arts at Paris were further divided into four nations according to their geographical provenance: the French nation (including

[37] Haskins, *Rise of Universities*, p. 75.

French, Italians, and Spaniards), the Picard (including natives of the Low Countries), the Norman and the English (including Germans), and northern and eastern Europe. This organization was imitated by the German universities; the Italian universities were generally content with the simpler classification of natives and foreigners. Together the four nations elected the head of the university, the rector, through their own elected procurators. The organization by nations, which prevailed also at Bologna, influenced the organization of Church councils in the fifteenth century.

Once organized as a gild, the university sought the same kind of *University* autonomy as any other medieval gild. Since university students were *autonomy* ordinarily clerks—that is, celibates who had taken the tonsure—the university came to insist that its members, when they violated secular law, should be tried in Church courts, not in the civil courts of prince or king; that is, they should, as clergy, enjoy benefit of clergy. Then the universities tried to secure the same complete freedom from the supervision of the Church. Although they were never quite able to reach their goal, they did attain a considerable degree of autonomy; German universities still have their own jails, and English universities their own representatives in Parliament.

The original term for a university was *studium generale*. It admitted students from everywhere, and its graduates had the right to teach anywhere (*ius ubique docendi*). It offered instruction in at least one of the professional subjects, law, medicine, and theology, entrance into which—a requirement no longer insisted upon in all our universities—depended upon completion of the course in arts. The degrees authorized by the various faculties were all teaching degrees, which signified that their holders had become full-fledged members of the *University* teaching gild, and ordinarily required them, as part of their obligation *courses and* in taking the degree, to continue for a while in the university as teach- *degrees* ers. To become a bachelor of arts, a degree of no distinction, the candidate after four or five years of study passed an examination on the trivium. To obtain the degree of master of arts or a doctor's degree in one of the professions he remained three or four more years; for the former he completed the study of the quadrivium, with special attention to Aristotle, and for the latter special texts and commentaries on his chosen subject. The theological course was very long; at Paris the minimum was eight years, later extended to fourteen, and no student less than thirty-five years of age could be made a doctor. Finally, the candidate made a public defense of his thesis from six in the morning until six in the evening against a succession of examiners (in theory any person was at liberty to question him), and formally inaugurated his teaching career by giving a specimen lecture.

His degree was then conferred upon him—at Paris in the cathedral —and he donned the biretta, or master's cap. There followed a banquet for the masters at the candidate's expense. Students were known to be obliged to promise that if they failed in their examinations they would not attack their examiners with knife or dagger. Some university regulations refer to the practice of the candidate's furnishing wine for the examiners. To put them in good humor for the examination students were advised in college manuals to send such invitations as the following: "Reverend master, may we ask Your Reverence not to refuse to accept the entertainment of Master N.'s collation, and that you be mindful of us in the disputation, and we shall always be most studious to please you." "Reverend master, does it please Your Grace to enter the bath? For I am going to pay the fee for you. I pray, moreover, that you accept it with good will. Indeed, if I could show you greater reverence or honour, I would do so most eagerly." [38] After it was all over the young master could write home to his parents: "Sing unto the Lord a new song, praise him with stringed instruments and organs, rejoice upon the high-sounding cymbals, for your son has held a glorious disputation, which was attended by a great number of teachers and scholars. He answered all questions without a mistake, and no one could get the better of him or prevail against his arguments. Moreover, he celebrated a famous banquet, at which both rich and poor were honoured as never before, and he has duly begun to give lectures which are already so popular that others' classrooms are deserted and his own are filled." [39]

Students and faculties of medieval universities enjoyed the discomforts of real Gothic rather than the luxury of American pseudo-Gothic; a confessional was a confessional to them, not a telephone booth. The earliest universities had no buildings at all. Classes met in any available church buildings around the cathedral, or in rooms or halls rented by the master himself. In the bare classroom the master possibly had a desk. The students sat on the floor, with perhaps trusses of straw under them, or later on benches, where they were admonished to sit "quiet as girls" without "shouting, playing and interrupting." The language of the classroom and of all academic exercises was Latin, and even in social intercourse with one another students were often required to use Latin in so far as possible.

*Methods
of study*

[38] Quoted by Haskins, *Studies in Mediæval Culture*, p. 87.
[39] *Ibid.*, p. 28.

Courses were based on textbooks which the master read and elaborated in lecture. He was expected to present his commentary *ex tempore*, not to read it. Sometimes the pace of his utterance was set by rule; he was to lecture not "drawingly" (*tractim*) but "rapidly" (*raptim*), "bringing out his words as rapidly as if no one was taking them down." There was no paper, and the expense of parchment was so great as to be prohibitive for the ordinary student; those who had books in manuscript had to take great care lest they be stolen. Students might club together to buy a text, and at least at Paris many volumes were rented to students long before the establishment of libraries. For the student without a text it was important to take full notes on the lecture on wax tablets, or, if he could afford it, on parchment. Without notes the student could only rely on memory to retain what he heard. Students might also club together to buy parchment, and after the lecture hie themselves to a near-by pothouse, of which there were always plenty, to set down what they remembered of the lecture. The resulting notebook, created with plenty of hot discussion on the side, was then common property and was passed from hand to hand for study.

With lectures and notes the work of learning was still incomplete. On late afternoons and week-ends students met to discuss subjects recently covered in their lectures. These discussions were formal disputations, where they had every opportunity to exercise the mental agility that their training in logic gave them. Indeed, skill in debate was often considered more important than soundness of learning. It was the opinion of Robert de Sorbon, for example, that disputation "is much more advantageous than reading, because it results in clearing up doubts. Nothing is known perfectly which has not been masticated by the teeth of disputation." Our debating societies are at best pale reflections of the prominence in medieval education of the disputation. The grand climax of the student's career was the disputation in defense of his thesis, for which he was prepared by countless earlier disputations throughout his whole course of study.

It is from this same Robert de Sorbon, a chaplain of St. Louis's, that the University of Paris is commonly called the Sorbonne, because of his foundation of a college to furnish board and room for students of theology. The first college was accordingly an endowed home for poor *Colleges* students. Now the presence of so many students, all immune from arrest by lay authority and most of them very young, obviously created a peculiar situation. The students of the several nations were always ready to fight with each other, and they all made common cause against the citizenry; riots between town and gown were sometimes truly

formidable. Flogging, of which there was plenty in elementary schools
—as there still is in some English schools—had no part in university

*Discipline in a school for the sons
of noblemen*

discipline. This serious disciplinary and social problem, it was soon
perceived, could best be solved by the organization of more colleges.
As time went on colleges began to be endowed by rich prelates, nobles,
and burghers, whose names they often bore. Finally the colleges swallowed up the university. Students were obliged to live in some college,
and the faculty of the university was divided into groups attached to
the respective colleges. All instruction thenceforth was given within
the college, and the university was left to give examinations and grant
degrees. In the thirteenth century eight colleges were founded at Paris,
in the fourteenth century twenty-seven, and before 1500 there were
sixty-eight. At Bologna one may still visit the college for Spanish
students. Oxford with twenty-three colleges and Cambridge with nineteen still retain the federal organization of a medieval university; on
the continent the colleges were generally abolished after the French
Revolution.

Student life　　Of the life of individual students at the universities we know little
enough, but of their life as a class we know a good deal. Our knowledge
has been garnered from the regulations of various colleges; from
manuals prepared to help students over all difficulties; from collections
published by professors of rhetoric of form letters to be sent home to
parents or written by fathers to sons at the university; from the comments of contemporary preachers; from accounts of fights between

students and citizens; from the records of the nations at Paris; and from the Latin poetry of the wandering scholars. The life of the student of the thirteenth century seems to us rough, primitive, and violent, even as in many ways the thirteenth century seems, and yet the differences are superficial compared with the fundamental similarity; by and large the medieval students were much like twentieth-century students, of all kinds and all degrees of kinds.

New students at Leipzig in the fifteenth century were treated as greenhorns, who after the horseplay of "dehorning" had to give a party for the older students. An Oxford student wrote home: "The city is expensive and makes many demands; I have to rent lodgings, buy necessaries, and provide for many other things which I cannot now specify. Wherefore I respectfully beg your paternity that by the prompting of divine pity you may assist me, so that I may be able to complete what I have well begun. For you must know that without Ceres and Bacchus Apollo grows cold." [40] One father wrote back to his son: "I have recently discovered that you live dissolutely and slothfully, preferring license to restraint and play to work, and strumming a guitar while the others are at their studies, whence it happens that you have read but one volume of law while your more industrious companions have read several." [41] Oxford students "went through the streets with swords and bows and arrows shortly before the hour of curfew and assaulted all who passed by." [42] Students at Rome went "wandering armed from tavern to tavern and other unhonest places; sometimes going on to quarrel or fight in arms with laymen; committing manslaughter, thefts, robberies and very many other things that are far from honesty." [43] "They are so litigious and quarrelsome that there is no peace with them; wherever they go, be it Paris or Orleans, they disturb the country, their associates, even the whole university. Many of them go about the streets armed, attacking the citizens, breaking into houses, and abusing women. They quarrel among themselves over dogs, women, or what not, slashing off one another's fingers with their swords, or, with only knives in their hands and nothing to protect their tonsured pates, rush into conflicts from which armed knights would hold back. Their compatriots come to their aid, and soon whole nations of students may be involved in the fray." [44]

"The student is much more familiar," says Robert de Sorbon, "with

[40] *Ibid.*, p. 10.
[41] *Ibid.*, p. 15.
[42] Quoted by Coulton, *Life in the Middle Ages*, II, 74.
[43] *Ibid.*, p. 88.
[44] Haskins, *Studies in Mediæval Culture*, p. 60.

the text of the dice, which he recognizes at once, no matter how rapidly they are thrown, than with the text of the old logic." [45] Students at Paris even had to be warned to stop playing dice on the altar of Notre Dame after one of their festival processions. From their records we learn how the English nation drank up their surplus funds, and incidentally learn a good deal about the taverns of medieval Paris. At every university there was always considerable "feasting and free indulgence in the wine-cup, as well as wild carouses in the streets and the visiting of disreputable resorts. Many of the students led a life that was by no means celibate, and there were allusions to the darkest of monastic vices." [46] Students at Leipzig were fined for throwing stones at the masters, the fines being carefully graduated, for "hitting without wounding" and "wounding without mutilation." At Oxford "playing with a ball or a bat" was considered an "insolent" game, and at New College chess was forbidden as a "noxious, inordinate and unhonest game." At other colleges there were rules against "dancing or jumping in the chapel," and against "struggling, chorus-singing, dancing, leaping, singing, shouting, tumult and inordinate noise, pouring forth of water, beer and all other liquids, and tumultuous games in the Hall, on the ground that they were likely to disturb the occupants of the chaplain's chamber below." [47]

While they always—as they aim to do—attract a disproportionate amount of attention, the rowdies no more dominated medieval universities than they dominate our universities today. Far more typical, no doubt, were the boys at Orléans, who wrote home: "We occupy a good and comely dwelling, next door but one to the schools and market-place, so that we can go to school every day without wetting our feet." [48] There was the student who "studies too much—who rises before the morning bell, is first to enter and last to leave the schools, spends the day in his room reading, ponders his lectures at meal-time, and even reviews and argues in his sleep." There was "the poor student, with no friend but St. Nicholas, seeking such charity as he can find or earning a pittance by carrying holy water or copying for others, in a fair but none too accurate hand,—as thin as if he had just come from hell, or poor enough to sell his soul to the Devil,—sometimes too poor to buy books or afford the expense of a course in theology, yet usually surpassing his more prosperous fellows, who, with every opportunity,

The serious student

[45] *Ibid.*, p. 58.
[46] *Ibid.*, p. 59.
[47] Rashdall, *op. cit.*, II, 672–73.
[48] Quoted by Haskins, *Studies in Mediæval Culture*, p. 17.

have an abundance of books at which they never look." [49] Chaucer's Oxford clerk was not

> "too fat, I'll undertake,
> But he looked hollow and went soberly.
> Right threadbare was his overcoat; for he
> Had got him yet no churchly benefice,
> Nor was so worldly as to gain office.
> For he would rather have at his bed's head
> Some twenty books, all bound in black and red,
> Of Aristotle and his philosophy
> Than rich robes, fiddle, or gay psaltery.
> Yet, and for all he was philosopher,
> He had but little gold within his coffer;
> But all that he might borrow from a friend
> On books and learning he would swiftly spend,
> And then he'd pray right busily for the souls
> Of those who gave him wherewithal for schools.
> Of study took he utmost care and heed.
> Not one word spoke he more than was his need;
> And that was said in fullest reverence
> And short and quick and full of high good sense.
> Pregnant of moral virtue was his speech;
> And gladly would he learn and gladly teach."

Nicholas, the Oxford clerk who lived at the carpenter's house, was in more fortunate circumstances, but a serious fellow too. He was

> "All garnished with sweet herbs of good repute;
> And he himself sweet-smelling as the root
> Of licorice, valerian, or setwall.
> His *Almagest*, and books both great and small,
> His astrolabe, belonging to his art,
> His algorism stones—all laid apart
> On shelves that ranged beside his lone bed's head;
> His press was covered with a cloth of red.
> And over all there lay a psaltery
> Whereon he made an evening's melody,
> Playing so sweetly that the chamber rang;
> And *Angelus ad virginem* he sang;

[49] *Ibid.*, pp. 29 and 63.

> And after that he warbled the *King's Note:*
> Often in good voice was his merry throat." [50]

The Latin poetry of the wandering scholars, one of the richest sources of our knowledge of the medieval student, will be considered in the following chapter.

[50] Translations of J. U. Nicolson.

Chapter 24

THE MEDIEVAL RENAISSANCE

LITERATURE, ART, MUSIC

IN LITERATURE, art, and music we find the happiest expressions of medieval culture. These by their very perfection can never fail to call forth the warm emotional response of appreciation and enjoyment. They are at the same time the sort of authentic and complete representation of their time that stands out forever after to mark the culmination of an epoch. Properly studied, any one of the greatest products of medieval artistry—the *Romance of the Rose*, the *Divine Comedy*, the *Canterbury Tales*, the Cathedral of Chartres—is in itself astonishingly close to a complete textbook of the middle ages.[1] Like such wholly typical artistic monuments of any period, those of the twelfth and thirteenth centuries embody together with influences from many sources a dominant spirit of their own; the result is something that seems natural and inevitable, sometimes almost familiar, yet always novel and unmistakable. From the older and more advanced civilizations of Roman and Saracen in southern Europe the vigorous young peoples of northern Europe, Germans, Scandinavians, and Celts, borrowed what they needed to speak out their minds and hearts on what had become of most vital importance to them, their Christianity. But while Christianity was the mold into which all their artistic expression was poured, their youthful spirit could not be restrained from breaking its bonds.

In medieval literature, art, and music there is, therefore, alongside the disciplined forms imposed by the Latin and Christian tradition, a wealth of new forms, to express the spontaneous, gay, youthful, curious spirit of peoples who were discovering that it was fun to be alive,

[1] The best exemplification of this is no doubt Henry Adams's *Mont-Saint-Michel and Chartres.*

and that this world can be as interesting as the next. At the cost of no little grief to the Church they reduced their religion to an intimate part of their daily life; it had its place, to be sure, and the largest place, but it was no longer the only part of his life in which a man might find satisfaction. For our purpose this amounts to saying that, while always predominantly Christian, medieval culture at its height began to assert a secular spirit born outside the Church, even though it was the Church that contributed most to make its birth possible. From the Christian point of view this secular spirit was associated, or identified, with paganism, particularly with classical paganism. We must therefore first ask what classical element there really was in the secular spirit of medieval culture. To what extent was what we have called the medieval renaissance a renaissance in the stricter sense of the term, namely, a rebirth of interest in, and cultivation of, Latin letters?

In this connection it should be still further emphasized that the revival of the study of Roman law in the twelfth century was just such a source of secular influence. In the sixth century Justinian's new codes of Roman law, together called the *Corpus Iuris Civilis*,[2] were useless for the western empire, already occupied by barbarian German kingdoms that had brought with them their own customary personal law. In accord with the basic principle of this law, however, the old Roman population and the clergy were permitted to retain their own law.[3] The Church, as we have seen, developed its canon law into a body of principles, rules, and procedures, codified at length by Gratian and

Roman law from the sixth to the eleventh century

his successors under the influence of the revived study of Roman law.[4] In Italy, Spain, and southern France the Roman peoples continued to live under Roman law itself, not, however, as codified by Justinian but as contained in the Theodosian Code of a century earlier, reissued as a special code for their Roman subjects by the various German kings.[5] In the course of time Roman law in the various regions of southern Europe thus developed into a body of local custom, adapted to the vicissitudes of time and place and circumstance. Just so the old German customary law, which under the influence of Roman law had been written down in simple codes, developed back again into a body of unwritten feudal and manorial custom. In the earlier middle ages, accordingly, whether Roman or Germanic in source, law in

[2] See p. 128.
[3] See p. 189.
[4] See pp. 654–55.
[5] See p. 189.

western Europe had become the unwritten custom of an agricultural, feudal society.

In fact, although the authentic tradition of Roman law was never wholly lost in Italy, the Justinian Code was unheard of in western Europe until the eleventh century. Then it began to be cited in local Italian courts, manuscripts of it became available, and henceforth until the sixteenth century Italy remained the source of the spread of the *Corpus Iuris Civilis* throughout western Europe. In reality this revival marks the first step in that recovery of the whole classical tradition, beginning in the fourteenth century, which has been called the Italian renaissance. Although other men in other places preceded him, the first notable student of the Justinian Code in Italy was Irnerius at Bologna (*c.* 1060–1125). It was largely because of his teaching and writing that a university specializing in Roman law grew up at Bologna. It was through his students, with the enthusiasm characteristic of the later Italian humanists, that Roman law was carried beyond the Alps to the new French universities at Montpellier, Orléans, and Paris, and directly to England. *The revival of Roman law in Italy in the eleventh century*

The first task of these early students of the *Corpus* was that of every scholar who gets hold of a new manuscript, namely, to understand and explain. Their writings took the natural form of explanatory comments, or glosses, on the text of the *Corpus,* or more usually of the *Digest* in particular, and as a group they are called glossators. By the middle of the thirteenth century the important earlier glosses were combined into one large gloss by the Italian Accursius. Henceforth, just as the study of Peter Lombard's *Sentences* tended to displace the study of the Bible, so the study of the glosses tended to supplant the study of the actual text of the *Corpus.* In the universities Roman law was studied by the usual dialectical method. Together with the study of canon law, with the early development of English common law hammered out by Henry II, and with the various codifications of local feudal custom undertaken under the influence of Roman law, the revival of Roman law represented a legal renaissance in the twelfth century.

Without considerable knowledge of both Roman law and feudal law it is difficult for us to conceive of the civilian's wonder and reverence for the Justinian Code.[6] Here he found ready for use the legal system of a highly complex and civilized society, principles of jurisprudence applicable anywhere. His adoration for the code was like the student's worship of Aristotle; here was the essence of legal wis- *Enthusiasm for Roman law*

⁶ See p. 128.

dom, "written reason," the law of nature. Europe in the twelfth century happened to be ready to receive Roman law. The revival of the medieval empire under the Hohenstaufens called for its support; as we have already pointed out, Italian lawyers were in the service of Frederick Barbarossa at Roncaglia,[7] and he regarded some of his own pronouncements as additions made to Roman law by a legitimate Roman emperor. At the same time western Europe was witnessing the growth of old and new towns. The customary law of a simple agrarian society no longer met the needs of commerce, trade, and finance, which appealed to Roman law. Finally, local princes and kings, in their earliest efforts to consolidate their diverse feudal dominions, found in Roman law the common written law that was needed to supplant the old local customary law. To a Europe badly in need of unity Roman law promised, in support of such real unity as had been imparted by the Church and the specious unity of the Holy Roman empire, at least the same legal unity that it had given to the wide dominions of Rome.

To be sure, there were obstacles to the acceptance of Roman law. It consecrated the absolutism of the emperor on the ground that the Roman people had surrendered their original sovereignty to him. Since the medieval emperor was a German king, this doctrine was *Opposition* anathema to Italian cities, to the popes, and to the kings of the ris-
to Roman ing national states of France and England. On the other hand, once
law the power of the German emperors was no longer real, this same doctrine redounded to the benefit of every prince and king, to whom the absolutism of the emperor was now transferred. When there was no strong emperor, the Italian cities were quick to resort to Roman law to defend themselves against their other enemy, the papacy. The popes, having encouraged the appropriation by canon law of whatever in Roman law the Church could turn to use, had no further use for it; they even forbade its study at Paris at the beginning of the thirteenth century. Theologians, such as Thomas Aquinas, preferred to emphasize rather that sovereignty lay in the people than that it had been absorbed by the king. The old customary laws of Europe obstinately resisted attempts to supplant them by one common written law. English common law fought Roman law successfully after some English kings had tried to introduce it and lawyers and judges of the common law had borrowed from it. In northern France, after being accepted for a time as a written supplement to local customary law, it was later opposed. But in spite of all obstacles, because of its in-

[7] See p. 401.

herent superiority Roman law continued to gain ground in numerous subtle ways. It was received by Scotland and Germany in the sixteenth century, and remained the common law of Germany until 1900. Its influence in France was hardly impaired until the Napoleonic Code of 1804; in Italy not until 1866. On the development of international law it had great influence. In recovering and transmitting Roman law the middle ages did more than once again preserve a precious ancient heritage. In particular, Roman law provided the legal argument for the destruction of the feudal system by the national states, and at the same time facilitated the formulation of the people's right, implicit in the feudal notion of government by contract, to take back from an unjust prince the sovereignty committed to him by the people.

There can be little doubt that the study of the Roman law fostered *The* in its devotees a rationalistic temper that may be characterized as *secular* secular. Instructed in a law whose principles were based on reason *spirit of* and experience, not on revealed religion, it was the hard-headed Ro- *Roman* man practicality that they brought to bear on the solution of Europe's *law* legal problems. It was at this time that the trained lawyer made his first appearance in medieval Europe. He was immediately drawn into the service of the kings and princes of national and territorial states, who were no longer (as was, for example, Charles the Great) interested in theocracy, but in forging instruments of wealth and power adequate to crush feudalism and weld all classes of society into some sort of unity. Religion, to be sure, might be of use here too, but lawyers, like bureaucrats and armies, spoke more loudly. The merely secular needs of the state were now sufficient motivation for all political action. The political expediency and "reasons of state" of the newer type of princes and kings, like Philip IV of France, were blandly indifferent to Christian morality.

We would not, for all that we have said about the influence of the study of Roman law, suggest that the sort of rationalism exemplified by the legal mind could have any direct appeal for the scholars and *The attitude* poets of the twelfth and thirteenth centuries, who had been brought *of the uni-* up on the tradition of the Latin classics. So far from it, indeed, that *versities and* they resented the emphasis the universities were putting upon logic *the Church* and upon professional training, much as faculties of liberal arts to- *towards* day resent the professionalizing of education by schools of educa- *classical* tion. For, what with Aristotle, Peter Lombard, Galen, Gratian, and *literature* the *Corpus*, the universities discriminated strongly against the study of the Latin classics, represented by grammar and rhetoric in the arts course. For that matter, even yet the middle ages had not completely resolved the problem inherited from the early Church Fathers, whether it was even proper for a Christian scholar to occupy himself with classical literature. Aside from some monks and zealots, however, most churchmen were ready to acquiesce in the decision of Gratian. While certain authorities, he admits, argue that "knowledge of profane literature is not to be sought after by churchmen," yet "we read that Moses and Daniel were learned in *all* the wisdom of the Egyptians and Chaldeans. We read also that the Lord ordered the children of Israel to spoil the Egyptians of their gold and silver; the moral interpretation of this teaches that, should we find in the poets either the gold of wisdom or the silver of eloquence, we should turn it to the profit of salutary learning." [8]

Classical study in the cathedral schools before the victory of the universities

Before the universities were surcharged with the study of logic and professional training there were classical scholars in the schools who needed no such justification nor felt any necessity to put their learning to such a noble purpose. The study and enjoyment of the Latin classics for their own sake, a dim sense of what Rome actually stood for, the writing of good Latin prose and of good Latin poetry in classical meters are all associated with the cathedral schools of the twelfth century, especially those of Chartres and Orléans. Hildebert of Le Mans, trained in the cathedral school there and later Bishop and Archbishop of Tours, who died about 1130, wrote such excellent verse that for a while some of his work was mistaken for classical poetry. He for one did not visit medieval Rome without wondering what it must have been like before it crumbled into ruins. The classical tradition at Chartres went back to Fulbert.[9] Its greatest representative was the extraordinary Englishman, John of Salisbury, who died as bishop there in 1180. No one in his age was better acquainted with the Latin classics, and no one loved them better. Virgil, Ovid, Horace, Juvenal, Persius, Lucan, Statius, Martial, Cicero, Seneca, Pliny the Elder, if not also Tacitus, Livy, Lucretius, and Catullus, were read at Chartres and ardently imitated.

While often, particularly in the scholar-poets, acquaintance with these authors engendered a frankly pagan and humanistic state of mind, they were in fact more often concerned to find what use there might be for Gratian's "salutary learning." Most of them felt bound to hide their enjoyment, or—still worse—to justify it by seeking for the allegorical meaning; in other words, they sought to Christianize their classics as the theologians Christianized their Aristotle. The

[8] Quoted by Haskins, *The Renaissance of the Twelfth Century*, p. 97.
[9] See p. 692.

scholar who complained that the rules of Ovid's *Art of Love* were being neglected by his contemporaries was an exception, not the rule.

Orléans as a center of classical study developed somewhat later than Chartres. It was here especially that rhetoric was transformed into the art of letter writing, and even the letters of students indicate that their teachers had some acquaintance with Latin authors. The battle between logic and literature continued on into the thirteenth century. It is reflected in contemporary poems in which Orléans, defending the side of literature, loses the battle with the logic of Paris.

> "Withers the Latin tongue.
> The springtime fields of the old poets are bare.
> Across the flowering fields the North Wind blows,
> And they are winter-starved." [10]

In the growing vernacular tongues of western Europe Latin poetry had to face a more relentless rival, whose triumph was foreordained and irrevocable. But before this conflict was decided, in the thirteenth century—the same century that witnessed the victory of the universities—poets, both secular and religious, wrought miracles with the old Latin language. The Latin poetry of the twelfth century abandoned completely the traditional classical forms of quantitative verse, although many of the classical meters continued to be used. It employed a variety of verse forms, based on stress and on number of syllables, whether long or short, together with rime, which had first appeared as early as the fourth century and was by now thoroughly established. It is hard to say whether the religious or the secular lyric was prior in the use of the new forms, since a poet passed easily from one theme to another. There can be no doubt, however, that Latin poetry influenced the form of the nascent vernacular poetry, which, for example, borrowed rime from it, and as little doubt that the latter breathed its own fresh spirit into the Latin. The history of modern lyric poetry stems from both together at this very period.

Latin poetry of the twelfth century

It is in the secular lyric of the twelfth and early thirteenth centuries that the full humanistic flavor of a classical revival is best discerned. The authors of these poems knew their Latin poets, and had imbibed from them something of the old frank enjoyment of this world. Their poetry is sensuous, gay, satirical, sometimes downright rowdy. They had learned their mythology well, and learned it from Ovid, but their humanism is no mere learned resuscitation of Venus and

The spirit of the secular lyric

[10] Quoted by Waddell, *The Wandering Scholars*, p. xiii.

Bacchus and choruses of dancing maidens. It is rather the attitude of gifted men whom knowledge and wit have made sophisticated enough to smile or laugh at the conventional world about them, and to proclaim with enthusiasm the values of a natural instead of a supernatural world. Their poetry seems so new and original, it is written with such verve and freedom from restraint, that one who has known only the pages of monastic chroniclers and scholastic theologians is driven to conclude that he hardly knew the middle ages at all. Through this poetry blows the fresh springtide of an age just coming to maturity.

> "Jocund Spring is with us,
> Come, virgins, all;
> Come, lads, join the revel,
> Answer Spring's call.
> Hurray, hurray! O happy day!
> With love I'm all on fire;
> To have a maid beside me laid
> Is now my one desire." [11]

As Miss Waddell puts it, it is the expression of the wish "that all times were April and May, and every month renew all fruits again, and every day fleurs de lis and gillyflower and violets and roses wherever one goes, and woods in leaf and meadows green, and every lover should have his lass, and they to love each other with a sure heart and true, and to every one his pleasure and a gay heart."

The Goliardic poets

For the most part the authors of these poems are unknown to us. From the fact that they were fond of referring to their wholly mythical patron, Bishop Golias, "a certain parasite . . . notorious alike for his intemperance and his wantonness . . . a tolerable scholar but without morals or discipline," they have been called Goliards and their poetry Goliardic. A few among them have been identified. There was Hugh the Primate, possibly at one time a canon of Orléans, "an unmitigated scoundrel, but of amazing verve, who begged and lectured and vilified and versed from Sens . . . to Orleans to Paris, and very subject to being kicked downstairs by enraged ecclesiastics." [12] The great genius among them, called the Archpoet, we know had the distinguished Rainald of Dassel [13] as his patron. Reginald of Châtillon we know, and a few others. Many of them came from the cathedral

---

[11] *Ibid.*, pp. 200–1.
[12] *Ibid.*, p. 150.
[13] See p. 395.

schools and the early universities in France. They wandered up and down the highways of central and western Europe; learned tramps they were, "needy, poverty-stricken, suffering," as one of them says, "broken in reputation, consumed with hunger and thirst, shivering with cold, stiff with frost, swollen with wind, beggarly in habit, a linen clout on our bare backs, one foot forever unshod, driven out from the houses of the laity, turned away from the doors of the clergy, bats that can find no place either with beast or bird." [14] Some, however, were cloistered monks, others even ecclesiastics in high position, who were likely to be subject to disciplinary action by synods. To parody the growing prevalence of monastic orders they liked to refer to themselves as an order, who

> "In our wandering,
> Blithesome and squandering,
>
> . . . . .
>
> Eat to satiety,
> Drink with propriety;
>
> . . . . .
>
> Laugh till our sides we split,
> Rags on our hides we fit
>
> . . . . .
>
> Jesting eternally,
> Quaffing infernally." [15]

Their order had no rules of eligibility.

> "This our sect doth entertain
> Just men and unjust ones;
> Halt, lame, weak of limb or brain,
> Strong men and robust ones;
> Those who flourish in their pride,
> Those whom age makes stupid;
> Frigid folk and hot folk fried
> In the fires of Cupid.

[14] Waddell, *op. cit.*, pp. 240–41.
[15] Symonds, *Wine, Women and Song*, pp. 61–62.

"Tranquil souls and bellicose,
　　Peacemaker and foeman;
Czech and Hun, and mixed with those
　　German, Slav, and Roman;
Men of middling size and weight,
　　Dwarfs and giants mighty;
Men of modest heart and state,
　　Vain men, proud and flighty." [16]

*The "Con-
fession of
Golias"*

　　The Archpoet produced one of the truly great poems of the middle
ages in his "Confession of Golias," addressed to the Archbishop of
Cologne.

"Æstuans intrinsecus
　ira vehementi
　in amaritudine
　loquar meæ menti:
　factus de materia
　levis elementi
　similis sum folio
　de quo ludunt venti.

"Boiling in my spirit's veins
　　With fierce indignation,
From my bitterness of soul
　　Springs self-revelation:
Framed am I of flimsy stuff,
　　Fit for levitation,
Like a thin leaf which the wind
　　Scatters from its station.[17]

·　　·　　·　　·　　·　　·　　·　　·

"Feror ego veluti
　sine nauta navis,
　ut per vias æris
　vaga fertur avis;
　non me tenent vincula,
　non me tenet clavis;
　quæro mihi similes
　et adiungor pravis.

"Carried am I like a ship
　　Left without a sailor,
Like a bird that through the air
　　Flies where tempests hale her;
Chains and fetters hold me not,
　　Naught avails a jailer;
Still I find my fellows out
　　Toper, gamester, railer.

·　　·　　·　　·　　·　　·　　·　　·

"Via lata gradior
　more iuventutis,
　implico me vitiis
　inmemor virtutis;
　voluptatis avidus
　magis quam salutis,

"Down the broad road do I run,
　　As the way of youth is;
Snare myself in sin, and ne'er
　　Think where faith and truth is;
Eager far for pleasure more
　　Than soul's health, the sooth is,

[16] *Ibid.*, p. 52.
[17] *Ibid.*, pp. 65 ff.

mortuus in anima
curam gero cutis.

For this flesh of mine I care,
    Seek not ruth where ruth is.

"Præsul discretissime,
    veniam te precor;
morte bona morior,
    dulci nece necor;
meum pectus sauciat
    puellarum decor,
et quas tactu nequeo
    saltem corde mœchor.

"Prelate, most discreet of priests,
    Grant me absolution!
Dear's the death whereof I die,
    Sweet my dissolution;
For my heart is wounded by
    Beauty's soft suffusion;
All the girls I come not nigh,
    Mine are in illusion.

"Res est arduissima
    vincere naturam,
in aspectu virginis
    mentem esse puram;
iuvenes non possumus
    legem sequi duram,
leviumque corporum
    non habere curam.

" 'Tis most arduous to make
    Nature's self surrender;
Seeing girls, to blush and be
    Purity's defender!
We young men our longings ne'er
    Shall to stern law render,
Or preserve our fancies from
    Bodies smooth and tender.

"Secundo redarguor
    etiam de ludo.
Sed cum ludus corpore
    me dimittat nudo,
frigidus exterius
    mentis estu sudo,
tunc versus et carmina
    meliora cudo.

"In the second place, I own
    To the vice of gaming:
Cold indeed outside I seem,
    Yet my soul is flaming:
But when once the dice-box hath
    Stripped me to my shaming,
Make I songs and verses fit
    For the world's acclaiming.

"Tertio capitulo
    memoro tabernam;
Illam nullo tempore
    sprevi, neque spernam,
donec sanctos angelos
    venientes cernam,
cantantes pro mortuis
    Requiem eternam.

"In the third place, I will speak
    Of the tavern's pleasure;
For I never found nor find
    There the least displeasure;
Nor shall find it till I greet
    Angels without measure,
Singing requiems for the souls
    In eternal leisure.

.   .   .   .

"Meum est propositum
in taberna mori,

"In the public-house to die
    Is my resolution;

ut sint vina proxima
morientis ori;
tunc cantabunt lætius
angelorum chori:
'Deus sit propitius
huic potatori!' "

Let wine to my lips be nigh
    At life's dissolution:
That will make the angels cry,
    With glad elocution,
'Grant this toper, God on high,
    Grace and absolution!' "

The pleasures of the dance the Archpoet seems to have overlooked, but not so another Goliardic poet.

Other
Goliardic
poems

"Cast aside dull books and thought;
    Sweet is folly, sweet is play;
Take the pleasure Spring hath brought
    In youth's opening holiday!
Right it is old age should ponder
    On grave matters fraught with care;
Tender youth is free to wander,
    Free to frolic light as air.
       Like a dream our prime is flown,
          Prisoned in a study;
       Sport and folly are youth's own,
          Tender youth and ruddy.

"Live we like the gods above;
    This is wisdom, this is truth:
Chase the joys of tender love
    In the leisure of our youth!
Keep the vows we swore together,
    Lads, obey that ordinance;
Seek the fields in sunny weather,
    Where the laughing maidens dance.
       Like a dream our prime is flown,
          Prisoned in a study;
       Sport and folly are youth's own,
          Tender youth and ruddy.

"There the lad who lists may see
    Which among the maids is kind;
There young limbs deliciously
    Flashing through the dances wind;
While the girls their arms are raising,

> Moving, winding o'er the lea,
> Still I stand and gaze, and gazing
> They have stolen the soul of me!
>   Like a dream our prime is flown,
>   Prisoned in a study;
>   Sport and folly are youth's own,
>   Tender youth and ruddy." [18]

Still another sings the glory of poetry itself.

> "Should a tyrant rise and say,
>   'Give up wine!', I'd do it;
> 'Love no girls!', I would obey,
>   Though my heart should rue it.
> 'Dash thy lyre!', suppose he saith,
>   Naught should bring me to it;
> 'Yield thy lyre or die!' My breath,
>   Dying, should thrill through it." [19]

The Goliardic poets were masters of satire. There was nothing they *Goliardic* would not parody; they wrote Masses for topers and services for gam- *satire* blers; they changed hymns to the Virgin into praises of wine. Reginald of Châtillon wrote a Gospel according to the Mark of Silver, in which the venality of the Roman *Curia* is pilloried unmercifully. Philip de Grève in a dialogue makes Diogenes ask Aristippus how to get along at Rome, being no liar and no flatterer. "Diogenes, what do you want?" Aristippus answers. "Do you want office, do you want prefer-ment? You must first of all make this clear. For the churches are gov-erned by those who will have nothing to do with you unless you in-volve yourself in their vices. You will be welcome if you praise the prelates for the things which disfigure their lives. For the consecrated bishops love above all men those who are partners of their guilt and servants of their sins." [20] Here is the dying scholar's parody of the Creed: [21]

> "*Credo*—in dice I well believe,
>   That got me often bite and sup,

---

[18] *Ibid.*, pp. 99–101.
[19] *Ibid.*, p. 163.
[20] Raby, *History of Secular Latin Poetry*, II, 234.
[21] *Credo in Deum patrem omnipotentem, creatorem cœli et terræ, et in Jhesum Christum filium eius unicum.* ("I believe in God the father almighty, maker of heaven and earth, and in Jesus Christ, his only son.")

And many a time hath had me drunk,
And many a time delivered me
From every stitch and every penny.
In Deum—never with my will
Gave Him a thought nor ever will.

. . . .

Patrem—at St. Denis in France,
Good Sir, I had a father once,
Omnipotentem in his having,
Money and horses and fine wearing.

. . . .

Creatorem who made all
I've denied— He has his will
Of me now. . . .
Cœli—of heaven ever think?
Nay, but the wine that I could drink.
Et terræ—there was all my joy.
Do you think that I believe
More in *Jhesum* than the tavern?
Better love I him who's host
There than *Christum filium eius.*
Watch the roast turn on the spit,
And the wine that's clear and green,
Orleans, Rochelle, Auxerre—
That's the joy that's *unicum.*" [22]

Goliardic satire, however, was not all parody and blasphemy and bitterness. The following specimen strikes a genuine evangelical note.

"O Truth of Christ,
O most dear rarity,
O most rare charity,
Where dwell'st thou now?

. . . .

Then Love replied:
'Man, wherefore didst thou doubt?
Not where thou wast wont to find

[22] Waddell, *Wandering Scholars,* pp. 192–93.

My dwelling in the southern wind,
Not in court and not in cloister,
Not in casque nor yet in cowl,
Not in battle nor in bull,
But on the road from Jericho
I come with a wounded man.' " [23]

For even the Goliard had his serious moments. He could promise to

"Seek a better mind;
Change, correct, and leave behind
What I did with purpose blind;
From vice sever, with endeavour
Yield my soul to serious things,
Seek the joy that virtue brings.

.   .   .   .

"Therefore bind,
Tread down and grind
Fleshly lusts that blight us;
So heaven's bliss
'Mid saints that kiss
Shall for aye delight us." [24]

Religious poetry, both in its own right and as a part of the liturgy of the Church, achieved the same independence of classical form, the same grace and perfection, as the secular lyric. It may express the mysticism of such men as St. Bernard and the monks of St. Victor at Paris, or such personal devotion to Christ and the Blessed Virgin and grief for their sufferings as were fostered by the evangelical religion preached by the Franciscans. It may be an elaboration of a dogma of the Church, or merely tell or retell a saint's legend. Religious poetry is generally, and naturally, because of the limitations imposed by the subject matter, less personal in inspiration than the carefree fancy or raillery of the scholar. And yet St. Bernard could lay aside his pompous prose with his austerity, and write as simply as a child of Jesus, whose memory was sweet and filled the heart with joy, but whose presence was sweeter than honey.

The religious lyric

[23] Waddell, *Mediæval Latin Lyrics*, pp. 193–95.
[24] Symonds, *op. cit.*, 185.

"Jesu dulcis memoria,
Dans vera cordi gaudia,
Sed super mel et omnia
Eius dulcis præsentia." [25]

Again he says: "None other, whether angel or man, but Himself I ask that He kiss me with the kisses of his mouth."

Abélard's famous love songs have unhappily not survived, but some of his religious verse has. In "David's Lament for Jonathan" something of the tragedy of his love for Héloïse still lingers:

"Low in thy grave with thee
Happy to lie,
Since there's no greater thing left Love to do:
And to live after thee
Is but to die,
For with but half a soul what can Life do?

"So share thy victory,
Or else thy grave,
Either to rescue thee, or with thee lie:
Ending that life for thee,
That thou didst save,
So Death that sundereth might bring more nigh.

"Peace, O my stricken lute!
Thy strings are sleeping.
Would that my heart could still
Its bitter weeping!" [26]

A monk at Cluny in the twelfth century, named Bernard, wrote a poem, *De Contemptu Mundi*, "On Contempt for the World," in three thousand hexameter lines. Each line is divided into three parts with the first two riming, and the lines themselves rime in couplets, a *tour de force* so extraordinary that we have the author's word for it that "unless the spirit of wisdom and understanding had been with him he could not have composed so long a work in so difficult a metre." A small part of it, beginning

Bernard of Cluny's De Contemptu Mundi

[25] Part of this poem has been made into the favorite hymn beginning "Jesus, the very thought of thee."
[26] Waddell, *Mediæval Latin Lyrics*, p. 169.

"Urbs Sion aurea, patria lactea, cive decora,
    omne cor obruis, omnibus obstruis et cor et ora.
    Nescio, nescio, quæ iubilatio, lux tibi qualis,
    quam socialia gaudia, gloria quam specialis"
has been pretty closely translated as the well-known hymn "Jerusalem
the Golden."

"Jerusalem the Golden,
    With milk and honey blest,
    Beneath thy contemplation
        Sink heart and voice oppressed.
    I know not, O I know not,
        What social joys are there,
    What radiancy of glory,
        What light beyond compare!"

The form of both religious and secular Latin lyric was influenced
by the development of a new type of verse called the sequence. In the *The*
service of the Mass between the Epistle and the Gospel there may oc- *sequence*
cur two chants, called the gradual and the alleluia. It was customary
in singing the alleluia to prolong the final *a* of the last "alleluia" with
a complicated melody. When it became the practice to replace the
chanted vowel by a special prose text written to fit the melody, this
text was called the sequence, i.e., a continuation of the alleluia chant.
Who wrote the first sequence is a matter of dispute; it has been attributed to an eighth-century French author and to Notker, a monk of
St. Gall in the ninth century. The early sequence, then, was written in
prose to accompany a given melody; prose later gave way to poetry,
and melody and sequence were written together by the same person.
By the twelfth century, in the hands of the monk Adam of St. Victor
in Paris, the sequence reached its perfection as an entirely original
verse form. Adam's two best known sequences were written for the
offices of St. Stephen and Easter; others were composed for Masses in
some saint's honor, and especially to enrich the services for the Virgin
Mary.

In the increasingly popular cult of the Queen of Heaven was incorporated all the wealth of allegory and symbolism that reached its
height in the ecclesiastical writers and poets of the twelfth and thir- *Sequences*
teenth centuries. Mary was prefigured in the Shulamite of the Song of *in honor*
Solomon, whose breasts were as fragrant as wine, whose lovely skin *of the*
surpassed the whiteness of milk and of lilies, with whose perfume no *Virgin*
flower or balsam could compare.

"Tua sunt ubera
Vino redolentia,
Candor superat lac et lilia,
Odor flores vincit et balsama."

She is the saving ark of Noah in the floods of this world, the dove with the olive branch showing the way of peace.

"Tu es archa Noe viva
Per mundi diluvia,
Tu columba cum oliva
Veræ pacis prævia."

She is the Star of the Sea, the Portal of Heaven. Above all, she is Christ's dear Mother and ours, who lays our prayers before Him and gathers us into her bosom.

"Ave maris stella,	"Hail, thou Star of ocean!
Dei mater alma,	Portal of the sky!
Atque semper Virgo,	Ever Virgin Mother
Felix cœli porta.	Of the Lord most high!

.　　.　　.　　.　　.　　.

"Monstra te esse matrem,	"Show thyself a Mother;
Sumat per te preces,	Offer Him our sighs,
Qui pro nobis natus	Who for us Incarnate
Tulit esse tuus.	Did not thee despise.

"Virgo singularis,	"Virgin of all virgins!
Inter omnes mitis,	To thy shelter take us.
Nos culpis solutos	Gentlest of the gentle!
Mites fac et castos."	Chaste and gentle make us." [27]

The Stabat Mater

On the other hand, as the tortured mother of a crucified son the Virgin cried out for the sympathy of all human hearts. Franciscan devotion of the purest kind produced in the thirteenth century that tender and tragic hymn, *Stabat Mater Dolorosa*, whose lovely Latin hardly needs translation to be felt, even if not understood and appreciated, by those so unfortunate as to know no Latin. It is still sung as a sequence in one of the Good Friday services in honor of the Seven Dolors of the Virgin.

[27] The translation of the Roman Missal, p. 279.

The Last Judgment from the Cathedral of Bourges

The Saved

The Damned

Thirteenth century capitals from the Marienkirche at Mühlhausen

A capital from the choir of the Marienkirche

Equestrian statue in the Cathedral at Bamberg

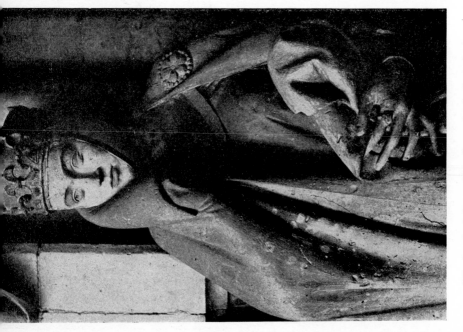

The lovely Princess Uta, from the Cathedral of Naumburg (See p. 826)

"Stabat Mater dolorosa
 Iuxta crucem lacrymosa,
 Dum pendebat Filius

  .   .   .

"Quis est homo qui non fleret,
 Matrem Christi si videret
 In tanto supplicio?
 Quis non posset contristari,
 Christi Matrem contemplari
 Dolentem cum Filio?

"Pro peccatis suæ gentis
 Vidit Iesum in tormentis
 Et flagellis subditum;
 Vidit suum dulcem natum
 Morientem, desolatum,
 Dum emisit spiritum.

"Eia Mater, fons amoris,
 Me sentire vim doloris
 Fac, ut tecum lugeam.

 .   .   .   .

"Sancta Mater, istud agas,
 Crucifixi fige plagas

Cordi meo valide;
 Tui nati vulnerati,
 Tam dignati pro me pati,
 Pœnas mecum divide.

 .   .   .   .

"Fac me plagis vulnerari,
 Fac me cruce inebriari,
 Et cruore Filii;
 Inflammatus et accensus,
 Per te, Virgo, sim defensus
 In die iudicii."

²⁸ *Ibid.*, pp. 368–70.

"Next the cross in tears unceasing,
 Worn by sorrow aye increasing,
 Stood the Mother 'neath her Son.

"Hard the man his tears refraining,
 Watching Mary uncomplaining
 Bear a sorrow like to none.
 Hard the man that shares no sorrow
 With a Mother fain to borrow
 Every pang that writhes her Son.

"Tortured, scourged in expiation
 Of the sins that marred his nation,
 Mary watched his every pang.
 She beheld her dear Begotten
 Stretched in death by all forgotten,
 As on hoisted rood he hung.

"Mother, fount of Love, the purest,
 Floods of sorrow thou endurest;
 Turn them towards this heart of
   mine.

"Hallowed Mother, do this favour,
 Those five wounds that gored my
   Saviour
 Deeply on my heart engrave.
 Pains thou gladly with him sharest,
 Anguish that thou bravely bearest,
 Fully share with me, I crave.

"May his scars my body carry!
 May his cross and blood not tarry
 Soul of mine to satiate!
 Thus inflamed with love consuming,
 Shall I not, thy aid presuming,
 Safe the reck'ning day await?" ²⁸

In the hands of Thomas Aquinas the sequence was even used to expound with extreme poetic economy the strict scholastic doctrine on the mystery of transubstantiation. His sequence, from which we quote, is still sung in the service for the Feast of Corpus Christi ("Body of Christ").

"Dogma datur Christianis,
    Quod in carnem transit panis
    Et vinum in sanguinem;
    Quod non capis, quod non vides,

Animosa firmat fides,

Præter rerum ordinem."

"Christian truth uncontroverted
    Is that bread and wine converted
    Sacred flesh and blood become.
    Mind and eye whilst unperceiving,

What's beyond their own conceiving

Strenuous faith to them brings home." [29]

And certainly it was fitting that the sequence, which had grown out of the liturgy of the Church, should be employed for the Church's benefit. It was the form taken by many of the greatest Latin hymns of the middle ages. Of the so-called seven great hymns, we have referred to two, *De Contemptu Mundi* and *Stabat Mater*. The greatest of all Latin hymns may have been written by Thomas of Celano, St. Francis's first biographer and one of his earliest disciples; whoever wrote it felt the authentic inspiration of Franciscan realism, simplicity, and austerity. The *Dies Iræ* has been called the "greatest of all hymns and one of the greatest of all poems." Indeed, it is saying too little to call it—what it certainly is—"the most majestic of medieval sequences . . . perfect in form . . . the most sublime and poignant expression of the terror of the day" (i.e., the Day of Judgment).[30] It is still sung in all Masses for the dead, and one hears its words in Mozart's stupendous *Requiem*. "No English translation," says Helen Waddell, "has even come near it."

The Dies Iræ

"Dies iræ, dies illa
    Solvet sæclum in favilla,

Teste David cum Sibylla.

"Dreaded day, that day of ire,
    When the world shall melt in fire,

Told by Sybil and David's lyre.

[29] *Ibid.*, p. 665.
[30] Raby, *Christian Latin Poetry*, p. 443.

"Quantus tremor est futurus,

Quando iudex est venturus,

Cuncta stricte discussurus!

"Fright men's hearts shall rudely shift,
As the judge through gleaming rift
Comes each soul to closely sift.

"Tuba, mirum spargens sonum

Per sepulchra regionum,
Coget omnes ante thronum.

"Then the trumpet's shrill refrain,
Piercing tombs by hill and plain,
Souls to judgment shall arraign.

"Mors stupebit et natura,
Cum resurget creatura
Iudicanti responsura.

"Death and nature stand aghast,
As the bodies rising fast
Hie to hear the sentence passed.

"Liber scriptus proferetur,
In quo totum continetur

Unde mundus iudicetur.

"Then before Him shall be placed
That whereon the verdict's based,
Book wherein each deed is traced.

"Iudex ergo cum sedebit,

Quidquid latet, apparebit;
Nil inultum remanebit.

"When the Judge his seat shall gain,
All that's hidden shall be plain,
Nothing shall unjudged remain.

"Quid sum miser tunc dicturus,

Quem patronum rogaturus,
Cum vix iustus sit securus?

"Wretched man, what can I plead?
Whom to ask to intercede.
When the just much mercy need?

"Rex tremendæ majestatis,
Qui salvandos salvas gratis,
Salva me, fons pietatis!

"Thou, O awe-inspiring Lord,
Saving e'en when unimplored,
Save me, mercy's fount adored.

"Recordare, Iesu pie,
Quod sum causa tuæ viæ:

Ne me perdas illa die.

"Ah! Sweet Jesus, mindful be,
That thou cam'st on earth for me:
Cast me not this day from thee.

"Quærens me sedisti lassus;

Redemisti crucem passus:
Tantus labor non sit cassus.

. . . .

"Qui Mariam absolvisti,
Et latronem exaudisti,
Mihi quoque spem dedisti.

. . . .

"Oro supplex et acclinis,

Cor contritum quasi cinis:
Gere curam mei finis.

"Seeking me thy strength was
spent,
Ransoming thy limbs were rent:
Is this toil to no intent?

. . . .

"Mary's soul thou madest white,
Didst to heaven the thief invite,
Hope in me these now excite.

. . . .

"Prostrate, suppliant, now no
more
Unrepenting as of yore,
Save me dying, I implore." [31]

In addition to the sequence, which influenced so much religious and secular poetry, the Latin liturgy of the Church produced also the germ of the medieval and therefore the modern drama. There was a complete break between classical drama and medieval drama. Medieval drama began with the introduction into the liturgy for special feast days, such as Easter and Christmas, of the trope, an addition in the form of a dialogue, sung antiphonally by the choir. The earliest tropes may have been introduced into the liturgy at St. Gall in the ninth century, or more probably in France at a somewhat earlier time. They took the form, for example, of the conversation between the angels and the Marys at the tomb of the risen Lord, or of the three Magi on the way to behold the Child in the manger. Originally a part of the service, in the course of time, with an increase in the amount of dialogue and the personification of the characters, they were separated from the liturgy itself though performed in the church by priests and clerks. As they became more elaborate they were moved outside of the church to the church porch or yard, and finally to the market place. The place of the clergy as participants was gradually relinquished to lay actors, until at last special corporations or gilds were made responsible for their production. The history of the drama is therefore, like everything else medieval, a story of gradual secularization. Likewise the vernaculars, in the twelfth and thirteenth centuries, came gradually to supplant the Latin of the liturgy.

The earliest medieval drama was the mystery play, whose subject

Medieval drama

[31] Roman Missal, pp. 219–20.

matter was taken from the dramatic tales of the Old and New Testaments and whose purpose was religious edification and instruction. The twelfth century witnessed the rise of the miracle play, that is, of a dramatic representation of the intervention of the Virgin or some saint (St. Nicholas and St. Catherine were favorites) in the daily life of the world. Finally, in the fourteenth and fifteenth centuries, with the prevalent influence of the towns, emerged the morality play, whose characters and subject matter were allegorical. But once freed from Latin and the Church, the miracle and morality plays by no means necessarily retained either a religious or an ethical purpose; at times they introduced political questions and were put on for the sake of amusing town audiences. In the form of the oratorio and the passion play (notably that at Oberammergau, in Bavaria) the medieval drama survives in our midst in a form close to the original.

The history of medieval drama is an epitome of the history of medieval languages and literature. In all fields can be traced the same emancipation of the vernacular from Latin, the same triumph of secular and worldly interests over religious and ascetic interests. The history of medieval literature is inevitably a record of the political, economic, social, and intellectual development of the middle ages. The preeminence of Latin as an international language lasted about as long as the domination of the international ideal of the Holy Roman empire and the Roman Church. The triumph of the vernacular was coincident with the substitution of the ideal of a national state and a national church, with the growth of the towns, and with the emergence of the new internationalism of trade, commerce, and industry. In subject matter we should expect the young literatures to cater to the tastes not only of the feudal aristocracy but of the new bourgeoisie. The war waged against feudalism and manorialism by ambitious townsmen and peasants we should expect to find mirrored in literature. The earlier lack of concern for the peasant we should expect to see rectified as the peasant took his fate into his own hands, and as the majority of men acquired a more civilized and decent attitude. It would be strange if there were no giant in the literary domain; no writer whose typical, all-inclusive, and panoramic career meant for literature what Innocent III meant for the papacy, St. Francis for the monastery, St. Louis for the state; no poet whose work Henry Adams might have compared to the Gothic cathedral, as he compares the mighty intellectual edifice constructed by St. Thomas Aquinas.

The significance of the development of vernacular languages

One of the most important facts in the history of the middle ages we have been inclined so far to take for granted, namely, the formation of the languages used today by the peoples of western Europe, and by them carried to all quarters of the globe. There is perhaps no more fascinating pursuit, and no more accurate measure of the development of any civilization, than to study the growth of its spoken and written language. In the course of her expansion Rome imposed her language upon the native peoples of Italy, Spain, Gaul, Britain, parts of the Alps, and the province of Dacia, north of the lower Danube. We are not now interested in the literary language of Rome, but in the colloquial or vulgar Latin (Latin *vulgus,* "the common people") spoken by the soldiers, petty officials, colonists, and traders from whom the barbarian peoples learned their Latin. Except in Britain, where Celtic persisted, the spoken language in all these areas became this kind of Latin. What the conquered peoples learned naturally depended upon the time of the conquest: the language of Spain began as the Latin of the second century B.C., whereas the natives of Dacia learned the Latin of three hundred years later. The way in which the different peoples spoke Latin was naturally determined by many influences. For one thing, what kind of language had they previously spoken? Again, what other languages did they hear about them? In later times Arabic was spoken in Spain for many centuries, while the Latin-speaking Dacians were surrounded, and almost submerged, by Slavic invaders; indeed, one may well marvel that in these countries Latin survived at all. Finally, it was inevitable that Latin everywhere should be profoundly affected by the whole political and economic history of each of the Latin-speaking peoples; by the twelfth century northern French was a fairly well unified language, whereas in the actual speech even of educated people Italian is hardly yet a unified language. When the first Europeans settled in America, the printing press was already a hundred and fifty years old, and yet we know how many different varieties of English are still spoken in America, ranging all the way from Harvard English to Yiddish English, from Montana English to Negro English. In the course of use by illiterate people the originally somewhat different dialects of vulgar Latin so changed as to become finally—though it is not possible to say just when —the Latin or Romance languages (*linguæ Romanæ*). These include not only the major Latin languages of today—Italian, French, Spanish, Portuguese, and Rumanian—but numerous dialects, ranging in importance from Catalan and Provençal to those spoken in the eastern Alps.

Roman expansion did not embrace the Celts of Ireland or Scotland, or the Teutonic peoples of Germany and Scandinavia. On the contrary, the expansion of the Germans in the fourth, fifth, and sixth centuries enlarged the area speaking a German tongue. Except for Wales and Cornwall the invasion of Angles, Saxons, and Jutes into Britain destroyed both the vulgar Latin spoken by the Britons and what remained of their Celtic speech. On the continent the expansion of Franks and Alemanni to the left bank of the Rhine made this area, and part of Switzerland as well, German-speaking. But those Germans *The spread of* who wandered in comparatively small numbers far from home into *the German* areas speaking a dialect of vulgar Latin—the Visigoths in Spain and *language* southern Gaul, the Burgundians in the Rhone valley, and the Lombards in Italy—lost their language and took on that of the natives, just as the second and third generations of American immigrants lose their language. Their only influence on the vulgar Latin dialects was to add some words to their vocabularies, and possibly to delay their appearance as written languages. In addition to pushing the Celtic Britons back into Wales, the German invasions into Britain led to an exodus of Britons to the continent, which made again of Brittany a Celtic-speaking area after the threatening victory there of vulgar Latin. The expansion and colonization of the Franks north of the Loire in Gaul, although it did not lead to the extension of German speech to this area, nevertheless did influence the vulgar Latin dialect of the region more than the Visigothic conquest influenced that of southern Gaul. This accounts for the fact that the dialect of this region, which became the literary language of France, differs more from the parent Latin than the other Romance languages.

Although the Roman empire did not carry Latin to the Celts of Ireland and Scotland or to Germany and Scandinavia, the expansion of Christianity with its monasteries and organized Church served the same purpose. Christianity, however, could introduce Latin only as *Emergence* the written and spoken language of religion and learning; it was un- *of the written* able to influence at all the Celtic and German spoken by these peoples. *vernacular* Therefore, alongside of the Romance languages there developed, originally from a parent Teutonic tongue, a group of Germanic languages: German proper, Swedish, Norwegian, Danish, Dutch, and Flemish. Irish (Gaelic) was the earliest Celtic language to reach the dignity of a written language in the middle ages, because, as a spoken language, it had no competition with either Latin or German. Welsh and Breton were practically identical and were written as well as spoken. The Germanic languages, because of no competition with Latin, were written before the Romance languages. Anglo-Saxon poetry appeared in the eighth century, and prose in the ninth. The first

French we have was written in the Strassburg Oath (842). The first examples of Spanish and Italian come from the tenth century. English occupies a peculiar place in this development because of the Norman conquest in 1066. Then the Anglo-Saxon speech of the preconquest period, influenced to some extent by Celtic and Latin, became the language of the uneducated peasant and townsman, while the Norman-French of the conqueror became the language of the government, of the aristocracy, of some small groups in the towns, and of literature. The essentially Germanic language of the English people was consequently much enriched by the Romance language of the conquerors, so that although it was retarded in achieving literary perfection it remains the most composite and the richest of all European languages.

Medieval Latin

At the same time that vulgar Latin was developing into the Romance tongues the written and spoken Latin of educated men was also undergoing its last transformation as a living language. In a sense the tendencies are quite parallel. As long as men studied Latin in the schools and read the classical authors there could not be a complete breakdown of the forms of classical Latin. And when such a breakdown actually threatened, the revivals inspired by Charles the Great and by some cathedral schools helped to stop it. Yet it was impossible to keep using Latin as a learned and professional language and at the same time maintain the classical perfection of Cicero. For Latin to be kept useful it must be adapted to a society very different from that of the first century B.C. The Latin of a Roman republic, of a pagan religion, of an urban society, could scarcely be applied to feudalism, Christianity, and a primitive agricultural society. The Latin vocabulary had to take on new meanings or adopt new words from the vernaculars. Grammar and syntax had to become less rigid and simpler to be employed by men who had less satisfactory opportunities for schooling, and who aimed to appeal to an audience perhaps even less fortunate than they. Moreover, in the written speech scholars were inevitably influenced by the popular speech about them. Latin had to conform to the simpler usages and forms of the vernaculars.

To the dyed-in-the-wool classicist all this is a sign of degeneration, barbarism, and ignorance. Indeed, some medieval Latin was written by ignorant men who had no more knowledge of spelling and grammar than many freshmen in our universities. But in many cases deviations—for example, in spelling—are to be explained by differences in pronunciation rather than by ignorance. In any case, there was no slavish subservience on the part of the ordinary medieval scholar to the forms of what would have been an archaic language to him. He bent Latin to his own needs in all fields of pursuit, and thus kept it alive and growing. In fact, medieval Latin developed such a vitality that in spite of the more common use of the vernaculars after the twelfth century, and in spite of the demand of the humanists of the Italian renaissance that all Latin writing should conform to the Ciceronian canon, it continued to be used as an international scholarly language down into the seventeenth century. Many have been the pleas that it be restored to that position today in order to avoid the necessity of having to learn to read the language of any scholar whose works one wishes to consult. The Canon of the Cathedral of Palermo today, when he wishes to write a priest in New York City to thank him for money sent for commemorative Masses, does not need to have someone write in English for him. He simply writes a letter in Latin, still a living language for the Church.

The final development of the vernaculars into literary form reflects in some ways the actual political development of western Europe. Feudalism as a political system was essentially local, and had to be destroyed by monarchy if the larger needs of a more complicated society *Competition* were to be met. Vernacular speech likewise took form as local dialects, *between the* and before there emerged a literary language recognized as standard, *vernacular* a long battle was fought between the dialects themselves. In France, *dialects* for example, the dialect that triumphed south of the Loire was originally that of the region of Limousin, which, when used by the troubadours of the south for their poetry, was generally called Provençal. North of the Loire, the dialect that was spoken in the Capetian Île de France won out over many others. The dialect of the Capetian domain expanded with that domain into the south and ultimately crowded out Provençal as a literary language. The language of the French kings destroyed the dialects as literary media just as the French kings themselves destroyed feudalism.

Politics alone, however, cannot explain the victory of one dialect over the other. In case one particular dialect was used by an artist in a masterpiece widely admired and imitated, such an example might prove as powerful as kings. In Italy it was the dialect of Tuscany that became the literary language, because Dante made such superb use of it in the *Divine Comedy*. In Spain the kings of Castile helped to assure the victory of Castilian; in Germany, Luther's translation of the Bible made for the victory of the language of the Saxon court; Chaucer laid the foundation for modern English. In spite of the victory of one particular dialect in the literary language, the others continued to exist as local patois for familiar speech, and of course still exist. Although possessed of a common literary language, the Berliner today has difficulty in understanding the patois of the Bavarian in Munich, and both would have difficulty in understanding the speech of an Alsatian peasant.

The epic tradition

The vernacular literatures of the middle ages are so rich and varied that it is somewhat bold to try to summarize them briefly. Until the thirteenth century they expressed themselves almost exclusively in poetry, and, as is usually the case with primitive peoples, that poetry was epic in form. It was the German and Viking of the heroic periods of their expansion who founded the epic tradition in European vernacular literature. Of the earlier epics in Germanic tongues there were the Anglo-Saxon *Beowulf*, the German *Hildebrandslied*, and the Norse sagas.[32] They take us back into the world of the hardy German warrior of superb stature and of his equally magnificent gods and goddesses. They are thoroughly pagan in spirit. In a new version of one of the German sagas, the *Song of the Niebelungs (Niebelungenlied)*, written around the turn of the twelfth and thirteenth centuries, it is evident how much the Christian and chivalric ideals have modified the old pagan, heroic sentiment. The setting is historic, the royal

The Niebelungenlied

court of the Burgundians at Worms and Attila's court in modern Hungary. In its recital of the hostility between Kriemhild and Brunhild, of the death of Siegfried, and of the frightful slaughter of the Burgundian court by the Huns, it preserves much of the stern, brooding, elemental passions of the earlier sagas, but at the same time it is a Christian and feudal German atmosphere into which this older theme is placed. If Kriemhild became the wild and raging queen of the Hunnic king, she was to begin with the gentle lady wooed by the brave knight Siegfried. Richard Wagner, the German composer of the nineteenth century, rewrote the old German sagas and set them to music of far more stirring quality than the tales themselves for the four music dramas that make up his *Ring der Niebelungen*.

The Song of Roland

The German epic tradition caught hold of the Romance vernaculars in France and Spain in the late eleventh and twelfth centuries in the two poems with which the history of French and Spanish literature begins, the *Song of Roland* and the *Poem of My Cid*. With them we leave the earlier heroic German world for the epoch of the first crusades, yet the actual theme of these poems is not the crusades to the east but the struggle between Christian and Moslem in Spain. It is curious that the eastern crusades supplied nothing more than gen-

[32] See pp. 227, 261, 271.

eral atmosphere for western epic poetry. In the *Song of Roland* a patriarchal Charlemagne assumes heroic proportions as a crusader for "sweet France." The historic incident around which the poem was built by clerks aiming to furnish amusement for pilgrims to St. James of Compostella was the fatal attack by Christian Basques on the Frankish rear guard that cost the life of Roland, Margrave of Brittany.[33] But the author of the *Roland* was no more able than any other medieval artist to give any historical perspective to his tale, even had he wanted to. It is an army of powerful, brave, and loyal Christian vassals under their suzerain, the venerable French king of the late eleventh century, who are lording it over the Moslems in Spain. For the *Roland* is French in its patriotism, and it is a faithful reflection of an aristocratic feudal society in which women as yet have no very large place. The historical figure back of the *Poem of My Cid* is Ruy Diaz de Bivar (d. 1099), who played a conspicuous part in the struggle of the kings of Castile with the Moors in the late eleventh century but who never managed to keep the good graces of his king and fought with the Moslems as well as with the Christians. In the earliest Spanish epic he is already a figure of heroic legend, the faithful vassal, the loving husband and father, the Castilian crusader warring against the Infidel.

The Poem of My Cid

Around Charles the Great and his knights, especially Roland, there developed a whole cycle of no less than eighty epic *chansons de geste* (songs of deeds) of undying popularity in all countries of western Europe for the rest of the middle ages. In Germany the figure of Roland erected in the town square became the symbol of the town's freedom. In Italy, with no proper epic tradition of its own, Roland (Orlando) became a great favorite, changing in type with changes in literary fashion. In the late fifteenth century Boiardo in his *Orlando Innamorato* is writing "of great Orlando caught by Love's delight," in what is a combination of the legends of Charles the Great and Arthur. In the next century Ariosto was writing in his *Orlando Furioso* of a Roland mad with jealousy, who at the same time is enough of a sophisticated man of the world not to take love too tragically.

The Carolingian cycle of chansons de geste

An example of the transformation of the older *chansons de geste* of the Charlemagne legend with humor, extravagant fantasy, and romance is the *Pilgrimage of Charlemagne to Jerusalem*. Charlemagne, in fine mettle, challenges his wife with the question, "Dame . . . hast thou ever seen a king beneath Heaven whose crown and sword became him so well?" and receives the unexpected answer that King Hugon the Strong, Emperor of Greece and Constantinople, is far

The Pilgrimage of Charlemagne to Jerusalem

[33] See pp. 243-44.

more accomplished in wearing his crown and sword. The emperor, accompanied by his twelve peers, felt it necessary to test out this opinion for himself by going to see Hugon. They rode on "strong and gentled-paced" mules, taking with them throne chairs and tents of silk. But first they paid a visit to Jerusalem, and in the church where "God did once chant mass, and eke the apostles," Charles sat down in the chair in which God had sat, and his peers occupied the chairs of the twelve apostles, with the result that it was announced to the patriarch that God and the twelve apostles had come to visit him. After four months they left Jerusalem for Constantinople, taking with them precious relics which the patriarch had given them, "some sweat from the brow of Jesus at the time when He was put down and laid in the Sepulchre," "the holy crown that God wore on His head," "the knife that God held at meat," "some of the beard of St. Peter besides, and some of the hairs of his head," and "milk of the holy Virgin, with which she suckled Jesus when He was come down to earth in our midst."

When they approached Constantinople they saw "twenty thousand knights . . . clad in silk and white ermine, and great martin-furs falling down to their very feet" and "three thousand maidens in gleaming gold embroideries." The emperor they found at a plow whose "yokes were of fine gleaming gold, and the axles and wheels and plowshares of bronze." King Hugon was very glad to see them and took them into the wondrous palace "veined with azure; very beautiful it was with painted semblances of beasts and serpents, of flying birds and all created things." After feasting them with "venison and boar's meat, wild goose and crane, and peppered peacocks," while "jongleurs sang and fiddled and played on the rote," he conducted them to sumptuous quarters for the night and gave them plenty of wine. As a result of it Charles and the Franks took to boasting of what they would do on the morrow, boasts varying from feats of super-human strength to extraordinary sexual prowess. When these boasts were reported to Hugon by a spy, he vowed that the Franks should perform them on the following day. This they did after an angel of God appeared before Charles saying, "Charles, be not dismayed, Jesus commands thee! The boastings thou madest last evening were great folly; Christ bids thee never do the like to any man again. Go and begin them, for not one of them will fail." When they threatened to ruin Hugon's empire, he had them stopped and became Charles's vassal. Thereupon a crown-wearing contest was staged, and it was concluded by all the Franks that "Our lady the Queen spoke wrong and foolishly." The Franks then mounted their mules for home. Oliver left his fair Byzantine princess behind with the unchivalrous remark, "Fair one . . . my love must leave thee behind. I go hence to France with my lord Charles." It was such a fine trip that Charles pardoned his dame when he got home, "for the love of the Sepulchre unto which he hath prayed." [34]

In the twelfth and thirteenth centuries France was the source of literary inspiration for western Europe. At the same time that poets in northern France were developing the taste for epic poetry with the *chansons de geste,* poets in southern France, writing in Provençal, were perfecting the lyric. Corresponding to the poet of northern France, the trouvère, whose works were sung by the wandering jongleur, was the southern French troubadour, who gave his poems to be sung to the joglar. It is difficult to explain why there should have arisen in southern France in the twelfth century such a great amount of troubadour poetry of such great technical excellence and variety. About five hundred troubadours are known by name who wrote in some nine hundred stanza forms. Our general books have not yet made clear enough to us the particular features of the history of the region south of the Loire that would explain the sudden appearance of a well-developed school of lyric poetry by the end of the eleventh century. Nor have we had sufficiently well pointed out to us the extent to which northwestern Italy, southern France, and northern Spain were controlled by closely related feudal families, and bound together by trade with each other and with Mohammedan Spain and North Africa. This whole area formed a kind of cultural unity with a strong Roman tradition under Moslem influence. It nourished heretics as well as poetry. The unity was broken by the Albigensian crusade, which opened up the way for northern French influences and the deadening effect of religious conformity. *The Provençal troubadour*

Before this catastrophe, southern France had enriched European literature with a poetry belonging neither to the German nor to the Latin tradition, whose imitation was widespread and whose influence on lyric poetic forms has never ceased. Although the troubadours themselves were not necessarily of noble birth (indeed, they frequently were of obscure or bourgeois origin, and some of them were clergy) they addressed themselves to the feudal courts of the south, among which they wandered, those among others of Poitiers, Orange, Montpellier, Toulouse, Marseilles, Béziers, Carcassonne, and Roussillon. And, what was new, they addressed themselves as lovers to the *The troubadour and his lady*

[34] The quotations are from the translation by Margaret Schlauch in *Medieval Narrative,* pp. 77 ff.

married ladies who presided over these courts, whose inexhaustible virtues they never wearied of extolling, and whose haughty aloofness, they said, they were struggling with great pains to unbend. When "your noble, graceful form, your fair light-brown hair, your brow whiter than the lily, your gay laughing eyes, your straight well-formed nose, your fresh complexion, whiter and redder than any flower, your little mouth, your fair teeth, whiter than pure silver . . . your fair white hands with the smooth and slender fingers" [35] became subjects for lyric poetry, something had happened to the harsh, crude, feudal world. Love and my lady entered elegantly into the scene.

Yet, allowing for the normal weakness of mortal flesh, the love which the troubadour bore his mistress was a purely formal, conventional love according to rules couched in the language of feudalism. The troubadour was the vassal of the lady, owing service in her court of love. His homage and fealty were rendered in his poetry, as much a matter of rule as courtly love itself. In fact love was poetry. Becoming a lady's troubadour was a matter of ceremonial contract. What he pretended to crave was the favor of his lady's smile, worth more than the smiles of four hundred angels, a nod of recognition, a lock of her hair, a ribbon, gloves, or a ring. What he was most interested in was food and drink and lodging for a while, some generous acknowledgment of his talent. The poetry of the troubadours celebrated courtly love in courtly poetry, and developed and popularized the intellectual adoration of women. In so doing it formulated some of the rules of knightly chivalry. But it was also the outcome of a peculiar system of patronage.

The troubadour arranged his intricate metrical and rime schemes into poems of a definite subject matter and form. Some authors prided themselves on the obscurity of their verse and were blamed for it by those who wrote in the clear style. The ordinary love song was the *chanso,* and as sung by Bernard de Ventadour, Eleanor of Aquitaine's troubadour and one of the greatest of them all, it laments the indifference of all ladies.

A chanso of Bernard de Ventadour

> "Whene'er the lark's glad wings I see
> Beat sunward 'gainst the radiant sky
> Till, lost in joy so sweet and free,
> She drops, forgetful how to fly,—
> Ah, when I view such happiness
> My bosom feels so deep an ache,

[35] Arnaut de Mareiul in Chaytor, *The Troubadours,* p. 51.

Meseems for pain and sore distress
My longing heart will straightway break.

"Alas, I thought I held the key
To love! How ignorant am I!
For her that ne'er will pity me
I am not able to defy;
My loving heart, my faithfulness,
Myself, my world, she deigns to take,
Then leaves me bare and comfortless
To longing thoughts that ever wake.

"Henceforth all ladies I will flee,—
No more in hope or trust I'll sigh;
Oft have I been their guarantee,
But now for champion let them hie
Where'er they will; for one could bless
My life, yet binds me to the stake;
They're all alike, and I profess
That all alike I now forsake." [36]

The *salut d'amor*, or greeting of love, was cast in the form of a letter to the lady, and at least in the verses of Arnaut de Mareiul goes beyond the bonds of mere conventionality.

A salut d'amor of Arnaut de Mareiul

"When I shall see you, who can say?
But my true heart, which chose to stay
With you the very day I learned
Your loveliness, hath ne'er returned;
Hath ne'er returned to me again,
But e'er hath dwelt with you since then.
Where'er you be 'tis there with you
Both day and night your love to woo. . . .
O lovely lady, would I might
For all my truth see day or night
Ere life departs, when—free and bold
Or even in secret—I could fold
Within my arms your fair, sweet form,
And gaze and lavish kisses warm
On lips, on eyes, until in one

[36] Smith, *The Troubadours at Home*, II, 162–65.

We melt a hundred,—still not done,
And faints for joy my blissful soul!
I've said too much, but self-control
Cannot forbid me once to say
The wish I've thought this many a day. . . ." [37]

A sirventes of Raimbaut de Vaqueiras   In the *sirventes* the troubadour expressed his feelings on all subjects not concerned with love and gave vent to political and moral satire. Raimbaut de Vaqueiras puts the difficulty of having to go on a crusade and thus leave his lady.

"The Maker of air and heaven, earth and sea,
And heat and cold, and wind and rain and sky,
Bids all the pious raise their sails and fly,
And he will guide us as the magian Three
Were led to Bethlehem; the Turks, elated,
Seize plain and mountain; God checks not the loss,
For we are bound, as He endured our cross,
To fight for Him; to live despised and hated
And die in shame choose they who do not go;
For we are slaves to sin, as all should know,
But he that Jordan bathes is liberated.

. . . .

Shall I, Fair Knight, account my soul as dross
For your sake whom I sing, or take the cross?
To go, to stay—in vain have I debated;
Your beauty, while I see you, lays me low,
And, lonely though the company o'erflow,
I seem to die when we are separated." [38]

Peire Cardinal   Peire Cardinal in a *sirventes* suggests that it would not do for God to turn him down on the Judgment Day, nor anyone else for that matter.

"A new sirvente I have resolved to make,
Which I will offer at the Judgment-Day
To Him that formed me of the lifeless clay,
If, when 1 come, His anger should awake;

[37] *Ibid.*, I, 174.
[38] *Ibid.*, I, 72–73.

And if He wish to send me to perdition,
'So be it not,' I'll say with all submission,
'An evil world I've had to undergo,
So shelter me, I pray, from endless woe.'

"The court of heaven shall marvel and shall quake
To hear the pleas that I shall then array,
For I declare God doth His own betray
If He destroy them in the burning lake;
To lose what He could gain is an admission
That He should lack, since that is His ambition,
For He should sweetly make His heaven grow
By taking all whom death permits to go.

"To close the door would be a sad mistake,
And how 't would shame Lord Peter to obey
(For Peter keeps the gate) and turn away
A single guest that would God's cheer partake;
For every court is open to suspicion
If some fare ill, while some have glad fruition;
And though God be a mighty king, we know,
If closed His portal, we shall cry 'What, ho!'" [39]

In other of his *sirventes* he is indignant at the clergy. "Kings and emperors, dukes, counts and knights used to rule the world: now the priests have the power which they have gained by robbery and treachery, by hypocrisy, force and preaching." "Eagles and vultures smell not the carrion so readily as priests and preachers smell out the rich." [40] He is equally outspoken against social evils: "Many a man builds walls and palaces with the goods of others and yet the witless world says that he is on the right path, because he is clever and prosperous." "As silver is refined in the fire, so the patient poor are purified under grievous oppression: and with what splendour the shameless rich man may feed and clothe himself, his riches bring him naught but pain, grief and vexation of spirit." Guillem Fiqueira in his *sirventes* attacks Rome bitterly: "I wonder not, Rome, that men go astray, for thou hast cast the world into strife and misery; virtue and good works die and are buried because of thee, treacherous Rome, thou guiding-star, thou root and branch of all iniquity. . . . Rome, thou

Criticism in the sirventes

[39] *Ibid.,* II, 46.
[40] Quoted in Chaytor, *op. cit.,* p. 85.

hast the outward semblance of a lamb, so innocent is thy countenance, but within thou art a ravening wolf, a crowned snake begotten of a viper and therefore the devil greeteth thee as the friend of his bosom."

The *tenso* was a form of poetical debate such as was used in Latin poetry. It debated such questions as: Is it better to have wisdom or be irresistible to the ladies? Which should a lady prefer, the man who avows his love or the man who dares not avow it? Which is the harder to bear, debt or lovesickness? Are the joys or the ills of love the greater? The *planh* was a funeral lament for a patron, the most famous of which is Gaucelm Faidit's lament over the death of Richard Lion-hearted. The *pastorela* recounted the conversation between knight and shepherdess wherein the maiden is not always so cold to love's overtures as she sometimes is. The *alba* announced to the lovers at dawn in the words of a watching friend that the pleasures of the night must, alas, be put aside. In one of Guiraut de Borneil's *albas*, the watching friend says:

> "I have not slept, fair friend, since you were there,
> But on my knees have made unceasing prayer
> That Mary's Son would grant you His protection,
> And give you back to my sincere affection,
> And soon will come the morning."

He even in the first stanza calls upon God himself to guard this clandestine love.

> "O glorious king, true radiance and light,
> Lord, powerful God, be pleased with gracious might
> To guard my friend, for since the night descended
> He turns not back from perils where he wended,
> And soon will come the morning."

In the evening song, or *serena*, the lover contemplates expectantly the joys of the coming night. In a song of Bertran de Born, whom Dante puts in hell for causing strife between Henry II of England and his sons, the pageantry as well as the brutality of feudal warfare is glorified.

> "I love the blithesome Eastertide,
> That brings the leaves and flowers back;

I love the merry birds that glide
  Through blooming copses, with no lack
  Of gay and happy singing;
    I love to see fair tents arrayed
    Across the meadow and the glade,
    And then, while spurs are stinging,
    To see, with gonfanons displayed,
    The armored knights and steeds parade.

" 'Tis pleasant when the scout and guide
  Drive herds and people from their track,
And when behind them swiftly ride
  A host of lances to attack,
    Like eagles fiercely winging;
    'Tis pleasant when assaults are made,
    Walls broken, garrisons dismayed,—
Fresh soldiers ever springing,
    And no attacking knight afraid
    To try the ditch and palisade.

"We see the work of strength and pride,
  Swords, maces, helmets blue and black,
And broken shields on every side;
  Brave struggling knights that hew and hack,
    And horses madly flinging
    The wounded riders they obeyed;
    While all the men of noble grade
Their brands and axes swinging,
    Lop arms and heads, unmoved, unstayed,—
    Defeat not death should one evade.

"I prize no meat or drink beside
  The cry 'On, on!' from throats that crack;
The neighs when frightened steeds run wide,
  A riderless and frantic pack,
    And set the forest ringing;
    The calls 'Help, help!'; the warriors laid
    Beside the moat with brows that fade,
To grass and stubble clinging;
    And then the bodies, past all aid,
    Still pierced with broken spear or blade.

"Come, barons, haste ye, bringing
Your vassals for the daring raid;
Risk all, and let the game be played!" [41]

*Spread of
Provençal
poetry*

The Albigensian crusade either scattered the troubadours into neighboring countries or destroyed their means of livelihood. In truth, they had by that time well-nigh exhausted the possibilities of the theme of romantic love and chivalrous service to the lady. But individual poets continued to write, and often enough wrote under the influence of the intensified post-crusade orthodoxy. They simply substituted for Our Lady of the Castle, Our Lady, the Mother of Christ, preserving all the elegant and superficial formality of their verse. By the middle of the fourteenth century (1356) it was possible for the few remaining troubadours to formulate the rules of their art into a definite code, the *Leys d'amors*. Like the *chansons de geste* troubadour poetry spread everywhere in the west. Through the influence of Eleanor of Aquitaine, herself the granddaughter of the first notable troubadour, William IV, Count of Poitiers, and her daughter the Countess of Champagne, it spread into northern France and England. In northern Spain, Provençal was preferred for a while to local dialects, and troubadour poetry was the stimulus for an important outpouring of Portuguese poetry. In Italy the court of Frederick II was only too glad to welcome gifted men whom a papal crusade had ousted. In northern and central Italy also, Provençal poetry was the source in both form and subject matter of Italian poetry. It was upon its

*The
minnesinger
Walter von der
Vogelweide*

tradition that the young Dante fed. In Germany Provençal poetry stimulated the minnesinger to song, although, as was the case in Italy, the theme of romantic love (*Minne*) was handled with greater freshness and depth. The greatest of the German minnesingers was Walter von der Vogelweide. In one of his poems he dreams of meeting his lady at a dance.

" 'Take this wreath,' I said, 'they are only wild flowers, but the best I can give you; and I know where there are more gay flowers, yonder upon the heath they grow, where the little birds sing. Come, let us break the flowers.' She took what I offered her, like a bashful maiden she flushed, her cheeks were like roses blooming amid lilies, she cast down her lovely eyes, it seemed to me that never did I have

[41] Smith, *op. cit.*, II, 238–39.

greater joy. The air was heavy with blossoms falling from the trees, I was woven around with delight; then it dawned and I awoke." [42]

As a sincere German patriot he blamed Innocent III for ruining Germany with the civil war between Welf and Hohenstaufen, and one of the earliest of a long line of such complaints pictures Innocent saying: "All the while I fill my chests. I have led them about by my stick: their riches will all be mine, their German silver flows into my Roman shrine. Feast on fowl, ye priests, and drink your wine, and let the witless German laymen fast!" [43] The great writers of troubadour poetry, while concerned chiefly with the theme of the lady, could not refrain from expressing themselves upon what they regarded as the evils of their own times.

France was again the center for the spread of a third important type of literature for the aristocratic feudal classes—the courtly epic centering about King Arthur and his Knights of the Round Table. But France was not the source of these tales. They were Celtic, either Breton or Welsh in origin. Their hero, Arthur, who with his knights came now to threaten the popularity of Charles the Great and his twelve peers, was the early sixth-century Celtic hero of Britain in the fight against the Saxon invaders. The cycle of legend about Arthur preserved in the Welsh vernacular was first introduced to a wider reading public by Geoffrey of Monmouth, a half-Norman, half-Welsh writer who in about 1135 finished his *History of the Kings of Britain*, in the composition of which he says he used Welsh material. On the continent the *lais* of the Anglo-Norman poet Marie de France introduced the Arthurian cycle to northern French feudal society. Her poem *Lanval* presented Arthur, and *La Chevrefeuille* the immortal lovers Tristram and Iseult. *The Arthurian cycle*

It was as if with great relief that the poets and their aristocratic audiences turned from those *chansons de geste* which pictured the realistic world of turmoil about them to the wholly imaginary and fantastic realm of adventurous romance enshrined in the Arthurian legends, to "these enchanted castles from which gentle maidens are to be rescued; these miraculous mountains in the wilderness near which terrific battles are to be fought for nothing; these giants and dwarfs defying courtly manners; these lions with lamb-like obedience following their masters; these caves of love and fairy groves; these bold abductions and strange deliverances." Here are "incessant descriptions

---

[42] Francke, *History of German Literature*, p. 74.
[43] Francke, *Personality in German Literature before Luther*, p. 16, n. 1.

of armaments and garments; of hairdress and complexion; of the striding, riding, sitting and curtseying of the knights and ladies; of horses, hounds, and monsters; of precious stones and stately halls; of rocky defiles and impenetrable forests." [44] In fact, with the Arthurian legend was blended the contemporaneous cult of women and courtly love from southern France to make of the courtly epics the literary expressions of the ideal world of perfect chivalry. In France the classic writer of the romances of chivalry was Chrétien de Troyes.

The Grail legend

The two essentially unchristian themes of romantic love and chivalry were modified to include the best idealism of the crusading orders of the twelfth century. The ideal of the perfect knight was enlarged to include service to the helpless and oppressed, service to the Church, and seeking communion with the mystic power of God. The legends growing about the Holy Grail Christianized the essentially secular Celtic and Provençal material, and were attached to the earlier Arthurian material in the prose romances of the thirteenth century. The ideal knight, the embodiment of all Christian virtues, became a saintly figure in *Perceval,* taking as his adventure the search for the holy vessel which was used at the Last Supper or caught the blood from the wounds of the Savior on the cross. Galahad, the son of Lancelot, marks the end of the development: the pure, chaste, ascetic monk-knight. In this form the Arthurian legend mirrored the eternal struggle for salvation and the mystic's flight into the unknown. Of course the Arthurian cycle was as widespread in popularity as the

Spread of the Arthurian legend

chansons de geste or the poetry of the troubadour. It spread into Spain and Italy. In the hands of German poets it received in some instances a treatment much superior to that of the French poets. Hartmann von Aue adapted Chrétien's *Erec and Yvain.* Wolfram von Eschenbach completed and adapted Chrétien's *Perceval* in his *Parzival,* a humanly conceived drama of spiritual liberation, "the most interesting individual work of modern European literature prior to the *Divina Commedia.*" [45] In the writing of Gottfried of Strassburg the story of Tristram and Iseult reached its classic form. Richard Wagner has done over the legends of Tristram and Perceval and set them to priceless and imperishable music. In the late fifteenth century Sir Thomas Malory summarized the whole Arthurian cycle in fine English prose in his *Morte d'Arthur.* Most students have read parts of it in Tennyson's *Idylls of the King.* From the late twelfth century on Charlemagne, Arthur, and the spirit of the Provençal lyric kept close com-

[44] *Ibid.,* pp. 20–21.
[45] Quoted in Lawrence, *Medieval Story,* p. 123.

pany and spread to an ever widening audience. For a short while there followed in their wake the heroes of a classical cycle—Alexander, Æneas, and others of Troy and Thebes—but in spite of their medieval dress they were unable to stand the competition.

Such literature as the heroic *chansons de geste*, the Provençal lyrics, or the Arthurian romances, sung by wandering minstrels in castle halls or in milady's boudoir, was hardly for the bourgeoisie. They took to prose renderings of these tales, to be sure, or to such half-prose, half-verse tales of Byzantine origin as that telling of the love of noble young Aucassin for Nicolette, a captive purchased from the Saracens. In this charming story no threat of hell deters Aucassin from pursuing his beloved. Of paradise, in fact, he had no very high opinion: *Literature for the bourgeoisie*

"For into Paradise go none but such people as I will tell you of. There go those agèd priests, and those old cripples, and the maimed, who all day long and all night couch before the altars, and in the crypts beneath the churches; those who go in worn old mantles and old tattered habits; who are naked, and barefoot, and full of sores; who are dying of hunger and of thirst, of cold and of wretchedness. Such as these enter in Paradise, and with them have I nought to do. But in Hell will I go. For to Hell go the fair clerks and the fair knights who are slain in the tourney and the great wars, and the stout archer and the loyal man. With them will I go. And there go the fair and courteous ladies, who have friends, two or three, together with their wedded lords. And there pass the gold and the silver, the ermine and all rich furs, harpers and minstrels, and the happy of the world. With these will I go, so only that I have Nicolette, my very sweet friend, by my side." [46]   *Aucassin and Nicolette*

Together with Nicolette he fled across the sea to the realm of Torelore, whose king lay ill in childbed and whose queen was out fighting the enemies of the realm with "roasted crab-apples and eggs and fresh cheeses." After many adventures they were separated but finally happily reunited. But this even was too romantic for shrewd and earthy bourgeois taste. The burgher preferred the collection of animal stories going back through Rome to Æsop which had been gathered together in the *Romance of Renard*. Renard the Fox was sharp-witted, cunning, and without principle. He needed to be to survive; for this literature seemed to say that society is ruled by evil and brute strength, only to be overcome by an unscrupulous cunning. The authors of these *The Romance of Renard*

[46] The translation of E. Mason in Everyman's Library, p. 6.

tales parodied with telling cynicism the feudal world of the *chansons* or the romances.

The townsman relished, in addition, those amusing stories gathered from all sources and put into verse that are called the *fabliaux*. Herein was no restraint of good form or good taste. The only thing necessary was to appeal to a rather undeveloped sense of humor, usually at the expense of the housewife, who is generally unfaithful, or of the clergy, who are frequently the cause of her infidelity. In one of them the town prostitute tells a noble, a burgher, a priest, and several peasants that each is the father of her child and each contributes to its support. In another a "fair and savory, gay, joyous and amorous" wife, while entertaining "a fair and well-instructed clerk," was called upon by "a comely varlet." The clerk having been put behind a chest, she had only commenced to entertain the varlet when her husband came home. The varlet had to hide under the table. They were both discovered, but nothing much happened, for the husband was "debonair and frank . . . a long-suffering cuckold," and the wife "was not too greatly embarrassed, for of a necessity she was made aware that her husband was a true cuckold." In a third, a Paris clerk is refused hospitality by a burgher's wife, only to pass, as he continued on his way, "a priest wrapped up in his black cape," who was welcomed into the house at which he had just been turned down. But the clerk met the husband and was taken back home with him, the priest this time having to hide in the stable. The priest was at last discovered, after the clerk made known the feast that had been prepared for him but was being denied to the husband and clerk. The priest was roughly handled and his coat and hood turned over to the student.[47] These bourgeois women are the paler forerunners of Chaucer's grand wife of Bath.

The medieval childlike love for a story was fed also on such fantastic and moralized tales as those collected in the *Gesta Romanorum*, which were translated into the vernaculars and furnished tales and plots to many later writers, or in collections of stories from the lives of the saints, the most famous of which was the thirteenth-century *Legenda aurea* (the *Golden Legend*) made by a Dominican Archbishop of Genoa. Many other collections of tales were made by famous preachers, usually friars, for use as sermon-stories (*exempla*).

It must be noted too that although there was no written literature for the peasant, since he was illiterate, his song and tale passed from mouth to mouth, and were occasionally written down. Moreover, in the thirteenth and fourteenth centuries the peasant came to be an ob-

[47] These *fabliaux* are translated in Schlauch, *op. cit.*, pp. 433 ff.

ject of sympathetic treatment by clerical or lay writers. In England the Robin Hood ballads of the fourteenth century, born of the democratic spirit of the peasantry, made clear that knights and ladies were not the only ones who possessed manners. They pay scant respect to the clergy. In the same century William Langland, in his allegorical *Vision of Piers Plowman*, voices strong protest against the sufferings of the English peasantry, which indeed broke out into open revolt towards the end of the century. "It is not only the first authentic voice of the English people, it is the first and almost the only utterance in literature of the cry of the poor," of

The peasant in literature

> "Old men and hoar . that be helpless and needy,
> And women with child . that cannot work,
> Blind men and bed ridden . and broken in their members,
> And all poor sufferers . patient under God's sending,
> As lepers and mendicants . men fallen into mischief,
> Prisoners and pilgrims . and men robbed perchance,
> Or brought low by liars . and their goods lost,
> Or through fire or through flood . fallen to poverty,
> That take their mischiefs meekly . and mildly at heart." [48]

The rich may talk about God, but he is really among lowly men:

> "Thus they drivel on their dais . the Deity to know
> And gnaw God in their gullet . when their guts are full.
> But the careful may cry . and complain at the gate
> Both a-hungered and a-thirst . quaking with cold
> Is none to call him near . to help his need.
> But they hue him away like a hound . and order him off.
>
> .   .   .   .
>
> God is much in the mouths . of these great masters,
> But among mean men . His mercy and works." [49]

More particularly from southern Germany, however, came works of the thirteenth century treating sympathetically of the lives and ambitions of the wealthier peasants. In Hartmann von Aue's *Der arme Heinrich (Poor Henry)*, Heinrich, the lord of the manor, is stricken low with leprosy and cared for by a faithful peasant, a free

Der arme Heinrich

[48] Dawson, *Mediæval Religion*, pp. 170–71.
[49] *Ibid.*, pp. 176–77.

Meier
Helmbrecht

renter. The young daughter of the peasant insists upon offering up her life for the health of her father's lord. Ultimately, after Heinrich is cured through the self-sacrifice of the maid and with the realization of his own perverse attitude, he marries her. The locale is Swabian, and the relationship pictured between peasant and lord is harmonious.

The locale of Wernher's *Meier Helmbrecht* is southeastern Bavaria, the region about Burghausen. It is the tale of a prosperous peasant's whippersnapper son, who leaves his father's farm to seek the adventurous life of decadent knighthood. That life consists chiefly in robbing the wayfarer, merchant, and priest and despoiling Meier Helmbrecht's own peasant neighbors. The son finally comes to a bad end with the law. Blinded and maimed, he seeks the refuge of his father's home, only to be turned out on the mercy of peasants he has robbed and pillaged, to be clubbed to death and hanged. In the early part of the poem the old father, proud of the work to which God has called him, and convinced that it is more honorable and useful than the wayward frivolities and plunderings of the nobility, pleads with his son to stay at home and help with the farm.

> "Dear son, you drive the steer for me,
> Or take the plow while I drive. We
> Shall thus get all our acres plowed.
> And you will near your grave and shroud
> With fullest honor, as I do.
>
> .   .   .   .
>
> My son, if you would noble be,
> I counsel you most faithfully
> Be noble, then, in what you do!
> Good conduct, this is always true,
> Is crown of all true nobleness."

It is a fine and sympathetic picture that Wernher draws of the sturdy old Bavarian peasant father, and in striking contrast with the decadent knight.

> "Of yore the worthy knights were seen
> Where pretty ladies lingered round.
> Today they're always to be found
> Where wine is kept for sale.
>
> .   .   .   .

This is the minnesong they sing:
'Come, barmaid, pretty little thing,
Our cups must overflowing be!
A monkey and a fool were he
Whose body ever should incline
To worship women more than wine!' "

The rage with which the plundered peasants seize upon the maimed
young Helmbrecht after he is turned out of his father's house fore-
shadows the fury of many peasant revolts to come.

"A peasant saw him going past
As he was seeking out a nest
Within the woods where he could rest.
The man was cutting wood that day
For fire, as is a peasant's way.
'Twas of a morning. Helmbrecht, now,
Had taken his best calving cow—
As fine a beast as one could find;
And now the peasant saw him blind!
He called his neighbors round about
And asked if they would help him out.
'In truth I will,' said one with lust,
'I'll shred him into bits of dust
Like those one sees in sunlight fly,
If I'm not stopped by passers-by.
Me and my wife he once roped in
And stripped us to the very skin—
Took every garment we had on;
So now he is my proper pawn.'
The third one then spoke up with vim:
'And were there even three of him,
With my sole hand I'd kill all three!
That unclean, thieving devil, he
Once split apart my cellar door
And pillaged all I had in store.'
A fourth, who'd been splitting wood for fire,
Shook like a leaf with his desire.
'I'll wring his chicken's neck for spite!
None can deny I have the right!
He stuck my child into a sack

While it lay sleeping on its back;
Wrapped a bed round the little one—
'Twas night when this foul deed was done.
When it awoke and wailed in woe,
He shook it out upon the snow.
Ere morn it surely would have died
Had I not heard it as it cried.'
'In faith,' a fifth one said in wrath,
'I'm glad he's fallen in our path!
My heart will find a great delight
Today in feasting on his sight.
The villain outraged my poor girl!
And were he thrice as blind, the churl,
I'd hang him to the nearest limb!
And I myself escaped from him
But barely, naked forced to flee.
Though bigger than a house were he,
I'd have revenge on him this day,
Since he has come to creep away
Within this wood so deep and wide.' " [50]

After a century and a half to two centuries of preparation the Italian, French, and English vernaculars, with the help of the intellectual ferment of the medieval renaissance and the economic and social revolution brought about by the towns, were in a position to be used by men of great talent to create three medieval masterpieces. These *The master-* are the *Divine Comedy* of Dante Alighieri, the *Romance of the Rose* *pieces of the* of William of Lorris and John of Meun, and the *Canterbury Tales* of *vernacular* Geoffrey Chaucer. Each is, in its own way, an almost perfect sum-*literatures* mary of the middle ages at their height, and each is at the same time a reminder that the great writers always withstand classification, for while they are incorporating in their works those points of view that are predominant in their environment, they are so sensitively aware of the minor currents that point to a new development that they are often taken to be what essentially they are not, the heralds of a new day. The medievalist and the student of the Italian renaissance are both inclined to claim these men for their very own. If we remember that no age is static, and that every artist who is not a hopeless conservative or a reactionary must not only come to terms with the culture available to him but must find a way out of the eternal *impasse* of

[50] Bell, *Peasant Life in Old German Epics*, pp. 86–87.

every contemporary scene, then we shall not expect him to belong to what we call one age or another but to belong to all ages.

Dante we should choose to call the best exemplification possible of *Dante* what we have described as the ecclesiastical culture of the middle *Alighieri* ages, and yet all books on the Italian renaissance begin with him as its founder. If we look at him as students of history rather than as literary critics we shall find evidence to support the former point of view. It is easy to point out that he emerged from that most important of medieval economic changes, the urban revolution. A citizen of Florence, the son of a lawyer, he was as convinced as any Greek of the fifth century of the necessity for the well-rounded life, of actively participating in the political life, which in Florence amounted to the political strife of his native city-state. He was therefore enrolled in one of the greater gilds of Florence, the apothecaries' gild; he belonged to one of the major political parties of the city, the Whites, who struggled with the Blacks for the control of the city. His political views were Ghibelline rather than Guelf,[51] and he became a bitter opponent of the political ambitions of Pope Boniface VIII[52] in his native city. His ability was recognized sufficiently to bring him to public office, and because of his decided views, with the victory of the Blacks he was exiled in 1302, and henceforth, until his death in 1321 at Ravenna, was obliged to lead the abject and pathetic life of the political exile, refusing to return to Florence as one who had been forgiven for the error of his ways. But in spite of his active life Dante found time to master and to make an intimate part of himself the intellectual and literary culture available to his generation, so that it is possible to say of him that no one in his day was more learned. Yet, as we might expect, there did not come from his austere mind a poetry and a philosophy that could be called expressive of the emancipated secular spirit of a capitalistic Italian town. On the contrary, Dante's study and his own personal character, combined with a delicate sensitivity, forced him to create a poetic encyclopedia, the *Divine Comedy*, which is a classic and complete statement of the medieval outlook.

Dante, we should therefore say, was a product of the medieval renaissance. In our discussion of that movement the emergence of the vernacular languages as suitable vehicles for literature occasioned emphasis. Italian was the last of the Romance languages to reach literary maturity. At the court of Frederick II the first school of Italian

[51] See p. 392.
[52] See pp. 955 ff.

poets was to be found, singing of the romantic love so thoroughly exploited by the Provençal troubadours. But in central and northern Italy groups of poets sprang up who wrote in their own peculiar dialects. Dante took a decided attitude towards this new development in Italian literature. In his *De vulgari eloquentia* (*On the Vernacular Tongue*), written in Latin to appeal to the sophisticated literati of Italy, he pleaded for some simplification of the medley of fourteen dialects into which Italian speech was divided, and attested his conviction that Italian, for its simple beauty, was quite well suited to the uses that any man of literary inclination might see fit to put it. Moreover, in his own Italian, whether prose or poetry, but especially in the *Divina Commedia,* he so perfected the idiom of his native Tuscan dialect that it became the literary language of Italy. It has been pointed out that Dante did such a masterful job that the Italian of the *Divine Comedy* is less removed from the literary Italian of today than the language of Shakespeare is removed from twentieth-century English.

We have tried to insist, too, that another feature of the medieval renaissance was the working out on the part of the Provençal troubadours of the theory and practice of romantic love. From this point of view, also, Dante may be considered as the culmination of a characteristic development of medieval poetry. The Italians gave to this theme an emotional depth unknown to but a few of the poets of southern France. It was a poet of Bologna, Guido Guinizelli, who raised the rather formal and artificial devotion of the French troubadour into a love of mystic potency. Woman was a messenger sent by God to shed the radiance of her divine beauty and goodness among all those in whose midst she moved, and particularly to ennoble with her mere presence and, one is tempted to say, her Mona Lisa smile, that one individual who became enamored of her. Dante carried this Italian development to its finest heights in his *Vita Nuova* (*The New Life*), a collection of poems, with prose commentary, written in honor of Beatrice, the lady of his sublimest devotion. She was a real person and his a real love. He had been first transfigured by her as a child of nine, when she was only eight, and as a youth he had been blessed by her gracious smile, the full significance of which he expresses in a sonnet.

> "My lady carries love within her eyes;
> All that she looks on is made pleasanter;
> Upon her path men turn to gaze at her;

He whom she greeteth feels his heart to rise,
And droops his troubled visage, full of sighs,
And of his evil heart is then aware:
Hate loves, and pride becomes a worshipper.
O women, help to praise her in somewise.
Humbleness, and the hope that hopeth well,
By speech of hers into the mind are brought,
And who beholds is blessed oftenwhiles.
The look she hath when she a little smiles
Cannot be said, nor holden in the thought;
'Tis such a new and gracious miracle." [53]

As he indeed promises in the *Vita Nuova*, Dante carried his devotion to far loftier heights. In the *Divine Comedy*, Beatrice, as one of the blessed, directs Virgil to lead Dante on the pilgrimage through hell and purgatory. And she it is, who, in the terrestrial paradise, situated on the mount of purgatory, relieves Virgil of his task, and as the symbol of divine revelation leads Dante on through the planetary spheres of paradise to the ultimate empyrean, where she gives over her guidance to St. Bernard and resumes her place amongst the blessed. When Dante finds her gone, he prays to her: *Beatrice in the Divine Comedy*

" 'O Lady, in whom my hope is strong and sweet,
And who for my salvation didst endure
In Hell to leave the imprint of thy feet,
Of all the things presented to my sight
I recognize the virtue and the grace
As coming from thy goodness and thy might.
To freedom thou hast brought me from a slave
By all those paths, by all the gentle arts
Thou hadst within thy power thus to save.
May thy magnificence watch over me
So that my soul, which thou hast remade sound,
Be from the body loosed, pleasing to thee.'
And thus I prayed; and she from that far place
Smiled, as it seemed, and looked once more at me." [54]

In contrast with the troubadours, to Dante the consummation of romantic love took place in paradise, where beloved and lover were to-

---

[53] Wilkins, *Dante: Poet and Apostle*, pp. 7-8.
[54] Fletcher (tr.), *The Divine Comedy*, pp. 459-60.

Dante
and Virgil

gether bathed and blessed in the dazzling radiance of the divine light.

We have noticed that a third feature of the medieval renaissance was the feeble beginning of a study and appreciation of the Latin classics for their own sake, free from the naïve obsession that they were written by dangerous pagans. Dante himself was widely familiar with those Latin writers most popular in the middle ages. Moreover, in choosing Virgil as his guide through hell and purgatory he associated himself in part with the classical and imperial tradition. In the very first canto of the *Divine Comedy*, when Dante comes across Virgil he greets him with a reverent acknowledgment of his great dependence upon him.

> " 'Art thou that Virgil then, that fountainhead
> Which pours abroad so wide a stream of speech?'
> In answer, with awe-stricken brow, I said.
> 'O of all other poets light and glory,
> May the long zeal avail me, the great love
> That made me meditate on thy high story!
> My master and my author verily,
> Thou only art the one from whom I took
> The seemly style for which men honor me.' " [55]

In the *Comedy* Virgil is more than the poet-guide to a fellow poet. He is the symbol of that reason, that philosophy, that love of all learning which should guide one in the search for peace and happiness on this earth, the counterpart of Beatrice, Dante's guide through the heavens of paradise. And just as Beatrice is more than a symbol—she is, indeed, a real person whom Dante has loved—so Virgil is, too, the intimate and beloved friend of the poet.

Dante
and the
imperial
tradition

Dante's relationship to the twelfth-century revival of Roman law and the attendant revival of the Roman empire under the Hohenstaufen emperors is well illustrated by his fervid devotion to the imperial tradition and his rather pathetic and futile hope in the possibilities of the restoration of that German empire which had already been destroyed by the popes. His faith in empire was grounded in his pacifism, which in turn was based upon the high demands that he made of government. "The proper business of the human race," he says in his treatise *On Monarchy*, wherein he defends the empire, "is to actualize constantly the total potentiality of the possible intellect," in other words, to make possible the fullest development of which the

[55] *Ibid.*, p. 5.

human being is capable. War interfered with such a purpose, and in order to do away with it he argues in the *Convivio* (*The Banquet*), his unfinished encyclopedia aiming to popularize the learning he had acquired, for the necessity of a world state in the form of a monarchy, "a single prince, who possessing all things, and having nothing left to desire, may keep kings confined within the borders of their kingdoms so that peace may reign between them; in which peace the cities may have rest; in which rest the neighborhoods may love each other; in which love the households may satisfy all their wants; and when these are satisfied, man may attain joy, which is the end whereunto man was born." [56] In essence this is the argument of Thomas Aquinas for a monarchical head of a universal church.

In his *On Monarchy* he reverts to the earlier Christian theorists, such as Ambrose, on the relationship between Church and state by insisting that in no sense at all is the empire dependent upon the papacy. It is an institution whose origin is as divine as that of the papacy. It cannot accept any dictation in temporal affairs from the head of the Church. For such heretical doctrine the work was burned in the early fourteenth century and put on the Index in the sixteenth. Dante is therefore unsparing of those popes who meddle in political affairs, and he does not hesitate to put popes in hell who have been guilty of simony and thus corrupted their high calling. Of the German kings Albrecht and Henry VII he expected the most in the re-establishment of empire, and when they failed utterly his disillu-sionment and condemnation knew no bounds. Indeed, Dante's trust in the power of the enfeebled empire was closely bound up with an Italian patriotism that detested the raging strife between Italian towns and thought that only under the German emperors could Italy hope for the unification that would bring peace. In the *Purgatory* he cries out: *Dante, a patriot*

> "Slavish Italy, guesthouse of rue,
> Ship without steersman in the stress of storm,
> Of provinces not mistress, but of stew!
>
> .   .   .   .
>
> And now in thee abide not without brawl
> Thy living ones, and each the other gnaws
> Of those shut in behind one moat, one wall.
> .   .   .   .

[56] Wilkins, *op. cit.*, pp. 35–36.

Ah, folk from whom is all devotion due,
Who in that saddle would let Cæsar sit,
Heeded ye well what God hath bidden you,
Look ye how brutal is become this beast
For being not corrected by the spurs,
Since on its bridle-rein laid hand the priest.
O German Albert, who hast put aside
Her that is grown intractable and wild,
Whose saddle-bows thou oughtest to bestride,
May a just judgment from the stars above
Fall on thy blood, so manifest and strange
That thy successor may have fear thereof!" [57]

Dante and
medieval
religion

Finally, in a still more significant way than any of these was Dante related to the medieval renaissance. For he had profited much from the translations from the Arabic of Greek philosophy and Moslem science, from the syntheses of Albertus Magnus, Aquinas, and Peter Lombard, and from the mysticism of Dionysius, Bernard, Richard of St. Victor, and Bonaventura. Of all this the *Divine Comedy* is a closely woven re-expression. For Dante is here not only a supreme poet, but the seer of visions, the preacher of justice (*vir prædicans iustitiam*), the writer of allegory, the orthodox theologian, and the mystic. While conceived in part as a tribute to Beatrice and accordingly to the ennobling influence of women, Dante states clearly that his purpose in writing it was a moral one, namely, "to remove those living in this life from the state of misery and lead them to the state of felicity." Therefore his hell was made so horrible, his purgatory so painful and hopeful, his paradise so joyous and resplendent, that men in reading his poem must be driven through fear and hope and longing to seek to avoid eternal pain and strive for eternal joy. Moreover, Dante has made perfectly clear that in writing the *Divine Comedy* he was doing something more than portraying the actual state of souls after death; he was writing an allegory of the destiny of man.

The "subject of the Paradise in a literal sense is the state of the blessed after death, in the allegorical sense, man according as by meriting he is subject to Justice rewarding." In other words the *Comedy* is an artistic and orthodox explanation of how and why God punishes man for the demerits accumulated in the abuse of his free will, and rewards him for the merits acquired in its proper use. The whole scheme, argument, and setting of the *Divine Comedy* is with

[57] Fletcher, *op. cit.*, pp. 183–84.

slight exception strictly in accordance with the orthodoxy of Thomas Aquinas, whose great authority, Aristotle, was to Dante "the master of them that know." Dante's astronomy, in the arrangement of earth, planets, and fixed stars, is strictly Ptolemaic and learned from the Arabs. The influence of the stars is explained in accordance with a Christianized astrology. This is all very clear in Dante's mind. At one moment in the *Paradise* he looks back to survey the heavens and earth, sees the seven planets in their proper relation and "this orb of ours," "the threshing-floor which maketh men so fierce," and he cannot keep from smiling "to see how mean it seemed and small." But its insignificance was viewed from the vast import of heavenly bliss and not from the meaningless collection of staggering solar systems that make up the universe of the modern sceptic.

His hell, while fashioned in detail from his vivid visual and auditory imagination, punishes the seven deadly sins [58] from the moment that he steps through the gate of hell with its dread motto, "Leave ye all hope behind who enter here," until at the very pit the three-headed Lucifer, frozen to his waist in ice, flaps his bat-like wings to make a freezing wind, weeps with his six eyes, and "down three chins the tears were trickling, and a bloody slaver," mangles in the mouth of his red face the traitor of Christ, Judas Iscariot, and gnaws Brutus and Cassius, the traitors of Cæsar and empire in his black and yellow mouths. The mount of purgatory, likewise, with its seven terraces, frees man from the remaining stains of the seven deadly sins and restores him to his original state of innocence in the Garden of Eden, the terrestrial paradise at the top of the mount.

Henceforth, through the Ptolemaic heavens, peopled with souls of varying degree of blessedness and organized according to the celestial hierarchy of Dionysius,[59] it is a matter of instruction in the orthodox doctrines of the Faith, including predestination and grace, the theological virtues of faith, hope, and charity, until through the intercession of the Virgin in a prayer of great beauty the climax of the whole pilgrimage is reached in the beatific vision of the Trinity, the mystic's infrequent rapturous ecstasy, which in paradise is made continuous.

> "But as were strengthened more and more mine eyes
>   By gazing, so that semblance ever one,
>   Even as I altered, altered its own guise.
> Within the deep and luminous extension

[58] See pp. 41–42.
[59] See p. 257.

Of the High Light three circles showed themselves,
　　Of threefold color and of one dimension;
One by the other, as Iris by Iris wreathed,
　　Appeared reflected, and the third seemed fire
　　Which equally the one and other breathed.
Oh, how fall short the words! how recreant
　　To my conception! and this, to what I saw,
　　Is such 'tis not enough to call it scant.
Oh Light Eternal, that in thyself alone
　　Abidest, alone thyself dost understand,
　　And lovest and smilest, self-knowing and self-known!
That circle which as radiance reflected
　　Appeared to be conceived within thyself,
　　When for some little by mine eyes inspected,
Within itself, with color of its own
　　Was painted with our image, as it seemed;
　　Wherefore I gave mine eyes to it alone.
As the geometer who fain would tax
　　His wits to square the circle, and finds not,
　　By taking thought, the principle he lacks,
Such at that wondrous sight was I; for trace
　　I would how to the circle was conformed
　　The image, and how there it found a place;
But wings had not been mine for the high aim,
　　Save that my mind was smitten suddenly
　　As by a lightning-flash,—and its will came.
Here power failed to the high fantasy;
　　But my desire and will now from afar
　　Was turning—as a wheel turned evenly—
The Love that moves the sun and every star." [60]

At the moment when the poets of Bologna were modifying with the "sweet new style" the romantic themes of the poets of Provence—a fusion that was to reach its climax in the poetry of Dante—the *Romance of the Rose* was written in France. It has been called a general encyclopedia of knowledge, a "treasure-house of amorous doctrine" for medieval lay society, and even a "long-winded, metrical rumination about all things under heaven." [61] The poem was begun around

The Romance of the Rose

[60] Fletcher, *op. cit.*, pp. 470–71.
[61] Pound, *The Spirit of Romance*, p. 84.

1230 by William of Lorris, who composed the first four thousand lines. John of Meun continued it forty years later for fourteen thousand lines more, and probably finished it before 1265, the year of Dante's birth. Very little is known of either of these men, save that both came from the Loire country, and that John of Meun spent most of his life in Paris. Together, the two very different parts of the poem began a series of love visions, lyrics, and love allegories, to say nothing of unending debates over the merits of womankind, which lasted more than two centuries.

Allegory had long been a familiar device with both theologians and Christian poets. It was taken up by the troubadours into the system of courtly love, and was used by trouvères in their blending of Arthurian *Allegory and* legend with the Provençal tradition. To this use Ovid and the cathe- *the* Romance dral schools made their contributions. The result had been to perfect from these various elements the literary treatment of the religion of love. Before the *Romance of the Rose* was started this religion had been summarized by Andreas Capellanus in definite rules in his *De Arte Honeste Amandi* (*Concerning the Art of Loving Honestly*) and fully carried out in the poetry of Chrétien of Troyes.[62] In his brief part of the poem William of Lorris shows how profoundly he was bound by the conventions of these earlier writers. The form of the dream vision which he used may have been in origin an imitation of Christian apocalyptic writings. The time chosen for the poem is that "amorous month of May" which all medieval poets loved; the place is a beautiful garden transformed into a terrestrial paradise by trees from Arabic lands, green grass, flowering plants, and singing birds. The chief character is a comely youth who becomes a servant of the God of Love after having been pierced through the eye by Beauty, an arrow in Love's quiver. The youth's heart by some transcendental process leaves his own breast to be possessed by his beloved, whose love is embodied in the Rose. He suffers many trying, agonizing situations; his face grows pale; he becomes careless in dress and goes sleepless for many a long night. Yet in spite of all this he remains faithful to the God of Love. In all this William of Lorris but follows the rules, and writes a compendium of the system of courtly love. But he adjusted allegory to romantic love more ingeniously than had other poets, and infused emotion into his personifications of abstract qualities. He restated in a refreshing and graceful manner the old conventions, and could be original and pleasing in detail, as in these lines on the charms of May:

[62] See p. 778.

"O month of joy
That knows all nature to decoy
To mirth and pleasure; bush and brake
Alike their fresh spring raiment take
Of leaves that long in swaddlings lay
Close shrouded from the light of day,
While woods and thickets don their green
Rich mantling of resplendent sheen.

. . . .

The merry birds that silence kept
While all the world 'neath winter slept,
And wild winds roared, and skies were grey
With rain, break forth, when cometh May
In lusty note, and let sweet song
Proclaim their joy that winter's wrong
Is past, and now once more doth reign
Sweet spring-tide o'er old earth's domain." [63]

William of Lorris's part of the Romance

The character of William of Lorris's allegory can be seen from an all too brief summary. The dreamer is admitted one fine May morning into the garden of Mirth. Love, who stalks him for some time with his deadly arrows, is able finally to pierce him as he stands gazing into a marble fountain. An inscription identifies the fountain as that into which Narcissus wept himself away. Two crystal stones at the bottom signify the eyes of the beloved, and they reflect from a rosebush near-by very lovely rosebuds, one of which is especially beautiful. The dreamer declares himself now to be the vassal of the God of Love, and hears the commandments of Love dictated to him. He finds himself passionately desirous of overcoming the thorny hedge enclosing the rosebush reflected in the fountain, and of plucking the most beautiful of the buds. He is befriended by Fair-Welcome (the lady's natural good nature), but Danger (her equally natural fear of love and possession by a lover) at length chases them both away from the enclosure. Reason approaches and advises the lover to forsake the nonsense of love, but this, he says, he cannot do, and finds solace in his best friend, who suggests that there are ways of avoiding Danger. At length, upon the intervention of Venus he is granted permission to kiss the Rose; but his helper, Fair-Welcome, is now imprisoned in a high tower by Jealousy (perhaps a personifica-

[63] Ellis (tr.), *The Romance of the Rose*, I, 3.

tion of the lady's family), and the lover is left to mourn the fate of his erstwhile friend. Here the tale as told by William of Lorris ends abruptly at line 4203.[64] Some eighty lines giving it a happy ending were interpolated by some other contemporary poet or poets, but actually John of Meun took up the work at this point.

John of Meun, true sophisticated Parisian that he became, treats the courts of love, and in fact all other contemporary institutions, in a rational and often cynical spirit. His long "conclusion" is therefore vastly different in tone and temper from the idyllic, gracious revery of William of Lorris. Although perhaps too much is made of this, yet he did re-enforce the cynical and satirical trends of the *fabliaux* and *Renard the Fox;* and although his literary talents are considerable, his part of the work is, as poetry, much inferior to Lorris's. "Jean de Meung in the latter and larger part of the poem simply stuffs into it stock satire on women, stock learning, and stock semi-pagan morality." [65]

John of Meun's part of the Romance

He begins his part of the poem by having Reason appear once more. She speaks for several hundred lines, using all sorts of historical examples to show the caprice of Fortune, but the lover rejects her logic, and for over three thousand lines listens to his friend discoursing on the miseries connected with poverty, the evils that accompany marriage, domestic troubles caused by a jealous husband, and a general railing against all womankind. Finally, when the friend has departed and the lover is wandering in despair about the garden, Love decides to call together his barons and come to his aid. In their discussion of the plans for attack, one of the barons, False-Seeming, is given a chance to speak, and there ensues a very long digression on various aspects of hypocrisy. John of Meun here has an opportunity to flay the begging friars, echoing the thirteenth-century Parisian "doctors frought with learning in divinity," who had denounced them.

> "Monkish mendicants, those stout
> And thriving blades, the begging friars,
> Who show themselves as rough as briars
> In open street, but love to win,
> With oily tongues, their way within
> The goodmen's houses whom they cheat
> With lying words, while drink and meat
> They batten on: and though they sing

---

[64] Ellis's translation.
[65] Saintsbury, *The Flourishing of Romance*, p. 302.

Their poverty, they're gathering
Fat livelihood, and many a heap
Of deniers have they dolven deep
Beneath the earth." [66]

The digression continues long enough to give advice to women on dress and table deportment. Chaucer's Madam Eglantine made use of the latter.

" 'Tis well she take especial care
That in the sauce her fingers ne'er
She dip beyond the joint, nor soil
Her lips with garlick, sops, or oil,
Nor heap up gobbets and then charge
Her mouth with pieces overlarge,
And only with the finger point
Should touch the bit she'd fain anoint
With sauce, white, yellow, brown, or green,
And lift it towards her mouth between
Finger and thumb with care and skill,
That she no sauce or morsel spill
About her breast-cloth." [67]

The lover finally gains admittance to the tower where Fair-Welcome is confined. But this accomplishes nothing, for he is ejected by Danger, and the poet has opportunity to hold forth on the art of love. Venus at last decides to come to the aid of Love, her son, his barons, and, ultimately, of the lover. At this point Nature, who is represented as forever busy at furthering procreation, begins a confession to her priest, Genius, after the latter has delivered a long digression of his own. What a confession it is! Its chief function is to display the author's learning. Among other topics it discusses cosmography, astronomy, optics, the elements, death, man's folly, free will, necessity, destiny, visions, dreams, sleepwalking, effects of fever, the soul, evaluations of mankind, the contrariness of man towards nature and her laws, the qualities of a gentleman, the insignificance of a man's ancestry, astrology, Plato, alchemy, the birth of Christ, bad mothers-in-law, woman's wiles and arts in capturing her victims, Manfred of

[66] Ellis, *op. cit.*, II, 31–32.
[67] *Ibid.*, II, 220.

Sicily, and the death of Conradino at the hands of Charles of Anjou! Genius is at length enthroned by Love, after which he makes a long speech which seems to be dedicated to the fecundity of all the creatures of the planet. Finally, after digressions which William of Lorris could not have dreamed of, Venus directs the attack on the tower, and after a time the lover possesses his Rose—that is, the love of the lady, who herself nowhere enters the poem in the flesh.

It is plain that John of Meun was not particularly interested in the idyllic fancy of William of Lorris. In the main, his purpose was to instruct in the current dogmas of history, religion, science, and philosophy. He was a rationalist; he hated superstition; and he ridiculed what he considered destructive to the society of which he was a part. He is not extremely original, for in what he has to say he is in the main a cataloguer. Satire on women, on the Church, on everything that was important to the men of the age had been written before him and was to be written after him. Certainly it is not true to say that in any real sense the ideas of courtly love came to an end with him—their discussion went on for centuries—but his discussion of them had no little effect upon his successors. And it is true that the *Romance* is a kind of guidebook to the middle ages: all the ideas of the time are recorded there; but they are not tied together in the kind of synthesis that was to come with Dante. One feels secure, however, in repeating the statement that "to comprehend a Gothic cathedral the *Rose* should be as familiar as the *Dies Iræ*." [68]

The impor-tance of the Romance

To turn from Dante, William of Lorris, and John of Meun to Chaucer is at first glance to come into another world. To be sure, in all external appearances it is another world. Chaucer belonged to the fourteenth century (*c.* 1340–1400), to England, and to London. But not much is said by remarking that Chaucer belongs to another world if by that we mean to imply that his world was essentially different from that of these earlier writers. It was not. Chaucer simply happened to be interested most in aspects of his world that did not interest these other men so much. He was interested in the story-loving, earthy, realistic world of real people which he saw constantly about him. This surrounding of colorful personalities existed for Dante and the authors of the *Romance of the Rose* as well as for Chaucer, and as indeed for all men who take care to observe it. Chaucer may be said therefore to be no less medieval, if we have left any meaning to this word, than the others. Moreover, he is far more than merely English, for the personalities that he creates in the *Canterbury Tales* belong to

[68] Saintsbury, *op. cit.*, p. 303.

no one country or period. They are types as well as individuals, and their appeal knows no national limitation.

Geoffrey Chaucer

Like Dante, Chaucer was a townsman and the son of a bourgeois father, a vintner. Like Dante, too, he remained a layman and led a very active life in the service of the English monarchy. For a while he was a page at the court of Elizabeth of Ulster, wife of the Duke of Clarence, the third son of Edward III. As yeoman or esquire he served in the household of Edward III. He fought in the Hundred Years' War, and went for his king on many diplomatic missions to Flanders, France, and Italy. For eleven years he served as the controller of the customs and subsidies on wools, hides, and woolfells in the port of London, during which time he lived over the Aldgate. In 1385 he was justice of the peace for Kent, and served later in such various capacities as clerk of the works for Westminster Palace, the Tower of London, and other castles and manors, and as a member of a surveying commission "to inspect walls, ditches, gutters, sewers, bridges, roads, ponds and trenches along the Thames between Greenwich and Woolwich." He finally became a member of Parliament. His active career as a civil servant of the English monarchy provided him with ample opportunity to know the various classes of fourteenth-century English society and to appreciate the colorful variety of human personality.

Chaucer's reading

Like Dante, however, Chaucer found time to read extensively in all types of medieval literature. He was as devoted to Boethius as Dante, and in fact translated the *Consolation of Philosophy* into English. As well as any medieval author he knew Ovid's *Art of Love* and the *Metamorphoses*. He was well read in the classical romances of Troy and Thebes and in the large store of collections of tales that the middle ages so readily devoured. The *Romance of the Rose* he admired so much that he translated part of it into English. From his diplomatic missions to Italy he brought back manuscripts of Dante, Boccaccio, and Petrarch.[69] He knew his French contemporaries Guillaume de Machaut, Jean Froissart, and Eustache Deschamps.[70] These he adapted freely to his own purposes in his own works. Dante is much in evidence in the *House of Fame;* in *Troilus and Criseyde,* which has been called "the first great poem in English" and "one of the very great and beautiful poems of the world," [71] there is much reliance on Boccaccio's *Filostrato*. But in Chaucer's use of other literary sources it can never be said that he stooped to mere reproduction and imitation.

[69] See p. 1009.
[70] See p. 1019.
[71] Lowes, *Chaucer*, p. 165.

His own peculiar talent transcended his material, and his style set a standard for literary English. As Dante raised the dialect of Florence and Tuscany to literary predominance, Chaucer did likewise for the Anglo-French dialect of the Londoner.

In the *Canterbury Tales*, as in the *Divine Comedy*, we are taken on a pilgrimage; but what a different pilgrimage it is! Here is no sophisticated Dante being led by Virgil and Beatrice as symbols of philosophy and theology to salvation through hell, purgatory, and paradise. Rather, it is the very human Chaucer accompanying a band of thirty pilgrims on a very jolly journey from London to Canterbury to visit the shrine of St. Thomas à Becket. The leader of this pilgrimage was Harry Bailey, the owner of the Tabard Inn at Southwark, which dispensed very powerful ale, as some of the travelers well knew. Chaucer proposed to retell the tales that these pilgrims narrated in turn in order to pass the time away. In so doing he emerges the master of all medieval storytellers. His high purpose was not to give moral instruction, but to amuse. Gathered together in his pilgrim band were representatives of all classes of English society except royalty, a thoroughly democratic gathering who afforded him in the prologue to the tales, through the tales themselves, and in the dialogue that binds them together, the chance to paint in detail his inimitable portraits of warm human beings. It is no allegory which Chaucer is writing; rather he is an uncontrollable realist, so much so that at times he feels called upon to apologize to his reader for it. Yet after all, he had to tell what these people looked like, and wore, and said, and thought. But like Dante, Chaucer is also a critic of his own society and particularly of the Church. Unlike Dante he does not rise to heights of righteous indignation in condemning men and institutions. He prefers merely to let the items of his portraiture do the damning. Yet what could be more scathing than his picture of the decadent friar:

The Canterbury Tales

> "He heard confession gently, it was said,
> Gently absolved too, leaving naught of dread.
> He was an easy man to give penance
> When knowing he should gain a good pittance;
>
> .   .   .   .
>
> His tippet was stuck always full of knives
> And pins, to give to young and pleasing wives.
> And certainly he kept a merry note;
> Well could he sing and play upon the rote.

At balladry he bore the prize away.
His throat was white as lily of the May;
Yet strong he was as ever champion.
In towns he knew the taverns, every one,
And every good host and each barmaid too—
Better than begging lepers, these he knew.

. . . .

And so, wherever profit might arise,
Courteous he was and humble in men's eyes.

. . . .

Of double worsted was his semi-cope,
That rounded like a bell, as you may guess.
He lisped a little, out of wantonness,
To make his English soft upon his tongue;
And in his harping, after he had sung,
His two eyes twinkled in his head as bright
As do the stars within the frosty night.
This worthy limiter was named Hubert." [72]

Chaucer may be quoted almost at random with delight. But it would not be fair to him to pass him by without some reference, at least, to his remarkable portraits of women, omitting, however, Dame Prudence, who knew far too much of the Fathers of the Church and the Stoics for the peace of mind of any husband, and patient Griselda, whose slavish deference to her husband inspired envy in the merchant's heart and who would have been, in Harry Bailey's opinion, a woman whom his wife might profitably have imitated. There is the prioress at dinner:

Chaucer's women

"At table she had been well taught withal,
And never from her lips let morsels fall,
Nor dipped her fingers deep in sauce, but ate
With so much care the food upon her plate
That never driblet fell upon her breast.
In courtesy she had delight and zest.
Her upper lip was always wiped so clean
That in her cup was no iota seen
Of grease, when she had drunk her draught of wine.
Becomingly she reached for meat to dine." [73]

[72] Nicolson (tr.), *The Canterbury Tales*, pp. 8–9.
[73] *Ibid.*, p. 5.

And the poor widow:

> "For she'd small goods and little income-rent;
> By husbanding of such as God had sent
> She kept herself and her young daughters twain.
> Three large sows had she, and no more, 'tis plain,
> Three cows and a lone sheep that she called Moll.
> Right sooty was her bedroom and her hall,
> Wherein she'd eaten many a slender meal.
> Of sharp sauce, why she needed no great deal,
> For dainty morsel never passed her throat;
> Her diet well accorded with her coat.
> Repletion never made this woman sick;
> A temperate diet was her whole physic,
> And exercise, and her heart's sustenance.
> The gout, it hindered her nowise to dance,
> Nor apoplexy spun within her head;
> And no wine drank she, either white or red;
> Her board was mostly garnished, white and black,
> With milk and brown bread, whereof she'd no lack,
> Broiled bacon and sometimes an egg or two,
> For a small dairy business did she do." [74]

Of the wives, there is the carpenter's young wife:

> "And she was come to eighteen years of age.
> Jealous he was and held her close in cage.
> For she was wild and young and he was old,
> And deemed himself as like to be cuckold.
>
> .   .   .   .
>
> Fair was this youthful wife, and therewithal
> As weasel's was her body slim and small.
> A girdle wore she, barred and striped, of silk,
> An apron, too, as white as morning milk
> About her loins, and full of many a gore;
> White was her smock, embroidered all before
> And even behind, her collar round about,
> Of coal-black silk, on both sides, in and out;
> The strings of the white cap upon her head

[74] *Ibid.*, p. 265.

Were, like her collar, black silk worked with thread;
Her fillet was of wide silk worn full high:
And certainly she had a lickerish eye.
She'd thinned out carefully her eyebrows two,
And they were arched and black as any sloe.
She was a far more pleasant thing to see
Than is the newly budded young pear-tree;
And softer than the wool is on a wether.
Down from her girdle hung a purse of leather,
Tasselled with silk, with latten beading sown.
In all this world, searching it up and down,
So gay a little doll, I well believe,
Or such a wench, there's no man can conceive.
Far brighter was the brilliance of her hue
Than in the tower the gold coins minted new.
And songs came shrilling from her pretty head
As from a swallow's sitting on a shed.
Therewith she'd dance too, and could play and sham
Like any kid or calf about its dam.
Her mouth was sweet as bragget or as mead
Or hoard of apples laid in hay or weed.
Skittish she was as is a pretty colt,
Tall as a staff and straight as cross-bow bolt.
A brooch she wore upon her collar low,
As broad as boss of buckler did it show;
Her shoes laced up to where a girl's legs thicken.
She was a primrose, and a tender chicken
For any lord to lay upon his bed,
Or yet for any good yeoman to wed." [75]

The miller's wife unfortunately was the daughter of "the parson of the town," "had been bred up in a nunnery," and

"Besides, because she was a dirty bitch,
She was as high as water in a ditch;
And full of scorn and full of back-biting.
She thought a lady should be quite willing
To greet her for her kin and culture, she
Having been brought up in that nunnery." [76]

[75] *Ibid.*, pp. 89–90.
[76] *Ibid.*, p. 110.

Most extraordinary of all is the precious wife of Bath, "who—sad to say—was deaf in either ear."

> "In all the parish there was no goodwife
> Should offering make before her, on my life;
> And if one did, indeed, so wroth was she
> It put her out of all her charity.
> Her kerchiefs were of finest weave and ground;
> I dare swear that they weighed a full ten pound
> Which, of a Sunday, she wore on her head.
> Her hose were of the choicest scarlet red,
> Close gartered, and her shoes were soft and new.
> Bold was her face, and fair, and red of hue.
> She'd been respectable throughout her life,
> With five churched husbands bringing joy and strife,
> Not counting other company in youth;
> But thereof there's no need to speak, in truth.
>
> . . . .
>
> Gap-toothed was she, it is no lie to say.
> Upon an ambler easily she sat,
> Well simpled, aye, and over all a hat
> As broad as is a buckler or a targe;
> A rug was tucked around her buttocks large
> And on her feet a pair of sharpened spurs.
> In company well could she laugh her slurs.
> The remedies of love she knew, perchance,
> For of that art she'd learned the old, old dance." [77]

As a prologue to her tale the wife of Bath felt inclined to justify the title of Ovid's favorite work, and to tell of her experiences with her five husbands, the last of whom, a former student at Oxford, she had some difficulty in subduing after he continued to infuriate her by reading from books about submissive and mischievous wives. But she did finally, after tearing three leaves out of the "cursed book" and knocking him into the fireplace. After the tale she prays:

> ". . . and Jesus to us send
> Meek husbands, and young ones, and fresh in bed,
> And good luck to outlive them that we wed.

[77] *Ibid.*, p. 15.

And I pray Jesus to cut short the lives
Of those who'll not be governed by their wives;
And old and querulous niggards with their pence,
And send them soon a mortal pestilence!" [78]

Architecture

In proceeding now with the architectural history of the medieval renaissance it must be our purpose to re-emphasize by use of new material the same general development of medieval culture that is illustrated by the philosophic, scientific, educational, and literary trends. Obviously there were similar inheritances from the Roman past; obviously, if the architectural development paralleled the others in inventiveness, it must show a similar emancipation from this past, taking form in a new architectural style expressive of a new age. Since our concern must be wholly with ecclesiastical architecture, we should expect in the churches a particular glorification of medieval Christianity; if what has been said about the progressive dilution of an ecclesiastical by a secular culture has any validity, some evidence for this feature should be found even in the houses of God. So far we have mentioned only that style of architecture perfected at Constantinople by Justinian in the Church of Santa Sophia.[79] The architects of that church did so well in exploiting the possibilities of the domed church that little further development of Byzantine architecture as such can be traced. Its history, like that of Byzantine culture in general, remained essentially static. Nor can more be written here of the possible influences of Moslem architecture upon western architecture than has been written elsewhere.[80]

In fact, aside from the exceptional early influences of Byzantine architecture,[81] the architecture of western Europe, built upon certain structural features inherited from Rome, appears to have had a perfectly logical and independent development of its own. For the sake of convenience rather than accuracy it has been divided into two styles, Romanesque and Gothic, Romanesque indicating the earlier dependence upon Roman architecture, and Gothic indicating an entirely new style somehow evolved by the Germanic peoples of northern Europe. The term "Gothic" as applied to architecture was first used in derision by architects of the Italian renaissance, who thought that the only possible way to build was in the manner of Rome, and not in the Gothic,

*Romanesque
and Gothic
architecture*

[78] *Ibid.*, p. 344.
[79] See pp. 146 ff.
[80] See p. 181.
[81] See pp. 149–50.

i.e., barbaric and Germanic, style of northern Europe. Subsequent study leading to an appreciation of the subtlety of Gothic architecture, combined with a whole change in attitude towards the middle ages, has transformed a term of derision into one of highest praise.

Since so-called Romanesque architecture underwent a constant development, and merged into so-called Gothic architecture without there being any very clear-cut line of division, it is perhaps better to speak simply of the gradual perfection of Christian architecture. The real break came with the classical revival of Italian architects in the fifteenth century, as the Church, the chief living force in medieval art, lost its primacy. At that, the rout of Gothic by the classical style of the Italian renaissance was slow. Gothic persisted in France until the middle of the sixteenth century and in England to about 1600. Since Gothic there has been no really great architecture in the west except it be the American skyscraper.

When Christian art emerged from the catacombs, it possessed nothing much more of its own than the beginnings of a complicated symbolism which requires the very special study of iconography to understand. It was inevitable that Christians should take over pagan temples for their own, and that in building new churches they should use whatever materials in the form of columns and capitals that they could. Just so long as there were Roman materials to be used the originality of western architecture was curbed. Neither is it surprising that the *The* new Christian churches copied the form of that Roman building *Roman* called the basilica, which was used for large public gatherings. The *basilica* basilica was in ground plan a rectangle divided into three aisles, a central, main aisle, or nave, separated from the two side aisles by two arcades of semicircular arches, capitals, and columns. The arcades supported the walls of the nave and the clearstory, or upper rows of windows in the nave walls. The nave proper was terminated by a semi-circular apse, extending beyond the rectangle of the ground plan. Ordinarily the basilica was covered with a wooden roof. But the Romans had used as roofing not only wood but stone and concrete, in the form of the barrel or tunnel and the groined or cross vault. The barrel vault is simply a heavy stone roof arched in the form of a semicircle. The groined vault is a roof formed by the intersection of two barrel vaults at right angles. Strictly speaking, it is the use or imitation of classical materials, the adoption of the basilican ground plan, experimentation with the round arch in the building of barrel and cross vaults that give to Romanesque its specific literal meaning.

The barbarian invasions of the fourth and fifth centuries, combined with the decay of Roman society, checked all advance in building. The general disorder of the Merovingian period was followed after the brief Carolingian revival by the confusion of new barbarian invasions and civil wars. Under such conditions nothing more could be expected than that men should erect buildings as quickly and cheaply as possible to protect themselves. Not only the older Roman population lost its skill in the art of building, but the new barbarian peoples had as yet acquired none. The art of western Europe accordingly suffered an almost total eclipse. The Merovingians built mostly in wood, and what little they built in stone was made up of the moldings, capitals, and other fragments from Roman ruins. Except for a rugged and attractive goldsmith work they produced almost no lasting art. The late eighth century witnessed, nevertheless, the beginning of an architectural revival that may well be considered a part of the Carolingian renaissance.[82] Charles the Great's palace church at Aachen was an imitation of the Byzantine Church of San Vitale at Ravenna, whence he transported classical columns to adorn it. It set the example for many round churches of the Carolingian period. Yet the round church was hardly suited to the new needs of the Christian ritual, which was requiring an augmented clergy and some kind of provision in the church for the growing cult of saint and relic worship.

Merovingian and Carolingian architecture

Carolingian architects took some steps along this direction that pointed to the future. By this time the usual rectangular basilican form had been modified by the addition, between apse and nave and side aisles, of a transverse aisle called the transept. Since the transept extended beyond the side aisles it transformed the ground plan into the shape of a T.[83] Carolingian architects also enlarged the apse of the earlier basilica to provide for a choir. The side aisles of the basilica were in some instances continued around the choir and apse to form an ambulatory. The apse itself was occasionally raised. To house the relics of saints little chapels or absidioles were built off the ambulatory. Here was the whole eastern end, or *chevet*, of the fully developed Gothic church in the germ: choir, apse, ambulatory, and chapels. To provide further places for relics absidioles were added to the transept. For the same purpose a crypt was added under the whole eastern end of the church. Sometimes too a second or western apse was built with a corresponding transept. This double apsidal termination became an especial feature of later German, notably Rhenish, Romanesque. At the sides of the front, or façade, of the church appeared in some in-

[82] See p. 252.
[83] T-shaped basilicas date from the early Christian period,

stances two towers, the forerunners of the later Romanesque or Gothic towers, and spires of the western façade. Because columns of classical buildings were used up during the Carolingian period, and stonecutters were not yet skillful enough to reproduce them, stone piers began to appear in place of the columns of the nave arcade. When it is noted how many of the modifications to the basilica plan became permanent features of later building, it must be allowed that the Carolingian period was by no means stagnant. Most of the Carolingian buildings, however, even the palaces of Charlemagne, were of wood. Though not unknown, glass was rare; brickmaking was practically unknown; but lead plates and tiles were used for roofing, and bells were made with some skill. Frescoes decorated the greater churches and monasteries.

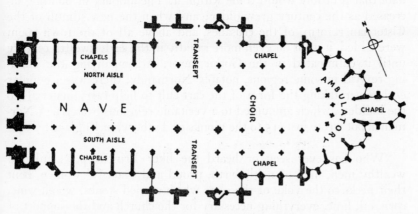

The ground plan of Amiens, showing the typical arrangement of the Gothic cathedral

The ninth and tenth centuries were in general a period of destruction rather than construction. New barbarian invasions and the civil and feudal wars accompanying the collapse of the Carolingian empire were ruinous to all wooden buildings, and of course to all churches built with wooden roofs. The mere enumeration of the repeated burnings of towns and churches is enough to make clear of what builders were, of course, soon convinced: that the prime necessity was henceforth a fireproof building, that is, one built entirely of stone. Meanwhile too, by the end of the period, with the cessation of the invasions, the relative settling down of feudal chaos, and the growing monastic reform associated with Cluny, forces were set in motion making possible the first real architectural revival in the west in the eleventh century.

*The archi-
tectural revival
of the eleventh
century*
To a French monk writing at the beginning of the eleventh century the large amount of new building in stone made it seem "as though the world were throwing off its decrepitude to clothe itself anew in an array of white sanctuaries." It was to be a new age of stone. Building became an exciting passion; prelates were struck by what the chronicles call the disease of building (*morbus ædificandi*). One French archeologist enumerates by name some one thousand five hundred and eighty-seven church buildings for France alone in the eleventh century, a figure that excludes all monastic buildings. There are at least three hundred and forty-five feudal châteaux that can definitely be placed within the period, and innumerable more of unascertainable date that probably would come within it. The amount of building increased as the century grew older; and when the new stimuli of the Cistercian reform, of the crusades, and above all of the town boom were added, it went on even more rapidly in the early twelfth century until it culminated in the Gothic furor. Accompanying the building revival in some regions, notably Normandy, there was a popular

The cart cult
enthusiasm taking the form of the cart cult to help carry materials to the builders, which amounted to a veritable religious hysteria. A Norman abbot wrote in 1115 to the monks of Tutbury, in England:

"Who has ever seen or heard the like? Princes, powerful and wealthy men, men of noble birth, proud and beautiful women, bent their necks to the yoke of the carts which carried stones, wood, wine, corn, oil, lime, everything necessary for the church and the support of those working at it. One saw as many as a thousand people, men and women, attached to the reins drawing a wagon so heavy was its burden and a profound silence reigned among the crowd pressing forward with difficulty in the emotion which filled their hearts.

"At the head of the long procession, minstrels of the highest sounded their brazen trumpets and the sacred banners in their brilliant colors swayed in the wind. Nothing proved an obstacle. The ruggedness of the mountains, the depths of the streams, the waves of the sea at Sainte Marie du Pont could not delay the march. To the carts there were yoked even old men bent under the weight of their years; and children tied to the reins had no need to stoop. They would march upright under the traces. . . .

"When they have reached the church they arrange the wagons

about it like a spiritual camp and during the whole of the following night the army of the Lord keeps watch with psalms and canticles. The carts are emptied by the light of ruddy torches and the relics of the saints are brought for the relief of the sick and the weak, for whom priests in procession implore the clemency of the Lord and his Blessed Mother. If healing does not follow at once they cast aside their garments, men and women alike and drag themselves from altar to altar . . . begging the priests to scourge them for their sins."

It was, roughly speaking, during the century and a half following 1000 that the characteristic features of what we call the Romanesque style were evolved. Yet it is difficult to be accurate in defining the particular features that distinguish Romanesque from earlier and later *The Roman-* styles. It is hardly possible to say that the use of the round arch dis- *esque style* tinguishes it because it borrowed the round arch from the Romans, and there are pointed arches in Romanesque churches in southern France. Buildings in various parts of western Europe, although contemporaneous, are widely different. In fact, the historians of Romanesque proceed to enumerate the various schools of Romanesque: the Lombard school, the Rhenish school, the Norman school, the Anglo-Norman school, and some dozen French schools. There are fundamental differences between such Romanesque churches as Sant' Ambrogio at Milan, the cathedral at Pisa, the cathedral at Worms, St. Michael's at Hildesheim, Ely Cathedral, the Abbaye-aux-hommes at Caen, the Cluniac church at Vézelay, and St. Trophime at Arles. It is even difficult to say, as is so often said, that Romanesque architecture is essentially a monastic architecture, since obviously the above enumeration is by no means chiefly limited to monastic churches. Yet it is true that among the most impressive of the Romanesque churches are Benedictine, and above all reformed Benedictine, i.e. Cluniac, houses, and that the architects and builders of the period were preponderantly abbots, monks, and lay brothers who were summoned from their own cloisters to do work elsewhere.

Some unity was given to these various schools by traveling workmen and conquest. The Lombard school influenced the Rhenish Romanesque, and Italian influence is noticeable elsewhere in Germany, partly at least as a result of the establishment of the Holy Roman empire in 962. Italian building abbots such as William of Volpiano and Anselm of Bec, called to Normandy by the dukes, brought with them or summoned Italian workmen and influenced certainly Norman

Romanesque. The Norman conquest of England in 1066 introduced into England the Norman style, which was only slightly conditioned by Anglo-Saxon architecture.

Ordinarily the Romanesque church was inclined to be low and poorly lighted, to employ predominantly the round Roman arch, and to emphasize horizontal lines. It preserved and improved upon the modifications of the Carolingian basilican ground plan. The church became larger, and the approach to the altar from the nave more impressive, and as at Caen and Vézelay with a certain vast horizontal sweep. The enlargement of both *chevet* and transept transformed the originally rectangular basilica into the form of a Latin cross. The nave was of course for the congregation with its ground plan left open for the vista and for processions. The side or true aisles were the approaches; the transepts provided space for the officiating clergy and their assistants and for part of the communicants. In the feudal age the wings of the transept were reserved for the clergy and the aristocracy. Romanesque interiors were sometimes, especially in Italy, richly decorated with frescoes and mosaics under Byzantine influence. Carved stone and wood in moldings, wooden ceilings, capitals, and plain wall surfaces were brightly colored in strong reds, blues, greens, and gold. The façade was as yet undeveloped except for the sometimes extraordinary Norman western towers. Yet, as the façade of the Abbaye-aux-hommes reveals, the three round-arched entrances between the heavy buttresses supporting the towers and façade wall emphasize the vertical division of the church into nave and side aisles; and the row of entrances surmounted by the two round-arched blind arcades emphasizes the horizontal division of the church into ground floor, gallery or triforium built over the side aisles (a new feature of Romanesque structure), and the clearstory.

This tendency at Caen to reveal internal by external structural features was developed to its limit by the Gothic architects. In southern France the recessed portals of the façades were covered with an elaborate and often symbolic sculpture of great vitality and originality. Romanesque capitals are usually as exciting a joy to present beholders as they were not to St. Bernard.[84] Indeed, some of the Romanesque interiors, improved by structural features that we must next consider, are as moving as some Gothic interiors. It is to be hoped that no one who has stood in the nave of the recently restored Cathedral of Mainz while the sun was yet high enough to enter through small windows, to pierce the dimness of its somber atmosphere and set the red lime-

[84] See p. 616.

The Abbaye-aux-hommes at Caen

stone of its walls on fire, will come away without having felt at least the strength, vigor, and surpassing nobility of the great Romanesque churches.

To illustrate those improvements made in Romanesque construction that led straight to the Gothic church, it will be sufficient to limit our-

selves to two rather revolutionary churches—Sant' Ambrogio at
Milan, and St. Stephen at Caen, elsewhere called the Abbaye-aux-
hommes.[85] These improvements derived directly from the desire to
remove the danger of fire by substituting stone vaults for wooden
roofs, and in northern France and Europe, without the bright sunlight of the south, to introduce more light into the church. Better
times, increased wealth, heightened religious emotion in general demanded bigger and better churches. The Romans had built three kinds
of stone vaults, the domed, barrel, and groined vaults.[86] During the
early middle ages it appears that knowledge of how to build these
stone vaults was lost in the west. But during the Romanesque period
it was regained, and these three kinds of stone vaults began to be used.

The domed vault was the least popular. Rarely was it used as roofing
for the nave, but it is usually found at the crossing of nave and tran-

Barrel and
groined vaults
septs in Norman churches. To build a barrel vault over nave or side
aisles requires an elaborate preliminary scaffolding for the whole area
to be vaulted in order to center the arch of the vault until the mortar
or cement hardens. The vault itself must be of considerable weight to
spring successfully over any considerable area. To support it, therefore,
the walls upon which it rests must be of corresponding weight, and it
is dangerous to pierce them with anything but relatively small windows for fear they will collapse. Moreover, every stone vault contains
a force called a thrust, a tendency to bulge outwards, which, if the
walls are not strong enough to contain it as well as hold the weight
of the vault, causes them to collapse. The thrust of the barrel vault
is strongest at the haunches of the arch and is, of course, continuous
for its whole length.

In the groined vault, however, the continuous thrust of the barrel
vault is disassociated into individual thrusts which are concentrated
along the lines of the intersections or groins of the vault, and brought
down to a definite point at the four corners of the vault. In the groined
vault, therefore, there are two points of thrust, the haunch and springing point of the arch, but they are isolated along the lines of intersection of the two barrel vaults which go to make up the groined vault.
If some external support to the walls of the nave or side aisles could
be applied at those points where, in a groined vault, the thrust is concentrated, then the function of the walls would be limited to support-

[85] The Abbaye-aux-hommes and the Abbaye-aux-dames (see pp. 814–15) were
built by William the Conqueror and Mathilda to make amends for their marriage
within the prohibited degrees.
[86] See p. 805.

ing the weight of the vault, rather than both supporting the weight and containing the thrust; they could accordingly be made lighter, and could less dangerously be opened up with windows. Thus, from the point of view of a well-lighted interior, groined vaults were superior to barrel vaults. All this knowledge was learned by the Romanesque architects only after costly and sometimes disastrous experiment with actual buildings.

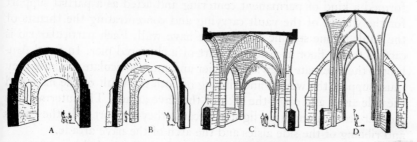

The evolution of vaulting in medieval architecture. A. A very early Romanesque barrel vault. B. Section through piers of an early Romanesque round-arched groin vault. C. Section through window showing later round-arched and ribbed groin vault. D. Section through window bay showing typical Gothic pointed arch vault with ribs, piers, and flying buttresses.

Stone vaults were first of all thrown over the narrower spaces of the side aisles. Skill and knowledge had to be acquired before the builders dared put them over the wider areas of nave and transepts; some Romanesque churches never got stone vaults for their naves and transepts. Likewise greater difficulty in building groined vaults kept them for a while from being used for the nave, so that there are many Romanesque churches with groined vaults for the side aisles and barrel vaults for the nave and transepts. One of the first Romanesque churches to have a groined vault for the nave was Sant' Ambrogio. The building of a groined vault necessitates the division of the area to be vaulted into squares called bays, for obviously the intersection of two barrel vaults of equal height can only cover a square. To intersect two barrel vaults of unequal heights is a very difficult and dangerous thing to do, besides producing an unattractive irregular groin. To keep the bays of the nave square at Sant' Ambrogio, one bay of the nave was made to equal two bays of the side aisles. The construction of barrel vaults is also simplified by dividing the area to be covered into bays, which can then be vaulted one at a time with less expense in less time, because scaffolding for centering needs to be for one bay only.

The vaulting at Sant' Ambrogio

For both barrel vaulting (as at St. Sernin at Toulouse) and groined vaulting, builders found it advantageous to mark the limits of the bay by spanning the area to be vaulted with arches of masonry, called ribs, that could be used as partial supports of the vaults themselves. At Sant' Ambrogio the builders discovered the utility of sending ribs along the diagonal groins of the vault, and longitudinally along the wall of the nave. The framework of transverse, diagonal, and longitudinal ribs formed a kind of permanent centering and acted as a partial support for the weight of the vault carrying and concentrating the thrusts of the vault to one specific spot on the nave wall. Each particular rib is carried to the floor as a distinct part of a clustered pier. In Sant' Am- brogio the alternate piers are heavier and more articulate, because they must support the weight and ribbing of both the vault of the nave and the side aisles and carry the arch of the nave arcade. The intermediate piers are correspondingly lighter, because they support only the vaults and ribbing of the side aisles and the arch of the nave arcade.

But the problem of light was not satisfactorily settled here, because the builders did not dare to raise the very heavy vault of the nave so high as to admit a clearstory. Light had to come in, therefore, only from the windows of the well-developed triforium gallery and of the side aisles. Without a clearstory the concentrated thrust of the nave vaulting could be met by the vaults of the triforium gallery, which carried them to the strong pilaster buttresses built on the outside walls of the side aisles and triforium, at those points where the thrusts of their own vaults were concentrated by ribbing. Thus already at Sant' Ambrogio the church was beginning to consist of a skeletal framework of buttresses, piers, and ribbing supporting a stone vault. But if the problem of the support of a stone vault was solved, the architects were not bold enough to utilize it to make the church lighter.

In St. Stephen's, however, the Norman architects were bold enough. They not only introduced an extra transverse rib between the diag- onal ribs of the nave vault, but they raised the vaulting of the nave high enough above the triforium gallery to permit a clearstory. To support the thrust of the nave vault the triforium gallery was vaulted not as in Milan with a groined vault, but with a half-barrel vault which was thrown up against the wall of the nave. Since the thrusts of the nave vault were concentrated by means of ribbing at the points where they met the piers, so much buttressing by a continuous half-barrel vault was unnecessary. This the architects realized, and when they built a similar church, the Abbaye-aux-dames at Caen, they removed all the buttressing except that running from the side walls to the exact

New features in St. Stephen's at Caen

points of stress on the nave walls. In this way a rudimentary flying buttress made its appearance, but under the wooden roof which kept it from public view. Except for differences in proportion the interior of St. Stephen's is in other respects similar to that of Sant' Ambrogio. But the Normans had taken another step in preparing for Gothic by

E A E B

Two bays in the Romanesque S. Ambrogio at Milan, showing how individual members of the clustered piers (A B E) receive the ribs supporting the vaults of nave and side aisles, as well as the arches of the nave arcade.

combining ribbed vaulting with clearstory and elementary flying buttresses.

In fact there remained, except for the perfection and refinement of details, only one major problem left for the Gothic architect, namely, that of raising the height of the church, of lifting it skyward. Gothic architects of the Île de France soon found out that as long as the round arch continued to be used in arcading, fenestration, ribbing, and vaulting, all aspiration to soar into the heavens was limited by the simple,

The pointed arch

inescapable fact that the radius of a circle is only one-half the diameter, and hence that the height of a semicircular arch could be only one-half of its width. If therefore the pointed arch were introduced into the very structure of the whole building, as something more than an item of decoration, then the building could immediately be raised, because the height of the pointed arch is not determined by its width. The possibilities of the use of the pointed arch in the building of the ribbing for the groined vault was first made evident in connection with Romanesque vaulting. Even in the case where the bay to be ribbed and

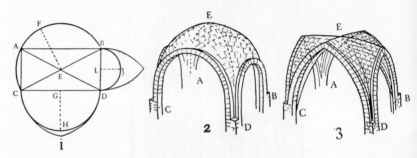

The advantages in vaulting with a pointed arch. (1) ABCD is an oblong bay to be vaulted. BC is the diagonal rib; DC, the transverse; and BD, the longitudinal. If circular ribs are erected, their heights will be EF, GH, and IJ. The result will be a domical vaulting (2) irregular in shape because of the unequal heights of the ribs, and with the longitudinal arch too low to admit of a clearstory. A building so vaulted is low and dark, like Sant' Ambrogio. The problem, then, is to bring the crowns of all the ribs to the same height as that of the diagonal rib E. This can be done by pointing the lower ribs. The result is a lighter, more flexible system, affording ample space for a clearstory (3).

vaulted was square, as at Sant' Ambrogio, a difficulty presented itself in that the height of the arch of the two diagonal ribs was naturally greater than that of the two transverse, and two wall or longitudinal ribs. Some Romanesque architects simply flattened out the diagonal ribs so that their crowns equaled in height the crowns of the other ribs, giving to the whole vault an elliptical form. At Sant' Ambrogio, however, the builders made no adjustment of the height of the diagonal ribs, so that the vault took a slightly domical shape. In neither case was the problem of height solved.

Quite obviously if the builders wished to retain in the nave bays of equal size with the bays of the side aisles, in view of the fact that the nave was usually twice the width of the side aisles, to retain the use of the unaltered round-arched ribbing would produce a vault of queer and almost impossible domical shape. It therefore occurred to the Gothic architects that if the arch of the transverse and longitudinal or wall ribs were pointed enough to make their crowns equal in height the crown of the diagonal ribs, the ungainly domical vault would be avoided, the vault would be higher, and more window space would be allowed in the clearstory. If at the same time the diagonal ribs were pointed and the other ribs pointed or stilted to an equal height, the

Gothic structure and the pointed arch

Showing the skeleton framework of ribs over a nave bay. A, transverse rib. B, diagonal rib. C, cross ridge. D, longitudinal ridge. E, wall or longitudinal rib. This also shows the stonework filling between ribs in a finished vault.

vault would be still higher. And if the arches of the nave arcade and of the triforium were pointed the nave would rise even higher still. The only limit to the height of the church was henceforth safety. When the pointed arch was introduced into the structure of the ribbing, vaulting, triforium, and nave arcade, the Gothic was established.

The experiments made leading to the structural use of the pointed arch were conducted by architects of the Île de France. They produced

in a short time the great Gothic cathedrals of Notre Dame, Chartres,
Amiens, Rheims, Beauvais, and many others which were only a gradual refinement, along all lines, of the principles of Romanesque and
Gothic construction mentioned above. The chief new structural addition made by Gothic architects was to bring the primitive flying buttress of the Romanesque from under cover of the lean-to roof of the
side aisles, and to raise it to meet the higher thrust of a higher nave
vault and carry it to the ground. Thus what the Gothic cathedral was
from a structural point of view was a skeletal framework of side-aisle

*Cross section of a Gothic cathe-
dral, showing the arrangement of
the nave and side aisles, the flying
buttresses, and buttress piers supporting the nave vaulting.*

wall buttresses, flying buttresses, clustered piers, and ribbing in perfect
equilibrium, built to support the weight of and counterbalance and
carry to the ground the thrusts of the stone vaults of the side aisles
and the nave. With such a framework, walls as such served no purpose except to keep out the light. Gothic architects then proceeded to
remove all the flat wall surfaces and to substitute for them windows
of colored glass. Hence the walls of the side aisles tended to become
mere glass interrupted only by the outside wall buttresses. The clearstory became in effect one continuous sheet of colored glass interrupted only by ribs running down from vault to pier or to the floor.
When a gabled roof was substituted for a lean-to roof over the side
aisles, the triforium could be transformed into glass. In total effect,

therefore, the Gothic church is a soaring glass house held together by a skeletal framework of stone, or a vast "vaulted glass cage." [87]

"This century, 1140 to 1250, was the most momentous in architectural history and the one that most thoroughly repays study. Nothing has been done since then that can be set beside its achievements." [88] It was of course the century of the perfection of the Gothic style, wholly attributable to the genius of French architects of the original Capetian domain. But as fascinating as Gothic is as a logical development from certain structural discoveries, to the general student it must be all the more interesting as the embodiment of the essential features of the medieval renaissance, and indeed of the civilization of the middle ages at its height—French civilization, we should be obliged to say, but that Gothic architecture spread from western Europe to all parts of Europe as no other architecture ever has. It is no mere coincidence that during the reign of Philip Augustus new cathedrals were started at Paris, Chartres, Bourges, Laon, Soissons, Rheims, Meaux, Noyon, Amiens, Rouen, Cambrai, Arras, Tours, Séez, Coutances, Bayeux, and that nearly all of them were completed before the end of the thirteenth century. It is certainly a reflection of the consolidating work of the Capetians that in its spread throughout France, no such variety can be traced in the few schools of Gothic as existed in the many schools of French Romanesque, and what differences there were are not fundamental. The spread of Gothic to the rest of Europe is but another bit of evidence of that preponderance of French culture in Europe that we have noted in connection with the French universities and French literature.

Gothic as an expression of medieval civilization

It is of interest that Gothic architecture is not predominantly the architecture of the monastery but of the cathedral, the bishop's church, of those bishops indeed who were bound together in an international church directed by the pope, of the power of which Gothic architecture must be considered an expression. Gothic flourished when the papacy and Church were at their height. But it is no less instructive that the Cistercians and the Friars carried a knowledge of and an enthusiasm for Gothic from France throughout Europe. It is of course significant that the cathedral was a product of the town, placed on the public square, surrounded by the homes of its builders, "the religious, civic, social centre of everything . . . at once church, picture gallery, library, school, even in a sense, theatre." It was built by the wealth of

---

[87] The phrase is that of Professor Smith of the department of architecture of the University of Nebraska.

[88] Sturgis and Frothingham, *History of Architecture*, III, xxix–xxx.

the bishop, which was the wealth of the merchant, banker, and gilds-man. The gilds at Chartres contributed many of the precious windows of the cathedral: the bakers' gild gave a window depicting a medieval bakeshop in operation; the clothmakers, the interior of one of their shops.

Moreover, the cathedral was often the outcome of town rivalry in

Notre Dame de Paris

the building of bigger and better churches. Siena became quite dis-satisfied with her church after the Cathedral of Florence was built, so she decided to use her present church merely as the transept for a new cathedral really indicative of her importance. But the larger church remains still to be done. The burghers of Beauvais would erect the highest of all French cathedrals, but unfortunately it collapsed. Even so, with modifications in structure they went ahead to build the highest of all French Gothic cathedrals, but they never got more than the choir and transept completed. Architects, as at Chartres, planned for many more soaring towers than were ever finished. In most instances the main towers of the western façades are still unfinished, or were only finished after a long period of delay.

Again it was not the monk as builder or architect who raised the Gothic cathedral. The architect was the lay professional master builder, a person of considerable importance, who often competed with others of his craft for the honor of building a new church, and was in charge of its actual construction. The workers were members of the gilds, masons, stonecutters, carpenters, sculptors, metalworkers, and stained glass workers, many of them artists of genius, proud of their work. Indeed, the architect emerged with the lawyer as a new professional man. The whole building of the church by laymen was a phase of medieval secularization.

It can well be seen, too, that Gothic architecture reflects some of the intellectual features of the medieval renaissance. The architects themselves were mathematicians who knew how to draw logical deductions from newly established premises. They made models for their buildings and drew plans; anyone who has tried to understand the drawings for the complicated ribbing of a choir with a winding ambulatory and adjoining chapels will realize how much of a geometer he must be. The vibrant and tense skeletal framework of the Gothic church, with its logical balance of thrust and counterthrust, so true that not even constant bombardment by modern artillery in the recent war of such a cathedral as Rheims caused it to collapse, has often been compared to the logic of the *Summa* of a scholastic theologian. The experimental temper of thirteenth-century science is repeated in the experiments of the Romanesque and Gothic builders with ribbing and vaulting to get proper height and light, to solve problems of weight and thrust, and to achieve suitable æsthetic effects. *Gothic and the medieval renaissance*

The tendency of the medieval scientist to observe the world of nature about him was the same as that of the Gothic sculptor, who introduced into his capitals and his moldings delicate reproductions of a wide variety of plant life that he perhaps saw in his own garden. In fact, the very abundance of sculpture on the cathedral has been shown to express in detail the general contents of such a medieval encyclopedia as Vincent of Beauvais's *Speculum Naturale*, and to have been arranged very probably after consultation with learned men. This did not prevent it from being used for popular instruction, and makes it possible to refer to the cathedral as an encyclopedia in stone. Yet after all this is said, it must not be forgotten that the cathedral is a church, and that if it failed to supply an adequate milieu for the relief of religious emotion it would be essentially false. In the complicated allegory of its sculpture, in the mysticism of its lofty colored interior, and in its devotion to such figures as the Virgin and the saints with their relics, it incorporated what we have repeatedly emphasized were features of medieval religion. None the less, as a supreme and unified work of art it inspired men's hearts to seek their God and Savior.

Gothic architecture remains a joy to most architects not only because the period gave the architect such complete authority in the building of the whole, not only because it so realistically revealed the features of its structure, but also because all the other arts were so completely subordinated to the total architectural effect of the building. Such arts as sculpture and stained glass were not permitted to usurp an independent place calling attention to themselves. When they did, the period of Gothic was over. It remains now to illustrate this feature by pointing out some of the refinements made by Gothic architects in the main principles mentioned above.

Development of ground plan The steady development of the ground plan is to be noticed by comparing the plan of the simple Roman basilica that was its origin with the ground plan of typical thirteenth-century cathedrals. The nave became larger and wider, and was adjoined by correspondingly enlarged side aisles that were occasionally doubled. Adjoining the outer side aisles were often regular series of chapels for the saints. The transept became larger and wider. In English cathedrals a second transept was frequently added, transforming the general plan into an archiepiscopal cross. The choir was elongated to provide for a larger number of participating clergy. When there were double side aisles they were continued about the choir in a double ambulatory. Off the ambulatory, continuing the series of chapels of the side aisles, was a second series of choir or apsidal chapels. English cathedrals commonly ended in a square apse, the importation probably of Cistercian monks.

Development of the flying buttress The development of flying buttresses and the façade shows the same march forward. Originally but a half-barrel vault hidden by a roof, when once roof and the unnecessary sections of this vault were removed, the buttress leapt upward to meet the thrust of the higher nave vault. Then a work of art was made of it without depriving it of its structural features. The pier buttress of the side-aisle wall from which it sprang receded gracefully in oblique stone planes until topped with a pinnacle and crockets. Sculpture was introduced into niches on its face. The flying buttress itself was decorated in various ways: it was made to carry off the water from a copper or lead roof covering the vault, the water running down a groove made on the top face of the buttress and through the mouth of a fantastic gargoyle which threw it clear of the wall of the side aisle. When the architects discovered that the thrust of the vault was greatest not only at the haunch but at the point where the piers receive the ribbing of the vault, they then sent up a double flying buttress to meet this double point of stress. At Chartres the lower wing of the double flying but-

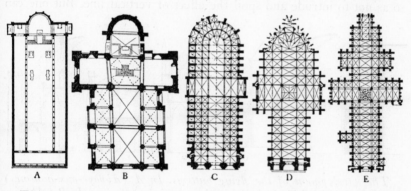

A   B   C   D   E

The development of the ground plan of the medieval cathedral. From the simple basilican plan of A (Santa Maria Maggiore at Rome—fourth century) transept and apse have developed in B (San Michele at Povia—twelfth century) to give the church the form of a Latin cross. In C (Paris—thirteenth century) the side aisles have been doubled, and continued, in a double ambulatory around the lengthened choir apse, the whole being flanked by chapels. In D (Amiens—thirteenth century) the transept is tripartite and the whole chevet beautifully articulated. In E (Salisbury, England) there are two transepts and a square choir and apse, giving the church the form of an archiepiscopal cross.

tresses was transformed into a curved colonnade. When the church had two side aisles, the flying buttress first had to span the outside aisle and then spring to the vaulting from the pier buttresses of the inside aisle. English architects never took much to this employment of the flying buttress. They preferred the solidity of their earlier Romanesque construction.

The development of the Gothic façade can best be understood by comparing the façade of St. Stephen's at Caen with the façade of Notre Dame of Paris, the most graceful and symmetrical of all Gothic façades, and then with such a façade as Rheims or Amiens. What

Development of the façade

happened was the elimination of all plain surfaces on the façade without at the same time hiding the structure of the interior of the building. The portals to nave and side aisles were widened at Paris and elsewhere to include all the space between the buttresses of the façade. The portals were then more deeply recessed and filled in lavishly with sculpture pertaining first of all to those persons to whom the portals were dedicated, usually Christ, the Virgin, and the patron saint of the church. The figure sculpture of the portals was strictly subordinated to the architecture of the portal. It was often elongated so as not to intrude and spoil the effect of vertical line. But one can

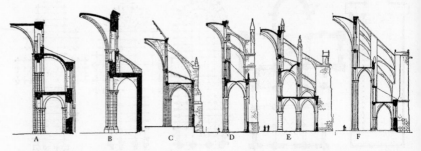

A   B   C   D   E   F

The development of the flying buttress. In A (Abbaye-aux-hommes) the thrust is carried by the half-barrel vault of the triforium. In B (Abbaye-aux-dames) the simple flying buttress, a segment of the half-barrel in A, is still covered with a roof. In C (English Gothic) the wall buttress begins to be decorated, the flying buttress is clear and reaches to a greater height. In D (Amiens) a double buttress spans a single side aisle; in E (Paris) two side aisles with the top buttress ending in a gargoyle. In F (Bourges) a triple buttress spans two side aisles.

find almost anything in the sculpture of the portals: saints, kings, knights, virtues, scenes from Scripture, scenes from the lives of the saints, devils, demons, grotesques, plants, and animals, some of it frankly symbolical, some frankly realistic, and all arranged in a definite sequence. In the tympanum of the main portal was often a representation of the Last Judgment showing freakish devils driving, poking, and jamming with evident delight the condemned souls into the mouth of hell, and in contrast angels guiding to paradise the saved, who sometimes wear very self-satisfied smiles.

After studying this sculpture in detail one becomes aware of its lovely and gentle humanity, and its superb mastery in portraying the ideal figure of Christ or a saint, or the distorted anatomy of a devil. In its own way medieval sculpture is quite on a par with Greek sculpture.

Surmounting the portals was ordinarily a dignified row of the kings of Judah, and above this the rose window. The development of the two western towers paralleled that of the rest of the façade in intricacy, dignity, and grace. At Paris they are joined by a beautiful arcade that reveals the gabled roof of the nave. It is to be noticed that whatever uncarved surfaces are left on the façade of Notre Dame are removed from the façades of Rheims and Amiens.

The particular transformation wrought by the Gothic in the interior was the change of emphasis from the horizontal to the vertical line and the addition of color through the medium of stained glass. *Stained glass* The soaring effect was of course given by the use of the pointed arch and slender clustered piers, from whose very base rise the ribs which carry the vault at Beauvais to one hundred and fifty-three feet above the pavement of the nave. The stained glass windows of side aisles, triforium gallery, and clearstory have taken the place of the frescoed walls of Romanesque churches. The glass is one of the most priceless creations of medieval art; modern artists are at a loss to recapture it. The glass was colored while in a molten state and not simply painted over; enamel colors were often fused with it to give it its peculiar depth and tone. It was then cut into very small pieces, from one to six inches long, which were fitted into a leaden framework, itself the chief means of design. The windows were thus essentially glass mosaics. Some additional lines were added in neutral color for detail. The colored glass in its leaden framework was then fitted into plate tracery, made by piercing geometrical designs into thin plates of stone. But plate tracery was quickly supplanted by bar tracery, thinly cut mullions of stone fitted together on the principles of the arch. Bar tracery made possible such *tours de force* as the rose windows. The designer of the window had so to fit together his small pieces of differently colored glass that the human eye at considerable distance would blend them into an harmonious color scheme, the very principle that French impressionists used in the nineteenth century with oil paints.

Moreover, the window had to be so designed that no harm would be done to the architectural lines of the building by a figure or illustration that would call attention to the window rather than put it into an architectural setting. Extremely small figures set in squares, circles, and lozenges with large embroidered borders were therefore the rule in the best windows of the school at Chartres. The later school of stained glass artists at Paris tended to spoil the architectural propriety of the early windows by making the figures in the windows unduly prominent. The basic color tone of the best early windows was a deep, unearthly, translucent blue such as is seen in the lancet windows of the façade at Chartres. With time, this verged into deep red and then violet. Finally the style of the earlier glass was ruined when it was painted rather than stained with a predominating yellow of ocher and silver chloride. A greenish white glass called grisaille came to be used with colored glass for some effects, and it was used alone (as at Chartres) for whole windows to offset windows of colored glass.

The combination of large figures, painted glass, and even ordinary white glass ruined the earlier art in the fourteenth century. The subject matter of the figures in the glass, like that of the sculpture, was often complicated by symbolism, or again reproduced simple scenes to illustrate Scripture, saints' lives, or the trades of the town. Together sculpture and glass may have exercised some influence as instruments of popular education. Metalworkers and wood carvers added their handiwork to the furniture and plate of the church. Wrought iron was made into candelabra, screens, gates, and intricate hinges for the great wooden doors. The shrines, altars, tombs, and statues glowed with color. On the altars were vessels of precious metals and cloths of fine lace or rich embroidery. The wooden choir stalls, lecterns, pulpits, and screens were carved with delicacy and humorous charm. The wood carver too took his models from nature, from medieval lore of legendary creatures, or just from the grotesqueries of his own imagination. In brightly painted stone and wood imps peeped out from the most unexpected places. Yet good taste forbade the introduction into the interior of the profusion of sculpture placed on the main portals and porches of the transepts. The series of moving life-sized figures of real persons introduced into the choir of the cathedral at Naumburg, Germany, is unique.

The Gothic spirit

After all, it is nearly impossible, except perhaps for the talented literary artist, to convey in words the total overwhelming effect of the Gothic cathedral. One must be on the spot to see and study and feel before one appreciates the need of superlatives in describing it. Fortunately, this is still possible. The cathedrals are still in use, and are graciously open to any who care to go in. One may still visit Chartres on a gala feast day when the church is crowded to the limit, as it ordinarily was in the middle ages, or walk about its triforium gallery or climb its towers, help toll its bells, peer down on its vaulting, sit on its buttresses, and notice that no matter how far removed from the public eye below, the medieval artist never resorted to anything shoddy. One may spend days in its interior going from window to window of a church completely filled with the best of medieval glass. One may watch the different effects in the interior according as it is early morning, high noon, or early afternoon light that comes through the jeweled windows to make all the stone surfaces a mosaic of colored light. Or most suitably, perhaps, to get the proper impression of the mystic moods of the Gothic interior, one may steal into the church late in the afternoon when it is quite empty and shadows have begun to fill the high vaults, while the light fades from the windows. Standing at the crossing of nave and transept one may gaze upon the darkened glory of three rose windows. If one is lucky the organist will climb to the loft and fill the whole church with music for him, until that moment when in the somber quietness of dusk it is necessary to leave.

In music the middle ages achieved the same distinction of special form and mood as in the other arts, and prepared the whole groundwork for the development of modern music. Here too there is no definite break between antiquity and the middle ages, nor between them and the subsequent period. There is only a gradual change in emphasis and form. The Church took music into its service as eagerly as it did the other arts. It not only gave practical training in singing to choirboys in its singing schools (*scholæ cantorum*), but in the monastic and episcopal schools and universities musical theory was studied as a part of the quadrivium in close relationship to mathematics, and praised as such by men like Grosseteste and Roger Bacon. In the development of both practice and theory it has given to us such things as our whole system of musical notation, consisting of staves and bars, clefs and notes, sharps, flats, and naturals. These were definitely the inventions of medieval composers, and depended in no way upon the musical notation of classical antiquity. They were the outgrowth of experiments in writing a kind of music unknown to the ancient world, music written for several voices or parts rather than as a simple melody for one voice or part. *Medieval music*

From antiquity, apparently by way of Byzantium, the early middle ages inherited, in addition to the Greek modes and a number of musical instruments including the organ, the unison song, or, as it was called in Latin, *musica plana*. This plain music, or plain song, or plain chant was adopted by the Church to form the musical setting for its Latin liturgy. Inasmuch as tradition ascribes the first organization of Christian liturgical music to Pope Gregory the Great,[89] plain chant is often called Gregorian chant. It is to be found, as the official music *Gregorian chant*

[89] See p. 200.

of the organized liturgy, embodied in the Roman Antiphonal. In Gregorian chant the melody, sung in unison by the choir or chanted by the priest, is allowed no independent value of its own, but is closely subordinated to the sacred words of the service it accompanies. It flows on in the unmeasured rhythms of the stately prose of the Latin liturgy, where each syllable is of approximately equal duration. In the earliest manuscripts only signs called neumes, marking the general upward or downward motion of the chant, were used as notation. Of course thousands of these Gregorian melodies have been preserved. Despite subsequent developments, Gregorian chant remained and is still the unchangeable foundation and main body of the music of the Church, and many of the melodies survive in the Lutheran chorales of the Protestants.

More, however, than simply to adapt the classical tradition of unison song to the form and mood of the liturgy of the Church, western music went ahead to develop a characteristic form of its own. *Diaphony and organum* To the one-voiced or homophonic chant, composers began to add more voices, and the result was what is called polyphonic, or more precisely many-voiced, music. They began by adding to the simple melody of the chant at an interval of an octave, a fifth, or a fourth, that is, eight, five, or four notes away from the basic melody, one more voice part running, however, quite parallel to the melodic line of the chant. This type of parallel writing, amounting to a lateral extension of the original melody, was called diaphony. The number of voices was soon increased to three and even four, and the collective name given to this species of many-voiced music was organum. By the end of the tenth century experiments in many-voiced music had been sufficiently advanced to lead to their general acceptance in the music of the Church.

Organum necessarily called attention to problems unconnected with the composition of simple plain song. There was first of all the necessity of keeping the various voices together, of introducing a time relationship between them. This became especially serious when singers and composers refused to limit themselves to simple parallel melodies, and introduced decorative notes into individual voices, or wrote in voices that were in no sense parallel. Definite rhythms adopted from poetic meters were introduced, and to keep them simultaneous in all the voices a new system of musical notation, indicating *Musica mensurata and consonance* the relative length of time each note was to be held, had to be devised. The unmeasured melody of the chant became measured polyphony; *musica plana* became *musica mensurata*. Then, too, while the emphasis in polyphonic music was always on the horizontal line, as in Romanesque architecture, the singing together of tones at a fourth, or fifth, or eighth from the melody inevitably brought up the possibility of the chord, or consonance, or harmony of these simultaneous tones, or one might say their vertical or Gothic relationship. In other words, music by beginning to have a warp of several threads called attention to the necessity of a woof as well. Therewith began that chief characteristic of western music, harmony.

What was responsible for the new trend, and whether other factors than those mentioned above contributed to the general development, it is difficult to say. It may have been the influence of the literature on Arabic music coming in with the twelfth-century renaissance. It may have been the repercussion of the strong rhythmical music used to accompany popular dances or metrical poetry in Latin or vernacular tongues. It may have been the difficulty of singing in unison in choirs of mixed men's and boys' voices of different pitches. Paris and northern France, as in other fields, led this development in the twelfth and thirteenth centuries.

The trend started with diaphony and organum knew no end. On the basis of the original melody of the chant additional voice parts could easily be added in a contrary rather than a parallel motion. Or the tenor (the holder) could be made to keep to the chant, while quite independent melodies were made to accompany, care being taken, however, to relate the secondary melody note by note, or point by point (*punctus contra punctum*; the Latin term for note was *punctus*), according to the intervals that the ear had become accustomed to, and therefore regarded as pleasant and authoritative. Such composition *Composition* is called counterpoint and constitutes, when written with the accept- *in counterpoint* able measured rhythms, the typical music of the twelfth and thirteenth centuries. It is best expressed in the compositions of the French composers Léonin and Pérotin, who were in the service of the Cathedral of Notre Dame of Paris. In spite of the early rules of contrapuntal composition, which limited the consonances to the octave, the fourth, and the fifth, composers could not avoid, in their complicated interweaving of melodies, actual discords and consonances of a third or a sixth. The ear was trained to like a variety of chords, and composers could make a feeble beginning in the vertical relationship of chords to chords, to vary the prevalent horizontal relationship of melody to melody.

An innovation of great consequence for subsequent musical form *The canon,* was made when, for the sake of variety, the basic melody of the com- *or round* position was repeated in second or third parts at some time after the first melody had been begun, in the manner of the rounds, such as "Three Blind Mice," which we all have sung. In contemporary writings such a round was called a canon, or fugue, or *rota*, and when used, forced special attention upon questions of measured rhythm and consonance. Complicated rounds were composed by the thirteenth century, the most famous of them being the English "Sumer is icumen in." The form of the round thus introduced reached the height of its development in the complicated fugues of John Sebastian Bach in the early eighteenth century.

As the title of "Sumer is icumen in" indicates, composition according to the rules of counterpoint was not limited to the music meant for the liturgy. It led to the production of several kinds of organum, and also to such secular forms as the cantilena or rondel and the motet. Of these, the motet had a notable development in the twelfth and thirteenth centuries. Originally its basic melody was taken from the plain chant of the liturgy and was sung to the Latin words or *The motet* phrases accompanying it. To this was added one or more melodies, each sung with its own appropriate words, so that sometimes both French words and Latin words would be sung with these additional tunes written to accompany the fundamental melody. In time, however, the basic melody with its words was taken from popular songs, and the whole motet was completely secularized. When the melodies were measured according to given rhythmical patterns and written with the required consonances, the motet approached a definite art form. This whole development of polyphonic or contrapuntal composition, in whatever form composed, one may describe as scholastic music. The plain song melody was the authoritative theme, the counterpart of Christian dogma in philosophy and theology. The subsidiary melodies weaving themselves about the authoritative theme, according to definite rules of composition in counterpoint, one could compare with the Aristotelian dialectics of scholastic philosophy. The logic of the completed composition was therefore the logic of the *summæ* or of the Gothic church.

Composers of the middle of the fourteenth century complained that the older forms of organum were being abandoned for the cantilena and the motet. When the efforts to build up a complicated *Late medieval* pattern of independent melodies around the theme melody were *counterpoint* applied to the music of the liturgy, the results inevitably detracted from the actual Latin text of the liturgy, and might well obscure the basic melody of the chant. This was to neglect the religious purpose of the liturgy for mere cleverness in composition. Indeed, music in counterpoint, as written by Netherlandish composers of the fourteenth and fifteenth centuries, became a competitive game in mere dexterity. These composers of the Low Countries, and we know the names and works of hundreds of them, went to the limit of adding five, twelve, sixteen, or even occasionally twenty-four additional voices to the theme of the chant. Moreover, the themes of secular songs, of the *chansons* of the trouvères, were introduced outright to take the place of the melody of the chant. Masses came to be known from the names of the songs whose melodies they incorporated, such as the Mass of the "Armed Men," or the "Good-bye my Love" Mass.

The reaction to this form of excessively complicated and secularized music did not come until the sixteenth century, with the Protestant reformation and the counterreformation of the Church. It was carried out originally by pupils of the Netherlandish composers in Italy. Protest against the elaborate counterpoint of Church music at the Council of Trent went so far as to demand a return to pure and unadulterated Gregorian chant. Fortunately no such radical step was taken. But in the music of Giovanni Pierluigi da Palestrina (1526– *Palestrina* 94), certainly one of the greatest of all composers, the return was made to the ideal of plain chant: the supremacy of the liturgy and of the religious mood, with simplicity in style, without returning to the literal single melody itself. His music is contrapuntal in nature, but the forced canonic (i.e., in the nature of the round) polyphony of the Flemish composers gave way to a fluent, singable, and relatively simple vocal setting which represents the beginnings of a true *a cappella* style.

Much less is known of secular music than of Church music, and it *Secular music* is just as difficult to speak of the interrelations between the music of the liturgy and of the people as it is to speak of the interrelations between Latin and vernacular poetry. The Celts and other peoples of western Europe of course sang and danced long before the arrival of the Germans and the Norse. The Germans were already singing in Tacitus, and the heroic tales of Norse legend were sung by bards and scalds to the accompaniment of the harp. Troubadours and trouvères composed melodies for their poetry, sometimes inferior to the poetry itself, if we may believe their contemporary critics. The jongleur, viol on his back and a sheaf of musical manuscripts in his wallet, traveled from castle to castle to sing the songs of the troubadour. Should a castle door be shut in his face, the jongleur sang in the public square. The music was nothing more than simple melodies, like plain chant, but fitted to a poetry of great metrical variety it gave to the songs a rhythm and allure so like our own music that it is difficult to believe them eight hundred years old. They were passed on everywhere by pilgrims and mendicants. St. Francis, it will be remembered, knew his French songs, and his lesser brothers were urged as jongleurs of the Lord (*joculatores Domini*) to praise him in song. The students, too, we have seen, sang their songs as they played on their Spanish guitars. Secular song was taken up by Church composers and given additional voice parts according to the rules of counterpoint. In the madrigals of the sixteenth century these part songs were perfected, but they never lost the gaiety and rhythm of their source.

Instrumental music

Because the musical instruments inherited from antiquity and introduced from Spain [90] were, even by the end of the fifteenth century, relatively simple in construction, they limited the possible skill of the performer. In comparison, therefore, with the amount of choral music written, not much attention was given to instrumental music. Yet by the beginning of the sixteenth century independent music for the organ and the lute had been written in abundance, and some indeed for other instruments. But the development of an independent instrumental music, with special dance forms of its own, was really of later date, and was retarded by the attempts of composers to transfer the methods of counterpoint from the medium of choral music to instruments not suited to it.

[90] See pp. 182–83.

Chapter 25

THE DEVELOPMENT OF THE ENGLISH STATE
(1272–1485) *

* The author of this chapter is Dr. Glenn W. Gray.

WHEN the petulant and pious Henry III died in 1272 his heir was in Palestine upon a crusade. Since the council considered that a period of lawlessness lasting until Edward reached England might be too long they broke all precedents by immediately proclaiming the new king's peace [1] and thus inaugurating the reign of Edward I. Although Edward Plantagenet's contemporaries frequently named him "Longshanks" and he himself ordered "Hammer of the Scots" engraved upon his tomb, yet today he is usually called "the English Justinian," with Robert Burnell for his Tribonian; and none of the names lacks justification. If his motto *"Pactum Serva"* could be translated as "Keep your rights" as well as "Keep your promises," although disregarding his great ability, it would give a fair measure of the man. He loved venery and war, like his ancestors. He possessed to a marked degree the vile temper, insatiable ambition, desire for order, keen observation, and fearlessness of change of his great-grandfather Henry II. He attempted to unite the British Isles in one monarchy; created towns as did no other English monarch; quarreled, successfully, with the Church; limited the independence and power of the feudal classes; and added to the stature of the common law. Yet as Henry II, the great founder of the Angevin dynasty, is remembered primarily for the growth of the common law, so his great descendant Edward I is remembered for the growth of the English Parliament. Edward I made a new institution, the Parliament, that was eventually to supersede kings, a customary feature of the English state.

Edward I (1272–1307)

The word *"parliamentum"* gradually came into popular usage in western Europe between 1200 and 1250. For several generations the English chroniclers used it as a somewhat slangy equivalent to *col-*

The word "parliamentum" and law

[1] For the significance of the king's peace in England see pp. 446, 452.

833

loquium or *tractatum,* applying it to meetings and assemblies of any kind. Neither conference nor gabfest carries quite the same connotation today. By the second quarter of the century chroniclers and clerks, again throughout western Europe, were using the word to denote a meeting of a king's feudal court, more fully attended than customary, at which petitions and complaints against the king and his officials were heard. The semiannual assembly of the *curia* ordered by Frederick II in 1234 was to present and remedy complaints against officials and was called a *parlemento.* A great meeting of Henry III's *curia* in 1236 was called the Parliament of Merton [2] and another of 1258 the Oxford Parliament.[3] In France during the same years meetings of the *curia* for judicial purposes became known as *parlements.*[4] In England, however, the judicial functions of Parliament and the name itself were merged in a second institution.

The appearance of representative assemblies

This second institution was apparently the result of a belief, widespread throughout the feudal world, that any unusual grant of money to the king, or the undertaking by a king of any extremely hazardous enterprise, ought to be consented to by more than the feudal and official classes. The growing wealth and power of towns and merchants were thus recognized, and probably the tremendous wealth, organization, and influence of the clergy, which reached to the remotest parish, were also being taken into consideration by the rulers of the west. Although certainty concerning the motives of the thirteenth-century kings and princes who convoked these larger assemblies is impossible, it is known that throughout western and central Europe, during a few generations, the practice of summoning groups of representatives to reinforce the normal feudal meetings began. Between 1250 and 1350 *Cortes* appeared in the numerous kingdoms of the Spanish peninsula, *États-Généraux* and provincial estates in Paris and the French provinces, Diet and *Landtage* in the Germanies, the Diet in Bohemia, and Parliament in England.[5] Characteristic of them all was the appearance of new classes in feudal assemblies and the pos-

[2] At this parliament, or great council, the barons made their famous declaration of adherence to the common law. Asked by the king to change English law to conform to the canon law they replied, *"Nolumus leges Angliæ mutare."*

[3] See p. 459.

[4] The *Parlemento* founded in the Spanish peninsula was a meeting of an enlarged *curia* to select a new king after a dynasty became extinct.

[5] In general, these institutions appeared first in the south and southwest and latest in the north and northeast of Europe. A *cortes* was called in Aragon as early as 1188 and the *Parlemento* of Frederick II mentioned above in southern Italy was to be attended by municipal representatives, but the *Riksdag* of Sweden did not appear until about 1435.

session by the enlarged groups of some control over taxation and legislation. Yet the continental institutions were to wither away (although seldom as spectacularly as the *États-Généraux* or the Polish Diet), while the English Parliament, becoming a permanent instrument of state in the thirteenth century and combining functions elsewhere separated, was to create limited monarchy and to become the progenitor of the representative legislatures of the world today.[6]

The core of an early English parliament was the small council of the *curia regis*. Despite the attempts made by the baronage in Henry III's reign [7] it still remained a generalized institution, possessing neither defined functions nor specific membership. In an English parliament the small council was absorbed within the feudal great council of royal officials, prelates, or lords spiritual, and magnates, or lords temporal. The officials were, of course, frequently members of one of the other classes as well, as Robert Burnell was both Chancellor of England and Bishop of Bath and Wells. Moreover, the merging of these various elements in Parliament did not end their separate lives, for the great council met occasionally as a council of the magnates in the fourteenth and fifteenth centuries, and the small council as the continual or privy council continued to be the progenitor of specialized institutions of government well into modern times.

The English curia and Parliament

The officials of the *curia regis* were a small group of technically trained administrators and judges. By the end of the thirteenth century they formed a group of heads of departments and a sort of permanent civil service. Since the nobles were intensely jealous of the right to control the great offices of state, and repeatedly asserted in the later middle ages that they alone were the natural advisers and ministers of the king, the influence and number of officials in the great council depended almost entirely upon the ability of the reigning monarch, with the result that a feeble king was always forced to watch the authority of his personal staff in the great council decrease. Edward I raised his officials to an unprecedented importance, which they were unable to retain. It has been estimated that in 1305 approx-

The officials of the curia

---

[6] Pollard has best stated the importance to the world of English parliamentary institutions. "Parliamentary institutions have, in fact, been incomparably the greatest gift of the English people to the civilization of the world. Civilized man has drawn his religious inspirations from the East, his alphabet from Egypt, his Algebra from the Moors, his art and literature mainly from Greece, and his laws from Rome. But his political organization he owes mostly to English conceptions, and constitutional systems all over the world are studded with words and phrases which can only be explained by reference to the medieval English parliament." *Evolution of Parliament* (2d ed.), p. 3.

[7] See pp. 459–60.

imately seventy persons were his councillors, of whom about thirty were neither lords spiritual nor lords temporal. Among the officials whom he summoned to Parliament were his lord chancellor, lord treasurer, chancellor of the exchequer, lord privy seal, keeper of the wardrobe, the two chief justices, and about ten judges. During his reign the greater part of the work of any parliament, the hearing of complaints and petitions and the drafting of statutes, was performed by the small council. The class lost its position of equality, however, during the feudal reaction of the following reigns. Although still summoned, they became servants and technical advisers of the House of Lords rather than members; thus the lord chancellor became chairman of the lords and the judges their legal experts. Thereafter an official in order to vote, and perhaps even to participate unasked in debate, had also to be either a lord spiritual or a lord temporal.

The lords spiritual

The lords spiritual of the great council included the two archbishops, the bishops, mitred abbots, cathedral deans and priors, and the grand masters of the Templars, Hospitalers, and the Order of Sempringham.[8] The English were never able to formulate an acceptable theory to account for the presence of the lords spiritual in Parliament; the best was that they were the king's tenants-in-chief and owed attendance to his *curia* as a feudal obligation. Those who owed military service especially had no excuse for withdrawal, yet others were summoned and attended. Apparently Edward I was calling the great men of his kingdom before him, regardless of his right to do so, and few dared refuse.

The lords temporal

The lords temporal were the powerful lay vassals of the king, owing attendance to his court as a part of the feudal contract, and demanding summons as his "natural" advisers. During the reign of Edward I they were divided into two social ranks of about ten earls and approximately one hundred barons. By 1400, however, the modern classes of dukes, marquises, earls, viscounts, and barons had developed.[9] Edward I summoned to his parliaments those lords temporal whom he wished, and omitted the others. No one possessed a right to a parliamentary summons, although the duty to attend if summoned lay apparently upon all tenants-in-chief. When Parliament later gained independence the lords established the rules that a person

---

[8] The Templars were arrested in England in 1308. For that order and the Hospitalers see pp. 533–34. For the Order of Sempringham see p. 613.

[9] An additional class, that of the bannerets of the later years of Edward III's reign, was of only ephemeral importance. The continental title of count never became an English title, probably because the Latin term *comes* was appropriated for the English earls.

once called as a lord temporal thereafter had a right to be called, and that membership was hereditary under the strict rules of primogeniture. The creation of parliamentary lords temporal by a formal grant embodied in a charter rather than by a simple summons to Parliament began late in Edward III's reign. The parliamentary character assumed by the English nobility in England during the fourteenth century allowed only the eldest male heir of a noble to become a noble, and that only upon his predecessor's death, while other children remained commoners. As a result the English nobility was always numerically insignificant, although usually more wealthy, when compared with continental nobility, each of whose legitimate children inherited his father's titles and nobility.

As the House of Lords developed from one specialized use of the three classes attending the *curia regis*, so the House of Commons represented one more use of the sworn inquest. Henry I called sworn inquests from all the vills and hundreds of one county together, but did so infrequently. His grandson Henry II made it a regular practice to do so before his itinerant justices. Henry II's son John first ordered inquests from several counties to meet together. In the reign of John's son Henry III they were first called together from all England. Henry III's son Edward I called them so frequently before his *curia* that they became a customary part of his parliaments. Under Edward III they became a necessary part of any parliament. *The sworn inquest and the House of Commons*

One of the first of the larger assemblies that were to become parliaments was held in 1254 when two knights from each county were called before the *curia* to grant a special tax for war in France. The great parliamentary precedent of Henry III's reign, however, was Simon de Montfort's Parliament of 1265. In that year Montfort, holding the king and Prince Edward captive, wished to secure popular support for his proposed reforms.[10] At his command writs were issued summoning not only two knights from each shire but also two burgesses from each of many of the English cities and boroughs. Thus representatives from both rural and urban areas met together before the great council in Parliament for the first time. During the following thirty years many parliaments were held to which representatives from the shires and boroughs were sometimes summoned and sometimes not. At times representatives from the shires alone were summoned and at other times only those from the towns, while at still other times representatives of the minor clergy were summoned before the *curia*. Although the number demanded from each constituency *Henry III's parliaments*

[10] See p. 460.

varied between one and six, two became customary, perhaps from the
existing requirement that two knights be sent to the central law courts
to verify acts of the county court.

In 1295 Edward I summoned the Model Parliament, at which
every element ever called to a medieval English parliament was
present. In addition to the three classes composing the *curia* three
groups were present by representatives. Two knights were called from
each shire. In feudal parlance probably some of these were tenants-
in-chief who might be considered to represent those lesser tenants-in-
chief whom the king had promised in Chapter Fourteen of Magna
Carta to summon by the sheriff to the great council, yet the majority
were mesne tenants. By feudal custom the suzerain could summon
only the former to his court, but the English kings were powerful
enough and had already limited feudalism enough to disregard feudal
ties and, as kings, to summon their subjects before them in Parliament.
This step was the easier to take since in the reign of Henry III the
resentment of those mesne tenants called bachelors against their immediate overlords had played a part in the revolt led by Simon de
Montfort. The knights elected to Parliament were elected in the
county court and their elections certified by the sheriffs to the chancery.
The right to vote in these elections was so unimportant that it was left
undefined until 1430, when a statute limited it to those owning freehold estates in the county that returned an income of at least forty
shillings annually. Qualifications for election were defined from the
first by the requirement in the king's writ demanding the election
of knights, a requirement that could normally be met only by those
possessing land worth twenty pounds a year. A similar requirement
that those elected be residents of the county for which they were returned was disregarded by the fifteenth century. In Edward III's
reign sheriffs were made ineligible, but an attempt to exclude lawyers
failed.

The second group of representatives in the Model Parliament was
the burgesses. Two burgesses were summoned from each of many cities
and boroughs.[11] According to feudal law, of course, the king had a
legal right to summon his own towns before his court quite as he
summoned any tenant-in-chief, and a vassal town would naturally
appear by representatives. A great majority of the cities and boroughs
summoned to Parliament were royal, just as a great majority of all

[11] The English called a municipality containing a cathedral a city and its inhabitants citizens, while one without a cathedral was called a borough and its
inhabitants burgesses.

English municipalities were royal. Since the English kings, however, both did not summon some of their municipal tenants-in-chief and did summon boroughs belonging to their tenants-in-chief, the monarchs again were enforcing their authority as kings rather than as suzerains. The method by which burgesses were elected probably varied from borough to borough, with the majority being chosen by the borough councils. The expense of paying their members, since every member was paid a daily wage for attendance by his constituency, caused many boroughs to attempt to escape from parliamentary representation.

Clerical proctors, the third element among the representatives, represented the Church as the burgesses did the towns and the knights *The proctors* the landowners. This group was composed of the archdeacons and representatives of the parochial clergy of each diocese and of each cathedral chapter. The proctors preferred their own assembly, Convocation, to the new assembly of the state, Parliament, and consequently slowly ceased attending the latter. Since by 1400 they were accustomed to ignore the royal summons little is known of proctors in Parliament. The Model Parliament, attended by three conciliar groups and three types of representatives, was not an invariable example in composition for later parliaments, since the king's discretion remained for several generations the determining factor in any meeting of this sort; yet the assembly of 1295 provided an example that later rulers customarily observed.

During the century that followed the calling of the Model Parlia- *Formation* ment the five classes which permanently attended gradually coalesced *of the House* into groups, or houses. The lords spiritual were required to attend *of Lords* Parliament, although they were also members of Convocation. Their previous membership in the *curia*, the fact that many of them were officials, and the feudal liability of many to attend the court of their overlord prevented their following the example of their fellow churchmen, the proctors, of withdrawing from Parliament. Their traditional association with the great lay vassals in the *curia* together with the family bond that arose from many bishops' being chosen from the younger sons of the nobility furnished a tie uniting the lords temporal and spiritual. The lords temporal, whether required to attend or not (the kings until the fifteenth century were usually powerful enough to secure any attendance they desired), found in Parliament the device for controlling the king that they had sought,[12] and also effective aid upon many occasions from their companions the

[12] See pp. 458 ff.

lords spiritual in using that device. The less able kings who followed Edward I were unable to prevent the nobles from minimizing the importance of the officials, with the result that the officials as a class lost their full membership, retaining it only in so far as they were either lords spiritual or lords temporal. In this way the House of Lords was born.

Formation of the House of Commons

The formation of the lower house is more difficult to understand. The clerical proctors withdrew because they preferred to grant taxes in their own assembly [13] and because their constant claim to exemption from secular jurisdiction made the right of petition in Parliament somewhat anomalous. The knights of the shire were by birth and membership in the feudal order more closely connected with the lords temporal than with any other class in Parliament, and had the same desire to diminish the king's exactions. Moreover, the younger children of the nobles, by grants of land and by marriages, constantly entered the class from which the knights were chosen. Perhaps the fact that the knights had not been members of the *curia*, the possible discontent existing between mesne tenants and their overlords, and the lords temporal's feeling of social superiority all united to prevent any junction of the two classes as Parliament developed.[14] The burgesses, representing the merchants, were considered throughout the middle ages to be a social class inferior to the knights. Edward I succeeded in bargaining separately with them,[15] but similar attempts by Edward III finally failed because of protests made by knights and burgesses united in Parliament. The merchants undoubtedly gained political influence from their association with the knights. The common economic interests of both classes in the wool trade, the willingness of the burgesses to accept the leadership of the knights of the shire, a minority in numbers in Parliament, the former exclusion of both classes from the *curia*, and their both being composed of paid representatives, were probably the primary causes for the final union. By the close of Edward III's reign the knights and burgesses, meeting together in the chapter house of Westminster Abbey and with their own clerk and speaker, had united to form the House of Commons.

The dual grouping that was taking place in England during the fourteenth century was contemporaneous with similar developments in the continental institutions whose births had accompanied that of

---

[13] Parliament nevertheless regularly taxed the temporalities of the clergy.

[14] "The question whether the knights of the shire would permanently cast their lot with the lords or with the burgesses was perhaps the most critical in the whole history of Parliament." White, *Constitutional History*, p. 380.

[15] See p. 854.

the English Parliament; yet none duplicated the English. The French *Continental* États-Généraux divided into three houses or estates—nobles, clergy, *divisions of* and townsmen—and the French provincial estates followed their ex- *assemblies* ample. The *Cortes* of the Spanish peninsula and Sicily, with the exception of Aragon, used a similar grouping, as did the Diet of Bohemia. The German Diet of electors,[16] princes, and high clergy and the provincial *Landtage* likewise had three houses. Two examples of four houses developed: in Aragon, where clergy, nobles, knights, and townsmen met separately, and in Sweden, with its estates of clergy, nobles, townsmen, and peasants. Two houses were found in Hungary, clergy and nobles, and in Poland, nobles and townsmen. The Scots could afford but one house, whose duties were soon delegated, perhaps for the sake of further economy, to a committee.

The number of persons attending the two houses of an English parliament varied from one meeting to another. This was particularly *Composition* true of Parliament in its formative period under Edward I, who in *of Parliament* his second parliament in 1305 summoned thirty-seven persons, after having called over six hundred to the first parliament of the same year. Edward I summoned as many as a hundred and ten lords tem- poral or as few as nine, with the other classes in proportion. Since the variations became far smaller in the reign of Edward III, approxi- mate figures for the subsequent portion of the middle ages are possible. During the latter half of the fourteenth and fifteenth centuries two archbishops, nineteen bishops, and the grand masters of the two orders regularly attended. The abbots and priors attempted to duplicate the withdrawal of the proctors with such success that the eighty frequently called by Edward I had decreased to less than thirty by the begin- ning of the fifteenth century. Nevertheless, since the lords temporal after the death of Edward III were seldom more than fifty in num- ber, the lords spiritual customarily possessed a majority in the upper chamber. Edward I summoned as many as seventy officials to some parliaments. His grandson's officials in Parliament were, as a class, unimportant. The medieval House of Commons was regularly at- tended by seventy-four knights of the shire from the thirty-seven counties. The number of towns represented never became fixed, and the one hundred and sixty-six towns summoned at one time or another by Edward I, although not to any one meeting, had diminished by the end of the century to ninety-nine returning two hundred members, London having four.

The English Parliament was at first what the French *Parlement*

[16] See p. 909.

continued to be, primarily a law court. A legal author of Edward I's
reign correctly wrote, "The king has his court in his council in his
parliament." Before the reign of Edward I began the English king
held his court in his *curia* for his vassals, as did any feudal overlord.
To a king, however, was attached the further duty of doing justice
to his subjects, and this duty was performed in the English *curia* as
well as in the royal law courts. Just as justice from the king's law
courts was preferable, for its greater power and impartiality, to justice
from local or feudal courts, so justice from the king himself was
preferred to that of his law courts. Royal justice was at such a premium
in France that the French *Parlement* sat almost continuously. To
obtain the king's justice was the primary reason why throughout the
fourteenth century the English demanded parliaments three times,
twice, or at least once a year. The baronial demand at Oxford in 1258
for parliaments thrice annually was an attempt to secure meetings of
the council, although they called it Parliament, at which complaints
against the royal government might be heard and redressed. In the
later years of Henry III's reign and throughout the reign of Edward I
there was apparently an attempt to hold parliaments three times a
year. Although during some years the English Parliament met as
many as four times, the average number from 1265 to 1399 was little
more than three meetings every two years.

The king's justice in Parliament was obtained by petition. Before
the first meeting of any parliament the king appointed from his clerks
receivers of petitions, who sorted all petitions by subject matter and
sent all those that could be answered by any permanent department
of state to that department. Thus the exchequer or the court of common pleas was expected to answer petitions within its jurisdiction.
After the formal opening of Parliament, at which the king frequently
described to his lords and commons the reasons for their meeting and
the exceptional circumstances that caused him to ask for financial aid,
committees of triers or auditors of petitions were appointed. There
were usually two committees of auditors, one for petitions from the
British Isles and one for those from Gascony. In Edward I's reign
the auditors were primarily officials, but in the following century the
lords spiritual and temporal assumed control of this function. After
some conclusion had been reached concerning a money grant, the
second and last formal meeting of Parliament was held. Again the
commons came before the lords to listen to the king or his chancellor.
One of the king's clerks read the petitions, another the royal answers.
"The king wishes it" was acceptance of a general or public petition;

"Let it be done as is desired," acceptance of a private petition; "The king will think it over," a veto; and "The king thanks his gracious subjects," etc., the royal gratitude for a subsidy.

While the knights and burgesses, in the interval between the two formal meetings of Parliament, were discussing royal extravagance and the inferior quality of London beer at the numerous taverns around Westminster, they soon discovered that many of their number carried similar complaints and petitions. Complaints of the extortions of sheriffs, of the misdeeds of escheators, or of the privileges of alien merchants came from all portions of the realm, and each had greater likelihood of a favorable response if complained of by the entire group. Upon such matters of general concern the commons began petitioning as a unit during the reign of Edward II, even before they had succeeded in borrowing a common meeting place from Westminster Abbey. Petitions of this type, called group or commons' petitions, became a new method of initiating legislation. They were examined by the entire *curia* or House of Lords instead of by a committee of auditors, whence, with the lords' recommendation, they were sent to the king. His answer at the formal closing of Parliament now ended a legislative rather than a judicial process. *Commons' petitions*

The great statutes [17] of Edward I, however, were drafted by his officials after a parliament had been dismissed. Edward's legislation was as royal in origin and sanction as that of Henry II. After commons' petitions became customary in Edward III's reign a statute was still drafted by officials after a parliament, by changing any commons' petition that had received royal consent from the form of a request into the form of a declaration. After Parliament gained the king's promise to alter no basic law without parliamentary consent many bills were introduced into Parliament for him by his officials. The commons' petitions of Edward III's reign made possible the popular initiation of statutes, but did not destroy royal initiation, nor did parliamentary statutes immediately become more valid than royal ordinances. When Parliament under the Lancastrian kings reached the highest point in its power during the middle ages nearly all *Statute making*

[17] Legislation in England during the middle ages was called by a variety of names. "Doom," the Anglo-Saxon term, applied to both laws and judicial decisions. "Constitution" and "assize" were the terms customarily employed in the twelfth century. They were replaced, however, by the terms "provision," "ordinance," and "statute." In the fourteenth century "statute," which had become fashionable during the reign of Edward I, was already restricted in meaning to legislation by the king in Parliament, while "ordinance" became the customary term for legislation by the king and his council. The comparable names "act" and "proclamation" became fashionable at the close of the middle ages.

statutes were initiated by commons' petitions; but both before and after the Lancastrian period bills introduced by the government were important. Nevertheless the invention of a new method of legislating, together with the requirement that all basic legislation be enacted by that method, both of which appeared under the three Edwards, gave the English Parliament a stability and authority necessary for its survival.

The powers of Parliament

Increases in the power of Parliament were greatly aided by the political situation in England. The English kings' possession of French territories involved them in constant wars. Edward I and his successors tried many expedients to secure the money necessary to protect or reconquer their continental possessions.[18] One of the most frequently used was to request a special grant from Parliament that soon had to be purchased by a redress of grievances and by additions to the power of Parliament. Moreover, the old conflict between king and baronage aided Parliament. As early as the reign of Edward I the great vassals sought to use Parliament to check the power of the monarch. In this new institution they were to discover before their disappearance the machinery that they had sought vainly in Magna Carta and the Provisions of Oxford.

Financial powers

One of the first powers gained by Parliament resulted from the transfer to it of the ancient quarrel between the king and the landed classes over taxation. The counsel of the great council for the levy of aids, promised by the original grant of Magna Carta and, although withdrawn, regularly observed during the reign of Henry III,[19] became in that reign the counsel of Parliament, as the great council itself was becoming a part of the larger body. Then in a great constitutional crisis in 1297 Edward I, in order to gain any support from his rebellious barons, was forced to confirm the charters and to promise to exact no aid or prize without the common assent of all the realm. Another version of this Confirmation of Charters promised to exact no tallage or aid without the assent of "archbishops, bishops, earls, barons, knights, burgesses, and other freemen." Although Edward I later succeeded in securing the pope's cancellation of this promise, Edward II was forced by the barons to accept the Ordinances of 1311, in which he promised, among other things, to cease taking new prizes. This he successfully revoked in the Parliament of 1322, but with a proviso that matters touching the king and realm be established in Parliament. In 1340 Edward III, to meet the expenses of the French

[18] See pp. 879 ff.
[19] See pp. 459–60.

wars,[20] was forced to agree that no tax be levied without the consent of Parliament. In 1340 and 1343 he was forced to promise to make no additions to the traditional customs duties without the consent of Parliament and not to treat with the merchants outside Parliament. Although these statutes were frequently evaded, in less than two generations Parliament had gained control over the great sources of public revenue.

By similar methods Parliament gained some control over officials. *Parliamentary control over officials* Complaints concerning local officials were brought to the first parliaments, as they had been to the *curia*. Provisions of the Ordinances of 1311 continued the thirteenth-century [21] dispute by providing for the appointment of the major officials in Parliament. Although these were repealed, Edward III was compelled in 1340 to make similar promises. But this statute was revoked without protest in 1341. Like demands were made in 1376 and 1377. At the close of Edward III's reign parliaments, regardless of whether lords or commons were primarily responsible, were making strenuous efforts to control the appointment of royal officials, just as the great councils had done in the reign of Henry III. Of greater permanent importance, however, was the invention in the Good Parliament of 1376 of impeachment. At that time the commons accused great ministers of state to the lords, with the result that several were removed, fined, and imprisoned. Although the medieval attempts to secure parliamentary appointment of major officials proved unsuccessful, yet impeachment and attainder secured in large part the objects desired.

Miscellaneous powers were gained during the same period. In 1322 *Miscellaneous powers* and in 1377 the king limited his power to legislate outside of Parliament. Various statutes directed against the clergy were of parliamentary origin and furnished precedents for similar action in time to come. Many regulations concerning trade and industry, such as the Statutes of the Staple,[22] were passed as the result of demands in Parliament and likewise furnished precedents. Parliament assumed the task of increasing the scope of the common law which had been denied the chancellor by the Statute of Westminster II.[23] Hundreds of statutes were devoted to correcting and chastising local officials. Once

[20] See pp. 880 ff.
[21] See pp. 459–60.
[22] The many Statutes of the Staple enacted in the fourteenth and fifteenth centuries were attempts to regulate the export of wool and similar commodities. The majority of them established some city or cities as the place through which all such exports should pass. Calais was frequently called the seat of the staple.
[23] See p. 847.

some control of the purse had been gained, few indeed were the func
tions of government left unregulated by Edwardian parliaments.

*Reasons for
the growth of
Parliament*

Any description of parliamentary origins must include reasons for
its unique growth in England. This was largely due to the fact that
the institution met needs of all influential classes. Although knights
and burgesses had no desire for a new tax-granting institution they did
desire the great court of law, and while using the law court they
discovered its utility for keeping both officials and financial exactions
under control. The nobility found in parliaments a permanent means
of enforcing the great charters that carried with it an appearance of
popular support. The paraphrase from Justinian's Code, "It is fitting
that that which concerns all should be consented to by all," which fre
quently appeared in connection with the summoning of parliaments,
was probably of little importance. The kings, however, discovered new
sources of revenue as well as a method of testing the opinion of the
nation. No continental institution served so many purposes.

*Variations be-
tween Parlia-
ment and the
continental
assemblies*

Moreover, a number of minor variations between the English
Parliament and the analogous continental institutions may account for
their dissimilar fates. Many of the continental assemblies were com
posed of representatives with limited powers. That is, their constitu
encies instructed them, as modern ambassadors are instructed by their
governments, to grant or consent only to certain things. Edward I
before the end of the thirteenth century, ordered his sheriffs to secure
the return of representatives with full power to act for their constit
uencies, and this became the English custom. Again, several of the
continental bodies, particularly some of the powerful *Cortes* in the
Spanish peninsula, were hampered by the requirement of an unani
mous vote. Consent by a simple majority was the English practice.
Others, notably the *États-Généraux*, were hindered by the custom of
sending substitutes or proxies, which never became prevalent in Eng
land. The frequent continental practice of exempting the feudal classes
from taxation was prevented from becoming important in England
by the division of the feudal classes between two houses in each of
which they formed only a minority, and by the small number of nobles.
The Hundred Years' War alone caused a divergence between the
English and French assemblies. As a war for conquest the English
parliaments granted money for it only grudgingly, and as the pay
ment for limitations upon royal authority; while the French, strength
ening the executive to repel devastating invasions, granted more
permanent financial resources to their kings. Finally, the growth of
the common law in England, the formation of its schools, and its al

iance with Parliament [24] prevented the civilians, who upon the continent were among the greatest advocates of absolute monarchy, from ever becoming influential in medieval England.

Although the story of Parliament bulks large in any modern study of the development of the English state, it was little regarded by contemporaries. Instead, they noted wars, pestilences, and statutes. Under the three Edwards they were cursed with many of each.

The age of Edward I compares with that of Queen Victoria alone in the number of its great statutes. The unregulated growth of the common law under Henry III was carefully pruned and trained by great codifying laws drafted by the king's officials. The Statute of Westminster II created entailed estates, established new circuit courts, and limited strictly the power of the chancery to create new writs. The Statute of Gloucester destroyed the importance of the local, non-royal, courts by limiting their jurisdiction to cases involving less than forty shillings. The Statute of Westminster III, by forbidding sub-infeudation, prevented any further lengthening of the feudal chain and eventually made nearly all freeholders tenants-in-chief of the king. The Statute of Winchester provided for supervision of strangers in cities, the clearing of highroads, and the closing and guarding of city gates and walls, and refurbished Henry II's Assize of Arms by again establishing a minimum of armor and weapons to be owned by each man according to his wealth. The Statute of Acton Burnell enabled merchants to use the royal courts to collect their debts. The Statute of Wales extended the English system of shires and legal officials to Wales. And these were only a few of the more important acts passed. The Statute of Westminster II alone contained fifty separate chapters, each a statute in itself.

The statutes of Edward I

Edward I had also to carry on the English medieval king's perpetual struggle with a feudal baronage and with the Roman Church. He began his reign with a careful scrutiny of the royal properties and rights throughout the land in which his justices were directed to discover all illegal diminutions of them. In 1278 the Statute of Gloucester enabled the king to begin a thorough inquiry into public courts held in private hands, in which he attempted to destroy all courts existing without specific royal charter. Baronial unrest, however, compelled him to recognize as legal those that had been in existence at the coronation of Richard I. The investigation prevented

Edward I and feudalism

---

[24] The English Parliament probably gained additional strength from the common law by borrowing parts of its procedure. Several of the continental institutions suffered from defective procedure.

any further seizure of local courts by the baronage. The years that fol lowed were ostensibly quiet, yet the king's increasing financial de mands, made necessary by wars in Wales, Scotland, and France steadily added to baronial unrest. The culmination in 1297 was a revolt similar to that which had forced John to sign Magna Carta.[25] Edward was compelled not only to accept the Confirmation of Char ters, but also during the following four years to agree to other sup plementary limitations. Magna Carta and the Charters of the Forest were reissued. No new taxation without the consent of all concerned was promised.[26] Edward's financial exactions before 1297 were de clared to be no precedents. Although Edward was freed by the pope from these promises in 1305 it is somewhat to his credit that he sub sequently evaded only the Forest Charters.

The relations between state and Church were equally troubled. The common-law courts by writs of prohibition were slowly under mining the jurisdiction of the canon law, which Edward permitted as much as he dared. English kings, however, were frequently ham pered by archbishops who wished to follow in the footsteps of St. Thomas of Canterbury. Both Peckham and Winchelsey were of this type. Yet Edward's greatest officials were bishops who aided in the conflict against the Church. Robert Burnell, Bishop of Bath and Wells, was probably the creator of the great statutes made between 1272 and 1292. The pope twice refused, because of his immoral life, to translate him to Canterbury. Walter Langton, Bishop of Lichfield and Coven try, who later became Edward's treasurer and trusted adviser, was suspended from his ecclesiastical functions by the pope when charged with adultery, concubinage, simony, and intercourse with the devil.

Edward I and the Church

Archbishop Peckham as early as 1279 ordered his clergy to explain Magna Carta to their parishioners, and to describe the excommunica tion issued against those employing writs of prohibition. Edward re torted by compelling the archbishop to withdraw his orders and by making the Statute *de Religiosis,* which forbade the further acquisi tion of land by the Church without the consent of the king. The conflict continued, largely over prohibitions and the king's financial demands. Six years later, by the writ *circumspecte agatis,* directed to his judges, Edward described the jurisdiction to be allowed the ecclesi astical courts. They were to retain control over matters solely spiritual,

---

[25] At this time Edward, demanding foreign service of Earl Bigod, said, "By God, Sir Earl, you shall either go or hang." And Edward's loyal vassal replied, "By God, O King, I shall neither go nor hang." Bigod was correct.

[26] See p. 459.

matters punishable by penance, injuries to clerks, perjury, and defamation. The conflict continued after Peckham's death and the accession of Winchelsey. Simultaneous wars in Scotland, Wales, and France increased the king's demands for money from the clergy. In 1294 he demanded, and received, a half of the clergy's revenue. Edward's visage while making this request was so terrible that the Dean of St. Paul's died of fright. In 1296 Boniface VIII issued the bull *Clericis laicos*,[27] to which Edward's answer was to withdraw all protection of the law from the Church. The "open season" that followed was a great success for the king since excommunications failed and the clergy paid. Edward's last statute, that of Carlisle, forbade the payment of tallages on monastic property through which money was sent abroad. Parliament's petition to the king at that time for legislation against provisors,[28] alien churchmen, and the financial exactions of the papacy betrayed a rising popular discontent with the papacy, centuries before the reformation.

The wars of Edward I

Edward's great failures were in his foreign wars, wars so costly that they almost stultified his domestic policy. The costly attempts to protect his French possessions were only partially successful. His plan to unite the British Isles under one monarch led to the conquest of Wales, although rebellions continued there for more than another century. He twice conquered Scotland and carried away the Stone of Scone to be placed in the coronation chair of English kings, but his attempts aroused the two national heroes of Scotland, William Wallace and Robert Bruce. Edward defeated and executed the first, but died just south of the border while leading a great host to an attempted third conquest. His son Edward II failed completely, for the Battle of Bannockburn in 1314 re-established the independence of the northern kingdom with Robert Bruce as its king. Edward I's attempt to annex Scotland made that state a faithful ally of France for the remainder of the middle ages [29] and prevented the English conquest of Ireland. Not until 1603 were the English and Scotch to recognize a common king, and he was a Scot.

Edward II (1307-27)

Edward II had none of his father's strength. The quiet growth of Parliament and of the administrative departments continued. The great nobles forced the king to accept the Ordinances of 1311, which gave the baronage for a time control of the great offices of state, although, by use of the household departments, Edward minimized

[27] See p. 956.
[28] See p. 970.
[29] See p. 880.

their importance.[30] He succeeded in revoking the ordinances, but a
alliance between the barons and his wife dethroned him. He was soo
thereafter murdered.

Edward III
(1327–77)

Edward III was to his contemporaries the pattern of a perfec
monarch. He delighted in hunting, jousting, and warfare. The grea
feasts and stately pageantry of his court pleased his subjects. The
victor of Sluys and Crécy, the captor of Calais,[31] the king whose long
bowmen ravaged western Europe, killed a King of Bohemia, tool
captive the kings of Scotland and of France, and exacted ransom fron
a pope, Edward Plantagenet dazzled the eyes of Europe. The splendo
of his reign blinded his age to the permanent losses of royal authority
that were taking place. Edward III, trusting to recoup all by the con
quest of France, continually secured money soon spent, in return fo
the grant of powers permanently retained by Parliament. At the end
of his reign the king's right to tax had been practically destroyed, hi
power to legislate by ordinance made inferior to parliamentary statute
and parliaments had shown both willingness and ability to punish roya
officials.

Transfor-
mation of
feudalism

The third Edward had little trouble with his great vassals. The
old feudal taxation was fast disappearing, while the glory and loo
of foreign wars pleased many. Moreover, the character of English
feudalism was rapidly changing at this time. The victories of the Eng
lish archers at Crécy, Poitiers, and scores of other battles destroyed
the value of the purely feudal army. In fact many of Edward's noble
contracted to furnish archers and men-at-arms for his armies quite a
any captain of mercenaries. The ravages of the Black Death turned
many landowners from users of serfs to employers of sheepherders, tc
the detriment of both the quantity and quality of their retainers. Ed
ward himself secured wide possessions for his younger children
through which they entered the baronage.[32] The English rule o
primogeniture for the inheritance of both nobility and lands decreased
the numbers of the feudal magnates while increasing their individua
wealth. All these things created a small class of powerful barons whc
were both closely related to the royal family and leaders of bands o
mercenaries. This new feudalism henceforth, and even in the last year
of Edward III, was to attempt to capture for its own nominee the

---

[30] See p. 458, n. 44.
[31] See p. 882.
[32] For the somewhat similar creation of appanages that occurred at the same time
in France see p. 503.

oyal machinery of state, while the old feudalism had attempted to
lestroy it.

The rising tide of resentment against the Church was increased *Edward III*
>oth by the financial demands of the popes at Avignon [33] and by the *and the Church*
ncreasing luxury of the clergy. Edward III once bluntly informed the
>ope that His Holiness was commissioned to feed his Master's sheep,
1ot to fleece' them. Popular discontent led to several attempts to bar
hurchmen from the great offices of state. The passage of the Statutes
>f Provisors (1351 and 1390), forbidding papal appointment to Eng-
ish benefices, and of the Statutes of Præmunire (1353 and 1393), for-
>idding appeals to courts outside England, were both the result of
1ational rather than royal sentiment. Finally, in the closing years of
he reign, Wyclif and his followers the Lollards secured support from
ll classes in their opposition to the papacy.[34]

Yet there were various constitutional changes of a less spectacular *The Inns*
ort. During this period the legal profession created its own great *of Court*
1niversity in London, the Inns of Court. There, between the law
ourts and the City, apprentices to the common law were trained.
[heir legal education was given by lectures, oral disputation, and by
.ttendance at the courts. Their graduates became sergeants-at-law, with
 monopoly of practice before the court of common pleas. They were
he first numerous body of educated laymen in western Europe. From
he sergeants, the judges of both the circuit courts and the great
ommon-law courts in London were chosen, while some, called king's
ergeants, were permanently retained by the state for other legal serv-
ce. It soon became customary for landowners both great and small to
end their heirs to the Inns of Court that they might obtain the legal
nowledge necessary to protect their inheritances. There, in addition to
he common law, they could be taught, among other things, Scripture,
lancing, and music. Although it was not customary for such students
o become sergeants-at-law they did obtain the knowledge that en-
.bled them to draft bills as members of the House of Commons and
o administer their own districts as justices of the peace. The Inns of
Court were the only permanent schools to be developed by any Ger-
nanic law,[35] and the "tough law" they taught is one reason for the
urvival of the English system.

[33] See pp. 971-72.
[34] See pp. 978 ff.
[35] The schools at Pavia which taught Lombard law for about two hundred years
fter 1000 were the only other schools developed by a Germanic law. They failed to
vithstand the revival of the study of civil law. See p. 741.

During Edward III's reign the third and last of the great central courts of the common law slowly separated itself from the exchequer quite as the exchequer had separated itself from the *curia* two centuries previously. The officials of the exchequer of account decided semijudicial questions concerning revenue at least as early as the thirteenth century. In difficult cases the king's council meeting in the exchequer aided them. Slowly the judicial work of the exchequer was separated from that of accounting for revenue, and quite as gradually the council ceased to attend the court. During the reign of Edward III the new institution became known as the court of the exchequer. Its judges, called barons of the exchequer, gained a recognized jurisdiction, while they lost the major portion of their right to a procedure differing from that of the common law. Their primary functions were to decide questions involving money owed the king; but since they were paid in the customary manner by fees, they soon devised means of increasing their jurisdiction. As in other instances, adding to business added to salaries. The most famous means of increasing their jurisdiction was the writ *quo minus*. Any person wishing to collect a debt could purchase this writ by alleging that because of the debt owed him he was less able (*quo minus*) to pay money he owed the king. The court of exchequer would thereupon employ the effective process devised to collect money owed the king for the benefit of the plaintiff, collect their fees, and amiably overlook the plaintiff's allegation that he owed the king. Armed by this effective writ the court of exchequer became the ordinary recourse of creditors and one of the great courts of the common law.[36]

A third development that centered around the reign of Edward III was the evolution of justices of the peace. Although the attempts made after 1349 by the Ordinance and Statutes of Laborers to fix wages and prices at the scale in force before the Black Death were foredoomed to failure, yet the officials created to enforce the laws, the justices of labor, were to have an eventful history. Their functions were slowly combined with those of earlier officials, the keepers or conservators of the peace.[37] The result was an official, called the justice of the peace, who fulfilled the fondest hopes of any medieval ruler. He was appointed and dismissed by the king; he was unpaid; he was chosen from the lesser landowners who possessed enough property to

[36] The court of king's bench later secured a similar device, the Bill of Middlesex, and thereafter the jurisdiction of the three great courts was in part concurrent.
[37] See p. 462.

The Annunciation on the Marienkapelle at Wurzburg. A very German Gabriel is making the important announcement to a very German Virgin Mary with full cheeks and with her hair down her back.
God sits above with bare feet. From God's mouth to Mary's left ear runs a tube, terminating in the figure
of a dove, symbol for the Holy Ghost. The future baby Jesus is sliding down the tube head first on his
stomach with arms in front of him. The sculptor has tried to make very clear an event very difficult, under any circumstances, to explain.

Jan Arnolfini, the Flemish Merchant, and his lady, by Jan van Eyck (1434) (See p. 1024)

The Virgin and the Infant Jesus, by Jean Fouq (about 1450) (See p. 1025)

The boar hunt (miniature from the Duc de Berry's Book of Hours, painted by Pol de Limbourg)

be held responsible and yet not enough to be able to escape punishment, while the office carried enough honor and social prestige to make the best seek it. The natural result was that justices of the peace, either to act separately or in groups, were entrusted by fifteenth- and sixteenth-century governments with almost complete control of local police and administration. Their courts replaced those of shire and hundred, of manor and of feudal lord. The justices of the peace governed rural England until the late nineteenth century. Their attenuated shadows live on in both England and the United States.

The decline of feudalism, the growth of Parliament, and the constant wars together made necessary extensive changes in public finance. The prevalent theory throughout the middle ages demanded that the king ordinarily "live of his own"; that is, that the customary revenue from crown lands, forfeitures, fines, fees, and licenses, the coinage, feudal dues, and customs duties should pay the costs of king and government. Certain feudal customs and prerogatives were also supposed to make this more possible: thus in theory the king still had either a force of six thousand men provided him free of charge for forty days annually or an equivalent in money, and a large number of his officials were paid by the fees they received from the public. Likewise, the king could rightfully demand a certain amount of free transportation and had the right, called purveyance, to buy first and at less than the ordinary prices.[38]

Failure of the old public revenues

Although it is possible that these sources, carefully used, would have met peacetime expenses during the first half of the fourteenth century, yet in general they proved unsatisfactory. English crown manors were probably administered by the sheriffs and exchequer more efficiently than elsewhere in Europe. The English kings, however, quite as their continental contemporaries, believed it necessary to grant such lands as rewards to faithful servants and, especially, as establishments for their younger children. A regency was also disastrous to public revenue, for the guardians of the state invariably rewarded themselves well during their terms of office. Forfeitures, which might have replenished the crown lands, were only too frequently regarded as lucky windfalls and granted to the king's favorite of the moment. Carucage was discontinued before the accession of Edward I, while the last attempt to impose tallage failed from parlia-

[38] It also included caption, the right to take with no payment whatsoever. Purveyance formed one of the major grievances of the middle ages, no less than ten statutes being passed during the single reign of Edward III to regulate it.

mentary opposition in 1332. Feudal dues decreased rapidly, despite frequent investigations, as lawyers taught vassals methods of evading them. The feudal army had never been satisfactory, since it was provided for only a limited time and could not be used outside the realm; moreover it was almost entirely displaced by the new English military tactics of the fourteenth century. The money substitute, scutage, proved so cumbersome and irritating that, despite extreme financial need, Edward III abandoned it permanently. Finally, although the older sources of revenue might possibly have paid peacetime expenses, there were very few years of peace.

The new public revenues

To meet the recurrent deficits many experiments were tried; one of the most successful was taxation of imports and exports. The principle of taxation of trade was not new, for several attempts to use it had been made by Anglo-Saxon as well as by Norman and Angevin kings, but none hitherto had been successful. Edward I in 1275 secured in the Old or Great Customs a duty upon wool, woolfells, and leather that continued to be a source of revenue throughout the remainder of the middle ages. In 1303, in return for the privileges granted foreign merchants in England by the *Carta Mercatoria*, he obtained from them both a fifty-per-cent increased rate upon the Old Customs and a duty of two shillings per tun on imported wine and of three pence in the pound value on all other imports and exports. This New and Small Customs became in 1373, after two generations of acrimonious dispute between the three Edwards and their parliaments, the tonnage and poundage thereafter granted by Parliament upon all traders domestic and foreign.[39] The rates were increased at various times, some articles were exempted, and in the fifteenth century it became customary for Parliament to grant it to a king for his life. Customs duties have remained, except for the century 1830–1930, one of the primary sources of public revenue in England.

Somewhat less successful experiments were made upon the precedents for taxation of income and of personal property. These, consisting of a grant of some fraction of the nation's wealth in chattels, were always controlled by Parliament and granted only for some exceptional need. A tenth of personal property in the towns and royal demesne and a fifteenth of other personal property became the accepted fraction, but in 1334 the assessments were stabilized at the figures of 1332. Thereafter a grant of a tenth and fifteenth was the grant of the fixed sum of approximately thirty-eight thousand pounds,

[39] The controller of the petty customs from 1374 to 1386 was the busy civil servant and poet Geoffrey Chaucer. See pp. 798 ff.

and rapidly became a tax upon real estate.[40] It was at times granted both in multiples and fractionally. Other experiments were usually failures; thus the simple and graduated poll taxes of 1377, 1379, and 1380 were instrumental in causing the Peasants' Revolt of 1381, and a proposed hearth tax was never voted.

With revenues insufficient the three Edwards relied increasingly upon credit. Earlier monarchs had been able to extract money regularly from the Jews,[41] but Edward I in 1290 expelled these royal chattels from the kingdom in return for a fifteenth from Parliament, which paid him £116,346, 12s., 11½d. Henry III dealt regularly with Italian bankers, whom the English rather incorrectly called the Caorsini. The three Edwards also borrowed great sums from Italian bankers until 1345, when Edward III, by repudiating his debts to the Peruzzi and Bardi, destroyed those great financial houses and gave a terrific blow to the credit of all Florence. Flemish lenders were somewhat more fortunate, for they demanded better security, having the English crown and an Archbishop of Canterbury in pawn at different times. A number of English merchants, like the Pole family, found loans to Edward III somewhat speculative. The exchequer itself, reorganized in 1290 and again in 1323, discovered methods of anticipating payments by means of assignments and began dealing largely with credit instead of cash. The proceeds of taxes were regularly anticipated by pledging them as security for loans. It was not, however, until the reign of Richard II that the forced loan was invented. In this the lender was given no choice about the lending and ordinarily was repaid upon the Greek Kalends.

The use of public credit

The senile Edward III was succeeded in 1377 by his eleven-year-old grandson Richard II, whose uncles, powerful magnates (from the generosity of their father), attempted to dominate the young king and his government. As Richard came of age he tried to create a following of his own supporters. Faction thereafter fought faction. Richard's first and second attempts to secure his independence failed. The first led the magnates in Parliament to impeach his chancellor, procure the dismissal of his treasurer, and appoint a committee to control the government. After the second attempt the magnates, led by the king's relatives and now called the lords appellant, forced the king to summon the Merciless Parliament of 1388. This was shamelessly packed and proceeded by judicial forms to destroy the king's

Richard II (1377-99)

---

[40] The yield was decreased by exemptions to about £30,000 before the end of the middle ages. It was last levied in 1624.

[41] The royal methods were infrequently so drastic as those of John's treatment of the Jew of Bristol who was condemned to lose a tooth a day until he presented the king with 10,000 marks. He guarded his treasure for six days.

officials and friends. Richard's third and successful attempt was followed by the ten years of his personal rule. His character has been an enigma to historians. He displayed great bravery and cowardice. He acted with petulance and rashness, yet controlled himself for seven years to take his vengeance upon the lords appellant. Influenced by the new continental political theories which exalted the prerogative of kings,[42] he attempted to regain the powers lost to Parliament by his predecessors. In his attempt to limit Parliament and magnates he exploited old and discovered new sources of revenue. Thus he extorted fines and confiscations and, by the privy seal, secured forced loans and compulsory gifts. He created his own private military force, gave new life to the council, and extended the use of prerogative courts. The revolution of 1399 defeated his efforts, yet the methods he employed were refurbished a century later to create the despotism of the Tudors.

The small or privy council

The small council as something more than a number of officials of various departments had almost vanished during the rise of Parliament. Despite the fact that both magnates and Parliament had attempted to control it since the days of Henry III, Richard revived it to free himself from dependence. He enlarged his council by appointing persons of minor rank. He employed it to supervise the general administration and to exercise the ordinance-making power which the kingship retained after the making of statutes had fallen under the control of Parliament. Most disliked, however, was its judicial power, for particularly it tried cases to which the king was a party or in which the parties were too powerful for a just trial to be obtained in the ordinary courts of justice. Since the council was not a common-law court it used the subpœna and procedure from the civil law. During Richard's reign the council secured the department of the privy seal for its secretariat and the use of the privy seal itself to validate documents.[43]

The court of admiralty

A second prerogative court of permanent importance was the court of admiralty. Since the king's council for a century had at intervals heard cases involving alien merchants, the transfer of maritime cases to a separate court was comparatively easy. The wars between Edward I and Philip IV compelled the English government to face the problem of piracy, for Edward's allies would have been soon lost if English seamen continued their practice of unlimited looting. Ad-

---

[42] The Merciless Parliament in 1388 expressly asserted its supremacy in legislative matters and expressly denied the validity of the civil law in England.

[43] The king's secretary having charge of the signet became the household official. See p. 458. From the king's secretary the various secretaries of state of the present English cabinet have developed.

mirals [44] were first appointed in England by Edward I to command English shipping during the French wars. They soon were given the maritime jurisdiction formerly exercised by the council, and thereafter borrowed wholeheartedly from both the law merchant and the civil law. The lord admirals claimed jurisdiction over the high seas, national waters to the high tide mark, and harbors and navigable rivers. They heard cases involving piracy, wreck, salvage, bills of lading, and average. Parliament, by two statutes of Richard's reign, attempted to define and limit their jurisdiction. As in the case of probate and divorce, which were later seized from the canon law, admiralty law has never been thoroughly absorbed by the common law, but retains today marks of its separate origin.

The reign of Richard II witnessed the great lords' continuing the *Richard II* practice, discovered in previous reigns, of associating themselves with *and Par-* Parliament to secure their wishes. The device of controlling elections *liament* was used by them in packing parliaments to give an appearance of national consent to their acts. Richard's insistence upon the powers of the king quite naturally caused his opponents to magnify the powers of Parliament. During his minority the nobles in Parliament governed England, there appointing the great officials and quarreling among themselves. The first parliament of the reign secured the promise that no law made in Parliament should be revoked or altered outside of it. On the occasion of Richard's first attempt to escape tutelage the magnates threatened him successfully with two apocryphal statutes: one that if a king failed to appear at a parliament for forty days the members had a right to dissolve it, and another that Parliament could legally depose an incompetent king.

Richard's dislike of parliaments expressed itself in many bitter remarks. Thus, in 1386 he declared that he would not dismiss his humblest scullion at its request and several times asserted the supremacy of the royal prerogative. He procured a declaration by his judges that royal officials could be punished by parliaments only with the king's permission, that parliaments could be dissolved at the king's will, and that they had no right to discuss subjects other than those submitted to them by the king. These judicial opinions, however, he was able to put into effect only after 1397. When able, he packed parliaments as thoroughly as any of his barons, and on one occasion ostentatiously massed his military forces around its meeting place. On the other hand, the impeachments of 1386 and 1388 were purely political

[44] The name and original functions of the admiral were copied from Genoa and Spain, where the name at least had been borrowed from the Moslems.

excuses to justify the baronial destruction of royal officials.[45] The successful revolution in 1399 was led by the greatest of the magnates, and was justified by his first parliament. This revolution, however, was more than the replacement of one dynasty by another; among other things it marked the defeat of the first major attempt to check the rise of Parliament.

Political history (1399–1485)

The deposition of Richard II and the accession of Henry IV in 1399 established the dynasty of Lancaster. Henry IV suppressed baronial revolts only to be troubled by dissensions within his own family. His son Henry V, although troubled by rebellions, successfully distracted his baronage by a revival of the French wars.[46] His son Henry VI, who succeeded to the throne when nine months old, found neither his piety nor strong-willed wife enough to counteract his inheritance. The appearance of Joan of Arc in 1429 was followed by twenty-four years of English military reverses, which terminated only when a last English army was broken and its leaders killed in the fire of French artillery at Castillon.[47] England retained only Calais upon the continent. Meanwhile the country became financially exhausted, its officials unpaid, corrupt, and the sport of faction. The descendants of John of Gaunt busied themselves with fraternal quarrels, while the mercenaries expelled from France continued their lawlessness in their homeland. Henry became insane.

Baronial revolts led by another descendant of Edward III began. These, known as the Wars of the Roses, led to Henry's deposition in 1461 and his murder ten years later. In the former year Edward IV, of the house of York, became king. He loved his own ease and the maids of London too greatly to be entirely successful as an English ruler. Many of the governmental devices employed during his reign, however, were used to support the strong monarchy of the succeeding dynasty. Edward left two male children, who were murdered by their uncle Richard III. The vindictiveness of Richard's rule led to the revolt in 1485 that ended the Wars of the Roses and the kings of the house of York, and began the period of the Tudors.

The Lancastrian parliamentary monarchy

During the first half of the century England was governed by a parliamentary monarchy. Since the best claim of the Lancastrian kings to the English throne was their recognition by Parliament and since they continually were in abject need of money, Parliament gained a

[45] One of the charges upon which Brembre, a former Mayor of London, was convicted and executed was that he desired to change the name of London to Troynovant. This is the only occasion known of an execution for a mistake in archeology.

[46] See p. 887.

[47] See p. 894.

control over the state under them that it was not to exercise again until 1688. During the first forty years of the century the rulers retained only such officials as were acceptable to Parliament. In several instances high officials explained and justified their conduct to it, and at times officials were appointed in Parliament. The commons, having secured official recognition that they were the originators of money grants, at times made grants for specific purposes and frequently provided for a parliamentary audit of accounts. It became customary for the commons to present separate bills during a session rather than a comprehensive commons' petition containing all their requests near its close. The commons' presentation of bills rather than the former preferment of petitions prevented judges and kings from altering the wording of a parliamentary request when drafting the statute. Such alterations had frequently been to the advantage of the monarchs of the previous century. An unsuccessful attempt was made to secure the royal answers to requests before any money grants were made. Several statutes regulating elections and qualifications were passed. All these furnished invaluable precedents two centuries later, but in the fifteenth century the power of feudalism was too great to allow successful government by Parliament.

Second only to Parliament at this time was the king's council. Since its members were frequently appointed in Parliament and at all times lay under danger of impeachment, council and Parliament usually worked hand in hand. Its members, varying between six and thirty in number, were salaried officials chosen primarily from the noble and clerical classes. It exercised a general supervision over the administration, but its judicial functions were largely, although never entirely, transferred to the lord chancellor. The failure of Lancastrian government was largely the failure of its council. At a time when the king was a child and later when he was intermittently insane, the noble members of the council were rent by faction, and used it to add to their private fortunes, even though frequently absent. *The Lancastrian council*

In the Lancastrian period the lord chancellor added the leadership of a great judicial department to his other duties. The chancellor had been frequently delegated in the past to act as a judge in special cases, for his department was closely allied to both the council and the law courts. He himself, invariably a churchman in the fifteenth century, was always trained in the canon law and frequently in the civil law as well. Both the decreased frequency of parliaments and their greater concentration upon statutes and supervision of the executive departments prevented their answering as many private petitions as formerly. *The lord chancellor and equity*

The court of exchequer was likewise ceasing to administer extraordinary justice at a time when the absence of Henry V in France and the minority of his son prevented the king from administering the personal justice given in previous reigns. The rules and formalities of the common law were preventing as well as securing justice. The great magnates of the Lancastrian councils were unwilling to devote time to the examination of private petitions. All of these factors combined to make the lord chancellor the head of a great judicial institution and to add to his department, the chancery, the duty of administering equity.

The chancellor, now known as the "keeper of the king's conscience," was untrammeled by the precedents, the writs, and the juries of the common law, and borrowed his methods from common, canon, or civil law impartially. In the ability to use the subpœna, the injunction, and the mandamus he possessed procedural advantages denied the common law. His willingness to protect the beneficiary of property held in trust, unrecognized by the common law, enabled the clergy to evade the Statute *de Religiosis* and vassals to evade certain feudal obligations. Thus the chancery as a court of equity came into existence to give, by its corrections and additions to the common law, a sturdier growth to the entire administration of justice.

The Lancastrians and the Church

The Lancastrian kings worked in closest harmony with the Church. Henry IV had been a crusader against the Lithuanians,[48] and both he and his son dreamed of expelling the Infidels from the Holy Land. The Lancastrian kings secured the passage of the Statute *de hæretico comburendo* which authorized the state to burn at the stake those convicted of heresy by the Church, successfully resisted all of the many popular attempts to confiscate Church property, and destroyed the Lollards.

Fifteenth-century feudalism

The Lancastrian dynasty was destroyed by the dying struggles of the new feudalism in England. The many descendants of Edward III [49] scattered among the baronage furnished claimants for the throne. Increasingly after 1430 parliaments became the instruments of first one baronial faction and then another. The length of time taken by impeachments led to the invention of bills of attainder as a more expeditious method of executing the defeated. The weakness of the central government allowed private warfare to flourish as never since the reign of Stephen. Unpaid judges and bribed or intimidated juries led to the temporary failure of the common law. The king was

[48] See pp. 939–40.
[49] See p. 1050.

reduced to begging his nobles to attend the council. In 1450 the first great uprising occurred, and five years later open warfare broke out between the families of Lancaster and York. Edward IV, the only king of the house of York to really govern England, ruled with the absolute minimum of councils and parliaments. His quest for non-parliamentary sources of revenue and his encouragement of the mercantile interests both foreshadowed the methods of the Tudors. The civil wars between 1450 and 1458 destroyed a feudalism that had passed its usefulness, in large part because the English nation grew tired of its wars and inefficiency.

In 1485 over a thousand years had passed since the Roman eagles *Recapitulation* ceased guarding their British provinces: twice as great an interval as that which separates Edward of York and Henry of Tudor from ourselves. The thousand years is the English middle ages in which barbaric Anglo-Saxons lived and fought and died for six centuries, dividing the land into the fields and villages and shires that Henry Tudor knew, but failing to unite their England. Upon their failure the mailed Normans had erected a feudal system more efficient than in its homeland. Henry the Norman and Henry the Angevin then began building, within the order that their feudalism produced, the institutions we today consider essential to our governments. That process of institutional elaboration once begun continued almost of its own momentum, although requiring every few generations a strong king, an Edward Longshanks or a Henry Tudor, to prune and guide its wild growth.

The same forces of growth still operate today. In medieval England they created law court after law court, writ after writ, tax after tax, and local official and royal secretary almost as regularly as the succession of the seasons. During the last three centuries of that thousand years a combination of circumstances, each seemingly petty in itself but each the result of an English modification of a general European need and idea, produced the English Parliament with its combination of judicial, financial, and legislative functions elsewhere unduplicated. Moreover, these functions were entrusted to a more perfectly balanced group of representatives and councillors than the continental states produced. Together they guaranteed the survival of the representative institutions that we have seen taken over by democracy in the last century. Parliament arose in company with the increased importance of the lesser landholder, the English knight, and of the merchant. In England it could minimize the mighty institutions of the earlier period, the Church and feudalism, for it grew within the administrative and judicial machinery created by strong kings. But English parliaments found themselves used as a tool by feudalism to destroy the strong kings; and, when strong kings were destroyed, feudalism and misused parliaments together failed in the bloody rioting of the Wars of the Roses.

Despite the more advanced evolution of its political institutions England was never immune to continental influence; the widespread feudal reaction of the fifteenth century took place in England just as did the revolt from the Roman Catholic Church in the sixteenth. Louis XI of France, Ferdinand of Spain, and Henry Tudor were all cast in the same mold and put to uses in large part similar. But in England the medieval institutions of government were more able to resist the pressure of absolutism that followed the combination between townsmen and kings with which the middle ages ended.

Chapter 26

WESTERN EUROPE IN THE FOURTEENTH AND FIFTEENTH CENTURIES

THE fourteenth and fifteenth centuries are sometimes referred to as the later middle ages in accordance with a subdivision which calls the period from about 400 to 800 the early middle ages, with its culmination in the empire of Charles the Great and the Carolingian renaissance; the period from about 800 to 1300 the high middle ages, or feudal age, with its climax in the medieval renaissance; while for the later middle ages the so-called Italian renaissance *The later* is regarded as its peak. We have steadily resisted—without much suc- *middle ages* cess—such periodization, inasmuch as the lines of division seem quite artificial, and where one thing appears to end it is usually clear that another has long since begun. Recently a book appeared which calls the period of the fourteenth and fifteenth centuries "The Dawn of a New Era." [1] The new era referred to is the so-called modern era, of which it used to be confidently supposed that the nineteenth and twentieth centuries were a culmination which itself would never culminate. From this point of view the period about to be outlined was a transitional period from a medieval to a modern world. Such terms assume that we know very definitely what "modern" and "medieval" mean, and can therefore easily detect when one merges into the other. Granted that we do, it yet remains certain that to give precise meanings to these terms involves choosing certain characteristic features and excluding quite as many others. By concentrating attention on the excluded features it is usually possible to show that such terms as "medieval" and "modern" have no real meaning.

We shall treat the fourteenth and fifteenth centuries not as a transition between this and that (every moment is such a transition), but simply as a further development of certain features of the preceding centuries. That much of the old persisted must not surprise anyone

[1] E. P. Cheyney, *The Dawn of a New Era, 1250–1453.*

who has come to realize the lethargic character of change; that there were new emphases will not surprise him who knows that at least change is possible.

Already in our discussion of feudalism and manorialism it has been necessary to show them as changing institutions. It remains but to emphasize in accordance with our original analysis those changes that appear to characterize these two centuries. Feudalism as a system of local and private government controlled by the landed magnate was certainly on the wane everywhere in central and western Europe before the precise beginning of the fourteenth century. There was little to stop its further decline. The superior efficiency of royal and princely courts of justice, and of a centralized and paid administrative and financial organization composed of individuals of obscure or middle-class lineage, conspired to reveal the futility of relying longer upon the local nobility to establish the conditions of an orderly existence. The general continued prevalence of war, whether local private war or war on a territorial or national scale, tended to concentrate power in the hands of the prince who could best deal with it. The most energetic, efficient, and scheming feudal princes, and often the luckiest, were about to crush out their competitors in the struggle for the capture of the resources of lands and people. Whether it was the territorial prince in Germany, the despot of the city-state in Italy, or the monarch in England, France, Spain, and Portugal who did it, the inherited right of the local landowner to govern in his own name was being slowly swept away.

That is not to say that the independent-spirited feudal lords gave way easily (the revolts of feudal nobles against the central government continued), nor that they disappeared as political agents. But they entered the service of the state, to compete with the middle classes, in the hope of controlling the policy of the state in their own interests. There they remain in European governments to this day. Their right to govern was and has been limited to a right to help to govern. Nor must it be assumed that in losing political independence the noble lost too certain privileges with which that independence was associated. The feudal maxim that tax-paying was ignoble, that the noble rendered services but paid no taxes, remained valid until a comparatively recent date in the general exemption of noble classes from direct taxation. It is still practiced everywhere in a modified form.

The political decline of feudalism lessened its influence as a system of dependent land tenure or fiefs involving the personal relationships of homage and fealty and service in the tie of vassalage. English

he decline of feudalism as a system of government

The economic decline of feudalism

feudalism since the Norman conquest had fixed all land tenure as from the king, and had transferred to him the associated personal ties and services. Subinfeudation in England was forbidden as early as 1285. A lord might alienate his land, but the new owner held of the lord of the donor and not of the lord from whom the land was acquired. Continental feudalism recognized in principle that all land was held from the king, but it took longer there to translate that theory, under the influence of Roman law, into fact. In England, however, the fief, even though held of the king, remained and still remains the fundamental principle of English land law. On the continent, where absolute monarchy established itself, the principle was maintained that the king owned all the land of the kingdom: there was no such thing as private property within the state. This was still the old feudal principle. But the vassal was changing actually into the subject of the king and the fief into actual private property, although it must not be thought that the large landed estates of the nobility were seriously touched by either the political or the economic decline of feudalism. The tenure of some burghers in the towns might become a freehold, that of some serfs a rent-paying tenure, some peasants might even buy land for themselves; but in the main the land stayed in the hands of the aristocracy, or of those few rich bourgeois who bought out impoverished noble families and themselves entered the ranks of the aristocracy. And there, except for such countries as France, Czechoslovakia, the Baltic states, and Russia, where either pre-war or post-war revolutions broke up large estates owned by the nobility, it remains today. In such countries as England, Italy, and Hungary the problems involved in the medieval inheritance of the large estate are yet to be solved.

Likewise it may be said that feudalism as a military system, the rendering of cavalry service in return for a fief, was made obsolete during this period. Long before this time the limitations of feudal military service caused monarchs and princes to supplement it with a mercenary infantry as quickly as they secured the necessary money. The ineffectiveness of feudal cavalry before urban militias was well demonstrated in such battles as Legnano and Bouvines.[2] The knowledge of gunpowder led to the manufacture of firearms and cannon, and these together with the English long bow and the Swiss pikes made the mounted, heavily armored knight a military anachronism, and a reliance solely upon cavalry foolhardy. Yet such changes were slow. Although the English armies in the early fourteenth century

The military decline of feudalism

[2] See pp. 404, 488.

used the long bow with deadly effectiveness and possessed cannon, it
was another century before the French began to consider seriously
the utilization of archers and artillery. The early cannon did little
serious damage to town and castle walls. They were frightening more
than anything else. Not until the latter half of the fifteenth century
were they really destructive. It took long before the monarchs and
princes were convinced of the necessity of doing without the feudal
levy and the temporary hiring of mercenary troops and of substituting for them the standing army.

Early standing armies such as the French army were small. They
had to be supplemented by mercenary troops. In fact, until the late
seventeenth century mercenaries constituted the main bulk of European armies. Nor must it be forgotten that even though the peculiar
feudal military system gradually disappeared the tradition of the
aristocracy as the fighting caste did remain. The officers at least of the
new standing armies were still the nobility, and this remains the case
to a large extent in many European countries of today.

*The growing
strength of
chivalry*

Feudalism as the social code of chivalry by no means paralleled
the waning of feudalism in its other aspects. In fact, it was quite the
opposite in the fourteenth and fifteenth centuries, an age "notable for
the ruthlessness of its warfare, the butchery of prisoners, the breaking of promises, for conspiracy, assassination, treachery, torture and
general license," and at the same time the age that saw "the foundation of the most celebrated orders of Knighthood, the age in which
the tournament and the joust reached the height of their popularity
and magnificence, the age in which more was written in praise of
chivalry than ever before or since." [3] The less men acted as chivalrous
knights, the more deliberately they preserved the external forms of
the code of knighthood and talked and wrote about its ethical program. The old international brotherhood of knights dissolved into
territorial or national orders of knighthood—the luxurious and brilliant Burgundian Order of the Knights of the Golden Fleece, the
French Order of the Knights of the Star, and the English Knights
of the Garter. Secular mystery cults they were, the equivalent of our
aristocratic and exclusive clubs. When the Ottoman Turks threatened
central Europe,[4] the old chivalric ideal of the capture of Jerusalem
from infidel hands seized again the imaginations of king, pope, and
prince, all of whom felt that they must be off on a crusade, not so
much to block the advance of the Turk as to liberate the holy capital

[3] Waugh, *A History of Europe* (*1378–1494*), p. 303.
[4] See pp. 942 ff.

of Christendom. On the battlefield knights and kings went through the formalities of the military code of honor. Kings challenged each other to duels to decide a conflict and to spare the lives of their armies, but the duels were never fought. Proposals were made to the leaders of forces occupying favorable positions that they should abandon them and fight like true knights in the open field. While courteously entertained, such proposals were usually rejected in the interest of military tactics.

The historians of the period, not knowing how to interpret the conflict of political and economic forces raging about them, interpreted all from the point of view of honor, bravery, adventure, and revenge for injustice done. They lavished their praise on the knightly conduct of noble heroes making a fortune from the ransoms of noble prisoners and butchering the common people of the countryside. While princes were collecting the relics of chivalrous heroes, such as Tristram, and authors were preserving their saintly lives in a new type of biography, no one seemed to realize fully that the conduct of the nobility was a mockery, and that chivalrous ethics were gradually being supplanted by capitalistic ethics or no ethics at all. The feudal concept of society—namely, that of caste—still monopolized the minds of intelligent men. Despite all economic and social change, peasant and bourgeois were generally despised, and only the noble aristocrat was believed capable of the finer actions and sentiments. It is hardly necessary to point out that such a social attitude, in a more or less modified form, still prevails.

Manorialism experienced a development similar to that of feudalism in the fourteenth and fifteenth centuries. As the local unit of feudal government it suffered an eclipse comparable to that of feudal government. Yet manorial courts persisted here and there right down into recent centuries. As the means of livelihood for the nobility, Church, and peasantry its importance was not seriously diminished by the growth of towns and the increase in trade, commerce, and industry. In the neighborhood of the towns themselves there was some little specialization in the production of dairy products and garden produce. But Europe remained rather exclusively agricultural until the nineteenth century. As a peculiar system of cultivating the soil by a village community in accordance with the three-field and strip systems, manorialism underwent comparatively little change. In response to the demand for raw wool in the textile industry there was in England, Flanders, Champagne, Tuscany, Lombardy, and the region of Augsburg a tendency to enclose common waste, meadow, and some arable lands for the purpose of sheep raising, and in Flanders and England

Changes in manorialism

a rural textile industry grew up. In some regions, notably in Germany, this period witnessed the introduction of a more intensive agriculture under capitalistic methods leading to the liquidation of common rights of the villagers in behalf of the owner, who often justified this procedure with a Roman law that knew no common village rights to forest, waste, meadowland, and stream. Yet these changes were still too isolated to bring about anything like a general change.

Those conditions that we have previously described as leading to the liberation of the serf class in western Europe [5] were by no means subsequently altered. Serfdom continued to diminish. It was the exception rather than the rule by 1500, but it had not totally disappeared. In Germany and eastern Europe, however, it persisted and grew apace until the reforms and revolutions of the nineteenth century. The fixation of week work and boon work to definite amounts of time and of manorial taxes to definite amounts had made the lot of the serf less precarious. Yet it must not be supposed that manorial dues, customary payments, services, and monopolies disappeared. The change from a prevailingly natural to a prevailingly money economy led to the commutation of these items into their money value, that is all. That the serf became a renter did not mean that he escaped the burdens of the long-established property rights of the lord, and very few peasants became actual property owners. It is only within the last few years that in such a region as Quebec the manor in these aspects has disappeared. When such property rights came to be abolished, the nobility were of course paid for abandoning them, except when the process was accompanied by revolution, as in France.

Peasant
revolts

The peasant was no less terrified and harassed by famine, pestilence, and war than formerly; and these, when combined with the attempt to deprive him of long-established common rights and with the stiffening of the manorial system occasioned by the more costly life of the nobility and the decline in land values accompanying the urban revolution, led him into serious revolts either to improve his conditions or to remove additional obstacles to a status already improved. Not only were the revolts directed against secular lords but usually they were definitely anticlerical as well, the Church being among the most conservative of landlords.

Northern France was disturbed in 1251 by an insurrection of peasants moved by crusading fervor to rescue St. Louis from the Holy Land. It vented itself not only against the Church but against Jews and university students. Often these revolts were joined by the under-

[5] See pp. 348 ff.

privileged laborers in the towns. Flanders in 1323 was torn by a peasant revolt led by Nicolas Zannequin that not only attacked the manor houses of the lords, but helped to destroy unpopular patrician governments in the towns. Western Europe, and indeed all Europe, was decimated in 1348-49 and the years following by an epidemic of bubonic plague, called the Black Death, which was carried to Mediterranean ports from the Levant by the rats infesting ships. The effect of the great loss of life was a temporary dislocation of all forms of human existence, producing everything from the extremes of religious hysteria to riotous and spendthrift living. When the peasant attempted to take advantage of the scarcity of labor resulting from the plague by demanding higher wages and the commutation of services and dues into a definite money equivalent, legislation in England, France, and Spain tried in vain to force him to accept wages and conditions customary before the plague. But Europe quickly recovered from its horrible loss, and it is not likely that the Black Death had much to do with improving the lot of the peasant. At most it may have accelerated for a time an improvement explainable in other ways.

Throughout the fourteenth and first half of the fifteenth centuries, during the period of the so-called Hundred Years' War, the French peasant was at the mercy of an almost continuous ravaging of English troops and mercenary hordes. At a desperate moment of the war in 1358, a peasant uprising called the *Jacquerie* (the French peasant was commonly known as Jacques Bonhomme, James the Goodfellow) spread over much of France in furious protest against the sufferings of war, and strove to unite with a radical urban movement in Paris headed by Étienne Marcel, the leader of the merchants' gild. It was suppressed, however, with as much fury as it had been begun. England was torn in 1381 by a peasant revolt led by John Ball and Wat Tyler, joined by workingmen in the towns protesting against the attempt to treat them as if there had been no Black Death, strongly anticlerical in its temper, and demanding such things as the abolition of serfdom, of market tolls, lower rents, and rights to use the forests and streams. But it was quickly circumvented by the crown. The last part of the fifteenth century witnessed peasant revolts in Alsace and the Rhinelands.

It is difficult and dangerous to generalize about the condition of the peasantry as a whole during this period. In some regions there was a distinct improvement and in others a reversal. In Germany forces of peasant discontent were gathering sufficient strength to break out, under the stimulus of evangelical Lutheranism, into the widespread revolt of 1524-25. Yet if great masses of the peasant population of

western Europe had been freed from serfdom, agriculture was still
bound by the customary fetters of the manorial régime, and the great
problem of returning the land to the peasant was left for succeeding
generations to work out.

*Developments
in trade and
industry*

The revival of trade, commerce, and industry in the twelfth and
thirteenth centuries grew apace in the fourteenth and fifteenth, despite
all obstacles. The routes that it followed, except for the inauguration
by the Venetians in 1317 of an all-sea voyage from Venice to England
or the Low Countries, remained essentially the same. The commerce
of the Mediterranean was still largely in the control of the Italian
cities, and that of the Baltic and North Seas had come into the hands
of the merchants of the German cities comprising the Hanseatic
League. With the diminished importance of the Champagne fairs and
the outbreak of war between England and France, Augsburg and
Nuremberg, in southern Germany, became important centers of exchange and distribution. The towns of the Low Countries, notably
Bruges and, in the fifteenth century, Antwerp, remained the chief
centers of exchange for northern and southern wares. At the very end
of the period new fairs and more permanent commodity and credit
markets arose at Lyons, Geneva, Frankfurt am Main, Frankfurt an
der Oder, and Antwerp.

But the movement of goods was north and south, largely overland
and interregional and intermunicipal rather than international. Little
change can be noted, except in England, in regard to the earlier obstacles to a free-flowing internal, overland commerce. The roads were
still bad enough to make river transportation preferable, and river
transportation was still hampered by all too frequent toll stations.
Customs duties between provinces or petty states, tolls at roads and
bridges and at town gates impeded overland trade. A variety of local
mints and weights and measures continued to exist everywhere on the
continent. Only in England was there a uniform coinage and system
of weights and measures, and there too internal customs and tolls had
somewhat mysteriously disappeared in the fourteenth and fifteenth
centuries. While the commercial revival penetrated more deeply into
all parts of Europe, there were no spectacular changes that need mention here until the decline of the Hanseatic League [6] and the Portuguese and Spanish voyages of discovery at the end of the fifteenth
century.[7] The commercial revolution then introduced must be associated with the cumulative changes that had previously taken place,

[6] See pp. 932–33.
[7] See p. 1030.

leading to the comparatively sudden growth of commercial capitalism and the transfer of economic regulation from the town and gild to the territorial and city-states of Germany and Italy, or the monarchical governments of the more consolidated states of western Europe.

The earlier ubiquity of the Italian and later of the German merchant was somewhat diminished in northern Europe when English and French monarchs began to encourage their own merchants. When surplus capital began to accumulate in the hands of the German, English, and French merchants and manufacturers the earlier predominance of the Italian bankers in the north was likewise at an end. Yet the general prevalence of war in western Europe in the fourteenth and fifteenth centuries interfered somewhat with the development of an urban and cosmopolitan economy into a national economy. The national states themselves had first to be made.

It has been previously noticed that in England, France, and Spain *The decline* the medieval town never quite achieved that measure of autonomy *of town* characteristic of the towns of Flanders, Italy, and Germany. The *autonomy* towns of the former as well as the latter group, however, lost some *and of the* degree of their autonomy and their general significance in the four- *gilds* teenth and fifteenth centuries. Likewise the importance of merchant and craft gilds within the towns diminished. That is not to say that the towns everywhere did not continue to possess a large and important body of local privileges until they were completely merged into the polity of the state, nor that the gild system ceased to control most of industry, if not commerce, and persisted until destroyed by the revolutions of the eighteenth and nineteenth centuries. The quasi-independence of the town fell before the absolutism of prince and king, its economic policy was subordinated to the economic policy of the state. The organization, economic theory, and ethics of the gild were injured by the organization, economic theory, and ethics of what we call capitalism.

The accumulation of a mobile, fluid, surplus capital composed of *Accumulation* cash and what we should call commercial paper (letters of credit, *of surplus* bills of exchange, mortgages, and stocks), to supplement the im- *capital* mobile capital of the earlier period, notably land, was a slow process. Not until the end of the fifteenth and the beginning of the sixteenth century did such an accumulation begin to have far-reaching significance. That is not to say that its earlier history should therewith be minimized. The sources of the new surplus capital were undoubtedly many and varied. Part of it came from hoards of precious metals built up over long periods of time and drawn into use with new opportunities for investment. A large part of it came from the profits of the commercial and industrial revival and from the profits of exchanging, transporting, and storing money. Other services of the new bankers continued to pile it up—interest from loans to merchants, churchmen, princes, and kings and new types of maritime insurance. Increased rents from lands of increased value in the new towns with growing populations contributed their share. Fortunes were made in the holding of government office, and special economic privileges went to the creditors of kings. The stock of the precious metals was increased by the use of shaft mining to supplant surface mining. In general, it was the banker who made possible the spread of capitalism to commerce and industry. And at least in the earlier fourteenth century all merchants, especially goldsmiths, were engaged in banking activities.

Surplus capital belonging to individuals led to the formation of new types of organization wherewith to invest the surplus and thereby increase it. The specious game of making money for the sake of making more money was thus commenced. Pooling of surpluses by the members of a family developed into the well-known family banks of the Buonsignori of Siena, and the Bardi, Peruzzi, and Medici of Florence. Individual surpluses were pooled for a specific commercial voyage, or venture at sea. Opportunities for investment were made possible by the issuance of shares in trading, industrial, or banking firms.

New capitalistic organizations

The new types of organization were the antithesis in spirit of the regulated monopoly of the gilds. Huge fortunes instead of a comfortable income for the individual, production for profit instead of primarily for use, unlimited competition instead of regulation were the new rules. The newer organizations and spirit reduced, if they did not destroy, the importance of the earlier merchant gild. The craft gilds, while not destroyed, were harnessed to the new merchant-capitalist or the new company, which supplied raw materials for manufacture (this is true especially of the textile industries) and bought and disposed of the finished product, reducing the full-fledged master gildsman to the position of a wage-earner. For the most part industry was still centered in the shop of the gildsman, as formerly, or in the home of the peasant, as was the case when the textile industry spread into the countryside. It was therefore still domestic. The combination of merchant-capitalist and homework as a system of production is called the domestic system in contrast with a factory system, which then was in its merest beginnings.

The transformation of some craft gilds into associations of wage earners paralleled an aristocratic tendency in all the gilds that led to such things as hereditary membership, limitations on the number of masters within a gild, and lengthening the years of apprenticeship. To protect themselves journeymen organized within the same craft *The rise* widespread associations of their own, which tended to diminish the *of an urban* importance of the gilds proper. Together, the growth of a patrician *proletariat* group within the gilds and the capitalization of some industries were the reverse side of the same movement that brought about an increase in the numbers of dependent wage earners in the towns or the growth of what we call a proletariat. The struggles between the dominant merchant groups and the working classes for the control of the town governments in this later period we have already pointed to.[8] Here it is only necessary to add that the disturbances caused by these class conflicts in the fourteenth and fifteenth centuries made easier the intervention of prince and king in the interests of establishing order, but such intervention often as not brought with it a diminution of town liberties.

In general, it does not seem possible to say that the lot of the medieval workingman was at all improved by these new tendencies. The reverse was rather the case. A general feature of all the towns in central and western Europe towards the close of the fifteenth century was such a large increase in poverty that the older system of charity dispensed by the Church broke down, and poverty was recognized to be a problem of first importance crying for a new, intelligent solution. Such it has remained ever since. The ordinances of many towns in the late fifteenth century—at least in England, Switzerland, Germany, and Italy—made desperate efforts to keep the newfangled rich, in contrast to the growing number of the poor, from spending too much money on extravagant clothes (which usually had to be purchased abroad), luxurious and delicate food, lavish entertainments, and other pamperings of the flesh. In the Mediterranean countries slavery made its reappearance in merchant households, the slaves, both Christian and Saracen, being purchased from the Turks, Algerian or Moroccan slave traders, and at the very end of the period from Portuguese dealers in Negro slaves. In the towns of southern France homes were founded for the bastard children of the slaves of Christian merchants. At the end of the fifteenth century Rome itself became an important slave market. Pope Innocent VIII received one hundred Moors as a gift from Ferdinand the Catholic of Aragon and divided them among the cardinals and certain Roman nobles.

[8] See pp. 595–96.

Increased importance of the bourgeoisie

If towns and gilds as corporations were losing independence and importance during this period, the same cannot be said for individual members of the bourgeoisie or for the middle class as a whole. Money had become such an indispensable means of building up the power of princes and kings through armies and bureaucracies that those who had it were in a position of strategic importance. The alliance between the king or prince and the bourgeoisie to further the development of absolute government became more than ever a vital political force. The number and importance of bourgeois holding important governmental positions increased, even though central governments at least were predominantly aristocratic.

It is always necessary to ask, in regard to every major political accomplishment or war: Who is paying for it? The Rockefellers, Morgans, and Du Ponts of every period exercise a great influence on the course of events. When Edward III of England prepared for and began to fight with France in the Hundred Years' War he borrowed from such various sources as the German Tiedemann of Limburg, the Italian Bartholomew of Lucca, the Bardi and Peruzzi of Florence, the citizens of Mechlin, the citizens of Cologne, and the Archbishop of Trier. The popes borrowed from Orlando and Bonifazio Buonsignori of Siena to support the expedition of Charles of Anjou against the Hohenstaufens [9] and from bankers of Florence and Pistoia to support Rudolf of Hapsburg against Ottokar of Bohemia.[10] Philip the Fair used the money of the Guidi of Florence to smooth the way by bribery for his Flemish campaign [11] and of the Peruzzi to hire a mercenary captain to lead his band in the attack on Pope Boniface VIII.[12] Italian bankers supported the mercenary leaders and the new families rising to dictatorships in the Italian towns. Indeed, by treating the bankers and mercenary captains alone one could write a great deal of the history of this period.

Jacques Cœur

In France in the fifteenth century the makers of the new artillery, the Bureau brothers, helped to reform the French army. Already the makers of munitions have secured a hold on the state. At the same time the notorious Jacques Cœur of Bourges was having his dramatic career. As a merchant he made his fortune trading with the east, securing from the pope permission to deal with the Infidels, running a passenger service on board his galleys, and dealing in slaves. He was taken

[9] See p. 429.
[10] See p. 913.
[11] See p. 881.
[12] See p. 958.

into the service of the government of Charles VII as treasurer of the royal household, master of the mint of Paris and Bourges, and member of the king's council. These offices he used to good advantage in building up his fortune. He loaned money to everyone at court, and for the king bought back jewels presented to one mistress in order that they might be given to another. Royal privileges enabled him to exploit silver, copper, and lead mines near Lyons, where he established a benevolent if rigid paternalistic régime over his miners. He helped to reform French finances, and practically paid for the campaign that reconquered Normandy from the English.[13] He bought up the estates of impoverished nobles, married his daughter to a viscount, secured choice positions in the Church for his brothers and sons, and himself won a patent of nobility. But he cast his net too wide, and his scheming, grafting, and crooked methods tripped him up. Upon the instigation of his noble debtors a royal court ordered his goods confiscated, imposed a ruinous fine, and banished him for life for, among other things, the embezzlement of public funds. Cœur escaped and was starting to make another fortune when death caught him in 1456.

In Germany during the same century the famous Fugger family of Augsburg was building its fortunes. From mere textile workers to merchants dealing in linen, to modest bankers, and to speculators in mines, they became in the sixteenth century the bankers of the Hapsburgs and the popes, and entered the ranks of the nobility.

The political history of the fourteenth and fifteenth centuries is often summed up in the phrase "the rise of the national state," the point of departure in this connection being the feudal state of the earlier period. To be sure, as we shall point out in this chapter for western Europe, political boundaries at the end of the period corresponded more closely to those on a map of Europe today than they did at the beginning of the period: they include, that is, a larger number of the peoples whom today we call nations. But in using the term "national state" to describe the political development of the period it may be asked whether we are not reading into its history too much of the history of the last century, and with it using terms that are not strictly applicable. It is better to adhere to the terminology previously used to characterize the history of the earlier period, namely, the rise of the strong monarch within and above the feudal system. *The growth of strong monarchy*

In the previous chapter the history of England in these two centuries was concerned with the conflict between king and Parliament, or between king and feudalism. In the course of that struggle Parlia-

[13] See p. 894.

ment was permanently established as an institution limiting the powers of the king; but the immediate outcome of it, after a reappearance in the Wars of the Roses [14] of a period of feudal anarchy comparable to Stephen's reign, was a victory for the strong king which, with the Tudor dynasty, rapidly turned into absolutism. The political history of France during this period was, as it had earlier been, inseparably bound up with England. It was concerned with settling the issue raised when Aquitaine became a fief held by the English king of the French king, and it is quite possible to conceive of it as a feudal rather than a national struggle. The so-called Hundred Years' War, fought over this issue, strengthened for a time the States-General in France, as it strengthened the position of Parliament in England. That is to say, it strengthened the forces opposed to the crown at the same time that it let loose anarchic local feudal war. The immediate end of it all was a victory for the strong king, Louis XI, the eclipse of the States-General, and at least the temporary defeat of the French aristocracy.

During the fifteenth century, the French monarchy was also at the mercy of the new state of Burgundy, a wholly chivalrous and feudal creation, whose dukes were vassals of the French king. French kings were still fighting vassals in the fourteenth and fifteenth centuries. In the Spanish peninsula, the two kingdoms of Castile and Aragon continued and completed their crusade against the remnants of Mohammedan power. At the moment of victory the two monarchies were united by marriage. But the union was purely dynastic, like many a previous union of fiefs, and it is impossible to speak of a Spanish nation. During the period the influence of the *Cortes* of the Spanish kingdoms waned before that of the monarchs, duplicating the fate of the States-General and the Parliament.

The rise of the dynastic state

The growth of the absolute monarchy in these countries was only the reverse of the decline of political feudalism already spoken of. It is even helpful to conceive of it as but another phase in the development of feudalism itself. For after all, historically considered, the victory of king over feudal aristocracy was merely the victory of one feudal lord over the remaining feudal lords; the absolute monarch was in a way just the glorified feudal lord. Likewise, the enlargement of the royal domain to include other feudal domains, so that, as in France, the boundaries of the royal domain were coterminous with the boundaries of the kingdom, was, from one point of view, merely the enlargement of the original feudal holdings of the king. France therefore

[14] See pp. 860–61.

became just the glorified fief of a glorified feudal lord, the king. The territory comprising the kingdom was the personal holding of the king. He regarded it as his personal possession in the same way as the feudal lord regarded his fief as a personal possession. It was his private property, to be handed down to his eldest son as any other piece of private property. The state belonged to the family of the king, or, to use the conventional term, to the dynasty. It is therefore preferably called a dynastic rather than a national state.

The subjects of former feudal lords became now the direct subjects of the one feudal lord, the king. They looked to him for the kind of protection previously given them by the former feudal lords whom he had outpowered and outwitted. But it is difficult to see that their attitude towards their new lord was fundamentally different from their attitude towards their old lords. Loyalty to the king was but a step removed from loyalty to the local lord. The sentiment was not felt by large numbers of the aristocracy, who were only too willing still to thwart the king. It was more prevalent among the bourgeoisie. The peasantry was largely inaudible. The wars between the new strong kings resemble nothing more than the quarrels of rival feudal nobles. We may call the France that became the possession of one king a national state, but it is difficult to give it more than a feudal description. For that matter, the King of France in 1500 had two more centuries of hard fighting with the nobility ahead of him.

What we call today nationalism or patriotism was therefore in the fourteenth and fifteenth centuries largely loyalty to a royal dynasty. There was not too much even of that in western Europe. But we must not exaggerate. It is surely significant that the dream of a Europe united under a Holy Roman empire had even less validity during this period than it had previously. We shall have more occasion to point out also that the fact of a universal church was seriously changed by the emergence of what is ordinarily called national churches.[15] Actually, when looked at from the history of Church and state in the earlier middle ages, what took place was that a king or prince came to control the Church within the larger area of his territory or kingdom or his larger fief. The Universal Church under earlier local feudal control came to be subjected to local royal or princely control. It is ambiguous to call such a development national. Of course dynastic states and dynastic churches may be said to mark the widening of the political horizon away from the extreme earlier localism of feudalism.

The Church and the dynastic state

[15] See pp. 992–93.

But they, like feudalism itself, were only another species of provincialism, approaching from a great distance the provincialism that we now call nationalism.

Peoples whose institutions were threatened with extinction by neighboring states exhibited something more akin to what we may call nationalism. The successful defense of the Scots against England, of the Swiss against the Hapsburgs, of the Poles and Lithuanians against the Teutonic Knights, of the Hungarians and Balkan Slavs against the Ottoman Turks, of the Czechs or Bohemians against the Germans and the Church aroused a somewhat more patriotic spirit than can be demonstrated to have existed in Spain, France, or England.[16] Likewise, the opposition of the Swedes to the Union of Kalmar and the pride of the Portuguese in their brilliant fifteenth-century period of exploration are cases in point.[17] But it may be doubted just how far such sentiments may be called really national, how far they reached down into the hearts of the whole people, and whether they were more than expressions of the instinct of self-preservation by one aristocracy threatened with expropriation by another.

The first effect of the Hundred Years' War upon the development of strong absolute monarchy out of feudalism in France was utterly disastrous. The patient work of Philip Augustus, St. Louis, and Philip IV was seemingly brought to nought for over a century, while France suffered from regular foreign invasion and during the periods of truce from incessant devastation by bands of mercenary troops called the free companies. For of course there was not continuous warfare between England and France during the years from 1337 to 1453. At least sixty-eight of these years were formally years of truce, even if, under the circumstances, it was hard to distinguish between years of war and years of peace. In addition to foreign invasion and ravaging mercenaries, the country was victimized for a large part of the period by a civil war between rival factions, led by princes of the royal house struggling for the control of the government in their own purely selfish interests.

France from 1337 to 1453

A new feudalism, the feudalism of faction, which Louis VIII's original granting out of appanages to his sons made possible,[18] absorbed the traditions of the older feudalism of the local semi-independent lord that the Capetians had well-nigh destroyed, and arose to ruinous

[16] For Scotland see p. 849, for the Swiss p. 922, for the Poles p. 940, for the Hungarians and Slavs pp. 945–46, and for the Czechs p. 985.
[17] See pp. 934, 1030–31.
[18] See p. 503.

heights when royal incapacity and the opportunities of foreign war removed all obstacles. Add to this the terror of the Black Death, which after its original toll of death continued to reappear here and there at about ten-year periods, and one has a melancholy picture of a nation of some twenty million people, mostly peasants, buffeted by disease and war and at the mercy of an aristocracy composed mostly of wastrels. To make matters worse the persons of the new Valois kings were, to say the least, none too promising. Philip VI (1328–51) and John the Good (1351–64) were extravagant incompetents devoted to a fantastic and decadent code of chivalry. Between them and Charles VI (1380–1422) ruled the only king of ability and character, Charles V, the Wise. Charles VI was insane for increasingly long intervals after 1392, and his son Charles VII (1422–61) has been characterized as 'one of the most contemptible creatures that ever disgraced the title of king and actually under as sorry a set of knaves as ever abused the functions of government." [19]

Under such circumstances France lost the leadership of western civilization, which she was not to regain until the seventeenth century. In a sense she had to begin to build all over again upon the scaffolding set up by the Capetians. Despite the bitter experiences with the Valois kings there was yet no other way out than to rely on the leadership of the monarchy and the loyalty that it could inspire in the nobility, and chiefly in the reviving bourgeois class. Of this fact Louis XI (1461–83) was to be the proof, if Charles VII with the Bureau brothers and Jacques Cœur at his side had not been already.

The second Hundred Years' War between France and England was the direct outcome of the first.[20] The Treaty of Paris of 1259 had left to Henry III as the vassal of St. Louis all of southwestern France, known as the Duchy of Aquitaine, or Guienne and Gascony. The region was of the greatest economic importance as one of the chief wine-producing centers in all Europe. Aside from relying on it to help supply the increasing demand for wine, the English kings reaped a rich harvest from the wine trade in export taxes out of Bordeaux and import taxes into England. They were determined not to lose the advantages that the political and economic control over Aquitaine brought. The Valois kings, no less determined than the Capetians to complete the territorial unification of France, took every opportunity to make difficulties for the English in Aquitaine. The time-honored method was to encourage appeals from nobles of the region over the

The question of Aquitaine

[19] Waugh, *op. cit.*, p. 63.
[20] See pp. 485–86.

heads of their lord, the English king, to the *Parlement* at Paris, and then to cite the English kings as French vassals before the court of the French king. The indisposal of English kings to answer such summons opened the way for decrees of confiscation on the charge of contumacy, which, when not backed by force, were nothing but annoying and to disputes over the character of the homage, whether simple or liege, which the English kings owed their French lords.

The last such dispute occurred when Edward III went to Amiens in 1329 to do homage. The whole situation was anomalous and under the circumstances could be settled only by Aquitaine's becoming French. But the English kings were as determined to maintain their empire in France as the German kings had been to maintain their position in Italy. Moreover, they had never forgotten what John had lost to Philip Augustus in 1204, and when the fortunes of war seemed to raise hopes that the whole former Angevin empire in France might be reacquired, they determined to have all or nothing. The most important issue of the war was therefore what it had been in the earlier Capetian-Angevin struggle: Could the comparatively small English nation maintain its present or restore its ancient empire in France in the face of the determination of the Valois kings to complete the territorial unification of their kingdom?

The question of Flanders

Other difficulties helped to bring on a revival of the conflict. English and French towns on either side of the channel were engaged in almost constant private and half-piratical wars to settle disputes concerning the fisheries of the North Sea. The French were supporting the efforts of the Scotch to defend themselves from an English conquest, and in return received promises of aid in any war against the English. A more serious problem involved Flanders. The English were then, and have always been since, concerned with preventing any continental power from using the Flemish coast as a possible base for an invasion of England, and conversely with its possibilities as a base for an English invasion of the continent. Flanders was dominated by flourishing autonomous towns making woolen cloth. Most of the raw wool going into Flemish textiles came from the large estates of Cistercian monasteries in northern England, and a fair amount of Flemish cloth was sold to England. England and Flanders were thus economically interdependent, and the English kings enjoyed revenue from export taxes on raw wool and import taxes on Flemish cloth. It was therefore to their interests to see that nothing interfered with the normal trade relations with Flanders, while to Flanders the English market was a matter of life and death.

Flanders was, however, a fief held of the French crown by a count whose authority was in constant danger of being further limited by uprisings in the Flemish towns. To stop such audacity the count had recourse to his overlord, the French king, always on the lookout to incorporate Flanders more completely into the French state and thereby to profit from its wealth and industry. The later thirteenth and fourteenth centuries were a period of almost perpetual conflict in the Flemish towns between the artisans and smaller merchants and the merchant oligarchs for control of the town government. In these conflicts the merchant oligarchs sought the protection of the count and the French king, and their opponents looked most naturally to England. In 1302 an uprising in Flanders against the presence of French soldiers in the towns and against their allies, the patricians of the city, brought Philip the Fair with an army to Courtrai. He was overwhelmingly defeated by the town militias in the "Battle of the Spurs," so called from the rich harvest in golden spurs taken from the French knights. In 1326 the Count of Flanders, acting upon orders from his French overlord, arrested all Englishmen traveling or resident in Flanders and threw them into prison. The answer of Edward II of England was to ruin the Flemish textile industry by prohibiting the export of English wool and the importation of Flemish cloth. Peasant and urban revolutions in 1328 led to another intervention of the French army, which reversed its defeat at Courtrai by a victory at Cassel.

In these desperate circumstances a merchant of Ghent, Jacques van Artevelde, managed to organize a successful revolution against the patrician town governments and their aristocratic and French supporters, and to come to terms with England by offering neutrality in the event of war with France in return for removing the restrictions on the export of raw wool and the import of Flemish cloth. To make matters worse, Edward III of England had, since the accession of Philip VI in 1328, contested the legitimacy of Philip's kingship with the argument that although it had been decided that a woman could not succeed to the French throne it had by no means been decided that the throne could not be inherited through a woman. Since his mother Isabella was a daughter of Philip IV, he had a better claim to the French throne than Philip. In 1340, forsaking their neutrality, the Flemish towns accepted Edward's claim to the French throne, and at Ghent in January Edward assumed the title of King of the French.

Meanwhile, war had already begun. To carry on war in France the English must have control of the seas leading to the French and Flemish coasts. To thwart such control and to prevent an English

The Battle of Sluys

army from landing in Flanders, a French fleet consisting of Norman, Genoese, and Spanish ships gathered at Sluys, the harbor of Bruges. In June 1340, however, it was almost totally destroyed by the English fleet in a battle that gave England the mastery of the channel for about thirty years to come. (Fourteenth-century naval battles were essentially hand-to-hand conflicts between soldiers and sailors after the ships had succeeded in locking each other. At Sluys English long bowmen were much in evidence.)

Five years later an urban revolution in Ghent cost the life of Jacques van Artevelde and re-established French influence in the Flemish cities. Consequently the English had to seek another port of entry into France at Calais, the siege of which they began in 1346. Raids had already been begun on French territory from Aquitaine, and a large expedition was gathered for an invasion of northern France in the winter of 1345–46. Because the French troops were concentrated in Poitou to meet what they expected to be an attack from Aquitaine, Edward III landed without difficulty in Normandy in July 1346, and started a ravaging march northwards, intending to re-embark for home from Flanders. He was forced to take a stand at Crécy, where *Crécy* French troops hurriedly summoned from Poitou finally caught up with him. The result was such a defeat for the French feudal cavalry as to destroy the prestige that France had enjoyed since Bouvines as the first military power in Europe, and to render her for the time being helpless. The English had some cannon at Crécy and a large number of long bowmen. The cannon were not powerful enough to produce anything but terror, but the archers played havoc with the Genoese crossbowmen in the French front lines, and when they shot into the horses of the French knights forced them to dismount and fight in their cumbersome heavy armor. They were slaughtered and suffocated. Crécy may have demonstrated to the English the superiority of a combination of long bowmen and feudal cavalry, but the French were hardly so convinced. It was another century before they learned the lesson.

Crécy may also be called the first of a long series of continental victories for England over France that terminated with Waterloo, but in itself the battle was hardly decisive. More telling was the final capture of Calais in August of 1347, whither the English had moved after *Calais* Crécy. It proved to be the most permanent English conquest of the whole war, and was held until 1558. The French inhabitants were expelled from the town and for them were substituted English colonists. With Calais England had an open door into France that compensated for the loss of her influence in Flanders. Moreover, it gave the English a continental market for the disposal of their wool and manufactures and for the purchase of continental goods.

The English completed this brilliant inauguration of the war after the expiration of a truce (1347–55) and the horrors of the Black Death in France. The summer of 1356 was spent by Edward III's eldest son, the Black Prince, in harrowing with little opposition the rich cities of the valley of the Loire and the provinces of Berry, Touraine, and Anjou. Only in mid-September did a large French army make its appearance and force the prince to fight when it might have starved him into submission. The English victory at Maupertuis (Poitiers) was even more overwhelming than at Crécy. King John the *Poitiers* Good of France, three of his sons, two marshals, and a great many of those French nobles who had not fled were captured and held for ransom. The number of prisoners was so great that the Black Prince had the common soldiery slaughtered for fear the battle might be renewed. He wintered in Bordeaux, where "there was much feasting and merriment," returning to England in the spring of 1357 with his royal and noble prisoners. King John had a glorious time in England, where he was treated more as a guest than a prisoner. He was finally lodged in the Savoy Palace with a retinue of servants, a liberal allowance of spending money, and leave to hunt in the royal forests. From his haven it was difficult to get him to return.

John's capture at Poitiers put his eldest son, the Dauphin Charles, at the head of the government. The title dauphin, equivalent to the English Prince of Wales, was taken when Philip VI before his death secured from the last ruler of Dauphiné, in the Kingdom of Arles, the right of the king's eldest son to inherit the region. It was no mean task that the dauphin faced. France after Poitiers was not only without a king, but without an army, the nobility having been thoroughly discredited, and without a government. In the general misery the States-General, summoned frequently in 1356–57, attempted for the first time to secure control not only of the collection and expenditure of the taxes granted by them, but also of the supervision of the ministers and officials of the crown. The leading figure in the third estate was *The States-* Étienne Marcel,[21] who controlled a revolutionary government in *General and* Paris, allied with a disgruntled claimant of the French throne, Charles Jacquerie the Bad of Navarre, and went so far at the last moment as to admit free companies of English troops into the city. Meanwhile, in 1358 the infuriated peasantry, harassed by demands for payments of the ransoms

[21] See p. 869.

for nobles taken at Poitiers, with no protection from their lords against the well-organized companies of plundering mercenaries, broke out into the revolt already described as the *Jacquerie*.[22] Marcel did not actually ally with the peasants, but he co-operated with them. The dauphin was able to escape the tutelage of Marcel in Paris, and to capitalize on the fear aroused by the attempts to dictate to the royal government and by the peasants' revolt. Once out of Paris he summoned a meeting of the States for Compiègne, which granted him money; then he advanced on Paris. A reaction in Paris against the high-handed and extraordinary limits to which Marcel was willing to go cost him his life in July 1358, and the dauphin entered Paris and restored order.

The treaty of Bretigny

Two years later, after the States-General had refused to accept a treaty of King John's with the English that restored the old Angevin empire in France to the boundaries of 1200, and after an unsuccessful English campaign in 1359, the preliminaries for a settlement of the war were arranged at Bretigny in 1360 and confirmed later in the year at Calais. The Treaty of Bretigny (or Calais) turned over to Edward III, without obligation of feudal allegiance to the French crown, Guienne and Gascony (i.e., the Agenais, Périgord, Quercy, Rouerque, Bigorre, Limousin, Saintonge, Angoumois) and also Poitou. In the north the counties of Montreuil, Ponthieu, and Guines (Calais) were to be ceded to Edward. The English holdings were therefore substantially increased. Moreover, the ransom for King John was set at the handsome figure of three million gold crowns, or about thirty million dollars. Edward III was to renounce in turn all claims to the French throne. But like most treaties, this treaty was not a peace. King John, when once released from his enjoyable captivity, upon the payment of a first installment of the ransom, returned again in 1363 when his second son, Louis, Duke of Anjou, held as a hostage in England for the payment of the remainder, came home in violation of his parole. With the remark that "where good faith and honor vanished from the rest of the world, such virtues ought still to find their room in the breasts of kings," this happy-go-lucky, debonair, self-indulgent, and incapable king returned to England to gamble, hunt, and race horses, "in order to guarantee by his presence the execution of the treaty."

King John and Burgundy

Before his departure, however, he had taken a step of grave importance for the history of his kingdom. At the death without direct heirs of Philip of Rouvres, who held both the Duchy and Free County of Burgundy (Franche-Comté), he annexed the duchy to the crown, and as a reward to his son Philip, who had won the sobriquet of "the

---

[22] See p. 869.

Head of the condottiere, Gattamelata, by Donatello
(See p. 1028)

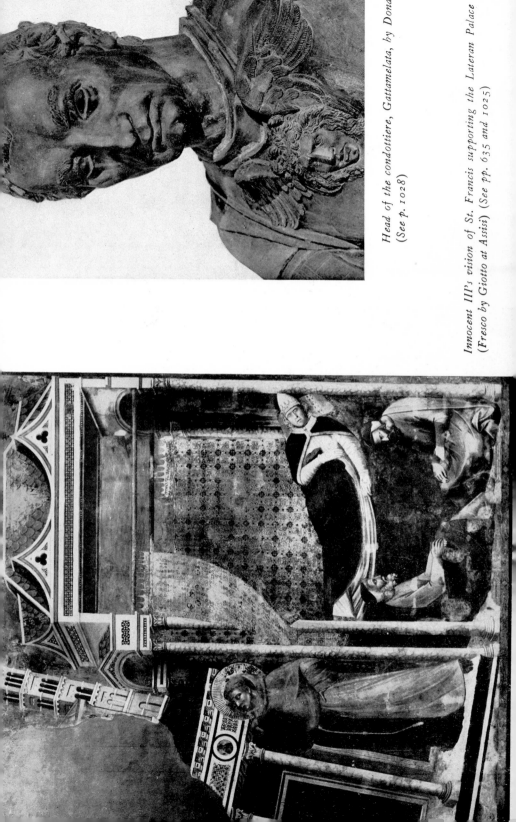

Innocent III's vision of St. Francis supporting the Lateran Palace
(Fresco by Giotto at Assisi) (See pp. 635 and 1025)

Ghirlandaio's portrait of an old man and his grandson
See pp. 998 and 1026)

Adam and Eve's expulsion from
Eden. Masaccio's fresco in the
Brancacci chapel (See p. 1026)

Piero de Medici, by Botticelli

Bold" at Poitiers, he made him its new duke and secured for him from the German emperor investiture with the Free County of Burgundy as well. The new royal appanage was the beginning of a mid-European

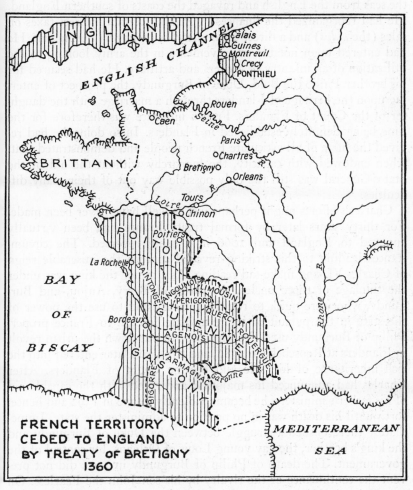

FRENCH TERRITORY
CEDED TO ENGLAND
BY TREATY OF BRETIGNY
1360

state that proved to be as dangerous to the French monarchy as the English fiefs had ever been.

In 1369 the war recommenced. When the thin, awkward, frail, and sickly Charles V died in 1380, he had with the aid of the renowned *The success* Bertrand du Guesclin, his tough Breton constable, and with his own *of Charles V* sharp intelligence, not only reduced the English holdings in France to Calais, Cherbourg, and Brest in the north, and a strip reaching from

Bordeaux to Bayonne in the southwest, but he had done much to free France from the curse of the free companies. Moreover, he had created a royal navy which, with Castilian aid, took the supremacy of the seas from the English and ravaged the coasts of southern England. He had reorganized the finances by making certain indirect taxes on sales (the *aides*) and a direct tax on hearths (*fouages*) permanent. He had entered upon notable improvements in the army looking to the utilization of an infantry of archers and artillery. He had secured for his brother Philip the Bold, Duke of Burgundy, the prospect of entering upon the heritage of Flanders through a marriage with the daughter of the Count of Flanders. French influence was therefore for the time being definitely established in Flanders. In so doing he had revived the hope of all articulate French people and demonstrated that, when endowed with capacity, the monarchy without the aid of the States-General was still the only possible way out of their many difficulties.

Charles's efforts might perhaps just as well have never been made. For thirty years later by formal treaty France had been virtually annexed to England and 1066 in a sense reversed. The circumstances leading to this striking reversal concern the miserable reign of Charles VI, and make sad reading. As a minor the king was under *Charles VI* the tutelage of three uncles, the dukes of Berry, Anjou, and Bur-*and the* gundy, who were quick to rob the treasury and to use the power of *Burgundian-* the state in the pursuit of interests quite foreign to France proper. *Armagnac* Philip of Burgundy used French troops to put down the urban revolt *struggle* in Flanders at Roosebeke in 1382, and two years later entered into the rich inheritance of his wife and became Count of Flanders. After Charles had announced his majority, and ruled with the capable aid of his father's ministers, he became violently insane in 1392 and henceforth until his death was in no position to administer the state. Immediately there ensued a struggle between the Duke of Burgundy and the king's brother, the gay young Louis of Orléans, for control of the government. The death of Philip of Burgundy in 1404 did not prevent the continuance of the rivalry by his son John the Fearless. On an evening in November 1407, while riding home on his mule from a visit to the queen, contentedly humming a tune, Louis of Orléans was murdered in cold blood by hired assassins of the Duke of Burgundy, who confessed to the deed quite openly and got away with it.

The murder produced a nasty civil war in France between the Burgundian faction, of northern and northeastern France, and the Orléanist or Armagnac (so called from the father-in-law of the new young Duke of Orléans, Count Bernard of Armagnac) faction, of southern and southeastern France. The two parties were not only struggling for control of the government of a mad king; they were divided too over the question of war with England and over which pope to support in the reigning schism.[23] Burgundy with its Flemish towns was inclined to maintain good relations with the new Lancastrian dynasty in England,[24] while the Armagnacs put on a pretense of patriotic support of the realm against the traditional enemy. Burgundy was neutral in the matter of the schism, while the Armagnacs supported the French pope at Avignon. But as a matter of fact each faction entered upon negotiations with England for support against the other in the civil war. It was a situation calculated to invite the active reopening of the war on the part of England. Henry V was not so securely seated on the English throne as not to wish for the support which a glorious foreign victory might bring him. In reviving the claim to the French throne, to which he had even less claim than Edward, he seemed to figure that the support of the English in securing the French throne might remove their opposition to his holding the English one.

The war was reopened in 1415 with the English in possession of a loose kind of alliance with the Burgundians. Henry V's aim was to open up another port of entry on the continent at Harfleur, to provide *The Battle* his army with a rich assortment of plunder by marching north through *of Agincourt* Normandy, and then to embark at Calais for England. The original aim was accomplished, but on the march northward the English were forced by an Armagnac army to take a stand at Agincourt. The Burgundians, while not definitely supporting the English, at least held aloof from the battle. It was another such slaughter as Crécy and Poitiers had been. Nothing had ever come of the military reforms of Charles V, and the French army was largely composed of heavy armored cavalry. The English repeated their traditional tactics, and more French knights were killed or suffocated than there were men in the English army.

There was now little to prevent an English occupation of practically all of northern France. It was begun in 1418 with the important and successful siege of Rouen. In that same year John the Fearless got control of Paris and the royal government, and those Armagnacs who were left in the city after a terrific slaughter managed

[23] See p. 973.
[24] See p. 858.

to escape with the dauphin, the future Charles VII, south of the Loire, where subsequently a rival government was set up for all Armagnac territory. The dauphin was now the virtual head of the Armagnac party.

The murder of John the Fearless, Duke of Burgundy

Despite his alliance with the English, the Duke of Burgundy began negotiations with the Armagnacs looking towards a cessation of the civil war and a common front against the English. A final conference was arranged for September 10, 1419, at the bridge of Montereau, but it ended in the unpremeditated murder of John the Fearless with an axe. The murder of course made all further attempts to come to terms with the dauphin-Armagnac party impossible. Philip the Good, John's son, immediately turned to the English and by Christmas had concluded an alliance with them. Moreover, being in charge of the government of Charles VI, he arranged with Henry V the Treaty of Troyes, signed in May 1420. The treaty amounted to a realization of the wildest English hopes. The dauphin was cast aside for Henry V, who was declared to be Charles VI's son, and the heir to his king-

The Treaty of Troyes

dom. During the lifetime of Charles, Henry V was to act as regent with the co-operation of the Duke of Burgundy. He was to retain all his conquests in northern France in full sovereignty, but they were to be returned to the Kingdom of France when Henry V succeeded Charles. Furthermore, Henry V married Catherine, Charles VI's daughter. The English then began to spread their conquest north of the Loire and to consolidate their position. But in 1422 both Henry V and Charles VI died. An infant Henry VI was King of France north of the Loire, with his uncle John, Duke of Bedford, as his regent, and with the support of the Duke of Burgundy. South of the Loire ruled the former dauphin, Charles VII, king but without benefit of corona-tion and consecration in Rheims Cathedral. Could the Treaty of Troyes be carried out?

We can now say no. At the moment, its enforcement depended chiefly upon two things—the continuance of the Anglo-Burgundian al-liance and of the listlessness of Charles VII. Should one or the other cease, it was but a question of how long the English could hold on. If

Bedford's rule in northern France

both should cease the withdrawal of the English would be speedy. Bedford did his best to make the conquered French territories con-tented. He made some little attempt to colonize Englishmen in Nor-mandy. His financial administration was superior to that of the Valois kings, but he could not establish law and order with the small number of troops that a faction-ridden English government supplied to him. The French under Bedford's regency were not sullen. But inasmuch as he could not supply them with the kind of decent government that might well have made them contented with the Treaty of Troyes, they were hopeful that a change to Charles VII might be for the better. Charles could therefore always count on this hope.

Meanwhile the English pushed their way into central France by defeating the French and Scotch forces at Verneuil (1424) and began preparations for an invasion of Charles's territory across the Loire by besieging Orléans. The king himself was hopeless. Aside from being a frail and sickly youth, he was abnormally fearful of the English, of the passions that raged among a disgusting set of courtiers about him, indeed of anything at all connected with war. While his officials grew rich by pilfering government funds, the king ate plain food, wore shabby clothes, and got wet feet because he could not afford decent shoes. In the Loire country that he loved he loitered in the châteaux of Bourges and Chinon, derisively dubbed by French and English alike the King of Bourges.

It was at this moment that Charles was temporarily and partially jolted out of his indifference by an illiterate peasant girl seventeen years of age named Joan of Arc. She was born at Domrémy in the *Joan of Arc* Castellany of Vaucouleurs, a region on the northeastern Lorraine frontier which had remained loyal to the Armagnac cause, and that was at the time fearing an attack from Bedford. Joan, like any other young girl of her time, was sincerely devoted to the saints whose images stood in the village parish church, and she became convinced that they were in turn devoted to her. She heard their voices, the voices of St. Michael, St. Catherine, and St. Margaret, speak to her and announce that they had a mission for her. She must go to the king, and lead him to Rheims to be crowned and anointed. Then she must expel the English from France. These voices were to her nothing less than direct commands from God upon which it was necessary to act immediately. For the rest of her short life it was her unquestioning belief that she was directly inspired by God and directed by the voices she always heard. She went to the commander of the garrison at Vaucouleurs, received a small escort, and managed in some way to get through three hundred miles of Anglo-Burgundian territory to Chinon, where, dressed as a man, she presented herself to Charles with the simple announcement that she had come on God's behalf to help him and his kingdom.

The extraordinary character of the incident made her suspected, and she was turned over to a commission of theologians at Poitiers, who pronounced her, after three weeks' time, simple, good, honest, and virtuous. She was then given a horse, a suit of white armor, and a banner with her own device, Jhesus Maria. In command of a small number of men, she was then permitted to join the forces going to the relief of Orléans. The moral tone of the army was not much to her liking. She tried to get rid of the crowd of prostitutes who followed the army, forbade her own men to curse, and encouraged them to confess and attend Mass. The French army felt that it was accompanied by a saint. She made up for her ignorance of military affairs by a reckless courage that inspired the troops, and in the relief of Orléans she played a conspicuous part and was wounded in the shoulder. Within a short while the English withdrew from the siege. The tide had been turned. "Before she came," wrote a French chronicler, "two hundred Englishmen used to drive five hundred Frenchmen before them. After her coming, two hundred Frenchmen could chase five hundred Englishmen."

After the siege of Orléans had been raised Joan was permitted with her men to join the troops engaged in freeing the Loire basin. It must not be supposed that she was in charge of the French army. In the victory at Patay she was in the rear, but she was with the army and in popular imagination that was enough. It might have been well had the French army made directly for Paris, but Joan's mission had been to lead the king to Rheims for his coronation, and she had her way. The king was brought to Rheims without great difficulty, and in July 1429 the coronation was held in the cathedral, with Joan and her banner standing behind the king during the ceremonies. At this particular point her rôle was really ended. She had been instrumental in securing the relief of Orléans and the coronation of the king. She had revived hopes for the ultimate victory of the French crown. That was considerable. The sudden turn in the war made the English and Burgundians believe that the French were being guided by a witch, and they could hardly be expected to fight against an agent of the devil.

To Joan her mission was only half completed: the English were not yet driven out. Charles VII, after so much exertion, was anxious to get back to the comfortable châteaux of the Loire country. His advisers preferred rather than to continue to fight to negotiate with the English and Burgundians. Under these circumstances Joan got out of hand; her voices were driving her on; she would not listen to advice or take orders, and became a nuisance. Charles is supposed to have remarked in a fit of annoyance, "Let her go hang herself." In fact she was permitted practically to go her own way as best she could with whatever troops she could get to follow her. All her succeeding exploits, including an attack on Paris in September, when she was wounded again, failed to accomplish anything more than to reveal quite clearly that the English hold on northern France was none too strong. Finally, in May 1430, she was taken prisoner by an archer in the Burgundian army besieging Compiègne, as she participated in a sortie out of the city to relieve a village that the Burgundians had taken. She was turned over to a Burgundian partisan, who sold her to the English for ten thousand pounds.

Joan had but one more year to live. She was quickly abandoned by her king, who did none of the things that he might have to secure her release from the English. Indeed, she was abandoned by everyone except, she thought, her God and her voices; and her faith in these put her into the hands of the Inquisition. For the English, resolved to de- *Joan in the* stroy the singular moral influence that Joan had wielded, were anxious *hands of the* to have her condemned to death as the witch they were convinced she *Inquisition* was, to prove that she was possessed of demoniac, not divine, power. But the Church too was much concerned over her claim to be the directly inspired agent of God. According to Church dogma that was impossible. In the course of long centuries the Church, i.e., the clergy, had interposed itself between God and man as the only possible mediator of divine grace. Personal communion with God did away with the necessity of the Church and smelled of the heresy of St. Francis, Peter Waldo, John Wyclif,[25] and John Hus.[26] The English therefore surrendered Joan to the Inquisition at Rouen, presided over by the Bishop of Beauvais, Pierre Cauchon, in whose diocese Joan had been taken prisoner. She was charged with heresy and sorcery, and a large array of legal and theological talent was employed to try her.

It is possibly true that Joan's trial was "no more unfair" than other trials by the Inquisition. But her condemnation was almost a foregone conclusion. "Joan had asserted that she was God's messenger, commissioned by Him through the voice of the saints and angels. It was possible, to say the least, that her inspiration was from the devil. Was she willing to leave the question to the Church? If she refused submission, her guilt was established, for to deny the authority of the Church was at once the commonest and deadliest of heresies. If she submitted, then the ecclesiastical tribunal before which she stood was ready to assume the functions of the Church, and to decide the question against her." [27] Yet hour after hour, day after day, through the ten long

---

[25] See p. 978.
[26] See p. 983.
[27] Lowell, *Joan of Arc*, p. 203.

weeks of the trial in the spring of 1431, the intrepid girl foiled her
enemies by the ingenuous candor of her speech or disarmed them by
the shrewdness of her retorts. When asked if she knew if she were in the
grace of God she replied, "May God bring me into His grace if I am
not; if I am in it, may He keep me there." Thus she avoided presuming on the authority of the Church by saying "Yes" and convicting
herself by saying "No."

The articles drawn up convicting her of sorcery and heresy were approved by no less an authority than the theological faculty of the
University of Paris. The Inquisition always pressed for a confession, and when Joan in May was brought to the churchyard of St.
Ouen in Rouen to hear the sentence committing her to the flames,
weary, deserted, heartsick, homesick, in pain of body and in mental
anguish, weakened by a year's imprisonment after a lifetime spent
in the open air, worn out by the strain of the long trial during the
Lenten fast, which she had faithfully kept even upon the meager
prison food, and horrified at the thought of her nice body, as she put
it, being burned to ashes, she confessed that she was guilty, that she
had lied about her voices, practiced sorcery, and sinned in claiming the
direct inspiration of God. Under such circumstances her sentence was
changed to life imprisonment and she resumed her feminine garb.

But once back in prison, she knew that she had been untrue to her
faith and herself. "Whatever I have said was from fear. . . . I told
you the truth of everything at the trial. . . . I did not understand
what was in the deed of abjuration." From the point of view of the
Inquisition this was clearly a relapse into heresy meriting capital punishment, and she was accordingly turned over to the English to be
burned. She died at the stake in the market place of Rouen on May
30, 1431, with the name of Jesus on her lips. An English soldier who
was present is reported to have remarked, "My God, we have burned
a saint." He spoke better than he knew. In 1456, in order to conciliate
Charles VII and free the French monarchy from the charge that it
had been assisted by a convicted sorceress and heretic, the papacy
ordered a rehearing of Joan's case, which pronounced the original
trial irregular and Joan's punishment unjustified. In 1909 Pius X declared her beatified; in 1919 Benedict XV canonized her. The poor
girl who was sentenced to be burned as a heretic and sorceress by the
Church in 1431 is today venerated as a saint by that same Church.

No more than her life did Joan's death change much the actual
military situation in France. The possibility of great change came
when, in 1435 at the Congress of Arras, the Duke of Burgundy aban-

doned his English alliance at a good price, and thus removed the second condition for the possible fulfillment of the Treaty of Troyes. At the congress England was offered the rather generous concession of both Guienne and Normandy as fiefs of the French crown, on condition that Henry VI renounce all claim to the French throne. The English not only refused to renounce the claim to the throne but demanded all France north of the Loire, to be held quite independently. They agreed to ask for no more than they already held only if Charles VII would become a vassal to Henry VI for all his territory. Under the circumstances, considering that the Burgundians had warned the English ambassadors that if they did not come to terms, the Burgundians themselves would make peace with France, these were extraordinary demands. When they were refused the English huffily quit the congress. The Duke of Burgundy withdrew from the English alliance after receiving the counties of Mâcon and Auxerre, and the *prévôtés* of Peronne, Montdidier, and Roye. In addition he was to receive "the towns of the Somme," although they might be repurchased by France. As long as Philip or Charles lived the duke was to perform no homage for his territory, and he was to aid Charles if the English renewed their attack.

At that the Burgundians did not participate much in fighting against the English, with whom they made a truce in 1439. Charles VII recovered Paris in 1436, and reconstituted the *Parlement* of Paris, but the next ten years were another period of great disorder. The kingdom was ravaged by the *écorcheurs* (the flayers), private bands of soldiers of foreign and French extraction; and the chief nobles of the kingdom, led by the impatient and wily dauphin, the future Louis XI, tried to prevent any recovery of the monarchy by organizing in 1440 a revolt called the *Praguerie*. In the face of the recrudescence of general anarchy the monarchy was in fact the only hope. *Military and tax reform* The States-General in 1439 gave to Charles alone the sole right to levy and organize troops and the means to carry out the military reorganization, namely, a taille, a direct tax on persons, the assessment and collection of which was to be entirely in the king's hands without any reference at all to the States-General. The monarchy thus provided with the means to make itself in time absolute was unable to take steps to inaugurate the military reform until 1445 and after. Then in preparation for a revival of war against the English, the king, with the financial aid of Jacques Cœur and the expert knowledge of the Bureau brothers, destroyed the private military companies in France and introduced many of them into the new companies of cavalry, the *compagnies d'ordonnance*, of which twenty of six hundred men each were set up and stationed in the towns. They were paid for by the proceeds of the taille and were the nucleus of a permanent standing army of the French king. Some attempt was made to provide an infantry by obliging every fifth hearth in France to supply an archer who could be called upon when summoned. Because immune from the taille they were called free archers, but in actual combat they proved of little use and were abandoned by Louis XI for the really formidable Swiss pikemen. Great attention, however, was given to both field and siege artillery, so that France possessed in a short time the best artillery in Europe.

The end of the war

The new military reforms, when combined with the money of Jacques Cœur, brought speedy results when war with England was resumed in 1449. Rouen, Caen, and Cherbourg fell in 1449–50, and the English rule in Normandy was gone for good. Without a stay the field of war was shifted to Guienne and Gascony. Bordeaux and Bayonne were taken in 1450–51. The Gascons organized a revolt against the newly introduced French government, supported by the English, who sent over England's greatest war dog, Talbot, a sixty-eight-year-old veteran of Agincourt. But the revolt was crushed in July 1453 at Castillon (Châtillon), and Guienne and Gascony were again added to the royal domain. Although this was not the official termination of the long war, since the English persisted in their claims and sent armies into France in 1475 and 1492, yet it was the real end. The later attempts were easily bought off, and after 1453 the English made no further efforts to acquire an empire on the continent. 1453 may be said therefore to be the end of the long struggle begun really in 1066. The attempt of the English to reverse 1066, to unite the English and French monarchies and to hold a large empire in France, was a dismal failure. At the end she held only Calais. The Valois kings had recovered Guienne and Gascony. After a frightful halt in the development of civilization, the monarchy, because of the impotence of all other elements, was able with bourgeois help to lay the foundations of absolutism with a standing army and a system of direct taxation which it itself controlled.

The growth of Burgundy

If the Hundred Years' War drove the English out of France, it also set up within France and on the northern and eastern frontiers of France a new state of Burgundy, which for the first three-quarters of the fifteenth century was much more dangerous to the Valois monarchy than ever the English would have been alone. No sooner, indeed, was the English conquest completed than Charles VII and especially his son and successor Louis XI (1461–83) were obliged to devote their attention to the possible eclipse of France by Burgundy. In 1363 John the Good founded the state by turning over to his son Philip the Bold (1363–1404) the Duchy of Burgundy and securing for him from the emperor investiture with the Free County of Burgundy. Philip was therefore a vassal of both the King of France and the German emperor. Thinking that it would help to assure French predominance in Flanders, Charles V paid its Count Louis de Mâle well to marry his sole heiress to Philip the Bold. At Louis's death in 1384 Philip came into possession of the inheritance of his wife, which included the County of Flanders, Artois, Franche-Comté, Nevers, and Rethel.

Burgundy, thus possessed of Flanders, one of the richest and most densely populated spots in all Europe, was ensconced on the English channel and in the Jura Mountains. Obviously the aim of the dukes was to join Flanders with the Burgundies. They were able to do this with extraordinary success chiefly by means of well-calculated marriage alliances made by Philip the Bold and John the Fearless (1404–19). During the reign of Philip the Good (1419–67) these earlier marriages brought into his hands the remainder of the Low Countries (Pays-Bas), namely, the duchies of Brabant and Limburg, and the counties of Holland, Zeeland, and Hainault. Moreover, Philip purchased the County of Namur and the Duchy of Luxemburg, had one of his bastard sons provided with the important Bishopric of Utrecht, and an eighteen-year-old nephew made Bishop of Liége. He controlled too the Bishopric of Cambrai. By allying with the English in the Treaty of Troyes,[28] he provided for himself a free hand in the development of the united Low Countries, and in breaking off that alliance in the Treaty of Arras [29] he increased his state notably but at the same time made possible the revival of what was to prove the ruin of Burgundy, that is, the French monarchy.

Clearly Charles V had made a serious miscalculation. This was a new state with an independent policy of its own, not an appanage of the French monarchy. Philip the Good, in identifying himself with the interests of the Low Countries he had unified, laid the early foundations for their modern successors on the map of Europe, Belgium and Holland. The Burgundian court became under Philip the richest and most elaborate in Europe, in fact the center of decadent chivalry. Its princes collected a fine library, created a Burgundian

[28] See p. 888.
[29] See. p. 892.

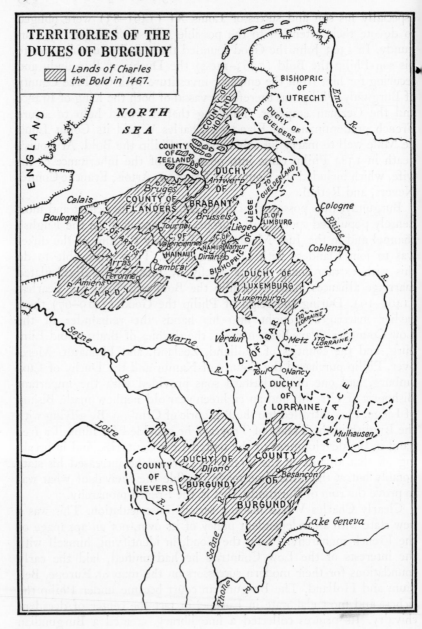

TERRITORIES OF THE
DUKES OF BURGUNDY

Lands of Charles
the Bold in 1467.

school of history, and patronized lavishly painting and sculpture.[30] They taught European courts for centuries to come the meaning of an involved ceremonial etiquette, and at least Philip the Good with his twenty-four mistresses put Charles VII's harem to shame. It was no wonder that the Duke of Burgundy, the vassal of the French king and the German emperor for all of his territory, aspired to be an independent king. His idea was to get the German emperor to revive the kingdom of Lothair of the Treaty of Verdun (843)[31] for him, and when thwarted refused the title of King of Brabant instead. But whether a kingdom or not, Burgundy was in fact a new independent state, a fifteenth-century revival of the old Lotharingia. Whether it any more than its predecessor could preserve a separate existence was the question of the moment.

While Louis XI was dauphin he had been obliged to throw him- *Louis XI* self on the mercy of the man who was to become Duke of Burgundy as Charles the Bold (1467–77). Louis had been an utterly faithless son. He simply could not wait until his father died. He had led the *Praguerie* in 1440, and his conduct in Dauphiné was so treasonable that his father drove him out and annexed the area to the royal domain in 1456. Charles VII in his later years was always afraid of being poisoned by his son. Deprived of Dauphiné he had accepted the favor of Charles the Bold. But once king, he forgot all obligations of gratitude.

In fact Louis XI was a very disagreeable king. He had not come into much by way of physical inheritance from his father and grandfather. A long nose and long legs made his appearance ungainly. He hated the pomp and circumstance of royalty and preferred to dress shabbily, partly in order to consort with ease with the bourgeois of the realm. For Louis was a complete break with the chivalrous past. He had no use for its pageantry in joust or tournament. He disliked to stake all his gains on the outcome of a battle and chose rather to negotiate when he could. He disliked Paris, and by choice stayed in the Loire country or went traveling about his realm, staying with the bourgeois families but detesting any kind of public welcomes or receptions. He was such a constant traveler that a clerk from Évreux had to follow him for sixty-five days before he could deliver a message. Religion he viewed with a cold practicality; he paid homage to the saints and their relics for what they could do for him. "He was expert in corrupting the saints of his enemies whom he sometimes induced

[30] See pp. 1024–27.
[31] See p. 281.

to be neutral or even to transfer their patronage." [32] He had no more love for his wife or his mistresses than he had for his children. The former were a means to produce children, whose chief reason for existence was to bring political gains to the state through marriage.

Louis XI was a new type of closeted, letter-writing monarch, carrying on a large correspondence with kings and princes and notably with his fellows in spirit, the Italian despots. He was in general a master diplomat, heralding a new era of wily international diplomacy in the skill with which he manipulated foreign ambassadors and his own agents. If there was one thing he was willing to spend money on it was in promoting his schemes through his agents. He was so much in his element when concocting conspiracies that he was known as "the universal spider." Louis's political views were of course those of absolute monarchy. "The Council," it was said, "rode on his mule." He made no demands of his political servitors except to be loyally served, and he was relentless and cruel in his punishment of disloyalty. He was fond of identifying himself with his kingdom and repeated often, "I am France."

A large part of his gains came after he had brought about the downfall of Burgundy. Charles the Bold was no match for him and the king knew it. The last Duke of Burgundy was like him in his zeal for hard work, a kind of foolishness that Charles's courtiers prayed that he would stop. Where Louis was not conspicuously incontinent, *The struggle between Louis XI and Charles the Bold* Charles to his court was painfully so; where Louis hated the game of chivalry and the ceremony of court, Charles was devoted to both and exhausted his court with his heavy drawn-out formality and his love for endless speech making. But Charles was stupid and Louis was not. The duke knew neither how to govern nor how to command an army. In his ambitious pursuit of the policy established by his predecessors, he knew not when to call a halt when obviously beaten or when circumstances obviously called for a temporary one. Until 1473 Charles was largely concerned in defending himself against Louis XI, since the king was patently intent on crippling Burgundian power. Louis had enraged the easily angered Charles by buying back the Somme towns in 1463 in accordance with the Treaty of Arras.

Two years later, while still the Count of Charolais, Charles directed a formidable group of French nobles, who called themselves the League of Public Weal, in a revolt against the king. Louis felt obliged to negotiate rather than prolong the fight, and Charles recovered the Somme towns. When the French king paid no attention to the treaties

---

[32] Waugh, *op. cit.*, p. 241.

made, Charles formed another league against his shifty foe and marched on Paris. At this point Louis begged for a personal interview with Charles at Péronne (October 1468). But the French king had forgotten to call off agents whom he had sent to Liége to stir up a rebellion against the duke, and in the midst of the interview Charles received the astounding news that because of the activity of his guest's agents, Liége had revolted and killed its bishop. The duke went into an uncontrollable rage and Louis was at his mercy. He was obliged to agree to anything. In addition to other gains, Charles got more territory on the Somme and Louis was obliged to accompany him to Liége to see just how thoroughly the Duke of Burgundy punished a city rebelling in the name of the King of France. Louis went along, but when once home he never forgot this humiliating experience.

A compliant assembly of nobles ruled that he was not bound by his treaties with a felonious duke, and the two were at war again in 1471. Charles allied with the English in an invasion of France in 1475,[33] which Louis, who meanwhile had completely gained the mastery of the situation within France, easily bought off. Charles, now abandoned by the English and engrossed in his schemes for completing the unification of Burgundy, made a nine-year truce with Louis in the same year. The French king fought henceforth with secret agents and money, until less than two years later he learned "the good and agreeable" news of Charles's death.

The first object of Charles's Burgundian policy was to remove the gap formed by Alsace and Lorraine between his Burgundian and lower Rhine territories. That done, he could look to further expansion at the expense of the empire and to raising his state to the dignity of a kingdom. The success of Burgundy was not only therefore a threat to France as she conceived it, but also a step in the diminution and decline of the German empire. In 1469, for fifty thousand florins advanced to the Hapsburg Duke Sigismund of Tyrol, he secured in pledge a bundle of rights, including those of count and landgrave, and a number of cities, in upper Alsace and Swabia, and began to act immediately as if he were lord and owner. In 1473, at the death of its duke, he annexed Guelders. In the same year, René of Lorraine by treaty recognized Charles as protector of his duchy and permitted him to send troops through Lorraine from one group of his territories to the other. Charles outraged the Lorrainers by putting garrisons in many of their towns.

Again in the same year the duke met the Emperor Frederick III at

The growth of Burgundian strength

[33] See p. 894.

Trier to complete the Burgundian edifice by entering into negotiations for the marriage of his daughter Mary with Frederick's son and heir Maximilian. Since there were many bids for Mary's hand Charles's demands had been high. He was to be elected King of the Romans—that is to say, made emperor elect. He even made it plain that he wouldn't mind having the imperial title immediately. Frederick countered with the suggestion that Burgundy might be made a kingdom, and at Trier it was agreed that Utrecht, Liége, Toul, Verdun, and the duchies of Cleves, Lorraine, and Savoy were to form a part of the new kingdom. Then when everything was thought to be arranged for this grand climax, Charles learned with astonishment that the emperor had left Trier on the night of November 24, was already way down the beautiful Moselle valley, and wouldn't come back. What happened nobody really knows. At least Louis XI had agents and money in Trier.

The harsh administration of Burgundian officials in upper Alsace, the aroused opposition of the Swiss to the growth of Burgundy, the dissatisfaction of René of Lorraine, the hope of Sigismund that he might get his rights and lands back, the cunning of Louis XI, all led *The end of Charles the Bold* to a series of alliances against Charles the Bold. A combination primarily of Alsatian towns formed the Lower Union in 1473. The next year it was joined by the Swiss, who were paid by Louis XI and Sigismund, and arrangements were made to redeem the latter's mortgage of his rights and lands to Charles the Bold. When Charles attacked the town of Neuss for the Archbishop of Cologne in 1474, the German emperor and Diet promised to help the Swiss against Charles. The Swiss declared war, defeated Charles in Alsace, and Sigismund was now recognized again in his Alsatian territory. Next spring, René of Lorraine joined the alliance.

Finally the duke began his offensive. After driving René from Nancy, the capital of Lorraine, he moved against the Swiss, who were harrowing Franche-Comté and the Vaud, belonging to Charles's ally, Savoy. At Granson, on Lake Neuchâtel, he was defeated once. After reorganizing his army at Lausanne he moved on towards Berne, but stopped to besiege Morat on the way. Here his army in its second defeat was slaughtered (June 1476) by an army of Swiss pikemen and halberdiers and German and Lorraine cavalry. Instead of stopping now to recover, and in spite of the fact that his allies and his own territories were deserting him, Charles took to more drink and determined to recapture Nancy from René, who had retaken it in October. But on January 5, 1477, before Nancy, half his army, thoroughly corrupted by French gold, deserted him, and the other half was badly beaten by an army of Lorrainers, Alsatians, and Swiss. Charles's naked body was later found frozen in the mud, his head split open by a Swiss halberd, his face eaten away by wolves.

The plans for a Burgundian middle kingdom were thus destroyed by a mixture composed chiefly of Louis XI's gold, Swiss troops, and the impetuous folly of Charles the Bold. Louis XI immediately claimed the inheritance of Burgundy's French fiefs on the theory that they could not be inherited by Charles's daughter or wife and more-over were confiscate because Charles was a rebellious vassal. In addi- *Expansion* tion he hoped to add Franche-Comté and Hainault to France. The *of the royal* Duchy of Burgundy he annexed without too much difficulty. The *domain under* Swiss had occupied Franche-Comté, but they sold out to Louis, and he *Louis XI* annexed it too after much greater difficulty. He proceeded then to take Picardy, and annexed Artois after forcing the resisting inhab-itants of Arras to get out and make way for new townsmen collected from the rest of France. Elsewhere in the Burgundian territories, i.e., in Flanders and Hainault, he failed. He confirmed his occupa-tion of Artois and Franche-Comté by arranging for the marriage of the dauphin with Margaret, the daughter of Maximilian and Mary of Burgundy, who was to bring as her dowry these two provinces. Be-sides these Burgundian additions Louis took advantage of a dynastic dispute in Aragon to conquer Roussillon and Cerdagne. He contem-plated the extinction of the house of Orléans by obliging Duke Louis to marry one of his daughters who he knew could never have any children. At the death of René of Anjou he joined Anjou and Bar to his royal domain and at the death of Charles of Maine, to whom René had left Provence, both Maine and Provence. At his death, therefore, which he could not prevent with either saints, miracles, or relics, Louis XI had the distinction of uniting more territory to the royal domain than any French king since Philip Augustus. The only large independent French fiefs that had not been added to the domain were Flanders and Brittany.

Flanders had been lost forever to France by the marriage of Mary of Burgundy to Maximilian in 1477. Brittany was brought into the domain through the marriage of Louis's son and successor Charles *The comple-* VIII (1483–98). When the last Duke of Brittany, Francis I, died in *tion of French* 1488, the local nobles, in a final effort to preserve the independence of *territorial uni-* the duchy, married his heiress Anne by proxy to Maximilian, who had *fication* been left a widower by the death of Mary of Burgundy in 1482. A French army invaded the duchy and obliged Anne to exchange her

Hapsburg husband for young Charles VIII. With this completion of the territorial unification of France, the king could now think, as German emperors and English kings had thought, of carrying France outside her boundaries, and of creating an empire in Italy. To prepare for the Italian campaign Charles abandoned some of the gains of his father. He gave back Roussillon and Cerdagne to Spain in 1493. Since, too, Charles VIII had had to break off his agreement to marry Margaret, Maximilian's daughter, in order to marry Anne of Brittany, her dowry of Artois and Franche-Comté was returned to her father. Louis XI and Charles both carried on and strengthened the administrative and military reform of the French monarchy inaugurated by Charles VII.

Viewed externally the task that the Capetians had set themselves may be considered accomplished. The civil and financial administration of the king was fixed in its main lines for centuries. Except for Artois and Flanders, the great fiefs of the old nobles, of the English, and of the newer appanaged princes of the blood had been annexed to the royal domain. The attempts of the older feudalism to preserve its local autonomy and of the newer feudalism to control the monarchy in its own interest had failed. The absolute king had triumphed, but his was only a superficial victory. For another century and a half the French kings had to fight the nobles before actually depriving them of political power, and after that fight had been won again, it took a period of equal length before they lost their social and economic privileges. In completing the territorial unification the Valois kings had at the same time been unable to prevent the rise of a strong Hapsburg power on their northern and eastern frontiers. The fight against England and Burgundy had no sooner been won at great cost than the fight with the Hapsburgs began.

We have noticed that that part of the Burgundian inheritance not added to France by Louis XI went to the Hapsburgs after the death in 1482 of Mary of Burgundy, wife of the Maximilian who became German emperor in 1493. The possibility of the union of these large territories with Spain was contained in the marriage of Philip the Fair, the son of Mary and Maximilian, with Joanna, the daughter of Ferdinand and Isabella, in 1496. We are scarcely concerned with the actual consummation of that union of territory in the person of Charles V, but rather in the fact that there was a Spain for Charles V to inherit. When last treated [34] the Spanish peninsula was divided between the four kingdoms of Portugal, Castile, Aragon, and Navarre,

Spain in the fourteenth and fifteenth centuries

[34] See pp. 551 ff.

FRANCE
SHOWING ADDITIONS TO THE MONARCHY
BETWEEN 1273 & 1494

Shaded Area shows
Possessions of the
English King in France
upon the Accession of
Henry VI, 1422

two of which, Castile and Aragon, had almost completed the crusade against the Mohammedans in Spain by the conquest of all the Moorish territory in the peninsula except the Kingdom of Granada. The period of the fourteenth and fifteenth centuries marked a halt in the advance against the Moors. By the monarchs of Castile, to whom they paid tribute, the rulers of Granada were regarded as quite harmless. Moreover, the internal history of both Castile and Aragon during this period incapacitated them somewhat for expansion in the south. In both kingdoms there was a never-ending succession of squabbles between the crown and a strongly entrenched local nobility striving to preserve its liberties against a monarchy growing in strength, and besides, regular struggles for the throne between the princes of the blood, the infantes. Dynastic struggles, feudal wars, disputes over the boundaries between the kingdoms altogether make melancholy reading.

In spite of them Aragon was able to establish a Mediterranean empire that included the Balearic Islands, nominal control over Sardinia and Corsica, and indirect control, through the dynasties of younger sons,[35] of Naples and Sicily. For a while the Aragonese were established as successors of several crusading states in the Morea in Greece. Altogether this gave them control over the western Mediterranean. But out of the internal chaos in both kingdoms there came nothing that we need report until in 1469; then Ferdinand, the son of King John II of Aragon, slipped away with a few companions disguised as merchants to Valladolid, in Castile, to marry Isabella, the half-sister of Henry the Impotent, King of Castile. The expenses of the ceremony had to be paid for with borrowed money. It made Louis XI furious, and he did what he could to undo it. For it happened to be the most important dynastic marriage of the century.

Isabella became Queen of Castile in 1474, and Ferdinand King of Aragon in 1479. Henceforth, although the kingdoms were joined in only a personal union, the two monarchs called themselves King and Queen of Spain. Indeed, they set about to make what we may truly call for the first time Spain. They completed, except for Portugal, the territorial union of the peninsula first by taking advantage of war in France to annex that part of the Kingdom of Navarre south of the Pyrenees. They next set about to complete the crusade against the Moors by taking the Kingdom of Granada. After the Moors refused tribute and captured a border fortress, the last campaign against them began in earnest. Málaga was taken in 1487, and a long siege of

[35] See p. 1007.

Granada terminated in 1491. By January 1492 negotiations over the *The comple-*
terms of the surrender were completed. The end of some seven hun- *tion of the*
dred years of warfare against the Mohammedans in Spain led to the *territorial*
forceful Christianizing of the Moors by means of the new Spanish *unification*
Inquisition, from which many fled. In gratitude to God for this suc- *of Spain*
cessful issue of the crusade Ferdinand and Isabella decreed the expulsion of the Jews from their kingdoms, thus driving out about two
hundred thousand people.

For some time they had been persecuted by the furious zeal of the
new Inquisition, which the monarchs had set up in 1478 free from all
papal control. Its personnel was supervised by the monarchs themselves, and under the terrible leadership of Torquemada it acted
chiefly as an instrument of state in leveling out all religious differences, confiscating the property of Jews and Moors, and terrifying
clergy and laymen into abject submission to the will of the monarchs.
The Inquisition may be regarded too as an instrument of the monarchs
in reducing the independent Spanish Church to obedience to the state.
When added to the control of appointments of the clergy, it was also
a means of instituting that reform of the Spanish Church under the
leadership of Cardinal Ximenes which set off the Spanish clergy from
those in the rest of western Europe and began the so-called counterreformation of the sixteenth century. That Ferdinand forced himself
upon the three great military orders in Spain as their grand master
reveals that here the monarchs were achieving the same control over
the Church that had been already accomplished elsewhere in western
Europe by this time.

The ecclesiastical policy of the new monarchs was but a part of
their larger effort to reduce the feudal elements in the state to the
will of the king. In Castile, where the crown was weakest, this was
undertaken as in France with the enthusiastic support of the towns.
The earlier *hermandades* were grouped into one large Holy Brotherhood, which brought two thousand horse into the royal army. Although the work of internal consolidation had to be followed up by
Ferdinand and Isabella's successors, enough was done to permit Spain
to enter into the area of international politics by contesting with
France for Italy. In October 1492 Columbus landed in the Bahamas.
The emergence of Spain and Portugal as world powers with far-flung
colonial empires is a theme that can best be considered elsewhere [36]
in its relation to earlier medieval expansion.

[36] See pp. 1030 ff.

Chapter 27

CENTRAL AND EASTERN EUROPE IN THE FOUR-
TEENTH AND FIFTEENTH CENTURIES

The nobility dominant in central and eastern Europe

THE chaotic history of central and eastern Europe in the fourteenth and fifteenth centuries witnessed no rise of the strong dynastic state, as did western Europe. Generally speaking, and with the exception of Muscovite Russia and the Ottoman empire, the feudal nobility and the territorial princes triumphed over monarchy. After all that has been said of the previous history of Germany, it would certainly be strange now to have to record that in this later period the whole trend of German history was bent in another direction. If attention is turned to the kingdoms outside of the German empire—to the Danish, Norwegian, Swedish, Polish-Lithuanian, Hungarian, Bulgarian, and Serbian kingdoms—it will be seen that the nobles rather than the kings really held the reins, and that they held them more firmly at the time chosen to close this account. Until the very end of the fifteenth century, Russia was a furor of warring princes, and the exception of the Ottoman Turks is not much to the point, inasmuch as the growth of their state was rather Asiatic than European in character.

The contrast between western and eastern Europe

It would be difficult, and hardly within our province, adequately to account for the political diversity between eastern and western Europe. To do so would necessitate describing the different levels of culture between west and east, and showing how the political needs of eastern Europe in the fourteenth and fifteenth centuries were similar to those of western Europe in the ninth, tenth, and eleventh centuries. The strong, efficient monarchy of the west was indubitably an improvement over feudalism. In the absence of a strong monarchy, the increasing strength of the German territorial prince was still an improvement over feudalism. If beyond the German empire, feudalism or its local equivalent raged rampant, that is perhaps another way of saying that eastern Europe was two centuries behind western Europe in political development and in all those phases that contributed to the peculiar political development of the west. Germany would therefore mark an intermediary stage.

From the point of view of general European development, therefore, the subject matter of this chapter gains significance as illustrative of the conflict between western and eastern Europe as represented chiefly by Latin-Roman and Greek-Byzantine Christianity. More particularly, it affords additional evidence of that extraordinary ability to expand, already noted as one of the chief characteristics of early western civilization.[1] Since the expansion of western civilization to northern and eastern Europe was almost exclusively the work of German secular and regular clergy, a German crusading order, German nobles, German merchants, and German peasants, in a narrower sense what took place was a Germanization of northern and eastern Europe. Because this expansion was in large part at the expense of Slavic peoples, and precipitated among them a resistance that may properly be called national, the history of this area may be held to demonstrate the old conflict between the Germanic and Slavic peoples. But German civilization spread also among non-Slavic peoples, among the Scandinavians, for example, and the Hungarians. Their resistance was in the end similar to the Slavic, and correspondingly as national.

The conflict between German and Slav

But whether conceived of as conflict between west and east, or between German and Slav, or as a kind of medieval national conflict, these issues are themselves diminished in general importance by the fact that both eastern and western Europe were threatened seriously by the renewed attacks of Mongolian peoples out of central Asia, notably the Tartars, already mentioned,[2] and the formidable Ottoman Turks. Since these Asiatic peoples took more readily to Islam than to Christianity, the old conflict between Asia and Europe and Mohammedanism and Christianity, already treated in connection with the expansion of the Arabs and the Seljuk Turks, was revived in a much more serious and permanent form. That is only to say that the crusades in Spain and in the Holy Land were but transferred in the fourteenth and fifteenth centuries to another front, the front of southeastern Europe. It is just since the last great war that the crusade against the Ottoman Turks has been brought to an end, if it really has been brought to an end, by their practical expulsion from Europe. Since, too, the Ottoman empire preserved rather than destroyed the main features of Byzantine civilization, and since, after freeing itself from

The revival of the crusades in southeastern Europe

[1] See pp. 1–2.
[2] See pp. 548–49.

the Tartar yoke, Russia, after the fall of Constantinople, emerged as a new Slav Byzantium, we may speak, in spite of all appearances to the contrary, of a revival of Byzantine influence. That means also a revival of the tradition of Roman imperialism. The shade of Justinian haunts the east at the end of this period as his living self had dominated it at the beginning.

A world or European state under the successor of the Roman emperor never became much of a reality in the middle ages. The growth of the dynastic states in the west pushed it more and more into the realm of those fine ideals to which the best men always cling even when circumstances are at their worst. In the particular form of the German Holy Roman empire, the ideal had come closer to realization. But we have already had to speak of the fall of the empire with the extinction of the Hohenstaufen family. The fourteenth and fifteenth centuries brought no revival. In the western borderlands French civilization pushed into the empire. The expansion of Burgundy was the growth essentially of a French state at the cost of the empire, and when it collapsed at the death of Charles the Bold, it was France that profited at the expense of the empire. Savoy, Dauphiné, and Provence were lost even more irretrievably than ever, and in this chapter the loss of those lands comprising Switzerland will be discussed.

The further decline of the Holy Roman empire

On the north and in the east the situation was the same. The former dependency of Denmark, Poland, and Hungary was lost. Although Bohemia and Austria remained within the formal boundaries of the empire they were to all intents and purposes independent states. The empire regained no hold on the Italian states after the collapse of Frederick II's empire. Yet the force of tradition and the actual need of some kind of larger political organization preserved the formal existence of the powerless German empire when but a few would have really missed it had it disappeared. The imperial title remained the prerogative of the German kings while few of them, no matter how interested in having the distinction of the title of Roman emperor, were very seriously interested in doing anything about the empire. The contrast between empire in theory and ideal and empire in fact became more glaring and ridiculous than ever.

The further decline of German kingship

As much might be said of the German kingdom. It almost disappeared during the period of the Interregnum (1256–73), and had it never been revived it would not have been seriously missed. Long before this actual period it had surrendered to the German secular and ecclesiastical princes most of the lands and regalian rights that would have made anything of it as a political power. There were at the end of the Hohenstaufen period few crown lands left. Frederick II in his privileges of 1220 and 1231 [3] had made the princes practically independent within their own small domains. All possibility of building up a royal financial and judicial administration, a royal army, and a royal system of taxation had disappeared. The kingship remained a dignity without the power inseparably connected with the imperial dignity, and was retained because it might prove useful for some things that had nothing to do with royal government. Indeed, the German princes and nobles had become so indifferent to it that they had long neglected to participate in royal elections, and abandoned their general right to a small group of electors composed finally of seven, the archbishops of Mainz, Trier, and Cologne, and the secular heads of the Palatinate, Brandenburg, Saxony, and Bohemia, four western and three eastern powers.

Out of the old feudal *Reichstag,* or *curia regis,* of the German kings the thirteenth century saw the development of the Diet, the German equivalent of the English Parliament and the French States-General. Composed first of two houses which usually met separately, the electors and the princes, it did not admit the German towns as a third house until 1489, although in fact individual towns were consulted as early as the thirteenth century. As late as the beginning of the sixteenth century, the Germans had shown so little general political capacity that no one was certain what this Diet could or could not do. Did a majority decision bind the minority? Were those who did not attend bound by the decisions of those who did attend? Did individual attendance depend upon royal summons? Could a Diet meet without the summons of the king? These questions were all unsettled. When the Diet did come to a decision, it negotiated with the king as with an independent power; and if there resulted some agreement, what was known as a recess was promulgated. When once promulgated, however, it was obeyed or not as the individual princes chose, for there was no royal power that could enforce a recess. In fact, the members of the German Diet were interested chiefly in only one thing—preventing the German kingdom and empire from ever amounting to anything that might interfere with their own independent positions within their little states. Every attempt to reform this situation, to provide some little means for acting as a whole, failed hopelessly.

This is only to say in a final way what we have repeatedly demonstrated to be the trend of German political history: it ended in the extreme localism of the German territorial noble. With an impotent em-

[3] See pp. 418–19.

peror and king, it might therefore be expected that the history of Germany during this period was even more chaotic than French history during the same period. And so at first sight it was. There were rivalries among the princes for the royal-imperial title, unashamed bribery of the electors, double elections and consequent civil wars, incessant squabbling among the princes themselves, wars between princes and nobles, between the nobles themselves, between princes and nobles and the unique survival in Germany of the free imperial knights, those robber-barons and professional kidnappers who professed allegiance to the emperor alone, between princes, nobles, knights and the towns, between the towns themselves. Within the towns there were constant clashes between the patrician merchants and the artisans, between rich and poor. Private warfare was rather generally unrestrained. The only way out of the general anarchy was the organization of private leagues of towns, or of towns and nobles. Some attempts were made to institute secular truces of God in the *Landfrieden,* regional agreements between nobles or nobles and towns, sometimes organized or supported by the emperors themselves, to preserve the peace for a definite period of time. Their great number must have had some effect in reducing private warfare, but on the whole it remained an unabated evil. Only within the walls of the German towns was there anything like peace, comfort, and prosperity.

Yet German history was not wholly without rime or reason during this period. From one point of view the chaotic political history may be viewed as a struggle between the older western ecclesiastical states along the Rhine, and the new eastern secular states formed as a result of German expansion. In the twelfth and thirteenth centuries the Rhenish ecclesiastical states had reached the height of their influence. Beginning on the lower Rhine with the bishoprics of Utrecht and Liége and continuing up the Rhine and its tributaries with the archbishoprics of Cologne, Trier, and Mainz and the bishoprics of Metz, Toul, Verdun, and Strassburg, to Basel and Constance, they kept down the small feudal princes of the Rhine valley and made it the heart of the empire, truly "the priest's road of the Holy Roman empire." The Hohenstaufens had relied to a great extent on their strength. The three archbishops had become the leaders in the electoral college. After the fall of the Hohenstaufens it was the intention of these princes to preserve their position of great importance in the state by controlling the elections to the German crown. Their method was always to elect small and harmless princelets of the Rhine valley who were obliged to pay heavily in money and favors for the title.

Yet the peculiar character of an ecclesiastical state whose head had no great incentive for expansion because unable to found a dynasty, and who was constantly at war with the rising power of his cathedral chapter, itself composed more and more of younger sons of the surrounding nobility, prevented the bishops and archbishops from retaining their earlier prestige. The balance of power within Germany gradually shifted eastwards to those large secular states, Brandenburg, Saxony, Bohemia, and Austria, carved out of eastern colonial territory. Brandenburg, Saxony, and Bohemia received admittance into the electoral college. But the churchmen of the west invariably fought these rising eastern powers, who themselves in turn supported the cathedral chapters against the bishops. The Archbishop of Mainz usually led the ecclesiastical princes of the west. When it was no longer possible to keep the eastern powers from securing the throne and using it to strengthen their own local positions, and to expand territorially, then the churchmen answered by broaching within the Diet programs of reform that would limit the powers of the eastern princes by saddling them with permanent advisory bodies of noble counsellors. The ultimate defeat of the Rhenish bishops and archbishops was but another evidence of the growing secularity of medieval society.

The best way, however, to understand German history in this period is to watch the individual territorial states themselves. Here indeed we may find a counterpart of the chief theme of western European history on a smaller scale. For it is in this period that the local *The growth* families which later dominated German history—the counts of Würt- *of the German* emberg and the Margrave of Baden, the Wittelsbach dukes of Ba- *territorial* varia, the Austrian Hapsburgs, and the Hohenzollerns of Branden- *state* burg—laid the foundations of their subsequent strength, and began the long rivalry between them which ultimately reduced itself to a struggle between Hohenzollerns and Hapsburgs for the mastery of Germany. Here we might, if we chose, trace the beginnings of an internal dynastic policy within the more important of these states similar in all its main features, even though on a smaller scale, to the policy of the Capetians. These territorial princes when once they had freed themselves from king and emperor were wholly preoccupied with making themselves masters within their states and with territorial expansion. Whatever national sentiment they possessed was directed primarily against the Church.[4] They were interested in the king-emperor for what there was still to get out of him, and they strove for the royal title because it was still useful in case local dynas-

[4] See pp. 991–92.

ties died out, to bring these territories into the control of their own families through the exercise of the feudal right of escheat. When powerful enough these local princes as kings could sometimes confiscate territory to their own advantage.

Their whole policy was directed in the interests of their dynasty their family, what the Germans call *Hauspolitik*. As in the case of the Capetians they had to solve the problem of partitioning their lands among heirs. But it was only in the fifteenth century that out side the electorates succession by primogeniture to the whole family inheritance was adopted here and there. Within the boundaries of their states they had to subdue a turbulent nobility and autonomous towns. They had also to contend with the interests of the nobility represented in the local *Landtage* or provincial estates that rose to great influence in the latter half of the thirteenth century in all Germany. Along these lines, particularly in the Hohenzollern and Hapsburg lands, advances were made by the end of the fifteenth century. The earlier tribal localism of the tribal duchy was transferred through the medium of feudalism into a territorial and dynastic localism that has remained to this date the cardinal fact in all German political history.

The first really foreign ruler to abandon Germany to her warring princes for the sake of his large imperial and Sicilian interests was Frederick II. What he left undone to throw Germany into confusion the popes, in their struggle with him, completed.[5] At the death of Frederick's son Conrad IV, in 1254, and that of the antiking, Count William of Holland two years later, the German princes had for so long enjoyed the freedom of being essentially without a king that they did not intend to reintroduce a German one. A small group of electors chose first as king an Englishman, Richard of Cornwall, and those who felt that they had not been sufficiently well bribed by Richard turned to Alfonso X, King of Castile. Neither candidate, of course, pretended to exercise any real influence in Germany. It is the ensuing anarchy, rather than the absence of a person holding the royal title, that justifies the term "Interregnum" for this period.

It was terminated formally by Pope Gregory X in 1273, after the death of Richard of Cornwall. At that moment, as at subsequent ones

The Interregnum

there were new foreign contestants for the throne; they were Philip III of France and the powerful Ottokar II of Bohemia. Seeing that Germany was sufficiently weakened, even to the point of diminishing Rome's income, and looking for someone to lead a new crusade and

[5] See pp. 427–28.

o help support him against the Angevin house at Naples, Gregory rdered the German electors to elect a king, or he would proceed o appoint one himself. The electors did the best they could under the ircumstances, and elected what they thought was a perfectly harmless mall German count, Rudolf of Hapsburg (1273–91). The Haps- urgs took their name from a castle, Hapsburg, or Hawk's Castle, in outhern Swabia. Although tracing their lineage back to the tenth entury, the fortunes of the family really began when in the twelfth entury they acquired the Landgraviate of Alsace, the County of Zurich, and the advocacy of several Swiss monasteries, to which they dded in the first half of the thirteenth century additional counties, ands, fiefs, and monasteries in Switzerland. But if "Interregnum" ndicates no more than the absence of strong royal authority in Ger- nany, the election of Rudolf can hardly be said to terminate it. It rent on for centuries.

Rudolf was quite indifferent to the imperial tradition, and didn't *Rudolf of* other to seek the title of emperor by a coronation in Rome. In fact *Hapsburg* one of his successors until Henry VII of Luxemburg troubled to go ɔ Italy. But Rudolf was very much interested in increasing the power f his own dynasty, and his royal title fortunately gave him, at the noment, an opportunity to increase the family holdings at the expense f Ottokar II, King of Bohemia. One of the powers still exercised by ne German king was his right to regrant imperial fiefs when there rere no longer heirs. In 1246 the Babenberg house in Austria and ne adjoining lands of Styria, Carinthia, and Carniola had died out. heir imperial lands were occupied without formal grant by Ottokar, nd when he refused to recognize Rudolf's election, the German king ot only declared him an outlaw and declared his Austrian lands orfeited but prepared to gather in this rich Babenberg inheritance. t took two military campaigns supported by papal money to do it, but y 1282 Rudolf had succeeded in adding to the southwestern lands of ne Hapsburgs this extensive area of colonial territory in the east. By se of his royal rights he had raised his family almost overnight to ne of the most important among all those of Germany. At Vienna, n the Danube, the Hapsburgs were to remain until 1918.

Somewhat stunned by this unexpected turn of Hapsburg fortune nd determined to preserve their electoral rights, the electors refused ɔ hear of electing Rudolf's son Albrecht to succeed him, but chose nstead—and were well paid for it—a second harmless count of the hine valley, Adolf of Nassau (1292–98). The history of Rudolf's *Adolf of* ːign threatened to repeat itself. The new *Pfaffenkönig* (priests' *Nassau*

king), as he was called, tried to use his royal power to gather in th
inheritance of the Wettin family in the Margraviate of Meissen, an
the Landgraviate of Thuringia as well, and to establish his house o
the eastern frontier as the Hapsburgs had done. But his military suc
cesses in Meissen and Thuringia cost him the support of the elector
who, when he was no longer content to play their game, deposed hir
and summoned Albrecht of Austria into the field against him. Nea
Göllheim, the Hapsburg duke slashed his rival in the face with hi
sword and left him to perish in a battle that raised him, the second o
his family, to the German throne.

The grounds of the hostility of the Rhenish electoral prince
towards any strong king were thoroughly revealed during the cours

Albrecht of
Austria

of Albrecht's reign (1298–1308). One of the archbishops as he wa
about to go hunting might say of the danger of Albrecht's power tha
it wasn't much to worry about, since he had many little kings in hi
hunting jacket, but events proved otherwise. Albrecht was determine
to support the Rhenish cities against the electoral princes in the de
mand that the numerous new toll stations set up along the Rhin
since the days of Frederick II be abolished. The right to regulat
tolls was a regalian right. When the three ecclesiastical electors o
Mainz, Trier, and Cologne and the Count of the Palatinate organize
a revolt against him, the Hapsburg king defeated them in successior
and had no more trouble from them for the rest of his short reigr
He too attempted to take heirless fiefs for his family. When th
family of the counts of Holland and Zeeland died out, he prepare
to gather in these areas, just as the revolt of the Rhenish elector
broke out. Bohemia and Moravia he actually turned over to his so
Rudolf, at the death in 1306 of Wenzel III, the last of the Premsy
dynasty. He was preparing to take up Adolf of Nassau's claim t
Meissen and Thuringia when, not far from the original Castle c
Hapsburg, in southern Swabia, he was murdered by a gang of cor
spirators that included his own nephew.

The electors returned again to their old policy of choosing a wea
Rhenish prince as king. Their choice was the French-speaking brothe

Henry of Lux-
emburg

of Archbishop Baldwin of Trier, Henry, Count of Luxemburg (1308–
13), who was thus repaid by his brother for getting him the Arch
bishopric of Trier to begin with. Once again, however, the royal titl
was of great advantage to a petty western house whose territory ha
come completely under the domination of France, and once again thi
advantage came from the east, in Bohemia. Internal difficulties i
Bohemia gave Henry his chance. An opposition party there supportin

AUSTRIAN LANDS
TO 1527

Acquired 1282
Acquired 1282-1521
Acquired 1521-1526
Acquired after 1526
Temporary possessions

the claims of Elizabeth, the younger sister of Wenzel III, to the Bohemian throne, over and against King Henry of Carinthia, invited the new German king to marry his son John to Elizabeth and invest them both with the Bohemian crown. Only too glad to forestall the Hapsburg claims to Bohemia, Henry married John to Elizabeth in 1310, and invested him with a Bohemia that he was obliged to conquer. The Luxemburgers were now established in the east, where indeed they were to remain for over a century, wearing, in addition to the Bohemian, the German royal and imperial crowns. For more than a century, too, the internal history of Germany was to center around the rivalry between the Luxemburg and Hapsburg houses. With this success behind him Henry could turn to the realization of another fond dream, the restoration, after such long neglect by the German kings, of the imperial program in Italy.

Thereto he was originally urged by the first pope at Avignon, Clement V, who sought in Henry a convenient instrument for papal ends in the Italy that the popes themselves had abandoned. And thereto he was called by such passionate Ghibellines as Dante, who tried to convince the Italians just how necessary the empire was as a peace bringer to a strife-ridden country. Henry received both the Lombard crown at Milan and the imperial crown in Rome; but when his plans for the re-establishment of empire became so realistic as to lead him into war with what he regarded as the usurping French King of Naples, both pope and Philip IV of France did what they could to thwart him. Henry never returned to Germany. He died near Siena when about to start his campaign against Naples. To us his imperial dream has a curious anachronistic touch. To him, however, and to Dante it meant the salvation of the world.

Louis of Bavaria

To some of the electors in 1314, Louis, the Duke of Upper Bavaria, seemed a less dangerous candidate than either the Luxemburg King John of Bohemia or the Hapsburg Duke Frederick the Handsome. With the help of the Luxemburg party, Louis was elected. But the Hapsburgs were not so easily crowded out of the picture, and a second election made Frederick the Handsome king. Germany was torn for eight years by civil war, until at Mühldorf in 1322, with the aid of the Hohenzollern Burgrave of Nuremberg, Louis of Bavaria secured the upper hand. Not, however, until the death of Frederick in 1330 was the struggle for the throne really ended.

Louis was hampered during his whole reign by conflict with the French papacy at Avignon,[6] yet even this conflict did not prevent his

[6] See p. 960.

EUROPE

IN THE FOURTEENTH CENTURY

– – – *Boundary of the Holy Roman Empire*

Luxemburg dominions

Wittelsbach   *"*

Hapsburg   *"*

English Miles

0 100 200 300 400 500

Map labels:

Shetland Is

Orkney Is

Stavanger

Bergen

K. OF NORWAY

K. OF SCOTLAND

Edinburgh

IRELAND

Dublin

York

Boston

K. OF ENGLAND

London

NORTH SEA

K. OF DENMARK

Copenhagen

Calais

Holland

Utrecht

Bremen

Oldenburg

Westphalia

Cologne

Brun

Berlin

Branden burg

Leipzig

Dresden

Saxony

Bohemia

Channel Is

Brest

Paris

Seine

Orleans

Nantes

Loire

Aachen

Luxem

Treves

Mainz

Frankfort

Strasbg

Basel

Lorraine

Munich

Vienna

Salzburg

K. OF FRANCE

Duchy of Aquitaine

Bordeaux

Toulouse

Avignon

Provence

Marseille

Lyons

Rhone

Genoa

Tirol

Lands of the Visconti

Milan

Venice

Florence

PAPAL STATES

Rome

K. OF NAPLES

Naples

ATLANTIC OCEAN

Oporto

Burgos

Duero

Ebro

KINGD. OF CASTILE

Toledo

Tagus

Guadiana

Cordova

Lisbon

K. OF PORTUGAL

Saragossa

K. OF ARAGON

Barcelona

Balearic Is

Corsica

Sardinia

K. of Granada

Tangier

Gibraltar

MEDITERRANEAN

Algiers

Tunis

HAFSIDS

MARINIDS

ZIANIDS

Palermo

K. of Sicily

Malta

Tripoli

TRIPOL

Bothnia

SWEDEN

Viborg
Stockholm
G. of Finland
Reval
hland
Esthonia
Peipu Lake
Livonia
Riga
Cour- Uxküll
Dünamünde
land
Memel
Dūna
Samogitia Polotsk
Danzig
Königsberg Kovno
UTONIC
Prussia
Vilna
Kulm
Thorn
Brandenburg
Estula

PRINCIP. OF
RUSSIAN STATES

Viatka
Novgorod
Kostroma
Tver
Yaroslav
MOSCOW
Moscow Vladimir
Nijni Novgorod
Suzdal
Volga
Oka
Riazan

KHANATE OF

THE GOLDEN HORDE

50

Smolensk

GRD PRINC.

Pinsk
Chernigov
OF LITHUANIA
Kiev
Volhynia Ukraine
Dnieper

Sarai
Volga

Astrakhan

Koulikovo

KINGD OF
POLAND
Cracow
Podolia
Dniester
Bessarabia

Moldavia
Budapest
HUNGARY
Jassy
Transyl-
Hermannstadt vania
Wallachia
Bukharest
grade
SERBIA
Nish
Kossovo
Danube
BULGARIA
Sofia
Varna
Adrianople
Thessalonica
Gallipoli
Janina
Brusa
Adalia
Modon
(to Venice)
Crete (to Venice)

Rostov Don
Azov
(to Genoa)

Cherson
(to Genoa)

BLACK SEA

GEORGIA
Tiflis

40

Sinope
Trepizond
Emp. of Trepizond
Constantinople
Nicomedia
Nicaea
EASTERN EMP.
Nicopoli
Seljuk Turks
Erzerum
ARMENIA OF MOHAMMED ARTIN

DOMS OF THE JALAYRS

Kara Kuyunli

Smyrna
Chios
Turkomans
Mosul

D. of
Athens
Achaia

Aleppo
Euphrates
Tigris
Bagdad

RHODES

K. of
Cyprus

Beirut
Damascus

N
SEA

Jaffa
Jerusalem

Barca
Alexandria
MAMELUKE SULTANATES

Arabia

30

Cairo

working successfully in the interests of his family, the Wittelsbachs. At the death of Margrave Waldemar of Brandenburg, and that of his only heir, Louis, by giving large parts of the Brandenburg holdings to powerful neighbors, made possible turning over the march itself with its electoral vote to his nine-year-old son Louis. In 1340 he joined Lower Bavaria to his own lands. He subsequently added the Tyrol to his house lands at the cost of antagonizing the Luxemburgers. A son of King John of Bohemia had married the heiress of the Tyrol, but his undeveloped physical stature was not equal to satisfying the sensuousness of his wife, who in her search for a more adequate husband set her eyes upon Louis of Brandenburg. Louis, *père et fils*, appeared in the Tyrol in 1342. The king dissolved the marriage of Margaret of Tyrol and John Henry of Bohemia by virtue of his own imperial authority, since the pope refused to do it, blessed the new marriage of his son with Margaret, and invested the couple with the Tyrol. Finally, in 1346, as a result of his second marriage with the daughter and heiress of the Count of Holland, Louis turned over at the count's death the counties of Holland, Hainault, Zeeland, and Frisia to his wife. Louis's quarrel with the papacy, his break with the Luxemburgers, and his high-handed action with regard to the Tyrol cost him his crown in 1346, when he was deposed and succeeded by Charles IV of Bohemia, the son of King John. But the issue was hardly settled until Louis's death the next year.

The history of Charles IV's reign (1347–78) belongs in large part *Charles IV of* to the history of Bohemia proper.[7] No German king worked harder *Bohemia* in the interests of his own family, and none had more brilliant success. He acquired a large part of the Rhenish Upper Palatinate, the last of the local principalities in Silesia not recognizing Bohemian overlordship, and Lower Lusatia. When the Bavarian house in the Tyrol died out in 1363 he helped the Hapsburgs to acquire it, and they kept it until 1918. Taking advantage of a serious internal quarrel in the Wittelsbach family, he was able to transfer Brandenburg to his own son Sigismund. Of the acquisitions of Louis of Bavaria for the Wittelsbachs only the counties in the Low Countries were left to them. Friendship with the Hapsburgs led to the Treaty of Brünn in 1364, whereby Hapsburgs and Luxemburgers promised each other that in case either family died out the other should succeed to its inheritance.

At the moment it looked as if the Luxemburgers might soon enough come into possession of Austria, Styria, Carinthia, Carniola, and the Tyrol. In planning the marriage of Sigismund to the eldest daughter

[7] See p. 982.

of the King of Hungary-Poland, an even grander prospect seemed about to be realized. All the external glamour of titular honors came to Charles also. Like Louis IV, he was crowned emperor in Rome, though he made no attempt to interfere in Italian politics, contenting himself with only a day's stay in the Eternal City. In 1365 he was crowned King of Arles, the only German king since Barbarossa to be' interested in that title. Likewise, in 1368–69 he followed Urban V to Rome [8] and presented to the world again the picture of the ideal co-operation between pope and emperor. But his quick return to Germany was followed by as speedy a return of Urban V to Avignon.

Charles IV had, however, no illusions about either the German empire or the German kingdom. He knew perfectly well that nothing could really revive them. Accepting them for what they were, he had long before his death taken steps to render permanent the electoral system in Germany, to remove whatever doubts there still remained about the details of its procedure, and to guarantee to the electors themselves so pre-eminent and independent a position among the German princes that they would have nothing to fear from him and might therefore constitute a strong party within the German kingdom upon which the Luxemburgers could rest and continue to hold the crown after his death.

The Golden Bull

These steps were approved by the electors and published at Christmas in 1356 in the so-called Golden Bull. The right of election was confirmed to the three archbishops of the Rhine, and the four lay electors of Saxony-Wittenberg, Bohemia, Brandenburg, and the Bavarian Palatinate. The electoral right was to be inherited by primogeniture and the territory of an elector was not to be divided. For lesser princes than the electors an example was thus set of how to strengthen their dynasties. Elections were to be held in Frankfort and coronations in Aachen. The Bull contains no word of any papal participation in any stage of the proceedings. Each elector was made virtually sovereign in his own territory. He was given sole control of mining and minting rights and of all salt works. His subjects could not be summoned to a court outside of the electorate, nor could they appeal from a local to an outside court. Vassals who fought against their lords were to lose their fiefs, and three days' notice was to be given before the commencement of a private war. The Bull tried to protect the princes against the cities by forbidding urban leagues and requiring those who wished to enjoy the privileges of a town actually to reside in the town. In rank the electors were to precede all other

[8] See pp. 973 ff.

German princes. Lord Bryce in his *Holy Roman Empire* says that Charles in the Golden Bull "legalized anarchy and called it a constitution." The characterization will hardly hold. The Bull did not free Germany from feudal anarchy, as it itself confesses, but in giving strength to the electors it took a step in that direction. It did guarantee the throne to the house of Luxemburg for as long as that family lasted (until 1437). And it regulated elections until the empire was destroyed in 1806.

The century or so following the death of Charles IV saw no change in the character of the political development in Germany. In fact, the prevalence of private warfare and warfare between all classes of society was as serious as ever it had been. To take the place of the weak and indifferent emperor-kings, new leagues of cities, leagues of knights, and leagues of cities and knights combined, strove to secure for themselves the rights no longer guaranteed to them and to preserve some kind of order. But they were combated by the territorial princes and ultimately defeated in their attempts. The German town gradually succumbed to the territorial prince. The powerless emperor-kings were conspicuous for neither capacity, sobriety, nor activity; and whatever their good intentions, their interests were so confined to questions not directly concerned with Germany proper that internal anarchy increased. When they strove to institute some kind of reform they were defeated by the divided interests of the cities and classes in Germany, and by the fear that the king might succeed in amounting to something. At the end of the fifteenth century the princes themselves were finally convinced of the need for some reform of the constitution of the empire; but since it was to be reform taking what power was left from the king and transferring it to the princes, it was defeated this time by Maximilian.

Charles IV was succeeded by his son Wenzel of Bohemia (1378–1400), who spent most of his time in his own kingdom. His lack of concern with Germany, combined with his really remarkable devotion to liquor, led to his deposition in 1400, although he continued until his death to act as if he had never been deposed. For the last time the Rhenish electoral princes resorted to a small western prince to restore their influence in the realm, choosing one of their number, Ruprecht, the Count of the Palatinate (1400–10). The sight of this prince trying to revive the imperial program in Italy, and obliged to return home immediately after pawning his crown, convinced the electors that it was hopeless even for their own interests to rely on their old policy.

The only strength the crown had was what the king as a territorial

Wenzel of Bohemia

Ruprecht of the Palatinate

lord possessed, and the frightful conditions in Germany were revealing the need of some kind of central power. They returned therefore to the Luxemburgers with another son of Charles IV, Sigismund of Brandenburg (1410–37), who became King of Bohemia at Wenzel's death, and king of Hungary through marriage.[9] There were times when Sigismund was as impecunious as Ruprecht, forced now to pawn the insignia of his newly granted Order of the Garter, and now to pledge the imperial linen before the citizens of Constance would let him leave the city. His devotion to women was as conspicuous as Wenzel's to wine. Since his own election was soon followed by a second, that of Jobst of Moravia, and since Wenzel still claimed the German throne, the empire with its three heads looked as ridiculous as the Church with its three.[10]

Sigismund of Brandenburg   As emperor Sigismund was primarily concerned with settling the schism in the Church,[11] and with the attempts to reform the Church at the councils of Constance and Basel.[12] As King of Bohemia he was preoccupied with the heretical movement led first by John Hus, and after Hus's martyrdom at Constance, and its aftermath, with a fierce and heroic national rebellion against the Germans.[13] As King of Hungary he was obliged to defend this kingdom against the Turks. Obviously, with all these exterior concerns there was little time left to devote to the affairs of Germany proper. All his hesitant attempts to lead the reform party in Germany to some modification of the constitution that might correct the anomalous internal anarchy came to nothing. Two dynastic changes in northern Germany must, however, be mentioned. In 1423, when the Saxe-Wittenberg line of Saxony died out, Sigismund turned over the duchy and electorate to the strong Wettin family of Meissen and Thuringia. The union of all these lands under one family proved to be the foundation for the much later Kingdom of Saxony. When Brandenburg came into his hands Sigismund turned it over to Frederick of Hohenzollern, the Burgrave of Nuremberg who had been of considerable help to him at his election. In 1417 Frederick was formally invested with the March and Electorate of Brandenburg, thus bringing to the front rank of the German princes a family that had its inconspicuous beginnings at Zollern, in Swabia, and is perhaps now having its inconspicuous end at Doorn, Holland.

In Bohemia, Hungary, and Germany, Sigismund, the last of the

[9] See pp. 917–18.
[10] See p. 975.
[11] See p. 987.
[12] See p. 990.
[13] See p. 985.

Luxemburgers, was succeeded by his Hapsburg son-in-law, Albert II (1438–39). By this time the Hapsburgs were so strong that it was out of the question for the electors to choose anybody except a Hapsburg without causing civil war in Germany. With Albert, there- *Frederick III* fore, began a line of Hapsburg kings and emperors continuous until 'the dissolution of the empire in 1806. Albert's career was cut short during a campaign against the Turks in Hungary. His successor Frederick III (1440–93) was certainly no heroic figure to terminate the line of prereformation German emperors. In one instance he was described as "perhaps the most contemptible creature that ever pretended to govern the Holy Roman Empire"; in another, as a blockhead. One of his advisers characterized his policy by having him say that "we mean to conquer the world by sitting still." *Roi fainéant* that he was, and devoted to the study of alchemy and astrology and to his collections of plants and precious stones, by merely occupying the throne for many years, and refusing for decades on end to leave his own estates, by devoting himself to Hapsburg interests and meeting with complacent indifference all dangers to them, he built up and fortified the Hapsburg tradition and hope that ultimately the whole world would be subject to their power. He met the danger of the Burgundian state of Charles the Bold by marrying his son Maximilian to Charles's only daughter.[14]

While other lands on the southwestern, northern, and northeastern frontiers were falling to the Swiss Confederation, Denmark, and Poland, by a treaty with Ladislas of Bohemia and Hungary Maximilian *Maximilian* made possible the Hapsburg accession to these kingdoms in the early sixteenth century. As Sigismund was in 1433 the first German king after Frederick II to be crowned emperor by the pope in Rome, so Frederick III in 1452 was the last emperor ever so crowned. The capture of Constantinople by the Turks in 1453 left the German emperor for the first time since 800 without an eastern rival, but the event itself led to no imperial preparations to meet the onward march of the Turks into Europe. As early as 1454 and thenceforward almost constantly there were regular demands made that he be deposed. Hope in Germany for political and religious reform centered more and more on his gifted son Maximilian, whose election as Roman king Frederick was able to postpone until 1486. From then on until his father's death Maximilian was the real ruler of Germany. Gathering for the time being all Hapsburg possessions into his own hands, he was able, because of his Burgundian marriage, to plan for the unification of the

[14] See p. 900.

Hapsburg lands with the possessions of Ferdinand and Isabella, to make a new European empire. The history of that empire under Maximilian's grandson Charles V belongs, however, to an account of the sixteenth century.

Closely related to the growth of the Hapsburgs on the southeastern frontier of Germany was their inability to maintain a hold in south-western Germany over Switzerland. The successful effort of the peasant communities and towns of this Alpine territory in freeing themselves from the danger of incorporation into a Hapsburg state is one of the more remarkable episodes in German history. It is of interest to the general student as another example of the territorial dissolution of the German empire. The peculiar interest, however, of this formation of what by 1500 amounted to an independent state is that it did not follow the general tendency of the formation of a territorial state under princely auspices. The Swiss secured their independence by forming leagues among themselves, and in this they were doing no more than many other peasant communities and towns had done and were doing at the same time as they. But though similar to other leagues in origin, the Swiss Confederation enjoys the distinction of being the only important organization of its kind to maintain its independence against princes and kings, and thereupon to transform a simple and loosely formed league into a unique federal state of a republican and democratic character. Like the leagues of the Greek city-states, it has therefore always had a peculiar fascination for the student of federal government.

The Swiss Confederation

Switzerland is today composed of three nationalities, German, French, and Italian, whom a long history has fused into one. The work of liberation and expansion was performed by German Switzerland, originally a part of the Duchy of Swabia and the Kingdom of Burgundy. The heart of German Switzerland, the three original forest cantons of Uri, Schwyz, and Unterwalden, assumed an importance denied to the ordinary peasant community because they controlled the important pass of the St. Gotthard to Italy, which the German emperors were anxious to control. The towns of Switzerland shared in the revival of trade and commerce because of their location on the trade routes from Italy through the passes to Germany, and because too they were the markets for the products of the forest cantons themselves. In the twelfth century the most important family in German Switzerland was the Zähringer,[15] and when it died out in 1218 the Hapsburgs for the most part succeeded it. As early as 1231 the peasants

Early history of the Confederation

[15] See p. 587.

of the Canton of Uri had been freed by Frederick II's son, King Henry of Germany, from any jurisdiction of the Hapsburg counts, and made answerable alone to the imperial jurisdiction—a privilege granting Uri a considerable amount of freedom, since in general there was no such thing as an imperial jurisdiction. Access to the St. Gotthard may be considered the explanation. It is also probable that with the growing confusion in Germany during the last of Frederick's reign the three forest cantons of Uri, Schwyz, and Unterwalden joined together in an alliance of mutual help that included Lucerne. During the period of the Interregnum itself, Count Rudolf of Hapsburg expanded right and left under any pretense in central and northeastern Switzerland, and inaugurated a plan to centralize, make uniform, and exploit his lands typical of all the feudal princes of his age. When the Interregnum terminated by bringing the Hapsburgs to the German throne the forest cantons felt doubly insecure in their rights and liberties, inasmuch as their private lord, the Hapsburg count, was now their public ruler as well, and the latter position might well be used to carry through the policy of the Hapsburgs as territorial princes.

Henceforth for two hundred years the fate of the Swiss cantons followed the vicissitudes of German politics. When the Hapsburgs were kings the Swiss had to defend themselves against their encroachment. When any other German family occupied the German throne, the Swiss strove to use its opposition to the growth of Hapsburg power to secure important privileges from them circumscribing the expansion and consolidation of the Austrian family. Generally speaking, what the Swiss aimed at was the position that Uri had won in 1231, and which many German towns had or were to win, namely, the recognition of their land as a special imperial province owing no allegiance except to the emperor alone. They did not mind having the Hapsburgs for kings and emperors if at the same time they did not have to have them for counts and advocates. It is illustrative, therefore, of the general situation that, although unable and to some extent unwilling to take steps during the reign of Rudolf of Hapsburg, in fear of the much more disliked Albert the three forest cantons in 1291 joined together in what was essentially a declaration of peasant revolt. They formed the historical foundation of the Swiss Confederation, a league aiming at joint maintenance of the public peace, military assistance against aggressors, and exclusion of foreign officials.

The Swiss and the Hapsburgs

From Adolf of Nassau, Uri and Schwyz secured privileges recognizing their immediacy under the empire alone. After the Swiss had knuckled under the combined feudal and royal position of Albert of

Hapsburg, Henry of Luxemburg extended the same privilege to Unterwalden. The three forest cantons were now definitely recognized as a single unit exempt from all feudal control. In the struggle for the throne between Louis of Bavaria and the Hapsburg Frederick the Handsome of Austria, the forest cantons inevitably supported the former and were in turn encouraged by him. It was under these circumstances that the brother of Frederick, Duke Leopold of Austria, decided to bring matters to a head by crushing once and for all the presumption of these German peasant mountaineers. But at Morgarten (1315) his knightly army was so thoroughly routed or drowned in the Agerisee that they never had a chance to fight. The victory of Morgarten guaranteed to the forest cantons their freedom from the Hapsburgs. In December of the same year at Brunnen they renewed their alliance of 1291 with terms binding them still more closely together.

The expansion of the Swiss Confederation

Other Hapsburg subjects were attracted by the success of the forest cantons, who in their turn were willing to strengthen themselves by expanding their alliance. In 1332 the Hapsburg town of Lucerne joined the three forest cantons. In 1351, when threatened by Duke Albert of Austria, Zurich joined these four. In the next year two more peasant communities were added—Glarus, which had been governed by Hapsburg advocates of the monastery of Säckingen, and Zug, which united Zurich with the three forest cantons. In 1353 the town of Berne allied with Uri, Schwyz, and Unterwalden to complete the original confederation of five peasant and three urban cantons.

The final struggle with the Hapsburgs

The struggle of the cantons against the Hapsburgs lasted until the very end of the fifteenth century, and was kept alive by the constant new encroachments that the cantons made on Hapsburg territory. In 1386 at Sempach and two years later at Näfels the Swiss repeated their victory of Morgarten and spread and swelled their military reputation into legendary proportions. As part of his campaign against the Hapsburgs, Sigismund abolished all their feudal rights in the cantons, whose old imperial privileges he confirmed. Frederick III, however, strove to restore his family to their old position in the region, going so far as to encourage Charles VII of France to take Basel. The complicated negotiations, which brought not only the French but also Burgundy into the struggle, have already been discussed.[16] It was in part the successful diplomacy of Louis XI of France directed against Burgundy that brought final peace in 1474 between the Hapsburgs

[16] See p. 900.

and the Swiss cantons in the so-called Perpetual Peace. In it the Hapsburgs recognized the Swiss as entirely free from them, guaranteed
to them all their conquests, settled all their old difficulties, and promised to arbitrate new ones. The Swiss even promised their former
lords military aid.

Yet the Swiss, having now legally freed themselves from Hapsburg
feudal control, had gone so far as to wish to free themselves even
from any material recognition of the jurisdiction of the German empire. In 1495 the German Diet and the Hapsburg Emperor Maximilian agreed upon a recess reforming the constitution of the empire.
There was to be established a new imperial supreme court and a new
imperial standing army, and a new imperial system of taxation was to
pay for both of these. As long as a Hapsburg emperor was powerless,
the Swiss, like the German towns, did not mind being immediately
under him. Yet the prospect of a strong Hapsburg emperor backed by
money, an army, and a judicial administration, they would not stomach. They had, in fact, their own courts and their own army quite sufficient for all their needs. It was therefore necessary for Maximilian to
try to impose these reforms on the Swiss by force in what was for them
virtually a war of independence from the German empire. The Treaty
of Basel which ended it in 1499, by freeing the Swiss from the imperial
law courts and re-establishing all their old privileges, amounted to the
renunciation by the empire of any control over the Swiss, to their practical independence, in fact, although it was not until 1648 that the
public law of Europe actually recognized them as independent. Before this final war of independence the eight original cantons had been
enlarged in 1481 to include Fribourg and Solothurn, and after it, in
1501, Basel and Schaffhausen. The addition in 1513 of Appenzell
brought the total number of cantons to thirteen.

It can be imagined with what enthusiasm the success of the two-
hundred-year struggle of the Swiss was greeted by neighboring leagues
of towns and peasants, and with what consternation by the princes and
nobles of southern Germany. Of course, the actual events and causes
of the conflict were soon obscured by a legend, whose chief hero was *The Swiss as*
William Tell. That military prowess of Swiss pikemen and halberdiers *mercenaries*
whom no feudal army could crush so increased their reputation that
by the middle of the fifteenth century they were being used as mercenary soldiers by any who could afford to pay them. Since the mountains and valleys of their homeland did not afford an adequate sustenance for the whole population, mercenary service, in fact, became a

Swiss national industry, opposed as utterly demoralizing by her patriotic citizens, but yet continuing to flourish well on into the sixteenth century.

In addition to the actual members of the Swiss Confederation itself, the cantons allied themselves with such areas as the French Valais, or such persons as the Abbot of St. Gall. Besides these allies, each canton had subject regions of its own, and together they governed common districts or bailiwicks. In the course of their long struggle they had developed no very well organized federal institutions. Each canton was a law unto itself in so far as local affairs were concerned; and the *The organi-* contrast between the democratic institutions of the forest cantons and *zation of the* those of the city cantons, where there were constant difficulties be-*Confederation* tween the rich patricians and the artisans for control of the government, proved to be a disrupting force. In 1370 the cantons then federated came to an agreement respecting the jurisdiction of ecclesiastical courts in their midst. In 1393 they regulated together their common military obligations and questions concerning division of booty and causes for which they would fight. Each canton had two votes in a federal Diet, and each ally one. But like the German Diet, the decisions of the federal Diet were not necessarily binding on the individual cantons, inasmuch as there was no federal executive to enforce the decisions of the Diet. Each canton was left to itself to decide how it would enforce the decisions and how it would regulate its relations with other members of the Confederation.

Yet the Diet came to have more authority than the above statement would lead one to suppose, and in regard to mercenary service and foreign policy it exercised a well-respected public and federal authority. If one were to compare the Perpetual Pact of 1291 between the three original forest cantons with the complex relationships existing between the thirteen forest and city cantons at the beginning of the sixteenth century, it would be seen how far the Swiss had gone in two hundred years, in the face of enemies on all sides, in developing a common federal government and a community of interests and action which could defy any enemy.

At the same time that the Swiss were detaching themselves from the German empire by means of confederation, the towns of all northern Germany were by use of the same principle securing for themselves an almost complete monopoly of the export and import trade of the northern half of the European continent. While not actually thus expanding Germany territorially, they were doing something far more important in carrying western European civilization in German

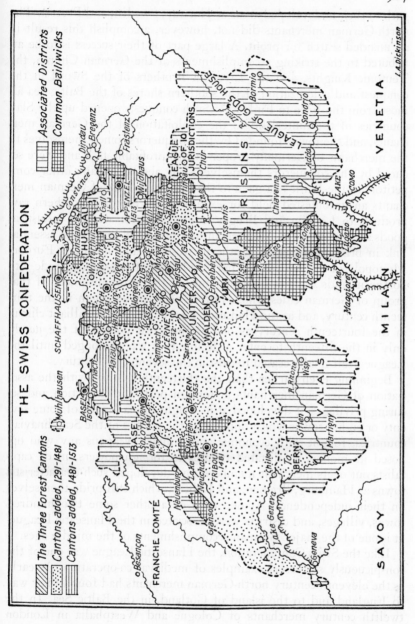

THE SWISS CONFEDERATION

The Three Forest Cantons
Cantons added, 1291–1481
Cantons added, 1481–1513

Associated Districts
Common Bailiwicks

I. A. Dickinson

VENETIA

MILAN

SAVOY

LEAGUE OF GODS HOUSE

GRISONS

VALAIS

garb to such undeveloped areas as Norway, Sweden, and Prussia. The north-German merchants did not, however, accomplish this result in *The Hanseatic* an unaided search for profit. A large part of their success is to be at-*League* tributed to the striking accomplishments of the German Church, the Teutonic Knights, and the Livonian Brothers of the Sword in the conquest and colonization of the southern shores of the Baltic Sea almost from the Elbe to Finland.[17] Such conquests opened up the Slav countries of the hinterland to the exploitation of the German merchants, and the towns founded by the conquerors joined themselves to the merchants of Germany proper in this profitable task and were secured by the conquerors themselves. The absence of any other competitors in the Baltic Sea gave to the resourcefulness of German merchants an uncontested field for expansion. In bringing northern raw products to London and Bruges to exchange for western industrial goods and the wares of Mediterranean trade, they formed an essential link in bringing together southern, western, and northern Europe. Monopoly of the northern export trade and of the import trade into northern lands was not only the aim but the accomplishment of that group of German cities whose history as a league began in the thirteenth century, and as the Hanseatic League reached a brilliant climax in the fourteenth century as one of the great powers of the north, only in the fifteenth to enter a decline that was prolonged until the League itself finally ceased to exist in the seventeenth century.

Beginning even earlier than the thirteenth century with the association of German merchants in foreign ports for protection and securing privileges, it developed at its height into a league of some seventy or eighty towns which dominated the politics of the Scandinavian countries, fought with economic and military weapons any who opposed its monopoly, dictated treaties to foreign powers, made capitalists out of its merchant members, and developed such characteristic towns as Hamburg, Bremen, and Lübeck, which still pride themselves on their independence. At one time or another some two hundred towns, villages, and districts were associated in the Hanseatic League. It is one of the major German accomplishments of the middle ages.

Like the Swiss Confederation, the Hanseatic League was one of the conspicuously successful examples of medieval co-operation. As early *The four* as the eleventh century north-German merchants had found their way *chief factories* to England and to the island of Gotland, in the Baltic Sea. In the *of the League* twelfth century merchants of Cologne and Westphalia in London banded together to secure privileges from Henry II. Lübeck, Ham-

[17] See pp. 935 ff.

burg, and Wismar acted together to secure privileges from Henry III, and before the end of the thirteenth century all German merchants in London were recognized as a corporate group whose life and business centered in their own gild hall. All the business of German merchants came to be concentrated in their special quarter or factory—the Steelyard—where they lived together a life of strict capitalistic asceticism, regulating their own affairs and armed for any outbreak of local hostility. Smaller steelyards were founded at Yarmouth, Boston, and Lynn. The merchant settlement at Wisby on Gotland became autonomous. From it before the end of the twelfth century another factory, "the court of St. Peter," was founded at Novgorod to tap the rich natural resources of Russia, consisting especially of furs. Under Haakon IV of Norway merchants of Lübeck and Hamburg were granted privileges at Bergen, where soon another rigid quasi-monastic settlement of some three thousand German merchants organized the monopoly of Norwegian trade. In 1252 the German merchants at Bruges secured special privileges and organized themselves as a self-governing group with their own aldermen, council, and ordinances.

The privileges that these merchants sought and secured had to do with freedom and security of trade, with the guarantee of as much monopoly as they were able to get, with special treatment in regard to import and export taxes, and with the right of regulating their own affairs. The factories at London, Bruges, Bergen, and Novgorod were the farthest outposts of the German trade. They were welcomed by the local authorities because they were not only the instruments of exchange of goods procurable in hardly any other way, but they brought income in the form of indirect taxes. They were, too, ready with their surpluses of mobile capital to loan money to impecunious kings and princes. From the Baltic and North Sea ports the German merchants poured into London, Bruges, and the west, furs, hides, leather, timber, pitch, tar, turpentine, potash, iron and copper ores, livestock, horses, hawks, amber, grain, beer, flax, wool, herring, cod, salt, and some textiles and drugs brought through Russia, to exchange for the wines, spices, sugar, fruits, textiles, and other industrial products of the west and the Mediterranean. For at least some three hundred years, from 1200 to 1500, this northern trade was almost completely in the hands of the merchants of the cities of the Hanseatic League, occupied with problems of a far different nature from those besetting the German king-emperors.

The necessity for the co-operation of German merchants abroad demonstrated the advisability of co-operation at home. To protect

trade routes on land from knightly highwaymen and on sea from pirates, to organize the force necessary to keep the merchants themselves
in line, to coerce recalcitrant governments, to facilitate trade by common legal codes and a common currency, to promote in every possible
way the interests of their merchants abroad, forced the home towns
themselves to experiment with some kind of organization. Long before
the term "Hanseatic League" appeared formally in documents (1344,
for the first time), ever shifting groups of north-German towns had,
like the towns elsewhere in Europe, formed alliances for the purpose
of meeting some specific danger to their trade. By the end of the
thirteenth century a considerable number of them had organized
themselves under the law of Lübeck. The new colonial towns tended
to adopt the law of Magdeburg.

When finally in 1366 trading privileges in the factories and settlements abroad were denied to those who could not prove citizenship in
the organized home towns, some kind of corporate unity resembling
a league was established. Yet it is inaccurate to speak of any very
highly and permanently organized Hanseatic League. It is impossible
to draw up a satisfactory list of members. There were no such things
as league officials, a league army or treasury, a common seal or common flag. Certain towns within larger groups of towns were recognized as the leaders. Among these Lübeck, the head of the Wendish
group, consisting of Hamburg, Rostock, Wismar, and Stralsund, always predominated. At least until the beginning of the fifteenth century the League always kept the appearance of a loose framework,
preserving the essential independence of its members in most matters, and functioning as a group only in matters of immediate and
serious danger. The members came together from time to time to consult in assemblies, whose decisions have been published; but these assemblies met infrequently, they were not well attended, and the una-
nimity of action required prevented their dealing with matters of great
importance. Not until 1418 was the recess of such an assembly meant
to be binding on all members and to lay down a scheme for the development of a firmer group action. By that time the best days of the
Hanse were really over. Meetings continued at intervals of from
twenty to thirty years, attended by fewer and fewer towns. When the
last assembly of the League met in 1669 only five towns were represented. Under such circumstances it is really surprising that the League
was able to accomplish so much.

The League could punish members acting out of harmony with its
general interests by depriving them of its privileges in foreign ports

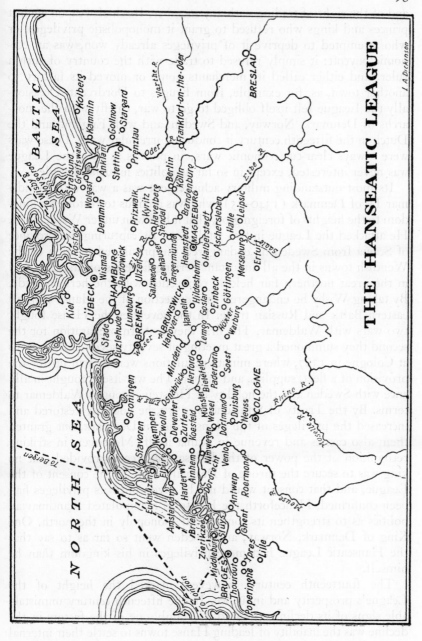

THE HANSEATIC LEAGUE

I. A. Dickinson

and of the right of trading with any member. Its chief weapon against princes and kings who refused to grant it monopolistic privileges, or who attempted to deprive it of privileges already won, was an economic boycott: it simply refused to trade with the country of such a ruler, and either called its merchants home or moved its factory to another town, as, for example, from Bruges to Dordrecht. Occasionally the League felt itself obliged to go to war, chiefly with the monarchs of Denmark, Norway, and Sweden, and with England and the Dutch in the fifteenth century it conducted irregular wars. These wars were always clear-cut economic wars; in politics as such the League was never interested, except in so far as politics influenced trade.

The League at war

Its most outstanding military achievement was a war with Waldemar IV of Denmark (1340–75), who was anxious to restore his kingdom to the heights of foreign glory that it had won under Waldemar I. He attacked the League in two vital spots. By capturing the province of Scania from Sweden he endangered the privileged position of the Wendish towns in the all-important herring fisheries off its coast, and in the great northern fair held in connection with the herring trade. By taking Wisby he endangered the connection of the Hanse with all eastern Baltic and Russian trade. In the seventies the Hanse fought two wars with Waldemar. The first they lost. In preparation for the second they summoned a great meeting of seventy-seven Hanse towns at Cologne in 1367, where minute regulations were drawn up for the provision of a fleet, supplies, and money. The war itself, fought in alliance with Sweden and the nobility of Holstein, brought Waldemar to terms. By the Treaty of Stralsund in 1370, he not only restored and increased the privileges of the Hanse cities in Denmark, but granted them also castles and revenue in Scania itself. Moreover, in striking recognition of the power of the Hanse, the treaty provided that no king was to secure the throne of Denmark without the consent of the League, and that consent would not be given until its privileges had been confirmed. Henceforth the Hanse so manipulated Scandinavian politics as to strengthen its commercial monopoly in the north. One King of Denmark, Norway, and Sweden went so far as to say that the Hanseatic League had more privileges in his kingdom than he himself.

The decline of the League

The fourteenth century, however, marked the height of the League's prosperity and influence. In the fifteenth century unmistakable signs of its decline appeared. Certainly one of the factors in the decline was the inability of leading Hanse towns to settle their internal political problems. In many Hanse towns, notably Lübeck, the rivalry between the patrician merchant class and the democratic gildsmen for the control of the government brought about prolonged disturbances. The League as a whole naturally took a stand against the democratic parties, going so far at one time as to threaten expulsion from the League for any town overthrowing its merchant government. In addition, intense rivalries developed among groups of the Hanse towns themselves. Cologne was at odds with the League in the fifteenth century and at one moment withdrew and formed a special league of her own. The predominance of Lübeck and the Wendish towns was resented by the Prussian towns, led by Danzig, and by German towns farther east. They finally welcomed merchants from England and Holland at the expense of those from Lübeck.

It was this entrance of new competitors into the North and Baltic Seas that was more serious. The Hanse was stubborn to a degree in the maintenance of its own monopoly. It refused, for example, to grant to English merchants in its own towns the same kind, or even any kind, of privileges that the Hanse merchants enjoyed in England. But the disturbed condition of northern politics, the prevalence of piracy in the North and Baltic Seas, and the growing opposition of Scandinavian kings to the privileged position of the Hanse opened the way for English, Scotch, and Dutch merchants. Although for a long time the Hanse succeeded in keeping them out, in the long run it failed and had to recognize them as equal participants in northern trade. The gradual rise of native merchant and industrial classes in England, Scandinavia, and Russia brought resentment against Hanse privileges. English merchants in the fifteenth century were clamoring for a diminution of privileges of the steelyards; at the end of the same century Scandinavian merchants were doing likewise. In the sixteenth century in both these regions the Hanse lost its privileges. In 1494 Ivan III destroyed the factory at Novgorod and ended the German monopoly there.

Other factors helped to destroy the predominance of the Hanse. The Hundred Years' War cost it dearly. The rise of Burgundy hampered its business at Bruges. The defeat of the Teutonic Order by Poland deprived it of a valuable ally in Prussia. The successful efforts of such princes as the Hohenzollerns of Brandenburg in depriving their towns of freedom deprived the League of important members. Moreover, as a final blow the strict control over the sea and land routes of northern Germany by the Hanse, combined with the disturbances caused by northern wars, led finally to the establishment by the cities of southern Germany of new trade routes between east and west and north and south. Nuremberg and Frankfort on the Main established their own connections with Flanders and Antwerp, with Breslau and Prague and eastern Europe. Leipzig succeeded Lübeck as the center of the fur trade. And all this took place before the dislocation of the trade routes caused by the discovery of America and new trade routes to the Far East had any noticeable effect upon northern Europe. Yet the Hanse lived on, and the prosperous descendants of its earlier great merchants still populate the rathskellers of its town halls, consuming the best of German wines.

Because of the importance of the Hanse in Scandinavian politics and trade it is not inaccurate to regard the history of Denmark, Norway, and Sweden in the fourteenth and fifteenth centuries as a chapter in the expansion of German influence. The prevalence of the German merchant in the north prevented until the very end of the fifteenth century in both Denmark and Sweden the growth of a native middle class, and in Norway such a development was postponed to an even *Denmark,* later date. Feudalism crept into Scandinavia for the most part from *Norway, and* Germany, from Germany to Denmark, and thence to Norway and *Sweden* Sweden. Throughout the period Scandinavian kings were sought from princes of German houses, from Mecklenburg and Pomerania, from Oldenburg and even Bavaria. German princes of Holstein dominated Danish politics and succeeded in securing control of Danish Schleswig. The growth of feudalism in Scandinavia made the nobles of the kingdoms the controlling force, against which the kings fought in vain. For the Danish and Swedish peasant feudalism brought considerable loss of freedom and prosperity. The power of the nobility in Denmark and Sweden was being challenged by middle classes at the end of the fifteenth century, but in Norway, where the free peasant maintained himself, the nobility was just reaching the height of its influence. In fact in all three countries there had been such an intermixture of noble families through immigration and intermarriage that there was hardly any national differentiation among the aristocracy of the three countries.

Such a lack of national sentiment among the Scandinavian nobility, combined with the internationalism of the Hanse interests, explains *The Union* the ease with which that "lady king," Margaret, who had become suc- *of Kalmar* cessively the ruler of Denmark, Norway, and Sweden, was able in 1397 to bring about what was calculated to be a perpetual union of the three kingdoms. She called together the noble councils of Denmark, Norway, and Sweden to a conference at the Swedish town of Kalmar, and as a reult of it there emerged a kind of dynastic union of the three countries that lasted a little over a century. But the Union of Kalmar was no organic linking together of the three kingdoms. It never intended to be more than a union under one king, since each kingdom preserved its own administration and law; and it never received the proper legal validity, since the Norwegian delegates refused to subscribe to it. Even the dynastic union was imperfectly preserved for the next century largely because of the opposition of the Swedes. The Union is indicative of the superior position of Denmark in Scandinavian affairs. Norway became a satellite of Denmark, losing her colonies of the Orkneys and Shetlands to the Scotch, and permitting her sons in Greenland to starve and degenerate. The Norwegian nobility voted a dynastic union in 1450 which lasted until 1814. Although Sweden colonized the eastern shores of the Gulf of Bothnia and Finland, and strove to enter upon the heritage of the Teutonic Order in the eastern Baltic, she did not succeed in breaking off from Denmark until the beginning of the sixteenth century. Denmark, having lost her earlier empire to the princes of northern Germany and the Teutonic Order, became essentially a domain of German culture.

Yet the Scandinavian kingdoms had secured the freedom of their Church from English and German control; Denmark had freed herself from the German empire; middle classes had begun to grow in Denmark and Sweden by the end of the fifteenth century; and in Sweden with the foundation of the University of Upsala in 1477, and in Denmark with the University of Cophenhagen in 1478, the groundwork had been laid for the development of a national culture.

Another great achievement of the German people in the later middle ages was the completion of their expansion into eastern and northeastern Europe. Many historians have pronounced this not only the most outstanding accomplishment of the German people during their whole history, but even one of the finest contributions made by any people during the whole middle ages. If that is so we have spent far too much time on other phases of German history, and particularly on that phase which had little or nothing to do with the colonization movement—namely, on imperial history. For it is rather interesting to note that the work of colonizing the shores of the Baltic from the Elbe-Saale to the Gulf of Finland, and of peopling other districts in central and eastern Europe, was done by those particularist forces the predominance of which in later medieval German history national historians take great pains to lament. German princes, German archbishops and bishops, and German crusading orders undertook and completed what the German emperor-kings were incapable of attempt-

German eastward expansion

ing. If one considers too that the Hanseatic League was the work of the German merchant, and the Swiss Confederation the combined work of peasant and townsman, one is likely to wonder just what great use German emperor-kings were in the fourteenth and fifteenth centuries.

Already some casual mention has been made of German eastward expansion at the cost of Slavic peoples. The earlier successes and failures of the tenth and eleventh centuries and the work of Adolf of Holstein, Henry the Lion, and Albert the Bear in the early twelfth century founded such important states as Lübeck, Mecklenburg, and Brandenburg.[18] Along the southern shores of the Baltic stretched a country inhabited by Slavs, Balts, and Finns, offering a fair prospect to missionaries, conquerors, and colonizers. Between the Oder and the Vistula were the Slavic Pomeranians; between the Vistula and the Niemen, the non-Slavic, Baltic Prussians. In the valley of the Niemen lived the Lithuanians, and northeastward reaching to Lake Peipus a complicated intermixture of Baltic Letts, and Finnish Kurs, Livs, and Esths. Among the three peoples who competed in the Christianization and conquest of these peoples—the Danes, Poles, and Germans—the Germans secured the most permanent results. The Danes were early crowded from the scene, leaving Germans and a combination of Poles and Lithuanians to fight out the issue between Teuton and Slav. The results of that conflict are the historical basis for the problems that still beset this troubled area of Europe.

At the end of the twelfth and the beginning of the thirteenth century Denmark, under her two kings Waldemar I and II, struck out for a strong Baltic empire. The Esths were converted and subjected to the bishop of the newly founded town of Reval, and closer home Holstein, Hamburg, Lübeck, Mecklenburg, and Pomerania acknowledged Danish overlordship. But a combination of north-German princes put an end to Danish hopes at Bornhörde in 1227, leaving to Denmark only far-removed Esthonia. In western Pomerania the Germans, in eastern Pomerania the Poles, took the leadership in conversion, even if the actual work of bringing Pomerania into line with western Europe was done by such Cistercian monasteries as Kolbatz and Oliva. The Poles began to convert the Prussians in co-operation with Cistercian monks from the Polish house of Lekno.

Before the Teutonic Order began its rigorous conquest of Prussia an example had been set in yet another Baltic area of the really effective manner in which to achieve permanent results. Before the end of

The peoples of the southern shore of the Baltic Sea

Early Christianization, conquest, and colonization

[18] See p. 394.

the twelfth century, under the stimulation of the Archbishop of Hamburg-Bremen, an Augustinian monk from Holstein went to convert the Livs at the mouth of the Düna and became the Bishop of Üxküll in order to carry on his work. His successor, Albert, set out from Lübeck in 1201 with far more grandiose plans. He founded at the mouth of the Düna the new German town of Riga. To assist in the conversion of the natives he founded a Cistercian house at Dünamünde, and to carry out the work of conquest he founded a new crusading order, the Livonian Brothers of the Sword. Not only was Livonia quickly conquered, converted, and subjected to Albert as independent Bishop of Livonia, and to the Brothers of the Sword, but with the co-operation of Livs and Letts an advance was made into Esthonia, and two new dioceses organized there. Word quickly spread to the nobles of Westphalia that lands were to be had on feudal tenure in large amounts in this new ecclesiastical state. The German nobles came, forming henceforth and to this day an upper crust of German aristocracy over the whole region that reduced the natives ultimately to serfdom. When Albert died in 1229 an entirely new state under German control had been founded on the eastern Baltic.

Already, however, the Teutonic Knights [19] had been introduced into the Baltic lands. The waning of crusading ardor in Syria and Palestine after the disastrous third and fourth crusades led to the transfer of some of the Knights into eastern Hungary in the early thirteenth century. Their welcome there had just worn out when they were invited in 1228 by a Polish prince, Conrad of Mazovia, to assist him in his campaign against the Prussians. The invitation offered lands in the neighborhood of Thorn and the right to hold all conquests made at the expense of the Prussians. The grand master of the Order, Herman of Salza, was quick to see the possibilities not only of giving new purpose to the Order in a fight against the heathen on the Baltic, but also of establishing his Knights as wealthy German lords in an area that was otherwise likely to become Polish. He lost no time in accepting Conrad's invitation and in securing from Frederick II a confirmation of all conquests to be made in Prussia. In a real sense therefore the Teutonic Order entered Prussia as veritable expanders of the German state as well as converters of the heathen at the point of the sword. The new prospects of the Order called into its ranks from central and southern Germany chiefly the younger sons of the German nobility.

The Teutonic Knights and Prussia

The Teutonic Order completed the conquest of Prussia in fifty years.

[19] See p. 534.

The conquest and coloniza- tion of East Prussia
From their earlier castles at Thorn and Kulm they pushed down the Vistula, founded castles in their wake such as the Marienburg, and when they reached the sea began the conquest of the Prussian tribes along the coast. With the conquest of the Sambians, which brought the Order the control of the amber trade, and with the founding of Königsberg, East Prussia belonged to the Knights. The conquest drove out Pomeranians and Poles and shifted the direction of Polish colonization to the south and southeast. East Prussia was quickly organized into four dioceses, and the combined efforts of the Order and the bishops introduced into Prussia early streams of colonists, for the most part from northern Germany. Yet these colonists were not confined, as elsewhere in this frontier land, to the German aristocracy, but included peasants and merchants who established themselves in the towns that soon sprang up about the castles of the Order.

The Order itself quickly prepared to sell the surplus from its large estates. It sought from the pope in 1263 the right to engage in trade, and when permitted to do so with the condition that it was not to be for profit, it later faked a privilege that did not contain this annoying restriction. The towns that grew up so quickly in Prussia joined the Hanseatic League, but they resented bitterly the competition from the Order itself. For that matter the character of the conversion and conquest by these hot-blooded young nobles from Germany created only hostility among the Prussians. The history of the conquest is a repetition of revolt, put down with extreme ferocity. Indeed, like the Slavs of the Elbe-Saale frontier, the native Prussians were practically exterminated and Germans introduced in their place. Yet the Order was no more successful in winning the confidence of the German immigrants than it had been in its dealings with the Prussians themselves. Before long German Prussia was in a ferment of discontent.

Meanwhile, because of its constant expansion the Order brought down on itself the hostility of Lithuania and Poland. In 1237 the Livonian Brothers of the Sword, already organized according to the
Further expan- sion of the Order
rule of the Knights, sought a union with the Teutonic Order to complete and extend its work in Livonia. The union was accomplished, and in the next few years the brothers of the combined orders made striking advances. An attempt to force the Russians out of the Greek Church and into the Latin Church failed, but in addition to securing Livonia, the combined orders completed the conversion and conquest of Kurland and founded the city of Memel to keep the Kurs and Letts in check. Quite obviously now the Order was forced to consider the grand project of joining Prussia with Kurland and Livonia by the con-

quest of Lithuania—the last important resort of paganism in Europe. Samogitia, the coastal region between Prussia and Kurland, was finally occupied. Yet the conquest of the Lithuanians was another matter. It was some hundred years before the issue was ultimately settled. Before that settlement, after very sharp dealings at the expense of the Poles, the Order had expanded on the west to include Pomerelia (i.e., eastern Pomerania or western Prussia) and Danzig, which soon became a flourishing German city. In 1326 the Order purchased Esthonia from Denmark. Now its holdings reached from the Oder to Lake Peipus, and the whole area was opened to German settlement. The creation of this German crusaders' state on the Baltic obliged the grand master of the Order to transfer his seat from Venice to the Marienburg in 1309.

The occupation of Pomerelia by the Teutonic Order shut off Poland from access to the sea and caused war between Poland and the Order, as a result of which in 1343 the Poles were obliged to recognize the conquest. For that matter the phenomenal success of the Order soon made the Poles see in it something more than a divine instrument *The Order* for the conversion of the heathen. Prussia was no longer an outlet for *and the* Polish colonization, and the advance of the Germans on the eastern *Poles* frontier of Brandenburg, and into Lusatia and Silesia, no less than the Germanization of Prussia, threatened to inundate Poland itself with the onward German push. Before the end of the fourteenth century German merchants and peasants were crowding into Poland itself. It has been estimated that some six hundred and fifty districts within Poland were colonized by Germans. The middle class in Poland was German. The German colonists retained their own law and language, and the rise of Poland in European affairs may be in large measure attributed to the infusion of this great German element. But the German expansion itself precipitated first in the minds of the Polish kings, and then more slowly in the minds of the Polish nobility, a national feeling that aimed finally to stop and throw back the German surge.

The Lithuania which the Teutonic Order threatened to absorb was *The Order* no inconsequential state. During the fourteenth century, under a line *and Lithuania* of native princes, Lithuania expanded from the Baltic to the Black Sea, defending her northeastern frontier against the princes of Muscovite Russia, becoming the protector of the Slavs of southwestern Russia against the Tartars, securing the overlordship of Bessarabia, Wallachia, and Moldavia, and launching a colonizing movement in the direction of the Black Sea that ultimately so mixed the Lithuanian and Russian Slavs that the former, like the Bulgars of an earlier date, became in effect a Slavic and not a Baltic people. It was the height of enthusiastic boldness for the Teutonic Order to hope to submerge this growing people. The occupation of Samogitia cut the Lithuanians off from the Baltic, and from Prussia the Knights advanced slowly through the wilderness between Prussia and Lithuania and down the Niemen to Kovno. Lithuania was stirred by a national spirit similar to that of the Poles. Lithuanians expelled from Prussia bore an undying hatred of the Order and the German. But the fact that the Lithuanians remained heathen sanctified the whole campaign of the Order and brought them the excited support of all Europe.

Then suddenly the brilliant prospects of the Order were rudely shattered by a wholly unexpected event. Through the manipulation chiefly of the Polish nobility, it was arranged in 1385 that the Grand Prince of Lithuania, Jagiello, was to come into the Latin Church of the west, convert his people to the same faith, and recover the lost *The union of* provinces from the Teutonic Order. In return he was to marry the *Poland and* ruling princess of Poland, Jadwiga, and become King of Poland, with *Lithuania* which henceforth Lithuania was to be united. The union of Poland and Lithuania took place in the next year. It must be looked upon as the common answer of Poles and Lithuanians to the threat of German expansion. The conversion of the Lithuanians to Catholic Christianity brought them within the circle of western European peoples and deprived the Teutonic Order of its very reason for existence as a crusading order on the Baltic. The union of the material resources of the two countries meant that the height of the Order's glory had been reached and that the Slav reaction had begun.

When it is remembered that the German inhabitants of Prussia were by no means satisfied with the government of the Order, and looked to Poland for relief, it is clear that it was only a matter of time, after 1386, until the Teutonic Order should have to fight for its very existence. War did not actually come until the beginning of the fifteenth century, after the Order had made further acquisitions on the Polish frontier. In 1410 a motley Polish-Lithuanian army of some one hundred thousand men that included Czech mercenaries, Tartar *The final de-* chieftains, Russian boyars, and skin-clad Samogitians invaded Prussia *feat and end* and met the army of the Order not far from the village of Tannen- *of the Order* berg (Grünwald), where they defeated it so thoroughly that the military power of the Knights was broken for good. In all Prussia only the fortress of Marienburg stood out against the invaders. Yet local difficulties within both Poland and Lithuania kept them from pursuing their victory to the end.

In the Peace of Thorn of 1411, which ended this first war, the Order was obliged to give up Samogitia and pay an indemnity. All efforts of the grand masters in the ensuing period to placate the German nobles, towns, and peasants in Prussia failed largely because of the resistance of the Knights themselves, whose discipline and spirit was in notable decay. The lesser officials of the Order were frankly insubordinate. By 1454 most of Prussia was in revolt against the Order and organized into a powerful Prussian League, which offered Casimir of Poland suzerainty over it. When the grand master himself appealed to Casimir for aid, the answer came in the form of a declaration of war; the war lasted for thirteen disastrous years. In the second Peace of Thorn, which ended it in 1466, the wings of the Order were finally clipped. Prussia was split into two parts. Western Prussia (i.e., Pomerelia, or eastern Pomerania), including Danzig, was ceded outright to the Poles, and along with it the region of Kulm, the Marienburg, Elbing, and Ermeland. Eastern Prussia, with its capital at Königsberg, was thus separated from Germany, and moreover the peace provided that it was to be held by the grand master as a Polish fief. Poland had therefore at last reached the Baltic. It was to the second Treaty of Thorn that the Poles returned again after the partitions of the eighteenth century had destroyed their state. The student will find instructive a comparison of the Treaty of Versailles (1919) for this area with the second Treaty of Thorn. After this humiliation the Order dragged on its existence until 1525, when its Hohenzollern grand master turned Lutheran and converted eastern Prussia into a secular hereditary duchy. The lands of the Livonian Brothers were likewise transformed into a secular Duchy of Kurland. After their victory Poland and Lithuania preserved at least a dynastic if not an organic union, although Lithuania usually had its own grand prince. The victory over the Germans was at the cost of the predominance of the nobility in each state. Before the end of the fifteenth century the Polish gentry, their chief military task completed, settled down on their estates and began the reduction of the Polish peasant to serfdom. Although a halt had been called to German colonization along the shores of the Baltic, nevertheless enough had been done to change the whole ethnographic character of the population. In addition to the colonization of Holstein, Mecklenburg, and Brandenburg which made these regions German instead of Slav, western Pomerania had been completely Germanized, and eastern Pomerania, although Slav in the countryside, was German in the towns. Germans had poured into Lusatia and Silesia. Prussia had been made completely German. In Kurland, Livonia,

Permanent effects of German expansion

and Esthonia Germans had taken the best of the land, and only since the last great war have their descendants lost their large estates to the native peasants whom they made serfs.

Impressive as is the work of the Germans along the shores of the Baltic, it must be remembered that it brought about the extermination or enslavement of Slavic, Baltic, and Finnish natives by and to German landlords. Nor must it be forgotten that much of the extermination and enslavement were done in the name of Christianity by German prelates and German crusading orders. Finally, to complete the picture of German expansion one should remember too that the colonization of the shores of the Baltic was but a small part of the whole. The infiltration of Germans into Poland, Bohemia,[20] and eastern Hungary (Transylvania) was preceded by the Germanization of Austria, Styria, Carinthia, Carniola, and northern Tyrol. The earlier fourteenth-century Slavic nationalism of the Pole, Lithuanian, and Czech directed against the first onward march of the Germans must be kept in mind when considering the recrudescence of Slavic nationalism in the nineteenth and twentieth centuries, again directed in large part against the Germans. When one considers all that the German expansion has brought in its wake, including the seemingly insoluble problems that still confront central and eastern Europe, it would be a bold, dogmatic, and biased historian indeed who would venture to boast of the glory and progress involved in the expansion to the Slavs of western European civilization under Christian and German auspices.

If the Poles, Lithuanians, and Czechs were able to maintain their political independence over and against the advancing Germans, as much cannot be said for their Slavic kinsmen of the Balkan peninsula in their struggle with the Mohammedan Ottoman Turks. From the general point of view the phenomenal rise of a new Turkish empire to take the place of the decadent Byzantine empire was but the appearance in Europe of the last wave of Mongolian nomads out of central Asia that began with the Huns, and followed with the Bulgars, Avars, Magyars, Seljuk Turks, and Tartars. Of these only the Bulgars and Magyars had succeeded in forming anything like a permanent state in Europe. The empires of the others vanished or dissolved almost as quickly as they were formed.

The Ottoman Turks

When looked at more closely, however, the rise of the Ottoman Turks was only superficially similar to these other invasions. They made no sudden and destructive inroads into southern Russia and central Europe. Their advance from Asia Minor was slow and carefully

[20] See p. 982.

prepared, and the conditions that they met, combined with the policies they adopted, permitted them to found a large and important state in western Asia and southeastern Europe which, although gradually diminished in size, has remained to date and is likely long to persist. If one were seeking for a better analogy than that between Ottoman Turks and the other Mongolian invasions, one would find it in comparing the expansion of the Arabs with that of the Ottoman Turks. Although different in race, they both had a nomadic background. Their historical careers consisted chiefly in occupying disaffected portions of the Byzantine empire. In the making of their states each employed the Byzantine institutions and personnel that they encountered, and each pursued towards Christianity and native customs a policy of tolerance which tended to make their conquest easy and secure. To be sure, under Ottoman patronage no such renaissance of Greek and oriental culture occurred as under the patronage of the caliphs of Bagdad. That was perhaps because the Arabs had already succeeded in doing so much, and because the Greek-Christian culture of Byzantium was dead.

The Ottoman Turks are so called from Osman, or Othman, the real founder of the dynasty that presided over their fortunes until 1918. They are Osmanli, or the sons of Osman, a name which in English has become Ottoman. Around the middle of the thirteenth century they were permitted by the Seljuks to settle with their herds and flocks in northeastern Asia Minor around Sugut. In a short time they were independent and began their attacks on the remnants of Byzantine territory in Bithynia. Under Osman and his son Orkan (1289–1359), the strong line of fortresses guarding the Sangarios was pierced and Brusa, Nicomedia, and Nicæa fell. What the Seljuk Turks had been unable to accomplish in two hundred and forty years, the Ottomans brought about in a single generation—the ruin of Greek dominion in Asia Minor. The Ottoman state then faced Constantinople across the Bosporus, and the revived Byzantine empire faced its doom. *The Turks occupy Byzantine Asia Minor*

Already the sultans had begun to fashion those military institutions that were to win for them a large empire. From the landowners of the conquered areas they required contingents of light-armed horsemen to form their cavalry. More important, however, was their realization, inspired by the Byzantine example, of the necessity of a strong standing army of infantry. These new troops, called *Yeni Cheri*, or Janisaries, they formed from the Christian boys of the conquered territories who were delivered up each year by their parents as a form of tribute. They were put into Moslem schools, separated from all home or family ties, brought up in the faith of Islam, and forbidden to *Turkish policy towards Christian subjects* marry. Imbued thus with an undivided allegiance to the Ottoman state and religion, upon which all their aspirations hung, when their training was completed they entered either the civil service or in greater numbers the infantry. They were in fact trained slaves of the state, but like the prætorian guards of the Roman emperors they soon became its masters.

Except for the conversion here and there of certain Christian churches into mosques, Greek Christianity and the Greek clergy were unmolested. In fact the Greek Church was treated so well that the change in rulers from Byzantine emperors to Ottoman sultans was not necessarily regarded by the Greek clergy as a calamity. These were often given increased authority enough to make them virtual rulers of their flocks. As in the case of the Arabs, the prospect of preferential treatment by the Turks brought many conversions to Islam. The Turks drew no color line. Very early they began to intermarry with the natives of Asia Minor and soon lost most of their peculiar Mongolian features. The only distinction made between Christian and Turk was that the former was not permitted to carry arms and was obliged to pay a special head tax, conditions resembling again those placed by the Arabs upon their Christian subjects. Native Greeks were quickly drawn into the service of the Turks and came to monopolize certain important branches of the government.

Under these conditions the Turks were not likely to find difficult the destruction of that feeble remnant of the Byzantine empire that *The obstacles* was restored in 1261 by the Palæologus family after the disastrous *to Turkish* fourth crusade. Headed by emperors who were so weak that they were *advance* willing to become the vassals of almost anybody, in the desperate hope of preserving their state, and who, in addition, usually had rival candidates for the throne with whom it was easy to ally, the Byzantine empire was at the mercy of the Turks whenever they were prepared to attack Constantinople. What the Turks had more to fear were the Serbs who were advancing towards Constantinople from the north west at the same time that the Turks were approaching from the south east. Constantinople was hemmed in as before the first crusade.[2] There was always, too, the possibility that the rise of another Mohammedan power in western Asia might arouse the languished crusading ardor of western Europe, if not to defend the holy places or the threatened Byzantine empire, then at least to protect Europe from possible invasion. Yet that was at the moment unlikely to any serious degree, inasmuch as western Europe was engaged in the Hundred

[21] See p. 143.

Years' War from the moment the Turks crossed into Europe until they took Constantinople. The same power that pushed the Turks from Persia into Asia Minor, namely, the Mongols, might also threaten the Turks from the rear with one of their terrifying outbursts of destructive fury.

Of those Slavs who settled in the Balkan peninsula in the sixth and seventh centuries, only the Bulgars had been able to establish an independent existence, which, we have already noticed,[22] was cut off from Constantinople at the beginning of the eleventh century. At the moment when the Ottoman Turks were about to cross over into Europe the situation in the Balkans had changed considerably. The Vlachs or Rumanians were organized into the two principalities of Moldavia and Wallachia. The Bulgars at the end of the twelfth century had set up a second independent state under a dynasty founded by two brothers, John and Peter Asen, and called accordingly the Asenid dynasty. The fourth crusade gave Venice many important islands in the Ægean and cities along the coast of the Peloponnesus. The same crusade established several principalities in the hands of nobles from western Europe on Greek soil, of which the chief remaining one was now the Duchy of Athens. The Byzantine empire retained at least a nominal hold on the rest of Greece, Macedonia, Thrace, Albania, and Serbia. *The situation in the Balkans*

It was the development of a Serbian state that changed the balance in the Balkans and provided the Serbs, after they had been crushed by the Turks, with a career of past glory upon which they could nourish their future hopes for an eventual liberation. The founder of the medieval Serb state was Stephen Nemania (1165–96), who as the great Zupan brought the Serbs under the general control of his family, the Nemania dynasty, which lasted until 1371 and was to be associated with the growth of an independent Serbia. It was Stephen's son who took and kept the title of King (Kral) of all Serbia. It was not, however, until the fourteenth century, under the rule of Stephen Dushan (1331–55), that the Serbs reached the height of their earlier glory and pushed the boundaries of their state to its farthest extent. Already in 1330 they had reduced the revived Bulgarian state to vassalage by the Battle of Velbuzd. Under Stephen the greater part of Albania was subdued, Thessaly and Epirus conquered, and a beginning made of the conquest of Macedonia. The Serbs controlled the Balkans from the Danube to the Ægean. Dushan, moreover, freed the Greek Church in Serbia from any dependence upon the Patriarch of Constantinople by setting up an independent Serbian patriarch, who was *Medieval Serbia*

[22] See pp. 140–41.

to crown him as emperor of a newly established Serbo-Byzantine state. No doubt he had set as his goal the capture of Constantinople and the destruction of the harmless Byzantine empire. He went so far as to take the title of *basileus*, or emperor. Yet before his death the Turks had crossed over into Europe, and before they actually met the Serbs on the field of battle, both the empire of Dushan and the Nemania dynasty itself had come to an inglorious end. It was therefore not only a helpless Byzantine empire but a chaotic Balkan peninsula with which the successors of Orkan had to deal.

As allies of a rival emperor at Constantinople and not as conquerors the Turks first entrenched themselves in Europe at Gallipoli around 1354. Their first subsequent move was to close in on Constantinople by occupying Adrianople, whither they moved their capital from Brusa in Asia Minor. Henceforth Constantinople lived in terror as a vassal state of the sultan, to whom she paid tribute and rendered military service. Once having surrounded Constantinople on both the Asiatic and European sides, the Turks could devote their energy to the completion of the conquest of Asia Minor and the reduction of Serbs, without having to bother first with the difficult siege of

The conquest of Serbia and Bulgaria

Constantinople itself. The attention of Sultan Murad I (1359–89) was first given to Bulgaria, Macedonia, and Albania and finally to the Serbs proper. At Kossovo on June 28, 1389, he delivered the death-blow to the Serbian state, which henceforth gradually sank to the level of a Turkish province. Not even the murder of Murad by a Serbian patriot could compensate the Serbs for this most tragic experience of their national legend. Four years later Bayezid I incorporated Bulgaria into the growing Ottoman state.

The defeat of western crusaders at Nicopolis

With the conquest of Serbia and Bulgaria the Turks had reached the Danube frontier. Hungary first, and then all central and western Europe were at the moment their potential victims. This was clearly realized by the Holy Roman Emperor Sigismund, who was also through marriage the King of Hungary; [23] with the co-operation of the pope he summoned Europe to a crusade. A crusading army composed largely of French struck at Bayezid's army at Nicopolis on the Danube, and was so badly beaten that western Europe had more cause than ever to fear the powerful military strength of the Turks. Under the circumstances it was strange that neither the Byzantine empire nor the Balkan peoples attempted to aid the crusaders. Both had had some experience with successful crusading armies.

The sultan began to prepare for the inevitable siege of Constanti-

[23] See p. 920.

nople after Nicopolis when there appeared in Asia Minor as an ally of Constantinople a far more serious rival in the hosts of the Mongolian chieftain Tamerlane, or Timur the Lame, the white-haired, seventy- *Tamerlane* year-old, crippled veteran of many wars intended to work the remnants of the empire of Jenghiz Khan and his successors into a new Mongolian empire. In rapid succession and with unspeakable ferocity (he once embedded two thousand rebellious soldiers in a pyramid of brick and mortar) he had conquered northern India, Persia, and Syria, and before advancing on China decided to add Asia Minor to his dominions. Bayezid met Tamerlane at the present Turkish capital of Angora in 1402, was defeated and taken captive, and died in his captor's train the next year. The Mongols did not follow up their victory. Tamerlane returned to Samarkand and died in 1405 in the midst of his Chinese campaign. Yet the onward march of the Turks had been stayed and the capture of Constantinople postponed for another fifty years.

Neither the Byzantine empire, the beaten Balkan peoples, nor the threatened Europeans took advantage of the Turkish weakness and confusion that followed upon the defeat at Angora. Consequently, *Defeat of the* under Murad II (1421–51) the Turks regained their former strength, *crusaders at* recovered and completed their conquests in Asia Minor, strengthened *Varna* their position in Europe, and successfully met a more serious attack from western crusading armies, led by Ladislas V, the King of Hungary and Poland, John Hunyadi, the Governor of Transylvania, and Cardinal Cesarini. The first attack of the crusaders at Nish was so successful that for a moment the Turks had to abandon their hold on Serbia; but in the hope of delivering a crushing blow on the Turks, the crusaders were urged by the cardinal to violate that term of the peace which precluded an advance beyond the Danube, and after a march to Varna on the Black Sea were hopelessly crushed by Murad in 1444. With the Danube frontier thus free for some time from further attack, the Turks could at last prepare for Constantinople.

The siege was planned and conducted by one of the most versatile of all the Turkish sultans, Mohammed II (1451–81). The large army that attacked Constantinople from the land side was quite adequately equipped with the most recent advances in firearms. Bronze cannons *The final* hurling shots weighing over half a ton battered down the walls of the *siege of Con-* city. Realizing full well, however, that without control of the ap- *stantinople* proach by sea to Constantinople, any siege would be extremely difficult, engineers in the Turkish army contrived to move some seventy ships over land from the Bosporus to the Golden Horn, the upper harbor of Constantinople. They thus hemmed in the Græco-Italian fleet defending the harbor between that part of the Turkish fleet now in the upper harbor and that on the other side of the chain which rendered impossible direct entrance into the harbor. The final assault on the city came on May 29, 1453, after a seven weeks' siege. The Turks greatly outnumbered the defenders of the city, who included, aside from the Greeks themselves, some papal, Genoese, Venetian, and other western soldiers. Without more adequate help from the west, which the emperors had tried in vain to secure, going so far as to agree to a union of Greek and Roman Churches under the pope,[24] no amount of courage could eventually overcome the superior Turkish artillery. In the final onslaught the last Byzantine emperor, Constantine VI, perished, and the capture of the city was followed by three days of costly pillage similar to that visited upon the city by the heroes of the fourth crusade in 1204. The two events are in themselves not unconnected. Although the mosaics in Santa Sophia were whitewashed in order to render it suitable for use as a mosque, the Patriarch of Constantinople preserved his dignity as head of the Greek Church. The Byzantine empire might be destroyed, but its tradition persisted in the living Greek Church.

The remaining years of Mohammed's rule were spent in completely reducing the whole Balkan peninsula. Further efforts of Hunyadi preserved the Danube frontier against the Turks; but within the peninsula, in addition to Serbia and Bulgaria, the remaining Greek, Slavic, and European states were overcome. The Duchy of Athens was destroyed, and the whole territory of the Peloponnesus became Turkish. Venice lost her possessions on the mainland and in the islands of the Ægean after a war of seventeen years. Bosnia and Herzegovina were incorporated, and after the death of the Albanian hero Scanderbeg, in 1468, also Albania. Before the end of the century the Montenegrins were dependent. There were still left to contest the control of the eastern Mediterranean with the Turks the Knights of St. John at Rhodes, the Genoese at Chios and Naxos, the Venetians at Cyprus and in the Adriatic. The issue of sea power was not settled until the next century.

Completion of the conquest of the Balkans

As the successors of the Byzantine emperors, the Ottoman sultans had begun to unify the eastern Mediterranean along the lines laid down by Justinian. By the end of the fifteenth century their task was by no means completed. For the Slavic and non-Slavic nationalities in the Balkan peninsula the Turkish conquest meant little more than a

[24] See p. 990.

EUROPE ABOUT 1500

- - - Boundary of the Holy Roman Empire

Possessions of the House of Hapsburg

Possessions of the House of Bourbon

English Miles
0   100   200   300   400   500

Torneå

SWEDEN

Finland

Helsingfors

Stockholm

Gotland

ockholm

RUSSIAN

BALTIC SEA

Esthonia

DOMAIN OF THE TEUTONIC ORDER

Riga

Novgorod

Volga

Moscow

Nijni Novgorod

Samara

EMPIRE

Tatars

50

Vilna

D. OF PRUSSIA

D. OF Warsaw

POLAND

Cracow

GRD PRINC.

OF LITHUANIA

Pinsk

Lemberg

Galicia

Kiev

Ukraine

Dnieper

Voronezh

KHANATE

OF THE

CRIMEA

KHAN.

OF

ASTRAKHAN

Volga

Sarai

Don

Astrakhan

CASPIAN S.

HUNGARY

Budapest

Moldavia

Jassy

Transyl-vania

Theiss

Belgrade

Servia

Nish

Wallachia

Bukharest

Danube

Bulgaria

Sofia

Adrianople

Yedisan

Crimea

Azov

Balaklava

BLACK SEA

Sinope

Constantinople

Kizil Irmak

Trebizond

Circassians

K. OF IMERETHI

Tiflis

Georgia

Erzerum

PERSIAN

40

Janina

OTTOMAN

Albania

Salonica

Rumelia

Morea

ÆGEAN S.

Chios (to Genoa)

Smyrna

Angora

Adalia

Rhodes

EMPIRE

Aleppo

Mosul

Tabriz

EMP.

Syria

Euphrates

Tigris

Bagdad

Cyprus (to Venice)

(to Venice) Crete

Beirut

Damascus

SEA

MEDITERRANEAN

change of masters. The rudiments of their culture had been supplied *The effects* early by the Byzantine empire, but the Byzantine stimulus had not *of the Otto-* been great and continuous enough to lead on the Balkan peoples to *man conquest* those rich beginnings of national cultures contemporaneous in the west. What they had on the eve of the Turkish conquest they were permitted to keep, until new stimuli from western Europe at the end of the eighteenth century roused them to build upon these foundations the turbulent Balkan nationalities of today. But their evanescent medieval independence, combined with the Turkish conquest, formed the chief element of their conscious national pride and humiliation. It is difficult to say what 1453 meant for the west as a whole aside from supplying, in place of a helpless Greek empire, an aggressive Mohammendan power from which it had to protect itself. Its influence upon the Italian renaissance has been grossly overemphasized.[25] The economic position of Genoa and Venice in the east was scarcely altered by it. They bargained for concessions as successfully as they ever had done. In a sense 1453 was for them a new opportunity. Causal connections between 1453 and the new Atlantic voyages of discovery have been largely discredited.[26] 1453 may have more definitely than ever severed the cultural links between the Near East and western Europe.

Although the Ottoman Turks actually succeeded the Byzantine em- *Russia and* pire in the eastern Mediterranean, it was rather the Grand Prince of *Byzantium* Moscow who adopted the theory that after 1453 Russia was the logical successor to Byzantium, the protector of all Greek Christians, and the very heir to Constantinople itself. This convenient justification for future Russian expansion towards Constantinople via the Balkans rested on a profound change in the course of Russian history. We have already noted [27] that it was Swedish Vikings who founded a Russian monarchy in the ninth century which came to center at Kiev, and that from Constantinople Kiev received its Christianity and the elements of its culture. The importance of Novgorod as the easternmost factory of the Hanseatic League has also been mentioned.[28] Why Moscow rather than Kiev or Novgorod should become the political and ecclesiastical center of a new Russia must now be explained.

Under the descendants of Rurik Kiev retained until the middle of the eleventh century its supremacy as the capital of an essentially com-

[25] See p. 1010.
[26] See pp. 1030 ff.
[27] See pp. 266 ff.
[28] See p. 929.

mercial state whose chief article of commerce was slaves. The grand princes of Kiev were able to organize with a fair degree of success a reasonably compact state. But after the death of Yaroslav in 1054, the peculiar Russian practice of having the eldest member of the reigning family succeed to the throne, rather than the eldest son, brought on a series of family wars and led to the establishment of numerous independent principalities under related ruling families. It was one of these princes from the northeastern provinces, Andrew of Suzdal, who destroyed Kiev in 1169 and took the title of grand prince with his capital at Vladimir. After a second siege in 1203 Kiev lost its earlier preponderance. But before its actual destruction it had suffered

The passing of Kiev

much from the inroads of Mongolian nomads into the southern Russian steppes, particularly from the Cumans in the late eleventh century. 1169 intensified a colonization movement which had already begun, northward in the direction of Suzdal, and into the upper valleys of the Volga and Oka rivers, where the immigrant Slavs quickly amalgamated with the resident Finns to form that group of Slavs called the Great Russians. A second wave of colonists moved to the valleys of the upper Dnieper and Dvina around Smolensk and Polotsk, and a third into southwestern Galicia and Volhynia. Moscow, first mentioned in 1147, was the least important of the new frontier principalities formed out of this movement of pioneer agriculturists into central and northern Russia. Suzdal, Tver, Riazan, Rostov, Vladimir, Smolensk, and Novgorod were far more prosperous. Among the princes of these states there ensued a rivalry for the position of leadership formerly held by the rulers from Kiev. That the Muscovite princes won out in the end is to be explained largely by the disastrous results of the Tartar invasion of southern Russia.

After his invasion of eastern and central Europe, Batu, the nephew of Jenghiz Khan,[29] established his group of western Tartars, or the Golden Horde, at Sarai on the lower Volga. In the course of their raids into Europe the Golden Horde had sacked, pillaged, or destroyed every important town in Russia except Novgorod. Yet after the first waves had subsided the khans of the Golden Horde, while

The Tartar conquest

maintaining their overlordship of Russia, did not attempt the impossible by trying to make so vast a land a part of a Mongolian state. They used the steppes of southern Russia as grazing lands for their flocks and herds and contented themselves elsewhere with making their conquest lucrative. The princes of the many Russian principalities were forced to become vassals of the khan at Sarai. In token of this subjec-

[29] See p. 549.

tion they supplied him with troops. They were obliged to make personal journeys to Sarai to receive official authorization, in the form of charters, to govern their respective states. These charters were not merely a matter of grant to the proper ruler: they were granted only after the expenditure of much time, money, and treasure at the Mongolian court and went naturally to the most unscrupulous and the richest applicants. Moreover, the khans demanded a head tax from the subjected Russians. In the thirteenth century the khans appointed their own collectors of this tribute; but subsequently they used the native princes themselves, who brought it with them to Sarai.

All Russia, therefore, except Novgorod and that part of western Russia conquered by Lithuania, slumped for some two long centuries in this miserable and hopeless subservience to its exploiting Moslem overlords, the independent khans of the Golden Horde. The traces of this subjection have remained ineffaceable. For one thing it raised to an independent, rich, and influential position the Greek clergy. The Mongols collected no tribute from the clergy, freed them by special charters from any jurisdiction except their own, and recognized them as individual vassals alongside the Russian princes. No Russian prince could henceforth hope to succeed without the support of the Russian clergy, both secular and regular.

The fixation of the Mongol dominion coincided with the expansion of the Lithuanian state in the thirteenth and fourteenth centuries. All of western Russia, including Smolensk, Pinsk, Podolia, Kiev, and a *Little Russia* large part of the neighboring Ukraine became a part of Lithuania and *and Great* a field for Lithuanian and Polish colonization. After the union of *Russia* Poland and Lithuania and the acceptance of Roman Christianity by the latter, this western Russia under Polish-Lithuanian tutelage, a mixture of Roman and Greek Christianity and of Polish, Jewish, Lithuanian, and Slav peoples, developed special characteristics of its own that have led to its being referred to as Little Russia. It moved in the orbit of western European society and was in contrast to that Great Russia under the Mongols upon which it bordered. Great Russia was held together by Greek Christianity, but it was a mixture of Finns and Slavs who cultivated the plains of central and northern Russia. It was starting to center about Moscow.

The beginnings of the rise of the princes of Moscow are to be asso- *The rise of* ciated with that Ivan Kalita (1328–41) who managed to have him- *Moscow* self made the sole collector of all the tribute due the Golden Horde from all the Russian princes. The princes of Moscow, by harnessing themselves to the treasury of the khan in this way, not only built up their own wealth, but in a very direct way made the other Russian princes financially dependent upon them. They could count on the help of the Mongols in any difficulties over collecting the tribute, or, for that matter, in any attempts of the princes to withdraw from Mongolian and therefore indirectly from Muscovite control. The khans of the Golden Horde themselves were even fatally dependent upon the loyalty of the princes of Moscow, when once this incalculable privilege had been securely lodged in their own family. That loyalty broke in 1380, when Dimitri Domskoi, the third in the line of Ivan, at the head of a group of princes defeated the Golden Horde for the first time at Koulikovo. To be sure, the Mongol dominion was reimposed in 1382, but the spell had been broken and it had been broken by the princes of Moscow. The Russian Church, the important bond of unity of Great Russia, whose metropolitan settled at Moscow in the next century, preached and encouraged the liberation of Russia under the leadership of the Muscovite house. The Golden Horde moreover was so weakened by the attacks of Tamerlane that Vasili II of Moscow could forgo, in 1412, the customary visit to Sarai with the Russian tribute. At the same time the Muscovite princes were expanding the boundaries of their principality, crushing out incipient feudalism, and founding upon the example of the Tartars themselves the tradition of autocratic absolute tyranny.

Ivan III

Soon after the middle of the fifteenth century Moscow had risen to a position of equality with such principalities as Tver, Rostov, Novgorod, Riazan, and Vladimir. Upon these foundations Ivan III (1462–1505) could raise his house and his principality to such superiority as to make his crippled self the founder of the Russian autocratic state. Tver, Yaroslav, Rostov, Viatka, and Novgorod were annexed to Moscow. Smolensk, Chernigov, and Kiev were recovered from Poland-Lithuania, and Russia began once more to move westward. By arousing Tartar against Tartar, Ivan destroyed the dominion of the Golden Horde in 1480. Diplomatic contact was established with western Europe by alliances with the Holy Roman empire against Poland and the Turks, and with Denmark against Sweden.

Ivan married the niece of the last Byzantine emperor, Constantine VI, thus transforming his own into a Byzantine court and giving grounds for the theory that Moscow had now succeeded Constantinople, as Constantinople had succeeded Rome, as the center of civilization. She was the third Rome, and with her resident independent metropolitan of the Greek Church the only orthodox monarchy and the protector of all Greek Christians everywhere. The autocracy learned from the Tartars was covered with the trappings of the ceremonial court etiquette of the Byzantine emperors. The double-headed eagle of the Cæsars was emblazoned on the Russian coat of arms. The nobility of Russia were subjected to the needs of the autocracy in such a way that the free colonial peasantry were soon deprived of freedom and fixed to the large estates as serfs. Claiming descent from the Cæsars, Ivan finally took as his title Gospodar, or Sovereign of all Russia. A thousand years of Russian history had produced the foundations of a Russian state, at the same time as men like Louis XI and Henry VII in western Europe were, along similar lines, forging the framework of national existence. Turkey and Russia as heirs to Byzantium were soon to begin a fight of centuries over their inheritance.

Chapter 28

THE CHURCH IN THE FOURTEENTH AND FIFTEENTH CENTURIES

The papacy in the fourteenth and fifteenth centuries

O
UR interest in the history of the Church in the fourteenth and fifteenth centuries must be confined to tracing those deviations from its earlier developments that led to the destruction of Christian unity in the Protestant revolt of the sixteenth century. From that point of view we are dealing with what perhaps might be called the second chapter in the history of the medieval reformation, between which and the Protestant revolt itself there was no actual historical separation. To trace these deviations effectively is to show how the papacy, in pursuit of its older ideals of dominion over the Church and state, met with an opposition of fact and theory that it was unable to subdue. Forced then to compromise with its enemies, it succeeded in offending those sterner spirits in its ranks who were least interested in compromise, and who, after discovering that the history of Christianity was but one great compromise between the difficult program of its earliest followers and the weakness of mortal flesh, sought in their indignation to restore the difficult program and to make it work. To be more specific, the papacy, in its attempts to carry on that tradition of Gregory VII and Innocent III which aimed at supremacy over the state, encountered the opposition of the young and vigorous dynastic monarchies of western Europe and had to acknowledge its defeat. In fact it became the virtual tool of one of them, namely, France, by withdrawing its residence from Rome to Avignon. Notwithstanding its compromise with France, it was able from Avignon to advance its program of monarchical control over the personnel and wealth of the Church to unheard-of heights.

The local opposition of clergy to the program of papal centralization joined with the opposition of kings and princes to papal interference in the internal affairs of their states. When the papacy itself destroyed its own theoretical program of unity by splitting into a

French and Roman, and for a time even a Spanish, papacy, it lost all claim to respect. Its friends as well as its enemies insisted on thorough-going reform of the Church by means of such general councils as had in its early history defined its theology. This blow at its authority the papacy successfully parried by allying with the strongest force in Europe at the moment, the kings and territorial princes, at the expense of the clergy within these kingdoms and territories. It thus preserved the principle of authority in the organization of the Church to the cost of its influence over these local churches. Its exclusive concern with saving its own hide at any price obliged it to neglect the accumulation of abuses in the Church to which men were objecting with increased vehemence. Under these circumstances the papacy was caught on all sides. It was caught by the princes with whom it was obliged to compromise. It was hated by the local clergy whom it had sacrificed to these princes. It was excoriated by reformers who saw no good either in its system of organization or in its peculiar system of salvation.

The attempts of the papacy to enforce its claims to temporal supremacy over the state resulted first in the difficult struggle with the German empire that we have already traced.[1] Even before the accession of Boniface VIII in 1294 the papacy had had skirmishes with the growing dynastic states of western Europe. Yet it was in the course of Boniface's pontificate (1294–1303) that the papacy, in trying to bring such states as the England of Edward I and the France of Philip IV, the Fair, under its tutelage, met a resistance that it could not handle. While it may be said to have won its earlier fight with the empire, it could not prevent these vigorous monarchs from forcing the Church within their states to support their policies. In fact, the conclusive victory of these kings over the aged and proud pope furnishes another bit of evidence for the growing secularization of western European society.

The issue which quite characteristically brought on the struggle was whether the Church might be taxed by these kings for the support of a war that they were about to wage against each other. The Church had long maintained that it was exempt from taxation except in so far as it was bound as a part of the feudal system to pay the regular feudal dues owed by a vassal to the king. The claim had been taken up by the papacy as early as 1215, when any other monetary grants to the state were forbidden except with the permission of the pope. The papacy, however, had secured for itself the right to tax the local clergy for the ostensible purpose of supporting the crusades, and by defining

Boniface VIII and the issue of taxation of the clergy

[1] See Chapters 13 and 14.

liberally what might be considered a crusade it managed pretty effectively to tax the clergy for support of many of its political ventures. It had also gone so far as to permit princes and monarchs to tax the clergy for the support of policies in which the popes themselves were directly interested. In this indirect way the states of western Europe had begun to tap the huge landed resources of the Church.

For Philip the Fair this was not enough. Although granted by the pope the privilege of taxing the clergy in the form of tenths, he went ahead to lay on them, pleading the necessity of national defense, new state taxes of his own. The Church in France, already taxed by the papacy, and indirectly through the papacy by the crown, resented this new taxation. Led by the wealthy Cistercians it protested vigorously to Boniface with the claim that new taxes could not be instituted by *The bull* the king. Boniface's answer was clear-cut in the bull *Clericis laicos* of Clericis laicos 1296. He announced again the old principle that the clergy were not to contribute to the support of the state without the consent of Rome, and he went further than a pope had ever gone before in saying that any persons who ventured to impose such taxes on the clergy "by their own act shall incur sentence of excommunication."

The answers of both Edward I and Philip IV to this annoying statement of papal policy were equally clear-cut. Edward simply outlawed the clergy who would not contribute to the defense of the realm, and except for his Archbishop of Canterbury brought the English clergy around, and made them pay for their temporary support *Boniface with-* of *Clericis laicos*. Philip IV threatened the whole papal financial struc- *draws the* ture and the security of the Italian banking houses who managed it, *claims of* by forbidding the export from France of all money, gold and silver, Clericis laicos jewels, and negotiable paper. Probably at the frantic insistence of Italian bankers Boniface withdrew gradually from the position taken in *Clericis laicos*. By it, he said in later bulls, he did not mean that the clergy were not to contribute to the defense of the realm in the event of crisis, but only that they were not to do so without papal consent. Finally he withdrew this limitation. The King of France need not wait for papal confirmation if an emergency were at hand, and whether or not an emergency were at hand was a matter for the king and not the pope to decide. The issue then was decided wholly in favor of the state; the Church could not escape the burden of supporting with its wealth what the king regarded as the best interests of the state. Under these circumstances Philip was quite willing to withdraw the prohibition of exporting money, and precarious peace was established between Paris and Rome.

The outward calm did not long persist. Within a few years another issue that had always produced trouble between Church and state arose between Boniface and Philip. It concerned the question of whether a member of the clergy could be tried in secular courts. In this instance Bernard Saisset, Bishop of Pamiers, was suspected of treasonable conduct in a southern France that had not yet accepted wholly northern French rule. In a rather high-handed fashion the king proceeded to collect evidence against the bishop, confiscated his property, arrested him, and would have had him tried and sentenced immediately but for the objections of the French clergy, who insisted that the case be remanded to Rome. Philip complied and sent the evidence to Rome, but Boniface was so outraged at the treatment the bishop had been subjected to by the king that he answered with a bull renouncing all the concessions made since *Clericis laicos* and reinstated its provisions in full. In another bull which quickly followed, the *Ausculta fili* (papal bulls are named from the Latin words with which they begin), the pope repeated high-sounding claims of the right of the pope to interfere in the local affairs of a state being mismanaged by an impious king. "Wherefore," he wrote to Philip, calling him dearest son, "let none persuade you that you have not a superior, and that you are not subordinate to the head of the ecclesiastical hierarchy, for he is a fool who so thinks, and who pertinaciously affirms it is convicted as an unbeliever, and is not within the fold of the good Shepherd." [2] Philip was then censured for his misgovernment, the abuses of which were listed in detail, and the pope announced a synod for the following year which the French clergy were to attend, and which among other things was to deal with the question of the reformation of France and the correction of its king. When this bull reached France it was probably burnt.

Philip set about to work up a violent reaction in public opinion against the bull. He prepared for circulation a shortened and garbled version of it with which was spread abroad the answer of the king, beginning, "Philip by the grace of God, King of the Franks, to Boniface who gives himself out for Supreme Pontiff, little or no greeting," and continuing, "Let your great fatuousness know that in temporalities we are subject to none. . . . Such as believe otherwise we account fools or madmen." [3] It was under these circumstances that Philip summoned the first meeting of the States-General.[4] Each house sent

The second quarrel between Boniface and Philip

[2] Quoted in Boase, *Boniface VIII*, p. 302.
[3] *Ibid.*, p. 305.
[4] See p. 511.

protests to Rome against Boniface's conduct. But cardinals and pope would not budge. The king was subject to the pope for his sinful acts, and Boniface reminded the French legates that "our predecessors have deposed three kings of France . . . and we will if need be depose Philip, most culpable of all princes as though he were a groom."

Philip's defeat at Courtrai in the same year [5] encouraged Boniface to announce, in terms that had never been so bold, the papal claims to temporal supremacy. They are contained in the bull *Unam sanctam*. Part of it is familiar language: [6] "Truly he who denies that the temporal sword is in the power of Peter, misunderstands the words of the Lord, 'Put up thy sword into the sheath.' Both are therefore in the power of the Church, the spiritual and the material. . . . The one sword then, should be under the other, and temporal authority subject to the spiritual power. . . . If, therefore, the earthly power err, it shall be judged by the spiritual power. . . . But if the supreme power err, it can only be judged by God, not by man." The last sentence of the bull for the first time made subjection to papal authority an article of faith and therefore necessary to salvation: "Furthermore we declare, state, define and pronounce that it is altogether necessary to salvation for every human creature to be subject to the Roman pontiff." [7] When Philip temporized with Boniface's legates over particulars the pope threatened to excommunicate him if he did not submit completely.

The bull Unam sanctam

This was too much for the king. Before Courtrai he had listened to the counsel of his one-eyed chancellor, Peter Flote, who was killed at Courtrai. Now he turned to another of his shrewd legists, William Nogaret, who had worked out a scheme to put an end to the loud-mouthed pope. Philip was first of all to summon a general council, which would try and depose the pope. Nogaret, together with some of Boniface's Italian enemies who had fled to France, was to go to Anagni, Boniface's home town in Italy, seize the pope, conduct him to France, and make him a prisoner of the king. To replace him a new papal election was to be held. It was an extraordinary piece of boldness. The French court drew up a list of accusations against Boniface making him out to be an archcriminal and heretic. Boniface's answer to these accusations was contained in the bull *Super Petri solio*. Philip had incurred excommunication, he was to have no power of appointing to any Church office, his subjects were released from obedience to him, and all his treaties with other princes were declared of no validity.

The conspiracy against Boniface

[5] See p. 881.
[6] See p. 645.
[7] Quoted in Laffan, *Select Documents of European History*, I, 117.

The bull was to have been published on September 8, 1303. But the day before, Nogaret and his Italian accomplices had forced their way into Anagni. They broke into the papal palace and Boniface's private chambers. The aged and sick pope had dressed himself in his pontifical robes, and to the insults of his Italian enemies and their demands that he abdicate he turned a deaf ear. There was danger of violence, even peril to the pope's life. He lay down on a couch with a cross clasped to his breast, saying, "Here is my head, here is my breast." When Nogaret entered the room the situation was calmed. He did not want a dead pope on his hands. Boniface was simply put under guard, and according to one English reporter it was believed that he had a bad night. In the following days the townsmen of Anagni who had originally betrayed Boniface took advantage of Nogaret's indecision over what to do next, to rally to Boniface's support and drive the conspirators out of town. The pope was conducted to Rome under special escort, where, the severe strain having been too much for him, he died quietly on October 12. If the original plan had not been carried out to perfection, at least the old pope was out of the way. *The incident at Anagni*

The aftermath of this crude personal attack on Boniface demonstrated how complete the victory of the French monarchy had been. After a long interim, and as the result of the manipulations of French diplomacy, the Frenchman Bertrand de Got, Archbishop of Bordeaux, was finally elected pope as Clement V (1305-14). He never got to Rome, though intending always to do so, but rather took up residence at Avignon, a town belonging to the French counts of Provence. Clement's new appointees to the College of Cardinals were practically all members of his family, or creatures of Philip IV, mostly Gascons from southwestern France. The papacy became suddenly French. In his dealings with Philip IV the French pope was excessively compliant. Such bulls as *Clericis laicos* and *Unam sanctam* were revoked. Although hesitant fully to co-operate with Philip's ruthless extermination of the Order of Templars, he did finally dissolve the Order in 1312. Philip was declared innocent of any complicity in the Anagni affair; Nogaret himself was absolved; and, more to the point, kingdoms were declared to be of divine foundation. The outcome of the first struggle between the new monarchy and the old papacy was the reverse of that between the old empire and the new papacy. *The papacy at Avignon*

It is characteristic of declining institutions that they push their claims to authority to excessive heights in order to cover up their real lack of power. The papacy, no sooner than it had been humiliated by France, itself become French, and moved close to the French frontier at Avignon, took up once more its old quarrel with the German empire. Herein it was supported by the French kings, who themselves wanted to escape from the theoretical claim to secular overlordship of Europe that the German emperors insisted upon. The result was the last and strange struggle between popes and emperors before the popes had to defend themselves from the attacks of the Church at large. Its protagonists were Louis IV of Bavaria, Pope John XXII, and his two immediate successors, Benedict XII and Clement VI. In general the issue at stake was the old one fought out during the investiture struggle and the Hohenstaufen period: Which was the superior institution in Christian Europe, the empire or the papacy, and which therefore must acknowledge the supremacy of the other? Yet the issue lacked any real vitality inasmuch as the German empire in the fourteenth century had seen its best days, was in no position to harm the papacy, and, moreover, the emperors themselves were interested in their own dynastic fortunes within Germany and not especially in the old imperial dreams.

The general issues in the struggle between Louis IV and the papacy

For the popes at Avignon to return to the program of Gregory VII and Innocent III and his successors was obviously absurd. The allies of the two parties helped to make the whole struggle strangely unreal. Ostensibly the French monarchs were supporting the popes in those temporal claims that they had just so vigorously rejected. Really they were using the papacy to weaken the German empire. Louis IV of Bavaria enjoyed the support of a radical party within the Franciscan Order, the Spirituals,[8] who had been declared heretics by Pope John XXII in 1323 for insisting that Christ and his apostles had possessed no common property, but had lived in the absolute poverty that they, the Spirituals, chose to imitate. When monastic poverty became a papal heresy something was radically wrong somewhere, and for a German emperor to support radical monks was equally strange. The monks wished to see an emperor so superior to the pope that he could take the papacy in hand and reform it. Back of all these curious alignments was the strong desire of the popes at Avignon to preserve the impotence of the empire in Italy, and to make up for the loss of revenue brought about by the removal of the papal court to Avignon, by reasserting papal authority in central and northern Italy. Italy then as in the earlier struggles remained one of the important real issues. Under these circumstances the main events of the struggle seem like so much shadow-boxing.

The particular issue over which Louis IV and John XXII were at

[8] See pp. 636 ff.

odds was whether, by the mere fact of election by the German princes *The particular* and subsequent coronation at Aachen, the new King of the Romans [9] *issue of the* was authorized to exercise the powers of German king and Holy *quarrel* Roman emperor, or whether he needed first the confirmation of the pope, and then the imperial coronation at Rome by the pope, before he could exercise legally the authority of these two offices. The position of John XXII was that the empire, being in fact a papal creation, the emperor elect (i. e., the King of the Romans) could not exercise the royal prerogatives without papal consent given after an oath of fidelity to the pope, and that, moreover, the exercise of imperial sovereignty was legalized only after the imperial coronation at Rome. The position of Louis IV and the German princes was that election by the German princes to the position of King of the Romans was quite enough, without papal confirmation, to entitle the person so elected to act as both German king and Holy Roman emperor. The imperial coronation at Rome gave the King of the Romans the right to use the title of emperor; it did not confer upon him any more power than he actually had from his election as King of the Romans.

The double election of Louis of Bavaria and Frederick the Handsome in 1314 [10] gave to John XXII an opening wedge to reassert the old papal claim that it was for the pope to decide between two candidates. When the Battle of Mühldorf, in 1322, gave Louis IV the victory, and when he then proceeded to enter into negotiations with the Ghibelline party in Italy, John announced in a bull of October 1323 that since Louis had not received papal confirmation of his title as King of the Romans, he would be excommunicated if he did not abdicate within three months, and his subjects would be excommunicated if they did not renounce their allegiance to him. When noth- *The incidents* ing happened, John excommunicated the king in the following March, *of the quarrel* summoned him to obey, and threatened again with excommunication all those who supported him. When still nothing happened the pope deposed Louis the following July, and promised to take Bavaria from him if he didn't submit by October.

Meanwhile the king defended himself in a document that denied all the papal claims, called John a heretic for proclaiming the absolute poverty of Christ a heresy, and appealed to a general council of the Church to settle the issues in dispute. In 1327 he went to Italy, where he was accompanied or joined by the leaders of the Spiritual Franciscan party, Marsiglio of Padua, William of Ockham, and Michael

[9] See p. 411.
[10] See p. 916.

of Cesena. After being proclaimed by John a heretic and ordered to give up all his titles and property, the king advanced to Rome. In order to make clear just how independent of the papacy the empire was, he received the imperial crown from four officials of the government of Rome. After Europe had been summoned to a crusade against the new emperor by a French pope, Louis, in order to demonstrate the true relationship between empire and papacy, declared John a heretic and a traitor, declared him deposed, appointed a Spiritual Franciscan as pope, invested him with the symbols of his office, and placed the papal tiara on his head.

This would all be very interesting if we could take it seriously. The emperor was obliged to leave Italy in 1330. Once home, he was anxious to pursue his own dynastic policy. For the sake of being freed from these annoying papal fulminations and their disturbing effect upon Germany, he was willing to make terms with Avignon at almost any price that did not recognize the right of the pope to interfere in purely temporal matters, or to question the validity of his election as King of the Romans. When with neither John XXII nor his successor Benedict XII peace could be purchased, Louis summoned the German electoral princes to his support. In July 1338 at Rense they took a stand against the pope's questioning their right of election by declaring that "when anyone has been elected King of the Romans by the *The declara-* prince electors of the Empire, or by a majority of them in the case of *tion of Rense* dispute, he does not need the nomination, approbation, or confirma- *and the decree* tion, assent or authority of the Apostolic See in order to assume the *Licet iuris* administration of the rights and property of the Empire or the royal title." [11] The next month Louis called a meeting of the Diet at Frankfort to confirm the declaration of Rense, and published the confirmation in a decree known as *Licet iuris*. It declared that "the imperial dignity and power proceeded in the beginning immediately from God alone" and therefore not from the pope. It restated the provisions of Rense in stronger language, going so far as to deny any validity at all to the imperial coronation. "The Emperor is made very Emperor solely by the election of those entitled to elect him." The papal claims are "iniquitous doctrines," "detestable assertions," and "pestiferous theories." Anyone denying the provisions of *Licet iuris* was guilty of treason.

These provisions would be a remarkable declaration of independence of the German kingdom and empire from the theocratic claims of the papacy if one could be sure that they were an expression of na-

[11] Laffan, *op. cit.*, I, 148.

tional sentiment and not the mere wish of the electors to preserve their own rights and those of the king to be free to pursue policies that were anything but nationalistic. They did not regulate the conduct of German kings towards the popes. Before Louis IV's death in 1347, his rival for the royal and imperial crowns, Charles of Bohemia, was perfectly willing to bargain with Clement VI for his approbation. He promised not to proceed with his coronation as King of the Romans, or exercise any royal authority in Germany or imperial authority in Italy, without receiving Clement's confirmation of his election. Yet when the electoral procedure was regularized by him in the Golden Bull of 1356,[12] the pope was left out of the document. Whether that is to be interpreted as a confirmation of *Licet iuris* or as an opportunity for future German kings to act as Charles himself had acted is an open question. At least the Golden Bull denied the claim of the papacy to rule the empire during a vacancy. The issue of papal confirmation of German royal elections remained henceforth a dead issue, crowded out by disputes of greater moment. Yet if the struggle between Louis IV and the papacy may not be interpreted in any national sense, it must take its place alongside of the Boniface VIII-Philip IV struggle to indicate the impotence of the papacy to make good its theocratic claims over and against the rising secular claims of the state.

Inconclusive character of the settlement of the quarrel

More interesting than the events of the struggles between Philip IV and Boniface VIII and Louis IV and John XXII is the large amount of political theory that appeared instantly in the defense of the pope, the King of France, and the Holy Roman emperor. In fact, for the political theorist the earlier decades of the fourteenth century constitute one of the most creative and important periods with which he has to deal. Those men defending the papacy worked out to a degree beyond which it was impossible to go the full implications of the doctrine of the *plenitudo potestatis* of the pope.[13] In the works of the defenders of the state, whether France or Germany, novel and daring claims were made, reflecting not only the actual political development in western Europe but enunciating also principles that were to guide political and religious reformers for centuries to come. Although beaten in practice, the papacy winged its way triumphantly still in theory. The victorious French monarchy, having established in fact its independence from the empire and papacy, now saw its victories completed in the realm of theory. The anomalous empire drew to

Church and state in political theory

12 See p. 918.
13 See p. 650.

itself foreign writers who now raised to a height never before dreamed of the secular and all-inclusive rights of the state, and destroyed in thought at least the imposing constitution of the medieval Church. Both sides wielded effectively the clean-cutting sword of logic. The papal writers drew into their service the Scriptures allegorically interpreted and the provisions of canon law. The French writers proclaimed the necessity of having done with allegory and symbolism and of adhering to a literal interpretation of Biblical texts. They opposed to canon law the Justinian Code. The writers in the imperial camp drew in the secular viewpoint of Aristotle, talked about natural law, and deduced ideas of their own of revolutionary import.

For our purposes the papal writers are less instructive, inasmuch as they elaborated points of view with which we have already become familiar in the striking proclamations of Gregory VII, Innocent III, and Boniface VIII.[14] Men who defended Boniface VIII, such as *The papal* Egidius Colonna in his *On Ecclesiastical Power*, and James of Viterbo *writers* in his *On Christian Governance*, or men who defended John XXII, such as Augustinus Triumphus in his *On the Power of the Pope*, argued at great length to prove that the governance of the world was theocratic in character and that in the hands of the pope was the absolute control over all temporal and spiritual affairs. Emperors, kings, and princes were his mere agents and secular governments only departments of a vast world-wide ecclesiastical state headed by the pope. These works we may regard as restatements in the early fourteenth century of a point of view expressed in the early fifth century by St. Augustine in his *City of God*. They took advantage of what had meanwhile actually happened.

The men who defended Philip IV were neither monks nor clerics, for the most part. They were professionally trained lawyers, expert *The French* in Roman law and in certain cases holding political office. In their *writers* search for some sort of principle that would free France from the generally acknowledged superiority of the empire, which popes like Boniface VIII were inclined to emphasize in moments of anti-Gallic choler, they hit upon the phrase "the king is emperor in his own kingdom" (*rex est imperator in regno suo*). They could thus avoid henceforth the apparent inconsistency of using the maxims of absolutism contained in the Justinian Code, pertaining only to the Roman emperor and therefore only to his medieval successor the Holy Roman emperor, to apply to the position of the French king. Nor did they hesitate to do so. When the French feudal king became a Roman

[14] See pp. 378 ff., 645–46, 958.

emperor as important a step was taken as when Charles the Great, a German king, became a Roman emperor. In this instance after more than four centuries, thought caught up with the facts in so far as the independence of France from the Holy Roman empire was concerned.

One of the more interesting of the French writers defending Philip was the Norman lawyer in his service, Pierre Dubois, known especially for his pamphlet *On the Recovery of the Holy Land*. For the feeble old popes with their claims to temporal power he had little patience. The world would be much better off, he argued, if the pope would surrender, as he should, his temporal possessions and power to the King of France and content himself with spiritual affairs. Indeed, it was advisable for all the clergy, regular and secular, to give up their property to secular persons. The King of France could use the temporal possessions of the papacy to establish a really effective overlordship of Europe, not to mention such minor tasks as recovering the Holy Land. The property of the Church could be used better to this end also. It were better that many nunneries and the priories of crusading orders be turned into schools for boys and girls. If given a chance, the King of France, the head of the superior French people, could establish peace in Europe. There should be set up some kind of machinery for the settlement of international disputes. Within his realm the King of France was supreme. He ought to be so in Europe as a whole, and one useful thing the Church and papacy could do was to contribute to that ideal end.

Pierre Dubois

There were German writers, such as Jordan of Osnabrück, who justified the possession by German kings of the title Roman emperor and strove to preserve his independence from the pope. But the more striking of the imperialist writers were not German, and they were interested not so much in particular claims of empire as in using the empire to reform the papacy. They were, as we have already mentioned, adherents of a radical party within the Franciscan Order, Spiritual Franciscans, who insisted on maintaining to the letter the evangelical counsels of St. Francis and were therefore opposed to all those compromises on questions of property ownership that had been approved by the papacy after St. Francis's death. They had been proclaimed heretics by John XXII, and under ordinary circumstances would have been so regarded by the German emperor, but he could make fine use of them in his struggle with the papacy. The classic exponent of imperial claims, Dante (in his *On Monarchy*),[15] who

The imperialist writers

[15] See pp. 788-89.

wrote not long after the death of Boniface VIII, should be grouped with the imperial theorists at the court of Louis IV.

One of these latter was the English Franciscan, William of Ockham, who wrote his chief works, *The Dialogue* and *Eight Questions Concerning the Power and Dignity of the Pope*, after coming to the *Marsiglio* Bavarian court. Another was the Italian Marsiglio of Padua, who not *of Padua* only had had actual experience with the turbulent politics of an Italian town, but had also studied at the University of Paris and had been its rector for a short while. In the preparation of his epoch-making treatise, the *Defensor Pacis* (*Defender of the Peace*), he associated with himself for the earlier part of the work another member of the university, the Frenchman John of Jandun. The *Defensor Pacis* was finished before the two left for the court of Louis IV, and in papal eyes it made its authors "pupils of damnation" "full of heresies." The opinions of William and Marsiglio are so similar in general import that it is permissible to discuss them together. Both men made extensive use of Aristotle's *Politics* and approached the whole question of the purpose, organization, and functioning of civil society without giving to God, heaven, and immortality a predominant place.

The purpose of the state was to obtain peace, prosperity, and security, immediate and earthly ends, and not to prepare mortals for their heavenly home. Marsiglio displays a preference for monarchy as the suitable form of organization of the state—not monarchy of the French type, i.e., hereditary absolute monarchy, but the elective monarchy victorious in Germany. He prefers elective monarchy in order that the king may be under the supervision and control of the electors, and subject to deposition if they deem it wise. Indeed, Marsiglio's king is a medieval approximation of what we should call a limited monarch. He gives an important rôle in the governance of this monarchy to what he calls the legislator, composed of the people and acting as a check through the vote of a majority. But what he means by people and majority is not what is today called democracy, but only the guidance of the wealthier and wiser among the citizens. He suggests that this control should be exercised in a representative assembly. The will of the people in this sense should determine what is law, to which the prince himself should be obedient. The prince is the servant and not the maker of law, and must act always in the interest of all. A state so organized is quite self-sufficient and independent, a perfect society in itself, with absolutely no need of or use for the Church.

If hitherto popes and papal writers had treated secular states as mere departments of the Church subservient to the dictation and purposes of the Church, now for the first time the situation was reversed and the Church was made a mere department of state. Its property, personnel, and organization were subject to the control of the state. Its clergy had no right to the special jurisdiction of the canon law. They had no right to exercise a coercive judgment of any kind, whether temporal or spiritual.

In fact, Marsiglio continues, the clergy should be restricted wholly to spiritual functions—to preaching and teaching Christian doctrine and to administering the sacraments. When so restricted they are to be supported by the state. The Church is not the clergy, anyway. Clergy should not be and are not a special privileged class distinct from the laity. The Church is composed of the community of the *Marsiglio on* faithful (*universitas fidelium*), of all believing Christians. Final *the Church* authority in this Church rests not with pope and clergy but with the representatives of all believers gathered together in a general council. The laity as well as the clergy should be represented in this council. Ockham recommends that even women be included. The council has authority to deal with any questions concerning the spiritual affairs of the Church. As the prince is the instrument of the legislator, so the pope is the mere instrument of the will of a general council. Councils should be summoned by the secular prince and not by the pope. The ultimate authority in the Church should be the Scriptures, not as interpreted by the pope or clergy, but as interpreted by a group of reasonable and learned men. The Petrine theory is a falsehood, and the present papacy an accident of history. The pope is not superior to any other bishop. The clergy do not forgive sins in the confessional: it is God who forgives sins, the clergy acting only as his agents.

It is hard to imagine any more sweeping statement of the rights and claims of the secular state. No sooner had the papacy worked out its right to supreme and absolute control of all Christian society than it was confronted for the first time by a theory that did as much for the secular state, and robbed the papacy at the same time of its spiritual power within the Church itself. This is, of course, the distinction of Marsiglio. He announced a program that was to be taken up after him by such heretics as Wyclif and Hus, and by the Protestant reformers of the sixteenth century. Western Europe has spent a good deal of time to date trying to realize the program, and it has only in part succeeded. By the time of Marsiglio's death, political theory as well as political fact had reached the point of reversing the part played by Church and state in medieval society: it was the state and not the Church which rightly directed the general course of affairs.

If the popes at Rome and Avignon were unable to make their claims to unlimited temporal sovereignty prevail over kingdoms and empire, with the result that their temporal supremacy remained merely an impressive theory, they were nevertheless not so impotent in translating into fact their claims to unlimited spiritual supremacy over the whole Western Church. What that amounted to in detail was the right to pronounce authoritatively on questions of the doctrine of the Church, to control the personnel of the clergy, and to discipline that clergy through its own system of courts based on the canon law, and finally the ownership of all ecclesiastical property and the right to use that property as it pleased by means of taxation of the clergy. The degree of success that Innocent III and his successors in the thirteenth century achieved in rendering actual their own spiritual supremacy has already been described.[16] They had won out on all sides against the clergy. The new dogmatic definitions of the thirteenth century were made by councils which were completely under the dictation of the pope. The judicial system of the Church came more than ever to be centralized in the papal *Curia*. The popes began successfully to supply their own appointees to certain classes of ecclesiastical benefices and to discipline almost as they chose refractory members of the clergy. They had also begun to devise a lucrative system of taxing the clergy for the support of the papacy.

The papacy and spiritual supremacy

These things had been done by adhering strictly to principles of absolutism and centralization learned from the example of the Roman empire. They had, moreover, been accomplished by elaborating within the *Curia* efficient financial, judicial, disciplinary, and secretarial departments, and at the same time fashioning instruments for the control of the local churches, such as legates and papal tax collectors. It is worth repeating that in these ways the popes were striving to do what the kings and princes of central and western Europe were at the same time trying to do. They were, that is, trying to destroy the localism and feudalism in the Church just as the kings were striving to destroy the localism and feudalism in the state. The institutional history of the Church parallels that of the state and can be understood best from that point of view. In general it may be said that the popes were, ultimately to their own cost, far in advance of most of their secular contemporaries.

The peak of centralized papal absolutism was reached during the fourteenth century while the popes were in residence at Avignon, two hundred years earlier, it might be said, than in England and Spain,

16 See Chapter 22.

and three centuries earlier than in France. This being the case, it is The character impossible to say of the seven French popes from Clement V to of the Avi- Gregory XI (1305–78) that they were the servile tools of the gnon papacy French monarchy, and that this period in papal history was "the Babylonian Captivity" of the Church that Petrarch [17] labeled it. The French popes were, in fact, superior men. They were all trained legists, some of them (such as John XXII and Clement VI [1342–52]) financial experts, and many of them personally of unexceptionable character. Benedict XII was an austere ascetic and John XXII, in spite of his other preoccupations, a mystic. They made no break with the past tradition of the papacy. Some of them made earnest efforts to remedy the undoubted evils in the Church. They maintained the idea of a crusade as the chief instrument of papal foreign policy, and were zealous to mediate in the Hundred Years' War in order to establish the peace necessary for a crusade.

That they did not return to Rome is to be explained in part at least by the fact that Rome was a turmoil of rival noble families in whose disputes they would have become involved, and central and northern Italy a battlefield for the rising despots of the Italian cities. By staying at Avignon, which they purchased for themselves and where they constructed a new papal palace, still extant, they assured themselves of independence of action and the protection, now that the German empire was impotent, of the French monarchy. Absence from Rome and the loss of the Papal States in Italy deprived them of the major sources of their income, which they were obliged to recoup by extending the papal system of taxation and creating new taxes. To be sure, in their mediation between England and France, French popes tended to lean towards the French kings and even went so far as to loan money to them. And it is true that the papal court at Avignon was soon surrounded with the pomp, luxury, and extravagance that at the same time characterized the secular courts of Europe. One cardinal at Avignon needed fifty-one houses or parts thereof to keep his large retinue, and another ten stables to house his horses. But the abuses outstanding in the Church, the incontinence of the clergy, simony, nepotism, the holding by one person of more than one benefice, the entrusting to vicars at a modest salary of the duties of a benefice and pocketing the income thereof, even though never putting in an appearance, and, finally, the laxity in the monasteries, were all of long standing and were not of papal manufacture. Legislation against them was abundant enough but it was difficult to enforce. It was none of these

[17] See p. 1008.

things so much as the shrewd, efficient, and unlimited way in which the Avignonese popes went ahead to impose their sovereignty on the Church that called forth the howls of discontent from clergy and to a lesser extent from the states. The popes knew how to compromise with the secular rulers, whose programs were identical with their own. The clergy themselves were caught between a relentless Church and a relentless state.

The Avignonese popes needed for the most part only to extend the administrative institutions, practices, and precedents of the thirteenth century in order to develop to its medieval height papal centralized absolutism. This they could do by virtue of the theory of the *plenitudo potestatis*, which subjected them to no limitation in the exercise of their powers as successors to Christ in the headship of the Church. And this they did by elaborating the already existing power of "reservation" by which they set aside for their own use rights and powers hitherto exercised by local clergy or laymen.

The Avignon papacy and papal absolutism

They reserved for themselves, for example, the right to collate to local Church offices. That is to say, they deprived local ecclesiastical groups, such as cathedral or monastic chapters, and local patrons, of the right to elect or appoint to a certain office, and themselves claimed the right to confer—that is, to collate or appoint to this benefice whomsoever they pleased. The number of benefices to which the papacy had reserved the right of collation at the end of the thirteenth century was extensively increased by Clement V and John XXII. Urban V (1362–70) even reserved to the papacy "all patriarchal, archiepiscopal and episcopal churches exceeding the value of 200 florins annually, and all monasteries of men exceeding the annual value of 100 florins, whenever and however they should become vacant." Later he included "all churches of the same types and also monasteries of women of whatever value, whenever he chose to dispose of them." [18] Ultimately, except for the parish priesthood, there was almost no benefice in the Church that the popes had not reserved for their own appointment, or, as it was more usually called, their own provision. In large measure, in spite of all local opposition they put through their claims, although often by accepting suggestions from local authorities as to whom they should provide. It is needless to insist on what appointment to all the major offices in the Church by the popes meant for papal centralization.

In addition to reserving benefices for their own provision, the French

[18] Lunt, *Papal Revenues in the Middle Ages*, I, 85.

popes continued the practice of reserving for themselves certain fees hitherto collected by the local clergy. The chief example of this kind of reservation during the Avignon papacy concerned the fees called procurations. They were collected by the bishop or archdeacon to cover the expenses involved in making a visitation of the churches and monasteries in the diocese. The popes had earlier claimed the right to collect procurations remaining unpaid at the death of a local prelate. Innocent VI (1352–62) went so far as to order papal collectors to perform the visitations and collect the procurations, a good example of both administrative and financial centralization. A third class of reservations consisted in setting aside for the decision of the judicial department of the papal *Curia* infractions of the canon law previously handled in local ecclesiastical courts.

The popes at Avignon did not permit to lapse those taxes and fees that had been established in the thirteenth century,[19] the income from which was now increased inasmuch as the number of benefices which the popes controlled was notably increased. In addition to the reservation of episcopal procurations, and the larger use made of other taxes such as spoils, the only really new tax developed at Avignon was the annate, and it was new only in that it had not hitherto been collected by and for the pope. Clement V was the first pope to reserve annates for himself. They were a portion of the revenues of a benefice for the first year of occupancy paid to the pope when he collated to the benefice, and paid only by those benefices not subject to services. The system of collecting papal taxes locally was completed by Clement VI (1342–52) when all those lands subjected to the Roman See that had not yet been divided into definite collectorates were so divided. The use of reservations of various kinds, the new taxes, the more efficient collection of the old taxes, brought to the papal *Curia* an increased amount of business that had to be taken care of by an expansion and reorganization of its departments. "The camera reached the height of its development" at this time. John XXII reorganized the chancery, which by 1331 collected four hundred and fifteen different fees for various services. The penitentiary granted dispensations from the exactions of canon law in greater number and for the appropriate fees. The judicial department split off into four branches. The average annual income of the pontificate of John XXII approximated 228,000 florins. At the middle of the fourteenth century it reached as high as 335,000 florins. The average annual income of the camera from 1316

The Avignon popes and papal finance

[19] See pp. 658–59.

to 1362, expressed in pounds, approximated from £24,000 to £42,000 when for about the same period the income of the kings of England ranged from £35,000 to £272,000 annually.

Naturally enough, such accomplishments made an impression upon those who thought that the main business of the papacy was to save souls. Edward III of England said as much to Clement VI: "The successor of the Apostles was commissioned to lead the Lord's sheep to the pasture, not to fleece them." It was no more possible to keep graft out of this machinery than it is out of any political machinery run by human beings. The temptation to receive gifts in return for a papal provision to a benefice expected to be vacant, the so-called expectatives, could not be resisted. The danger of providing more than one candidate for the same vacant or to be vacated benefice, all at the appropriate sums, could not be avoided. By the end of the fourteenth century offices in the papal administration were for sale, and it was easy to multiply the number of offices in order to have more offices to sell. Towards the end of the fifteenth century most of the offices in the chancery, camera, and penitentiary could be bought. By the beginning of the sixteenth century the income from the sale of offices amounted to one-sixth of the entire papal revenue.

Papal collectors could not be prevented from loaning out the money they collected and keeping the interest. What in an extreme case the opportunities of a papal collectorship might result in is well illustrated by the case of Jean de Palmis, a collector in southern France. "Beginning his collectorship as a poor man, he soon became wealthy. He clipped the coins belonging to the camera that passed through his hands; accepted a horse in payment of a debt owed to the camera, fed it at the expense of the camera, sold it at a profit and put the profit in his pocket; collected debts for creditors who would pay him, by asserting falsely that the debts were owed to the camera and using his exceptional powers of ecclesiastical censure to compel payment; usurped the jurisdiction of the local ecclesiastical court; lent money at interest; made fraudulent contracts; sold the goods of the camera secretly to his friends and not at open sale; made himself a general nuisance to the community by his boastful and overbearing conduct; and displayed remarkably loose ideas about sexual relationships." [20] Reservations, taxes, and corruption, when combined with the removal of the papacy from its traditional location to Avignon, were enough to stir up protest. A serious crisis in the papacy itself led to action.

The particular crisis that drove the Church to a revolutionary at-

[20] Lunt, *op. cit.*, p. 49.

tempt to solve the difficulties that beset it was the schism or the split *The schism*
of the Church into two and finally three definite factions. Hitherto
the German emperors had used the weapon of an antipope in their
struggles with Rome, but they had never been supported enough by
other governments to make such schisms, of purely political origin,
a really scandalous division of the Church. Now in 1378 the Church
split itself into a Roman and a French faction because, first of all, of
the deficiencies of the method of electing a pope by the College of
Cardinals. By 1377 Gregory XI was no longer able to withstand
pressure of many kinds from Italy demanding that the Holy See be
re-established in Rome, whither he returned amid the cheers of the
Roman populace. He died there the next year. By far the majority of
the cardinals then staying in Rome were French, and they would
undoubtedly have preferred to elect one of their number as pope and
return to Avignon. But the people and government of Rome were
determined to have a Roman or Italian pope. The officials of the city
told the cardinals, "Name a Roman or an Italian pope, otherwise your
lives and ours are in danger, so determined are the peoples to have
what they want." Under the circumstances the Sacred College chose
a compromise candidate in the person of the Archbishop of Bari, who
took the name of Urban VI.

They soon repented of their choice. Urban was a "short, stout,
swarthy, obstinate, arrogant, stiff-necked, hot-blooded, bigoted old
man without tact or prudence, lacking in even the common courtesies
of life and entirely too prone to give his ear to obsequious flatteries,
whimsical, haughty, suspicious, supercritical, and at times choleric in
his dealings with those about him." He at once endeavored to inaugurate most drastic reforms, threatening the personal luxuriousness
of the cardinals and their lucrative simoniacal practices. He threatened to reduce their power by creating Italian cardinals, and most of
all, a low-born man himself, he berated the aristocratic cardinals in
coarse and insulting terms. They therefore finally denounced him as
anti-Christ, a devil, and an apostate, declared his election void because
of intimidation by the Roman mob, and in a new election chose one
of their own number, the young French Bishop of Geneva, formerly a
fighter in the Papal States and related to the King of France. He took
the name of Clement VII, and after a futile attempt to dislodge
Urban VI from Rome returned to Avignon with his cardinals.

There were thus two popes, two colleges of cardinals, and two papal
courts, one at Rome and one at Avignon. In view of the fact that there
was no way to pronounce upon the validity of either election—and the

The results of schism Church has never officially done so—or to enforce such a decision if made, it was open to Europe to take sides between the two or to remain neutral. What determined the choice made was for the most part political considerations. Western Europe was at the moment divided over the Hundred Years' War. France, therefore, and those states that moved in the French orbit—Castile, Aragon, Navarre, Sicily, and Scotland—supported Clement VII. England, Flanders, the Scandinavian states, Hungary, and Poland supported Urban VI. The German emperor was an Urbanist, but the German princes and the towns and princes of northern Italy were hopelessly divided between Urban and Clement. In view of the pretensions of the Church to unity under the one Vicar of Christ, the pope, this was a preposterous situation. Europe was thrown into violent discussion and unparalleled confusion that soon became ludicrous.

From all sides, and particularly from the University of Paris, came demands that the schism be healed and union restored. Various contradictory suggestions as to the methods of cure were made. Among these was the proposal that one college of cardinals refuse to elect at the death of a pope, and join the second college at the death of its pope in a new election. Another was to have both popes resign so as to make possible a new election by the combined colleges. Every member of the two colleges of cardinals was forced by public opinion to promise individually that if he were next elected pope he would unite the Church, even if he had to abdicate to do so. This, however, was asking too much of the cardinals and popes. The schism was prolonged. Urban VI was followed by a line of three Roman popes, and Clement VII by the Spanish Benedict XIII.[21] Each pope, with the liveliest side-remarks, excommunicated the other. This meant that whichever pope was validly elected, the people of a great part of Europe were denied the consolation of true sacraments. Each pope tried to appoint his own adherents to every office, and resorted to all the old devices and some new ones to raise money for the support of luxurious courts, and for wars of propaganda and force against his rival. Europe had to support two sets of cardinals, two papal courts, and everywhere there were two sets of legates and papal collectors, each clamoring to be recognized and denouncing the other. All the abuses and corruption of the Avignon papacy were doubled. Most

21

Roman line:	Avignon line:
Urban VI (1378–89)	Clement VII (1378–94)
Boniface IX (1389–1404)	Benedict XIII (1394–1417)
Innocent VII (1404–06)	
Gregory XII (1406–15)	

disastrous of all was the influence upon the simple believer of the sight of the divided Church. Something had to be done if the organization and influence of the Church were to be preserved.

Learned opinion, led by doctors of the University of Paris, finally came to the conclusion that the only solution for the anomaly of the schism was to revert to the practice of a general council and entrust it with authority to deal with the stubborn rival popes who were ruining the Church.[22] In 1408, a majority of the Roman and French cardinals withdrew from their respective popes, and in an effort to give this suggestion a trial summoned a general council for Pisa, which met with abundant numbers in March 1409, and assumed the direction of the Church. It thought to cure the schism by deposing both Gregory XII and Benedict XIII as "notorious schismatics, prompters of schism and notorious heretics, errant from the faith, and guilty of the notorious and enormous crimes of perjury and violated oaths." The union cardinals then elected as the new pope the Greek-born Cardinal of Milan, reputed to be a lover of good food, who took the name of Alexander V. At his death in the next year, the cardinals made an extraordinary choice as his successor in the person of Cardinal Baldassare Cossa, who called himself Pope John XXIII. He had made a reputation as a pirate and soldier, and was, in the words of a Catholic historian, "worldly minded and completely engrossed by the temporal interests, an astute politician and courtier, not scrupulously conscientious and more of a soldier than a churchman." He was hardly the person to lead Christian Europe back to unity. In fact, the Council of Pisa succeeded only in adding another head to the Church, whose leadership became now properly triune. Neither of the deposed popes recognized the authority of the Council of Pisa, and John XXIII was unable to enforce their deposition. For John's benefit they would not abdicate. It was confusion worse confounded.

The Council of Pisa

The fact that the Council of Pisa met as a "universal synod representing the Church universal" was far more significant than the results that it was able to obtain. For a council to presume to direct the Church was a reversal of the trend of a thousand years of papal history that had culminated in the doctrine of *plenitudo potestatis* enshrined in the canon law of the Church. That it failed to accomplish its purpose did not prevent the further use of councils for the same and other purposes. Pisa was followed by a series of councils, especially those of Constance and Basel, claiming the right to steer the wind-tossed Church into a safe harbor. The first half of the fifteenth century

[22] See p. 987.

The conciliar period

is therefore known as the conciliar period; and back of the movement to make the council the supreme source of authority in the Church was, in addition to the fact of schism, the need for reform, and the growth of radical heresies, a revolutionary conciliar theory that aimed at nothing less than a remaking of the constitution of the Church and a justification of the acts of the councils. Facts and theory combined to give the new constitution an opportunity to justify itself in the councils themselves. The threatened papacy, however, conspired to ruin the councils and invalidate the conciliar theory, while doing little or nothing about the facts that had called them both forth. That it succeeded is proof that a thousand years of history cannot be easily passed over.

The conciliar theorists

The chief conciliar theorists were associated with the University of Paris at a time when universities such as Paris, Oxford, and Prague actually counted for something in public life. No sooner had the schism broken out than men like Henry of Langenstein, Conrad of Gelnhausen, and Cardinal Pierre d'Ailly, the Bishop of Cambrai, argued in their writings for the superiority of a council to the pope. Before and during the Council of Constance John Gerson, the chancellor of the University of Paris, continued the argument; and the German, Nicholas of Cusa, undertook to defend the Council of Basel in the last great work of the school, the *Concordantia Catholica* (*Catholic Unity*). They were in turn answered by papal supporters and a group of writers less radical than they, in what amounted to a continuation of the disputes aroused by the conduct of popes Boniface VIII and John XXII.

The conciliar theorists had back of them the political experience of Europe with parliaments, states-general, *cortes,* and diets and the general assemblies of the mendicant orders. These, by the beginning of the fifteenth century, were declining in power in competition with monarchy. The papacy, however, had developed an absolutism without such contacts with the general body of the Church, and from this point of view the theorists were attempting to apply to the papacy a form of limitation already outworn in the state. Yet in their search for fundamental principles of divine government these men enunciated principles not necessarily new, but of value to men who were later to attempt to destroy absolute monarchy in the state. They went back to what they regarded as the principles of natural law which guaranteed the equality of men. If there arose differences in power and influence within the hierarchy of the Church they must have originally arisen with the consent of the Church. Papal power therefore rested on the consent of the Church; it had no inherent rights of its own. As a delegated power, it must, when abused as it was obviously being abused, be subject to the control and limitation of the Church, from which it got its power. This Church was, as had been argued by Marsiglio and Ockham, the whole body of the faithful, or, as some argued, the body of the clergy. The institution best qualified to represent its interests was the council. If the pope were not subject to the supervision and control of a council it was possible for the Church to become the slave and tool of the pope in the pursuit of goals that had no relation to the needs of the Church at large. The pope must therefore be the minister of the Church, i.e., of a council, and not an autocrat. As one historian has put it, he must be the Vicar of the Church, not of Christ.

The papacy was a limited, not an absolute, monarchy, subject to the control of a body representative of the whole Church. If in such a crisis as the present one the pope refused to summon a council, the emperor could summon one, or if necessary the council could meet on its own accord for as long as it wished, with no fear of dissolution at the hands of the pope. In this council the sovereignty of the Church resided, and not in the pope. It could depose popes, review and cancel their decrees, determine all matters of faith and discipline, and elect new popes. It was in accordance with these principles that the Council of Constance declared itself "a General Council constituting and representing the Catholic Church" with "authority immediately from Christ which everyone in existence of whatsoever status or dignity, even of papal, is bound to obey in those things which pertain to the faith, the extirpation of the said schism, and the reform of the Church in head and in members." [23] Such a statement has been called "probably the most revolutionary official document in the history of the world . . . striving to turn into a tepid constitutionalism the Divine authority of a thousand years." [24]

Kings and princes interested in doing without parliaments, states-general, and diets could not be expected to be very sympathetic to the conciliar theory. At heart they were at one with the pope, whom in *Monarchy and* fact they were trying to imitate. They were interested in supporting *the conciliar* the conciliar theory to get rid of the annoying schism and especially to *theory* wrest from papal hands concessions that would give them greater power over their own local churches. This clear-cut trend towards the formation of local dynastic churches subservient to the state was destroying more than anything else the universal character of the me-

[23] McIlwain, *The Growth of Political Thought in the West*, p. 347.
[24] Figgis, *From Gerson to Grotius*, p. 35.

dieval Church. During the schism the French Church under the di
rection of the king withdrew its obedience from Benedict XIII and
set up its own organization, forming thus a Gallican or French Church
Although this withdrawal did not last, the monarchically controlled
French Church used the subsequent councils chiefly for the purpose of
maintaining the independence that it had begun to establish.

Similar attempts were made elsewhere during the schism. In Eng
land during the Avignon papacy Parliament protested over and over
against the interference of the popes in the affairs of the English
Church. In particular it refused to recognize any longer the subjection
to the papacy involved in the payment of the tribute levied on Eng
land by Innocent III when John became his vassal. It refused to
pay and refused to admit that it was in any sense obligated to pay
Parliament protested again and again and passed many statutes of
provisors against the practice of papal provision to English benefices
of foreigners who never bothered to come to England. It passed
too, statutes of præmunire trying to prevent cases from being appealed
from English ecclesiastical courts to the papal *Curia*. Royal limitation
of the circulation of papal bulls in England was constant. Yet there
came no break between England and the papacy, inasmuch as the pope
was wise enough not to challenge, and was in no position to challenge
the English state. Individual difficulties could always be adjudicated
and in such matters as provisions, candidates suggested by the king
and the universities were usually well taken care of.

The local protests were nevertheless strong enough to contribute to
the growing demand for a reform of the Church and, when the scanda
of the schism appeared, to strengthen the supporters of the genera
council. By the time the Council of Constance met, however, a much
more serious danger to the Church as a whole had appeared in heresies
associated definitely with local hostility to papal government, but go

New heresies

ing far beyond any program reformers and conciliar theorists had to
suggest, to a definite repudiation of the kind of Christianity repre
sented by the organized Church and the sacramental system. The two
leaders of the new radical heresies were the Englishman John Wyclif
(1320–84) and the Czech John Hus (1369–1415).

John Wyclif

Until the last few years of his life Wyclif was a master at Oxford
then at its prime as a center for liberal ideas. In what he wrote and
taught he was not an original thinker, nor was he a particularly warm
or attractive personality; but the combination of his ideas, ceaselessly
and forcefully put forward in both Latin and English, makes him as
thorough-going a radical as the conservative Protestant leaders of the

sixteenth century. There is little that separates him from them except time.

Philosophically Wyclif represents a reaction to the ideals of Thomas Aquinas, according to which the traditional faith could be harmonized with reason. Schoolmen after Thomas, under the influence of nominalism, had become quite sceptical as to the possibility of a union of the two, and in their scepticism turned to faith alone.[25] Wyclif was a realist, but whereas Thomas used Aristotle as the chief mediator between faith and reason, Wyclif championed a reconciliation based upon Scriptures, and indeed upon a literal interpretation of Scriptures. Such a point of view was a decided turn in medieval religious thought away from Aristotle and allegory. It marked a turn of broad implications, inasmuch as when once a return was made to a literal interpretation of Scriptures, the large contrast between the Christianity there contained and the Christianity of the fourteenth and fifteenth centuries was so glaring as to force consistent thinkers to try to modify the latter in terms of the former. In addition to Scriptures, Wyclif, like all the great subsequent reformers and Protestant leaders, was much influenced by St. Augustine. His emphasis upon Scriptures alone convinced him of the necessity of making them available to an audience beyond academic circles, and although he did not himself translate them into English he was responsible for their being translated into English for the first time. Together with his writings in English, this use of the vernacular tongue demonstrates the need he felt for an appeal to and satisfaction for popular religious feeling.

Until the papacy tried to get him in its grip in 1377 and the schism came in 1378, Wyclif was associated chiefly with the protests in Parliament against papal tyranny. He defended ardently the refusal to pay further tribute to the papacy. He opposed the papal provisions in England and served on a delegation to Bruges to negotiate with papal envoys over the matter. He brought down papal condemnation upon himself by his radical ideas on the subject of the right of the clergy to own property. Here Wyclif was in line with the radical party in the Franciscan Order as represented by the Englishman Ockham. It was Wyclif's adopted theory that all property was held in feudal *Wyclif and* fashion from God on condition of rendering service to God and being *Church* in his good grace. Theoretically every thoroughly righteous man *property* owned everything, and the only completely logical system of property holding was communism. He did not, however, push this to any practical extremes. That was left for certain leaders of the peasants' revolt of

[25] See p. 996.

1381 [26] to do. That property was held by unrighteous seculars was patent to all, but here again Wyclif did not convert his theory into any practical program.

In view, however, of the law of Christ contained in the Scriptures, it was quite impossible for the clergy to possess any property at all. The Church should live on the voluntary offerings of the faithful. For Church property to be possessed by clergy who did not use it for Godlike purposes was an intolerable scandal. Wyclif was frank and stubborn in his advocacy of the confiscation of all Church property by the state, to be divided among the lords so that the burden of dues and taxes might fall less heavily upon the poor. As he put it, "Secular lordships, that clerks have full falsely against God's law and spend so wickedly, shulden be given by the King and witty lords to poor gentlemen that wulden justly govern the people, and maintain the land against enemies. And then might our land be stronger by many thousand men of arms than it is now, without any new cost of lords, or talliage of the poor commons, and be discharged of great heavy rent, and wicked customs brought up by covetous clerks, and of many talliages and extorsions, by which they be now cruelly pilled and robbed." Such a program of confiscation of Church property was welcome enough to the king and witty lords, who when it was put into effect in the sixteenth century were not so much concerned about the remainder of Wyclif's program. For the medieval Church it meant nothing less than a revolution.

Because of his political influence and popular support by the Londoners Wyclif was able to ward off the papal attack on him. After the outbreak of schism, he went ahead for the remaining six years of his life to elaborate what we may properly call his Protestant views. The Church became for him the body of those predestined to be saved, whose head was Christ. The Church composed of the hierarchy headed by the pope was false. It might be convenient, but it was not necessary. The schismatic popes he branded as "monsters," "limbs of Lucifer," "men glowing with Satanic pride," and "sinful idiots"; their cardinals, "incarnate devils" and "hinges of Satan's house." He sought an organization similar to that of the earliest Church, when there was no differentiation between priest and bishop.

Wyclif on the Church and the sacramental system

Wyclif in fact sought for the realization of a religion of personal piety based on the direct dependence of the individual on God and a human Christ, wherein every man was his own priest and could do without the intervention of the clergy, the "fiends of hell." He re-

[26] See p. 869.

sented the suggestion that the sacrament of ordination alone could make a priest. "For crown [i.e., tonsure] and cloth make no priest . . . but power that Christ giveth and thus by life are priests known." He had no use for the specialized kind of Christianity practiced by the monastic orders. There were no grades of Christians, and as for the friars, whom he hated especially, they were "gluttonous idolaters." Everything in the sacramental system and other practices of the Church that tended to emphasize the mere external rites, the mechanics of the faith, at the expense of personal devotion he would exclude. He rejected the doctrine of transubstantiation. "Of all the heresies that have ever sprung up in the church, I think none was ever more cunningly brought in by hypocrites or cheats the people in more ways than this." His view was that the substance of the bread and wine remained after consecration by the priest, but was interfused with the spiritual presence of Christ. The sacrament of penance was unnecessary. Pardon from God could be secured by the penitent sinner himself. Except for marriage, there was no one of the seven sacraments that he did not attack. When it came to such popular practices as the worship of saints, pilgrimages to their shrines, veneration of their relics, he objected to them as mechanical and false substitutes for true piety. Indulgences he would not tolerate. With the puritanical spirit of a St. Bernard and a John Calvin he attacked the majesty of elaborate churches, gorgeous church furniture, and the use of the arts in religion.

Above all he trained at Oxford a band of poor priests, the Lollards, who were to spread his teachings among the people. It was no wonder that he was condemned by Rome, and that at Constance two hundred and fifty-one articles of his writings were condemned and his remains ordered disinterred and scattered on unconsecrated ground. The peasants' revolt of 1381 in England, for which he and his Lollards were in no way responsible, nevertheless discredited his movement, and the ensuing reaction killed it. Not until the sixteenth century was it to bear fruit in England, and then in much more conservative form than he would have wished.

Oddly enough at first sight, it was in Bohemia that Wyclif's ideas had their greatest influence. This was possible because of the establishment at Oxford, when Wyclif's writings were most popular, of scholarships for poor Bohemian students, who translated Wyclif's writings into their own tongue on returning home. While John Hus was still a student at the University of Prague he and the Czech masters at the university had probably come to know Wyclif. Jerome of Prague brought home from Oxford in the early years of the fifteenth century Wyclif's theo-

Wyclif and the Czech reform movement

logical writings. The Queen of England from 1382 to 1394 was a Bohemian, the sister of King Wenzel.

Wyclif's writings did not begin, however, the reform movement in Bohemia that brought the establishment of independent reformed churches there a hundred or so years earlier than elsewhere in Europe. The Bohemian Church had long been under the influence of the German Church, and German clergy were numerous in it. Not indeed until the reign of Charles IV did Bohemia have an independent archbishopric of its own at Prague. The Czechs were never satisfied with this situation. Nevertheless the Bohemian Church less than other churches in central and western Europe had been subjected to the dictates of the papacy, and the papal centralization of the fourteenth century had stirred up even more virulent protest there than elsewhere. Before John Hus became the leader of the reform movement a whole series of Czech reformers had begun to criticize, in their own language and upon the authority of the Bible, the luxury, immorality, and worldliness of the clergy, and the interference of the papacy in the affairs of the Czechish Church.

The writings of Wyclif acted as a powerful stimulus to this reform movement, and gave it a peculiar national turn, inasmuch as in the University of Prague, dominated at the moment by the German nations, the Czechish masters took up the doctrines of Wyclif with enthusiasm and were opposed by the German masters, who were in turn supported by the Bohemian Church. This peculiar anti-German start to Bohemian reform efforts has its larger setting in the history of German colonization in Bohemia in the thirteenth and fourteenth centuries, as a result of which the dominant elements in all the Bohemian towns were German and not Czech. Charles IV had limited German predominance in Bohemia by founding an independent archbishopric, a new University of Prague, and by using the Czech language and Czech advisers to stimulate a native self-conscious pride. The German-Czech rivalry was now to be augmented by religious differences.

It should be mentioned too that in addition to the earlier reform movement to which Wyclif's writings gave particular point, there was present in Bohemia among the peasants and artisans a much more radical background for the development of a national reform movement. In southern Bohemia the Waldensian heresy had taken firm root, had not been destroyed, and was still a potent force. It was reinforced by certain offshoots of the Cathari. Into Bohemia from northern France had recently come a group of exiled heretics called the Picards, who were prominent in the whole later movement. Among the peasants there was a strong belief, backed up by the preachings of some of the reformers, that the end of the world was nigh, and that soon after the appearances of anti-Christ, the millennial kingdom of Christ was to be established. Bohemia was fertile ground for a religious revolution.

The career of John of Husinec, or in short Hus, forced all this na- *John Hus* tional and religious discontent into a powerful movement of European import. He was first of all a patriot, devoted to his people and cultivating their language with care in his writings and sermons. The proud master in the new university succumbed wholly to the teachings and spirit of Wyclif. He did not, to be sure, agree with him on every point, differing especially on the question of transubstantiation, but his writings betray everywhere the influence of Wyclif, whom in many places he copied outright. As a forceful and popular preacher in the Bethlehem Chapel in Prague, he lashed unmercifully the failings of the clergy about him, and got himself into immediate difficulties with the archbishop, who excommunicated him more than once, sought to deprive him of his post, and worked constantly to rid Prague of the pernicious presence of Wyclif's books. He supported King Wenzel in his fight against the German masters of the university and the archbishop, who were favoring Gregory XII against the union cardinals and Council of Pisa. He rejoiced when Wenzel in 1409 destroyed the hold of the German masters on the policy of the university by giving the Czechish nation three votes to one for the three German nations. After the disgruntled German masters abandoned Prague to found the University of Leipzig, Hus was elected rector of the now completely national University of Prague. When John XXIII sent into Bohemia in 1412 a group of unscrupulous indulgence sellers to raise money for one of the all too frequent political crusades, this time against the King of Naples, Hus raised his voice in protest and subjected the whole theory of indulgences to question. For this he was excommunicated by the pope, and in the confusion caused by the appearance of the indulgence sellers withdrew from Prague for two years, devoting his time to study and writing.

He was anxious to vindicate himself and the Bohemian reform *The Council* movement before the Council of Constance when it met in 1414. He *of Constance* had no reason to be ignorant, however, of what the attitude of the *and Hus* council would be towards his Wyclifite ideas. It was interested in establishing its own supremacy within the Church, terminating the schism, reforming the papacy so as to free its own members from papal control, and introducing such general reform as might not be too hard on its clerical members. But heresy was the kind of rebellion that it would not tolerate. In fact it was anxious to prove its worth by solving the problem of heresy. Hus therefore thought to protect himself by securing from the Emperor Sigismund a safe-conduct to Constance and back again to Bohemia, and a guarantee of a public appearance before the full council assembled.

Hus was deceived. His Bohemian enemies at Constance had him summoned to a hearing before the cardinals, who arrested him and thrust him into the dark and foul dungeon of a local Dominican convent. Subsequently he was moved to another hole in a near-by castle, where he was chained day and night and inadequately nourished. The emperor was at first horrified at the council's disregard of his safe-conduct; but when for his support of a notorious heretic his own orthodoxy was put into question, and he was told that by supporting Hus he might ruin the prospects of the council itself, he broke his word and permitted it to do as it pleased with Hus.

The only thing the council wanted from Hus was a complete submission to itself in the form of a recantation of all the errors it chose to attribute to him. Although he knew his life was at stake Hus refused to go this far. He refused to recant errors which he said he never held, and refused to recant others which he admitted that he held until he should be convinced of their untruth on the basis of Scripture. Hus was therefore staking the right to believe what he thought true against the authority of the Church. For this he was condemned as a heretic to the loss of his priestly dignity and turned over to the secular arm for punishment. In early July 1415 he was led to a pyre outside of Constance and burned to death with the words of a hymn on his lips.

The council thus succeeded in making Hus a martyr of the Bohemian reform movement. A year later they pursued the same methods in dealing with his disciple, Jerome of Prague. He had originally recanted in proper fashion, but in spite of this was kept in custody and a new investigation ordered. When he saw clearly into the council's intentions, he renounced his former submission, pleaded the cause of Hus, and was burned on the same spot.

The burning of Hus and Jerome did not, of course, destroy the religious rebellion in Bohemia. It only raised it to the dignity of a powerful national movement. The Bohemians now were determined to remove from their cause the stigma of heresy, and knew that God had chosen them especially to fight in his cause against the Emperor Sigismund and the Council of Constance and the papacy. They rose in armed rebellion when the Church resorted to the methods it had used against the Albigensians and proclaimed the extermination of the Hussites by means of a crusade. Although torn by religious dissension among themselves, the Hussites from 1420 to 1434 resisted every attempt of Sigismund and others to invade their country and put down their new faith.

In the earlier part of their national struggle they were brilliantly organized by the one-eyed General Zizka, who before dying on the field of battle lost his other eye, and still went on striking terror into his foes. Zizka's armies were composed mostly of fanatical peasants and artisans. Armed with iron-tipped flails and hand guns, and in possession of cannons, from behind their barricades of wagons they broke up every attack ever made on them. The German crusading armies got so that they did not care to see a Hussite heretic face to face and often fled before ever entering battle. Under Zizka's successor, the bald-headed priest Prokop, who like many another medieval cleric would not actually fight himself but would lead an army, the Bohemian armies took the offensive, and spread not only the terror of their arms, but their doctrine as well, into Silesia, Thuringia, and Franconia. By the time the Council of Basel met in 1431 it was clear to all that the idea of a crusade against the Hussites must be given up, and they were invited to send delegates to Basel to negotiate, being promised that while they were there prostitutes would be kept off the streets and the members of the council urged to refrain from drunkenness, gambling, and dancing. *The failure of crusades against the Hussites*

Now that the question of national defense was no longer pressing, the Hussites tended to split more hopelessly into various sects. In 1420 they had united upon the program of the Four Articles of Prague, which insisted that there was to be absolute freedom in preaching the word of God, that the sacrament of communion was to be administered in both kinds,[27] that the property of the clergy was to be confiscated, and that all mortal sin and violations of the divine law were to be properly punished. Of these the most important came to be the second, which was felt to be prescribed by Scriptures and absolutely necessary to remove one difference between the priesthood and the laity. The cup used in the administration of communion became the symbol of the most conservative of the Hussite groups, the Utraquists or Calixtines. The most radical of the Hussites were the Taborites, whom Prokop represented. They were thoroughly Protestant in wishing to bring the doctrines and services of the Church completely in line *The Utraquists and Taborites*

[27] See p. 680.

with Scripture; but, composed largely of peasants, they had radical social and political ideals which included the abolition of royal power, taxes, peasant dues, and services, and the destruction of private property. They went to the complete limits of organizing an independent church of their own. The Taborites were, however, defeated in battle by an alliance of Utraquists and Catholics at Lipan in 1434, where Prokop was killed. Subsequently their group diminished to insignificant numbers.

For the sake of internal and external peace and their own security the Utraquists, composed mostly of the nobility and the rich townsmen, now pushed forward the negotiations with the Council of Basel that resulted in the Compacts of 1436. By them little more was granted to the Hussites than a limited communion in both kinds. In their final negotiations with Sigismund, however, the Utraquists provided for the organization of an autonomous Hussite Church even though within the framework of the Christian Church at large. Yet these agreements did not terminate the religious struggle within Bohemia. The papacy subsequently denounced the Compacts, forcing the Hussites into a compromise arrangement with the orthodox Catholics in Bohemia. The period after 1436 witnessed the growth of a new independent Hussite Church, the "New Unity of Brotherhood," "the first reformed church which consciously and expressly renounced the Catholic principle of the apostolic succession, and created its own priesthood by independent election." In this state of general revolt against Rome the various Hussite churches lasted until merged with the Lutheran revolt of the sixteenth century.

In addition to religious revolt, the Hussite movement brought other significant social, economic, and political changes in Bohemia. The Czech national movement against the Germans was successful not only in the university but in the towns, where in many instances the

Bohemia after the Hussite movement

German merchants and industrialists lost control. The orthodox Church and the monasteries in Bohemia suffered from an almost complete confiscation of their property, the first of its kind in Europe. The property went for the most part to the nobles and gentry, and in part to the towns, and their anxiety to get it accounts in large measure for their support of the Hussites. The nobles too, because of the lack of regular royal government over long periods of time, secured a much more important position in political affairs. The efforts of the peasants to seize upon religious discontent to improve their own economic position went for nought. The powerful nobility was able by the end of the fifteenth century to bring it about that the Bohemian peasants, like the peasants elsewhere in eastern Europe, were tied to the soil and made serfs by law. To be thoroughly familiar with the Protestant revolt of the sixteenth century, one should master the history of fifteenth-century Bohemia.

The councils of Constance and Basel thus failed to do anything more than increase rather than decrease—not to say destroy—the danger of heresy in Europe. The only effective attack on heresy would have been the inauguration and enforcement of a rigid program of reform. But the existence of the schism pushed into the background the question of reform when Constance met in November 1414; and the supporters of the supremacy of a council, who were not necessarily reformers, had their hands full in solving this problem according to their own ideas. The Council of Constance was called together primarily because of the initiative of the Emperor Sigismund, who was seriously concerned with the chaotic state of the Church and wished to imitate the Roman emperors in their initiative in trying to solve the problem of heresy in the fourth and fifth centuries. He practically *The Council* forced John XXIII, the second Pisan pope, to summon the magnifi- *of Constance* cent assembly of patriarchs, bishops, archbishops, abbots, doctors, and representatives of the lay princes who, together with their retinues, contemporaries estimated increased the population of Constance by forty thousand. Among these there were enough prostitutes to equal the total number of about seven hundred clergy attending the council at its height.

It is unfortunate that the historian is unable to relate how reformers, conciliar theorists, princes, and popes worked together in the councils to bring about changes in the Church that staved off the impending break in the religious unity of western Europe. Human nature being what it is, that was never done. The vested interests of the clergy, *The council* popes, and princes of western Europe conspired to take advantage of *and schism* the too radical proposals of the reformers and to leave unsatisfied the awakening conscience of large numbers of the intelligentsia and bourgeoisie of central and western Europe, who, when they discovered that they had been cheated, only too willingly took the whole matter into their own hands. With some difficulty the fathers at Constance did succeed in getting rid of the schism. John XXIII came to Constance hoping to keep his office, to organize the council so as to give his party control, and then speedily to dismiss it. He was foiled on all sides. The council organized itself on the basis of nations, following the organization of the University of Paris, and by thus defeating John's plan to vote by head prevented the Italians from having a majority. When John perceived that the council would not abandon its tasks and regarded him as one of three candidates to be somehow got rid of, he tried to break it up by escaping from Constance disguised as a messenger.

When the council recovered its composure it acted decisively and promptly. After a series of revolutionary decrees claiming superiority in all spheres of Church government,[28] it had the escaped pope arrested and imprisoned and brought him to trial for a long array of offenses. He was finally deposed when fifty-four of these charges, among them those of fornication, adultery, incest, and sodomy, were considered proved, and he was moreover obliged to ratify his own deposition. A little later Gregory XII came to terms with the council, and abdicated for an important position in Italy. There was thus only one of the three schismatic popes left, the stubborn Spaniard Benedict XIII. Sigismund left the council in the summer of 1415 to negotiate with him in southern France, and did not return until January 1417, leaving the council meanwhile to its own devices. With Benedict personally there was nothing to be done, but by agreement with those few states which adhered to him, the way was prepared for his deposition by the council in June 1417, as "a heretic and an incorrigible promoter of schism." The council was now free to elect a pope for the reunited Church. In co-operation with the cardinals at Constance, it elected in November, as Pope Martin V, the Italian cardinal, Otto Colonna.

The council and reform

There had been a good deal of discussion in the council as to whether it should proceed to the election of a new pope or institute the program of reform proclaimed as one of its chief purposes. The rivalries among the nations caused by the reopening of the Hundred Years' War in 1415, combined with the simple fact that the clergy at Constance were interested in reforming everyone but themselves, made it impossible to achieve anything of importance. With unity restored in the Church after the election of Martin V, there was even less interest in reform. The pope himself was an avowed enemy of councils, and took it as his chief task to restore the lost prestige of the papacy. Before the council was over he declared that "no one may appeal from the superior judge, that is the Apostolic See, or the Roman pontiff, vicar on earth of Jesus Christ, or may decline his authority in matters of faith." His attitude towards the reform of the *Curia* is well illustrated by the fact that the day after his election he issued new regulations for the chancery which increased rather than dimin-

[28] See p. 977.

ished the claims of his predecessors with regard to reservations and provisions.

In addition to proclaiming its supremacy over the pope and within the Church, the council in the decree *Frequens* of October 9, 1417, had taken care to perpetuate the institution of general councils by declaring that one should be held in five years after Constance, a second seven years later, and then at regular intervals of ten years. It had taken steps, besides, to deprive the pope of procurations and spoils. Martin V was prevailed upon to abandon the claim to income from vacant benefices and to limit his demands for clerical tenths. In his desire to bring the council quickly to an end he made with the respective nations at Constance individual concordats which were to last for a period of five years. The concessions by way of reform were not great and their contents of no importance, since they were never enforced. They do show the way out for the popes in their difficulties with the radical conciliarists and reformers: private negotiations with the individual nations concerned. They so satisfied the council as a whole that Martin was able to dissolve it in April 1418. It thought it had intimidated heretics, and it had removed the schism. The question of reform had been hardly touched, and what was to be the constitution of the Church was still in doubt.

In the interim between the Council of Constance and the opening of the Council of Basel in 1431, the attention of Martin V was riveted on securing a return to Rome and recovering the Papal States. He showed no conversion to the program of reform or of conciliar supremacy. The papal *Curia* went on as before. German envoys wrote home for money, "for here at court all friendships end with the last penny"; "greed reigns supreme in the Roman court and day by day finds new devices and artifices for extorting money from Germany under pretext of ecclesiastical fees." The English ambassador informed Martin that "if the abuses of the Church are not removed by your Holiness, the necessary reforms will be taken in hand by the secular powers." Public opinion prevented Martin from refusing, in accordance with the provision of Constance, to call a council at Pavia in 1423. It was quickly moved to Siena, but when the French nation proposed that the papacy should be confined to levying taxes only on the laity of the Papal States, Martin had the legates to the council dismiss it as soon as possible. Before his death in 1431 he had made the necessary arrangements for the opening of the Council of Basel under papal auspices.

The Council of Pavia

The new pope, the Venetian Eugenius IV, pursued with even more

The Council
of Basel

vigor the opposition of the papacy to the conciliar idea and to an adequate program of reform. The history of the Council of Basel resolves
itself in fact into so fierce a battle between the council and the papacy
for control of the Church that any possibility of a satisfactory reform
program was precluded. Dissatisfied with the council's reassertion of
the decree *Frequens* and its willingness to negotiate with Hussite heretics, Eugenius opened the struggle by dissolving the council not long
after it had met, and calling a new council for 1433 at Bologna. But
the council refused to dissolve, declared its immunity from any interference, and summoned the pope and cardinals to appear at Basel or
suffer the consequences dictated by the inspiration of the Holy Ghost.
For two years a battle of decrees and bulls went on, until finally, failing in an appeal to the princes of Europe against the council, Eugenius
capitulated and withdrew his bull of dissolution. Elated at this success
the council went ahead to pass radical decrees subjecting bishops and
archbishops to the control of local synods, and ordering that under
no circumstances was money to be paid out to Rome for an appointment to any benefice, for the issue of any papal bull, or in the form
of papal taxes. If enforced such decrees would have meant the total
destruction of the medieval papacy.

At this point pope and council took to fighting over which of the
two should conduct the negotiations with the Greek Church over the
proposed union of the Greek and Roman Churches. The emperors of
Constantinople were interested in union as a means of bringing military support from the west against the Ottoman Turks. Both pope
and council saw in the prospective union a fine chance to score against
the other. None of the parties concerned was much interested in the

The question
of the union
of the Greek
and Roman
Churches

principles of Christian unity. On this score Eugenius outwitted the
Fathers at Basel and succeeded in splitting the council. When the
issue came to a head at Basel over whether the Greeks were to come
where Eugenius or where the council wished them to come, the rival
parties drew swords and struck blows in the cathedral at Basel, and
the papal party stole the seal of the council in order to validate its
decrees. The delegation of Greeks headed by the emperor and the
patriarch came to the council summoned by Eugenius for Ferrara in
1438, which was thence transferred to Florence. After over a year's
discussion, agreement was reached on the question of the procession
of the Holy Spirit,[29] and of the leadership of the pope in the unified
Church, and an act of union was signed by both the Greek and Roman
delegates.

[29] See p. 135.

It did not effect a union between east and west, because the Greek clergy as a whole ignored the results of the council and the west was not unified to begin with. But it was a great victory for papal prestige and ruined the hopes of Basel. There the enraged council declared the conciliar theory a dogma of the Church, and first suspended and then deposed Eugenius IV from the papacy. It then went on in 1439 to elect in his place Amadeus VIII, the Duke of Savoy, a widower with several children, who, they hoped, was rich enough to cost the council nothing. Amadeus VIII took the name of Felix V. The Council of Basel had now succeeded in creating anew a schism that the Council of Constance had with such great difficulty removed. It remained to be seen if Europe would tolerate a new schism, and whether Eugenius IV was clever enough to manipulate the situation to the ruination of all conciliar programs and reforming hopes.

The council had gone too far and so discredited itself in the eyes of European princes, who now took matters in their own hands or resorted to private negotiation with Eugenius IV. In 1438 a synod of *The end of* the French Church assembled by Charles VII at Bourges had pro- *the Council* claimed in the Pragmatic Sanction the supremacy of a council to a *of Basel* pope, but had gone on to establish the liberties of the French Church —the Gallican liberties, they were called—which forbade papal appointment to French benefices, and prohibited the payment of annates to Rome and all judicial appeals to the Roman *Curia* before the resources of French courts had been exhausted. This declaration of independence, following upon the earlier withdrawal of obedience from Benedict XIII, was in effect nothing more than turning over the French Church to the control of the French monarchy. The kings and popes could subsequently negotiate at the expense of the French Church itself.

In the following year a German diet at Mainz followed the French suit in abolishing annates, papal reservations, and provisions. Except for a few universities and Hungary, the only support the Council of Basel received after the election of Felix V was from a few German princes. In 1444 at a diet of Nuremberg the princes adopted a policy of neutrality between pope and council, but demanded the restoration of unity within a year or they would summon a new council in Germany to solve the question themselves. Under these circumstances the Emperor Frederick III came to terms with Eugenius IV in 1445, and in return for recognition by the emperor the pope granted him large sums of money and the right to appoint to a large number of benefices in Hapsburg territory. By his death in 1447 Eugenius had succeeded

in reconciling a large number of the German princes, and his successor
Nicholas V completed the pacification by the Concordat of Vienna in
1448 between the pope and emperor in which were included subsequently the German princes. The concordat was a bargain over papal
provisions and reservations. It left the pope more control over the
German Church than he had elsewhere in Europe, but at the expense
of surrendering to Frederick for his Hapsburg territory, and to other
German princes, a large measure of control over their territorial
churches. The papal reconciliation with Germany deprived the Council of Basel of its last supporters. After being ordered out of Basel it
held a few sessions at Lausanne, where, after finally arranging for the
resignation of Felix V, it made its peace with Eugenius IV and dissolved itself in April 1449.

What had really happened was that the pope and the princes and
kings of western Europe, in their competition with each other for
control of the local churches in the interests of papal or royal absolutism, compromised with each other at the expense of the conciliar
theorists and of reform. No more was heard of a general council until
the papacy, faced with the rebellion of the Protestant revolt in the sixteenth century, was obliged in the Council of Trent to try to set the
The out-   Church's house in order. The popes after Basel found it simple to
come of the   restore their ancient claims and powers, to preserve the monarchical
conciliar   organization of the Church, and to nullify and anathematize the works
movement   and theories of the councils and their supporters. By concerning themselves with re-establishing their temporal power in the Papal States in
Italy, and by advertising their victory over the councils in a lavish
support of Italian scholars and artists, they failed to realize the importance of general reform, and thus made the Protestant revolt inevitable. If the Church would not reform, reform would have to be
thrust on it.

Meanwhile, in the course of the fifteenth century the monarchs,
princes, and even the town governments had tightened their grips on
their local churches, and used the councils and the reformers in order
to gain concessions from Rome that strengthened their holds. The
papacy's victory was thus only a phantom; it had lost to the state the
power it exercised in the thirteenth and fourteenth centuries. When
the actual revolt came in the sixteenth century, the princes had learned
enough from the history of the fifteenth to use the revolt to complete the transformation of western Christianity into state churches,
whether Catholic or Protestant. The reformers themselves had learned

as well that this was the only way out. The transition from the international church-state of medieval Christianity to the national and territorial churches of the sixteenth century was slowly accomplished during the fourteenth and fifteenth.

as well that this was the only way out. The transition from the in-
territorial church state of medieval Christianity to the national and
territorial churches of the sixteenth century was slowly accomplished
during the fourteenth and fifteenth.

Chapter 29

LEARNING AND ART IN THE FOURTEENTH
AND FIFTEENTH CENTURIES

F OR the same reasons that the terms "dark ages," "middle ages,"
and "medieval" have served for so long to mark the period
covered by this book, it has long been customary to treat the
cultural history of the fourteenth and fifteenth centuries as centered
in Italy and to speak, accordingly, of an Italian renaissance, which in
its spread stimulated a transalpine renaissance. Such a view is essentially
The so-called   narrow and unhistorical. It is narrow because to concentrate on Italy
Italian ren-   and the spread of Italian influence is to ignore the independent ac-
aissance   complishments elsewhere and to fail to show that the direction of influence was often into and not from Italy. It is unhistorical because
it emphasizes novelty rather than continuity. The cultural history of
western Europe and Italy was interwoven, and in every essential respect was the outcome of the medieval renaissance of the twelfth and
thirteenth centuries. In this chapter, therefore, rather than discuss the
cultural history of the period as if it were but the reflected radiance
of the rising Italian star, an attempt will be made to trace the aftermath of the earlier medieval renaissance. It will of course be necessary to show modifications that these later centuries introduced. In this
case again we must escape from catchwords of long standing that have
become meaningless and false.

The earlier renaissance was a response to the growing complexity
and diversity of western European society brought about by the growth
of towns; the simplicity of the earlier agricultural society was transformed by the introduction of new commercial, industrial, and urban
The growth   institutions. The chief intellectual expression of this change was the
of the secular growth of a secular or worldly spirit, contrasting with the earlier re-
spirit   ligious spirit. There is no reason to abandon this contrast for the fourteenth and fifteenth centuries. There was no interruption in the growth
of towns. Town life in northern Italy and Flanders, the two areas which

first displayed the specific characteristics of urban development, became more intensified, varied, and turbulent. It is therefore no mere accident that in these towns especially the secular spirit grew. It must not be supposed, however, that in any sense it completely triumphed. Western European civilization has not even yet gone so far. For the great masses in the towns and countryside the world was still too much of a puzzle. They needed and demanded, as they still need and demand, the simple and comforting teachings of a religion.

Intellectually the chief feature of the earlier renaissance was the rather sudden acquisition of Aristotelian logic and philosophy and Hellenistic and Moslem science, medicine, and mathematics. This remarkable addition to the knowledge of western Europe led to the formation of universities that assimilated, interpreted, and taught it. The process of assimilation, interpretation, and dissemination was not completed by the end of the thirteenth century. The number of universities continued to increase, and has, of course, never ceased to increase; the number of educated laymen grew correspondingly. In fact, one phase of *The growth* the increasing secularism has to do with the larger number of educated *of an edu-* laymen in proportion to the clergy, although no serious inroads were *cated laity* made upon the illiteracy of the masses. While the clergy remained the preponderant educated class, they no longer had a monopoly on learning. Dante, the well-educated layman of the end of the thirteenth century, was an exception. Such exceptions became more numerous with the increase in wealth and leisure of the bourgeois class. University education, however, preserved its professional character in training men for the schools, the Church, the law, and medicine. The larger share of scholarly work had still to do with writing summaries and digests, commentaries and glosses upon the books of the twelfth and thirteenth centuries.

The introduction of Greek and Moslem science and philosophy forced the scholar to consider the problem of the relationship of the new learning to the commonly accepted Faith. The courageous scholar rejected the suggestion that the new learning was essentially inimical to the Faith, and undertook to reconcile the two by use of the philosophy and logic of Aristotle. The revealed dogmas of Christianity were then buttressed by the rigid logic of the schoolmen; the unbelievers and those who would depend alone upon faith were defeated. Theology remained the queen of the sciences, and philosophical realism [1] the dominant school of thought.

Men like Albert the Great, Thomas Aquinas, and Roger Bacon were

[1] See pp. 694–95.

*The revival of
the controversy
between reason
and faith*
nevertheless extremely distrustful of authority, talked about natural causes, natural theology, a new experimental science, and in fact implied that philosophy and science might pursue their own independent ways. The body of knowledge was already too large to be confined by the concepts of earlier Christian learning. The leading scholastics were thus self-contradictory: they unified faith and knowledge at the risk of their separation. It was the task of the later schoolmen to reveal this contradiction. A revival of nominalism [2] led to an attack on the demonstrations of revealed truths undertaken by the schoolmen. Once again the incompatibility of reason and faith was insisted upon. The hopeful spirits went ahead to clear the way for a secular philosophy and a secular experimental science. Those who now adhered to the truth alone of revealed knowledge cleared the way for a revival of mysticism. Some scholars were pessimistic about the possibility of any human knowledge.

*The interest in
the classics
continued*
The medieval renaissance was characterized by a better understanding of the form and spirit of classical Latin literature. Lupus of Ferrières, John of Salisbury, Hildebert of Le Mans, some cathedral schools, and the poetry of the Goliards clearly illustrate this phase. The revival of the study of Roman law in Italy and its gradual spread elsewhere emphasized the classical side of the earlier learning. Long before the opening of the fourteenth century western Europe had thus begun to regain some historical perspective with regard to the classical period. Scholars, most of them Italian, now pursued the study of the ancient world with an ever growing enthusiasm that amounted to a cult.

*The revival
of Greek*
The west, moreover, had always regretted, even if it had not done much about, the loss of the Greek language. There were, to be sure, always a few men who knew Greek or some smattering of Greek, but they were very few indeed. Others, such as Roger Bacon, had stressed the importance of knowing Greek if only for the purpose of getting behind the Latin translations of the twelfth century. Scholars had pointed out that for Christian scholarship Greek was necessary to read the New Testament in the original and Hebrew to read the Old Testament. Circumstances made possible the gradual recovery of Greek in the west beginning with fifteenth-century Italy. In addition now to Aristotle in the original, a new stream of philosophy was introduced with Plato's *Dialogues*. There ensued violent controversies over the relative merits of Plato and Aristotle as philosophers. But the more serious of the Italian classical scholars inclined to neither Plato nor Aristotle, but rather to the third-century mystic, the Egyptian Plotinus, whom they

[2] See pp. 694–95.

used to interpret Plato and to bring about a new fusion of Christianity with the pagan tradition. To Greek philosophy was now added the whole wealth of Greek literature. Therewith the mission of Byzantium was completed for the west. Western Europe, having been first brought to maturity by contact with the civilization of Islam, was now put into possession of the whole classical tradition with the addition of Greek. Her intellectual task was the same as ever. She must come to terms with this classical outlook by first understanding it and then relating it to her own Christian experience. In the excitement of recovering the entire classical world she lost her perspective with regard to the intervening world, and the consequent intellectual upset has now only begun to be righted.

The literary history of these two centuries is again but a continuation, with new emphasis, of the earlier renaissance. Before the fourteenth century the vernacular languages had reached the point of development where they expressed themselves in both prose and poetry with great skill. In so doing they had perfected the use of allegory and *The earlier* symbolism in treating the themes of chivalry. The glamorous world of *literary* romantic adventure was, however, subjected to criticism and ridicule *tradition* by bourgeois authors. The romantic allegory of the first half of the *Romance of the Rose* became the satire and realism of the second half. The *Romance of Renard the Fox* took feudal society to task, and the *fabliaux* did the same for the Church.

No more great Latin poetry was written either in the form of hymns or students' songs after the thirteenth century. The classical scholars who wrote and patronized poetry in the classical style killed a living Latin poetry. In the vernacular tongues the old themes of the trouba- *Later medieval* dours, the trouvères, and the minnesingers continued to be worked *literature* over with perhaps greater finish in new verse forms. The ladies of romantic literature corresponded more closely to real ladies of the flesh. But allegory and symbolism soon exhausted themselves. As in the case of Chaucer's *Canterbury Tales*, there was nothing for authors to do but to return to the plain facts of real life. This, except for the most distinguished of them, they did very slowly. At the same time the world of nature, never really absent from earlier literature, received more adequate treatment. The homely virtues of rustic life, in the midst of an ingratiating countryside, were emphasized in pastoral poetry. The older feudal world was treated with greater abuse. But in general, as some of the writers complained, they had no new ideas to write about. The restored classical tradition brought no new life to vernacular literature. In the person of François Villon, writing at the middle of the fifteenth century, there arose a poet with no affection for either the romantic or the classical tradition. He concerned himself with the hard facts of life and the meaning of death.

*The develop-
ment of
Gothic art*

Gothic architecture had rather effectually subordinated all art to the cathedral. Although it had used allegory and symbolism as principles of decoration, it introduced too the natural world of flowers, plants, beasts, birds, and even men in sculpture. As an artistic form Gothic continued to dominate the fourteenth and fifteenth centuries, but not so exclusively in subordination to architecture. Gothic architecture itself ended its logical development in the virtuosity of the perpendicular or flamboyant style developed in England and transferred to the continent in the course of the Hundred Years' War. The new churches in England and France were not so much the bold pronouncements of logical structure as formerly; structure was rather concealed by an intricate encasement with stone lace and an extraordinary refinement of detail. Town and gild halls, the residences of the new rich bourgeoisie, and the more elegant private châteaux of the nobility took their places alongside of churches.

*Sculpture
and painting*

Sculpture, while still used to decorate both secular and religious buildings, finally freed itself from architecture and began to reassume the position occupied during the classical period. It began to decorate the tombs of the great, and to reproduce in independent portraits the features of the living. In so doing it gradually abandoned allegory and symbolism and contented itself with a realistic, and often melodramatic, treatment of its subject that reminds one of Hellenistic sculpture. In the same way painting emancipated itself from any necessary connection with architecture either in the form of fresco or stained glass or mosaic. The painting of miniatures in manuscripts and service books went on unhindered until the printed book. In books of private devotions it attained an astounding fidelity to the world of nature. In new altar pieces for the chapels of saints it retained the use of architectural settings for its subjects; but the world of nature was introduced in the form of landscape into the backgrounds, and the persons and objects of the main composition were painted with photographic exactness. As much can be said for the portraits of the easel painters. In fact the meticulous details of the miniatures of manuscripts were enlarged into independent pictures. It was not so much change in subject matter or improvement in technique that marked the new in sculpture and painting. It was the secular point of view with which the matter was treated that was novel. Painters were as interested in describing the wart on a man's nose as Chaucer was.

Italy during this period reached the height of her medieval culture. *The arts in Italy* She freed herself from the tradition of Byzantium in the arts. Until the beginning of the fifteenth century she was influenced very strongly by the Gothic art of western Europe. Henceforth, however, under the guidance of her own genius she returned to the native tradition of Rome, and under the stimulation of the classical enthusiasm of scholars she made use of the wealth of Italian princes, popes, and businessmen to produce an extraordinary display of exciting works in all the arts. With the disappearance of the Byzantine and Gothic traditions in architecture, she succumbed at last almost wholly to the Roman style and took to the most stubborn kind of servile imitation. But in sculpture and painting the classical tradition was in no sense confining or even very important, and with the gradual achievement of technical mastery, with an almost incomparable native talent, she went ahead in the sixteenth century, whither we must not follow her to reach a full maturity of genius.

In yet another aspect did the fourteenth and fifteenth centuries but *Western Europe continues to expand* mark the continuation of earlier history. Western European civilization was always remarkably expansive,[3] as witness both the Vikings and the crusades. The desire to know and to win fortunes drove on the adventurous during this later period not only to seek the Far East via land routes through central Asia, but also to seek it over the sea. The mysterious Atlantic Ocean began to yield its secrets.

From the scientific and mathematical Franciscan school at Oxford came the main attack on the earlier scholasticism in the fourteenth century. The later schoolmen, in fact, divided themselves into two groups: the ancients, who defended St. Thomas, and the moderns, who took up the new challenge of Duns Scotus (*c.* 1270–1308) and William of Ockham (*c.* 1300–49), both English Franciscans, the latter of whom we have met at the court of Louis IV of Bavaria.[4] In these men the *The ancients and moderns* evangelical piety of the Franciscan Order took the form of extreme dissatisfaction with the Thomist rationalism that would prove, rather than feel or believe, the existence of a supreme God, that would demonstrate logically, rather than accept on faith, his divine attributes, and that ventured to such boldness as to reason out the doctrine of the immortality of the soul. Divinely revealed truth, they argued, is not understandable by the human intellect, and what the human reason can hope to attain is so far removed from divine truth as to be quite uncertain. Such a challenge to a rational theology emphasized the separation

[3] See pp. 1–2.
[4] See p. 961.

of faith and reason implicit in St. Thomas. It led to a further specialization of knowledge demanded by the increase in men's information
and the growing maturity of their minds. Philosophy henceforth was
to go on separating itself from theology, until it became with Descartes
in the distant seventeenth century an independent discipline founded
on logic. To this the moderns further contributed by sharpening the
tools of logic handed down by the thirteenth-century scholastics.

The moderns did not succeed in routing the ancients from the universities. Even the old school of Averroists [5] held on at the University
of Padua. The fact that few doctrines of the Church had been officially
pronounced upon left ample opportunity still for the rationalists to
build up a rounded system of belief. Of this opportunity they did not
take advantage in any important way. Making use of a keener logic,

*The later
schoolmen*

they continued to dispute with each other, but the subjects of dispute
were not matters of great moment. Such questions, for example, as
whether the individual must come to the sacrament of penance with a
good disposition or merely with the absence of a bad disposition were
not too fundamental. They, and others like them, reveal the tendency
of later scholastics to make the economy of salvation more mechanical
and indulgent than ever, and to reduce theological speculation to clever
logical calisthenics. Martin Luther called these later schoolmen "sow
theologians."

The mystics

Men of a deep religious nature turned either to a mysticism that had
little patience with this kind of theology or sought moral inspiration
in the writers of classical antiquity. No more than the scholars of antiquity, therefore, could the scholars of this period answer conclusively
questions concerning the purpose of man's life and his relation to his
own world and the universe. In despair, the ancient world adopted
faith in Christianity. The medieval world, after trying to rationalize
that faith with Aristotelian logic, abandoned the attempt. It returned
either to the emotional satisfaction of the mystic, or the simple reliance
upon personal faith in God's revelation as contained in Scripture that
was to culminate in Protestantism; in some cases it returned as a last
desperate expedient to Plato and Plotinus, and to the moral earnestness
of the Stoic.

Eventually the development of experimental science was to transform the struggle between faith and knowledge. Building again upon
the foundations of the earlier Oxford school, the moderns made small

*The moderns
and science*

contributions also to this end. They brought about a revival of nominalism, which preferred to emphasize the individual fact, object, detail,

[5] See p. 707.

and person of the external world of sensible experience rather than the ideas, abstractions, and generalizations of the mind. If divine revelation could not be proved, let it rest unargued to be believed. What the human mind can know and understand, if it can really know and understand anything, must be based on the details that the senses can observe. To such a thoroughgoing conclusion they did not come. The whole corpus of Greek and Arabic science was still too formidable an authority to reject.

Yet under the stimulation of Ockham the moderns did look forward to that end. A group of men at Paris, John Buridan, Albert of Saxony, and Nicholas of Oresme, and in the fifteenth century Nicholas of Cusa,[6] did concern themselves with some of the fundamental problems of physics, such as the laws of falling objects, the principle of inertia, and the center of gravity. Nicholas of Oresme and Nicholas of Cusa reached the point of doubting the geocentric theory of the universe and of suggesting that the earth moves in an eternal rhythm with the heavens. Oresme protested against the prevalent belief in astrology and magic. Coming to terms finally with Greek and Arabic mathematics, definite advances were made in this field during these two centuries. Oresme has been called the founder of analytical geometry. The Italian Pozzo Toscanelli, the friend of Cusa, was an important mathematician, and Cusa himself stimulated the scientific curiosity of Leonardo da Vinci.

In the latter half of the fifteenth century the scientific center of Europe was Nuremberg, where under the patronage of the Pirckheimer family Johann Müller of Königsberg (Regiomontanus) established a scientific school of the first caliber. Müller's work in mathematics has been called the basis of subsequent trigonometry. The fifteenth-century scientists were extremely interested in cartography, another new specialized profession. If the nominalists called attention to detail, and the artists, as we shall see, put that detail into their pictures and sculpture, the scientists were removing geography from the imagination and putting it on maps. The world of nature, as well as of the intellect, was being more adequately described. Yet these were only tentative beginnings on the road to an experimental science that as yet was not understood by the best minds. From the strictly scientific point of view, the discoveries of artists and craftsmen were perhaps more important. It is enough, however, to point out that these two centuries were not unrelated to the scientific and mathematical advances of a subsequent century.

[6] See p. 976.

At the extreme opposite to these nominalist scientists were the mystics, some of whom were as indifferent to the conventional popular religion of the day as Nicholas of Cusa. The sources of mysticism in western Europe were Neo-Platonism as systematized by the Pseudo-Dionysius [7] and interpreted by St. Augustine. John the Scot [8] had made Dionysius available in a Latin translation, and during the earlier renaissance Bernard and the monastery of St. Victor at Paris had been powerful influences in the spread of mystical practices. The Dominicans proved to be severe intellectual mystics. Albert the Great founded a German mystical school in the Rhinelands, and Thomas Aquinas was almost as interested in Augustine as in Aristotle. The attack of the moderns—Franciscans and nominalists that they were—brought the school of Dominican Rhineland mystics to its height in the fourteenth century. The preparation for a more popular reception of mystical doctrines had already been prepared by such lay religious associations as mendicant tertiaries [9] and others of a similar stamp. The Beguines and Beghards, founded by Lambert le Bègue at Liége as early as the end of the twelfth century, were organized in thousands of houses in the Rhinelands and elsewhere, and the Brethren of the Free Spirit were widespread. The decline of the Church gave additional impulse to the cultivation of an earnest personal and evangelical religion seeking the inspiration of immediate contact with God.

The growth of mysticism

The fountainhead of learned Dominican mysticism was Master John Eckhart (*c.* 1260–1327) and his two disciples, John Tauler (*c.* 1290–1361) and Henry Suso (*c.* 1300–66), all of whose activity was concentrated in the Rhinelands, with Cologne as a center. It was the familiar theme of the union of the soul with God that these mystics wrote and preached about. Eckhart writes of God's drawing the soul into himself, "so that it is entirely absorbed in him, even as the sun draws the morning red into itself so that it is entirely absorbed by light." Suso writes of that joy of heaven which consists in gazing "upon the clear pure mirror of the godhead in which all things become known." Tauler describes man's flinging himself "into the divine abyss in which he dwelt eternally before he was created," and "then, when God finds the man thus simply and nakedly turned towards him, the godhead bends down and descends into the depths of the pure, waiting soul, and transforms the created soul, drawing it up into the uncreated essence, so that the spirit becomes one with him. Could such a man behold himself, he

The Rhineland mystics

[7] See p. 257.
[8] See pp. 257–58.
[9] See p. 636.

would see himself so noble that he would fancy himself God, and see himself a thousand times nobler than he is in himself, and would perceive all the thoughts and purposes, words and works, and have all the knowledge of all men that ever were."

These men did not, however, appeal simply to the learned. They preached to the masses in the towns and gave personal religious instruction and guidance. Tauler and Suso were both very active in the new association of the Friends of God, a popular adaptation of mysticism. In their writings they expressed too the intense realism of popular religion. When Suso makes Christ say of his sufferings on the cross, "My right hand was pierced by nails, my left hand was hammered through. My right arm was stretched out of joint, my left arm was drawn out of shape. My right foot was sore with open wounds and my left foot was cruelly mangled. The blood was breaking forth from all over my body, making it a gory mass and a horrible sight. I was covered with sores and ulcers," [10] one recognizes instantly the same kind of description that contemporary painters in the Rhinelands were putting into their treatment of that subject. The mysticism of the Rhinelands was definitely related to German Protestantism both in creed and in spirit. Luther read eagerly the summary of the teachings of the Friends of God contained in the *Theologica Germanica,* or *German Theology;* and of Tauler he said, "Although John Tauler is ignored and held in contempt in theological schools, I have found in him more solid and true theology than is to be, or can be found in all the scholastic doctors of the Universities."

From the upper Rhinelands mysticism spread into the Low Countries. Here its first influential teacher was the Dutchman John Ruysbroeck, who, like many of these later mystics, systematized the quest for God into practical exercises. His seventh degree, for example, "is attained when, beyond all knowledge and all knowing, we discover in ourselves a bottomless not-knowing; when beyond all names given to God and to creatures, we come to expire and pass over in eternal namelessness, where we lose ourselves. . . . God deprives us of all images and brings us back to the initial state where we find only wild and waste absoluteness, void of all form or image, forever corresponding with eternity." [11]

But Ruysbroeck succeeded in influencing other men to a much more practical mysticism. Another Dutchman, Gerard Groote of Deventer (1340–89), founded, in his semimonastic Brethren of the Common

The Brethren of the Common Life

---

[10] Francke, *Personality in German Literature Before Luther,* p. 68.
[11] Huizinga, *Waning of the Middle Ages,* p. 203.

Life, an association of practical mystics who, more than anyone else, succeeded in instituting religious and educational reform in the fourteenth and fifteenth centuries. Without taking monastic vows they lived together, sharing expenses and income. They specialized in the writing and copying of religious and moral works which were to inject a new personal element in contemporary religion. Especially, however, by the founding of schools, or by acting as teachers in already established schools, did they hope to stimulate in the youth new standards of scholarship and new religious values. From the famous schools at Deventer and Zwolle the educational reform of the Brethren spread widely into northern Germany, the upper Rhinelands, and Alsace. Using the texts of both Christian and pagan classics, they quickly became the best schoolmasters of northern Europe and trained many of the outstanding scholars of the late fifteenth and early sixteenth centuries. Under Hegius the school at Deventer reached its height. Here Erasmus began his schooling, and Luther attended for a while a school in Magdeburg in which Brethren taught.

They emphasized not only higher standards of learning but adopted a sharp critical attitude towards the abuses of later medieval religion. Their mystical leanings gave a definite personal and evangelical note to religious and moral instruction. From the pens of the Brethren, or of men under their influence, came the leading mystical works of the fifteenth century. The *Imitation of Christ,* ascribed to Thomas à Kempis of the Diocese of Cologne, became at once and has remained ever since the most popular of mystical tracts. For centuries it has retained, next to the Bible, the position of supreme importance in all devotional literature. Other writings of the school stimulated such a man as the founder of the Jesuits, Ignatius Loyola. The *Spiritual Ascensions* of Gerard Zerbolt has been called the pattern of Loyola's *Spiritual Exercises.* Out of the environment of the Brethren came the most extreme of the religious radicals after the death of Hus, Wessel Gansfort (1420–89). If there ever was a protestant before the Protestants, it was certainly he. There was little in the theology or the practice of the Church that he did not attack. Erasmus admitted that "Wessel had taught all that Luther was teaching, only in much less violent and offensive manner," and Luther himself confessed that "If I had read his works earlier my enemies might think that Luther had absorbed everything from Wessel, his spirit is so in accord with mine."

The only increase in the knowledge of western Europe during this period at all comparable to the increase of the twelfth and thirteenth centuries was the recovery in the form of books or manuscripts, and at least a beginning of a recovery in the mind, of the civilizations of Greece and Rome. Educated men had never ceased to admire, revere, and therefore to be curious about ancient civilization. But there had always existed impediments to a direct appropriation of the classics for their own sake. Christianity had so far constituted such an impediment. The wisdom and beauty of the ancients were to be exploited for Christian purposes, and if need be pagan literature Christianized by allegory; but only a few had arrived at a point of view that saw no danger to the Faith in an appreciative and sympathetic appropriation of the ancient world. The centuries of Christianity's fight with paganism were still not far enough behind. Because, too, the scholars of an earlier period had arrived at no method for studying the documents of antiquity so as to place them in their proper historical setting, like curious and entranced children they were obliged to regard the classical world through the colorful mist of romance. These two handicaps therefore prevented all but a very few from realizing the true significance of the classical period.

The impediments to the study of antiquity

That the handicaps were removed for a much larger number is one of the fine things about the fourteenth and fifteenth centuries, but it is not easy to explain. One can say that for a larger number of men with the leisure and inclination to pursue the paths of scholarship, the extreme rationality and subtlety of earlier and later scholasticism no longer satisfied their curiosity, and that the problems with which it dealt no longer seemed to be applicable to the society of which they were a part. The necessity for assimilating a large amount of Greek and Arabic science and philosophy had crowded out of the schools and universities the liberation of the spirit that comes with the study of literature. The things that the medieval world had for the learned to do were intensely practical, and the schools were accordingly intensely practical. A civilization that had to be built out of the wilderness by men who began as simple barbarians had not yet had time enough to devote to the full appropriation of its classical heritage. To be sure, it made possible that appropriation in so far as it was contained in the written documents. The monks had copied and preserved all of the Latin half of the heritage that had survived. It was not necessary for these later scholars to go off to Spain as earlier scholars had done. They needed only to go to the monastic libraries.

But once preserved, a great many considerations had prevented the manuscripts' being perused, studied, and thoroughly digested by any very large number of men. From the monks, whom he was inclined to despise, the scholar now took the carefully copied manuscripts and set

New interest in a study of antiquity

to work on the yet uncompleted task of restoring ancient civilization in its historical setting and using it to stimulate the human mind and imagination. That learned men felt the need of doing this must mean in part that scholasticism for them was dated. The enlarged, more active, varied, complicated, and refined life made possible by the advent of an urban element in medieval society could no longer find its justification in scholasticism. It was incapable at that moment of working out a new and original justification of its own. Its only recourse, therefore, was to go back to a civilization that was as complicated as it was itself beginning to be, and which exalted values that it now felt were of the greatest importance.

Although this new enthusiasm for classical studies was not confined even in its origins to Italy, nevertheless it is in Italy that its most typical expressions are to be found and the implications of the new passion most easily seen. This was perhaps only inevitable. The Roman tradition had been best preserved in the land of its origin. The papacy had continued its political and imperial phase. That Italy in whole or in part had been for so long a part of the Byzantine empire preserved the Greek part of the classical heritage. The public monuments of both the Greek and Roman past covered the whole peninsula and Sicily. The Holy Roman emperors were a constant stimulus to the recapture of bygone imperial glories. Out of Bologna had proceeded the enthusiasm for the recovered *Corpus Iuris Civilis*. The early growth of the Italian towns and their struggles for emancipation from feudal, ecclesiastical, or German control was often accompanied by a return in the imagination to Rome in the days of the republic. It required little to seize hold directly of this Rome that was everywhere present. That little was supplied mostly by the surplus wealth of the Italian towns through the patronage of their despots and unreformed higher clergy.

Italy and the classical tradition

Italian politics

Our last concern with Italian politics left the peninsula in confusion with the collapse of the Hohenstaufen empire. We need now only refer to the fact that before that event a reorganization had already begun.[12] There can be little real value in pursuing here the details of that reorganization in the violent political history of the fourteenth and fifteenth centuries. It will be enough to point out that the political history was generally similar in tendency to that which has elsewhere been described in more detail for central and western Europe. In Italy the counterpart of the German territorial princes and the strong dynasts of western Europe was the despots of the newly formed city-states. Once the towns had secured their autonomy or independence, they were

[12] See p. 426.

faced, as were the towns elsewhere in Europe, with the problems of self-government and interurban relations. Every Italian town of any importance was torn by the struggle between the new rich merchants and industrialists and the less favored bourgeoisie, gildsmen, and unorganized workingmen for control of the power and favor the government wielded. A complicating factor was always the peculiar position of the Italian nobility in the towns. This struggle in the towns, transforming the old Guelf and Ghibelline issues, was never successfully composed, except in Venice, without resort to an extraordinary power in the form of an outside podesta, *signor,* successful military captain or *condottiere,* or a local merchant prince, to whom was entrusted absolute power to enforce a régime necessary to prosperity.

The exigencies of urban economy forced the towns to expand over the surrounding country in order to control the sources of foodstuffs, or force economic rivals into the orbit of their trade. Venice expanded landwards to include Padua. Florence subjugated Pisa. The towns were developing into city-states, or better, into territorial states governed from the most important urban center. Combined with the interminable internal difficulties, the chronic state of war between the towns made way for the strong man or despot, whose government was always in the interests of the wealthier bourgeoisie.

Into this picture the papacy fits perfectly. Once rid of the annoying councils, the popes set themselves to recovering their position as temporal princes in central Italy, a position threatened by the expanding towns of Venice, Milan, and Florence. Henceforth until the Papal States were reacquired, the popes were no whit different from any other Italian princes in either policies or methods. In at least one instance they countenanced murder as a political method. By the end of the fifteenth century the papacy was completely secularized. *The popes*

Into southern Italy and Sicily the French house of Anjou had been introduced to take the place of the Hohenstaufens.[13] They were driven out of Sicily in 1282 by an uprising and wholesale massacre of the French known as the Sicilian Vespers. Henceforth Sicily remained in the hands of the kings of Aragon. In southern Italy the Angevins maintained themselves with varying success until 1435, when Alfonso the Magnanimous of Aragon joined it to Sicily, calling himself King of the Two Sicilies, and ruled Aragon, Valencia, Catalonia, Majorca, Corsica, and Sardinia as well. It was the Italy of the secularized popes and of the despots, the Visconti and Sforza of Milan, the Scaligers of Verona, the Carraras of Padua, the Gonzagas of Mantua, the Estes of Ferrara, and *The despots and antiquity*

[13] See p. 429.

above all the Medici of Florence, who created a society so different
from the earlier one that it sent its scholars back to the ancient period
for its prototype. The new enthusiasm of the scholars became an adornment of tyrannical governments and an unregenerate Church. Before
succumbing to outside invasion and to a papacy struck dumb by the
Protestant revolt, Italian town life, when once it achieved a balance of

ITALY
IN THE XVTH CENTURY

internal and external power, spent its surplus energy and wealth in the
elaboration of a culture based to some extent on antique models.

The typical classical scholar of the fourteenth and fifteenth centuries is often called a humanist, and his philosophy, humanism. In the
careers of the two fourteenth-century Italian humanists, Petrarch and
Boccaccio, and of Lorenzo Valla (1406–56) can be observed some of
the features of the classical revival in Italy. Both Petrarch and Boccaccio began their literary careers as distinguished users of the Italian

language,[14] but abandoned the vernacular for Latin. The turn to Latin *The human-* was in part the expression of an aristocratic disdain for the language of *ists and the* the people. As one humanist, Niccolò Niccoli, remarked, "I leave Dante *cult of style* to butchers and bakers and suchlike folk, for by his choice of language he seems to have wished to be their intimate." The Latin held up for emulation by these men was not the living Latin of the contemporary learned person and the Church, but the classical Latin of Cicero and his contemporaries. The humanists instituted therefore a cult of style, writing according to the Ciceronian and Virgilian canon, which in the long run killed the Latin prose and poetry that had been written for centuries, and made Latin the "dead" language that it has been called ever since. For substance they substituted form, for rigid analysis the elegance of rhetoric. As writers of an anachronistic Latin humanists were immediately called upon to serve as secretaries in the chancelleries of the Italian despots and the popes.

Both Petrarch and Boccaccio were enthusiastic searchers in monastic libraries for the manuscripts of classical authors, and eager transcribers of them when once found. Petrarch knew no Greek, but he was aware from his study of Latin authors of the necessity for encouraging Greek studies, and he encouraged Boccaccio to learn Greek. Boccaccio did so, *Petrarch* taught it at Florence, and introduced Greek studies among the Italian *and* humanists. With their personal interests and their Latin writings both *Boccaccio* men inaugurated the specialized study of classical antiquity. Petrarch was a collector of gems, coins, fragments of sculpture, and inscriptions from the ancient past. Boccaccio wrote a work on ancient geography. Both, in their writings on famous men and women of the classical period, produced early dictionaries of classical biography. Boccaccio in his work on the *Genealogy of the Gods* inaugurated an intensive study of classical mythology. Petrarch hoped to revive the epic with his Latin poem *Africa.* In their romantic devotion to the unqualified glory of the ancient world, they falsified the history of western Europe by choosing to condemn and reject the middle ages, which made possible their rather shallow enthusiasm.

Neither Petrarch nor Boccaccio was a first-rate classicist. That is hardly to be expected of the first generation of Italian humanists. They had little if any critical sense and were unable to escape the allegorical *The acqui-* interpretation of classical literature. Theirs was the contagious enthu- *sition of* siasm of the amateur and dilettante, of the literary dandy. But succes- *manuscripts* sors continued their work. The search for manuscripts in monastic libraries went on. In the hands of Niccolò Niccoli, the agent for Cosimo

[14] See p. 1018.

dei Medici, it became a profitable business. Poggio Bracciolini acquired such manuscripts as Quintilian's *Institutio Oratorica,* the textbook of the new classical education, Vitruvius on architecture, Columella on agriculture, and works of Ammianus, the Roman historian, Petronius, and Plautus. By the second quarter of the fifteenth century practically all of the Latin authors now known were available for a larger public and humanists had stopped Petrarch's practice of writing to dead authors, whose works he had uncovered, letters intended for public consumption.

Lorenzo Valla

In Valla a humanist of critical stamp appeared whose equal was not to be found until Erasmus. As a result of his critical study of the Scriptures he maintained that under no circumstances could they be regarded as verbally inspired. The Latin of Jerome's Vulgate he ridiculed, and Augustine he accused of heresy. The Apostles' Creed he showed could not have been written by the apostles, and the writings long attributed to Dionysius the Areopagite [15] could not possibly have been written that early. Men had long wished that the Donation of Constantine were a forgery, and Nicholas of Cusa had suspected it; but after Valla published his study of it, showing that its Latin could not possibly have been written in the early fourth century, nobody has ventured to suggest that it was not a forgery.

After Boccaccio the accumulation of manuscripts of Greek literature and philosophy, and the direct study of these, went on apace. Italians sought Greek manuscripts in Constantinople and brought them home.

Greek studies

Greeks came west with manuscripts and accepted teaching positions made available by the despots and popes. The great number of Greeks who came to Florence for the Council of 1438 stimulated the enthusiasm for Greek studies. Some of them stayed in Italy. One of their number, Bessarion, was made a cardinal of the Roman Church, became the leader of Greek studies in Rome, and with others was entrusted with the large task of translating the Greek classics into Latin. After the conquest of Constantinople by the Turks in 1453 the number of Greeks in Italy and the west increased, but they were on the whole second-rate men. By 1515 the most important Greek works in all fields had been published by the printing press.

Meanwhile in the field of classical studies such men as Ciriaco of Ancona and Flavio Biondo of Forli had opened up new fields of specialized study. Ciriaco, an early founder of epigraphy, traveled widely in the lands of the eastern Mediterranean searching for inscriptions. Biondo was an early student of archæology. The idea that Rome

[15] See p. 257.

glorious past could be literally unearthed by digging out her remains *New fields of* was a revelation. By 1462 the pope was induced to prohibit the despoil- *classical study* ing of classical monuments and buildings in Rome for use as lime and building stone. To house the newly assembled manuscripts and archæo- logical finds new museums and new libraries had to be founded. The despots and popes were generous with funds for setting up new li- braries. Lorenzo dei Medici founded the Laurentian Library at Flor- ence, with the library of Niccolò Niccoli as its beginning. Pope Nicho- las V founded the Vatican Library. The library of Frederigo of Montefeltro, the Duke of Urbino, prided itself on the exclusion of printed books. The Visconti founded a library at Pavia. The emergence of new libraries, formed from the contents of the monastic libraries, founded and supported by secular persons, and available to a wide cir- cle of secular scholars, marks a step in the secularization of scholarship. By 1500 the enthusiasm for a direct study of the classics, rather com- plete materials, and the beginnings of the technical and critical equip- ment necessary for their study were available in Italy and to a lesser extent in western Europe. The long, arduous, and glorious task upon which humanists are still engaged had begun.

It is to be asked what the more intensive study of classical civilization did for the humanists; what effect, through them, did it have upon the society and religion of which they were a part? These are not easy questions. Since the western world today has begun again to abandon the tradition taken up by the humanists, we are less well prepared to judge of the liberalizing and emancipatory effects of the enthusiastic study of the classics. It has different effects upon different men. By it some are left and some are made pedants, and of these effects there are adequate evidences in the fourteenth and fifteenth centuries. A con- temporary humanist has defined his kind: "A humanist is one who has a *The influence* love of things human, one whose regard is centered on the world about *of humanism* him and the best that man has done; one who cares more for art and letters, particularly the art and letters of Greece and Rome than for the dry light of reason, or the mystic's flight into the unknown; one who distrusts allegory; one who adores critical editions with variants and variorum notes; one who has a passion for manuscripts which he would like to discover, beg, borrow or steal; one who has an eloquent tongue which he frequently exercises, one who has a sharp tongue, which on occasion can let free a flood of good billingsgate or sting an opponent with an epigram." [16] If we judge the Italian humanists by this high standard then it is to be feared that few of them would qualify.

[16] Rand, *Founders of the Middle Ages,* pp. 102–3.

It is certain that there were features in Italian and western European society which alone could have called forth reactions from intelligent and sensitive men, and had in fact been doing so, without the renewal of the study of the classics. The alarming condition of the Church did not need the study of the classics to make men aware of it. The relations between cities, territories, and monarchies, the extravagant courts of kings, despots, and popes, and the intensive throb of a nascent capitalism did not need the revival of a study of the classics to teach men that it was not always the Christian virtues that were successful, that life on this earth was colorful and profitable enough to live to the full without too much consideration of its aftermath. It was evident enough that the go-getter, the self-made man, the *condottiere,* the despot, the unscrupulous prince or king, and the ambitious capitalist forged ahead without any especial respect for the moral values that Christianity insisted upon. Nor was a revival of the classics necessary to make men critical of the reigning scholasticism of the thirteenth century. Yet in the glaring contrast between what men professed to believe and what they did, the humanists thought they saw a compromise in the experience and thought of the classical world. Once again, as in the twelfth and thirteenth centuries, the more serious humanists sought to bring to bear the new learning upon the Faith in such a way that Christianity might be enlarged to include more than a dogma rationalized by logic. To the less serious the classics offered an escape into a comparatively new world—and novelty always has its victims—in which they might be daring, clever, and nimble with pen and tongue in a vague praise of a new form of sophistication.

Humanism and thought

Without bothering to read, not to say understand, the scholastics Petrarch brushed them aside for the conglomerate philosophy of Cicero, the religious Stoicism of Seneca; and, moreover, although he did not understand Plato, he called himself a Platonist. That is hardly an improvement upon St. Thomas. By their contemporaries both Petrarch and Boccaccio were looked upon as great moral philosophers, which is hardly complimentary to their contemporaries. The resurrection of Plato to take the place of Aristotle aroused violent controversy in the following century, stimulated and taken up by the Greek teachers and scholars who immigrated to Italy. But all the better humanists sought to give Christianity a wider philosophic basis as a result of their enlarged studies. They talked and wrote about a religion common and natural to all particular forms of faith, of which Christianity, if broadened, was best calculated to absorb the others.

Especially in Florence, under the leadership of Lorenzo dei Medici, were definite attempts made to provide this wider basis for Christianity *The Platonic* or to make a new amalgam of the Faith with the classical tradition. *academy* Lorenzo founded an academy for the study of Plato. Its two most distinguished members were Marsiglio Ficino and Pico della Mirandola. To Ficino was entrusted the task of translating the Platonic *Dialogues* into Latin, and when he came back to a study of religious questions he had come to the conclusion that the best interpretation of Plato was to be found in the Neo-Platonism of Plotinus and Proclus. This we know was a return to philosophical mysticism, to that late classical school of philosophy that was the chief enemy of Christianity. Ficino's Christian Platonism resolved itself therefore into mysticism, with which were combined some St. Paul and a profound belief in the truth of magic.

Mirandola was a more interesting figure. He was intoxicated by the desire to know everything there was to know. He studied the scholastics, which was unusual for a humanist; he studied Arabic in order to read the Koran; he studied Hebrew in order to read the Hebrew Scriptures in the original, and became very interested in the Jewish Kabbala, a theosophical and mystical interpretation of the Old Testament. After this preliminary study Pico announced to the world that he had nine hundred propositions that he was willing to argue against all comers in Rome and that he was willing to pay the expenses of any who would come to argue. One of the propositions was, "No science yields greater proof of the divinity of Christ than magic and the Kabbala." Of this St. Thomas would hardly have been capable. The pope judged thirteen of the propositions to be heretical, remarked that Pico seemed desirous of ending his life in the fires of the Inquisition, and obliged him to flee to France for his life. When he returned to Florence he followed the way of Ficino, became an extremely pious and ascetic devotee of the Faith, and succumbed wholly to that Dominican opponent of humanism in Florence, Savonarola. He died at thirty-one, before he had time to work out his new synthesis.

In both Ficino and Mirandola there is the element of the fantastic. It was present also in the extravagances of other humanists and their patrons. These men could not extricate themselves completely from the world about them. It is difficult to see how they were any improvement over the best that the earlier centuries had produced. In fact it is the opinion of another contemporary humanist that "it is not true to say . . . that the humanists introduced freedom of thought. They destroyed some medieval prejudices which blocked the way; they broke some old shackles but introduced new ones; they questioned the authority of dogmas but accepted the authority of the ancients. They tore down cumbersome restraints but replaced them by something in finitely worse, spiritual anarchy; they smothered scholasticism but pu in its stead literary ideals too vague to be effective. They looked back ward not forward. They created beauty, plenty of it, but not truth, and without truth, everything becomes arbitrary and insecure, and what ever freedom there is, is a sham." [17]

If there was any danger to Christianity from the humanists, the papacy, and the Church as a whole, saw to it that that danger should not become real. With this kind of danger they had had considerable experience in previous centuries, and Christianity had never to fear the accretions to western Europe's knowledge. The popes and higher clergy became in the fifteenth century the most enthusiastic patrons of the new classical studies and the new art. Humanistic sympathies were almost a qualification for the episcopate. The price that humanism had to pay for this support was ready willingness to keep hands off the dogma of the Church and to be sparing of its criticism of Church organization and papal power. This the humanists were content to do. They displayed a notable tendency to abandon in later life their earlier waywardness, or to give up a youthful boldness in thought to find peace, quiet, and employment in the service of the Church. Most of the humanists were in some kind of orders. Classical learning and the new art of the period became the decoration of a faith and an organization that remained unchanged and unreformed.

Humanism and the Church

There is no better example of this than in the progressive secularization of the papacy between the time of its victory over the councils and the reformers and when it was confronted by a man who was not a humanist and who would not make his peace—Martin Luther. The first good example of a pope as patron of the humanists was Nicholas V (1447–55). Lorenzo Valla, we have seen, was no unsparing critic of the Church. In writings other than those mentioned above he criticized Christian asceticism by exclaiming, "Would that man had fifty senses, since five give such delight!" or "Courtesans and street-women deserve better of the human race than nuns and virgins." [18] Yet Nicholas made Valla a papal secretary and set him to teaching rhetoric in Rome. In Poggio Bracciolini's *Facetiæ* all the earthiness of the medieval *fabliaux* is present at the expense of monks and clergy, but Nicholas made him a papal secretary, and he kept his job for fifty years. Franceso Filelfo, who boasted, "I am one of those who, celebrating with eloquence illustrious deeds make immortal them that by nature are mortal," was forgiven

The papacy and humanism

[17] Sarton, in *The Civilization of the Renaissance*, p. 94.
[18] Fletcher, *Literature of the Italian Renaissance*, p. 99.

for satires of a quality that outdid Bracciolini and given a job if only he would translate the *Iliad* and *Odyssey* into Latin. It was Nicholas who founded the Vatican Library and advised Lorenzo dei Medici concerning the founding of his library at Florence. If he failed to put a stop to the plundering of classical monuments at Rome, he began to rebuild St. Peter's—in its way, when finally completed, a complete summary of the secularized and somewhat vulgar papacy of the early sixteenth century.

From Nicholas to Alexander VI, who closed the century, we have to do with popes like Pius II, a humanist himself, although he scorned the empty rhetoric of the Ciceronians; Sixtus IV, who was primarily interested in promoting his nephews in the Church, and participated in a conspiracy to murder the Medici brothers; Paul II, who collected gems and *objets d'art* and took them to bed with him; Innocent VIII, whose illegitimate children, begotten before he took orders, were publicly acknowledged and married during his pontificate, and who was quite willing to accept money from the Turks in lieu of a crusade. To look at Raphael's picture of the last of this line, Alexander VI, is to know him quite well enough. He is famous for his two children Cæsar and Lucretia Borgia, not to mention the other six. This pope, known for the splendor of the bullfights he supported and attended in Rome, was ultimately responsible for the death of that stern reformer and hater of the excesses of humanism, Savonarola.

If we were to go on into the sixteenth century there would be Julius II, a bearded, hard-swearing leader of papal armies, and that Leo X, the Medici on the throne of St. Peter, who is credited with saying when he heard of his election to the papacy, "Let us enjoy the papacy since God has given it to us." There can be no doubt that he did enjoy it, when not occupied with the stubborn Martin Luther. The popes then had become Italian despots themselves, fighting to build up the Papal States; with their patronage of humanism and the arts they made Rome the successor of Florence in the leadership of the movement. The papal court continued in its old way, with simony, nepotism, and corruption more prevalent than ever. Unreformed and too indulgent of the new culture of urban Italy, it gave men who already had much to criticize, their final arguments. The papacy, become all too human, paid with the Protestant reformation.

The new enthusiasm for classical studies appeared somewhat later in France and Germany than in Italy, and in England last of all. In part the revival in these countries was but the continuation of an earlier tradition, and in part the influence of Italian scholars upon scholars

Humanism beyond the Alps

from the north who traveled in Italy. Men like Pierre d'Ailly and John Gerson, Nicolas of Clemanges and Jean de Montreuil are to be associated with its earliest manifestations in France, and in the fifteenth century William Fichet and Robert Gaguin were directly under the influence of Italian humanism. Nicholas of Cusa was an ardent early German humanist. In the fifteenth century among scholarly circles in the German towns, in some German universities, and among the German clergy an excited interest in the classics was evident. This was especially so at the universities of Heidelberg and Erfurt. At Cologne, Strassburg, Basel, Nuremberg, and Augsburg groups of humanists spread the new gospel. One of them, Rudolph Huysman (Agricola), when informed that he had been made an abbot on the same day that his concubine had presented him with a son, asked God to bless his double paternity.

The character of northern humanism

It was, however, more the serious than the bombastic phase of humanistic study that appealed to northern scholars. In Italy such men as Ficino and Mirandola were concerned above all with reconciling Christianity with the new stream of Platonic idealism through the use of Neo-Platonism and the Jewish Kabbala. Many Italian humanists of the fifteenth century were interested in the Latin and Greek Christian as well as pagan classics. Among these, of course, the Bible in the original tongues was foremost. There was much criticism of Jerome's Vulgate. Ficino was especially interested in St. Paul. Manuscript collectors included works of the early Latin and Greek Fathers in their libraries, and thence they got into the new state and papal libraries. In western Europe the realization of the importance of a knowledge of Greek and Hebrew in the study of the Scriptures, and of early Christian literature for a study of the growth of Christianity, was already present in learned circles in the thirteenth century. In addition to Bacon, Grosseteste should also be mentioned in this connection, inasmuch as he brought many Greek manuscripts of a pre-Christian and apostolic date to Oxford. This emphasis was taken up by the Brethren of the Common Life, who trained themselves and their pupils in early Christian as well as in secular literature. The learned mysticism of the Rhinelands combined with the Brethren to give to northern humanism its serious bent. What kept the scholars attentive to the Scriptures and early Greek and Latin literature was the fact that they saw therein ample justification for their dissatisfaction with the Christianity of their day. Such study brought the history of Christianity into perspective: it was quite obvious that it had gone through a tremendous change, and could be purified by going back to its sources.

The men who best of all represent this trend in northern humanism are the Frenchman Lefèvre d'Étaples, the German John Reuchlin, the Dutchman Desiderius Erasmus, and the Englishman Sir Thomas More. Since, for the most part, only their formative years belong to the fifteenth century, we can only indicate here the general character of their outlook. In so far as they were influenced by Italy they were chiefly the pupils, either in person or through reading, of Ficino, Mirandola, and Valla. They represent as a whole therefore a reaction from the rationality of the earlier schoolmen and the logical subtlety of the later schoolmen. From Aristotle they turned to Stoic ethics, Plato, and Neo-Platonic mysticism. As critical scholars of ancient literature they turned their attention to the Scriptures and to the early Greek and Latin Fathers. They insisted that these works must be studied in the original tongues, Greek and Hebrew, and not in translation, certainly not Jerome's translation, of which like many others they were extremely critical. They were accordingly interested in publishing critical editions of the Scriptures and the Fathers in the original tongues. They advocated the translation of Scriptures into the vernacular tongues. In their study of Scriptures and of early Christian literature they emphasized the necessity of abandoning wherever possible the allegorical method and of substituting for it an out-and-out historical and literal interpretation of the texts. The Bible, that is, must be put into its historical setting, and taken to mean just exactly what its text says, not what it signifies. They conceived of this kind of study as the best way to inject new life into what they regarded as a decadent Christianity seriously in need of reform.

The program of the northern humanists

It was to the historical and human Jesus of the New Testament and to the ardent St. Paul that they returned in an attempt to restore a measure of deep personal feeling into religion. Acquaintance with the historical sources of Christianity revealed to them the explanation for the discontent that they felt with the historical Church and its religious system. They could therefore argue that the Christianity of their day was not early Christianity, that the best method of reform was to go back to early Christianity. In saying this they were only repeating what men had said for centuries, but they now had a learned justification for their attitude that earlier centuries had lost, and riper scholarship polished their wit and indignation. As moral, ethical, and educational reformers, they would purge and not destroy. They were traditionalists and not revolutionaries; only they wished to recapture the whole tradition. They were horrified when the Protestant reformers proceeded to action. Later men said of Erasmus that he laid the egg that Luther hatched. His retort was: "Yes, but the egg I laid was a hen and Luther hatched a gamecock."

Before turning to the classics both Petrarch and Boccaccio had distinguished themselves as writers of Italian. In his sonnets Petrarch had celebrated with great elegance and charm the virtues of a Laura somewhat less blessed than Dante's Beatrice; he established therewith the sonnet form as a permanent poetic favorite. Boccaccio's Fiammetta was a step further away from the kind of love treated in the "sweet new style." This "little flame" was an object of physical passion. What

Vernacular literature: Italian

Dante and Petrarch succeeded in doing for Italian poetry, Boccaccio in his *Decameron* did for Italian prose. The *Decameron* is in spirit of a piece with the second half of the *Romance of the Rose* and with Chaucer's *Canterbury Tales*. It continued the tradition of the *fabliaux*. The stories with which a gay and conventionally pious party amused themselves while escaping from the plague in Florence may carry some readers "back to the sweltering world of pagan sensuality," but it is to be feared that actually they only reflect the kind of tales that the best society of fourteenth-century Italy found amusing. Boccaccio gathered his tales from all sources; he invented few of them. He told them with grace and without any comment except a gentle ironic style. Even Petrarch, from the lofty heights of humanism, had to admit: "My hasty perusal afforded me much pleasure. If the humor is a little too free at times, this may be excused at the age at which you wrote, the style and language [*sic*] which you employ, and the frivolity of the subjects, and of the persons who are likely to read such tales." [19] The example set by Boccaccio was taken up by many of his countrymen in the next two centuries.

In spite of the censures of the humanists, the Italian vernacular showed great vitality in the following century in developing and adapting to the cultivated society of Italian towns the romantic themes of earlier medieval poets. The good-natured satire of chivalry in Boiardo [20] was carried still further in the next century in Ariosto's *Orlando Furioso*. Meanwhile Italian historians were portraying with vivid detail the conflict of social forces in the towns, which the humanists did not bother to notice. The kind of realistic history that the Villanis wrote in their chronicle of Florence was continued and rationalized by Machiavelli in the next century.

Neither the French, German, nor English (i.e., after Chaucer) vernacular literatures displayed the same vigor as the Italian during

[19] *Ibid.*, p. 93.
[20] See p. 767.

his period. Nor were they influenced any more by the anachronistic *Vernacular literature beyond the Alps* return of the humanists to the classics. The chronicles of German towns catch the colorful life within their walls, and there was a notable development of folk song, but one searches in vain for talent comparable to that of the thirteenth century. In England Malory's *Morte d'Arthur* summarized the Arthurian legend in a vigorous prose. Chaucer's French contemporaries, Guillaume Machaut and Eustache Deschamps, carried on further the accomplishments of the troubadours in working out new verse forms in the ballade and rondeau, but aside from occasional glimpses into the chaos wrought by the Hundred Years' War they had little or nothing new to say. Allegorical romance had to play itself out. The early history of the war itself was treated as an adventure in chivalry by Froissart in his *Chronicles;* but by the end of the fifteenth century, in the *Memoirs* of Philippe de Comines French history had lost all contact with chivalry. There the ruthless character of Franco-Burgundian politics is treated with a regard for particulars and detail that makes nothing of moralizing sentiment. Louis XI, the realist in politics, had found the historian he needed.

The kind of history that Comines wrote was comparable to the poetry *François Villon* of François Villon. Villon's, however, is not the realism of high politics but rather the realism of his disillusioned mind and of the sordid life of the narrow streets of Paris. He was born in the year of Joan of Arc's execution, and lived on through the victorious years culminating the Hundred Years' War. Some time after 1462 he disappeared from public view. Little is known of his life, and that little is not complimentary. He took a degree from the University of Paris, but henceforth was to be found trying to escape the police in the alleys, wine-shops, and brothels of the city. He participated in a murderous brawl that resulted in the death of a monk, was a member of a gang that robbed the College of Navarre, for which he was imprisoned, and the last known incident of his life involved him in a street fight that caused the wounding of an official of the city, for which after torture he was finally sentenced to be hanged, although the sentence was afterwards commuted to exile. It was not in the jocund mood of the goliard's "from his bitterness of soul springs self-revelation" that he wrote. He seems to have cared little for anything or anybody, and to have suffered all the vicissitudes of a life of misery, poverty, and degradation. Obviously for this man the empty phrases of courtly poetry and the hearkening back to classical antiquity could have no attraction. His language was the hard-boiled language of the streets, his themes the futility, meanness, and degradation of human existence, the decay of old age, and the cruelty and imminence of death. These he wrote of in his Little and Great Testaments, and in his miscellaneous ballades and rondeaux, perhaps as he ate his heart out in spite and spleen, alone in the taverns.

He is almost savage as he pays his compliments to the envious and slanderous backbiters:

"In arsenic crystals and realgar red,
In orpiment, saltpetre, quicklime too;
And—better thus to clean—in boiling lead;
In tallow, pitch and lye, the which imbue
With excrement of some old female Jew;
In washings from the legs of men with pox;
In toejam and the scrapings of old sox;
In blood of snakes, in drugs whence men have died;
In gall of badger and of wolf and fox:
Let envious tongues be fricasseed and fried!" [21]

And he is pitiless as he describes the broken-down prostitute:

"Now—forehead seamed, locks grey like chaff,
Brows broken, eyes red-rimmed with rain—
Who looks at me now looks to laugh,
Where many a merchant paid to gain;
Nose like a beak, its beauty slain;
Ears lopped and grown with moss-like hair;
Face pale like death and sharp like pain;
Chin fallen, furred lips no more fair." [22]

He does not hesitate to describe his life as a pimp with his Fat Margot:

"Because I love and serve her of my heart,
Must you then call me villain, fool or sot?
Her love more fills my need than any art,
Hence I bear sword and shield for this harlot.
When men come here, I hop and hand the pot,
Run to fetch wine, nor grumble nor dispute,
And serve them water, cheese and bread and fruit;
If they are paying well, I expatiate,
And cry, 'return when you are roused to root
Here in this brothel where we hold our state!'

[21] Nicolson, *François Villon*, p. 299.
[22] *Ibid.*, p. 215.

"But soon thereafter calm is driven apart
When silverless comes Margot to our cot:
I hate her then like bitter death and swart,
And snatch robe, cloak and bonnet knot from knot,
Swearing to pawn them or to sell the lot.
She beats my ribs, this antichrist, to refute,
And swears by God's death I shall take no loot
From gear of hers—until I end debate
When my good fist to her big nose I shoot,
Here in this brothel where we hold our state." [23]

Unrelenting is his treatment of death:

"I know this well, that rich and poor,
    Fools, sages, laymen, friars in cowl,
    Large-hearted lords and each mean boor,
    Little and great and fair and foul,
    Ladies in lace, who smile or scowl,
    From whatsoever stock they stem,
    Hatted or hooded, prone to prowl,
    Death seizes every one of them.

"And Paris dying, or Helen, still
    Who dies, dies wretchedly and apart.
    Whoever loses breath and will,
    The black gall breaks upon his heart;
    He sweats—God knows how sweat will start!—
    Nor gains aid as his eyes grow dim:
    Child, brother, none will play the part
    Of hostage in death's hands for him.

"Death makes him shudder and turn pale,
    Pinches his nose, distends his veins,
    Swells out his throat, his members fail,
    Tendons and nerves grow hard with strains.
    O female flesh, like silken skeins,
    Smooth, tender, precious, in such wise
    Must you endure so awful pains?
    Aye, or go living to the skies." [24]

[23] *Ibid.*, pp. 319–20.
[24] *Ibid.*, pp. 191–92.

Humanism and the arts

As in literature, so in the architecture, sculpture, and painting of the fourteenth and fifteenth centuries, whenever the artists permitted their talents to develop in the older traditions, rather than to transform them in the light of Greece and Rome, they did their best work. In northern and western Europe, where there was as yet no stimulus from humanism, Gothic architecture in the flamboyant or perpendicular style exhausted itself in an extraordinary variety of decorative detail. In Italy, however, where there had been no great building comparable to the Gothic since Roman days, ecclesiastical, as contrasted with secular, architecture gradually reverted to the dictates of Roman architecture as laid down in the rediscovered book of the Roman Vitruvius, *On Architecture*. The lamentable practice of making over older churches to conform to the new classical style began, and such originality as men like Brunelleschi and Alberti possessed was soon stifled in the anachronistic academic return to antiquity. The laws of building with the various classical orders ruled for centuries.

On neither sculpture nor painting did humanism in its strict classical sense have any influence beyond the Alps by the end of this period. In Italy, where the remains of classical sculpture were numerous, its influence was not directive—certainly not to the extent that the influence of French Gothic sculpture was directive. For Italy there were no remains of classical painting. When once artists had freed themselves from the influence of Byzantine mosaics and frescoes, they were free to learn from the advances made in northern Europe and to develop in accordance with their own lights. Painting quickly supplanted architecture as the dominant art, and in it the Italians developed their genius to its highest limits.

The breakdown of medieval unity

The breakdown in the unity of the arts as assembled around the Gothic cathedral, and the emergence of the independent arts of sculpture, painting, and the so-called minor arts, can well be associated with the breakdown in the political, ecclesiastical, and intellectual unities of the twelfth and thirteenth centuries. It is at the same time another example of the further specialization and professionalism that accompanied the increase in western Europe's knowledge, the growing maturity of its mind, and the refinement of its tastes. The medieval empire and the medieval Church were dissolving into dynastic states and dynastic churches. The predominance of theology was ending with the development of an independent philosophy and science. As the Church was losing its grip on the minds and consciences of the educated classes, while a new philosophy and science, together with humanism, were gaining strength, so it was losing its power to direct

he course of literature and the arts. The earlier simplicity of medieval
ulture was giving way to complexity and diversity. In addition to
he Church the new princes and wealthy bourgeoisie were demand-
1g the services of the artists for purposes that had not necessarily to
.o with religion. The new professionalism of the twelfth and thir-
eenth centuries, to which was being added the new disciplines of the
umanists, was now increased by a new professionalism in the arts.

The freedom of the arts from architecture meant of course that
ainting and sculpture, to mention no others, now had thrust upon
hem a number of new problems that their subjection to architecture
ad enabled them to avoid. Each had to do for itself alone what
itherto it had done in conjunction with architecture. Entirely new
venues of development were opened up. These, together with a
artial emancipation from the spiritual and moral values always in-
isted upon by the Church, determined the general course of develop-
nent of these independent arts in the fourteenth and fifteenth cen-
uries. Since many phases of this emancipation were already present
n the best Gothic art, painting and sculpture had only to follow up
hese leads, until they in their turn were exhausted.

It is possible to say, for example, that earlier Romanesque and
Gothic art are characterized by the conventions dictated by an iconog-
aphy that used symbolism and allegory to reveal religious doctrine.
t is possible to show too that in these particular centuries this system
y no means died out. At the same time, however, it is undeniable
hat Gothic art, even in the service of this iconography, quit symbol-
sm, allegory, and myth for the world of fact. Its God and Christ, its
aints and Virgin, lost at times their austere, supernatural quality to
ecome simple, human, natural, smiling, and weeping human beings.
t is also true that for decorative uses, especially in Gothic capitals, the
arvers copied the literal facts of nature. All this can be labeled natu-
alism or realism or humanism in a larger sense. Yet symbolism and
bstraction rather than literalism and fact remain characteristic of
he earlier period. And just as one can say that in the vernacular litera-
ures of this period the earlier themes and their allegorical treatment
vere exhausted, and that there was nothing for the author to do ex-
ept to retreat to the classics or dwell on the variety of fact concerning
eal human beings about him, just as one can say that in philosophy
he earlier realism was abandoned for nominalism and scientists turned
o the objective fact, so we can say that in sculpture and painting there
vas nothing much left for the original artist to do in the field of conventional symbolism. He turned to the world of human and natural

*Realism
in art*

fact. This was the world in which his new patrons were interested. They wanted his work for their new palaces and gardens. In transalpine Europe the new realism of fact and feeling was not touched by classical reminders during this period. In Italy, humanism in the fifteenth century did succeed in imposing on it unessential details. The important new emphasis, however, was everywhere the same— the secular spirit expressing itself in realistic detail.

Architecture used painting to cover its walls with frescoes and mosaics. Gothic architecture, however, converted its walls into glass windows, and used painting to stain them and thus had little use for fresco or mosaic. Since the window was part of a building, Gothic architects had taken care that the decoration of the windows should not spoil the total architectural effect by calling attention too much to themselves.[25] Painters had also found employment in illuminating

*Northern
painting*

manuscripts and illustrating them with miniatures. Books used for the service of the Church and for private devotions were also elaborately decorated. By the beginning of the fifteenth century, in northern France such painters as Jacquemart de Hesdin and Pol de Limbourg, who decorated books of private devotions for the Duke of Berry (d. 1416), had produced miniatures that copied the world of nature with its human and architectural setting with an extraordinary and meticulous detail. When rich patrons or gilds began to order panels to decorate private chapels or chapels of patron saints, this minute reproduction of material fact was carried over from the miniature into the larger independent picture. The portraits of the patrons, whether included in the altar panels or in separate pictures, and the interiors used as settings, reveal this passion for including every detail.

Around the courts of the dukes of Burgundy this enlarged miniature painting reached a climax in Flanders in the first half of the fifteenth century with the van Eyck brothers, Hubert and John. Henceforth in the fifteenth century the center of western European art was Flanders. Improving on the long-known use of oil as a

Flemish art

medium in which to mix pigment, the van Eycks achieved an exciting perfection all their own. The portraiture, whether of Virgin or patron, is strong and living and scrupulous in the rendering of detail. The clothes of the subjects are rich and extravagant and painted almost to the individual threads. The rooms that contain the subjects are furnished with nothing that is not as carefully painted as the subject itself. If one can ever finish examining the details in the foreground, one may let one's eyes wander through the open window to

[25] See p. 825.

the natural landscape of the background and linger on the same meticulous detail or else follow the landscape into infinity. The window opening out on the natural scene is the ever present device of all painters of these centuries.

Chief among the painters working in Flanders after the van Eycks were Roger van der Weyden, Dierick Bouts, Hugo van der Goes, and Hans Memling. German painting in the fifteenth century centered about Cologne, where Stefan Lochner was working at the middle of the century. Rhineland mysticism, with its emotional realism, exercised some influence on the painting done. The chief representative of the French school was Jean Fouquet, whose "Virgin and Child" is a striking example of the secular treatment of this subject. No matter, then, what the subject matter, whether religious or secular, the camera-like representation of the human face and figure, and of the surrounding scene, either interior or landscape, together with an indifference to the religious implications of the subject matter and a mastery of technique, constitutes a triumph of secularism and realism in the art of western Europe. Here was founded the great tradition of the subsequent Flemish and Dutch schools of the sixteenth and seventeenth centuries, and of the work of the Holbeins and Dürer.

Italy was not uninfluenced by the painting done across the Alps. But long before the maturity of the Flemish school, Italian painting had started on its own liberation. Before the thirteenth century the chief inspiration of Italian painting had been Byzantine frescoes and mosaics. Because Italy did not adopt the highly developed Gothic cathedral, fresco painting was not crowded out by stained glass, and the mosaic tradition remained alive if not dominant. Nor did Italian architecture ever so completely control the other arts as in France. Byzantine painting used a symbolic iconography of austere grace to give a flat, one-planed surface a colorful and decorative pattern or design. The background for its figures was often one-toned, blue or gold. Thirteenth-century Italian painting is a faithful reflection of this spirit.

In the work of the Florentine painter Giotto (1266-1336) and his *Giotto* slightly older Sienese contemporary, Duccio di Buoninsegna, a definite break was made with this tradition, partly under inspiration from beyond the Alps. Giotto's painting is known to us chiefly in his frescoes in the Church of St. Francis at Assisi and in the Arena Chapel at Padua. It is not the work of one who achieved complete technical mastery of his craft, but is rather that of one who broke ground which subsequent painters were to cultivate to the very limit. It has been

remarked that "Giotto was the first mural painter to knock a hole i
the wall." [26] That is to say, he was interested in the third dimensior
in perspective, which is to speak of a mathematical interest inasmuc
as its ultimate solution depended upon the development of a nev
branch of mathematics. Giotto began to remove the simple one-tonec
background of Byzantine painting by putting things in their prope
position in space. He had therefore to concern himself with the thirc
dimension of the things, human beings and buildings for the mos
part, that he was relating in space. This brought up questions of the
harmonious composition of three-dimensional masses in space, and o
the use of light, shade, and color in this composition. In his treatment
of most of these problems Giotto is generally acknowledged a master
of great subsequent influence. Moreover, he was interested in giving
expression to the emotions of his figures, and did it with great force
and restraint. Perspective in art was certainly related to the better
perspective with regard to the classical period, and to the perspective
of the cartographers. These men were trying to set the natural, human
world in order.

The impetus given to painting by Giotto reached the height of perfection in the first half of the sixteenth century with such men as
Raphael, Leonardo da Vinci, Michelangelo, Giorgione, and Titian.

Florentine
painting

Meanwhile, especially in fifteenth-century Florence, further developments in technique gave to the native talent of the artist complete
freedom of artistic expression. Delight in the mastery of perspective
was displayed in the works of Uccello and Mantegna. The study of
the nude, which for the middle ages was confined to Adam and Eve,
became all-absorbing. To master it thoroughly required a knowledge
of human anatomy based on dissection. The paintings of Castagno and
Pollaiuolo glory in the revelation of muscle and bodily movement.
The frescoes of the young Masaccio (1401–28) in the Brancacci
Chapel in Florence are an almost premature accomplishment. In the
"Adam and Eve driven from the Garden" there is a mastery of the
rendering of the nude figure, a powerful rendering of human emotion, and a complete freedom given to great talent through the solution of technical problems. The paintings of Ghirlandaio (1449–94)
are masterpieces of realistic portraiture and of colorful and opulent
Florentine life.

The old religious as well as the new secular subject matter is treated
by many artists with perfect indifference to spiritual implications.
Madonna and child are often attractive young Italian matrons with

[26] *Cambridge Medieval History,* VIII, 258.

their *bambini*, and the models used were frequently the mistresses of the artists, even when the artists were monks. But the older reverence was not entirely displaced by the new gaiety, nor the older allegory by the new realism. Classical mythology crept in, in the works of Botticelli (1444–1510), and Mantegna faithfully reproduced the inscriptions on the buildings for his classical backgrounds. But it was not a major influence. In the paintings of the three Bellinis at Venice the knowledge and use of deep, hot, oriental color was added to the scientific development of the Florentines. By the end of the fifteenth century there was little that the Italian painter could not learn to do, and his only limitations were his talent, intelligence, and personality. Supported by a Church that always knew how to employ art, and by patrons who had new uses for it, Italian genius overflowed with a remarkable fecundity. Tardier in its origins than the artistic revival that came with Gothic art, and developing under Gothic influence, it was less the product of classical humanism than of the broader humanism that was born of the Italian town.

While it is true that not all medieval sculpture was related to the cathedral, by far the largest part of it was. The use of sculpture to decorate the portals and piers required that it should subordinate itself to the vertical lines of the Gothic church. It had no opportunity *Northern* to develop its own possibilities, and there was no call to exploit the *sculpture* beauty of the nude figure. The fourteenth century witnessed the emancipation of sculpture from architecture, and set it to working out its own limitations as an independent art. As the Flemish school of painting was associated with the dukes of Burgundy, so the most original sculpture in northern Europe at the end of the fourteenth and the beginning of the fifteenth centuries was done under their patronage. The Burgundian school was dominated by the striking work of Claus Sluter, done for the Carthusian monastery of Champmol in Burgundy and for the tomb of Philip the Bold. The contrast with Gothic sculpture is striking. The figures have no particular relation to architecture; they exist for themselves and are carved on a monumental scale. The prophets for the well of the cloister garden are individuals of inspiring stature rather than types. The mourners of the tomb are tortured with poignant grief. Figures and drapery are done in free, bold, and sweeping lines. As with the painting of the van Eycks, sculpture here seems suddenly to have come to maturity, and the restlessness and strain of the figures, reminiscent of Michelangelo's work, already betrays evidence of the need for a further breaking of all restraints.

*Italian
sculpture*

The sculpture of medieval Italy took a new turn at the court of Frederick II, the man responsible for so many of the innovations of later Italian culture.[27] Its inspiration was classical. It was probably from southern Italy that Niccola Pisano came, and in the pulpit that he did for the baptistery at Pisa the influence of Roman sarcophagi is predominant. But Niccola and especially his son Giovanni in their later work were strongly stimulated by Gothic sculpture. The work of the Burgundian school was not without its effect on the finest of the Italian sculpture of the fifteenth century. Donatello reveals it as well as the spell of classical sculpture. In him Italian sculpture reached a precocious maturity and sensitivity. The casting of bronze doors had been done early in the middle ages, and was continued by Ghiberti in his north doors for the baptistery of Florence, but Donatello in his "David" cast the first free-standing bronze figure of a nude since Roman days. His equestrian statue of the *condottiere* Gattamelata at Padua, while not the first of its kind (there are equestrian figures in medieval cathedrals), was a landmark of permanent influence. His realistic portrait busts revived the great talent of the Romans in this particular field. Together with the della Robbias, who worked in terra cotta, his Madonnas and his treatment of children are of extraordinary grace, delicacy, and fresh gaiety. Indeed, sculpture had so perfected itself with Donatello that Michelangelo to express his genius had to break with classical restraint in form and expression.

If adventurous scholars and artists were giving a better perspective to history and the natural world about them in their writings and pictures and statuary, adventurous mariners through their discoveries were putting in better order the fantastic imaginings of centuries concerning the glamorous Far East and the unknown Atlantic. Quite definitely the beginnings of discoveries in the Atlantic are to be associated with the crusades. The crusades were in the main an economic offensive directed against Moslem control of the Mediterranean. As such they had failed by the end of the thirteenth century, and they had never succeeded in even threatening the monopoly held by Mohammedan merchants of trade with eastern Africa, India, and the Far East over the Red Sea and Indian Ocean. The expansion of the Mongols in the early thirteenth century gave new hope to the religious and economic aspirations of western Europe. Possibly they could be converted to Christianity and with them as allies, Islam, in the Near East, crushed in a vise. Certainly for Venice and Genoa, the expan-

*Travels to
the Far East*

[27] See p. 718.

sion of the Mongols combined with the demise of the Byzantine empire compensated amply for the losses in Syria and Palestine. For over a century after about 1245 continuous attempts were made by popes and kings to establish good relations between the khans and the west. The religious envoys were usually Franciscans. St. Francis himself was active for a while in the Near East. In 1245 Pope Innocent IV sent the Franciscan friar John of Plano-Carpini on a mission to the khan, and his account of his travels opened up to western Europe entirely new vistas. In 1252 St. Louis sent the Franciscan William of Ruysbroeck to the khan, and he too wrote an account of his experiences.

Between the years 1260 and 1269 the brothers Nicolo and Maffeo Polo, Venetian merchants, journeyed all the way to the court of Kubla Khan on the outskirts of Peiping, bringing back with them from the khan an invitation to the pope to send emissaries to him who might discuss the superiority of Christianity over the religion of his own people. In 1271 the brothers started out for the khan's court again, leaving behind two Franciscans who had not the courage to make the trip, but taking along young Marco Polo, Nicolo's son, then seventeen years old. Traveling overland from Ormuz to Shangtu, they arrived at the court of the khan in 1275 and spent seventeen years in his service, becoming thus thoroughly acquainted with the richest and most populous and most civilized area in the known world. In 1292 they started home by sea from Zaitum, passing through the East Indies, Ceylon, and up the west coast of India back to Ormuz. They were back in Venice in 1295. Three years later Marco was taken prisoner in a naval battle with the Genoese, and while in prison dictated to a fellow prisoner an account of his travels. Western Europe had never had such an experience before. Now for the first time was revealed the actual character of the Far East. Here were the China, Japan, East Indies, and India hitherto only dreamed of. The book was subsequently read by Portuguese navigators, and a certain Christopher Columbus made marginal notations in his copy.

But the Mongols of western Asia turned to Islam rather than to Christianity, and the rise of the Ottoman Turks promised none too well for shattered Christian hopes. Meanwhile, however, the Franciscan effort made exceptional progress. John of Montecorvino, a contemporary of Marco, founded missions in Persia, India, and China. He became the first Archbishop of Peiping, with seven suffragan bishops, and by the end of the fourteenth century Franciscan houses in China numbered about fifty.

Events of this kind stimulated the desire of some to reach the Far East by sailing westward out of the Mediterranean and down the west coast of Africa. In the last decade of the thirteenth century Genoese sailors made the attempt but were never heard from. In the fourteenth century the Canary, Madeira, and Azores islands were discovered or rediscovered. Improvements in shipbuilding, better coastal maps, the mariner's compass, the astrolabe, and clocks made voyages into unknown waters less hazardous. Venice and Genoa, however, were bound to be concerned with maintaining the overland routes to the Far East, the outlets of which they tapped in the Near East. It was a comparatively new dynastic state of the Atlantic seaboard, Portugal, that was destined to pursue the idea of an African route to the east to its realization. Ostensibly this was but a continuation of the long crusade against the Moors in the Spanish peninsula, not yet completed. In 1415 Portugal carried the offensive to Africa by taking Ceuta, and then tried to pursue the offensive by turning the flank of Moslem North Africa, by continuing down the western African coast and possibly finding a means of moving into the interior. The Portuguese talked a good deal about the conversion of Infidels and natives to Christianity, but their chief interest was rather trade, and particularly trade in slaves, which were needed in Spain to work the regions devastated by the constant war against the Moors.

The man who took Ceuta for John I of Portugal was his younger son, Henry. Henceforth until his death in 1460, Prince Henry the Navigator, as he is called—although the amount of navigation he did was precious little, he being interested primarily in his own fortune—directed from his castle at Sagres, on Cape St. Vincent, the course of Portuguese exploration. The Canaries were disputed for with Castile, to whom they eventually went in 1496. The Madeiras were annexed and colonized. The Azores were settled with Portuguese and Netherlanders. Farther and farther down the west coast of Africa crept Portuguese ships searching for more numerous and stronger slaves, and hoping to find the interior route to Abyssinia or to the Far East. Only towards the end of his life did the prince seem to realize the possibility of discovering the all-sea route to India by continuing down the west African coast until it came to an end. By 1446 Cape Verde had been reached and in the year of his death the Cape Verde Islands discovered.

After his death the advance went on. In 1471 the equator was crossed, and fifteen years later Bartholomew Diaz rounded the Cape of Good Hope. It was only in 1497, however, that the Portuguese

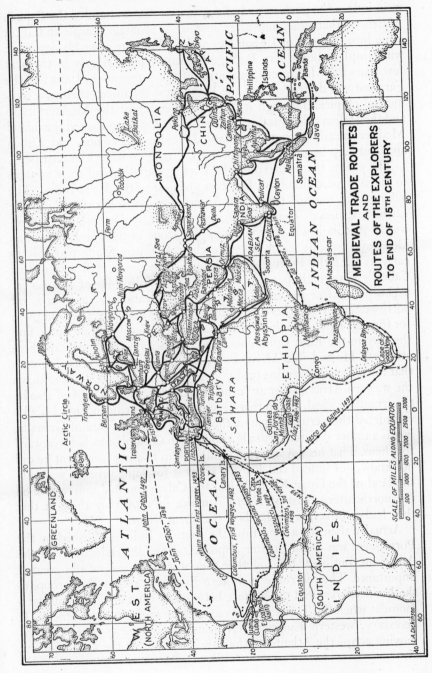

were induced to push on to India. Vasco da Gama rounded the Cape in March of that year, and after loading a profitable cargo at Calicut came into the port of Lisbon two and a half years after his departure with ample proof where Portugal's fortune lay. Quickly in the next few years the Mohammedan control of the sea routes to India and the Far East was destroyed, and the Portuguese organized their new commercial empire. Through it the predominance of the Mediterranean and the Italian cities was destroyed. The Atlantic supplanted the inland Mediterranean, Portugal supplanted Venice and Genoa, and Lisbon and Antwerp became the centers of the new capitalistic enterprise.

Columbus

The events that spurred on the Portuguese to extend their voyages to India were Columbus's first two voyages to the West Indies. The Vikings had touched the North American coast in the course of their earliest expansion. That there was land to be found by sailing due westward—Antilla it was called—a stepping-stone to the Far East, was an idea never wholly given up since classical times. Quite probably as early as 1448 the Portuguese had touched the coast of Brazil, so that Cabral's voyage thither in 1500 was but a follow-up of this earlier expedition. After the rediscovery and colonization of the islands off northwestern Africa there were rather aimless searchings beyond them for the new land. Into the north Atlantic Bristol sailors went out to find the way to the East. Columbus himself was acquainted with all these attempts. He had read Marco Polo; as a Genoese he was familiar with that town's great maritime tradition. He had been to Iceland and down the western African coast as far as the equator. He was moved also by the crusading ideal. But in that very year when Ferdinand and Isabella completed their crusade against the Moors by the capture of Granada, it was a rather different crusade upon which Columbus sailed westward for them. That his voyages had brought him to a new continent he did not know, nor indeed did Europe know it for some time. It was only the land of the Great Khan. When the Cabots touched somewhere on the northeastern coast of North America in 1496 they thought that they had come across the lands of the Great Khan.

Actually then for a long time the route to India established by the Portuguese was of far greater importance than the rediscovery of the American continent. But together they were of course of the greatest importance. The control by a western European nation of the route to the Far East restored the balance between Islam and Christianity at a moment when the Turks were invading Europe from the southeast. If necessary, western European civilization could escape the Turk by moving across the Atlantic to the new continent. At the very moment, too, when western Europe had begun to recover her full heritage from Greece and Rome, she was faced with the prospect of transmitting her newly enriched civilization both to older and richer, if less vigorous, civilizations of the Far East, and to a new continent inhabited sparsely by Indians. Western European civilization had finally succeeded in breaking for all time its European limitations and, still youthful and vigorous, was ready to begin its gradual conquest of the whole globe. What had been in the beginning but a local civilization confined to a small area in western Europe had expanded to northern, central, and certain parts of eastern Europe. In the process it had emerged from relative barbarism to full maturity along many lines. It was now about to transcend the limits of its locality and become a world civilization. That transformation is still going on.

If western Europe had gone a long way, it is well to remember that in many respects it had still a long way to travel. The exciting events that seem to crowd the history of the latter half of the fifteenth century do not seem so glamorous when it is remembered that at the very end of the century western Europe was suffering from what it regarded as its first epidemic of syphilis and from recurring ravages of the plague. How far its mentality was liberated is revealed by the fact that Savonarola was first to be tried for heresy by an ordeal of fire in the most enlightened city of the age, that alchemy and astrology reigned still supreme, and that Europe was beginning to be tortured by a mania for discovering and persecuting witches. What western Europe had to offer the rest of the world was not altogether a blessing.

The chronicle of Cologne reports for the year 1499 that "the eternal God has out of his unfathomable wisdom brought into existence the laudable art, by which men now print books, and multiply them so greatly that every man may for himself read or hear read the way of salvation." [28] Under just what circumstances this "laudable art" first came into existence in western Europe is a matter of considerable doubt. Printing with wooden blocks and with movable type was known at an early date in China, but it did not spread westward. The knowledge of paper making, however, did spread westward from China through the Islamic world. By the end of the twelfth century paper was made in Spain and southern France, and thence it spread into Italy. By the end of the fourteenth century Cologne and Nuremberg were producing it. But the printed book needed more than paper. In the early fourteenth century engraving on wood led to the making of a few prints, after a suitable ink had been discovered. The earliest date for a book

The invention of printing

[28] Usher, *A History of Mechanical Inventions*, p. 204.

printed with engraved wooden blocks, one for each page, is about 1440. To make wooden blocks for printing purposes was, however, more expensive than to have the pages written by hand. A movable metal type was needed that could be used indefinitely for any number or kind of books until it wore out. Printing thus depended on successful type founding. The problems of the press itself and of its manipulation were not so difficult, since the principles of the press were well known from its use in the making of wine.

It seems probable that the first books printed with movable metal type came from Holland in the second quarter of the fourteenth century. But the man who perfected the technique, if he did not invent it, was the printer of Mainz, John Gutenberg (c. 1398–1468). There was a printing shop at Mainz as early as 1450, and 1454 is the date for the first piece preserved from Gutenberg's press—an indulgence. Fust and Schöffer are to be associated with Gutenberg in putting the printing press on a sound foundation. Its use spread quickly to other German towns, and traveling German printers introduced it into Italy, Spain, and France. William Caxton, the first printer of English books, learned his art in Cologne and Bruges. German printers used the handwriting of the time, Gothic script, as model for their type, and it has persisted until recently in German books. They carried Gothic script with them on their journeys. In Italy, however, the humanists were using the script of the Carolingian scribes [29] to copy their classical manuscripts, and had little taste for Gothic. The type that was made to conform to Carolingian minuscule was the Roman type, which quickly supplanted Gothic, except in Germany, and is the type used in the printing of this book.

By the end of the fifteenth century the works of humanists, religious radicals, and classical authors could thus be printed and quickly disseminated throughout Europe. But printing was from the first not a philanthropy for the benefit of learning or revolution; it was a business. It quickly became one of the new capitalistic industries. The books that paid in the early decades of printing were not the new but the old learning, books that had to do with the "way of salvation." The works of St. Thomas and other theologians, the works of medieval encyclopedists such as Vincent of Beauvais and Bartholomew the Englishman, service books for the Church, textbooks for the schools, especially those on canon law, devotional tracts, collections of the stories of Troy and books on chess—these were what the public were buying.

By the beginning of the sixteenth century, however, the new as well

[29] See p. 254.

as the old learning was being printed in abundance. The Manutius press at Venice devoted itself to publishing the Greek classics. Italic type was first used then. The works of the religious reformers came to be in some instances best sellers. Erasmus's *Praise of Folly* was such a success, and together with Luther's *Ninety-five Theses* revealed the power of the new invention in spreading new ideas as well as in preserving old ones. The press did away with the progressive corruption of texts at the hands of a succession of copyists. It made, of course, for a wider and quicker dissemination of every kind of information. It changed the methods of instruction in the schools by minimizing the emphasis upon oral instruction. But as long as the vast majority of people did not know how to read its influences were severely limited. And since it cast a magic spell upon the printed page leading to the popular belief that what is printed must be true, its effects, when people read at all, were not necessarily beneficial. But there are very few who would wish to do without the printing press, despite all the difficulties that its gradual improvement has introduced. It is, at last, after considerable reluctance, restoring to those so-called middle ages that introduced it, a more accurate place in the history of western European civilization.

Genealogical Tables

The Lombard Kings in Italy

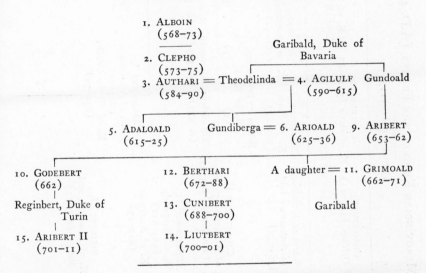

1. ALBOIN
   (568–73)

2. CLEPHO
   (573–75)

Garibald, Duke of Bavaria

3. AUTHARI = Theodelinda = 4. AGILULF   Gundoald
   (584–90)   (590–615)

5. ADALOALD   Gundiberga = 6. ARIOALD   9. ARIBERT
   (615–25)   (625–36)   (653–62)

10. GODEBERT   12. BERTHARI   A daughter = 11. GRIMOALD
    (662)   (672–88)   (662–71)

Reginbert, Duke of   13. CUNIBERT   Garibald
    Turin   (688–700)

15. ARIBERT II   14. LIUTBERT
    (701–11)   (700–01)

Kings not connected with this house were (7) Rothari, 636–52; (8) Rodoald, 652–53; (16) Ansprand, 712; (17) Liutprand, 712–44; (18) Hildebrand, 743–44; (19) Ratchis, 744–49; (20) Aistulf, 749–56; (21) Desiderius, 756–74.

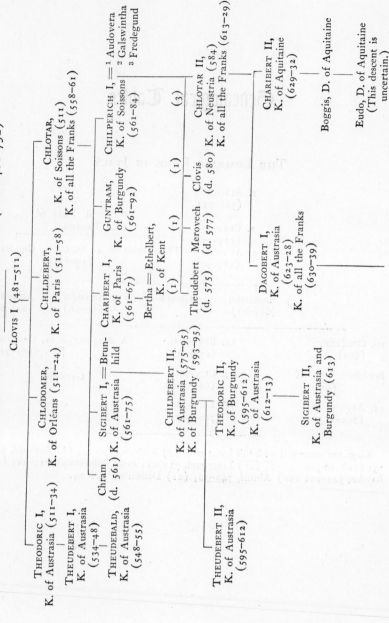

The Merovingian Kings of the Franks (A.D. 481–752)

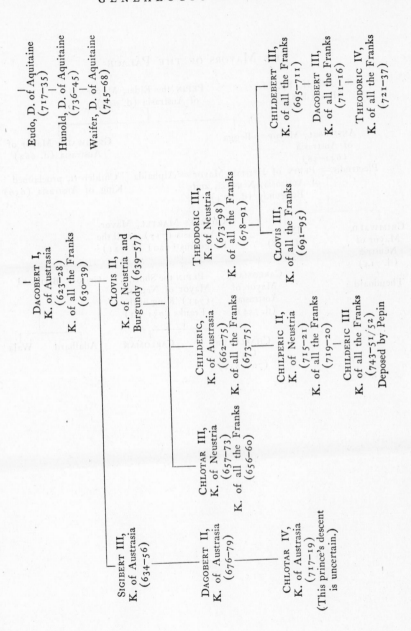

The Mayors of the Palace

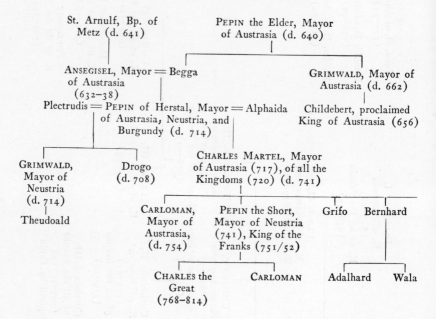

THE DESCENDANTS OF CHARLES THE GREAT

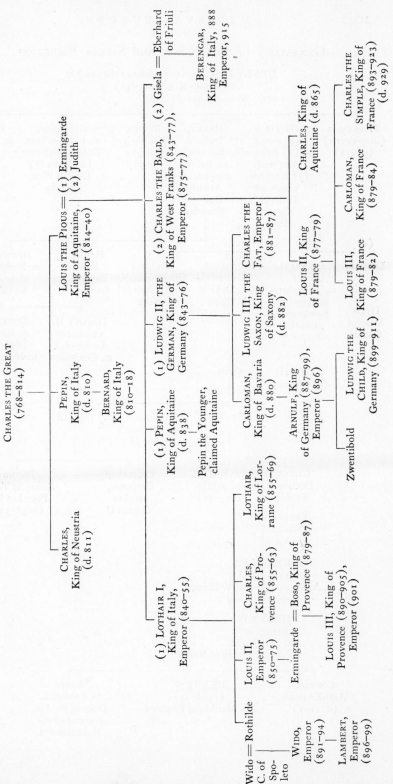

GENEALOGY OF THE SAXON AND SALIAN EMPERORS

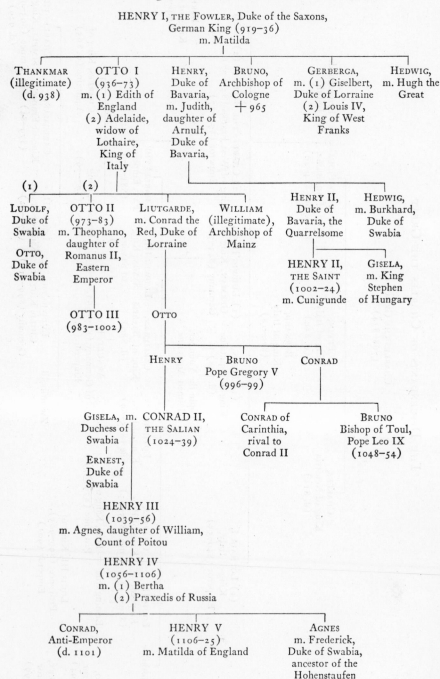

HENRY I, THE FOWLER, Duke of the Saxons,
German King (919–36)
m. Matilda

THANKMAR (illegitimate) (d. 938)

OTTO I (936–73) m. (1) Edith of England (2) Adelaide, widow of Lothaire, King of Italy

HENRY, Duke of Bavaria, m. Judith, daughter of Arnulf, Duke of Bavaria,

BRUNO, Archbishop of Cologne +965

GERBERGA, m. (1) Giselbert, Duke of Lorraine (2) Louis IV, King of West Franks

HEDWIG, m. Hugh the Great

(1)

(2)

LUDOLF, Duke of Swabia | OTTO, Duke of Swabia

OTTO II (973–83) m. Theophano, daughter of Romanus II, Eastern Emperor | OTTO III (983–1002)

LIUTGARDE, m. Conrad the Red, Duke of Lorraine | OTTO

WILLIAM (illegitimate), Archbishop of Mainz

HENRY II, Duke of Bavaria, the Quarrelsome | HENRY II, THE SAINT (1002–24) m. Cunigunde

HEDWIG, m. Burkhard, Duke of Swabia | GISELA, m. King Stephen of Hungary

HENRY | BRUNO Pope Gregory V (996–99) | CONRAD

GISELA, m. Duchess of Swabia | ERNEST, Duke of Swabia

CONRAD II, THE SALIAN (1024–39)

CONRAD of Carinthia, rival to Conrad II

BRUNO Bishop of Toul, Pope Leo IX (1048–54)

HENRY III (1039–56) m. Agnes, daughter of William, Count of Poitou | HENRY IV (1056–1106) m. (1) Bertha (2) Praxedis of Russia

CONRAD, Anti-Emperor (d. 1101)

HENRY V (1106–25) m. Matilda of England

AGNES m. Frederick, Duke of Swabia, ancestor of the Hohenstaufen

GENEALOGY OF THE HOUSE OF TANCRED OF HAUTEVILLE

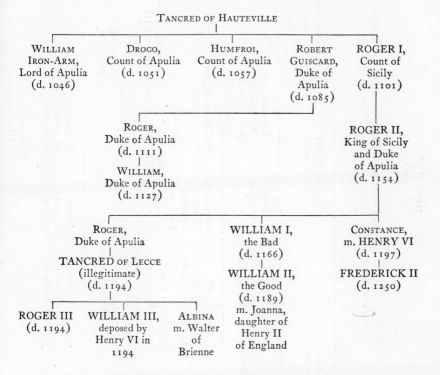

TANCRED OF HAUTEVILLE

WILLIAM IRON-ARM, Lord of Apulia (d. 1046)

DROGO, Count of Apulia (d. 1051)

HUMFROI, Count of Apulia (d. 1057)

ROBERT GUISCARD, Duke of Apulia (d. 1085)

ROGER I, Count of Sicily (d. 1101)

ROGER, Duke of Apulia (d. 1111)

WILLIAM, Duke of Apulia (d. 1127)

ROGER II, King of Sicily and Duke of Apulia (d. 1154)

ROGER, Duke of Apulia

TANCRED OF LECCE (illegitimate) (d. 1194)

WILLIAM I, the Bad (d. 1166)

WILLIAM II, the Good (d. 1189) m. Joanna, daughter of Henry II of England

CONSTANCE, m. HENRY VI (d. 1197)

FREDERICK II (d. 1250)

ROGER III (d. 1194)

WILLIAM III, deposed by Henry VI in 1194

ALBINA m. Walter of Brienne

The Welfs and the Hohenstaufens

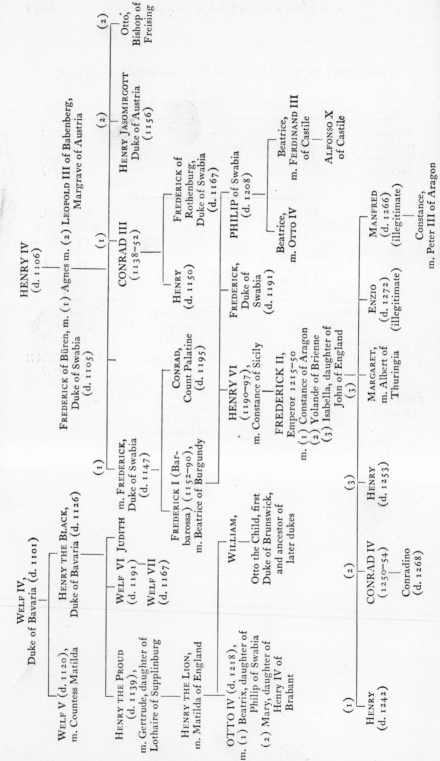

THE NORMAN AND ANGEVIN KINGS OF ENGLAND

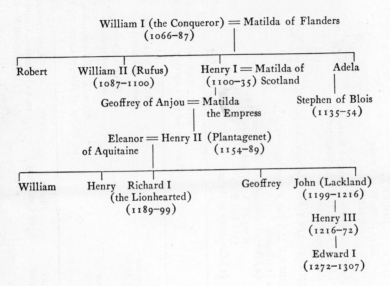

William I (the Conqueror) = Matilda of Flanders
(1066–87)

Robert   William II (Rufus)   Henry I = Matilda of   Adela
(1087–1100)   (1100–35) Scotland

Geoffrey of Anjou = Matilda   Stephen of Blois
the Empress   (1135–54)

Eleanor = Henry II (Plantagenet)
of Aquitaine   (1154–89)

William   Henry   Richard I   Geoffrey   John (Lackland)
(the Lionhearted)   (1199–1216)
(1189–99)

Henry III
(1216–72)

Edward I
(1272–1307)

THE CAPETIAN KINGS OF FRANCE

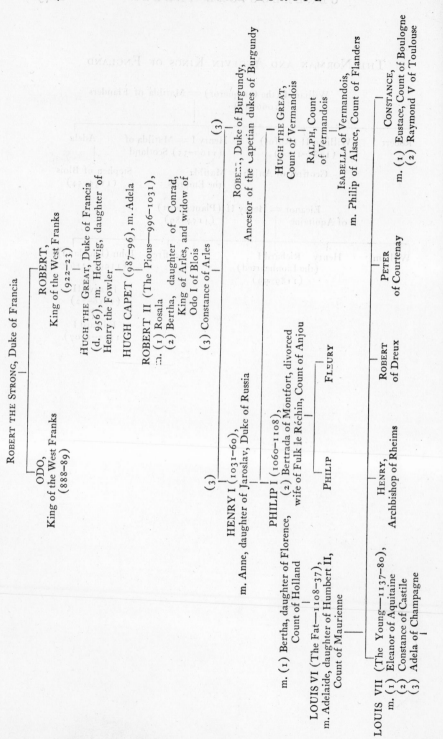

ROBERT THE STRONG, Duke of Francia

ODO, King of the West Franks (888–89)

ROBERT, King of the West Franks (922–23)

HUGH THE GREAT, Duke of Francia (d. 956), m. Hedwig, daughter of Henry the Fowler

HUGH CAPET (987–96), m. Adela

ROBERT II (The Pious—996–1031), m. (1) Rosala (2) Bertha, daughter of Conrad, King of Arles, and widow of Odo I of Blois (3) Constance of Arles

(3) HENRY I (1031–60), m. Anne, daughter of Jaroslav, Duke of Russia

PHILIP I (1060–1108), m. (1) Bertha, daughter of Florence, Count of Holland (2) Bertrada of Montfort, divorced wife of Fulk le Réchin, Count of Anjou

PHILIP

FLEURY

LOUIS VI (The Fat—1108–37), m. Adelaide, daughter of Humbert II, Count of Maurienne

LOUIS VII (The Young—1137–80), m. (1) Eleanor of Aquitaine (2) Constance of Castile (3) Adela of Champagne

HENRY, Archbishop of Rheims

ROBERT of Dreux

PETER of Courtenay

ROBERT, Duke of Burgundy, Ancestor of the Capetian dukes of Burgundy

HUGH THE GREAT, Count of Vermandois

RALPH, Count of Vermandois

ISABELLA of Vermandois, m. Philip of Alsace, Count of Flanders

CONSTANCE, m. (1) Eustace, Count of Boulogne (2) Raymond V of Toulouse

(1)

MARY, m. Henry I of Champagne

ALICE, m. Theobald I of Blois

(2)

MARGARET, m. Henry of Anjou (d. 1183)

ALICE

(3)

PHILIP II (Augustus) (1180–1223), m. (1) Isabella of Hainault (2) Ingeborg of Denmark (3) Agnes of Meran

AGNES, m. (1) Alexius Comnenus (2) Andronicus Comnenus

(3) PHILIP, Count of Boulogne

(3) MARY, m. Henry I, Duke of Brabant

(1) LOUIS VIII (1223–26), m. Blanche of Castile, granddaughter of Henry II

ROBERT (d. 1250), Count of Artois, m. Maud of Brabant

ALPHONSE (d. 1271), Count of Poitou, m. Joan, daughter of Raymond VII, Count of Toulouse

CHARLES (d. 1285), Count of Anjou and King of Sicily, m. Beatrice, fourth daughter of Raymond Berengar of Provence

LOUIS IX (St. Louis) (1226–70), m. Margaret, eldest daughter of Raymond Berengar, Count of Provence

ROBERT II (d. 1302), m. (1) BLANCHE, Henry I, King of Navarre and Count of Champagne (2) Edmund, Earl of Lancaster

PHILIP III (the Bold) (1270–85), m. (1) Isabel, daughter of James I of Aragon (2) Mary, daughter of Henry III, Duke of Brabant

JOHN, Count of Nevers (d. 1270)

PETER, Count of Alençon (d. 1284)

ROBERT, Count of Clermont (d. 1318), m. Beatrice of Burgundy, heiress of Bourbon

ISABELLA, m. Theobald V (the Young), King of Navarre and Count of Champagne

BLANCHE, m. Ferdinand of la Cerda, son of Alfonso X of Castile

MARGARET, m. John I, Duke of Brabant

AGNES, m. Robert II, Duke of Burgundy

LOUIS I, Duke of Bourbon (d. 1342), (ancestor of house of Bourbon)

PHILIP IV (the Fair) (1285–1314), m. Joan of Navarre

CHARLES, Count of Valois

LOUIS, Count of Évreux

(2)

MARGARET, m. Edward I

ISABELLA, m. Edward II

PHILIP VI of Valois, King in 1328

(1)

LOUIS X (1314–16)

PHILIP V (1316–22)

CHARLES IV (1322–28)

The Succession in France in 1328

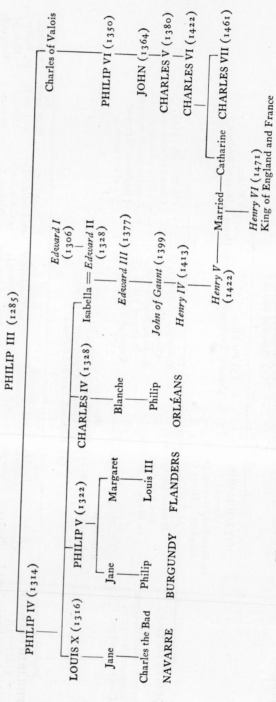

The dates, years of death. French kings, in capitals. Descendants of Edward I, in italics.

THE KINGS OF JERUSALEM

A

Godfrey the Bearded,
Duke of Lower Lorraine (d. 1069),
m. (1) Doda; (2) Beatrice, mother of Countess Matilda

Godfrey the Hunchback,
Duke of Lower Lorraine
(d. 1076)

Ida,
m. Eustace II,
Count of Boulogne

GODFREY DE BOUILLON,
Duke of Lower Lorraine, and
Baron of the Holy Sepulcher
(d. 1100)

Eustace III
of Boulogne

BALDWIN I,
Count of Edessa and
King of Jerusalem
(1100–18)

B

BALDWIN II,
cousin of Baldwin I
(1118–30)

MILLICENT,
m. FULK OF ANJOU
(1130–43)

BALDWIN III
(1143–63)

AMALRIC I
(1163–74)

BALDWIN IV
(1174–85)

Sibyl,
m. (1) William of Montferrat
(2) GUY OF LUSIGNAN
(1186–92)

Isabella,
m. (2) CONRAD OF MONTFERRAT
(1192)
(3) HENRY OF CHAMPAGNE
(1192–97)
(4) AMALRIC II OF CYPRUS
(1197–1205)

(1)
BALDWIN V
(1185–86)

(2)
Mary,
m. JOHN OF BRIENNE
(1210–22)

(4)
AMALRIC III
(d. 1206)

Yolande,
m. EMPEROR FREDERICK II
(d. 1250)

The Lancaster Dynasty in England

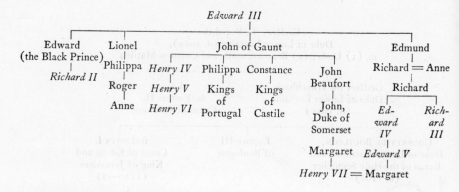

The names of the English kings are italicized. The diagram is extremely simplified. In 1450 at the outbreak of the Wars of the Roses many of the lords temporal were either descendants of Edward III or married to descendants. Excellent tables can be found in J. H. Ramsay, *Lancaster and York*.

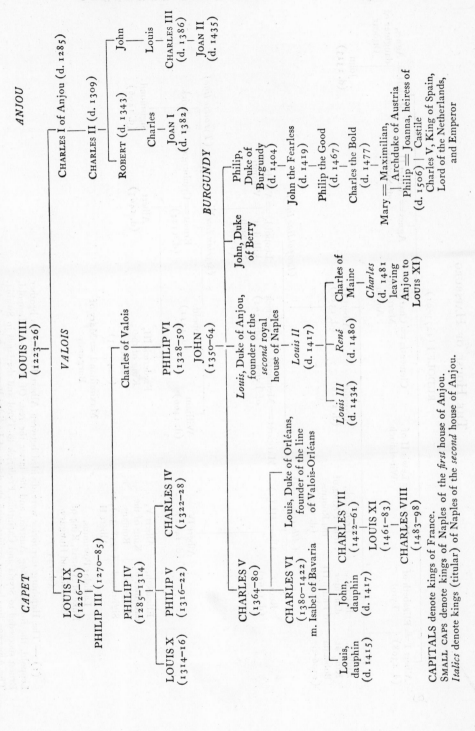

FRANCE, BURGUNDY, AND NAPLES

CAPET

LOUIS VIII
(1223–26)

ANJOU

CHARLES I of Anjou (d. 1285)

CHARLES II (d. 1309)

ROBERT (d. 1343)

Charles

JOAN I
(d. 1382)

John

Louis

CHARLES III
(d. 1386)

JOAN II
(d. 1435)

VALOIS

LOUIS IX
(1226–70)

PHILIP III (1270–85)

PHILIP IV
(1285–1314)

LOUIS X
(1314–16)

PHILIP V
(1316–22)

CHARLES IV
(1322–28)

Charles of Valois

PHILIP VI
(1328–50)

JOHN
(1350–64)

Louis, Duke of Anjou,
founder of the
second royal
house of Naples

Louis II
(d. 1417)

Louis III
(d. 1434)

René
(d. 1480)

Charles of
Maine

Charles
(d. 1481
leaving
Anjou to
LOUIS XI)

BURGUNDY

John, Duke
of Berry

Philip,
Duke of
Burgundy
(d. 1404)

John the Fearless
(d. 1419)

Philip the Good
(d. 1467)

Charles the Bold
(d. 1477)

Mary = Maximilian,
| Archduke of Austria
Philip = Joanna, heiress of
(d. 1506) | Castile
Charles V, King of Spain,
Lord of the Netherlands,
and Emperor

CHARLES V
(1364–80)

CHARLES VI
(1380–1422)
m. Isabel of Bavaria

Louis, Duke of Orléans,
founder of the line
of Valois-Orléans

Louis,
dauphin
(d. 1415)

John,
dauphin
(d. 1417)

CHARLES VII
(1422–61)

LOUIS XI
(1461–83)

CHARLES VIII
(1483–98)

CAPITALS denote kings of France.
SMALL CAPS denote kings of Naples of the *first* house of Anjou.
Italics denote kings (titular) of Naples of the *second* house of Anjou.

The House of Hapsburg

RUDOLF I (1273–91)

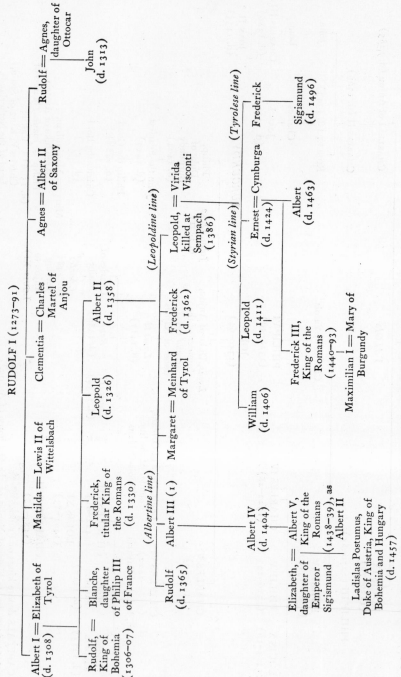

(1) — The Hapsburg territories were divided between Albert III and his brother Leopold, the former taking Austria, and the latter the rest. Of the sons of Leopold, Ernest succeeded to Styria and Carinthia, Frederick to Tyrol and the lands in Swabia. The Albertine line became extinct with the death of Ladislas Postumus, when Austria passed to Frederick III, and the latter's son, Maximilian I, reunited all the territories of the house.

REFERENCES FOR FURTHER READING

The student should become acquainted with textbooks other than this one devoted to the middle ages. In each of the following titles, chapters corresponding to those of this book can easily be found:

ADAMS, G. B., *Civilization During the Middle Ages* (New York, 1914).

AULT, W. O., *Europe in the Middle Ages* (New York, rev. ed., 1937).

BROWN, S. M., *Medieval Europe* (New York, rev. ed., 1935).

COLLINS, R. W., *A History of Medieval Civilization in Europe* (Boston, 1936).

HULME, E. M., *The Middle Ages* (New York, 1929).

MUNRO, D. C., and SONTAG, R. J., *The Middle Ages (395 to 1500)* (New York, rev. ed., 1928).

PREVITÉ-ORTON, C. W., *Outlines of Medieval History* (Cambridge [Eng.], 1929).

ROBINSON, J. H., *An Introduction to the History of Western Europe*, vol. I (1929).

SELLERY, G. C., and KREY, A. C., *Medieval Foundations of Western Civilization* (New York, 1929).

STEPHENSON, C., *Mediaeval History* (New York, 1935).

THATCHER, O. J., and McNEAL, E. H., *Europe in the Middle Ages* (New York, 1920).

THORNDIKE, L., *The History of Medieval Europe* (Boston, 1917).

In addition students would do well to investigate in the following books, which are collections of extracts from contemporary writers and noted historians, those chapters and excerpts, for the most part easily located, which correspond to the chapters of this book:

COULTON, G. G., *Life in the Middle Ages* (Cambridge [Eng.], 1931).

HENDERSON, E. F., *Select Historical Documents of the Middle Ages* (New York, 1892).

LAFFAN, R. G. D., *Select Documents of European History*, vol. I (London, 1930).

MUNRO, D. C., and SELLERY, G. C., *Medieval Civilization* (New York, 1904).

OGG, F. A., *A Source Book of Medieval History* (New York, 1907).

ROBINSON, J. H., *Readings in European History*, vol. I (Boston, 1906).

SCOTT, J. H., HYMA, A. H., and NOYES, A. H., *Readings in Medieval History* (New York, 1933).

THATCHER, O. J., and McNEAL, E. H., *A Source Book of Medieval History* (New York, 1905).

WEBSTER, H., *Historical Selections* (Boston, 1929).

Inasmuch as most instructors prefer to make their own suggestions for reading to their students, the following informal lists are meant to be helpful only, and to indicate some of the material used in the writing of the chapters.

CHAPTER 1

THE GRÆCO-ORIENTAL CONQUEST OF THE ROMAN EMPIRE

S. ANGUS, *The Mystery Religions and Christianity* and *The Religious Quests of the Græco-Roman World*; J. B. BURY, *Later Roman Empire*, I, bk. i, chaps. iii–iv; V. CHAPOT, *The Roman World*; *Cambridge Medieval History*, I, chaps. i–ii, xix; F. V. CUMONT, *The Oriental Religions in Roman Paganism*; S. DILL, *Roman Society from Nero to Aurelius*, bk. iv, and *Roman Society in the Last Century of the Western Empire*; T. R. GLOVER, *The Conflict of Religions in the Early Roman Empire*; H. STUART JONES, *The Roman Empire*; F. S. MARVIN, *Western Races and the World*, chap. iv (by H. STUART JONES); M. ROSTOVTZEFF, *Social and Economic History of the Roman Empire*, and *History of the Ancient World*, chaps. xx–xxv; J. E. SANDYS, *Companion to Latin Studies*, secs. 542–63; J. W. THOMPSON, *Economic and Social History of the Middle Ages* (300–1500), chap. i.

CHAPTERS 2 AND 3

THE CHRISTIAN CONQUEST OF THE ROMAN EMPIRE

S. ANGUS, *The Mystery Religions and Christianity*; J. F. BETHUNE-BAKER, *An Introduction to the Early History of Christian Doctrine*; W. K. B. BOYD, *The Church in the Theodosian Code*; J. B. BURY, *Later Roman Empire*, I, bk. i, chaps. i–ii; *Cambridge Medieval History*, I, chaps. iv–vi; C. B. COLEMAN, *Constantine and Christianity*; S. DILL, *Roman Society in the Last Century of the Western Empire*, bk. i, chaps. i–iv, bk. ii, chap. i; J. B. FIRTH, *Constantine*; ALICE GARDNER, *Julian*; T. R. GLOVER, *Conflict of Religions in the Early Roman Empire*; E. R. GOODENOUGH, *The Church in the Roman Empire*; C. GUIGNEBERT, *Christianity*; E. G. HARDY, *Christianity and the Roman Government*; EDWIN HATCH, *Organization of the Early Christian Church*, and *Growth of Church Institutions*; EDWIN PEARS, "The Campaign Against Paganism," *English Historical Review*, XXIV (January, 1909), 1 ff.; W. RAMSAY, *The Church and the Roman Empire*; J. W. THOMPSON, *Economic and Social History of the Middle Ages* (300–1500), chap. ii; E. L. WOODWARD, *Christianity and Nationalism in the Later Roman Empire*; H. B. WORKMAN, *The Evolution of the Monastic Ideal*.

CHAPTERS 4 AND 5

THE GERMAN CONQUEST OF THE ROMAN EMPIRE

P. BOISSONADE, *Life and Work in Medieval Europe*, bk. i, chap. i; J. B. BURY, *The Invasions of Europe by the Barbarians*, and *The Later Roman Empire*, I, bk. ii, chaps. vi–vii, bk. iii, chaps. iv–v; *Cambridge Medieval History*, I, chaps. vii–xv; S. DILL, *Roman Society in the Last Century of the Western Empire*, bk. iv; F. B. GUMMERE, *Germanic Origins*; C. J. H. HAYES, *Introduction to Sources Relating to the Germanic Invasions*; T. HODGKIN, *Dynasty of Theodosius*, chaps. iii–vii; *Theodoric the Ostrogoth*; "Visigothic Spain," in *English Historical Review*, II, 209; C. W. C. OMAN, *The Dark Ages*, chaps. i–ii, iv–vii, and *England Before the Norman Conquest*; W. FLINDERS PETRIE, "Migrations," in *Journal of the Anthropological Institute*, XXXVI (1906), 189 ff. (with remarkable maps); R. D. SHAW, "The Fall of the Visigothic Power in Spain," in *English Historical Review*, XXI, 209; TACITUS, *Germania*, in *Translations and Reprints of the University of Pennsylvania*, VI, no. 3; H. O. TAYLOR, *The Mediæval Mind* (1930), I, chap. viii; J. W. THOMPSON, *Economic and Social History of the Middle Ages* (300–1500), chaps. iii–iv.

CHAPTER 6

THE BYZANTINE EMPIRE

W. F. ADENEY, *The Greek and Eastern Churches*; N. H. BAYNES, *The Byzantine Empire*; C. R. BEAZLEY, *Dawn of Modern Geography*, II, 467–514 (on Slav invasions); J. B. BURY, *The Eastern Roman Empire*, II, chaps. xiv–xxiii, and *The Later Roman Empire*, vol. II; ROBERT BYRON, *The Byzantine Achievement*; R. BYRON and D. T. RICE, *The Birth of Western Painting*, chap. iii; *Cambridge Medieval History*, II, chaps. i–ii, ix, xiii–xiv; O. M. DALTON, *Byzantine Art and Archaeology*; CHARLES DIEHL, *History of Byzantine Empire* and *Byzantine Portraits*; W. G. HOLMES, *Justinian and Theodora*; W. H. HUTTON, *The Church in the Sixth Century*; C. W. C. OMAN, *The Dark Ages*, chaps. iii, v, vi, ix; J. W. THOMPSON, *Economic and Social History of the Middle Ages* (300–1500), chaps. vi, xiv; A. A. VASILIEV, *History of the Byzantine Empire*.

CHAPTER 7

THE EMPIRE OF THE ARABS

W. T. ARNOLD, *Preaching of Islam*; SIR T. ARNOLD and A. GUILLAUME (eds.), *The Legacy of Islam*; L. BARSAU-DIHIGO, *The Advance of Islam*; CARL H.

BECKER, *Christianity and Islam*; R. BELL, *The Origin of Islam in Its Christian Environment*; E. R. BEVAN and C. SINGER (eds.), *The Legacy of Israel*; J. B. BURY, *The Eastern Roman Empire*, chaps. viii, ix, and *The Later Roman Empire*, II, 308–19, 380–86, 401–7; A. J. BUTLER, *The Arab Conquest of Egypt*; *Cambridge Medieval History*, II, chaps. x–xiii; E. DOUTTÉ, *Islam and Mohamet*; D. G. HOGARTH, *Arabia*; C. I. HUART, *History of the Arabs*; C. S. HURGRONGE, *Mohammedanism*; G. LeSTRANGE, *Baghdad during the Abassid Caliphate*; D. S. MARGOLIOUTH, *Mohammed and the Rise of Islam*; E. H. PALMER, *Life of Haran-al-Rashid*; J. W. THOMPSON, *Economic and Social History of the Middle Ages* (300–1500), chap. vii; C. C. TORREY, *The Jewish Foundation of Islam*.

CHAPTER 8

THE CIVILIZATION OF EARLY WESTERN EUROPE

P. S. ALLEN and H. M. JONES, *The Romanesque Lyric*, chaps. viii–x; E. BREHAUT, *Isidore of Seville*; G. F. BROWNE, *Boniface of Crediton and His Companions*; J. B. BURY, *History of the Later Roman Empire*, II, bk. ii, chap. v, and *St. Patrick*; E. C. BUTLER, *Benedictine Monachism*; *Cambridge Medieval History*, I, chap. xviii, II, chaps. iv, v, vii, viii, xvi, xvii; J. B. CARTER, *Religious Life of Ancient Rome*, chap. vii; O. M. DALTON, *Gregory of Tours' History of the Franks*; C. DAWSON, *The Making of Europe*, chap. xi; *Dictionary of National Biography* (on Boniface); S. DILL, *Roman Society in Gaul in the Merovingian Age*; L. DUCHESNE, *Early History of the Christian Church*, II, chap. xiv, and *The Beginnings of the Temporal Sovereignty of the Popes*; F. H. DUDDEN, *Gregory the Great*; L. GOUGAUD, *Christianity in Celtic Lands*; F. GREGOROVIUS, *Rome in the Middle Ages*, II, 59–61, 194, 247, 251–58, 359–69; I. C. HANNAH, *Christian Monasticism*; E. F. HENDERSON, *Select Historical Documents of the Middle Ages*, pp. 176–89, 274–319; T. HODGKIN, *Italy and Her Invaders*, IV, bk. v, chap. xvi, vols. V–VII; T. S. HOLMES, *History of the Church in Gaul*; R. G. D. LAFFAN, *Select Documents of European History*, I, 1–6; M. C. W. LAISTNER, *Thought and Letters in Western Europe, A.D. 500 to 900*, chaps. i–vi; C. W. C. OMAN, *The Dark Ages*, chaps. xvii–xviii; F. J. E. RABY, *Christian Latin Poetry*, chaps. iii–v; E. K. RAND, *Founders of the Middle Ages*, chap. vii; E. SPEARING, *The Patrimony of the Roman Church in the Time of Gregory the Great*; E. SULLIVAN, *The Book of Kells*; *Translations and Reprints from the Original Sources of European History*, vol. II (*Life of St. Columban*); J. W. THOMPSON, *Economic and Social History of the Middle Ages* (300–1300), chaps. v, viii; HELEN WADDELL, *Medieval Latin Lyrics*, pp. 48–77, and *The Wandering Scholars*, chap. ii; H. B. WORKMAN, *The Evolution of the Monastic Ideal*; H. ZIMMER, *The Irish Element in Medieval Culture*.

CHAPTER 9

The Frankish State Under the Carolingians

P. S. Allen and H. M. Jones, *The Romanesque Lyric*, pp. 214–44; J. Bryce, *The Holy Roman Empire*, chaps. iv–v; *Cambridge Medieval History*, II, chaps. xix–xxi, III, chaps. i–iii; H. W. C. Davis, *Charlemagne*; E. Emerton, *Medieval Europe*, chaps. i, ii; T. Hodgkin, *Charles the Great*; R. G. D. Laffan, *Select Documents of European History*, I, 6–7; M. L. W. Laistner, *Thought and Letters in Western Europe, A.D. 500 to 900*, pp. 147–330; J. H. Mombert, *Charles the Great*; C. W. C. Oman, *The Dark Ages*, chaps. xx–xxv; H. O. Taylor, *The Mediæval Mind* (1930), I, 207–39; J. W. Thompson, *Economic and Social History of the Middle Ages* (300–1300), pp. 220–39, and chap. ix; *Translations and Reprints from the Original Sources of European History*, IV, no. 3, pp. 3–4, 12–13; S. E. Turner, *Life of Charlemagne by Einhard*; Helen Waddell, *Medieval Latin Lyrics*, pp. 78–125, 309–20.

CHAPTER 10

The Collapse of the Carolingian Empire

P. S. Allen and H. M. Jones, *The Romanesque Lyric*, pp. 216–43; C. R. Beazley, *The Dawn of Modern Geography*, II, 17–111; C. R. Beazley, N. Forbes, and G. A. Birkett, *Russia from the Varangians to the Bolsheviks*, pp. 1–50; J. B. Bury, *History of the Eastern Roman Empire*, I, chap. xiii; *Cambridge Medieval History*, I, chap. xiii, III, chaps. i–iv, IV, chap. i, 738–46; R. W. Chambers, *England before the Norman Conquest*, chaps. vi–viii; G. W. Dasent, *The Northmen in Iceland*; C. Dawson, *The Making of Europe*, chap. xiii; E. Emerton, *Medieval Europe*, chaps. i–ii; A. C. Flick, *Rise of the Medieval Church*, chaps. xv, xvi; F. Funck-Brentano, *The Middle Ages*, chap. i; K. Gjerset, *History of the Norwegian People*, vol. I; C. H. Haskins, *The Normans in European History*; E. Joranson, *The Danegeld in France*; C. F. Keary, *The Vikings in Western Christendom*; T. D. Kendrick, *A History of the Vikings*; R. G. D. Laffan, *Select Documents of European History*, pp. 8, 9–11, 13–15; D. Laing, *Heimskringla*; A. Mawer, *The Vikings*; J. R. Moreton-MacDonald, *History of France*, I, chaps. v–vii; Axel Olrik, *Viking Civilization*; C. W. C. Oman, *The Dark Ages*, chaps. xiii–xxv; H. A. Taine, *The Ancient Regime*, bk. i, chaps. i–ii; J. W. Thompson, *Economic and Social History of the Middle Ages* (300–1300), chaps. ix, x, and *Feudal Germany*, pp. 5–10, 167–75; V. Thomsen, *Relations between Ancient Russia and Scandinavia*; T. F. Tout, *The Empire and Papacy*, chaps. i–ii; G. Vigfusson, *Sturlunga Saga*, 2 vols.; Mary W. Williams, *Social Scandinavia in the Viking Age*.

CHAPTER 11

Feudalism

G. B. Adams, *Civilization during the Middle Ages*, chap. ix; Marc Bloch, "Feudalism," in *Encyclopedia of the Social Sciences*; G. C. Crump and E. F. Jacob (eds.), *The Legacy of the Middle Ages*, chap. vii; W. S. Davis, *Life on a Medieval Barony*; G. T. Denison, *History of Cavalry*, pp. 97–184; E. W. Dow and C. Seignobos, *The Feudal Regime*; Viollet Le Duc, *Annals of a Fortress*, and *Story of a House*; E. Emerton, *Medieval Europe*, chap. xiv; Joan Evans, *Life in Medieval France*, chap. ii; L. Gautier, *Chivalry*; Hubert Hall, *Court Life Under the Plantagenets*; A. Luchaire, *Social France at the Time of Philip Augustus*, chaps. viii–xi; W. C. Meller, *A Knight's Life in the Days of Chivalry*; C. W. C. Oman, *The Art of War in the Middle Ages*; Edgar Prestage (ed.), *Chivalry* (in *History of Civilization* series); H. O. Taylor, *The Mediæval Mind* (1930), I, 521–603; O. J. Thatcher and E. H. McNeal, *A Source Book for Medieval History*, pp. 341–87, 410–17; J. W. Thompson, *Economic and Social History of the Middle Ages* (300–1300), chap. xxvi, and *The Middle Ages*, II, chap. xxiv; *Translations and Reprints from European History*, vol. IV, no. 3; P. Vinogradoff, *English Society in the Eleventh Century*.

CHAPTER 12

Manorialism

W. J. Ashley, *English Economic History*, vol. I; E. P. Cheyney, "The Medieval Manor," in *Annals of the American Academy of Political and Social Sciences*, vol. IV (Sept., 1893); G. G. Coulton, *The Medieval Village*, chaps. iv, vii, viii; Joan Evans, *Life in Medieval France*, chaps. ii, iii; N. S. B. Gras, *History of Agriculture*, chap. iv, and *Introduction to Economic History*, chap. iii; N. J. Hone, *The Manor and Manorial Records*; Rudolphe Kötzschke, "Manorialism," in *Encyclopedia of the Social Sciences*; I. E. Lipson, *Introduction to the Economic History of England*, I, chaps. i–iii; A. Luchaire, *Social France at the Time of Philip Augustus*, chap. xiii; F. W. Maitland, *Domesday and Beyond*; E. Power, *Medieval People*, chap. i; J. E. T. Rogers, *Six Centuries of Work and Wages: The History of English Labor*, chaps. ii–iv; J. W. Thompson, *Economic and Social History of the Middle Ages* (300–1300), chap. xxvii; *Translations and Reprints from the Original Sources of European History*, vol. III, no. 5; P. Vinogradoff, *Growth of the Manor*.

CHAPTER 13

The Revival of the Empire

J. Bryce, *The Holy Roman Empire*, chaps. v, vii–ix; *Cambridge Medieval History*, V, chaps. i–iii; E. Curtis, *Roger of Sicily and the Normans of Lower Italy*; E. Emerton, *The Correspondence of Gregory VII*, and *Medieval Europe*, chaps. iii–viii; J. Evans, *Cluny*; H. Fisher, *The Medieval Empire*, I, chaps. i–iii; J. Haller, *Epochs of German History*, chaps. i–iii; C. H. Haskins, *The Normans in European History*, chaps. vii, viii; E. F. Henderson, *Select Historical Documents of the Middle Ages*, bk. ii, no. 5, bk. iii, no. 4, bk. iv, nos. 1, 2; A. J. Macdonald, *Hildebrand, Pope Gregory VII*; A. Mawer, *The Vikings*, chaps. xi–xii; C. H. McIlwain, *The Growth of Political Thought in the West*, pp. 201–20; E. Richard, *Germanic Civilization*, chaps. xii, xvi–xix; L. M. Smith, *The Early History of the Monastery of Cluny*; H. O. Taylor, *The Mediæval Mind* (1930), I, 298–306; J. W. Thompson, *Economic and Social History of the Middle Ages* (300–1300), chap. xi, and *Feudal Germany*, chaps. i–iii, xii–xiv; T. F. Tout, *The Empire and the Papacy*, chap. v.

CHAPTER 14

The Apex and the Decline of the Holy Roman Empire

U. Balzani, *The Popes and the Hohenstaufen*; W. F. Butler, *Lombard Communes*; *Cambridge Medieval History*, V, chaps. x–xiv; H. B. Cotterill, *Medieval Italy*, pp. 413 ff.; E. Emerton, *Medieval Europe*, chap. ix; H. Fisher, *Medieval Empire*, I, chaps. iv–vii, II (entire); F. Gregorovius, *Rome in the Middle Ages*, vols. IV–V; C. H. Haskins, *The Normans in European History*, chap. vii; L. Hutchinson, "The Oriental Trade and the Rise of the Lombard Communes," in *Quarterly Journal of Economics*, XVI, 413; E. Kantorowicz, *Frederick the Second*; T. E. May, *Democracy in Europe*, chap. vii; S. R. Packard, *Europe and the Church Under Innocent III*, chap. i; A. L. Poole, *Henry the Lion*; O. J. Thatcher and E. H. McNeal, *A Source Book for Medieval History*, pp. 189–259; J. W. Thompson, *Economic and Social History of the Middle Ages* (300–1300), chaps. xix–xx, and *Feudal Germany*, chaps. vii–xi; P. Villari, *Medieval Italy*, pp. 197–286.

CHAPTER 15

The Development of the English State (1066–1272)

A general introduction to English history during the period covered by this chapter is found in *England Under the Normans and Angevins* by H. W. C. Davis (London, 1909). The best brief description of the growth of the constitution is W. A. Morris's *The Constitutional History of England to 1216* (New York,

1930). It is well organized and contains excellent bibliographies. No less scholarly and perhaps more pleasantly written, although both longer and more specialized, is *The History of English Law before the Time of Edward I* by Sir Frederick Pollock and F. W. Maitland (2 vols., 2nd ed., Cambridge, Eng., 1923). *Local Government in Francia and England* by Helen Cam (London, 1912) is an excellent comparison between Anglo-Saxon and Carolingian institutions that should be consulted. The two essays by W. S. Corbett on the Norman kings, published in *The Cambridge Medieval History* (vol. V, chaps. xv and xvi), are the result of years of research. A detailed bibliography is given. F. M. Stenton, probably the greatest living scholar upon the Norman period, has embodied his conclusions in *The First Century of English Feudalism, 1066–1166* (Oxford, 1932). It is rather technical for elementary students. *The Domesday Inquest* by Adolphus Ballard (2nd ed., London, 1923) is both pleasingly written and scholarly. Stenton's *William the Conqueror* (New York and London, 1908) is still the best biography of the first Norman king. *Council and Courts in Anglo-Norman England* by G. B. Adams (New Haven, 1926) is a series of studies describing the evolution of the law courts. Mrs. Stenton's chapter on the reign of Henry II in *The Cambridge Medieval History* (vol. V, chap. xvii) is excellent. *Magna Carta* by W. S. Mc-Kechnie (2nd ed., Glasgow, 1914) is more than the best study of that document, for it contains excellent descriptions of both the Angevin innovations and of the later history of the charter. *The King's Council in England During the Middle Ages* by J. F. Baldwin (Oxford, 1913), *The Exchequer in the Twelfth Century* by R. L. Poole (Oxford, 1912), and *The Medieval English Sheriff to 1300* by W. A. Morris (Manchester, 1927) are excellent institutional studies. R. F. Treharne in *The Baronial Plan of Reform, 1258–1263* (Manchester, 1932) draws an unforgettable picture of Henry III and describes extremely sympathetically the aims of the baronial opposition. Miss Cam's *The Hundred and Hundred Rolls* (London, 1930), although in form a description of the great inquests with which the reign of Edward I began, is almost entirely a description of English local government during the thirteenth century. Few if any other books describe the impact of government, and misgovernment, upon ordinary human beings as does this volume of Miss Cam's. The works in previous generations of Bishop Stubbs, Frederick Maitland, Paul Vinogradoff, and J. H. Round created the English medieval history we are taught today. Their publications are listed in the bibliographies mentioned above.

CHAPTERS 16 AND 17

France Under the Capetian Kings

Henry Adams, *Mont-Saint-Michel and Chartres*, chap. xi; W. Barry, *The Papal Monarchy*, pp. 391–420; *Cambridge Medieval History*, V, chaps. xvii, xix, VI, chaps. ix, x; M. Creighton, *History of the Papacy*, I, Introduction, chap. i; E. Emerton, *Beginnings of Modern Europe*, pp. 106–27, nd *Medieval Europe*, chap. xii; JOAN EVANS, *Life in Medieval France*; F. FUNCK-BRENTANO, *The Middle Ages*, chap. xvii; C. H. HASKINS, *The Normans in European History*, chaps. iv, v; W. H. HUTTON, *Philip Augustus*; H. C. LEA, *The Inquisition*, III, chap. v; R. LODGE, *Close of the Middle Ages*, chaps. ii, iii; A. LUCHAIRE, *Social France at the Time of Philip Augustus*; J. R. MORETON-MacDONALD, *History of France*, I, chaps. xi, xii; E. NYS, *History of Economics*, chap. iv; F. PERRY, *St. Louis*; *Memoirs of the Sieur de Joinville* (Everyman's Library); F. M. POWICKE, *The Loss of Normandy*; H. D. SEDGEWICK, *Italy in the Thirteenth Century*, II, chaps. xviii, xix; J. W. THOMPSON, *Economic and Social History of the Middle Ages* (300–1300), chap. xviii, and *The Middle Ages*, II, chap. xxx; A. TILLEY, *Medieval France*, chaps. i–iii; T. F. TOUT, *Empire and Papacy*, chaps. xii–xv, xvii; P. VILLARI, *Medieval Italy*, bk. iii, chap. vii.

CHAPTER 18

THE CRUSADES

T. A. ARCHER, *The Crusade of Richard I*; T. A. ARCHER and C. L. KINGSFORD, *The Crusades*; E. BARKER, *The Crusades*; N. H. BAYNES, *The Byzantine Empire*; J. BRYCE, *The Holy Roman Empire*, chap. xvii; J. B. BURY, *The Eastern Roman Empire from Irene to Basil*; U. R. BURKE, *History of Spain*, vol. I; *Cambridge Medieval History*, IV, chap. xiv; V, chap. ix; C. E. CHAPMAN, *History of Spain*; E. GIBBON, *Decline and Fall of the Roman Empire*, vols. V–VI (J. B. BURY edition); S. HEATH, *Pilgrim Life in the Middle Ages*; JOINVILLE, *The Crusade of St. Louis* (Everyman's Library); E. JORANSON, "German Pilgrimage of 1064–1065," in *Essays Presented to D. C. Munro*; A. C. KREY, *The First Crusade*; J. LA MONTE, *Feudal Monarchy in the Latin Kingdom of Jerusalem*; R. B. MERRIMAN, *Spanish Empire*, vol. I; D. C. MUNRO, *The Kingdom of the Crusaders*; D. C. MUNRO and others, *Essays on the Crusades*; R. A. NEWHALL, *The Crusades*; C. W. C. OMAN, *A History of the Art of War*, bk. v; E. PEARS, *The Latin Kingdom of Constantinople*; F. SCHEVILL, *History of the Balkan Peninsula*, chaps. viii–x; W. B. STEVENSON, *The Crusaders in the East*; J. W. THOMPSON, *Economic and Social History of the Middle Ages* (300–1300), chap. xvi, and *The Middle Ages*, I, chaps. xix–xx; *Translations and Reprints*, I, nos. 2 and 4, III, no. 1; A. A. VASILIEV, *History of the Byzantine Empire*, II, 29–61, 68–74, 109–35; VILLEHARDOUIN, *The Fourth Crusade* (Everyman's Library); B. and E. WISHAW, *Arabic Spain*; F. WOODHOUSE, *The Military Religious Orders*.

CHAPTERS 19 AND 20

THE REVIVAL OF TRADE AND INDUSTRY. THE URBAN REVOLUTION. THE GILDS

W. J. ASHLEY, "Beginnings of Town Life in the Middle Ages," *Quarterly Journal of Economics*, X, 359; *Cambridge Medieval History*, V, chap. xix; G.

G. Coulton, *The Medieval Scene*; G. C. Crump and E. F. Jacob, *Legacy of the Middle Ages*, pp. 435–64; W. Cunningham, *Western Europe in its Economic Aspects: Middle Ages*, secs. 86–88; Clive Day, *History of Commerce*, chaps. v–x; *Encyclopedia of the Social Sciences*, articles on Commune, Guild, Law Merchant, Maritime Law, and Fairs; Joan Evans, *Life in Medieval France*; Giry and Reville, *Emancipation of the Towns* (trans. E. W. Dow); L. Halphen in *Medieval France*, chap. v (A. Tilley, ed.); F. J. C. Hearnshaw (ed.), *Medieval Contributions to Modern Civilization*, chaps. viii–ix; Bede Jarrett, *Social Theories in the Middle Ages*, chaps. v–vi; F. W. Keutgen, "The Medieval Commune," *Encyclopedia Britannica* (11th ed.), VI, 784; E. Lipson, *Economic History of England*, vol. I; H. Pirenne, *Medieval Cities*; E. Power, *Medieval People*, chaps. iv–v; L. F. Salzman, *English Life in the Middle Ages, English Woolen Industry, Medieval English Industries*; Carl Stephenson, *Borough and Town*; J. W. Thompson, *Economic and Social History of the Middle Ages (300–1300)*, chap. xxviii; *Translations and Reprints*, II, no. 1.

CHAPTER 21

The Medieval Reformation

E. L. Cutts, *Scenes and Characters of the Middle Ages*, chap. iv; E. S. Davison, *Forerunners of St. Francis*; *Encyclopedia of the Social Sciences*, articles on St. Francis and St. Dominic; G. R. Galbraith, *The Constitution of the Dominican Order*; J. Herkless, *Francis and Dominic and the Mendicant Orders*; J. Jörgensen, *St. Francis of Assisi*; P. Sabatier, *Life of St. Francis of Assisi*; V. D. Scudder, *The Franciscan Adventure*; H. O. Taylor, *The Mediæval Mind* (1930), I, chap. xx; E. Vancandard, *The Inquisition*; H. J. Warner, *The Albigensian Heresy*, 2 vols.

CHAPTER 22

The Triumph of the Church

G. G. Coulton, *St. Francis to Dante*, chaps. i, ii; H. W. C. Davis, *The Church as a World Power*; E. Emerton, *Medieval Europe*, chap. xvi; Fortesque, *The Mass*; H. C. Lea, *The Inquisition*, I, chap. i, and *Sacerdotal Celibacy*, chaps. xx–xxi; A. Lagarde, *The Latin Church in the Middle Ages*; A. Luchaire, *Social France at the Time of Philip Augustus*; S. R. Packard, *Europe and the Church Under Innocent III*; H. D. Sedgewick, *Italy in the Thirteenth Century*, I, chaps. ii, v–viii, xxv; A. L. Smith, *Church and State in the Middle Ages*; T. F. Tout, *Empire and Papacy*, pp. 433–49.

CHAPTER 23

The Medieval Renaissance: Philosophy, Science, Education

The universities:

R. W. Church, *St. Anselm*; Compayre, *Abelard and the Origin of the*

arly Universities; E. EMERTON, *Medieval Europe*, chap. xiii; C. GROSS, "Po-
itical Influence of the University of Paris in the Middle Ages," *American His-
orical Review*, VI, 440; C. H. HASKINS, *Rise of the Universities*; F. J. C. HEARN-
HAW (ed.), *Medieval Contributions to Modern Civilization*, chap. vii; J.
McCABE, *Peter Abelard*; J. B. MULLINGER, *Schools of Charles the Great*;
A. O. NORTON, *Readings in the History of Medieval Universities*; R. S. RAIT,
Life in the Medieval University; H. RASHDALL, *The Universities of Europe in
the Middle Ages*; H. O. TAYLOR, *The Mediæval Mind* (1930), 2 vols.;
M. DE WULF, *History of Medieval Philosophy*.

Science and philosophy:

H. ADAMS, *Mont-Saint-Michel and Chartres*; H. A. BELLOWS (tr.) *Abelard's The Story of My Misfortunes*; J. H. BRIDGES, *Life and Works of
Roger Bacon*; E. G. BROWNE, *Arabian Medicine*; C. G. CUMSTON, *Introduction
to the History of Medicine*, chaps. xiii, xiv; W. C. D. DAMPIER-WHETHAN,
A History of Science; C. H. HASKINS, *Studies in the History of Mediæval Science*,
and *Studies in Mediæval Culture*; A. J. MacDONALD, *Authority and Reason in
the Early Middle Ages*; A. C. McGIFFERT, *A History of Christian Thought*,
vol. II; R. P. McKEON (ed. and tr.), *Selections from Medieval Philosophers*,
2 vols.; J. RANDALL, *The Making of the Modern Mind*; W. T. SEDGWICK and
H. W. TYLER, *A Short History of Science*, chaps. vii, viii, ix; C. SINGER, *From
Magic to Science*; L. THORNDIKE, *A History of Magic and Experimental Science*;
T. O. WEDEL, *The Mediæval Attitude Toward Astrology*.

CHAPTER 24

THE MEDIEVAL RENAISSANCE: LITERATURE, ART, MUSIC

HENRY ADAMS, *Mont-Saint-Michel and Chartres*; P. S. ALLEN and H. M.
JONES, *The Romanesque Lyric*; CLAIR H. BELL, *Peasant Life in Old German
Epics*; J. D. BRUCE, *The Arthurian Legend*; A. J. DE H. BUSHNELL, *Storied
Windows*; E. K. CHAMBERS, *Arthur of Britain* and *The Mediæval Stage*;
H. J. CHAYTOR, *The Troubadours*; D. COMPARETTI, *Virgil in the Middle Ages*;
RALPH ADAMS CRAM, *The Substance of Gothic*; G. C. CRUMP and E. F. JACOB
(eds.), *Legacy of the Middle Ages*; O. M. DALTON, *Byzantine Art*; CHRISTOPHER
DAWSON, *Mediæval Religion*; E. DICKINSON, *Music in the History of the Western
Church*; EDWARD DILLON, *Stained Glass*; F. S. ELLIS (tr.), *The Romance
of the Rose*; LORD ERNLE, *The Light Reading of Our Ancestors*; JEFFERSON
BUTLER FLETCHER (tr.), *The Divine Comedy of Dante Alighieri*; KUNO
FRANCKE, *History of German Literature*, and *Personality in German Litera-
ture Before Luther*; A. L. FROTHINGHAM, *Monuments of Christian Rome*;
HELEN GARDNER, *Art Through the Ages*; CECIL GRAY, *History of Music*;
C. H. HASKINS, *Renaissance of the Twelfth Century*; R. C. HOPE, *Medieval
Music*; SIR THOMAS GRAHAM JACKSON, *Gothic Architecture in France, England,
and Italy*; W. P. KER, *Epic and Romance* and *Essays in Medieval Literature*;

WILLIAM LAWRENCE, *Medieval Story*; W. R. LETHABY, *Westminster Abbey an*
the King's Craftsmen; JOHN L. LOWES, *Geoffrey Chaucer*; E. MÂLE, *Religio*
Art in France in the Thirteenth Century; EUGENE MASON (tr.), *Aucassin an*
Nicolette (Everyman's Library); H. MORELY, *Medieval Tales*; D. C. MUNR
and G. SELLERY, *Medieval Civilization*, pp. 277–347; J. U. NICOLSON (tr.)
CHAUCER's *Canterbury Tales*; *Oxford History of Music*, vol. I; G. PARIS
Medieval French Literature (Everyman's Library); A. K. PORTER, *Medieva*
Architecture, its Origins and Development, and *Lombard Architecture*; E. S.
PRIOR, *A History of Gothic Architecture*; F. J. RABY, *Christian Latin Poetry*, and
History of Secular Latin Poetry, 2 vols.; *Roman Missal*; MARGARET SCHLAUCH,
Medieval Narrative; J. H. SMITH, *The Troubadours at Home*, vols. I, II;
R. STURGIS and A. L. FROTHINGHAM, *History of Architecture*, vol. III; J. A.
SYMONDS, *Wine, Women, and Song*; J. W. THOMPSON, *The Middle Ages*, II,
chap. xxviii; PAUL VINOGRADOFF, *Roman Law in Medieval Europe*; KARL
VOSSLER, *Medieval Culture*, vols. I, II; HELEN WADDELL, *Mediæval Latin Lyrics*
and *The Wandering Scholars*; A. W. WARD, *History of English Drama*, vol. I;
E. H. WILKINS, *Dante: Poet and Apostle*; K. YOUNG, *The Drama of the Medieval*
Church.

CHAPTER 25

THE DEVELOPMENT OF THE ENGLISH STATE (1272–1485)

A general introduction to the last two centuries of medieval England is given
in *England in the Later Middle Ages* by K. VICKERS (London, 1921), but no
constitutional studies like those of Morris and of Pollock and Maitland for
the earlier period exist for the later middle ages. Probably the most satisfactory
substitute is the various introductions in *English Constitutional Documents, 1307–*
1485 by E. C. LODGE and G. A. THORNTON (Cambridge, Eng., 1935). It contains
good bibliographies. G. H. MCILWAIN's chapter in the *The Cambridge Medi-*
eval History (vol. XII, chap. xxii) is an invaluable synopsis of the general European evolution of representative institutions, with a bibliography attached. Research upon the history of the English Parliament has progressed so rapidly in
the last generation that the results are still in the form of scattered monographs.
Of these *An Essay on the Origin of the House of Commons* by D. PASQUET
(translated by G. Lapsley, Cambridge, Eng., 1925), *The Influence of the Com-*
mons on Early Legislation by H. L. GRAY (Cambridge, 1932), and *The Parlia-*
mentary Representation of the English Boroughs During the Middle Ages by
M. MCKISACK (Oxford, 1932) are both good and usually accessible. MISS MC-
KISACK's bibliography can be used as a guide to other studies, of which those by
RICHARDSON and SAYLES are especially valuable. A. F. POLLARD's *The Evolu-*
tion of Parliament (2nd ed., London, 1926) is stimulating but can be accepted
only as subject to revision from the later monographic material. *The Chancery*
under Edward III by B. WILKINSON (Manchester, 1929) and A. M. KERLY's

Historical Sketch of the Equitable Jurisdiction of the Court of Chancery (Cambridge, Eng., 1890) describes the chancery. *The Office of Justice of the Peace in England in Its Origin and Development* by C. A. BEARD (New York, 1904) is still the best single account of that office, although the studies by BERTHA PUTNAM should be consulted wherever possible. *The Revenues of the Kings of England* by J. R. RAMSAY (2 vols., Oxford, 1925) covers the entire medieval period. *The Early English Customs System* by N. S. B. GRAS (Cambridge, 1918) and *Parliamentary Taxes on Personal Property, 1290 to 1334* by J. WILLARD (Cambridge, 1934) are excellent studies of public revenues. *Early Tudor Governments, Henry VII* by K. PICKTHORN (Cambridge, Eng., 1934) describes the organization of the English state at the close of the middle ages.

CHAPTER 26

WESTERN EUROPE IN THE FOURTEENTH AND FIFTEENTH CENTURIES

J. S. C. BRIDGE, *A History of France from the Death of Louis XI*; *Cambridge Medieval History*, VII, chaps. xii, xiii, xx, VIII, chaps. vii, viii, ix, x, xv, xvi; *Cambridge Modern History*, I, Introduction; W. CUNNINGHAM, *Western Civilization in its Economic Aspects: Middle Ages*, pp. 146–61; E. P. CHEYNEY, *The Dawn of a New Era*, chaps. i–v; V. DURUY, *History of France*, chaps. xxxiv, xxv; E. EMERTON, *Beginnings of Modern Europe*, Preface; H. A. L. FISHER, *A History of Europe*, I, chaps. xxvi, xxvii, xxviii, xxxi; R. LODGE, *Close of the Middle Ages*; R. PUTNAM, *Charles the Bold*; W. T. WAUGH, *A History of Europe from 1387 to 1494*, chaps. i–iii, x, xi, xii, xvi.

CHAPTER 27

CENTRAL AND EASTERN EUROPE IN THE FOURTEENTH AND FIFTEENTH CENTURIES

C. R. BEAZLEY, *Dawn of Modern Geography*, II, chap. v, III, 333–77; J. BRYCE, *The Holy Roman Empire*, chaps. xiii–xv; *Cambridge Medieval History*, IV, chaps. xv, xvii–xxi, VII, chaps. iii–v, vii, viii, ix, xxi, VIII, chaps. iv, xvii, xviii, xix; *Cambridge Modern History*, I, chaps. iii, ix, x; E. P. CHEYNEY, *The Dawn of a New Era*, chap. x; E. EMERTON, *Beginnings of Modern Europe*, chap. ii; H. A. L. FISHER, *A History of Europe*, I, chaps. xxix, xxxii, xxxiv; E. GIBBON, *Decline and Fall of the Roman Empire* (ed. J. B. BURY), VII, 43–70, chaps. lxiv–lxvii; E. F. HENDERSON, *Short History of Germany*, pp. 122–251; W. KING, *Chronicles of Three Free Cities*; R. LODGE, *Close of Middle Ages*, chaps. v–vii; W. D. McCRACKEN, *The Rise of the Swiss Republic*; F. NOWAK, *Medieval Slavdom and the Rise of Russia*; F. SCHEVILL, *History of the Balkan Peninsula*, chaps. xii, xiii; H. TUTTLE, *History of Prussia*, I, chap. i; A. A. VASILIEV, *History of the Byzantine Empire*,

II, chap. ix; W. T. Waugh, *A History of Europe from 1398 to 1494*, chaps. iv, vi, xiii–xv, xvii, xviii; H. Zimmern, *Hanse Towns.*

CHAPTER 28

The Church in the Fourteenth and Fifteenth Centuries

W. Barry, *Papal Monarchy*, pp. 391–428; T. S. R. Boase, *Boniface the Eighth*; H. Bruce, *The Age of the Schism*; *Cambridge Medieval History*, VII, chaps. x, xvi, VIII, chaps. i, ii, iii, xx; M. Creighton, *History of the Papacy*, vols. I–IV; M. Deansley, *History of the Medieval Church*, chaps. xiv–xviii; W. Dunning, *History of Political Theory* (medieval); E. Emerton, *Beginnings of Modern Europe*, chaps. iii, vii; J. N. Figgis, *From Gerson to Grotius*, chaps. i–ii; A. Flick, *Decline of the Medieval Church*; C. Guignebert, *Christianity*, chap. xviii; F. J. C. Hearnshaw, *Social and Political Ideas of Some Great Medieval Thinkers*, chap. viii; E. J. Kitts, *In the Days of the Councils*; G. Krüger, *The Papacy*, chap. vii; W. Lindsay, *History of the Reformation*, I, chap. i; R. Lodge, *Close of the Middle Ages*, pp. 196–242; W. Lunt, *Papal Revenues in the Middle Ages*, vol. I; C. H. McIlwain, *The Growth of Political Thought in the West*; L. Pastor, *History of the Popes*, vol. I; R. L. Poole, *Wycliffe and Movements for Reform*, and *Illustrations of the History of Medieval Thought*; G. M. Trevelyan, *England in the Age of Wycliffe*, chaps. iv, v; W. T. Waugh, *Europe, 1378–1494*, chaps. v, vii, ix; J. H. Wylie, *The Council of Constance.*

CHAPTER 29

Learning and Art in the Fourteenth and Fifteenth Centuries

W. C. Abbott, *Expansion of Europe*, I, chaps. ii–iii; J. N. L. Baker, *A History of Geographical Discovery and Exploration*; A. C. Barnes, *The Art in Painting*; C. R. Beazley, *Dawn of Modern Geography*, II, chaps. i–vi, III, chaps. i–ii; W. E. Brown, *The Achievement of the Middle Ages*; O. Browning, *Age of the Condottieri*; J. Burckhardt, *The Renaissance* (Leipzig, 1908); *Cambridge Medieval History*, VII, chap. xxv, VIII, chaps. xxiii, xxiv, xxv, and Epilogue; *Cambridge Modern History*, I, chaps. xvi–xvii; E. P. Cheyney, *European Background of American History*, chaps. i–iii, and *The Dawn of a New Era*, chaps. viii, ix; H. B. Cotterill, *Italy from Dante to Tasso*; M. Creighton, *History of the Papacy*, vol. V; E. Emerton, *Beginnings of Modern Europe*, chaps. v, viii, ix; J. B. Fletcher, *Literature of the Italian Renaissance*; K. Francke, *Personality in German Literature*, chap. ii; J. E. Gillespie, *A History of Geographical Discovery, 1400–1800*; J. Huizinga, *The Waning of the Middle Ages*; E. Hutton, *Giovanni Boccaccio*; A. Hyma, *The Christian Renaissance*, and *The Youth of Erasmus*; R. M. McKeon (ed. and tr.), *Selec-*

tions from Mediæval Philosophers, vol. II; R. LODGE, *Close of the Middle Ages*, chaps. viii, xii, xiv; H. S. LUCAS, *The Renaissance and the Reformation*; F. J. MATHER, JR., *History of Italian Painting*; A. MARQUAND and A. L. FROTHINGHAM, *History of Sculpture*, chaps. xviii–xxiii; F. MOLMENTI, *Venice: the Golden Age*; C. H. MOORE, *Character of Renaissance Architecture*; C. R. MOREY, *Christian Art*; J. U. NICOLSON, *The Complete Works of François Villon*; P. NOLHAC, *Petrarch and the Ancient World*; L. PASTOR, *History of the Popes*, I, Introduction; A. K. PORTER, *Beyond Architecture*; E. PRESTAGE, *The Portuguese Pioneers*; S. REINACH, *Apollo, a Manual of the History of Art*; J. H. ROBINSON and H. W. ROLFE, *Petrarch, the First Modern Scholar and Man of Letters*; J. E. SANDYS, *History of Classical Scholarship*, II, bk. i; W. B. SCAIFE, *Florentine Life During the Renaissance*; F. SCHEVILL, *A History of Florence*; EDITH SICHEL, *The Renaissance*; W. H. O. SMEATON, *The Medici and the Italian Renaissance*; P. SMITH, *Age of the Reformation*; J. A. SYMONDS, *The Age of the Despots*; *The Revival of Learning: Italian Literature*; *The Fine Arts*; H. O. TAYLOR, *Thought and Expression in the Sixteenth Century*; J. W. THOMPSON, F. SCHEVILL, G. SARTON, and G. RAWLEY, *The Civilization of the Renaissance*; A. A. TILLEY, *Renaissance Types*; A. P. USHER, *A History of Mechanical Inventions*, chap. viii; H. M. VAUGHAN, *The Medici Popes*; P. VILLARI, *Life and Times of Savonarola*; W. T. WAUGH, *A History of Europe from 1378 to 1494*, chaps. xix–xxii.

Index